AMERICAN HISTORY

RECONSTRUCTION TO THE PRESENT

Educational Advisory Panel

The following educators provided ongoing review during the development of prototypes and key elements of this program.

Contents

Module 1

★

Module 2

---- ★ ----

Module 3

---- ★ ----

Module 4

---- ★ ----

Module 5

Module 6

Module 7

★

Module 8

★

Module 9

⭐

Module 10

⭐

Module 11

Module 12

Module 13

Module 14

★

Module 15

★

Module 16

Module 17

Module 18

Module 19

Reference Section

——————————————— ★ ———————————————

Available Online

Biographical Dictionary
Close-Read Screencasts
Facts About the States
Presidents of the United States
Economics Handbook
Geography and Map Skills Handbook
Skillbuilder Handbook

 Multimedia Connections

HISTORY

▶ These online lessons feature award-winning content and
include short video segments, maps and visual materials,
primary source documents, and more.

Ponce de León

The American Revolution

Lewis and Clark

The Real West: Rush
   for Gold

Days of Darkness: The
   Gettysburg Civilians

Ellis Island

Dear Home: Letters from
   World War I

Henry Ford

Memories of World War II

October Fury: The Cuban
   Missile Crisis

HISTORY
MADE EVERY DAY.

HISTORY® is the leading destination for revealing, award-winning, original non-fiction series and event-driven specials that connect history with viewers in an informative, immersive and entertaining manner across multiple platforms. HISTORY is part of A+E Networks, a global entertainment media company that includes, among others, A&E®, HISTORY®, Lifetime®, H2®, FYI™, and LMN®.

HISTORY programming greatly appeals to educators and young people who are drawn into the visual stories our documentaries tell. Our Education Department has a long-standing record in providing teachers and students with curriculum resources that bring the past to life in the classroom. Our content covers a diverse variety of subjects, including American and world history, government, economics, the natural and applied sciences, arts, literature and the humanities, health and guidance, and even pop culture.

The HISTORY website, located at **www.history.com**, is the definitive historical online source that delivers entertaining and informative content featuring broadband video, interactive timelines, maps, games, podcasts and more.

"We strive to engage, inspire and encourage the love of learning..."

Since its founding in 1995, HISTORY has demonstrated a commitment to providing the highest quality resources for educators. We develop multimedia resources for K–12 schools, two- and four-year colleges, government agencies, and other organizations by drawing on the award-winning documentary programming of A&E Television Networks. We strive to engage, inspire and encourage the love of learning by connecting with students in an informative and compelling manner. To help achieve this goal, we have formed a partnership with Houghton Mifflin Harcourt.

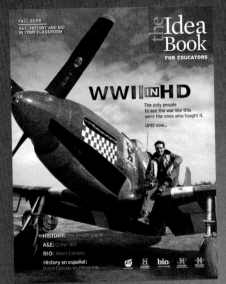
The Idea Book for Educators

Classroom resources that bring the past to life

Live webcasts

HISTORY Take a Veteran to School Day

In addition to premium video-based resources, **HISTORY** has extensive offerings for teachers, parents, and students to use in the classroom and in their in-home educational activities, including:

▶ **The Idea Book for Educators** is a biannual teacher's magazine, featuring guides and info on the latest happenings in history education to help keep teachers on the cutting edge.

▶ **HISTORY Classroom (www.history.com/classroom)** is an interactive website that serves as a portal for history educators nationwide. Streaming videos on topics ranging from the Roman aqueducts to the civil rights movement connect with classroom curricula.

▶ **HISTORY email newsletters** feature updates and supplements to our award-winning programming relevant to the classroom with links to teaching guides and video clips on a variety of topics, special offers, and more.

▶ **Live webcasts** are featured each year as schools tune in via streaming video.

▶ **HISTORY Take a Veteran to School Day** connects veterans with young people in our schools and communities nationwide.

In addition to **Houghton Mifflin Harcourt**, our partners include the *Library of Congress,* the *Smithsonian Institution, National History Day, The Gilder Lehrman Institute of American History,* the Organization of American Historians, and many more. HISTORY video is also featured in museums throughout America and in over 70 other historic sites worldwide.

HMH Social Studies
Dashboard

Designed for today's digital natives, **HMH® Social Studies** offers you an informative and exciting online experience.

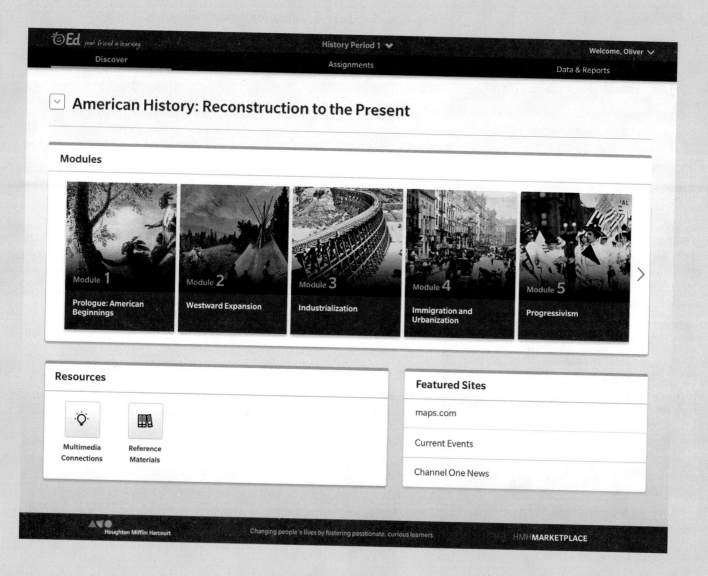

Your personalized Dashboard is organized into three main sections:

1. **Discover**—Quickly access content and search program resources

2. **Assignments**—Review your assignments and check your progress on them

3. **Data & Reports**—Monitor your progress on the course

Explore Online ▷
to **Experience** the **Power** of
American History
Reconstruction to the Present

Houghton Mifflin Harcourt™ is **changing** the way you **experience** social studies.

By delivering an immersive experience through compelling narratives enriched with media, we're connecting you to history through experiences that are energizing, inspiring, and memorable. The following pages highlight some digital tools and instructional support that will help you approach history through active inquiry, so you can connect to the past while becoming active and informed citizens for the future.

The Student eBook is the primary learning portal.

More than just the digital version of a textbook, the Student eBook serves as the primary learning portal for you. The narrative is supported by a wealth of multimedia and learning resources to bring history to life and give you the tools you need to succeed.

Bringing Content to Life

HISTORY® videos and Multimedia Connections bring content to life through primary source footage, dramatic storytelling, and expert testimonials.

In-Depth Understanding

Close Read Screencasts model an analytical conversation about primary sources.

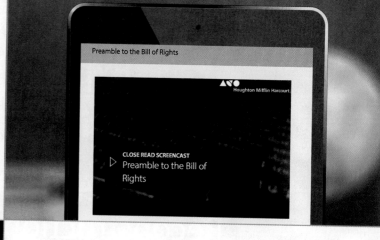

Content in a Fun Way

Interactive Features, Maps, and **Games** provide quick, entertaining activities and assessments that present important content in a fun way.

Investigate Like a Historian

Document-Based Investigations in every lesson build to end-of-module DBI performance tasks so you can examine and assess primary sources as historians do.

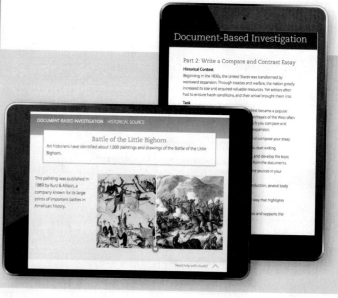

Full-Text Audio Support

You can listen while you read.

Skills Support

Point-of-use support is just a click away, providing instruction on critical reading and social studies skills.

Personalized Annotations

My Notes encourages you to take notes while you read and allows you to customize them to your study preferences. You can easily access them to review later as you prepare for exams.

Interactive Lesson Graphic Organizers

Graphic organizers help you process, summarize, and keep track of your learning for end-of-module performance tasks.

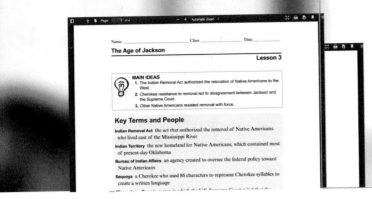

The **Guided Reading Workbook** and **Spanish/English Guided Reading Workbook** offer you lesson summaries with vocabulary, reading, and note-taking support.

Map Connections connects you with history and geography through interactive maps, games, and data.

Current Events features trustworthy articles on today's news that connect what you learn in class to the world around you.

No Wi-Fi®? No problem!

With the **HMH Player®** app, you can connect to content and resources by downloading when online and accessing when offline.

 HMH**PLAYER**® also allows you to:

Work Offline

Download lesson content and resources to work offline.

Communicate

"Raise a Hand" to ask or answer questions without having to be in the same room as your teacher.

Collaborate

Collaborate with your teacher via chat and in-lesson teamwork.

Unpacking the Florida Next Generation Sunshine State Standards

As you read the following pages and work through the unpacking of the Florida Next Generation Sunshine State Standards for High School American History, you will discover the big ideas and key concepts that you are expected to learn and understand.

You will see two things:

1. What the standard actually says
2. **What does it mean?** an explanation to help you understand the big ideas within the standard

ENGLISH LANGUAGE DEVELOPMENT

ELD.K12.ELL.SI.1 English language learners communicate for social and instructional purposes within the school setting. **What does it mean?** English language learners communicate for everyday and educational situations at school.

ELD.K12.ELL.SS.1 English language learners communicate information, ideas and concepts necessary for academic success in the content area of Social Studies. **What does it mean?** English language learners communicate about social studies content.

HEALTH EDUCATION

HE.912.C.2.4 Evaluate how public health policies and government regulations can influence health promotion and disease prevention. **Remarks/Examples:** Seat-belt enforcement, underage alcohol sales, reporting communicable diseases, child care, and AED availability. **What does it mean?** Evaluate how the government can affect health promotion and disease prevention. Go to Modules 4, 5, 7, 14, 17, and 18 for help.

LANGUAGE ARTS

LAFS.1112.RH.1.1 Cite specific textual evidence to support analysis of primary and secondary sources, connecting insights gained from specific details to an understanding of the text as a whole. **What does it mean?** Use ideas and details from primary and secondary sources to analyze the main idea and significance of the source and gain an understanding of the source as a whole. Go to the Skillbuilder Handbook in the Online Student Edition for help.

LAFS.1112.RH.1.2 Determine the central ideas or information of a primary or secondary source; provide an accurate summary that makes clear the relationships among the key details and ideas. **What does it mean?** Analyze the main ideas of both primary and secondary sources. Understand how main ideas and key events relate to each other throughout the text in order to summarize these concepts. Go to the Skillbuilder Handbook in the Online Student Edition for help.

LAFS.1112.RH.1.3 Evaluate various explanations for actions or events and determine which explanation best accords with textual evidence, acknowledging where the text leaves matters uncertain. **What does it mean?** Examine several explanations of events and decide which explanation is best supported by written evidence. Identify areas where the evidence leaves room for interpretation. Go to the Skillbuilder Handbook in the Online Student Edition for help.

LAFS.1112.RH.2.4 Determine the meaning of words and phrases as they are used in a text, including analyzing how an author uses and refines the meaning of a key term over the course of a text (e.g., how Madison defines *faction* in *Federalist* No. 10). **What does it mean?** Analyze specific words and phrases in a text to determine their meaning and how an author refines key terms in a text. Go to the Skillbuilder Handbook in the Online Student Edition for help.

LAFS.1112.RH.2.5 Analyze in detail how a complex primary source is structured, including how key sentences, paragraphs, and larger portions of the text contribute to the whole. **What does it mean?** Examine the organization of a complex primary source and how smaller parts (sentences, paragraphs, and chapters) contribute to the overall organization. Go to Module 1 Lesson 2 Enrichment in the Online Student Edition for help.

LAFS.1112.RH.2.6 Evaluate authors' differing points of view on the same historical event or issue by assessing the authors' claims, reasoning, and evidence. **What does it mean?** Examine the reasoning and evidence presented by different authors on the same topic to determine which is more compelling. Go to the Skillbuilder Handbook in the Online Student Edition for help.

LAFS.1112.RH.3.7 Integrate and evaluate multiple sources of information presented in diverse formats and media (e.g., visually, quantitatively, as well as in words) in order to address a question or solve a problem. **What does it mean?** Assess and use multiple sources from different media to answer questions. Go to the Document-Based Investigation activities that appear at the end of each module in the Online Student Edition for help.

LAFS.1112.RH.3.8 Evaluate an author's premises, claims, and evidence by corroborating or challenging them with other information. **What does it mean?** Judge an author's work by finding supporting evidence or challenge it using other sources. Go to the Skillbuilder Handbook in the Online Student Edition for help.

LAFS.1112.RH.3.9 Integrate information from diverse sources, both primary and secondary, into a coherent understanding of an idea or event, noting discrepancies among sources. **What does it mean?** Use primary and secondary sources to form a complete picture of an event and take note of where sources disagree. Go to the Document-Based Investigation activities that appear at the end of each module in the Online Student Edition for help.

LAFS.1112.RH.4.10 By the end of grade 12, read and comprehend history/social studies texts in the grades 11–CCR text complexity band independently and proficiently. **What does it mean?** Demonstrate the ability to read and understand grade-level appropriate social studies texts by the end of grade 12. Go to the American Literature features that appear in Modules 2, 4, 5, 8, 11, 12, 15, and 16 for help.

LAFS.1112.SL.1.1 Initiate and participate effectively in a range of collaborative discussions (one-on-one, in groups, and teacher-led) with diverse partners on grades 11–12 topics, texts, and issues, building on others' ideas and expressing their own clearly and persuasively.

a. Come to discussions prepared, having read and researched material under study; explicitly draw on that preparation by referring to evidence from texts and other research on the topic or issue to stimulate a thoughtful, well-reasoned exchange of ideas.

b. Work with peers to promote civil, democratic discussions and decision-making, set clear goals and deadlines, and establish individual roles as needed.

c. Propel conversations by posing and responding to questions that probe reasoning and evidence; ensure a hearing for a full range of positions on a topic or issue; clarify, verify, or challenge ideas and conclusions; and promote divergent and creative perspectives.

d. Respond thoughtfully to diverse perspectives; synthesize comments, claims, and evidence made on all sides of an issue; resolve contradictions when possible; and determine what additional information or research is required to deepen the investigation or complete the task.

What does it mean? Begin and participate in different types of discussions with different people on appropriate topics. Build on other people's ideas and express yourself with clear and persuasive language. Go to Module 1 Lesson 2 Enrichment in the Online Student Edition for help.

LAFS.1112.SL.1.2 Integrate multiple sources of information presented in diverse formats and media (e.g., visually, quantitatively, orally) in order to make informed decisions and solve problems, evaluating the credibility and accuracy of each source and noting any discrepancies among the data. **What does it mean?** Include several sources of different formats and analyze their credibility and accuracy. Go to the Skillbuilder Handbook in the Online Student Edition for help.

LAFS.1112.SL.1.3 Evaluate a speaker's point of view, reasoning, and use of evidence and rhetoric, assessing the stance, premises, links among ideas, word choice, points of emphasis, and tone used. **What does it mean?** Evaluate a speaker's argument and analyze the nature of the speaker's style, reasoning, and evidence. Go to the Skillbuilder Handbook in the Online Student Edition for help.

LAFS.1112.SL.2.4 Present information, findings, and supporting evidence, conveying a clear and distinct perspective, such that listeners can follow the line of reasoning, alternative or opposing perspectives are addressed, and the organization, development, substance, and style are appropriate to purpose, audience, and a range of formal and informal tasks. **What does it mean?** Organize and present information to listeners in a logical sequence and style that are appropriate to the task and audience. Go to the Document-Based Investigation activities in Modules 1, 2, 4, and 13 and the Skillbuilder Handbook in the Online Student Edition for help.

LAFS.1112.WHST.1.1 Write arguments focused on *discipline-specific content*.

a. Introduce precise, knowledgeable claim(s), establish the significance of the claim(s), distinguish the claim(s) from alternate or opposing claims, and create an organization that logically sequences the claim(s), counterclaims, reasons, and evidence.

b. Develop claim(s) and counterclaims fairly and thoroughly, supplying the most relevant data and evidence for each while pointing out the strengths and limitations of both claim(s) and counterclaims in a discipline-appropriate form that anticipates the audience's knowledge level, concerns, values, and possible biases.

c. Use words, phrases, and clauses as well as varied syntax to link the major sections of the text, create cohesion, and clarify the relationships between claim(s) and reasons, between reasons and evidence, and between claim(s) and counterclaims.

d. Establish and maintain a formal style and objective tone while attending to the norms and conventions of the discipline in which they are writing.

e. Provide a concluding statement or section that follows from or supports the argument presented.

What does it mean? Write and develop arguments with strong evidence and valid reasoning about topics relevant to social studies. Go to the Document-Based Investigation activities in Modules 3, 18, and 19 and the Skillbuilder Handbook in the Online Student Edition for help.

LAFS.1112.WHST.1.2 Write informative/explanatory texts, including the narration of historical events, scientific procedures/experiments, or technical processes.

a. Introduce a topic and organize complex ideas, concepts, and information so that each new element builds on that which precedes it to create a unified whole; include formatting (e.g., headings), graphics (e.g., figures, tables), and multimedia when useful to aiding comprehension.

b. Develop the topic thoroughly by selecting the most significant and relevant facts, extended definitions, concrete details, quotations, or other information and examples appropriate to the audience's knowledge of the topic.

c. Use varied transitions and sentence structures to link the major sections of the text, create cohesion, and clarify the relationships among complex ideas and concepts.

d. Use precise language, domain-specific vocabulary and techniques such as metaphor, simile, and analogy to manage the complexity of the topic; convey a knowledgeable stance in a style that responds to the discipline and context as well as to the expertise of likely readers.

e. Provide a concluding statement or section that follows from and supports the information or explanation provided (e.g., articulating implications or the significance of the topic).

What does it mean? Write clear, well-organized, and thoughtful informative and explanatory texts and narratives. Go to the Document-Based Investigation activities in Modules 5, 6, 7, 8, 9, 10, 11, 12, 14, 15, 16, and 17 and the Skillbuilder Handbook in the Online Student Edition for help.

LAFS.1112.WHST.2.4 Produce clear and coherent writing in which the development, organization, and style are appropriate to task, purpose, and audience. **What does it mean?** Produce texts that are appropriate to the task, purpose, and audience for whom you are writing. Go to the Focus on Writing activities in each Module Assessment in the Print Student Edition and the Skillbuilder Handbook in the Online Student Edition for help.

LAFS.1112.WHST.2.5 Develop and strengthen writing as needed by planning, revising, editing, rewriting, or trying a new approach, focusing on addressing what is most significant for a specific purpose and audience. **What does it mean?** Plan, revise, and refine your writing to address what is most important for your purpose and audience. Go to Enrichment writing activities, such as Module 3 Lesson 4, Module 7 Lesson 4, and Module 16 Lesson 4, and the Skillbuilder Handbook in the Online Student Edition for help.

LAFS.1112.WHST.2.6 Use technology, including the Internet, to produce, publish, and update individual or shared writing products in response to ongoing feedback, including new arguments or information. **What does it mean?** Use

technology to share writing products and to provide links to other relevant information. Go to Module 1 Lesson 3 Enrichment and Module 2 Lesson 1 Enrichment in the Online Student Edition for help.

LAFS.1112.WHST.3.7 Conduct short as well as more sustained research projects to answer a question (including a self-generated question) or solve a problem; narrow or broaden the inquiry when appropriate; synthesize multiple sources on the subject, demonstrating understanding of the subject under investigation. **What does it mean?** Engage in short and more complex research tasks that include answering a question or solving a problem by using multiple sources. The product of your research should demonstrate your understanding of the subject. Go to Enrichment activities, such as Module 4 Lesson 5, Module 6 Lesson 3, and Module 15 Lesson 4, and the Skillbuilder Handbook in the Online Student Edition for help.

LAFS.1112.WHST.3.8 Gather relevant information from multiple authoritative print and digital sources, using advanced searches effectively; assess the strengths and limitations of each source in terms of the specific task, purpose, and audience; integrate information into the text selectively to maintain the flow of ideas, avoiding plagiarism and overreliance on any one source and following a standard format for citation. **What does it mean?** Conduct effective searches and carefully analyze the relevance of sources in order to gather useful information from a variety of sources, while following a standard citation format to avoid plagiarism. Go to Module 17 Lesson 5 Enrichment and the Skillbuilder Handbook in the Online Student Edition for help.

LAFS.1112.WHST.3.9 Draw evidence from informational texts to support analysis, reflection, and research. **What does it mean?** Paraphrase, summarize, quote, and cite primary and secondary sources to support analysis, reflection, and research. Go to Enrichment activities, such as Module 2 Lesson 2, Module 11 Lesson 4, and Module 17 Lesson 6, in the Online Student Edition for help.

LAFS.1112.WHST.4.10 Write routinely over extended time frames (time for reflection and revision) and shorter time frames (a single sitting or a day or two) for a range of discipline-specific tasks, purposes, and audiences. **What does it mean?** Write for many different purposes and audiences both over short and extended periods of time. Go to the Focus on Writing activities in each Module Assessment in the Print Student Edition and the Skillbuilder Handbook in the Online Student Edition for help.

MATHEMATICS

MAFS.K12.MP.1.1 Make sense of problems and persevere in solving them. Mathematically proficient students start by explaining to themselves the meaning of a problem and looking for entry points to its solution. They analyze givens, constraints, relationships, and goals. They make conjectures about the form and meaning of the solution and plan a solution pathway rather than simply jumping into a solution attempt. They consider analogous problems, and try special cases and simpler forms of the original problem in order to gain insight into its solution. They monitor and evaluate their progress and change course if necessary. Older students might, depending on the context of the problem, transform algebraic expressions or change the viewing window on their graphing calculator to get the information they need. Mathematically proficient students can explain correspondences between equations, verbal descriptions, tables, and graphs or draw diagrams of important features and relationships, graph data, and search for regularity or trends. Younger students might rely on using concrete objects or pictures to help conceptualize and solve a problem. Mathematically proficient students check their answers to problems using a different method, and they continually ask themselves, "Does this make sense?" They can understand the approaches of others to solving complex problems and identify correspondences between different approaches. **What does it mean?** Understand the problems put in front of you and work through them until a solution is found. Applying math skills in social studies course work often takes the form of analyzing data in tables, graphs, and models. Go to the many graphs in the text, such as in Module 1 Lesson 6 Segment 1, Module 7 Lesson 3 Segment 1, and Module 11 Lesson 4 Segment 3, and the Skillbuilder Handbook in the Online Student Edition for help.

MAFS.K12.MP.3.1 Construct viable arguments and critique the reasoning of others. Mathematically proficient students understand and use stated assumptions, definitions, and previously established results in constructing arguments. They make conjectures and build a logical progression of statements to explore the truth of their conjectures. They are able to analyze situations by breaking them into cases, and can recognize and use counterexamples. They justify their conclusions, communicate them to others, and respond to the arguments of others. They reason inductively about data, making plausible arguments that take into account the context from which the data arose. Mathematically proficient students are also able to compare the effectiveness of two plausible arguments, distinguish correct logic or reasoning from that which is flawed, and—if there is a flaw in an argument—explain what it is. Elementary students can construct arguments using concrete referents such as objects, drawings, diagrams, and actions. Such arguments can make sense and be correct, even though they are not generalized or made formal until later grades. Later, students learn to determine domains to which an argument applies. Students at all grades can listen or read the arguments of others, decide whether they make sense, and ask useful questions to clarify or improve the arguments. **What does it mean?** Use logic and evidence to construct reasoned arguments and analyze the arguments of others using those same skills. Application of this skill in social studies course work most often comes in the form of written essays. However, direct application of math skills can be used when determining the story behind the numbers on a graph or critiquing someone else's conclusions about a set of data. Go to the Difficult Decisions features that appear in Modules 5, 8, 9, 16, and 17 and the Skillbuilder Handbook in the Online Student Edition for help.

MAFS.K12.MP.5.1 Use appropriate tools strategically. Mathematically proficient students consider the available tools when solving a mathematical problem. These tools might include pencil and paper, concrete models, a ruler, a protractor, a calculator, a spreadsheet, a computer algebra system, a statistical package, or dynamic geometry software. Proficient students are sufficiently familiar with tools appropriate for their grade or course to make sound decisions about when each of these tools might be helpful, recognizing both the insight to be gained and their limitations. For example, mathematically proficient high school students analyze graphs of functions and solutions generated using a graphing calculator. They detect possible errors by strategically using estimation and other mathematical knowledge. When making mathematical models, they know that technology can enable them to visualize the results of varying assumptions, explore consequences, and compare predictions with data. Mathematically proficient students at various grade levels are able to identify relevant external mathematical resources, such as digital content located on a website, and use them to pose or solve problems. They are able to use technological tools to explore and deepen their understanding of concepts. **What does it mean?** When approaching a problem, use the tools best suited to the job. In social studies course work, some of those tools are written essays, maps, graphs, and models. For example, a graph is often a better tool for visualizing the historical trends of a nation's economy than trying to describe those trends in an essay. Go to the many graphs in the text, such as in Module 1 Lesson 6 Segment 1, Module 7 Lesson 3 Segment 1, and Module 11 Lesson 4 Segment 3, and the Skillbuilder Handbook in the Online Student Edition for help.

MAFS.K12.MP.6.1 Attend to precision. Mathematically proficient students try to communicate precisely to others. They try to use clear definitions in discussion with others and in their own reasoning. They state the meaning of the symbols they choose, including using the equal sign consistently and appropriately. They are careful about specifying units of measure, and labeling axes to clarify the correspondence with quantities in a problem. They calculate accurately and efficiently, express numerical answers with a degree of precision appropriate for the problem context. In the elementary grades, students give carefully formulated explanations to each other. By the time they reach high school they have learned to examine claims and make explicit use of definitions. **What does it mean?** Be precise when communicating ideas and answers to others. In social studies as in math, precision avoids uncertainty and ensures the meaning and intent of arguments and solutions are understood. Go to Enrichment activities, such as Module 2 Lesson 3, Module 6 Lesson 2, and Module 18 Lesson 5, and the Skillbuilder Handbook in the Online Student Edition for help.

UNITED STATES HISTORY

SS.912.A.1 Use research and inquiry skills to analyze American history using primary and secondary sources. **What does it mean?** Develop the necessary skills to expand your understanding of American History. Understand the important role that primary and secondary sources play in researching and analyzing American history. Go to the Skillbuilder Handbook in the Online Student Edition for help.

SS.912.A.1.1 Describe the importance of historiography, which includes how historical knowledge is obtained and transmitted, when interpreting events in history. **What does it mean?** Understand that historiography refers to the study of how history is recorded and interpreted over time. Know why historiography is important when examining different topics of American history. Go to the Skillbuilder Handbook in the Online Student Edition for help.

SS.912.A.1.2 Utilize a variety of primary and secondary sources to identify author, historical significance, audience, and authenticity to understand a historical period. **What does it mean?** Develop a better understanding of the different periods of American history by using a variety of primary and secondary sources. Identify who created the source, why it was created, and why it is historically significant to better understand events of American history. Go to the Skillbuilder Handbook in the Online Student Edition for help.

SS.912.A.1.3 Utilize timelines to identify the time sequence of historical data. **What does it mean?** Examine timelines to gain a better grasp of the sequence of historical events. Go to the timelines that appear at the beginning of each module and the Skillbuilder Handbook in the Online Student Edition for help.

SS.912.A.1.4 Analyze how images, symbols, objects, cartoons, graphs, charts, maps, and artwork may be used to interpret the significance of time periods and events from the past. **What does it mean?** Explore how visuals can enhance your understanding of significant events and time periods of American history. Go to the Skillbuilder Handbook in the Online Student Edition for help.

SS.912.A.1.5 Evaluate the validity, reliability, bias, and authenticity of current events and Internet resources. **Remarks/Examples:** Students should be encouraged to utilize FINDS (Focus, Investigate, Note, Develop, Score), Florida's research process model accessible at: http://www.fldoe.org/bii/Library_Media/pdf/12TotalFINDS.pdf **What does it mean?** Analyze how reliably various Web sites portray current events. Learn how to identify the characteristics of credible Internet resources. Go to the HMH Current Events website and the Skillbuilder Handbook in the Online Student Edition for help.

SS.912.A.1.6 Use case studies to explore social, political, legal, and economic relationships in history. **What does it mean?** Carry out in-depth investigations of events in American history by using case studies. Go to the Historic Decisions of the Supreme Court features that appear in Modules 1, 5, 7, 10, 11, 14, 15, 17, and 18 for help.

SS.912.A.1.7 Describe various socio-cultural aspects of American life including arts, artifacts, literature, education, and publications. **What does it mean?** Understand the important role that arts, artifacts, literature, education, and publications have played throughout American history. Go to the American Literature features that appear in Modules 2, 4, 5, 8, 11, 12, 15, and 16 for help.

SS.912.A.2 Understand the causes, course, and consequences of the Civil War and Reconstruction and its effects on the American people. **What does it mean?** Trace the events that eventually led the Northern and Southern states to go to war with one another. Explain how the war and Reconstruction affected the American people. Go to Module 1 for help.

SS.912.A.2.1 Review causes and consequences of the Civil War. **Remarks/Examples:** Examples may include, but are not limited to, slavery, states' rights, territorial claims, abolitionist movement, regional differences, Reconstruction, 13th, 14th, and 15th amendments. **What does it mean?** Explain the key events leading to the outbreak of war between the Union and the Confederacy, and what consequences flowed from that conflict. Go to Module 1 for help.

SS.912.A.2.2 Assess the influence of significant people or groups on Reconstruction. **Remarks/Examples:** Examples may include, but are not limited to, Andrew Johnson, Radical Republicans, Jefferson Davis, Frederick Douglass, Ulysses S. Grant, Robert E. Lee, William T. Sherman, Buffalo Soldiers, Harriet Tubman, and Sojourner Truth. **What does it mean?** Evaluate how Reconstruction was affected by significant people and groups such as Andrew Johnson, the Radical Republicans, Frederick Douglass, and the Buffalo Soldiers. Go to Module 1 for help.

SS.912.A.2.3 Describe the issues that divided Republicans during the early Reconstruction era. **Remarks/Examples:** Examples may include, but are not limited to, the impeachment of Andrew Johnson, southern whites, blacks, black legislators and white extremist organizations such as the KKK, Knights of the White Camellia, The White League, Red Shirts, and Pale Faces. **What does it mean?** Identify the events and issues that divided the Republican Party during Reconstruction, such as the impeachment of Andrew Johnson and the actions of extremist organizations like the Ku Klux Klan. Go to Module 1 for help.

SS.912.A.2.4 Distinguish the freedoms guaranteed to African Americans and other groups with the 13th, 14th, and 15th Amendments to the Constitution. **Remarks/Examples:** Examples may include, but are not limited to, abolition of slavery, citizenship, suffrage, equal protection. **What does it mean?** Understand the purposes of these three Reconstruction amendments: ban slavery (Thirteenth Amendment), guarantee citizenship of all persons born in the United States (Fourteenth Amendment), and protect the right of freedmen to vote (Fifteenth Amendment). Go to Modules 1 and 5 for help.

SS.912.A.2.5 Assess how Jim Crow Laws influenced life for African Americans and other racial/ethnic minority groups. **What does it mean?** Describe the efforts made to restrict the newly won rights of freedpeople. Explain the purpose of Jim Crow laws and how those laws restricted the rights of African Americans and other minority groups. Go to Module 5 for help.

SS.912.A.2.6 Compare the effects of the Black Codes and the Nadir on freed people, and analyze the sharecropping system and debt peonage as practiced in the United States. **What does it mean?** Understand how Black Codes curtailed the civil liberties of African Americans during Reconstruction and afterward during the Nadir. Describe how the practices of sharecropping and debt peonage restricted the economic freedom of many African Americans. Go to Modules 1 and 5 for help.

SS.912.A.2.7 Review the Native American experience. **Remarks/Examples:** Examples may include, but are not limited to, westward expansion, reservation system, the Dawes Act, Wounded Knee Massacre, Sand Creek Massacre, Battle of Little Big Horn, Indian Schools, government involvement in the killing of the buffalo. **What does it mean?** Explain why the population in the West grew rapidly after Reconstruction and how that population growth affected Native Americans living there. Understand that significant events and issues in the Native American experience include the reservation system, the Dawes Act, the massacres at Sand Creek and Wounded Knee, and the Battle of Little Big Horn. Go to Modules 1, 2, 10, and 15 for help.

SS.912.A.3 Analyze the transformation of the American economy and the changing social and political conditions in response to the Industrial Revolution. **What does it mean?** Explain how industrial growth changed America's economy. Describe how those changes affected groups in the United States, such as immigrants and industrial workers. Go to Modules 1, 2, 3, 4, 5 and 8 for help.

SS.912.A.3.1 Analyze the economic challenges to American farmers and farmers' responses to these challenges in the mid to late 1800s. **Remarks/Examples:** Examples may include, but are not limited to, creation of agricultural colleges, Morrill Land Grant Act, gold standard and Bimetallism, the creation of the Populist Party. **What does it mean?** Identify the economic challenges faced by farmers in the mid- to late 1800s. Explore the issues and events related to agriculture during this period, including the creation of agricultural colleges, the Morrill Land Grant Act, the gold standard and bimetallism, and the rise of the Populist Party. Go to Modules 2, 3, and 4 for help.

SS.912.A.3.2 Examine the social, political, and economic causes, course, and consequences of the second Industrial Revolution that began in the late 19th century. **What does it mean?** Trace the development of the Second Industrial Revolution, and describe its social, political, and economic effects. Go to Module 3 for help.

SS.912.A.3.3 Compare the first and second Industrial Revolutions in the United States. **Remarks/Examples:** Examples may include, but are not limited to, trade, development of new industries. **What does it mean?** Understand that the Second Industrial Revolution is sometimes referred to as the Technological Revolution because it was characterized by the development of new technologies such as electricity and the internal combustion engine. Go to Modules 1 and 3 for help.

SS.912.A.3.4 Determine how the development of steel, oil, transportation, communication, and business practices affected the United States economy. **Remarks/Examples:** Examples may include, but are not limited to, railroads, the telegraph, pools, holding companies, trusts, corporations, contributed to westward expansion, expansion of trade and development of new industries, vertical and horizontal integration. **What does it mean?** Describe how the rapid technological and industrial changes of the late 1800s (such as railroads, the telegraph, corporations, and trusts) affected the American economy. Go to Modules 1, 2, and 3 for help.

SS.912.A.3.5 Identify significant inventors of the Industrial Revolution including African Americans and women. **Remarks/Examples:** Examples may include, but are not limited to, Lewis Howard Latimer, Jan E. Matzeliger, Sarah E. Goode, Granville T. Woods, Alexander Graham Bell, Thomas Edison, George Pullman, Henry Ford, Orville and Wilbur Wright, Elijah McCoy, Garrett Morgan, Madame C.J. Walker, George Westinghouse. **What does it mean?** Name American inventors of the Industrial Revolution (such as Thomas Edison, Lewis Latimer, and Jan E. Matzeliger), and describe the significance of their inventions. Go to Modules 1, 3, and 4 for help.

SS.912.A.3.6 Analyze changes that occurred as the United States shifted from agrarian to an industrial society. **Remarks/Examples:** Examples may include, but are not limited to, Social Darwinism, laissez-faire, government regulations of food and drugs, migration to cities, urbanization, changes to the family structure, Ellis Island, angel Island, push-pull factors. **What does it mean?** Describe how the shift from an agrarian society to an industrial society affected the nation. Recognize that this shift led to new developments such as the rise of Social Darwinism and the creation of government regulations for food and drugs. Go to Modules 1, 2, 3, and 4 for help.

SS.912.A.3.7 Compare the experience of European immigrants in the east to that of Asian immigrants in the west (the Chinese Exclusion Act, Gentlemen's Agreement with Japan). **Remarks/Examples:** Examples may include, but are not limited to nativism, integration of immigrants into society when comparing "Old" [before 1890] and "New" immigrants [after 1890], Immigration Act of 1924. **What does it mean?** Understand how the immigration experience of people from Asia differed from that of immigrants from Europe. Identify the impact of nativism, the Chinese Exclusion Act, and the Immigration Act of 1924. Go to Modules 1, 4, and 8 for help.

SS.912.A.3.8 Examine the importance of social change and reform in the late 19th and early 20th centuries (class system, migration from farms to cities, Social Gospel movement, role of settlement houses and churches in providing services to the poor). **What does it mean?** Explore social change and reform around the turn of the 20th century. Understand how the explosive growth of cities affected the people living there. Describe how American churches and reformers such as Jane Addams responded to these social changes. Go to Modules 4 and 5 for help.

SS.912.A.3.9 Examine causes, course, and consequences of the labor movement in the late 19th and early 20th centuries. **Remarks/Examples:** Examples may include, but are not limited to, unions, Knights of Labor, American Federation of Labor, socialist Party, labor laws. **What does it mean?** Understand that the Industrial Revolution profoundly changed the lives of American workers, and consider how these changes led to the rise of the labor movement. Explain the goals of the labor movement and how the movement affected the relationship between employers and employees. Go to Module 3 for help.

SS.912.A.3.10 Review different economic and philosophic ideologies. **Remarks/Examples:** Economic examples may include, but are not limited to, market economy, mixed economy, planned economy and philosophic examples are capitalism, socialism, communism, anarchy. **What does it mean?** Understand that economic ideologies include market, mixed, and planned economies, and that philosophic ideologies include capitalism, socialism, communism, and anarchy. Go to Modules 3 and 5 for help.

SS.912.A.3.11 Analyze the impact of political machines in United States cities in the late 19th and early 20th centuries. **Remarks/Examples:** Examples may include, but are not limited to, Boss Tweed, Tammany Hall, George Washington Plunkitt, Washington Gladden, Thomas Nast. **What does it mean?** Explore why political machines in American cities arose, why they thrived during the late 19th and early 20th centuries, and why many people struggled to dismantle them. Go to Modules 4 and 5 for help.

SS.912.A.3.12 Compare how different nongovernmental organizations and progressives worked to shape public policy, restore economic opportunities, and correct injustices in American life. **Remarks/Examples:** Examples may include, but are not limited to, NAACP, YMCA, Women's Christian Temperance Union, National Women's Suffrage Association, National Women's Party, Robert LaFollette, Florence Kelley, Ida M. Tarbell, Eugene Debs, Carrie Chapman Catt, Alice Paul, Theodore Roosevelt, William Taft, Woodrow Wilson, Upton Sinclair, Booker T. Washington, W.E.B. DuBois, Gifford Pinchot, William Jennings Bryan. **What does it mean?** Investigate how progressive individuals and nongovernmental organizations such as Florence Kelley, Ida M. Tarbell, W.E.B. DuBois, and the National Association for the Advancement of Colored People (NAACP) affected the lives of Americans in the late 19th century and early 20th century. Go to Module 5 for help.

SS.912.A.3.13 Examine key events and peoples in Florida history as they relate to United States history. **Remarks/Examples:** Examples may include, but are not limited to, the railroad industry, bridge construction in the Florida Keys, the cattle industry, the cigar industry, the influence of Cuban, Greek and Italian immigrants, Henry B. Plant, William Chipley, Henry Flagler, George Proctor, Thomas DeSaille Tucker, Hamilton Disston. **What does it mean?** Explore the relationship between American history and key people and events in Florida such as Henry B. Plant, Hamilton Disston, and bridge construction in the Florida Keys. Go to Modules 1, 3, and 5 for help.

SS.912.A.4 Demonstrate an understanding of the changing role of the United States in world affairs through the end of World War I. **What does it mean?** Trace the increasing role that the United States began to play in world affairs in the late 19th century and early 20th century. Go to Modules 6 and 7 for help.

SS.912.A.4.1 Analyze the major factors that drove United States imperialism. **Remarks/Examples:** Examples may include, but are not limited to, the Monroe Doctrine, Manifest Destiny, *The Influence of Sea Power Upon History*, Turner's thesis, the Roosevelt Corollary, natural resources, markets for resources, elimination of spheres of influence in China. **What does it mean?** Identify the factors that led to American imperialism, including Manifest Destiny, the Roosevelt Corollary, and the elimination of spheres of influence in China. Go to Module 6 for help.

SS.912.A.4.2 Explain the motives of the United States acquisition of the territories. **Remarks/Examples:** Examples may include, but are not limited to, Alaska, Hawaii, Puerto Rico, Philippines, Guam, Samoa, Marshall Islands, Midway Island, Virgin Islands. **What does it mean?** Identify why the United States wanted to acquire new territories such as Puerto Rico, Hawaii, Guam, and the Virgin Islands. Go to Module 6 for help.

SS.912.A.4.3 Examine causes, course, and consequences of the Spanish American War. **Remarks/Examples:** Examples may include, but are not limited to, Cuba as a protectorate, Yellow Journalism, sinking of the *Maine*, the Philippines, Commodore Dewey, the Rough Riders, acquisition of territories, the Treaty of Paris. **What does it mean?** Explain the reasons why the United States and Spain went to war and how the conflict was waged in the Caribbean and in the Philippines. Identify the new territories acquired by the United States as a result of the conflict. Go to Module 6 for help.

SS.912.A.4.4 Analyze the economic, military, and security motivations of the United States to complete the Panama Canal as well as major obstacles involved in its construction. **Remarks/Examples:** Examples may include, but are not limited to, disease, environmental impact, challenges faced by various ethnic groups such as Africans and indigenous populations, shipping routes, increased trade, defense and independence for Panama. **What does it mean?** Tell why U.S. leaders were determined to complete the Panama Canal, and describe the health risks and other challenges faced by those constructing the canal. Go to Module 6 for help.

SS.912.A.4.5 Examine causes, course, and consequences of United States involvement in World War I. **Remarks/Examples:** Examples may include, but are not limited to, nationalism, imperialism, militarism, entangling alliances vs. neutrality, Zimmerman Note, the *Lusitania*, the Selective Service Act, the homefront, the American Expeditionary Force, Wilson's Fourteen Points, the Treaty of Versailles (and opposition to it), isolationism. **What does it mean?** Trace the path that the United States took on the way to becoming involved in World War I and the key events that occurred as a result of American involvement. Go to Module 7 for help.

SS.912.A.4.6 Examine how the United States government prepared the nation for war with war measures (Selective Service Act, War Industries Board, war bonds, Espionage Act, Sedition Act, Committee of Public Information). **What does it mean?** Explain the role that the Selective Service Act, War Industries Board, and war bonds played in preparing the United States for World War I. Identify why government leaders thought it necessary to pass the Espionage Act and the Sedition Act. Go to Module 7 for help.

SS.912.A.4.7 Examine the impact of airplanes, battleships, new weaponry and chemical warfare in creating new war strategies (trench warfare, convoys). **What does it mean?** Describe how new technologies such as airplanes, battleships, machine guns, and deadly chemicals affected the course of the fighting during World War I. Go to Module 7 for help.

SS.912.A.4.8 Compare the experiences Americans (African Americans, Hispanics, Asians, women, conscientious objectors) had while serving in Europe. **What does it mean?** Understand that the experiences of American ethnic and racial groups serving in Europe often differed widely from those of other Americans overseas. Explain how the experiences of women and conscientious objectors also varied from that of other Americans. Go to Module 7 for help.

SS.912.A.4.9 Compare how the war impacted German Americans, Asian Americans, African Americans, Hispanic Americans, Jewish Americans, Native Americans, women and dissenters in the United States. **What does it mean?** Explore how women, opponents of the war, and different ethnic and racial groups were affected by World War I. Compare how their experiences were similar to and different from those of other Americans. Go to Module 7 for help.

SS.912.A.4.10 Examine the provisions of the Treaty of Versailles and the failure of the United States to support the League of Nations. **Remarks/Examples:** Examples may include, but are not limited to, self-determination, boundaries, demilitarized zone, sanctions reparations, and the League of Nations (including Article X of the Covenant). **What does it mean?** List the key aspects of the Treaty of Versailles and describe the goals of the proposed League of Nations. Explain how Congress and the nation reacted to President Woodrow Wilson's post-war plan. Go to Module 7 for help.

SS.912.A.4.11 Examine key events and peoples in Florida history as they relate to United States history. **Remarks/Examples:** Examples may include, but are not limited to, the Spanish-American War, Ybor City, Jose Marti. **What does it mean?** Explore the relationship between American history and key people and events in Florida during the late 19th and early 20th centuries, including the Spanish-American War, Ybor City, and José Martí. Go to Module 6 for help.

SS.912.A.5 Analyze the effects of the changing social, political, and economic conditions of the Roaring Twenties and the Great Depression. **What does it mean?** Describe the major political, economic, and social developments that followed the conclusion of World War I. Go to Modules 5, 7, 8, 9, 10, and 11 for help.

SS.912.A.5.1 Discuss the economic outcomes of demobilization. **What does it mean?** Explain how the demobilization of thousands of troops after World War I affected the U.S. economy and the lives of many Americans. Go to Module 8 for help.

SS.912.A.5.2 Explain the causes of the public reaction (Sacco and Vanzetti, labor, racial unrest) associated with the Red Scare. **Remarks/Examples:** Examples may also include, but are not limited to, Palmer Raids, FBI, J. Edgar Hoover. **What does it mean?** Identify why communism and socialism gained supporters and detractors in the United States in the early 20th century. Describe some of the events (the Sacco and Vanzetti trial, labor unrest, race riots), and explain how the federal government reacted to these events. Go to Module 8 for help.

SS.912.A.5.3 Examine the impact of United States foreign economic policy during the 1920s. **Remarks/Examples:** Examples may include, but are not limited to, the Depression of 1920-21, "The Business of America is Business," assembly line, installment buying, consumerism. **What does it mean?** Identify the effects of the federal government's economic policies during the 1920s, such as tax cuts, a reduction in federal spending, and high tariffs. Go to Module 8 for help.

SS.912.A.5.4 Evaluate how the economic boom during the Roaring Twenties changed consumers, businesses, manufacturing, and marketing practices. **What does it mean?** Explore how the economic boom of the 1920s led to the rise of automobile ownership, the mass production of goods, and the expanded use of marketing. Go to Module 8 for help.

SS.912.A.5.5 Describe efforts by the United States and other world powers to avoid future wars. **Remarks/Examples:** Examples may include, but are not limited to, League of Nations, Washington Naval Conference, London Conference, Kellogg-Briand Pact, the Nobel Prize. **What does it mean?** Identify examples of how the United States and other nations tried to avoid future wars, including the League of Nations, the Washington Naval Conference, the London Conference, and the Kellogg-Briand Pact. Go to Modules 7, 8, and 11 for help.

SS.912.A.5.6 Analyze the influence that Hollywood, the Harlem Renaissance, the Fundamentalist movement, and prohibition had in changing American society in the 1920s. **What does it mean?** Trace the rapidly increasing popularity of radio and movies in the years following World War I, and explain the significance of the Harlem Renaissance. Describe the rise of American fundamentalism during this period. Know the origins of the prohibition movement, what the Eighteenth Amendment prohibited, and why it was later repealed. Go to Module 8 for help.

SS.912.A.5.7 Examine the freedom movements that advocated civil rights for African Americans, Latinos, Asians, and women. **What does it mean?** Trace the women's suffrage movement to describe how women in the United States gained the right to vote. Describe other movements that called for the protection of the civil rights of African Americans, Latinos, and Asians. Go to Modules 5 and 8 for help.

SS.912.A.5.8 Compare the views of Booker T. Washington, W.E.B. DuBois, and Marcus Garvey relating to the African American experience. **What does it mean?** Explore the ideas of Booker T. Washington, W.E.B. DuBois, and Marcus Garvey, and identify in what ways these leaders agreed and disagreed with one another. Go to Modules 5 and 8 for help.

SS.912.A.5.9 Explain why support for the Ku Klux Klan varied in the 1920s with respect to issues such as anti-immigration, anti-African American, anti-Catholic, anti-Jewish, anti-women, and anti-union ideas. **Remarks/Examples:** Examples may include, but are not limited to, 100 Percent Americanism. **What does it mean?** Analyze what factors boosted the popularity of the Ku Klux Klan during the 1920s and how its criminal activities led to its decline. Go to Module 8 for help.

SS.912.A.5.10 Analyze support for and resistance to civil rights for women, African Americans, Native Americans, and other minorities. **What does it mean?** Describe the civil rights efforts of the early 20th century. Identify efforts to bolster and hinder the civil rights of women, African Americans, Native Americans, and other minorities. Go to Modules 5 and 8 for help.

SS.912.A.5.11 Examine causes, course, and consequences of the Great Depression and the New Deal. **What does it mean?** Recognize the causes of the Great Depression, such as drought, inflation, and the stock market crash, and the consequences, such as the New Deal plan for relief, recovery, and reform. Go to Modules 9 and 10 for help.

SS.912.A.5.12 Examine key events and people in Florida history as they relate to United States history. **Remarks/Examples:** Examples may include, but are not limited to, Rosewood, land boom, speculation, impact of climate and natural disasters on the end of the land boom, invention of modern air conditioning in 1929, Alfred DuPont, Marjorie Kinnan Rawlings, Zora Neale Hurston, James Weldon Johnson. **What does it mean?** Explore the relationship between American history and key people and events in Florida during the 1920s and 1930s, including Rosewood, the land boom, the impact of climate and natural disasters on the end of the land boom, the invention of modern air conditioning, Alfred DuPont, Marjorie Kinnan Rawlings, Zora Neale Hurston, and James Weldon Johnson. Go to Modules 9 and 10 for help.

SS.912.A.6 Understand the causes and course of World War II, the character of the war at home and abroad, and its reshaping of the United States role in the post–war world. **What does it mean?** Explain the causes of World War II, how the war was fought, how the war affected the lives of Americans back home, and why the war greatly expanded the U.S. economy, the federal government, and America's role in the post-war world. Go to Modules 11, 12, and 16 for help.

SS.912.A.6.1 Examine causes, course, and consequences of World War II on the United States and the world. **Remarks/Examples:** Examples may include, but are not limited to, rise of dictators, attack on Pearl Harbor, Nazi party, American neutrality, D-Day, Battle of the Bulge, War in the Pacific, internment camps, Holocaust, Yalta. **What does it mean?** Describe the causes and course of World War II and how the war affected the lives of Americans at home and abroad. Identify how the Cold War arose after the end of World War II. Go to Module 11 for help.

SS.912.A.6.2 Describe the United States response in the early years of World War II (Neutrality Acts, Cash and Carry, Lend Lease Act). **What does it mean?** Explain why, in the late 1930s and early 1940s, the United States refrained from offering direct military assistance to Great Britain. Describe the programs it did put in place to assist Britain during this period. Go to Module 11 for help.

SS.912.A.6.3 Analyze the impact of the Holocaust during World War II on Jews as well as other groups. **What does it mean?** Trace the course of the Holocaust in Germany and in German-controlled lands, identify which groups were targeted by the Nazis, and explain how the Holocaust affected these people. Go to Module 11 for help.

SS.912.A.6.4 Examine efforts to expand or contract rights for various populations during World War II. **Remarks/Examples:** Examples may include, but are not limited to, women, African Americans, German Americans, Japanese Americans and their internment, Native Americans, Hispanic Americans, Italian Americans. **What does it mean?** Understand that during World War II some groups in American society enjoyed greater opportunities while others found their opportunities and rights restricted. Describe how the rights of the following were affected during the war: women, African Americans, German Americans, Japanese Americans, Native Americans, Hispanic Americans, and Italian Americans. Go to Module 11 for help.

SS.912.A.6.5 Explain the impact of World War II on domestic government policy. **Remarks/Examples:** Examples may include, but are not limited to, rationing, national security, civil rights, increased job opportunities for African Americans, women, Jews, and other refugees. **What does it mean?** Explore how the war affected the federal government's domestic policies, including the implementation of a rationing program and increased job opportunities for African Americans, women, and Jews and other refugees. Go to Module 11 for help.

SS.912.A.6.6 Analyze the use of atomic weapons during World War II and the aftermath of the bombings. **What does it mean?** Consider why the United States used atomic weapons against Japan during World War II, and describe the destruction caused by these weapons. Go to Module 11 for help.

SS.912.A.6.7 Describe the attempts to promote international justice through the Nuremberg Trials. **What does it mean?** Understand that Nazi war crimes were tried during the Nuremberg Trials as a way to promote international justice. Go to Module 11 for help.

SS.912.A.6.8 Analyze the effects of the Red Scare on domestic United States policy. **Remarks/Examples:** Examples may include, but are not limited to, loyalty review program, House Un-American Activities Committee, McCarthyism (Sen. Joe McCarthy), McCarran Act. **What does it mean?** Examine the post–World War II Red Scare and identify some results of the scare, such as the activities of the House Un-American Activities Committee, McCarthyism, and the McCarran Act. Go to Module 12 for help.

SS.912.A.6.9 Describe the rationale for the formation of the United Nations, including the contribution of Mary McLeod Bethune. **Remarks/Examples:** Examples may include, but are not limited to, the Declaration of Human Rights. **What does it mean?** Identify that the United Nations was formed as an international organization to keep world peace and Mary McLeod Bethune was involved in developing the organization's charter. Go to Module 11 for help.

SS.912.A.6.10 Examine causes, course, and consequences of the early years of the Cold War (Truman Doctrine, Marshall Plan, NATO, Warsaw Pact). **What does it mean?** Explain why the United States developed the Marshall Plan and why it committed itself to stopping the spread of Soviet control in Europe. Describe how the Truman Doctrine and the so-called containment policy were both aimed at stopping communist aggression. Explain why the West and the Soviet Union each formed military alliances after World War II. Go to Module 12 for help.

SS.912.A.6.11 Examine the controversy surrounding the proliferation of nuclear technology in the United States and the world. **What does it mean?** Explore why opposition to the development and use of nuclear technology arose after World War II, and offer reasons why nuclear technology continues to be used. Go to Module 12 for help.

SS.912.A.6.12 Examine causes, course, and consequences of the Korean War. **Remarks/Examples:** Examples may include, but are not limited to, Communist China, 38th parallel, cease fire, firing of Gen. Douglas McArthur. **What does it mean?** Describe the origins, course, and consequences of the Korean War, including how the conflict related to the larger conflict of the Cold War. Go to Module 12 for help.

SS.912.A.6.13 Analyze significant foreign policy events during the Truman, Eisenhower, Kennedy, Johnson, and Nixon administrations. **Remarks/Examples:** Examples may include, but are not limited to, the Domino Theory, Sputnik, space race, Korean Conflict, Vietnam Conflict, U-2 and Gary Powers, Bay of Pigs invasion, Cuban Missile Crisis, Berlin Wall, Ping Pong Diplomacy, opening of China. **What does it mean?** Identify significant post–World War II foreign policy events, such as the Cuban missile crisis, the Gulf of Tonkin Resolution, the conflict in Vietnam, and relations with China. Go to Modules 12 and 16 for help.

SS.912.A.6.14 Analyze causes, course, and consequences of the Vietnam War. **Remarks/Examples:** Examples may include, but are not limited to, Geneva Accords, Gulf of Tonkin Resolution, the draft, escalating protest at home, Vietnamization, the War Powers Act. **What does it mean?** Understand how the United States became involved in the ongoing conflict between North Vietnam and South Vietnam. Describe the increasing role played by the United States in the region, and explain the consequences of the conflict. Go to Module 16 for help.

SS.912.A.6.15 Examine key events and peoples in Florida history as they relate to United States history. **Remarks/Examples:** Examples may include, but are not limited to, Mosquito Fleet, "Double V Campaign", construction of military bases and WWII training centers, 1959 Cuban coup and its impact on Florida, development of the space program and NASA. **What does it mean?** Explore the relationship between American history and key people and events in Florida during and after World War II, including the Mosquito Fleet, the "Double V Campaign," the construction of military bases and World War II training centers in Florida, the 1959 Cuban coup and its effect on Florida, and the development of the space program and NASA. Go to Modules 11, 12, and 16 for help.

SS.912.A.7 Understand the rise and continuing international influence of the United States as a world leader and the impact of contemporary social and political movements on American life. **What does it mean?** Describe how the United States changed in the decades following World War II. Understand that the nation took on a more visible role in the international community, experienced rapid economic growth, and expanded civil rights protections. Go to Modules 12, 13, 14, 15, 16, 17, 18, and 19 for help.

SS.912.A.7.1 Identify causes for Post-World War II prosperity and its effects on American society. **Remarks/Examples:** Examples may include, but are not limited to, G.I. Bill, Baby Boom, growth of suburbs, Beatnik movement, youth culture, religious revivalism (e.g., Billy Graham and Bishop Fulton J. Sheen), conformity of the 1950s and the protest in the 1960s. **What does it mean?** Analyze why the United States experienced increased prosperity after World War II. Examine the causes and effects of this prosperity, such as the G.I. Bill, the baby boom, and the growth of suburbs. Go to Module 13 for help.

SS.912.A.7.2 Compare the relative prosperity between different ethnic groups and social classes in the post-World War II period. **What does it mean?** Understand that although the nation as a whole experienced economic prosperity in the years following World War II, different ethnic groups and social classes benefited unequally from the economic boom. Go to Module 13 for help.

SS.912.A.7.3 Examine the changing status of women in the United States from post-World War II to present. **Remarks/Examples:** Examples may include, but are not limited to, increased numbers of women in the workforce, Civil Rights Act of 1964, *The Feminine Mystique*, National Organization for Women, *Roe* v. *Wade*, Equal Rights Amendment, Title IX, Betty Freidan, Gloria Steinem, Phyllis Schlafly, Billie Jean King, feminism. **What does it mean?** Identify ways that the role of women in the United States has changed since World War II, such as having more women in the workforce and politics. Go to Modules 13 and 15 for help.

SS.912.A.7.4 Evaluate the success of 1960s era presidents' foreign and domestic policies. **Remarks/Examples:** Examples may include, but are not limited to, civil rights legislation, Space Race, Great Society, War on Poverty. **What does it mean?** Describe how successful various foreign and domestic policies of the 1960s were, including civil rights legislation, the Space Race, and the Great Society. Go to Modules 12, 14, and 16 for help.

SS.912.A.7.5 Compare nonviolent and violent approaches utilized by groups (African Americans, women, Native Americans, Hispanics) to achieve civil rights. **Remarks/Examples:** Examples may include, but are not limited to, sit-ins, Freedom Rides, boycotts, riots, protest marches. **What does it mean?** Explore how various groups acted in violent and nonviolent ways to protect and expand their civil rights in the years following World War II. Go to Module 15 for help.

SS.912.A.7.6 Assess key figures and organizations in shaping the Civil Rights Movement and Black Power Movement. **Remarks/Examples:** Examples may include, but are not limited to, the NAACP, National Urban League, SNCC, CORE, James Farmer, Charles Houston, Thurgood Marshall, Rosa Parks, Constance Baker Motley, the Little Rock Nine, Roy Wilkins, Whitney M. Young, A. Philip Randolph, Dr. Martin Luther King, Jr., Robert F. Williams, Fannie Lou Hamer, Malcolm X [El-Hajj Malik El-Shabazz], Stokely Carmichael [Kwame Ture], H. Rap Brown [Jamil Abdullah Al-Amin], the Black Panther Party [e.g., Huey P. Newton, Bobby Seale]. **What does it mean?** Examine the influence of key persons and organizations in the Civil Rights Movement and Black Power Movement, such as Martin Luther King, Rosa Parks, the NAACP, and Malcolm X. Go to Module 15 for help.

SS.912.A.7.7 Assess the building of coalitions between African Americans, whites, and other groups in achieving integration and equal rights. **Remarks/Examples:** Examples may include, but are not limited to, Freedom Summer, Freedom Rides, Montgomery Bus Boycott, Tallahassee Bus Boycott of 1956, March on Washington. **What does it mean?** Trace the way that African Americans, whites, and other groups worked together to achieve integration and equal rights, and understand what occurred at landmark events such as Freedom Summer, the Freedom Rides, the Montgomery Bus Boycott, the Tallahassee Bus Boycott of 1956, and the March on Washington. Go to Module 15 for help.

SS.912.A.7.8 Analyze significant Supreme Court decisions relating to integration, busing, affirmative action, the rights of the accused, and reproductive rights. **Remarks/Examples:** Examples may include, but are not limited to, Plessy v. Ferguson [1896], Brown v. Board of Education [1954], Swann v. Charlotte-Mecklenburg Board of Education [1971], Regents of the University of California v. Bakke [1978], Miranda v. Arizona [1966], Gideon v. Wainwright [1963], Mapp v. Ohio [1961], and Roe v. Wade [1973]. **What does it mean?** Identify the importance of landmark Supreme Court rulings on issues such as integration (*Brown v. Board of Education*), affirmative action (*Regents of the University of California v. Bakke*), rights of the accused (*Miranda v. Arizona*), and reproductive rights (*Roe v. Wade*). Go to Modules 14, 15, and 17 for help.

SS.912.A.7.9 Examine the similarities of social movements (Native Americans, Hispanics, women, anti-war protesters) of the 1960s and 1970s. **What does it mean?** Describe social movements of the 1960s and 1970s, such as reimbursement for Native American lands, working conditions of Hispanics and bilingual and bicultural education, and women's rights. Go to Modules 14, 15, and 16 for help.

SS.912.A.7.10 Analyze the significance of Vietnam and Watergate on the government and people of the United States. **Remarks/Examples:** Examples may include, but are not limited to, mistrust of government, reinforcement of freedom of the press, as well as checks and balances, *New York Times v. Nixon*. **What does it mean?** Explain why many Americans objected to American involvement in Vietnam, how protestors expressed their objections, and what effect their protests had on political support for the war. Describe how the Watergate scandal affected Americans' attitude toward government. Go to Modules 16 and 17 for help.

SS.912.A.7.11 Analyze the foreign policy of the United States as it relates to Africa, Asia, the Caribbean, Latin America, and the Middle East. **Remarks/Examples:** Examples may include, but are not limited to, Haiti, Bosnia-Kosovo, Rwanda, Grenada, Camp David Accords, Iran Hostage Crisis, Lebanon, Iran-Iraq War, Reagan Doctrine, Iran-Contra Affair, Persian Gulf War. **What does it mean?** Evaluate the foreign policy that the United States developed in regard to Africa, Asia, the Caribbean, Latin America, and the Middle East. Go to Module 17 for help.

SS.912.A.7.12 Analyze political, economic, and social concerns that emerged at the end of the 20th century and into the 21st century. **Remarks/Examples:** Examples may include, but are not limited to, AIDS, Green Revolution, outsourcing of jobs, global warming, human rights violations. **What does it mean?** Identify and explore the political, economic, and social issues that the country confronted during the late 1900s to early 2000s. Go to Modules 17, 18, and 19 for help.

SS.912.A.7.13 Analyze the attempts to extend New Deal legislation through the Great Society and the successes and failures of these programs to promote social and economic stability. **Remarks/Examples:** Examples may include, but are not limited to, Civil Rights Act of 1964, Voting Rights Act of 1965, War on Poverty, Medicare, Medicaid, Headstart. **What does it mean?** Describe President Lyndon Johnson's anti-poverty policies (such as Medicare and Medicaid, urban development, housing, and transit), and evaluate how effective they were at promoting social and economic stability. Go to Module 14 for help.

SS.912.A.7.14 Review the role of the United States as a participant in the global economy (trade agreements, international competition, impact on American labor, environmental concerns). **Remarks/Examples:** Examples may include, but are not limited to, NAFTA, World Trade Organization. **What does it mean?** Identify ways the United States participates in the global economy, such as by trading with other countries and making trade agreements, and describe how this participation has affected American labor and the environment. Go to Modules 18 and 19 for help.

SS.912.A.7.15 Analyze the effects of foreign and domestic terrorism on the American people. **Remarks/Examples:** Examples may include, but are not limited to, Oklahoma City bombing, attack of September 11, 2001, Patriot Act, wars in Afghanistan and Iraq. **What does it mean?** Describe how foreign and domestic terrorism (such as the Oklahoma City bombing and the attacks of September 11, 2001) have affected the American people. Explain the relationship between the attacks of September 11, 2001, and the wars in Afghanistan and Iraq. Go to Modules 18 and 19 for help.

SS.912.A.7.16 Examine changes in immigration policy and attitudes toward immigration since 1950. **What does it mean?** Recognize that immigration policy and attitudes toward immigration have changed since 1950, and describe some of those key changes. Go to Modules 14, 15, and 18 for help.

SS.912.A.7.17 Examine key events and key people in Florida history as they relate to United States history. **Remarks/Examples:** Examples may include, but are not limited to, selection of Central Florida as a location for Disney, growth of the citrus and cigar industries, construction of Interstates, Harry T. Moore, Pork Chop Gang, Claude Pepper, changes in the space program, use of DEET, Hurricane Andrew, the Election of 2000, migration and immigration, Sunbelt state. **What does it mean?** Explore the relationship between American history and key people and events in Florida during and after World War II, including the selection of Central Florida as the location for Walt Disney World, the growth of the citrus and cigar industries, the construction of interstates, changes in the space program, the use of DEET, Hurricane Andrew, the 2000 election, and migration and immigration. Go to Modules 17, 18, and 19 for help.

GEOGRAPHY

SS.912.G.1 Understand how to use maps and other geographic representations, tools, and technology to report information. **What does it mean?** Explore how maps and other geographic representations can help you understand the ways that geography has affected American history. Go to the Geography Handbook and the Skillbuilder Handbook in the Online Student Edition for help.

SS.912.G.1.2 Use spatial perspective and appropriate geographic terms and tools, including the Six Essential Elements, as organizational schema to describe any given place. **What does it mean?** Use spatial perspective (where something is located) and geographic terms and tools to organize and identify information about a particular location. Go to Modules 1, 2, 6, 11, and 12 for help.

SS.912.G.1.3 Employ applicable units of measurement and scale to solve simple locational problems using maps and globes. **What does it mean?** Use appropriate units of measurement and scale to determine the distance between two places on a map or globe to solve simple problems. Go to maps in Module 7 Lesson 1 Segment 2 and Module 12 Lesson 5 Segment 2 in the Print Student Edition and Module 18 Lesson 4 Enrichment and Module 19 Lesson 6 Enrichment in the Online Student Edition for help.

SS.912.G.2 Understand physical and cultural characteristics of places. **What does it mean?** Describe the physical and cultural characteristics of a particular location. Go to the Geography Handbook in the Online Student Edition for help.

SS.912.G.2.1 Identify the physical characteristics and the human characteristics that define and differentiate regions. **Remarks/Examples:** Examples of physical characteristics are climate, terrain, resources. Examples of human characteristics are religion, government, economy, demography. **What does it mean?** Identify physical characteristics (such as climate and terrain), and human elements (such as religion and economy) that explain settlement patterns in various regions of the United States over time. Go to Modules 2 and 9 for help.

SS.912.G.4 Understand the characteristics, distribution, and migration of human populations. **What does it mean?** Describe the causes and effects of the movement and settlement of human populations in the United States over time. Go to the Geography Handbook in the Online Student Edition for help.

SS.912.G.4.2 Use geographic terms and tools to analyze the push/pull factors contributing to human migration within and among places. **What does it mean?** Understand how to use geographic terms and tools to describe how human migration has been affected by push/pull factors. Go to Modules 4, 9, and 18 for help.

SS.912.G.4.3 Use geographic terms and tools to analyze the effects of migration both on the place of origin and destination, including border areas. **What does it mean?** Understand how to use geographic terms and tools to examine the effects of migration on both where people migrate from and where they migrate to. Go to Module 4 Lesson 1 Enrichment and Module 18 Lesson 5 Enrichment in the Online Student Edition for help.

HUMANITIES

SS.912.H.1 Identify and analyze the historical, social, and cultural contexts of the arts. **What does it mean?** Understand how the arts have affected the people of the United States over time. Go to Historical Source features that appear throughout the text, such as in Modules 1, 5, and 13, for help.

SS.912.H.1.1 Relate works in the arts (architecture, dance, music, theatre, and visual arts) of varying styles and genre according to the periods in which they were created. **Remarks/Examples:** Examples are Bronze Age, Ming Dynasty, Classical, Renaissance, Modern, and Contemporary. **What does it mean?** Identify works in the arts, including architecture, music, and visual arts, from different time periods of American history. Go to Historical Source features that appear throughout the text, such as in Modules 1, 5, and 13, for help.

SS.912.H.1.3 Relate works in the arts to various cultures. **Remarks/Examples:** Examples are African, Asian, Oceanic, European, the Americas, Middle Eastern, Egyptian, Greek, Roman. **What does it mean?** Understand that artistic works are created by various cultures. Examples of cultures include African, Asian, Oceanic, European, the Americas, Middle Eastern, Egyptian, Greek, and Roman. Go to Modules 8, 13, and 14 for help.

SS.912.H.1.5 Examine artistic response to social issues and new ideas in various cultures. **Remarks/Examples:** Examples are Victor Hugo's Les Miserables, Langston Hughes' poetry, Pete Seeger's Bring 'Em Home. **What does it mean?** Understand that artists' works (such as Langston Hughes' poetry) are often created in response to social issues and new ideas. Go to the American Literature features that appear in Modules 2, 4, 5, 8, 11, 12, 15, and 16 for help.

SS.912.H.3 Understand how transportation, trade, communication, science, and technology influence the progression and regression of cultures. **What does it mean?** Understand that cultural changes are often strongly affected by developments in transportation, trade, communication, science, and technology. Go to Modules 18 and 19 for help.

SS.912.H.3.1 Analyze the effects of transportation, trade, communication, science, and technology on the preservation and diffusion of culture. **What does it mean?** Identify the effects of transportation, trade, communication, science, and technology on the preservation of a culture and its diffusion to other locations. Go to Modules 18 and 19 for help.

Module 1
Prologue: American Beginnings

★

Essential Question
How has early American history shaped our lives today?

About the Painting: This painting depicts the arrival of English explorer Henry Hudson in the Bay of New York in 1609. Native Americans watch as the ship moves toward the shore.

In this module you will learn about the earliest years of the United States, from the arrival of the first Europeans through independence and expansion to the Civil War and its aftermath.

▶ Explore ONLINE!

HISTORY

VIDEOS, including...
- The Declaration of Independence
- Saratoga: Force Surrender
- America Gets a Constitution
- The Invention of the Telegraph
- Frederick Douglass
- Independence for Texas
- Underground Railroad
- The South Secedes
- After the Assassination
- President Grant: The Celebrity
- **Multimedia Connections**

☑ Document-Based Investigations

☑ Graphic Organizers

☑ Interactive Games

☑ Animation: The Cotton Gin

☑ Image with Hotspots: The Attack on Fort Sumter

SS.912.A.1.2 Utilize a variety of primary and secondary sources to identify author, historical significance, audience, and authenticity to understand a historical period. **SS.912.A.1.4** Analyze how images, symbols, objects, cartoons, graphs, charts, maps, and artwork may be used to interpret the significance of time periods and events from the past. **SS.912.A.1.6** Use case studies to explore social, political, legal, and economic relationships in history. **SS.912.A.2.1** Review causes and consequences of the Civil War. **SS.912.A.2.2** Assess the influence of significant people or groups on Reconstruction. **SS.912.A.2.3** Describe the issues that divided Republicans during the early Reconstruction era. **SS.912.A.2.4** Distinguish the freedoms guaranteed to African Americans and other groups with the 13th, 14th, and 15th Amendments to the Constitution. **SS.912.A.2.6** Compare the effects of the Black Codes and the Nadir on freed people, and analyze the sharecropping system and debt peonage as practiced in the United States. **SS.912.A.2.7** Review the Native American experience. **SS.912.A.3.3** Compare the first and second Industrial Revolutions in the United States. **SS.912.A.3.4** Determine how the development of steel, oil, transportation, communication, and business practices affected the United States economy. **SS.912.A.3.5** Identify significant inventors of the Industrial Revolution including African Americans and women. **SS.912.A.3.6** Analyze changes that occurred as the United States shifted from agrarian to an industrial society. **SS.912.A.3.7** Compare the experience of European immigrants in the east to that of Asian immigrants in the west. **SS.912.A.3.13** Examine key events and peoples in Florida history as they relate to United States history. **SS.912.G.2.1** Identify the physical characteristics and the human characteristics that define and differentiate regions. **SS.912.G.4.2** Use geographic terms and tools to analyze the push/pull factors contributing to human migration within and among places. **SS.912.G.4.3** Use geographic terms and tools to analyze the effects of migration both on the place of origin and destination, including border areas. **SS.912.H.1.1** Relate works in the arts of varying styles and genre according to the periods in which they were created.

Timeline of Events 1439–1878

▶ *Explore ONLINE!*

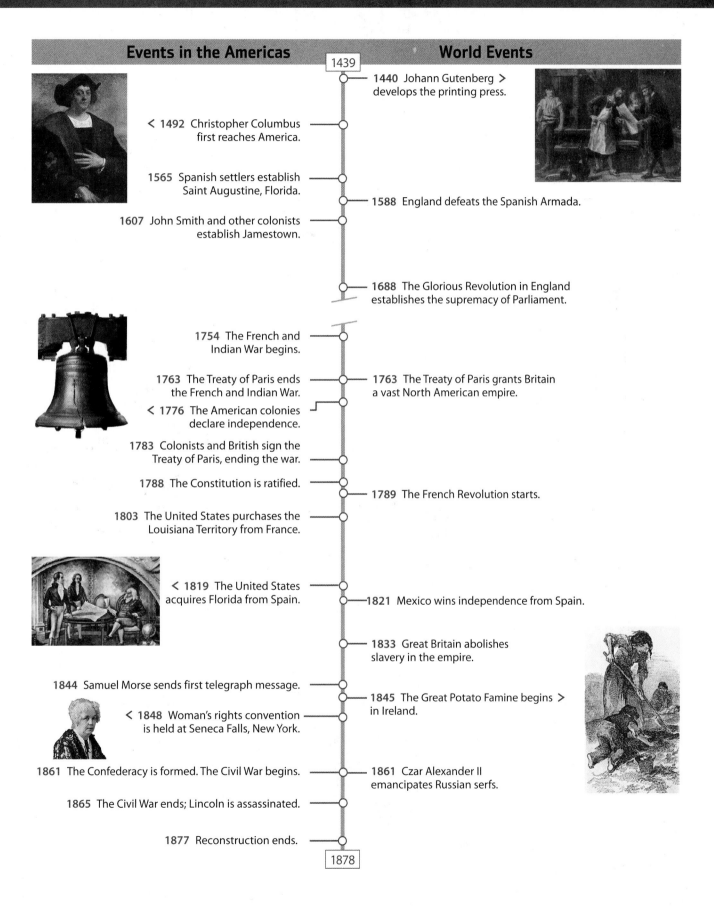

Events in the Americas		World Events

1439

1440 Johann Gutenberg ❯ develops the printing press.

❮ **1492** Christopher Columbus first reaches America.

1565 Spanish settlers establish Saint Augustine, Florida.

1588 England defeats the Spanish Armada.

1607 John Smith and other colonists establish Jamestown.

1688 The Glorious Revolution in England establishes the supremacy of Parliament.

1754 The French and Indian War begins.

1763 The Treaty of Paris ends the French and Indian War.

1763 The Treaty of Paris grants Britain a vast North American empire.

❮ **1776** The American colonies declare independence.

1783 Colonists and British sign the Treaty of Paris, ending the war.

1788 The Constitution is ratified.

1789 The French Revolution starts.

1803 The United States purchases the Louisiana Territory from France.

❮ **1819** The United States acquires Florida from Spain.

1821 Mexico wins independence from Spain.

1833 Great Britain abolishes slavery in the empire.

1844 Samuel Morse sends first telegraph message.

1845 The Great Potato Famine begins ❯ in Ireland.

❮ **1848** Woman's rights convention is held at Seneca Falls, New York.

1861 The Confederacy is formed. The Civil War begins.

1861 Czar Alexander II emancipates Russian serfs.

1865 The Civil War ends; Lincoln is assassinated.

1877 Reconstruction ends.

1878

The Colonial Era

The Big Idea

Beginning in the late 1400s, European monarchs sponsored exploration to find new trade routes and establish colonies in the Americas.

Why It Matters Now

European colonization of the Americas led to the founding of the United States.

Key Terms and People

Christopher Columbus

Juan Ponce de León

encomienda

joint-stock companies

Jamestown

William Penn

mercantilism

triangular trade

Enlightenment

Great Awakening

French and Indian War

SS.912.A.1.2; SS.912.A.1.4; SS.912.A.1.7; SS.912.A.2.7; SS.912.A.3.13; SS.912.G.1.2; SS.912.G.2.1; LAFS.1112.RH.3.8; LAFS.1112.RH.4.10

One European's Story

In January 1492 the Genoese sailor **Christopher Columbus** stood before the Spanish court with a daring plan: he would find a route to Asia by sailing west across the Atlantic Ocean. The plan was accepted, and on August 3, 1492, Columbus embarked on a voyage that changed the course of history. He began his journal by restating the deal he had struck with Spain.

Christopher Columbus, around 1519

"Based on the information that I had given Your Highnesses about the land of India and about a Prince who is called the Great Khan [of China], which in our language means 'King of Kings,' Your Highnesses decided to send me . . . to the regions of India, to see . . . the peoples and the lands, and to learn of . . . the measures which could be taken for their conversion to our Holy Faith. . . . Your Highnesses . . . ordered that I shall go to the east, but not by land as is customary. I was to go by way of the west, whence until today we do not know with certainty that anyone has gone. . . ."

—Christopher Columbus, from his log

Although Columbus did not find a route to Asia, his voyage set in motion a process that brought together the American and European worlds.

Spanish Colonies

The European interest in overseas expansion probably began in the 1200s with Marco Polo's journey to China. His published account in 1477 renewed interest. At that time, merchants had to travel to Asia by land, a costly and dangerous journey. Europeans wanted to find alternative routes. Merchants and explorers studied travelers' reports and reexamined maps drawn by ancient geographers.

SAILING TECHNOLOGY IMPROVES The explorers also used the advanced technology of the period. European ship captains in the 1400s tried new sailing vessels such as the caravel and navigating tools such as the compass and the astrolabe, which helped sailors plot direction at sea. One leader in these developments was Prince Henry the Navigator of Portugal, who sent ships to explore the west coast of Africa.

Portuguese explorations continued after Prince Henry died. Bartolomeu Dias rounded the southern tip of Africa in 1488. Vasco da Gama reached India ten years later. This new route around Africa to eastern Asia reduced traders' costs and increased their profits. While cartographers redrew their maps to show this new route, an Italian sea captain named Christopher Columbus believed there was a shorter route west across the Atlantic.

COLUMBUS CROSSES THE ATLANTIC In October 1492, roughly two months after leaving Spain, Columbus's ships, the *Niña*, the *Pinta*, and the *Santa María*, reached land, which he claimed for Spain. Columbus explored islands in the Bahamas and the coastlines of present-day Cuba and Hispaniola. Believing that these were islands off Asia known to Europeans as the Indies, Columbus called the people he met *los indios*.

Historical Source

Columbus Describes the Taino

On the first day of their encounter, the generosity of the Taino startled Columbus. "They are friendly and well-dispositioned people who bear no arms," he wrote in his log. "They traded and gave everything they had with good will." But after only two days, Columbus offered an assessment of the Taino that had dark implications for the future.

> *"It would be unnecessary to build . . . [a fort here] because these people are so simple in deeds of arms. . . . If Your Highnesses order either to bring all of them to Castile or to hold them as captivos [slaves] on their own island it could easily be done, because with about fifty men you could control and subjugate them all, making them do whatever you want."*
>
> —Christopher Columbus, quoted in Columbus: *The Great Adventure*

Analyze Historical Sources
Why do you think Columbus and other Spanish explorers would want to "subjugate" the Taino people?

Vocabulary
colonize to establish settlements under the control of a parent country

Hernándo Cortés

Reading Check
Analyze Motives
Why did the Spanish support exploration and colonization?

THE SPANISH CLAIM A NEW EMPIRE The Spanish monarchs funded three more of Columbus's voyages to colonize the newly claimed lands. Other Spanish explorers claimed more colonies for Spain. These *conquistadors* (kŏng-kē′stə-dôrz′) imagined vast lands filled with gold and silver. Hernándo Cortés landed in Mexico in 1519 and led troops inland to the Aztec Empire, where they found gold and silver. By 1521 Cortés had conquered the Aztecs. In 1532 Francisco Pizarro plundered the Inca Empire on the western coast of South America. Both lands became part of a Spanish Empire that included Mexico, parts of Central and South America, and much of the Caribbean.

Spain also sent explorers into what is now the southern United States. They set up outposts to protect their holdings and to spread their culture and religion to the Native Americans. Beginning with the efforts of **Juan Ponce de León** in 1513, the Spanish settled in present-day Florida. In 1565 they founded St. Augustine on the Florida coast. It became the oldest European-founded city in what is now the United States.

In building their American Empire, Spanish men tended to intermarry with native women. This practice eventually created a large *mestizo* (mĕs-tē′zō)—or mixed Spanish and Native American—population. However, the Spanish also oppressed the Native Americans, forcing them to work as slave labor in the **encomienda** (ĕng-kô-myĕn′dä) system. A number of Spanish priests demanded an end to the harsh encomienda system. In 1542 the Spanish monarchy abolished it. To meet their labor needs, the Spaniards began to use enslaved Africans.

SPAIN EXPLORES THE SOUTHWEST AND WEST Throughout the mid-1500s the Spanish also explored and settled in what are now the southwest and west regions of the United States. In 1540 Francisco Vasquez de Coronado traveled throughout what are now Texas, Oklahoma, Arizona, New Mexico, and Kansas in search of another wealthy empire to conquer. Failing to find gold and other treasures, the dejected conquistador returned home.

Some 50 years later, the Spanish returned to the modern-day Southwest—in search not of riches but of Christian converts. Spanish priests arrived in the Americas to spread Roman Catholicism. In the winter of 1609–1610, Pedro de Peralta, governor of Spain's northern holdings called New Mexico, built a capital called Santa Fe, or "Holy Faith." An 1,800-mile trail known as El Camino Real, or "the Royal Road," was established to carry goods between Santa Fe and Mexico City. In the next two decades, a string of Catholic missions arose among the Pueblos in the area. Other Spanish missionaries established missions in modern-day Texas and California.

English Colonies

Unlike Spanish colonies funded by the country's rulers, the English colonies were often funded by **joint-stock companies**. Joint-stock companies allowed investors to pool their wealth in support of a colony that they hoped would yield a profit. One joint-stock company, the Virginia Company, sent colonists to settle in North America.

THE ENGLISH SETTLE AT JAMESTOWN In April 1607 the Virginia Company colonists reached the North American shore and sailed partway up a river leading into Chesapeake Bay. Led by John Smith and others, the colonists selected a small, defensible peninsula where they established the settlement of **Jamestown**, named for their king.

Investors in the Jamestown colony demanded a quick return on their investment, and the colonists hoped to find gold to satisfy them. Consequently, they neglected farming and suffered the consequences. Disease from contaminated river water struck them first, followed soon by hunger.

John Smith held the colony together by forcing the colonists to farm and by securing food and support from the native Powhatan peoples. When Smith returned to England, the colony deteriorated to the point of famine. The settlement was saved, however, by the arrival of new colonists and by the development of a highly profitable crop, tobacco.

PURITANS CREATE A "NEW ENGLAND" A second permanent English colony came about for a very different reason. The Church of England had separated from the Catholic Church. However, one religious group, the Puritans, felt that the church had kept too much Catholic ritual. They wanted to "purify," or reform, the church by eliminating all traces of Catholicism. Some Puritans, called Separatists, wanted to separate from the English Church. They often met in secret to avoid the punishment inflicted upon those who did not follow the Anglican form of worship.

One congregation of Separatists, known today as the Pilgrims, eventually migrated to America. There, in 1620 this small group of families founded the Plymouth Colony. Their Mayflower Compact, or agreement, named for the ship on which they sailed, stated that the purpose of their government in America would be to frame "just and equal laws . . . for the general good of the colony." The document became an important landmark in the development of American democracy.

Vocabulary
repression
the act of putting
down by force

Other Puritans who were not Separatists felt the burden of increasing religious persecution, political repression, and dismal economic conditions. In 1630 a group of Puritans established the Massachusetts Bay Colony along the upper coast of North America. The port town of Boston soon became the colony's thriving capital. Settlers eventually incorporated the Plymouth Colony into the Massachusetts Bay Colony.

The Puritans had come to America to follow their own form of worship, but they were intolerant of people who had dissenting religious beliefs. One such dissenter was Roger Williams, an extreme Separatist, who expressed two controversial views. First, he declared that the English settlers had no rightful claim to the land unless they purchased it from Native Americans. Second, Williams argued that every person should be free to worship according to his or her conscience.

When officials tried to deport Williams back to England, he fled Massachusetts and traveled south. He negotiated with a local Native American group for a plot of land and set up a new colony, which he called Providence. In Providence, later the capital of Rhode Island, Williams guaranteed religious freedom and separation of church and state.

SETTLEMENT OF THE MIDDLE COLONIES While English Puritans were establishing colonies in New England, the Dutch were founding one to the south. The Dutch established a fur trade with the Iroquois and built trading posts on the Hudson River. In 1621 the Dutch government granted the newly formed Dutch West India Company permission to colonize New Netherland and expand the thriving fur trade. New Amsterdam (now New York City), became the capital of the colony. In 1664 the English took over the colony without a fight. The Duke of York, the new owner of the colony, renamed it New York. He later gave a portion of this land to two of his friends, naming this territory New Jersey for the British island of Jersey.

The acquisition of New Netherland was one step in England's quest to extend its American empire after 1660. King Charles II owed a debt to the father of a young man named **William Penn**. As payment, Charles gave the younger Penn a large area of land that the king insisted be called Pennsylvania, or "Penn's Woods," after the father.

William Penn belonged to the Society of Friends, or Quakers, a Protestant sect that held services without formal ministers, allowing any person to speak as the spirit moved him or her. They dressed plainly, refused to defer to persons of rank, and opposed war. Penn wanted to establish a good and fair society in keeping with Quaker ideals. His plan for government called for a representative assembly and freedom of religion. Like Roger Williams before him, Penn believed that the land belonged to the Native Americans, and he saw to it that they were paid for it.

Reading Check
Contrast
How did the English colonies differ from the Spanish colonies?

Colonial Economies

During the 1600s and 1700s, more British colonies in North America were founded as kings granted land to various supporters. By 1733 there were 13 British colonies that existed primarily for the benefit of England. The colonies exported to England a rich variety of raw materials, such as lumber and furs. In return, they imported the manufactured goods that England produced.

ENGLAND AND ITS COLONIES PROSPER Beginning in the 16th century, the nations of Europe competed for wealth and power under a new economic system called **mercantilism** (mûr'kən-tē-lĭz'əm). According to mercantilism, a nation could increase its power in two ways: by obtaining as much gold and silver as possible, and by establishing a favorable balance of trade, in which it sold more goods than it bought. A nation's ultimate goal was to become self-sufficient so that it did not have to depend on other countries for goods.

The key to becoming economically independent was the establishment of colonies. Colonies provided products, especially raw materials, and they bought goods manufactured in the home country. The American colonies were fulfilling this role, but some of the colonial merchants sold their products to Spain, France, and Holland. England viewed the colonists' pursuit of foreign markets as an economic threat. In 1651 England's Parliament, the country's legislative body, moved to tighten control of colonial trade by passing the Navigation Acts. Among the rules established by the acts was the

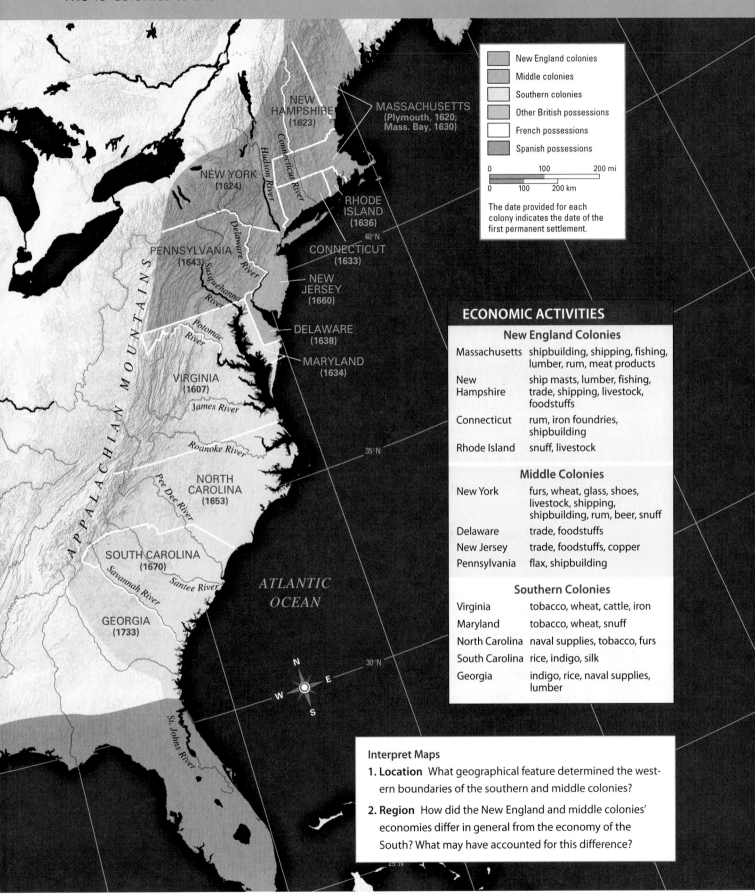

The 13 Colonies to the 1700s

New England colonies
Middle colonies
Southern colonies
Other British possessions
French possessions
Spanish possessions

| 0 | 100 | 200 mi |
| 0 | 100 | 200 km |

The date provided for each colony indicates the date of the first permanent settlement.

MASSACHUSETTS
(Plymouth, 1620;
Mass. Bay, 1630)

NEW HAMPSHIRE
(1623)

NEW YORK
(1624)

Connecticut River

Hudson River

RHODE ISLAND
(1636)

40°N

CONNECTICUT
(1633)

Delaware River

PENNSYLVANIA
(1643)

Susquehanna River

NEW JERSEY
(1660)

DELAWARE
(1638)

Potomac River

MARYLAND
(1634)

VIRGINIA
(1607)

James River

Roanoke River

35°N

APPALACHIAN MOUNTAINS

Pee Dee River

NORTH CAROLINA
(1653)

SOUTH CAROLINA
(1670)

Savannah River

Santee River

ATLANTIC OCEAN

GEORGIA
(1733)

30°N

St. Johns River

ECONOMIC ACTIVITIES

New England Colonies

Massachusetts	shipbuilding, shipping, fishing, lumber, rum, meat products
New Hampshire	ship masts, lumber, fishing, trade, shipping, livestock, foodstuffs
Connecticut	rum, iron foundries, shipbuilding
Rhode Island	snuff, livestock

Middle Colonies

New York	furs, wheat, glass, shoes, livestock, shipping, shipbuilding, rum, beer, snuff
Delaware	trade, foodstuffs
New Jersey	trade, foodstuffs, copper
Pennsylvania	flax, shipbuilding

Southern Colonies

Virginia	tobacco, wheat, cattle, iron
Maryland	tobacco, wheat, snuff
North Carolina	naval supplies, tobacco, furs
South Carolina	rice, indigo, silk
Georgia	indigo, rice, naval supplies, lumber

Interpret Maps

1. **Location** What geographical feature determined the western boundaries of the southern and middle colonies?

2. **Region** How did the New England and middle colonies' economies differ in general from the economy of the South? What may have accounted for this difference?

requirement that only English or colonial ships be used for the colonies' trading activity. Also, all goods traded between the colonies and Europe had to first pass through an English port. This benefited England, but it also spurred a boom in the colonial shipbuilding industry and supported the development of many other colonial industries.

A PLANTATION ECONOMY ARISES IN THE SOUTH As the colonies prospered, however, the southern and northern colonies developed distinct societies, based on sharply contrasting economic systems. While there were cities in the South, on the whole, the region developed as a rural society of self-sufficient plantations. Each plantation specialized in raising a single cash crop—one grown primarily for sale rather than for food or livestock feed—such as tobacco or rice. Plantation owners produced much of what they needed on their property. For that reason, they did not often need the shops, bakeries, and markets that would be found in cities.

While small farmers made up the majority of the southern population, prosperous plantation owners controlled much of the South's economy as well as its political and social institutions. In the 18th century, southerners turned increasingly to slavery to fill the labor needs of their agricultural economy. During the 17th century, Africans had become part of a transatlantic trade network described as the **triangular trade**. In this system, New England merchants shipped rum and other goods across the Atlantic Ocean and exchanged them for enslaved Africans. Africans were then transported to the West Indies where they were sold for sugar and molasses. These goods were then sold to rum producers in New England, and the cycle began again. Later, enslaved Africans were brought to North America as well. Between 1690 and 1750 the number of slaves working in the southern colonies increased from 13,000 to around 200,000. The plantation economy had come to depend on the institution of slavery.

COMMERCE GROWS IN THE NORTH The development of commercial cities and diverse economic activities gradually made the North radically different from the South. Grinding wheat, harvesting fish, and sawing lumber became thriving industries in the North. Many colonists prospered, and merchants became one of the most powerful groups in the North. The expansion of trade caused port cities such as Boston, New York, and Philadelphia to grow.

The northern colonies attracted a variety of immigrants. During the 18th century, about 463,000 Europeans migrated to America. Before 1700 most immigrants came from England, but by 1755 over half of all European immigrants were from other countries. They included large numbers of Germans and Scots-Irish. Other ethnic groups included the Dutch in New York, Scandinavians in Delaware, and Jews in cities like Newport and Philadelphia.

Unlike southern plantations, farms in New England and the middle colonies typically produced several cash crops. Northerners relied less on slave labor for farming, because growing wheat and corn did not require as much labor as the crops grown in the South did. However, slavery did exist in New England and was extensive throughout the middle colonies, as was racial prejudice against blacks—free or enslaved. As in the South, women in the North had extensive work responsibilities but few legal or social rights.

Reading Check
Contrast What were the main differences between the economies of the North and the South?

New Social Movements

During the 1700s the Enlightenment—an intellectual movement that began in Europe—and the Great Awakening—a colonial religious movement—influenced people's thinking throughout the 13 colonies.

THE ENLIGHTENMENT During the 1400s Europe experienced a cultural awakening known as the Renaissance (rĕn´ĭ-säns´)—a term meaning "rebirth." Scientists began using observation and reason, or rational thought, to determine some of the natural laws and principles governing the world and human behavior. The work of Nicolaus Copernicus, Galileo Galilei, and Sir Isaac Newton established that the earth revolved around the sun. This observation, which challenged the traditional assumption that the earth was the center of the universe, was at first fiercely resisted. It was thought to contradict the Bible and other religious teachings. These scientists also concluded that the world is governed by fixed mathematical laws rather than solely by the will of God. These ideas about nature led to a movement called the **Enlightenment**, in which philosophers tried to apply reason and scientific methods to politics and social concerns.

Enlightenment ideas spread from Europe to the colonies, where people such as Benjamin Franklin embraced the notion of obtaining truth through experimentation and reason. For example, Franklin's most famous experiment—flying a kite in a thunderstorm—demonstrated that lightning is a form of electrical power.

Enlightenment ideas spread quickly through the colonies by means of books and pamphlets. Literacy was particularly high in New England because the Puritans had long supported public education. However, Enlightenment views were disturbing to some people. The Enlightenment suggested that people could use science and logic—rather than the pronouncements of church authorities—to arrive at truths.

The Enlightenment also had a profound effect on political thought in the colonies. Colonial leaders such as Thomas Jefferson reasoned that human beings are born with natural rights that governments must respect. Enlightenment principles eventually would lead many colonists to question the authority of the British monarchy.

THE GREAT AWAKENING By the early 1700s the Puritans had lost some of their influence. Under the new Massachusetts charter of 1691, Puritans were required to practice religious tolerance. Furthermore, as Puritan merchants prospered, they developed a taste for fine houses, stylish clothes, and good food and wine. As a result, their interest in maintaining the strict Puritan code declined. A series of religious revivals aimed at restoring the intensity and dedication of the early Puritan church swept through the colonies. These religious changes came to be known collectively as the **Great Awakening**.

While the Great Awakening, which lasted throughout the 1730s and 1740s, restored many colonists' Christian religious faith, the movement also challenged the authority of established churches. As a result, independent denominations, such as the Baptists and Methodists, gained new members.

Vocabulary
revival a time of reawakened interest in religion

Reading Check
Analyze Effects
What effects did the Great Awakening have on organized religion in the colonies?

The Great Awakening and the Enlightenment caused people to question traditional authority. Both stressed the importance of the individual: the Enlightenment by emphasizing human reason, and the Great Awakening by de-emphasizing the role of church authority. Because these movements helped lead the colonists to question Britain's authority over their lives, they were important in creating the intellectual and social atmosphere that eventually led to the American Revolution.

The French and Indian War

While the British colonies in North America were growing and prospering, French traders and explorers were establishing colonies of their own in Canada and the Mississippi River valley. Together these colonies were known as New France. As the French Empire in North America expanded, it collided with the growing British Empire.

—— BIOGRAPHY ——

Benjamin Franklin (1706–1790)

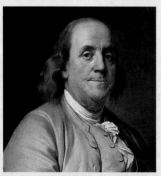

Benjamin Franklin was one of the leading champions of Enlightenment ideas in America. Like other scientists and philosophers of the Enlightenment, Franklin believed that human beings could use their intellectual powers to improve their lot.

Franklin's observations and experiments led to a number of inventions, including the lightning rod, bifocals, and a new kind of heating system that became known as the Franklin stove. Inventions like these proved that knowledge derived from scientific experiments could be put to practical use.

Franklin's achievements brought him world renown. In 1756 British scholars elected him to the Royal Society, and in 1772 France honored him with membership in the French Academy of Sciences.

Jonathan Edwards (1703–1758)

Descended from a long line of Puritan ministers, Jonathan Edwards denied that humans had the power to perfect themselves. He believed that "however you may have reformed your life in many things," as a sinner you were destined for hell unless you had a "great change of heart."

Edwards was a brilliant thinker who entered Yale College when he was only 13. His preaching was one of the driving forces of the Great Awakening. Ironically, when the religious revival died down, Edwards's own congregation rejected him for being too strict about doctrine. Edwards moved to Stockbridge, Massachusetts, in 1751, where he lived most of his remaining years as a missionary to a Native American settlement.

The French usually enjoyed good relations with Native Americans, in part because they needed the local people as partners in the fur trade. In fact, several military alliances developed out of the trade relationship between the French and Native Americans.

WAR ERUPTS Since the late 17th century, France and Britain had fought three inconclusive wars that spread to their overseas colonies. In 1754 the French-British friction reignited in a conflict known as the **French and Indian War**. It began when the French built Fort Duquesne in the Ohio River valley region. This led to conflict with the Virginia government, which had already granted 200,000 acres of land in the Ohio country to a group of wealthy planters. In response, Virginia's governor sent militia to evict the French. In the first battle of the war, the French delivered a crushing defeat to the outnumbered Virginians and their leader, an ambitious 22-year-old officer named George Washington.

A year after his defeat, Washington returned to battle as an aide to the British general Edward Braddock. Braddock's first task was to capture Fort Duquesne. As Braddock and nearly 1,500 soldiers neared the fort, French soldiers and their Native American allies ambushed them. The startled British soldiers turned and fled. The weakness of the British army surprised Washington. He and many other colonists began to question the competence of the British military, which suffered defeat after defeat during 1755 and 1756.

BRITAIN DEFEATS AN OLD ENEMY Angered by French victories, Britain's King George II selected new government leaders in 1757. One of these was William Pitt, an energetic, self-confident politician. Under Pitt's governance, the British and colonial troops finally began winning battles. These successes earned Britain the support of the powerful Iroquois, giving Britain some Native American allies to counterbalance those of France.

In September 1759, British troops defeated the French in a surprise attack near Quebec. This triumph brought the British victory in the war, which officially ended in 1763 with the signing of the Treaty of Paris. Great Britain claimed Canada and virtually all of North America east of the Mississippi River. Britain also took Florida from Spain, which had allied itself with

In this scene from the French and Indian War, British general Edward Braddock meets defeat and death on his march to Fort Duquesne in July 1755. The colonists and the British fought side by side in this conflict for nine years.

France. The treaty permitted Spain to keep possession of its lands west of the Mississippi and the city of New Orleans, which it had gained from France in 1762. France retained control of only a few islands and small colonies near Newfoundland, in the West Indies, and elsewhere.

CHANGES FOR NATIVE AMERICANS Native Americans resented the growing number of British settlers crossing the Appalachian Mountains and feared the settlers would soon drive away the game they depended on for survival. In the spring of 1763, the Ottawa leader Pontiac recognized that the French loss was a loss for Native Americans and decided to take action.

Led by Pontiac, Native Americans captured eight British forts in the Ohio valley and the Great Lakes area and laid siege to another. In response, British officers deliberately presented blankets contaminated with small-pox to two Delaware chiefs during peace negotiations, and the virus spread rapidly among the Native Americans. Weakened by disease and tired of fighting, most Native American groups negotiated treaties with the British by the summer of 1766.

To avoid further costly conflicts with Native Americans, the British government prohibited colonists from settling west of the Appalachian Mountains. The Proclamation of 1763 established a Proclamation Line along the Appalachians, which the colonists were not allowed to cross. However, the colonists, eager to expand westward from the increasingly crowded Atlantic seaboard, ignored the proclamation and continued to stream onto Native American lands.

**Reading Check
Summarize** How did Great Britain's victory over France affect Native Americans?

Lesson 1 Assessment

1. **Organize Information** Use a chart to identify the main effect of each of the causes listed.

Causes	Effects
Sailing technology improves.	
The Puritans are persecuted in England.	
Mercantilism grows in Europe.	
The French build Fort Duquesne.	

2. **Key Terms and People** For each key term or person in the lesson, write a sentence explaining its significance.

3. **Analyze Effects** What do you think were the most important long-term consequences of the Spanish and English colonies in the Americas?

Think About:
• conquering and claiming land
• forced labor of Native Americans and Africans
• the impact on Europe and the Americas

4. **Summarize** How did the Enlightenment affect the colonies?

5. **Draw Conclusions** How did the differences between the northern and southern economies lead to the development of two distinct cultural regions?

6. **Make Inferences** In 1774 African American poet Phyllis Wheatley wrote that each human possessed a God-given love of freedom. How does this idea express both religious belief and Enlightenment thought?

The American Revolution

The Big Idea

Conflicts between Great Britain and the American colonies escalated until the colonists declared their independence and won victory in the American Revolutionary War.

Why It Matters Now

The Declaration of Independence embodies guiding principles of the United States today, and the American Revolution remains a symbol of the fight for freedom.

Key Terms and People

Sugar Act

Stamp Act

Boston Tea Party

John Locke

Common Sense

Thomas Jefferson

Loyalists

Patriots

Valley Forge

Charles Cornwallis

Yorktown

Treaty of Paris

SS.912.A.1.2; SS.912.A.1.4; SS.912.A.1.7; SS.912.A.2.7; SS.912.G.1.2; LAFS.1112.RH.1.2; LAFS.1112.RH.4.10

One American's Story

Crispus Attucks was a sailor of African and Native American ancestry. On the night of March 5, 1770, he was part of a large and angry crowd that had gathered at the Boston Customs House to harass the British soldiers stationed there. More soldiers soon arrived, and the mob began hurling stones and snowballs at them. Attucks then stepped forward.

"This Attucks . . . appears to have undertaken to be the hero of the night; and to lead this army with banners . . . up to King street with their clubs. . . . [T]his man with his party cried, 'Do not be afraid of them. . . .' He had hardiness enough to fall in upon them, and with one hand took hold of a bayonet, and with the other knocked the man down."
—John Adams, quoted in *The Black Presence in the Era of the American Revolution*

Crispus Attucks

Attucks's action ignited the troops. Ignoring orders not to shoot, one soldier and then others fired on the crowd. Five people were killed; several were wounded. Crispus Attucks was, according to a newspaper account, the first to die.

The Road to Revolution

The conflict at the Boston Customs House in which Crispus Attucks was killed was part of a growing protest against British rule. The Proclamation of 1763 and later British actions convinced the colonists that the British government did not care about their needs.

THE COLONIES ORGANIZE TO RESIST BRITAIN In order to reduce its debt from the French and Indian War, in 1764 the British Parliament enacted the **Sugar Act**. The law placed duties on certain imports, such as sugar, that had not been taxed before. It also provided that colonists accused of violating the act would be tried in a vice-admiralty court rather than a colonial court. There, each case would be decided by a single judge rather than by a jury of sympathetic colonists. In March 1765 Parliament passed the **Stamp Act**, which imposed a tax on documents and printed items.

Enraged by the new acts, the colonial assemblies declared that Parliament lacked the power to impose taxes on the colonies because the colonists were not represented in Parliament. In October 1765, merchants in New York, Boston, and Philadelphia agreed to boycott British goods until the Stamp Act was repealed. The widespread boycott worked, and in March 1766 Parliament repealed the law.

On the same day, however, Parliament passed the Declaratory Act, which asserted Parliament's full right "to bind the colonies and people of America in all cases whatsoever." Then in 1767 Parliament passed the Townshend Acts, which taxed goods imported from Britain. The acts also imposed a tax on tea, the most popular drink in the colonies. Led by men such as Samuel Adams, the colonists again boycotted British goods.

TENSION MOUNTS IN MASSACHUSETTS As hostilities between the colonists and the British mounted, the atmosphere in Boston grew increasingly tense. On March 5, 1770, a mob gathered in front of the Boston Customs

Vocabulary
boycott
a collective refusal to use, buy, or deal with, especially as an act of protest

---

NOW & THEN

Recent Tax Revolts

Citizen action to affect tax policies continues to this day. On June 6, 1978, California residents voted in a tax reform law known as Proposition 13. By the late 1970s, taxes in California were among the highest in the nation. The property tax alone was 52 percent higher than the national norm. Proposition 13, initiated by ordinary citizens, limited the tax on real property to 1 percent of its assessed value in 1975–1976. It passed with 65 percent of the vote. Many state agencies were scaled down or cut due to the resulting loss of revenue, so in 1984 California voters approved a state lottery that provides supplemental funds for education.

Residents of other states have also initiated ballot measures to reduce taxes, though not all are successful. In 2010 Massachusetts voters defeated a sales tax reduction issue that opponents argued would result in cuts to education and public safety services. In 2012 Alaskans approved a measure that reduced property taxes by increasing the amount of a home's value that is exempt from property tax. Citizens in California have also placed a property tax exemption increase on the state ballot for 2016.

Proposition 13 and similar tax initiatives still generate heated debate, as Americans across the country struggle with conflicting desires: more government services versus less taxes.

House and taunted the British soldiers standing guard there. Shots were fired and five colonists, including Crispus Attucks, were killed. Colonial leaders quickly labeled the confrontation the Boston Massacre. To relieve some of the growing tension, Parliament repealed the Townshend Acts—except the tax on tea—in 1770. However, strong feelings remained on both sides.

Tensions rose again in 1772 when a group of Rhode Island colonists destroyed a British customs schooner that patrolled the coast for smugglers. In response, King George III named a special commission to find the suspects and bring them to England for trial.

The plan to haul Americans to England for trial ignited widespread alarm. The assemblies of Massachusetts and Virginia set up committees of correspondence, groups that were organized to exchange information about British threats to American liberties. By 1774 such committees formed a communication network linking leaders in nearly all the colonies.

In 1773 the British prime minister, Lord Frederick North, devised the Tea Act to save the nearly bankrupt British East India Company. The company gained the right to sell tax-free tea directly to consumers for less than colonial tea sellers. North hoped the American colonists would simply buy the cheaper tea; instead, they protested dramatically. On December 16, 1773, a large group of Boston rebels disguised themselves as Native Americans, boarded three British ships, and dumped 18,000 pounds of the East India Company's tea into Boston Harbor. This incident became known as the **Boston Tea Party**.

The incident infuriated King George. In 1774, in response to pressure from the king, Parliament enacted what colonists called the Intolerable Acts. One law shut down Boston Harbor. Another authorized British commanders to house soldiers in vacant private homes. In addition, General Thomas Gage, Commander-in-Chief of British forces in North America, was appointed governor of Massachusetts. He promptly placed Boston under martial law, or rule imposed by military forces.

Document-Based Investigation Historical Source

Mob Rule
This British cartoon portrays the events of the Boston Tea Party from the Loyalist perspective. While Patriots are dumping tea, a British tax collector, having been tarred and feathered, is having tea poured down his throat. The "Liberty Tree," where a copy of the Stamp Act has been nailed upside down, has been converted into a gallows, a device used for hanging people.

Analyze Historical Sources
1. How does the cartoonist make the mob look sinister?

2. What kind of comment does the cartoonist make by suspending a hangman's noose from the "Liberty Tree"? Explain.

In response to Britain's actions, the committees of correspondence assembled the First Continental Congress in Philadelphia. The 56 delegates drew up a declaration of colonial rights. They defended the colonies' right to run their own affairs and stated that if the British used force against the colonies, the colonies should fight back.

THE STIRRINGS OF REBELLION After the First Continental Congress met, minutemen—civilian soldiers who pledged to be ready to fight against the British on a minute's notice—quietly stockpiled firearms and gunpowder. General Gage learned about these activities, and he ordered troops to march from Boston to nearby Concord, Massachusetts, to seize illegal weapons. On the night of April 18, 1775, Paul Revere, William Dawes, and Samuel Prescott rode out from Boston to spread word that 700 British troops were headed for Concord. Church bells and gunshots—prearranged signals sent from town to town—warned that the British were coming.

As the king's troops, known as "redcoats" because of their uniforms, reached Lexington, Massachusetts, they saw 70 minutemen on the village green. The British commander ordered the minutemen to lay down their arms and leave. The minutemen started to move out without laying down their muskets. Then someone fired, and the British soldiers shot into the departing militia. Eight minutemen were killed and ten more were wounded, while only one British soldier was injured. The Battle of Lexington, the first battle of the Revolutionary War, lasted only 15 minutes.

The British marched on to Concord, where they found an empty arsenal. After a brief skirmish with minutemen, they began marching back to Boston. Between 3,000 and 4,000 minutemen fired on the troops from behind stone walls and trees. British soldiers fell by the dozens. Bloodied and humiliated, the remaining British soldiers returned to Boston.

In May 1775, colonial leaders called the Second Continental Congress in Philadelphia to debate their next move. Some delegates called for independence, while others argued for reconciliation with Great Britain. Despite their differences, the Congress agreed to recognize the colonial militia as the Continental Army and appointed George Washington as its commander.

General Gage decided to strike at militiamen north of Boston on Breed's Hill, near Bunker Hill. On June 17, 1775, Gage sent 2,400 British soldiers up the hill. The colonists held their fire until the last minute and then began to mow down the redcoats before finally retreating. In this deadliest battle of the war, the colonists lost 450 men, while the British troops suffered more than 1,000 casualties.

By July the Second Continental Congress was preparing for war though still hoping for peace. Most delegates, like most colonists, were loyal to George III and blamed the bloodshed on the king's ministers. On July 8 Congress sent the king the so-called Olive Branch Petition, urging a return to "the former harmony" between Britain and the colonies.

King George flatly rejected the petition, and he issued a proclamation that the colonies were in rebellion. He urged Parliament to order a naval blockade to isolate ships headed for the American coast.

Vocabulary
reconciliation
the restoration of
a former state of
harmony or friendship

Reading Check
Make Inferences
What do you think
King George set out
to achieve when
he pressed for the
Intolerable Acts?

Declaring Independence

Despite the growing crisis, many colonists were uncertain about the idea of independence. Following the Olive Branch Petition, public opinion in the colonies began to shift.

THE IDEAS BEHIND THE REVOLUTION This shift in public opinion was greatly influenced by Enlightenment ideas. A key Enlightenment thinker, English philosopher **John Locke** had maintained that people have natural rights to life, liberty, and property. Furthermore, he had contended, every society is based on a social contract—an agreement in which the people choose and obey a government so long as it safeguards their natural rights. If the government takes away or interferes with those rights, people have the right to resist and even overthrow the government.

Locke's ideas were rooted in the traditions of limited government and civil rights that had been basic to English law for centuries. The English nobility had forced King John to sign the Magna Carta in AD 1215. The Magna Carta acknowledged certain rights of the barons, including due process, a speedy trial, and trial by a jury of one's peers. Its main significance was to recognize that the sovereign did not have absolute authority but was subject to the rule of law. The English Bill of Rights reaffirmed this principle.

To the colonists, the various acts of Parliament between 1763 and 1775 had violated their rights as Englishmen. Those rights included taxation only by consent of property owners, a presumption of innocence, no standing army in peacetime without consent, no quartering of troops in private homes, freedom of travel, and the guarantee of regular legislative sessions.

Just as important as Locke's ideas in influencing the colonists were the ideas of Thomas Paine. In a widely read pamphlet titled ***Common Sense***, Paine declared that independence would allow America to trade more freely. He argued that freedom would give American colonists the chance to create a better society—one free from tyranny, with equal social and economic opportunities for all. *Common Sense* sold nearly 500,000 copies in 1776.

THE PATRIOTS DECLARE INDEPENDENCE By the early summer of 1776, the wavering Continental Congress finally decided to urge each colony to form its own government. On June 7 Virginia delegate Richard Henry Lee made a formal motion that "these United Colonies are, and of a right ought to be, free and independent States."

Virginia lawyer **Thomas Jefferson** was chosen to prepare the final draft of a Declaration of Independence. Drawing on Locke's ideas of natural rights, Jefferson's document declared the rights of "Life, Liberty, and the pursuit of Happiness" to be "unalienable" rights—ones that can never be taken away. Jefferson asserted that a government's legitimate power can only come from the consent of the governed, and that when a government denies citizens' unalienable rights, the people have the right to "alter or abolish" that government. Jefferson provided a long list of violations committed by the king and Parliament against the colonists' unalienable rights. On that basis, the American colonies declared their independence from Britain.

Background
Paine had supported reconciliation with Britain until the battles at Lexington and Concord. He placed responsibility for British tyranny on the shoulders of the king, calling him "the royal brute of Britain."

Reading Check
Summarize What reasons did Jefferson give to justify revolt by the colonies?

The Revolutionary War

As they took on the mighty British Empire, the colonists suffered initial losses. In time, however, the colonists would battle their way back.

THE WAR BEGINS Americans found themselves on different sides as the war began. **Loyalists**—those who opposed independence and remained loyal to the British king—included a number of judges and governors, as well as people of more modest means. Many Loyalists thought that the British were going to win and wanted to avoid punishment as rebels. Others thought that the Crown would protect their rights more effectively than the new colonial governments would. **Patriots**—the supporters of independence—saw political and economic opportunity in an independent America. In addition, many Americans remained neutral.

Many African Americans fought on the side of the Patriots, but others joined the Loyalists because the British promised freedom to slaves who would fight for the Crown. Many Native Americans supported the British because they viewed colonial settlers as a greater threat to their lands.

Early in the war, as part of the British plan to isolate New England, the British tried to seize New York City. The British sailed into New York harbor in the summer of 1776 with about 32,000 soldiers, including thousands of

▶ Explore ONLINE!

Revolutionary War, 1775–1778

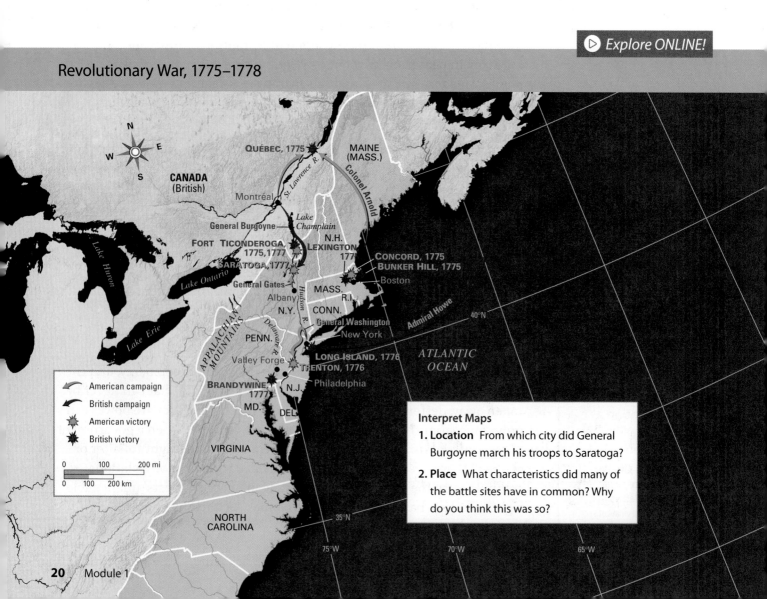

Interpret Maps

1. **Location** From which city did General Burgoyne march his troops to Saratoga?

2. **Place** What characteristics did many of the battle sites have in common? Why do you think this was so?

German mercenaries, or hired soldiers. Although the Continental Army attempted to defend New York, the untrained and poorly equipped colonial troops soon retreated. By late fall, the British had pushed Washington's army across the Delaware River into Pennsylvania.

Desperate for an early victory, Washington risked everything on one bold stroke planned for Christmas night 1776. In the face of a fierce storm, he led 2,400 men in small rowboats across the ice-choked Delaware River. They then marched to their objective—Trenton, New Jersey—and defeated a garrison of German mercenaries in a surprise attack. The British soon regrouped, however, and in September 1777 they captured the American capital at Philadelphia.

In the meantime, British general John Burgoyne planned to lead an army down a route of lakes from Canada to Albany, where he would meet British troops as they arrived from New York City. The two regiments would then join forces to complete their plan and isolate New England from the rest of the colonies. As Burgoyne traveled through forested wilderness, militiamen and soldiers from the Continental Army gathered. While he was fighting off the colonial troops, Burgoyne didn't realize that his fellow British officers were preoccupied with holding Philadelphia and weren't coming to meet him. American troops finally surrounded Burgoyne at Saratoga, where he surrendered on October 17, 1777.

The surrender at Saratoga was critically important. The French had secretly aided the Patriots since early 1776, and the Saratoga victory bolstered France's belief that the Americans could win the war. As a result, the French signed an alliance with the Americans in February 1778 and openly joined them in their fight.

— BIOGRAPHY

George Washington (1732–1799)

During the Revolutionary War, Commander in Chief George Washington became a national hero. An imposing man, Washington stood six feet two inches tall. He was broad-shouldered, calm, and dignified, and he was an expert horseman. But it was Washington's character that won hearts and, ultimately, the war.

Washington roused dispirited men into a fighting force. At Princeton, he galloped on his white horse into the line of fire, shouting and encouraging his men. At Valley Forge, he bore the same cold and privation as every suffering soldier. Time and again, Washington's tactics saved his smaller, weaker force to fight another day. By the end of the war, the entire nation idolized General Washington. Adoring soldiers crowded near him just to touch his boots when he rode by.

Molly Pitcher was the heroine of the Battle of Monmouth in New Jersey, which was fought in 1778. Afterward, General Washington appointed her as a noncommissioned officer to honor her brave deeds.

While this hopeful turn of events took place in Paris, Washington and his Continental Army—desperately low on food and supplies—fought to stay alive at winter camp in **Valley Forge**, Pennsylvania. More than 2,000 soldiers died, yet the survivors didn't desert.

LIFE DURING THE REVOLUTION One huge problem that the Continental Congress faced was paying the troops. When the Congress ran out of hard currency—silver and gold—it printed paper money called Continentals (like the Revolutionary soldiers). As the Congress printed more and more money, its value plunged, causing rising prices, or inflation. The Congress also struggled against great odds to equip the beleaguered army.

In 1781 the Congress appointed Robert Morris, a rich Philadelphia merchant, as superintendent of finance. Morris and his associate Haym Salomon borrowed on their own credit to provide salaries for the Continental Army.

Civilians also contributed to the war effort. When men marched off to fight, many wives began managing farms and businesses as well as households and families. Hundreds of women followed their husbands to the battlefield, where they washed and cooked for the troops—while some, including Molly Pitcher, even risked their lives in combat.

The war opened some doors for African Americans. Thousands of slaves escaped to freedom in the chaos of war. About 5,000 African Americans served in the Continental Army, where their courage, loyalty, and talent impressed white Americans. In general, Native Americans remained on the fringes of the Revolution. Although many supported the British cause, most preferred to remain apart from the conflict.

WINNING THE WAR In the midst of the frozen winter of 1778 at Valley Forge, American troops began an amazing transformation. Friedrich von Steuben, a Prussian captain and talented drillmaster, helped train the Continental Army. He helped turn farmers and workers into real soldiers.

Other foreign military leaders, such as the Marquis de Lafayette (mär-kē′ də lăf′ē-ĕt′), also offered their help. Lafayette lobbied France for French reinforcements and led a command in the last years of the war. With the help of such European military leaders, the raw Continental Army became an effective fighting force.

After their devastating defeat at Saratoga, the British shifted their operations to the South. At the end of 1778, a British expedition easily took Savannah, Georgia. In their greatest victory of the war, the British under generals Henry Clinton and **Charles Cornwallis** captured Charles Town, South Carolina, in May 1780. Clinton then left for New York, while Cornwallis conquered land throughout the South.

In early 1781, despite several defeats, the colonists continued to battle Cornwallis, hindering his efforts to take the Carolinas. The British general then chose to move the fight to Virginia. He stationed his army of 7,500 at **Yorktown**, on a peninsula between the James and York rivers. Cornwallis planned to fortify Yorktown, take Virginia, and then move north to join Clinton's forces.

Shortly after learning of Cornwallis's actions, Lafayette and Washington led their armies south toward Yorktown. Meanwhile, a French naval force blocked British sea routes to the Chesapeake Bay. By late September, French

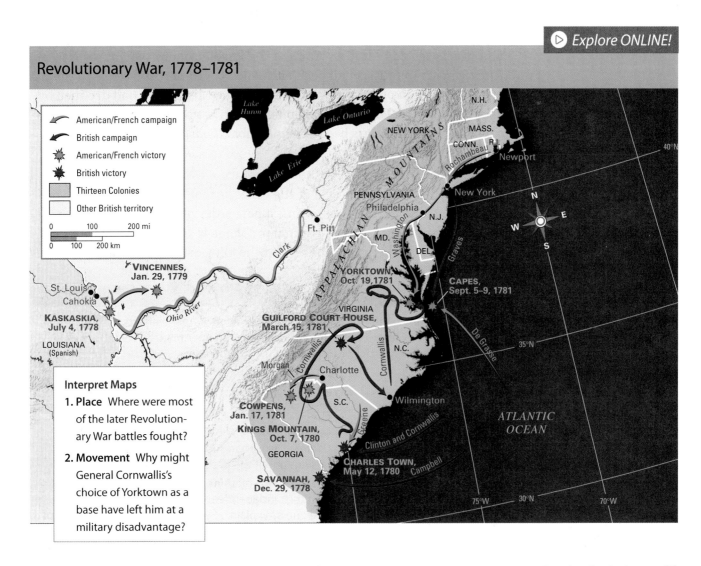

▶ Explore ONLINE!

Revolutionary War, 1778–1781

Legend:
- American/French campaign
- British campaign
- American/French victory
- British victory
- Thirteen Colonies
- Other British territory

0 100 200 mi
0 100 200 km

VINCENNES, Jan. 29, 1779
St. Louis
Cahokia
KASKASKIA, July 4, 1778
LOUISIANA (Spanish)
Ohio River
Clark
Ft. Pitt
N.H.
NEW YORK
MASS.
CONN. R.I.
Rochambeau
Newport
PENNSYLVANIA
Philadelphia
New York
N.J.
Washington
MD.
DEL.
Graves
YORKTOWN, Oct. 19, 1781
CAPES, Sept. 5–9, 1781
VIRGINIA
GUILFORD COURT HOUSE, March 15, 1781
De Grasse
N.C.
Morgan
Cornwallis
Charlotte
Cornwallis
Greene
COWPENS, Jan. 17, 1781
S.C.
Wilmington
KINGS MOUNTAIN, Oct. 7, 1780
Clinton and Cornwallis
ATLANTIC OCEAN
GEORGIA
CHARLES TOWN, May 12, 1780
Campbell
SAVANNAH, Dec. 29, 1778

40°N
35°N
30°N
75°W
70°W

Interpret Maps
1. **Place** Where were most of the later Revolutionary War battles fought?
2. **Movement** Why might General Cornwallis's choice of Yorktown as a base have left him at a military disadvantage?

and American troops surrounded the British and began bombarding them day and night. Less than a month later, on October 19, 1781, Cornwallis surrendered. The Americans had shocked the world by defeating the British.

Peace talks began in Paris in 1782. The American negotiating team included John Adams, John Jay, and Benjamin Franklin. In September 1783 the delegates signed the **Treaty of Paris**, which confirmed U.S. independence and set the boundaries of the new nation. The United States now stretched from the Atlantic Ocean to the Mississippi River and from Canada to the Florida border.

THE WAR BECOMES A SYMBOL OF LIBERTY Revolutionary ideals set a new course for American society. During the war, social distinctions had begun to blur as the wealthy wore homespun clothing and as military leaders showed respect for all of their soldiers. Changes like these stimulated the rise of egalitarianism (ĭ-găl′ĭ-târ′ē-ə-nĭz′əm)— a belief in the equality of all people. This belief fostered a new attitude: the idea that ability, effort, and virtue, not wealth or family background, defined one's worth.

English potter Josiah Wedgwood designed this anti-slavery cameo and sent copies of it to Benjamin Franklin.

The egalitarianism of the 1780s, however, applied only to white males. It did not bring any new political rights to women. Moreover, most African Americans were still enslaved, and even those who were free usually faced discrimination and poverty.

For Native Americans, the Revolution brought uncertainty. During both the French and Indian War and the Revolutionary War, many Native American communities had been either destroyed or displaced, and the Native American population living east of the Mississippi had declined by about 50 percent. Postwar developments further threatened Native American interests, as settlers began taking tribal lands left unprotected by the Treaty of Paris.

Reading Check
Analyze Effects
How had the American Revolution affected the lives of Native Americans?

The Continental Congress chose a quotation from the Roman poet Virgil as a motto for the reverse side of the Great Seal of the United States. The motto, *Novus Ordo Seclorum,* means "a new order of the ages." Establishing a government and resolving internal problems in that new order would be a tremendous challenge for citizens of the newborn United States.

Lesson 2 Assessment

1. **Organize Information** Fill in a cluster diagram with events that demonstrate the conflict between Great Britain and the American colonies before the war.

Choose one event to explain further in a paragraph.

2. **Key Terms and People** For each key term or person in the lesson, write a sentence explaining its significance.

3. **Analyze Effects** What were the effects of the Revolutionary War on the American colonists?
   Think About:
   • political effects
   • economic effects
   • social effects

4. **Make Inferences** Why do you think Thomas Paine's *Common Sense* had such a large impact on people's feelings about the need for independence?

5. **Evaluate** Do you think the colonists could have won their independence without assistance from foreigners? Explain.

The Declaration of Independence

Thomas Jefferson's Declaration of Independence is one of the most important and influential legal documents of modern times. Although the text frequently refers to 18th-century events, its Enlightenment philosophy and politics have continuing relevance today.

For more than 200 years, the Declaration of Independence has inspired leaders of other independence movements and has remained a crucial document in the struggle for democratic ideals of civil rights and human rights. For example, the Declaration of Independence quickly became very influential in France. Soon after the American Revolution ended, the French Revolution began based on the ideals set forth in the Declaration of Independence.

In Congress, July 4, 1776.

A Declaration by the Representatives of the United States of America, in General Congress assembled.

Jefferson begins the Declaration by attempting to legally and philosophically justify the revolution that was already underway. Here Jefferson is saying that, now that the colonists have begun to separate themselves from British rule, it is time to explain why the colonists have taken this course of action.

When in the Course of human events, it becomes necessary for one people to dissolve the political bands which have connected them with another, and to assume among the powers of the earth, the separate and equal station to which the Laws of Nature and of Nature's God entitle them, a decent respect to the opinions of mankind requires that they should declare the causes which impel them to the separation.

These passages reveal the influence of the English philosopher John Locke. In *Two Treatises of Government* (1690), Locke argued that if a government does not allow its citizens to enjoy certain rights and freedoms, the people have a right to replace that government. This argument is part of the Enlightenment idea of a natural social contract in which people must give their consent to being ruled by a government.

We hold these truths to be self-evident, that all men are created equal, that they are endowed by their Creator with certain unalienable Rights, that among these are Life, Liberty and the pursuit of Happiness; that, to secure these rights, Governments are instituted among Men, deriving their just powers from the consent of the governed; that whenever any Form of Government becomes destructive of these ends, it is the Right of the People to alter or to abolish it, and to institute new Government, laying its foundation on such principles and organizing its powers in such form, as to them shall seem most likely to effect their Safety and Happiness. Prudence, indeed, will dictate that Governments long established should not be changed for light and transient causes; and accordingly all experience hath shewn that mankind are more disposed to suffer, while evils are sufferable, than to right themselves by abolishing the forms to which they are accustomed. But when a long train of abuses and usurpations, pursuing invariably the same Object, evinces a design to reduce them under absolute Despotism, it is their right, it is their duty, to throw off such Government, and to provide new Guards for their future security.

Such has been the patient sufferance of these Colonies; and such is now the necessity which constrains them to alter their former Systems of Government. The history of the present King of Great Britain is a history of repeated injuries and usurpations, all having in direct object the establishment of an absolute Tyranny over these States. To prove this, let facts be submitted to a candid world.

Here begins the section in which Jefferson condemns the behavior of King George, listing the king's many tyrannical actions that have forced his American subjects to rebel.

He has refused his Assent to Laws, the most wholesome and necessary for the public good.

He has forbidden his Governors to pass Laws of immediate and pressing importance, unless suspended in their operation till his assent should be obtained; and, when so suspended, he has utterly neglected to attend to them.

He has refused to pass other Laws for the accommodation of large districts of people, unless those people would relinquish the right of Representation in the Legislature, a right inestimable to them, and formidable to tyrants only.

He has called together legislative bodies at places unusual, uncomfortable, and distant from the depository of their public Records, for the sole purpose of fatiguing them into compliance with his measures.

He has dissolved Representative Houses repeatedly, for opposing with manly firmness his invasions on the rights of the people.

He has refused for a long time, after such dissolutions, to cause others to be elected; whereby the Legislative powers, incapable of Annihilation, have returned to the people at large for their exercise; the State remaining in the mean time exposed to all the dangers of invasions from without, and convulsions within.

He has endeavoured to prevent the population of these States; for that purpose obstructing the Laws for Naturalization of Foreigners; refusing to pass others to encourage their migration hither, and raising the conditions of new Appropriations of Lands.

He has obstructed the Administration of Justice, by refusing his Assent to Laws for establishing Judiciary powers.

He has made Judges dependent on his Will alone, for the tenure of their offices, and the amount and payment of their salaries.

This is a reference to the 10,000 troops that the British government stationed in North America after the French and Indian War. Although the British government saw the troops as protection for the colonists, the colonists themselves viewed the troops as a standing army that threatened their freedom.

Here Jefferson condemns both the king and Parliament for passing the Intolerable Acts. Most of these laws were intended to punish the people of Massachusetts for the Boston Tea Party. For example, the Quartering Act of 1774 forced colonists to provide lodging for British troops. Another act allowed British soldiers accused of murder to be sent back to England for trial. The Boston Port Bill closed the port of Boston, "cutting off our Trade with all parts of the world."

Here Jefferson refers to the Quebec Act, which extended the boundaries of the province. He then refers to another act that changed the charter of Massachusetts and restricted town meetings.

He has erected a multitude of New Offices, and sent hither swarms of Officers to harass our people and eat out their substance.

He has kept among us, in times of peace, Standing Armies, without the Consent of our legislatures.

He has affected to render the Military independent of and superior to the Civil power.

He has combined with others to subject us to a jurisdiction foreign to our constitution and unacknowledged by our laws; giving his Assent to their Acts of pretended Legislation:

For quartering large bodies of armed troops among us;

For protecting them, by a mock Trial, from punishment for any Murders which they should commit on the Inhabitants of these States;

For cutting off our Trade with all parts of the world;

For imposing Taxes on us without our Consent;

For depriving us, in many cases, of the benefits of Trial by Jury;

For transporting us beyond Seas to be tried for pretended offenses;

For abolishing the free System of English Laws in a neighboring Province, establishing therein an Arbitrary government, and enlarging its Boundaries so as to render it at once an example and fit instrument for introducing the same absolute rule into these Colonies;

For taking away our Charters, abolishing our most valuable laws, and altering fundamentally the Forms of our Governments;

For suspending our own Legislatures, and declaring themselves invested with power to legislate for us in all cases whatsoever.

He has abdicated Government here, by declaring us out of his Protection and waging War against us.

He has plundered our seas, ravaged our Coasts, burnt our towns, and destroyed the lives of our people.

He is at this time transporting large Armies of foreign Mercenaries to compleat the works of death, desolation, and tyranny, already begun with circumstances of Cruelty & perfidy scarcely paralleled in the most barbarous ages, and totally unworthy the Head of a civilized nation.

He has constrained our fellow Citizens, taken Captive on the high Seas, to bear Arms against their Country, to become the executioners of their friends and Brethren, or to fall themselves by their Hands.

He has excited domestic insurrections amongst us, and has endeavoured to bring on the inhabitants of our frontiers the merciless Indian Savages, whose known rule of warfare is an undistinguished destruction of all ages, sexes and conditions.

In every stage of these Oppressions We have Petitioned for Redress in the most humble terms; Our repeated Petitions have been answered only by repeated injury. A Prince, whose character is thus marked by every act which may define a Tyrant, is unfit to be the ruler of a free people.

Here Jefferson turns his attention away from the king and toward the British people. Calling the British the "common kindred" of the colonists, Jefferson reminds them how often the Americans have appealed to their sense of justice. Reluctantly, the colonists are now forced to break their political connections with their British kin.

Nor have We been wanting in attentions to our British brethren. We have warned them from time to time of attempts by their legislature to extend an unwarrantable jurisdiction over us. We have reminded them of the circumstances of our emigration and settlement here. We have appealed to their native justice and magnanimity, and we have conjured them by the ties of our common kindred, to disavow these usurpations, which would inevitably interrupt our connections and correspondence. They too have been deaf to the voice of justice and of consanguinity. We must, therefore, acquiesce in the necessity, which denounces our Separation, and hold them, as we hold the rest of mankind, Enemies in War, in Peace Friends.

In this final paragraph, the delegates declare independence.

We, therefore, the Representatives of the United States of America, in General Congress, Assembled, appealing to the Supreme Judge of the world for the rectitude of our intentions, do, in the name, and by the Authority of the good People of these Colonies solemnly publish and declare, That these United Colonies are, and of Right ought to be, Free and Independent States; that they are Absolved from all Allegiance to the British Crown, and that all political connection between them and the State of Great Britain is, and ought to be, totally dissolved; and that as Free and Independent States, they have full Power to levy War, conclude Peace, contract Alliances, establish Commerce, and do all other Acts and Things which Independent States may of right do.

The Declaration ends with the delegates' pledge, or pact. The delegates at the Second Continental Congress knew that, in declaring their independence from Great Britain, they were committing treason—a crime punishable by death. "We must all hang together," Benjamin Franklin reportedly said, as the delegates prepared to sign the Declaration, "or most assuredly we shall all hang separately."

And for the support of this Declaration, with a firm reliance on the protection of divine Providence, we mutually pledge to each other our Lives, our Fortunes, and our sacred Honor.

[SIGNED BY]

John Hancock [**President of the Continental Congress**]

[GEORGIA]
Button Gwinnett
Lyman Hall
George Walton

[RHODE ISLAND]
Stephen Hopkins
William Ellery

[CONNECTICUT]
Roger Sherman
Samuel Huntington
William Williams
Oliver Wolcott

[NORTH CAROLINA]
William Hooper
Joseph Hewes
John Penn

[SOUTH CAROLINA]
Edward Rutledge
Thomas Heyward, Jr.
Thomas Lynch, Jr.
Arthur Middleton

[MARYLAND]
Samuel Chase
William Paca
Thomas Stone
Charles Carroll

[VIRGINIA]
George Wythe
Richard Henry Lee
Thomas Jefferson
Benjamin Harrison
Thomas Nelson, Jr.
Francis Lightfoot Lee
Carter Braxton

[PENNSYLVANIA]
Robert Morris
Benjamin Rush
Benjamin Franklin
John Morton
George Clymer
James Smith
George Taylor
James Wilson
George Ross

[DELAWARE]
Caesar Rodney
George Read
Thomas McKean

[NEW YORK]
William Floyd
Philip Livingston
Francis Lewis
Lewis Morris

[NEW JERSEY]
Richard Stockton
John Witherspoon
Francis Hopkinson
John Hart
Abraham Clark

[NEW HAMPSHIRE]
Josiah Bartlett
William Whipple
Matthew Thornton

[MASSACHUSETTS]
Samuel Adams
John Adams
Robert Treat Paine
Elbridge Gerry

A New Nation

The Big Idea

With a new Constitution as a blueprint for government, the United States grew in both size and prestige.

Why It Matters Now

The Constitution remains the nation's guiding document for government, and the nation's leaders still follow precedents set by its early leaders.

Key Terms and People

Federalists

Antifederalists

Bill of Rights

Alexander Hamilton

cabinet

sectionalism

nullification

Louisiana Purchase

Missouri Compromise

Andrew Jackson

Trail of Tears

One American's Story

Although John Dickinson had once opposed American independence, he later worked hard to help create a government for the new United States. In 1779 John Dickinson returned to the Continental Congress as a delegate from Delaware. At that time he explained the principles that guided his political decisions.

John Dickinson

"Two rules I have laid down for myself throughout this contest . . . first, on all occasions where I am called upon, as a trustee for my countrymen, to deliberate on questions important to their happiness, disdaining all personal advantages to be derived from a suppression of my real sentiments . . . openly to avow [declare] them; and, secondly, . . . whenever the public resolutions are taken, to regard them though opposite to my opinion, as sacred . . . and to join in supporting them as earnestly as if my voice had been given for them."

—John Dickinson, quoted in *The Life and Times of John Dickinson, 1732–1808*

Dickinson's two rules became guiding principles for the leaders who faced the formidable task of starting a new nation.

SS.912.A.1.2; SS.912.A.1.4; SS.912.A.1.7; SS.912.A.2.4; SS.912.A.2.7; SS.912.A.3.13; SS.912.G.1.2; SS.912.G.2.1; SS.912.G.4.2; LAFS.1112.RH.1.1; LAFS.1112.RH.1.2; LAFS.1112.RH.4.10

Forming a New Government

After the Revolution, fears and concerns about the form of government deeply affected the planning of the new government.

EXPERIMENTING WITH CONFEDERATION The Second Continental Congress set up a plan of government by adopting the Articles of Confederation, which went into effect in March 1781. The plan established a confederation, or alliance, among the 13 states. Under the Articles, each state had one vote in the Congress. Most power lay with individual states, but the national government—which included only Congress—was to handle large matters, such as declaring war and determining how to handle new territory. In one of its early actions, Congress passed two ordinances that governed how the lands west of the Appalachians would be surveyed and eventually admitted as states. These two ordinances were the Confederation's greatest successes.

Overshadowing these successes, however, were the Confederation's many problems. The Articles of Confederation created a weak central government and little unity among the states. To prevent abuses of power, the states had placed such severe limits on the national government that it was unable to solve many of the nation's problems. In May 1787, 12 states sent delegates to a convention called by Congress to discuss changes to the government.

CREATING A NEW GOVERNMENT Most of the delegates at the Constitutional Convention quickly gave up the idea of fixing the Articles of Confederation. They decided instead to form an entirely new government.

One major issue facing the delegates was giving fair representation to both large and small states. After much debate, Roger Sherman suggested the Great Compromise, which offered a two-house Congress. Each state would have equal representation in the Senate, which satisfied small states. Population size would determine representation in the House of Representatives, which satisfied larger states.

The Great Compromise settled one major issue but led to conflict between states about whether to count slaves in a state's population. The delegates eventually agreed to the Three-Fifths Compromise, which called for three-fifths of a state's slaves to be counted as part of the population.

Weaknesses of the Articles of Confederation
• Congress could not enact and collect taxes.
• Congress could not regulate interstate or foreign trade.
• Regardless of population, each state had only one vote in Congress.
• Two-thirds majority—9 out of 13 states—needed to agree to pass any law.
• Articles could be amended only if all states approved.
• There was no executive branch to enforce the laws of Congress.
• There was no national court system to settle legal disputes.
• There were 13 separate states that lacked national unity.

With major conflicts resolved, the delegates divided power between the states and the national government. This system of dividing power among multiple levels of government is called federalism. It was intended to keep the federal government from becoming too powerful. To further limit the possibility of anyone abusing power, the Founders created three branches of government: a legislative branch to make laws; an executive branch to carry out laws; and a judicial branch to interpret the laws and settle disputes. Then the delegates established a system of checks and balances to prevent any one branch from dominating the other two. Finally, the delegates also provided a means of changing the Constitution through the amendment process.

RATIFYING THE CONSTITUTION George Washington adjourned the Constitutional Convention on September 17, 1787. The new government could not become a reality until at least nine states ratified, or approved, the Constitution. Thus, the battle over ratification began.

Supporters of the Constitution called themselves **Federalists**, because they favored the new Constitution's balance of power between the states and the national government. Their opponents became known as **Antifederalists**, because they opposed having such a strong central government.

Both sides waged a war of words in the public debate over ratification. The writers of *The Federalist,* a series of 85 essays defending the Constitution, acknowledged defects in the new Constitution but argued that a stronger central government was superior to the weak Congress provided by the Articles of Confederation.

The Antifederalists' main opposition to the new Constitution was that it contained no bill of rights—a formal summary of citizens' rights and freedoms. In the end, the Federalists yielded and promised to add such a bill if the states would ratify the Constitution. In June 1788 New Hampshire became the ninth state to approve the Constitution, making it the new law of the land.

By December 1791 the states also had ratified ten amendments to the Constitution, which became known as the **Bill of Rights**. The first eight amendments spell out personal liberties. The Ninth and Tenth Amendments impose general limits on the powers of the federal government.

Document-Based Investigation Historical Source

A View of the New Government
Here is John Dickinson's description of an ideal American government:

> *"Let our government be like that of the solar system. Let the general government be like the sun and the states the planets, repelled yet attracted, and the whole moving regularly and harmoniously in their several orbits."*
>
> —John Dickinson, from The Records of the Federal Convention of 1787

Analyze Historical Sources
How does Dickinson's view of the new government reflect Enlightenment ideals?

The protection of rights and freedoms did not apply to all Americans at the time the Bill of Rights was adopted. Native Americans and slaves were excluded from its guarantees. Likewise, women were not mentioned in or protected by the Constitution. It would require many struggles—and many years—before all Americans were adequately protected.

CONTINUING RELEVANCE OF THE CONSTITUTION The United States Constitution is the oldest written national constitution still in use. One reason for its longevity lies in Article I, Section 8, which includes an "elastic clause." It gives Congress the power "To make all laws which shall be necessary and proper for carrying into execution" the powers enumerated by the Constitution. This clause stretches the power of the government to meet unforeseen circumstances.

Reading Check
Analyze Issues In what ways did the Great Compromise resolve certain problems even as it created new ones?

The Constitution also can be formally changed when necessary through amendments. The writers of the Constitution made the amendment process difficult in order to avoid arbitrary changes. In more than 200 years, only 27 amendments have been added to the Constitution.

Shaping the New Nation

Although the Constitution provided a strong foundation, it was not a detailed blueprint for governing. To create a working plan for the day-to-day governing of the country, President George Washington and Congress had to make many practical decisions.

WASHINGTON HEADS THE NEW GOVERNMENT When Washington took office as the first president of the United States under the Constitution, he and Congress faced a daunting task: creating an entirely new government. The momentous decisions that these early leaders made have resounded throughout American history.

One of the first tasks Washington and Congress faced was the creation of a judicial system. The Judiciary Act of 1789 provided for a Supreme Court and federal circuit and district courts. It also guaranteed that federal laws would remain "the supreme law of the land."

The nation's leaders also faced the task of building an executive branch. To help the president govern, Congress created three executive departments: the Department of State, to deal with foreign affairs; the Department of War, to handle military matters; and the Department of the Treasury, to manage finances. To head these departments, Washington chose Thomas Jefferson as secretary of state, **Alexander Hamilton** as secretary of the treasury, and Henry Knox as secretary of war. These department heads soon became part of the president's **cabinet**, or chief advisers.

As secretary of the treasury, Hamilton's job was to put the nation's economy on a firm footing. He proposed the establishment of a national bank that would be funded by both the federal government and wealthy private investors. This bank would issue paper money and handle taxes and other government funds.

Opponents of a national bank argued that since the Constitution made no provision for such an institution, Congress had no right to authorize it. This argument began the debate between those who favored a loose interpretation of the Constitution and those who favored a strict interpretation—a vital debate that has continued throughout U.S. history.

The differences within Washington's cabinet intensified and soon helped give rise to a two-party system. Those who shared Hamilton's vision of a strong central government (mostly northerners) called themselves Federalists. Those who supported Jefferson's vision of strong state governments (mostly southerners) called themselves Democratic-Republicans.

THE WHISKEY REBELLION During Washington's second term, an incident occurred that reflected the tension between federal and regional interests. In 1789 Congress had passed a protective tariff, an import tax on goods produced abroad meant to encourage American production. To generate even more revenue, Secretary Hamilton pushed through an excise tax—a tax on a product's manufacture, sale, or distribution—to be levied on the manufacture of whiskey.

In 1794 furious whiskey producers in western Pennsylvania refused to pay the tax and attacked the tax collectors. The federal government responded by sending some 13,000 militiamen to end the conflict. The Whiskey Rebellion, as it came to be known, marked the first use of armed force to assert federal authority.

CHALLENGES AT HOME AND ABROAD In addition to problems on the western frontier, the new government faced critical challenges overseas. In 1793 France was at war with Great Britain and other European countries. In the United States, the Democratic-Republicans supported France, while the Federalists wanted to back the British. President Washington, wary of foreign involvement, issued a declaration of neutrality, a statement that the United States would support neither side in the conflict.

In another significant foreign matter, Thomas Pinckney negotiated a treaty with Spain in 1795. Under Pinckney's Treaty, Spain gave up all land east of the Mississippi except Florida and gave Americans access to the Mississippi River and the port of New Orleans. The treaty helped pave the way for U.S. expansion west of the Appalachians.

Meanwhile, Americans faced trouble along their western border, where the British still maintained forts and Native Americans continued to resist white settlers. After numerous skirmishes in the area, John Jay, the Chief Justice of the Supreme Court, negotiated a treaty, known as Jay's Treaty, with Great Britain. Although the treaty was a diplomatic victory, it provoked outrage at home. Western settlers were angry that it allowed the British to continue their fur trade on the American side of the U.S.-Canadian border. The bitter political fight over Jay's Treaty, along with the growing division between the Federalists and Democratic-Republicans, convinced Washington not to seek a third term.

Portrait of a young John Adams by Joseph Badger

ADAMS PROVOKES CRITICISM In the election of 1796, the United States faced for the first time a contest between opposing parties. The Federalists nominated Vice-President John Adams for president, while the Democratic-Republicans chose Thomas Jefferson. Adams won the election by a small margin of electoral votes. Because the Constitution stated that the runner-up should become vice-president, the country found itself with a Federalist president and a Democratic-Republican vice-president.

The election of 1796 underscored the growing danger of **sectionalism**—placing the interests of one region over those of the nation as a whole. Almost all the electors from the southern states voted for Jefferson, while all the electors from the northern states voted for Adams. Some feared that people would care more about regional issues than what was best for the country as a whole.

Soon after taking office, President Adams faced the threat of war with France. Under Jay's Treaty, Britain had ceded control of the Northwest Territory to the United States but retained the right to continue its fur trade there. The French government regarded Jay's Treaty as a violation of the French-American alliance. In retaliation for this violation, the French began to seize American ships bound for Britain. Adams sent a three-man team to Paris to negotiate a solution.

This team planned to meet with the French foreign minister, Charles-Maurice de Talleyrand. Instead, the French sent three low-level officials, whom Adams in his report to Congress called X, Y, and Z. The French officials demanded a $250,000 bribe as payment for seeing Talleyrand. News of this insult, which became known as the XYZ Affair, provoked a wave of anti-French feeling at home. The Federalists called for war against France, but Adams refused. Through diplomacy, the two countries smoothed over their differences. Adams damaged his standing among the Federalists, but he kept the United States out of war.

Although Democratic-Republicans cheered Adams for avoiding war with France, they criticized him on many other issues. Some of the most vocal critics were foreign-born. In response, the Federalists in 1798 pushed through Congress four measures that became known as the Alien and Sedition Acts. The federal government then used the acts to prosecute and jail a number of Democratic-Republican editors, publishers, and politicians who they believed expressed "false, scandalous, and malicious statements" against the government. Outraged Democratic-Republicans called the laws a violation of freedom of speech guaranteed by the First Amendment.

The two main Democratic-Republican leaders, Thomas Jefferson and James Madison, saw the Alien and Sedition Acts as a serious misuse of power by the federal government. They appealed to the states for support. Virginia and Kentucky adopted resolutions warning of the danger that the Alien and Sedition Acts posed.

The Kentucky Resolutions asserted the principle of **nullification**: the states had the right to nullify, or consider void, any act of Congress that they deemed unconstitutional. No other states adopted similar resolutions, but the balance of power between the states and the federal government remained a controversial issue.

Reading Check
Contrast How did Jefferson's and Hamilton's views of government differ?

The Jeffersonian Era

The election of 1800 again pitted Democratic-Republican Jefferson against President John Adams and his Federalist Party. It was a hard-fought struggle. In the balloting in the Electoral College, Jefferson received eight more electoral votes than Adams. However, Jefferson's running mate, Aaron Burr, received the same number of votes as Jefferson himself. As a result, the House of Representatives was called upon to break the tie between the two. For six feverish days, the House took one ballot after another. On the 35th ballot, Jefferson received a majority of two votes. Burr then became vice-president.

JEFFERSON'S PRESIDENCY Jefferson's theory of government, often called Jeffersonian republicanism, held that the people should control the government and that a simple government best suited the needs of the people. Jefferson tried to shrink the government and cut costs wherever possible. For example, he rolled back Hamilton's economic program by eliminating all internal taxes and reducing the influence of the Bank of the United States.

One of Jefferson's first actions as president led to one of the most important Supreme Court decisions of all time. Just before leaving office, President Adams had tried to influence future judicial decisions by filling federal judgeships with Federalists. But the signed documents authorizing some of the appointments had not been delivered by the time Adams left office. Jefferson argued that these appointments were invalid.

This argument led to the Supreme Court case *Marbury* v. *Madison* (1803). In deciding the case, the Court, led by Chief Justice John Marshall, declared part of the Judiciary Act of 1789 unconstitutional. This decision strengthened the Supreme Court by establishing the principle of judicial review—the ability of the Supreme Court to declare a law—in this case an act of Congress—unconstitutional.

THE LOUISIANA PURCHASE In 1800 Napoleon Bonaparte of France persuaded Spain to return to France the Louisiana Territory, the land spanning from the Mississippi River west to the Rocky Mountains. Many Americans were alarmed by this transfer, as they feared that a strong French presence in North America would force the United States into an alliance with Britain.

Napoleon had dreamed of creating an American empire. However, by 1803 he had abandoned his ideas and offered to sell the Louisiana Territory to the United States at a price of $15 million. The **Louisiana Purchase** more than doubled the size of the United States. Under the direction of President Jefferson, Meriwether Lewis and William Clark organized and led a group to explore the new territory. The explorers brought back valuable information about the West and showed that transcontinental travel was possible.

MADISON AND THE WAR OF 1812 James Madison was elected president in 1808 during a period of increased tension between the French and British. This tension had begun to threaten American shipping. Although France and Britain both threatened U.S. ships between 1805 and 1814, Americans focused their anger on the British. Under the policy of impressment, the British seized Americans at sea and "impressed," or drafted, them into the British navy.

Background
To correct the flaw in the Constitution revealed by the election of 1800, Congress passed the Twelfth Amendment, which requires electors to cast separate ballots for president and vice-president. This system is still in effect today.

Thomas Jefferson

Background
Napoleon Bonaparte seized control of the French government in 1799 and expanded French territory until his defeat at Waterloo in Belgium in 1815.

Reading Check
Draw Conclusions
Why was the principle of judicial review important for the future of the Supreme Court?

By the spring of 1812, President Madison decided on war against Britain, and Congress approved the war declaration. When the fighting ended and the Treaty of Ghent was signed in 1814, the status of the United States as a free and independent nation was confirmed. The war also led to the growth of American industries to manufacture products previously obtained from Britain. In addition, it brought an end to the Federalist Party, whose members generally opposed the war.

Nationalism and Sectionalism

As with James Madison, foreign affairs dominated the first term of President James Monroe, who was elected in 1816. His secretary of state, John Quincy Adams, established a foreign policy based on nationalism—a belief that national interests should be placed ahead of regional concerns, such as slavery in the South or tariffs in the Northeast.

NATIONALISM SHAPES FOREIGN POLICY High on Adams's list of national interests were the security of the nation and the expansion of its territory. Under his leadership, the boundaries of the United States expanded, even reaching the Pacific Ocean. For example, in 1819 Adams persuaded the Spanish minister to the United States to agree to the Adams-Onís Treaty, which transferred possession of Florida to the United States.

▷ *Explore ONLINE!*

U.S. Boundary Settlements, 1803–1819

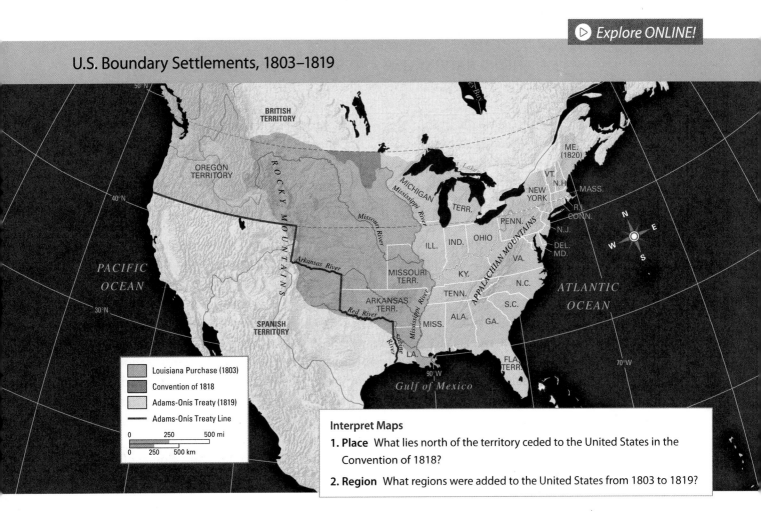

Legend:
- Louisiana Purchase (1803)
- Convention of 1818
- Adams-Onís Treaty (1819)
- Adams-Onís Treaty Line

0   250   500 mi
0   250   500 km

Interpret Maps
1. **Place** What lies north of the territory ceded to the United States in the Convention of 1818?
2. **Region** What regions were added to the United States from 1803 to 1819?

The formal transfer of Florida to the United States took place in 1821, two years after the signing of the treaty. The next year, Florida became an official U.S. territory. At the time, it extended as far west as the Sabine River, which today forms the boundary between Texas and Louisiana. The territorial capital was established at Tallahassee, approximately halfway between the former Spanish capitals of Pensacola and St. Augustine. Florida would remain a territory until 1845, by which time its population had grown large enough to allow it to apply for statehood.

James Monroe

THE MONROE DOCTRINE Monroe's greatest achievement in foreign policy came about because of conflicts in Europe and on the West Coast. In 1807 Spain and Portugal had been forced to give up territories in Latin America because a war with France had made the colonies too hard to govern. With the war over, the Spanish and Portuguese wanted to reclaim their lost colonies. At the same time, Russia was pushing south from trading posts it had established in Alaska into U.S. territory. Monroe knew that he needed to take action to protect American interests.

As a result, in his 1823 message to Congress, President Monroe warned European powers not to interfere with affairs in the Western Hemisphere. At the same time, the United States would not involve itself in European affairs or interfere with existing colonies. These principles became known as the Monroe Doctrine. The doctrine became a foundation for future American policy and represented an important step onto the world stage by the young nation. At home, however, sectional differences soon arose and challenged national unity.

BALANCING NATIONALISM AND SECTIONALISM As the United States focused on its national interests, sections of the country developed different economies—industries in the North, agriculture and slavery in the South, and small farms in the West. President Madison developed a plan to move the United States toward economic independence from Britain and other European powers. In 1815 he presented a plan to Congress that included establishing a protective tariff, rechartering the national bank, and sponsoring the development of transportation systems and other internal improvements.

Most northeasterners welcomed protective tariffs. However, people in the South and West, whose livelihoods did not depend on manufacturing, were less eager to tax European imports. Nevertheless, Henry Clay from Kentucky and John C. Calhoun from South Carolina convinced congressmen from their regions to approve the Tariff of 1816. Also in 1816, Congress voted to charter the Second Bank of the United States and to create a unified currency.

Reading Check
Analyze Effects
Do you think that the Monroe Doctrine would be a source of peace or conflict for the United States? Why?

Despite these efforts to unify the national economy, sectional conflicts remained part of American politics. In 1818 settlers in Missouri requested admission to the Union. However, northerners and southerners could not agree whether it should be a free state or a slave state. Under the **Missouri Compromise**, orchestrated by Henry Clay, Maine was admitted as a free state and Missouri as a slave state. The rest of the Louisiana Territory was split into two parts. The dividing line was set at 36°30' north latitude. South of the line, slavery was legal. North of the line—except in Missouri—slavery was banned.

The Age of Jackson

Despite these sectional tensions, America in the early 19th century was expanding. The man who best embraced the spirit of that expansion was **Andrew Jackson**, who captured the presidency in 1828.

THE ELECTION OF ANDREW JACKSON During John Quincy Adams's presidency, most states had eased property requirements for voting, thereby enlarging the voting population. In the election of 1824, approximately 350,000 white males voted for the presidency. In 1828 more than three times that number voted. Many of these new voters were common people who viewed the rugged westerner and war hero Jackson as their champion. This new voting bloc gave Jackson victory in the election of 1828.

Jackson's ideal was political power for all classes. He sought to give common people a chance to participate in government through the spoils system, in which new administrations hire their supporters to replace supporters of the previous administration. Jackson gave away huge numbers of jobs to friends and political allies.

JACKSON AND NATIVE AMERICANS However, political power did not extend to everyone in the United States. In 1830 Congress, with Jackson's support, passed the Indian Removal Act. Under this law, the federal government forced Native Americans to move west, out of their traditional homelands. Many groups signed removal treaties and began the long journey westward.

However, the Cherokee Nation refused to sign such a treaty and pledged to fight the government. They pressed their claim all the way to the Supreme Court. Although the Court ruled in favor of the Cherokee Nation, Jackson refused to abide by the decision, and the Cherokee were forced out of their lands. By 1840 about 16,000 Cherokee had been forcibly moved 800 miles west on routes afterward called the **Trail of Tears**. Because of the suffering they endured from cold, hunger, and diseases, one-fourth died.

When the U.S. Army similarly attempted to force the Seminole to leave Florida in 1835, however, they met resistance. The Seminole refused to give up their land and reacted with armed force. Seminole men conducted hit-and-run attacks on American soldiers, while women and children hid in the dense Florida swamps. About 3,000 Seminole were eventually forced to move to Indian Territory, but many more continued to resist. They were never officially defeated, and their descendants still live in Florida today.

NULLIFICATION AND THE BANK WAR Jackson's vice-president, John C. Calhoun of South Carolina, blamed tariff increases in 1824 and 1828 for economic problems in the South. From the South's point of view, the North was getting rich at the expense of the South.

To try to free South Carolinians from the tariff, Calhoun proposed a theory of nullification. He believed that because South Carolinians viewed the tariff as unconstitutional, they could declare it invalid within their state. South Carolina eventually threatened to secede, or withdraw from the Union, if customs officials tried to collect duties.

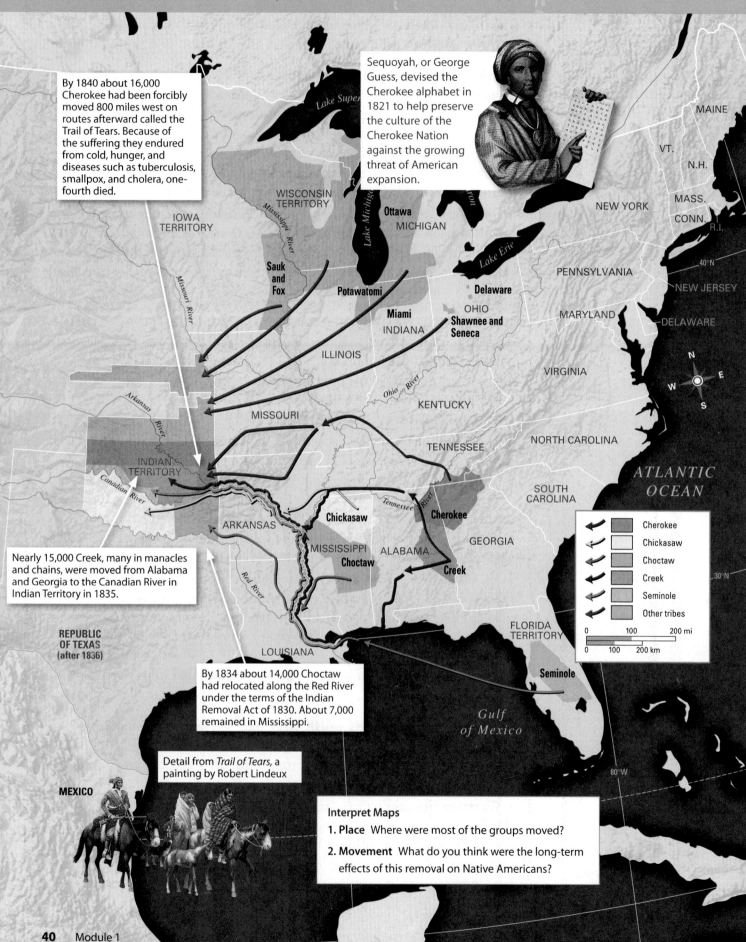

Effects of the Indian Removal Act, 1830s–1840s

By 1840 about 16,000 Cherokee had been forcibly moved 800 miles west on routes afterward called the Trail of Tears. Because of the suffering they endured from cold, hunger, and diseases such as tuberculosis, smallpox, and cholera, one-fourth died.

Sequoyah, or George Guess, devised the Cherokee alphabet in 1821 to help preserve the culture of the Cherokee Nation against the growing threat of American expansion.

Nearly 15,000 Creek, many in manacles and chains, were moved from Alabama and Georgia to the Canadian River in Indian Territory in 1835.

By 1834 about 14,000 Choctaw had relocated along the Red River under the terms of the Indian Removal Act of 1830. About 7,000 remained in Mississippi.

Detail from *Trail of Tears*, a painting by Robert Lindeux

MEXICO

Legend:
- Cherokee
- Chickasaw
- Choctaw
- Creek
- Seminole
- Other tribes

0   100   200 mi
0   100   200 km

REPUBLIC OF TEXAS (after 1836)

Interpret Maps

1. **Place** Where were most of the groups moved?

2. **Movement** What do you think were the long-term effects of this removal on Native Americans?

In response, an outraged Jackson urged Congress to pass the Force Bill to allow the federal government to use the military if state authorities resisted paying proper duties. Henry Clay forged a compromise, and the tension between states' rights and federal authority subsided—temporarily.

Although Jackson defended federal power in the nullification crisis, he tried to decrease federal power when it came to the Second Bank of the United States. He believed that the national bank was an agent of the wealthy. Jackson withdrew all government deposits and placed them in state banks loyal to the Democratic Party. As a result, the Bank of the United States became just another bank. Jackson had won the bank war, but many accused him of acting more like a king than a president. In 1832 his opponents formed a new political party, which they later called the Whig Party.

SUCCESSORS DEAL WITH JACKSON'S LEGACY Jackson's successor, Martin Van Buren, inherited the consequences of Jackson's bank war. Many of the state banks he had supported were wildcat banks that printed bank notes in excess of the gold and silver they had on deposit. Such banks were doomed to fail. In the bank panic of 1837, bank closings and the collapse of the credit system cost many people their savings, bankrupted hundreds of businesses, and put more than a third of the population out of work.

The recently formed Whig Party blamed Democrat Van Buren for the weak economy, and its candidate, William Henry Harrison, won the 1840 election. When President Harrison died just a month after his inauguration, Vice-President John Tyler became president.

The Democrat and Whig parties dominated national politics until the 1850s. The style of politics in America had changed drastically since the 1790s. Politicians appealed more to passion than reason. Political speeches became a form of mass entertainment, involving far more Americans in the political process. Also, western states like Missouri were playing an increasing role in national politics.

Reading Check
Analyze Causes
How did the Seminole respond to federal actions under the Indian Removal Act?

Lesson 3 Assessment

1. **Organize Information** Use a table to write newspaper headlines that tell the significance of each date.

Dates	Headlines
1781	
1788	
1796	
1803	
1828	
1838	

2. **Key Terms and People** For each key term or person in the lesson, write a sentence explaining its significance.

3. **Evaluate** In what ways do you think the Missouri Compromise and the nullification crisis might be considered important milestones in American history?
   Think About:
   • effects on slavery in the West
   • Calhoun's nullification theory
   • Jackson's reactions to South Carolina's actions

4. **Analyze Issues** Several states ratified the Constitution only after being assured that a bill of rights would be added to it. In your opinion, what is the most important value of the Bill of Rights? Why?

5. **Evaluate** Why was the War of 1812 a turning point for the early United States?

The Land Ordinance of 1785

Aerial photograph showing how the Land Ordinance transformed the landscape into a patchwork of farms

When states ceded, or gave up, their western lands to the United States, the new nation became "land rich" even though it was "money poor." Government leaders searched for a way to use the land to fund such services as public education.

The fastest and easiest way to raise money would have been to sell the land in huge parcels. However, only the rich would have been able to purchase land. The Land Ordinance of 1785 made the parcels small and affordable.

The Land Ordinance established a plan for dividing the land. The government would first survey the land, dividing it into townships of 36 square miles, as shown on the map below. Then each township would be divided into 36 sections of 1 square mile, or about 640 acres, each. An individual or a family could purchase a section and divide it into farms or smaller units. A typical farm of the period was equal to one-quarter section, or 160 acres. The minimum price per acre was one dollar.

Government leaders hoped the buyers would develop farms and establish communities. In this way, settlements would spread across the western territories in an orderly way. Government surveyors repeated the process thousands of times, imposing frontier geometry on the land.

In 1787 the Congress further provided for the orderly development of the Northwest Territory by passing the Northwest Ordinance, which established how states would be created out of the territory.

The map below shows how an eastern section of Ohio has been subdivided into townships and sections, according to the Land Ordinance of 1785.

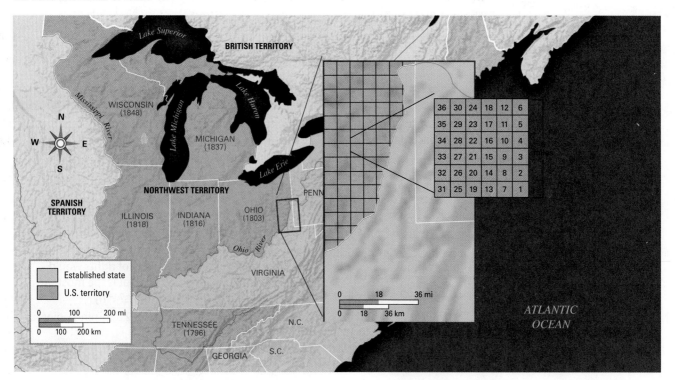

This map shows how a township, now in Meigs County, Ohio, was divided in 1787 into full square-mile sections and smaller, more affordable plots. The names of the original buyers are written on the full sections.

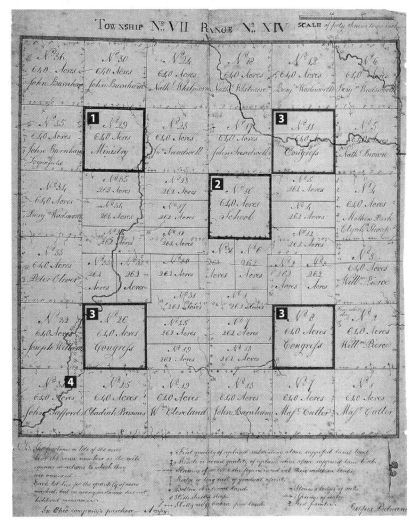

1 RELIGION

To encourage the growth of religion within the township, the surveyors set aside a full section of land. Most of the land within the section was sold to provide funds for a church and a minister's salary. This practice was dropped after a few years because of concern about the separation of church and state.

2 EDUCATION

The ordinance encouraged public education by setting aside section 16 of every township for school buildings. Local people used the money raised by the sale of land within this section to build a school and hire a teacher. This section was centrally located so that students could reach it without traveling too far.

3 REVENUE

Congress reserved two or three sections of each township for sale at a later date. Congress planned to sell the sections then at a tidy profit. The government soon abandoned this practice because of criticism that it should not be involved in land speculation.

4 WATER

Rivers and streams were very important to early settlers, who used them for transportation. Of most interest, however, was a meandering stream, which indicated flat bottomland that was highly prized for its fertility.

Critical Thinking

1. **Analyze Distributions** How did the Land Ordinance of 1785 provide for the orderly development of the Northwest Territory? How did it make land affordable?

2. **Create a Chart** Create a chart that organizes and summarizes the information in the map above. To help you organize your thoughts, pose questions that the map suggests and that a table could help answer.

The Constitution of the United States

"The Constitution was not made to fit us like a straightjacket. In its elasticity lies its chief greatness."

—President Woodrow Wilson

Purposes of the Constitution

The official charge to the delegates who met in Philadelphia in 1787 was to amend the Articles of Confederation. They soon made a fateful decision, however, to ignore the Articles and to write an entirely new constitution. These delegates—the "framers"—set themselves five purposes to fulfill in their effort to create an effective constitution.

1. ESTABLISH LEGITIMACY

First, the framers of the Constitution had to establish the new government's legitimacy—its right to rule. The patriots' theory of government was set out in the Declaration of Independence, which explained why British rule over the colonies was illegitimate. Now the framers had to demonstrate that their new government met the standards of legitimacy referred to in the Declaration.

For the framers of the Constitution, legitimacy had to be based on a contract among those who are to be ruled. The framers held to the principle called rule of law: Every member of the United States, both citizens and government, must follow its laws. This made a legitimate constitution absolutely necessary.

2. CREATE APPROPRIATE STRUCTURES

The framers' second purpose was to create appropriate structures for the new government. The framers were committed to the principles of representative democracy. They also believed that any new government must include an important role for state governments and ensure that the states retained some legitimacy to rule within their borders.

To achieve their goals, the framers created the Congress, the presidency, and the judiciary to share the powers of the national government. They also created a system of division of powers between the national government and the state governments.

3. DESCRIBE AND DISTRIBUTE POWER

The framers had as their third purpose to describe governmental powers and to distribute them among the structures they created. The powers of the legislative branch, which are those of Congress, are listed in Article I, Section 8, of the Constitution. Many of the executive powers belonging to the president are listed in Article II, Sections 2 and 3. The courts are given judicial powers in Article III. The words of Article IV imply that the states retain authority over many public matters.

4. LIMIT GOVERNMENT POWERS

The fourth purpose of the framers was to limit the powers of the structures they created. Limits on the Congress's powers are found in Article I, Section 9. Some of the limits on the powers of state governments are found in Article I, Section 10. There the framers enumerate functions that are delegated to the national government and so cannot be directed by the states.

5. ALLOW FOR CHANGE

The framers' fifth purpose was to include some means for changing the Constitution. Here they faced a dilemma: they wanted to make certain that the government endured by changing with the times, but they did not want to expose the basic rules of government to so many changes that the system would be unstable. So in Article V, they created a difficult, but not impossible, means for amending the Constitution.

The original manuscript of the Constitution is now kept in the National Archives in Washington, DC.

HOW TO READ THE CONSTITUTION

The Constitution, starting on the next page, appears in the major column, while the explanatory notes next to each article, section, or clause appear in the minor column. Each article is divided into sections, and the sections are subdivided into clauses. Headings have been added and the spelling and punctuation modernized for easier reading. Portions of the Constitution no longer in use have been crossed out. The Constitutional Insight questions and answers will help you understand significant issues related to the Constitution.

PREAMBLE

Constitutional Insight Why does the Preamble say "We the people of the United States . . . ordain and establish" the new government? The Articles of Confederation was an agreement among the states. But the framers of the Constitution wanted to be sure its legitimacy came from the American people, not from the states, which might decide to withdraw their support at any time. This is a basic principle of the Constitution.

ARTICLE I, SECTION 1

Constitutional Insight Why does the first article of the Constitution focus on Congress rather than on the presidency or the courts? The framers were intent on stressing the central role of the legislative branch in the new government because it is the branch that most directly represents the people and is most responsive to them.

Critical Thinking
Do you think Congress is still the branch of the federal government that is most directly responsible to the people? Why or why not?

ARTICLE I, SECTION 2.1

Constitutional Insight Why are members of the House of Representatives elected every two years? The House of Representatives was designed to be a truly representative body, with members who reflect the concerns and sentiments of their constituents as closely as possible. The framers achieved this timely representation by establishing two years as a reasonable term for members of the House to serve.

Critical Thinking
Do you think electing members of the House of Representatives every two years is a good idea? Why or why not?

The Constitution

PREAMBLE. PURPOSE OF THE CONSTITUTION

We the People of the United States, in Order to form a more perfect Union, establish Justice, insure domestic Tranquility, provide for the common defense, promote the general Welfare, and secure the Blessings of Liberty to ourselves and our Posterity, do ordain and establish this Constitution for the United States of America.

ARTICLE I. THE LEGISLATURE

Section 1. Congress

All legislative Powers herein granted shall be vested in a Congress of the United States, which shall consist of a Senate and House of Representatives.

Section 2. The House of Representatives

1. Elections The House of Representatives shall be composed of Members chosen every second Year by the People of the several States, and the Electors in each State shall have the Qualifications requisite for Electors of the most numerous Branch of the State Legislature.

2. Qualifications No Person shall be a Representative who shall not have attained to the Age of twenty five Years, and been seven Years a Citizen of the United States, and who shall not, when elected, be an Inhabitant of that State in which he shall be chosen.

3. Number of Representatives Representatives and direct Taxes shall be apportioned among the several States which may be included within this Union, according to their respective Numbers, ~~which shall be determined by adding to the whole Number of free Persons, including those bound to Service for a Term of Years, and excluding Indians not taxed, three fifths of all other Persons~~. The actual Enumeration shall be made within three Years after the first Meeting of the Congress of the United States, and within every subsequent Term of ten Years, in such Manner as they shall by Law direct. The Number of Representatives shall not exceed one for every thirty Thousand, but each State shall have at Least one Representative; ~~and until such enumeration shall be made, the State of New Hampshire shall be entitled to choose three, Massachusetts eight, Rhode-Island and Providence Plantations one, Connecticut five, New York six, New Jersey four, Pennsylvania eight, Delaware one, Maryland six, Virginia ten, North Carolina five, South Carolina five, and Georgia three.~~

4. Vacancies When vacancies happen in the Representation from any State, the Executive Authority thereof shall issue Writs of Election to fill such Vacancies.

5. Officers and Impeachment The House of Representatives shall choose their Speaker and other Officers; and shall have the sole Power of impeachment.

Section 3. The Senate

1. Number of Senators The Senate of the United States shall be composed of two Senators from each State, ~~chosen by the Legislature thereof,~~ for six Years; and each Senator shall have one Vote.

2. Classifying Terms Immediately after they shall be assembled in Consequence of the first Election, they shall be divided as equally as may be into three Classes. The Seats of the Senators of the first Class shall be vacated at the Expiration of the second Year, of the second Class at the Expiration of the fourth Year, and of the third Class at the Expiration of the sixth Year, so that one third may be chosen every second Year; ~~and if Vacancies happen by Resignation, or otherwise, during the Recess of the Legislature of any State, the Executive thereof may make temporary Appointments until the next Meeting of the Legislature, which shall then fill such Vacancies.~~

3. Qualifications No Person shall be a Senator who shall not have attained to the Age of thirty Years, and been nine Years a Citizen of the United States, and who shall not, when elected, be an Inhabitant of that State for which he shall be chosen.

4. Role of Vice President The Vice President of the United States shall be President of the Senate, but shall have no Vote, unless they be equally divided.

5. Officers The Senate shall choose their other Officers, and also a President pro tempore, in the Absence of the Vice President, or when he shall exercise the Office of President of the United States.

ARTICLE I, SECTION 3.1
Constitutional Insight Why are members of the Senate elected every six years? The framers feared the possibility of instability in the government. So they decided that senators should have six-year terms and be elected by the state legislatures rather than directly by the people. The Seventeenth Amendment, as you will see later, changed this. The framers also staggered the terms of the senators so that only one-third of them are replaced at any one time. This stabilizes the Senate still further.

Critical Thinking
Do you think it is important today for the Senate to have more stability than the House of Representatives? If so, why?

Requirements for Holding Federal Office

Position	Minimum Age	Residency	Citizenship
Representative	25 years	state in which elected	7 years
Senator	30 years	state in which elected	9 years
President	35 years	14 years in the United States	natural-born
Supreme Court Justice	none	none	none

Constitutional Insight Must an impeached president step down from office? Not necessarily. An impeachment is a formal accusation of criminal behavior or serious misbehavior. By impeaching the president, the U.S. House of Representatives is officially accusing the nation's chief executive of one or more wrong-doings that warrant possible removal from office. It is then the responsibility of the Senate to conduct a trial to determine whether the president is guilty or not guilty of the charges—and thus whether or not the president must step down. Conviction requires a two-thirds vote of the Senate.

Critical Thinking
Do you think a president should be put on trial for a crime while he or she is still in office? Explain.

ARTICLE I, SECTION 5.2
Constitutional Insight What kinds of rules does Congress make for itself? The Constitution gives each house control over most of its rules of procedure and membership. Rules are important, for they help shape the kinds of laws and policies that pass each body. Senate rules allow a filibuster, whereby a senator holds the floor as long as he or she likes in order to block consideration of a bill he or she dislikes. In recent years, a "cloture" rule has been used to end debate if 60 or more members vote to do so.

In contrast, the House of Representatives has rules to limit debate. The Rules Committee has the primary task of determining how long a bill on the floor of the House may be discussed and whether any amendments can be offered to the bill. In recent years, the power of the Rules Committee has been limited, but being able to shape the rules remains a powerful tool of members of Congress.

Critical Thinking
Why do you think the chair of the Rules Committee is in a powerful position?

6. Impeachment Trials The Senate shall have the sole Power to try all Impeachments. When sitting for that Purpose, they shall be on Oath or Affirmation. When the President of the United States is tried, the Chief Justice shall preside: And no Person shall be convicted without the Concurrence of two thirds of the Members present.

7. Punishment for Impeachment Judgment in Cases of Impeachment shall not extend further than to removal from Office, and disqualification to hold and enjoy any Office of honor, Trust or Profit under the United States: but the Party convicted shall nevertheless be liable and subject to Indictment, Trial, Judgment and Punishment, according to Law.

Section 4. Congressional Elections

1. Regulations The Times, Places and Manner of holding Elections for Senators and Representatives, shall be prescribed in each State by the Legislature thereof; but the Congress may at any time by Law make or alter such Regulations, except as to the Places of choosing Senators.

2. Sessions ~~The Congress shall assemble at least once in every Year, and such Meeting shall be on the first Monday in December, unless they shall by Law appoint a different Day.~~

Section 5. Rules/Procedures

1. Quorum Each House shall be the Judge of the Elections, Returns and Qualifications of its own Members, and a Majority of each shall constitute a Quorum to do Business; but a smaller Number may adjourn from day to day, and may be authorized to compel the Attendance of absent Members, in such Manner, and under such Penalties as each House may provide.

2. Rules and Conduct Each House may determine the Rules of its Proceedings, punish its Members for disorderly Behaviour, and, with the Concurrence of two thirds, expel a Member.

3. Records Each House shall keep a Journal of its Proceedings, and from time to time publish the same, excepting such Parts as may in their Judgment require Secrecy; and the Yeas and Nays of the Members of either House on any question shall, at the Desire of one fifth of those Present, be entered on the Journal.

4. Adjournment Neither House, during the Session of Congress, shall, without the Consent of the other, adjourn for more than three days, nor to any other Place than that in which the two Houses shall be sitting.

Section 6. Payment

1. Salary The Senators and Representatives shall receive a Compensation for their Services, to be ascertained by Law, and paid out of the Treasury of the United States. They shall in all Cases, except Treason, Felony and Breach of the Peace, be privileged from Arrest during their Attendance at the Session of their respective Houses, and in going to and returning from the same; and for any Speech or Debate in either House, they shall not be questioned in any other Place.

2. Restrictions No Senator or Representative shall, during the Time for which he was elected, be appointed to any civil Office under the Authority of the United States, which shall have been created, or the Emoluments whereof shall have been increased during such time; and no Person holding any Office under the United States, shall be a Member of either House during his Continuance in Office.

Section 7. How a Bill Becomes a Law

1. Tax Bills All Bills for raising Revenue shall originate in the House of Representatives; but the Senate may propose or concur with Amendments as on other Bills.

ARTICLE I, SECTION 7.1
Constitutional Insight Why must all bills to raise revenue originate in the House? Because its members all stand for election every two years, the House was expected to be more directly responsive to the people. The tradition of restricting the powers of taxation to the people's representatives dates prior to the English Bill of Rights (1689), which granted to Parliament and withheld from the king the right to raise taxes. When colonists protesting the Stamp Act and the Intolerable Acts protested "no taxation without representation," they were appealing to a longstanding right codified in the English Bill of Rights.

How a Bill in Congress Becomes a Law

1
A bill is introduced in the House or the Senate and referred to a standing committee for consideration.

2
A bill may be reported out of committee with or without changes—or it may be shelved.

3
Either house of Congress debates the bill and may make revisions. If passed, the bill is sent to the other house.

4
If the House and the Senate pass different versions of a bill, both versions go to a conference committee to work out the differences.

5
The conference committee submits a single version of the bill to the House and the Senate.

6
If both houses accept the compromise version, the bill is sent to the president to be signed.

7
If the president signs the bill, it becomes law.

8
If the president vetoes the bill, the House and the Senate may override the veto by a vote of two thirds of the members present in each house, and then the bill becomes law.

Interpret Visuals
How is the constitutional principle of checks and balances reflected in the process of a bill's becoming a law?

ARTICLE I, SECTION 7.2
Constitutional Insight How often do presidents use the veto, and how often is that action overridden? The use of the veto, which is the refusal to approve a bill, depends on many factors, especially the political conditions of the time. Until 1865 only nine presidents exercised the veto for 36 pieces of legislation, including Andrew Jackson who used it 12 times. Since 1865 every president has used the veto power, some on relatively few occasions, others as frequently as over a hundred times. Usually Congress is unable to produce the votes (those of two-thirds of the members present in each house) needed to override presidential vetoes.

Critical Thinking
Do you think it should be easier for Congress to override a president's veto? Why or why not?

ARTICLE I, SECTION 8
Constitutional Insight The powers given to Congress are in Section 8 of Article I. The first 17 clauses of Section 8 are often called the enumerated powers because they name individually Congress's specific powers. These powers deal with issues ranging from taxation and the national debt to calling out the armed forces of the various states to governing the nation's capital district (Washington, DC).

Critical Thinking
Why do you think it is important to spell out the powers specifically granted to Congress?

2. Lawmaking Every Bill which shall have passed the House of Representatives and the Senate, shall, before it become a Law, be presented to the President of the United States: If he approve he shall sign it, but if not he shall return it, with his Objections to that House in which it shall have originated, who shall enter the Objections at large on their Journal, and proceed to reconsider it. If after such Reconsideration two thirds of that House shall agree to pass the Bill, it shall be sent, together with the Objections, to the other House, by which it shall likewise be reconsidered, and if approved by two thirds of that House, it shall become a Law. But in all such Cases the Votes of both Houses shall be determined by yeas and Nays, and the Names of the Persons voting for and against the Bill shall be entered on the Journal of each House respectively. If any Bill shall not be returned by the President within ten Days (Sundays excepted) after it shall have been presented to him, the Same shall be a Law, in like Manner as if he had signed it, unless the Congress by their Adjournment prevent its Return, in which Case it shall not be a Law.

3. Role Of The President Every Order, Resolution, or Vote to which the Concurrence of the Senate and House of Representatives may be necessary (except on a question of Adjournment) shall be presented to the President of the United States; and before the Same shall take Effect, shall be approved by him, or being disapproved by him, shall be repassed by two thirds of the Senate and House of Representatives, according to the Rules and Limitations prescribed in the Case of a Bill.

Section 8. Powers Granted to Congress

1. Taxation The Congress shall have Power To lay and collect Taxes, Duties, Imposts and Excises, to pay the Debts and provide for the common Defense and general Welfare of the United States; but all Duties, Imposts and Excises shall be uniform throughout the United States;

2. Credit To borrow Money on the credit of the United States;

3. Commerce To regulate Commerce with foreign Nations, and among the several States, and with the Indian Tribes;

4. Naturalization and Bankruptcy To establish an uniform Rule of Naturalization, and uniform Laws on the subject of Bankruptcies throughout the United States;

5. Money To coin Money, regulate the Value thereof, and of foreign Coin, and fix the Standard of Weights and Measures;

6. Counterfeiting To provide for the Punishment of counterfeiting the Securities and current Coin of the United States;

7. Post Office To establish Post Offices and post Roads;

ARTICLE I, SECTION 8.18

Constitutional Insight How is the last clause different? The 18th and final clause gives Congress the power to do what is "necessary and proper" to carry out the enumerated powers. Thus, the enumerated powers of Congress "to lay and collect taxes," "to borrow money," "to regulate commerce," and "to coin money" imply the power to create a bank in order to execute these powers. Early in the country's history, this "elastic clause," as it has been called, was used by Congress to establish the controversial Bank of the United States in 1791 and the Second Bank of the United States in 1816.

Critical Thinking
Why do you think the elastic clause is still important today?

8. Patents and Copyrights To promote the Progress of Science and useful Arts, by securing for limited Times to Authors and Inventors the exclusive Right to their respective Writings and Discoveries;

9. Courts To constitute Tribunals inferior to the supreme Court;

10. International Law To define and punish Piracies and Felonies committed on the high Seas, and Offences against the Law of Nations;

11. War To declare War, grant Letters of Marque and Reprisal, and make Rules concerning Captures on Land and Water;

12. Army To raise and support Armies, but no Appropriation of Money to that Use shall be for a longer Term than two Years;

13. Navy To provide and maintain a Navy;

14. Regulation of the Military To make Rules for the Government and Regulation of the land and naval Forces;

15. Militia To provide for calling forth the Militia to execute the Laws of the Union, suppress Insurrections and repel Invasions;

16. Regulation of the Militia To provide for organizing, arming, and disciplining, the Militia, and for governing such Part of them as may be employed in the Service of the United States, reserving to the States respectively, the Appointment of the Officers, and the Authority of training the Militia according to the discipline prescribed by Congress;

17. District of Columbia To exercise exclusive Legislation in all Cases whatsoever, over such District (not exceeding ten Miles square) as may, by Cession of particular States, and the Acceptance of Congress, become the Seat of the Government of the United States, and to exercise like Authority over all Places purchased by the Consent of the Legislature of the State in which the Same shall be, for the Erection of Forts, Magazines, Arsenals, dock-Yards, and other needful Buildings;—And

18. Necessary and Proper Clause To make all Laws which shall be necessary and proper for carrying into Execution the foregoing Powers, and all other Powers vested by this Constitution in the Government of the United States, or in any Department or Officer thereof.

Constitutional Insight Why
didn't the framers include a bill
of rights in the original Constitution?   Actually, they did. Article I,
Section 9, defines limits on the powers
of Congress, just as the first ten amendments (which we call the Bill of Rights)
do. While some of the provisions focus
on such issues as slavery and taxation,
there are three explicit prohibitions
dealing with citizens' rights:

- *Writ of habeas corpus.* Section 9,
  Clause 2, says that, except in time of
  rebellion or invasion, Congress cannot suspend people's right to a writ
  of habeas corpus. This means that
  people cannot be held in prison or jail
  without being formally charged with
  a crime.

- *Bill of attainder.* Clause 3 prohibits
  the passage of any law that convicts
  or punishes a person directly and
  without a trial. Any legislative action
  that would punish someone without
  recourse to a court of law is called a
  bill of attainder.

- *Ex post facto law.* The same clause
  prohibits ex post facto laws. Such a
  law would punish a person for an act
  that was legal when it was performed.

The fact that these particular rights
were protected by the original document issued by the framers reflects
both the framers' experiences during
the Revolution and their fear of excessive government power.

Critical Thinking
Why are American citizens today so
intent on having protections against
government violations of their rights?

Section 9. Powers Denied Congress

1. Slave Trade ~~The Migration or Importation of such Persons as any of the States now existing shall think proper to admit, shall not be prohibited by the Congress prior to the Year one thousand eight hundred and eight, but a Tax or duty may be imposed on such Importation, not exceeding ten dollars for each Person.~~

2. Habeas Corpus The Privilege of the Writ of Habeas Corpus shall not be suspended, unless when in Cases of Rebellion or Invasion the public Safety may require it.

3. Illegal Punishment No Bill of Attainder or ex post facto Law shall be passed.

4. Direct Taxes No Capitation, or other direct, Tax shall be laid, unless in Proportion to the Census or enumeration herein before directed to be taken.

5. Export Taxes No Tax or Duty shall be laid on Articles exported from any State.

6. No Favorites No Preference shall be given by any Regulation of Commerce or Revenue to the Ports of one State over those of another; nor shall Vessels bound to, or from, one State, be obliged to enter, clear, or pay Duties in another.

7. Public Money No Money shall be drawn from the Treasury, but in Consequence of Appropriations made by Law; and a regular Statement and Account of the Receipts and Expenditures of all public Money shall be published from time to time.

8. Titles of Nobility No Title of Nobility shall be granted by the United States: And no Person holding any Office of Profit or Trust under them, shall, without the Consent of the Congress, accept of any present, Emolument, Office, or Title, of any kind whatever, from any King, Prince, or foreign State.

Section 10. Powers Denied the States

1. Restrictions No State shall enter into any Treaty, Alliance, or Confederation; grant Letters of Marque and Reprisal; coin Money; emit Bills of Credit; make any Thing but gold and silver Coin a Tender in Payment of Debts; pass any Bill of Attainder, ex post facto Law, or Law impairing the Obligation of Contracts, or grant any Title of Nobility.

2. Import and Export Taxes No State shall, without the Consent of the Congress, lay any Imposts or Duties on Imports or Exports, except what may be absolutely necessary for executing it's inspection Laws: and the net Produce of all Duties and Imposts, laid by any State on Imports or Exports, shall be for the Use of the Treasury of the United States; and all such Laws shall be subject to the Revision and Control of the Congress.

3. Peacetime and War Restraints No State shall, without the Consent of Congress, lay any Duty of Tonnage, keep Troops, or Ships of War in time of Peace, enter into any Agreement or Compact with another State, or with a foreign Power, or engage in War, unless actually invaded, or in such imminent Danger as will not admit of delay.

ARTICLE II. THE EXECUTIVE

Section 1. The Presidency

1. Terms of Office The executive Power shall be vested in a President of the United States of America. He shall hold his Office during the Term of four Years, and, together with the Vice President, chosen for the same Term, be elected, as follows:

2. Electoral College Each State shall appoint, in such Manner as the Legislature thereof may direct, a Number of Electors, equal to the whole Number of Senators and Representatives to which the State may be entitled in the Congress: but no Senator or Representative, or Person holding an Office of Trust or Profit under the United States, shall be appointed an Elector.

3. Former Method of Electing President The Electors shall meet in their respective States, and vote by Ballot for two Persons, of whom one at least shall not be an Inhabitant of the same State with themselves. And they shall make a List of all the Persons voted for, and of the Number of Votes for each; which List they shall sign and certify, and transmit sealed to the Seat of the Government of the United States, directed to the President of the Senate. The President of the Senate shall, in the Presence of the Senate and House of Representatives, open all the Certificates, and the Votes shall then be counted. The Person having the greatest Number of Votes shall be the President, if such Number be a Majority of the whole Number of Electors appointed; and if there be more than one who have such Majority, and have an equal Number of Votes, then the House of Representatives shall immediately choose by Ballot one of them for President; and if no Person have a Majority, then from the five highest on the List the said House shall in like Manner choose the President. But in choosing the President, the Votes shall be taken by States, the Representation from each State having one Vote; A quorum for this purpose shall consist of a Member or Members from two thirds of the States, and a Majority of all the States shall be necessary to a Choice. In every Case, after the Choice of the President, the Person having the greatest Number of Votes of the Electors shall be the Vice President. But if there should remain two or more who have equal Votes, the Senate shall choose from them by Ballot the Vice President.

ARTICLE II, SECTION 1.1

Constitutional Insight What exactly is "executive power"? We know the president has it, but nowhere is it explicitly defined. It is most often defined as the power to carry out the laws of the land, but of course no one person can handle such a chore alone. A more appropriate definition is found in Section 3 of this article, which empowers the president to "take care that the laws be faithfully executed." In this sense, the president is the chief administrator.

Critical Thinking
Why is it important to have an executive who is the chief administrator?

ARTICLE II, SECTION 1.6

Constitutional Insight What happens when the vice-president succeeds a dead or incapacitated president? Section 1.6 provides that the vice-president shall assume the powers and duties of the presidential office. But until the Twenty-Fifth Amendment was added to the Constitution in 1967, there was no explicit statement in the document that the vice-president is to become president. That procedure owes its origin to John Tyler, the tenth president of the United States, who in 1841 succeeded William Henry Harrison—the first president to die in office. Tyler decided to take the oath of office and assume the title of president of the United States. Congress voted to go along with his decision, and the practice was repeated after Lincoln was assassinated. It would take another century for the written provisions of the Constitution to catch up with the practice.

Critical Thinking
Why is it important to know the order of succession if a president dies in office?

4. Election Day The Congress may determine the Time of choosing the Electors, and the Day on which they shall give their Votes; which Day shall be the same throughout the United States.

5. Qualifications No Person except a natural born Citizen, ~~or a Citizen of the United States, at the time of the Adoption of this Constitution~~, shall be eligible to the Office of President; neither shall any Person be eligible to that Office who shall not have attained to the Age of thirty five Years, and been fourteen Years a Resident within the United States.

6. Succession In Case of the Removal of the President from Office, or of his Death, Resignation, or Inability to discharge the Powers and Duties of the said Office, the Same shall devolve on the Vice President, and the Congress may by Law provide for the Case of Removal, Death, Resignation or Inability, both of the President and Vice President, declaring what Officer shall then act as President, and such Officer shall act accordingly, until the Disability be removed, or a President shall be elected.

7. Salary The President shall, at stated Times, receive for his Services, a Compensation, which shall neither be increased nor diminished during the Period for which he shall have been elected, and he shall not receive within that Period any other Emolument from the United States, or any of them.

8. Oath of Office Before he enter on the Execution of his Office, he shall take the following Oath or Affirmation: —"I do solemnly swear (or affirm) that I will faithfully execute the Office of President of the United States, and will to the best of my Ability, preserve, protect and defend the Constitution of the United States."

ARTICLE II, SECTION 2.1

Constitutional Insight Just how much authority does the president have as "Commander in Chief" of the armed forces?   The president has the power to give orders to American military forces. There have been several instances in U.S. history when presidents have used that authority in spite of congressional wishes.

President Harry Truman involved U.S. armed forces in the Korean War from 1950 to 1953 without a congressional declaration of war.

Reacting to criticism of the Vietnam War, Congress in 1973 enacted the War Powers Resolution, making the president more accountable to Congress for any military actions he or she might take. Every president since Richard Nixon has called the resolution unconstitutional. Nevertheless, every president has reported to Congress within 48 hours of sending troops into an international crisis, as is required by the resolution.

Critical Thinking
Why is it important that the Commander in Chief of the U.S. armed forces be a civilian (the president) rather than a military general?

ARTICLE II, SECTION 3

Constitutional Insight Is it necessary for the president to deliver a State of the Union address before a joint session of Congress at the start of each legislative year?   The Constitution requires only that the president report to Congress on the state of the Union from time to time, and nowhere does it call for an annual address. In 1913 President Woodrow Wilson wanted to influence Congress to take action without delay on some legislation that he thought was important. Wilson revived the tradition—which had been discontinued by Jefferson—of delivering the State of the Union address in person.

Critical Thinking
How does the president use the State of the Union address today?

Section 2. Powers of Presidency

1. Military Powers The President shall be Commander in Chief of the Army and Navy of the United States, and of the Militia of the several States, when called into the actual Service of the United States; he may require the Opinion, in writing, of the principal Officer in each of the executive Departments, upon any Subject relating to the Duties of their respective Offices, and he shall have Power to grant Reprieves and Pardons for Offences against the United States, except in Cases of Impeachment.

2. Treaties and Appointments He shall have Power, by and with the Advice and Consent of the Senate, to make Treaties, provided two thirds of the Senators present concur; and he shall nominate, and by and with the Advice and Consent of the Senate, shall appoint Ambassadors, other public Ministers and Consuls, Judges of the supreme Court, and all other Officers of the United States, whose Appointments are not herein otherwise provided for, and which shall be established by Law: but the Congress may by Law vest the Appointment of such inferior Officers, as they think proper, in the President alone, in the Courts of Law, or in the Heads of Departments.

3. Vacancies The President shall have Power to fill up all Vacancies that may happen during the Recess of the Senate, by granting Commissions which shall expire at the End of their next Session.

Section 3. Presidential Duties

He shall from time to time give to the Congress Information of the State of the Union, and recommend to their Consideration such Measures as he shall judge necessary and expedient; he may, on extraordinary Occasions, convene both Houses, or either of them, and in Case of Disagreement between them, with Respect to the Time of Adjournment, he may adjourn them to such Time as he shall think proper; he shall receive Ambassadors and other public Ministers; he shall take Care that the Laws be faithfully executed, and shall Commission all the Officers of the United States.

ARTICLE II, SECTION 4

Constitutional Insight Have high-level public officials ever been impeached? The House has impeached only two presidents, and neither had to leave office. In 1868 the Senate found President Andrew Johnson not guilty by one vote after the House impeached him, charging him with violating a congressional act. In 1999 senators acquitted President Bill Clinton after the House impeached him with charges of lying under oath and obstructing justice in the attempted cover-up of a White House scandal.

The only other president to come close to impeachment was Richard Nixon. In 1974 the House Judiciary Committee, in what is the first step of the impeachment process, recommended three articles of impeachment against Nixon for his role in the infamous Watergate scandal. Before the full House could vote for or against the articles of impeachment, however, Nixon resigned from office.

Critical Thinking
Why do you think the framers of the Constitution created such an elaborate procedure for removing a sitting president?

ARTICLE III, SECTION 2.1

Constitutional Insight What is judicial review? Is it the same as judicial power? No. Judicial power is the authority to hear cases involving disputes over the law or the behavior of people. Judicial review, in contrast, is a court's passing judgment on the constitutionality of a law or government action that is being disputed. Interestingly, nowhere does the Constitution mention judicial review. There are places where it is implied (for example, in Section 2 of Article VI), but the only explicit description of the responsibility of the courts is the reference to judicial power in Section 1 of Article III. The Supreme Court's power to review laws passed by Congress was explicitly affirmed by the Court itself in *Marbury v. Madison*.

Critical Thinking
Why is judicial review, although not mentioned in the Constitution, an important activity of the Supreme Court?

Section 4. Impeachment

The President, Vice President and all civil Officers of the United States, shall be removed from Office on Impeachment for, and Conviction of, Treason, Bribery, or other high Crimes and Misdemeanors.

ARTICLE III. THE JUDICIARY

Section 1. Federal Courts and Judges

The judicial Power of the United States shall be vested in one supreme Court, and in such inferior Courts as the Congress may from time to time ordain and establish. The Judges, both of the supreme and inferior Courts, shall hold their Offices during good Behavior, and shall, at stated Times, receive for their Services a Compensation, which shall not be diminished during their Continuance in Office.

Section 2. Authority of the Courts

1. General Authority The judicial Power shall extend to all Cases, in Law and Equity, arising under this Constitution, the Laws of the United States, and Treaties made, or which shall be made, under their Authority;—to all Cases affecting Ambassadors, other public Ministers and Consuls;—to all Cases of admiralty and maritime Jurisdiction;—to Controversies to which the United States shall be a Party;—to Controversies between two or more States—between a State and Citizens of another State; —between Citizens of different States;—between Citizens of the same State claiming Lands under Grants of different States, and between a State, or the Citizens thereof, and foreign States, Citizens or Subjects.

2. Supreme Authority In all Cases affecting Ambassadors, other public Ministers and Consuls, and those in which a State shall be Party, the supreme Court shall have original Jurisdiction. In all the other Cases before mentioned, the supreme Court shall have appellate Jurisdiction, both as to Law and Fact, with such Exceptions, and under such Regulations as the Congress shall make.

3. Trial by Jury The Trial of all Crimes, except in Cases of Impeachment, shall be by Jury; and such Trial shall be held in the State where the said Crimes shall have been committed; but when not committed within any State, the Trial shall be at such Place or Places as the Congress may by Law have directed.

Section 3. Treason

1. Definition Treason against the United States, shall consist only in levying War against them, or in adhering to their Enemies, giving them Aid and Comfort. No Person shall be convicted of Treason unless on the Testimony of two Witnesses to the same overt Act, or on Confession in open Court.

2. Punishment The Congress shall have Power to declare the Punishment of Treason, but no Attainder of Treason shall work Corruption of Blood, or Forfeiture except during the Life of the Person attainted.

ARTICLE IV. RELATIONS AMONG STATES

Section 1. State Acts and Records

Full Faith and Credit shall be given in each State to the public Acts, Records, and judicial Proceedings of every other State. And the Congress may by general Laws prescribe the Manner in which such Acts, Records and Proceedings shall be proved, and the Effect thereof.

Section 2. Rights of Citizens

1. Citizenship The Citizens of each State shall be entitled to all Privileges and Immunities of Citizens in the several States.

2. Extradition A Person charged in any State with Treason, Felony, or other Crime, who shall flee from Justice, and be found in another State, shall on Demand of the executive Authority of the State from which he fled, be delivered up, to be removed to the State having Jurisdiction of the Crime.

3. Fugitive Slaves No Person held to Service or Labour in one State, under the Laws thereof, escaping into another, shall, in Consequence of any Law or Regulation therein, be discharged from such Service or Labour, but shall be delivered up on Claim of the Party to whom such Service or Labour may be due.

ARTICLE IV, SECTION 2.1

Constitutional Insight Why do college students attending public universities outside their state of residence have to pay higher tuition fees? The Supreme Court has interpreted the "privileges and immunities" clause to allow higher tuition fees (and fees for hunting permits, etc.) for nonresidents when a state can give a "substantial reason" for the difference. Since state colleges and universities receive some financial support from the states' taxpayers, the difference is regarded as justified in most states. If a student establishes residency in the state, he or she can pay in-state tuition after one year.

Critical Thinking
Do you think it is fair that a nonresident must pay higher tuition fees at a state college than a resident of the state must pay? Explain.

ARTICLE IV, SECTION 3.1

Constitutional Insight Should there be a West Virginia? The Constitution states that "no new state shall be formed or erected within the jurisdiction of any other state" without the permission of the legislature of the state involved and of the Congress. Vermont, Kentucky, Tennessee, and Maine were created from territory taken from existing states, with the approval of the sitting legislatures.

West Virginia, however, is a different story. During the Civil War, the residents of the westernmost counties of Virginia were angry with their state's decision to secede from the Union. They petitioned Congress to have their counties declared a distinct state. Congress agreed, and so the state of West Virginia was created. After the Civil War, the legislature of Virginia gave its formal approval, perhaps because it was in no position to dispute the matter.

Critical Thinking
Suppose a section of Texas should decide to become a new state today. Could it do this? Why or why not?

Section 3. New States

1. Admission New States may be admitted by the Congress into this Union; but no new State shall be formed or erected within the Jurisdiction of any other State; nor any State be formed by the Junction of two or more States, or Parts of States, without the Consent of the Legislatures of the States concerned as well as of the Congress.

2. Congressional Authority The Congress shall have Power to dispose of and make all needful Rules and Regulations respecting the Territory or other Property belonging to the United States; and nothing in this Constitution shall be so construed as to Prejudice any Claims of the United States, or of any particular State.

Section 4. Guarantees to the States

The United States shall guarantee to every State in this Union a Republican Form of Government, and shall protect each of them against Invasion; and on Application of the Legislature, or of the Executive (when the Legislature cannot be convened), against domestic Violence.

ARTICLE V. AMENDING THE CONSTITUTION

The Congress, whenever two thirds of both Houses shall deem it necessary, shall propose Amendments to this Constitution, or, on the Application of the Legislatures of two thirds of the several States, shall call a Convention for proposing Amendments, which, in either Case, shall be valid to all Intents and Purposes, as Part of this Constitution, when ratified by the Legislatures of three fourths of the several States, or by Conventions in three fourths thereof, as the one or the other Mode of Ratification may be proposed by the Congress; Provided that no Amendment which may be made prior to the Year One thousand eight hundred and eight shall in any Manner affect the first and fourth Clauses in the Ninth Section of the first Article; and that no State, without its Consent, shall be deprived of its equal Suffrage in the Senate.

Section 1. Valid Debts

All Debts contracted and Engagements entered into, before the Adoption of this Constitution, shall be as valid against the United States under this Constitution, as under the Confederation.

Section 2. Supreme Law

This Constitution, and the Laws of the United States which shall be made in Pursuance thereof; and all Treaties made, or which shall be made, under the Authority of the United States, shall be the supreme Law of the Land; and the Judges in every State shall be bound thereby, any Thing in the Constitution or Laws of any State to the Contrary notwithstanding.

Section 3. Loyalty to Constitution

The Senators and Representatives before mentioned, and the Members of the several State Legislatures, and all executive and judicial Officers, both of the United States and of the several States, shall be bound by Oath or Affirmation, to support this Constitution; but no religious Test shall ever be required as a Qualification to any Office or public Trust under the United States.

ARTICLE VI, SECTION 2

Constitutional Insight Just how "supreme" is the "law of the land"? The Constitution and all federal laws and treaties are the highest law of the land. (To be supreme, federal laws must be constitutional.) All state constitutions and laws and all local laws rank below national law and cannot be enforced if they contradict national law. For example, if the United States enters into a treaty protecting migratory Canadian birds, the states must change their laws to fit the provisions of that agreement. That was the decision of the Supreme Court in the case of *Missouri v. Holland* (1920). The state of Missouri argued that the national government could not interfere with its power to regulate hunting within its borders, but the Supreme Court concluded that the treaty was a valid exercise of national power and therefore took priority over state and local laws. The states had to adjust their rules and regulations accordingly.

Critical Thinking
What would happen if the national law were not supreme?

Constitutional Insight Why was ratification by only nine states sufficient to put the Constitution into effect? In taking such a momentous step as replacing one constitution (the Articles of Confederation) with another, the framers might have been expected to require the agreement of all 13 states. But the framers were political realists. They knew that they would have a difficult time winning approval from all 13 states. But they also knew that they had a good chance of getting nine or ten of the states "on board" and that once that happened, the rest would follow. Their strategy worked, but just barely. Although they had the approval of nine states by the end of June 1788, two of the most important states—Virginia and New York—had not yet decided to ratify. Without the approval of these influential states, the new government would have had a difficult time surviving. Finally, by the end of July, both had given their blessing to the new constitution, but not without intense debate.

Then there was the last holdout—Rhode Island. Not only had Rhode Island refused to send delegates to the Constitutional Convention in 1787, but it turned down ratification several times before finally giving its approval in 1790 under a cloud of economic and even military threats from neighboring states.

Critical Thinking
Do you think all 50 states would ratify the Constitution today? Why or why not?

ARTICLE VII. RATIFICATION

The Ratification of the Conventions of nine States, shall be sufficient for the Establishment of this Constitution between the States so ratifying the Same.

Done in Convention by the Unanimous Consent of the States present the Seventeenth Day of September in the Year of our Lord one thousand seven hundred and Eighty seven and of the Independence of the United States of America the Twelfth In witness whereof We have hereunto subscribed our Names,

George Washington—President and deputy from Virginia

Delaware
George Read
Gunning Bedford, Jr.
John Dickinson
Richard Bassett
Jacob Broom

Maryland
James McHenry
Dan of St. Thomas Jenifer
Daniel Carroll

Virginia
John Blair
James Madison, Jr.

North Carolina
William Blount
Richard Dobbs Spaight
Hugh Williamson

South Carolina
John Rutledge
Charles Cotesworth Pinckney
Charles Pinckney
Pierce Butler

Georgia
William Few
Abraham Baldwin

New Hampshire
John Langdon
Nicholas Gilman

Massachusetts
Nathaniel Gorham
Rufus King

Connecticut
William Samuel Johnson
Roger Sherman

New York
Alexander Hamilton

New Jersey
William Livingston
David Brearley
William Paterson
Jonathan Dayton

Pennsylvania
Benjamin Franklin
Thomas Mifflin
Robert Morris
George Clymer
Thomas FitzSimons
Jared Ingersoll
James Wilson
Gouverneur Morris

Attest:
William Jackson,
Secretary

AMENDMENT I

Constitutional Insight Do Americans have an absolute right to free speech? The right to free speech is not without limits. In the case of *Schenck v. United States* (1919), Justice Oliver Wendell Holmes wrote that this right does "not protect a man in falsely shouting fire in a theatre and causing a panic." Thus, some forms of speech are not protected by the First Amendment, and Congress is allowed to make laws regarding certain types of expression.

Critical Thinking
Why is there controversy over freedom of speech today?

AMENDMENT IV

Constitutional Insight Can the police search your car without a court-issued search warrant when they stop you for speeding? The answer, according to Supreme Court decisions, depends on whether they have good reasons—called "probable cause"—for doing so. If a state trooper notices bloody clothing in a vehicle that has been stopped for a traffic violation, there might be probable cause for a search of the vehicle. There is probably not sufficient reason for a search if the trooper is merely suspicious of the driver's behavior. In such cases, the trooper may make a casual request to perform a search. If the driver agrees, then according to the Court, he or she has waived his or her constitutional right against unreasonable searches.

Critical Thinking
Why do you think the right against unreasonable searches and seizures is highly important to most people?

AMENDMENT V

Constitutional Insight Can you be tried twice for the same offense? The prohibition against "double jeopardy" protects you from having the same charge brought against you twice for the same offense, but you can be tried on different charges related to that offense.

Critical Thinking
What do you think could happen if a person could be tried twice for the same offense?

Amendments I–X: The Bill of Rights
PROPOSED BY CONGRESS SEPTEMBER 25, 1786.
RATIFIED DECEMBER 15, 1791.

AMENDMENT I   RELIGIOUS AND POLITICAL FREEDOM (1791)

Congress shall make no law respecting an establishment of religion, or prohibiting the free exercise thereof; or abridging the freedom of speech, or of the press; or the right of the people peaceably to assemble, and to petition the Government for a redress of grievances.

AMENDMENT II   RIGHT TO BEAR ARMS (1791)

A well regulated Militia, being necessary to the security of a free State, the right of the people to keep and bear Arms, shall not be infringed.

AMENDMENT III   QUARTERING TROOPS (1791)

No Soldier shall, in time of peace be quartered in any house, without the consent of the Owner, nor in time of war, but in a manner to be prescribed by law.

AMENDMENT IV   SEARCH AND SEIZURE (1791)

The right of the people to be secure in their persons, houses, papers, and effects, against unreasonable searches and seizures, shall not be violated, and no Warrants shall issue, but upon probable cause, supported by Oath or affirmation, and particularly describing the place to be searched, and the persons or things to be seized.

AMENDMENT V   RIGHTS OF ACCUSED PERSONS (1791)

No person shall be held to answer for a capital, or otherwise infamous crime, unless on a presentment or indictment of a Grand Jury, except in cases arising in the land or naval forces, or in the Militia, when in actual service in time of War or public danger; nor shall any person be subject for the same offence to be twice put in jeopardy of life or limb; nor shall be compelled in any criminal case to be a witness against himself, nor be deprived of life, liberty, or property, without due process of law; nor shall private property be taken for public use, without just compensation.

AMENDMENT VI

Constitutional Insight What are the Miranda rights? The term comes from the Supreme Court's decision in *Miranda* v. *Arizona* (1966), in which the justices established rules police must follow when questioning a suspect. If suspected of a crime, you must be told that you have a right to remain silent and that anything you say "can and will" be used against you. You also need to be informed that you have a right to an attorney and that the attorney may be present during questioning.

Critical Thinking
How do Miranda rights protect you?

AMENDMENT VII

Constitutional Insight What are the "rules of the common law"? The common law is the body of legal practices and decrees developed in England and English-speaking America from AD 1066 through the present. It includes the Magna Carta (1215), which acknowledges versions of rights affirmed in the Fifth, Sixth, and Seventh Amendments, as well as the English Bill of Rights (1689), which codified rights asserted in the First, Second, Seventh, and Eighth Amendments. It also includes the decisions and published opinions of state and federal appeals courts, including the U.S. Supreme Court.

AMENDMENT IX

Constitutional Insight Do you have a right to privacy? Until 1965 no such right had ever been explicitly stated by the courts. That year, in the case of *Griswold* v. *Connecticut,* the Court said there is an implied right of American citizens to make certain personal choices without interference from the government; this case concerned the right to use birth control. Years later, in *Roe* v. *Wade* (1973), the same logic was used to declare unconstitutional a Texas law restricting a woman's right to an abortion in the first stages of pregnancy. Since that decision, both the right to privacy and abortion rights have become major political controversies.

Critical Thinking
How do you define the right to privacy?

AMENDMENT VI   RIGHT TO A SPEEDY, PUBLIC TRIAL (1791)

In all criminal prosecutions, the accused shall enjoy the right to a speedy and public trial, by an impartial jury of the State and district wherein the crime shall have been committed, which district shall have been previously ascertained by law, and to be informed of the nature and cause of the accusation; to be confronted with the witnesses against him; to have compulsory process for obtaining witnesses in his favor, and to have the Assistance of Counsel for his defence.

AMENDMENT VII   TRIAL BY JURY IN CIVIL CASES (1791)

In suits at common law, where the value in controversy shall exceed twenty dollars, the right of trial by jury shall be preserved, and no fact tried by a jury, shall be otherwise reexamined in any Court of the United States, than according to the rules of the common law.

AMENDMENT VIII   LIMITS OF FINES AND PUNISHMENTS (1791)

Excessive bail shall not be required, nor excessive fines imposed, nor cruel and unusual punishments inflicted.

AMENDMENT IX   RIGHTS OF PEOPLE (1791)

The enumeration in the Constitution, of certain rights, shall not be construed to deny or disparage others retained by the people.

AMENDMENT X   POWERS OF STATES AND PEOPLE (1791)

The powers not delegated to the United States by the Constitution, nor prohibited by it to the States, are reserved to the States respectively, or to the people.

Amendments XI–XXVII

AMENDMENT XI

Article III, Section 2, of the Constitution was modified by the Eleventh Amendment.

AMENDMENT XII

A portion of Article II, Section 1, of the Constitution was superseded by the Twelfth Amendment.

Constitutional Insight **How did the election of 1800 lead to the Twelfth Amendment?** The election ended in a tie vote between the Republican running mates. The election was decided in Jefferson's favor on the House's 36th ballot. Almost immediately, Alexander Hamilton and others designed an amendment that established that the presidential electors would vote for both a presidential and a vice-presidential candidate. This amendment prevents a repeat of the problem experienced in the 1800 election.

Critical Thinking
Why is the Twelfth Amendment important?

AMENDMENT XI   LAWSUITS AGAINST STATES (1795)
PASSED BY CONGRESS MARCH 4, 1794. RATIFIED FEBRUARY 7, 1795.

The Judicial power of the United States shall not be construed to extend to any suit in law or equity, commenced or prosecuted against one of the United States by Citizens of another State, or by Citizens or Subjects of any Foreign State.

AMENDMENT XII   ELECTION OF THE EXECUTIVES (1804)
PASSED BY CONGRESS DECEMBER 9, 1803. RATIFIED JUNE 15, 1804.

The Electors shall meet in their respective states and vote by ballot for President and Vice-President, one of whom, at least, shall not be an inhabitant of the same state with themselves; they shall name in their ballots the person voted for as President, and in distinct ballots the person voted for as Vice-President, and they shall make distinct lists of all persons voted for as President, and of all persons voted for as Vice-President, and of the number of votes for each, which lists they shall sign and certify, and transmit sealed to the seat of the government of the United States, directed to the President of the Senate;—the President of the Senate shall, in the presence of the Senate and House of Representatives, open all the certificates and the votes shall then be counted;—The person having the greatest number of votes for President, shall be the President, if such number be a majority of the whole number of Electors appointed; and if no person have such majority, then from the persons having the highest numbers not exceeding three on the list of those voted for as President, the House of Representatives shall choose immediately, by ballot, the President. But in choosing the President, the votes shall be taken by states, the representation from each state having one vote; a quorum for this purpose shall consist of a member or members from two-thirds of the states, and a majority of all the states shall be necessary to a choice. ~~And if the House of Representatives shall not choose a President whenever the right of choice shall devolve upon them, before the fourth day of March next following, then the Vice-President shall act as President, as in case of the death or other constitutional disability of the President.~~—The person having the greatest number of votes as Vice-President, shall be the Vice-President, if such number be a majority of the whole number of Electors appointed, and if no person have a majority, then from the two highest numbers on the list, the Senate shall choose the Vice-President; a quorum for the purpose shall consist of two-thirds of the whole number of Senators, and a majority of the whole number shall be necessary to a choice. But no person constitutionally ineligible to the office of President shall be eligible to that of Vice-President of the United States.

AMENDMENT XIII

A portion of Article IV, Section 2, of the Constitution was superseded by the Thirteenth Amendment.

AMENDMENT XIV

Article I, Section 2, of the Constitution was modified by Section 2 of the Fourteenth Amendment.

Constitutional Insight Which personal status takes priority— that of U.S. citizen or that of state citizen? The Fourteenth Amendment firmly notes that Americans are citizens of both the nation and the states, but that no state can "abridge the privileges or immunities" of U.S. citizens, deprive them "of life, liberty, or property, without due process of law," or deny them "equal protection of the laws."

What does it mean to have "equal protection of the laws"? "Equal protection of the laws" means that the laws are to be applied to all persons in the same way. The legal system may discriminate between persons—treat them differently, or unequally—if there are relevant reasons to do so. For example, a person's income and number of dependents are relevant for how much income tax the person should pay; a person's gender is not. The Supreme Court's 1954 decision in *Brown* v. *Board of Education of Topeka,* which declared segregated public schools unconstitutional, was based on an Equal Protection claim; a child's race is not a relevant reason for the state to assign that child to a particular school.

Critical Thinking
Do you agree or disagree with the Supreme Court's decision that separate educational facilities are unequal? Explain your position.

AMENDMENT XIII   SLAVERY ABOLISHED (1865)
PASSED BY CONGRESS JANUARY 31, 1865. RATIFIED DECEMBER 6, 1865.

Section 1 Neither slavery nor involuntary servitude, except as a punishment for crime whereof the party shall have been duly convicted, shall exist within the United States, or any place subject to their jurisdiction.

Section 2 Congress shall have power to enforce this article by appropriate legislation.

AMENDMENT XIV   CIVIL RIGHTS (1868)
PASSED BY CONGRESS JUNE 13, 1866. RATIFIED JULY 9, 1868.

Section 1 All persons born or naturalized in the United States, and subject to the jurisdiction thereof, are citizens of the United States and of the State wherein they reside. No State shall make or enforce any law which shall abridge the privileges or immunities of citizens of the United States; nor shall any State deprive any person of life, liberty, or property, without due process of law; nor deny to any person within its jurisdiction the equal protection of the laws.

Section 2 Representatives shall be apportioned among the several States according to their respective numbers, counting the whole number of persons in each State, ~~excluding Indians not taxed~~. But when the right to vote at any election for the choice of electors for President and Vice-President of the United States, Representatives in Congress, the Executive and Judicial officers of a State, or the members of the Legislature thereof, is denied to any of the ~~male~~ inhabitants of such State, ~~being twenty-one years of age~~, and citizens of the United States, or in any way abridged, except for participation in rebellion, or other crime, the basis of representation therein shall be reduced in the proportion which the number of such ~~male~~ citizens shall bear to the whole number of ~~male~~ citizens ~~twenty-one years of age~~ in such State.

Section 3 No person shall be a Senator or Representative in Congress, or elector of President and Vice-President, or hold any office, civil or military, under the United States, or under any State, who, having previously taken an oath, as a member of Congress, or as an officer of the United States, or as a member of any State legislature, or as an executive or judicial officer of any State, to support the Constitution of the United States, shall have engaged in insurrection or rebellion against the same, or given aid or comfort to the enemies thereof. But Congress may by a vote of two-thirds of each House, remove such disability.

AMENDMENT XV

Constitutional Insight Can you be denied the right to vote?   The Fifteenth Amendment prohibits the United States or any state from keeping citizens from voting because of race or color or because they were once slaves. However, a person convicted of a crime can be denied the right to vote, as can someone found to be mentally incompetent.

Critical Thinking
Why do you think so many people do not exercise the right to vote?

AMENDMENT XVI

Article I, Section 9, of the Constitution was modified by the Sixteenth Amendment.

Constitutional Insight How has the ability of Congress to impose taxes been amended?   The Sixteenth Amendment permits a federal income tax and in so doing changes Article I, Section 9, Clause 4, by stating that Congress has the power to levy an income tax—which is a direct tax—without apportioning such a tax among the states according to their populations.

Critical Thinking
Do you think Congress should have the power to impose an income tax on the people of the nation? Explain your answer.

AMENDMENT XVII

Article I, Section 3, of the Constitution was modified by the Seventeenth Amendment.

Constitutional Insight How has the way senators are elected been changed?   The Seventeenth Amendment changes Article I, Section 3, Clause 1, by stating that senators shall be elected by the people of each state rather than by the state legislatures.

Critical Thinking
Why is the direct election of senators by the people of each state important?

Section 4 The validity of the public debt of the United States, authorized by law, including debts incurred for payment of pensions and bounties for services in suppressing insurrection or rebellion, shall not be questioned. But neither the United States nor any State shall assume or pay any debt or obligation incurred in aid of insurrection or rebellion against the United States, or any claim for the loss or emancipation of any slave; but all such debts, obligations and claims shall be held illegal and void.

Section 5 The Congress shall have the power to enforce, by appropriate legislation, the provisions of this article.

AMENDMENT XV   RIGHT TO VOTE (1870)
PASSED BY CONGRESS FEBRUARY 26, 1869. RATIFIED FEBRUARY 3, 1870.

Section 1 The right of citizens of the United States to vote shall not be denied or abridged by the United States or by any State on account of race, color, or previous condition of servitude.

Section 2 The Congress shall have the power to enforce this article by appropriate legislation.

AMENDMENT XVI   INCOME TAX (1913)
PASSED BY CONGRESS JULY 2, 1909. RATIFIED FEBRUARY 3, 1913.

The Congress shall have power to lay and collect taxes on incomes, from whatever source derived, without apportionment among the several States, and without regard to any census or enumeration.

AMENDMENT XVII   DIRECT ELECTION OF SENATORS (1913)
PASSED BY CONGRESS MAY 13, 1912. RATIFIED APRIL 8, 1913.

Clause 1 The Senate of the United States shall be composed of two Senators from each State, elected by the people thereof, for six years; and each Senator shall have one vote. The electors in each State shall have the qualifications requisite for electors of the most numerous branch of the State legislatures.

Clause 2 When vacancies happen in the representation of any State in the Senate, the executive authority of such State shall issue writs of election to fill such vacancies: *Provided*, That the legislature of any State may empower the executive thereof to make temporary appointments until the people fill the vacancies by election as the legislature may direct.

Clause 3 ~~This amendment shall not be so construed as to affect the election or term of any Senator chosen before it becomes valid as part of the Constitution.~~

AMENDMENT XVIII   PROHIBITION (1919)

PASSED BY CONGRESS DECEMBER 18, 1917. RATIFIED JANUARY 16, 1919. REPEALED BY AMENDMENT XXI.

Section 1 ~~After one year from the ratification of this article the manufacture, sale, or transportation of intoxicating liquors within, the importation thereof into, or the exportation thereof from the United States and all territory subject to the jurisdiction thereof for beverage purposes is hereby prohibited.~~

Section 2 ~~The Congress and the several States shall have concurrent power to enforce this article by appropriate legislation.~~

Section 3 ~~This article shall be inoperative unless it shall have been ratified as an amendment to the Constitution by the legislatures of the several States, as provided in the Constitution, within seven years from the date of the submission hereof to the States by the Congress.~~

AMENDMENT XIX   WOMEN'S SUFFRAGE (1920)

PASSED BY CONGRESS JUNE 4, 1919. RATIFIED AUGUST 18, 1920.

Clause 1 The right of citizens of the United States to vote shall not be denied or abridged by the United States or by any State on account of sex.

Clause 2 Congress shall have power to enforce this article by appropriate legislation.

AMENDMENT XX   "LAME DUCK" SESSIONS (1933)

PASSED BY CONGRESS MARCH 2, 1932. RATIFIED JANUARY 23, 1933.

Section 1 The terms of the President and the Vice President shall end at noon on the 20th day of January, and the terms of Senators and Representatives at noon on the 3d day of January, of the years in which such terms would have ended if this article had not been ratified; and the terms of their successors shall then begin.

Section 2 The Congress shall assemble at least once in every year, and such meeting shall begin at noon on the 3d day of January, unless they shall by law appoint a different day.

Section 3 If, at the time fixed for the beginning of the term of the President, the President elect shall have died, the Vice President elect shall become President. If a President shall not have been chosen before the time fixed for the beginning of his term, or if the President elect shall have failed to qualify, then the Vice President elect shall act as President until a President shall have qualified; and the Congress may by law provide for the case wherein neither a President elect nor a Vice President shall have qualified, declaring who shall then act as President, or the manner in which one who is to act shall be selected, and such person shall act accordingly until a President or Vice President shall have qualified.

AMENDMENT XIX

Constitutional Insight When did women first get the right to vote in the United States?   Women had the right to vote in the state of New Jersey between 1776 and 1807. In the late 19th century, some states and territories began to extend full or limited suffrage to women. Then, in 1920 the Nineteenth Amendment prohibited the United States or any state from denying women the right to vote.

Critical Thinking
How does the right of women to vote affect politics today?

AMENDMENT XX

Article I, Section 4, of the Constitution was modified by Section 2 of this amendment. In addition, a portion of the Twelfth Amendment was superseded by Section 3.

Constitutional Insight Why is the Twentieth Amendment usually called the "Lame Duck" amendment?   A lame duck is a person who continues to hold office after his or her replacement has been elected. Such a person is called a lame duck because he or she no longer has any strong political influence. The Twentieth Amendment reduces the time between the election of a new president and vice-president in November and their assumption of the offices, which it sets at January 20 instead of March 4. It also reduces the time new members of Congress must wait to take their seats from four months to about two months. They are now seated on January 3 following the November election. As a result, the lame duck period is now quite short.

Critical Thinking
Why may the framers have specified a longer lame duck period?

Section 4 The Congress may by law provide for the case of the death of any of the persons from whom the House of Representatives may choose a President whenever the right of choice shall have devolved upon them, and for the case of the death of any of the persons from whom the Senate may choose a Vice President whenever the right of choice shall have devolved upon them.

Section 5 ~~Sections 1 and 2 shall take effect on the 15th day of October following the ratification of this article.~~

Section 6 ~~This article shall be inoperative unless it shall have been ratified as an amendment to the Constitution by the legislatures of three-fourths of the several States within seven years from the date of its submission.~~

AMENDMENT XXI   REPEAL OF PROHIBITION (1933)
PASSED BY CONGRESS FEBRUARY 20, 1933. RATIFIED DECEMBER 5, 1933.

Section 1 The eighteenth article of amendment to the Constitution of the United States is hereby repealed.

Section 2 The transportation or importation into any State, Territory, or Possession of the United States for delivery or use therein of intoxicating liquors, in violation of the laws thereof, is hereby prohibited.

Section 3 ~~This article shall be inoperative unless it shall have been ratified as an amendment to the Constitution by conventions in the several States, as provided in the Constitution, within seven years from the date of the submission hereof to the States by the Congress.~~

AMENDMENT XXII   LIMIT ON PRESIDENTIAL TERMS (1951)
PASSED BY CONGRESS MARCH 21, 1947. RATIFIED FEBRUARY 27, 1951.

Section 1 No person shall be elected to the office of the President more than twice, and no person who has held the office of President, or acted as President, for more than two years of a term to which some other person was elected President shall be elected to the office of President more than once. ~~But this Article shall not apply to any person holding the office of President when this Article was proposed by Congress, and shall not prevent any person who may be holding the office of President, or acting as President, during the term within which this Article becomes operative from holding the office of President or acting as President during the remainder of such term.~~

Section 2 ~~This article shall be inoperative unless it shall have been ratified as an amendment to the Constitution by the legislatures of three-fourths of the several States within seven years from the date of its submission to the States by the Congress.~~

AMENDMENT XXI

Constitutional Insight What is unique about the Twenty-First Amendment?   Besides being the only amendment that explicitly repeals another, it was the first, and is so far the only one, to have been ratified by the state convention method outlined in Article V. Congress, probably fearing that state legislatures would not deal swiftly with the issue of repeal, chose to have each state call a special convention to consider the amendment. The strategy worked well, for the elected delegates to the conventions represented public opinion on the issue and ratified the amendment without delay.

Critical Thinking
Why is it necessary to pass another amendment to revoke or remove an existing amendment?

AMENDMENT XXIII

Constitutional Insight Why were residents of the District of Columbia without a vote in presidential elections? First, the district was merely an idea at the time the Constitution was written. Second, no one expected the district to include many residents. Third, the framers designed the electoral college on a state framework. By 1960, however, the fact that nearly 800,000 Americans living in the nation's capital could not vote in presidential elections was an embarrassment. The Twenty-Third Amendment gives Washington, DC, residents the right to vote in presidential elections by assigning them electoral votes.

Critical Thinking
Do you think the District of Columbia should be made a separate state?

AMENDMENT XXIV

Constitutional Insight Why was the poll tax an issue important enough to require an amendment? The poll tax was used in some places to prevent African American voters—at least the many who were too poor to pay the tax—from participating in elections. As the civil rights movement gained momentum, the abuse of the poll tax became a major issue, but the national government found it difficult to change the situation because the constitutional provisions in Article I, Section 4, leave the qualifications of voters in the hands of the states. The Twenty-Fourth Amendment changed this by prohibiting the United States or any state from including payment of any tax as a requirement for voting.

Critical Thinking
What impact do you think the Twenty-Fourth Amendment has had on elections?

AMENDMENT XXV

Article II, Section 1, of the Constitution was affected by the Twenty-Fifth Amendment.

AMENDMENT XXIII VOTING IN DISTRICT OF COLUMBIA (1961)
PASSED BY CONGRESS JUNE 16, 1960. RATIFIED MARCH 29, 1961.

Section 1 The District constituting the seat of Government of the United States shall appoint in such manner as Congress may direct:

A number of electors of President and Vice President equal to the whole number of Senators and Representatives in Congress to which the District would be entitled if it were a State, but in no event more than the least populous State; they shall be in addition to those appointed by the States, but they shall be considered, for the purposes of the election of President and Vice President, to be electors appointed by a State; and they shall meet in the District and perform such duties as provided by the twelfth article of amendment.

Section 2 The Congress shall have power to enforce this article by appropriate legislation.

AMENDMENT XXIV ABOLITION OF POLL TAXES (1964)
PASSED BY CONGRESS AUGUST 27, 1962. RATIFIED JANUARY 23, 1964.

Section 1 The right of citizens of the United States to vote in any primary or other election for President or Vice President, for electors for President or Vice President, or for Senator or Representative in Congress, shall not be denied or abridged by the United States or any State by reason of failure to pay poll tax or other tax.

Section 2 The Congress shall have power to enforce this article by appropriate legislation.

AMENDMENT XXV PRESIDENTIAL DISABILITY, SUCCESSION (1967)
PASSED BY CONGRESS JULY 6, 1965. RATIFIED FEBRUARY 10, 1967.

Section 1 In case of the removal of the President from office or of his death or resignation, the Vice President shall become President.

Section 2 Whenever there is a vacancy in the office of the Vice President, the President shall nominate a Vice President who shall take office upon confirmation by a majority vote of both Houses of Congress.

Section 3 Whenever the President transmits to the President pro tempore of the Senate and the Speaker of the House of Representatives his written declaration that he is unable to discharge the powers and duties of his office, and until he transmits to them a written declaration to the contrary, such powers and duties shall be discharged by the Vice President as Acting President.

AMENDMENT XXVI

Amendment XIV, Section 2, of the Constitution was modified by Section 1 of the Twenty-Sixth Amendment.

Constitutional Insight **Why was the Twenty-Sixth Amendment passed?** Granting 18-year-olds the right to vote became a major issue in the 1960s, during the Vietnam War, when people questioned the justice of requiring 18-year-old men to submit to the military draft but refusing them the right to vote in federal elections. In 1970 Congress passed a voting rights act giving 18-year-olds the right to vote in elections. When the constitutionality of this act was challenged, the Supreme Court decided that states had to honor the 18-year-old vote for congressional and presidential elections but could retain higher age requirements for state and local elections. To avoid confusion at the polls, the Twenty-Sixth Amendment was passed. It guarantees 18-year-olds the right to vote in national and state elections.

Critical Thinking
Do you think 18-year-olds should have the right to vote? Why or why not?

AMENDMENT XXVII

Constitutional Insight **How long did it take to ratify this amendment?** Although the Twenty-Seventh Amendment was one of the 12 amendments proposed in 1789 as part of the Bill of Rights, it was not ratified until 1992. This amendment, which deals with congressional compensation, allows the members of Congress to increase congressional pay, but delays the increase until after a new Congress is seated.

Critical Thinking
Do you think members of Congress should be able to vote themselves a pay increase? Explain your answer.

Section 4 Whenever the Vice President and a majority of either the principal officers of the executive departments or of such other body as Congress may by law provide, transmit to the President pro tempore of the Senate and the Speaker of the House of Representatives their written declaration that the President is unable to discharge the powers and duties of his office, the Vice President shall immediately assume the powers and duties of the office as Acting President.

Thereafter, when the President transmits to the President pro tempore of the Senate and the Speaker of the House of Representatives his written declaration that no inability exists, he shall resume the powers and duties of his office unless the Vice President and a majority of either the principal officers of the executive department or of such other body as Congress may by law provide, transmit within four days to the President pro tempore of the Senate and the Speaker of the House of Representatives their written declaration that the President is unable to discharge the powers and duties of his office. Thereupon Congress shall decide the issue, assembling within forty-eight hours for that purpose if not in session. If the Congress, within twenty-one days after receipt of the latter written declaration, or, if Congress is not in session, within twenty-one days after Congress is required to assemble, determines by two-thirds vote of both Houses that the President is unable to discharge the powers and duties of his office, the Vice President shall continue to discharge the same as Acting President; otherwise, the President shall resume the powers and duties of his office.

AMENDMENT XXVI 18-YEAR-OLD VOTE (1971)
PASSED BY CONGRESS MARCH 23, 1971. RATIFIED JULY 1, 1971.

Section 1 The right of citizens of the United States, who are eighteen years of age or older, to vote shall not be denied or abridged by the United States or by any State on account of age.

Section 2 The Congress shall have power to enforce this article by appropriate legislation.

AMENDMENT XXVII CONGRESSIONAL PAY (1992)
PROPOSED BY CONGRESS SEPTEMBER 25, 1789. RATIFIED MAY 7, 1992.

No law, varying the compensation for the services of the Senators and Representatives, shall take effect, until an election of representatives shall have intervened.

Economic and Social Changes

One American's stroy

In 1837 painter and scientist **Samuel F. B. Morse,** with Leonard Gale, built an electromagnetic telegraph. Morse's first model could send signals ten miles through copper wire. Morse asked Congress to fund an experimental telegraphic communication that would travel for 100 miles.

The Big Idea

Inventions and economic developments in the early 19th century helped transform American society.

Why It Matters Now

The market revolution and free enterprise system that took hold during this period still drive the nation's economy today.

Key Terms and People

Samuel F. B. Morse

entrepreneurs

strike

Ralph Waldo Emerson

abolition

William Lloyd Garrison

Frederick Douglass

Elizabeth Cady Stanton

Seneca Falls Convention

"This mode of instantaneous communication must inevitably become an instrument of immense power, to be wielded for good or for evil. . . . Let the sole right of using the Telegraph belong, in the first place, to the Government, who should grant . . . the right to lay down a communication between any two points for the purpose of transmitting intelligence."

—Samuel F. B. Morse, quoted in *Samuel F. B. Morse: His Letters*

Samuel Morse was a painter before he became famous as an inventor.

Congress granted Morse $30,000 to build a 40-mile telegraph line between Baltimore and Washington, DC. In 1844 Morse tapped out in code the words "What hath God wrought?" The message sped from Washington, DC, over a metal wire in less than a second. As new communication links began to put people into instant communication with one another, new transportation links carried goods and people across vast regions.

SS.912.A.1.2; SS.912.A.1.4; SS.912.A.1.7; SS.912.A.3.3; SS.912.A.3.4; SS.912.A.3.5; SS.912.A.3.6; SS.912.A.3.7; LAFS.1112.WHST.2.6

Regional Economies

In the early decades of the 19th century, the economies of the various regions of the United States developed differently. The Northeast began to industrialize, while the South and West continued to be more agricultural.

EARLY INDUSTRY IN THE UNITED STATES The Industrial Revolution—large-scale production resulting in massive change in social and economic organization—began in Great Britain in the 18th century and gradually reached the United States.

Industry took off first in New England, where the economy depended on shipping and foreign trade. New Englanders embraced new forms of manufacturing. Prime among these were mechanized textile, or fabric, mills.

Farmers in the North began to specialize in one or two crops or types of livestock (such as corn and cattle), sell what they produced to urban markets, and then purchase what they needed from stores. Often the items purchased were made in northern factories. As a result, a market economy began to develop in which agriculture and manufacturing each supported the growth of the other.

THE SOUTH REMAINS AGRICULTURAL Meanwhile, the South continued to grow as an agricultural power. Eli Whitney's invention of a cotton gin (short for "engine," or machine) in 1793 made it possible for southern farmers to

---

Document-Based Investigation Historical Source

Slater's Mill

This painting from around 1790 shows Samuel Slater's mill, the first cotton mill in the United States. The mill, located in Pawtucket, Rhode Island, drew its power from the Blackstone River.

Analyze Historical Sources
How does this painting illustrate the changing nature of the American economy in the 1790s?

produce cotton more profitably. The emergence of a Cotton Kingdom in the South—and thus the need for more field labor—contributed to the expansion of slavery. Between 1790 and 1820 the enslaved population increased from less than 700,000 to over 1.5 million. In the North, things were different. By 1804 states north of Delaware had either abolished slavery or had enacted laws for gradual emancipation. Slavery declined in the North, but some slaves remained there for decades.

Reading Check Analyze Causes How did agriculture and industry support a market economy in the North?

Vocabulary free enterprise the freedom of private businesses to operate competitively for profit with little government regulation

The Market Revolution

During the first half of the 19th century in the United States, the market economy sparked by the Industrial Revolution developed in a period known as the market revolution. People increasingly bought and sold goods rather than making them for themselves. Inventions like the cotton gin and steamboat fueled economic growth.

Over a few decades, buying and selling multiplied, while incomes rose. In the 1840s alone, the national economy grew more than it had in the first 40 years of the century. The quickening pace of U.S. economic growth coincided with the growth of free enterprise—the freedom of private businesses to operate competitively for profit with little government regulation.

In their pursuit of profit, businessmen called **entrepreneurs**, from a French word that means "to undertake," invested their own money in new industries. In doing this, entrepreneurs risked losing their investment if a venture failed, but they also stood to earn huge profits if it succeeded.

INVENTIONS AND IMPROVEMENTS Inventor-entrepreneurs began to develop goods to make life more comfortable for more people. While some inventions simply made life more enjoyable, others fueled the economic revolution and transformed manufacturing, transportation, and communication.

New communication links began to put people into instant contact with one another. In 1837 Samuel F. B. Morse patented the telegraph, which sent messages in code over a wire in a matter of seconds. Businesses used the telegraph to transmit orders and relay up-to-date information on prices and sales. Railroads employed the telegraph to keep trains moving regularly and to warn engineers of safety hazards. By 1854, 23,000 miles of telegraph wire crossed the country.

Meanwhile, better transportation systems improved the movement of people and goods. In 1807 Pennsylvanian Robert Fulton had ushered in the steamboat era when his boat, the *Clermont,* made the 150-mile trip up the Hudson River from New York City to Albany in 32 hours, a remarkable speed for that era. By 1830, 200 steamboats traveled the nation's western rivers that flowed into the Mississippi River. Steamboats slashed freight rates as well as voyage times.

Water transport was particularly important in moving raw materials such as lead, copper, and heavy machinery. Where waterways didn't exist, Americans made them by building canals. By the 1840s America boasted more than 3,300 miles of canals.

From Telegraph to Internet

What do the telegraph and the Internet have in common? They are both tools for instant communication. The telegraph relied on a network of wires that spanned the country. The Internet—an international network of smaller computer networks—allows any computer user to communicate instantly with any other computer user in the world.

MORSE CODE

In 1837 Samuel Morse patents the telegraph, the first instant electronic communicator. Morse taps on a key to send bursts of electricity down a wire to the receiver. An operator "translates" the coded bursts into understandable language within seconds.

TELEPHONE

In 1876 Alexander Graham Bell invents the telephone. It relies on a steady stream of electricity, rather than electrical bursts, to transmit sounds. By 1900 there are over 1 million telephones in the United States.

MARCONI RADIO

In 1895 Guglielmo Marconi, an Italian inventor, sends telegraph code through the air as electromagnetic waves. By the early 1900s "the wireless" makes voice transmissions possible. Commercial radio stations are broadcasting music and entertainment programs by the 1920s.

TELEVISION

In the late 1800s scientists begin to experiment with transmitting pictures as well as words through the air. In 1923 Vladimir Zworykin, a Russian-born American scientist, files a patent for the iconoscope, the first television camera tube suitable for broadcasting. In 1924 he files a patent for the kinescope, the picture tube used in receiving television signals. In 1929 Zworykin demonstrates his new television.

COMPUTERS

Scientists develop electronically powered computers during the 1940s. In 1951 UNIVAC I (UNIVersal Automatic Computer) becomes the first commercially available computer. In 1964 IBM initiates System/360, a family of mutually compatible computers that allow several terminals to be attached to one computer system.

INTERNET

Today, on the Internet, through email (electronic mail) or online conversation, any two people can have instant dialogue. The Internet becomes the modern tool for instant global communication not only of words but also of images.

Canals, however, soon gave way to railroads, which were faster and allowed for winter travel. Developed in England in the early 1800s, steam-powered locomotives began operating in the United States in the 1830s. By 1850 over 9,000 miles of track had been laid across the United States.

THE MARKET REVOLUTION TRANSFORMS THE NATION Although most Americans during the early 1800s still lived in rural areas and only 14 percent of workers had manufacturing jobs, these workers produced more and better goods at lower prices than ever before. Many of these goods became affordable for ordinary Americans, and improvements in transportation allowed people to purchase items manufactured in distant places. By the 1840s improved transportation and communication also made America's regions more interdependent.

Heavy investment in canals and railroads transformed the Northeast into the center of American commerce. As the Northeast began to industrialize, many people moved to the Midwest to farm its fertile soil. They employed new machines, such as the John Deere steel plow, for cultivating the tough prairie sod, and Cyrus McCormick's reaper for harvesting grain. Meanwhile, most of the South remained agricultural and relied on such crops as cotton, tobacco, and rice.

CHANGING WORKPLACES The new market economy in the United States also changed the ways Americans worked. Moving production from the home to the factory split families, created new communities, and transformed relationships between employers and employees. By the mid-19th century, new machines allowed unskilled workers to perform tasks that once had taken the effort of trained artisans. To do this work, though, workers needed factories.

In the 1820s a group of entrepreneurs built several large textile mills in Lowell, Massachusetts. The Lowell textile mills soon became booming enterprises. Thousands of people, mostly women, left family farms to find work in Lowell. Mill owners sought female employees because women provided an abundant source of labor and owners could pay lower wages to women than men. To the girls in the mills, though, textile work offered better pay than their main alternatives: teaching, sewing, and domestic work. Before long, however, work conditions deteriorated. The workday at Lowell was more than 12 hours long. In addition, mills often were dark, hot, and cramped. Factory owners often showed little sympathy for the plight of workers.

WORKERS SEEK BETTER CONDITIONS As industry grew, strikes broke out as workers protested poor working conditions and low wages. In 1834 the Lowell mills announced a 15 percent wage cut, and 800 mill girls organized a **strike**, a work stoppage to force an employer to respond to demands. Criticized by the Lowell press and clergy, most of the strikers agreed to return to work at reduced wages. The mill owners fired the strike leader.

Although only 1 or 2 percent of workers in the United States were organized, the 1830s and 1840s saw dozens of strikes—many for higher wages, but some for shorter hours. Employers defeated most of these strikes because they could easily replace unskilled workers with people recently arrived from Europe who desperately needed jobs.

This trade union banner was made for the glass cutters organization around 1840.

Vocabulary
immigration leaving one country and settling in another

Background
During the Great Potato Famine of 1845–1849, about 1 million Irish died of starvation and disease.

Reading Check
Summarize Why were most strikes of the 1830s and 1840s ineffective?

European immigration—leaving one country and settling in another—rose dramatically in the United States between 1830 and 1860. Between 1845 and 1854 alone, nearly 3 million immigrants moved to the United States. More than 1 million were Irish immigrants, who fled their homeland after a disease on potatoes caused the Great Potato Famine. As millions of Irish men and women faced the threat of mass starvation, many decided to try to find new lives in America.

Irish immigrants faced prejudice, both because they were Roman Catholic and because they were poor. Frightened by allegations of a Catholic conspiracy to take over the country, Protestant mobs in big cities constantly harassed them. Other workers resented the Irish for their willingness to work as cheap labor, a willingness that made them more desirable to employers.

Amid the growing labor unrest in the 1830s, trade unions in different towns began to join together to expand their power. The national trade union movement faced fierce opposition from bankers and owners. In addition, workers' efforts to organize were at first hampered by court decisions declaring strikes illegal. In 1842, however, the Massachusetts Supreme Court supported the workers' right to strike in the case of *Commonwealth* v. *Hunt*.

Reforming American Society

The workplace was not the only area of American life that experienced unrest in the mid-19th century. Indeed, a series of religious and social reform movements went hand in hand with these economic changes.

During the 19th century, Americans embarked on a widespread effort to solve problems in society. Abolition, the movement to abolish slavery, became the most important of a series of reform movements in America.

A SPIRITUAL AWAKENING INSPIRES REFORM Many of these movements had their roots in a spiritual awakening that swept the nation after 1790. Known as the Second Great Awakening, it was a widespread Christian movement to awaken religious sentiments that lasted from the 1790s to the 1830s. People caught up in the Second Great Awakening began to emphasize individual responsibility for seeking salvation and insisted that people could improve themselves and society. These religious attitudes stressed the importance and power of the common person.

The primary forum for the changes of the Second Great Awakening was the revival meeting, where participants attempted to revive religious faith through impassioned preaching. Revival meetings might last for days as participants studied the Bible, reflected on their lives, and heard emotional sermons. Revivalism had a strong impact on the American public. According to one estimate, just 1 in 15 Americans belonged to a church in 1800, but by 1850 that number had risen to 1 in 6.

Another growing religious movement during this period was Unitarianism. The Unitarians shared with revivalism a faith in the individual. But instead of appealing to emotions, Unitarians emphasized reason as the path to perfection.

As the Second Great Awakening reached its maturity in the 1830s, another kind of awakening led by a writer, philosopher, and former Unitarian minister named **Ralph Waldo Emerson** began in New England. In 1831 Emerson traveled to England, where he discovered romanticism, an artistic and intellectual movement that emphasized nature, human emotions, and the imagination. From these romantic ideals, Emerson, along with other thinkers, developed a philosophy called transcendentalism. Transcendentalists believed that truth could be discovered intuitively by observing nature and relating it to one's own emotional and spiritual experience.

The call of religious reform was growing among African Americans, too. In the North, free African Americans formed their own churches. These churches often became political, cultural, and social centers for African Americans by providing schools and other services that whites denied free blacks. In the rural South, slaves heard the same sermons and sang the same hymns as did their owners, but they often interpreted the stories they heard, especially those describing the exodus from Egypt, as a promise of freedom. The goal of ending slavery grew not only among African Americans but among many white activists as well.

SLAVERY AND ABOLITION By the 1820s **abolition**—the movement to free African Americans from slavery—had taken hold. More than 100 antislavery societies had been advocating that African Americans be resettled in Africa. In 1817 the American Colonization Society had been founded to encourage black emigration. Other abolitionists, however, demanded that African Americans remain in the United States as free citizens.

The most radical white abolitionist was a young editor named **William Lloyd Garrison**. Active in religious reform movements in Massachusetts, Garrison became the editor of an antislavery paper in 1828. Three years later he established his own paper, *The Liberator,* to deliver an uncompromising demand: immediate emancipation.

Frederick Douglass, 1851

Before Garrison's call for the immediate emancipation of slaves, support for that position had been limited. In the 1830s, however, it gained support. Whites who opposed abolition hated Garrison. In 1835 a Boston mob paraded him through town at the end of a rope. Nevertheless, Garrison enjoyed widespread black support; three out of four early subscribers to *The Liberator* were African Americans.

One of those eager readers was **Frederick Douglass**, who escaped from bondage to become an eloquent and outspoken critic of slavery. Garrison heard him speak and was so impressed that he sponsored Douglass to speak for various antislavery organizations. Hoping that abolition could be achieved without violence, Douglass broke with Garrison, who believed that abolition justified whatever means necessary to achieve it. In 1847 Douglass began his own antislavery newspaper. He named it *The North Star,* after the star that guided runaway slaves to freedom.

Slave quarters, from a photograph taken around 1865

LIFE UNDER SLAVERY Despite the efforts of Garrison, Douglass, and others, millions of African Americans remained slaves. In the 18th century, most slaves were male, had recently arrived from the Caribbean or Africa, and spoke one of several languages other than English. By 1830, however, the numbers of male and female slaves had become more equal. The majority had been born in America and spoke English.

Most slaves worked as house servants, farm hands, or in the fields. Some states allowed masters to free their slaves and even allowed slaves to purchase their freedom over time. But these "manumitted" or freed slaves were very few. The vast majority of African Americans in the South were enslaved and endured lives of suffering and constant degradation.

Some slaves rebelled against their condition. One rebellion was led by Virginia slave Nat Turner. In August 1831 Turner and more than 50 followers attacked four plantations and killed about 60 whites. Whites eventually captured and executed many members of the group, including Turner.

The Turner rebellion frightened and outraged slaveholders. In some states, people argued that the only way to prevent future slave revolts was through emancipation. Others, however, chose to tighten restrictions on all African Americans to prevent them from plotting insurrections. Some proslavery advocates even began to argue that slavery was a benevolent institution. They used the Bible to defend slavery and cited passages that counseled servants to obey their masters. Nevertheless, opposition to slavery refused to disappear.

WOMEN AND REFORM In the early 19th century, women had limited economic or social opportunities. Prevailing customs encouraged women to restrict their activities after marriage to the home and family. Although young unmarried women could work outside the home, they were expected to contribute their earnings to their families and to give up their work if they married. They were denied full participation in the larger community.

Despite such pressures, women actively participated in all the important reform movements of the 19th century. For many, their efforts to improve society had been inspired by the Second Great Awakening. From abolition to education, women worked for reform despite the cold reception they got from many men.

Perhaps the most important reform effort that women participated in was abolition. Women abolitionists raised money, distributed literature, and collected signatures for antislavery petitions to Congress. Women also played key roles in the temperance movement, the effort to prohibit the drinking of alcohol. Some women, most notably Dorothea Dix, fought to improve treatment for the mentally disabled. Dix also joined others in the effort to reform the nation's harsh and often inhumane prison system.

EDUCATION FOR WOMEN Work for abolition and temperance accompanied gains in education for women. Until the 1820s, American girls had few educational opportunities beyond elementary school. As Sarah Grimké complained in *Letters on the Equality of the Sexes and the Condition of Woman* (1838), a woman who knew "chemistry enough to keep the pot boiling, and geography enough to know the location of the different rooms in her house" was considered learned enough. Grimké believed that increased education for women was a better alternative.

Throughout the 1800s, more and more educational institutions for women began to appear. In 1821 Emma Willard opened one of the nation's first academically oriented schools for girls in Troy, New York. In addition to classes in domestic sciences, the Troy Female Seminary offered classes in math, history, geography, languages, art, music, writing, and literature. It became the model for a new type of women's school. Despite tremendous ridicule, Willard's school prospered.

In 1833 the first class of Ohio's Oberlin College included four women, thereby making Oberlin the nation's first fully coeducational college. In 1837 Mary Lyon surmounted heated resistance to found another important institution of higher learning for women, Mount Holyoke Female Seminary (later Mount Holyoke College) in South Hadley, Massachusetts.

Unfortunately, black women enjoyed even fewer educational opportunities than their white counterparts. In 1831 Prudence Crandall, a white Quaker, opened a school for girls in Canterbury, Connecticut. Two years later, she admitted an African American girl named Sarah Harris. The townspeople protested so vigorously that Crandall decided to enroll only African Americans. This aroused even more opposition, and in 1834 Crandall was forced to close the school and leave town. Only after the Civil War would the severely limited educational opportunities for black women slowly begin to expand.

Improvement in women's education began to improve women's lives, most notably in health reform. Elizabeth Blackwell, who in 1849 became the first woman to graduate from medical college, later opened the New York Infirmary for Women and Children. In the 1850s Catharine Beecher, sister of novelist Harriet Beecher Stowe, undertook a national survey of women's health. To her dismay, Beecher found three sick women for every healthy one. Amelia Bloomer helped pioneer changes in women's fashion. She often wore a costume with loose-fitting pants tied at the ankles and covered with a short skirt. Many women followed her example and took to wearing pants.

WOMEN'S RIGHTS MOVEMENT EMERGES The reform movements of the mid-19th century fed the growth of the women's movement by providing women with increased opportunities to act outside the home. **Elizabeth Cady Stanton** and Lucretia Mott had been ardent abolitionists. At the World's Anti-Slavery Convention in 1840, male abolitionists discriminated against them. All the women delegates were barred from participation in the convention and were forced to sit and listen from a curtained gallery. Stanton and Mott, angered by their inability to express their opinions, vowed "to hold a convention as soon as we returned home, and form a society to advocate the rights of women." Eight years later, the **Seneca Falls Convention** fulfilled that vow.

With her dignified bearing and powerful voice, Sojourner Truth made audiences snap to attention. Truth fought for women's rights, abolition, prison reform, and temperance.

In 1848 more than 300 women convened in Seneca Falls, New York. Among the convention's resolutions was one calling for women to have the right to vote.

In spite of all the political activity among middle-class white women, African American women found it difficult to gain recognition of their problems. A former slave named Sojourner Truth did not let that stop her, however. At a women's rights convention in 1851, Truth, an outspoken abolitionist, refuted the arguments that because she was a woman she was weak, and because she was black she was not feminine.

As Truth showed, hard work was a fact of life for most women. But she also pointed to the problem of slavery that continued to vex the nation. As abolitionists intensified their attacks, proslavery advocates strengthened their defenses. Before long, the issue of slavery threatened to destroy the Union.

Reading Check
Analyze Issues
What were some of the areas of society that women worked to reform?

Lesson 4 Assessment

1. **Organize Information** Use a graphic organizer to fill in historical events or key figures related to reforming American society in the 19th century.

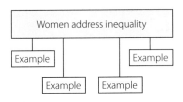

Write a paragraph about one of the examples you chose, explaining its significance.

2. **Key Terms and People** For each key term or person in the lesson, write a sentence explaining its significance.

3. **Evaluate** Which do you think was a more effective strategy—violence or nonviolence—for eliminating slavery? Why?

   Think About:
   - Frederick Douglass
   - Nat Turner
   - William Lloyd Garrison
   - Sojourner Truth

4. **Analyze Effects** How do you think the people you have read about in this lesson would have responded to the changes taking place during the market revolution?

5. **Make Inferences** Consider the philosophical and religious ideas expressed in the Second Great Awakening. How did they influence the activities of the 19th-century reformers?

Westward Expansion

The Big Idea

The United States expanded its boundaries during the mid-1800s, but disagreements over slavery led to the breakup of the Union.

Why It Matters Now

This period's events established the current borders of the 48 contiguous states and gave rise to the modern Democratic and Republican parties.

Key Terms and People

manifest destiny

Stephen F. Austin

Sam Houston

Treaty of Guadalupe Hidalgo

popular sovereignty

Stephen Douglas

Underground Railroad

Harriet Tubman

Dred Scott

Abraham Lincoln

Confederacy

Jefferson Davis

SS.912.A.1.2; SS.912.A.1.3; SS.912.A.1.4; SS.912.A.1.6; SS.912.A.1.7; SS.912.A.2.1; SS.912.A.3.13; SS.912.G.1.2; SS.912.G.2.1; SS.912.G.4.2; SS.912.G.4.3; SS.912.H.1.1; LAFS.1112.RH.1.1; LAFS.1112.RH.1.2; LAFS.1112.RH.2.6; LAFS.1112.RH.4.10; MAFS.K12.MP.5.1

One American's Story

With all their belongings loaded into wagons, Celinda Hines and her family set off for Oregon from their home in New York in 1853. She kept a record of nearly every day of the journey in a diary. She described how the group came to a crossroads one day in what is now Wyoming.

An estimated 350,000 pioneers—equal to 1.5 percent of the total American population in 1850—followed overland trails to the West.

"*Friday, June 24—Warm. Came to the Black Hills. Laramie Peak has been in sight for a week. Some of the road was very rough, some very good. Landscape wild and romantic. On the bluffs we were by cedar and pine trees. Was advised by a trader to take a cut-off, thereby shunning the Black Hills and also 20 miles where there was neither wood or water. He represented that by going this new way we should have good water at intervals of four or five miles also a better road and 30 miles nearer. We took it.*"

—Celinda Hines, quoted in *Transactions of the 46th Annual Reunion of the Oregon Pioneer Association*, 1918

Celinda Hines' family was just one of thousands to journey across the continent in the mid-1800s. They faced crossroads similar to the one the Hines family encountered. Making the wrong decision could mean becoming lost or stranded or running out of food and water. Why were they willing to take such risks? Like many Americans at the time, they had a dream that new opportunities and a better life awaited them in the West.

Manifest Destiny

As various presidents established policies in the early 19th century that expanded U.S. territory, American settlers pushed first into the Northwest Territory and then headed farther west.

SETTLING THE FRONTIER In the 1840s expansion fever gripped the country. The abundance of land invited some people to seek new lives. Others moved west to escape economic problems in the East. As the number of settlers climbed, merchants and manufacturers followed, seeking new markets. Whatever their reasons, these pioneers believed they were helping fulfill the country's **"manifest destiny,"** the belief that the United States was ordained to expand to the Pacific Ocean and into Mexican and Native American territory.

The settlers used old Native American trails as well as new routes. One of the busiest was the Santa Fe Trail, which stretched 780 miles from Independence, Missouri, to Santa Fe in the Mexican province of New Mexico. Each spring from 1821 through the 1860s, American traders loaded their covered wagons with goods and set off toward Santa Fe. The Oregon Trail stretched from Independence, Missouri, to Oregon City, Oregon. It was blazed in 1836 by two Methodist missionaries. They proved that wagons could travel on the Oregon Trail, although the trip took months.

Unlike those pursuing economic opportunity, the Mormons migrated west to escape persecution. They were a religious community founded by Joseph Smith in upstate New York in 1827, moving to Ohio and then Illinois to escape persecution. After an anti-Mormon mob murdered Smith, Brigham Young urged the Mormons to move farther west. In 1847 the Mormons stopped at the edge of the desert near the Great Salt Lake, in what is now Utah. Soon, settlements and farms flourished in the land they called Deseret.

SETTING BOUNDARIES In 1842 the Webster–Ashburton Treaty settled border disputes between the United States and British North America in the East and the Midwest. However, the two nations continued the "joint occupation" of the Oregon Territory that they had first established in 1818. In 1846 they agreed to extend the mainland boundary westward from the Rocky Mountains to Puget Sound, establishing the current boundary between the United States and Canada.

New Territories in the West

After 300 years of Spanish rule, only a few thousand Mexican settlers had migrated to what is now Texas. After Mexico won independence from Spain in 1820, the new Mexican government encouraged Americans to settle in Texas to make the land more secure and stable.

TEXAN INDEPENDENCE Many Americans rushed at the chance to buy inexpensive land in Texas. The population of Anglo, or English-speaking, settlers from the United States soon surpassed the population of Tejanos, or Mexican settlers in Texas.

Background
The Mormon religion was controversial in part for its belief in polygamy, a practice that allowed a man to have more than one wife

Reading Check
Analyze Motives
Why did the Mormons move farther west in their search for a new home?

Explore ONLINE!

Blackfoot

ROCKY

Portland   Columbia R.

Yakima

Nez Perce

Crow

CASCADE RANGE

The interior of a covered wagon may have looked like this on its way west.

Snake River

Fort Hall

Cheyenne

MOUNTAINS

Missouri River

GREAT

N. Platte River

Pawnee

Mississippi River

Great Salt Lake

Salt Lake City

Sacramento

Council Bluffs

PLAINS

Nauvoo

San Francisco

SIERRA NEVADA

Colorado River

Ute

St. Louis

Independence

Arkansas River

Cimarron Cutoff

Navajo

Los Angeles

Santa Fe

Cherokee
Creek
Seminole
Choctaw
Chickasaw

Fort Smith

Red River

Mississippi River

Rio Grande

El Paso

A Navajo man and woman in photographs taken by Edward S. Curtis

▬▬▬	Butterfield Overland Trail
▬▬▬	California Trail
▬▬▬	Mormon Trail
▬▬▬	Old Spanish Trail
▬▬▬	Oregon Trail
▬▬▬	Sante Fe Trail

0   100   200 mi
0   100   200 km

N
W   E
S

Interpret Maps

1. Location Approximately how long was the trail from St. Louis to El Paso?

2. Movement At a wagon train speed of about 15 miles a day, approximately how long would that trip take?

In 1821 **Stephen F. Austin** established a colony in Texas. By 1825 he had issued 297 land grants to the group that later became known as Texas's Old Three Hundred. By 1830 there were more than 20,000 Americans in Texas.

Differences over cultural issues created tension between Anglos and the Mexican government. The overwhelmingly Protestant Anglo settlers spoke English instead of Spanish. Furthermore, many of the settlers were southerners, who had brought slaves with them. Mexico had abolished slavery in 1829 and insisted in vain that the Texans free their slaves.

Late in 1833 Austin traveled to Mexico City to petition Mexican president Antonio López de Santa Anna for greater self-government for Texas, but Santa Anna had him imprisoned for inciting revolution. By the time Austin returned to Texas in 1835, he had become convinced that war was its "only resource." Determined to force Texas to obey Mexican law, Santa Anna marched his army toward San Antonio. Austin and his followers called for Texans to arm themselves, beginning the Texas Revolution. Lieutenant Colonel William Travis, the commander at the mission and fort called the Alamo, believed that his troops could prevent Santa Anna's movement farther north.

On February 23, 1836, Santa Anna and his troops began attacking the rebels holed up in the Alamo. The 13-day siege finally ended on March 6, 1836, when Mexican troops scaled the Alamo's walls. All 187 Anglo defenders and hundreds of Mexicans died. Even as the Alamo defenders were fighting for their lives, Texan leaders were declaring their independence from Mexico and creating a constitution based on that of the United States.

Six weeks later, 900 soldiers led by **Sam Houston** surprised a group of Mexicans near the San Jacinto River. With shouts of "Remember the Alamo!" the Texans killed 630 of Santa Anna's soldiers in 18 minutes and captured Santa Anna himself. The Texans set Santa Anna free only after he signed the Treaty of Velasco, which granted independence to Texas. In September 1836 Houston was elected president of the new Republic of Texas.

Document-Based Investigation Historical Source

Annexing Texas

Debates on the westward expansion of the United States were at the center of the 1844 presidential election. The man who would win, slaveholder James K. Polk, firmly favored annexation of Texas "at the earliest practicable period." With the annexation question settled by the time he took office in 1845, Polk again expressed his support of Texas statehood at his inauguration.

> *"The Republic of Texas has made known her desire to come into our Union, to form a part of our Confederacy and enjoy with us the blessings of liberty secured and guaranteed by our Constitution. Texas . . . possesses an undoubted right to dispose of a part or the whole of her territory and to merge her sovereignty as a separate and independent state in ours."*
>
> —James K. Polk, from his Inaugural Address, 1845

Analyze Historical Sources
How does Polk's statement reflect the ideas behind manifest destiny?

Most Texans hoped that the United States would annex their republic, but U.S. opinion divided along sectional lines. Southerners wanted Texas in order to extend slavery. Northerners feared that the annexation of more slave territory would tip the uneasy balance in the Senate in favor of slave states—and prompt war with Mexico. The winner of the 1844 U.S. presidential election, slaveholder James K. Polk, firmly favored the annexation of Texas. On December 29, 1845, Texas entered the Union.

THE WAR WITH MEXICO In March 1845, angered by U.S.-Texas negotiations on annexation, the Mexican government recalled its ambassador from Washington. Events moved quickly toward war.

President Polk believed that war with Mexico would also bring New Mexico and California into the Union. Hence, he supported Texan claims in border disputes with Mexico. While Texas insisted that its southern border extended to the Rio Grande, Mexico maintained that the border stopped at the Nueces River, 100 to 150 miles northeast of the Rio Grande. Polk sent a representative to negotiate the boundary dispute and the purchase of California and New Mexico. The Mexican government refused to receive him. When Polk heard this news, he ordered U.S. troops into the territory between the Rio Grande and the Nueces River that the United States claimed.

In 1845 John C. Frémont led an American exploration party into California, violating Mexico's territorial rights. In response, Mexican troops crossed the Rio Grande. In a skirmish near Matamoros, Mexican soldiers killed 11 U.S. soldiers. Polk immediately called for war, and Congress approved.

In California, a group of American settlers seized the town of Sonoma in June 1846. Hoisting a flag that featured a grizzly bear, the rebels proudly declared their independence from Mexico and proclaimed the nation of the Republic of California. After a brief battle, the Mexican troops gave way, leaving U.S. forces in control of California.

Meanwhile, American troops in Mexico, led by generals Zachary Taylor and Winfield Scott, scored one victory after another until Mexico conceded defeat. On February 2, 1848, the United States and Mexico signed the **Treaty of Guadalupe Hidalgo**. Mexico agreed to the Rio Grande as the border between the United States and Mexico. It also ceded the New Mexico and California territories to the United States for $15 million. The area included present-day California, Nevada, New Mexico, Utah, most of Arizona, and parts of Colorado and Wyoming.

In 1853 President Franklin Pierce authorized James Gadsden to pay Mexico an additional $10 million for another piece of territory to secure a southern railroad route to the Pacific Ocean. Along with the settlement of the Oregon boundary and the Treaty of Guadalupe Hidalgo, the Gadsden Purchase established the current borders of the contiguous 48 states.

THE CALIFORNIA GOLD RUSH The United States quickly benefited from its new territories when gold was discovered in California. On January 24, 1848, a carpenter named James Marshall discovered a few particles of gold lying near John Sutter's sawmill in the Sierra Nevada mountains. Soon, more gold was found at Sutter's Mill, and news of the chance discovery began to spread with lightning speed.

When the news reached San Francisco, virtually the whole town hustled to the Sacramento valley to pan for gold. As gold fever traveled eastward, overland migration to California rose from 400 in 1848 to 44,000 in 1850. The discovery also attracted people from Asia, South America, and Europe. By the end of 1849, California's population exceeded 100,000.

The discovery of gold revolutionized California's economy. Gold financed the development of farming, manufacturing, shipping, and banking. Mining continued in California throughout the 1850s. By 1857 the total value of gold production in California approached $2 billion.

Reading Check
Summarize What disagreement led to the Texas Revolution?

The Conflict over Slavery

Over time, the northern and southern sections of the United States had developed into very different cultural and economic regions. However, it was the South's dependence on slavery that eventually brought them into conflict.

DIFFERENCES BETWEEN NORTH AND SOUTH The South's plantation economy relied on an enslaved labor force. In the increasingly industrialized North, opposition to slavery grew more intense. The controversy over slavery worsened as new territories and states were admitted to the Union. Supporters of slavery saw an opportunity to create more slave states, while opponents remained equally determined that slavery should not spread.

SLAVERY IN THE TERRITORIES The issue of slavery in California and in the western territories led to heated debates in Congress. Because of the gold rush, California had grown quickly and applied for statehood in December 1850. California's constitution forbade slavery, even though it lay south of the 36°30' line set by the Missouri Compromise. This alarmed and angered many southerners, who wanted the compromise to apply to all territories.

As the 31st Congress opened in December 1849, the question of statehood for California topped the agenda. Of equal concern was a border dispute in which the slave state of Texas claimed the eastern half of the New Mexico Territory, where the issue of slavery had not yet been settled.

Senator Henry Clay of Kentucky worked to shape a compromise that both the North and the South could accept. After obtaining the support of the powerful Massachusetts senator Daniel Webster, Clay presented to the Senate a series of resolutions later called the Compromise of 1850. To please the North, the compromise provided that California be admitted to the Union as a free state. To please the South, the compromise proposed a new and more effective fugitive slave law. To placate both sides, a provision allowed **popular sovereignty**, the right of people in an area to decide issues for themselves, to settle the question of slavery in the New Mexico and Utah territories.

Reading Check
Analyze Motives Why did southerners want to increase the number of slave states?

The Senate rejected the proposed compromise in July, and Clay left Washington. Senator **Stephen Douglas** of Illinois unbundled the package of resolutions and reintroduced them one at a time, hoping to obtain a majority vote for each measure individually. After the death of President Taylor, his successor, Millard Fillmore, made it clear that he supported the compromise, and the Compromise of 1850 became law.

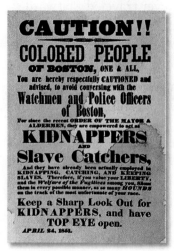

This abolitionist poster distributed in 1851 encouraged northerners not to cooperate with the Fugitive Slave Act.

Protest, Resistance, and Violence

The Fugitive Slave Act of 1850 infuriated many opponents of slavery. The act denied fugitive slaves the right to a trial by jury, and anyone convicted of helping a fugitive was liable for a fine of $1,000 and imprisonment for up to six months. Some northerners resisted the law by organizing "vigilance committees" to send endangered African Americans to safety in Canada. Others worked to help slaves escape, sometimes resorting to violence.

THE UNDERGROUND RAILROAD Attempting to escape from slavery was dangerous. It meant traveling on foot at night, with only the North Star and other natural signs for guidance. It meant avoiding patrols of armed men on horseback and struggling through forests and across rivers. Often it meant going without food for days at a time.

As time went on, free African Americans and white abolitionists developed a secret network of people who would help runaway slaves. The escape routes these abolitionists used became known as the **Underground Railroad**. "Conductors" on the routes hid fugitives, provided them with food and clothing, and escorted or directed them to the next "station."

One of the most famous conductors was **Harriet Tubman**, who had been born a slave in Maryland in 1820 or 1821. In 1849 she decided to make a break for freedom and succeeded in reaching Philadelphia. Shortly after the passage of the Fugitive Slave Act, Tubman became a conductor on the Underground Railroad. She made 19 trips back to the South and is said to have helped 300 slaves—including her own parents—flee to freedom.

UNCLE TOM'S CABIN Meanwhile, another woman brought the horrors of slavery into the homes of Americans. In 1852 Harriet Beecher Stowe published her novel *Uncle Tom's Cabin,* which told of the troubles faced by slaves on a southern plantation. Stowe's novel put human faces on the stories of the inhumanity suffered by slaves. Her writing stressed that slavery was not just a political contest but also a great moral struggle. The book stirred northern abolitionists to increase their protests against the Fugitive Slave Act, while southerners criticized it as an attack on the South.

TENSION IN KANSAS AND NEBRASKA Despite Tubman's and Stowe's efforts, the debate over slavery in the West continued. The Kansas and Nebraska territory lay north of the Missouri Compromise line and therefore was legally closed to slavery. Stephen Douglas introduced a bill in Congress on January 23, 1854, to divide the area into two territories: Nebraska in the north and Kansas in the south. The bill would repeal the Missouri Compromise and establish popular sovereignty for both territories. Congressional debate was bitter, but the Kansas-Nebraska Act was finally passed.

Both supporters and opponents of slavery attempted to populate Kansas in order to win the vote on slavery in the territory. By March 1855 Kansas had enough settlers to hold an election, but thousands of "border ruffians" from the slave state of Missouri had crossed into Kansas to vote illegally. It wasn't long before bloody violence surfaced in the struggle for Kansas, earning the territory the name "Bleeding Kansas."

Free and Slave States and Territories, 1820–1854

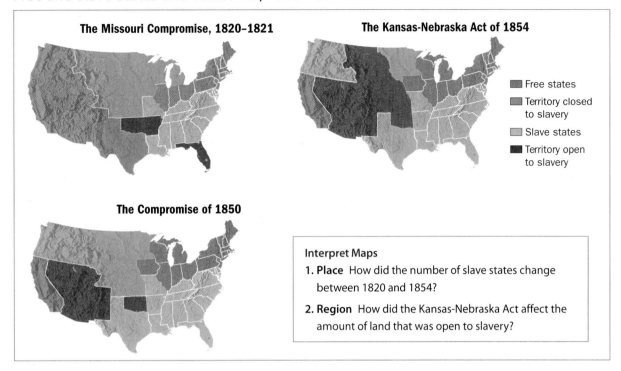

The Missouri Compromise, 1820–1821

The Kansas-Nebraska Act of 1854

- ■ Free states
- ■ Territory closed to slavery
- ▢ Slave states
- ■ Territory open to slavery

The Compromise of 1850

Interpret Maps

1. **Place** How did the number of slave states change between 1820 and 1854?
2. **Region** How did the Kansas-Nebraska Act affect the amount of land that was open to slavery?

NEW POLITICAL PARTIES EMERGE The gulf between the North and the South affected party politics. The Kansas-Nebraska Act finished the Whigs. The southern faction splintered as its members looked for a proslavery, pro-Union party to join. Whigs in the North sought an alternative of their own.

One alternative was the American Party, also called the Know-Nothings. Its members were devoted to nativism, the favoring of American-born citizens over immigrants. Two antislavery parties had also emerged during the 1840s. The Liberty Party aimed to abolish slavery with new laws. The Free-Soil Party opposed slavery in the territories. However, northerners could be Free-Soilers without being abolitionists. Free-Soilers objected to slavery's competition with free white workers, or a wage-based labor force. They feared that it would drive down wages.

In 1854 opponents of slavery in the territories formed the Republican Party. The Republicans opposed the Kansas-Nebraska Act and wanted to keep slavery out of the territories, but otherwise they held a wide range of opinions.

Conflict Leads to Secession

Political conflicts intensified after the election of President James Buchanan. The first controversy arose on March 6, 1857, two days after he took office.

THE *DRED SCOTT* DECISION A major Supreme Court case was brought about by **Dred Scott**, a slave whose owner took him from the slave state of Missouri to free territory in Illinois and Wisconsin and back to Missouri. Scott appealed to the Supreme Court for his freedom on the grounds that living in free areas—Illinois and Wisconsin—had made him a free man.

On March 6, 1857, the Supreme Court ruled against Scott, saying that he could not sue in federal court because he was not a citizen. The Court ruled

Reading Check
Summarize How did the Underground Railroad operate?

Background
The *Dred Scott* case was only the second one in American history in which the Supreme Court reversed a federal legislative act.

that living in free territory did not free a slave and that the Fifth Amendment protected people from losing their property, including slaves. Territories could not deprive slaveholders of their property by excluding slavery.

LINCOLN-DOUGLAS DEBATES Several months after the *Dred Scott* decision, the 1858 race for the U.S. Senate in Illinois began. The race was a contest between Democratic incumbent Stephen Douglas and Republican challenger **Abraham Lincoln**, at the time a representative in Congress. Lincoln challenged Douglas to a series of debates on the issue of slavery in the territories. Douglas accepted the challenge, and the stage was set for some of the most celebrated debates in U.S. history.

Neither man wanted slavery in the territories, but they disagreed on how to keep it out. Douglas believed in popular sovereignty. Lincoln believed that slavery was immoral. However, he did not expect individuals to give up slavery unless Congress abolished slavery with a constitutional amendment. In their second debate, Lincoln asked his opponent a crucial question: Could the settlers of a territory vote to exclude slavery before the territory became a state? The *Dred Scott* decision said no, so popular sovereignty was an empty phrase. Douglas replied that the people of a territory could just elect representatives who would not enforce slave property laws in that territory, thus getting around *Dred Scott*. Douglas won the Senate seat, but Lincoln's attacks on the "vast moral evil" of slavery drew national attention.

HARPER'S FERRY While politicians debated the slavery issue, abolitionist John Brown decided to act. On the night of October 16, 1859, Brown led a band of 21 men—black and white—into Harpers Ferry, Virginia (now West Virginia). He planned to seize the federal arsenal there and start a general slave uprising. However, his plan was not successful. Instead, federal troops put down the rebellion. Later, Brown was tried and executed.

Public reaction to Brown's execution was immediate and intense in both sections of the country. In the North, bells tolled and crowds gathered to hear speeches denouncing the South. The southern response included mobs assaulting whites whom they suspected of antislavery views.

LINCOLN IS ELECTED PRESIDENT
As the 1860 presidential election approached, the Republicans nominated Abraham Lincoln. Lincoln pledged to halt the further spread of slavery, but he also tried to reassure southerners that he would not abolish slavery. Three major candidates besides Lincoln vied for office. Lincoln won with less than half the popular vote and with no electoral votes from the South.

John Brown Going to His Hanging (1942), Horace Pippin. Oil on canvas, 24 1/8" × 30 1/4". Courtesy of the Museum of American Art of the Pennsylvania Academy of the Fine Arts, Philadelphia, Pennsylvania. John Lambert Fund [1943.11]

SOUTHERN SECESSION Southerners had viewed the struggle over slavery partly as a conflict between the states' right of self-determination and federal government control. Lincoln's victory convinced them that they had lost their voice in the national government. Some southern states decided to act. First, South Carolina seceded from the Union on December 20, 1860. When the news reached northern-born William Tecumseh Sherman, superintendent of the Louisiana State Seminary of Learning and Military Academy (now Louisiana State University), he poured out his fears for the South.

> "This country will be drenched in blood. . . . [T]he people of the North . . . are not going to let this country be destroyed without a mighty effort to save it. . . . Besides, where are your men and appliances of war to contend against them? . . . You are rushing into war with one of the most powerful, ingeniously mechanical and determined people on earth—right at your doors. . . . Only in spirit and determination are you prepared for war. In all else you are totally unprepared."
>
> —William Tecumseh Sherman, quoted in *None Died in Vain*

Soon Mississippi seceded, followed by Florida, Alabama, Georgia, Louisiana, and Texas. In February 1861, delegates from the secessionist states met in Montgomery, Alabama. They formed the Confederate States of America, or **Confederacy** and drew up a constitution that closely resembled that of the United States but with a few notable differences. The most important difference was that it "protected and recognized" slavery in new territories.

The Confederates then unanimously elected former senator **Jefferson Davis** of Mississippi as president. The North had heard threats of secession before. When it finally happened, no one was shocked. But everyone wondered if the North would allow the South to leave the Union without a fight.

Reading Check
Compare and Contrast Compare and contrast Lincoln's and Douglas's views on slavery.

Lesson 5 Assessment

1. **Organize Information** Use a timeline to show the events that heightened the tensions between the North and the South.

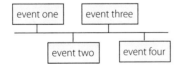

Select one event and explain its significance.

2. **Key Terms and People** For each key term or person in the lesson, write a sentence explaining its significance.

3. **Analyze Effects** What were the benefits and drawbacks of westward expansion? Use specific references to the lesson to support your response.

   Think About:
   • the belief in Manifest Destiny
   • the challenges that new settlers faced
   • the impact on the nation as a whole

4. **Evaluate** Would you have supported war with Mexico? Why or why not? Explain your answer, including details from the lesson.

5. **Evaluate** John Brown, Harriet Tubman, Harriet Beecher Stowe, and Stephen Douglas all opposed slavery. Who do you think had the greatest impact on American history and why?

6. **Develop Historical Perspective** How did the tension between states' rights and national government authority manifest itself in the events leading up to the Civil War?

Mapping the Oregon Trail

In 1841 Congress appropriated $30,000 for a survey of the Oregon Trail. John C. Frémont was named to head the expeditions. Frémont earned his nickname "the Pathfinder" by leading four expeditions—which included artists, scientists, and cartographers, among them German-born cartographer Charles Preuss—to explore the American West between 1842 and 1848. When Frémont submitted the report of his second expedition, Congress immediately ordered the printing of 10,000 copies, which were widely distributed.

The "Topographical Map of the Road from Missouri to Oregon," drawn by Preuss, appeared in seven sheets. Though settlers first used this route in 1836, it was not until 1846 that Preuss published his map to guide them. The long, narrow map shown here is called a "strip" map, a map that shows a thin strip of the earth's surface—in this case, the last stretch of the trail before reaching Fort Wallah-Wallah.

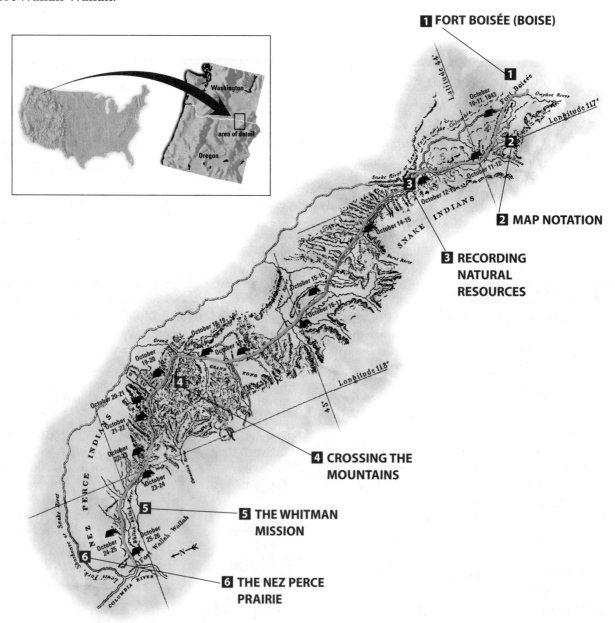

1 FORT BOISÉE (BOISE)

2 MAP NOTATION

3 RECORDING NATURAL RESOURCES

4 CROSSING THE MOUNTAINS

5 THE WHITMAN MISSION

6 THE NEZ PERCE PRAIRIE

1 FORT BOISÉE (BOISE)

This post became an important stopping point for settlers along the trail. Though salmon were plentiful in the summer, Frémont noted that in the winter Native Americans often were forced to eat "every creeping thing, however loathsome and repulsive," to stay alive.

2 MAP NOTATION

Preuss recorded dates, distances, temperatures, and geographical features as the expedition progressed along the trail.

3 RECORDING NATURAL RESOURCES

On October 13, Frémont traveled through a desolate valley of the Columbia River to a region of "arable mountains," where he observed "nutritious grasses" and good soil that would support future flocks and herds.

4 CROSSING THE MOUNTAINS

Pioneers on the trail cut paths through the Blue Mountains, a wooded range that Frémont believed had been formed by "violent and extensive igneous [volcanic] action."

5 THE WHITMAN MISSION

The explorers came upon the Whitmans' missionary station. They found thriving families living primarily on potatoes of a "remarkably good quality."

6 THE NEZ PERCE PRAIRIE

Chief Looking Glass (right, in 1871) and the Nez Perce had "harmless" interactions with Frémont and his expedition.

Critical Thinking

1. **Analyze Patterns** Use the map to identify natural obstacles that settlers faced on the Oregon Trail.

2. **Create a Geographic Model** Do research to find out more about early mapping efforts for other western trails. Then create a settler's map of a small section of one trail. To help you decide what information you should show in your model, pose some questions that a settler might have and that your model will answer. Then, sketch and label your map.

Dred Scott v. Sandford (1857)

ORIGINS OF THE CASE

Slave Dred Scott's master had brought him from the slave state of Missouri to live for a time in free territory and in the free state of Illinois. Eventually they returned to Missouri. Scott believed that because he had lived in free territory, he should be free. In 1854 he sued in federal court for his freedom. The court ruled against him, and he appealed to the Supreme Court.

THE RULING

The Supreme Court ruled that African Americans were not and could never be citizens. Thus, Dred Scott had no right even to file a lawsuit and remained enslaved.

LEGAL REASONING

The Court's decision, based primarily on Chief Justice Roger Taney's written opinion, made two key findings. First, it held that because Scott was a slave, he was not a citizen and had no right to sue in a United States court.

"We think they [slaves] . . . are not included, and were not intended to be included, under the word 'citizens' in the Constitution, and can therefore claim none of the rights and privileges which that instrument provides for and secures to citizens of the United States."

This could have been the end of the matter, but Taney went further. He said that by banning slavery, Congress was, in effect, taking away property. Such an action, he wrote, violated the Fifth Amendment, which guarantees the right not to be deprived of property without due process of law (such as a hearing). Thus, all congressional efforts to ban slavery in the territories were prohibited.

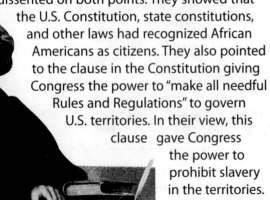

Justices John McLean and Benjamin Curtis strongly dissented on both points. They showed that the U.S. Constitution, state constitutions, and other laws had recognized African Americans as citizens. They also pointed to the clause in the Constitution giving Congress the power to "make all needful Rules and Regulations" to govern U.S. territories. In their view, this clause gave Congress the power to prohibit slavery in the territories.

Chief Justice
Roger Taney

LEGAL SOURCES

U.S. CONSTITUTION

U.S. Constitution, Article 4, Section 2 (1789)
"No Person held to Service or Labor in one State, . . . escaping into another, shall, in Consequence of any Law or Regulation therein, be discharged from such Service or Labor. . . ."

U.S. Constitution, Article 4, Section 3 (1789)
"The Congress shall have Power to dispose of and make all needful Rules and Regulations respecting the Territory or other Property belonging to the United States. . . ."

U.S. Constitution, Fifth Amendment (1791)
"No person shall be . . . deprived of life, liberty, or property, without due process of law. . . ."

RELATED CASES

Ableman v. Booth (1858)
The Court decided that the Fugitive Slave Act was constitutional and that laws passed in northern states that prohibited the return of fugitive slaves were unconstitutional.

WHY IT MATTERED

Taney's opinion in *Dred Scott* had far-reaching consequences. Legally, the opinion greatly expanded the reach of slavery. Politically, it heightened the sectional tensions that would lead to the Civil War.

Before the Court decided *Dred Scott,* Americans widely accepted the idea that Congress and the states could limit slavery. As the dissenters argued, many previous acts of Congress had done just that—for example, the Northwest Ordinance had banned slavery in the Northwest Territory—and no one had claimed that those acts violated property rights.

Taney's opinion in Dred Scott, however, was a major change. This expansion of slaveholders' rights cast doubt on whether free states could prevent slave owners from bringing or even selling slaves into free areas.

As a result, Dred Scott intensified the slavery debate as no single event had before. In going beyond what was needed to settle the case before him, Taney's ruling became a political act and threw into question the legitimacy of the Court. Further, Taney's opinion took the extreme proslavery position and installed it as the national law. It not only negated all the compromises made to date by proslavery and antislavery forces, but it seemed to preclude any possible future compromises.

HISTORICAL IMPACT

It took four years of bitter civil war to find out if Taney's opinion would stand as the law of the land. It would not. Immediately after the Civil War, the federal government moved to abolish slavery with the Thirteenth Amendment (1865) and then to extend state and national citizenship with the Fourteenth Amendment (1868) to "[a]ll persons born or naturalized in the United States." The wording of

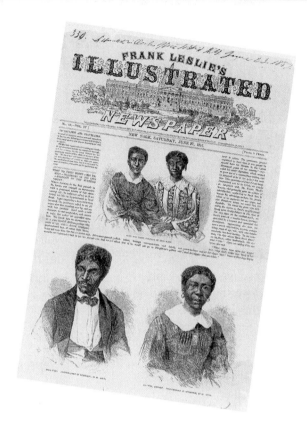

Contemporary newspaper article describing the *Dred Scott* case

these amendments was expressly intended to nullify *Dred Scott*

These amendments meant that *Dred Scott* would no longer be used as a precedent, an earlier ruling that can be used to justify a current one. Instead, it is now pointed to as an important lesson on the limits of the Supreme Court's power, as a key step on the road to the Civil War, and as one of the worst decisions the Supreme Court ever made.

Critical Thinking

1. **Connect to History** Use the library or online resources to find commentaries on *Dred Scott* written at the time the decision was made. Read two of these commentaries and identify which section—North or South—the writer or speaker came from. Explain how each person's regional background shaped his or her views

2. **Connect to Today** Consider what it means to be a citizen of the United States and what rights that citizenship extends. Do Internet research to learn which constitutional amendments, U.S. laws, and Supreme Court decisions guarantee the rights of citizens. Prepare an oral presentation or annotated display to summarize your findings.

★
The Civil War

The Big Idea
The Civil War brought about dramatic social and economic changes in American society.

Why It Matters Now
The federal government established supreme authority, and no state has threatened secession since.

Key Terms and People
Stonewall Jackson

Ulysses S. Grant

Robert E. Lee

Emancipation Proclamation

conscription

income tax

Gettysburg

William Tecumseh Sherman

Appomattox Court House

Thirteenth Amendment

John Wilkes Booth

One American's Story

Mary Chesnut, a wellborn southerner whose husband served in the Confederate government, kept a diary describing key war events, such as the attack on Fort Sumter. Her diary paints a vivid picture as well of the marriages and flirtations, hospital work, and dinner parties that comprised daily life in the South.

In 1864 Chesnut found that her social standing could no longer protect her from the economic effects of the war.

"September 19th . . . My pink silk dress I have sold for six hundred dollars, to be paid in installments, two hundred a month for three months. And I sell my eggs and butter from home for two hundred dollars a month. Does it not sound well—four hundred dollars a month, regularly? In what? 'In Confederate money.' Hélas! [Alas!]"
—Mary Chesnut, quoted in *Mary Chesnut's Civil War*

The Confederate money Chesnut received—once a small fortune—had been rendered almost worthless by the war. Inflation, or a sharp increase in the cost of living, had devalued Confederate currency to such an extent that $400 was worth only a dollar or two compared to prewar currency. Across both the South and the North, civilians found their lives profoundly changed by the ongoing conflict.

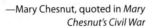

SS.912.A.1.4; SS.912.A.1.7; SS.912.A.2.1; SS.912.A.2.4; SS.912.A.3.13; SS.912.G.1.2; LAFS.1112.RH.3.7; MAFS.K12.MP.1.1; MAFS.K12.MP.3.1; MAFS.K12.MP.5.1

The War Begins

As soon as the Confederacy was formed, Confederate soldiers began seizing federal forts. On April 12, 1861, they fired on Fort Sumter in Charleston harbor, and the next day the Union garrison surrendered. News of Fort Sumter's fall united the North, and the response to Lincoln's call for volunteers was overwhelming. In the South, Virginia, Arkansas, North Carolina, and Tennessee seceded, bringing the number of Confederate states to 11. The western counties of Virginia opposed slavery, so they seceded from Virginia and were admitted into the Union as West Virginia in 1863. The four remaining slave states—Maryland, Delaware, Kentucky, and Missouri—remained in the Union.

UNION AND CONFEDERATE FORCES CLASH Although civilians on both sides felt that victory was assured, in reality the two sides were unevenly matched. The Union had more people, more factories, greater food production, and a more extensive railroad system. The Confederacy's advantages included "King Cotton," first-rate generals, and highly motivated soldiers.

Both sides adopted military strategies suited to their objectives and resources. The Union, which had to conquer the South to win, devised a three-part plan: (1) the Union navy would blockade southern ports, so the South could neither export cotton nor import much-needed manufactured goods; (2) Union riverboats and armies would move down the Mississippi River and split the Confederacy in two; and (3) Union armies would capture the Confederate capital at Richmond, Virginia. The Confederacy's strategy was mostly defensive, although southern leaders encouraged their generals to attack the North if the opportunity arose.

The first bloodshed occurred about three months after Fort Sumter fell, near Bull Run, a creek 25 miles from Washington, DC. In the morning, the Union army gained the upper hand, but the Confederates held firm, inspired

Northern and Southern Resources, 1861

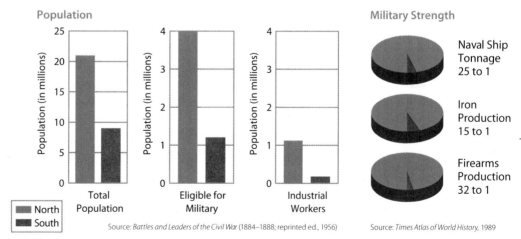

Population

Military Strength

North
South

Source: *Battles and Leaders of the Civil War* (1884–1888; reprinted ed., 1956)

Source: *Times Atlas of World History*, 1989

Interpret Graphs

1. Which side—North or South—had the advantage in terms of industrial production?

2. What do the overall data suggest about the eventual outcome of the war?

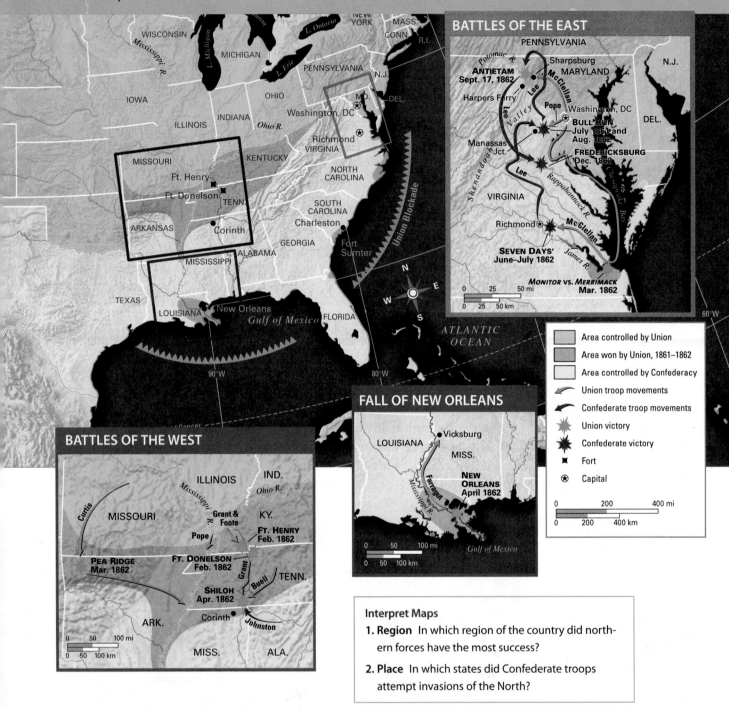

Civil War, 1861–1862

Explore ONLINE!

BATTLES OF THE EAST

PENNSYLVANIA

ANTIETAM
Sept. 17, 1862

Sharpsburg
McClellan
MARYLAND
N.J.

Harpers Ferry
Pope
Washington, DC
DEL.

BULL RUN
July 1861 and
Aug. 1862

Manassas
Jct.
FREDERICKSBURG
Dec. 1862

VIRGINIA

Richmond
McClellan

SEVEN DAYS'
June–July 1862

MONITOR vs. MERRIMACK
Mar. 1862

0   25   50 mi
0   25   50 km

Legend:
- Area controlled by Union
- Area won by Union, 1861–1862
- Area controlled by Confederacy
- Union troop movements
- Confederate troop movements
- Union victory
- Confederate victory
- Fort
- Capital

0   200   400 mi
0   200   400 km

FALL OF NEW ORLEANS

LOUISIANA
Vicksburg
MISS.

Farragut

NEW
ORLEANS
April 1862

0   50   100 mi
0   50   100 km

Gulf of Mexico

BATTLES OF THE WEST

ILLINOIS   IND.

Curtis

MISSOURI

Grant &
Foote

KY.

Pope
FT. HENRY
Feb. 1862

PEA RIDGE
Mar. 1862
FT. DONELSON
Feb. 1862

Grant
Buell
TENN.

SHILOH
Apr. 1862

ARK.
Corinth
Johnston

0   50   100 mi
0   50   100 km
MISS.   ALA.

Interpret Maps

1. **Region** In which region of the country did northern forces have the most success?

2. **Place** In which states did Confederate troops attempt invasions of the North?

by General Thomas J. Jackson, who earned the nickname **Stonewall Jackson** for his strong defense. In the afternoon, Confederate reinforcements helped win the first southern victory, but they were too exhausted to follow up with an attack on Washington. Still, Confederate morale soared.

Lincoln responded to the defeat at Bull Run by appointing General George McClellan to lead the Union forces encamped near Washington. While McClellan drilled his troops, the Union forces in the west began the fight for control of the Mississippi River.

In February 1862 a Union army headed by General **Ulysses S. Grant** invaded western Tennessee. In just 11 days, Grant's forces captured two Confederate forts: Fort Henry on the Tennessee River and Fort Donelson on the Cumberland River. Two months later, Grant led his troops into Tennessee, where they faced a Confederate army in a bloody battle at Shiloh. Nearly one-fourth of the 100,000 men who fought in the battle were killed, wounded, or captured.

As Grant pushed toward the Mississippi River, David G. Farragut, commanding a Union fleet of about 40 ships, seized New Orleans, the Confederacy's largest city and busiest port. By June, Farragut had taken control of much of the lower Mississippi. Between Grant and Farragut, the Union had nearly achieved its goal of cutting the Confederacy in two. Only Port Hudson, Louisiana, and Vicksburg, Mississippi, still stood in the way.

In the spring of 1862, while General McClellan was leading his army toward Richmond, he met Confederate troops commanded by General Joseph E. Johnston. After a series of battles, Johnston was wounded, and command passed to **Robert E. Lee**. Determined to save the Confederate capital, Lee drove McClellan away from Richmond.

In September, troops led by Robert E. Lee crossed the Potomac into Maryland. McClellan ordered his men to pursue Lee. The two sides fought on September 17 near a creek called the Antietam (ăn-tē'təm). The clash was the bloodiest single-day battle in American history, with casualties totaling more than 26,000. The next day, instead of pursuing the battered Confederate army into Virginia and possibly ending the war, McClellan did nothing. As a result, Lincoln removed him from command.

THE POLITICS OF WAR After secession, many southerners believed that dependence on southern cotton would force Great Britain to recognize the Confederacy as an independent nation. However, not only had Britain accumulated a huge cotton inventory just before the outbreak of war, it also found new sources of cotton in Egypt and India. Due to European crop failures, Britain now needed northern wheat and corn. Britain remained neutral.

As the Confederacy struggled to gain foreign recognition, abolitionist feeling grew in the North. Although Lincoln disliked slavery, he did not believe that the federal government had the power to abolish it. Lincoln did find a way to use his constitutional war powers to end slavery. As Commander in Chief, Lincoln could order his troops to seize enemy resources, which in the South included slaves. Therefore, he decided that, just as he could order the Union army to take Confederate supplies, he could also authorize the army to emancipate slaves. Emancipation was not just a moral issue; it became a weapon of war.

On January 1, 1863, Lincoln issued his **Emancipation Proclamation**. It stated that all slaves in areas currently under rebellion would be freed immediately. The proclamation did not actually free any slaves, because it applied only to areas behind Confederate lines, outside Union control. Nevertheless, for many, the proclamation gave the war a moral purpose by turning the struggle into a fight to free the slaves. It also enraged the South and ensured that compromise was no longer possible.

Reading Check
Analyze Motives
In what way was the Emancipation Proclamation a part of Lincoln's military strategy?

Neither side in the Civil War was completely unified. There were thousands of Confederate sympathizers in the North and thousands of Union sympathizers in the South. For example, south Florida cattlemen who sympathized with the Union sold their cattle at Union-held Fort Myers.

Lincoln dealt forcefully with dissent. He suspended the writ of habeas corpus, which prevents the government from holding citizens without formally charging them with crimes. Jefferson Davis did the same.

Life During Wartime

The war led to social upheaval and political unrest in both the North and the South. As the fighting intensified, heavy casualties and widespread desertions led each side to impose **conscription**, a draft that forced men to serve in the army. Sweeping changes occurred in the wartime economies of both sides as well as in the roles played by African Americans and women.

SOLDIERS SUFFER Both Union and Confederate soldiers had marched to war thinking it would be a glorious affair. They were soon disillusioned, not only by battlefield casualties but also by filthy surroundings, poor diets, and inadequate medical care. Body lice, dysentery, and diarrhea were common.

Conditions in war prisons were atrocious. The Confederate camps were especially overcrowded and unsanitary. Prison camps in the North were only slightly better. Historians estimate that 15 percent of Union prisoners in southern prisons died, while 12 percent of Confederate prisoners died in northern prisons.

African Americans made up only 1 percent of the North's population, but by war's end, about 180,000 African Americans had fought for the Union—about 10 percent of the northern army. In spite of their dedication, African American soldiers in the Union army faced discrimination. They served in separate regiments commanded by white officers and earned lower pay.

Background
After the war, Clara Barton became the first woman to head a U.S. government agency, whose employees helped family members to track down missing soldiers.

Although women did not fight, many contributed to the war effort. Thousands of women on both sides served as army nurses. One dedicated Union nurse was Clara Barton, who went on to found the American Red Cross after the war. Barton cared for the sick and wounded, often at the front lines.

THE WAR AFFECTS REGIONAL ECONOMIES In general, the war expanded the North's economy and shattered the South's. The Confederacy soon faced a food shortage due to the drain of manpower into the army, the Union occupation of food-growing areas, and the loss of enslaved field workers. Food prices skyrocketed, and the inflation rate rose 7,000 percent.

Reading Check
Analyze Effects
What effects did the Civil War have on the economies of the North and the South?

Overall, the war's effect on the economy of the North was much more positive. The army's need for supplies supported northern industries. However, wages did not keep up with prices. When workers went out on strike, employees hired free blacks, immigrants, and women to replace them for lower wages. As the northern economy grew, Congress imposed the nation's first **income tax**, a tax that takes a percentage of an individual's income, to help pay for the war.

The North Takes Charge

In December 1862 Lee's army had defeated the Union Army of the Potomac at Fredericksburg, Virginia. Then, in May, the South defeated the North again at Chancellorsville, Virginia. The North's only consolation after Chancellorsville came when a wounded Stonewall Jackson caught pneumonia and died on May 10.

THE TIDE TURNS Despite Jackson's death, Lee decided to invade the North. He needed supplies, and he also thought a major Confederate victory on northern soil might sway public opinion in the Union in the South's favor. In addition, he hoped that the presence of a Confederate army in the North would force the Union to move troops out of southern territory to defend its own territory. Accordingly, Lee crossed the Potomac into Maryland and pushed on into Pennsylvania.

Historical Source

Mathew Brady's Photographs

The Civil War marked the first time in U.S. history that photography, a resource since 1839, played a major role in a military conflict. Hundreds of photographers traveled with the troops, working both privately and for the military. The most famous Civil War photographer was Mathew Brady, who employed about 20 photographers to meet the public demand for pictures from the battlefront. This was the beginning of American news photography, or photojournalism. Images like this, showing the wounded or the dead, brought home the harsh reality of war to the civilian population.

Analyze Historical Sources
How does this photograph compare with more heroic imagery of traditional history paintings?

The most decisive battle of the war was fought near **Gettysburg**, in southern Pennsylvania, beginning on July 1. The Union soldiers fired on approaching Confederate troops from defensive positions on the hills and ridges surrounding the town. Both sides called for reinforcements. By the end of that day, 90,000 Union troops under General George Meade had fought against 75,000 Confederates led by General Lee.

Fighting went on for three days. For two hours on July 3, the two armies fired at one another in a vicious exchange that could be heard in Pittsburgh. Then the Confederates charged the lines, but Union artillery renewed its barrage. Devastated, the Confederates staggered back to their lines. The three-day battle produced huge losses: 23,000 Union men and 28,000 Confederates were killed or wounded.

In November 1863 President Lincoln spoke at the dedication of a cemetery in Gettysburg. According to some contemporary historians, Lincoln's Gettysburg Address "remade America." The speech helped the country realize that it was not just a collection of individual states; it was one unified nation.

While Meade's Army of the Potomac was destroying Confederate hopes in Gettysburg, Union general Ulysses S. Grant fought to take Vicksburg, one of the two remaining Confederate strongholds on the Mississippi River. Vicksburg itself was particularly important because it rested on bluffs above the river from which guns could control all water traffic. In the winter of 1862–1863, Grant tried several schemes to reach Vicksburg and take it from the Confederates. Nothing seemed to work—until the spring of 1863.

Grant launched his new strategy by weakening the Confederate defenses that protected Vicksburg. He was able to land his troops south of Vicksburg on April 30 and immediately sent his men in search of Confederate troops in Mississippi. In 18 days, Union forces had sacked Jackson, the capital of the state. Grant and his troops then made two unsuccessful attacks on Vicksburg. Finally, in the last week of May 1863, Union troops began shelling the city from both the river and from land for several hours a day, forcing the city's residents into caves that they dug out of the yellow clay hillsides.

After food supplies ran so low that people were reduced to eating dogs and mules, the Confederate command of Vicksburg asked Grant for terms of surrender. The city fell on July 4. Five days later, the last Confederate holdout on the Mississippi also fell. The Union had achieved another of its major military objectives, and the Confederacy was cut in two.

THE CONFEDERACY WEARS DOWN The twin defeats at Gettysburg and Vicksburg cost the South much of its limited manpower. The Confederacy was already low on food, shoes, uniforms, guns, and ammunition. No longer able to attack, it could hope only to hang on long enough to destroy northern morale and work toward an armistice.

That plan proved increasingly unrealistic, however, in part because southern morale was weakening. Many Confederate soldiers had deserted, and newspapers, state legislatures, and individuals throughout the South began to call openly for peace. Worse yet for the Confederacy, Lincoln finally found not just one but two generals who would fight.

In March 1864 President Lincoln appointed Ulysses S. Grant commander of all Union armies. Grant then appointed **William Tecumseh Sherman** as commander of the military division of the Mississippi. Both Grant and Sherman believed in waging total war. If the Union could destroy the southern population's will to fight, the Confederacy would collapse. Grant's overall strategy was to decimate Lee's army in Virginia, while Sherman raided Georgia. Even if his casualties ran twice as high as those of Lee—and they did—the North could afford it; the South could not.

In the spring of 1864, Sherman began a march through Georgia to the sea, creating a wide path of destruction. His army burned almost every house in its path and destroyed livestock and railroads. By mid-November he had captured and burned most of Atlanta, one of the South's largest cities. After reaching the ocean, Sherman's forces—followed by 25,000 former slaves—turned north to help Grant "wipe out Lee."

Despite the war, politics in the Union went on as usual. As the 1864 presidential election approached, Lincoln faced heavy opposition from the Democrats and from a faction within his own party. A growing number of northerners were dismayed at the war's length and its high casualty rates. Lincoln was pessimistic about his chances to remain president. News of General Sherman's victories, however, inspired the North and helped Lincoln win reelection.

On April 9, 1865, in the town of **Appomattox** (ăp´ə-măt′əks) **Court House**, Virginia, Lee and Grant met at a private home to arrange a Confederate surrender. At Lincoln's request, the terms were generous. Grant paroled Lee's soldiers and sent them home with their possessions and three days' worth of rations. After four long years, the Civil War was over.

Reading Check
Analyze Motives
Why did Sherman and Grant want to wage "total war"?

Thomas Lovell's *Surrender at Appomattox* is a modern rendering of Lee's surrender to Grant.

Legacy of the Civil War

The Civil War caused tremendous political, economic, technological, and social change in the United States. It also exacted a high price in terms of human life. Approximately 360,000 Union soldiers and 260,000 Confederates died, nearly as many American combat deaths as in all other major American wars combined.

THE WAR CHANGES THE NATION The Civil War greatly increased the federal government's power and authority. During the war, the federal government passed laws, including income tax and conscription laws, that gave it much more control over individual citizens. In addition, after the war, no state ever threatened secession again.

The Civil War dramatically widened the economic gap between North and South. During the war, the economy of the northern states boomed. The southern economy, on the other hand, was devastated. The war not only marked the end of slavery as a labor system but also wrecked most of the region's industry and farmland. The economic gulf between the regions would not diminish until the 20th century.

Technological improvements during the war also made battles bloodier. The two deadliest improvements of the Civil War were the rifle and the minié ball, a soft lead bullet that was more destructive than earlier bullets. Hand grenades and land mines became more lethal. Another technological improvement was the ironclad ship, which could splinter wooden ships by ramming them, withstand cannon fire, and resist burning.

The Costs of the Civil War

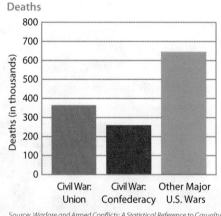

Deaths

Deaths (in thousands)

800
700
600
500
400
300
200
100
0

Civil War: Union — Civil War: Confederacy — Other Major U.S. Wars

Source: *Warfare and Armed Conflicts: A Statistical Reference to Casualty and Other Figures, 1500-2000*; U.S. Department of Defense

Economics

- Union war costs totaled $2.3 billion.
- Confederate war costs ran to $1 billion.
- Union war costs increased the national debt from $65 million in 1860 to $2.7 billion in 1865.
- Confederate debt ran over $1.8 billion in 1864.
- Union inflation peaked at 182% in 1864.
- Confederate inflation rose to 7,000%.

Interpret Graphs
1. Based on the bar graph, how did the combined Union and Confederate losses compare with those of other wars?
2. Why was inflation worse in the Confederacy than in the Union?

A store in Richmond, Virginia, decorated in celebration of Liberation Day, the anniversary of the Emancipation Proclamation.

THE WAR CHANGES LIVES The war not only revolutionized weaponry but also changed people's lives throughout the country. Perhaps the biggest change came for African Americans.

The Emancipation Proclamation had freed only those slaves who lived in states that were behind Confederate lines and not yet under Union control. The government still had to decide what to do about the border states, where slavery still existed. The president believed that the only solution was a constitutional amendment abolishing slavery.

After some political maneuvering, the **Thirteenth Amendment** was ratified at the end of 1865. The U.S. Constitution now stated, "Neither slavery nor involuntary servitude, except as a punishment for crime whereof the party shall have been duly convicted, shall exist within the United States."

Whatever further plans Lincoln had to reunify the nation after the war, he never got to implement them. On April 14, 1865, five days after Lee surrendered to Grant, Lincoln and his wife went to Ford's Theatre in Washington to see a British comedy, *Our American Cousin.* During its third act, a man crept up behind Lincoln and shot the president in the back of his head. The assassin, **John Wilkes Booth**, a 26-year-old actor and southern sympathizer, then leaped down from the presidential box to the stage and escaped. Twelve days later, Union cavalry trapped him in a Virginia tobacco shed and shot him dead.

Lincoln never regained consciousness and died on April 15. It was the first time a president of the United States had been assassinated. The journey of the funeral train that carried Lincoln's body from Washington to his hometown of Springfield, Illinois, took 14 days. Approximately 7 million Americans—almost one-third of the entire Union population—turned out to mourn publicly their martyred leader.

The Civil War had ended. Slavery and secession were no more. Now the country faced two new problems: how to restore the southern states to the Union and how to integrate approximately 4 million newly freed African Americans into national life.

**Reading Check
Summarize** What were some effects that the war had on individuals?

Lesson 6 Assessment

1. **Organize Information** Use a multiple-effects chart to identify major consequences of the Civil War.

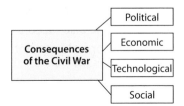

2. **Key Terms and People** For each key term or person in the lesson, write a sentence explaining its significance.

3. **Analyze Effects** What effects did the Civil War have on women and African Americans?
   Think About:
   • the impact of the Emancipation Proclamation
   • women's role in the war effort

4. **Contrast** What advantages did the Union have over the South?

5. **Summarize** How did Lincoln abolish slavery in all states?

6. **Draw Conclusions** Why did the Union's victory strengthen the power of the national government?

★
Reconstruction

The Big Idea

Congress opposed Lincoln's and Johnson's plans for Reconstruction and instead implemented its own plan to rebuild the South.

Why It Matters Now

Reconstruction was an important step in African Americans' struggle for civil rights.

Key Terms and People

Andrew Johnson

Reconstruction

Radical Republicans

Freedmen's Bureau

black codes

Fourteenth Amendment

Fifteenth Amendment

carpetbagger

scalawag

Hiram Revels

sharecropping

Ku Klux Klan (KKK)

SS.912.A.1.2; SS.912.A.1.4; SS.912.A.1.7; SS.912.A.2.1; SS.912.A.2.2; SS.912.A.2.3; SS.912.A.2.4; SS.912.A.2.6; SS.912.A.3.13

One American's Story

As a young man, **Andrew Johnson**—who succeeded Abraham Lincoln as president—entered politics in Tennessee. He won several important offices, including those of congressman, governor, and U.S. senator.

After secession, Johnson was the only senator from a Confederate state to remain loyal to the Union. A former slave owner, by 1863 Johnson supported abolition. He hated wealthy southern planters, whom he held responsible for dragging poor whites into the war. Early in 1865 he endorsed harsh punishment for the rebellion's leaders.

"The time has arrived when the American people should understand what crime is, and that it should be punished, and its penalties enforced and inflicted. . . . Treason must be made odious . . . traitors must be punished and impoverished . . . their social power must be destroyed. I say, as to the leaders, punishment. I say leniency, conciliation, and amnesty to the thousands whom they have misled and deceived."

—Andrew Johnson, quoted in *Reconstruction: The Ending of the Civil War*

Andrew Johnson, the 17th president of the United States

On becoming president, Johnson faced the issue of whether to punish or pardon former Confederates. He also faced the larger problem of how to bring the defeated Confederate states back into the Union.

The Politics of Reconstruction

The need to help former slaves was just one of many issues the nation confronted after the war. In addition, the government, led by Andrew Johnson, Lincoln's vice-president and eventual successor, had to determine how to bring the Confederate states back into the Union. **Reconstruction**, the period during which the United States began to rebuild after the Civil War, lasted from 1865 to 1877. The term also refers to the process the federal government used to readmit the defeated Confederate states to the Union. Complicating the process was the fact that Abraham Lincoln, Andrew Johnson, and the members of Congress all had different ideas about how Reconstruction should be handled.

LINCOLN'S PLAN Lincoln made it clear that he favored a lenient Reconstruction policy. In December 1863 Lincoln announced his Proclamation of Amnesty and Reconstruction, also known as the Ten-Percent Plan. Under this plan, the government would pardon all Confederates—except high-ranking officials and those accused of crimes against prisoners of war—who would swear allegiance to the Union. As soon as ten percent of those who had voted in 1860 took this oath of allegiance, a Confederate state could form a new state government and send representatives and senators to Congress. Under Lincoln's terms, Arkansas, Louisiana, and Tennessee moved toward readmission to the Union.

However, Lincoln's Reconstruction plan angered a minority of Republicans in Congress, known as **Radical Republicans**. The Radicals, led by Senator Charles Sumner of Massachusetts and Representative Thaddeus Stevens of Pennsylvania, wanted to destroy the political power of former slaveholders. Most of all, they wanted African Americans to be given full citizenship and the right to vote.

Southern soldiers returning from the Civil War found much of the region in ruins.

JOHNSON'S RECONSTRUCTION PLAN

Lincoln was assassinated before he could fully implement his Reconstruction plan. He was succeeded by Andrew Johnson, a Tennessee Democrat and a states' rights advocate. Johnson had been selected to be Lincoln's running mate in the 1864 election as a way to broaden the base of the Republican Party. Less than six weeks after his inauguration as vice-president, Johnson succeeded to the presidency. His tenure was marked by constant conflict with Radical Republicans in Congress, whose views on the treatment of the defeated South differed sharply from his.

In May 1865 Johnson announced his own plan, which differed little from Lincoln's. The major difference was that Johnson tried to break the planters' power by excluding high-ranking Confederates and wealthy southern landowners from taking the oath needed for voting privileges. However, Johnson also pardoned more than 13,000 former Confederates because he believed that "white men alone must manage the South."

The remaining ex-Confederate states quickly agreed to Johnson's terms. In the following months, all these states except Texas set up new state governments and elected representatives to Congress. In December 1865 the new southern legislators arrived in Washington to take their seats. Congress, however, refused to admit them. At the same time, moderate Republicans pushed for new laws to remedy weaknesses they saw in Johnson's plan.

In February 1866 Congress voted to continue and enlarge the **Freedmen's Bureau**. Congress had established the bureau in the last month of the war. It assisted former slaves and poor whites in the South by distributing clothing and food. In addition, the Freedmen's Bureau set up more than 40 hospitals, approximately 4,000 schools, 61 industrial institutes, and 74 teacher-training centers. Two months after enlarging the Freedmen's Bureau, Congress passed the Civil Rights Act of 1866. The new law gave African Americans citizenship and forbade states from passing discriminatory laws—**black codes**—that severely restricted African Americans' lives.

Johnson shocked everyone when he vetoed both the Freedmen's Bureau Act and the Civil Rights Act. Congress, Johnson contended, had gone far beyond anything "contemplated by the authors of the Constitution."

CONGRESSIONAL RECONSTRUCTION Angered by Johnson's actions, radical and moderate Republican factions decided to work together to shift the control of the Reconstruction process from the executive branch to the legislature. In mid-1866 they overrode the president's vetoes of the Civil Rights Act and Freedmen's Bureau Act. In addition, Congress drafted the **Fourteenth Amendment**, which prevented states from denying rights and privileges to any U.S. citizen, now defined as "all persons born or naturalized in the United States." This definition was expressly intended to overrule and nullify the *Dred Scott* decision.

In the 1866 elections, moderate and radical Republicans gained control of Congress. They joined together to pass the Reconstruction Act of 1867, which did not recognize any of the state governments formed under the Lincoln and Johnson plans, except Tennessee. The act divided the former Confederate states into five military districts. The states were required to grant African American men the vote and to ratify the Fourteenth Amendment in order to reenter the Union. When Johnson vetoed the Reconstruction legislation, Congress promptly overrode the veto.

JOHNSON IMPEACHED The Radical Republicans thought Johnson was blocking Reconstruction and looked for a reason to impeach him. They found grounds when Johnson removed Secretary of War Edwin Stanton, their ally in the Cabinet, from office in 1868. Johnson's removal of the cabinet member violated the Tenure of Office Act, which stated that a president could not remove cabinet officers without the Senate's approval. The House impeached Johnson, but he remained in office after the Senate voted not to convict.

U. S. GRANT ELECTED In the 1868 presidential election, Civil War hero Ulysses S. Grant won by a margin of only 306,000 votes out of almost 6 million ballots cast. More than 500,000 southern African Americans had voted. Of this number, 9 out of 10 voted for Grant. The importance of the African American vote to the Republican Party was obvious.

After the election, the Radicals introduced the **Fifteenth Amendment**, which states that no one can be kept from voting because of "race, color, or previous condition of servitude." The Fifteenth Amendment, which was ratified by the states in 1870, was an important victory for the Radicals. It was aimed not only at the South. At the time it was passed, African American men could not vote in 16 states. One Radical Republican wrote, "We have no moral right to impose an obligation on one part of the land which the rest will not accept."

Reading Check
Make Inferences
How did the views of presidents Lincoln and Johnson on Reconstruction differ from the views of Radical Republicans?

Reconstructing Society

Under the congressional Reconstruction program, state constitutional conventions met and southern voters elected new, Republican-dominated governments. By 1870 all of the former Confederate states had completed the process. However, even after all the states were back in the Union, the Republicans did not end the process of Reconstruction because they wanted to make economic changes in the South.

CONDITIONS IN THE POSTWAR SOUTH The war had devastated the South economically. Southern planters returned home to find that the value of their property had plummeted. Throughout the South, many small farms were ruined. The region's population was also devastated. Hundreds of thousands of southern men had died in the war. Republican governments began public works programs to repair the physical damage and to provide social services.

Florida was not as damaged as the rest of the South, because not much fighting had taken place there. In addition, cattle helped the state recover from the Reconstruction era depression. No longer hindered by Union coastal blockades, Florida cattlemen resumed trade with Cuba. From 1868 to 1878, 1.6 million cattle were exported to the island, adding millions of dollars to the state's economy.

POLITICS IN THE POSTWAR SOUTH The southern Republican Party during Reconstruction consisted of three groups who worked together to achieve their goals. The first group was the **carpetbaggers**, the northerners who moved to the South after the war. This negative name came from the misconception that they arrived with so few belongings that they carried everything in small traveling bags made of carpeting. Some were Freedmen's Bureau agents who felt a moral duty to help former slaves. They wanted to help rebuild the war-torn region, but others were dishonest and greedy people who hoped to profit from southerners' misfortunes. Despite these varied motives, most white southerners believed that the newcomers wanted to exploit the South's postwar turmoil for their own profit.

"Unwelcome Guest"

Of all the political cartoonists of the 19th century, Thomas Nast (1840–1902) had the greatest and most long-lasting influence. This Nast cartoon from a southern Democratic newspaper depicts Carl Schurz, a liberal Republican who advocated legal equality for African Americans. Schurz is shown as a carpetbagger trudging down a dusty southern road as a crowd of people watch his arrival.

Analyze Historical Sources

Is Schurz shown in a positive or negative light? How can you tell?

Why do you think the cartoonist portrays the southern people standing in a group, far away from Schurz?

A second group was made up of white southerners who joined the Republican Party to have greater political opportunities. Democrats who opposed the Republicans' plan for Reconstruction called these white southerners who changed parties **scalawags**. They considered scalawags traitors to their southern heritage. Some of these new Republicans hoped to win a high office and gain wealth and power. Others believed that a Republican government offered the best chances for the South to rebuild and industrialize. The majority were small farmers who wanted to improve their economic and political position. They also hoped to prevent the formerly wealthy southern planters from regaining power.

The third and largest group of southern Republicans—African Americans—gained voting rights as a result of the Fifteenth Amendment. They overwhelmingly supported the Republican Party, because it was the party of Lincoln—the same party that had freed them from servitude. During Reconstruction, African American men registered to vote for the first time. Although many former slaves could neither read nor write and were politically inexperienced, they were eager to exercise their voting rights. As a result, the voting rates among African Americans were incredibly high during Reconstruction.

The alliance of the three Republican groups was often an uneasy one. Despite their shared party affiliation, the three groups did not always agree on issues. Few scalawags, for example, shared the Republican commitment to civil rights and suffrage for African Americans. Over time, many of them returned to the Democratic Party.

The new status of African Americans required fundamental changes in the attitudes of most southern whites. However, many white southerners refused to accept blacks' new status and resisted the idea of equal rights. Some even left the South rather than accept the new reality.

FORMER SLAVES IMPROVE THEIR LIVES Before the Civil War, African Americans had been denied many opportunities in their lives. Most did not have the rights to marry or keep their families intact. When they gained freedom, many immediately took steps to change those circumstances. They threw wedding ceremonies and tracked down long-lost family members.

Slaves had also been denied full membership in many churches. During Reconstruction, African Americans founded their own churches, which often became the center of the African American community and the only institutions that African Americans fully controlled. Many African American ministers emerged as influential community leaders who also played an important role in the broader political life of the country.

With 95 percent of former slaves illiterate, the freed African Americans required education to become economically self-sufficient. In most of the southern states, the first public school systems were established by the Reconstruction governments. The new African American churches, aided by missionaries from northern churches and by $6 million from the Freedmen's Bureau, worked to create and run these and other schools. Atlanta, Fisk, and Howard universities, for instance, were all founded by religious groups such as the American Missionary Association.

Thousands of African Americans also took advantage of their new freedom by migrating to reunite with family members or to obtain jobs in southern towns and cities.

AFRICAN AMERICANS IN POLITICS After the war, African Americans took an active role in the political process. Not only did they vote, but for the first time they held office in local, state, and federal government.

Although there were almost as many black citizens as white citizens in the South, African American officeholders remained in the minority. Of 125 southerners elected to Congress during Reconstruction, only 16 were black. Among them was **Hiram Revels**, the first African American senator.

— BIOGRAPHY

Hiram Revels (1822–1901)

Hiram Revels of Mississippi (pictured on the far left, with—left to right—African American representatives Benjamin S. Turner of Alabama, Robert C. De Large of South Carolina, Josiah T. Walls of Florida, Jefferson M. Long of Georgia, Joseph H. Rainey of South Carolina, and Robert Brown Elliott of South Carolina) was born of free parents in Fayetteville, North Carolina. Because he could not obtain an education in the South, he attended Knox College in Illinois. As an African Methodist Episcopal minister, he recruited African Americans to fight for the Union during the Civil War and also served as an army chaplain.

In 1865 Revels settled in Mississippi. He served on the Natchez city council and then was elected to Mississippi's state senate in 1869. In 1870 Revels became the first African American elected to the U.S. Senate. Ironically, he held the seat that had once belonged to Jefferson Davis.

SHARECROPPING AND TENANT FARMING In January 1865 General Sherman had promised the former slaves who followed his army 40 acres of land per family and the use of army mules. For the most part, however, former slaves received no land. Most Republicans considered private property a basic American right, and thus refused to help redistribute it. As a result, many plantation owners in the South retained their land.

Without their own land, freed African Americans, as well as poor white farmers, could not grow crops to sell or to use to feed their families. Therefore, economic necessity forced many former slaves and impoverished whites to become sharecroppers. In the system of **sharecropping**, landowners divided their land and assigned each head of household a few acres, along with seed and tools. Sharecroppers kept a small share of their crops and gave the rest to the landowners. In theory, "croppers" who saved a little might even rent land and keep their harvest in a system known as tenant farming.

Reading Check
Form Generalizations
How did southern African Americans respond to their new status?

The Collapse of Reconstruction

Most white southerners swallowed whatever resentment they felt over African American suffrage and participation in government. Some whites expressed their feelings by refusing to register to vote. Others were frustrated by their loss of political power and by the South's economic stagnation. These were the people who formed vigilante groups and used violence to intimidate African Americans.

Although it began as a social group, the Ku Klux Klan became a white supremacist organization whose members attacked African Americans. Members wore costumes to conceal their identities and to appear more menacing.

OPPOSITION TO RECONSTRUCTION The most notorious and widespread of the southern vigilante groups was the **Ku Klux Klan (KKK)**. The Klan's goals were to destroy the Republican Party, to throw out the Reconstruction governments, to aid the planter class, and to prevent African Americans from exercising their political rights. In addition to the Ku Klux Klan, groups such as Knights of the White Camellia, The White League, Red Shirts, and Pale Faces were making efforts to intimidate African Americans and whites that supported them. Many of these groups worked more openly than the Ku Klux Klan, directing their efforts at political goals. To achieve these goals, the Klan and other groups killed perhaps 20,000 men, women, and children. In addition to violence, some white southerners refused to hire or do business with African Americans who voted Republican.

To curtail Klan violence and Democratic intimidation, Congress passed a series of Enforcement Acts in 1870 and 1871. One act provided for the federal supervision of elections in southern states. Another act gave the president the power to use federal troops in areas where the Klan was active.

Although Congress seemed to shore up Republican power with the Enforcement Acts, it also passed legislation that severely weakened the power of the Republican Party in the South. In May 1872 Congress passed the Amnesty Act, which returned the right to vote and the right to hold federal and state offices to about 150,000 former Confederates. In the same year Congress allowed the Freedmen's Bureau to expire. These actions allowed southern Democrats to regain political power.

SUPPORT FOR RECONSTRUCTION FADES Eventually, support for Reconstruction weakened. The breakdown of Republican unity made it even harder for the Radicals to continue to impose their Reconstruction plan on the South. In addition, a series of bank failures known as the panic of 1873 triggered a five-year depression, which diverted attention in the North away from the South's problems. The Supreme Court also began to undo some of the social and political changes that the Radicals had made. Although political violence continued in the South and African Americans ere denied their civil and political rights, Republicans gradually retreated from the policies of Reconstruction.

DEMOCRATS "REDEEM" THE SOUTH As the Republicans' hold on the South loosened, southern Democrats began to regain control of the region. As a result of "redemption"—as the Democrats called their return to power—and a political deal made during the national election of 1876, congressional Reconstruction came to an end.

In the election of 1876, Democratic candidate Samuel J. Tilden won the popular vote, but was one vote short of the electoral victory. Three southern states and Oregon reported two different sets of results. Congress appointed a 15-member electoral commission to award the votes. The commission—eight Republicans and seven Democrats—voted along party lines, giving all the votes to Republican Rutherford B. Hayes. Conflict still seemed likely, until southern Democrats in Congress agreed to accept Hayes if federal troops were withdrawn from the South. After Republican leaders agreed to the demands, Hayes was elected, and Reconstruction ended in the South.

Reconstruction ended without much real progress in the battle against discrimination. However, the Thirteenth, Fourteenth, and Fifteenth Amendments remained part of the Constitution. In the 20th century, these amendments provided the necessary constitutional foundation for important civil rights legislation.

Background
The Twelfth Amendment (1804) gives the House of Representatives the power to elect the president if no candidate has a majority of electoral votes.

Reading Check
Summarize How did southern Democrats regain political power?

Lesson 7 Assessment

1. **Organize Information** Use a table to list problems facing the South after the Civil War and at least one attempted solution for each problem.

Problems	Attempted Solution

2. **Key Terms and People** For each key term or person in the lesson, write a sentence explaining its significance.

3. **Draw Conclusions** Do you think that Reconstruction had positive effects on southern society? Why or why not?

   Think About:
   • the formation of the Ku Klux Klan
   • the establishment of African American churches and schools
   • why so many African Americans turned to sharecropping

4. **Summarize** How did black codes and the system of sharecropping affect freed African Americans?

5. **Analyze Motives** Why did the Radical Republicans want to impeach Andrew Johnson?

Module 1 Assessment

Key Terms and People

For each key term or person below, write a sentence explaining its connection to America's early history.

1. Great Awakening
2. John Locke
3. Federalists
4. Missouri Compromise
5. Seneca Falls Convention
6. popular sovereignty
7. Harriet Tubman
8. Ulysses S. Grant
9. Robert E. Lee
10. John Wilkes Booth

Main Ideas

Use your notes and the information in the module to answer the following questions.

The Colonial Era

1. Why did the Spanish want to colonize the Americas?
2. How did the goals of the Jamestown colonists differ from those of the Puritan colonists in Massachusetts?
3. How did the differences between the northern and southern economies lead to the development of two distinct cultural regions?
4. How did Enlightenment ideas affect political thinking in the colonies?
5. What did Britain gain from its victory in the French and Indian War?

The American Revolution

6. How did the first Continental Congress prepare the way for an armed uprising against Britain?
7. Why did so many colonists remain loyal to Britain during the Revolutionary War?
8. How did the American victory at Saratoga affect the course of the war?

A New Nation

9. What were some of the problems with the kind of government set up by the Articles of Confederation?
10. How did the United States gain Florida from Spain?
11. How did the Louisiana Purchase affect the United States?
12. What was the Missouri Compromise?
13. How did the Seminole respond to attempts to force them to leave Florida?

Economic and Social Changes

14. How did the inventions and innovations of the mid-19th century help fuel the nation's economy?
15. Why did workers go on strike and begin to form trade unions in the 1830s?
16. What new religious ideas set the stage for the reform movements of the mid-19th century?

Westward Expansion

17. Why was the concept of manifest destiny such an appealing one to Americans in the 1840s?
18. What were the terms of the Treaty of Guadalupe Hidalgo?
19. What was the Compromise of 1850?
20. Why did Lincoln's election as president convince southerners that they had lost their voice in the national government?

The Civil War

21. What were the military strategies of the North and the South at the onset of the Civil War?
22. What role did African Americans and women play in the Civil War?
23. What effect did Lincoln's Gettysburg Address have on the country?
24. Which northern tactic helped destroy morale in the South after Gettysburg and Vicksburg?
25. What effect did the war have on the economies of the North and the South?

Reconstruction

26. How did President Johnson try to influence Reconstruction?

27. Why did the Radical Republicans want to impeach Andrew Johnson?

28. In what ways did emancipated slaves exercise their freedom?

29. How did the scalawags differ from other Republicans on issues related to African Americans?

30. How did southern whites regain political power during Reconstruction?

Critical Thinking

1. **Contrast** Create a chart listing the ideological differences between the Federalists and the Democratic-Republicans.

Federalists	Democratic-Republicans

2. **Compare and Contrast** How were English and Spanish policies toward Native Americans similar and different?

3. **Interpret Maps** Look at the map in Lesson 1. Compare and contrast the types of economic activities of the three regions of British colonies in the Americas—New England, Middle, and Southern.

4. **Form Opinions** Review France's role in helping the colonies rebel against Great Britain. Under what conditions, if any, do you think the United States should help other countries?

5. **Evaluate** In your view, which compromise during the Constitutional Convention was more important: the Great Compromise or the Three-Fifths Compromise? Explain your choice.

6. **Predict** How might manifest destiny later affect U.S. relations with Native Americans?

7. **Analyze Effects** In what ways did the reform movement of the mid-19th century affect the lives of women—both white and black, both free and enslaved? Support your answer with examples.

8. **Analyze Issues** Why was the Kansas-Nebraska Act so controversial?

9. **Make Inferences** Why were northern factories and railroads so advantageous to the Union's war effort?

10. **Develop Historical Perspective** How close did African Americans come to gaining full civil rights during Reconstruction? Explain your answer.

Engage with History

Imagine that you are a U.S. citizen during the Civil War and Reconstruction. Consider the Thirteenth, Fourteenth, and Fifteenth Amendments to the Constitution that were ratified during that period. Write a paragraph that explains the freedoms guaranteed by each amendment.

Focus on Writing

Imagine you will be attending the Seneca Falls Convention. Write a formal list of grievances to be presented at the convention. Include grievances about the treatment of women, the lack of opportunities for women, slavery, and any other reforms that society should consider.

Multimedia Activity

Choose a technological development of the early 1800s and create a website to advertise it. Possible inventions include the steam engine, the spinning mule, the telegraph, and the sewing machine. Use vivid language to describe how the invention works, how it relates to the shift to an industrial society, and its effects on how people live or work. Include an image of the invention.

Module 2

Westward Expansion

★

Essential Question
Was the "settlement" of the American western frontier inevitable?

About the Photograph: Until the 1860s the migratory Native Americans of Montana followed the buffalo herds and traded peacefully with whites in the region.

In this module you will learn about continued westward expansion and its effect on Native Americans of the Great Plains. You will also learn about the settlers who moved into the new frontier to mine, ranch, and farm.

▷ Explore ONLINE!

HISTORY.

VIDEOS, including...
- Settling the Great Plains
- Sitting Bull: Chief of the Lakota Nation
- Wild West Cattle Drive

☑ Document-Based Investigations

☑ Graphic Organizers

☑ Interactive Games

☑ Carousel: Importance of the Buffalo

☑ Interactive Map: Railroads Change the Nation

SS.912.A.1.2 Utilize a variety of primary and secondary sources to identify author, historical significance, audience, and authenticity to understand a historical period. **SS.912.A.1.4** Analyze how images, symbols, objects, cartoons, graphs, charts, maps, and artwork may be used to interpret the significance of time periods and events from the past. **SS.912.A.1.7** Describe various sociocultural aspects of American life including arts, artifacts, literature, education, and publications. **SS.912.A.2.7** Review the Native American experience. **SS.912.A.3.1** Analyze the economic challenges to American farmers and farmers' responses to these challenges in the mid to late 1800s. **SS.912.A.3.4** Determine how the development of steel, oil, transportation, communication, and business practices affected the United States economy. **SS.912.A.3.6** Analyze changes that occurred as the United States shifted from agrarian to an industrial society. **SS.912.G.1.2** Use spatial perspective and appropriate geographic terms and tools, including the Six Essential Elements, as organizational schema to describe any given place. **SS.912.G.2.1** Identify the physical characteristics and the human characteristics that define and differentiate regions. **SS.912.G.4.2** Use geographic terms and tools to analyze the push/pull factors contributing to human migration within and among places. **SS.912.G.4.3** Use geographic terms and tools to analyze the effects of migration both on the place of origin and destination, including border areas. **SS.912.H.1.1** Relate works in the arts of varying styles and genre according to the periods in which they were created. **SS.912.H.3.1** Analyze the effects of transportation, trade, communication, science, and technology on the preservation and diffusion of culture. **LAFS.1112.RH.2.4** Determine the meaning of words and phrases as they are used in a text, including analyzing how an author uses and refines the meaning of a key term over the course of a text. **LAFS.1112.WHST.3.7** Conduct short as well as more sustained research projects to answer a question or solve a problem; narrow or broaden the inquiry when appropriate; synthesize multiple sources on the subject, demonstrating understanding of the subject under investigation.

Timeline of Events 1868–1901 ▶ *Explore ONLINE!*

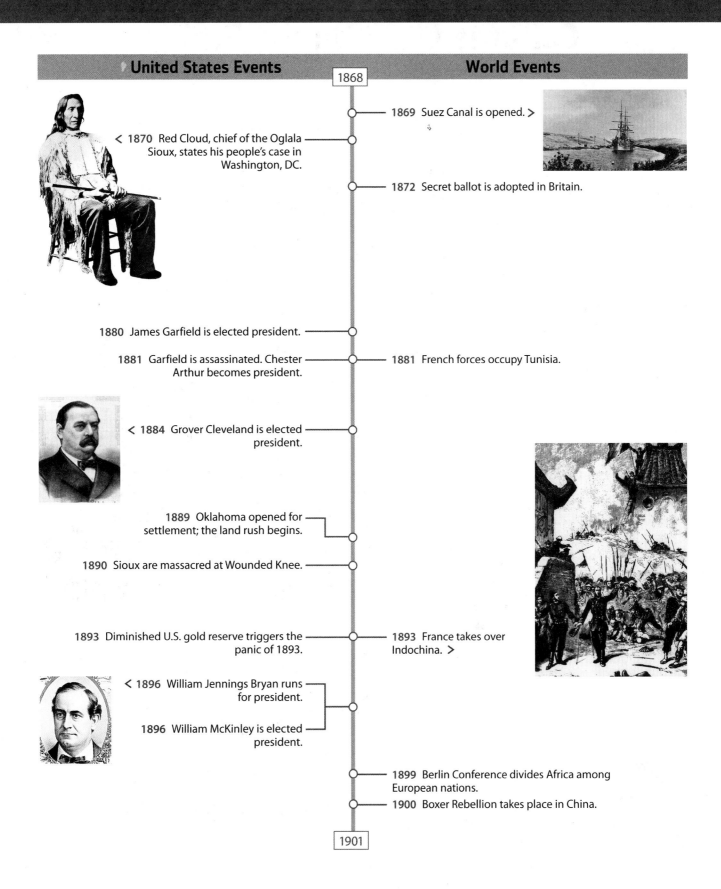

| **United States Events** | 1868 | **World Events** |

1869 Suez Canal is opened. ❯

< 1870 Red Cloud, chief of the Oglala Sioux, states his people's case in Washington, DC.

1872 Secret ballot is adopted in Britain.

1880 James Garfield is elected president.

1881 Garfield is assassinated. Chester Arthur becomes president.

1881 French forces occupy Tunisia.

< 1884 Grover Cleveland is elected president.

1889 Oklahoma opened for settlement; the land rush begins.

1890 Sioux are massacred at Wounded Knee.

1893 Diminished U.S. gold reserve triggers the panic of 1893.

1893 France takes over Indochina. ❯

< 1896 William Jennings Bryan runs for president.

1896 William McKinley is elected president.

1899 Berlin Conference divides Africa among European nations.

1900 Boxer Rebellion takes place in China.

1901

Cultures Clash on the Prairie

The Big Idea

The culture of the Plains Indians declined as the government encouraged white settlers to move West.

Why It Matters Now

Today, Plains Indians work to preserve their cultural traditions.

Key Terms and People

Great Plains

Treaty of Fort Laramie

Sitting Bull

George A. Custer

assimilation

Dawes Act

Battle of Wounded Knee

One American's Story

Zitkala-Ša was born a Sioux in 1876. As she grew up on the Great Plains, she learned the ways of her people. When Zitkala-Ša was eight years old, she was sent to a Quaker school in Indiana. Though her mother warned her of the "white men's lies," Zitkala-Ša was not prepared for the loss of dignity and identity she experienced, which was symbolized by the cutting of her hair.

"I cried aloud . . . and heard them gnaw off one of my thick braids. Then I lost my spirit. Since the day I was taken from my mother I had suffered extreme indignities. . . . And now my long hair was shingled like a coward's! In my anguish I moaned for my mother, but no one came. . . . Now I was only one of many little animals driven by a herder."
—Zitkala-Ša,
from *The School Days of an Indian Girl*

Zitkala-Ša

During this time, white settlers were beginning to push westward. The U.S. government felt that the vast expanses of fertile land that native peoples used as communal hunting grounds would be put to better use if it were farmed and settled. Many felt that it was the Americans' "manifest destiny" to spread across the entire North American continent. Zitkala-Ša experienced firsthand the clash of two very different cultures that occurred as ever-growing numbers of these settlers moved onto the Great Plains. In the resulting struggle, the Native American way of life was changed forever.

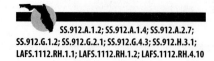

SS.912.A.1.2; SS.912.A.1.4; SS.912.A.2.7; SS.912.G.1.2; SS.912.G.2.1; SS.912.G.4.3; SS.912.H.3.1; LAFS.1112.RH.1.1; LAFS.1112.RH.1.2; LAFS.1112.RH.4.10

The Culture of the Plains Indians

Zitkala-Ša knew very little about the world east of the Mississippi River. Most easterners knew equally little about the West, picturing a vast desert occupied by savage people. That view could not have been more inaccurate. In fact, distinctive and highly developed Native American ways of life existed on the **Great Plains**, the grassland extending through the west-central portion of the United States.

To the east, near the lower Missouri River, nations such as the Osage and Iowa had, for more than a century, hunted and planted crops and settled in small villages. Farther west, nomadic nations such as the Sioux and Cheyenne gathered wild foods and hunted buffalo. Peoples of the plains, abiding by tribal law, traded and produced beautifully crafted tools and clothing.

THE HORSE AND THE BUFFALO After the Spanish brought horses to New Mexico in 1598, the Native American way of life began to change. As the native peoples acquired horses—and then guns—they were able to travel farther and hunt more efficiently. By the mid-1700s almost all the nations on the Great Plains had left their farms to roam the plains and hunt buffalo.

Their increased mobility often led to war when hunters in one nation trespassed on other nations' hunting grounds. For the young men of a nation, taking part in war parties and raids was a way to win prestige. A Plains warrior gained honor by killing his enemies, as well as by "counting coup." This practice involved touching a live enemy with a coup stick and escaping unharmed. And sometimes warring nations would call a truce so that they could trade goods, share news, or enjoy harvest festivals. Native Americans made tepees from buffalo hides and also used the skins for clothing, shoes, and blankets. Buffalo meat was dried into jerky or mixed with berries and fat to make a staple food called pemmican. While the horse gave Native Americans speed and mobility, the buffalo provided many of their basic needs and was central to life on the plains.

FAMILY LIFE Native Americans on the plains usually lived in small extended family groups with ties to other bands that spoke the same language. Young men trained to become hunters and warriors. The women helped butcher the game and prepared the hides that the men brought back to the camp; young women sometimes chose their own husbands.

The Plains Indians believed that powerful spirits controlled events in the natural world. Men or women who showed particular sensitivity to the spirits became medicine men or women, or shamans. Children learned proper behavior and culture through stories and myths, games, and good examples. Despite their communal way of life, however, no individual was allowed to dominate the group. The leaders of a group ruled by counsel rather than by force, and land was held in common for the use of the whole group.

Vocabulary
coup a feat of bravery performed in battle

This Yankton Sioux coup stick was used by warriors.

Reading Check
Summarize
How did the horse influence Native American life on the Great Plains?

The Government Restricts Native Americans

The culture of the white settlers who streamed westward differed in many ways from that of the Native Americans on the plains. Unlike Native Americans, who believed that land could not be owned, the settlers believed that owning land, making a mining claim, or starting a business would give them a stake in the country. They argued that the Native Americans had forfeited their rights to the land because they hadn't settled down to "improve" it. Concluding that the plains were "unsettled," migrants streamed westward along railroad and wagon trails to claim the land.

The expansion of the railroads allowed more settlers to move westward and also influenced the government's policy toward the Native Americans who lived on the plains. In 1834 the federal government had passed an act that designated the entire Great Plains as one enormous reservation, or land set aside for Native American nations. In the 1850s, however, the U.S. government, needing more land for railroads, changed its reservation policy and created treaties that defined specific boundaries for each nation. Most Native Americans spurned the government treaties and continued to hunt on their traditional lands, clashing with settlers and miners—with tragic results.

MASSACRE AT SAND CREEK One of the most tragic events occurred in 1864. Most of the Cheyenne, assuming they were under the protection of the U.S. government, had peacefully returned to Colorado's Sand Creek Reserve for the winter. Yet General S. R. Curtis, U.S. Army commander in the West, sent a telegram to militia colonel John Chivington that read, "I want no peace till the Indians suffer more." In response, Chivington and his troops descended on the Cheyenne and Arapaho—about 200 warriors and 500 women and children—camped at Sand Creek. The attack at dawn on November 29, 1864, killed over 150 inhabitants, mostly women and children.

DEATH ON THE BOZEMAN TRAIL The Bozeman Trail ran directly through Sioux hunting grounds in the Bighorn Mountains. The Sioux chief, Red Cloud (Mahpiua Luta), had unsuccessfully appealed to the government to end white settlement on the trail. In December 1866 the warrior Crazy Horse ambushed Captain William J. Fetterman and his company at Lodge Trail Ridge. Over 80 soldiers were killed.

——— BIOGRAPHY ———

Sitting Bull (1831–1890)

As a child, Sitting Bull was known as Hunkesni, or Slow; he earned the name Tatanka Iyotanka (Sitting Bull) after a fight with the Crow, a traditional enemy of the Sioux.

Sitting Bull led his people by the strength of his character and purpose. He was a warrior, spiritual leader, and medicine man, and he was determined that whites should leave Sioux territory. His most famous fight was at the Little Bighorn River. About his opponent, George Armstrong Custer, he said, "They tell me I murdered Custer. It is a lie. . . . He was a fool and rode to his death."

After Sitting Bull's surrender to the federal government in 1881, his dislike of whites did not change. Native American police at Standing Rock Reservation killed him in December 1890.

Native Americans called this fight the Battle of the Hundred Slain. Whites called it the Fetterman Massacre.

Skirmishes continued until the government agreed to close the Bozeman Trail. In return, the **Treaty of Fort Laramie**, in which the Sioux agreed to live on a reservation along the Missouri River, was forced on the leaders of the Sioux in 1868. **Sitting Bull** (Tatanka Iyotanka), leader of the Hunkpapa Sioux, had never signed it. Although the Ogala and Brule Sioux did sign the treaty, they expected to continue using their traditional hunting grounds.

Reading Check
Analyze Issues
What was the government's policy toward Native American land?

▷ Explore ONLINE!

Shrinking Native American Lands, and Battle Sites

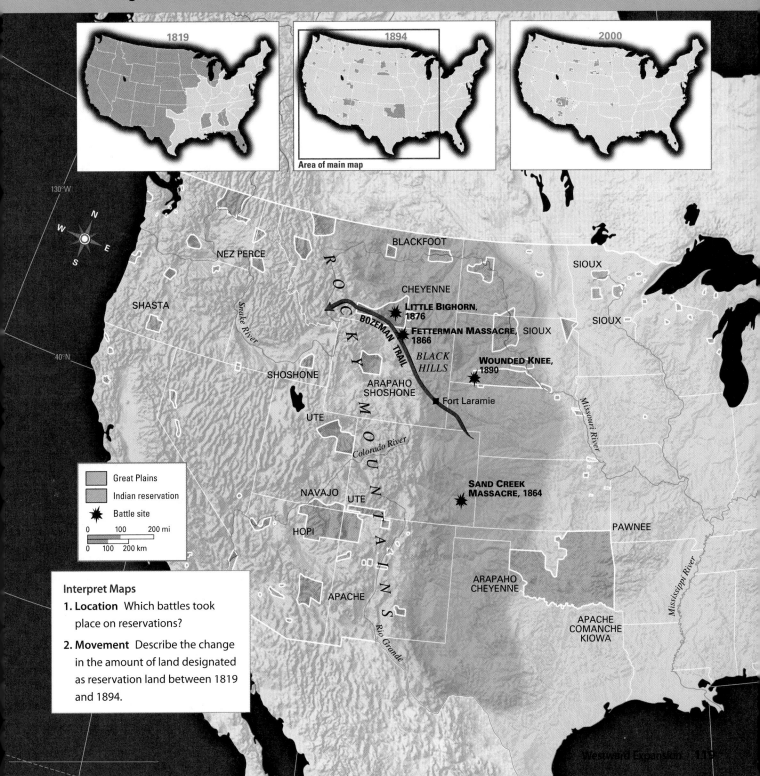

Interpret Maps

1. **Location** Which battles took place on reservations?

2. **Movement** Describe the change in the amount of land designated as reservation land between 1819 and 1894.

Westward Expansion 151

Bloody Battles Continue

The Treaty of Fort Laramie provided only a temporary halt to warfare. The conflict between the two cultures continued as settlers moved westward and Native American nations resisted the restrictions imposed upon them. A Sioux warrior explained why.

> "[We] have been taught to hunt and live on the game. You tell us that we must learn to farm, live in one house, and take on your ways. Suppose the people living beyond the great sea should come and tell you that you must stop farming, and kill your cattle, and take your houses and lands, what would you do? Would you not fight them?"
> —Gall, a Hunkpapa Sioux, quoted in *Bury My Heart at Wounded Knee*

RED RIVER WAR In late 1868 war broke out yet again as the Kiowa and Comanche engaged in six years of raiding that finally led to the Red River War of 1874–1875. The U.S. Army responded by herding the people of friendly nations onto reservations, while opening fire on all others. General Philip Sheridan, a Union army veteran, gave orders "to destroy their villages and ponies, to kill and hang all warriors, and to bring back all women and children." With such tactics, the army crushed resistance on the southern plains.

Colonel George Armstrong Custer, 1865

Reading Check
Analyze Effects
What were the results of Custer's last stand?

GOLD RUSH Within four years of the Treaty of Fort Laramie, miners began searching the Black Hills for gold. The Sioux, Cheyenne, and Arapaho protested the encroachment on their lands to no avail. In 1874, when Colonel **George A. Custer** reported that the Black Hills had gold "from the grass roots down," a gold rush was on. Red Cloud and Spotted Tail, another Sioux chief, vainly appealed again to government officials.

CUSTER'S LAST STAND In early June 1876 the Sioux and Cheyenne held a sun dance, during which Sitting Bull had a vision of soldiers and some Native Americans falling from their horses. When Colonel Custer and his troops reached the Little Bighorn River, the Native Americans were ready for them.

Led by Crazy Horse, Gall, and Sitting Bull, the warriors—with raised spears and rifles—outflanked and crushed Custer's troops. Within an hour, Custer and all of the men of the Seventh Cavalry were dead. By late 1876, however, the Sioux were beaten. Sitting Bull and a few followers took refuge in Canada, where they remained until 1881. Eventually, to prevent his people's starvation, Sitting Bull was forced to surrender. Later, in 1885 he appeared in William F. "Buffalo Bill" Cody's Wild West Show.

The Government Supports Assimilation

The Native Americans still had supporters in the United States, and debate over the treatment of Native Americans continued. Starting in about 1870, the government began moving toward a new strategy, encouraging Native Americans to abandon their traditional cultures and religions and live like white Americans.

Native American students attend class in an assimilation school.

AMERICANIZATION Many reformers who were sympathetic to the Native Americans' plight supported the government's idea of **assimilation**, a plan under which Native Americans would give up their beliefs and way of life and become part of the white culture. As part of this plan, the government built schools for Native American children, often hundreds of miles away from the students' homes. In these schools, students could only speak English and could not wear their traditional clothing. Every effort was made to discourage students from practicing their own culture so that they might be "Americanized," learning to live like white Americans. The Carlisle Indian Industrial School was a school for assimilation in Pennsylvania. Boys and girls were taught to read, write, and learn industrial and domestic activities of white American culture.

However, not all reformers agreed that the government's policies were helping Native Americans. The well-known writer Helen Hunt Jackson, for

---

Document-Based Investigation Historical Source

Chief Satanta

Known as the Orator of the Plains, Chief Satanta represented the Kiowa people in 1867 negotiations with the U.S. government.

Analyze Historical Sources
What do Chief Satanta's words reveal about the changing frontier?

"*All the land south of the Arkansas belongs to the Kiowas and Comanches, and I don't want to give away any of it. I love the land and the buffalo and will not part with it. I want you to understand well what I say. Write it on paper. Let the Great Father [U.S. president] see it, and let me hear what he has to say. I want you to understand also, that the Kiowas and Comanches don't want to fight, and have not been fighting since we made the treaty. I hear a great deal of good talk from the gentlemen whom the Great Father sends us, but they never do what they say. I don't want any of the medicine lodges [schools and churches] within the country. I want the children raised as I was. When I make peace, it is a long and lasting one—there is no end to it. . . . A long time ago this land belonged to our fathers; but when I go up to the river I see camps of soldiers on its banks. These soldiers cut down my timber; they kill my buffalo; and when I see that, my heart feels like bursting; I feel sorry. I have spoken.*"
—Chief Satanta, from a speech at the Medicine Lodge Creek Council of 1867

example, exposed the government's many broken promises in her 1881 book *A Century of Dishonor*. Jackson was a vocal critic of government officials and their inconsistent policies toward Native Americans. She was a passionate advocate for Native American land rights and legal protection, working in California with groups whose rights were restricted and threatened in the wake of the mining boom. Rather than encouraging Native Americans to change their lifestyle, she focused on increasing public awareness about the problems that Native Americans faced. Her work succeeded in increasing awareness and inspired other advocacy groups to form, but it had little impact on the government's policies or treatment of Native Americans.

THE DESTRUCTION OF THE BUFFALO Perhaps the most significant blow to tribal life on the plains was the destruction of the buffalo. Tourists and fur traders shot buffalo for sport. The transcontinental railroad, which impacted Native American life in many ways, also contributed to the loss of the buffalo. Trains slowed down—and sometimes stopped—to allow railroad passengers to shoot buffalo from the train windows. Large herds were wiped out in this

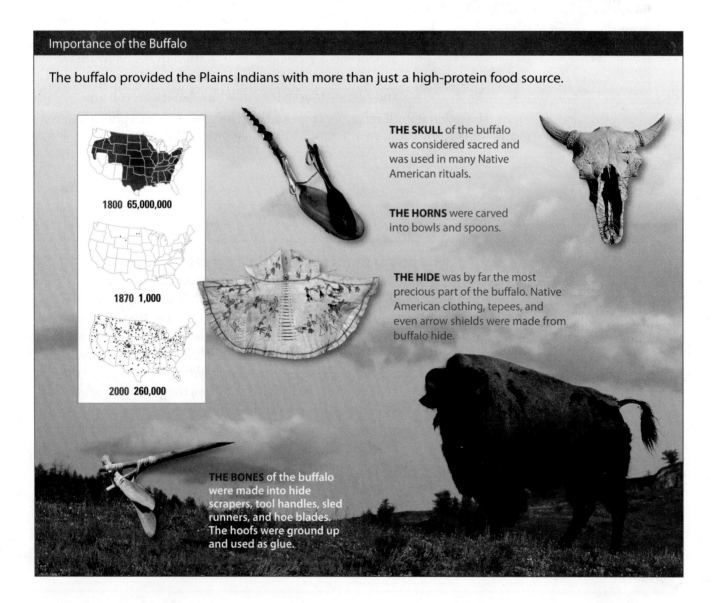

Importance of the Buffalo

The buffalo provided the Plains Indians with more than just a high-protein food source.

1800 65,000,000

1870 1,000

2000 260,000

THE SKULL of the buffalo was considered sacred and was used in many Native American rituals.

THE HORNS were carved into bowls and spoons.

THE HIDE was by far the most precious part of the buffalo. Native American clothing, tepees, and even arrow shields were made from buffalo hide.

THE BONES of the buffalo were made into hide scrapers, tool handles, sled runners, and hoe blades. The hoofs were ground up and used as glue.

way. U.S. general Sheridan noted with approval that buffalo hunters were destroying the Plains Indians' main source of food, clothing, shelter, and fuel. In 1800 approximately 65 million buffalo roamed the plains; by 1890 fewer than 1,000 remained. In 1900 the United States sheltered a single wild herd of buffalo, in Yellowstone National Park.

As the buffalo disappeared from the plains, surviving nomadic Native American groups needed to roam even greater distances to find food. The land set aside for reservations was not adequate to meet the needs of groups who survived by hunting and gathering. The government's solution to this problem was to turn some Native Americans into farmers. Farming required less land than hunting and gathering, and the government hoped that the change in lifestyle would encourage Native Americans to assimilate into white culture.

THE DAWES ACT In 1887 Congress passed the **Dawes Act**, which broke up the reservations and gave some of the reservation land to individual Native Americans to farm—160 acres to each head of household and 80 acres to each unmarried adult. These pieces of land were known as allotments. The government would sell the remainder of the reservations to settlers, and the resulting income would be used by Native Americans to buy farm implements.

Many Native Americans did not understand the terms of the Dawes Act. Their cultures and traditions did not include the concept of private land ownership. Some resisted assimilation, such as Kiowa leader Lone Wolf, who lost his court battle challenging the land allotments. By 1932 whites had taken about two-thirds of the territory that had been set aside for Native Americans. In the end, the Native Americans received no money from the sale of these lands.

Reading Check
Analyze Effects
How did the destruction of the buffalo affect the lifestyle of the Native Americans?

The Battle of Wounded Knee

The Sioux continued to suffer poverty and disease. In desperation, they turned to a Paiute prophet who promised that if the Sioux performed a ritual called the Ghost Dance, Native American lands and way of life would be restored.

The Ghost Dance movement spread rapidly among the 25,000 Sioux on the Dakota reservation. Alarmed military leaders ordered the arrest of Sitting Bull. In December 1890 about 40 Native American police were sent to arrest him. Sitting Bull's friend and bodyguard, Catch-the-Bear, shot one of them. The police then killed Sitting Bull. In the aftermath, Chief Big Foot led the fearful Sioux away.

On December 28, 1890, the Seventh Cavalry—Custer's old regiment—rounded up about 350 starving and freezing Sioux and took them to a camp at Wounded Knee Creek in South Dakota. The next day, the soldiers demanded that the Native Americans give up all their weapons. A shot was fired; from which side, it was not clear. The soldiers opened fire with deadly cannon.

Within minutes, the Seventh Cavalry slaughtered as many as 300 mostly unarmed Native Americans, including several children. The soldiers left the

Nez Perce in Oregon

Forced off their tribal lands in Wallowa County, Oregon, in 1877, the Nez Perce are returning almost 120 years later. Population figures from 1999 put the number of Nez Perce in the Oregon area at around 3,000.

In 1997 Wallowa community leaders obtained a grant to develop the Wallowa Band Nez Perce Trail Interpretive Center—a cultural center that hosts powwows and other activities to draw tourists.

"I never thought I'd see the day," said Earl (Taz) Conner, a direct descendant of Chief Joseph, the best known of the Nez Perce. And, in the words of Soy Redthunder, another tribe member, "[We] look at it as homecoming."

corpses to freeze on the ground. This event, the **Battle of Wounded Knee**, brought the Indian wars—and an entire era—to a bitter end.

> *"I did not know then how much was ended. When I look back . . . I can still see the butchered women and children lying heaped and scattered all along the crooked gulch. . . . And I can see that something else died there in the bloody mud, and was buried in the blizzard. A people's dream died there. It was a beautiful dream."*
>
> —Black Elk, quoted in *Black Elk Speaks*

The events of this period changed the demographic makeup of the American West. Lured by new opportunities and supported by government policies that sought to force Native Americans onto reservations and convince them to abandon their traditional culture, white Americans moved in and settled these lands. The land occupied by Native Americans decreased dramatically.

Reading Check
Analyze Causes
What events led to the Battle of Wounded Knee?

Lesson 1 Assessment

1. **Organize Information** Use a diagram to record supporting details about the culture of the Plains Indians.

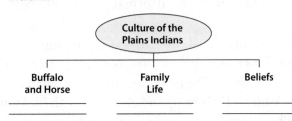

2. **Key Terms and People** For each key term or person in the lesson, write a sentence explaining its significance.

3. **Make Inferences** Why do you think the assimilation policy of the Dawes Act failed? Support your opinion with information from the text and details about how Native Americans reacted.

   Think About:
   - the experience of Native Americans such as Zitkala-Ša
   - the attitudes of many white leaders toward Native Americans
   - the merits of owning property
   - the importance of cultural heritage

4. **Analyze Events** What environmental, cultural, and economic factors influenced Native American reservations in the West?

Mining and Ranching

The Big Idea
Many people sought fortunes during the mining and cattle booms of the American West.

Why It Matters Now
The mining and cattle booms built cities that continue to be important centers of commerce today.

Key Terms and People
Comstock Lode

placer mining

hydraulic mining

hard-rock mining

longhorn

Chisholm Trail

long drive

SS.912.A.1.2; SS.912.A.1.4; SS.912.A.1.7; SS.912.A.3.1; SS.912.G.1.2; SS.912.G.4.2; SS.912.G.4.3; SS.912.H.1.1; LAFS.1112.RH.1.1; LAFS.1112.RH.2.4; LAFS.1112.RH.4.10; LAFS.1112.WHST.3.7

One American's Story

Tappan Adney was one of tens of thousands who struck out for Alaska's Yukon Territory during the Klondike gold rush of the late 1890s. However, unlike most of the adventurers making the journey, Adney wasn't seeking unimaginable riches. He was a journalist for *Harper's Weekly* in search of a compelling story. He published his observations, including this account of the scene at the bay in Skagway, where miners arrived from various West Coast ports.

"I go ashore . . . and such a scene as meets the eye! It is simply bewildering, it is all so strange. There are great crowds of men. . . . Tents there are of every size and kind, and men cooking over large sheet-iron stoves set up outside. Behind these are more tents and men, and piles of merchandise and hay, bacon smoking, men loading bags and bales of hay upon horse and starting off. . . . Everybody is on the move, excepting those just arrived, and each is intent upon his own business. There are said to be twenty-five hundred people along the road between the bay and the summit. . . ."

—Tappan Adney, from *The Klondike Stampede*

Miners bound for the Klondike goldfields climb the Chilkoot Pass in 1898.

The men and women braving the Alaskan wilderness were just some of those headed west in search of a new life, spurred on by the promise of adventure and opportunity.

The Lure of Silver and Gold

The prospect of striking it rich was one powerful attraction of the West. The California gold rush of 1849 had captured the imaginations of many Americans. Between the Civil War and the turn of the century, deposits of the precious yellow metal were discovered in scattered sites from the Black Hills of South Dakota and Cripple Creek, Colorado, to Nome, Alaska. The dream of riches lured hundreds of thousands of prospectors into territories that were previously inhabited only by native peoples. They came from all walks: grizzled veterans from the California gold rush of 1849, youths seeking adventure, middle-class professionals, and even some families.

THE MINING BOOM After the California gold rush, the first promising discovery occurred in 1858 in Colorado. The discovery of gold near Pikes Peak drew tens of thousands of miners to the region. Most left disappointed. In 1859 prospectors found silver in Carson River valley of present-day Nevada. Thousands of miners rushed to this mine, which became known as the **Comstock Lode**. Over the next 20 years, miners took about $500 million from the Comstock Lode.

Almost as soon as gold was discovered somewhere, prospectors would swarm into the region. Most mining camps and tiny frontier towns had filthy, ramshackle living quarters. Rows of tents and shacks with dirt "streets" and wooden sidewalks had replaced unspoiled picturesque landscapes.

Fortune seekers of every description—including Irish, German, Polish, Chinese, and African American—crowded the camps and boomtowns. Most prospectors were men, but a few hardy, business-minded women tried their luck, too, working as laundresses, freight haulers, or miners. Cities such as Virginia City, Nevada, and Helena, Montana, originated as mining camps on Native American land. The commercial lumbering industry also expanded into the West to meet the demands of the mining industries and boomtowns, which also took an ecological toll. Vast forests were cut down, leaving only seas of stumps.

Some of the sprawling mining camps grew into towns. Stores and saloons sprang up, seemingly overnight. As towns developed, more women and children came to join the men. The arrival of families often turned rough-and-tumble towns into prosperous, respectable communities. Townspeople established churches, schools, newspapers, even opera houses. Gold-rush towns could blossom out of the wilderness virtually overnight, but they could also die out just as quickly. Only some were able to survive and develop into full-fledged cities.

DIFFICULT WORK Some surface gold could be extracted by **placer mining**, in which minerals are found in loose sand and gravel. Panning was the simplest form of placer mining. It was a cheap but tedious way for an individual to try to make money. Some miners also tried sluicing—a technique that used a trough to separate gold from gravel.

Most gold was located in veins in underground rock. When the surface deposits of gold ran out, miners needed more sophisticated equipment to

A mother and her son prospecting in Fairbanks, Alaska, in 1898

extract the gold from these veins deep within the earth. Large companies were formed to invest in this expensive equipment. Mining companies used two methods to extract the ore. **Hydraulic mining** used water under high pressure to blast away dirt, exposing the minerals underneath. This method sent sediment into rivers, choking them and causing floods. The other method, **hard-rock mining**, involved digging tunnels along the veins of gold and breaking up tons of ore—hard and dangerous work.

By the 1880s mining was dominated by these big companies, and most miners became employees rather than lone prospectors. For some, it was better than relying on their own luck, but it still carried plenty of risks. Tunnels often collapsed, and miners who weren't killed were trapped in utter darkness for days. Heat was a problem, too. As miners descended into the earth, the temperature inside the mine soared. At a depth of about 2,000 feet, the temperature of the water that invariably flooded the bottom of a mine could be 160°F. Sometimes, the pressure in the underground rock became so intense that it caused deadly explosions. An estimated 7,500 people died while digging for gold and silver during the western gold rushes. That was more than the total number of people who died in the Indian wars.

INJUSTICES OF THE WEST Conditions were also dangerous in the camps, which had no law enforcement. Since miners were competing against each other for gold, the intense rivalry frequently led to violence. Some people formed their own vigilante committees to combat theft and violence, but their methods were often excessively violent. An accused criminal could be hanged after a speedy and unofficial "trial" of sorts. It was a dark period for the many immigrants who were often wrongly blamed for crimes and faced this kind of vigilante justice. It was also a time when the legal rights of Native Americans and Mexican Americans were swept aside as they faced continual loss of lands.

Mexican Americans had lived in the southwest for generations on land that formerly belonged to Mexico. The Treaty of Guadalupe Hidalgo, which ended the Mexican-American War, allowed the United States to pay Mexico a

Reading Check
Form Generalizations
What were the advantages and the disadvantages of the mining boom?

little more than $15 million for the area known as the Mexican Cession. This included California, Nevada, Utah, and parts of Arizona, New Mexico, Colorado, and Wyoming. The treaty had provisions that were intended to protect the legal rights and property rights of the Mexican American landowners, who became full American citizens as part of the treaty. However, white settlers took advantage of many Mexican Americans who did not understand American laws. Many Mexican Americans lost their land because they could not prove ownership or did not understand the American tax system.

American Literature

Literature of the West

The American humorist Samuel Clemens—better known as Mark Twain—was a would-be gold and silver miner who penned tales of frontier life. "The Celebrated Jumping Frog of Calaveras County" is set in a California mining camp. Most of the tale is told by Simon Wheeler, an old-timer given to exaggeration.

The Celebrated Jumping Frog of Calaveras County

"Well, Smiley kep' the beast in a little lattice box, and he used to fetch him downtown sometimes and lay for a bet. One day a feller—a stranger in the camp, he was—come acrost him with his box, and says:

"'What might it be that you've got in the box?'

"And Smiley says, sorter indifferent-like, 'It might be a parrot, or it might be a canary, maybe, but it ain't—it's only just a frog.'

"And the feller took it, and looked at it careful, and turned it round this way and that, and says, 'H'm—so 'tis. Well, what's he good for?'

"'Well,' Smiley says, easy and careless, 'he's good enough for one thing, I should judge—he can outjump any frog in Calaveras County.'

"The feller took the box again, and took another long, particular look, and give it back to Smiley, and says, very deliberate, 'Well,' he says, 'I don't see no p'ints about that frog that's any better'n any other frog.'

"'Maybe you don't,' Smiley says. 'Maybe you understand frogs and maybe you don't understand 'em; maybe you've had experience, and maybe you ain't only a amature, as it were. Anyways, I've got my opinion, and I'll resk forty dollars that he can outjump any frog in Calaveras County".

—from "The Celebrated Jumping Frog of Calaveras County" (1865)

MARK TWAIN

Analyze American Literature
Why do you think Twain deliberately misspells words in the passage above, such as writing "acrost" instead of "across" and "sorter" instead of "sort of"? Use details from the selections to help explain your answer.

Cattle Becomes Big Business

As the great herds of buffalo disappeared, and Native Americans were forced onto smaller and less desirable reservations, horses and cattle flourished on the plains. As cattle ranchers opened up the Great Plains to big business, ranching from Texas to Kansas became a profitable investment.

VAQUEROS AND COWBOYS American settlers had never managed large herds on the open range, and they learned from their Mexican neighbors how to round up, rope, brand, and care for the animals. The animals themselves, the Texas **longhorns**, were sturdy, short-tempered breeds accustomed to the dry grasslands of southern Spain. Unlike other breeds, longhorns were hardy, could travel long distances without much water, and could live on grass alone. They adjusted well to life on the plains. Spanish settlers raised longhorns for food and brought horses to use as work animals and for transportation.

As American as the cowboy seems today, his way of life stemmed directly from that of those first Spanish ranchers in Mexico. The cowboy's clothes, food, and vocabulary were heavily influenced by the Mexican *vaquero,* who was the first to wear spurs, which he attached with straps to his bare feet and used to control his horse. His *chaparreras,* or leather overalls, became known as chaps. He ate *charqui,* or "jerky"—dried strips of meat. The Spanish *bronco caballo,* or "rough horse" that ran wild, became known as a bronco or bronc. The strays, or *mesteños,* were the same mustangs that the American cowboy tamed and prized. The Mexican *rancho* became the American ranch. Finally, the English words *corral* and *rodeo* were borrowed from the Spanish. In his skills, dress, and speech, the Mexican vaquero was the true forerunner of the American "buckaroo," or cowboy.

Despite the plentiful herds of western cattle, cowboys were not in great demand until the railroads reached the Great Plains. Before the Civil War, ranchers for the most part didn't stray far from their homesteads with their cattle. There were, of course, some exceptions. During the California gold rush in 1849, some hardy cattlemen on horseback braved a long trek, or drive, through Apache territory and across the desert to collect $25 to $125 a head for their cattle. In 1854, two ranchers drove their cattle 700 miles to Muncie, Indiana, where they put them on stock cars bound for New York City. When the cattle were unloaded in New York City, the stampede that followed caused a panic on Third Avenue. Parts of the country were not ready for the mass transportation of animals.

GROWING DEMAND FOR BEEF After the Civil War, the demand for beef skyrocketed, partly due to the rapidly growing cities in the East. The Chicago Union Stock Yards opened in 1865, and by spring 1866 the railroads were running regularly from Sedalia, Missouri. From there, Texas ranchers could ship their cattle to Chicago and markets throughout the East. They found, however, that the route to Sedalia presented several obstacles, including thunderstorms and rain-swollen rivers. Also, in 1866 farmers angry about trampled crops blockaded cattle in Baxter Springs, Kansas, preventing them from reaching Sedalia. Some herds then had to be sold at cut-rate prices, and others died of starvation.

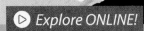

Cattle Trails and the Railroads, 1870s–1890s

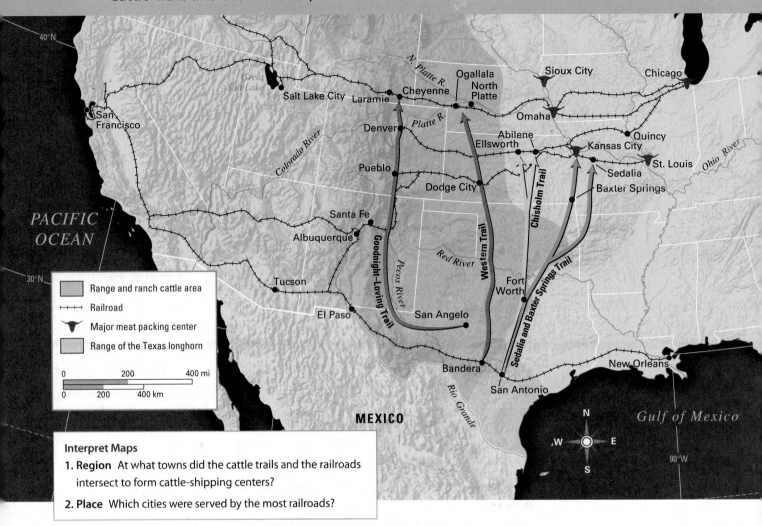

Range and ranch cattle area

Railroad

Major meat packing center

Range of the Texas longhorn

0   200   400 mi

0   200   400 km

Interpret Maps

1. **Region** At what towns did the cattle trails and the railroads intersect to form cattle-shipping centers?

2. **Place** Which cities were served by the most railroads?

THE COW TOWN The next year, cattlemen found a more convenient route. Illinois cattle dealer Joseph McCoy approached several western towns at railheads—places where the trails and rail lines came together—with plans to create shipping yards. The tiny Kansas town of Abilene enthusiastically agreed to the plan. McCoy built cattle pens, a three-story hotel, and helped survey the **Chisholm Trail**—the major cattle route from San Antonio, Texas, through Oklahoma to Kansas. Thirty-five thousand head of cattle were shipped out of the yard in Abilene during its first year in operation. The following year, business more than doubled, to 75,000 head. More and more ranchers began hiring cowboys to drive their herds to these cow towns, where they were shipped to meatpacking centers such as Chicago. Within a few years, the Chisholm Trail had worn wide and deep.

Reading Check
Summarize What developments led to the rapid growth of the cattle industry?

A Day in the Life of a Cowboy

The meeting of the Chisholm Trail and the railroad in Abilene ushered in the heyday of the cowboy. As many as 55,000 worked the plains between 1866 and 1885. Although folklore and postcards depicted the cowboy as Anglo-American, about 25 percent of them were African American, and at least 12 percent were Mexican. The romanticized American cowboy of myth rode the open range, herding cattle and fighting villains. Meanwhile, the real-life cowboy was doing nonstop work.

A DAY'S WORK A cowboy worked 10 to 14 hours a day on a ranch and 14 or more on the trail, always alert for dangers that might harm or upset the herds. Some cowboys were as young as 15; most were broken down by the time they were 40. A cowboy might own his saddle, but his trail horse usually belonged to his boss. He was an expert rider and roper. His gun might be used to protect the herd from wild or diseased animals rather than to fend off outlaws.

ROUNDUP The cowboy's season began with a spring roundup, in which he and other hands from the ranch herded all the longhorns they could find on the open range into a large corral. They kept the herd penned there for several days, until the cattle were so hungry that they preferred grazing to running away. Then the cowboys sorted through the herd, claiming the cattle that were marked with the brand of their ranch and calves that still needed to be branded. After the herd was gathered and branded, the trail boss chose a crew for the long drive.

THE LONG DRIVE This overland transport, or **long drive**, of the animals often lasted about three months. A typical drive included one cowboy for every 250 to 300 head of cattle; a cook who also drove the chuck wagon and set up camp; and a wrangler who cared for the extra horses. A trail boss earned $100 or more a month for supervising the drive and negotiating with settlers and Native Americans.

During the long drive, the cowboy was in the saddle from dawn to dusk. He slept on the ground and bathed in rivers. He risked death and loss every day of the drive, especially at river crossings, where cattle often hesitated and were swept away. Because lightning was a constant danger, cowboys piled

Painter and sculptor Frederic Remington is best known for his romantic and spirited depictions of the western frontier, such as this painting titled *Stampeded by Lightning* (1908). Remington liked to paint in a single dominant color. Native Americans, cowboys at work, and other familiar western scenes were all subjects of Remington's work.

their spurs, buckles, and other metal objects at the edge of their camp to avoid attracting lightning bolts. Thunder, or even a sneeze, could cause a stampede.

LEGENDS OF THE WEST In the 1880s William F. Cody toured the country with a show called Buffalo Bill's Wild West. The show featured trick riding and roping exhibitions. It thrilled audiences with mock battles between cowboys and Native Americans. The touring show featured famous figures of the West—including sharpshooter Annie Oakley and the leader of the Hunkpapa Sioux, Sitting Bull. These touring performances helped make western life a part of American mythology. Some legendary performers like James Butler "Wild Bill" Hickok and Martha Jane Burke (Calamity Jane) actually never dealt with cows. Hickok served as a scout and a spy during the Civil War and, later, as a marshal in Abilene, Kansas. He was a violent man who was shot and killed while holding a pair of aces and a pair of eights in a poker game, a hand still known as the "dead man's hand." Calamity Jane was an expert sharpshooter who dressed as a man. She may have been a scout for Colonel George Custer.

Reading Check
Compare How did the cowboy's life differ from the myth about it?

The End of the Open Range

Almost as quickly as cattle herds multiplied and ranching became big business, the cattle frontier met its end. Ranchers had overstocked the range. As a result, there was a shortage of good grazing land and a surplus of beef, which drove down prices.

Document-Based Investigation Historical Source

Changes on the Range

Teddy Abbott was born in England, but he moved to Nebraska with his family when he was ten years old. Shortly after arriving, his father bought a herd of cattle in Texas and drove the herd to Nebraska, allowing Teddy to join. Even as a young boy, he loved the life of a cowhand and continued to work as a cowboy after his father and brothers became farmers.

"*Most of southeastern Nebraska and the whole state west of Lincoln was open range when we got there in '71, but about 1876 a flock of settlers took the country, and after that there was only a few places where you could hold cattle. Father was lucky. There was a lot of rough country adjoining him that did not get settled until '79 or '80, and he run cattle until then, but afterwards he went to farming like the rest of them. That was how I come to leave home for good when I was eighteen. . . . I stayed with the cattle and went north with them. You see, environment—that's a big word for me but I got onto it—does everything for a boy. I was with cowpunchers from the time I was eleven years old. And then my father expected to make a farmer of me after that! It couldn't be done.*"

—Teddy Abbott, from *We Pointed Them North: Recollections of a Cowpuncher*

Analyze Historical Sources
What does Abbott's recollection tell you about the changing frontier?

The introduction of barbed wire allowed farmers and ranchers to keep cattle from wandering across property lines to damage crops or graze on neighbors' land.

Farmers were glad to see the end of the open range. Cattle herds often trampled farmer's crops. The farmers also feared that free-roaming herds would infect their dairy cows with a disease called "Texas fever." However, traditional fencing materials—stone and wood—were scarce on the plains. After the invention of barbed wire, patented by Illinois farmer Joseph F. Glidden, farmers had a new way to protect their fields and ranchers could enclose their grazing lands.

The enclosure of the open range led to conflicts between landless cattle owners and the ranchers and farmers who enclosed the lands. In the foothills of the Rockies, sheepherders squared off against local cattle ranchers because sheep cropped the grass so close that cattle could no longer graze. Many range wars broke out between cattle ranchers and sheep ranchers for control of the grasslands. Some ranchers were reckless with their enclosures, stringing barbed wire across public lands or other people's property, even blocking public roads. This set off a wave of fence cutting in 1883, which slowed the next year when the Texas legislature made fence cutting a felony.

Between 1883 and 1887 alternating patterns of dry summers and harsh winters wiped out whole herds, bringing staggering losses to the cattle industry. Most ranchers then downsized, raising smaller herds of high-grade stock that would yield more meat per animal. They fed their fenced-in herds hay in the winter. The days of the long cattle drives came to an end. The era of the wide-open West was over.

Reading Check
Analyze Causes
How did geographical factors lead to the end of the cattle boom?

Lesson 2 Assessment

1. **Organize Information** Using an idea web, list the geographical features of the West that contributed to the mining boom and cattle boom in the mid-1800s.

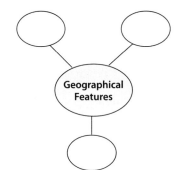

2. **Key Terms and People** For each key term in the lesson, write a sentence explaining its significance.

3. **Draw Conclusions** Analyze the reasons for the rise and the decline of the cattle industry.

   Think About:
   • the growth of urban areas
   • access to natural resources
   • changes in the market and trade
   • the end of the open range

4. **Analyze Causes** What economic opportunities drew large numbers of people to the Great Plains beginning in the mid-1800s?

The Klondike Gold Rush

"Gold! Gold! Gold!" shouted the headline of the *Seattle Post Intelligencer* on July 17, 1897. A huge gold strike had been made along the Klondike River in Canada's remote Yukon Territory near the Alaska border. Soon, gold was discovered on the Alaska side of the border as well. The lure of gold soon inspired thousands of people to rush to the West. Over the next year, about 100,000 Americans stampeded to the Klondike in search of fortune.

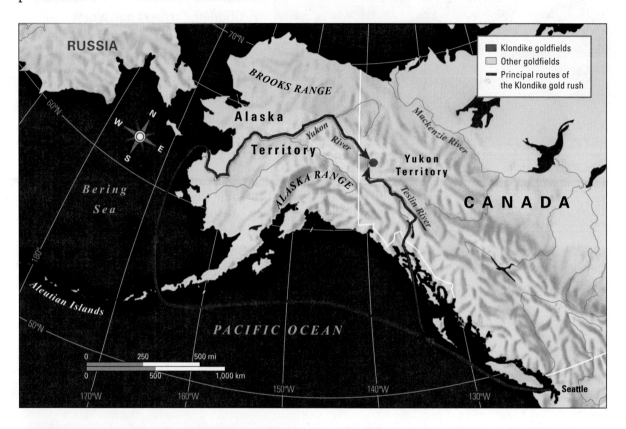

TRANSPORTATION
As word spread, people began to flock to Seattle, hoping to make it north to the goldfields before winter. From Seattle, there were two main routes: one mostly by water, through the Bering Sea to the Yukon River, and one primarily over land, involving a boat to Skagway, Alaska, followed by a trek along the Dyea Trail over Chilkoot Pass or the White Pass Trail over White Pass. Unfortunately, the water route was expensive, so many miners were forced to use the grueling overland routes. Both trails were steep, and the trip was long, cold, and difficult. Conditions were harsh, and starvation, malnutrition, and exposure to cold were serious problems. Many gave up, and several died.

PREPARATION
Miners' efforts to reach the Klondike goldfields were further complicated by the supplies they had to bring with them. Canadian officials required that miners bring enough provisions for a year, or nearly a ton of goods. Prospectors brought groceries, clothing, hardware, tents, packsaddles, stoves, bedding, and sleds. Prospectors made slow progress on their journeys north, having to move a year's worth of supplies over rough terrain. This image shows miners with their supplies preparing to tackle Chilkoot Pass around 1898.

ECONOMIC DEVELOPMENT AND POPULATION SHIFTS

Unfortunately, the odds of striking it rich were not good, as the graphic shows. Most of the prospectors who reached the Klondike came away disappointed. The best gold-bearing creeks had already been claimed, and the reports of "gold for the taking" had been greatly exaggerated. The greatest economic impact was on the towns in the region. For instance, as many as three-fourths of the prospectors passed through Seattle, and the money from the supplies they purchased there boosted the economy considerably. Cities also developed near the goldfields. About 30,000 people settled in Dawson City in the Yukon Territory. The population of Vancouver doubled, and in Edmonton, it tripled.

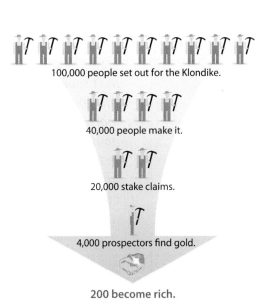

100,000 people set out for the Klondike.

40,000 people make it.

20,000 stake claims.

4,000 prospectors find gold.

200 become rich.

Critical Thinking

1. **Draw Conclusions** What physical and human geographic factors impacted the Klondike gold rush? What effects did these factors have?

2. **Research Mining Towns** Research the history of a mining town that developed due to the Klondike gold rush. Does the town still benefit from its period as a boomtown? Present a short report on how the gold rush influenced the town's development.

Settling on the Great Plains

The Big Idea

Settlers on the Great Plains transformed the land despite great hardships.

Why It Matters Now

The Great Plains region remains the breadbasket of the United States.

Key Terms and People

Homestead Act

exoduster

soddy

Morrill Acts

bonanza farm

One American's Story

When Esther Clark Hill was a girl on the Kansas prairie in the 1800s, her father often left the family to go on hunting or trading expeditions. His trips left Esther's mother, Allena Clark, to take care of the farm.

Esther remembered her mother holding on to the reins of a runaway mule team, "her black hair tumbling out of its pins and over her shoulders, her face set and white, while one small girl clung with chattering teeth to the sides of the rocking wagon." The men in the settlement spoke admiringly about "Leny's nerve," and Esther thought that daily life presented a challenge even greater than driving a runaway team.

"I think, as much courage as it took to hang onto the reins that day, it took more to live twenty-four hours at a time, month in and out, on the lonely and lovely prairie, without giving up to the loneliness."

—Esther Clark Hill, quoted in *Pioneer Women*

Plains settlers, like this woman depicted in Harvey Dunn's painting *Pioneer Woman,* had to be strong and self-reliant.

As the railroads penetrated the frontier and the days of the free-ranging cowboy ended, hundreds of thousands of families migrated west, lured by vast tracts of cheap, fertile land. In their effort to establish a new life, they endured extreme hardships and loneliness.

SS.912.A.1.3; SS.912.A.1.4; SS.912.A.3.1; SS.912.A.3.6; SS.912.G.2.1; SS.912.G.4.2; SS.912.G.4.3

Settlers Move Westward to Farm

Workers on the transcontinental railroad

It took over 250 years—from the first settlement at Jamestown until 1870—to turn 400 million acres of forests and prairies into flourishing farms. Settling the second 400 million acres took only 30 years, from 1870 to 1900. Federal land policy and the completion of transcontinental railroad lines made this rapid settlement possible.

RAILROADS OPEN THE WEST From 1850 to 1871 the federal government made huge land grants to the railroads—170 million acres, worth half a billion dollars—for laying track in the West. In one grant, both the Union Pacific and the Central Pacific received ten square miles of public land for every mile of track laid in a state. This grant also gave the railroads 20 square miles of land for every mile of track laid in a territory.

In the 1860s the two companies began a race to lay track. The Central Pacific moved eastward from Sacramento, and the Union Pacific moved westward from Omaha. The vast majority of railroad workers were Chinese and Irish immigrants. They did most of the grueling labor, along with Civil War veterans, African Americans, and Mexican Americans. In late 1868 workers for the Union Pacific cut their way through the solid rock of the mountains, laying up to eight miles of track a day. Both companies had reached Utah by the spring of 1869. Fifteen years later, the country boasted five transcontinental railroads. The rails to the East and West Coasts were forever linked.

The railroad companies sold some of their land to farmers for two to ten dollars an acre. Some companies successfully sent agents to Europe to recruit buyers. By 1880, approximately 44 percent of the settlers in Nebraska and more than 70 percent of those in Minnesota and Wisconsin were immigrants.

GOVERNMENT SUPPORT FOR SETTLEMENT Another powerful attraction of the West was the land itself. In 1862 Congress passed the **Homestead Act**. This act offered 160 acres of land free to any citizen or intended citizen who was head of the household. Similar laws had been proposed in the past but had been blocked by southern states, who didn't want the western territories to gain political power. However, the Civil War had begun a year earlier, in 1861, and the southern states had seceded. The remaining states were eager to populate the western states and territories.

The government wanted the land to be used, contributing to a nationwide economy. Each homesteader, or settlers on this free land, had to build a home on the land, make improvements, and farm the land for five years before being granted full ownership of the land by the government. The act offered land to farmers regardless of race for as little as $1.25 an acre. From 1862 to 1900 up to 600,000 families took advantage of the government's offer. During this period, many territories gained statehood. These states included Nevada (1864), Nebraska (1867), Colorado (1867), North Dakota and South Dakota (1889), Montana (1889), Washington (1889), Idaho (1890), and Wyoming (1890).

In the late 1870s African Americans began a massive migration West from the post-Reconstruction South. This migration came to be called the "Great Exodus." Those who made the journey were called **exodusters**. Some were inspired by the words of Benjamin "Pap" Singleton, a community builder and former slave. Singleton established settlements in Kansas, which had been admitted to the Union as a state in 1861. He urged African Americans to move to his settlements to build their own communities. The withdrawal of federal troops from the South in 1877 had led to segregation laws and violent attacks from groups such as the Ku Klux Klan. The Homestead Act gave African Americans the chance to own their own land and start new lives in the West, where their freedoms would not be restricted. By 1900 African American farmers owned more than 1 million acres of western land. Often, African American townships developed near these farming communities, providing jobs for black professionals and shopkeepers.

Despite the massive response by homesteaders, private speculators and railroad and state government agents sometimes used the law for their own gain. Cattlemen fenced open lands, while miners and woodcutters claimed national resources. Only about 10 percent of the land was actually settled by the families for whom it was intended. In addition, not all plots of land were of equal value. Although 160 acres could provide a decent living in the fertile soil of Iowa or Minnesota, settlers on drier western land required larger plots to make farming worthwhile.

Eventually, the government strengthened the Homestead Act and passed more legislation for state land grants to encourage settlers. In 1889 a major land giveaway in what is now Oklahoma attracted thousands of people. In less than a day, land-hungry settlers claimed 2 million acres in a massive land rush. Some took possession of the land before the government officially declared it open. Because these settlers claimed land sooner than they were supposed to, Oklahoma came to be known as the Sooner State.

Vocabulary
speculator a person who buys or sells something that involves a risk on the chance of making a profit

Posters like the one shown here drew hundreds of thousands of settlers to the West. Among the settlers were thousands of exodusters—freed slaves who had left the South.

THE CLOSING OF THE FRONTIER These federal policies provided significant economic incentives that changed the country forever as settlers gobbled up western land. The transcontinental railroad made it easier than ever for settlers to reach points further west. The Homestead Act, with its offer of free land, also had a huge impact as nearly 2 million people applied for claims.

In the face of this expansion, General Henry D. Washburn and fellow explorer Nathaniel P. Langford asked Congress to help preserve natural resources and protect the wilderness from settlement. In 1870 Washburn, who was surveying land in northwestern Wyoming, described the area's geysers and bubbling springs as "objects new in experience . . . possessing unlimited grandeur and beauty." Fueled by General Washburn's enthusiasm for the natural wonders near the Yellowstone River, Congress created Yellowstone National Park there in 1872. Seven years later, the Department of the Interior forced railroads to give up their claim to western landholdings that were equal in area to New York, New Jersey, Pennsylvania, Delaware, Maryland, and Virginia combined. Even so, by 1880 individuals had bought more than 19 million acres of government-owned land.

For decades, the U.S. Census Bureau had monitored the extent of American settlement. The frontier, according to the bureau, existed at the point where the population totaled fewer than two people per square mile. In 1890 the Census Bureau declared that the country no longer had a continuous frontier line. The frontier no longer existed. To many, the frontier was what had made America unique. In an 1893 essay entitled "The Significance of the Frontier in American History," historian Frederick Jackson Turner agreed.

> *"American social development has been continually beginning over again on the frontier. This perennial rebirth, this fluidity of American life, this expansion westward with its new opportunities, its continuous touch with the simplicity of primitive society, furnish the forces dominating American character."*
>
> —Frederick Jackson Turner, from "The Significance of the Frontier in American History"

Today, many historians question Turner's view. They think he gave too much importance to the frontier in the nation's development and in shaping a special American character.

Settlers Meet the Challenges of the Plains

The frontier settlers faced extreme hardships. The environment offered one of the biggest challenges. In the winter, blizzards roared out of Canada. In the summer, the thermometer frequently soared above 100 degrees. Tornadoes sometimes swept across the plains. Pests such as large swarms of locusts descended on the land, eating everything in sight. There were also the social problems of living in the West—loneliness, boredom, and isolation—and the

Background
The U.S. Census Bureau is the permanent collector of timely, relevant data about the people and economy of the United States.

Reading Check
Summarize What was Turner's view of the role of the American frontier in 1893?

Vocabulary
locust any of numerous grasshoppers that travel in large swarms, often doing great damage to crops

danger of occasional raids by outlaws and Native Americans. Although many settlers, including the thousands of immigrants who journeyed West, had come in search of a better quality of life, they found that life on the frontier was very difficult. And the work involved in farming the frontier was grueling and dangerous. Yet the number of people living west of the Mississippi River grew from 1 percent of the nation's population in 1850 to almost 30 percent by the turn of the century.

DUGOUTS AND SODDIES Since trees were scarce, most settlers built their homes from the land itself. Many pioneers dug their homes into the sides of ravines or small hills. A stovepipe jutting from the ground was often the only clear sign of such a dugout home.

Those who moved to the broad, flat plains often made freestanding houses by stacking blocks of prairie turf. Like a dugout, a sod home, or **soddy**, was warm in winter and cool in summer. Soddies were small, however, and offered little light or air. They were havens for snakes, insects, and other pests. Although they were fireproof, they leaked continuously when it rained.

WOMEN'S WORK Virtually alone on the flat, endless prairie, homesteaders had to be almost superhumanly self-sufficient. Women often worked beside the men in the fields, plowing the land and planting and harvesting the

Document-Based Investigation Historical Source

Life on the Plains

Most pioneers' first homes were soddies, like the one pictured here, which were built out of bricks of sod—dense prairie grass with the roots and soil attached. This is a photograph of a pioneer family in front of their soddy near Merna, Nebraska, in 1886.

Analyze Historical Sources
What details in the photograph help you understand the challenges this family faced as they attempted to build a life on the plains?

predominant crop, wheat. They sheared the sheep and carded wool to make clothes for their families. They hauled water from wells that they had helped to dig, and made soap and candles from tallow. At harvest time, they canned fruits and vegetables. They were skilled in doctoring—from snakebites to crushed limbs. Women also sponsored schools and churches in an effort to build strong communities.

The women in the West were not only equals in the fields. The frontier states and territories led the rest of the nation in extending to women the right to vote and hold elected office. In 1869 Wyoming granted women full voting rights. This was 50 years before the Nineteenth Amendment would guarantee the right for all women in the United States. Colorado followed in 1893. By 1912 women could vote and hold office in Utah, Idaho, Washington, California, Oregon, Kansas, and Arizona.

TECHNICAL SUPPORT FOR FARMERS Establishing a homestead was challenging. Once accomplished, it was farming the prairie, year in and year out, that became an overwhelming task. In 1837 John Deere had invented a steel plow that could slice through heavy soil. In 1847 Cyrus McCormick began to mass-produce a reaping machine. But a mass market for these devices didn't fully develop until the late 1800s, with the migration of farmers onto the plains.

Other new and improved devices made farm work speedier. These included the spring-tooth harrow to prepare the soil (1869), the grain drill to plant the seed (1841), barbed wire to fence the land (1874), and the corn binder (1878). Then came a reaper that could cut and thresh wheat in one pass. By 1890 there were more than 900 manufacturers of farm equipment. In 1830 producing a bushel of grain took about 183 minutes. By 1900, with the use of these machines, it took only ten minutes. These inventions made more grain available for a wider market.

AGRICULTURAL EDUCATION The federal government supported farmers by financing agricultural education. The **Morrill Acts** of 1862 and 1890 gave federal land to the states to help finance agricultural colleges. Many states sold most of the land and used the proceeds to fund education. The Morrill Act of 1862 was significant because it was the first time the federal government provided assistance for higher education. The 1890 act withheld money from states that did not admit nonwhite students, which encouraged states to found colleges for African Americans and Native Americans. Students of these land grant colleges were given the opportunity to study agriculture and mechanics, learning new skills. Although many brought what they learned back to the farm, these colleges provided the option of learning new trades and professions. Today, land grant colleges such as Michigan State and Texas A&M continue to make higher education widely accessible. In 1887 the Hatch Act provided more funding to the colleges to establish agricultural experiment stations. Researchers at these stations worked to find innovative solutions to the agricultural problems of the plains. They developed new grains that could grow in arid soil and improved irrigation techniques that helped the dry land retain moisture.

One of the biggest problems facing the farmers of western Nebraska, Kansas, and the Dakotas was the lack of annual rainfall. In some years, there was plenty of rain to grow wheat and other grain crops. Often, however, there were dry years and even droughts, when no rain fell. Hardy W. Campbell, a farmer in Dakota Territory, promoted a technique called dry farming, that made it possible to raise certain crops with very little water. Campbell plowed the land deeply and repeatedly. This allowed the rain to be absorbed into the soil, reaching the roots of the plants. Campbell also planted special varieties of wheat that needed less water than other types. By learning and using dry-farming methods, farmers could raise crops in dry years. These innovations enabled the dry eastern plains to flourish and become "the breadbasket of the nation."

FARMERS IN DEBT Elaborate machinery was expensive, and farmers often had to borrow money to buy it. When prices for wheat were higher, farmers could usually repay their loans. When wheat prices fell, however, farmers needed to raise more crops to make ends meet. This situation gave rise to a new type of farming in the late 1870s. Railroad companies and investors created **bonanza farms**, enormous single-crop spreads of 15,000–50,000 acres.

Inventions that Tamed the Prairie

On the Great Plains, treeless expanses, root-filled soil, and unpredictable weather presented challenges to farming.

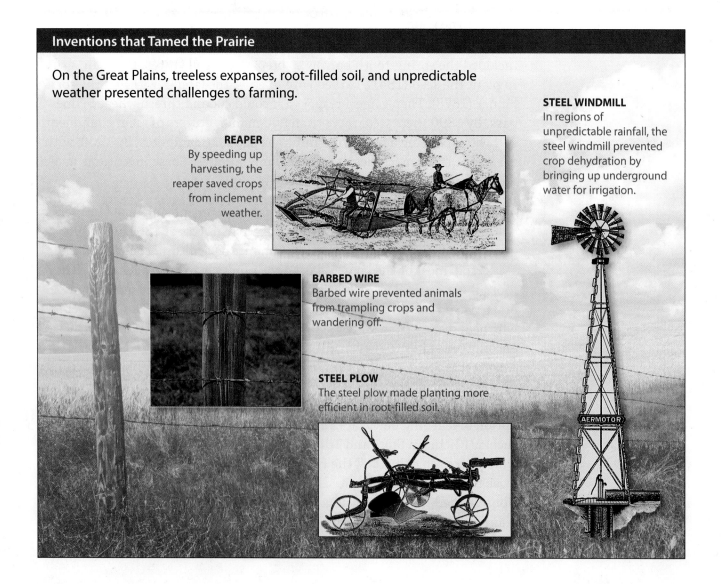

REAPER
By speeding up harvesting, the reaper saved crops from inclement weather.

STEEL WINDMILL
In regions of unpredictable rainfall, the steel windmill prevented crop dehydration by bringing up underground water for irrigation.

BARBED WIRE
Barbed wire prevented animals from trampling crops and wandering off.

STEEL PLOW
The steel plow made planting more efficient in root-filled soil.

Reading Check
Summarize How did new inventions change farming in the West?

The Cass-Cheney-Dalrymple farm near Cassleton, North Dakota, for example, covered 24 square miles. By 1900 the average farmer had nearly 150 acres under cultivation. Some farmers mortgaged their land to buy more property, and as farms grew bigger, so did farmers' debts. Between 1885 and 1890 much of the plains experienced drought. The large single-crop operations couldn't compete with smaller farms, which could be more flexible in the crops they grew. The bonanza farms slowly folded into bankruptcy.

Farmers also felt pressure from the rising cost of shipping grain. Railroads charged western farmers a higher fee than they did farmers in the East. Also, the railroads sometimes charged more for short hauls, for which there was no competing transportation, than for long hauls. The railroads claimed that they were merely doing business, but farmers resented being taken advantage of. "No other system of taxation has borne as heavily on the people as those extortions and inequalities of railroad charges" wrote Henry Demarest Lloyd in an article in the March 1881 edition of *Atlantic Monthly*.

Many farmers found themselves in a cycle of overproduction, growing as much grain as they could grow, on as much land as they could acquire, which resulted in going further into debt. But they were not defeated by these conditions. Instead, these challenging conditions drew farmers together in a common cause.

Lesson 3 Assessment

1. **Organize Information** Create a timeline of four events that shaped the settling of the Great Plains.

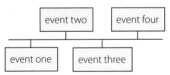

   How might history be different if one of these events hadn't happened?
2. **Key Terms and People** For each key term in the lesson, write a sentence explaining its significance.

3. **Evaluate** How successful were government efforts to promote settlement of the Great Plains? Give examples to support your answer.
   Think About:
   • the growth in population on the Great Plains
   • the role of railroads in the economy
   • the Homestead Act
4. **Draw Conclusions** Review the changes in technology that influenced the life of settlers on the Great Plains in the late 1800s. Explain how you think settlement of the plains would have been different without these inventions.
5. **Identify Problems** What were the social problems faced by the farmers?

Farmers and the Populist Movement

The Big Idea
Farmers united to address their economic problems, giving rise to the Populist movement.

Why It Matters Now
Many of the Populist reform issues, such as income tax and legally protected rights of workers, are now taken for granted.

Key Terms and People
Oliver Hudson Kelley

Grange

Farmers' Alliances

populism

gold standard

bimetallism

William McKinley

William Jennings Bryan

One American's Story

As a young adult in the early 1870s, Mary Elizabeth Clyens left home to teach school on the Kansas plains. After marrying farmer Charles Lease, she joined the growing Farmers' Alliance movement and began speaking on issues of concern to farmers. Lease joked that her tongue was "loose at both ends and hung on a swivel," but her golden voice and deep blue eyes hypnotized her listeners.

"What you farmers need to do is to raise less corn and more Hell! We want the accursed foreclosure system wiped out. . . . We will stand by our homes and stay by our firesides by force if necessary, and we will not pay our debts to the loan-shark companies until the Government pays its debts to us."
—Mary Elizabeth Lease, quoted in "The Populist Uprising"

Mary Elizabeth Lease, the daughter of Irish immigrants, was a leader of the Populist Party.

Farmers had endured great hardships in helping to transform the plains from the "Great American Desert" into the "breadbasket of the nation," yet every year they reaped less and less of the bounty they had sowed with their sweat.

SS.912.A.1.4; SS.912.A.3.1; SS.912.A.3.4; SS.912.A.3.6

Farmers Unite to Address Common Problems

In the late 1800s many farmers were trapped in a vicious economic cycle. Prices for crops were falling. Farmers often mortgaged their farms so that they could buy more land and produce more crops. Good farming land was becoming scarce, though. And banks were foreclosing on the mortgages of increasing numbers of farmers who couldn't make payments on their loans. Moreover, the railroads were taking advantage of farmers by charging excessive prices for shipping and storage.

ECONOMIC DISTRESS The troubles of the farmers were part of a larger economic problem affecting the entire nation. During the Civil War, the United States had issued almost $500 million in paper money, called greenbacks. Greenbacks could not be exchanged for silver or gold money. They were worth less than hard money of the same face value. Hard money included both coins and paper money printed in yellow ink that could be exchanged for gold. After the war, the government began to take the greenbacks out of circulation.

Retiring the greenbacks caused some discontent. It increased the value of the money that stayed in circulation. It meant that farmers who had borrowed money had to pay back their loans in dollars that were worth more than the dollars they had borrowed. At the same time, they were receiving less money for their crops. Between 1867 and 1887, for example, the price of a bushel of wheat fell from $2.00 to 68 cents. In effect, farmers lost money at every turn.

Throughout the 1870s, the farmers and other debtors pushed the government to issue more money into circulation. Those tactics failed—although the Bland-Allison Act of 1878 required the government to buy and coin at least $2 million to $4 million worth of silver each month. It wasn't enough to support the increase in the money supply that the farmers wanted. The Sherman

---

Document-Based Investigation Historical Source

The Plight of the Farmers

Farmers were particularly hard hit in the decades leading to the financial panic of 1893. They regarded big business interests as insurmountable enemies who were bringing them to their knees and leaving them with debts at every turn. This cartoon is a warning of the dangers confronting not only the farmers but the entire nation.

Analyze Historical Sources

1. How does this cartoon depict the plight of the farmers?

2. Who does the cartoonist suggest is responsible for the farmers' plight?

Silver Purchase Act of 1890 tried again to address the farmers' concerns. This act increased the amount of silver the government purchased each month by about 50 percent. To pay for these additional purchases, the U.S. Treasury began to issue special paper notes that could be redeemed for silver or gold.

PROBLEMS WITH THE RAILROADS Meanwhile, farmers paid outrageously high prices to transport grain. Lack of competition among railroads meant that it might cost more to ship grain from the Dakotas to Minneapolis by rail than from Chicago to England by boat. Also, railroads made secret pacts with middlemen, such as grain brokers and merchants. The deals allowed the railroads to control grain storage prices and influence the market price of crops.

Many farmers mortgaged their farms for credit with which to buy seed and supplies. Suppliers charged high rates of interest, sometimes charging more for items bought on credit than they did for cash purchases. Farmers got caught in a cycle of credit that meant longer hours and more debt every year. It was time for reform.

THE FARMERS' ALLIANCES To push effectively for reforms, however, farmers needed to organize. In 1867 **Oliver Hudson Kelley** started the Patrons of Husbandry, an organization for farmers that became popularly known as the **Grange**. Its original purpose was to provide a social outlet and an educational forum for isolated farm families. By the 1870s, however, Grange members spent most of their time and energy fighting the railroads. The Grange's battle plan included teaching its members how to organize, how to set up farmers' cooperatives, and how to sponsor state legislation to regulate railroads.

The Grange gave rise to other organizations, such as **Farmers' Alliances**. These groups included others who sympathized with farmers. Alliances sent lecturers from town to town to educate people about topics such as lower interest rates on loans and government control of railroads and banks. Spellbinding speakers such as Mary Elizabeth Lease helped get the message across.

Membership grew to more than 4 million—mostly in the South and the West. The Southern Alliance, made up of white southern farmers, was the largest. About 250,000 African Americans belonged to the Colored Farmers' National Alliance. This organization was founded in Houston, Texas, in 1886 by R. M. Humphrey, a white Baptist missionary. Like their counterparts in the white alliances, members of the local colored farmers' alliances promoted cooperative buying and selling. Unlike white organizations, however, the black alliances had to work mostly in secret to avoid racially motivated violence at the hands of angry landowners and suppliers. Some alliance members promoted cooperation between black and white alliances. But most members accepted the separation of the organizations.

The Rise and Fall of Populism

Leaders of the alliance movement realized that to make far-reaching changes, they would need to build a base of political power. **Populism**—the movement of the people—was born with the founding of the Populist, or People's, Party, in 1892. On July 2, 1892, a Populist Party convention in Omaha, Nebraska,

A poster depicting the Grange

Vocabulary
regulate to control or direct according to a rule or law

Reading Check
Analyze Causes
What were some of the causes of farmers' economic problems?

demanded reforms to lift the burden of debt from farmers and other workers and to give the people a greater voice in their government.

THE POPULIST PARTY PLATFORM The economic reforms proposed by the Populists included an increase in the money supply. This would produce a rise in prices received for goods and services. The Populists also wanted bank regulation, a graduated income tax, and a federal loan program. They further called for government ownership and regulation of railroad and telegraph companies. The proposed governmental reforms included the election of U.S. senators by popular vote, single terms for the president and the vice-president, and a secret ballot to end voter fraud. Finally, the Populists called for an eight-hour workday and restrictions on immigration.

The proposed changes were so attractive to struggling farmers and desperate laborers that in 1892 the Populist presidential candidate won almost 10 percent of the total vote. In the West, the People's Party elected 5 senators, 3 governors, and about 1,500 state legislators. The Populists' programs eventually became the platform of the Democratic Party. Populists kept alive the concept that the government is responsible for reforming social injustices.

THE PANIC OF 1893 During the 1880s farmers were overextended with debts and loans. Railroad construction had expanded faster than markets. In February 1893 the Philadelphia and Reading Railroad went bankrupt, followed by the Erie, the Northern Pacific, the Union Pacific, and the Santa Fe. The government's gold supply had worn thin, partly due to its obligation to purchase silver under the Sherman Silver Purchase Act. People panicked and traded their paper money for gold. This put a huge strain on the Treasury's gold reserves. The panic also spread to Wall Street, where the prices of stocks fell rapidly. The price of silver then plunged. This caused silver mines to close. To protect the **gold standard**—backing dollars solely with gold—and to restore confidence in the economy, President Cleveland called for Congress to repeal the Sherman Silver Purchase Act. Congress did so, but it was too late. By the end of the year, over 15,000 businesses and 500 banks had collapsed.

Investments declined, and consumer purchases, wages, and prices also fell. Panic deepened into depression as 3 million people lost their jobs. By December 1894 a fifth of the work force was unemployed. Many farm families suffered both hunger and unemployment.

SILVER OR GOLD Populists watched as the two major political parties became deeply divided in a struggle taking place between different regions and economic interests. Business owners and bankers of the industrialized Northeast were Republicans. The farmers and laborers of the agrarian South and West were Democrats.

The central issue of the campaign was which metal would be the basis of the nation's monetary system. On one side were the "silverites," who favored **bimetallism**, a monetary system in which the government would give citizens either gold or silver in exchange for paper currency or checks. On the other side were President Cleveland and the "gold bugs." They favored the gold standard.

The backing of currency was an important campaign issue because people saw paper money as worthless if it could not be turned in for gold or silver.

William Jennings Bryan (1860–1925)

William Jennings Bryan might be considered a patron saint of lost causes. This is largely because he let beliefs, not politics, guide his actions. He resigned his position as secretary of state (1913–1915) under Woodrow Wilson, for example, to protest the president's movement away from neutrality regarding the war in Europe.

Near the end of his life, he went to Tennessee to assist the prosecution in the Scopes "monkey trial," contesting the teaching of evolution in public schools. He is perhaps best characterized by a quote from his own "Cross of Gold" speech: "The humblest citizen in all the land, when clad in the armor of a righteous cause, is stronger than all the hosts of error."

Because silver was more plentiful than gold, backing currency with both metals, as the silverites advocated, would make more currency (with less value per dollar) available. Supporters of bimetallism hoped that this measure would stimulate the stagnant economy. On the other hand, retaining the gold standard would provide a more stable, but expensive, currency.

BRYAN AND THE "CROSS OF GOLD" Stepping into the debate, the Populist Party called for bimetallism and free coinage of silver. Yet their strategy was undecided: should they join forces with sympathetic candidates in the major parties and risk losing their political identity? Or should they nominate their own candidates and risk losing the election?

As the 1896 campaign progressed, the Republican Party stated its firm commitment to the gold standard and nominated Ohioan **William McKinley** for president. After much debate, the Democratic Party came out in favor of a combined gold and silver standard. This included unlimited coinage of silver. At the Democratic convention, former Nebraska congressman **William Jennings Bryan**, editor of the *Omaha World-Herald*, delivered an impassioned address to the assembled delegates. An excerpt of what has become known as the "Cross of Gold" speech follows.

> *"Having behind us the producing masses of this nation and the world, supported by the commercial interests, the laboring interests, and the toilers everywhere, we will answer their demand for a gold standard by saying to them: You shall not press down upon the brow of labor this crown of thorns, you shall not crucify mankind upon a cross of gold."*
> —William Jennings Bryan, from his Democratic convention speech, Chicago, July 8, 1896

Bryan won the Democratic nomination. When the Populist convention met two weeks later, the delegates were both pleased and frustrated. They liked Bryan and the Democratic platform, but they detested the Democratic vice-presidential candidate, Maine banker Arthur Sewall. Nor did they like giving up their identity as a party. They compromised by endorsing Bryan, but nominating their own candidate, Thomas Watson of Georgia, for vice-president. The Populists kept their party organization intact.

Gold Bugs and Silverites

	Gold Bugs	Silverites
Who They Were	bankers and businessmen	farmers and laborers
What They Wanted	gold standard less money in circulation	bimetallism more money in circulation
Why	Loans would be repaid in stable money.	Products would be sold at higher prices.
Effects	DEFLATION • Prices fall. • Value of money increases. • Fewer people have money.	INFLATION • Prices rise. • Value of money decreases. • More people have money.

THE END OF POPULISM Bryan faced a difficult campaign. His free-silver stand had led gold bug Democrats to nominate their own candidate. It also weakened his support in cities, where consumers feared inflation because it would make goods more expensive. In addition, Bryan's meager funds could not match the millions backing McKinley. Bryan tried to make up for lack of funds by campaigning in 27 states. He sometimes made 20 speeches a day. McKinley, on the other hand, campaigned from his front porch. Meanwhile, thousands of well-known people toured the country speaking on his behalf.

McKinley got approximately 7 million votes and Bryan about 6.5 million. As expected, McKinley carried the East. Bryan carried the South and the farm vote of the Middle West. The voters of the industrial Middle West, with their fear of inflation, brought McKinley into office.

With McKinley's election, the Populist Party collapsed, burying the hopes of the farmers. The movement left two powerful legacies, however: a message that the downtrodden could organize and have political impact, and an agenda of reforms, many of which would be enacted in the 20th century.

Reading Check
Summarize
What was the Populist Party platform?

Lesson 4 Assessment

1. **Organize Information** Identify the causes of the rise of the Populist Party and the effects the party had.

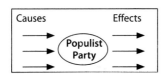

   Which effect has the most impact today? Explain.

2. **Key Terms and People** For each key term or person in the lesson, write a sentence explaining its significance.

3. **Evaluate** What do you think were the most significant factors in bringing an end to the Populist Party? Explain why you think some factors were more important than others.
   Think About:
   • monetary policy
   • third-party status
   • source of popular support
   • popular participation policy

4. **Make Inferences** How did the Grange and the Farmers' Alliances pave the way for the Populist Party?

5. **Analyze Issues** Why did farmers think that an increased money supply would help solve their economic problems?

Module 2 Assessment

Key Terms and People

For each key term or person below, write a sentence explaining its connection to changes on the Great Plains.

1. Homestead Act
2. Sitting Bull
3. assimilation
4. Comstock Lode
5. exoduster
6. George A. Custer
7. William Jennings Bryan
8. William McKinley
9. populism
10. Grange

Main Ideas

Use your notes and the information in the module to answer the following questions.

Cultures Clash on the Prairie

1. Identify three differences between the culture of the Native Americans and the culture of the white settlers on the Great Plains.
2. What effect did the transcontinental railroad have on the culture of Native Americans?
3. How effective was the Dawes Act in promoting the assimilation of Native Americans into white culture?
4. How did the destruction of the buffalo affect the culture and migration patterns of Native Americans?

Mining and Ranching

5. How did mining lead to the establishment of new towns in the West?
6. What difficulties did miners face?
7. Why did the cattle industry become a big business in the late 1800s?

8. How did cowboy culture reflect the ethnic diversity of the United States?
9. How did the invention of barbed wire change the western frontier?

Settling on the Great Plains

10. How did the railroads help open the West?
11. In what ways did government policies encourage settlement of the West?
12. Why did African Americans migrate West from southern states in the late 1870s?
13. Why was the Morrill Act significant?
14. How did settlers overcome the challenges of living on the Great Plains?

Farmers and the Populist Movement

15. What economic problems confronted American farmers in the 1890s?
16. According to farmers and other supporters of free silver, how would bimetallism help the economy?
17. What caused the panic of 1893?
18. Why was the metal that backed paper currency such an important issue in the 1896 presidential campaign?

Critical Thinking

1. **Analyze Causes and Effects** Create a cause/effect diagram identifying the reasons that agricultural output from the Great Plains increased during the late 1800s.

2. **Draw Conclusions** Explain how Native Americans felt about the concept of land ownership. How might that have influenced their patterns of migration and settlement?

3. **Analyze Motives** In 1877 Nez Perce Chief Joseph said, "My people have always been the friends of white men. Why are you in such a hurry?" Why do you think white people hurried to settle the West, with so little regard for Native Americans? How do you think the way in which the white settlers saw the West differed from the way Native Americans viewed the same land? Give evidence from the module to support your position.

4. **Analyze Causes** Explain the ways in which the geography of the West was a factor in its settlement.

5. **Compare** Describe the expanded rights that women and African Americans had in the West as opposed to other parts of the country during this time.

6. **Compare and Contrast** How did farmers and ranchers on the Great Plains compete with each other? Explain what you've learned about competition between farmers and how it was similar to and/or different from competition between ranchers.

7. **Analyze Issues** Explain the causes of economic differences between farmers and industrial capitalists such as railroad owners. What consequences did farmers face because of those differences?

8. **Analyze Issues** Explain how farmers' economic choices were affected by the scarcity of the resources available to them.

9. **Summarize** What was the Grange movement? Explain how it began and how it changed to represent the interests of farmers.

10. **Interpret Tables** Review the table of gold bugs and silverites in Lesson 4. What would be the result of the policies favored by the gold bugs? by the silverites?

Engage with History

Imagine you are a frontier settler. Write a letter to the family members you left behind describing your journey west and how you are living now. Use information from the module to provide some vivid impressions of life on the frontier.

Focus on Writing

Imagine you are a historian studying the development of the American West. Write an essay explaining how Americans settled the West in the late 1800s and the ways in which the region changed as a result. Use specific examples to support your main idea. In your closing, include details about how the events you've discussed continue to be important today.

Collaborative Learning

Working in small groups, use the Internet to find the complete text of William Jennings Bryan's Cross of Gold speech. Take turns reading sections of the speech aloud, listening for the arguments he makes regarding monetary policy and the gold standard. Choose one argument that your group feels is powerful and effective. Write a few sentences to explain what Bryan is expressing—citing the speech—and explain why your group thinks the argument might have helped Bryan win the Democratic nomination.

Module 3
Industrialization

★

Essential Question
Did rapid industrialization benefit economic and social systems in the United States?

About the Photograph: Chinese laborers from the Central Pacific Railroad blast tunnels and construct bridges in a race to lay track through the Sierra Nevada. Blasting tunnels was difficult; sometimes laborers progressed less than a foot a day.

▶ *Explore ONLINE!*

HISTORY

VIDEOS, including...
- Great Minds in Business: Andrew Carnegie
- Oil
- Setting Time Zones
- The Rise of J. P. Morgan
- Traits of a Titan
- Homestead Strike

☑ Document-Based Investigations

☑ Graphic Organizers

☑ Interactive Games

☑ Animation: Early Refrigerated Railroad Cars

☑ Image with Hotspots: Triangle Shirtwaist Fire

In this module you will learn about the industrial revolution of the late 1800s, sometimes referred to as the second industrial revolution, and the impact it had on American businesses and workers.

SS.912.A.1.2 Utilize a variety of primary and secondary sources to identify author, historical significance, audience, and authenticity to understand a historical period. **SS.912.A.1.3** Utilize timelines to identify the time sequence of historical data. **SS.912.A.1.4** Analyze how images, symbols, objects, cartoons, graphs, charts, maps, and artwork may be used to interpret the significance of time periods and events from the past. **SS.912.A.3.1** Analyze the economic challenges to American farmers and farmers' responses to these challenges in the mid to late 1800s. **SS.912.A.3.2** Examine the social, political, and economic causes, course, and consequences of the second Industrial Revolution that began in the late 19th century. **SS.912.A.3.3** Compare the first and second Industrial Revolutions in the United States. **SS.912.A.3.4** Determine how the development of steel, oil, transportation, communication, and business practices affected the United States economy. **SS.912.A.3.5** Identify significant inventors of the Industrial Revolution including African Americans and women. **SS.912.A.3.6** Analyze changes that occurred as the United States shifted from agrarian to an industrial society. **SS.912.A.3.9** Examine causes, course, and consequences of the labor movement in the late 19th and early 20th centuries. **SS.912.A.3.10** Review different economic and philosophic ideologies. **SS.912.A.3.13** Examine key events and peoples in Florida history as they relate to United States history. **SS.912.G.1.2** Use spatial perspective and appropriate geographic terms and tools, including the Six Essential Elements, as organizational schema to describe any given place. **SS.912.G.2.1** Identify the physical characteristics and the human characteristics that define and differentiate regions. **LAFS.1112.RH.1.2** Determine the central ideas or information of a primary or secondary source; provide an accurate summary that makes clear the relationships among the key details and ideas. **LAFS.1112.RH.4.10** By the end of grade 12, read and comprehend history/social studies texts in the grades 11–CCR text complexity band independently and proficiently.

▶ *Explore ONLINE!*

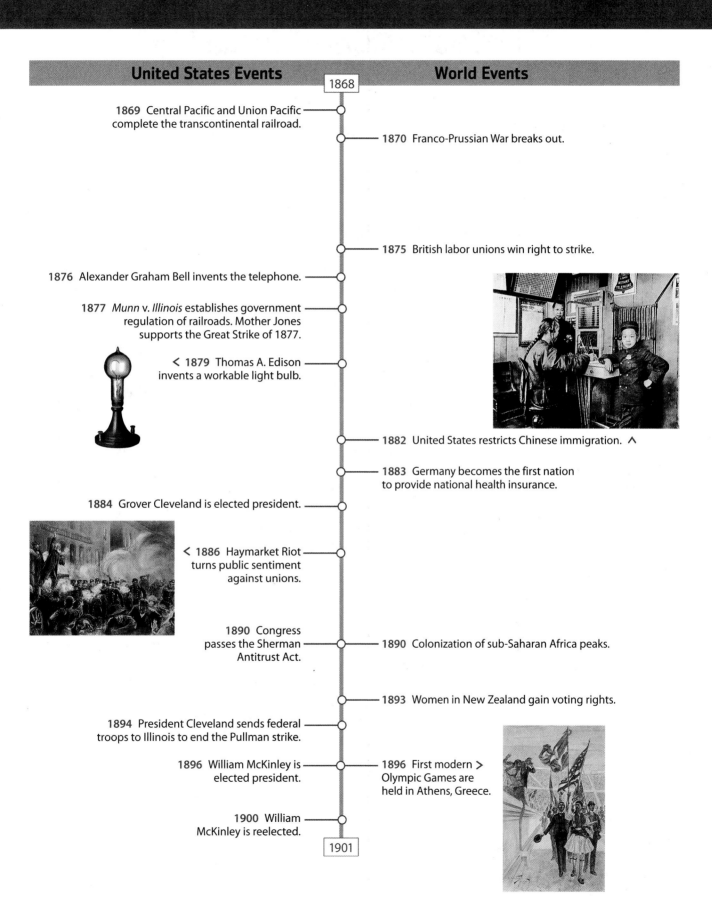

United States Events		World Events

1868

1869 Central Pacific and Union Pacific complete the transcontinental railroad.

1870 Franco-Prussian War breaks out.

1875 British labor unions win right to strike.

1876 Alexander Graham Bell invents the telephone.

1877 *Munn* v. *Illinois* establishes government regulation of railroads. Mother Jones supports the Great Strike of 1877.

< **1879** Thomas A. Edison invents a workable light bulb.

1882 United States restricts Chinese immigration. ∧

1883 Germany becomes the first nation to provide national health insurance.

1884 Grover Cleveland is elected president.

< **1886** Haymarket Riot turns public sentiment against unions.

1890 Congress passes the Sherman Antitrust Act.

1890 Colonization of sub-Saharan Africa peaks.

1893 Women in New Zealand gain voting rights.

1894 President Cleveland sends federal troops to Illinois to end the Pullman strike.

1896 William McKinley is elected president.

1896 First modern > Olympic Games are held in Athens, Greece.

1900 William McKinley is reelected.

1901

The Expansion of Industry

The Big Idea
At the end of the 19th century, natural resources, creative ideas, and growing markets fueled an industrial boom.

Why It Matters Now
Technological developments of the late 19th century paved the way for the continued growth of American industry.

Key Terms and People
Edwin L. Drake

Bessemer process

Thomas Alva Edison

Lewis H. Latimer

Christopher Sholes

Alexander Graham Bell

One American's Story

One day, Pattillo Higgins noticed bubbles in the springs around Spindletop, a hill near Beaumont in southeastern Texas. This and other signs convinced him that oil was underground. If Higgins found oil, it could serve as a fuel source around which a vibrant industrial city would develop.

Higgins, who had been a mechanic and a lumber merchant, couldn't convince geologists or investors that oil was present, but he didn't give up. A magazine ad seeking investors got one response. It was from Captain Anthony F. Lucas, an experienced prospector who also believed that there was oil at Spindletop. When other investors were slow to send money, Higgins kept his faith, not only in Spindletop, but in Lucas.

"Captain Lucas, . . . these experts come and tell you this or that can't happen because it has never happened before. You believe there is oil here, . . . and I think you are right. I know there is oil here in greater quantities than man has ever found before."
—Pattillo Higgins, quoted in *Spindletop*

Pattillo Higgins

In 1900 the two men found investors, and they began to drill that autumn. After months of difficult, frustrating work, on the morning of January 10, 1901, oil gushed from their well. The Texas oil boom had begun.

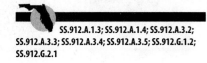

SS.912.A.1.3; SS.912.A.1.4; SS.912.A.3.2; SS.912.A.3.3; SS.912.A.3.4; SS.912.A.3.5; SS.912.G.1.2; SS.912.G.2.1

Natural Resources Fuel Industrialization

During the early 1800s an industrial revolution brought new technology and industries to the United States. Factories and machines began to do much of the work that had previously been done by hand. By the end of the Civil War, however, the nation was still largely agricultural. In the late 1800s another period of industrial growth and technological development occurred in the United States. By the 1920s it had become the leading industrial power in the world. This immense industrial boom is sometimes called the Second Industrial Revolution. It was due to several factors, including new uses of natural resources, government support for business and innovation, and a growing urban population that provided both cheap labor and markets for new products.

BLACK GOLD Though eastern Native American tribes had made fuel and medicine from crude oil long before Europeans arrived on the continent, early American settlers had little use for oil. In the 1840s, Americans began using kerosene to light lamps after the Canadian geologist Abraham Gesner discovered how to distill the fuel from oil or coal.

It wasn't until 1859, however, when **Edwin L. Drake** successfully used a steam engine to drill for oil near Titusville, Pennsylvania, that removing oil from beneath the earth's surface became practical. This breakthrough started an oil boom that spread to Kentucky, Ohio, Illinois, Indiana, and, eventually, Texas. Petroleum refining industries arose in Cleveland and Pittsburgh as entrepreneurs rushed to transform the oil into kerosene. Gasoline, a byproduct of the refining process, originally was thrown away. But after the automobile became popular, gasoline became the most important form of oil.

BESSEMER STEEL PROCESS Oil was not the only natural resource that was plentiful in the United States. There were also abundant deposits of coal and iron. In 1887 prospectors discovered iron ore deposits more than 100 miles long and up to 3 miles wide in the Mesabi Range of Minnesota. At the same time, coal production skyrocketed—from 33 million tons in 1870 to more than 250 million tons in 1900.

Iron is a dense metal, but it is soft and tends to break and rust. It also usually contains other elements, such as carbon. Removing the carbon from iron produces a lighter, more flexible, and rust-resistant metal—steel. The raw materials needed to make steel were readily available. All that was needed was a cheap and efficient manufacturing process. The **Bessemer process** was developed independently by both the British manufacturer Henry Bessemer and American ironmaker William Kelly around 1850. It soon became widely used. This technique involved injecting air into molten iron to remove the carbon and other impurities. By 1880 American manufacturers were using the new method to produce more than 90 percent of the nation's steel. In that age of rapid change and innovation, even the successful Bessemer process was improved by the 1860s. It was eventually replaced by the open-hearth process. This process enabled manufacturers to produce quality steel from scrap metal as well as from raw materials.

Vocabulary
entrepreneur a person who organizes, operates, and assumes the risk for a business venture

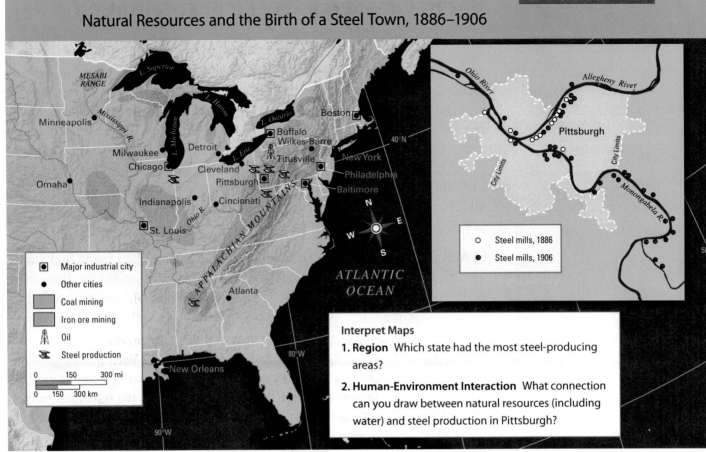

Natural Resources and the Birth of a Steel Town, 1886–1906

Interpret Maps

1. **Region** Which state had the most steel-producing areas?

2. **Human-Environment Interaction** What connection can you draw between natural resources (including water) and steel production in Pittsburgh?

NEW USES FOR STEEL The railroads, with thousands of miles of track, became the biggest customers for steel, but inventors soon found additional uses for it. Cyrus McCormick and John Deere used steel to create mechanical farming equipment such as reapers and plows. This equipment helped transform the plains region into the food producer of the nation. These improvements in technology made farming more efficient, but it also meant that fewer laborers were needed to work the land. As a result, many people had to move from rural areas to cities to find work.

Steel changed the face of the nation as well. It made innovative construction possible. One of the most remarkable structures was the Brooklyn Bridge. Completed in 1883, it spanned 1,595 feet of the East River in New York City. Its steel cables were supported by towers higher than any man-made and weight-bearing structure except the pyramids of Egypt. Like those ancient marvels, the completed bridge was called a wonder of the world.

Around this time, William Le Baron Jenney designed the first skyscraper with a steel frame—the Home Insurance Building in Chicago. This set the stage for a new era of expansion upward as well as outward. Before Jenney had his pioneering idea, the weight of large buildings was supported entirely by their walls or by iron frames, which limited the buildings' height. With a steel frame to support the weight, however, architects could build as high as they wanted. As structures soared into the air, not even the sky seemed to limit what Americans could achieve.

Reading Check
Summarize
What natural resources were most important for industrialization?

Inventions Promote Change

By capitalizing on natural resources, their own ingenuity, and government support for innovation in the form of patents, inventors changed more than the landscape. Their inventions affected the very way people lived and worked.

THE POWER OF ELECTRICITY In 1876 **Thomas Alva Edison** became a pioneer on the new industrial frontier when he established the world's first research laboratory in Menlo Park, New Jersey. There Edison and his associates worked to perfect the incandescent light bulb, applying for a patent for his version of the bulb in 1880. **Lewis H. Latimer**, an African American inventor, played a key role in improving the light bulb when he invented a carbon filament in 1881. This filament lasted longer than filaments made from other materials that had been used in the past. Latimer later went to work for Edison's company. Eventually, Edison and his team improved the light bulb even further by using tungsten filaments, which are still used today.

Thomas Edison also invented an entire system for producing and distributing electrical power. Another inventor, George Westinghouse, along with Edison, added innovations that made electricity safer and less expensive. The harnessing of electricity completely changed the nature of business in America. By 1890 electric power ran numerous machines, from fans to printing presses. This inexpensive, convenient source of energy soon became available in homes and spurred the invention of time-saving appliances. Electric streetcars made urban travel cheap and efficient and also promoted the outward spread of cities.

More important, electricity allowed business owners greater freedom in deciding where to locate their plants. Many factories in the past, including textile mills, were powered by water. That meant they had to be located near rivers or streams. The availability of electric power meant that

Vocabulary
incandescent giving off visible light as a result of being heated

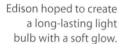

Edison hoped to create a long-lasting light bulb with a soft glow.

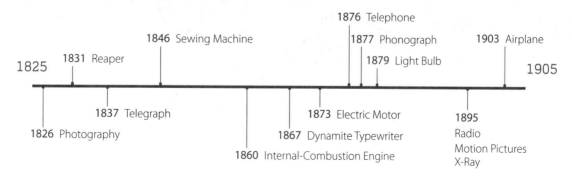

The Technological Explosion, 1825–1905

1825

1826 Photography
1831 Reaper
1837 Telegraph
1846 Sewing Machine
1860 Internal-Combustion Engine
1867 Dynamite Typewriter
1873 Electric Motor
1876 Telephone
1877 Phonograph
1879 Light Bulb
1895 Radio Motion Pictures X-Ray
1903 Airplane

1905

manufacturers could consider other factors such as population and the availability of natural resources when determining where to locate their plants. Many automobile manufacturers, for example, chose to locate their plants in Detroit, Michigan. There rail and water shipping routes were easily accessible and coal and iron mines were nearby. Greater flexibility enabled industries to grow as never before.

INVENTIONS CHANGE LIFESTYLES Edison's light bulb was only one of several revolutionary inventions of the late 1800s. **Christopher Sholes** invented the typewriter in 1867 and changed the world of work. Next to the light bulb, however, perhaps the most dramatic invention was the telephone. **Alexander Graham Bell** and Thomas Watson unveiled this invention in 1876. It allowed people to talk to each other over long distances and opened the way for a worldwide communications network. Companies quickly found the telephone to be an essential business tool.

The typewriter and the telephone particularly affected office work and created new jobs for women. Businesses began to hire women as typists to manage company correspondence. Women made up less than 5 percent of all office workers in 1870. By 1910 they accounted for nearly 40 percent of the clerical work force.

The typewriter shown here dates from around 1890.

New inventions also had a tremendous impact on factory work, as well as on jobs that traditionally had been done at home. For example, women had previously sewn clothing by hand for their families. With industrialization, clothing could be mass-produced in factories. This created a need for garment workers, many of whom were women.

Industrialization freed some factory workers from backbreaking labor and helped make their jobs easier. Shoemaker Jan Ernst Matzeliger designed a machine that could attach the upper part of shoes to the soles, helping to automate the shoe man-ufacturing process. Mar-garet E. Knight invented several machines that made the shoemaking process more efficient. Matzeliger's and Knight's contributions to the footwear industry helped lower the cost of production. Automation made it possible to make larger quantities of shoes in a shorter amount of time.

By 1890 the average workweek in the United States had been reduced by about ten hours. However, many laborers felt that the mechanization of so many tasks reduced human workers' worth. As consumers, though, workers regained some of their lost power in the marketplace.

The inventions and processes of the late 1800s and early 1900s increased the standard of living in the United States and created notable wealth for business owners. The increased living standards attracted new immigrants seeking opportunities for a better life.

The rise of immigration brought a new set of challenges and concerns to the democratic system of the United States. It also brought new workers and potential consumers to the economy. The country's expanding urban population provided a vast potential market for the new inventions and products of the late 19th century.

Reading Check
Analyze Effects How did electricity change American life?

Lesson 1 Assessment

1. **Organize Information** Use a chart to list resources, ideas, and markets that affected the industrial boom of the 19th century. In the second column, note how each item contributed to industrialization.

Resources, Ideas, Markets	Impact

2. **Key Terms and People** For each key term or person in the lesson, write a sentence explaining its significance.

3. **Analyze Effects** Which invention or development described in this lesson had the greatest impact on society? Justify your choice.

   Think About:
   • the applications of inventions
   • the impact of inventions on people's daily lives
   • the effect of inventions on the workplace

4. **Make Inferences** Do you think consumers gained power as industry expanded in the late 19th century? Why or why not?

5. **Hypothesize** If the United States had been poor in natural resources, how would industrialization have been affected?

Industry Changes the Environment

By the mid-1870s, new ideas and technology were well on the way to changing almost every aspect of American life. The development of waterways enabled people and goods to move quickly across the United States, promoting the growth of a nationwide economy. The location of Cleveland, Ohio, on the shores of Lake Erie, gave the city access to raw materials and made it ripe for industrialization. What no one foresaw were the undesirable side effects of rapid development and technological progress.

1 FROM HAYSTACKS TO SMOKESTACKS

In 1874 parts of Cleveland were still rural, with farms like the one pictured dotting the landscape. The smokestacks of the Standard Oil refinery in the distance, however, indicate that industrialization had begun.

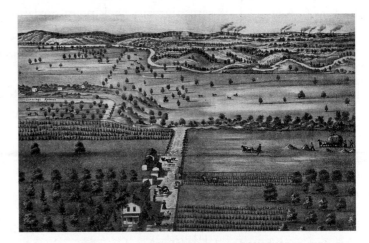

2 REFINING THE LANDSCAPE

Industries like the Standard Oil refinery shown in this 1889 photo soon became a source of prosperity for both Cleveland and the entire country. The pollution they belched into the atmosphere, however, was the beginning of an ongoing problem: how to balance industrial production and environmental concerns.

3 A RIVER OF FIRE

Industrial pollution would affect not only the air but also the water. Refineries and steel mills discharged so much oil into the Cuyahoga River that major fires broke out on the water in 1936, 1952, and 1969. The 1952 blaze (pictured at right) destroyed three tugboats, three buildings, and the ship-repair yards. In the decade following the 1969 fire, changes in the way industrial plants operated, along with the construction of wastewater treatment plants, helped restore the quality of the water.

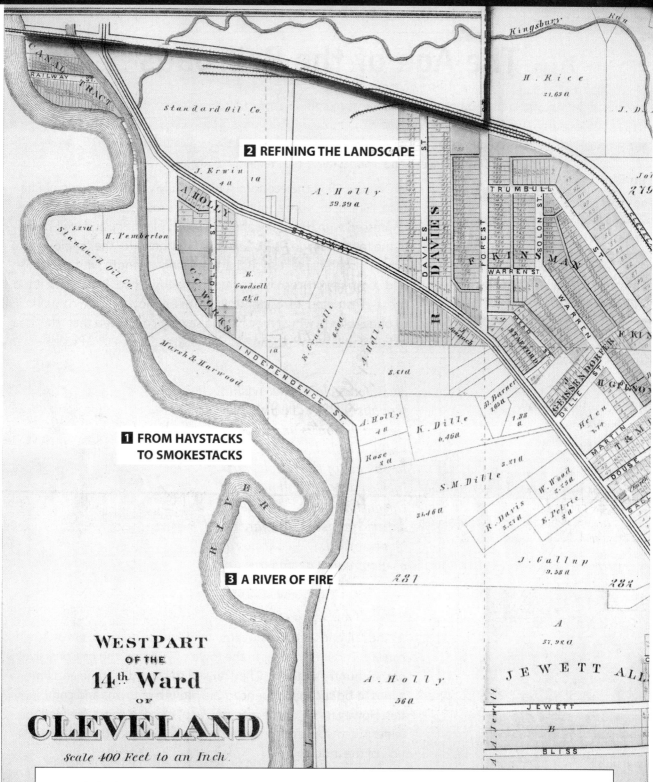

2 REFINING THE LANDSCAPE

1 FROM HAYSTACKS TO SMOKESTACKS

3 A RIVER OF FIRE

WEST PART
OF THE
14th Ward
OF
CLEVELAND

Scale 400 Feet to an Inch.

Critical Thinking

1. Analyze Patterns Locate the Standard Oil Company on the map of Cleveland. What can you conclude about where industry was located as compared with the location of residential neighborhoods?

2. Create a Thematic Map Pose a historical question about the relationship between industry and areas of the Midwest. For example, what types of industry developed near Chicago and why? Then research and create a map that answers your question.

The Age of the Railroads

The Big Idea

The growth and consolidation of railroads benefited the nation but also led to corruption and required government regulation.

Why It Matters Now

Railroads made possible the expansion of industry across the United States.

Key Terms and People

George M. Pullman

transcontinental railroad

Cornelius Vanderbilt

Crédit Mobilier

Munn v. *Illinois*

Interstate Commerce Act

One American's Story

In October 1884 the economist Richard Ely visited the town of Pullman, Illinois, to write about it for *Harper's* magazine. At first Ely was impressed with the atmosphere of order, planning, and well-being in the town **George M. Pullman** had designed for the employees of his railroad-car factory. But after talking at length with a dissatisfied company officer, Ely concluded the town had a fatal flaw: it too greatly restricted its residents. Pullman employees were compelled to obey rules in which they had no say. Ely concluded that "the idea of Pullman is un-American."

The town of Pullman was carefully laid out and strictly controlled.

"It is benevolent, well-wishing feudalism [a medieval social system of nobles and peasants], which desires the happiness of the people, but in such way as shall please the authorities. . . . If free American institutions are to be preserved, we want no race of men reared as underlings."

—Richard Ely, from "Pullman: A Social Study"

As the railroads grew, they came to influence many facets of American life. This included, as in the town of Pullman, the personal lives of the country's citizens. They caused the standard time and time zones to be set and influenced the growth of towns and communities. However, the unchecked power of railroad companies led to widespread abuses that spurred citizens to demand federal regulation of the industry.

SS.912.A.1.2; SS.912.A.1.4; SS.912.A.3.1; SS.912.A.3.2; SS.912.A.3.4; SS.912.A.3.6; SS.912.A.3.13; SS.912.G.1.2

Railroads Span Time and Space

Rails made local transit reliable and westward expansion possible for business as well as for people. Realizing how important railroads were for settling the West and developing the country, the government made huge land grants and loans to the railroad companies.

A NATIONAL NETWORK By 1856 the railroads extended west to the Mississippi River. Three years later, they crossed the Missouri. Just over a decade later, crowds across the United States cheered as the Central Pacific and Union Pacific Railroads met at Promontory, Utah, on May 10, 1869. A golden spike ceremony marked when the first **transcontinental railroad** spanned the nation. Other transcontinental lines followed, and regional lines multiplied as well. At the start of the Civil War, the nation had about 30,000 miles of track. By 1890 that figure was nearly six times greater.

Cornelius Vanderbilt of New York was one of the key figures in the expansion of regional railroads. After the Civil War, Vanderbilt purchased several small railroads in the New York area. Like most regional railroads of the time, each of them was very short, linking only two cities. Vanderbilt, however, chose to link these small railroads into a larger network. Over time, he expanded his network westward from New York into the Midwest, greatly improving interstate travel. Before Vanderbilt's consolidation, a train trip from New York City to Chicago required a passenger to change trains 17 times and took at least 50 hours. On Vanderbilt's new network, the same trip took place on a single train and took less than half the time. By the time he died, Vanderbilt controlled more than 4,500 miles of track and was one of the wealthiest men in the country.

ROMANCE AND REALITY The railroads brought the dreams of available land, adventure, and a fresh start within the grasp of many Americans. This romance was made possible, however, only by the harsh lives of railroad workers.

The Central Pacific Railroad employed thousands of Chinese immigrants. The Union Pacific hired Irish immigrants and desperate, out-of-work Civil War veterans. Although the railroads paid all their employees poorly, Asians usually earned less than whites. The average pay for whites working a ten-hour day was $40 to $60 a month plus free meals. Chinese immigrants hired by the Central Pacific performed similar tasks from dawn to dusk for about $35 a month—and they had to supply their own food.

The working conditions for all immigrants, though, were equally horrendous. Accidents and diseases disabled and killed thousands of men each year. In 1888, when the first railroad statistics were published, the casualties totaled more than 2,000 employees killed and 20,000 injured.

Chinese immigrants and other railroad laborers worked in grueling conditions and all kinds of weather.

RAILROAD TIME In spite of these difficult working conditions, the railroad laborers helped to transform the diverse regions of the country into a united nation. Though linked in space, each community still operated on its own time, with noon when the sun was directly overhead. Noon in Boston, for example, was almost 12 minutes later than noon in New York. Travelers riding from Maine to California might reset their watches 20 times.

In 1869, to remedy this problem, Professor C. F. Dowd proposed that the earth's surface be divided into 24 time zones, one for each hour of the day. Under his plan, the United States would contain four zones: the Eastern, Central, Mountain, and Pacific time zones. The railroad companies endorsed Dowd's plan enthusiastically, and many towns followed suit.

Finally, on November 18, 1883, railroad crews and towns across the country synchronized their watches. In 1884 an international conference set worldwide time zones that incorporated railroad time. The U.S. Congress, however, didn't officially adopt railroad time as the standard for the nation until 1918. As strong a unifying force as the railroads were, however, they also opened the way for abuses that led to social and economic unrest.

Reading Check **Summarize** How did the railroads affect the growth of cities and industires?

Opportunities and Opportunists

The growth of the railroads influenced the industries and businesses in which Americans worked. Iron, coal, steel, lumber, and glass industries grew rapidly as they tried to keep pace with shortages as the railroads' demand for materials and parts increased. The rapid spread of railroad lines also fostered the growth of towns, helped establish new markets, and offered rich opportunities for both visionaries and profiteers.

ANOTHER PERSPECTIVE

On the Wrong Track

While the railroads captured the imagination of most 19th-century Americans, there were those who didn't get on the bandwagon. The writer Herman Melville raged against the smoke-belching iron horse and the waves of change it set in motion as vehemently as his character Captain Ahab raged against the white whale and the sea in *Moby-Dick*. "Hark! here comes that old dragon again—that gigantic gadfly . . . snort! puff! scream! Great improvements of the age," Melville fumed. "Who wants to travel so fast? My grandfather did not, and he was no fool."

SUPPLY AND DEMAND The increased output of iron, coal, and other railway materials was in response to the economic principles of supply and demand. In economics, the term *supply* refers to the amount of a good or service that companies are willing to produce for sale. *Demand* is the amount of that product that consumers are willing or able to purchase. The two concepts are linked. In general, as the demand for a product rises, companies produce more of it, hoping to increase their sales and profits. Miners, smelters, and lumberers were happy to increase their output as railroad construction increased. The increased demand caused their profits to skyrocket.

NEW TOWNS AND MARKETS By linking previously isolated cities, towns, and settlements, the railroads promoted trade and interdependence. As part of a nationwide network of suppliers and markets, individual towns began to specialize in particular products.

Chicago soon became known for its stockyards and Minneapolis for its grain industries. These cities prospered by selling large quantities of their products to the entire country. In Florida railroads helped create a tourism industry. Henry Flagler purchased and built railroad lines to link Florida, including the Florida Keys, to the rest of the country. He hoped to capitalize on the state's warm climate to attract northern visitors.

New towns and communities also grew up along the railroad lines. As a result, parts of the country that had been sparsely populated began to fill with residents. Cities as diverse as Abilene, Kansas; Flagstaff, Arizona; Denver, Colorado; and Seattle, Washington, owed their prosperity, if not their very existence, to the railroads.

Pullman cars brought luxury to the rails, as shown in this advertisement from around 1890.

PULLMAN The railroads helped cities not only grow up but branch out. In 1880, for example, George M. Pullman built a factory for manufacturing sleepers and other railroad cars on the Illinois prairie. His Pullman Palace Car Company was known for creating sleeper cars that made long-distance travel more comfortable.

The nearby town that Pullman built for his employees followed in part the models of earlier industrial experiments in Europe. Whereas New England textile manufacturers had traditionally provided housing for their workers, the town of Pullman provided for almost all of workers' basic needs. Pullman residents lived in clean, well-constructed brick houses and apartment buildings with at least one window in every room—a luxury for city dwellers. In addition, the town offered services and facilities such as doctors' offices, shops, and an athletic field.

As Richard Ely observed, however, the town of Pullman remained firmly under company control. Residents were not allowed to loiter on their front steps or to drink alcohol. Pullman hoped that his tightly controlled environment would ensure a stable work force. However, Pullman's refusal to lower rents after cutting his employees' pay led to a violent strike in 1894.

CRÉDIT MOBILIER Pullman was driven to create his company town by profit motive. This economic principle states that the main goal of a business is to make money. For some other railroad magnates, or powerful and influential industrialists, this profit motive turned into self-serving corruption. In one of the most infamous schemes, stockholders in the Union Pacific Railroad formed, in 1864, a construction company called **Crédit Mobilier** (krĕd'ĭt mō-bēl'yər). The stockholders gave this company a contract to lay track at two to three times the actual cost—and pocketed the profits. They donated shares of stock to about 20 representatives in Congress in 1867.

A congressional investigation of the company, spurred by reports in the *New York Sun,* eventually found that the officers of the Union Pacific had taken up to $23 million in stocks, bonds, and cash. Testimony implicated such well-known and respected federal officials as Vice-President Schuyler Colfax and Congressman James Garfield, who later became president. Although these public figures kept their profits and received little more than a slap on the wrist, the reputation of the Republican Party was tarnished.

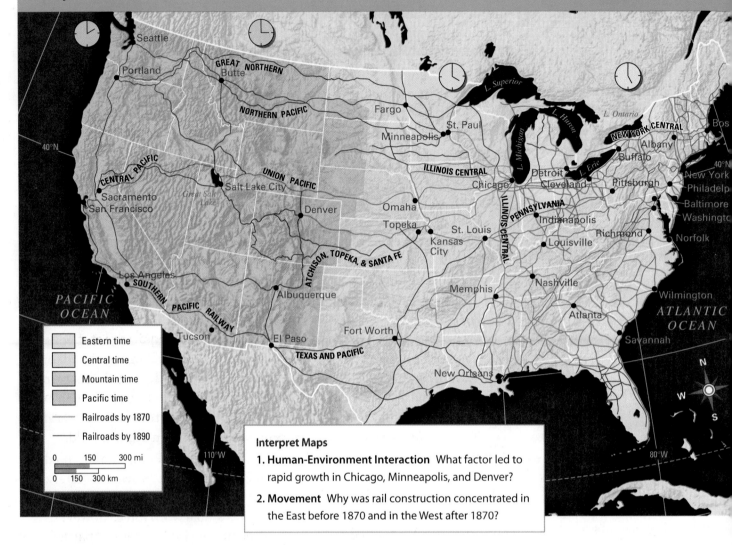

Major Railroad Lines, 1870–1890

Explore ONLINE!

Interpret Maps

1. **Human-Environment Interaction** What factor led to rapid growth in Chicago, Minneapolis, and Denver?

2. **Movement** Why was rail construction concentrated in the East before 1870 and in the West after 1870?

The Grange and the Railroads

Farmers were especially disturbed by what they viewed as railroad corruption. The Grangers were members of the Grange, a farmers' organization founded in 1867. They began demanding governmental control over the railroad industry.

RAILROAD ABUSES Farmers were angry with railroad companies for a host of reasons. They were upset by misuse of government land grants, which the railroads sold to other businesses rather than to settlers, as the government intended. The railroads also entered into formal agreements to fix prices, which helped keep farmers in their debt. In addition, they charged different customers different rates. They often demanded more for short hauls—for which there was no alternative carrier—than they did for long hauls.

GRANGER LAWS In response to these abuses by the railroads, the Grangers took political action. They sponsored state and local political candidates, elected legislators, and successfully pressed for laws to protect their interests. In 1871 Illinois authorized a commission "to establish maximum freight and

Background
Price fixing occurs when companies within an industry all agree to charge the same price for a given service, rather than competing to offer the lowest price.

passenger rates and prohibit discrimination." Grangers throughout the West, Midwest, and Southeast convinced state legislators to pass similar laws, called Granger laws.

The railroads fought back, challenging the constitutionality of the regulatory laws. In 1877, however, in the case of **Munn v. Illinois**, the Supreme Court upheld the Granger laws by a vote of seven to two. The states thus won the right to regulate the railroads for the benefit of farmers and consumers. The Grangers also helped establish an important principle—the federal government's right to regulate private industry to serve the public interest.

INTERSTATE COMMERCE ACT The Grangers' triumph was short-lived, however. In 1886 the Supreme Court ruled, in *Wabash* v. *Illinois*, that a state could not set rates on interstate commerce—railroad traffic that either came from or was going to another state. This overturned their earlier decision in *Munn* v. *Illinois*. In response to public outrage, Congress passed the **Interstate Commerce Act** in 1887. This act reestablished the right of the federal government to supervise railroad activities and set up a five-member Interstate Commerce Commission (ICC). The ICC's objective was to make railroad rates fair for all customers by requiring rates to be "reasonable and just." However, due to poorly defined language in the act and resistance from the railroads, the ICC had difficulty regulating rates. The law had the most success in preventing the railroads from arranging special rates among themselves, which offered consumers some protection.

The final blow to the commission came in 1897. After several court cases challenged the act, the Supreme Court ruled that the ICC could not set maximum railroad rates. Not until 1906, under President Theodore Roosevelt, did the ICC gain the power it needed to be effective. Still, the law was a historic milestone, marking the first time that the federal government had regulated an industry. It served as a model for later attempts.

Document-Based Investigation Historical Source

"The Modern Colossus of (Rail) Roads"

Joseph Keppler drew this cartoon in 1879, featuring the railroad "giants" William Vanderbilt (top), Jay Gould (bottom right), and Cyrus W. Fields (bottom left). The three magnates formed a railroad trust out of their Union Pacific, New York Central, and Lake Shore & Dependence lines. The title of this cartoon is a pun on the Colossus of Rhodes, a statue erected in 282 BC on an island near Greece. According to legend, the 100-foot-tall statue straddled Rhodes's harbor entrance.

Analyze Historical Sources
The reins held by the railroad magnates attach not only to the trains but also to the tracks and the railroad station. What does this convey about the magnates' control of the railroads?

PANIC AND CONSOLIDATION Although the ICC presented few problems for the railroads, corporate abuses, mismanagement, overbuilding, and competition pushed many railroads to the brink of bankruptcy. Their financial problems played a major role in a nationwide economic collapse known as the panic of 1893.

Economic downturns like the one that occurred in 1893 are part of a cycle of growth and contraction that all industrial societies experience. Economists call this pattern the business cycle. After a period of expansion, during which overall industrial production increases and prices rise, a country will experience a crisis. The crisis will often result in widespread bankruptcy and the closing of many businesses, as happened in 1893. By the end of that year, around 600 banks and 15,000 businesses had failed. By 1895, 4 million people had lost their jobs. An economic crisis will generally be followed by a recession, during which time the country's overall productivity drops. Prices fall, and banks raise interest rates, making it more difficult for many people to repay loans.

The panic of 1893 caused the worst recession in American history up to that time, and it was particularly hard on the railroad industry. By the middle of 1894 a quarter of the nation's railroads had been taken over by financial companies. Large investment firms such as J. P. Morgan & Company reorganized the railroads. As the 20th century dawned, seven powerful companies held sway over two-thirds of the nation's railroad tracks.

However, no recession lasts forever. In the business cycle, a recession is followed by a period of recovery as new businesses open, production increases, and consumers begin to spend more money. By 1897 the U.S. economy had begun to recover from the downturn. The next decade would witness a new period of rapid expansion and success.

Reading Check
Analyze Issues How did the Grangers, who were largely poor farmers, do battle with the giant railroad companies?

Lesson 2 Assessment

1. **Organize Information** Create a web diagram and fill in effects of the rapid growth of railroads.

How did the growth of railroads affect people's everyday lives? How did it affect farmers?

2. **Key Terms and People** For each term or person in the lesson, write a sentence explaining its significance.

3. **Make Inferences** Do you think the government and private citizens could have done more to curb the corruption and power of the railroads? Give examples to support your opinion.

   Think About:
   • why the railroads had power
   • the rights of railroad customers and workers
   • the scope of government regulations

4. **Synthesize** The federal government gave land and made loans to the railroad companies. Why was the government so eager to promote the growth of railroads? What effects did this eagerness have on average citizens, such as farmers and workers?

5. **Analyze Motives** Reread "Another Perspective" on railroads. Why do you think that some Americans disliked this new means of transportation?

Big Business

One American's Story

Born in Scotland to penniless parents, **Andrew Carnegie** came to this country in 1848 at age 12. Six years later he was the private secretary to the local superintendent of the Pennsylvania Railroad. One morning, Carnegie single-handedly relayed messages that unsnarled a tangle of freight and passenger trains. His boss, Thomas A. Scott, rewarded Carnegie by giving him a chance to buy stock. Carnegie's mother mortgaged the family home to make the purchase possible. Soon Carnegie received his first dividend.

The Big Idea

The expansion of industry resulted in the growth of big business.

Why It Matters Now

Many of the strategies used today in industry, such as consolidation, have their origins in the late 19th century.

Key Terms and People

Andrew Carnegie

laissez-faire

Social Darwinism

vertical and horizontal integration

J. P. Morgan

John D. Rockefeller

trust

monopoly

Sherman Antitrust Act

"One morning a white envelope was lying upon my desk, addressed in a big John Hancock hand, to 'Andrew Carnegie, Esquire.' . . . All it contained was a check for ten dollars upon the Gold Exchange Bank of New York. I shall remember that check as long as I live. . . . It gave me the first penny of revenue from capital— something that I had not worked for with the sweat of my brow. 'Eureka!' I cried. 'Here's the goose that lays the golden eggs.'"
—Andrew Carnegie, from
Autobiography of Andrew Carnegie

Nineteenth-century industrialist Andrew Carnegie gave money to build public libraries, hoping to help others write their own rags-to-riches stories.

Andrew Carnegie was one of the first industrial moguls to make his own fortune. His rise from rags to riches made him a model of the American success story.

SS.912.A.1.2; SS.912.A.1.4; SS.912.A.3.1; SS.912.A.3.2; SS.912.A.3.3; SS.912.A.3.4; SS.912.A.3.6; SS.912.A.3.10; LAFS.1112.RH.1.2

A Favorable Climate

The economic climate of the United States in the late 1800s was ripe for ambitious individuals like Carnegie to build huge companies and amass great fortunes. Americans of the time believed that a strong work ethic could make someone successful. The business world welcomed new entrepreneurs willing to take risks in search of profits. They were driven by the idea that individuals could better themselves and society through their own efforts.

BELIEF IN FREE MARKETS The positive view of entrepreneurship grew out of the American economic system. The U.S. economy is based on a form of capitalism called free enterprise. As in any capitalist economy, individuals and private businesses run most industries. Companies in some capitalistic countries have to follow strict government policies about pricing and wages. However, those in a free enterprise system are free to set their own. Generally, their decisions are driven by such factors as competition and consumer demand.

By the late 1800s most business leaders believed in **laissez-faire** (lĕs´ā fâr′) capitalism. The term laissez-faire is French for "to let do." Laissez-faire capitalism allows companies to conduct business without intervention by the government. Business leaders believed that government regulation would destroy individual self-reliance, reduce profits, and harm the economy. And by and large, the government maintained a hands-off attitude toward business.

Even though business owners generally wanted the government to stay away, at times they still turned to the government for help. Some railroad builders, for example, accepted grants of land and money from the government. Hoping to eliminate foreign competition, many business leaders also were in favor of protective tariffs that the government placed on imported goods.

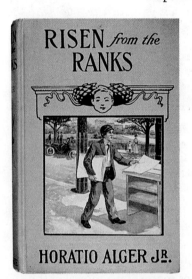

Popular literature promoted the possibility of rags-to-riches success for anyone who was virtuous and hard-working.

SOCIAL DARWINISM Americans understood that there were inequalities in the free enterprise system. Some people became very rich while others remained very poor. But many thinkers believed that inequalities were part of the social order. To explain why some people prospered and others did not, economists, social philosophers, and business leaders embraced the philosophy of **Social Darwinism**. This philosophy adapted the ideas of the British naturalist Charles Darwin and applied them to human society. Darwin had studied plants and animals and concluded that members of a species compete for survival. Those best adapted to their environment thrive and pass their traits to the next generation. Less-suited members gradually die out. Darwin called this process natural selection.

The English philosopher Herbert Spencer used Darwin's biological theories to explain the evolution of human society. Economists found in Social Darwinism a way to justify the doctrine of laissez-faire. Stronger people, businesses, and nations would prosper. Weaker ones would fail. According to Social Darwinists, the market should not be regulated because no one had the right to interfere with this process.

The premise of the survival and success of the most capable naturally made sense to the 4,000 millionaires who had emerged since the Civil War. Because the theory supported the notion of individual responsibility and blame, it also appealed to the Protestant work ethic of many Americans. According to Social Darwinism, riches were a sign of God's favor. Therefore the poor must be lazy or inferior people who deserved their lot in life.

Some people found fault with the attitude of the rich toward the working class. Walter Rauschenbusch, a minister who lived among the poor in New York City, said, "Competitive commerce exalts selfishness to the dignity of a moral principle. It pits men against one another in a gladiatorial game in which there is no mercy and in which ninety percent of the combatants finally strew the arena. . . . If the rich had only what they earned, and the poor had all that they earned, . . . Life would be more sane."

Reading Check
Find Main Ideas
What conditions created a favorable climate for business during the late 1800s?

New Business Strategies

Although some entrepreneurs endorsed the "natural law" in theory, in practice many business owners did everything they could to gain dominance. They tried new ways to maximize profits, get rid of competition, and control production. As they did so, business organizations became more and more complex.

MAXIMIZING PROFITS By 1865 Carnegie was so busy managing the money he had earned in dividends that he happily left his job at the Pennsylvania Railroad. He entered the steel business in 1873 after touring a British steel mill and witnessing the awesome spectacle of the Bessemer process in action. By 1899 the Carnegie Steel Company manufactured more steel than all the factories in Great Britain. Carnegie's success was due in part to management practices that he initiated and that soon became widespread. First, he continually searched for ways to make better products more cheaply. He incorporated new machinery and techniques, such as accounting systems that enabled him to track precise costs. Second, he attracted talented people by offering them stock in the company, and encouraged competition among his assistants.

In addition to improving his own manufacturing operation, Carnegie attempted to control as much of the steel industry as he could. He did this mainly by **vertical integration**. Using this process, he bought out his suppliers—coal fields and iron mines, ore freighters, and railroad lines—in order to control the raw materials and transportation systems. Carnegie also pursued mergers with competing steel producers as a form of **horizontal integration**, a process that joins together companies producing similar products. A merger usually occurred when one corporation bought out the stock of another. Having gained control over his suppliers and having limited his

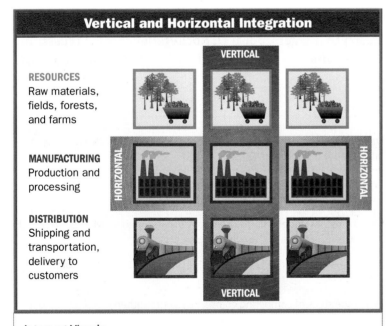

Vertical and Horizontal Integration

VERTICAL

RESOURCES
Raw materials, fields, forests, and farms

MANUFACTURING
Production and processing

DISTRIBUTION
Shipping and transportation, delivery to customers

HORIZONTAL

HORIZONTAL

VERTICAL

Interpret Visuals
How is vertical integration different from horizontal integration? How are they related?

competition, Carnegie controlled almost the entire steel industry. By the time he sold his business in 1901, Carnegie's companies produced, by far, the largest portion of the nation's steel.

Steel was not the only industry to embrace the business practices that made Carnegie so rich. Chicago meatpackers, for example, used vertical integration to drive their own success. In the 1870s Gustavus Swift, owner of the Swift & Company packing plant, tried to convince railroad manufacturers to build refrigerated boxcars that he could use to ship beef over long distances. The manufacturers refused. So Swift decided to build the cars himself, hiring an engineer to design them, a production company to build them, and a rail line to pull them. Before long he was able to ship meat anywhere in the country, changing the meat industry forever and earning himself a vast fortune. One of Swift's major rivals, Philip Danforth Armour of Armour & Company likewise looked for ways to increase his company's profits. He bought a factory near his packing plant and hired scientists to research new uses for the animal byproducts the plant produced. Before long, Armour was selling a wide range of products besides meat, from soap and glue to leather and brushes.

ELIMINATING THE COMPETITION Carnegie made his fortune building a single business. Some tycoons, such as banker **J. P. Morgan**, made theirs by taking over and merging other people's businesses. Morgan created holding companies—corporations that did nothing but buy out the stock of other companies. Morgan used his holding companies to gain control of the railroad, steel, and farm equipment industries. In 1901 he merged the Carnegie Steel Company and other steel companies to form the United States Steel Corporation. It was the world's largest business at the time. Morgan was known for his dedication to efficiency. Although he didn't build his own businesses, many believe that his consolidation methods made some mismanaged and inefficient companies better.

In another approach to mergers, **John D. Rockefeller** formed **trusts**. In a trust, competing companies put control of their businesses under a single

New Business Organizations

corporation	A business owned by investors who buy part of the company through shares of stock. Selling stock was a way for business owners to raise money to invest back into the company.
monopoly	A single seller of a product, good, or service. Without competition, a company that has a monopoly can raise prices higher or reduce the quality of its products lower than it otherwise might.
trust	Competing companies put control of their businesses under a single group of trustees—people who run the separate companies as one corporation. The trust can manage the companies without owning them.
pool	An arrangement whereby companies in the same industry divide up the businesses. Each takes a share of the market and agrees not to compete for a larger share.
holding company	A corporation that does nothing but buy out the stock of competing companies to strengthen their control over the market. Operates in much the same way as trusts.

John D. Rockefeller (1839–1937)

At the height of John Davison Rockefeller's power, an associate noted that he "always sees a little farther than the rest of us —and then he sees around the corner."

Rockefeller's father was a flashy peddler of phony cancer cures with a unique approach to raising children. "I cheat my boys every chance I get. . . . I want to make 'em sharp," he boasted.

It seems that this approach succeeded with the oldest son, John D., who was sharp enough to land a job as an assistant bookkeeper at the age of 16. Rockefeller was very proud of his own son, who succeeded him in the family business. At the end of his life, Rockefeller referred not to his millions, but to John D. Jr. as "my greatest fortune."

group of trustees. The trustees run the separate companies as one large corporation. Rockefeller's company, Standard Oil, began as a refinery. He then acquired companies that supplied his business, buying barrel factories, oil fields, oil-storage facilities, pipelines, and railroad cars. These companies were all placed under the control of a trust agreement. This trust allowed Rockefeller to eventually gain total control of the oil industry in America. In 1870 his company processed about three percent of the country's crude oil. Within a decade, Standard Oil controlled 90 percent of the refining business. Businessmen in other industries followed Rockefeller's example. Trusts were formed in the sugar, cottonseed oil, and lead-mining industries.

Sometimes business owners in the same industry would pool their businesses to eliminate competition. The businesses would then be divided amongst the owners. Each owner would take a share of the market and fix prices, agreeing to not compete with the others in the pool.

FEWER CHOICES Carnegie, Morgan, and Rockefeller had achieved nearly complete **monopolies**, or complete control over an industry's production, wages, and prices. These monopolies meant that consumers had fewer choices in the marketplace. Without competition, a company that had a monopoly could raise prices on its products or lower quality much more freely than it otherwise might. Consumers either have to accept the company's price for its product or choose not to buy it. For example, Rockefeller drove his competitors out of business by selling his oil at a lower price than it cost to produce it. Then, when he controlled the market, he hiked prices far above original levels. The public had to pay the price because they couldn't buy oil from anyone else. Monopolies also meant that workers had fewer choices in the companies they could work for. If a company paid low wages, a worker could not easily find a better paying job.

A MIXED LEGACY Many Americans admired Carnegie, Morgan, Rockefeller, and other "captains of industry." They credited these entrepreneurs with using their business skills to make the American economy more productive and, in turn, stronger. Andrew Carnegie said that he and his fellow tycoons were "the bees that make the most honey, and contribute most to the hive even after they have gorged themselves full."

Carnegie and other wealthy industrialists felt they had a duty to put their fortunes towards the public good. While they generally opposed financial handouts, they supported philanthropy. In the name of Social Darwinism, they built libraries and funded colleges and other institutions. These institutions provided opportunities for the fittest to succeed, regardless of their financial background. Carnegie explained his philosophy in an 1889 article called "The Gospel of Wealth." He wrote, "This, then, is held to be the duty of the man of Wealth . . . to consider all surplus revenues which come to him simply as trust funds . . . to produce the most beneficial result for the community." Carnegie donated about 90 percent of the wealth he accumulated during his lifetime. His fortune still supports the arts and learning today. John D. Rockefeller gave away over $500 million, establishing the Rockefeller Foundation. His foundation provided funds to found the University of Chicago, and created a medical institute that helped find a cure for yellow fever.

Despite these charitable contributions, some Americans came to view industrialists more as robber barons than as revered "captains of industry." They believed that these tycoons were taking advantage of workers and consumers. Critics argued that these tycoons profited unfairly by squeezing out competitors and using other tough tactics. Their huge mansions and luxurious lifestyles seemed like ill-gotten rewards.

Reading Check Summarize What strategies enabled big businesses to eliminate competition?

Government and Business

For a time, the government was content to allow the laissez-faire system to continue unregulated for fear of harming the economy. Industrialization was raising the standard of living, but income inequality was also increasing. Eventually, the government grew uneasy about the power of big corporations and stepped in to regulate some of the business practices of the industrialists.

GOVERNMENT REGULATION The government was concerned that expanding corporations would stifle free competition. In 1890 Congress passed the **Sherman Antitrust Act**, which made it illegal to form a trust that interfered with free trade between states or with other countries. It also prohibited monopolies and other activities that hindered competition.

Prosecuting companies under the Sherman Act was not easy. The act didn't clearly define terms such as trust. Also, if firms such as Standard Oil felt pressure from the government, they simply reorganized into single corporations. The Supreme Court threw out seven of the eight cases the federal government brought against trusts. Eventually, the government stopped trying to enforce the Sherman Act. The consolidation of businesses continued.

The Sherman Act was also unclear about whether it could outlaw monopolies in the *manufacturing* of a good, as well as in the trade of it. The question had to be decided in 1894 by the Supreme Court. In *United States* v. *E. C. Knight Co.*, the court ruled that the government could not enforce the Sherman Act against the manufacturing operations of the E. C. Knight Company, which had control of 98 percent of the sugar refining industry. The decision meant that the Sherman Act could do little to stop most monopolies.

"What a Funny Little Government!"

This 1900 cartoon—captioned "What a funny little government!"—is a commentary on the power of the Standard Oil empire. John D. Rockefeller holds the White House in his hand.

Analyze Historical Sources
What is the cartoonist suggesting by showing the White House in the hands of a tycoon like Rockefeller?

Reading Check
Draw Conclusions
Were the Sherman Antitrust Act and other government actions effective in responding to the challenges associated with rapid industrialization? Explain.

BUSINESS BOOM BYPASSES THE SOUTH Industrial growth concentrated in the North, where natural and urban resources were plentiful. In contrast, the South was still trying to recover from the Civil War. It was hindered by a lack of capital—money for investment. After the war, people were unwilling to invest in risky ventures. Northern businesses already owned 90 percent of the stock in the most profitable southern enterprise—the railroads—thereby keeping the South in a stranglehold. The South remained mostly agricultural, with farmers at the mercy of railroad rates. Entrepreneurs suffered not only from excessive transportation costs, but also from high tariffs on raw materials and imported goods, and from a lack of skilled workers. The post-Reconstruction South seemed to have no way out of economic stagnation. However, growth in forestry and mining, and in the tobacco, furniture, and textile industries, offered hope.

Lesson 3 Assessment

1. **Organize Information** Create a cause and effect chart. For each item in the "Cause" column, list some effects.

Cause	Effects
Laissez-faire capitalism	
Businesses consolidate through mergers	
Big businesses become very powerful	

2. **Key Terms and People** For each key term or person in this lesson, write a sentence explaining its significance.

3. **Evaluate** Do you think that the tycoons of the late 19th century are best described as ruthless robber barons or as effective captains of industry?

   Think About:
   - their management tactics and business strategies
   - their contributions to the economy and society
   - their attitude toward competition

4. **Compare** Compare Andrew Carnegie's business practices to the philosophy of Social Darwinism. Do they support or counter each other? Explain.

5. **Analyze Effects** How did new business structures such as corporations, pools, trusts, and holding companies lead to the growth of an industrialized economy? What was their impact on consumers and workers?

6. **Synthesize** How did economic factors limit industrialization in the South?

The Rise of the Labor Movement

The Big Idea

The expansion of industry prompted laborers to form unions to better their lives.

Why It Matters Now

Many of the strategies used today in the labor movement, such as the strike, have their origins in the late 19th century.

Key Terms and People

Samuel Gompers

collective bargaining

American Federation of Labor (AFL)

Eugene V. Debs

Industrial Workers of the World (IWW)

Mary Harris Jones

One American's Story

The son of Jewish immigrants, **Samuel Gompers** came to the United States with his parents at age 13. He worked as a cigar maker and joined a local union, eventually becoming its president. Gompers would go on to become a key figure in the labor movement, dedicating his life to helping working Americans. He campaigned for basic trade-union rights, such as the right to picket and to organize boycotts and strikes. His efforts on behalf of workers helped organized labor gain national recognition and respect. Samuel Gompers had this to say in response to the question: *What does labor want?*

Labor leader Samuel Gompers worked tirelessly to improve working conditions and wages for American workers.

"We want more school-houses and less jails; more books and less arsenals; more learning and less vice; more constant work and less crime; more leisure and less greed; more justice and less revenge; in fact, more of the opportunities to cultivate our better natures, to make manhood more noble, womanhood more beautiful and childhood more happy and bright. . . . These are the demands made by labor upon modern society and in their consideration is involved the fate of civilization."
—Samuel Gompers, from a speech before the International Labor Congress, 1893

Gompers' ideas were shared by thousands of workers across the country. Soon they would join the rising labor movement to help turn these ideas into reality.

SS.912.A.1.2; SS.912.A.1.3; SS.912.A.1.4; SS.912.A.3.2; SS.912.A.3.3; SS.912.A.3.4; SS.912.A.3.9; SS.912.A.3.10; LAFS.1112.RH.1.2; LAFS.1112.RH.4.10

Labor Unions Emerge

As business leaders merged and consolidated their forces, it seemed necessary for workers to do the same. Although northern wages were generally higher than southern wages, exploitation and unsafe working conditions drew workers together across regions in a nationwide labor movement. Laborers—skilled and unskilled; female and male; black, brown, and white; immigrant and non-immigrant—joined together in unions to try to improve their lot.

This 1917 photograph shows a 14- year-old boy linking bed springs at a factory in Boston, Massachusetts.

LONG HOURS AND DANGER One of the largest employers, the steel mills, often demanded a seven-day workweek. Seamstresses, like factory workers in most industries, worked 12 or more hours a day, six days a week. Employees were not entitled to vacation, sick leave, unemployment compensation, or reimbursement for injuries suffered on the job.

Yet injuries were common. In dirty, poorly ventilated factories, workers had to perform repetitive, mind-dulling tasks, sometimes with dangerous or faulty equipment. In 1882 an average of 675 laborers were killed in work-related accidents each week. In addition, wages were so low that most families could not survive unless everyone held a job. Between 1890 and 1910, for example, the number of women working for wages doubled, from 4 million to more than 8 million. Twenty percent of the boys and ten percent of the girls under age 15 also held full-time jobs. Some were as young as five years old. With little time or energy left for school, child laborers forfeited their futures to help their families make ends meet.

Not surprisingly, jobs for women and children paid the lowest wages. The pay was often as little as 27 cents for a child's 14-hour day. In 1899 women earned an average of $267 a year, nearly half of men's average pay of $498. In contrast, the very next year Andrew Carnegie made $23 million—with no income tax.

Document-Based Investigation Historical Source

Sweatshops

In sweatshops, or workshops in tenements rather than in factories, workers had little choice but to put up with the conditions. Sweatshop employment, which was tedious and required few skills, was often the only avenue open to women and children. Jacob Riis described the conditions faced by "sweaters."

Analyze Historical Sources
According to Jacob Riis, how were working conditions for children in sweatshops?

> "The bulk of the sweater's work is done in the tenements, which the law that regulates factory labor does not reach. . . . In [them] the child works unchallenged from the day he is old enough to pull a thread. There is no such thing as a dinner hour; men and women eat while they work, and the 'day' is lengthened at both ends far into the night."
>
> —Jacob Riis, from *How the Other Half Lives*

EARLY LABOR ORGANIZING Skilled workers had formed small, local unions since the late 1700s. The first large-scale national organization of laborers, the National Labor Union (NLU), was formed in 1866 by ironworker William H. Sylvis. The refusal of some NLU local chapters to admit African Americans led to the creation of the Colored National Labor Union (CNLU). Isaac Meyers, a caulker from Baltimore, led the CNLU. Nevertheless, NLU membership grew to 640,000. In 1868 the NLU persuaded Congress to legalize an eight-hour day for government workers.

NLU organizers concentrated on linking existing local unions. In 1869 Uriah Stephens focused his attention on individual workers and organized the Noble Order of the Knights of Labor. Its motto was "An injury to one is the concern of all." Membership in the Knights of Labor was officially open to all workers, regardless of race, gender, or degree of skill. Like the NLU, the Knights supported an eight-hour workday and advocated "equal pay for equal work" by men and women. They saw strikes, or refusals to work, as a last resort and instead advocated arbitration. At its height in 1886, the Knights of Labor had about 700,000 members. Although the Knights declined after the failure of a series of strikes, other unions continued to organize.

Vocabulary
arbitration a method of settling disputes in which both sides submit their differences to a mutually approved judge

THE POWER OF UNIONS As more and more workers joined, the unions were able to exert increased power on business leaders. Unions concentrated on bread-and-butter issues—higher wages, shorter hours, better working conditions. Many union leaders felt that the best way to obtain these benefits was through **collective bargaining**. In collective bargaining, union officials representing the workers negotiate with management. If negotiation fails, workers may strike or organize a boycott to support union demands.

Some businesses had union contracts that stated that only members of the union could work there. In order to be hired at such a business, which was called a closed shop, workers had to join the union. An open shop could hire anyone. Even the threat of a strike at a closed shop could give a union much more negotiating power with management.

With increased union membership also came increased political power. Each union member was a potential voter. Unions could leverage this fact to influence sympathetic politicians. These politicians would in turn draft and pass laws favorable to labor. In addition, unions could use their influence among members to raise money for and run their own political candidates. Still, divergent ideas among union leadership managed to keep some unions from working together.

Reading Check
Analyze Issues How did industrial working conditions contribute to the growth of the labor movement?

Union Movements Diverge

As labor activism spread, it diversified. Two major types of unions made great gains under forceful leaders.

CRAFT UNIONISM One form of labor organization was craft unionism, which included skilled workers from one or more trades. Samuel Gompers led the Cigar Makers' International Union to join other craft unions in 1886. The **American Federation of Labor (AFL)**, with Gompers as its president, was

able to reach written agreements on wages, hours, and working conditions. Unlike the Knights of Labor, the AFL used strikes as a major tactic. Successful strikes helped the AFL win higher wages and shorter workweeks. Between 1890 and 1915, the average weekly wages in unionized industries rose from $17.50 to $24. The average workweek fell from almost 54.5 hours to just under 49 hours.

INDUSTRIAL UNIONISM Some labor leaders felt that unions should include all laborers—skilled and unskilled—in a specific industry. This concept captured the imagination of **Eugene V. Debs**, who attempted to form such an industrial union—the American Railway Union (ARU). Most of the new union's members were unskilled and semiskilled laborers, but skilled engineers and firemen joined too. Debs believed that the strike was "the weapon of the oppressed." In 1894 the new union won a strike for higher wages. Within two months, its membership climbed to 150,000, dwarfing the 90,000 enrolled in the four skilled railroad brotherhoods. Though the ARU, like the Knights of Labor, never recovered after the failure of a major strike, it added to the momentum of union organizing.

SOCIALISM AND THE IWW In an attempt to solve the problems faced by workers, Eugene Debs and some other labor activists eventually turned to socialism. Socialism is an economic and political system based on government control of business and property and equal distribution of wealth. Socialism carried to its extreme form is communism, as advocated by the German philosopher Karl Marx. Socialism would result in the overthrow of the capitalist system. Most socialists in late-19th-century America drew back from this goal, however, and worked within the labor movement to achieve better conditions for workers. In 1905 a group of radical unionists and socialists in Chicago organized the **Industrial Workers of the World (IWW)**, or the Wobblies. Headed by William "Big Bill" Haywood, the Wobblies included miners, lumberers, and cannery and dock workers. Unlike the ARU, the IWW welcomed African Americans, but membership never topped 100,000. Its only major strike victory occurred in 1912. Yet the Wobblies, like other industrial unions, gave dignity and a sense of solidarity to unskilled workers.

In New York City's Union Square in 1914, IWW members protest violence against striking coal miners in Colorado.

Reading Check
Compare and
Contrast How did
craft unions and
industrial unions
differ?

OTHER LABOR ACTIVISM IN THE WEST In April 1903 about 1,000 Japanese and Mexican immigrant workers organized a successful strike in the sugar-beet fields of Ventura County, California. They formed the Sugar Beet and Farm Laborers' Union of Oxnard. In Wyoming, the State Federation of Labor supported a union of Chinese and Japanese immigrant miners who sought the same wages and treatment as other union miners. These small, independent unions increased both the overall strength of the labor movement and the tension between labor and management.

Strikes Turn Violent

Industry and government responded forcefully to union activity, which they saw as a threat to the entire capitalist system.

THE GREAT STRIKE OF 1877 In July 1877 workers for the Baltimore and Ohio Railroad (B&O) struck to protest their second wage cut in two months. The work stoppage spread to other lines. Most freight and even some passenger traffic, covering over 50,000 miles, was stopped for more than a week. Several state governors asked President Rutherford B. Hayes to intervene, saying that the strikers were impeding interstate commerce. Federal troops ended the strike.

THE HAYMARKET AFFAIR Encouraged by the impact of the 1877 strike, labor leaders continued to press for change. On the evening of May 4, 1886, 3,000 people gathered at Chicago's Haymarket Square to protest police brutality. A striker had been killed and several had been wounded at the McCormick Harvester plant the day before. Rain began to fall at about 10 o'clock, and the crowd was dispersing when police arrived. Then someone tossed a bomb into the police line. Police fired on the workers. Seven police officers and several workers died in the chaos that followed. No one ever learned who threw the bomb, but the three speakers at the demonstration and five other radicals were charged with inciting a riot. All eight were convicted; four were hanged and one committed suicide in prison. The three surviving men were later pardoned by the governor of Illinois. He justified the pardon because he believed that the accused had not received a fair trial. After Haymarket, the public began to turn against the labor movement.

THE HOMESTEAD STRIKE Despite the violence and rising public anger, workers continued to strike. On June 29, 1892, after company president Henry Clay Frick announced his plan to cut wages, workers at the Carnegie Steel Company's Homestead plant in Pennsylvania called a strike. Frick hired armed guards from the Pinkerton Detective Agency to protect the plant so that he could hire scabs, or strikebreakers, to keep it operating. In a pitched battle, at least three detectives and nine workers died. The steelworkers forced out the Pinkertons and kept the plant closed until the Pennsylvania National Guard arrived on July 12. The strike continued until November, but by then the union had lost much of its support and gave in to the company. It would take 45 years for steelworkers to mobilize once again.

THE PULLMAN COMPANY STRIKE Strikes continued in other industries, however. During the panic of 1893 and the economic depression that followed, the Pullman company laid off more than 3,000 of its 5,800 employees. It cut the wages of the rest by 25 to 50 percent, without cutting the cost of its employee housing. After paying their rent, many workers took home less than $6 a week. A strike was called in the spring of 1894, when the Pullman company failed to restore wages or decrease rents. Eugene Debs asked for arbitration, but Pullman refused to negotiate with the strikers. So the ARU began boycotting Pullman trains.

After Pullman hired strikebreakers, the strike turned violent. President Grover Cleveland sent in federal troops. In the bitter aftermath, Debs was jailed. Pullman fired most of the strikers, and the railroads blacklisted many others, so they could never again get railroad jobs.

WOMEN ORGANIZE Although women were barred from many unions, they united behind powerful leaders to demand better working conditions, equal pay for equal work, and an end to child labor. Perhaps the most prominent organizer in the women's labor movement was **Mary Harris Jones**. Jones supported the Great Strike of 1877 and later organized for the United Mine Workers of America (UMW). She endured death threats and jail with the coal miners, who gave her the nickname Mother Jones. In 1903, to expose the cruelties of child labor, she led 80 mill children—many with hideous injuries—on a march to the home of President Theodore Roosevelt. Their crusade influenced the passage of child labor laws.

 — BIOGRAPHY

Eugene V. Debs (1855–1926)

Born in Indiana, Eugene V. Debs left home at the age of 14 to work for the railroads. In 1875 he helped organize a local lodge of the Brotherhood of Locomotive Firemen. After attempts to unite the local railroad brotherhoods failed, Debs organized the American Railway Union.

While in prison following the Pullman strike in 1894, Debs read the works of Karl Marx. He became increasingly disillusioned with capitalism. He became a spokesperson for the Socialist Party of America and was its candidate for president five times. In 1912 he won about 900,000 votes—an amazing 6 percent of the total.

Mother Jones (1830–1930)

Mary Harris "Mother" Jones was a native of Ireland who immigrated to North America as a child. She became involved in the American labor movement after receiving assistance from the Knights of Labor. According to a reporter who followed "the mother of the laboring class" on her children's march in 1903, "She fights their battles with a Mother's Love." Jones continued fighting until her death at age 100.

Jones was definitely not the kind of woman admired by industrialists. "God almighty made women," she declared, "and the Rockefeller gang of thieves made ladies."

The fire department's ladders reached only to the sixth floor, two floors below the burning Triangle Shirtwaist Company.

Other organizers also achieved significant gains for women. In 1909 Pauline Newman, just 16 years old, became the first female organizer of the International Ladies' Garment Workers' Union (ILGWU). A garment worker from the age of eight, Newman also supported the "Uprising of the 20,000." This 1909 seamstresses' strike won labor agreements and improved working conditions for some strikers.

The public could no longer ignore conditions in garment factories after a fire broke out at the Triangle Shirtwaist factory in New York City on March 25, 1911. The fire spread swiftly through the oil-soaked machines and piles of cloth, engulfing the eighth, ninth, and tenth floors. As workers, mostly immigrant women, attempted to flee, they discovered that the company had locked all but one of the exit doors to prevent theft. The unlocked door was blocked by fire. The factory had no sprinkler system, and the single fire escape collapsed almost immediately. In all, 146 women died. Some were found huddled with their faces raised to a small window. Public outrage flared after a jury acquitted the factory owners of manslaughter. In response, the state of New York set up a task force to study factory working conditions.

During the Paterson Silk Strike of 1913, women actually gained a place among male union leadership. Encouraged by the IWW, local leaders, such as Italian immigrant Carrie Golzio and Jewish immigrant Hannah Silverman, held "women only" meetings for female weavers. The silk workers were demanding a halt to the new four-loom system, which required a worker to run four room-sized looms, instead of two. For nearly five months, striking

The Growth of Union Membership, 1878–1904

Members in Thousands

- Total Nationwide Union Membership
- American Federation of Labor
- Knights of Labor
- American Railway Union

Haymarket Riot

Wabash Railroad Strike

Pullman Strike

Interpret Graphs

1. Which union's membership increased in 1889–1890?

2. What effect(s) did the Haymarket Riot have on union membership?

workers shut down all 300 silk mills and dye houses in Paterson, New Jersey, the center of the American silk industry. Even though the strike was ultimately a failure, the strikers did manage to put aside their differences in gender, ethnicity, and skill level to unite for a common cause.

MANAGEMENT AND GOVERNMENT PRESSURE UNIONS The more powerful the unions became, the more employers came to fear them. Management refused to recognize unions as representatives of the workers. Many employers forbade union meetings and fired union members. They also forced new employees to sign "yellow-dog contracts," swearing that they would not join a union.

Business leaders, mainly in the South, also took advantage of state laws that allowed them to hire prison laborers at much lower wages than free laborers. In Tennessee, this led to the Coal Creek Saga. When mine owners at Coal Creek replaced free workers with prisoners, armed miners, over the course of a year, repeatedly attacked the company's buildings, freeing hundreds of convicts. Although the uprising was ultimately put down in 1892, and many of the armed miners arrested, the events did fuel public outrage. By 1896 Tennessee ended its practice of allowing businesses to hire prison laborers.

Finally, industrial leaders, with the help of the courts, turned the Sherman Antitrust Act against labor. All a company had to do was say that a strike, picket line, or boycott would hurt interstate trade, and the state or federal government would issue an injunction against the labor action. Legal limitations made it more and more difficult for unions to be effective. Despite these pressures, workers—especially those in skilled jobs—continued to view unions as a powerful tool. By 1904 the AFL had about 1,700,000 members in its affiliated unions. By the eve of World War I, AFL membership would climb to over 2 million.

Reading Check
Summarize What factors made the Triangle Shirtwaist fire so lethal?

Lesson 4 Assessment

1. **Organize Information** Make a timeline of the notable achievements and setbacks of the labor movement between 1876 and 1913.

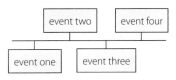

In what ways did strikes threaten industry?

2. **Key Terms and People** For each term or person in the lesson, write a sentence explaining its significance.

3. **Evaluate** What influence do you think unions and labor leaders had in improving working conditions and wages for American workers?

   Think About:
   • their tactics and strategies
   • their organizational abilities
   • their influence on public opinion

4. **Make Inferences** How might things have turned out differently if Eugene Debs had succeeded in pushing for arbitration before the Pullman Strike?

5. **Hypothesize** If the government had supported unions instead of management in the late 19th century, how might the lives of workers have been different?

Module 3 Assessment

Key Terms and People

For each term or person below, write a sentence explaining its connection to the industrialization of the late 19th century.

1. Thomas Alva Edison
2. Alexander Graham Bell
3. George M. Pullman
4. transcontinental railroad
5. Interstate Commerce Act
6. Andrew Carnegie
7. Sherman Antitrust Act
8. Samuel Gompers
9. American Federation of Labor (AFL)
10. Mary Harris Jones

Main Ideas

Use your notes and the information in the module to answer the following questions.

The Expansion of Industry

1. How did the growth of the steel industry influence the development of other industries?
2. What effects did the introduction of mechanical farming equipment have on some rural areas?
3. In what ways did the invention of the telephone impact the United States?
4. How did inventions and developments in the late 19th century change the way people worked?

The Age of the Railroads

5. What impact did Cornelius Vanderbilt have on transportation networks in the United States?
6. What affect did the principles of supply and demand have on businesses and industries during this time period?
7. How did railroad owners use Crédit Mobilier to make huge, undeserved profits?
8. Why did people, particularly farmers, demand regulation of the railroads in the late 19th century?

9. Why were attempts at railroad regulation often unsuccessful?

Big Business

10. How did American economic principles and the ideas of Social Darwinists encourage the growth of big business?
11. Why did business leaders oppose government regulation?
12. Why were business leaders such as John D. Rockefeller called robber barons?
13. Why did the South industrialize more slowly than the North did?

The Rise of the Labor Movement

14. Why did workers form unions in the late 19th century?
15. What factors limited the success of unions?
16. What were the results of the Homestead Strike for steelworkers?
17. How was the Paterson Silk Strike different from other labor strikes?

Critical Thinking

1. **Categorize** In a chart, list what you see as the overall costs and benefits of industrialization.

Industrialization	
Costs	Benefits

2. **Develop Historical Perspective** In 1902 George Baehr, head of the Philadelphia and Reading Railway Company, said, "The rights and interests of the labor man will be protected and cared for not by the labor agitators but by the Christian men to whom God in his infinite wisdom has given the control of the property interests of the country." What bias does this statement reveal? How does Baehr's view reflect Social Darwinism?

3. **Identify Problems** Consider the problems that late-19th-century workers faced and the problems that workers face today. How important do you think unions are for present-day workers? Support your answer.

4. **Compare** In 1903, Mother Jones led a march of 80 children to expose the cruelties of child labor. In 1911, 146 women died in the Triangle Shirtwaist factory fire. How did the government respond to each of these events?

5. **Evaluate** Think about all of the tactics used by unions. Which tactics do you think were the most successful?

6. **Synthesize** How did the growth of capitalism and industrialization affect American democracy in the late 1800s? Consider such factors as the debate over government involvement in the economy, the role of labor unions in politics, and the increase in immigration in your answer.

Engage with History

Imagine that you are a journalist during the industrial age. Write a newspaper editorial about the Great Strike of 1877, supporting the position of either the railroad owners or the striking workers. Be sure to discuss the effects of railroad expansion and business consolidation on society and the economy and how they support your point of view.

Focus on Writing

Imagine you are a union leader in a factory. If your demands for better working conditions are not met, all of the employees will stop work and go on strike. Write a persuasive letter in which you urge your employer to adopt specific reforms to improve working conditions.

Multimedia Activity

In a small group read and discuss the "One American's Story" at the beginning of Lesson 1. Consider the following question: What qualities did Pattillo Higgins have that made him successful? Then make a poster describing Pattillo Higgins's personal qualities and how they helped him to achieve his dream. What present-day figures share Higgins's traits? Add images of these people, with captions, to the poster and display it in your classroom.

Module 4
Immigration and Urbanization

★

Essential Question
Did the benefits of immigrating to the United States at the turn of the century outweigh the challenges?

About the Photograph: This photo shows the intersection of Orchard and Hester Streets on New York City's Lower East Side, a center of Jewish immigrant life in 1905.

In this module you will explore the immigrant experience. You will also learn about the rapid growth of cities, advances in technology, and the rise of mass culture.

▶ Explore ONLINE!

HISTORY

VIDEOS, including...
- Arrival at Ellis Island
- Angel Island: Ellis Island of the West
- Italians in America: Old World, New Land
- Irish in America
- Jacob Riis
- Captured Light
- Roller Coasters

☑ Document-Based Investigations

☑ Graphic Organizers

☑ Interactive Games

☑ Carousel: Immigrant Workers

☑ Image with Hotspots: Skyscrapers

SS.912.A.1.2 Utilize a variety of primary and secondary sources to identify author, historical significance, audience, and authenticity to understand a historical period. **SS.912.A.1.4** Analyze how images, symbols, objects, cartoons, graphs, charts, maps, and artwork may be used to interpret the significance of time periods and events from the past. **SS.912.A.1.7** Describe various sociocultural aspects of American life including arts, artifacts, literature, education, and publications. **SS.912.A.3.1** Analyze the economic challenges to American farmers and farmers' responses to these challenges in the mid to late 1800s. **SS.912.A.3.5** Identify significant inventors of the Industrial Revolution including African Americans and women. **SS.912.A.3.6** Analyze changes that occurred as the United States shifted from agrarian to an industrial society. **SS.912.A.3.7** Compare the experience of European immigrants in the east to that of Asian immigrants in the west. **SS.912.A.3.8** Examine the importance of social change and reform in the late 19th and early 20th centuries. **SS.912.A.3.11** Analyze the impact of political machines in United States cities in the late 19th and early 20th centuries. **SS.912.G.1.2** Use spatial perspective and appropriate geographic terms and tools, including the Six Essential Elements, as organizational schema to describe any given place. **SS.912.G.4.2** Use geographic terms and tools to analyze the push/pull factors contributing to human migration within and among places. **SS.912.G.4.3** Use geographic terms and tools to analyze the effects of migration both on the place of origin and destination, including border areas. **SS.912.H.1.1** Relate works in the arts of varying styles and genre according to the periods in which they were created. **SS.912.H.1.5** Examine artistic response to social issues and new ideas in various cultures. **HE.912.C.2.4** Evaluate how public health policies and government regulations can influence health promotion and disease prevention. **LAFS.1112.RH.1.1** Cite specific textual evidence to support analysis of primary and secondary sources, connecting insights gained from specific details to an understanding of the text as a whole. **LAFS.1112.RH.2.6** Evaluate authors' differing points of view on the same historical event or issue by assessing the authors' claims, reasoning, and evidence.

Timeline of Events 1876–1917

▶ *Explore ONLINE!*

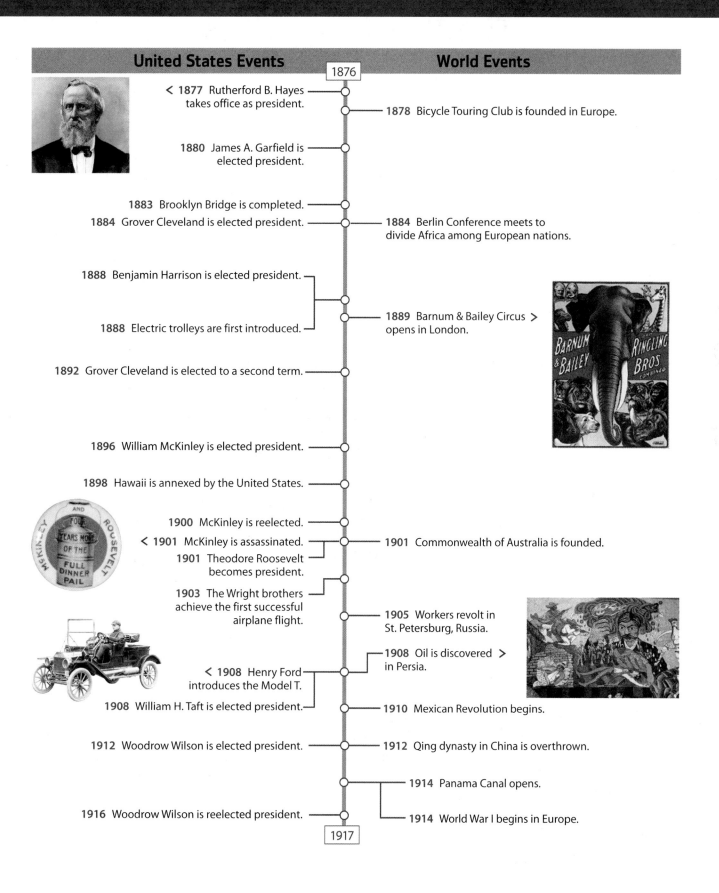

United States Events	1876	World Events

< **1877** Rutherford B. Hayes takes office as president.

1878 Bicycle Touring Club is founded in Europe.

1880 James A. Garfield is elected president.

1883 Brooklyn Bridge is completed.

1884 Grover Cleveland is elected president.

1884 Berlin Conference meets to divide Africa among European nations.

1888 Benjamin Harrison is elected president.

1889 Barnum & Bailey Circus > opens in London.

1888 Electric trolleys are first introduced.

1892 Grover Cleveland is elected to a second term.

1896 William McKinley is elected president.

1898 Hawaii is annexed by the United States.

1900 McKinley is reelected.

< **1901** McKinley is assassinated.

1901 Commonwealth of Australia is founded.

1901 Theodore Roosevelt becomes president.

1903 The Wright brothers achieve the first successful airplane flight.

1905 Workers revolt in St. Petersburg, Russia.

1908 Oil is discovered > in Persia.

< **1908** Henry Ford introduces the Model T.

1908 William H. Taft is elected president.

1910 Mexican Revolution begins.

1912 Woodrow Wilson is elected president.

1912 Qing dynasty in China is overthrown.

1914 Panama Canal opens.

1916 Woodrow Wilson is reelected president.

1914 World War I begins in Europe.

1917

The New Immigrants

The Big Idea

Immigration from Europe, Asia, the Caribbean, and Mexico reached a new high in the late 19th and early 20th centuries.

Why It Matters Now

This wave of immigration helped make the United States the diverse society it is today.

Key Terms and People

Ellis Island

Angel Island

melting pot

nativism

Chinese Exclusion Act

Gentlemen's Agreement

One American's Story

In 1871, 14-year-old Fong See came from China to "Gold Mountain"—the United States. Fong See stayed, worked at menial jobs, and saved enough money to buy a business. Despite widespread restrictions against the Chinese, he became a very successful importer and was able to sponsor many other Chinese who wanted to enter the United States. Fong See had achieved the American Dream. However, as his great-granddaughter Lisa See recalls, he was not satisfied.

"He had been trying to achieve success ever since he had first set foot on the Gold Mountain. His dream was very 'American.' He wanted to make money, have influence, be respected, have a wife and children who loved him. In 1919 when he traveled to China, he could look at his life and say he had achieved his dream. But once in China, he suddenly saw his life in a different context. In America, was he really rich? Could he live where he wanted? . . . Did Americans care what he thought? . . . The answers played in his head—no, no, no."
—Lisa See, from *On Gold Mountain*

Despite Fong See's success, he could not, upon his death in 1957, be buried next to his Caucasian wife because California cemeteries were still segregated.

SS.912.A.1.2; SS.912.A.1.4; SS.912.A.3.7; SS.912.G.4.2; SS.912.G.4.3; LAFS.1112.RH.1.1; LAFS.1112.RH.1.2; LAFS.1112.RH.2.6; LAFS.1112.RH.4.10; MAFS.K12.MP.1.1; MAFS.K12.MP.5.1

Through the "Golden Door"

Millions of immigrants, like Fong See, entered the United States in the late 19th and early 20th centuries. They were drawn by pull factors, such as the promise of a better life. Others wanted to escape push factors, such as famine, land shortages, or religious or political persecution. Still others, known as "birds of passage," intended to immigrate temporarily. They wanted to earn money and then return to their homelands.

EUROPEANS Between 1870 and 1920, approximately 20 million Europeans arrived in the United States. Before 1890 most immigrants came from countries in western and northern Europe. Beginning in the 1890s, however, increasing numbers came from southern and eastern Europe. In 1907 alone, about a million people arrived from Italy, Austria-Hungary, and Russia.

Why did so many leave their homelands? Many of these new immigrants left to escape religious persecution. Whole villages of Jews were driven out of Russia by pogroms. These were organized attacks often encouraged by local authorities. Other Europeans left because of rising population. Between 1800 and 1900, the population in Europe doubled to nearly 400 million, resulting in a scarcity of land for farming. Farmers competed with laborers for too few industrial jobs. In the United States, jobs were supposedly plentiful. In addition, a spirit of reform and revolt had spread across Europe in the 19th century. Influenced by political movements at home, many young European men and women sought independent lives in America.

Background
From 1815 to 1848, a wave of revolutions shook Europe. Most were sparked by a desire for constitutional governments. In 1830, for example, the Polish people rose up against their Russian rulers.

American Literature

A Poem for Liberty

In 1883 poet Emma Lazarus was asked to write a poem that would be auctioned to raise funds to build a pedestal for the Statue of Liberty. Lazarus was a descendant of Jewish immigrants. She wanted her poem to reflect the hopes, dreams, and fears of immigrants and the promise of a better life offered by the American Dream. The sonnet she wrote, called "The New Colossus," summed up this feeling in these now-famous lines.

The New Colossus

"Keep ancient lands, your storied pomp!" cries she
With silent lips. "Give me your tired, your poor,
Your huddled masses yearning to breathe free, The
wretched refuse of your teeming shore. Send these,
the homeless, tempest-tost to me, I lift my lamp
beside the golden door!"

—Emma Lazarus, from "The New Colossus"

Analyze American Literature
What do you think Emma Lazarus is saying about the United States, as compared to other countries at the time?

CHINESE AND JAPANESE While waves of Europeans arrived on the shores of the East Coast, Chinese immigrants came to the West Coast in smaller numbers. Between 1851 and 1883, about 300,000 Chinese arrived. Many came to seek their fortunes after the discovery of gold in 1848 started the California gold rush. Chinese immigrants helped build the nation's railroads, including the first transcontinental line. When the railroads were completed, they turned to farming, mining, and domestic service. Some, like Fong See, started businesses. However, Chinese immigration was sharply limited by an act of Congress in 1882.

The United States annexed Hawaii in 1898. This resulted in increased Japanese immigration to the West Coast. Immigration continued to increase as word of comparatively high American wages spread. The wave peaked in 1907, when 30,000 left Japan for the United States. By 1920 more than 200,000 Japanese lived on the West Coast.

THE WEST INDIES AND MEXICO Between 1880 and 1920, about 260,000 immigrants arrived in the eastern and southeastern United States from the West Indies. They came from Jamaica, Cuba, Puerto Rico, and other islands. Many West Indians left their homelands because jobs were scarce. The industrial boom in the United States seemed to promise work for everyone.

U.S. Immigration Patterns, as of 1900

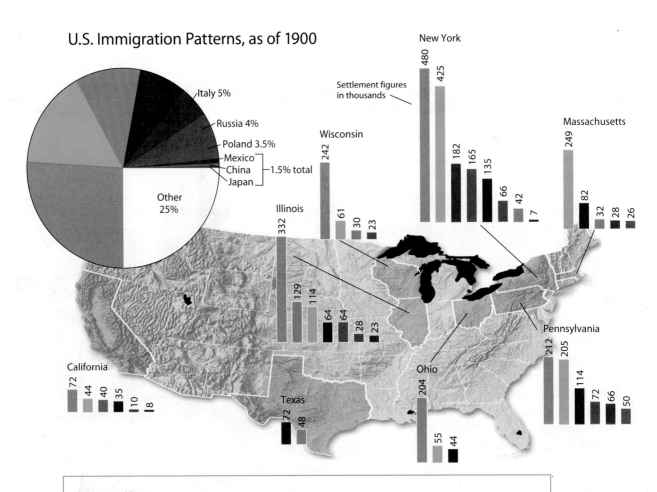

Interpret Maps

1. **Movement** Where did the greatest number of Italian immigrants settle?

2. **Movement** From which country did the smallest percentage of immigrants come?

Reading Check
Analyze Causes
What reasons did
people from other
parts of the world
have for immigrating
to the United States?

Mexicans, too, immigrated to the United States to find work and to flee political turmoil. The 1902 National Reclamation Act encouraged the irrigation of arid land and created new farmland in western states. This drew Mexican farm workers northward. After 1910 political and social upheavals in Mexico prompted even more immigration. About 700,000 people—7 percent of the population of Mexico at the time—came to the United States over the next 20 years.

A Difficult Journey

By the 1870s almost all immigrants traveled by steamship. The trip across the Atlantic Ocean from Europe took approximately one week. The Pacific crossing from Asia took nearly three weeks. Many immigrants traveled in steerage, the cheapest accommodations in a ship's cargo holds. Immigrants were crowded together in the gloom. They were rarely allowed on deck, so they could not exercise or catch a breath of fresh air. They often had to sleep in bunks infested with lice and share toilets with many other passengers. Under these conditions, disease spread quickly. Some immigrants died before they reached their destination. For those who survived, the first glimpse of America could be breathtaking.

ELLIS ISLAND After initial moments of excitement, the immigrants faced the anxiety of not knowing whether they would be admitted to the United States. They had to pass inspection at immigration stations, such as the one at Castle Garden in New York City. That station was later moved to **Ellis Island** in New York Harbor. From 1892 to 1924, Ellis Island was the chief immigration station in the United States. An estimated 17 million immigrants passed through its noisy, crowded facilities.

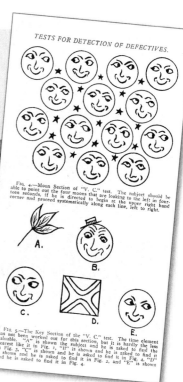

Many immigrants, like these arriving at Ellis Island, were subjected to tests such as the one shown here. To prove their mental competence, they had to identify the four faces looking left in 14 seconds. Can you do it?

Immigration

Immigrants faced difficult and sometimes dangerous conditions just to make it to Ellis Island or Angel Island. However, there still was no guarantee that they would be admitted into the United States.

"America! . . . We were so near it seemed too much to believe. Everyone stood silent—like in prayer. . . . Then we were entering the harbor. The land came so near we could almost reach out and touch it. . . . Everyone was holding their breath. Me too. . . . Some boats had bands playing on their decks and all of them were tooting their horns to us and leaving white trails in the water behind them."

—Rosa Cavalleri, quoted in *Rosa: The Life of an Italian Immigrant*

"When I saw Ellis Island, it's a great big place, . . . We all had to gather your bags, and the place was crowded with people and talking, and crying, . . . And we passed through some of the halls there, big open spaces there, and there was bars, and there was people behind these bars, and they were talking different languages, and I was scared to death. I thought I was in jail."

—Mary Mullins Gordon, from Ellis Island Oral History Project

Analyze Historical Sources
How was the experience of arriving in the United States different for Rosa Cavalleri and Mary Mullins Gordon?

Vocabulary
tuberculosis a bacterial infection, characterized by fever and coughing, that spreads easily

felony any one of the most serious crimes under the law, including murder, rape, and burglary

About 20 percent of the immigrants at Ellis Island were held for a day or more before being inspected. However, only about 2 percent of those were denied entry. The processing of immigrants on Ellis Island was an ordeal that might take five hours or more. First, they had to pass a physical examination by a doctor. Anyone with a serious health problem or a contagious disease, such as tuberculosis, was promptly sent home. Those who passed the medical exam then reported to a government inspector. The inspector checked documents and questioned immigrants. He had to determine whether they met the legal requirements for entering the United States. The requirements included proving they had never been convicted of a felony, demonstrating that they were able to work, and showing that they had some money (at least $25 after 1909).

Women traveling alone had to remain on the island until a male relative came for them. If they had no male relative in the country, they would often be deported, or sent back to their home country. Under an 1891 rule, inspectors could turn away single women and widows. Officials thought that they would "likely become public charges," or require public assistance, such as welfare.

ANGEL ISLAND While European immigrants arriving on the East Coast passed through Ellis Island, Asians—primarily Chinese—arriving on the West Coast gained admission at **Angel Island** in San Francisco Bay. Between 1910 and 1940, about 50,000 Chinese immigrants entered the United States through Angel Island. Processing at Angel Island was different from the procedure at Ellis Island. Immigrants endured harsh questioning. They were kept in dirty, run-down buildings while they waited to find out whether they would be admitted or rejected.

Life in the New Land

No matter what part of the globe immigrants came from, they faced many adjustments to a foreign—and often unfriendly—culture.

COOPERATION FOR SURVIVAL Once admitted to the country, immigrants faced many challenges. They had to find a place to live and get a job. They had to get along in daily life, while trying to learn an unfamiliar language and culture. Many immigrants tried to find people who shared their cultural values, practiced their religion, and spoke their native language. They settled in ethnic neighborhoods that served as life rafts for immigrants. In these communities, they could speak their native language. In New York City, for example, Jewish immigrants founded a theater that gave performances in Yiddish. This was the language spoken by Jews from central and eastern Europe. They even published newspapers in their own languages.

These ethnic neighborhoods also allowed immigrants to practice their own customs and traditions, which had often been passed down from generation to generation through families. People pooled their money to build churches or synagogues. They formed schools and social clubs to help preserve their customs. Ethnic neighborhoods also provided the comfort foods immigrants craved. These foods included Chinese dumplings, Italian pasta, Jewish latkes, and Polish perogies.

Immigrants also opened local shops and small businesses in these neighborhoods. Established business owners often helped new arrivals by offering credit and giving small loans. Such aid was important for newcomers because there were few commercial banks in immigrant communities.

Immigrants were committed to their own cultures, but they also tried to take on new identities. Many immigrants began to think of themselves as "hyphenated" Americans. They tried hard to fit in. However, these new Polish- and Italian- and Chinese-Americans felt increasing friction as they rubbed shoulders with people born and raised in the United States. Native-born people often disliked the immigrants' unfamiliar customs and languages. Ironically, the descendants of earlier immigrants often viewed these new groups of immigrants as a threat to the American way of life.

This Italian immigrant sells fresh oysters from a cart on the streets of New York City.

SEEKING OPPORTUNITIES The majority of European immigrants settled in cities. Most were unskilled workers, so they took low-paying jobs in factories and mills. However, unskilled southern and eastern European immigrants were also recruited to work in the mining industry. These jobs usually paid the same low wages as factory jobs, but they were much more dangerous. Miners worked in dark, cramped conditions under the constant threat of cave-ins. Worse still was the presence of gases, such as methane, that could kill if breathed in an enclosed space. On top of that, miners had to deal with pools of stagnant dirty water, coal dust, and swarms of rats. In the early 1900s, mine accidents killed three out of every ten miners in the United States each year.

In 1884 the Japanese government allowed Hawaiian planters to recruit Japanese workers. This caused a boost in Japanese emigration. By 1886 the majority of farm workers in the United States were of Asian descent. These workers included Chinese, Japanese, Indians, and Filipinos. Often they were barred from labor unions because of their race or status as unskilled workers. These immigrants had few protections and suffered terrible working conditions. They usually worked 16 hours a day in the hot sun. Low wages and unsanitary conditions in workers' camps made life for these immigrants even more difficult.

Reading Check
Summarize How did immigrants deal with challenges they faced?

Immigration Restrictions

Many native-born Americans thought of their country as a **melting pot**, a mixture of people of different cultures and races who blended together by abandoning their native languages and customs. Many new immigrants, however, did not wish to give up their cultural identities. As immigration increased, strong anti-immigrant feelings emerged.

THE RISE OF NATIVISM One response to the growth in immigration was **nativism**, or overt favoritism toward native-born Americans. Nativism gave rise to anti-immigrant groups and also led to a growing demand for immigration restrictions.

Many nativists believed that Anglo-Saxons—the Germanic ancestors of the English—were superior to other ethnic groups. These nativists did not object to immigrants from the "right" countries.

Prescott F. Hall, a founder in 1894 of the Immigration Restriction League, identified desirable immigrants as "British, German, and Scandinavian stock, historically free, energetic, progressive." Nativists thought that problems were caused by immigrants from the "wrong" countries—"Slav, Latin, and Asiatic races, historically down-trodden . . . and stagnant."

Nativists sometimes objected more to immigrants' religious beliefs than to their ethnic backgrounds. Many native-born Americans were Protestants and thought that Roman Catholic and Jewish immigrants would undermine the democratic institutions established by the country's Protestant founders. The American Protective Association, a nativist group founded in 1887, launched vicious anti-Catholic attacks, and many colleges, businesses, and social clubs refused to admit Jews.

In 1897 Congress, influenced by the Immigration Restriction League, passed a bill requiring a literacy test for immigrants. Those who could not read 40 words in English or their native language would be refused entry. Although President Cleveland vetoed the bill, it was a powerful statement of public sentiment. In 1917 a similar bill would be passed into law in spite of President Woodrow Wilson's veto.

Vocabulary
progressive favoring advancement toward better conditions or new ideas

Fear and resentment of Chinese immigrants sometimes resulted in mob attacks, like the one shown here.

ANTI-ASIAN SENTIMENT Nativism also found a foothold in the labor movement, particularly in the West, where native-born workers feared that jobs would go to Chinese immigrants, who would accept lower wages. The depression of 1873 intensified anti-Chinese sentiment in California. Work was scarce, and labor groups exerted political pressure on the government to restrict Asian immigration. The founder of the Workingmen's Party, Denis Kearney, headed the anti-Chinese movement in California. He made hundreds of speeches throughout the state, each ending with the message, "The Chinese must go!"

In 1882 Congress essentially slammed the door on Chinese immigration for ten years by passing the **Chinese Exclusion Act**. This act banned entry to all Chinese except students, teachers, merchants, tourists, and government officials. In 1892 Congress extended the law for another ten years. In 1902 Chinese immigration was restricted indefinitely; the law was not repealed until 1943.

THE GENTLEMEN'S AGREEMENT The fears that had led to anti-Chinese agitation were extended to Japanese and other Asian people in the early 1900s. In 1906 the local board of education in San Francisco segregated Japanese children by putting them in separate schools. When Japan raised an angry protest at this treatment of its emigrants, President Theodore Roosevelt worked out a deal. Under the **Gentlemen's Agreement** of 1907–1908, Japan's government agreed to limit emigration of unskilled workers to the United States in exchange for the repeal of the San Francisco segregation order.

Although doorways for immigrants had been all but closed to Asians on the West Coast, cities in the East and the Midwest teemed with European immigrants—and with urban opportunities and challenges.

Reading Check
Analyze Causes
How did nativism influence United States' policy on immigration?

Lesson 1 Assessment

1. **Organize Information** Create a two-column chart, and list two or more causes of each effect.

Causes	Effects
1. 2. 3.	Immigrants leave their home countries.
1. 2. 3.	Immigrants face hardships in the United States.
1. 2. 3.	Some nativists want to restrict immigration.

2. **Key Terms and People** For each key term in the lesson, write a sentence explaining its significance.

3. **Evaluate** What arguments can you make against nativism and anti-immigrant feelings?
   Think About:
   • the personal qualities of immigrants
   • the reasons for anti-immigrant feelings
   • the contributions of immigrants to the United States

4. **Identify Problems** Which group of immigrants do you think faced the greatest challenges in the United States? Why?

5. **Analyze Effects** What were the effects of the massive influx of immigrants to the United States in the late 1800s?

The Challenges of Urbanization

One American's Story

In 1870, at age 21, Jacob Riis left his native Denmark for the United States. Riis found work as a police reporter, a job that took him into some of New York City's worst slums, where he was shocked at the conditions in the overcrowded, airless, filthy tenements. Riis used his talents to expose the hardships of New York City's poor.

"Be a little careful, please! The hall is dark and you might stumble over the children pitching pennies back there. Not that it would hurt them; kicks and cuffs are their daily diet. They have little else. . . . Close [stuffy]? Yes! What would you have? All the fresh air that ever enters these stairs comes from the hall-door that is for-

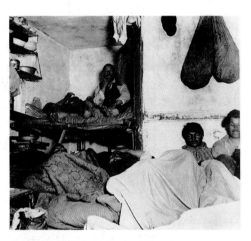

As many as 12 people slept in rooms such as this one in New York City, photographed by Jacob Riis around 1889.

ever slamming. . . . Here is a door. Listen! That short hacking cough, that tiny, helpless wail—what do they mean? . . . The child is dying with measles. With half a chance it might have lived; but it had none. That dark bedroom killed it."

—Jacob Riis, from *How the Other Half Lives*

Making a living in the late 19th and early 20th centuries was not easy. Natural and economic disasters had hit farmers hard in Europe and in the United States, and the promise of industrial jobs drew millions of people to American cities. The urban population exploded from 10 million to 54 million between 1870 and 1920. This growth revitalized the cities but also created serious problems that had a powerful impact on the new urban poor.

SS.912.A.1.2; SS.912.A.1.4; SS.912.A.3.1; SS.912.A.3.6; SS.912.A.3.8; SS.912.G.1.2; SS.912.G.4.3; HE.912.C.2.4; LAFS.1112.RH.1.2

Urban Opportunities

The technological boom in the 19th century contributed to the growing industrial strength of the United States. The result was rapid **urbanization**, or growth of cities, mostly in the regions of the Northeast and Midwest.

IMMIGRANTS SETTLE IN CITIES Most of the immigrants who streamed into the United States in the late 19th century became city dwellers because cities were the cheapest and most convenient places to live. As a result, many of the large, established cities—such as New York City and Chicago—got larger. Cities also offered unskilled laborers steady jobs in mills and factories. By 1890 there were twice as many Irish residents in New York City as in Dublin, Ireland. By 1910 immigrant families made up more than half the total population of 18 major American cities.

The **Americanization movement** was designed to assimilate people of wide-ranging cultures into the dominant culture. This social campaign was sponsored by the government and by concerned citizens. Schools and voluntary associations provided programs to teach immigrants skills needed to participate in American democracy, such as English literacy and American history and government. Subjects such as cooking and social etiquette were included to help the newcomers learn the ways of native-born Americans.

Despite these efforts, many immigrants did not wish to abandon their traditions. Ethnic communities provided the social support of others from the same country. This enabled immigrants to speak their own language and practice their customs and religion. In time, the customs, traditions, literature, arts, and foods of ethnic communities began to influence the national culture. A new American culture began to develop in diverse American cities, such as New York City. After the turn of the century, new movements in art, music, and literature were inspired by the ethnic diversity of American cities. These movements would bring fresh ideas, such as jazz music, to the world stage. People from America's rural areas moved to these cities, and they added even more to the cultural mix.

MIGRATION FROM COUNTRY TO CITY Rapid improvements in farming technology during the second half of the 19th century were good news for some farmers but bad news for others. Inventions such as the McCormick reaper and the steel plow made farming more efficient but meant that fewer laborers were needed to work the land. As industrialization continued to move the U.S. economy away from agriculture and toward manufacturing, many rural people moved to cities to find whatever work they could. Rural areas, especially in the South, continued to struggle with poverty well into the 20th century.

Many of the southern farmers who lost their livelihoods were African Americans. Between 1890 and 1910, about 200,000 African Americans moved to northern and midwestern cities, such as Chicago and Detroit, in an effort to escape racial violence, economic hardship, and political oppression. Many found conditions only somewhat better than those they had left behind. Segregation and discrimination also existed in northern cities. Job competition

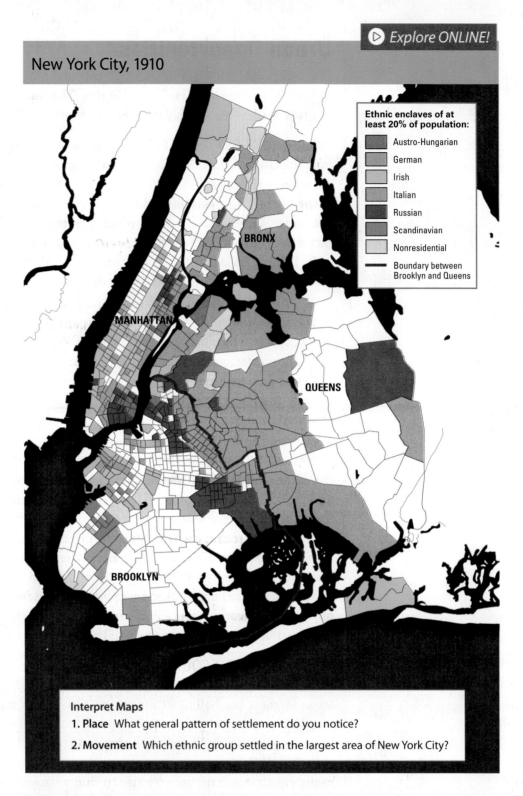

New York City, 1910

Explore ONLINE!

Ethnic enclaves of at least 20% of population:
- Austro-Hungarian
- German
- Irish
- Italian
- Russian
- Scandinavian
- Nonresidential
- Boundary between Brooklyn and Queens

BRONX

MANHATTAN

QUEENS

BROOKLYN

Interpret Maps

1. **Place** What general pattern of settlement do you notice?

2. **Movement** Which ethnic group settled in the largest area of New York City?

between blacks and white immigrants caused further racial tension. These social and economic pressures helped divide many northern and midwestern cities along racial lines. African Americans settled in mostly black neighborhoods in much the same way, and for some of the same reasons, that immigrants settled in ethnic neighborhoods.

The West also attracted African American migrants looking to escape discrimination and build better lives for themselves and their families. Instead of settling in cities, though, many African American migrants in Kansas and other western states continued to farm.

Urban Problems

As the urban population skyrocketed, city governments faced the problems of how to provide residents with needed services and safe living conditions.

HOUSING When the industrial age began, working-class families in cities had two housing options: They could either buy a house on the outskirts of town, where they would face transportation problems, or rent cramped rooms in a boarding house in the central city. As the urban population increased, however, new types of housing were designed. For example, row houses, single-family dwellings that shared side walls with other similar houses, packed many single-family residences onto a single block.

After working-class families left the central city, immigrants often took over their old housing. Sometimes two or three families occupied a one-family residence. As Jacob Riis pointed out, these multifamily urban dwellings, called **tenements**, were overcrowded and unsanitary. In some cases, these tenement neighborhoods turned into ghettos. In a ghetto, people of a certain ethnic or racial group live together because of social, political, or economic pressure. In many cities, residents were not only divided along ethnic and racial lines but also along class lines. This **social stratification**, or organization of people into social classes by wealth, was clearly on display in New York City. The city was home to grand mansions, modest working-class neighborhoods, and sprawling slums.

In 1867 New York City passed the first in a series of laws to improve such slum conditions. These laws set minimum standards for plumbing, safety, and ventilation in apartments. However, landlords found creative ways to get around the new building requirements. The second law, passed in 1879, required a window for each bedroom to provide fresh air. In many buildings, though, this window opened onto a dark, interior air shaft. Because garbage was picked up infrequently, people sometimes dumped it into the air shafts, where it attracted vermin. Residents nailed the windows shut to keep out the smell. The final law, passed in 1901, included a key element the other two laws did not have. It set up the Tenement House Department to inspect and enforce the laws. Although landlords continued to resist reform, these laws are still in effect today. The new tenements were established with good intent, but they soon became even worse places to live than the converted single-family residences.

POVERTY Working conditions in cities were often no better than living conditions. Having come mainly from rural areas, few new immigrants were skilled in modern manufacturing or industrial work. They often had no choice but to take low-paying, unskilled jobs in factories, mills, and sweatshops. Often, entire families had to work just to make ends meet.

In New York City, the garment, or clothing, industry employed mainly immigrant women. Long hours and dangerous conditions were common. Many of these immigrant women joined the International Ladies' Garment Workers' Union. They organized a series of successful strikes. The longest strike lasted 133 days. Afterward, the workers won new contracts for increased wages and fewer working hours.

TRANSPORTATION Innovations in **mass transit**, transportation systems designed to move large numbers of people along fixed routes, enabled workers to go to and from jobs more easily. Streetcars were introduced in San Francisco in 1873 and electric subways in Boston in 1897. By the early 20th century, there were mass-transit networks in many urban areas. They linked city neighborhoods to one another and to outlying communities. Cities tried to meet the transportation demands of their growing populations. They struggled to repair old transit systems and to build new ones.

WATER Cities also faced the problem of supplying safe drinking water. As the urban population grew in the 1840s and 1850s, cities such as New York and Cleveland built public waterworks to handle the increasing demand. As late as the 1860s, however, the residents of many cities had inadequate piped water—or none at all. Even in large cities like New York, homes seldom had indoor plumbing. Residents had to collect water in pails from faucets on the street and heat it for bathing. There was a clear need to improve water quality to control diseases such as cholera and typhoid fever. To make city water safer, filtration was introduced in the 1870s. Chlorination was introduced in 1908. However, in the early 20th century, many people in cities still had no access to safe water.

SANITATION As the cities grew, so did the challenge of keeping them clean. Horse manure piled up on the streets, and sewage flowed through open gutters. Factories released foul smoke into the air. People dumped garbage on the streets because they had no dependable trash collection. Private contractors called scavengers were hired to sweep the streets, collect garbage, and clean outhouses. But they often did not do the jobs properly. By 1900 many cities had developed sewer lines and created sanitation departments. However, providing healthful living conditions was an ongoing challenge for city leaders.

Vocabulary
chlorination a method of purifying water by mixing it with the chemical chlorine

Sanitation problems in big cities were overwhelming. It was not unusual to see a dead horse in the street.

The San Francisco Earthquake of 1906

At 5:12 on the morning of April 18, 1906, while many in the city slept, a massive earthquake struck San Francisco, California. The force of the earthquake and the fires that followed destroyed much of the city. Jack London described the fires that raged after the earthquake.

> *"On Wednesday morning at a quarter past five came the earthquake. A minute later the flames were leaping upward. In a dozen different quarters south of Market Street, in the working-class ghetto, and in the factories, fires started. There was no opposing the flames. . . . And the great water-mains had burst. All the shrewd contrivances and safeguards of man had been thrown out of gear by thirty seconds' twitching of the earth-crust."*
>
> —Jack London, from "The Story of an Eye-witness"

Analyze Historical Sources
According to Jack London, how did the earthquake undo the safeguards the city had put into place to fight fires?

CRIME As the populations of cities increased, pickpockets and thieves flourished. New York City organized the first full-time, salaried police force in 1844. However, most city law enforcement units were too small to have much impact on crime.

FIRE The limited water supply in many cities contributed to another risk: the spread of fires. Major fires occurred in almost every large American city during the 1870s and 1880s. In addition, most cities had many wooden buildings. These structures were like kindling waiting for a spark. The use of candles and kerosene heaters also created a fire hazard.

At first, most city firefighters were volunteers and not always available when they were needed. Cincinnati, Ohio, established the nation's first paid fire department in 1853. By 1900 most cities had full-time professional fire departments. Cities were made safer by the introduction of a practical automatic fire sprinkler in 1874. In addition, brick, stone, or concrete began to replace wood as a building material.

Reading Check
Analyze Effects
How did conditions in cities affect people's health?

Reformers Mobilize

As problems in cities mounted, concerned Americans worked to find solutions. Social reformers focused their efforts on relieving urban poverty.

THE SETTLEMENT HOUSE MOVEMENT An early reform program, the **Social Gospel movement**, preached salvation through service to the poor. One of the founders of this movement was a Protestant minister named Washington Gladden. As an editor of the *New York Independent*, Gladden helped to expose the greed and corruption caused by industrialization. He also focused public attention on the living and working conditions of the poor. Members of the movement believed that churches had a moral duty to help solve society's problems. They also believed that religious faith should be expressed through good works.

Inspired by the message of the Social Gospel movement, 19th-century reformers responded to the call to help the urban poor. In the late 1800s a few reformers established **settlement houses**, community centers in slum neighborhoods that provided assistance to people in the area, especially immigrants. London reformers had founded the first settlement houses in 1884.

Settlement houses in the United States were founded by Charles Stover and Stanton Coit in New York City in 1886. **Jane Addams**—one of the most influential members of the movement—and Ellen Gates Starr founded Chicago's Hull House in 1889. In 1890 Janie Porter Barrett established the Locust Street Social Settlement in Hampton, Virginia—the first settlement house for African Americans.

Run largely by middle-class, college-educated women, settlement houses provided educational, cultural, and social services. Many settlement workers lived at the houses so that they could learn firsthand about the problems caused by urbanization and help create solutions.

"Keenly conscious of the social confusion all about us and the hard economic struggle, we at times believed that the very struggle itself might become a source of strength. . . . We fatuously hoped that we might pluck from the human tragedy itself a consciousness of a common destiny which should bring its own healing, that we might extract from life's very misfortunes a power of cooperation which should be effective against them."

—Jane Addams, quoted in *Twenty Years at Hull House*

Jane Addams (1860–1935)

During a trip to England, Jane Addams visited Toynbee Hall, the first settlement house. Addams believed that settlement houses could be effective because there, workers would "learn from life itself" how to address urban problems. She cofounded Chicago's Hull House in 1889.

Addams was also an antiwar activist and a spokesperson for racial justice. She advocated for quality-of-life issues, from infant mortality to better care for the aged. In 1931 she was a co-winner of the Nobel Peace Prize.

Until the end of her life, Addams insisted that she was just a "very simple person." But many familiar with her accomplishments consider her a source of inspiration.

This art class for children, at Hull House, is just one example of the many services settlement houses provided to their communities.

Settlement houses provided classes in such subjects as English, health, and painting, and offered college extension courses. They also sent visiting nurses into the homes of the sick and provided whatever aid was needed to secure "support for deserted women, insurance for bewildered widows, damages for injured operators, furniture from the clutches of the installment store." Reformers hoped that these services would help immigrants claim the benefits of living in a democracy and help them increase **social mobility**. Social mobility refers to the ability of families or individuals to move into a higher social class.

Settlement houses also sought political solutions by lobbying state and local governments to resolve social and economic problems. By 1910 about 400 settlement houses were operating in cities across the country. These settlement houses helped cultivate a sense of social responsibility toward the urban poor.

Reading Check
Analyze Motives
What motivated social reformers to tackle the problems of urban poverty?

Lesson 2 Assessment

1. **Organize Information** Use a spider map to organize information about urban problems. List urban problems on the vertical lines. Fill in details about attempts that were made to solve each problem.

Solutions to Urban Problems

2. **Key Terms and People** For each key term or person in the lesson, write a sentence explaining its significance.

3. **Analyze Effects** What effects did the migration from rural areas to the cities in the late 19th century have on urban society?

   Think About:
   • why people moved to cities
   • the problems caused by rapid urban growth
   • the differences in the experiences of whites and blacks

4. **Analyze Motives** Why did immigrants tend to group together in cities?

5. **Evaluate** Which solution (or attempted solution) to an urban problem discussed in this lesson do you think had the most impact? Why?

★
Politics in the Gilded Age

The Big Idea
Local and national political corruption in the 19th century led to calls for reform.

Why It Matters Now
Political reforms paved the way for a more honest and efficient government in the 20th century and beyond.

Key Terms and People
political machine

graft

Boss Tweed

patronage

civil service

Rutherford B. Hayes

James A. Garfield

Chester A. Arthur

Pendleton Civil Service Act

Grover Cleveland

Benjamin Harrison

One American's Story

Mark Twain described the excesses of the late 19th century in a satirical novel, *The Gilded Age,* a collaboration with the writer Charles Dudley Warner. The title of the book has since come to represent the period from the 1870s to the 1890s. Twain mocks the greed and self-indulgence of his characters, including Philip Sterling.

A luxurious apartment building rises behind a New York City shantytown in 1889.

"There are many young men like him [Philip Sterling] in American society, of his age, opportunities, education and abilities, who have really been educated for nothing and have let themselves drift, in the hope that they will find somehow, and by some sudden turn of good luck, the golden road to fortune. . . . He saw people, all around him, poor yesterday, rich to-day, who had come into sudden opulence by some means which they could not have classified among any of the regular occupations of life."
—Mark Twain and Charles Dudley Warner, from *The Gilded Age*

Twain's characters find that getting rich quick is more difficult than they had thought it would be. Investments turn out to be worthless; politicians' bribes eat up their savings. The glittering exterior of the age turns out to hide a corrupt political core and a growing gap between the few rich and the many poor.

SS.912.A.1.2; SS.912.A.1.4; SS.912.A.3.11; SS.912.H.1.1

The Emergence of Political Machines

In the late 19th century, cities experienced rapid growth under inefficient government. In a climate influenced by dog-eat-dog Social Darwinism, cities were receptive to a new power structure, the political machine, and a new politician, the city boss.

THE POLITICAL MACHINE The **political machine** was an organized group that controlled the activities of a political party in a city. It also offered services to voters and businesses in exchange for political or financial support. In the decades after the Civil War, political machines gained control of local government in Baltimore, New York, San Francisco, and other major cities.

The machine was organized like a pyramid. At the pyramid's base were local precinct workers and captains who reported to a ward boss. They tried to get voters' support on a city block or in a neighborhood. At election time, the ward boss worked to secure the vote in all the precincts in the ward, or electoral district. Ward bosses helped the poor and gained their votes by doing favors or providing services. As Martin Lomasney, elected ward boss of Boston's West End in 1885, explained, "There's got to be in every ward somebody that any bloke can come to . . . and get help. Help, you understand; none of your law and your justice, but help." At the top of the pyramid was the city boss, who controlled the activities of the political party throughout the city. Precinct captains, ward bosses, and the city boss worked together to elect their candidates and guarantee the success of the machine.

A corrupt 19th-century boss robs the city treasury by easily cutting government red tape, or bureaucracy.

THE ROLE OF THE POLITICAL BOSS Whether or not the boss officially served as mayor, he controlled access to municipal jobs and business licenses. He also influenced the courts and other municipal agencies. Bosses like Roscoe Conkling in New York City used their power to build parks, sewer systems, and waterworks. They also gave money to schools, hospitals, and orphanages. Bosses could also provide government support for new businesses, a service for which they were often paid extremely well.

It was not only money that motivated city bosses. By solving urban problems, bosses could reinforce voters' loyalty, gain additional political support, and extend their influence.

IMMIGRANTS AND THE MACHINE Many precinct captains and political bosses were first-generation or second-generation immigrants. Few were educated beyond grammar school. They entered politics early and worked their way up from the bottom. They could speak to immigrants in their own language and understood the challenges that newcomers faced. More important, the bosses were able to provide solutions. The machines —such as New York City's powerful Democratic political machine Tammany Hall—helped immigrants with naturalization (attaining full citizenship). They also helped immigrants find housing and jobs, the newcomers' most important needs. In return, the immigrants provided the votes that the political bosses needed.

"Big Jim" Pendergast, an Irish American saloonkeeper, worked his way up from precinct captain to Democratic city boss in Kansas City, Missouri. He did this by helping Italian, African, and Irish American voters in his ward. By 1900 he controlled Missouri state politics as well.

> *"I've been called a boss. All there is to it is having friends, doing things for people, and then later on they'll do things for you. . . . You can't coerce people into doing things for you—you can't make them vote for you. I never coerced anybody in my life. Wherever you see a man bull-dozing anybody he don't last long."*
>
> —James Pendergast, quoted in *The Pendergast Machine*

Reading Check
Summarize In what way did the structure of the political machine resemble a pyramid?

Municipal Graft and Scandal

While the well-oiled political machines provided city dwellers with services, many political bosses fell victim to corruption as their influence grew.

ELECTION FRAUD AND GRAFT When the loyalty of voters was not enough to carry an election, some political machines turned to fraud. Party members used fake names to cast as many votes as were needed to win.

Once a political machine got its candidates into office, it could take advantage of numerous opportunities for **graft**, the illegal use of political influence for personal gain. For example, by helping a person find work on a construction project for the city, a political machine could ask the worker to bill the city for more than the actual cost of materials and labor. The worker then "kicked back" a portion of the earnings to the machine. Taking these kickbacks, or illegal payments for their services, enriched the political machines—and individual politicians.

Political machines also granted favors to businesses in return for cash. They accepted bribes to allow illegal activities, such as gambling, to flourish. Politicians were able to get away with dishonest deals because the police rarely interfered. Until about 1890, police forces were hired and fired by political bosses.

THE TWEED RING SCANDAL William M. Tweed, known as **Boss Tweed**, became head of Tammany Hall in 1868. Between 1869 and 1871, Boss Tweed led the Tweed Ring. This group of corrupt politicians defrauded New York City.

One scheme, the construction of the New York County Courthouse, involved extravagant graft. The project cost taxpayers $13 million, but the actual construction cost was $3 million. The difference went into the pockets of Tweed and his followers.

Boss Tweed, head of Tammany Hall

"The Tammany Tiger Loose"

Political cartoonist Thomas Nast ridiculed Boss Tweed and his machine in the pages of *Harper's Weekly*. Nast's work threatened Tweed, who reportedly said, "I don't care so much what the papers write about me—my constituents can't read; but . . . they can see pictures!" In this cartoon, under the Tammany tiger's victim, is a torn paper that reads "LAW." Boss Tweed and his cronies are portrayed as noblemen. They watch from the stands on the left. The cartoon's caption reads: "What are you going to do about it?

Analyze Historical Sources
What effect do you think Nast wanted this political cartoon to have on his audience?

Thomas Nast, a political cartoonist, helped provoke public outrage against Tammany Hall's graft. The Tweed Ring was finally broken in 1871. Tweed was indicted on 120 counts of fraud and extortion and was sentenced to 12 years in jail. His sentence was reduced to one year, but after leaving jail, Tweed was quickly arrested on another charge. While serving a second sentence, Tweed escaped. He was captured in Spain when officials identified him from a Thomas Nast cartoon. By that time, political corruption had become a national issue.

Civil Service Replaces Patronage

The desire for power and money made local politics corrupt in the industrial age. It also infected state and national politics.

PATRONAGE SPURS REFORM Since the beginning of the 19th century, presidents had complained about the problem of **patronage**. This was the practice of giving government jobs to people who had helped a candidate get elected. In Andrew Jackson's administration, this policy was known as the spoils system. People from cabinet members to workers who scrubbed the steps of the Capitol owed their jobs to political connections. As might be expected, some government employees were not qualified for the positions they filled. In addition, political appointees sometimes used their positions for personal gain.

Reformers began to push for the elimination of patronage. They wanted a merit system of hiring. Reformers believed that jobs in **civil service**—government administration—should go to the most qualified persons. It should not matter what political views they held or who recommended them.

Vocabulary
extortion illegal use of one's official position to obtain property or funds

Reading Check
Draw Conclusions
What finally prompted the government to take action against Boss Tweed and Tammany Hall?

Rutherford B. Hayes
(1877–1881)

James A. Garfield
(1881)

Chester A. Arthur
(1881–1885)

REFORM UNDER HAYES, GARFIELD, AND ARTHUR Civil service reform made gradual progress under Presidents Hayes, Garfield, and Arthur. Republican president **Rutherford B. Hayes**, elected in 1876, could not convince Congress to support reform, so he used other means. Hayes named independents to his cabinet. He also set up a commission to investigate the nation's customhouses, which were well-known centers of patronage. On the basis of the commission's report, Hayes fired two of the top officials of New York City's customhouse, where jobs were controlled by the Republican Party. These firings enraged the Republican New York senator and political boss Roscoe Conkling and his supporters, the Stalwarts.

When Hayes decided not to run for reelection in 1880, a free-for-all broke out at the Republican convention, between the Stalwarts—who opposed changes in the spoils system—and reformers. Neither Stalwarts nor reformers could win a majority of delegates. As a result, the convention settled on an independent presidential candidate, Ohio congressman **James A. Garfield**. To balance out Garfield's ties to reformers, the Republicans nominated for vice-president **Chester A. Arthur**, one of Conkling's supporters. Despite Arthur's inclusion on the ticket, Garfield angered the Stalwarts by giving reformers most of his patronage jobs once he was elected.

On July 2, 1881, President Garfield walked through the Washington, DC, train station. There he was shot two times by a mentally unbalanced lawyer named Charles Guiteau, whom Garfield had turned down for a job. Guiteau announced, "I did it and I will go to jail for it. I am a Stalwart and Arthur is now president." Garfield ultimately died from his wounds on September 19. Despite his ties to the Stalwarts, Chester Arthur turned reformer when he became president. His first message to Congress urged legislators to pass a civil service law. The resulting **Pendleton Civil Service Act** of 1883 authorized a bipartisan civil service commission. This group was to make appointments to federal jobs through a merit system based on candidates' performance on an examination.

GOVERNOR THEODORE ROOSEVELT Reforms also took place at the state level. In 1898 the New York State Republican political machine, run by Thomas C. Platt, chose to back Rough Rider and Spanish-American War hero Theodore Roosevelt for governor. Roosevelt was up against the Tammany Hall candidate, Augustus Van Wyck. With Platt's help and influence, Roosevelt won a close victory to become New York's 33rd governor in 1899.

Roosevelt had campaigned on putting public interest ahead of partisan politics. Once in office, he went against tradition and refused to fill civil service jobs through patronage. When Roosevelt also began to ignore the state Republican machine's wishes on policy matters, donors began to doubt Platt's influence over Roosevelt. Before Roosevelt's reforms could hurt the Republican state machine further, Platt devised a clever plan. With the help of national Republican Party leaders, Roosevelt was nominated to replace Vice-President Garret Hobart, who had just died in office. Roosevelt accepted, hoping that this might be a step toward winning a nomination to run for president. As president, Roosevelt hoped to continue reforming the political system. However, by leaving the governorship, Roosevelt left New York in the hands of the machine.

Reading Check
Analyze Causes
How did patronage contribute to government incompetence and fraud?

Business Buys Influence

By 1901 more than 40 percent of all federal jobs had been classified as civil service positions. But the Pendleton Act had mixed consequences. On the one hand, public administration became more honest and efficient. On the other hand, officials could no longer pressure employees for campaign contributions. Consequently, politicians turned to other sources for donations— wealthy business owners. Therefore, the alliance between government and big business became stronger than ever.

Big business leaders hoped the government would preserve, or even raise, the tariffs that protected domestic industries from foreign competition. The Democratic Party, however, opposed high tariffs because they increased prices. In 1884 the Democratic Party won a presidential election for the first time in 28 years with candidate **Grover Cleveland**. As president, Cleveland tried to lower tariff rates, but Congress refused to support him.

Benjamin Harrison

In 1888 Cleveland ran for reelection on a low-tariff platform. His opponent was former Indiana senator **Benjamin Harrison**, the grandson of President William Henry Harrison. Harrison's campaign was financed mostly by large contributions from companies that wanted even higher tariffs. Although Cleveland won about 100,000 more popular votes than his opponent, Harrison took a majority of the electoral votes and the presidency. He signed the McKinley Tariff Act of 1890, which raised tariffs on manufactured goods to their highest level yet.

In 1892 Cleveland was elected again—the only president to serve two nonconsecutive terms. He supported a bill for lowering the McKinley Tariff but refused to sign it because it also provided for a federal income tax. Despite his opposition, the Wilson-Gorman Tariff became law in 1894 without the president's signature. In 1897 William McKinley was inaugurated president and raised tariffs once again.

Reading Check
Analyze Effects
What were the positive and the negative effects of the Pendleton Civil Service Act?

The attempt to reduce the tariff had failed, but the spirit of reform was not dead. New developments in areas ranging from technology to mass culture would help redefine American society as the United States moved into the 20th century.

Lesson 3 Assessment

1. **Organize Information** Use a web diagram to list examples of corruption in 19th-century politics.

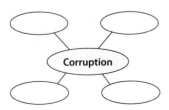

Corruption

2. **Key Terms and People** For each key term or person in the lesson, write a sentence explaining its significance.

3. **Predict** How do you think politics in the United States would have been different if the Pendleton Civil Service Act had not been passed?

   Think About:
   • the act's impact on federal workers
   • the act's impact on political fundraising
   • Republican Party conflicts

4. **Evaluate** Reread the quotation from James Pendergast. Explain whether you agree or disagree that machine politicians did not coerce people.

5. **Analyze Causes** Why do you think tariff reform failed? Support your response with evidence from the lesson.

New Technologies

One American's Story

The Brooklyn Bridge, connecting Brooklyn to the island of Manhattan in New York City, opened in 1883. It took 14 years to build. Each day, laborers descended to work in a caisson, or watertight chamber, that took them deep beneath the East River. E. F. Farrington, a mechanic who worked on the bridge, described the working conditions.

In 1883 New Yorkers celebrated the opening of the world's longest suspension bridge, the 1,595-foot-long Brooklyn Bridge.

"Inside the caisson everything wore an unreal, weird appearance. There was a confused sensation in the head. . . . What with the flaming lights, the deep shadows, the confusing noise of hammers, drills, and chains, the half-naked forms flitting about . . . one might, if of a poetic temperament, get a realizing sense of Dante's Inferno."

—E. F. Farrington, quoted in *The Great Bridge*

Four years later, trains ran across the bridge 24 hours a day and carried more than 30 million travelers each year.

The Big Idea

Advances in science and technology helped solve urban problems, including overcrowding.

Why It Matters Now

American cities continue to depend on the results of scientific and technological research.

Key Terms and People

Louis Sullivan

Daniel Burnham

Frederick Law Olmsted

Orville and Wilbur Wright

George Eastman

SS.912.A.1.4; SS.912.A.3.5; SS.912.H.1.1

Technology and City Life

Engineering innovations, such as the Brooklyn Bridge, laid the groundwork for modern American life, and they also helped fuel the imaginations of those chasing the American Dream. Through technology, innovation, and hard work, it seemed that even the impossible could be achieved. Cities in every industrial area of the country expanded both outward and upward. In 1870 only 25 American cities had populations of 50,000 or more; by 1890, 58 cities could make that claim. By the turn of the 20th century, due to the increase of industrial jobs, four out of ten Americans made their homes in cities.

In response to these changes, technological advances began to meet the nation's needs for communication, transportation, and space. One remedy for more urban space was to build toward the sky.

SKYSCRAPERS Architects were able to design taller buildings because of two factors: the invention of elevators and the development of internal steel skeletons to bear the weight. In 1890–1891, architect **Louis Sullivan** designed the ten-story Wainwright Building in St. Louis. He called the new breed of skyscraper a "proud and soaring thing." The tall building's appearance was graceful because its steel framework supported both floors and walls.

The Flatiron Building, shown here under construction, stands at the intersection of Fifth Avenue and 23rd Street in New York City.

The skyscraper became America's greatest contribution to architecture, "a new thing under the sun," according to architect Frank Lloyd Wright, who studied under Sullivan. Skyscrapers solved the practical problem of how to make the best use of limited and expensive space. The unusual form of another skyscraper, the Flatiron Building, seemed perfect for its location at one of New York City's busiest intersections. **Daniel Burnham** designed this slender 285-foot tower in 1902. The Flatiron Building and other new buildings served as symbols of a rich and optimistic society.

ELECTRIC TRANSIT As skyscrapers expanded upward, changes in transportation allowed cities to spread outward. Before the Civil War, horses had drawn the earliest streetcars over iron rails embedded in city streets. In some cities during the 1870s and 1880s, underground moving cables powered streetcar lines. Electricity, however, transformed urban transportation.

In 1888 Richmond, Virginia, became the first American city to electrify its urban transit. Other cities followed. By the turn of the 20th century, networks of electric streetcars—also called trolley cars—ran from outlying neighborhoods to downtown offices and department stores.

New railroad lines also fed the growth of suburbs, allowing residents to commute to downtown jobs. New York's northern suburbs alone moved 100,000 commuters each day to the central business district.

A few large cities moved their streetcars far above street level, creating elevated or "el" trains. Other cities, like New York, built subways by moving their rail lines underground. These streetcars, elevated trains, and subways enabled cities to annex suburban developments that emerged along the advancing transportation routes.

ENGINEERING AND URBAN PLANNING Steel-cable suspension bridges, like the Brooklyn Bridge, also brought cities' sections closer together. Sometimes these bridges provided recreational opportunities. In his design for the Brooklyn Bridge, for example, John Augustus Roebling provided an elevated promenade whose "principal use will be to allow people of leisure, and old and young invalids, to promenade over the bridge on fine days." This need for open spaces in crowded commercial cities inspired the new science of urban planning.

City planners tried to restore serenity to the environment by designing recreational areas. Landscape architect **Frederick Law Olmsted** led the movement for planned urban parks.

In 1857 Olmsted, along with English-born architect Calvert Vaux, helped draw up a plan for "Greensward." It was selected to become Central Park, in New York City. Olmsted envisioned the park as a rustic haven in the center of the busy city. The finished park featured boating and tennis facilities, a zoo, and bicycle paths. Olmsted hoped that the park's beauty would soothe the city's inhabitants and let them enjoy a "natural" setting.

> *"The main object and justification [of the park] is simply to produce a certain influence in the minds of people and through this to make life in the city healthier and happier. The character of this influence . . . is to be produced by means of scenes, through observation of which the mind may be more or less lifted out of moods and habits."*
>
> —Frederick Law Olmsted, quoted in *Frederick Law Olmsted's New York*

In the 1870s Olmsted planned landscaping for Washington, DC, and St. Louis. He also drew the initial designs for "the Emerald Necklace," Boston's parks system. Boston's Back Bay area had originally been a 450-acre swamp. It was drained and developed by urban planners into an area of elegant streets and cultural attractions, including Olmsted's parks.

CITY PLANNING By contrast, Chicago, with its explosive growth from 30,000 people in 1850 to 300,000 in 1870, represented uncontrolled expansion. Fortunately for the city, a local architect, Daniel Burnham, was intrigued by the prospect of remaking the city. His motto was "Make no little plans. They have no magic to stir men's blood." He oversaw the transformation of a swampy area near Lake Michigan. He transformed it into a glistening White City for Chicago's 1893 World's Columbian Exposition. Majestic

Vocabulary
promenade a public place for walking

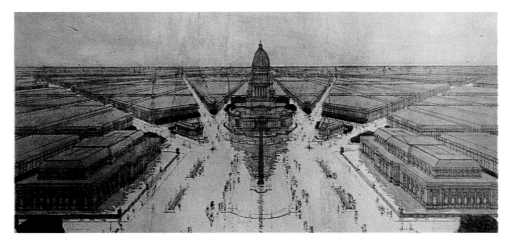

Unity was architect Daniel Burnham's goal for Chicago's city center. Major thoroughfares converge at a central grand plaza to help create a unified city.

exhibition halls, statues, the first Ferris wheel, and a lagoon greeted more than 21 million visitors who came to the city.

Many urban planners saw visions of future cities in Burnham's White City. Burnham, however, left Chicago an even more important legacy. It was an overall plan for the city, crowned by elegant parks strung along Lake Michigan. As a result, Chicago's lakefront today has curving banks of grass and sandy beaches instead of a jumbled mass of piers and warehouses.

FEEDING CITIES To feed their populations, large cities needed a reliable food supply. The same new agricultural technologies that pushed many rural workers off of farms and into cities made it possible for cities to supply large, growing populations with food. New technologies and ideas allowed farmers to produce more crops on the same amount of land with fewer workers.

The ideas of George Washington Carver helped revolutionize farming in the South. By repeatedly planting cotton crops season after season, southern farmers were wearing out the soil. To combat this, Carver promoted the idea of crop rotation. This practice restored nitrogen, an important nutrient for growing crops, to the soil. Carver even developed and promoted ways to use crops that restored soil nutrients, such as peanuts. By promoting new uses for these crops, Carver provided farmers with new markets.

Another important breakthrough in agriculture occurred in 1905. Chemist Fritz Haber discovered a way to extract nitrogen from the air. This discovery led to the Haber-Bosch process, which made it possible to create chemical fertilizers. With chemical fertilizers, farmers could provide nutrients directly to crops. By 1909 farmers were using more than 3 million tons of chemical fertilizer a year.

Even though farmers could produce plenty of food for the growing population, they still needed a way to get their products to market before they spoiled. One solution was refrigerated railroad cars. Another was chemical preservatives, such as borax. These chemicals did extend the freshness of food, but many were harmful to human health. By 1906 the government would enact regulations to ensure the safety of the U.S. food supply.

Reading Check
Summarize List three major changes in cities near the turn of the century. What effect did each have?

Advances in Communication

New developments in communication brought the nation closer together. In addition to a railroad network that now extended across the nation, further advances in printing, aviation, and photography helped to speed the transfer of information.

A REVOLUTION IN PRINTING By 1890 the literacy rate in the United States had risen to nearly 90 percent. Publishers turned out ever-increasing numbers of books, magazines, and newspapers to meet the growing demand of the reading public. A series of technological advances in printing facilitated their efforts.

American mills began to produce huge quantities of cheap paper from wood pulp. The new paper proved durable enough to withstand high-speed presses. The electrically powered web-perfecting press, for example, printed on both sides of a continuous paper roll, rather than on just one side. It then cut, folded, and counted the pages as they came down the line. Faster production and lower costs made newspapers and magazines more affordable. People could now buy newspapers for a penny a copy.

AIRPLANES In the early 20th century, brothers **Orville and Wilbur Wright**, bicycle manufacturers from Dayton, Ohio, experimented with new engines powerful enough to keep "heavier-than-air" craft aloft. First the Wright brothers built a glider. Then they commissioned a four-cylinder internal combustion engine, chose a propeller, and designed a biplane with a 40-foot 4-inch wingspan. Their first successful flight—on December 17, 1903, at Kitty Hawk, North Carolina—covered 120 feet and lasted 12 seconds. Orville later described the take-off.

Vocabulary
internal combustion engine an engine in which fuel is burned within the engine rather than in an external furnace

Document-Based Investigation Historical Source

The Wright Flyer

The Wright Flyer had a wooden frame covered in canvas. It measured 9 feet 4 inches high and just over 21 feet long, with a wingspan of 40 feet 4 inches. Powered by a 4-cylinder 12-horsepower piston engine, the total weight of the airplane was 605 pounds. The engine, at 180 pounds, was the heaviest component in the airplane. The design of lighter, more powerful engines was the most important development in early aviation history.

Analyze Historical Sources
Examine the photo of the Wright Flyer. Why do you think the Wright brothers did not paint their airplane?

"After running the motor a few minutes to heat it up, I released the wire that held the machine to the track, and the machine started forward into the wind. Wilbur ran at the side of the machine . . . to balance it. . . . Unlike the start on the 14th, made in a calm, the machine, facing a 27-mile wind, started very slowly. . . . One of the life-saving men snapped the camera for us, taking a picture just as the machine had reached the end of the track and had risen to a height of about two feet."

—Orville Wright, quoted in *Smithsonian Frontiers of Flight*

Within two years, the Wright brothers had increased their flights to 24 miles. By 1920, convinced of the great potential of flight, the U.S. government had established the first transcontinental airmail service.

A Kodak camera

PHOTOGRAPHY EXPLOSION Before the 1880s, photography was a professional activity. Because of the time required to take a picture and the weight of the equipment, a photographer could not shoot a moving object. In addition, photographers had to develop their shots immediately.

New techniques eliminated the need to develop pictures right away. **George Eastman** developed a series of more convenient alternatives to the heavy glass plates previously used. Now, instead of carrying their darkrooms around with them, photographers could use flexible film, coated with gelatin emulsions, and could send their film to a studio for processing. When professional photographers were slow to begin using the new film, Eastman decided to aim his product at the masses.

In 1888 Eastman introduced his Kodak camera. The purchase price of $25 included a 100-picture roll of film. After taking the pictures, the photographer would send the camera back to Eastman's Rochester, New York, factory. For $10, the pictures were developed and returned with the camera reloaded. Easily held and operated, the Kodak prompted millions of Americans to become amateur photographers. The camera also helped to create the field of photojournalism. Reporters could now photograph events as they occurred.

Reading Check
Draw Conclusions
How did new technologies help improve communication and bring the nation closer together?

Lesson 4 Assessment

1. **Organize Information** Use a three-column chart to list three important changes in city design, communication, and transportation.

City Design	Communication	Transportation
1.	1.	1.
2.	2.	2.
3.	3.	3.

Which change had the greatest impact on urban life? Why?

2. **Key Terms and People** For each key term or person in the lesson, write a sentence explaining its significance.

3. **Predict** If you had been an urban planner at the turn of the century, what new ideas would you have included in your plan for the ideal city?
   Think About:
   - Olmsted's plans for Central Park
   - Burnham's ideas for Chicago

4. **Evaluate** Which scientific or technological development described in this lesson had the greatest impact on American culture? Use details from the text to justify your choice.

5. **Summarize** How did bridge building contribute to the growth of cities?

The Dawn of Mass Culture

The Big Idea

As Americans had more time for leisure activities, a modern mass culture emerged.

Why It Matters Now

Today the United States has a worldwide impact on mass culture.

Key Terms and People

Ashcan school

pragmatism

Mark Twain

Joseph Pulitzer

William Randolph Hearst

rural free delivery (RFD)

One American's Story

Along the Brooklyn seashore, on a narrow sandbar just nine miles from busy Manhattan, rose the most famous urban amusement center, Coney Island. In 1886 its main developer, George Tilyou, bragged, "If Paris is France, then Coney Island . . . is the world." Indeed, tens of thousands of visitors mobbed Coney Island after work each evening and on Sundays and holidays. When Luna Park, a spectacular amusement park on Coney Island, opened in May 1903, reporter Bruce Blen described the scene.

"[Inside the park was] an enchanted, storybook land of trellises, columns, domes, minarets, lagoons, and lofty aerial flights. And everywhere was life—a pageant of happy people; and everywhere was color—a wide harmony of orange and white and gold. . . . It was a world removed—shut away from the sordid clatter and turmoil of the streets."
—Bruce Blen, quoted in *Amusing the Million*

The sprawling amusement center at Coney Island became a model for urban amusement parks.

Coney Island offered Americans a few hours of escape from the hard workweek. A schoolteacher who walked fully dressed into the ocean explained her unusual behavior by saying, "It has been a hard year at school, and when I saw the big crowd here, everyone with the brakes off, the spirit of the place got the better of me." The end of the 19th century saw the rise of a "mass culture" in the United States.

SS.912.A.1.2; SS.912.A.1.4; SS.912.A.1.7;
SS.912.H.1.1; SS.912.H.1.5

American Leisure

Vocabulary

consumer a person who purchases goods or services for direct use or ownership

standard of living the measure of wealth and goods an individual needs to belong to a certain social class

Middle-class Americans from all over the country had shared experiences. They enjoyed new leisure activities and experienced nationwide advertising campaigns. The rise of a consumer culture began to level regional differences. As the 19th century drew to a close, many Americans could forget city congestion and dull industrial work by enjoying amusement parks, bicycling, new forms of theater, and spectator sports. Many Americans saw their standard of living rise. As members of the carpenters' union of Worcester, Massachusetts, proclaimed, "eight hours for work, eight hours for rest, eight hours for what we will."

AMUSEMENT PARKS Cities worked to meet the recreational needs of their residents. Chicago, New York City, and other cities began setting aside precious green space for outdoor enjoyment. Many built small playgrounds and playing fields in neighborhoods for their citizens' enjoyment.

Some amusement parks were constructed on the outskirts of cities. Often trolley-car companies built them to attract more passengers. The parks featured picnic grounds and a variety of rides. The roller coaster drew adventurous customers to Coney Island in 1884. The first Ferris wheel drew enthusiastic crowds to the World's Columbian Exposition in Chicago in 1893. Clearly, many Americans were ready for new forms of entertainment—and a variety of recreational activities soon became available.

BICYCLING AND TENNIS The first American bicycles had huge front wheels and solid rubber tires. It was a challenge to ride them. A bump might throw the cyclist over the handlebars. As a result, bicycling began as a male-only sport. However, in 1885 the first commercially successful "safety bicycle" was built. It had smaller wheels and air-filled tires. This bicycle made the activity more popular. The Victor safety bicycle had a dropped frame and no crossbar, which appealed to women.

Instead of tight corsets, women bicyclists wore tailored blouses called shirtwaists and "split" skirts. This clothing allowed them to cycle more comfortably. This outfit soon became popular for daily wear. The bicycle also freed women from the ever-present chaperone. Suffragist Susan B. Anthony declared, "I think [bicycling] has done more to emancipate women than anything else in the world. . . . It gives women a feeling of freedom and self-reliance." About 50,000 men and women had begun cycling by 1888. Two years later, 312 American companies produced 10 million bikes in one year.

Bicycling and other new sports became fads in the late 1800s.

Americans took up the sport of tennis as enthusiastically as they had taken up cycling. The modern version of this sport originated in North Wales in 1873. A year later, the United States saw its first tennis match. Socialite Florence Harriman recalled that in the 1880s her father returned from England with one of New York's first tennis sets. At first, neighbors thought the elder Harriman had installed the nets to catch birds.

Hungry or thirsty after tennis or cycling? Turn-of-the-century Americans began eating new snacks with recognizable brand names. They could munch on a Hershey chocolate bar, first sold in 1900, and wash down the chocolate with a Coca-Cola®. An Atlanta pharmacist originally formulated the drink as a cure for headaches in 1886. The ingredients included extracts from Peruvian coca leaves as well as African cola nuts.

SPECTATOR SPORTS Americans not only participated in new sports but became eager fans of spectator sports, especially boxing and baseball. These two sports had begun as popular informal activities. By the turn of the 20th century, they were profitable businesses. Fans who couldn't attend an important boxing match crowded into barbershops and hotel lobbies. There they listened to the contest's highlights sent out by telegraph.

BASEBALL New rules changed baseball into a professional sport. In 1845 Alexander J. Cartwright, an amateur player, organized a club in New York City. He set down regulations using elements of an English sport called rounders. Five years later, 50 baseball clubs had sprung up in the United States. New York alone had 12 clubs in the mid-1860s.

In 1869 a professional team named the Cincinnati Red Stockings toured the country. Other clubs soon followed. This led to the formation of the National League in 1876 and the American League in 1900. In the first World Series, held in 1903, the Boston Pilgrims beat the Pittsburgh Pirates. African American baseball players were excluded from both leagues because of racial discrimination. They formed their own clubs and two leagues—the Negro National League and the Negro American League.

The Negro leagues were first formed in 1920.

Novelist Mark Twain called baseball "the very symbol . . . and visible expression of the drive and push and rush and struggle of the raging, tearing, booming nineteenth century." By the 1890s baseball had a published game schedule, official rules, and a standard-sized diamond.

The Spread of Mass Culture

As increasing numbers of Americans attended school and learned to read, their cultural opportunities expanded. More people had access to art galleries, libraries, books, and museums. Other advances promoted mass entertainment. New media technology led to the release of hundreds of motion pictures. Mass-production printing techniques generated thousands of books, magazines, and newspapers.

PROMOTING FINE ARTS By 1900 every large city had at least one art gallery. Some American artists, including Philadelphian Thomas Eakins, began to embrace realism. This was an artistic school that tried to portray life as it is really lived. Eakins had studied anatomy with medical students. He used exacting geometric perspective in his work. By the 1880s Eakins was also using photography to make realistic studies of people and animals.

Reading Check
Draw Conclusions
Why do you think sports were so popular among Americans at the turn of the century?

Document-Based Investigation Historical Source

Realism

This 1871 painting, *The Champion Single Sculls (Max Schmitt in a Single Scull),* by Thomas Eakins is an example of the realist movement. This artistic school focused on representing people and environments as they really are.

Analyze Historical Sources
What realistic details do you see portrayed in this painting?

In the early 20th century, the **Ashcan school** of American art was led by Eakins's student Robert Henri. He painted urban life and working people with gritty realism and no frills. However, both Eakins and the Ashcan school soon were challenged by the European development known as abstract art. This was a direction that most people found difficult to understand.

In many cities, people could walk from a new art gallery to a new public library. Libraries were sometimes called "the poor man's university." By 1900 free circulating libraries in America numbered in the thousands.

PHILOSOPHY As industrialization, mass immigration, and technological innovation pushed the boundaries of American society, scholars tried to make sense of it all. **Pragmatism** was a school of philosophical thought developed in the United States in the 1870s by Charles Peirce and William James. Its main goal was to help reconcile the tensions between science and morality and religion. Science was based on facts and observed evidence, but religion and morality were based on faith, feelings, and beliefs. For pragmatists, the value of a theory, idea, or innovation was based on its practical application. For example, the practical application of electricity is to provide light and power for homes and businesses. According to pragmatists, the purpose of thought was to promote action in solving problems. Ideas that were not practical should be rejected. Over time, pragmatic ideals would influence and be adopted by government officials. Their job was to develop and run programs that served citizens.

PERFORMING ARTS As Americans moved from rural areas to cities, they looked for new ways to spend their weekend and evening leisure time. Audiences could choose from a wide range of music, drama, circus, and the latest in entertainment—motion pictures.

Vaudeville theater performances included song, dance, juggling, and slapstick comedy. It sometimes featured chorus lines of female performers. In October 1899, actor Edwin Milton Royle wrote in *Scribner's Magazine* that vaudeville theater was "an American invention" that offered something to attract nearly everyone. However, in many towns, the biggest spectacle of all was often the annual visit of the Barnum & Bailey Circus. Its founders—P.T. Barnum and Anthony Bailey— advertised it as the "Greatest Show on Earth."

In time, motion pictures would become more widespread than live performances. A film could be shown as often as 16 times a day. This produced greater profits than a costly stage production. In 1888 Edison Company engineer William Dickson developed the first successful motion picture camera—the Kinetograph. The first films were one-reel, ten-minute sequences. They consisted mostly of vaudeville skits or faked newsreels. In 1903 the first modern film debuted in five-cent theaters called nickelodeons. It was an eight-minute silent feature called *The Great Train Robbery*. By 1907 an estimated 3,000 nickelodeons dotted the country.

Around the turn of the century, a new style of music also began to sweep the nation. Called ragtime, it was a blend of African American spirituals and European musical forms. Ragtime led later to jazz, rhythm and blues, and rock 'n' roll. Sheet music, and later phonograph records, helped these forms of popular music spread worldwide. Thomas Edison invented the phonograph

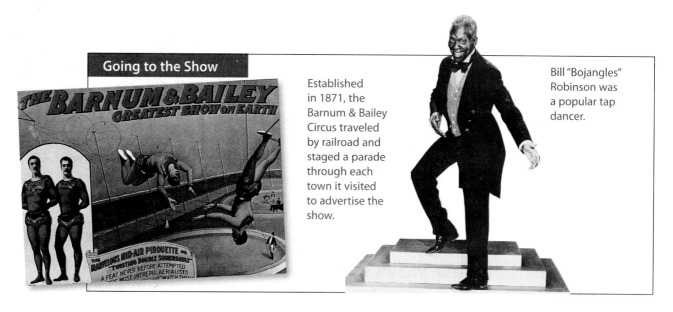

Established in 1871, the Barnum & Bailey Circus traveled by railroad and staged a parade through each town it visited to advertise the show.

Bill "Bojangles" Robinson was a popular tap dancer.

in 1877. It used a tinfoil cylinder and needle to record the human voice or other sounds. A second needle played back the recording. Edison often said that of all his inventions, the phonograph was his favorite. Though it took some time to catch on, phonograph production reached into the millions by the end of the 1920s.

POPULAR FICTION As literacy rates rose, scholars debated the role of literature in society. Some felt that literature should uplift America's literary tastes, which tended toward crime tales and western adventures.

Most people preferred to read light fiction. Such books sold for a mere ten cents. For this reason, they were called "dime novels." Dime novels typically told glorified adventure tales of the West and featured heroes like Edward Wheeler's Deadwood Dick. Wheeler published his first *Deadwood Dick* novel in 1877. In less than a decade, he produced over 30 more.

Some readers wanted a more realistic portrayal of American life. Successful writers of the time included Sarah Orne Jewett, Theodore Dreiser, Stephen Crane, Jack London, and Willa Cather. Most wrote about characters less polished than the upper-class men and women of Henry James's and Edith Wharton's novels. Samuel Langhorne Clemens was the novelist and humorist better known as **Mark Twain**. He inspired a host of other young authors when he declared his independence of "literature and all that bosh." Yet, some of his books have become classics of American literature. *The Adventures of Huckleberry Finn,* for example, remains famed for its description of life along the Mississippi River.

Although art galleries and libraries tried to raise cultural standards, many Americans had little interest in high culture. Others did not even have access to it. African Americans, for example, were excluded from visiting many museums and other white-controlled cultural institutions.

MASS-CIRCULATION NEWSPAPERS American newspapers, looking for ways to captivate readers' attention, began using sensational headlines. For example, to introduce its story about the horrors of the Johnstown, Pennsylvania flood of 1889, in which more than 2,000 people died, one newspaper used the headline "THE VALLEY OF DEATH."

Reading Check
Draw Conclusions
How did the *World*
and the *Journal*
attract readers?

Joseph Pulitzer, a Hungarian immigrant who had bought the *New York World* in 1883, pioneered popular innovations, such as a large Sunday edition, comics, sports coverage, and women's news. Pulitzer's paper emphasized "sin, sex, and sensation" in an attempt to outdo his main competitor, the wealthy **William Randolph Hearst**. Hearst had purchased the New York *Morning Journal* in 1895, and already owned the San Francisco Examiner. He tried to outdo Pulitzer by filling the *Journal* with exaggerated stories. These tales featured personal scandals, cruelty, hypnotism, and even an imaginary conquest of Mars. The escalation of their circulation war drove both papers to even more sensational news coverage. By 1898 the circulation of each paper had reached more than 1 million copies a day.

New Ways to Sell Goods

Along with enjoying new activities, Americans also changed the way they shopped. At the beginning of the 19th century, many Americans, especially in rural areas, produced their own goods or traded with neighbors for what they needed. Americans at the turn of the 20th century witnessed the beginnings of the shopping center, the development of department and chain stores, and the birth of modern advertising. These steps in the market revolution made it even easier for people around the country to buy goods.

URBAN SHOPPING Growing city populations made promising targets for enterprising merchants. The nation's earliest form of a shopping center opened in Cleveland, Ohio, in 1890. The glass-topped arcade contained four levels of jewelry, leather goods, and stationery shops. The arcade also provided band music on Sundays so that Cleveland residents could spend their Sunday afternoons strolling through the elegant environment and gazing at the window displays.

Retail shopping districts formed where public transportation could easily bring in shoppers. To anchor these retail shopping districts, ambitious merchants started something quite new: the modern department store.

THE DEPARTMENT STORE Marshall Field of Chicago first brought the department store concept to America. While working as a store clerk, Field found that paying close attention to women customers could increase sales considerably. In 1865 Field opened his own store, featuring several floors of specialized departments. Field's motto was "Give the lady what she wants." Field also pioneered the bargain basement, selling bargain goods that were "less expensive but reliable."

THE CHAIN STORE Department stores prided themselves on offering a variety of personal services. New chain stores—retail stores offering the same merchandise under the same ownership—sold goods for less by buying in quantity and limiting personal service. In the 1870s F. W. Woolworth found that if he offered an item at a very low price, "the consumer would purchase it on the spur of the moment" because "it was only a nickel." By 1911 the Woolworth chain boasted 596 stores and sold more than a million dollars in goods a week.

NOW	&	THEN

Catalog Shopping

Catalogs were a novelty when Sears and Montgomery Ward arrived on the scene. However, by the mid-1990s, more than 13 billion catalogs filled the mailboxes of Americans.

Today, the world of mail-order business is changing. After over 100 years of operation, Montgomery Ward filed for bankruptcy on December 28, 2000.

Online shopping is challenging mail-order commerce today. Online retail sales grew from $500 million in 1998 to nearly $305 billion in 2014. What do online shoppers order? Clothing, computer hardware, and electronics make up about 30 percent of online spending.

ADVERTISING Advertising exploded with consumerism. Expenditures for advertising were under $10 million a year in 1865 but increased to $95 million by 1900. Patent medicines took the largest number of advertising lines, followed by soaps and baking powders. In addition to newspapers and magazines, advertisers used creative methods to push products. Passengers riding the train between New York and Philadelphia in the 1870s might see signs for Dr. Drake's Plantation Bitters on barns, houses, billboards, and even rocks.

CATALOGS AND RFD Montgomery Ward and Sears Roebuck brought retail merchandise to small towns. Ward's catalog, launched in 1872, grew from a single sheet the first year to a booklet with ordering instructions in ten languages. Richard Sears started his company in 1886. Early Sears catalogs stated that the company received "hundreds of orders every day from young and old who never [before] sent away for goods." By 1910 about 10 million Americans shopped by mail. In 1896 the post office introduced a **rural free delivery (RFD)** system that brought packages directly to every home.

The turn of the 20th century saw prosperity that caused big changes in Americans' daily lives. At the same time, the nation's growing industrial sector faced problems that called for reform.

Reading Check
Summarize What innovations in retail methods changed the way urban and rural Americans shopped during this time?

Lesson 5 Assessment

1. **Organize Information** Use a spider diagram to organize information about mass culture.

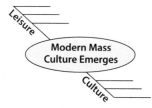

Leisure

Modern Mass Culture Emerges

Culture

Why is mass culture often described as a democratic phenomenon?

2. **Key Terms and People** For each key term or person in the lesson, write a sentence explaining its significance.

3. **Summarize** How did American methods of selling goods change at the turn of the 20th century?

Think About:
- how city people shopped
- how rural residents bought goods
- how merchants advertised their products

4. **Analyze Primary Sources** According to the cartoonist, where were the masters of the "new journalism," Pulitzer and Hearst, leading American journalists?

Module 4 Assessment

Key Terms and People

For each key term or person below, write a sentence explaining its significance to immigration and urbanization.

1. Ellis Island
2. Gentlemen's Agreement
3. Americanization movement
4. Jane Addams
5. patronage
6. Rutherford B. Hayes
7. Pendleton Civil Service Act
8. Louis Sullivan
9. Orville and Wilbur Wright
10. rural free delivery (RFD)

Main Ideas

Use your notes and the information in the module to answer the following questions.

The New Immigrants

1. What pull factors and push factors prompted people to move to the United States in the late 19th and early 20th centuries?
2. After 1890 from where did most of the European immigrants come?
3. How did immigrants deal with challenges they faced?
4. Why did nativists want the government to bar entry to Chinese immigrants?
5. What compromise did the governments of the United States and Japan reach on immigration?

The Challenges of Urbanization

6. How did mass immigration and migration help accelerate urbanization?
7. Why did many immigrants choose to settle in cities?
8. How did many farm workers in the South react to technological and economic changes in the late 1800s?

9. What problems did rapid growth pose for cities?
10. What solutions to urban problems did the settlement house movement propose?

Politics in the Gilded Age

11. Why did machine politics become common in big cities in the late 19th century?
12. Why did immigrants support political machines?
13. What government problems arose as a result of patronage?
14. Summarize the views of Grover Cleveland and Benjamin Harrison on tariffs.

New Technologies

15. How did new technologies make the building of skyscrapers practical?
16. How did new technologies promote urban growth around the turn of the century?
17. How did the ideas of George Washington Carver improve farming in the South?

The Dawn of Mass Culture

18. How did the mass production of bicycles change women's lives?
19. What factors contributed to the popularity of dime novels?
20. Ragtime was a blend of what two musical styles?

Critical Thinking

1. **Categorize** Use a diagram to list one result of and one reaction against (a) the increase in immigration and (b) the increase in machine politics.

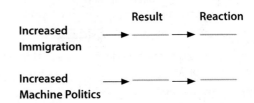

2. **Evaluate** The United States government set up two ports of entry to process immigrants and passed laws to limit immigration. What do you think of the effectiveness of the government's response to the mass immigration in the late 1800s? Use facts and details from the module to support your answer.

3. **Categorize** Nativism was a reaction to the massive influx of immigrants at the turn of the 20th century. What groups, ideas, laws, and agreements grew out of this movement?

4. **Analyze Effects** Many new immigrants resisted the Americanization movement, holding on to their traditions, beliefs, values, language, and customs. What impact do you think this has had on American culture and the arts?

5. **Evaluate** In the 1860s Horace Greeley—editor of the *New York Tribune*—remarked, "We cannot all live in the cities, yet nearly all seem determined to do so." Why do you think this was true at the end of the 19th century? Do you think it is still true? Why or why not?

6. **Contrast** The philosophy of Social Darwinism embraced the idea that society could gradually fix itself if left alone. Stronger people, businesses, and nations would prosper. Weaker ones would fail. How were the ideas of Social Darwinism different from the ideas of the Social Gospel movement?

7. **Synthesize** Many immigrants came to the United States in search of the American Dream—a better life for themselves and their families. What were some of the impediments and opportunities presented to immigrants in search of the American Dream?

8. **Compare** How were politicians like Boss Tweed similar to industrial magnates like Carnegie and Rockefeller?

9. **Draw Conclusions** How did changes in technology affect urban life at the turn of the 20th century?

10. **Analyze Effects** How did new technology and advances in agriculture become both a push- and pull-factor for the growth of cities?

11. **Develop Historical Perspective** In what way was pragmatism a reaction to rapid industrialization?

Engage with History

With what you have learned about the challenges faced by immigrants in the 19th century, consider the following question: What were the best solutions attempted by government and reformers in the 1800s? Create a pamphlet promoting one of the reforms, improvements, or government solutions you chose.

Focus on Writing

Imagine you are a senator and the Senate is about to vote on the Chinese Exclusion Act. Prepare a persuasive speech arguing against the new law. For the first part of your speech, explain why this law is unjust and unfair to the Chinese. For the second part, address the concerns of those in favor of the act and provide an alternate solution for the issues prompting it.

Collaborative Learning

Organize into small groups and discuss stories of immigration or the experiences of recent immigrants to the United States that you have heard or read about. With the group, create a multimedia presentation of these stories. Use pictures, text, and sound to represent the stories.

Ellis Island

For most European immigrants, Ellis Island was the first stop. Between 1892 and 1954, the immigration station processed over 12 million immigrants. These immigrants went through an inspection before they were allowed to enter the United States. Those with serious health problems were sent home, as were those who did not meet various legal requirements. Others were sent home because they exceeded immigration quotas.

However, if immigrants could clear these hurdles, they were free to enter the United States and begin their new lives.

Go online to explore some of the personal stories and recollections of immigrants who made the journey to America and passed through Ellis Island. You can find a wealth of information, video clips, primary sources, activities, and more through your online textbook.

1. Doctors examined immigrants as they headed upstairs to the Great Hall.
2. Lines were long, but the inspection often lasted only a few minutes.
3. Immigrants who passed the inspection could exchange money, send mail or telegrams, or buy train tickets.
4. Immigrants then met relatives or loved ones.
5. Immigrants who had to stay overnight were assigned to dormitories.

Go online to view these and other **HISTORY®** resources.

The Golden Door

Watch the video to see how and why immigrants traveled to the United States.

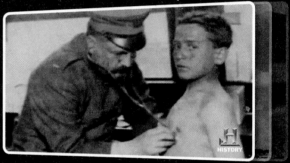

Examination

Watch the video to see the physical examination that immigrants experienced at Ellis Island.

Quotas

Watch the video to see how immigration quotas affected immigrants trying to come to the United States.

Module 5

Progressivism

Essential Question
Was the progressive movement successful?

About the Photograph: In the late 1800s women began to form organizations to push for equal rights. This women's suffrage parade took place in New York City in 1912.

In this module you will explore the progressive movement that grew during the late 1800s and learn how individuals and groups worked for political and social changes.

▶ Explore ONLINE!

VIDEOS, including...
- Henry Ford's Motor Company
- W.E.B. DuBois
- Teddy Roosevelt vs. Big Industry
- Teddy Roosevelt's Acts and Legacy
- T.R. and the Bull Moose Party
- Woodrow Wilson

 Document-Based Investigations

 Graphic Organizers

 Interactive Games

 Image Compare: Ford Factory Workers

 Image with Text Slider: Suffrage Victories

SS.912.A.1.6 Use case studies to explore social, political, legal, and economic relationships in history. **SS.912.A.1.7** Describe various sociocultural aspects of American life including arts, artifacts, literature, education, and publications. **SS.912.A.2.4** Distinguish the freedoms guaranteed to African Americans and other groups with the 13th, 14th, and 15th Amendments to the Constitution. **SS.912.A.2.5** Assess how Jim Crow Laws influenced life for African Americans and other racial/ethnic minority groups. **SS.912.A.2.6** Compare the effects of the Black Codes and the Nadir on freed people, and analyze the sharecropping system and debt peonage as practiced in the United States. **SS.912.A.3.8** Examine the importance of social change and reform in the late 19th and early 20th centuries. **SS.912.A.3.10** Review different economic and philosophic ideologies. **SS.912.A.3.11** Analyze the impact of political machines in United States cities in the late 19th and early 20th centuries. **SS.912.A.3.12** Compare how different nongovernmental organizations and progressives worked to shape public policy, restore economic opportunities, and correct injustices in American life. **SS.912.A.3.13** Examine key events and peoples in Florida history as they relate to United States history. **SS.912.A.5.7** Examine the freedom movements that advocated civil rights for African Americans, Latinos, Asians, and women. **SS.912.A.5.8** Compare the views of Booker T. Washington, W.E.B. DuBois, and Marcus Garvey relating to the African American experience. **SS.912.A.5.10** Analyze support for and resistance to civil rights for women, African Americans, Native Americans, and other minorities. **SS.912.A.7.8** Analyze significant Supreme Court decisions relating to integration, busing, affirmative action, the rights of the accused, and reproductive rights. **SS.912.G.2.1** Identify the physical characteristics and the human characteristics that define and differentiate regions. **SS.912.H.1.1** Relate works in the arts of varying styles and genre according to the periods in which they were created. **SS.912.H.1.5** Examine artistic response to social issues and new ideas in various cultures. **HE.912.C.2.4** Evaluate how public health policies and government regulations can influence health promotion and disease prevention.

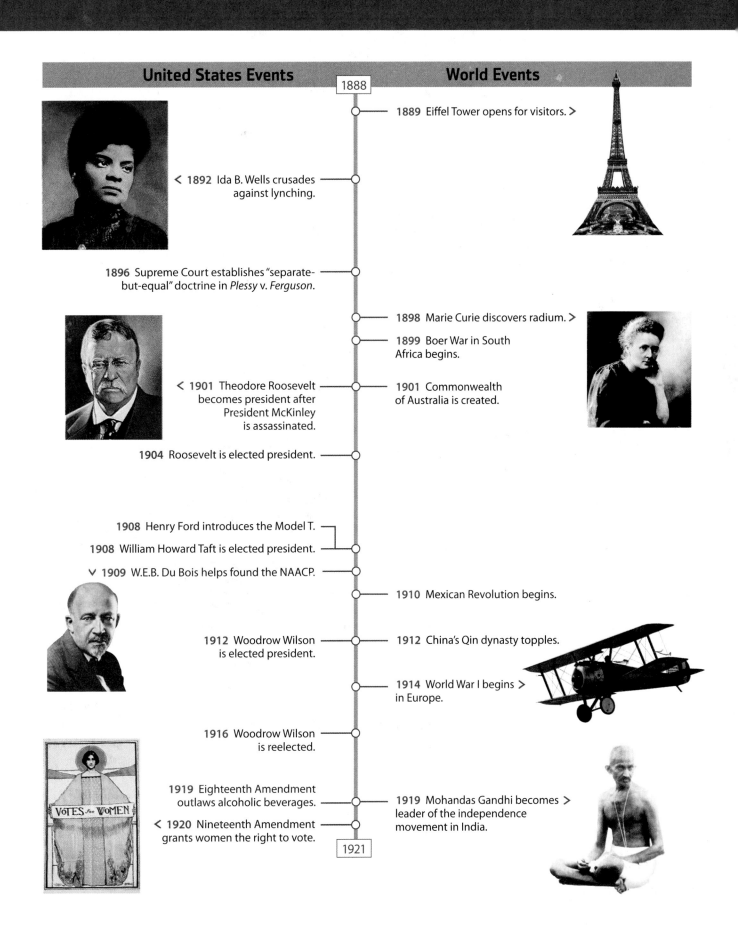

United States Events

1888

1921

< 1892 Ida B. Wells crusades against lynching.

1896 Supreme Court establishes "separate-but-equal" doctrine in *Plessy* v. *Ferguson*.

< 1901 Theodore Roosevelt becomes president after President McKinley is assassinated.

1904 Roosevelt is elected president.

1908 Henry Ford introduces the Model T.

1908 William Howard Taft is elected president.

∨ 1909 W.E.B. Du Bois helps found the NAACP.

1912 Woodrow Wilson is elected president.

1916 Woodrow Wilson is reelected.

1919 Eighteenth Amendment outlaws alcoholic beverages.

< 1920 Nineteenth Amendment grants women the right to vote.

World Events

1889 Eiffel Tower opens for visitors. >

1898 Marie Curie discovers radium. >

1899 Boer War in South Africa begins.

1901 Commonwealth of Australia is created.

1910 Mexican Revolution begins.

1912 China's Qin dynasty topples.

1914 World War I begins > in Europe.

1919 Mohandas Gandhi becomes > leader of the independence movement in India.

VOTES for WOMEN

The Origins of Progressivism

The Big Idea
Political, economic, and social change in late 19th-century America led to broad progressive reforms.

Why It Matters Now
Progressive reforms in areas such as labor and voting rights reinforced democratic principles that continue to exist today.

Key Terms and People
progressive movement

Florence Kelley

prohibition

muckraker

scientific management

Henry Ford

Robert M. La Follette

initiative

referendum

recall

Seventeenth Amendment

SS.912.A.1.2; SS.912.A.1.4; SS.912.A.1.7; SS.912.A.3.8; SS.912.A.3.10; SS.912.A.3.11; SS.912.A.3.12; SS.912.H.1.5; HE.912.C.2.4; LAFS.1112.RH.1.1; LAFS.1112.RH.1.2; LAFS.1112.RH.4.10

One American's Story

Camella Teoli was just 12 years old when she began working in a Lawrence, Massachusetts, textile mill to help support her family. Soon after she started, a machine used for twisting cotton into thread tore off part of her scalp. The young Italian immigrant spent seven months in the hospital and was scarred for life.

Three years later 20,000 Lawrence mill workers went on strike for higher wages. Camella was selected to testify before a congressional committee investigating labor conditions. These conditions included workplace safety and underage workers. When asked why she had gone on strike, Camella answered simply, "Because I didn't get enough to eat at home." She explained how she had gone to work before reaching the legal age of 14.

Mill workers on strike in 1912 in Lawrence, Massachusetts

"I used to go to school, and then a man came up to my house and asked my father why I didn't go to work, so my father says I don't know whether she is 13 or 14 years old. So, the man say: You give me $4 and I will make the papers come from the old country [Italy] saying [that] you are 14. So, my father gave him the $4, and in one month came the papers that I was 14. I went to work, and about two weeks [later] got hurt in my head."

—Camella Teoli, from testimony at congressional hearings, March 1912

After nine weeks of striking, the mill workers won the sympathy of the nation as well as pay raises. Stories like Camella's set off a national investigation of labor conditions. Reformers organized to address the problems of industrialization.

Four Goals of Progressivism

At the dawn of the new century, middle-class reformers addressed many of the problems that had contributed to the social upheavals of the 1890s. Journalists and writers exposed the unsafe conditions often faced by factory workers, including women and children. Intellectuals questioned the dominant role of large corporations in American society. Political reformers struggled to make government more responsive to the people. Together, these reform efforts formed the **progressive movement**. This movement aimed to restore economic opportunities and correct injustices in American life.

Reformers never completely agreed on the problems or solutions. However, each of their progressive efforts shared at least one of the following goals:

- protecting social welfare
- promoting moral improvement
- creating economic reform
- fostering efficiency

PROTECTING SOCIAL WELFARE Many social welfare reformers worked to soften some of the harsh conditions of industrialization. The Social Gospel and settlement house movements of the late 1800s aimed to help the poor through community centers, churches, and social services. These movements continued during the Progressive Era and inspired more reform activities.

The Young Men's Christian Association (YMCA), for example, opened libraries, sponsored classes, and built swimming pools and handball courts. The Salvation Army fed poor people in soup kitchens and cared for children in nurseries. It also sent "slum brigades" to instruct poor immigrants in middle-class values of hard work and temperance.

Vocabulary
temperance
refraining from
alcohol consumption

In addition, many women were inspired by the settlement houses to take action. **Florence Kelley** became an advocate for improving the lives of women and children. She helped to win passage of the Illinois Factory Act in 1893. The act, which prohibited child labor and limited women's working hours, soon became a model for other states. That same year, Kelley was appointed chief inspector of factories for Illinois.

– BIOGRAPHY –

Florence Kelley (1859–1932)

Florence Kelley was the daughter of an antislavery Republican congressman from Pennsylvania. She became a social reformer who sympathized with the powerless, especially working women and children. Kelley pushed the government to solve America's social problems.

In 1899 Kelley became general secretary of the National Consumers' League, where she lobbied to improve factory conditions. "Why," Kelley asked while campaigning for a federal child labor law, "are seals, bears, reindeer, fish, wild game in the national parks, buffalo, [and] migratory birds all found suitable for federal protection, but not children?"

PROMOTING MORAL IMPROVEMENT Other reformers felt that morality, not the workplace, held the key to improving the lives of poor people. These reformers wanted immigrants and poor city dwellers to uplift themselves by improving their personal behavior. **Prohibition**, the banning of alcoholic beverages, was one such program.

Prohibitionist groups feared that alcohol was undermining American morals. Founded in Cleveland in 1874, the Woman's Christian Temperance Union (WCTU) spearheaded the crusade for prohibition. Members advanced their cause by entering saloons, singing, praying, and urging saloonkeepers to stop selling alcohol. As momentum grew, Frances Willard transformed the union from a small midwestern religious group in 1879 to a national organization. Boasting 245,000 members by 1911, the WCTU became the largest women's group in the nation's history.

WCTU members followed Willard's "do everything" slogan. They began opening kindergartens for immigrants, visiting inmates in prisons and asylums, and working for suffrage. The WCTU reform activities provided women with expanded public roles, which they used to justify giving women voting rights.

Sometimes efforts at prohibition led to trouble with immigrant groups. Quietly founded by progressive women in 1895, the Anti-Saloon League called itself "the Church in action against the saloon." Early temperance efforts had asked individuals to change their ways. In contrast, the Anti-Saloon League worked to pass laws to force people to change and to punish those who drank. As members sought to close saloons to cure society's problems, tensions arose between them and many immigrants. Immigrant customs often included the consumption of alcohol. Additionally, saloons filled a number of roles within the immigrant community such as cashing paychecks and serving meals.

The Anti-Saloon League endorsed politicians of any party who opposed "Demon Rum." It also organized statewide referendums to ban alcohol. Between 1900 and 1917 voters in nearly half of the states prohibited the sale, production, and use of alcohol. Individual towns, city wards, and rural areas also voted themselves "dry."

CREATING ECONOMIC REFORM As moral reformers sought to change behavior, a severe economic panic in 1893 prompted some Americans to question the capitalist economic system. As a result, some Americans, especially workers, embraced socialism. Labor leader Eugene V. Debs helped organize the American Socialist Party in 1901. He commented on the uneven balance among big business, government, and ordinary people under free-market capitalism.

> *"Competition was natural enough at one time, but do you think you are competing today? Many of you think you are competing. Against whom? Against [oil magnate John D.] Rockefeller? About as I would if I had a wheelbarrow and competed with the Santa Fe [railroad] from here to Kansas City."*

—Eugene V. Debs, from *Debs: His Life, Writings and Speeches*

Though most Progressives distanced themselves from socialism, they saw the truth of many of Debs's criticisms. Big business often received favorable treatment from government officials and politicians. Business could use its economic power to limit competition.

Journalists who wrote about the corrupt side of business and public life in mass circulation magazines during the early 20th century became known as **muckrakers** (mŭk′rāk´r). (The term refers to John Bunyan's *Pilgrim's Progress*. In this book, a character is so busy using a rake to clean up the muck of this world that he does not raise his eyes to heaven.) In her "History of the Standard Oil Company," a monthly serial in *McClure's Magazine,* writer Ida M. Tarbell described the company's cutthroat methods of eliminating competition. "Mr. Rockefeller has systematically played with loaded dice," Tarbell charged, "and it is doubtful if there has been a time since 1872 when he has run a race with a competitor and started fair." Other muckraking journalists worked to expose dangerous working conditions. These conditions included the use of child labor, unsafe products, and political corruption.

FOSTERING EFFICIENCY Many progressive leaders put their faith in experts and scientific principles to make society and the workplace more efficient. An Oregon law limited women factory and laundry workers to a ten-hour workday. When lawyer Louis D. Brandeis defended this law, he paid little attention to legal argument. Instead, he focused on data produced by social scientists showing the high costs of long working hours for both the individual and society. This type of argument—the "Brandeis brief"—would become a model for later reform litigation.

Within industry, Frederick Winslow Taylor began using time and motion studies to improve efficiency by breaking manufacturing tasks into simpler parts. "Taylorism" became a management fad. Industry reformers applied these **scientific management** studies to see just how quickly each task could be performed.

One of the champions of efficiency in the workplace was automobile pioneer Henry Ford. In the early 1900s **Henry Ford** revolutionized manufacturing with the production and sale of the Ford Model T automobile. By making his cars simple and identical, Ford was able to introduce mass production through a large-scale assembly line. In this system, the product moved along a conveyor belt as each worker performed one specific job. This new and efficient way of manufacturing automobiles made them more affordable for the general public. What was once viewed as a luxury for the rich soon became the main form of transportation. As Ford stated, "everybody will be able to afford [a car], and about everyone will have one." Cars flew out of Ford's manufacturing plant. His company was soon the largest automobile manufacturer in the world.

However, not all workers could work at the same rate. The introduction of the assembly lines did speed up production, but the system required people to work like machines. This caused a high worker

Workers at the Ford flywheel factory cope with the demanding pace of the assembly line to earn five dollars a day—a good wage in 1914.

The Muckrakers

The muckraking movement spilled over from journalism as writers made use of the greater dramatic effects of fiction to bring about reform. Ida M. Tarbell's "The History of the Standard Oil Company" exposed the ruthlessness of John D. Rockefeller and added force to the trustbusting reforms of the early 20th century. Lincoln Steffens is usually named as a leading figure of the muckraking movement. He published exposés of business and government corruption in various magazines. These articles were then collected in two books: *The Shame of the Cities* and *The Struggle for Self-Government.*

IDA M. TARBELL

Mr. Hanna had been refining since July, 1869. . . . Some time in February, 1872, the Standard Oil Company asked [for] an interview with him and his associates. They wanted to buy his works, they said. "But we don't want to sell," objected Mr. Hanna. "You can never make any more money, in my judgment," said Mr. Rockefeller. "You can't compete with the Standard. We have all the large refineries now. If you refuse to sell, it will end in your being crushed." Hanna and Baslington were not satisfied. They went to see . . . General Devereux, manager of the Lake Shore road. They were told that the Standard had special rates; that it was useless to try to compete with them. General Devereux explained to the gentlemen that the privileges granted the Standard were the legitimate and necessary advantage of the larger shipper over the smaller. . . . General Devereux says they "recognised the propriety" of his excuse. They certainly recognised its authority. They say that they were satisfied they could no longer get rates to and from Cleveland which would enable them to live, and "reluctantly" sold out. It must have been reluctantly, for they had paid $75,000 for their works, and had made thirty per cent. a year on an average on their investment, and the Standard appraiser allowed them $45,000.

—from "The History of the Standard Oil Company" (1904)

LINCOLN STEFFENS

The police are forbidden by law to stand within thirty feet of the polls, but they are at the box and they are there to see that the [Republican political] machine's orders are obeyed and that repeaters whom they help to furnish are permitted to vote without "intimidation" on the names they, the police, have supplied. The editor of an anti-machine paper who was looking about for himself once told me that a ward leader who knew him well asked him into a polling place. "I'll show you how it's done," he said, and he had the repeaters go round and round voting again and again on the names handed them on slips. . . . The business proceeds with very few hitches; there is more jesting than fighting. Violence in the past has had its effect; and is not often necessary nowadays, but if it is needed the police are there to apply it.

—from *The Shame of the Cities* (1904)

Analyze American Literature

State the main idea of each of these selections. What role do details play in making the passages convincing?

turnover, often due to injuries suffered by fatigued workers. To keep automobile workers happy and to prevent strikes, Henry Ford reduced the workday to eight hours and paid workers five dollars a day. This incentive attracted thousands of workers, but they exhausted themselves. As one homemaker complained in a letter to Ford in 1914, "That $5 is a blessing—a bigger one than you know but oh they earn it."

Such efforts at improving efficiency, an important part of progressivism, targeted not only industry but government as well.

Cleaning Up Local Government

Cities faced some of the most obvious social problems of the new industrial age. In many large cities, political bosses rewarded their supporters with jobs and kickbacks. Bosses also openly bought votes with favors and bribes. Efforts to reform city politics stemmed in part from the desire to make government more efficient and more responsive. But those efforts also grew from distrust of immigrants' participation in politics.

REFORMING LOCAL GOVERNMENT Natural disasters sometimes played an important role in prompting reform of city governments. In 1900 a hurricane and tidal wave almost demolished Galveston, Texas. The politicians on the city council botched the huge relief and rebuilding job. The Texas legislature then appointed a five-member commission of experts to take over. Each expert took charge of a different city department, and soon Galveston was rebuilt. This success prompted the city to adopt the commission idea as a form of government. By 1917, 500 cities had followed Galveston's example.

A flood in Dayton, Ohio, in 1913 led to the widespread adoption of the council-manager form of government. Staunton, Virginia, had already pioneered this system, in which people elected a city council to make laws. The council, in turn, appointed a manager, typically a person with training and experience in public administration, to run the city's departments. By 1925 managers were administering nearly 250 cities.

REFORM MAYORS In some cities, mayors such as Hazen Pingree of Detroit, Michigan (1890–1897), and Tom Johnson of Cleveland, Ohio (1901–1909), introduced progressive reforms without changing how their city governments were organized.

Concentrating on economics, Pingree instituted a fairer tax structure and lowered fares for public transportation. He also rooted out corruption and set up a system of work relief for the unemployed. Detroit city workers built schools, parks, and a municipal lighting plant.

Johnson was only one of 19 socialist mayors who worked to institute progressive reforms in America's cities. In general, these mayors focused on dismissing corrupt and greedy private owners of utilities and converting the utilities to publicly owned enterprises. Johnson believed that citizens should play a more active role in city government. He held meetings in a large circus tent and invited them to question officials about how the city was managed.

Reading Check
Contrast Contrast the goals of scientific management with other progressive reforms.

Reading Check
Summarize How did city government change during the Progressive Era?

Reform at the State Level

Local reforms coincided with progressive efforts at the state level. Spurred by progressive governors, many states passed laws to regulate railroads, mines, mills, telephone companies, and other large businesses.

REFORM GOVERNORS Under the progressive Republican leadership of **Robert M. La Follette**, Wisconsin led the way in regulating big business. "Fighting Bob" La Follette served three terms as governor before he entered the U.S. Senate in 1906. Under his leadership, Wisconsin became a laboratory for progressivism. He developed a program called the Wisconsin Idea to recruit the help of professors at the University of Wisconsin in writing laws and providing expert advice. All of La Follette's reforms and progressive experiments revolved around the idea that government should be controlled by voters rather than business leaders. He explained that he did not mean to "smash corporations, but merely to drive them out of politics, and then to treat them exactly the same as other people are treated."

James S. Hogg

La Follette's major target was the railroad industry. He taxed railroad property at the same rate as other business property. He also set up a commission to regulate rates and forbade railroads to issue free passes to state officials. Other reform governors who attacked big business interests included Charles B. Aycock of North Carolina and James S. Hogg of Texas.

PROTECTING WORKING CHILDREN As the number of child workers rose dramatically, reformers worked to protect workers and to end child labor. Businesses hired children because they performed unskilled jobs for lower wages. Children's small hands also made them more adept at handling small parts and tools. Immigrants and rural migrants often sent their children to work because they viewed their children as part of the family economy. Wages were usually so low for adults that every family member needed to work.

In industrial settings, however, children were more prone to accidents caused by fatigue. Many developed serious health problems and suffered from stunted growth.

Formed in 1904, the National Child Labor Committee sent investigators to gather evidence of children working in harsh conditions. They then organized exhibitions with photographs and statistics to dramatize the children's plight. Labor union members joined in this effort. They argued that child labor lowered wages for all workers. These groups pressured national politicians to pass the Keating-Owen Act in 1916. The act prohibited the transportation across state lines of goods produced with child labor.

Two years later the Supreme Court declared the act unconstitutional due to interference with states' rights to regulate labor. However, muckrakers, unions, and other reformers did ultimately succeed in convincing nearly every state to enact legislation that banned child labor and set maximum hours. By removing children from the workforce, Progressives were able to place them in public schools. By 1900 more than half the states had laws requiring children to attend school. By 1918 all states had enacted compulsory school attendance laws.

Lewis Hine

In 1908 Lewis Hine quit his teaching job to document child labor practices. He believed in the power of photography to move people to action. His compelling images of exploitation—such as these spindle boys and girls who were forced to climb atop moving machinery to replace parts—helped to convince the public of the need for child labor regulations.

Hine devised a host of clever tactics to gain access to his subjects. He learned shop managers' schedules and arrived during their lunch breaks. While talking casually with the children, he secretly scribbled notes on paper hidden in his pocket.

Analyze Historical Sources

1. What elements of this photograph do you find most striking?

2. Why do you think Hine was a successful photographer?

EFFORTS TO LIMIT WORKING HOURS The Supreme Court sometimes took a more sympathetic view of the plight of workers. In the 1908 case of *Muller* v. *Oregon,* Louis D. Brandeis argued that poor working women were much more economically insecure than large corporations. Asserting that women required the state's protection against powerful employers, Brandeis convinced the Court to uphold an Oregon law limiting women to a ten-hour workday. Other states responded by enacting or strengthening laws to reduce women's hours of work. A similar Brandeis brief in *Bunting* v. *Oregon* in 1917 persuaded the Court to uphold a ten-hour workday for men.

Progressives also succeeded in winning workers' compensation to aid the families of workers who were hurt or killed on the job. Beginning with Maryland in 1902, more states passed laws requiring employers to pay benefits in death cases.

REFORMING ELECTIONS In some cases, ordinary citizens won state reforms. William S. U'Ren prompted his state of Oregon to adopt the secret ballot (also called the Australian ballot), the initiative, the referendum, and the recall. These reforms were also a key part of the Wisconsin Idea to give citizens a more direct say in government.

By the late 1880s each party produced their own ballots for elections. In most states the job of printing and distributing these ballots fell to political bosses in each ward. This made it nearly impossible for voters to cast secret ballots. It also made it much easier for political bosses to manipulate elections. The presidential election of 1888 helped focus the public's attention on vote rigging and other corrupt practices. Muckraking journalists, aided by Democrats, exposed the Republican Party's bold practice of openly buying votes in Indiana. This practice handed the presidency to Benjamin Harrison.

By the next presidential election in 1892, all states had adopted a secret ballot to help stop voter corruption.

The initiative and referendum gave citizens the power to create laws. Citizens could petition to place an **initiative**—a bill originated by the people rather than lawmakers—on the ballot. Then voters accepted or rejected the initiative by **referendum**, a vote on the initiative. The **recall** enabled voters to remove public officials from elected positions by forcing them to face another election before the end of their term if enough voters asked for it. By 1920, 20 states had adopted at least one of these procedures.

In 1899 Minnesota passed the first mandatory statewide primary system. This enabled voters, instead of political machines, to choose candidates for public office through a special popular election. About two-thirds of the states had adopted some form of direct primary by 1915.

DIRECT ELECTION OF SENATORS It was the success of the direct primary that paved the way for the **Seventeenth Amendment** to the Constitution. Before 1913 each state's legislature had chosen its own United States senators. This practice put even more power in the hands of party bosses and wealthy heads of corporations. To force senators to be more responsive to the public, Progressives pushed for the popular election of senators. Popular election would also limit the power of state political machines. At first, the Senate refused to go along with the idea. Gradually more and more states began allowing voters to nominate senatorial candidates in direct primaries. As a result, Congress approved the Seventeenth Amendment in 1912. Its ratification in 1913 made direct election of senators the law of the land.

Government reform—including efforts to give Americans more of a voice in electing their legislators and creating laws—drew increased numbers of women into public life. It also focused renewed attention on the issue of woman suffrage.

Reading Check
Summarize
Summarize the impact of the direct election of senators.

Lesson 1 Assessment

1. **Organize Information** Fill in a web with examples of organizations that worked for economic, moral, political, and social welfare reform.

Which group was most successful and why?

2. **Key Terms and People** For each key term or person in the lesson, write a sentence explaining its significance.

3. **Form Generalizations** In what ways might Illinois, Wisconsin, and Oregon all be considered trailblazers in progressive reform? Support your answers.

   Think About:
   - legislative and electoral reforms at the state level
   - the leadership of William U'Ren and Robert La Follette
   - Florence Kelley's appointment as chief inspector of factories for Illinois

4. **Analyze Primary Sources** This cartoon shows Carry Nation inside a saloon that she has attacked. Do you think the cartoonist had a favorable or unfavorable opinion of this prohibitionist? Explain.

★ Education Reform

SS.912.A.1.2; SS.912.A.1.4; SS.912.A.1.7; SS.912.A.2.5; SS.912.A.3.8; SS.912.A.3.10; SS.912.A.3.12; SS.912.A.3.13; SS.912.A.5.7; SS.912.A.5.8; SS.912.A.5.10; LAFS.1112.RH.1.2; LAFS.1112.RH.4.10; MAFS.K12.MP.1.1; MAFS.K12.MP.3.1; MAFS.K12.MP.5.1

The Big Idea

Reforms in public education led to a rise in national literacy and the promotion of public education.

Why It Matters Now

The public education system is a foundation of the democratic ideals of American society.

Key Terms and People

Booker T. Washington

Tuskegee Normal and Industrial Institute

W.E.B. Du Bois

Niagara Movement

One American's Story

William Torrey Harris was an educational reformer who saw the public schools as a great instrument "to lift all classes of people into . . . civilized life." As U.S. commissioner of education from 1889 to 1906, Harris promoted the ideas of great educators like Horace Mann and John Dewey. Harris advanced the belief that schools exist for the children and not the teachers. Schools, according to Harris, should properly prepare students for full participation in community life.

"Every [educational] method must . . . be looked at from two points of view: first, its capacity to secure the development of rationality or of the true adjustment of the individual to the social whole; and, second, its capacity to strengthen the individuality of

Compulsory attendance laws, though slow to be enforced, helped fill classrooms at the turn of the 20th century.

the pupil and avoid the danger of obliterating the personality of the child by securing blind obedience in place of intelligent cooperation, and by mechanical memorizing in place of rational insight."

—William Torrey Harris, quoted in *Public Schools and Moral Education*

Many other middle-class reformers agreed with Harris. They viewed the public schools as training grounds for employment and citizenship. People believed that economic development depended on scientific and technological knowledge. As a result, they viewed education as a key to greater security and social status. Others saw the public schools as the best opportunity to assimilate immigrants entering American society. Most people also believed that public education was necessary for a stable and prosperous democratic nation.

Expanding Public Education

Although most states had established public schools by the Civil War, many school-age children still received no formal schooling. The majority of students who went to school left within four years. Few went to high school. However, as the United States moved from an agricultural economy to a more modern industrial economy, formal education grew in importance.

SCHOOLS FOR CHILDREN Between 1865 and 1895 states passed laws requiring 12 to 16 weeks annually of school attendance by students between the ages of 8 and 14. The curriculum emphasized reading, writing, and arithmetic. However, the emphasis on rote memorization and the uneven quality of teachers drew criticism. Strict rules and physical punishment made many students miserable.

In spite of such problems, children began attending school at a younger age. Kindergartens had been created outside the public school system to offer childcare for working mothers. Kindergartens became increasingly popular. Their numbers surged from 200 in 1880 to 3,000 in 1900. Under the guidance of William Torrey Harris, public school systems began to add kindergartens to their programs.

Although public education grew, opportunities differed sharply for white and black students. In 1880 about 62 percent of white children attended elementary school. This compared to about 34 percent of African American children. Not until the 1940s would public school education become available to the majority of black children living in the South.

THE GROWTH OF HIGH SCHOOLS In the new industrial age, the economy demanded advanced technical and managerial skills. Moreover, business leaders like Andrew Carnegie pointed out that keeping workers loyal to capitalism required society to "provide ladders upon which the aspiring can rise."

By early 1900 more than half a million students attended high school. The curriculum expanded to include courses in science, civics, and social studies.

Document-Based Investigation Historical Source

Early Immigrant Education

By 1895 most states passed laws requiring children under age 14 to attend school. One 13-year-old boy explained to a Chicago school inspector why he hid in a warehouse basement instead of going to school.

> "They hits ye if yer don't learn, and they hits ye if ye whisper, and they hits ye if ye have string in yer pocket, and they hits ye if yer seat squeaks, and they hits ye if ye don't stan' up in time, and they hits ye if yer late, and they hits ye if ye ferget the page."
>
> —anonymous schoolboy, quoted in *The One Best System*

Analyze Historical Sources
What reason does the Chicago schoolboy give for not wanting to attend school?

Expanding Education/Increasing Literacy

Year	Students Enrolled	Literacy in English (% of Population age 10 and over)
1871	7.6 million	80%
1880	9.9 million	83%
1890	12.7 million	87%
1900	15.5 million	89%
1910	17.8 million	92%
1920	21.6 million	94%

= 1,000,000 students

Sources: *Statistical Abstract of the United States, 1921; Historical Statistics of the United States*

Interpret Graphs
1. Which year reported the greatest gain in the literacy rate?
2. What do you think were the implications on society of a more literate population?

New vocational courses in drafting, carpentry, and mechanics prepared male graduates for industrial jobs. Courses in stenography and bookkeeping prepared female graduates for office work.

RACIAL DISCRIMINATION African Americans were mostly excluded from public secondary education. In 1890 fewer than 1 percent of black teenagers attended high school. More than two-thirds of these students went to private schools, which received no government financial support. By 1910 about 3 percent of African Americans between the ages of 15 and 19 attended high school. However, a majority of these students still attended private schools.

Mary McLeod Bethune started one such private school in Daytona Beach, Florida. With less than $20 in her budget, Bethune rented a house and built desks. She opened a school for African American girls. Through her work in education and civil rights, Bethune attracted help from wealthy donors, such as John D. Rockefeller and Eleanor Roosevelt. In time, Bethune's school grew and merged with a local African American boys school to become Bethune-Cookman College.

EDUCATION FOR IMMIGRANTS Unlike African Americans, immigrants were encouraged to go to school. Nearly 10 million European immigrants settled in the United States between 1860 and 1890. Many were Jewish people fleeing poverty and systematic oppression in eastern Europe. Most immigrants sent their children to America's free public schools, where they quickly became "Americanized." Russian Jewish immigrant Mary Antin recalled the large numbers of non-English-speaking immigrant children. By the end of the school year, they could recite "patriotic verses in honor of George Washington and Abraham Lincoln . . . with plenty of enthusiasm."

Technology and Schools

In 1922 Thomas Edison predicted that motion pictures would eventually replace textbooks. More recently, it has been predicted that online learning will replace traditional classrooms and texts. Today, many students are able to read and interact with course materials on the Internet, using computers, tablets, and cell phones. MOOCs, or massive open online courses, allow students in many locations to participate in the same class. Students are also using the Internet to access and share scientific data and to communicate with peers around the world. Technology has begun to reshape traditional classrooms as well. Teachers are using electronic interactive whiteboards to help them lead and record presentations and discussions.

Vocabulary
parochial school a school supported by a church parish

Reading Check
Draw Conclusions
Why did American children begin attending school at a younger age?

Some people resented the suppression of their native languages in favor of English. Catholics were concerned that many public school systems had mandatory readings from the (Protestant) King James Version of the Bible. Catholic communities often set up parochial schools to give their children a Catholic education.

Thousands of adult immigrants attended night school to learn English and to qualify for American citizenship. Employers often offered daytime programs to Americanize their workers. At his Model T plant in Highland Park, Michigan, Henry Ford established a "Sociology Department." He believed "men of many nations must be taught American ways, the English language, and the right way to live." Ford's ideas were not universally accepted. Some labor activists argued that Ford's educational goals sought to weaken the trade union movement by teaching workers not to confront management.

Expanding Higher Education

Although the number of students attending high school had increased by the turn of the century, only a minority of Americans had high school diplomas. At the same time, an even smaller minority—only 2.3 percent—of America's young people attended colleges and universities.

CHANGES IN UNIVERSITIES Between 1880 and 1920 college enrollments more than quadrupled. And colleges instituted major changes in curricula and admission policies. Industrial development changed the nation's educational needs. The research university emerged—offering courses in modern languages, the physical sciences, and the new disciplines of psychology and sociology. Professional schools in law and medicine were established. Some state universities began to admit students by using the high school diploma as the entrance requirement. Other colleges and universities required entrance exams to help them identify the most qualified students.

HIGHER EDUCATION FOR AFRICAN AMERICANS After the Civil War, thousands of freed African Americans pursued higher education, despite their exclusion from white institutions. With the help of the Freedmen's Bureau and other groups, blacks founded Howard, Atlanta, and Fisk

Students at Hampton Institute in Virginia learn dressmaking.

universities. These schools opened between 1865 and 1868. Private donors could not, however, financially support enough black college graduates to meet the needs of the segregated communities. By 1900, out of about 9 million African Americans, only 3,880 attended colleges or professional schools.

The prominent African American educator, **Booker T. Washington**, believed that racism would end once blacks acquired useful labor skills and proved their economic value to society. Washington, who was born enslaved, graduated from Virginia's Hampton Institute. By 1881 he headed the **Tuskegee Normal and Industrial Institute**, now called Tuskegee University, in Alabama. Tuskegee aimed to equip African Americans with teaching diplomas and useful skills in agricultural, domestic, or mechanical work. "No race," Washington said, "can prosper till it learns that there is as much dignity in tilling a field as in writing a poem."

W.E.B. Du Bois, the first African American to receive a doctorate from Harvard, strongly disagreed with Washington's gradual approach. In 1905 Du Bois founded the **Niagara Movement**. This group insisted that blacks should seek a liberal arts education so that the African American community would have well-educated leaders.

The Niagara Movement was comprised of 29 black intellectuals. They met secretly in 1905 to compose a civil rights manifesto. Du Bois proposed that a group of educated blacks attempt to achieve immediate inclusion into mainstream American life. He wanted the group to be the most "talented tenth" of the community. "We are Americans, not only by birth and by citizenship," Du Bois argued, "but by our political ideals. . . . And the greatest of those ideals is that ALL MEN ARE CREATED EQUAL."

By the turn of the 20th century, millions of people received the education they needed to cope with a rapidly changing world. At the same time, however, racial discrimination remained a thorn in the flesh of American society.

Reading Check
Synthesize Describe the state of higher education for African Americans at the turn of the century.

Lesson 2 Assessment

1. **Organize Information** Create a chart to list three developments in education at the turn of the 20th century and their major results.

Development	Result
1.	
2.	
3.	

Which educational development do you think was most important? Explain your choice.

2. **Key Terms and People** For each key term or person in the lesson, write a sentence explaining its significance.

3. **Predict** How might the economy and culture of the United States have been different without the expansion of public schools?

   Think About:
   • public school goals and whether they have been met
   • why people supported expanding public education
   • the impact of public schools on the development of private schools

4. **Compare and Contrast** Compare and contrast the views of Booker T. Washington and W.E.B. Du Bois on the subject of the education of African Americans.

★
Segregation and Discrimination

The Big Idea
African Americans led the fight against voting restrictions and Jim Crow laws.

Why It Matters Now
Today, African Americans have the legacy of a century-long battle for civil rights.

Key Terms and People
Ida B. Wells

poll tax

grandfather clause

segregation

Jim Crow laws

Plessy v. *Ferguson*

debt peonage

One American's Story

Born into slavery shortly before emancipation, **Ida B. Wells** moved to Memphis in the early 1880s to work as a teacher. She later became an editor of a local paper. Racial justice was a persistent theme in Wells's reporting. The events of March 9, 1892, turned that theme into a crusade. Three African American businessmen, friends of Wells, were lynched—illegally executed without trial. Wells saw lynching for what it was.

"Thomas Moss, Calvin McDowell, and Lee Stewart had been lynched in Memphis . . . [where] no lynching had taken place before. . . . This is what opened my eyes to what lynching really was. An excuse to get rid of Negroes who were acquiring wealth and property and thus keep the race terrorized."

—Ida B. Wells, quoted in
Crusade for Justice

Ida B. Wells moved north to continue her fight against lynching by writing, lecturing, and organizing for civil rights.

African Americans were not the only group to experience violence and racial discrimination. Native Americans, Mexican residents, and Chinese immigrants also encountered bitter forms of oppression, particularly in the American West.

SS.912.A.1.2; SS.912.A.1.3; SS.912.A.1.6; SS.912.A.2.4; SS.912.A.2.5; SS.912.A.2.6; SS.912.A.3.8; SS.912.A.3.10; SS.912.A.3.12; SS.912.A.5.7; SS.912.A.5.10; SS.912.A.7.8; LAFS.1112.RH.1.1; LAFS.1112.RH.4.10; LAFS.1112.WHST.3.9

Legal Discrimination

As African Americans exercised their newly won political and social rights during Reconstruction, many at this time held onto the hope that life in America was changing for the better. However, African Americans faced hostile and often violent opposition from some whites. For at least ten years after the end of Reconstruction in 1877, African Americans in the South continued to vote and occasionally hold political office. By the turn of the 20th century, however, southern states had adopted a broad system of legal policies of racial discrimination. These states devised methods to weaken African American political power. This period between the late 19th and early 20th centuries was called *the nadir* by noted black historian Rayford Logan.

Vocabulary
nadir the worst or lowest point in an experience

VOTING RESTRICTIONS As the nadir wore on, the hopes of African Americans slowly eroded. All southern states imposed new voting restrictions and denied legal equality to African Americans. Some states, for example, limited the vote to people who could read. Registration officials administered a literacy, or reading, test. Blacks trying to vote were often asked more difficult questions than whites, or given a test in a foreign language. Officials could pass or fail applicants as they wished.

Another requirement was the **poll tax**, an annual tax that had to be paid before qualifying to vote. Black as well as white sharecroppers were often too poor to pay the poll tax. To reinstate white voters who may have failed the literacy test or could not pay the poll tax, several southern states added the **grandfather clause** to their constitutions. The clause stated that even if a man failed the literacy test or could not afford the poll tax, he was still entitled to vote if he, his father, or his grandfather had been eligible to vote before January 1, 1867. Before that date, freed slaves did not have the right to vote. The grandfather clause, therefore, did not protect voting rights for many African Americans.

JIM CROW LAWS During the 1870s and 1880s, the Supreme Court failed to overturn the poll tax or the grandfather clause. The laws stood even though they undermined all federal protections for African Americans' civil rights. At the same time that blacks lost voting rights, southern states passed racial **segregation** laws to separate white and black people in public and private facilities. This kind of segregation, enforced by laws, is known as *de jure* segregation. These laws came to be known as **Jim Crow laws** after a popular old minstrel song that ended in the words "Jump, Jim Crow."

Vocabulary
minstrel one of a troupe of entertainers in blackface presenting a comic variety show

The first Supreme Court decision to set a precedent for segregation appeared to have nothing to do with race relations at all. In 1873 three separate cases regarding the meatpacking industry in New Orleans were brought before the Court. Together, these cases were called the Slaughterhouse Cases. The state of Louisiana had decided to create a new corporation to run all slaughterhouses in the city of New Orleans. The slaughterhouse owners objected, stating that it would be an unlawful monopoly. They argued that Louisiana violated the Fourteenth Amendment, which stated that no state could impede the rights and privileges of its citizens. Unfortunately for the

This theater in Leland, Mississippi, was segregated under the Jim Crow laws.

plaintiffs, the Supreme Court did not agree. It said that the Fourteenth Amendment only protected the rights granted by the U.S. Constitution. It did not protect rights, such as business ownership, that had been granted by states.

Though they did not deal directly with segregation, the Slaughterhouse Cases were later used to justify the creation of separate facilities for blacks and whites. After all, schooling, housing, transportation, and the like were rights granted to citizens by states, not the federal government. Therefore, states had the right to determine how those rights were interpreted.

PLESSY v. FERGUSON Eventually a legal case reached the U.S. Supreme Court to test the constitutionality of segregation. In 1896, in ***Plessy v. Ferguson***, the Supreme Court ruled that the separation of races in public accommodations was legal and did not violate the Fourteenth Amendment. The decision established the doctrine of "separate but equal." This allowed states to maintain segregated facilities for blacks and whites as long as they provided equal service. The decision permitted legalized racial segregation for almost 60 years.

The implementation of Jim Crow laws and the decision in *Plessy* v. *Ferguson* chipped away at the rights of African Americans and other racial minorities. Democracy in the United States had been founded on a tradition of majority rule while at the same time protecting minority rights. The Bill of Rights was intended to protect the rights of all U.S. citizens, whether they are in the majority or the minority. In the late 1800s, however, the political majority—overwhelmingly white men—used legislation and court decisions to strip away the rights of minorities. Despite these roadblocks, African Americans continued to fight inequality through the courts and through the press. By the mid-1900s these efforts would begin to pay off. Strong, national civil rights organizations helped push for laws and protections to end racial discrimination.

Reading Check
Analyze Effects
How did the *Plessy* v. *Ferguson* ruling affect the civil rights of African Americans?

Turn-of-the-Century Race Relations

African Americans faced not only formal discrimination but also informal rules and customs, called racial etiquette, that regulated relationships between whites and blacks. Usually, these customs belittled and humiliated African Americans, enforcing their second-class status. For example, blacks and whites never shook hands, since shaking hands would have implied equality. Blacks also had to yield the sidewalk to white pedestrians. Black men always had to remove their hats for whites.

WASHINGTON VS. DU BOIS Some moderate reformers, like Booker T. Washington, earned support from whites. Washington suggested that whites and blacks work together for social progress. Washington hoped that improving the economic skills of African Americans would pave the way for long-term gains. He argued for a gradual approach to racial equality. Washington suggested that "it is at the bottom of life we must begin, and not at the top."

People like Ida B. Wells and W.E.B. Du Bois, however, thought that the problems of inequality were too urgent to postpone. W.E.B. Du Bois denounced Washington's view of gradual equality. Du Bois demanded full social and economic equality for African Americans. He declared that "persistent manly agitation is the way to liberty."

VIOLENCE African Americans and others who did not follow the racial etiquette could face severe punishment or death. All too often, blacks who were accused of violating the etiquette were lynched. Between 1882 and 1892 more than 1,400 African American men and women were shot, burned, or hanged without trial in the South. Lynching peaked in the 1880s and 1890s but continued well into the 20th century.

The Wilmington Race Riots revealed the lengths that some whites in the South would go to hold on to power. In 1896 white Populists and black Republicans in North Carolina had joined forces to defeat the Democrats that controlled state politics. In 1898 the Democrats won back control. But this did not pacify white radicals in Wilmington. They rioted, driving black community leaders from the city, burning black-owned businesses, and gunning down African Americans in the streets. By the next day, 14 African Americans had been killed, according to official records. However, the real number was likely much higher. In addition, many African Americans were banished from the city. Others fled, fearing for their lives.

Document-Based Investigation Historical Source

The Atlanta Compromise

On September 18, 1895, Booker T. Washington was invited to deliver a speech to the Cotton States and International Exposition in Atlanta. In the speech, he outlined his ideas about racial inequality and the shared responsibilities of African Americans and whites in improving society both socially and economically.

> "To those of the white race . . . I would repeat what I say to my own race. . . . Cast down your bucket among these people who have, without strikes and labour wars, tilled your fields, cleared your forests, builded your railroads and cities, and brought forth treasures from the bowels of the earth. . . . In all things that are purely social we can be as separate as the fingers, yet one as the hand in all things essential to mutual progress."
>
> —Booker T. Washington, from a speech to the Cotton States and International Exposition

Analyze Historical Sources
How do Washington's words represent a compromise?

AFRICAN AMERICAN PRESS With the erosion of federal protections for African Americans, many in the South turned to the press to help fight back against inequality. During the latter half of the 19th century, hundreds of black newspapers sprang up in communities across the South. While many of these newspapers did not last long, they provided a valuable service for communities that had few outlets to seek justice. Brave editors, such as Ida B. Wells of the *Free Speech and Headlight* in Memphis, Tennessee, documented lynching and other acts of violence. When a lynch mob attacked her newspaper office in 1892, Wells was fortunately out of town. Fearing for her safety, she did not return to the South for another 30 years. She did not give up on her work, however. She continued to fight back, hoping that one day the traditions of American democracy would be applied equally to all of the country's citizens.

DISCRIMINATION IN THE NORTH Most African Americans lived in the segregated South. By 1900, however, a number of blacks had moved to northern cities. Many blacks migrated to northern cities in search of better-paying jobs and social equality. But after their arrival, African Americans found that there was racial discrimination in the North as well. Many African Americans faced social and economic pressures that forced them into segregated neighborhoods. This kind of segregation is known as *de facto* segregation. Although not enforced by laws, *de facto* segregation had some of the same effects on African Americans in northern cities as *de jure* segregation had on African Americans in the South.

African Americans faced discrimination in the workplace as well. Labor unions often discouraged black membership. Employers hired African American labor only as a last resort and fired blacks before white employees. Sometimes the competition between African Americans and working-class whites became violent, as in the New York City race riot of 1900. Violence erupted after a young black man, believing that his wife was being mistreated by a white policeman, killed the policeman. Word of the killing spread, and whites retaliated by attacking blacks. Northern blacks, however, were not alone in facing discrimination. Nonwhites in the West also faced oppression.

Reading Check
Summarize What were Booker T. Washington's views about establishing racial equality?

Discrimination in the West

Western communities were home to people of many backgrounds working and living side by side. Native Americans still lived in the western territories claimed by the United States. Asian immigrants went to America's Pacific coast in search of wealth and work. Mexicans continued to inhabit the American Southwest. African Americans were also present, especially in former slave-holding areas, such as Texas. Still, racial tensions often made life difficult.

MEXICAN WORKERS In the late 1800s the railroads hired large numbers of Mexicans to construct rail lines in the Southwest. Mexicans were accustomed to the region's hot, dry climate. But the work was grueling, and the railroads made them work for less money than other ethnic groups.

Mexican track workers for the Southern Pacific Railroad posed for this group photo taken sometime between 1910 and 1915.

Mexicans were also vital to the development of mining and agriculture in the Southwest. When the 1902 National Reclamation Act gave government assistance for irrigation projects, many southwest desert areas bloomed. Mexican workers became the major labor force in the agricultural industries of the region.

Like other immigrant workers, Mexican farm workers often faced difficult working conditions for low pay. To help win improved conditions and higher pay, Mexican and Japanese farm workers formed the Japanese-Mexican Labor Association in 1903. This was the first farm labor union of its kind.

Some Mexicans, however, as well as African Americans in the Southwest, were forced into **debt peonage**. This system bound laborers into slavery in order to work off a debt to the employer. Not until 1911 did the Supreme Court declare involuntary peonage a violation of the Thirteenth Amendment.

Vocabulary
peon a worker bound in servitude to a landlord creditor

EXCLUDING THE CHINESE By 1880 more than 100,000 Chinese immigrants lived in the United States. White people's fear of job competition often pushed the Chinese into segregated schools and neighborhoods.

Discrimination against Chinese immigrants prompted some to return to China. Among them were the parents of Wong Kim Ark, who returned in 1890. Wong Kim Ark, though, decided to stay. Having been born in California, he considered the United States his home. After a brief visit with his parents in China in 1894, Wong was denied reentry to the United States and detained. To justify this action, government officials cited the Chinese Exclusion Act of 1882. Rather than abandon his homeland, Wong Kim Ark decided to fight back. After a four-year legal battle, the U.S. Supreme Court, citing the Fourteenth Amendment, ruled that because Wong was born in the United States, he was a citizen. *United States* v. *Wong Kim Ark* became a landmark case in determining citizenship status for the children of immigrants.

NATIVE AMERICANS Like other minority groups in the West, Native Americans faced discrimination and violence. Unlike other minority groups, though, most Native Americans were not U.S. citizens. As the United States

Native Americans of the Cheyenne and Arapaho tribes perform a Ghost Dance at the Indian Congress in 1898.

grew, Native Americans were pushed farther and farther west. Many had to give up their lands for homes on reservations. In addition, many whites felt that Native Americans lacked the intelligence to become citizens. Whites often opposed any naturalization efforts by the government.

The courts ruled that Native American citizenship was not granted by the Fourteenth Amendment. Because most were living on reservations, Native Americans were not under the jurisdiction, or rule, of the United States government at birth. After the Dawes Act in 1887, some Native American groups were able to trade reservation land for citizenship. However, even with full citizenship, many states still denied Native Americans the right to vote, serve on juries, or attend public schools.

Beginning in the late 19th century, groups formed to help Native Americans fight for their civil rights. One such group was the Women's National Indian Association. However, many of these groups believed that the only way for Native Americans to become full citizens was to assimilate into American culture. This pressure to assimilate led many Native Americans to embrace the Ghost Dance movement. The Ghost Dance movement encouraged Native Americans to return to their traditions. The movement's leader, Wovoka, claimed to have had a vision of the end of the world. At that point, Wovoka claimed, Native Americans would regain their lands and ways of life. Though the movement had been formed as a peaceful attempt to revitalize Native American culture, the federal Bureau of Indian Affairs feared it would encourage violent rebellion. The bureau banned the Ghost Dance.

Vocabulary
naturalization the formal process of becoming a United States citizen

Reading Check
Make Inferences
Why did some Native Americans resist offers of citizenship?

Lesson 3 Assessment

1. **Organize Information** Review the lesson, and find five key events to place on a timeline.

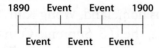

1890   Event   Event   1900

Event   Event   Event

Which of these events do you think was most important? Why?

2. **Key Terms and People** For each key term or person in the lesson, write a sentence explaining its significance.

3. **Contrast** How did the challenges and opportunities for Mexicans in the United States differ from those for African Americans?

Think About:
• the types of work available to each group
• the effects of government policies on each group
• the effect of the legal system on each group

4. **Identify Problems** How did segregation and discrimination affect the lives of African Americans at the turn of the 20th century?

5. **Compare** What did some African American leaders do to fight discrimination?

Plessy v. Ferguson (1896)

ORIGINS OF THE CASE

In 1892 Homer Plessy took a seat in the "Whites Only" car of a train and refused to move. He was arrested, tried, and convicted in the District Court of New Orleans for breaking Louisiana's segregation law. Plessy appealed, claiming that he had been denied equal protection under the law. The Supreme Court handed down its decision on May 18, 1896.

THE RULING

The Court ruled that separate-but-equal facilities for blacks and whites did not violate the Constitution.

LEGAL REASONING

Plessy claimed that segregation violated his right to equal protection under the law. Moreover, he claimed that, being "of mixed descent," he was entitled to "every recognition, right, privilege and immunity secured to the citizens of the United States of the white race."

Justice Henry B. Brown, writing for the majority, ruled:

"The object of the [Fourteenth] amendment was . . . undoubtedly to enforce the absolute equality of the two races before the law, but . . . it could not have been intended to abolish distinctions based upon color, or to enforce social, as distinguished from political equality, or a commingling of the two races upon terms unsatisfactory to either. Laws permitting, and even requiring, their separation in places where they are liable to be brought into contact do not necessarily imply the inferiority of either race to the other."

In truth, segregation laws did perpetrate an unequal and inferior status for African Americans. Justice John Marshall Harlan understood this fact and dissented from the majority opinion. He wrote, "In respect of civil rights, all citizens are equal before the law." He condemned the majority for letting "the seeds of race hate . . . be planted under the sanction of law." He also warned that "The thin disguise of 'equal' accommodations . . . will not mislead any one, nor atone for the wrong this day done."

Justice John Marshall Harlan

LEGAL SOURCES

LEGISLATION

U.S. Constitution, Fourteenth Amendment (1868)

"No state shall . . . deny to any person within its jurisdiction the equal protection of the laws."

Louisiana Acts 1890, No. 111

". . . that all railway companies carrying passengers in their coaches in this State, shall provide equal but separate accommodations for the white, and colored races."

RELATED CASES

Civil Rights Cases (1883)

The Court ruled that the Fourteenth Amendment could not be used to prevent private citizens from discriminating against others on the basis of race.

***Williams* v. *Mississippi* (1898)**

The Court upheld a state literacy requirement for voting that, in effect, kept African Americans from the polls.

***Cumming* v. *Board of Education of Richmond County* (1899)**

The Court ruled that the federal government cannot prevent segregation in local school facilities because education is a local, not federal, issue.

One result of Jim Crow laws was separate drinking fountains for whites and African Americans.

WHY IT MATTERED

In the decades following the Civil War (1861–1865), southern state legislatures passed laws that aimed to limit civil rights for African Americans. The Black Codes of the 1860s, and later Jim Crow laws, were intended to deprive African Americans of their newly won political and social rights granted during Reconstruction.

Plessy was one of several Supreme Court cases brought by African Americans to protect their rights against segregation. In these cases, the Court regularly ignored the Fourteenth Amendment and upheld state laws that denied blacks their rights. Plessy was the most important of these cases because the Court used it to establish the separate-but-equal doctrine.

As a result, city and state governments across the South—and in some other states—maintained their segregation laws for more than half of the 20th century. These laws limited African Americans' access to most public facilities, including restaurants, schools, and hospitals. Without exception, the facilities reserved for whites were superior to those reserved for nonwhites. Signs reading "Colored Only" and "Whites Only" served as constant reminders that facilities in segregated societies were separate but not equal.

HISTORICAL IMPACT

It took many decades to abolish legal segregation. During the first half of the 20th century, the National Association for the Advancement of Colored People (NAACP) led the legal fight to overturn Plessy. Although they won a few cases over the years, it was not until 1954 in *Brown* v. *Board of Education* that the Court overturned any part of Plessy. In that case, the Supreme Court said that separate-but-equal was unconstitutional in public education, but it did not completely overturn the separate-but-equal doctrine.

In later years, the Court did overturn the separate-but-equal doctrine, and it used the Brown decision to do so. For example, in 1955 Rosa Parks was convicted for violating a Montgomery, Alabama, law for segregated seating on buses. A federal court overturned the conviction, finding such segregation unconstitutional. The case was appealed to the Supreme Court, which upheld without comment the lower court's decision. In doing so in this and similar cases, the Court signaled that the reasoning behind *Plessy* no longer applied.

As secretary of the Montgomery chapter of the NAACP, Rosa Parks had protested segregation through everyday acts long before September 1955.

Critical Thinking

1. **Connect to History** Research and read Justice Harlan's entire dissent in *Plessy* v. *Ferguson*. Based on his position, what view might Harlan have taken toward laws that denied African Americans the right to vote? Write a paragraph or two expressing what Harlan would say about those laws.

2. **Connect to Today** Read the part of the Fourteenth Amendment reprinted in this feature. Write a paragraph explaining what you think "equal protection of the laws" means. Use evidence to support your ideas.

Women in Public Life

The Big Idea

As a result of social and economic change, many women entered public life as workers and reformers.

Why It Matters Now

Women won new opportunities in labor and education that are enjoyed today.

Key Terms and People

NACW

Susan B. Anthony

suffrage

Elizabeth Cady Stanton

NAWSA

One American's Story

In 1879 Susette La Flesche, a young Omaha woman, traveled east to translate into English the sad words of Chief Standing Bear, whose Ponca people had been forcibly removed from their homeland in Nebraska. Later, she was invited with Chief Standing Bear to go on a lecture tour to draw attention to the Ponca's situation.

Susette La Flesche

"We are thinking men and women. . . . We have a right to be heard in whatever concerns us. Your government has driven us hither and thither like cattle. . . . Your government has no right to say to us, Go here, or Go there, and if we show any reluctance, to force us to do its will at the point of the bayonet. . . . Do you wonder that the Indian feels outraged by such treatment and retaliates, although it will end in death to himself?"

—Susette La Flesche, quoted in *Bright Eyes*

La Flesche testified before congressional committees and helped win passage of the Dawes Act of 1887. This act allowed individual Native Americans to claim reservation land and citizenship rights. Her activism was an example of a new role for American women, who were expanding their participation in public life.

SS.912.A.1.2; SS.912.A.2.4; SS.912.A.3.8; SS.912.A.3.12; SS.912.A.5.7; SS.912.A.5.10; LAFS.1112.RH.4.10

Women in the Work Force

Before the Civil War, married middle-class women were generally expected to devote nearly all their time to the care of their homes and families. By the late 19th century, however, only middle-class and upper-class women could afford to do so. Poorer women usually had no choice but to work for wages outside the home.

FARM WOMEN On farms in the South and the Midwest, women's roles had not changed substantially since the previous century. In addition to household tasks such as cooking, making clothes, and laundering, farm women handled a host of other chores such as raising livestock. Often, the women had to help plow and plant the fields and harvest the crops.

WOMEN IN INDUSTRY As better-paying opportunities became available in towns and cities, women had new options for finding jobs. This occurred even though men's labor unions excluded them from membership. At the turn of the century, one out of five American women held jobs. One quarter of these women worked in manufacturing.

The garment trade claimed about half of all women industrial workers. They typically held the least skilled positions, however, and received only about half as much money as their male counterparts or less. Many of these women were single and were assumed to be supporting only themselves. Men were assumed to be supporting families.

Women also began to fill new jobs in offices, stores, and classrooms. These jobs required a high school education. By 1890 women high school graduates outnumbered men. Moreover, new business schools prepared bookkeepers and stenographers, as well as training female typists, to operate the new machines.

DOMESTIC WORKERS Many women without formal education or industrial skills contributed to the economic survival of their families by doing domestic work, such as cleaning for other families. After almost 2 million African American women were freed from slavery, poverty quickly drove nearly half of them into the work force. They worked on farms and as domestic workers. They also migrated by the thousands to big cities for jobs as cooks, laundresses, scrubwomen, and maids. Altogether, roughly 70 percent of women employed in 1870 were servants.

Unmarried immigrant women also performed domestic labor, especially when they first arrived in the United States. Many married immigrant women contributed to the family income by taking in piecework or caring for boarders at home.

Telephone operators manually connect phone calls in 1915.

Reading Check
Analyze Causes
What kinds of job opportunities prompted more women to complete high school?

PROPERTY RIGHTS Until the mid-1800s, women were not legally guaranteed the right to the fruits of their labor. In many states, for example, the wages earned by a married woman were legally the property of her husband. In 1839 Mississippi was the first state to pass a Married Women's Property Act. By 1900 every state had followed Mississippi's lead. Married women gained the right to own property in their own name, as well as keep any wages from their work. For women, gaining property rights was just one victory in a new push for equality.

Women Lead Reform

Dangerous conditions, low wages, and long hours led many female industrial workers to push for reforms. Their ranks grew after 146 workers, mostly Jewish and Italian immigrant girls, died in a 1911 fire in the Triangle Shirtwaist Factory in New York City. Middle- and upper-class women also entered the public sphere. By 1910 women's clubs, at which these women discussed art or literature, were nearly half a million strong. These clubs sometimes grew into reform groups that addressed issues such as temperance or child labor.

WOMEN IN HIGHER EDUCATION Many of the women who became active in public life in the late 19th century had attended the new women's colleges. Vassar College—with a faculty of 8 men and 22 women—accepted its first students in 1865. Smith and Wellesley colleges followed in 1875. Though Columbia, Brown, and Harvard colleges refused to admit women, each university established a separate college for women.

By the late 19th century, marriage was no longer a woman's only alternative. Many women entered the work force or sought higher education. In fact, almost half of all college-educated women in the late 19th century never married, retaining their own independence. Many of these educated women began to apply their skills to needed social reforms.

Document-Based Investigation Historical Source

Educational Opportunities

Although women were still expected to fulfill traditional domestic roles, women's colleges sought to grant women an excellent education. In her will, Smith College's founder, Sophia Smith, made her goals clear.

> "[It is my desire] to furnish for my own sex means and facilities for education equal to those which are afforded now in our College to young men. . . . It is not my design to render my sex any the less feminine, but to develop as fully as may be the powers of womanhood & furnish women with means of usefulness, happiness, & honor now withheld from them."
>
> —Sophia Smith, quoted in Alma Mater

Analyze Historical Sources
What do you think Sophia Smith hoped women would be able to accomplish through higher education?

WOMEN AND REFORM Uneducated laborers started efforts to reform workplace health and safety. The participation of educated women often strengthened existing reform groups and provided leadership for new ones. Because women were not allowed to vote or run for office, women reformers strove to improve conditions at work and home. Their "social housekeeping" targeted workplace reform, housing reform, educational improvement, and food and drug laws.

In 1896 African American women founded the National Association of Colored Women, or **NACW**, by merging two earlier organizations. Josephine Ruffin identified the mission of the African American women's club movement as "the moral education of the race with which we are identified." The NACW managed nurseries, reading rooms, and kindergartens.

After the Seneca Falls Convention of 1848, women split over the Fourteenth and Fifteenth Amendments. These amendments granted equal rights including the right to vote to African American men but excluded women. **Susan B. Anthony**, a leading proponent of woman **suffrage**, the right to vote, said "[I] would sooner cut off my right hand than ask the ballot for the black man and not for women." Anthony felt that she could not support suffrage for African American men while women were still denied their voting rights.

In 1869 Anthony and **Elizabeth Cady Stanton** had founded the National Woman Suffrage Association (NWSA). This group united with another group in 1890 to become the National American Woman Suffrage Association, or **NAWSA**. Other prominent leaders included Lucy Stone and Julia Ward Howe, the author of "The Battle Hymn of the Republic." Unlike Anthony, Lucy Stone supported the passage of the Fourteenth and Fifteenth Amendments. She saw the passage of these amendments as a positive sign that suffrage would eventually be extended to women as well.

Woman suffrage faced constant opposition. The liquor industry feared that women would vote in support of prohibition. The textile industry worried that women would vote for restrictions on child labor. Many men simply feared the changing role of women in society.

A THREE–PART STRATEGY FOR SUFFRAGE Suffragist leaders tried three approaches to achieve their objective. First, they tried to convince state legislatures to grant women the right to vote. They achieved a victory in the

Suffragists recruit supporters for a march.

Susan B. Anthony (1820–1906)

Born to a strict Quaker family, Susan B. Anthony was not allowed to enjoy typical childhood entertainment such as music, games, and toys. Her father insisted on self-discipline, education, and a strong belief system for all of his eight children. Anthony developed a positive view of womanhood from teacher Mary Perkins, who educated the children in their home.

After voting illegally in the presidential election of 1872, Anthony was fined $100 at her trial. "Not a penny shall go to this unjust claim," she defiantly declared. She never paid the fine.

territory of Wyoming in 1869. By the 1890s Utah, Colorado, and Idaho had also granted voting rights to women. After 1896 efforts in other states failed.

Second, women pursued court cases to test the Fourteenth Amendment, which declared that states denying male citizens the right to vote would lose congressional representation. Weren't women citizens, too? Susan B. Anthony and other women tested that question by attempting to vote at least 150 times in ten states. The Supreme Court ruled in 1875 that women were indeed citizens but then denied that citizenship automatically conferred the right to vote.

Third, women pushed for a national constitutional amendment to grant women the vote. Stanton succeeded in having the amendment introduced in California, but it was killed later. For the next 41 years, women lobbied to have it reintroduced, only to see it continually voted down.

Reading Check
Make Inferences
Why did suffragist leaders employ a three-part strategy for gaining the right to vote?

Before the turn of the century, the campaign for suffrage achieved only modest success. Later, however, women's reform efforts paid off in improvements in the treatment of workers and in safer food and drug products. President Theodore Roosevelt supported these efforts, along with his own plans for reforming business, labor, and the environment.

Lesson 4 Assessment

1. **Organize Information** Use a chart to list details about working women in the late 1800s.
   What generalizations can you make about women workers at this time?

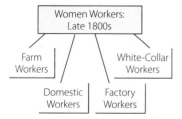

2. **Key Terms and People** For each key term or person in the lesson, write a sentence explaining its significance.

3. **Synthesize** What women and movements during the Progressive Era helped dispel the stereotype that women were submissive and nonpolitical?

4. **Make Inferences** Why do you think some colleges refused to accept women in the late 19th century?

5. **Analyze Issues** Imagine you are a woman during the Progressive Era. Explain how you might recruit other women to support the following causes: improving education, housing reform, food and drug laws, the right to vote.

   Think About:
   • the problems that each movement was trying to remedy
   • how women benefited from each cause

Teddy Roosevelt's Square Deal

The Big Idea
As president, Theodore Roosevelt worked to give citizens a Square Deal through progressive reforms.

Why It Matters Now
As part of his Square Deal, Roosevelt's conservation efforts made a permanent impact on environmental resources.

Key Terms and People
Upton Sinclair

The Jungle

Theodore Roosevelt

Square Deal

Meat Inspection Act

Pure Food and Drug Act

conservation

NAACP

One American's Story

When muckraking journalist **Upton Sinclair** began research for a novel in 1904, his focus was the human condition in the stockyards of Chicago. Sinclair intended his novel to reveal "the breaking of human hearts by a system [that] exploits the labor of men and women for profits." What most shocked readers in Sinclair's book *The Jungle* (1906), however, was the sickening conditions of the meatpacking industry.

Upton Sinclair poses with his son at the time of the writing of *The Jungle*.

"There would be meat that had tumbled out on the floor, in the dirt and sawdust, where the workers had tramped and spit uncounted billions of consumption [tuberculosis] germs. There would be meat stored in great piles in rooms; . . . and thousands of rats would race about on it. . . . A man could run his hand over these piles of meat and sweep off handfuls of the dried dung of rats. These rats were nuisances, and the packers would put poisoned bread out for them; they would die, and then rats, bread, and meat would go into the hoppers together."

—Upton Sinclair, from *The Jungle*

President **Theodore Roosevelt**, like many other readers, was nauseated by Sinclair's account. The president invited the author to visit him at the White House. Roosevelt promised Sinclair that "the specific evils you point out shall, if their existence be proved, and if I have the power, be eradicated."

SS.912.A.1.2; SS.912.A.1.4; SS.912.A.1.7; SS.912.A.3.12; SS.912.A.5.7; SS.912.A.5.8; SS.912.A.5.10; SS.912.G.1.2; SS.912.G.2.1; SS.912.H.1.1; SS.912.H.1.5; HE.912.C.2.4; LAFS.1112.RH.1.2

A Rough-Riding President

Theodore Roosevelt was not supposed to be president. Although born into a wealthy New York family in 1858, he was a sickly child. Young Teddy, however, drove himself to accomplish demanding physical feats. As a teenager, he mastered marksmanship and horseback riding. At Harvard College, Roosevelt boxed and wrestled.

ROOSEVELT'S RISE At an early age, the ambitious Roosevelt became a leader in New York politics. After serving three terms in the New York State Assembly, he became New York City's police commissioner. He later served as assistant secretary of the U.S. Navy. The aspiring politician grabbed national attention, advocating war against Spain in 1898. His volunteer cavalry brigade, the Rough Riders, won fame for its role in the battle at San Juan Hill in Cuba. Roosevelt returned a hero. He was soon elected governor of New York and then later won the vice-presidency. As vice-president, Roosevelt stood a heartbeat away from becoming president. Indeed, President McKinley had served barely six months of his second term before he was assassinated.

Theodore Roosevelt enjoyed an active lifestyle, as this 1902 photo reveals.

THE MODERN PRESIDENCY When Roosevelt was thrust into the presidency in 1901, he became the youngest president ever at 42 years old. Unlike previous presidents, Roosevelt soon dominated the news with his many exploits. While in office, Roosevelt enjoyed boxing, although one of his opponents blinded him in the left eye. On another day, he galloped 100 miles on horseback, merely to prove the feat possible.

In politics, as in sports, Roosevelt acted boldly. He used his personality and popularity to advance his programs. His leadership and publicity campaigns helped create the modern presidency. He became a model by which all future presidents would be measured. Roosevelt thought the federal government should assume control whenever states proved incapable of dealing with problems. He explained, "It is the duty of the president to act upon the theory that he is the steward of the people, and . . . to assume that he has the legal right to do whatever the needs of the people demand, unless the Constitution or the laws explicitly forbid him to do it."

Reading Check
Synthesize What actions and characteristics of Teddy Roosevelt contributed to his reputation as the first modern president?

Roosevelt saw the presidency as a "bully pulpit," from which he could influence the news media and shape legislation. If big business victimized workers, then President Roosevelt would see to it that the common people received what he called a **Square Deal**. This term was used to describe the various progressive reforms sponsored by his administration.

Using Federal Power

Roosevelt's study of history convinced him that modern America required a powerful federal government. "A simple and poor society can exist as a democracy on the basis of sheer individualism," Roosevelt declared, "but a rich and complex industrial society cannot so exist." The young president soon met several challenges to his assertion of federal power.

TRUSTBUSTING By 1900 trusts—legal bodies created to hold stock in many companies—controlled about four-fifths of the industries in the United States. Some trusts, like Standard Oil, had earned poor reputations with the public by the use of unfair business practices. Many trusts lowered their prices to drive competitors out of the market. They then took advantage of the lack of competition to jack prices up even higher. Congress had passed the Sherman Antitrust Act in 1890, but the act's vague language made enforcement difficult. As a result, nearly all the suits filed against the trusts under the Sherman Act were ineffective.

President Roosevelt did not believe that all trusts were harmful. But he did seek to curb the actions of those that hurt the public interest. The president concentrated his efforts on filing suits under the Sherman Antitrust Act. In 1902 Roosevelt made newspaper headlines as a trustbuster. That year he ordered the Justice Department to sue the Northern Securities Company. This company had established a monopoly over northwestern railroads. In 1904 the Supreme Court, ruling in favor of the government in *Northern Securities Co. v. United States,* dissolved the company. Although the Roosevelt administration filed 44 antitrust suits, winning a number of them, it was unable to slow the merger movement in business.

1902 COAL STRIKE In 1902, 140,000 coal miners in Pennsylvania went on strike and demanded a 20 percent raise and a nine-hour workday. They also wanted the right to organize a union. The mine operators, however, refused to bargain. Five months into the strike, coal reserves ran low. Roosevelt called both sides to the White House to talk and eventually settled the strike. The president was irked by the "extraordinary stupidity and bad temper" of the mine operators. He later confessed that only the dignity of the presidency had kept him from taking one owner "by the seat of the breeches" and tossing him out of the window.

Document-Based Investigation Historical Source

"The Lion-Tamer"

As part of his Square Deal, President Roosevelt aggressively used the Sherman Antitrust Act of 1890 to attack big businesses engaging in unfair practices. His victory over the Northern Securities Company earned him a reputation as a hard-hitting trustbuster committed to protecting the public interest. This cartoon shows Roosevelt trying to tame the wild lions that symbolize the great and powerful companies of 1904.

Analyze Historical Sources

1. What do the lions stand for, and why are they coming out of a door labeled "Wall St."?

2. What do you think the cartoonist thinks about trustbusting? Cite details from the cartoon that support your interpretation.

Vocabulary
collude to act together secretly to achieve an illegal or deceitful purpose

Reading Check
Analyze Effects
What was significant about the way the 1902 coal strike was settled?

Faced with Roosevelt's threat to take over the mines, the opposing sides finally agreed to submit their differences to an arbitration commission. This commission acted as a third party that would work to mediate the dispute. In 1903 the commission issued its compromise settlement. The miners won a 10 percent pay hike and a nine-hour workday. With this, however, they had to give up their demand for a closed shop—in which all workers must belong to the union—and their right to strike during the next three years.

President Roosevelt's actions had demonstrated a new principle. From then on, when a strike threatened the public welfare, the federal government was expected to intervene. In addition, Roosevelt's actions reflected the progressive belief that disputes could be settled in an orderly way with the help of experts. Members of the arbitration commission were examples of such experts.

RAILROAD REGULATION Roosevelt's real goal was federal regulation. In 1887 Congress had passed the Interstate Commerce Act. This law prohibited wealthy railroad owners from colluding to fix high prices. The Interstate Commerce Commission (ICC) was set up to enforce the new law but had little power. With Roosevelt's urging, Congress passed the Elkins Act in 1903. This law made it illegal for railroad officials to give, and shippers to receive, rebates for using particular railroads. The act also specified that railroads could not change set rates without notifying the public.

The Hepburn Act of 1906 strictly limited the distribution of free railroad passes, a common form of bribery. It also gave the ICC power to set maximum railroad rates. Although Roosevelt had to compromise with conservative senators who opposed the act, its passage boosted the government's power to regulate the railroads.

Health and the Environment

President Roosevelt's enthusiasm and his skill at compromise led to laws and policies that benefited both public health and the environment. He wrote, "We recognize and are bound to war against the evils of today. The remedies are partly economic and partly spiritual, partly to be obtained by laws, and in greater part to be obtained by individual and associated effort."

REGULATING FOODS AND DRUGS After reading *The Jungle* by Upton Sinclair, Roosevelt responded to the public's clamor for action. He appointed a commission of experts to investigate the meatpacking industry. The commission issued a scathing report backing up Sinclair's account of the disgusting conditions in the industry. True to his word, Roosevelt pushed for passage of the **Meat Inspection Act** in 1906. This law dictated cleanliness requirements for meatpackers and created the program of federal meat inspection. The program continued until replaced by more sophisticated techniques in the 1990s.

The compromise that won the act's passage, however, left the government paying for the inspections. The act also did not require companies to label their canned goods with date-of-processing information. The compromise moreover granted meatpackers the right to appeal negative decisions in court.

Government workers inspect meat as it moves through the packinghouse.

PURE FOOD AND DRUG ACT Before any federal regulations were established for advertising food and drugs, manufacturers made wild claims about their products. These ranged from curing cancer to growing hair. In addition, popular children's medicines often contained opium, cocaine, or alcohol. In a series of lectures across the country, Dr. Harvey Washington Wiley, chief chemist at the Department of Agriculture, criticized manufacturers for adding harmful preservatives to food. He brought needed attention to this issue.

In response to concerns about these practices, Congress passed the **Pure Food and Drug Act** in 1906. This law halted the sale of contaminated foods and medicines and called for truth in labeling. The act did not ban harmful products outright. But its requirement of truthful labels reflected the progressive belief that given accurate information, people would act wisely.

Along with the Meat Inspection Act, the Pure Food and Drug Act reflected the changing relationship between the federal government and private businesses during this period. This act marked the first general pure food and drug law at the federal level. The government's Bureau of Chemistry, which later became the Food and Drug Administration, took responsibility for enforcement of the law. Unfortunately, enforcement met with mixed results. On the whole, the law helped to protect consumers by improving product standards. It also reduced confusion about the benefits and dangers of various products. However, some critics point out that the law reduced marketplace competition by forcing out smaller producers. Also, efforts to regulate the patent medicine industry were largely unsuccessful until Congress passed new laws in 1938.

CONSERVATION AND NATURAL RESOURCES Before Roosevelt's presidency, the federal government had paid very little attention to the nation's natural resources. Despite the establishment of the U.S. Forest Bureau in 1887, the government stood by while private interests gobbled up the shrinking wilderness.

In the late 19th century, Americans had shortsightedly exploited their natural environment. Pioneer farmers leveled the forests and plowed up the prairies. Ranchers allowed their cattle to overgraze the Great Plains. Coal companies cluttered the land with refuse from mines. Lumber companies ignored the effect of their logging operations on flood control. They also neglected to plant trees to replace those they had cut down. Cities dumped untreated sewage and industrial wastes into rivers, poisoning streams and creating health hazards.

CONSERVATION MEASURES Roosevelt condemned the view that America's resources were endless. He made conservation a primary concern. John Muir, a naturalist and writer with whom Roosevelt camped in California's Yosemite National Park in 1903, persuaded the president to set aside 148 million acres of forest. Roosevelt also set aside 1.5 million acres of water-power sites and another 80 million acres of land that experts from the U.S. Geological Survey would explore for mineral and water resources. Roosevelt also established more than 50 wildlife sanctuaries and several national parks and monuments, including the Grand Canyon, Muir Woods, Crater Lake, and Mesa Verde National Park.

True to the progressive belief in using experts, in 1905 the president named Gifford Pinchot as head of the U.S. Forest Service. A professional conservationist, Pinchot had administrative skills as well as the latest scientific and technical information. He advised Roosevelt to conserve forest and grazing lands by exempting large tracts of federal land from private sale.

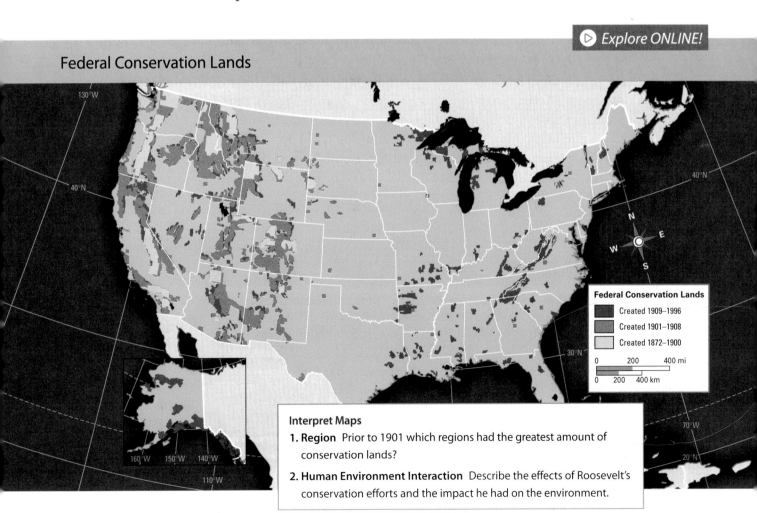

▶ Explore ONLINE!

Federal Conservation Lands

Federal Conservation Lands
- Created 1909–1996
- Created 1901–1908
- Created 1872–1900

0   200   400 mi
0   200   400 km

Interpret Maps

1. **Region** Prior to 1901 which regions had the greatest amount of conservation lands?

2. **Human Environment Interaction** Describe the effects of Roosevelt's conservation efforts and the impact he had on the environment.

Conservationists like Roosevelt and Pinchot, however, did not share the views of Muir, who advocated complete preservation of the wilderness. Instead, **conservation** to them meant that some wilderness areas would be preserved while others would be developed for the common good. Indeed, Roosevelt's federal water projects transformed some dry wilderness areas to make agriculture possible. Under the National Reclamation Act of 1902, known as the Newlands Act, the sale of public lands in the West funded large-scale irrigation projects such as the Roosevelt Dam in Arizona and the Shoshone Dam in Wyoming. The Newlands Act established the precedent that the federal government would manage the water resources of the West.

Reading Check
Analyze Causes
What caused President Roosevelt to enact measures to conserve the natural environment?

Roosevelt and Civil Rights

Roosevelt's concern for the land and its inhabitants was not matched in the area of civil rights. Though Roosevelt's father had supported the North, his mother, Martha, was a model southern belle. As president, Roosevelt—like most other Progressives—failed to support civil rights for African Americans. He did, however, support a few individual African Americans.

Despite opposition from whites, Roosevelt appointed an African American as head of the Charleston, South Carolina, customhouse. In another instance some whites in Mississippi refused to accept the black postmistress he had appointed. The president closed the station rather than give in. In 1906, however, Roosevelt angered many African Americans when he dismissed without question an entire regiment of African American soldiers accused of conspiracy in protecting others charged with murder in Brownsville, Texas.

As a symbolic gesture, Roosevelt invited Booker T. Washington to dinner at the White House. Washington—head of the Tuskegee Normal and Industrial Institute—was then the African American leader most respected by powerful whites. Washington faced opposition, however, from other African Americans for his accommodation of segregationists and for blaming black poverty on blacks and urging them to accept discrimination.

Vocabulary
accommodation adapting or making adjustments in order to satisfy someone else

– BIOGRAPHY –

W.E.B. Du Bois (1868–1963)

In 1909 W.E.B. Du Bois helped to establish the NAACP and entered into the forefront of the early U.S. civil rights movement. However, in the 1920s he faced a power struggle with the NAACP's executive secretary, Walter White.

Ironically, Du Bois had retreated to a position others saw as dangerously close to that of Booker T. Washington. Arguing for a separate economy for African Americans, Du Bois made a distinction, which White rejected, between enforced and voluntary segregation. By mid-century, Du Bois was outside the mainstream of the civil rights movement. His work remained largely ignored until after his death in 1963.

Persistent in his criticism of Washington's ideas, W.E.B. Du Bois renewed his demands for immediate social and economic equality for African Americans. In his 1903 book *The Souls of Black Folk*, Du Bois wrote of his opposition to Washington's position.

"So far as Mr. Washington preaches Thrift, Patience, and Industrial Training for the masses, we must hold up his hands and strive with him. . . . But so far as Mr. Washington apologizes for injustice, North or South, does not rightly value the privilege and duty of voting, belittles the emasculating effects of caste distinctions, and opposes the higher training and ambition of our brighter minds,—so far as he, the South, or the Nation, does this,—we must unceasingly and firmly oppose them."

— W.E.B. Du Bois, from *The Souls of Black Folk*

Du Bois and other advocates of equality for African Americans were deeply upset by the apparent progressive indifference to racial injustice. In 1905 they held a civil rights conference in Niagara Falls. In 1909 a number of African Americans joined with prominent white reformers in New York to found the **NAACP**—the National Association for the Advancement of Colored People. The next year, Du Bois founded *The Crisis*—the NAACP's magazine. As chief editor, Du Bois used *The Crisis* to highlight issues of race and inequality. He wrote, "We refuse to surrender . . . leadership . . . to cowards and trucklers. We are men; we will be treated as men." Within ten years of its founding, *The Crisis* reached a national audience with about 100,000 readers.

The NAACP, which had over 6,000 members by 1914, aimed for nothing less than full equality among the races. That goal, however, found little support in the Progressive movement. Progressives mostly focused on the needs of middle-class whites. The two presidents who followed Roosevelt also did little to advance the goal of racial equality.

Reading Check
Analyze Motives
Why did W.E.B. Du Bois found *The Crisis* magazine?

Lesson 5 Assessment

1. **Organize Information** Create five problem-solution diagrams to show how the following problems were addressed during Roosevelt's presidency: (a) 1902 coal strike, (b) Northern Securities Company monopoly, (c) unsafe meat processing, (d) exploitation of the environment, and (e) racial injustice.
   Write headlines announcing the solutions.

   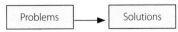
   Problems ➝ Solutions

2. **Key Terms and People** For each key term or person in the lesson, write a sentence explaining its significance.

3. **Evaluate** Research the coal strike of 1902. Do you think Roosevelt's intervention was in favor of the strikers or of the mine operators? Why?

4. **Analyze Issues** Why did W.E.B. Du Bois oppose Booker T. Washington's views on racial discrimination?

5. **Form Generalizations** In what ways do you think the progressive belief in using experts played a role in shaping Roosevelt's reforms? Refer to details from the text.

   Think About:
   • Roosevelt's use of experts to help him tackle political, economic, and environmental problems
   • how experts' findings affected legislative actions

Progressivism Under Taft

The Big Idea

Taft's ambivalent approach to progressive reform led to a split in the Republican Party and the loss of the presidency to the Democrats.

Why It Matters Now

Third-party candidates continue to wrestle with how to become viable candidates.

Key Terms and People

Gifford Pinchot

William Howard Taft

Payne-Aldrich Tariff

Bull Moose Party

Woodrow Wilson

One American's Story

Early in the 20th century, Americans' interest in the preservation of the country's wilderness areas intensified. Writers proclaimed the beauty of the landscape. New groups like the Girl Scouts gave city children the chance to experience a different environment. The desire for preservation clashed with business interests that favored unrestricted development. **Gifford Pinchot** (pĭn´shō´), head of the U.S. Forest Service under President Roosevelt, took a middle ground. He believed that wilderness areas could be scientifically managed to yield public enjoyment while allowing private development.

"The American people have evidently made up their minds that our natural resources must be conserved. That is good. But it settles only half the question. For whose benefit shall they be conserved—for the benefit of the many, or for the use and profit of the few? . . . There is no other question before us that begins to be so important, or that will be so difficult to straddle, as the great question between special interest and equal opportunity, between the privileges of the few and the rights of the many, between government by men for human welfare and government by money for profit."

—Gifford Pinchot, from *The Fight for Conservation*

Gifford Pinchot

President Roosevelt favored Pinchot's multi-use land program. However, when he left office in 1909, this approach came under increasing pressure from business people who favored unrestricted commercial development.

SS.912.A.3.12; MAFS.K12.MP.3.1

Taft Becomes President

After winning the election in 1904, Roosevelt pledged not to run for reelection in 1908. He handpicked his secretary of war, **William Howard Taft**, to run against William Jennings Bryan, who had been nominated by the Democrats for the third time. Under the slogan "Vote for Taft this time, You can vote for Bryan any time," Taft and the Republicans won an easy victory.

TAFT STUMBLES As president, Taft pursued a cautiously progressive agenda, seeking to consolidate rather than to expand Roosevelt's reforms. He received little credit for his accomplishments, however. His legal victories, such as busting 90 trusts in a four-year term, did not bolster his popularity. Indeed, the new president confessed in a letter to Roosevelt that he never felt like the president. "When I am addressed as 'Mr. President,'" Taft wrote, "I turn to see whether you are not at my elbow."

The cautious Taft hesitated to use the presidential bully pulpit to arouse public opinion. Nor could he subdue troublesome members of his own party. Tariffs and conservation posed his first problems.

THE PAYNE-ALDRICH TARIFF Taft had campaigned on a platform of lowering tariffs, a staple of the progressive agenda. When the House passed the Payne Bill, which lowered rates on imported manufactured goods, the Senate proposed an alternative bill. The Aldrich Bill, proposed by the Senate, made fewer cuts and increased many rates. Amid cries of betrayal from the progressive wing of his party, Taft signed the **Payne-Aldrich Tariff**, a compromise that only moderated the high rates of the Aldrich Bill. This angered Progressives, who believed Taft had abandoned progressivism. The president made his difficulties worse by clumsily attempting to defend the tariff. He called it "the best [tariff] bill the Republican party ever passed."

DISPUTING PUBLIC LANDS Next, Taft angered conservationists by appointing lawyer Richard A. Ballinger as his secretary of the interior. Ballinger, who disapproved of conservationist controls on western lands, removed 1 million acres of forest and mining lands from the reserved list and returned it to the public domain.

DIFFICULT DECISIONS

Controlling Resources

Historically, conservationists such as Gifford Pinchot have stood for the balanced use of natural resources, preserving some and using others for private industry. Free-market advocates like Richard Ballinger pressed for the private development of wilderness areas. Preservationists such as John Muir advocated preserving all remaining wilderness.

1. Examine the pros and cons of each position. With which do you agree? What factors do you think should influence decisions about America's wilderness areas?

2. If you were asked today to decide whether to develop or preserve America's remaining wilderness areas, what would you decide? Why? Use the views of Ballinger, Pinchot, or Muir to back up your point of view.

Reading Check
Analyze Issues
How did Taft's appointee Richard Ballinger anger conservationists?

When a Department of the Interior official was fired for protesting Ballinger's actions, the fired worker published a muckraking article against Ballinger in *Collier's Weekly* magazine. Pinchot added his voice. In congressional testimony, he accused Ballinger of letting commercial interests exploit the natural resources that rightfully belonged to the public. President Taft sided with Ballinger and fired Pinchot from the U.S. Forest Service.

The Republican Party Splits

Taft's cautious nature made it impossible for him to hold together the two wings of the Republican Party: Progressives who sought change and conservatives who did not. The Republican Party began to fragment.

PROBLEMS WITHIN THE PARTY Republican conservatives and Progressives split over Taft's support of the political boss Joseph Cannon, House Speaker from Illinois. A rough-talking, tobacco-chewing politician, "Uncle Joe" often disregarded seniority in filling committee slots. As chairman of the House Rules Committee, which decides what bills Congress considers, Cannon often weakened or ignored progressive bills.

Reform-minded Republicans decided that their only alternative was to strip Cannon of his power. With the help of Democrats, they succeeded in March 1910. A new resolution called for the entire House to elect the Committee on Rules, and it also excluded the Speaker from membership in the committee.

By the midterm elections of 1910, however, the Republican Party was in shambles. The Progressives were on one side and the "old guard" was on the other. Voters voiced concern over the rising cost of living, which they blamed on the Payne-Aldrich Tariff. They also believed Taft to be against conservation. The Republicans lost many seats. The Democrats gained control of the House of Representatives for the first time in 18 years.

Vocabulary
"old guard"
conservative members of a group

─ BIOGRAPHY ─────────────────────────────────────

William Howard Taft (1857–1930)

William Howard Taft never wanted to be president. After serving one term, Taft left the White House, which he called "the lonesomest place in the world." He then taught constitutional law at Yale for eight years.

In 1921 President Harding named Taft chief justice of the Supreme Court. The man whose family had nicknamed him "Big Lub" called this appointment the highest honor he had ever received. As chief justice, Taft wrote that "in my present life I don't remember that I ever was President."

However, Americans remember Taft for, among many other things, initiating in 1910 the popular presidential custom of throwing out the first ball of the Major League Baseball season.

THE BULL MOOSE PARTY After leaving office, Roosevelt headed to Africa to shoot big game. He returned in 1910 to a hero's welcome. He responded with a rousing speech proposing a "New Nationalism," under which the federal government would exert its power for "the welfare of the people." As he stated in a speech delivered in 1910, "I stand for the square deal. . . . I stand for having . . . rules changed so as to work for . . . equality of opportunity and of reward . . . our government, national and state, must be freed from the sinister influence or control of special interests."

By 1912 Roosevelt had decided to run for a third term as president. The primary elections showed that Republicans wanted Roosevelt. But Taft had the advantage of being the incumbent—that is, the holder of the office. At the Republican convention in June 1912, Taft supporters maneuvered to replace Roosevelt delegates with Taft delegates. Republican Progressives refused to vote and formed a new third party, the Progressive Party. They nominated Roosevelt for president.

The Progressive Party became known as the **Bull Moose Party**, after Roosevelt's boast that he was "as strong as a bull moose." Their platform called for the direct election of senators and the adoption in all states of the initiative, referendum, and recall. It also advocated woman suffrage, workmen's compensation, an eight-hour workday, a minimum wage for women, a federal law against child labor, and a federal trade commission to regulate business.

Reading Check
Contrast What were the differences between Taft's and Roosevelt's campaign platforms?

The split in the Republican ranks handed the Democrats their first real chance at the White House since the election of Grover Cleveland in 1892. In the 1912 presidential election, they put forward as their candidate a reform governor of New Jersey named **Woodrow Wilson**.

Woodrow Wilson

Democrats Win in 1912

Under Governor Woodrow Wilson's leadership, the previously conservative New Jersey legislature had passed a host of reforms. Now, as the Democratic presidential nominee, Wilson endorsed a progressive platform called the New Freedom. It demanded even stronger antitrust legislation, banking reform, and reduced tariffs.

The split between Taft and Roosevelt, former Republican allies, turned nasty during the fall campaign. Taft labeled Roosevelt a "dangerous egotist." Roosevelt branded Taft a "fathead" with the brain of a "guinea pig." Wilson distanced himself, quietly gloating, "Don't interfere when your enemy is destroying himself."

The election offered voters several choices: Wilson's New Freedom, Taft's conservatism, Roosevelt's progressivism, or the Socialist Party policies of Eugene V. Debs. Both Roosevelt and Wilson supported a stronger government role in economic affairs, but they differed over strategies. Roosevelt supported government action to supervise big business, but he did not oppose all monopolies. Debs called for an end to capitalism. Wilson supported small business and free-market competition. He characterized monopolies as evil.

Presidential Election of 1912

Party	Candidate	Electoral Votes	Popular Vote
■ Democratic	Woodrow Wilson	435	6,296,547
■ Progressive	Theodore Roosevelt	88	4,118,571
■ Republican	William H. Taft	8	3,486,720
Socialist	Eugene V. Debs	0	900,672

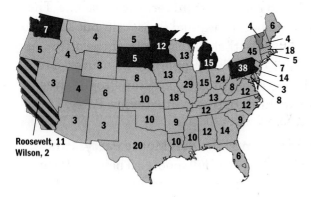

Roosevelt, 11
Wilson, 2

Reading Check
Make Inferences
What might be one of Wilson's first issues to address as president?

In a speech, Wilson explained why he felt that all business monopolies were a threat.

"If the government is to tell big business men how to run their business, then don't you see that big business men have to get closer to the government even than they are now? Don't you see that they must capture the government, in order not to be restrained too much by it? . . . I don't care how benevolent the master is going to be, I will not live under a master. That is not what America was created for. America was created in order that every man should have the same chance as every other man to exercise mastery over his own fortunes."
—Woodrow Wilson, quoted in *The New Freedom*

Although Wilson captured only 42 percent of the popular vote, he won an overwhelming electoral victory and a Democratic majority in Congress. Because Taft and Roosevelt split the Republican votes, Wilson was able to win the electoral votes of 40 states without winning even half of the popular vote. As a third-party candidate, Roosevelt defeated Taft in both popular and electoral votes.

But reform claimed the real victory. More than 75 percent of the vote went to reform candidates—Wilson, Roosevelt, and Debs. Americans clearly wanted change. In victory, Wilson could claim a mandate to break up trusts and to expand the government's role in social reform.

Lesson 6 Assessment

1. **Organize Information** Create a chart to organize information about the causes Taft supported that made people question his leadership.

Which causes do you think would upset most people today? Explain.

2. **Key Terms and People** For each key term or person in the lesson, write a sentence explaining its significance.

3. **Evaluate** Both Roosevelt and Taft resorted to mudslinging during the 1912 presidential campaign. Do you approve or disapprove of negative campaign tactics? Support your opinion.

4. **Predict** What if Roosevelt had won another term in office in 1912? Speculate on how this might have affected the future of progressive reforms. Support your answer.

   Think About:
   - Roosevelt's policies that Taft did not support
   - the power struggles within the Republican Party
   - Roosevelt's perception of what is required of a president

Wilson's New Freedom

The Big Idea

Woodrow Wilson established a strong reform agenda as a progressive leader.

Why It Matters Now

The passage of the Nineteenth Amendment during Wilson's administration granted women the right to vote.

Key Terms and People

Carrie Chapman Catt

Clayton Antitrust Act

Federal Trade Commission (FTC)

Federal Reserve System

Nineteenth Amendment

SS.912.A.1.2; SS.912.A.1.3; SS.912.A.1.4; SS.912.A.1.7; SS.912.A.2.6; SS.912.A.3.12; SS.912.A.5.7; SS.912.A.5.10; SS.912.H.1.1; MAFS.K12.MP.1.1; MAFS.K12.MP.5.1

One American's Story

On March 3, 1913, the day of Woodrow Wilson's inauguration, 5,000 woman suffragists marched through hostile crowds in Washington, DC. Alice Paul and Lucy Burns, the parade's organizers, were members of the National American Woman Suffrage Association (NAWSA). As police failed to restrain the rowdy gathering and congressmen demanded an investigation, Paul and Burns could see the momentum building for suffrage.

By the time Wilson began his campaign for a second term in 1916, the NAWSA's president, **Carrie Chapman Catt**, saw victory on the horizon. Catt expressed her optimism in a speech on September 7 of that year.

Carrie Chapman Catt

"I believe our victory hangs within our grasp, inviting us to pluck it out of the clouds and establish it among the good things of the world. . . . If this be true, the time is past when we should say: 'Men and women of America, look upon that wonderful idea up there; see, one day it will come down.' Instead, the time has come to shout aloud in every city, village and hamlet, and in tones so clear and jubilant that they will reverberate from every mountain peak and echo from shore to shore: 'The woman's Hour has struck.'"

—Carrie Chapman Catt, quoted in *The Crisis*

Catt called an emergency suffrage convention in September 1916. She invited President Wilson, who cautiously supported suffrage. He told those gathered at the convention, "There has been a force behind you that will . . . be triumphant and for which you can afford . . . to wait." They did have to wait. But within four years, the passage of the suffrage amendment became the capstone of the progressive movement.

Wilson Wins Financial Reforms

Like Theodore Roosevelt, Woodrow Wilson claimed progressive ideals. But he had a different idea for the federal government. He believed in attacking large concentrations of power to give greater freedom to average citizens. The prejudices of his southern background, however, prevented him from using federal power to promote civil rights for African Americans.

WILSON'S BACKGROUND Wilson spent his youth in the South during the Civil War and Reconstruction. The son, grandson, and nephew of Presbyterian ministers, he received a strict upbringing. Before entering politics, Wilson worked as a lawyer, a history professor, and later as president of Princeton University. In 1910 Wilson became the governor of New Jersey. As governor, he supported progressive legislation programs. These included a direct primary, workers' compensation, and the regulation of public utilities and railroads.

As America's newly elected president, Wilson moved to enact his program, the "New Freedom." He planned his attack on what he called the triple wall of privilege: the trusts, tariffs, and high finance.

TWO KEY ANTITRUST MEASURES "Without the watchful . . . resolute interference of the government," Wilson said, "there can be no fair play between individuals and such powerful institutions as the trusts. Freedom today is something more than being let alone." During Wilson's administration, Congress enacted two key antitrust measures. The first, the **Clayton Antitrust Act** of 1914, sought to strengthen the Sherman Antitrust Act of 1890. The Clayton Act prohibited corporations from acquiring the stock of another if doing so would create a monopoly. If a company violated the law, its officers could be prosecuted.

The Clayton Act also specified that labor unions and farm organizations had a right to exist. They also would no longer be subject to antitrust laws. Therefore, strikes, peaceful picketing, boycotts, and the collection of strike benefits became legal. In addition, injunctions against strikers were prohibited unless the strikers threatened damage that could not be remedied. Samuel Gompers, president of the American Federation of Labor (AFL), saw great value to workers in the Clayton Act. He called it a Magna Carta for labor. The statement referred to an English document, signed in 1215, in which the English king recognized that he was bound by the law and that the law granted rights to his subjects.

The second major antitrust measure, the Federal Trade Commission Act of 1914, set up the **Federal Trade Commission (FTC)**. This "watchdog" agency was given the power to investigate possible violations of regulatory statutes. It could also require periodic reports from corporations and put an end to a number of unfair business practices. Under Wilson, the FTC administered almost 400 cease-and-desist orders to companies engaged in illegal activity.

Critics of antitrust laws contend that the federal government should not regulate private businesses. They argue that such regulation punishes the businesses that have been most successful in outperforming their

Vocabulary
injunction a court order prohibiting a party from a specific course of action

competition. This leads to inefficiency. These critics believe such regulation also needlessly consumes government resources. Supporters argue that such regulation is necessary to ensure that markets stay competitive.

A NEW TAX SYSTEM In an effort to curb the power of big business, Wilson worked to lower tariff rates. He knew that supporters of big business hadn't allowed such a reduction under Taft.

Wilson lobbied hard in 1913 for the Underwood Act. This law would substantially reduce tariff rates for the first time since the Civil War. He summoned Congress to a special session to plead his case and established a precedent of delivering the State of the Union message in person. Businesses lobbied too, looking to block tariff reductions. When manufacturing lobbyists—people hired by manufacturers to present their case to government officials—descended on the capital to urge senators to vote no, passage seemed unlikely. Wilson denounced the lobbyists and urged voters to monitor their senators' votes. Because of the new president's use of the bully pulpit, the Senate voted to cut tariff rates even more deeply than the House had done.

FEDERAL INCOME TAX With lower tariff rates, the federal government had to replace the revenue that tariffs had previously supplied. Ratified in 1913, the Sixteenth Amendment legalized a federal income tax. This provided revenue by taxing individual earnings and corporate profits.

Under this graduated tax, larger incomes were taxed at higher rates than smaller incomes. The new income tax was limited to a modest tax on family incomes over $4,000. It ranged from 1 percent to a maximum of 6 percent on incomes over $500,000. Initially, few congressmen realized the potential of the income tax. By 1917, however, the government was receiving more money from the income tax than it had ever gained from tariffs. Today, income taxes on corporations and individuals represent the federal government's main source of revenue.

FEDERAL RESERVE SYSTEM Next, Wilson turned his attention to financial reform. The nation needed a way to strengthen the ways in which banks were run. Also needed was a way to quickly adjust the money supply, or the amount of money in circulation. Both credit availability and money supply had to keep pace with the economy.

Wilson's solution was to establish a decentralized private banking system under federal control. The Federal Reserve Act of 1913 divided the nation into 12 districts and established a regional central bank in each district. These "banker's banks" then served the other banks within the district.

The federal reserve banks could issue new paper currency in emergency situations.

Revenue from Individual Federal Income Tax, 1915–1995

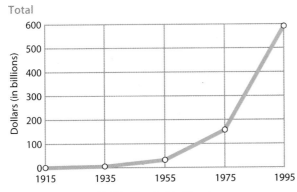

Total

Sources: *Historical Statistics of the United States; Statistical Abstract of the United States, 1987, 1995, 1999*

Interpret Graphs
1. About what year did income tax revenues first begin to rise sharply?
2. About how much revenue did the income tax bring in 1995?

Member banks could use the new currency to make loans to their customers. Federal reserve banks could transfer funds to member banks in trouble. This would save the banks from closing and protect customers' savings. In this way, the federal reserve banks could help the country avoid periods of financial panic by maintaining a steady and stable economy. Through its lending to other banks, the Federal Reserve could also influence interest rates to help "heat up" or "cool down" the economy. For example, low interest rates would encourage borrowing and spending to put more money into the economy. High interest rates would have the opposite effect, discouraging borrowing and taking money out of the economy. The Federal Reserve might raise interest rates to combat inflation, or sharply rising prices.

By 1923 roughly 70 percent of the nation's banking resources were part of the **Federal Reserve System**. This system still serves as the basis of the nation's banking system.

Women Win Suffrage

While Wilson pushed hard for his reforms, determined women intensified their push for the vote. The middle-class women who had been active in progressive movements had grown increasingly impatient about not being allowed to vote. As of 1910 women had federal voting rights only in Wyoming, Utah, Colorado, Washington, and Idaho.

Determined suffragists pushed on, however. They finally saw success come within reach as a result of three developments. These included the increased activism of local groups, the use of bold new strategies to build enthusiasm for the movement, and the rebirth of the national movement under Carrie Chapman Catt.

LOCAL SUFFRAGE BATTLES The suffrage movement was given new strength by growing numbers of college-educated women. Two Massachusetts organizations, the Boston Equal Suffrage Association for Good Government and the College Equal Suffrage League, used door-to-door campaigns to reach potential supporters. Founded by Radcliffe graduate Maud Wood Park, the Boston group spread the message of suffrage to poor and working-class women. Members also took trolley tours where, at each stop, crowds would gather to watch the unusual sight of a woman speaking in public.

Many wealthy young women who visited Europe as part of their education became involved in the suffrage movement in Britain. Led by Emmeline Pankhurst, British suffragists used increasingly bold tactics to advance their cause. They heckled government officials, endured hunger strikes, and even spat on policemen who tried to quiet them. For their activities, British suffragists were sometimes imprisoned. Inspired by their activism, American women returned to the United States armed with similar approaches in their suffrage campaigns.

CATT AND THE NATIONAL MOVEMENT Susan B. Anthony's successor as president of NAWSA was Carrie Chapman Catt. She served from 1900 to 1904 and resumed the presidency in 1915. When Catt returned to NAWSA

Vocabulary
interest rate the percentage of a loan that a borrower must pay back in addition to the amount borrowed

Reading Check
Summarize What was the impact of the two antitrust measures?

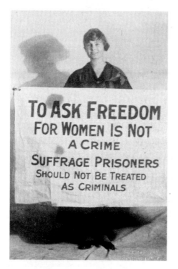

Some suffragists favored stronger forms of protest, which sometimes landed them in jail. This young woman is protesting the rough treatment received by these suffragists at the hands of the police and other government officials.

after organizing New York's Woman Suffrage Party, she concentrated on five tactics. These tactics were: (1) painstaking organization; (2) close ties between local, state, and national workers; (3) establishing a wide base of support; (4) cautious lobbying; and (5) gracious, ladylike behavior.

Although suffragists saw victories, the greater number of failures led some suffragists to try more radical tactics. Lucy Burns and Alice Paul formed their own more radical organization, the Congressional Union, and its successor, the National Woman's Party. They pressured the federal government to pass a suffrage amendment. By 1917 Paul had organized her followers to mount a round-the-clock picket line around the White House. Some of the picketers were arrested, jailed, and even force-fed when they attempted a hunger strike.

These efforts, and America's involvement in World War I, finally made suffrage inevitable. Patriotic American women who headed committees, knitted socks for soldiers, and sold Liberty Bonds now claimed their overdue reward for supporting the war effort. In 1919 Congress passed the **Nineteenth Amendment**, granting women the right to vote. The amendment won final ratification in August 1920. This was 72 years after women had first convened and demanded the vote at the Seneca Falls Convention in 1848.

Reading Check
Analyze Events Why do you think women won the right to vote in 1920, after earlier efforts had failed?

The Limits of Progressivism

Despite Wilson's economic and political reforms, he disappointed Progressives, who favored social reform. In particular, on racial matters Wilson appeased conservative southern Democratic voters. This disappointed his northern white and black supporters. Wilson placed segregationists in charge of federal agencies, thereby expanding racial segregation in the federal government, the military, and Washington, DC.

Vocabulary
appease pacify by granting concessions

WILSON AND CIVIL RIGHTS Like Roosevelt and Taft, Wilson retreated on civil rights once in office. During the campaign of 1912, he won the support of black intellectuals and white liberals by promising to treat blacks equally and to speak out against lynching.

As president, however, Wilson opposed federal anti-lynching legislation. He argued that these crimes fell under state jurisdiction. In addition, the Capitol and the federal offices in Washington, DC, which had been earlier desegregated, resumed the practice of segregation shortly after Wilson's election.

Wilson appointed to his cabinet fellow white southerners who extended segregation. Secretary of the Navy Josephus Daniels, for example, proposed at a cabinet meeting to do away with common drinking fountains and towels in his department. According to an entry in Daniels's diary, President Wilson agreed because he had "made no promises in particular to negroes, except to do them justice." Segregated facilities, in the president's mind, were just.

African Americans and their liberal white supporters in the NAACP felt betrayed. Oswald Garrison Villard, a grandson of the abolitionist William Lloyd Garrison, wrote to Wilson in dismay, "The colored men who voted and worked for you in the belief that their status as American citizens was safe in your hands are deeply cast down." Wilson's response—that he had acted "in the interest of the negroes" and "with the approval of some of the most influential negroes I know"—only widened the rift between the president and some of his former supporters.

On November 12, 1914, the president's reception of an African American delegation brought the confrontation to a bitter climax. William Monroe Trotter, editor-in-chief of the *Guardian*, an African American Boston newspaper, led the delegation. Trotter complained that African Americans from 38 states had asked the president to reverse the segregation of government employees. Instead, segregation had since increased. Trotter then commented on Wilson's inaction.

> *"Only two years ago you were heralded as perhaps the second Lincoln, and now the Afro-American leaders who supported you are hounded as false leaders and traitors to their race. . . . As equal citizens and by virtue of your public promises we are entitled at your hands to freedom from discrimination, restriction, imputation, and insult in government employ. Have you a 'new freedom' for white Americans and a new slavery for your 'Afro-American fellow citizens'? God forbid!"*
>
> —William Monroe Trotter, from an address to President Wilson, November 12, 1914

Historical Source

American Architecture

The progressive movement impacted the world of American architecture. One of the most prominent architects of the time was Frank Lloyd Wright, who studied under the renowned designer Louis Sullivan. In the spirit of progressivism, Wright sought to design buildings that were orderly, efficient, and in harmony with the world around them.

Wright's "prairie style" design features a low, horizontal, and well-defined structure made predominantly of wood, concrete, brick, and other simple materials.

Architecture of the Gilded Age featured ornate decoration and detail, as seen here in this Victorian-style house that was built between 1884 and 1886. Wright rejected these showy and decorative styles in favor of more simplistic designs.

Analyze Historical Sources

1. What are the most striking differences between the two houses? Cite examples that contrast the two buildings.

2. How does Wright's style reflect the progressive spirit?

Wilson found Trotter's tone infuriating. After an angry Trotter shook his finger at the president to emphasize a point, the furious Wilson demanded that the delegation leave. Wilson's refusal to extend civil rights to African Americans pointed to the limits of progressivism under his administration. America's involvement in the war that was raging in Europe would soon reveal other weaknesses.

THE TWILIGHT OF PROGRESSIVISM After taking office in 1913, Wilson had said, "There's no chance of progress and reform in an administration in which war plays the principal part." Yet he found that the outbreak of World War I in Europe in 1914 demanded America's involvement. Meanwhile, distracted Americans and their legislators allowed reform efforts to stall. As the pacifist and reformer Jane Addams mournfully reflected, "The spirit of fighting burns away all those impulses . . . which foster the will to justice."

International conflict was destined to be part of Wilson's presidency. During the early years of his administration, Wilson had dealt with issues of imperialism that had roots in the late 19th century. However, World War I dominated most of his second term as president. The Progressive Era had come to an end.

Reading Check
Analyze Effects
What actions of Wilson disappointed civil rights advocates?

Lesson 7 Assessment

1. **Organize Information** Create a timeline of key events relating to progressivism during Wilson's first term, from 1913 to 1916.

1913   1914   1915   1916

Write a paragraph explaining which event you think best demonstrates progressive reform.

2. **Key Terms and People** For each key term or person in the lesson, write a sentence explaining its significance.

3. **Analyze Motives** Why do you think Wilson failed to push for equality for African Americans, despite his progressive reforms?

4. **Analyze Primary Sources** Wilson said, "Without the watchful . . . resolute interference of the government, there can be no fair play between individuals and . . . the trusts." How does this statement reflect Wilson's approach to reform? Support your answer.

Think About:

• the government's responsibility to the public
• the passage of two key antitrust measures

Key Terms and People

For each key term or person below, write a sentence explaining its connection to late 19th-century American life.

1. progressive movement
2. muckraker
3. Niagara Movement
4. Ida B. Wells
5. Jim Crow laws
6. debt peonage
7. suffrage
8. NAACP
9. Carrie Chapman Catt
10. Federal Reserve System

Main Ideas

Use your notes and the information in the module to answer the following questions.

The Origins of Progressivism

1. What were the four goals that various progressive reform movements struggled to achieve?
2. Why did the prohibition movement appeal to so many women?
3. How did Henry Ford embrace progressive ideas?
4. What kind of state labor laws resulted from progressives lobbying to protect workers?
5. How did government change during the Progressive Era? How were these changes important?

Education Reform

6. How did late 19th-century public schools change?
7. What institutions encouraged European immigrants to become assimilated?
8. Why did some immigrants oppose sending their children to public schools?

Segregation and Discrimination

9. In what ways was racial discrimination reinforced by the federal government's actions and policies?

10. How did conditions for African Americans in the North differ from their circumstances in the South?
11. How did Mexicans help make the Southwest prosperous in the late 19th century?

Women in Public Life

12. In the late 1890s what job opportunities were available to uneducated women without industrial skills?
13. What social and economic effects did higher education have on women?
14. How did the views of Susan B. Anthony and Lucy Stone differ on the passage of the Fourteenth and Fifteenth Amendments?
15. Give two examples of national women's organizations committed to social activism. Briefly describe their progressive missions.

Teddy Roosevelt's Square Deal

16. What scandalous practices did Upton Sinclair expose in his novel *The Jungle*? How did the American public, Roosevelt, and Congress respond?
17. How did Roosevelt earn his reputation as a trustbuster?
18. How did Muir's views on conservation differ from those of Roosevelt and Pinchot?

Progressivism Under Taft

19. As a Progressive, how did Taft compare with Roosevelt?
20. Why did the Republican Party split during Taft's administration?
21. What progressive reforms did the platform of the Bull Moose Party support?

Wilson's New Freedom

22. How did the Clayton Antitrust Act benefit labor?
23. Why did Congress ratify the Sixteenth Amendment?

Module 5 Assessment, continued

24. How did the Federal Reserve System help keep the 1920's economy stable?

25. How did the tactics of Alice Paul and Lucy Burns differ from those of other suffragists?

26. Cite two examples of social welfare legislation that Wilson opposed during his presidency and the arguments he used to defend his position.

Critical Thinking

1. **Compare and Contrast** Create a Venn diagram to show some of the similarities and differences between Roosevelt's Square Deal and Wilson's New Freedom.

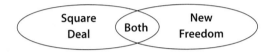

2. **Develop Historical Perspective** What social, political, and economic trends in American life do you think caused the reform impulse during the Progressive Era? Support your answer with details from the text.

3. **Draw Conclusions** How did the work of photojournalist Lewis Hines help lead to the passage of child labor laws?

4. **Evaluate** How effective do you think the muckrakers were in helping reform American society?

5. **Synthesize** Populists demanded that people have a greater say in government and sought to advance the interests of farmers and laborers over those of industrialists. How did the goals of Populists overlap with those of Progressives?

6. **Analyze Motives** Recall what you know about how democracy works in the United States. Why do you think suffrage was so important to many American women? What were the consequences for women of not gaining the right to vote?

7. **Compare and Contrast** In the 1900s there were two competing views about the environment that often pitted industrialist and conservationist against one another. How were these two competing views demonstrated by the environmental policies of President Roosevelt and President Taft?

8. **Compare** Compare the women's suffrage movement to the progressive movement. What were the limitations and accomplishments of each?

Engage with History

As a class, discuss what progressive reformers did to bring about changes in government and society. Consider what else they might have done to be more effective. Rank their efforts in order of effectiveness and offer suggestions for improvement.

Focus on Writing

Imagine you are a newspaper editor in 1896. Write an editorial explaining what you think of the Supreme Court ruling in *Plessy* v. *Ferguson*. Be sure to address the "separate but equal" argument.

Multimedia Activity

Imagine you are a reporter covering a 1912 congressional hearing investigating labor conditions in a textile mill. Work with a partner to write two newspaper articles—one that shows bias in favor of the mill workers, and one that shows bias in favor of the mill. Share the articles with the class, and analyze how language can affect the reporting of information.

Module 6
U.S. Imperialism

★

Essential Question
Did American imperialism have a positive or negative impact on the world and the United States?

About the Painting: This painting depicts Theodore Roosevelt leading the Rough Riders in the fight for Cuba's freedom on San Juan Hill. Though the painting shows the troops on horseback, they actually fought on foot.

In this module you will learn about factors that influenced U.S. imperialism, and about the transformation of the United States into a world power.

Explore ONLINE!

VIDEOS, including...
- TR and the Spanish-American War
- San Juan Hill
- China: Boxer Uprising
- The Peasant Revolution

✓ Document-Based Investigations

✓ Graphic Organizers

✓ Interactive Games

✓ Historical Source: Yellow Journalism

✓ Image with Hotspots: The Panama Canal

SS.912.A.1.2 Utilize a variety of primary and secondary sources to identify author, historical significance, audience, and authenticity to understand a historical period. **SS.912.A.1.4** Analyze how images, symbols, objects, cartoons, graphs, charts, maps, and artwork may be used to interpret the significance of time periods and events from the past. **SS.912.A.4.1** Analyze the major factors that drove United States imperialism. **SS.912.A.4.2** Explain the motives of the United States acquisition of the territories. **SS.912.A.4.3** Examine causes, course, and consequences of the Spanish American War. **SS.912.A.4.4** Analyze the economic, military, and security motivations of the United States to complete the Panama Canal as well as major obstacles involved in its construction. **SS.912.G.1.2** Use spatial perspective and appropriate geographic terms and tools, including the Six Essential Elements, as organizational schema to describe any given place. **LAFS.1112.RH.1.2** Determine the central ideas or information of a primary or secondary source; provide an accurate summary that makes clear the relationships among the key details and ideas. **LAFS.1112.RH.2.6** Evaluate authors' differing points of view on the same historical event or issue by assessing the authors' claims, reasoning, and evidence. **LAFS.1112.RH.4.10** By the end of grade 12, read and comprehend history/social studies texts in the grades 11–CCR text complexity band independently and proficiently. **MAFS.K12.MP.1.1** Make sense of problems and persevere in solving them. **MAFS.K12.MP.3.1** Construct viable arguments and critique the reasoning of others. **MAFS.K12.MP.5.1** Use appropriate tools strategically. **MAFS.K12.MP.6.1** Attend to precision.

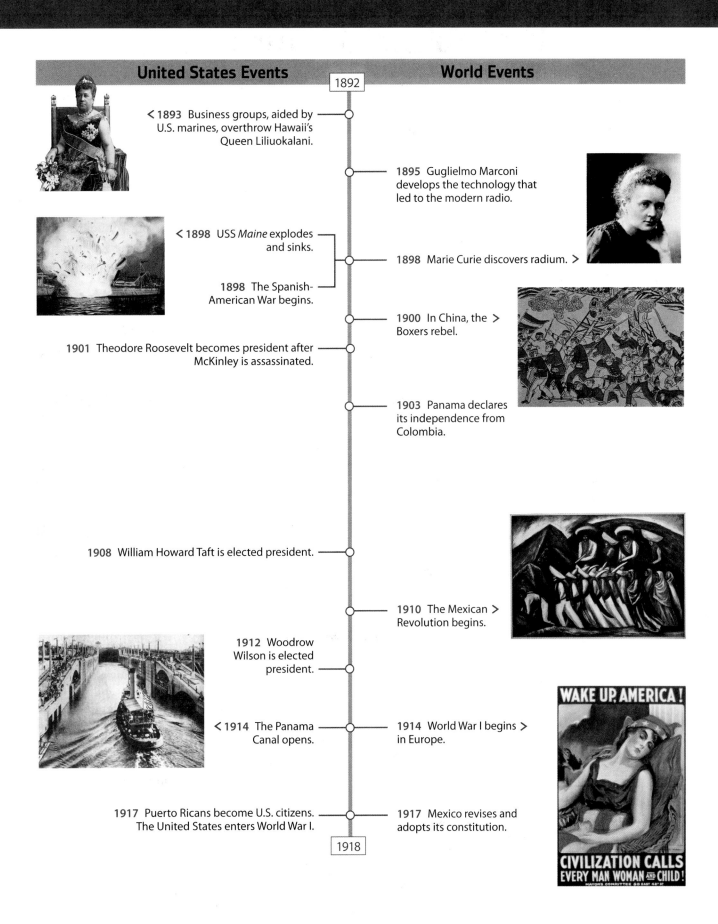

| United States Events | 1892 | World Events |

< 1893 Business groups, aided by U.S. marines, overthrow Hawaii's Queen Liliuokalani.

1895 Guglielmo Marconi develops the technology that led to the modern radio.

< 1898 USS *Maine* explodes and sinks.

1898 Marie Curie discovers radium. **>**

1898 The Spanish-American War begins.

1900 In China, the **>** Boxers rebel.

1901 Theodore Roosevelt becomes president after McKinley is assassinated.

1903 Panama declares its independence from Colombia.

1908 William Howard Taft is elected president.

1910 The Mexican **>** Revolution begins.

1912 Woodrow Wilson is elected president.

< 1914 The Panama Canal opens.

1914 World War I begins **>** in Europe.

1917 Puerto Ricans become U.S. citizens. The United States enters World War I.

1917 Mexico revises and adopts its constitution.

1918

WAKE UP, AMERICA!

CIVILIZATION CALLS EVERY MAN WOMAN AND CHILD!

★
Imperialism and America

The Big Idea

Beginning in 1867 and continuing through the century, global competition caused the United States to expand.

Why It Matters Now

During this time period, the United States acquired Hawaii and Alaska, both of which became states in 1959.

Key Terms and People

Queen Liliuokalani

imperialism

Alfred T. Mahan

William Seward

Pearl Harbor

Sanford B. Dole

One American's Story

In 1893 **Queen Liliuokalani** (lə-lē′ə-ō-kə-lä′nē) realized that her reign in Hawaii had come to an end. More than 160 U.S. sailors and marines stood ready to aid the *haoles* (white foreigners) who planned to overthrow the Hawaiian monarchy. In an eloquent statement of protest, the proud monarch surrendered to the superior force of the United States.

Hawaii's "Queen Lil" announced that if restored to power, she would behead those who had conspired to depose her.

"I, Liliuokalani, . . . do hereby solemnly protest against any and all acts done against myself and the constitutional government of the Hawaiian Kingdom. . . . Now, to avoid any collision of armed forces and perhaps the loss of life, I do under this protest . . . yield my authority until such time as the Government of the United States shall . . . undo the action of its representatives and reinstate me in the authority which I claim as the constitutional sovereign of the Hawaiian Islands."
—Queen Liliuokalani, quoted in *Those Kings and Queens of Old Hawaii*

U.S. ambassador to Hawaii John L. Stevens informed the State Department, "The Hawaiian pear is now fully ripe, and this is the golden hour for the United States to pluck it." The annexation of Hawaii was only one of the goals of America's empire builders in the late 19th century.

SS.912.A.1.2; SS.912.A.1.4; SS.912.A.4.1;
SS.912.A.4.2; SS.912.G.1.2; LAFS.1112.RH.1.2;
LAFS.1112.RH.4.10; MAFS.K12.MP.1.1; MAFS.K12.MP.3.1;
MAFS.K12.MP.5.1

American Expansionism

Americans had always sought to expand the size of their nation, and throughout the 19th century they extended their control toward the Pacific Ocean. Their successes in increasing trade and expanding territory in the 1840s and 1850s eventually led to even greater efforts to spread U.S. influence around the world.

EARLY ENCOUNTERS As the United States expanded west in the mid-19th century, new port cities on the Pacific coast gave the nation the opportunity to expand its global trade network as well. The potential for profits from trade with China and Japan motivated U.S. officials to extend the country's reach into the Pacific and attempt to formalize diplomatic relations. Though China initially resisted trade with Westerners, in the 1840s U.S. officials signed the Treaty of Wangxia to protect U.S. business interests in the region.

This Japanese print shows the arrival of Commodore Perry's warships in Japan.

Like China, Japan was resistant to trade with Western nations. Though British, French, Russian, and American ships occasionally anchored off the Japanese coast, Japan repeatedly refused to meet with their representatives. However, the appeal of trade with Japan proved too great for the United States to give up. In addition to wanting to open Japanese ports to trade, the United States also wanted to secure vital coaling stations that could be used to refuel U.S. trade ships and warships in the Pacific.

On July 8, 1853, Commodore Matthew Perry sailed into Tokyo Bay with four warships to open negotiations with the Japanese. This thinly veiled threat of military force convinced the Japanese government to negotiate. The next year, the two countries signed the Treaty of Kanagawa, which opened up two Japanese ports for refueling. In 1858 Japan signed the Harris Treaty, opening its ports to trade.

At the same time, some Americans were also looking for ways to increase U.S. involvement and territory in Central America and the Caribbean. They had little success until the Mexican-American War. After the land gains of the 1840s and 1850s, the idea of increasing U.S. territory appealed to many Americans. Over time, more and more Americans began to side with the interventionists, or those willing to interfere with the economic, political, or social affairs of other nations. By the 1880s U.S. leaders were convinced that the United States should join the imperialist powers of Europe, establishing overseas colonies and spreading America's global influence. **Imperialism**—the policy in which stronger nations extend their economic, political, or military control over weaker territories—was already a trend around the world.

GLOBAL COMPETITION European nations had been establishing colonies for centuries. In the late 19th century, Africa had emerged as a prime target of European expansionism. By the early 20th century, only two countries in all of Africa—Ethiopia and Liberia—remained independent.

Imperialists also competed for territory in Asia, especially in China. In its late 19th-century reform era, Japan replaced its old feudal order with a strong central government. Hoping that military strength would bolster industrialization, Japan joined European nations in competition for China in the 1890s.

Alfred T. Mahan (1840–1914)

Alfred T. Mahan joined the U.S. Navy in the late 1850s and served for nearly 40 years. In 1886 he became president of the newly established Naval War College in Newport, Rhode Island.

Throughout his lifetime, Mahan was one of the most outspoken advocates of American military expansion. In his book *The Influence of Sea Power upon History, 1660–1783* (published in 1890), Mahan called for the United States to develop a modern fleet capable of protecting American business and shipping interests around the world.

He also urged the United States to establish naval bases in the Caribbean, to construct a canal across the Isthmus of Panama, and to acquire Hawaii and other Pacific islands.

Feelings of nationalism, or national pride, in the United States grew as well. Many Americans believed in the superiority of America's political and cultural ideals. With a belief in manifest destiny, they already had pushed the U.S. border to the Pacific Ocean. Spreading America's ideals oversees was the next logical step. As Americans gradually warmed to the idea of overseas expansion, three factors fueled the new American imperialism:

- desire for military strength
- thirst for new markets
- belief in cultural superiority

DESIRE FOR MILITARY STRENGTH Seeing that other nations were establishing a global military presence, American leaders advised that the United States build up its own military strength. One such leader was Admiral **Alfred T. Mahan** of the U.S. Navy. Mahan urged government officials to build up American naval power in order to compete with other powerful nations. As a result of the urging of Mahan and others, the United States built nine steel-hulled cruisers between 1883 and 1890. The construction of modern battleships such as the *Maine* and the *Oregon* transformed the country into the world's third-largest naval power.

THIRST FOR NEW MARKETS In the late 19th century, advances in technology enabled American farms and factories to produce far more than American citizens could consume. For example, plows, harrows, threshing machines, and reapers increased corn production by 264 percent and the wheat harvest by 252 percent. Now the United States needed raw materials for its factories and new markets for its agricultural and manufactured goods. Imperialists viewed foreign trade as the

In the early 1900s the Navy's Great White Fleet, so named because its ships were painted white, was a sign of America's growing military power.

Vocabulary
xenophobia an unreasonable dislike or fear of people from another country

Reading Check
Analyze Effects
How did domestic tensions, such as overproduction, unemployment, racism, and the closing of the United States frontier to westward expansion, affect thoughts about imperialism?

Reading Check
Analyze Motives
How did time prove that the purchase of Alaska was not an act of folly?

solution to American overproduction and the related problems of unemployment and economic depression. They felt that a worldwide trade network anchored by U.S. colonies and trading posts could provide the country with the economic growth it needed.

BELIEF IN CULTURAL SUPERIORITY Cultural factors also were used to justify imperialism. The same xenophobia that helped pass the Chinese Exclusion Act in 1882, and led to its renewal in 1892 and 1902, fueled imperialist ideas about foreign nations. Some Americans combined the philosophy of Social Darwinism—a belief that free-market competition would lead to the survival of the fittest—with a belief in the racial superiority of Anglo-Saxons. They argued that the United States had a responsibility to spread Christianity and democracy to "civilize" the world's "inferior peoples." This viewpoint narrowly defined "civilization" according to the standards of only one culture.

The United States Acquires Alaska

An early supporter of American expansion was **William Seward**, Secretary of State under presidents Abraham Lincoln and Andrew Johnson. In 1867 Seward arranged for the United States to buy Alaska from the Russians for $7.2 million. Seward had some trouble persuading the House of Representatives to approve funding for the purchase. Some people thought it was silly to buy what they called "Seward's Icebox" or "Seward's folly." Time showed how wrong they were. In 1959 Alaska became a state. For about two cents an acre, the United States had acquired a land rich in timber, minerals, and, as it turned out, oil.

Document-Based Investigation Historical Source

Buying and Selling Alaska

While leaders in the United States government debated whether to buy Alaska, Russian officials were having a similar debate about the sale of their colony.

"In view of the straitened circumstances of State finances . . . I think we would do well to take advantage of the excess of money . . . in the Treasury of the United States of America and to sell our North American colonies. . . . we must not deceive ourselves and must forsee that the United States, . . . desiring to dominate undividedly the whole of North America, will take the . . . colonies from us and we shall not be able to regain them. . . . At the same time these colonies bring us very small profit and their loss to us would not be greatly felt. . . . These considerations I beg Your Excellency to report to His Majesty the Emperor."

—Grand Duke Konstantin, from a letter to Prince A.M. Gorchakov, March 22, 1857

Analyze Historical Sources
What reservations does Grand Duke Konstantin have about the United States' interest in Alaska?

The United States Takes Hawaii

In 1867, the same year in which Alaska was purchased, the United States took over the Midway Islands, which lie in the Pacific Ocean about 1,300 miles north of Hawaii. No one lived on the islands, so the event did not attract much attention.

Hawaii was another question. The Hawaiian Islands had been economically important to the United States for nearly a century. Since the 1790s American merchants had stopped there on their way to China and East India. In the 1820s Yankee missionaries founded Christian schools and churches on the islands. Their children and grandchildren became sugar planters who sold most of their crop to the United States.

THE CRY FOR ANNEXATION In the mid-19th century, American-owned sugar plantations accounted for about three-quarters of the islands' wealth. Plantation owners imported thousands of laborers from Japan, Portugal, and China. By 1900 foreigners and immigrant laborers outnumbered native Hawaiians about three to one.

White planters profited from close ties with the United States. In 1875 the United States agreed to import Hawaiian sugar duty-free. Over the next 15 years, Hawaiian sugar production increased nine times. Then the McKinley Tariff of 1890 provoked a crisis by eliminating the duty-free status of Hawaiian sugar. As a result, Hawaiian sugar growers faced competition in the American market. American planters in Hawaii called for the United States to annex the islands so they wouldn't have to pay the duty.

U.S. military and economic leaders already understood the value of the islands. In 1887 they pressured Hawaii to allow the United States to build a naval base at **Pearl Harbor**, the kingdom's best port. The base became a coaling station for refueling American ships.

THE END OF A MONARCHY Also in that year, Hawaii's King Kalakaua had been strong-armed by white business leaders. They forced him to amend Hawaii's constitution, effectively limiting voting rights to only wealthy landowners. But when Kalakaua died in 1891, his sister Queen Liliuokalani came to power with a "Hawaii for Hawaiians" agenda. She proposed removing the property-owning qualifications for voting. To prevent this from happening, business groups—encouraged by Ambassador John L. Stevens—organized a revolution. With the help of marines, they overthrew the queen and set up a government headed by **Sanford B. Dole**.

Vocabulary
annex to incorporate territory into an existing country or state

Hawaii's Changing Population, 1853–1920

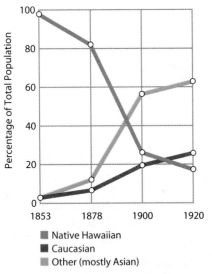

Source: Robert C. Schmitt, *Demographic Statistics of Hawaii, 1778-1965*

Interpret Graphs
1. What were the most dramatic changes in Hawaiian population between 1853 and 1920?
2. How might these changes have affected the political climate there?

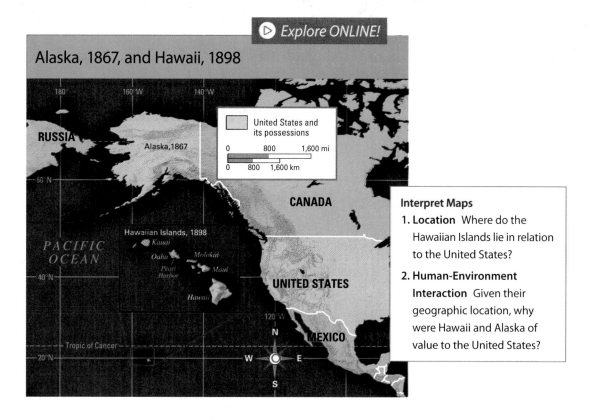

Alaska, 1867, and Hawaii, 1898

▷ *Explore ONLINE!*

Interpret Maps

1. **Location** Where do the Hawaiian Islands lie in relation to the United States?

2. **Human-Environment Interaction** Given their geographic location, why were Hawaii and Alaska of value to the United States?

President Cleveland directed that the queen be restored to her throne. When Dole refused to surrender power, Cleveland formally recognized the Republic of Hawaii. But he refused to consider annexation unless a majority of Hawaiians favored it.

In 1897 William McKinley, who favored annexation, succeeded Cleveland as president. On August 12, 1898, Congress proclaimed Hawaii an American territory, although Hawaiians had never had the chance to vote. In 1959 Hawaii became the 50th state of the United States.

Reading Check
Analyze Events
What factors led to the annexation of Hawaii in 1898?

Lesson 1 Assessment

1. **Organize Information** Fill in a web diagram with events and concepts that illustrate the roots of imperialism.

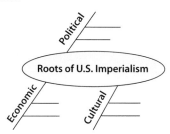

Choose one event to explain further in a paragraph.

2. **Key Terms and People** For each key term or person in the lesson, write a sentence explaining its significance.

3. **Draw Conclusions** Manifest destiny greatly influenced American policy during the first half of the 19th century. How do you think manifest destiny set the stage for American imperialism at the end of the century?

4. **Evaluate** In your opinion, did Sanford B. Dole and other American planters have the right to stage a revolt in Hawaii in 1893?

   Think About:
   • American business interests in Hawaii
   • the rights of native Hawaiians

5. **Analyze Primary Sources** At a meeting of Republicans in 1898, Indiana senator Albert J. Beveridge discussed his views on imperialism.

   "Fate has written our policy for us; the trade of the world must and shall be ours. . . . We will establish trading posts throughout the world as distributing points for American products. . . . Great colonies governing themselves, flying our flag and trading with us, will grow about our posts of trade."

   How does Beveridge explain the country's need to acquire new territories and expand its worldwide trade network?

The Spanish-American War

The Big Idea

In 1898 the United States went to war to help Cuba win its independence from Spain.

Why It Matters Now

U.S. involvement in Latin America and Asia increased greatly as a result of the war and continues today.

Key Terms and People

José Martí

Valeriano Weyler

yellow journalism

USS *Maine*

George Dewey

Rough Riders

San Juan Hill

Treaty of Paris

One American's Story

Early in 1896 James Creelman traveled to Cuba as a *New York World* reporter, covering the second Cuban war for independence from Spain. While in Havana, he wrote columns about his observations of the war. His descriptions of Spanish atrocities aroused American sympathy for Cubans.

Cuban rebels burn the town of Jaruco in March 1896.

"No man's life, no man's property is safe [in Cuba]. American citizens are imprisoned or slain without cause. American property is destroyed on all sides. . . . Wounded soldiers can be found begging in the streets of Havana. . . . The horrors of a barbarous struggle for the extermination of the native population are witnessed in all parts of the country. Blood on the roadsides, blood in the fields, blood on the doorsteps, blood, blood, blood! . . . Is there no nation wise enough, brave enough to aid this blood-smitten land?"
—James Creelman, from a *New York World* article, May 17, 1896

Newspapers during that period often exaggerated stories like Creelman's to boost their sales as well as to provoke American intervention in Cuba.

SS.912.A.1.2; SS.912.A.1.4; SS.912.A.4.1; SS.912.A.4.2; SS.912.A.4.3; SS.912.G.1.2; LAFS.1112.RH.1.2; LAFS.1112.RH.2.6; LAFS.1112.RH.4.10

Cubans Rebel Against Spain

By the end of the 19th century, Spain—once the most powerful colonial nation on earth—had lost most of its colonies. It retained only the Philippines and the island of Guam in the Pacific, a few outposts in Africa, and the Caribbean islands of Cuba and Puerto Rico in the Americas.

AMERICAN INTEREST IN CUBA The United States had long held an interest in Cuba, which lies only 90 miles south of Florida. In 1854 diplomats recommended to President Franklin Pierce that the United States buy Cuba from Spain. The Spanish responded by saying that they would rather see Cuba sunk in the ocean.

But American interest in Cuba continued. When the Cubans rebelled against Spain between 1868 and 1878, American sympathies went out to the Cuban people.

The Cuban revolt against Spain was not successful, but in 1886 the Cuban people did force Spain to abolish slavery. After the emancipation of Cuba's slaves, American capitalists began investing millions of dollars in large sugar cane plantations on the island.

THE SECOND WAR FOR INDEPENDENCE Anti-Spanish sentiment in Cuba soon erupted into a second war for independence. **José Martí**, a Cuban poet and journalist in exile in New York, launched a revolution in 1895. Martí organized Cuban resistance against Spain, using an active guerrilla campaign and deliberately destroying property, especially American-owned sugar mills and plantations. Martí counted on provoking U.S. intervention to help the rebels achieve *¡Cuba Libre!*—a free Cuba.

Public opinion in the United States was split. Many business people wanted the government to support Spain in order to protect their investments. Other Americans, however, were enthusiastic about the rebel cause.

Vocabulary
guerrilla a member of a military force that harasses the enemy

---

- BIOGRAPHY

José Martí (1853–1895)

The Cuban political activist José Martí dedicated his life to achieving independence for Cuba. Expelled from Cuba at the age of 16 because of his revolutionary activities, Martí earned a master's degree and a law degree. He eventually settled in the United States.

Wary of the U.S. role in the Cuban struggle against the Spanish, Martí warned, "I know the Monster, because I have lived in its lair." His fears of U.S. imperialism turned out to have been well-founded. U.S. troops occupied Cuba on and off from 1906 until 1922.

Martí died fighting for Cuban independence in 1895. He is revered today in Cuba as a hero and martyr.

Reading Check
Analyze Motives
Why did José Martí
encourage Cuban
rebels to destroy sugar
mills and plantations?

The cry "¡*Cuba Libre!*" was, after all, similar in sentiment to Patrick Henry's "Give me liberty or give me death!" Despite economic concerns and public opinion, President Grover Cleveland remained true to the Monroe Doctrine, which promised that the United States would not intervene in the affairs of existing European colonies in the Western Hemisphere. Soon, though, the promises of the Monroe Doctrine would be put to the test.

War Fever Escalates

In 1896 Spain responded to the Cuban revolt by sending General **Valeriano Weyler** to Cuba to restore order. Weyler tried to crush the rebellion by herding the entire rural population of central and western Cuba into barbed-wire concentration camps. Here, civilians could not give aid to rebels. An estimated 300,000 Cubans filled these camps, where thousands died from hunger and disease.

HEADLINE WARS Weyler's actions fueled a war over newspaper circulation that had developed between the American newspaper tycoons William Randolph Hearst and Joseph Pulitzer. To lure readers, Hearst's *New York Journal* and Pulitzer's *New York World* printed exaggerated accounts—by reporters such as James Creelman—of "Butcher" Weyler's brutality. Stories of poisoned wells and of children being thrown to the sharks deepened American sympathy for the rebels. This sensational style of writing, which exaggerates the news to lure and enrage readers, became known as **yellow journalism**.

Hearst and Pulitzer fanned war fever. When Hearst sent the gifted artist Frederic Remington to Cuba to draw sketches of reporters' stories, Remington informed the publisher that a war between the United States and Spain seemed very unlikely. Hearst reportedly replied, "You furnish the pictures and I'll furnish the war."

THE DE LÔME LETTER American sympathy for "¡*Cuba Libre!*" grew with each day's headlines. When President William McKinley took office in 1897, demands for American intervention in Cuba were on the rise. Preferring to avoid war with Spain, McKinley tried diplomatic means to resolve the crisis. At first his efforts appeared to succeed. Spain recalled General Weyler, modified the policy regarding concentration camps, and offered Cuba limited self-government.

In February 1898, however, the *New York Journal* published a private letter written by Enrique Dupuy de Lôme, the Spanish minister to the United States. A Cuban rebel had stolen the letter from a Havana post office and leaked it to the newspaper, which was thirsty for scandal. The de Lôme letter criticized President McKinley, calling him "weak" and "a bidder for the admiration of the crowd." The embarrassed Spanish government apologized, and the minister resigned. Still, Americans were angry over the insult to their president.

THE USS *MAINE* EXPLODES Only a few days after the publication of the de Lôme letter, American resentment toward Spain turned to outrage. Early in 1898 President McKinley had ordered the **USS *Maine*** to Cuba to bring home

American citizens in danger from the fighting and to protect American property. On February 15, 1898, the ship blew up in the harbor of Havana. More than 260 men were killed.

At the time, no one really knew why the ship exploded; however, American newspapers claimed that the Spanish had blown up the ship. The *Journal*'s headline read "The warship *Maine* was split in two by an enemy's secret infernal machine." Hearst's paper offered a reward of $50,000 for the capture of the Spaniards who supposedly had committed the outrage.

Reading Check
Summarize What events increased the tension between the United States and Spain?

The de Lôme letter and the constant stream of sensational headlines helped feed a growing jingoism, or extreme patriotism. When combined with the explosion of the *Maine,* these events had many Americans demanding war with Spain.

War with Spain Erupts

Until this time, the United States had remained largely isolationist, favoring a policy of avoiding foreign entanglements. Now there was no holding back the forces that wanted war. "Remember the *Maine!*" became the rallying cry for U.S. intervention in Cuba. It made no difference that the Spanish government agreed, on April 9, to almost everything the United States demanded, including a six-month cease-fire.

Despite the Spanish concessions, public opinion favored war. On April 11 McKinley asked Congress for authority to use force against Spain. After a week of debate, Congress agreed. On April 20 the United States declared war.

THE WAR IN THE PHILIPPINES The Spanish thought the Americans would invade Cuba. But the first battle of the war took place in a Spanish colony on the other side of the world—the Philippine Islands.

On April 30 the American fleet in the Pacific steamed to the Philippines. The next morning, Commodore **George Dewey** gave the command to open fire on the Spanish fleet at Manila, the Philippine capital. Within hours, Dewey's men had destroyed every Spanish ship there. Dewey's victory allowed U.S. troops to land in the Philippines.

Dewey had the support of the Filipinos who, like the Cubans, also wanted freedom from Spain. Over the next two months, 11,000 Americans joined forces with Filipino rebels led by Emilio Aguinaldo. In August Spanish troops in Manila surrendered to the United States.

Spain's fleet was not prepared to face the might of the U.S. Navy.

THE WAR IN THE CARIBBEAN In the Caribbean, hostilities began with a naval blockade of Cuba. Admiral William T. Sampson effectively sealed up the Spanish fleet in the harbor of Santiago de Cuba.

Dewey's victory at Manila had demonstrated the superiority of United States naval forces. In contrast, the army maintained only a small professional force, supplemented by a larger, inexperienced, and ill-prepared volunteer force. About 125,000 Americans had volunteered to fight. The new soldiers were sent to training camps that lacked adequate supplies and effective leaders. Moreover, there were not enough modern guns to go around, and

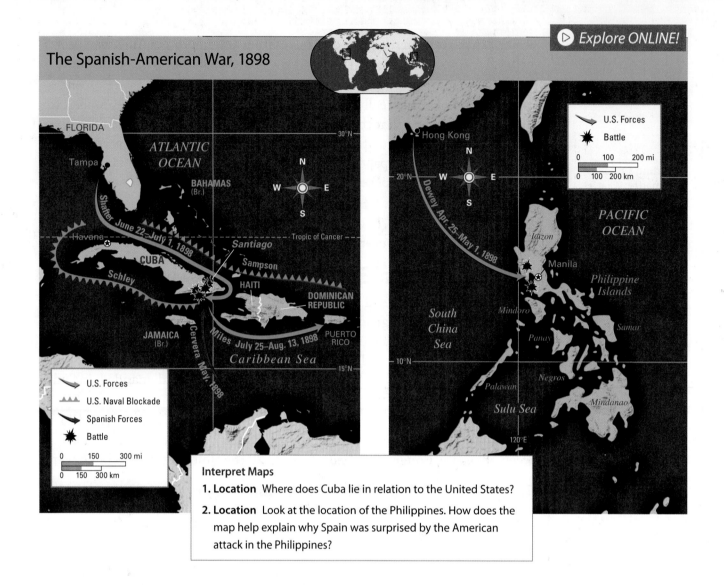

The Spanish-American War, 1898

Explore ONLINE!

FLORIDA
Tampa
ATLANTIC OCEAN
BAHAMAS (Br.)
Shafter June 22–July 1, 1898
Havana
CUBA
Schley
Santiago
Sampson
HAITI
Tropic of Cancer
30°N
DOMINICAN REPUBLIC
JAMAICA (Br.)
Cervera May 1898
Miles July 25–Aug. 13, 1898
PUERTO RICO
Caribbean Sea
15°N

U.S. Forces
U.S. Naval Blockade
Spanish Forces
Battle

0   150   300 mi
0   150   300 km

Hong Kong
20°N
Dewey Apr 25–May 1, 1898
Luzon
Manila
PACIFIC OCEAN
Philippine Islands
South China Sea
Mindoro
Samar
Panay
Palawan
Negros
Sulu Sea
Mindanao
10°N
120°E

U.S. Forces
Battle
0   100   200 mi
0   100   200 km

Interpret Maps
1. **Location** Where does Cuba lie in relation to the United States?
2. **Location** Look at the location of the Philippines. How does the map help explain why Spain was surprised by the American attack in the Philippines?

the troops were outfitted with heavy woolen uniforms unsuitable for Cuba's tropical climate. In addition, the officers—most of whom were Civil War veterans—had a tendency to spend their time recalling their war experiences rather than training the volunteers.

ROUGH RIDERS Despite these handicaps, American forces landed in Cuba in June 1898 and began to converge on the port city of Santiago. The army of 17,000 included four African American regiments of the regular army and the **Rough Riders**, a volunteer cavalry under the command of Leonard Wood and Theodore Roosevelt. Roosevelt, a New Yorker, had given up his job as assistant secretary of the navy to lead the group of volunteers. He would later become president of the United States.

The most famous land battle in Cuba took place near Santiago on July 1. The first part of the battle, on nearby Kettle Hill, featured a dramatic uphill charge by the Rough Riders and two African American regiments, the Ninth and Tenth Cavalries. Their victory cleared the way for an infantry attack on the strategically important **San Juan Hill**. Although Roosevelt and his units played only a minor role in the second victory, U.S. newspapers declared him the hero of San Juan Hill.

Two days later, the Spanish fleet tried to escape the American blockade of the harbor at Santiago. The naval battle that followed, along the Cuban coast, ended in the destruction of the Spanish fleet. On the heels of this victory, American troops invaded Puerto Rico on July 25.

TREATY OF PARIS The United States and Spain signed an armistice, a cease-fire agreement, on August 12, ending what Secretary of State John Hay called "a splendid little war." The actual fighting in the war had lasted only 15 weeks.

On December 10, 1898, the United States and Spain met in Paris to agree on a treaty. At the peace talks, Spain freed Cuba and turned over the islands of Guam in the Pacific and Puerto Rico in the West Indies to the United States. Spain also sold the Philippines to the United States for $20 million.

DEBATE OVER THE TREATY The **Treaty of Paris** touched off a great debate in the United States. Arguments centered on whether or not the United States had the right to annex the Philippines, but imperialism was the real issue.

Document-Based Investigation Historical Source

Interventionists vs. Noninterventionists

The issue of whether to annex the Philippines was part of a larger debate about U.S. imperialism. The novelist and anti-imperialist Mark Twain questioned the motives for U.S. intervention around the world in a satirical piece written in 1901. At a meeting of the Republican Party, Indiana senator Albert Beveridge made a case in favor of global intervention.

"Shall we go on conferring our Civilization upon the peoples that sit in darkness, or shall we give those poor things a rest? . . . Extending the Blessings of Civilization to our Brother who Sits in Darkness has been a good trade and has paid well, on the whole; and there is money in it yet . . . but not enough, in my judgment, to make any considerable risk advisable."

—Mark Twain, quoted in
To the Person Sitting in Darkness

"The Opposition tells us that we ought not to govern a people without their consent. . . . Would not the people of the Philippines prefer the just, humane, civilizing government of this Republic to the savage, bloody rule of pillage and extortion from which we have rescued them? Do not the blazing fires of joy and the ringing bells of gladness in Porto Rico prove the welcome of our flag? . . . do we owe no duty to the world? . . . Shall we abandon them, with Germany, England, Japan, hungering for them?"

—Albert Beveridge, from the March of the Flag speech,
September 16, 1898

Analyze Historical Sources

1. What reasons does Beveridge give for a foreign policy of intervention?

2. Why do you think Twain opposes intervention?

This lithograph criticizes American foreign policy in 1898. In the cartoon, Uncle Sam is riding a bicycle with wheels labeled "western hemisphere" and "eastern hemisphere." He has abandoned his horse, on whose saddle appears "Monroe Doctrine," because the horse is too slow.

Reading Check
Summarize What were the terms of the Treaty of Paris?

President McKinley told a group of Methodist ministers that he had prayed for guidance on Philippine annexation and had concluded "that there was nothing left for us to do but to take them all [the Philippine Islands], and to educate the Filipinos, and uplift and Christianize them." McKinley's need to justify imperialism may have clouded his memory—most Filipinos had been Christian for centuries.

Other prominent Americans presented a variety of arguments—political, moral, and economic—against annexation. Some felt that the treaty violated the Declaration of Independence by denying self-government to the newly acquired territories. The African American educator Booker T. Washington argued that the United States should settle race-related issues at home before taking on social problems elsewhere. The labor leader Samuel Gompers feared that Filipino immigrants would compete for American jobs.

On February 6, 1899, the annexation question was settled with the Senate's approval of the Treaty of Paris. The United States now had an empire that included Guam, Puerto Rico, and the Philippines. The next question Americans faced was how and when the United States would add to its dominion.

Lesson 2 Assessment

1. **Organize Information** In 1898 a debate raged in the United States over whether the United States had the right to annex the Philippines. Use a graphic organizer to summarize the pros and cons of this debate.

Which side do you support? Why?

2. **Key Terms and People** For each key term or person in the lesson, write a sentence explaining its significance.

3. **Make Inferences** What do you think were the unstated editorial policies of yellow journalism? Support your answer with evidence from the text.

   Think About:
   • James Creelman's account of Spanish atrocities against Cubans
   • Hearst's remark to Remington
   • the *Journal* headline about the explosion of the battleship *Maine*

4. **Analyze Effects** Many anti-imperialists worried that imperialism might threaten the American democratic system. How might this happen?

5. **Draw Conclusions** In 1898 Theodore Roosevelt resigned his post as assistant secretary of the navy to organize the Rough Riders. Why do you think Roosevelt was willing to take this risk? How do you think this decision affected his political career?

Acquiring New Lands

SS.912.A.1.2; SS.912.A.1.3; SS.912.A.1.4; SS.912.A.4.1; SS.912.A.4.2; SS.912.G.1.2; LAFS.1112.RH.1.2

The Big Idea

In the early 1900s the United States engaged in conflicts in Puerto Rico, Cuba, and the Philippines.

Why It Matters Now

Today the United States maintains a strong military and political presence in strategic worldwide locations.

Key Terms and People

Foraker Act

Platt Amendment

protectorate

Emilio Aguinaldo

John Hay

Open Door notes

Boxer Rebellion

One American's Story

When Puerto Rico became part of the United States after the Spanish-American War, many Puerto Ricans feared that the United States would not give them the measure of self-rule that they had gained under the Spanish. Puerto Rican statesman and publisher Luis Muñoz Rivera was one of the most vocal advocates of Puerto Rican self-rule. Between 1900 and 1916, he lived primarily in the United States and continually worked for the independence of his homeland. Finally, in 1916 the U.S. Congress, facing possible war in Europe and wishing to settle the issue of Puerto Rico, invited Muñoz Rivera to speak. On May 5, 1916, Muñoz Rivera stood before the U.S. House of Representatives to discuss the future of Puerto Rico.

Luis Muñoz Rivera

"You, citizens of a free fatherland, with its own laws, its own institutions, and its own flag, can appreciate the unhappiness of the small and solitary people that must await its laws from your authority. . . . when you acquire the certainty that you can found in Puerto Rico a republic like that founded in Cuba and Panama . . . give us our independence and you will stand before humanity as . . . a great creator of new nationalities and a great liberator of oppressed peoples."
—Luis Muñoz Rivera, quoted in *The Puerto Ricans*

Muñoz Rivera returned to Puerto Rico, where he died in November 1916. Three months later, the United States made Puerto Ricans U.S. citizens.

Ruling Puerto Rico

Not all Puerto Ricans wanted independence, as Muñoz Rivera did. Some wanted statehood, while still others hoped for some measure of local self-government as an American territory. As a result, the United States gave Puerto Ricans no promises regarding independence after the Spanish-American War.

MILITARY RULE During the Spanish-American War, United States forces, under General Nelson A. Miles, occupied the island. As his soldiers took control, General Miles issued a statement assuring Puerto Ricans that the Americans were there to "bring you protection, not only to yourselves but to your property, to promote your prosperity, and to bestow upon you the immunities and blessings of the liberal institutions of our government." For the time being, Puerto Rico would be controlled by the military until Congress decided otherwise.

RETURN TO CIVIL GOVERNMENT Although many Puerto Ricans had dreams of independence or statehood, the United States had different plans for the island's future. Puerto Rico was strategically important to the United States, both for maintaining a U.S. presence in the Caribbean and for protecting a future canal that American leaders wanted to build across the Isthmus of Panama. In 1900 Congress passed the **Foraker Act**, which ended military rule and set up a civil government. The act gave the president of the United States the power to appoint Puerto Rico's governor and members of the upper house of its legislature. Puerto Ricans could elect only the members of the legislature's lower house.

In 1901 in the *Insular* Cases, the U.S. Supreme Court ruled that the Constitution did not automatically apply to people in acquired territories. Congress, however, retained the right to extend U.S. citizenship, and it granted that right to Puerto Ricans in 1917. It also gave them the right to elect both houses of their legislature.

Reading Check
Analyze Issues Why was Puerto Rico important to the United States?

| NOW | & | THEN |

Puerto Rico

Ever since their transfer under the Treaty of Paris from Spain to the United States, Puerto Ricans have debated their status, as shown here. In 1967, 1993, and 1998, Puerto Ricans rejected both statehood and independence in favor of commonwealth, a status given the island in 1952.

As members of a commonwealth, Puerto Ricans are U.S. citizens. They can move freely between the island and the mainland and are subjected to the military draft but cannot vote in U.S. presidential elections. A majority of Puerto Ricans have rejected statehood because they fear it would mean giving up their Latino culture.

Cuba and the United States

When the United States declared war against Spain in 1898, it recognized Cuba's independence from Spain. It also passed the Teller Amendment, which stated that the United States had no intention of taking over any part of Cuba. The Treaty of Paris, which ended the war, further guaranteed Cuba the independence that its nationalist leaders had been demanding for years.

AMERICAN SOLDIERS Though officially independent, Cuba was occupied by American troops when the war ended. José Martí, the Cuban patriot who had led the movement for independence from Spain, had feared that the United States would merely replace Spain and dominate Cuban politics. In some ways, Martí's prediction came true. Under American occupation, the same officials who had served Spain remained in office. Cubans who protested this policy were imprisoned or exiled.

On the other hand, the American military government provided food and clothing for thousands of families, helped farmers put land back into cultivation, and organized elementary schools. Through improvement of sanitation and medical research, the military government helped eliminate yellow fever, a disease that had killed hundreds of Cubans each year.

PLATT AMENDMENT In 1900 the newly formed Cuban government wrote a constitution for an independent Cuba. The constitution, however, did not specify the relationship between Cuba and the United States. Consequently, in 1901 the United States insisted that Cuba add to its constitution several provisions, known as the **Platt Amendment**. The amendment stated that

- Cuba could not make treaties that might limit its independence or permit a foreign power to control any part of its territory,
- the United States reserved the right to intervene in Cuba,
- Cuba was not to go into debt that its government could not repay, and
- the United States could buy or lease land on the island for naval stations and refueling stations.

The United States made it clear that its army would not withdraw until Cuba adopted the Platt Amendment. In response, a torchlight procession marched on the residence of Governor-General Leonard Wood in protest. Some protestors even called for a return to arms to defend their national honor against this American insult. The U.S. government stood firm, though, and Cubans reluctantly ratified the new constitution. In 1903 the Platt Amendment became part of a treaty between the two nations, and it remained in effect for 31 years. Under the terms of the treaty, Cuba became a U.S. **protectorate**, a country whose affairs are partially controlled by a stronger power.

PROTECTING AMERICAN BUSINESS INTERESTS The most important reason for the United States to maintain a strong political presence in Cuba was to protect American businesses. U.S. companies had invested in the island's sugar, tobacco, and mining industries, as well as in its railroads and public utilities.

Background
Dr. Carlos Finlay discovered that yellow fever is carried by mosquitoes. Clearing out the mosquitoes' breeding places helped eliminate the disease in Cuba.

Vocabulary
ratify to make valid by approving

U.S. Intervention

Throughout the early 1900s, the United States intervened in the affairs of its Latin American neighbors several times. Not surprisingly, few Latin Americans welcomed United States intervention. As the cartoon shows, the United States had a different point of view.

Analyze Historical Sources

1. Which president does the waiter portray?

2. What is on the bill of fare, or menu, in this restaurant? What seems to be Uncle Sam's attitude toward the offerings on the menu?

WELL, I HARDLY KNOW WHICH TO TAKE FIRST!

Although many businesspeople were convinced that annexing and imposing colonial rule on new territories was necessary to protect American business interests, some were concerned about colonial entanglements. The industrialist Andrew Carnegie voiced his opposition to the taking of nations as colonies.

> "The exports of the United States this year [1898] are greater than those of any other nation in the world. Even Britain's exports are less, yet Britain 'possesses' . . . a hundred 'colonies' . . . scattered all over the world. The fact that the United States has none does not prevent her products and manufactures from invading . . . all parts of the world in competition with those of Britain."
> —Andrew Carnegie, quoted in *Distant Possessions*

Reading Check
Analyze Effects
What were the effects of the American occupation of Cuba?

Despite such concerns, the U.S. State Department continued to push for control of its Latin American neighbors. In the years to come, the United States would intervene time and again in the affairs of other nations in the Western Hemisphere.

Filipinos Rebel

In the Philippines, Filipinos reacted with outrage to the Treaty of Paris, which called for American annexation of the Philippines. The rebel leader **Emilio Aguinaldo** (ĕ-mēl′yō ä′gē-näl′dō) believed that the United States had promised independence. When he and his followers learned the terms of the treaty, they vowed to fight for freedom.

U.S. military action in the Philippines resulted in suffering for Filipino civilians. About 200,000 people died as a result of malnutrition, disease, and such guerrilla tactics as the burning of villages.

PHILIPPINE–AMERICAN WAR In February 1899 the Filipinos, led by Aguinaldo, rose in revolt. The United States assumed almost the same role that Spain had played, imposing its authority on a colony that was fighting for freedom. When Aguinaldo turned to guerrilla tactics, the United States forced Filipinos to live in designated zones, where poor sanitation, starvation, and disease killed thousands. This was the very same practice that Americans had condemned Spain for using in Cuba.

During the occupation, white American soldiers looked on the Filipinos as inferiors. However, many of the 70,000 U.S. troops sent to the Philippines were African Americans. When African American newspapers questioned why blacks were helping to spread racial prejudice to the Philippines, some African American soldiers deserted to the Filipino side and developed bonds of friendship with the Filipinos.

It took the Americans nearly three years to put down the rebellion. About 20,000 Filipino rebels died fighting for independence. The war claimed 4,000 American lives and cost $400 million—20 times the price the United States had paid to purchase the islands.

AFTERMATH OF THE WAR After suppressing the rebellion, the United States set up a government similar to the one it had established for Puerto Rico. The U.S. president would appoint a governor, who would then appoint the upper house of the legislature. Filipinos would elect the lower house of the legislature. Under American rule, the island nation moved gradually toward independence. On July 4, 1946, the Philippines finally became an independent republic.

Foreign Influence in China

U.S. imperialists saw the Philippines as a gateway to the rest of Asia, particularly to China. China was seen as a vast potential market for American products. It also presented American investors with new opportunities for large-scale railroad construction.

Weakened by war and foreign intervention, China had become known as the "sick man of Asia." France, Germany, Britain, Japan, and Russia had established prosperous settlements along the coast of China. They also had carved out spheres of influence, areas where each nation claimed special rights and economic privileges.

JOHN HAY'S OPEN DOOR NOTES The United States began to fear that the other foreign powers would carve China into colonies and American traders would be shut out. To protect American interests, U.S. Secretary of State **John Hay** issued, in 1899, a series of policy statements called the **Open Door notes**. The notes were letters addressed to the leaders of imperialist nations proposing that the nations share their trading rights with the United States. This would create an open door policy, meaning that no single nation would have a monopoly on trade with any part of China. The other imperialist powers reluctantly accepted this policy.

Reading Check
Contrast What were the consequences of the war for Filipinos? for the Americans?

U.S. Imperialism, 1867–1906

▶ *Explore ONLINE!*

Bering Sea, 1893 International tribunal denies U.S. claims to exclusive rights to waters of Bering Sea.

Open Door Policy, 1899 U.S. aims to prevent foreign powers in China from shutting out the United States from Chinese markets.

Pearl Harbor, 1887 Hawaii gives U.S. exclusive rights to build a naval base.

Alaskan Boundary Crisis, 1902–1903 After gold is discovered in Klondike, Canadians want to redraw boundary to Alaskan Panhandle. A tribunal settles in favor of the United States.

Algeciras Conference, 1906 Roosevelt offers U.S. "good offices" to settle Franco-German differences over Morocco.

Big Stick Diplomacy, 1904 Roosevelt sends warships to Morocco when local authorities detain a Greek citizen with disputed U.S. citizenship.

Samoa, 1889–1899 Hurricane destroys U.S., British, and German ships, preventing armed clash over control of Samoa. Ten years later, the U.S. splits islands with Germany.

Congo Conference, 1885 U.S. persuades European powers to agree to freedom of trade and abolition of slave trade in central Africa.

ASIA · CHINA · NORTH AMERICA · UNITED STATES · EUROPE · MOROCCO · AFRICA · CONGO · SOUTH AMERICA · AUSTRALIA

Alaska 1867 · Midway Island 1867 · Wake Island 1899 · Guam 1898 · Philippine Islands 1898 · Hawaiian Islands 1898 · Puerto Rico 1898 · Panama Canal Zone 1903 · PACIFIC OCEAN · ATLANTIC OCEAN · Equator

🚩 Territory and date of acquisition

0   1,500   3,000 mi
0   1,500   3,000 km

Interpret Maps

1. **Location** What territories were acquired by the United States during this time period?

2. **Human-Environment Interaction** What events show the United States acting as a mediator in international disputes? What does this role indicate about the status of the U.S. in the world?

THE BOXER REBELLION IN CHINA Although China kept its freedom, Europeans dominated most of China's large cities. Resentment simmered beneath the surface as some Chinese formed secret societies pledged to rid the country of "foreign devils." The most famous of these secret groups were the Boxers, so named by Westerners because members practiced martial arts.

The Boxers killed hundreds of missionaries and other foreigners, as well as Chinese converts to Christianity. Foreign citizens fled to Beijing to escape the Boxer onslaught. In August 1900 troops from Britain, France, Germany, and Japan joined about 2,500 American soldiers and marched on the Chinese capital. As the foreign armies took back territory, they pushed to secure their spheres of influence within China. Within two months, the international forces put down the **Boxer Rebellion**. Thousands of Chinese people died during the fighting.

Vocabulary
martial arts combat or self-defense arts that originated in East Asia, such as judo or karate

298 Module 6

During the Boxer Rebellion, shown here in this Chinese print, Chinese patriots demanded that all foreigners be expelled from the country. The Boxers surrounded the European section of Beijing and kept it under siege for several months.

On September 7, 1901, China and 11 other nations signed the Boxer Protocol—a final settlement of the Boxer Rebellion. The Qing government agreed to execute some Chinese officials, to punish others, and to pay about $332 million in damages. The United States was awarded a settlement of $24.5 million. It used about $4 million to pay American citizens for actual losses incurred during the rebellion. In 1908 the U.S. government returned the rest of the money to China to be used for the purpose of educating Chinese students in their own country and in the United States.

PROTECTING AMERICAN RIGHTS After the Boxer Rebellion, the United States feared that European nations would use their victory to take even greater control of China. To prevent this, John Hay issued a second series of Open Door notes, announcing that the United States would "safeguard for the world the principle of equal and impartial trade with all parts of the Chinese Empire." This policy paved the way for greater American influence in Asia.

The Open Door policy reflected three deeply held American beliefs about the United States industrial capitalist economy. First, Americans believed that the growth of the U.S. economy depended on exports. Second, they felt the United States had a right to intervene abroad to keep foreign markets open. Third, they feared that the closing of an area to American products, citizens, or ideas threatened U.S. survival. These beliefs became the bedrock of American foreign policy.

Reading Check
Analyze Causes
How did the policy statements known as the Open Door notes put an end to spheres of influence in China?

The Impact of U.S. Territorial Gains

In 1900 Republican William McKinley, a reluctant but confirmed imperialist, was elected to a second term against Democrat William Jennings Bryan, who staunchly opposed imperialism. McKinley's reelection confirmed that a majority of Americans favored his policies. Under McKinley, the United States had gained an empire.

Yet even before McKinley was reelected, an Anti-Imperialist League had sprung into being. The league included some of the most prominent people in America, such as former president Grover Cleveland, industrial leader Andrew Carnegie, labor leader Samuel Gompers, social worker Jane Addams, and many leading writers. Anti-imperialists had different and sometimes conflicting reasons for their opposition. For example, Gompers was concerned about the impact of imperialism on U.S. workers. Carnegie, on the other hand, worried that U.S. imperialism could lead to endless wars with European rivals. All anti-imperialists, though, agreed that it was wrong for the United States to rule other people without their consent. These beliefs were summed up by the vice-president of the New England Anti-Imperialist League, Moorfield Storey.

"We are here to insist that a war begun in the cause of humanity shall not be turned into a war for empire, that an attempt to win for Cubans the right to govern themselves shall not be made an excuse for extending our sway over alien peoples without their consent. The Fundamental principles of our government are at stake."

—Moorfield Storey, from a speech at Faneuil Hall, Boston, June 15, 1898

Despite the fame of some anti-imperialists, their pleas fell largely on deaf ears. In the early 20th century, the United States under President Theodore Roosevelt and President Woodrow Wilson would continue to exert its power around the globe.

Reading Check
Analyze Issues Why did some Americans oppose imperialism?

Lesson 3 Assessment

1. **Organize Information** Create a timeline of key events relating to U.S. relations with Cuba, Puerto Rico, and the Philippines.

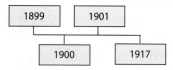

Which event do you think was most significant? Why?

2. **Key Terms and People** For each key term or person in the lesson, write a sentence explaining its significance.

3. **Evaluate** How did American rule of Puerto Rico harm Puerto Ricans? How did it help Puerto Ricans? Do you think the benefits outweighed the harmful effects? Why or why not?

4. **Compare** How was U.S. policy toward China different from U.S. policy toward the Philippines? To what can you attribute the difference?

5. **Analyze Issues** How did U.S. foreign policy at the turn of the century affect actions taken by the United States toward China?

   Think About:
   - why the United States wanted access to China's markets
   - the purpose of the Open Door notes
   - the U.S. response to the Boxer Rebellion

America as a World Power

One American's Story

Joseph Bucklin Bishop, a policy adviser to the canal's chief engineer, played an important role in the building of the **Panama Canal**. As editor of the *Canal Record,* a weekly newspaper that provided Americans with updates on the project, Bishop described a frustrating problem that the workers encountered.

The Big Idea

The Russo-Japanese War, the Panama Canal, and the Mexican Revolution added to America's military and economic power.

Why It Matters Now

American involvement in conflicts around 1900 led to involvement in World War I and later to a peacekeeper role in today's world.

Key Terms and People

Panama Canal

Roosevelt Corollary

dollar diplomacy

Francisco "Pancho" Villa

Emiliano Zapata

John J. Pershing

Workers digging the Panama Canal faced hazardous landslides and death from disease.

"The Canal Zone was a land of the fantastic and the unexpected. No one could say when the sun went down what the condition of the Cut would be when [the sun] rose. For the work of months or even years might be blotted out by an avalanche of earth or the toppling over of a mountain of rock. It was a task to try men's souls; but it was also one to kindle in them a joy of combat . . . and a faith in ultimate victory which no disaster could shake."

—Joseph Bucklin Bishop, quoted in
The Impossible Dream: The Building of the Panama Canal

The building of the Panama Canal reflected America's new role as a world power. As a technological accomplishment, the canal represented a confident nation's refusal to let any physical obstacle stand in its way.

SS.912.A.1.2; SS.912.A.1.4; SS.912.A.4.1; SS.912.A.4.4; MAFS.K12.MP.5.1; MAFS.K12.MP.6.1

Teddy Roosevelt and the World

The assassination of William McKinley in 1901 thrust Vice-President Theodore Roosevelt into the role of a world leader. Roosevelt was unwilling to allow the imperial powers of Europe to control the world's political and economic destiny. In 1905, building on the Open Door notes to increase American influence in East Asia, Roosevelt mediated a settlement in a war between Russia and Japan.

ROOSEVELT THE PEACEMAKER In 1904 Russia and Japan, Russia's neighbor in East Asia, were both imperialist powers, and they were competing for control of Korea. The Japanese took the first action in what would become the Russo-Japanese War with a sudden attack on the Russian Pacific fleet. To everyone's surprise, Japan destroyed it. Japan then proceeded to destroy a second fleet sent as reinforcement. Japan also won a series of land battles, securing Korea and Manchuria.

As a result of these battles, Japan began to run out of men and money, a fact that it did not want to reveal to Russia. Instead, Japanese officials approached President Roosevelt in secret and asked him to mediate peace negotiations. Roosevelt agreed, and in 1905 Russian and Japanese delegates convened in Portsmouth, New Hampshire.

The first meeting took place on the presidential yacht. Roosevelt had a charming way of greeting people with a grasp of the hand, a broad grin, and a hearty "Dee-lighted." Soon the opposing delegates began to relax and cordially shook hands.

The Japanese wanted Sakhalin Island, off the coast of Siberia, and a large sum of money from Russia. Russia refused. Roosevelt persuaded Japan to accept half the island and forgo the cash payment. In exchange, Russia agreed to let Japan take over Russian interests in Manchuria and Korea. The successful efforts in negotiating the Treaty of Portsmouth won Roosevelt the 1906 Nobel Peace Prize.

– BIOGRAPHY

Theodore Roosevelt (1858–1919)

Rimless glasses, a bushy mustache, and prominent teeth made Roosevelt easy for cartoonists to caricature. His great enthusiasm for physical activity—boxing, tennis, swimming, horseback riding, and hunting—provided cartoonists with additional material. Some cartoons portrayed Roosevelt with the toy teddy bear that he inspired.

Roosevelt had six children, who became notorious for their rowdy antics. Their father once sent a message through the War Department, ordering them to call off their "attack" on the White House. Roosevelt thrived on the challenges of the presidency. He wrote, "I do not believe that anyone else has ever enjoyed the White House as much as I have."

As U.S. and Japanese interests expanded in East Asia, the two nations continued diplomatic talks. In later agreements, they pledged to respect each other's possessions and interests in East Asia and the Pacific.

PANAMA CANAL By the time Roosevelt became president, many Americans, including Roosevelt, felt that the United States needed a canal cutting across Central America. Such a canal would greatly reduce travel time for commercial and military ships by providing a shortcut between the Atlantic and Pacific oceans. As early as 1850 the United States and Britain had agreed to share the rights to such a canal. In the Hay-Pauncefote Treaty of 1901, however, Britain gave the United States exclusive rights to build and control a canal through Central America.

Engineers identified two possible routes for the proposed canal. One, through Nicaragua, posed fewer obstacles because much of it crossed a large lake. The other route crossed through Panama (then a province of Colombia) and was shorter and filled with mountains and swamps. In the late 1800s a French company had tried to build a canal in Panama. After ten years, the company gave up. It sent an agent, Philippe Bunau-Varilla, to Washington to convince the United States to buy its claim. In 1903 the president and Congress decided to use the Panama route and agreed to buy the French company's route for $40 million.

Before beginning work on the Panama Canal, the United States had to get permission from Colombia, which then ruled Panama. When these negotiations broke down, Bunau-Varilla helped organize a Panamanian rebellion against Colombia. Aided by a U.S. naval blockade that stopped Colombian troops from landing in Panama, the rebels won independence. On November 3, 1903, nearly a dozen U.S. Navy warships were present as Panama declared its independence from Colombia.

This threat of military force by the United States was a prime example of gunboat diplomacy. Fifteen days later, Panama and the United States signed the Hay-Bunau-Varilla Treaty. The United States agreed to pay Panama $10 million plus an annual rent of $250,000 for an area of land across Panama, called the Canal Zone. The United States now controlled the canal route across the Isthmus of Panama and could begin construction on the Panama Canal.

CONSTRUCTING THE CANAL Construction of the Panama Canal ranks as one of the world's greatest engineering feats. Builders fought diseases, such as yellow fever and malaria, and soft volcanic soil, that proved difficult to remove from where it lay. Work began in 1904 with the clearing of brush and draining of swamps. By 1913, the height of the construction, more than 43,400 workers were employed. Some had come from Italy and Spain; three-quarters were blacks from the British West Indies. More than 5,600 workers on the canal died from accidents or disease. The total cost to the United States was about $380 million.

On August 15, 1914, the canal opened for business, and more than 1,000 merchant ships passed through during its first year. U.S.–Latin American relations, however, had been damaged by American support of the rebellion in Panama. The resulting ill will lasted for decades, despite Congress's paying Colombia $25 million in 1921 to compensate the country for its lost territory.

"The World's Constable"

This cartoon, drawn by Louis Dalrymple in 1905, shows Teddy Roosevelt implementing his new world diplomacy. The cartoon implies that Roosevelt has the right to execute police power to keep the countries of Europe (shown on the right) out of the affairs of Latin American countries (shown on the left).

THE WORLD'S CONSTABLE.

Analyze Historical Sources
How does the cartoonist portray President Roosevelt?

THE ROOSEVELT COROLLARY Financial factors drew the United States further into Latin American affairs. In the late 19th century, many Latin American nations had borrowed huge sums from European banks to build railroads and develop industries. Roosevelt feared that if these nations defaulted on their loans, Europeans might intervene. He was determined to make the United States the predominant power in the Caribbean and Central America.

Roosevelt reminded the European powers of the Monroe Doctrine, which had been issued in 1823 by President James Monroe. The Monroe Doctrine demanded that European countries stay out of the affairs of Latin American nations. Roosevelt based his Latin America policy on a West African proverb that said, "Speak softly and carry a big stick." In his December 1904 message to Congress, Roosevelt added the **Roosevelt Corollary** to the Monroe Doctrine. He warned that disorder in Latin America might "force the United States . . . to the exercise of an international police power." In effect, the corollary said that the United States would now use force to protect its economic interests in Latin America.

Vocabulary
corollary an additional statement that follows logically from the first one

DOLLAR DIPLOMACY During the next decade, the United States exercised its police power on several occasions. For example, when a 1911 rebellion in Nicaragua left the nation near bankruptcy, President William H. Taft, Roosevelt's successor, arranged for American bankers to loan Nicaragua enough money to pay its debts. In return, the bankers were given the right to recover their money by collecting Nicaragua's customs duties. The U.S. bankers also gained control of Nicaragua's state-owned railroad system and its national bank. When Nicaraguan citizens heard about this deal, they revolted against President Adolfo Díaz. To prop up Díaz's government, some 2,000 marines were sent to Nicaragua. The revolt was put down, but some marine detachments remained in the country until 1933.

Reading Check
Identify Problems
What problems did canal workers encounter in constructing the Panama Canal?

The Taft administration followed the policy of using the U.S. government to guarantee loans made to foreign countries by American businesspeople. This policy was called **dollar diplomacy** by its critics and was often used to justify keeping European powers out of the Caribbean.

Woodrow Wilson's Missionary Diplomacy

The Monroe Doctrine, issued by President James Monroe in 1823, had warned other nations against expanding their influence in Latin America. The Roosevelt Corollary asserted, in 1904, that the United States had a right to exercise international police power in the Western Hemisphere. In 1913 President Woodrow Wilson gave the Monroe Doctrine a moral tone.

According to Wilson's "missionary diplomacy," the United States had a moral responsibility to deny recognition to any Latin American government it viewed as oppressive, undemocratic, or hostile to U.S. interests. Prior to this policy, the United States recognized any government that controlled a nation, regardless of that nation's policies or how it had come to power. Wilson's policy pressured nations in the Western Hemisphere to establish democratic governments. Almost immediately, the Mexican Revolution put Wilson's policy to the test.

THE MEXICAN REVOLUTION Mexico had been ruled for more than three decades by a military dictator, Porfirio Díaz. A friend of the United States, Díaz had long encouraged foreign investments in his country. As a result, foreigners, mostly Americans, owned a large share of Mexican oil wells, mines, railroads, and ranches. While foreign investors and some Mexican landowners and politicians had grown rich, the common people of the country were desperately poor.

In 1911 Mexican peasants and workers led by Francisco Madero overthrew Díaz. Later that year Madero was elected president. He promised democratic reforms, but he proved unable to satisfy the conflicting demands of landowners, peasants, factory workers, and the urban middle class. After two years, General Victoriano Huerta took over the government. Within days, Madero was murdered. Wilson refused to recognize the government that Huerta formed. He called it "a government of butchers."

Intervention in Mexico

Most U.S. citizens supported American intervention in Mexico. Edith O'Shaughnessy, wife of an American diplomat in Mexico City, had another perspective. After touring Veracruz, O'Shaughnessy wrote to her mother:

"I think we have done a great wrong to these people; instead of cutting out the sores with a clean, strong knife of war . . . and occupation, . . . we have only put our fingers in each festering wound and inflamed it further."

INTERVENTION IN MEXICO Wilson adopted a plan of "watchful waiting," looking for an opportunity to act against Huerta. The opportunity came in April 1914, when one of Huerta's officers arrested a small group of American sailors in Tampico, on Mexico's eastern shore. The Mexicans quickly released them and apologized, but Wilson used the incident as an excuse to intervene in Mexico and ordered U.S. Marines to occupy Veracruz, an important Mexican port. Eighteen Americans and at least 200 Mexicans died during the invasion.

The incident brought the United States and Mexico close to war. The three most powerful countries in Latin America, known as the ABC powers—Argentina, Brazil, and Chile—stepped in to mediate the conflict. At the ABC Conference in Niagara Falls, New York, they proposed that Huerta step down and that U.S. troops withdraw without paying Mexico for damages. Mexico rejected the plan, and Wilson refused to recognize a government that had come to power as a result of violence. The Huerta regime soon collapsed, however, and Venustiano Carranza, a nationalist leader, became president in 1915. Wilson withdrew the troops and formally recognized the Carranza government.

REBELLION IN MEXICO Carranza was in charge, but like others before him, he did not have the support of all Mexicans. Rebels under the leadership of **Francisco "Pancho" Villa** (vē'ə) and **Emiliano Zapata** (ĕ-mēl-yä'nō zə-pä'tə) opposed Carranza's provisional government. Zapata—son of a mestizo peasant—was dedicated to land reform. "It is better to die on your feet than live on your knees," Zapata told the peasants who joined him. Villa, a fierce nationalist, had frequently courted the support and aid of the United States.

"[A]s long as I have anything to do with the affairs in Mexico there will be no further friction between my country and my friends of the north . . . To President Wilson, the greatest American, I stand pledged to do what I can to keep the faith he has in my people, and if there is anything he may wish I will gladly do it, for I know it will be for the good of my country."

—Pancho Villa, quoted in the *New York Times,* January 11, 1915

Despite Villa's talk of friendship, when President Wilson recognized Carranza's government, Villa threatened reprisals against the United States. In January 1916 Carranza invited American engineers to operate mines in northern Mexico. Before they reached the mines, however, Villa's men took the Americans off a train and shot them. Two months later, some of Villa's followers raided Columbus, New Mexico, and killed 17 Americans. Americans held Villa responsible.

Pancho Villa directs a column of his troops through northern Mexico in 1914.

CHASING VILLA With the American public demanding revenge, President Wilson ordered Brigadier General **John J. Pershing** and an expeditionary force of about 15,000 soldiers into Mexico to capture Villa dead or alive. For almost a year, Villa eluded Pershing's forces. Wilson then called out 150,000 National Guardsmen and stationed them along the Mexican border. In the meantime, Mexicans grew angrier over the U.S. invasion of their land. In June 1916 U.S. troops clashed with Carranza's army, resulting in deaths on both sides.

Carranza demanded the withdrawal of U.S. troops, but Wilson refused. War seemed imminent. However, in the end, both sides backed down. The United States, facing war in Europe, needed peace on its southern border. In February 1917 Wilson ordered Pershing to return home. Later that year, Mexico adopted a constitution that gave the government control of the nation's oil and mineral resources and placed strict regulations on foreign investors.

Although Carranza had called for the constitution of 1917, he failed to carry out its measures. Instead, he ruled oppressively until 1920, when a moderate named Alvaro Obregón came to power. Obregón's presidency marked the end of civil war and the beginning of reform.

U.S. intervention in Mexican affairs provided a clear model of American imperialist attitudes in the early years of the 20th century. Americans believed in the superiority of free-enterprise democracy, and the American government attempted to extend the reach of this economic and political system, even through armed intervention.

Reading Check
Analyze Motives
Why did President Wilson refuse to recognize Huerta's government?

The United States pursued and achieved several foreign policy goals in the early 20th century. First, it expanded U.S. access to foreign markets in order to ensure the continued growth of the domestic economy. Second, the United States built a modern navy to protect its interests abroad. Third, the United States exercised its international police power to ensure dominance in Latin America.

Lesson 4 Assessment

1. **Organize Information** In a two-column chart, list ways Teddy Roosevelt and Woodrow Wilson used American power around the world during their presidencies.

Using American Power	
Roosevelt	Wilson

   Choose one example and discuss its impact with your classmates.

2. **Key Terms and People** For each key term or person in the lesson, write a sentence explaining its significance.

3. **Compare and Contrast** What do you think were the similarities and differences between Roosevelt's Big Stick policy and Wilson's missionary diplomacy? Use evidence from the text to support your response.

4. **Evaluate** In your opinion, should the United States have become involved in the affairs of Colombia, Nicaragua, and Mexico during the early 1900s? Support your answer with details.

   Think About:
   • the effect of the Roosevelt Corollary
   • the results of dollar diplomacy
   • the implication of Wilson's missionary diplomacy

The Panama Canal: Linking East and West

By the late 19th century, the U.S. position in global trade was firmly established. A glance at a world map during that time revealed the trade advantages of cutting through the world's great landmasses at two strategic points. The first cut, or canal, through the Isthmus of Suez in Egypt was completed in 1869 and was a spectacular success. A second cut, this one through Panama, in Central America, would be especially advantageous to the United States. Such a cut would substantially reduce the sailing time between the nation's Atlantic and Pacific coasts. This was not only important for trade and travel but also for U.S. national security. During the Spanish-American War, U.S. warships in the Pacific had to sail around South America to join the fighting in the Caribbean. The Panama Canal would solve that problem.

It took the United States ten years, from 1904 to 1914, to build the Panama Canal. By 1999 more than 700,000 vessels, flying the flags of about 70 nations, had passed through its locks. On December 31, 1999, Panama assumed full control of the canal.

INTERCOASTAL TRADE
The first boat through the canal heralded the arrival of increased trade between the Atlantic and Pacific ports of the United States. New York City and other U.S. Atlantic ports accounted for about 60 percent of the traffic using the Panama Canal in the early decades of its existence.

NUMBERS TELL THE STORY
A ship sailing from New York to San Francisco by going around South America travels 13,000 miles; the canal shortens the journey to 5,200 miles. Ships must be no more than 106 feet across and 965 feet in length, with a draft (the depth of the vessel below the water line when fully loaded) of no more than 39.5 feet. Each ship pays a toll based on its size, its cargo, and the number of passengers it carries.

San Francisco

New York

13,000 mi.
5,200 mi.

WARSHIPS
The USS *Arizona* passes through the Panama Canal in 1921. In addition to being a valuable trade route, the Panama Canal also provided the U.S. Navy with a way to link the east and west coasts of the United States.

LOCKS
Locks are used to raise and lower ships a total of 170 feet during the 51-mile trip through the Panama Canal. For example, ships from the Atlantic Ocean are lifted by the Gatún Locks to the level of Gatún Lake. The ships cross the human-made lake, then move through another waterway, the Gaillard Cut. The Pedro Miguel and Miraflores locks then lower the ships to the level of the Pacific Ocean.

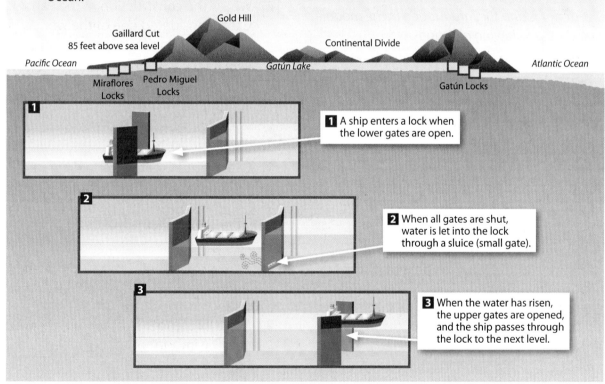

Gold Hill

Gaillard Cut
85 feet above sea level

Continental Divide

Pacific Ocean

Gatún Lake

Atlantic Ocean

Miraflores Locks

Pedro Miguel Locks

Gatún Locks

1 A ship enters a lock when the lower gates are open.

2 When all gates are shut, water is let into the lock through a sluice (small gate).

3 When the water has risen, the upper gates are opened, and the ship passes through the lock to the next level.

Critical Thinking
1. **Analyze Patterns** On a world map, identify the route that ships took to get from New York City to San Francisco before the Panama Canal opened. How did this route change after the opening of the canal?

2. **Create a Model** Use clay to shape a model of a cross-section of the Panama Canal. For the locks, use foam blocks or pieces of wood that you have glued together. Paint the model, and then label each part of the canal.

Module 6 Assessment

Key Terms and People

For each key term or person below, write a sentence explaining its significance to U.S. foreign policy between 1890 and 1920.

1. Queen Liliuokalani
2. imperialism
3. José Martí
4. yellow journalism
5. USS *Maine*
6. protectorate
7. Open Door notes
8. Boxer Rebellion
9. Panama Canal
10. Roosevelt Corollary

Main Ideas

Use your notes and the information in the module to answer the following questions.

Imperialism and America

1. What three factors spurred American imperialism?
2. How did European imperialism affect Africa?
3. Why did Admiral Alfred T. Mahan feel the United States should build up its naval power?
4. How was religion used to justify imperialism?
5. How did Queen Liliuokalani's main goal conflict with American imperialists' goals?

The Spanish-American War

6. Why was American opinion about Cuban independence divided?
7. How did the Spanish try to avoid war with the United States?
8. What event ultimately led the United States to change its foreign policy to one of intervention?
9. Briefly describe the terms of the Treaty of Paris of 1898.

Acquiring New Lands

10. Why was the United States interested in events in Puerto Rico?
11. What was the Teller Amendment?
12. How did the annexation of the Philippines expand America's global influence?
13. What sparked the Boxer Rebellion in 1900, and how was it crushed?
14. What three key beliefs about America's industrial capitalist economy were reflected in the Open Door policy?

America as a World Power

15. What conflict triggered the war between Russia and Japan?
16. What role did the United States play in the revolution in Panama?
17. Why is the construction of the Panama Canal considered one of the world's greatest engineering feats?
18. Explain the key difference between Woodrow Wilson's missionary, or moral, diplomacy and William Taft's dollar diplomacy.

Critical Thinking

1. **Categorize** Create a Venn diagram to show the similarities and differences between José Martí of Cuba and Emilio Aguinaldo of the Philippines.

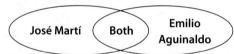

2. **Make Inferences** Why would a powerful navy be important to the imperialist ambitions of the United States?
3. **Analyze Causes** Imperialists, like Admiral Alfred T. Mahan, advocated for growing America's influence by increasing the strength and presence of its military. How might the growing global presence of the U.S. military have led to the Spanish-American War?

4. **Analyze Issues** At the turn of the century, African Americans and other racial minorities in the United States often faced discrimination and racism. How were the justifications for these practices similar to the cultural factors used to justify imperialism?

5. **Predict** Would Cuba have won its independence in the late 19th century if the United States had not intervened there? Support your opinion with details from the text.

6. **Analyze Motives** What economic, social, and political factors helped lead to the Spanish-American War?

7. **Analyze Events** How did the Spanish-American War mark the emergence of the United States as a world power?

8. **Analyze Effects** What effects did the Open Door policy have on U.S. interests in Asia?

Interact with History

Suppose you are a journalist at the end of the Spanish-American War. You work for William Randolph Hearst's *New York Journal.* Write a newspaper editorial that presents your point of view about whether or not the Senate should ratify the Treaty of Paris, thus annexing the Philippines.

Focus on Writing

Imagine you are a worker helping to build the Panama Canal. Write a diary entry giving details about the work you are doing, the hardships you face, and why you think the project is worthwhile.

Multimedia Activity

Use Internet resources to research opinions on imperialism between 1895 and 1920. Then, use your research to answer the question: Why did imperialism prevail over anti-imperialism in the United States? Create a presentation to deliver your findings. Use facts and details from your research to support your conclusion.

World War I

Essential Question

What was the most significant impact of World War I?

About the Photograph: This photograph depicts a battle on the western front during World War I. Brutal battles like this would make the war the bloodiest in history up to that time.

▶ Explore ONLINE!

HISTORY

VIDEOS, including...
- Death of Glory
- A Continent Mobilizes
- The Last Day of World War I

✓ Document-Based Investigations

✓ Graphic Organizers

✓ Interactive Games

✓ Image with Hotspots: Trench Warfare

✓ Carousel: Technology at War

In this module you will examine the causes and consequences of World War I. The conflict in Europe forced the United States to abandon its neutrality, and it spurred social, political, and economic change in the United States

SS.912.A.1.2 Utilize a variety of primary and secondary sources to identify author, historical significance, audience, and authenticity to understand a historical period. **SS.912.A.1.6** Use case studies to explore social, political, legal, and economic relationships in history. **SS.912.A.4.5** Examine causes, course, and consequences of United States involvement in World War I. **SS.912.A.4.6** Examine how the United States government prepared the nation for war with war measures. **SS.912.A.4.7** Examine the impact of airplanes, battleships, new weaponry and chemical warfare in creating new war strategies. **SS.912.A.4.8** Compare the experiences Americans had while serving in Europe. **SS.912.A.4.9** Compare how the war impacted German Americans, Asian Americans, African Americans, Hispanic Americans, Jewish Americans, Native Americans, women and dissenters in the United States. **SS.912.A.4.10** Examine the provisions of the Treaty of Versailles and the failure of the United States to support the League of Nations. **SS.912.A.5.5** Describe efforts by the United States and other world powers to avoid future wars. **SS.912.G.1.3** Employ applicable units of measurement and scale to solve simple locational problems using maps and globes. **SS.912.G.4.2** Use geographic terms and tools to analyze the push/pull factors contributing to human migration within and among places. **SS.912.G.4.3** Use geographic terms and tools to analyze the effects of migration both on the place of origin and destination, including border areas. **LAFS.1112.SL.1.1** Initiate and participate effectively in a range of collaborative discussions with diverse partners on grades 11–12 topics, texts, and issues, building on others' ideas and expressing their own clearly and persuasively. **LAFS.1112.SL.2.4** Present information, findings, and supporting evidence, conveying a clear and distinct perspective, such that listeners can follow the line of reasoning, alternative or opposing perspectives are addressed, and the organization, development, substance, and style are appropriate to purpose, audience, and a range of formal and informal tasks. **LAFS.1112.WHST.1.2** Write informative/explanatory texts, including the narration of historical events, scientific procedures/experiments, or technical processes.

Timeline of Events 1913–1920

span⏵ *Explore ONLINE!*

United States Events	1913	World Events

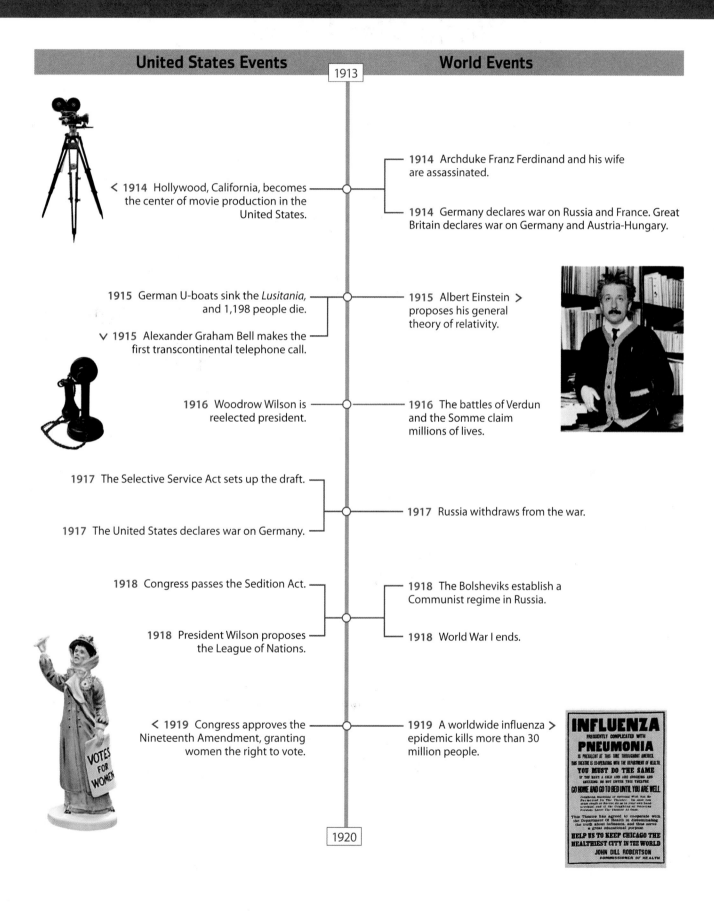

◄ 1914 Hollywood, California, becomes the center of movie production in the United States.

1914 Archduke Franz Ferdinand and his wife are assassinated.

1914 Germany declares war on Russia and France. Great Britain declares war on Germany and Austria-Hungary.

1915 German U-boats sink the *Lusitania,* and 1,198 people die.

1915 Albert Einstein ▶ proposes his general theory of relativity.

∨ 1915 Alexander Graham Bell makes the first transcontinental telephone call.

1916 Woodrow Wilson is reelected president.

1916 The battles of Verdun and the Somme claim millions of lives.

1917 The Selective Service Act sets up the draft.

1917 Russia withdraws from the war.

1917 The United States declares war on Germany.

1918 Congress passes the Sedition Act.

1918 The Bolsheviks establish a Communist regime in Russia.

1918 President Wilson proposes the League of Nations.

1918 World War I ends.

◄ 1919 Congress approves the Nineteenth Amendment, granting women the right to vote.

1919 A worldwide influenza ▶ epidemic kills more than 30 million people.

1920

INFLUENZA
FREQUENTLY COMPLICATED WITH
PNEUMONIA
IS PREVALENT AT THIS TIME THROUGHOUT AMERICA.
THIS THEATRE IS CO-OPERATING WITH THE DEPARTMENT OF HEALTH.
YOU MUST DO THE SAME
IF YOU HAVE A COLD AND ARE COUGHING AND SNEEZING DO NOT ENTER THIS THEATRE
GO HOME AND GO TO BED UNTIL YOU ARE WELL
Coughing, Sneezing or spitting Will Not Be Permitted In The Theatre. In case you must cough or Sneeze do so in your own hand kerchief, and if the Coughing or Sneezing Persists Leave The Theatre At Once.
This Theatre has agreed to co-operate with the Department Of Health in disseminating the truth about Influenza, and thus serve a great educational purpose.
HELP US TO KEEP CHICAGO THE HEALTHIEST CITY IN THE WORLD
JOHN DILL ROBERTSON
COMMISSIONER OF HEALTH

★
World War I Begins

The Big Idea
As conflict in Europe intensified, the United States was forced to abandon its neutrality.

Why It Matters Now
The United States remains involved in European and world affairs.

Key Terms and People
nationalism
militarism
Allies
Central powers
balance of power
Archduke Franz Ferdinand
trench warfare
"no man's land"
Lusitania
Sussex pledge
Zimmermann note

One American's Story

It was about 1:00 a.m. on April 6, 1917, and the members of the U.S. House of Representatives were tired. For the past 15 hours, they had been debating President Wilson's request for a declaration of war against Germany. There was a breathless hush as Jeannette Rankin of Montana, the first woman elected to Congress, stood up. Rankin declared, "I want to stand by my country but I cannot vote for war. I vote no." Later she reflected on her action.

"I believe that the first vote I cast was the most significant vote and a most significant act on the part of women, because women are going to have to stop war. I felt at the time that the first woman [in Congress] should take the first stand, that the first time the first woman had a chance to say no to war she should say it."
—Jeannette Rankin, quoted in *Jeannette Rankin: First Lady in Congress*

Jeannette Rankin was the only member of the House to vote against the United States entering both World War I and World War II.

After much debate as to whether the United States should join the fight, Congress voted in favor of U.S. entry into World War I. With this decision, the government abandoned the neutrality that America had maintained for three years. What made the United States change its policy in 1917?

SS.912.A.1.2; SS.912.A.1.4; SS.912.A.4.5; SS.912.A.4.9; SS.912.G.1.2; SS.912.G.1.3; LAFS.1112.RH.1.2; LAFS.1112.RH.4.10; MAFS.K12.MP.1.1; MAFS.K12.MP.5.1; MAFS.K12.MP.6.1

Causes of World War I

Although many Americans wanted to stay out of the war, several factors made American neutrality difficult to maintain. As an industrial and imperial power, the United States felt many of the same pressures that had led the nations of Europe into devastating warfare. Historians generally cite four long-term causes of World War I: nationalism, imperialism, militarism, and the formation of a system of alliances.

Vocabulary
alliance a formal agreement or union between nations

NATIONALISM Throughout the 19th century, politics in the Western world were deeply influenced by the concept of **nationalism**—a devotion to the interests and culture of one's nation. Often, nationalism led to competitive and antagonistic rivalries among nations. In this atmosphere of competition, many feared Germany's growing power in Europe.

In addition, various ethnic groups resented domination by others. They longed for their nations to become independent. Many ethnic groups looked to larger nations for protection. Russia regarded itself as the protector of Europe's Slavic peoples, no matter which government they lived under. Among these Slavic peoples were the Serbs. Serbia, located in the Balkans, was an independent nation. However, millions of ethnic Serbs lived under the rule of Austria-Hungary. As a result, Russia and Austria-Hungary were rivals for influence over Serbia.

IMPERIALISM For many centuries, European nations had been building empires. These nations had slowly extended their economic and political control over various peoples of the world. Colonies supplied the European imperial powers with raw materials and provided markets for manufactured goods. As Germany industrialized, it competed with France and Britain in the contest for colonies.

MILITARISM Empires were expensive to build and to defend. The growth of nationalism and imperialism led to increased military spending. Each nation wanted stronger armed forces than those of any potential enemy. The imperial powers followed a policy of **militarism**—the development of armed forces and their use as a tool of diplomacy.

By 1890 the strongest nation on the European continent was Germany. It had set up an army reserve system that drafted and trained young men. At first, Britain was not alarmed by Germany's military expansion. As an island nation, Britain had always relied on its navy for defense and protection of its shipping routes. In addition, the British navy was the strongest in the world. However, in 1897 Wilhelm II, Germany's kaiser, or emperor, decided that his nation should also become a major sea power in order to compete more successfully against the British. Soon, British and German shipyards competed to build the largest battleships and destroyers. France, Italy, Japan, and the United States quickly joined the naval arms race.

ALLIANCE SYSTEM By 1907 there were two major defense alliances in Europe. The Triple Entente, later known as the **Allies**, consisted of France, Britain, and Russia. The Triple Alliance consisted of Germany,

German emperor Wilhelm II *(center)* marches with two of his generals, Hindenburg *(left)* and Ludendorff, during World War I.

Reading Check
Analyze Causes
How did nationalism and imperialism lead to conflict in Europe?

Austria-Hungary, and Italy. Germany and Austria-Hungary, together with the Ottoman Empire—an empire of mostly Middle Eastern lands controlled by the Turks—were later known as the **Central powers**.

Some European leaders believed that these alliances created a **balance of power**, in which each nation or alliance had equal strength. Many leaders thought that the alliance system would help decrease the chances of war. They hoped that no single nation would attack another out of fear that the attacked nation's allies would join the fight.

War Breaks Out

Despite their hopes, the major European powers' long history of national tensions, imperial rivalries, and military expansion proved too great for alliances to overcome. As it turned out, a single spark set off a major conflict.

AN ASSASSINATION LEADS TO WAR That spark flared in the Balkan Peninsula. This area was known as "the powder keg of Europe." In addition to the ethnic rivalries among the Balkan peoples, Europe's leading powers had interests there. Russia wanted access to the Mediterranean Sea. Germany wanted a rail link to the Ottoman Empire. Austria-Hungary, which had taken control of Bosnia in 1878, accused Serbia of subverting its rule over Bosnia. The "powder keg" was ready to explode.

In June 1914 **Archduke Franz Ferdinand**, heir to the Austrian throne, visited the Bosnian capital, Sarajevo. As the royal entourage drove through the city, Serbian nationalist Gavrilo Princip stepped from the crowd and shot the Archduke and his wife, Sophie. Princip was a member of the Black Hand, an organization promoting Serbian nationalism. The assassinations touched off a diplomatic crisis. On July 28 Austria-Hungary declared what was expected to be a short war against Serbia.

Crisis in the Balkans

After World War I, Bosnia became part of a country that eventually became known as Yugoslavia. Although Yugoslavia included various religious and ethnic groups, the government was dominated by Serbs.

In 1991 Yugoslavia broke apart, and Bosnia declared independence in 1992. However, Serbs wanted Bosnia to remain part of Serbian-controlled Yugoslavia.

A bloody civil war broke out. This war became notorious for the mass murder and deportation of Bosnian Muslims. This process became known as "ethnic cleansing." In 1995 the United States helped negotiate a cease-fire.

But peace in the Balkans did not last. In the late 1990s Albanians in the province of Kosovo also tried to break away from Serbia. Serbia's violent response, which included the "ethnic cleansing" of Albanians, prompted NATO to intervene. Kosovo declared its independence in 2008, despite Serbia's opposition.

The alliance system pulled one nation after another into the conflict. On August 1 Germany, obligated by treaty to support Austria-Hungary, declared war on Russia. On August 3 Germany declared war on Russia's ally France. After Germany invaded Belgium, Britain declared war on Germany and Austria-Hungary. The Great War had begun.

THE FIGHTING STARTS On August 3, 1914, Germany invaded Belgium, following a strategy known as the Schlieffen Plan. This plan called for a holding action against Russia, combined with a quick drive through Belgium to Paris. After France had fallen, the two German armies would defeat Russia. European leaders were confident of a short war. Kaiser Wilhelm II even promised German soldiers that they would be home "before the leaves had fallen."

As German troops swept across Belgium, thousands of civilians fled in terror. In Brussels, the Belgian capital, an American war correspondent described the first major refugee crisis of the 20th century.

Vocabulary
refugee a person who flees in search of protection or shelter, as in times of war or religious persecution

"[We] found the side streets blocked with their carts. Into these they had thrown mattresses, or bundles of grain, and heaped upon them were families of three generations. Old men in blue smocks, white-haired and bent, old women in caps, the daughters dressed in their one best frock and hat, and clasping in their hands all that was left to them, all that they could stuff into a pillow-case or flour-sack. . . . Heart-broken, weary, hungry, they passed in an unending caravan."
—Richard Harding Davis, quoted in *Hooray for Peace, Hurrah for War*

Unable to save Belgium, the Allies retreated to the Marne River in France. There they halted the German advance in September 1914. After struggling to outflank each other's armies, both sides dug in for a long siege. By the spring of 1915, two parallel systems of deep, rat-infested trenches crossed France.

Explore ONLINE!

Tannenberg, August 1914 Germans stop Russian advance.

May 1915 *Lusitania* is sunk.

Gallipoli, April 1915–January 1916 Allied forces are defeated in bid to establish a supply route to Russia.

Sarajevo, June 1914 Archduke Franz Ferdinand is assassinated.

ATLANTIC OCEAN

British Blockade

NORWAY

Petrograd (St. Petersburg)

Moscow

North Sea

DENMARK

R U S S I A

IRELAND (Br.)

GREAT BRITAIN

NETHERLANDS

Baltic Sea

Berlin

TANNENBERG

Eastern Front Oct. 1917

London

Brussels

BELGIUM

GERMANY

Paris

LUXEMBOURG

Vienna

SWITZERLAND

AUSTRIA-HUNGARY

ROMANIA

Bay of Biscay

FRANCE

Black Sea

PORTUGAL

SPAIN

ITALY

Sarajevo

SERBIA

BULGARIA

Rome

MONTENEGRO

Adriatic Sea

B A L K A N   P E N I N S U L A

Constantinople (Istanbul)

ALBANIA

GALLIPOLI

Aegean Sea

GREECE

OTTOMAN EMPIRE

M e d i t e r r a n e a n   S e a

THE WESTERN FRONT, 1914–1916

English Channel

NETHERLANDS

Brussels

BELGIUM

Meuse

Somme

Oise

Aisne

Front on July 1, 1916

LUXEMBOURG

Marne

Metz

Lunéville

Rhine

Farthest German advance, Sept. 5, 1914

Paris

Seine

Meuse

Moselle

G E R M A N Y

N W E S

F R A N C E

SWITZERLAND

0   50   100 mi
0   50   100 km

A MARNE, 1st battle, Sept. 1914 Allies stop German advance on Paris

B YPRES, 2nd battle, May 1915 Germans use chemical weapons for the first time

C VERDUN, Feb.–July 1916 French hold the line in longest battle of the war

D SOMME, 1st battle, July–Nov. 1916 Disastrous British offensive

→ German troop movement

→ Allied troop movement

Allied Powers, 1916

Central Powers, 1916

Neutral countries

German submarine activity

★ Battle

0   250   500 mi
0   250   500 km

Interpret Maps

1. **Location** About how many miles separated the city of Paris from German forces at the point of their closest approach?

2. **Place** Consider the geographical location of the Allies in relation to the Central powers. What advantage might the Allies have had?

The trenches stretched from the Belgian coast to the Swiss Alps. German soldiers occupied one set of trenches, Allied soldiers the other. The scale of slaughter was horrific. During the First Battle of the Somme—which began on July 1, 1916, and lasted until mid-November—the British suffered 60,000 casualties the first day alone. Final casualties totaled about 1.2 million, yet only about seven miles of ground changed hands. This virtual stalemate lasted for more than three years. Elsewhere, the fighting was just as devastating and inconclusive.

IN THE TRENCHES The stalemate was mainly an effect of **trench warfare**, in which armies fought for mere yards of ground. On the battlefields of Europe, there were three main kinds of trenches—front line, support, and reserve. Soldiers spent a period of time in each kind of trench. Dugouts, or underground rooms, were used as officers' quarters and command posts. Between the trench complexes lay **"no man's land."** This was a barren expanse of mud pockmarked with shell craters and filled with barbed wire. Periodically, the soldiers charged enemy lines, only to be mowed down by machine-gun fire.

Life in the trenches was miserable. The soldiers were surrounded by filth, lice, rats, and polluted water that caused dysentery. Many soldiers suffered trench foot. This condition was caused by standing in cold, wet trenches for

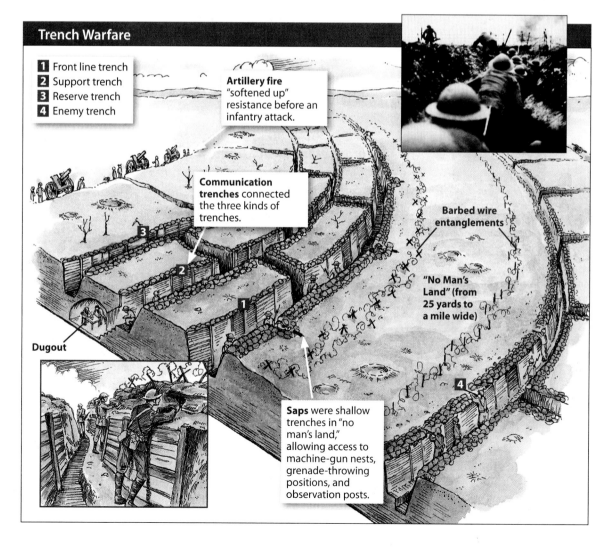

Trench Warfare

1 Front line trench
2 Support trench
3 Reserve trench
4 Enemy trench

Artillery fire "softened up" resistance before an infantry attack.

Communication trenches connected the three kinds of trenches.

Barbed wire entanglements

"No Man's Land" (from 25 yards to a mile wide)

Dugout

Saps were shallow trenches in "no man's land," allowing access to machine-gun nests, grenade-throwing positions, and observation posts.

long periods of time without changing into dry socks or boots. First, the toes would turn red or blue. Then, they would become numb, and finally, they would start to rot. The only solution was to amputate the toes, and in some cases, the entire foot. A painful infection of the gums and throat, called trench mouth, was also common among the soldiers.

The soldiers also suffered from lack of sleep. Constant bombardments and other experiences often led to battle fatigue and "shell shock." This term was coined during World War I to describe a complete emotional collapse from which many never recovered.

Reading Check
Analyze Effects
Why were so many European nations pulled into the conflict?

Americans Question Neutrality

Just after the fighting in Europe began, President Woodrow Wilson declared that the United States would remain neutral. His statement reflected a long-standing American commitment to isolationism. Most Americans agreed that there was no reason to join a struggle 3,000 miles away. The war did not threaten American lives or property. This did not mean, however, that certain groups and individuals in the United States were indifferent to who would win the war. Public opinion was strong—but divided.

The British spread the news of Germany's atrocious attacks on civilians through propaganda, but most Americans felt the war in Europe was not their fight.

Vocabulary
emigrate to leave one's country or region to settle in another; to move

DIVIDED LOYALTIES Socialists criticized the war as a capitalist and imperialist struggle between Germany and England to control markets and colonies in China, Africa, and the Middle East. Pacifists, such as lawyer and politician William Jennings Bryan, believed that war was evil and that the United States should set an example of peace to the world.

Many Americans simply did not want their sons to experience the horrors of warfare, as a hit song of 1915 conveyed.

"I didn't raise my boy to be a soldier,
I brought him up to be my pride and joy.
Who dares to place a musket on his shoulder,
To shoot some other mother's darling boy?"

Millions of naturalized U.S. citizens followed the war closely because they still had ties to the nations from which they had emigrated. For example, many Americans of German descent sympathized with Germany. Americans of Irish descent remembered the centuries of British oppression in Ireland. They saw the war as a chance for Ireland to gain its independence. Pressure from some of these ethnic groups in the United States contributed to American neutrality. Some immigrants created organizations to help the causes of their homelands. Some even advised the government on policies that affected the people of their homelands.

On the other hand, many Americans felt close to Britain because of a common ancestry and language as well as similar democratic institutions and legal systems. Germany's aggressive sweep through Belgium increased American sympathy for the Allies. The Germans attacked civilians, destroying villages, cathedrals, libraries, and even hospitals. Some atrocity stories—spread

U.S. Exports to Europe, 1912–1917

Dollars (in millions)

2,000
1,600
1,200
800
400
0

1912 1913 1914 1915 1916 1917

■ Great Britain   ■ All Other European Countries
■ France   ■ Germany

Interpret Graphs
1. By how much did total U.S. exports to Europe rise or fall between 1914 and 1917?
2. What trends does the graph show before the start of the war and during the war?

Reading Check
Analyze Motives
Why did the United States begin to favor Britain and France?

by British propaganda—later proved to be false. However, enough of them proved true that one American magazine referred to Germany as "the bully of Europe."

Maintaining neutrality proved difficult for American businesses. America's economic ties with the Allies were far stronger than its ties with the Central powers. Before the war, American trade with Britain and France was more than double its trade with Germany. With the start of the war, America's transatlantic trade became even more lopsided. The Allies flooded American manufacturers with orders for all sorts of war supplies. These included dynamite, cannon powder, submarines, copper wire and tubing, and armored cars. The United States shipped millions of dollars of war supplies to the Allies, but requests kept coming. By 1915 American factories were producing so many supplies for the Allies that the United States was experiencing a labor shortage.

Some businesses, seeking to remain neutral, tried to continue dealing with Germany, but this trade became increasingly risky. Shipments were often stopped by the British navy. In addition, President Wilson and others spoke out against German atrocities and warned of the threat that the German empire posed to democracy. From 1914 on, trade with the Allies quadrupled, while trade with Germany fell to near zero.

Also, by 1917 American banks had loaned $2.3 billion to the Allies, but only $27 million to the Central powers. Many U.S. leaders, including Treasury secretary William McAdoo, felt that American prosperity depended upon an Allied victory.

The War Hits Home

Although the majority of Americans favored victory for the Allies rather than the Central powers, they did not want to join the Allies' fight. By 1917, however, America had mobilized for war against the Central powers in order to ensure Allied repayment of debts to the United States and to prevent the Germans from threatening U.S. shipping.

THE BRITISH BLOCKADE As fighting on land continued, Britain began to make more use of its naval strength. It blockaded the German coast to prevent weapons and other military supplies from getting through. However, the British expanded the definition of *contraband* to include food. They also extended the blockade to neutral ports and mined the entire North Sea.

The results were twofold. First, American ships carrying goods for Germany refused to challenge the blockade and seldom reached their destination. Second, Germany found it increasingly difficult to import foodstuff and fertilizers for crops. By 1917 famine stalked the country. An estimated 750,000 Germans starved to death as a result of the British blockade.

Americans had been angry at Britain's blockade. It threatened freedom of the seas and prevented American goods from reaching German ports. However, Germany's response to the blockade soon outraged Americans.

GERMAN U-BOAT RESPONSE Germany responded to the British blockade with a counterblockade by U-boats (from *Unterseeboot,* the German word for *submarine*). Any British or Allied ship found in the waters around Britain would be sunk—and it would not always be possible to warn crews and passengers of an attack.

One of the worst disasters occurred on May 7, 1915, when a U-boat sank the British liner **Lusitania** (lōō′sĭ-ta′nē-ə) off the Irish coast. Of the 1,198 persons lost, 128 were Americans. The Germans defended their action on the grounds that the liner carried ammunition. Despite Germany's explanation, Americans became outraged with Germany because of the loss of life. American public opinion turned against Germany and the Central powers.

Despite this provocation, President Wilson ruled out a military response in favor of a sharp protest to Germany. Three months later, in August 1915, a U-boat sank another British liner, the *Arabic,* drowning two Americans. Again the United States protested, and this time Germany agreed not to sink any more passenger ships. But in March 1916 Germany broke its promise and torpedoed an unarmed French passenger steamer, the *Sussex.* The *Sussex* sank, and about 80 passengers, including Americans, were killed or injured. After this attack, Wilson threatened to end diplomatic relations with Germany unless it stopped killing innocent civilians. German officials feared that the United States might enter the war, so Germany issued the ***Sussex*** **pledge**, which included a promise not to sink merchant vessels "without warning and without saving human lives." But there was a condition: if the United States could not persuade Britain to lift its blockade against food and fertilizers, Germany would consider renewing unrestricted submarine warfare.

This image of a U-boat crew machine-gunning helpless survivors of the *Lusitania* was clearly meant as propaganda. In fact, U-boats seldom lingered after an attack.

"Peace Without Victory"

After the 1916 election, President Wilson tried to mediate between the warring alliances in Europe. The attempt failed. In a later speech, the president asked the Allied and Central powers to accept a "peace without victory," in which neither side would impose harsh terms on the other.

"The treaties and agreements which bring [the war] to an end must embody terms which will create a peace that is worth guaranteeing and preserving, a peace that will win the approval of mankind, not merely a peace that will serve the several interests and immediate aims of the nations engaged. . . . it must be a peace without victory . . . Victory would mean peace forced upon the loser, a victor's terms imposed upon the vanquished. It would be accepted in humiliation, under duress, at an intolerable sacrifice, and would leave a sting, a resentment, a bitter memory upon which terms of peace would rest, not permanently, but only as upon quicksand. Only a peace between equals can last."

—President Woodrow Wilson, from an address to the Senate, January 22, 1917

Analyze Historical Sources
How does this speech reflect Wilson's ideas about equality in a postwar world?

THE 1916 ELECTION In November 1916 came the U.S. presidential election. The Democrats renominated Wilson, and the Republicans nominated Supreme Court Justice Charles Evans Hughes. Wilson campaigned on the slogan "He Kept Us Out of War." Hughes pledged to uphold America's right to freedom of the seas but also promised not to be too severe on Germany.

The election returns shifted from hour to hour. In fact, Hughes went to bed believing he had been elected. When a reporter tried to reach him with the news of Wilson's victory, an aide to Hughes said, "The president can't be disturbed." "Well," replied the reporter, "when he wakes up, tell him he's no longer president."

Reading Check
Analyze Effects
How did the German U-boat campaign affect U.S. public opinion?

The United States Declares War

Despite Wilson's efforts on behalf of peace, hope seemed lost. The Allies were angered by Wilson's request for "peace without victory." They blamed the Central powers for starting the war and wanted them to pay for wartime damage and destruction. Germany, too, ignored Wilson's call for peace.

GERMAN PROVOCATION Germany's leaders hoped to defeat Britain by resuming unrestricted submarine warfare. On January 31 the kaiser announced that U-boats would sink all ships in British waters—hostile or neutral—on sight. Wilson was stunned. The German decision meant that the United States would have to go to war. However, the president held back, saying that he would wait for "actual overt acts" before declaring war.

The overt acts came. First was the **Zimmermann note**, a secret telegram from the German foreign minister to the German ambassador in Mexico that was intercepted and decoded by British agents. The telegram proposed an alliance between Mexico and Germany and promised that if war with the United States broke out, Germany would support Mexico in recovering "lost territory in Texas, New Mexico, and Arizona." The Germans hoped that an American war with Mexico would keep the United States out of the war in Europe. Excerpts of the telegram were printed in newspapers. The American public was outraged. On top of this, the Germans sank four unarmed American merchant ships, with a loss of 36 lives, further angering Americans.

Background
The Bolsheviks were led by Vladimir Ilich Lenin and Leon Trotsky.

A REVOLUTION IN RUSSIA Meanwhile, events in Russia also troubled the United States. By the end of 1915 Russia had suffered about 2.5 million casualties in the fight against the Central powers and was experiencing massive food shortages. Blaming the Russian czar for the nation's losses, revolutionaries ousted him in March 1917 and established a provisional government. In November, a group known as the Bolsheviks overthrew the provisional government and set up a Communist state. The new government withdrew the Russian army from the eastern front and signed a peace agreement with the Central powers.

With Russia out of the conflict, Germany was free to focus on fighting in the west. It looked as if Germany had a chance of winning the war. These events removed the last significant obstacle to direct U.S. involvement in the war. Now supporters of American entry into the war could claim that this was a war of democracies against brutal monarchies.

AMERICA ACTS A light drizzle fell on Washington on April 2, 1917, as senators, representatives, ambassadors, members of the Supreme Court, and other guests crowded into the Capitol to hear President Wilson deliver his war resolution.

Alliances During World War I

Allies		Central Powers
Australia	Italy	Austria-Hungary
Belgium	Japan	Bulgaria
British Colonies	Montenegro	Germany
Canada & Newfoundland	New Zealand	Ottoman Empire
France	Portugal	
French North Africa & French Colonies	Romania	
	Russia	
Great Britain	Serbia	
Greece	South Africa	
India	United States	

Although not all of the countries listed above sent troops into the war, they all joined the war on the Allied side at various times.

"Property can be paid for; the lives of peaceful and innocent people cannot be. The present German submarine warfare against commerce is a warfare against mankind. . . . We are glad . . . to fight . . . for the ultimate peace of the world and for the liberation of its peoples. . . . The world must be made safe for democracy. . . . We have no selfish ends to serve. We desire no conquest, no dominion. We seek no indemnities. . . . It is a fearful thing to lead this great peaceful people into war. . . . But the right is more precious than peace."

—President Woodrow Wilson, quoted in *American Voices*

Congress passed the resolution a few days later. With the hope of neutrality finally shattered, U.S. troops would follow the stream of American money and munitions that had been heading to the Allies throughout the war. But Wilson's plea to make the world "safe for democracy" wasn't just political posturing. Indeed, Wilson and many Americans truly believed that the United States had to join the war to pave the way for a future order of peace and freedom. A resolved but anxious nation held its breath as the United States prepared for war.

Reading Check
Make Inferences
Why did the Zimmermann note alarm the U.S. government?

Lesson 1 Assessment

1. **Organize Information** Use a web diagram to list the causes for the outbreak of World War I.

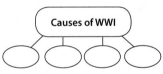

Which was the most significant cause? Explain your answer.

2. **Key Terms and People** For each key term or person in the lesson, write a sentence explaining its significance.

3. **Analyze Issues** Why do you think Germany escalated its U-boat attacks in 1917?

Think About:
- Germany's military buildup
- the effects of the British blockade
- Germany's justification for unrestricted submarine warfare

4. **Summarize** Why were America's ties with the Allies stronger than its ties with the Central powers?

5. **Analyze Events** How did the Russian Revolution change the course of the war?

6. **Analyze Causes** Why did the United States want to remain neutral in the conflict in Europe? What caused the shift from neutrality to involvement in the war?

7. **Form Opinions** Do you think the United States was justified to enter the war? Support your answer with details from the text.

The United States Joins the War

One American's Story

Eddie Rickenbacker, famous fighter pilot of World War I, was well known as a racecar driver before the war. He went to France as a driver but transferred to the aviation division. He learned to fly on his own time and eventually joined the U.S. Army Air Service. Rickenbacker repeatedly fought the dreaded Flying Circus—a German air squadron led by the "Red Baron," Manfred von Richthofen.

The Big Idea
The United States mobilized a large army and navy to help the Allies achieve victory.

Why It Matters Now
During World War I, the United States military evolved into the powerful fighting force that it remains today.

Key Terms and People
Eddie Rickenbacker

Selective Service Act

convoy system

American Expeditionary Force

John J. Pershing

Alvin York

conscientious objector

armistice

"I put in six or seven hours of flying time each day. . . . My narrowest escape came at a time when I was fretting over the lack of action. . . . Guns began barking behind me, and sizzling tracers zipped by my head. . . . At least two planes were on my tail. . . . They would expect me to dive. Instead I twisted upward in a corkscrew path called a 'chandelle.' I guessed right. As I went up, my two attackers came down, near enough for me to see their faces. I also saw the red noses on those Fokkers [German planes]. I was up against the Flying Circus again."
—Eddie Rickenbacker, from *Rickenbacker: An Autobiography*

World War I flying ace Eddie Rickenbacker

After engaging in 134 air battles and downing 26 enemy aircraft, Rickenbacker won fame as the Allied pilot with the most victories—"American ace of aces."

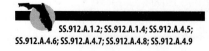

SS.912.A.1.2; SS.912.A.1.4; SS.912.A.4.5; SS.912.A.4.6; SS.912.A.4.7; SS.912.A.4.8; SS.912.A.4.9

America Mobilizes

The United States was not prepared for war. Only 200,000 men were in service when war was declared, and few officers had combat experience. Drastic measures were needed to build an army large and modern enough to make an impact in Europe.

RAISING AN ARMY To meet the government's need for more fighting power, Congress passed the **Selective Service Act** in May 1917. The act required men to register with the government in order to be randomly selected for military service. By the end of 1918, 24 million men had registered under the act. Of this number, almost 3 million were called up. About 2 million troops reached Europe before the truce was signed, and three-fourths of them saw actual combat. Most of the inductees had not attended high school, and about one in five was foreign-born.

The eight-month training period took place partly in the United States and partly in Europe. During this time, the men put in 17-hour days on target practice, bayonet drill, kitchen duty, and cleaning up the grounds. Since real weapons were in short supply, soldiers often drilled with fake weapons. They used rocks instead of hand grenades or wooden poles instead of rifles.

DIVERSITY IN THE MILITARY For the United States to effectively fight the Central powers, its military needed the cooperation of its minority population. Government publications appealed to all Americans, regardless of race or ethnicity, to support the war effort. One pamphlet reminded Americans that ". . . black men, yellow men, white men, from all quarters of the globe, are fighting side by side to free the world from the Hun peril. That's the patriotism of equality!"

Document-Based Investigation Historical Source

Uncle Sam the Recruiter

Before motion pictures and television were commonplace, the poster was an important visual medium. Easily produced and displayed, posters captured the immediate attention of the public.

In an effort to increase military recruitment, the U.S. government hired artists to create posters to appeal to a sense of patriotism in young men. James Montgomery Flagg's portrayal of a stern Uncle Sam became the most famous recruiting poster in American history.

Analyze Historical Sources
1. How does the poster use patriotic symbolism?

2. How effective do you think the poster was in convincing men to fight for the Allied cause?

The 369th Infantry Regiment, also known as the Harlem Hell Fighters, served a record 191 days in the trenches.

Many minorities hoped that by fighting for America, they would gain respect and be treated as equal citizens to whites. One lieutenant who served in the all-black 369th Infantry Regiment explained this perspective to a reporter.

"Now is the opportunity to prove what we can do. If we can't fight and die in this war just as bravely as white men, then we do not deserve equality with white men. . . . But if we can do things at the front; if we can make ourselves felt; if we can make America really proud . . . then it will be the biggest possible step toward our equalization as citizens."

—a U.S. Army lieutenant, from *The Crisis*,
August 1918

About 400,000 African Americans would ultimately serve in the armed forces. They generally did not get the equal treatment they wanted, however. They served in segregated units and were excluded from the navy and marines. Many white army officers and southern politicians objected to training African American soldiers to use weapons. They feared that these black soldiers might pose a threat after the war. Most African Americans were assigned to noncombat duties, although there were exceptions. The 369th Infantry Regiment saw more continuous duty on the front lines than any other American regiment. Two soldiers of the 369th, Henry Johnson and Needham Roberts, were the first Americans to receive France's highest military honor, the Croix de Guerre—the "cross of war."

Native Americans were required to register for the draft, but at the time were not generally considered to be citizens. Nonetheless, an estimated 10,000 Native Americans served in the military during the war. Many did so eager to gain war honors and maintain the warrior traditions of their peoples. The army used some Choctaw Indians to transmit messages in their native language. This was a strategy that the U.S. military would use more extensively in the next world war.

Other minority groups also contributed to the war effort. Like African Americans, many Asian Americans and Hispanic Americans saw military service as a way to gain equal rights. To accommodate Hispanic soldiers who did not speak fluent English, the military established programs in New Mexico and Georgia to help them learn the language. The Jewish Welfare Board established centers for Jewish servicemen in the United States and overseas. It also led enlistment and fundraising campaigns for the war effort.

Although women were not allowed to enlist, the army reluctantly accepted women in the Army Corps of Nurses. However, it denied them army rank, pay, and benefits. Meanwhile, some 13,000 women accepted noncombat positions in the navy and marines. There they served as nurses, secretaries, and telephone operators with full military rank. Some French-speaking American women served in the U.S. Army Signal Corps as switchboard operators. These "Hello Girls" served a crucial role by keeping communications open between the front line and the military headquarters. Some women went overseas to serve as volunteer ambulance drivers on the front lines.

Some shipyards were capable of building a war vessel in just over five days.

MASS PRODUCTION In addition to the vast army that had to be created and trained, the United States had to transport men, food, and equipment over thousands of miles of ocean. But German U-boat attacks on merchant ships in the Atlantic were a serious threat to the Allied war effort. By early 1917 German submarines had sunk twice as much ship tonnage as the Allies had built.

In response, the U.S. government took several steps to expand its fleet. First, the government exempted many shipyard workers from the draft. It gave others a "deferred" classification, delaying their participation in the draft. Second, the U.S. Chamber of Commerce joined in a public relations campaign to emphasize the importance of shipyard work. They distributed service flags to families of shipyard workers, just like the flags given to families of soldiers and sailors. Finally, shipyards used prefabrication techniques. Instead of building an entire ship in the yard, standardized parts were built elsewhere and then assembled at the yard. This method reduced construction time substantially.

Reading Check
Summarize How did the United States raise an army for the war?

The Fight "Over There"

After two and a half years of fighting, the Allied forces were exhausted, demoralized, and desperate for help. The Americans were able to provide fresh troops and much-needed supplies. But first they had to turn the tide in the battle against the German U-boats.

THE CONVOY SYSTEM Mass production techniques greatly increased the number of ships hauling materials and personnel to Europe. However, those ships remained easy targets for prowling U-boats. The United States needed to figure out a way to protect its transatlantic shipping. American vice-admiral William S. Sims convinced the British to try the **convoy system**. This method involved a heavy guard of destroyers escorting merchant ships back and forth across the Atlantic in groups. By fall of 1917 shipping losses had been cut in half.

The U.S. Navy also helped lay a 230-mile barrier of mines across the North Sea from Scotland to Norway. The barrier was designed to bottle up the U-boats that sailed from German ports in order to keep them out of the Atlantic Ocean.

By early 1918 the Germans found it increasingly difficult to replace their losses and to staff their fleet with trained submariners. Of the almost 2 million Americans who sailed to Europe during the war, only 637 were lost to U-boat attacks.

World War I Convoy System

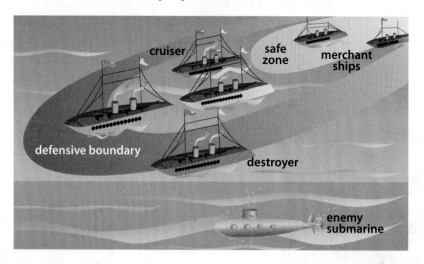

THE AMERICAN EXPEDITIONARY FORCE The first U.S. troops arrived in France in late June 1917. The American soldiers who went overseas formed the **American Expeditionary Force** (AEF), which was led by General **John J. Pershing**. The AEF included soldiers from the regular army, the National Guard, and a new larger force of volunteers and draftees. The men came from all over the country. Many had never traveled much beyond the farms or small towns where they lived. These American infantrymen were nicknamed doughboys, possibly because of the white belts they wore, which they cleaned with pipe clay, or "dough."

One of the main contributions that American troops made to the Allied war effort, besides their numbers, was their freshness and enthusiasm. They were determined to hit the Germans hard. Twenty-two-year-old Joseph Douglas Lawrence was a U.S. Army lieutenant. He remarked on the importance of the American soldier's enthusiasm when he described his first impression of the trenches.

— BIOGRAPHY —

John J. Pershing (1860–1948)

General Pershing was the commander of the American Expeditionary Force (AEF) in France. When he arrived there, he found that the Allies intended to use American troops simply as reinforcements. Pershing, however, urged that the AEF operate as an independent fighting force, under American command. He refused to have the AEF "scattered among the Allied forces where it will not be an American army at all." Pershing also wanted to give his troops more training. He believed that sending inexperienced soldiers into battle was the same as sending them to die. As a result, Pershing sent his troops to training camps in eastern France.

Pershing believed in aggressive combat. He felt that three years of trench warfare had made the Allies too defensive. Under Pershing, American forces captured important enemy positions and helped stop the German advance. After the war, Pershing was made General of the Armies of the United States. This was the highest rank an army officer could achieve. Many of Pershing's tactics would be used by the military in future wars.

"I have never seen or heard of such an elaborate, complete line of defense as the British had built at this point. There was a trench with dugouts every three hundred yards from the front line in Ypres back four miles to and including Dirty Bucket. Everything was fronted with barbed wire and other entanglements. Artillery was concealed everywhere. Railroad tracks, narrow and standard gauge, reached from the trenches back into the zone of supply. Nothing had been neglected to hold this line, save only one important thing, enthusiasm among the troops, and that was the purpose of our presence."

—Joseph D. Lawrence, quoted in *Fighting Soldier: The AEF in 1918*

Lieutenant Joseph D. Lawrence

A NEW KIND OF WAR Even the enthusiasm of the American doughboys often turned to shock upon experiencing the horrors of the European fronts. An American nurse named Florence Bullard described the deadly toll of modern warfare as she cared for soldiers in a hospital near the front in 1918.

"The Army is only twelve miles away from us and only the wounded that are too severely injured to live to be carried a little farther are brought here. . . . Side by side I have Americans, English, Scotch, Irish, and French, and apart in the corners are Boche [Germans]. They have to watch each other die side by side. I am sent for everywhere—in the . . . operating-room, the dressing-room, and back again to the rows of men. . . . The cannon goes day and night and the shells are breaking over and around us. . . . I have had to write many sad letters to American mothers. I wonder if it will ever end."

—Florence Bullard, quoted in *Over There: The Story of America's First Great Overseas Crusade*

Not only did World War I see the use of trench warfare, but it saw the first large-scale use of weapons that would become standard in modern war. Although some of these weapons were new, others, like the machine gun, had been so refined that they changed the nature of warfare. The new guns could hit targets that were miles away. And capable of firing 600 rounds a minute, machine guns could inflict heavy casualties on the enemy. In fact, they were responsible for 90 percent of Allied casualties at the Battle of the Somme in 1916.

The two most innovative weapons were the tank and the airplane. Together, they heralded mechanized warfare, or warfare that relies on machines powered by gasoline and diesel engines. Tanks ran on caterpillar treads and were built of steel so that bullets bounced off. The British first used tanks at Somme, but not very effectively. By 1917 the British had learned how to drive large numbers of tanks through barbed-wire defenses, clearing a path for the infantry. Because tanks were not damaged by either machine-gun or rifle fire, their use would mark the eventual end of trench warfare.

When the United States entered the war, its air power was weak. Congress eventually appropriated $675 million to build an air force. The early airplanes were so flimsy that at first both sides limited their use to scouting. After a while, the two sides used tanks to fire at enemy planes that were gathering information. Early dogfights, or individual air combats, like the one described by Eddie Rickenbacker, resembled duels. Pilots sat in their open cockpits and shot at each other with pistols. Because it was hard to fly a plane and shoot a pistol at the same time, planes began carrying mounted machine guns. But the planes' propeller blades kept getting in the way of the bullets. Then the Germans introduced an interrupter gear, which permitted the stream of bullets to avoid the whirring blades.

Meanwhile, airplanes were built to travel faster and carry heavy bomb loads. By 1918 the British had built up a strategic bomber force of 22,000 planes. This force attacked German weapons factories and army bases.

Technology at War

Both sides in World War I used new technology to attack more soldiers from greater distances than ever before. Aircraft and long-range guns were even used to fire on civilian targets. These included libraries, cathedrals, and city districts. The biggest guns could shell a city from 75 miles away.

MACHINE GUNS
Firepower increased to 600 rounds per minute.

AIRSHIPS AND AIRPLANES
The most famous World War I plane was the British Sopwith Camel. It had a front-mounted machine gun for "dogfights." Planes were also loaded with bombs, as were the floating gas-filled "airships" called zeppelins.

POISON GAS
The yellow-green fog of chlorine sickened, suffocated, burned, and blinded entrenched soldiers. Gas masks became standard issue.

TANKS
Tanks, like this French light tank, were used to "mow down" barbed wire and soldiers.

SHIPS
Even with the advantages of firepower and speed, dreadnoughts still faced threats from torpedo ships.

The Allies and the Central powers also poured valuable resources into building a new type of battleship called a dreadnought. These ships were more heavily armed than any other battleship. They also featured a revolutionary steam turbine propulsion system that gave them speed.

Observation balloons were widely used by both sides in the war in Europe. Balloons were so important strategically that they were often protected by aircraft. They became prime targets for Rickenbacker and other ace pilots.

Armies also used chemical warfare during World War I. Slow-moving clouds of poison gas could reach soldiers sheltered in the deepest of trenches. Toxic tear gas, mustard gas, chlorine, and phosgene were all used to deadly effect. This led some historians to call World War I the "chemists' war." Today the use of poison gas is a war crime.

Reading Check
Form Generalizations
How did World War I change the nature of warfare?

American Troops Go on the Offensive

When Russia pulled out of the war in 1917, the Germans shifted their armies from the eastern front to the western front in France. By May they were within 50 miles of Paris. The Americans arrived just in time to help stop the German advance at Cantigny. Several weeks later, U.S. troops played a major role in throwing back German attacks at Château-Thierry and Belleau Wood.

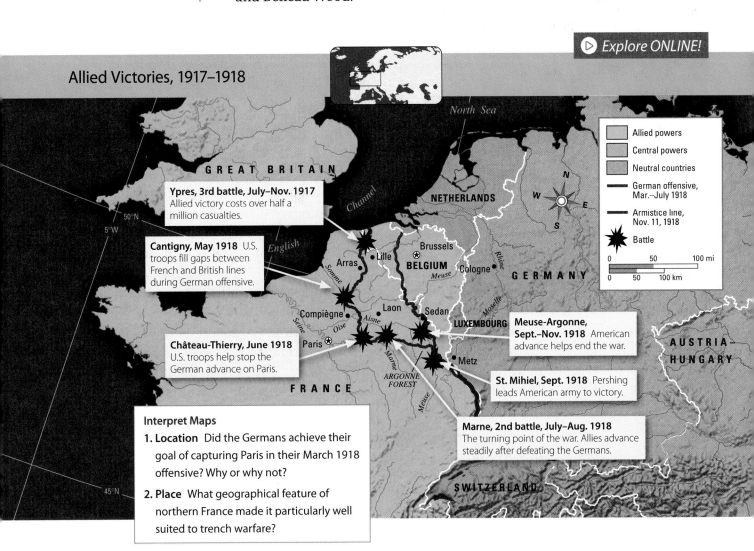

▶ Explore ONLINE!

Allied Victories, 1917–1918

Ypres, 3rd battle, July–Nov. 1917 Allied victory costs over half a million casualties.

Cantigny, May 1918 U.S. troops fill gaps between French and British lines during German offensive.

Château-Thierry, June 1918 U.S. troops help stop the German advance on Paris.

Meuse-Argonne, Sept.–Nov. 1918 American advance helps end the war.

St. Mihiel, Sept. 1918 Pershing leads American army to victory.

Marne, 2nd battle, July–Aug. 1918 The turning point of the war. Allies advance steadily after defeating the Germans.

Legend:
- Allied powers
- Central powers
- Neutral countries
- German offensive, Mar.–July 1918
- Armistice line, Nov. 11, 1918
- Battle

Map labels: North Sea, GREAT BRITAIN, Channel, NETHERLANDS, English, Brussels, Arras, Lille, BELGIUM, Cologne, GERMANY, Somme, Meuse, Rhine, Compiègne, Laon, Sedan, Moselle, Seine, Oise, Aisne, Paris, LUXEMBOURG, Metz, Marne, AUSTRIA-HUNGARY, ARGONNE FOREST, FRANCE, Meuse, SWITZERLAND

Interpret Maps

1. **Location** Did the Germans achieve their goal of capturing Paris in their March 1918 offensive? Why or why not?

2. **Place** What geographical feature of northern France made it particularly well suited to trench warfare?

On July 15, 1918, the Germans launched a last, desperate offensive at the Second Battle of the Marne. The German army suffered some 150,000 casualties and retreated on August 3. The Allies led a counterattack in September. The AEF defeated German troops at Mihiel, near the French-German border.

The Allies continued their advance toward the French city of Sedan. The railway there was the main supply line of German forces. For more than a month, the Allies pushed northward through the rugged Argonne Forest, facing artillery fire and deadly explosions every step of the way. The Americans suffered some 120,000 casualties in the Battle of the Argonne Forest, but by November they had occupied the hills around Sedan.

Sergeant Alvin York

AMERICAN WAR HERO During the fighting in the Meuse-Argonne area, one of America's greatest war heroes, **Alvin York**, became famous. York sought exemption as a **conscientious objector**, a person who opposes warfare on moral grounds, pointing out that the Bible says, "Thou shalt not kill."

York eventually decided that it was morally acceptable to fight if the cause was just. On October 8, 1918, armed only with a rifle and a revolver, York killed 25 Germans and—with 6 other doughboys—captured 132 prisoners. General Pershing called him the outstanding soldier of the AEF, while Marshal Foch, the commander of Allied forces in Europe, described his feat as "the greatest thing accomplished by any private soldier of all the armies of Europe." For his heroic acts, York was promoted to sergeant and became a celebrity when he returned to the United States.

THE COLLAPSE OF GERMANY By late 1918 the war was crippling the German economy; many civilians lacked food and supplies. Food riots and strikes erupted in Germany, and revolution swept across Austria-Hungary. The Central powers had difficulty encouraging their soldiers to fight.

On November 3, 1918, Austria-Hungary surrendered to the Allies. That same day, German sailors mutinied against government authority. The mutiny spread quickly. Everywhere in Germany, groups of soldiers and workers organized revolutionary councils. On November 9 socialist leaders in the capital, Berlin, established a German republic. The kaiser gave up the throne.

Although there were no Allied soldiers on German territory and no truly decisive battle had been fought, the Germans were too exhausted to continue fighting. So at the 11th hour, on the 11th day, in the 11th month of 1918, Germany agreed to a cease-fire and signed the **armistice**, or truce, that ended the war.

THE FINAL TOLL World War I was the bloodiest war in history up to that time. Deaths numbered about 22 million, more than half of them civilians. In addition, 20 million people were wounded, and 10 million more became refugees. The direct economic costs of the war may have been about $338 billion.

The United States lost 48,000 men in battle, with another 62,000 dying of disease. More than 200,000 Americans were wounded.

For the Allies, news of the armistice brought great relief. Private John Barkley described the reaction to the news.

> *"About 9 o'clock in the evening we heard wild commotion in the little town. The French people, old and young, were running through the streets. Old men and women we'd seen sitting around their houses too feeble to move, were out in the streets yelling, 'Vive la France! Vive la France! Vive l'America!'. . . .*
>
> *Down the street came a soldier. He was telling everybody the armistice had been signed. I said, 'What's an armistice?' It sounded like some kind of machine to me. The other boys around there didn't know what it meant either.*
>
> *When the official word came through that it meant peace, we couldn't believe it. Finally Jesse said, 'Well kid, I guess it really does mean the war is over.'*
>
> *I said, 'I just can't believe it's true.' But it was."*
>
> —John L. Barkley, quoted in *No Hard Feelings*

Reading Check
Draw Conclusions
How did American forces help the Allies win the war?

Across the Atlantic, Americans also rejoiced at the news. Many now expected life to return to normal. However, people found their lives at home changed almost as much as the lives of those who had fought in Europe.

Lesson 2 Assessment

1. **Organize Information** Fill in a web diagram to show how Americans responded to the war.

American Responses to World War I

Why was the entire population affected by America's entry into World War I?

2. **Key Terms and People** For each key term or person in the lesson, write a sentence explaining its significance.

3. **Draw Conclusions** In what ways did World War I represent a frightening new kind of warfare?

   Think About:
   - the casualty figures
   - the physical and psychological effects, such as shell shock, of warfare in World War I
   - how new weapons and new kinds of warfare affected the outcome of the war

4. **Contrast** Describe how the experiences of some groups of Americans serving overseas, such as women, African Americans, and Native Americans, differed from those of white soldiers.

5. **Analyze Primary Sources** This World War I poster shows the role of noncombatants overseas. What is the message in this poster? How effective do you think it was in influencing public opinion?

Back our girls over there
Y.W.C.A.
United War Work Campaign

The War at Home

The Big Idea

World War I spurred social, political, and economic change in the United States.

Why It Matters Now

Such changes increased government powers and expanded economic opportunities.

Key Terms and People

War Industries Board

Bernard M. Baruch

propaganda

Committee on Public Information

George Creel

Espionage and Sedition Acts

Great Migration

SS.912.A.1.2; SS.912.A.1.4; SS.912.A.1.6; SS.912.A.4.5; SS.912.A.4.6; SS.912.A.4.9; SS.912.G.4.2; SS.912.G.4.3; LAFS.1112.RH.1.1; LAFS.1112.RH.1.2; LAFS.1112.RH.2.6; LAFS.1112.RH.3.7; LAFS.1112.RH.4.10; LAFS.1112.SL.1.1; LAFS.1112.SL.2.4; LAFS.1112.WHST.1.2; MAFS.K12.MP.1.1; MAFS.K12.MP.5.1

One American's Story

The suffragist Harriot Stanton Blatch visited a munitions plant in New Jersey during World War I and proudly described women at work.

Harriot Stanton Blatch followed in the footsteps of her famous mother, Elizabeth Cady Stanton

"The day I visited the place, in one of the largest shops women had only just been put on the work, but it was expected that in less than a month they would be found handling all of the twelve hundred machines under that one roof alone. The skill of the women staggers one. After a week or two they master the operations on the 'turret,' gauging and routing machines. The best worker on the 'facing' machine is a woman. She is a piece worker, as many of the women are. . . . This woman earned, the day I saw her, five dollars and forty cents. She tossed about the fuse parts, and played with that machine, as I would with a baby."

—Harriot Stanton Blatch, quoted in *We, the American Women*

Before World War I, women had been excluded from many jobs. However, the wartime need for labor brought over a million more women into the work force. For women, as for the rest of society, World War I brought about far-reaching changes.

Government Oversees the War Effort

Winning the war was not a job for American soldiers alone. As Secretary of War Newton Baker said, "War is no longer Samson with his shield and spear and sword, and David with his sling. It is the conflict of smokestacks now, the combat of the driving wheel and the engine."

CONGRESS GIVES POWER TO WILSON Because World War I was such an immense conflict, the entire economy had to be refocused on the war effort. The shift from producing consumer goods to producing war supplies was too complicated and important a job for private industry to handle on its own, so business and government collaborated in the effort. In the process, the power of government was greatly expanded. Congress gave President Wilson direct control over much of the economy. It gave him the power to fix prices and to regulate—even to nationalize—certain war-related industries. One of the first industries to be nationalized was shipping. The government took over commercial and private ships and converted them for transatlantic war use.

The main regulatory body was the **War Industries Board** (WIB). It was established in 1917 and reorganized in 1918 under the leadership of **Bernard M. Baruch** (bə-rōōk'), a prosperous businessman. The board encouraged companies to use mass-production techniques to increase efficiency. It also urged them to eliminate waste by standardizing products—for instance, by making only 5 colors of typewriter ribbons instead of 150. The WIB set production quotas and allocated raw materials.

THE ECONOMY GROWS Under the WIB, industrial production in the United States increased by about 20 percent. However, the WIB applied price controls only at the wholesale level. As a result, retail prices soared. In 1918 they were almost double what they had been before the war.

Background
In 1913 Henry Ford speeded up factory production with a constantly moving assembly line. Wartime production spread this technique throughout the country.

The War Economy, 1914–1920

Average Annual Income

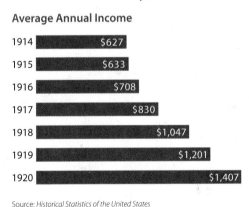

Year	Income
1914	$627
1915	$633
1916	$708
1917	$830
1918	$1,047
1919	$1,201
1920	$1,407

Source: *Historical Statistics of the United States*

Consumer Price Index*

*A measure of changes in the prices of goods and services commonly bought by consumers

Interpret Graphs
1. How did the rise in average annual income compare with the rise in prices from 1914 to 1920?
2. How might the combined change in wages and prices affect a working family?

Wages in most industries rose during the war years. For example, hourly wages for blue-collar workers in the metal trades, shipbuilding, and meat-packing rose by about 20 percent. However, rising food prices and housing costs undercut household income.

By contrast, corporate profits soared. This was especially true in industries such as chemicals, meatpacking, oil, and steel. One industrial manufacturer, the DuPont Company, saw its stock multiply in value 1,600 percent between 1914 and 1918. By that time, the company was earning $68 million in profits each year.

Unions boomed during the war years. One cause was the difference in pay between labor and management. Other causes were increasing work hours, child labor, and dangerously "sped-up" conditions. Union membership climbed from about 2.5 million in 1916 to more than 4 million in 1919. More than 6,000 strikes broke out during the war months. To deal with disputes between management and labor, President Wilson established the National War Labor Board in 1918. Workers who refused to obey board decisions could lose their draft exemptions. "Work or fight," the board told them. However, the board also worked to improve factory conditions. It pushed for an eight-hour workday, promoted safety inspections, and enforced the child labor ban.

OTHER AGENCIES The WIB was not the only federal agency to regulate the economy during the war. The Railroad Administration controlled the railroads. The Fuel Administration monitored coal supplies and rationed gasoline and heating oil. In addition, many people adopted "gasless Sundays" and "lightless nights" to conserve fuel. In March 1918 the Fuel Administration introduced another conservation measure. This was daylight-saving time, which had first been proposed by Benjamin Franklin in the 1770s as a way to take advantage of the longer days of summer.

To help produce and conserve food, Wilson set up the Food Administration under Herbert Hoover. Instead of rationing food, he called on people to follow the "gospel of the clean plate." He declared one day a week "meatless,"

A wartime poster encourages Americans to conserve resources.

A Japanese American family tends a victory garden in New York City in 1917.

another "sweetless," two days "wheatless," and two other days "porkless." Restaurants removed sugar bowls from the table and served bread only after the first course.

Homeowners planted "victory gardens" in their yards. Schoolchildren spent their after-school hours growing tomatoes and cucumbers in public parks. As a result of these and similar efforts, American food shipments to the Allies tripled. Hoover also set a high government price on wheat and other staples. Farmers responded by putting an additional 40 million acres into production. In the process, they increased their income by almost 30 percent.

Reading Check
Summarize What steps did the government take to manage the economy during the war?

Selling the War

Once the government had extended its control over the economy, it was faced with two major undertakings: raising money and convincing the public to support the war.

WAR FINANCING The United States spent about $35.5 billion on the war effort. The government raised about one-third of this amount through taxes. These taxes included a progressive income tax (which taxed high incomes at a higher rate than low incomes), a war-profits tax, and higher excise taxes on tobacco, liquor, and luxury goods. It raised the rest through public borrowing by selling "Liberty Loan" and "Victory Loan" bonds.

The government sold bonds through tens of thousands of volunteers. Movie stars spoke at rallies in factories, in schools, and on street corners. As Treasury Secretary William G. McAdoo put it, only "a friend of Germany" would refuse to buy war bonds.

Propaganda posters were designed to elicit emotional responses from viewers. This poster urged Americans to get involved in the war effort for the good of civilization.

INFLUENCING PUBLIC OPINION To popularize the war, the government set up the nation's first **propaganda** agency, the **Committee on Public Information** (CPI). Propaganda is a kind of biased communication designed to influence people's thoughts and actions. The head of the CPI was a former muckraking journalist named **George Creel**.

Creel persuaded the nation's artists and advertising agencies to create thousands of paintings, posters, cartoons, and sculptures promoting the war. He recruited some 75,000 men to serve as "Four-Minute Men." They spoke about everything relating to the war: the draft, rationing, bond drives, victory gardens, and topics such as "Why We Are Fighting" and "The Meaning of America."

Creel did not ignore the written word. He ordered a printing of almost 25 million copies of "How the War Came to America." It included Wilson's war message in English and other languages. He distributed some 75 million pamphlets, booklets, and leaflets, many with the enthusiastic help of the Boy Scouts. Creel's propaganda campaign was highly effective.

U.S. newspapers, too, became agents of public opinion during the war. Once U.S. soldiers joined the fight, newspapers ran fewer photographs from the battlefields. Instead, they printed patriotic images of parades and heroic portraits of President Wilson. The *New York Times* began including daily tallies of which states had contributed the most recruits and purchased the most war bonds. This started a friendly competition among readers to support the war effort.

Reading Check Summarize How did the government raise money for the war effort?

Attacks on Civil Liberties Increase

While the government's propaganda campaign promoted patriotism, it also inflamed hatred and violations of the civil liberties of certain ethnic groups and opponents of the war. Early in 1917 President Wilson expressed his fears about the consequences of war hysteria.

> *"Once lead this people into war and they'll forget there ever was such a thing as tolerance. To fight you must be brutal and ruthless, and the spirit of ruthless brutality will enter into the very fiber of our national life, infecting Congress, the courts, the policeman on the beat, the man in the street. Conformity would be the only virtue, and every man who refused to conform would have to pay the penalty."*
>
> —Woodrow Wilson, quoted in *Cobb of "The World"*

The president's prediction came true. As soon as war was declared, conformity indeed became the order of the day. Attacks on civil liberties, both unofficial and official, erupted.

Stripped! By J. H. Cassel

During the war, conspiracy theories flourished in the United States, and foreign spies were believed to be everywhere. Cartoons like this one from 1917 revealed the hysteria that gripped the nation and helped inflame prejudice against recent immigrants.

ANTI-IMMIGRANT HYSTERIA The main targets of these attacks were Americans who had emigrated from other nations, especially those from Germany and Austria-Hungary. The most bitter attacks were directed against the nearly 2 million Americans who had been born in Germany, but other foreign-born persons and Americans of German descent suffered as well.

Many Americans with German names lost their jobs. Orchestras refused to play the music of Mozart, Bach, Beethoven, and Brahms. Some towns with German names changed them. Schools stopped teaching the German language, and librarians removed books by German authors from the shelves. People even resorted to violence against German Americans. Some were flogged or smeared with tar and feathers. A mob in Collinsville, Illinois, wrapped a German flag around a German-born miner named Robert Prager and lynched him. A jury cleared the mob's leader.

Finally, in a burst of anti-German fervor, Americans changed the name of German measles to "liberty measles." Hamburger—named after the German city of Hamburg—became "Salisbury steak" or "liberty sandwich," depending on whether you were buying it in a store or eating it in a restaurant. Sauerkraut was renamed "liberty cabbage," and dachshunds turned into "liberty pups."

Vocabulary
sedition rebellion against one's government; treason

ESPIONAGE AND SEDITION ACTS In June 1917 Congress passed the Espionage Act, and in May 1918 it passed the Sedition Act. Under the **Espionage and Sedition Acts**, a person could be fined up to $10,000 and sentenced to 20 years in jail for interfering with the war effort or for saying anything disloyal, profane, or abusive about the government or the war effort.

Like the Alien and Sedition Acts of 1798, these laws clearly violated the spirit of the First Amendment. Their passage led to over 2,000 prosecutions for loosely defined antiwar activities; of these, over half resulted in convictions. Newspapers and magazines that opposed the war or criticized any of the Allies lost their mailing privileges. The House of Representatives refused to seat Victor Berger, a socialist congressman from Wisconsin, because of his antiwar views. Columbia University fired a distinguished psychologist because he opposed the war. A colleague who supported the war thereupon resigned in protest. He said, "If we have to suppress everything we don't like to hear, this country is resting on a pretty wobbly basis."

The Espionage and Sedition Acts targeted socialists and labor leaders. Eugene V. Debs was handed a ten-year prison sentence for speaking out against the war and the draft. The anarchist Emma Goldman received a two-year prison sentence and a $10,000 fine for organizing the No Conscription League. When she left jail, the authorities deported her to Russia. "Big Bill" Haywood and other leaders of the Industrial Workers of the World (IWW) were accused of sabotaging the war effort because they urged workers to strike for better conditions and higher pay. Haywood was sentenced to a long prison term. (He later skipped bail and fled to Russia.) Under such federal pressure, the IWW faded away.

Reading Check
Analyze Effects
What impact did the Espionage and Sedition Acts have on free speech?

The War Encourages Social Change

Wars often unleash powerful social forces. The period of World War I was no exception. Important changes transformed the lives of African Americans, immigrants, and women.

THE GREAT MIGRATION In concrete terms, the greatest effect of the First World War on African Americans' lives was that it accelerated the **Great Migration**, the large-scale movement of hundreds of thousands of southern blacks to cities in the North. This great population shift had already begun before the war in the late 19th century. At that time, African Americans trickled northward to escape the Jim Crow South. After the turn of the century, the trickle became a tidal wave.

Several factors contributed to the tremendous increase in black migration. First, many African Americans wanted to escape racial discrimination in the South. Discrimination made it hard for them to make a living and

African American Support of the War

Black public opinion about the war was divided. Some people—such as William Monroe Trotter, the founder of the Boston *Guardian*—believed that victims of racism should not support a racist government. Despite grievances over racial inequality in the United States, most African Americans, however, backed the war. They supported the opinions of W.E.B. Du Bois. He believed that African American support for the war would strengthen calls for racial justice. Du Bois explained his position.

> *"That which the German power represents today spells death to the aspirations of Negroes and all darker races for equality, freedom and democracy. . . . Let us, while this war lasts, forget our special grievances and close our ranks shoulder to shoulder with our own white fellow citizens and the allied nations that are fighting for democracy."*
>
> —W.E.B. Du Bois, from "Close Ranks"

Analyze Historical Sources
How does Du Bois try to convince African Americans to support the war effort?

often threatened their lives. Also, a boll weevil infestation, aided by floods and droughts, had ruined much of the South's cotton fields. In the North, there were more job opportunities. For example, Henry Ford opened his automobile assembly line to black workers in 1914. The outbreak of World War I and the drop in European immigration increased job opportunities for African Americans. There were jobs in steel mills, munitions plants, and stockyards. Northern manufacturers sent recruiting agents to distribute free railroad passes through the South. In addition, the publisher of the black-owned newspaper *Chicago Defender* bombarded southern blacks with articles contrasting Dixieland lynchings with the prosperity of African Americans in the North.

Between 1910 and 1930 hundreds of thousands of African Americans migrated to such cities as Chicago, New York, and Philadelphia. Author Richard Wright described the great exodus.

> *"We are bitter no more; we are leaving! We are leaving our homes, pulling up stakes to move on. We look up at the high southern sky and remember all the sunshine and all the rain and we feel a sense of loss, but we are leaving. We look out at the wide green fields which our eyes saw when we first came into the world and we feel full of regret, but we are leaving. We scan the kind black faces we have looked upon since we first saw the light of day, and, though pain is in our hearts, we are leaving. We take one last furtive look over our shoulders to the Big House—high upon a hill beyond the railroad tracks—where the Lord of the Land lives, and we feel glad, for we are leaving."*
>
> —Richard Wright, quoted in *12 Million Black Voices*

The Migration of the Negro, Panel No. 1 by Jacob Lawrence shows three of the most common destinations for African Americans leaving the South.

For the most part, the migrants' lives changed for the better in the North. As the artist Jacob Lawrence wrote, "the children were able to go to school, and their parents gained the freedom to vote. And the migrants kept coming." However, racial prejudice against African Americans existed in the North as it had in the South.

The press of new migrants to northern cities caused overcrowding and intensified racial tensions. Some cities passed zoning laws that segregated city streets by race. Sometimes the racial prejudice in northern cities took violent forms. In July 1917 a race riot exploded in East St. Louis, Illinois. White workers were furious over the hiring of African Americans as strike-breakers at a munitions plant, so they rampaged through the streets. Forty blacks and nine whites died.

Another riot erupted in July 1919 in Chicago when a 17-year-old African American swam from the water off a "black beach" to the water off a "white beach." There, white bathers threw rocks at him until he drowned. African Americans retaliated, and several riots broke out in the city. Order was restored after several days of violence that involved about 10,000 people. Racially motivated riots occurred in some two dozen other cities in 1919.

WOMEN IN THE WAR While African Americans began new lives, women moved into jobs that had been held exclusively by men. They became railroad workers, cooks, dockworkers, and bricklayers. They mined coal and took part in shipbuilding. At the same time, women continued to fill more traditional jobs as nurses, clerks, and teachers. In all, about 1 million women entered the work force during World War I. In addition, many women worked as volunteers, serving at Red Cross facilities and encouraging the sale of bonds and the planting of victory gardens. Others, such as Jane Addams, were active in the peace movement. Addams helped found the Women's Peace Party in 1915 and remained a pacifist even after the United States entered the war.

Women worked in a variety of jobs during the war. Here, women assemble an aircraft wing.

After the war ended, however, most women left the jobs they had taken. Many women left by choice; others were forced to leave by employers who wanted to give the jobs to returning servicemen.

The contributions that women made to the war effort, however, did not go unnoticed. President Wilson stated, "The services of women during the supreme crisis have been of the most signal usefulness and distinction; it is high time that part of our debt should be acknowledged." While acknowledgment of that debt did not include equal pay for equal work, it did help bolster public support for woman suffrage. In 1919 Congress finally passed the Nineteenth Amendment, granting women the right to vote. In 1920 the amendment was ratified by the states.

THE FLU EPIDEMIC In the fall of 1918, the United States suffered a home-front crisis. An international flu epidemic affected about one-quarter of the U.S. population. The epidemic had a devastating effect on the economy. Mines shut down, telephone service was cut in half, and factories and offices staggered working hours to avoid contagion. Cities ran short of coffins, and the corpses of poor people lay unburied for as long as a week. Death could come in a matter of days. Doctors did not know what to do, other than to recommend cleanliness and quarantine. One epidemic survivor recalled that "so many people died from the flu they just rang the bells; they didn't dare take [corpses] into the church."

New York City street cleaners wore masks to avoid catching influenza.

In the army, living conditions allowed contagious illnesses to spread rapidly. More than a quarter of the soldiers caught the disease. In some AEF units, one-third of the troops died. Germans fell victim in even larger numbers than the Allies. The illness may have been spread around the world by soldiers. The epidemic killed about 500,000 Americans before it disappeared in 1919. Historians believe that the influenza virus killed as many as 30 million people worldwide.

World War I brought death and disease to millions, but like the flu epidemic, the war also came to a sudden end. After four years of slaughter and destruction, the time had come to forge a peace settlement. Americans hoped that this "war to end all wars" would do just that. Leaders of the victorious nations gathered at Versailles outside Paris to work out the terms of peace, and President Wilson traveled to Europe to ensure it.

Reading Check
Make Inferences
How did the war open opportunities for African Americans and women?

Lesson 3 Assessment

1. **Organize Information** Use a graphic organizer to compare the impact of World War I on women, African Americans, immigrants, and dissenters in the United States.

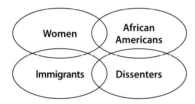

Explain how each group benefited from or was disadvantaged by changes brought about by the war.

2. **Key Terms and People** For each key term or person in the lesson, write a sentence explaining its significance.

3. **Evaluate** Do you think that the war had a positive or a negative effect on American society?

   Think About:
   • how the propaganda campaign influenced people's behavior
   • the new job opportunities for African Americans and women
   • how the government controlled industry
   • how the war affected individuals' civil liberties

4. **Make Inferences** Why would labor disputes affect the war effort?

5. **Draw Conclusions** How did the war affect government power? Do you think government actions such as creating the War Industries Board, the Food Administration, and the Fuel Administration, and passing the Espionage and Sedition Acts were necessary in wartime? Explain why or why not.

6. **Analyze Events** Why did many African Americans move to the North during the war? What effect did the Great Migration have on the North? What factors led to racial tension in northern cities?

Schenck v. United States (1919)

ORIGINS OF THE CASE

Charles Schenck, an official of the U.S. Socialist Party, distributed leaflets that called the draft a "deed against humanity" and compared conscription to slavery, urging conscripts to "assert your rights." Schenck was convicted of sedition and sentenced to prison, but he argued that the conviction, punishment, and even the law itself violated his right to free speech. The Supreme Court agreed to hear his appeal.

THE RULING

A unanimous court upheld Schenck's conviction, stating that under wartime conditions, the words in the leaflets were not protected by the right to free speech.

LEGAL REASONING

The Supreme Court's opinion in the *Schenck* case, written by Justice Oliver Wendell Holmes Jr., has become famous as a guide for how the First Amendment defines the right of free speech. Holmes wrote:

"The question in every case is whether the words used are used in such circumstances and are of such a nature as to create a clear and present danger that they will bring about the substantive evils that Congress has a right to prevent."

Justice Holmes noted that "in ordinary times" the First Amendment might have protected Schenck, but "[w]hen a nation is at war many things that might be said in time of peace . . . will not be endured."

The analogy that Holmes used to explain why Schenck could be punished for his words has become probably the best-known observation ever made about free speech:

"Protection of free speech would not protect a man in falsely shouting 'Fire!' in a theatre and causing a panic."

Writing for the Court, Holmes implied that during wartime, Schenck's leaflet was just that dangerous.

Oliver Wendell Holmes Jr., Supreme Court Justice 1902–1932

LEGAL SOURCES

LEGISLATION

U.S. Constitution, First Amendment (1791)

"Congress shall make no law . . . abridging the freedom of speech, or of the press."

The Sedition Act (1918)

"(W)hoever . . . shall willfully utter, print, write or publish any disloyal, profane, scurrilous, or abusive language about the form of government, . . . Constitution, . . . military or naval forces, . . . flag, . . . or the uniform of the Army or Navy of the United States . . . shall be punished by a fine of not more than $10,000 or imprisonment for not more than twenty years, or both."

RELATED CASES

Debs v. *United States* (1919)

The conviction against Eugene Debs for speaking against the war and the draft is upheld.

Frohwerk v. *United States* (1919)

The publisher of a newspaper that had criticized the war is sentenced with a fine and ten years in prison.

Abrams v. *United States* (1919)

Leaflets criticizing the U.S. expeditionary force in Russia are found to be unprotected by the First Amendment. Holmes writes a dissenting opinion calling for the "free trade of ideas."

WHY IT MATTERED

During the course of World War I, the federal government brought approximately 2,000 prosecutions for violations of the Espionage Act of 1917 or the Sedition Act of 1918, the same laws under which it convicted Schenck, Debs, and Frohwerk.

By the fall of 1919, however, Holmes had changed his mind. The case of *Abrams* v. *United States* concerned leaflets that criticized President Wilson's "capitalistic" government for sending troops to put down the Russian Revolution. Justice Holmes, joined by Justice Louis Brandeis, dissented from the majority of the Court, which upheld the conviction. In his dissent, Holmes emphasized the importance of a free exchange of ideas so that truth will win out in the intellectual marketplace. His reasoning won him acclaim as a protector of free speech.

The belief that truth will eventually win out in the marketplace of ideas has become important legal justification for promoting freedom of speech.

Eugene Debs was arrested for antiwar speeches like the one he gave at this 1916 presidential campaign stop.

HISTORICAL IMPACT

Disagreements about what kinds of speech are "free" under the First Amendment continue. During the 1950s, when people were jailed for supporting communism, and during the Vietnam War, when war protestors supported draft resistance, these issues again reached the Supreme Court.

The Court has also been asked to decide if young people in schools have the same First Amendment rights as adults. In *Tinker* v. *Des Moines School District* (1969), the Court ordered a school to readmit students who had been suspended for wearing black armbands in protest of the war in Vietnam.

This so-called symbolic speech, such as wearing an armband or burning a draft card or a flag to express an opinion, has sparked heated debate. In *Texas* v. *Johnson* (1989), the Court, by a narrow five to four vote, invalidated a law under which a man who burned an American flag to protest Reagan administration policies had been convicted. The decision so outraged some people that members of Congress considered amending the Constitution to prohibit any "physical desecration" of the flag. The amendment did not pass. Our freedoms of expression continue to depend upon the words in the first article of the Bill of Rights, written more than 200 years ago.

In 1965 Mary Beth Tinker and her brother, John, were suspended from school for wearing armbands that symbolically criticized the Vietnam War.

Critical Thinking

1. **Connect to History** Read Justice Holmes's dissent in *Abrams* v. *United States*. Compare it with the opinion he wrote in *Schenck* v. *United States*. Explain the major difference or similarity in the two opinions.

2. **Connect to Today** Use the library or Internet to research articles about recent free speech issues. Select an issue—such as whether the press should have freedom to publish information that could put national security at risk—to discuss as a class. Work in groups to propose a point of view on the issue, and develop as many arguments as you can to defend it. Then present a debate to the class.

Wilson Fights for Peace

The Big Idea

European leaders opposed most of Wilson's peace plan, and the U.S. Senate failed to ratify the peace treaty.

Why It Matters Now

Many of the nationalist issues left unresolved after World War I continue to trouble the world today.

Key Terms and People

Fourteen Points

self-determination

League of Nations

Georges Clemenceau

David Lloyd George

Treaty of Versailles

reparations

war-guilt clause

Henry Cabot Lodge

One American's Story

In January 1918, at the magnificent Palace of Versailles outside Paris, President Wilson tried to persuade the Allies to construct a just and lasting peace and to establish a League of Nations. Colonel E. M. House, a native of Texas and a member of the American delegation to Versailles, later wrote about the conference.

"How splendid it would have been had we blazed a new and better trail! . . . It may be that Wilson might have had the power and influence if he had remained in Washington and kept clear of the Conference. When he stepped from his lofty pedestal and wrangled with representatives of other states, upon equal terms, he became as common clay. . . .

Colonel Edward M. House was a friend and adviser to President Woodrow Wilson.

To those who are saying that the Treaty is bad and should never have been made and that it will involve Europe in infinite difficulties in its enforcement, I feel like admitting it. But I would also say in reply that empires cannot be shattered and new states raised upon their ruins without disturbance."
—Colonel E. M. House, quoted in *Hooray for Peace, Hurrah for War*

House saw what happened when Wilson's idealism ran up against practical politics. The Allied victors, vengeful toward Germany after four years of warfare, rejected most of Wilson's peace program.

SS.912.A.1.2; SS.912.A.1.4; SS.912.A.4.5; SS.912.A.4.10; SS.912.A.5.5; SS.912.G.1.2; LAFS.1112.RH.1.2; LAFS.1112.RH.2.6; LAFS.1112.RH.3.7; LAFS.1112.RH.4.10

Wilson Presents His Plan

Rejection was probably the last thing Wilson expected when he arrived in Europe. Everywhere he went, people gave him a hero's welcome. Italians displayed his picture in their windows. Parisians scattered flowers in the street. Representatives of one group after another, including Armenians, Jews, Ukrainians, and Poles, spoke to him. They appealed help in setting up independent nations for themselves.

FOURTEEN POINTS Even before the war was over, Wilson presented his vision for the postwar world. On January 18, 1918, he presented his **Fourteen Points** plan to Congress. The first several points were issues that Wilson believed had to be addressed to prevent another war. He suggested banning secret agreements between nations. He proposed lower tariffs to facilitate free trade. He also called for military cutbacks and freedom of the seas.

Several other points focused on the need to resolve national border disputes. His plan also proposed settlements for colonial peoples who wished to be independent. Wilson suggested that colonial policies should consider

---

Document-Based Investigation Historical Source

The Fourteen Points

In addition to outlining specific proposals for peace, the Fourteen Points marked a new philosophy—that the foreign policy of a democratic nation should be based on a sense of morality, not just national interests.

> "We entered this war because violations of right had occurred which touched us to the quick and made the life of our own people impossible unless they were corrected and the world secured once for all against their recurrence. What we demand in this war, therefore, is nothing peculiar to ourselves. It is that the world be made fit and safe to live in; and particularly that it be made safe for every peace-loving nation which, like our own, wishes to live its own life, determine its own institutions, be assured of justice and fair dealing by the other peoples of the world as against force and selfish aggression."
>
> —Woodrow Wilson, from the "Fourteen Points"

Goals of the Fourteen Points

1. Public diplomatic negotiations and an end to secret treaties
2. Freedom of navigation on the seas
3. Free trade among nations
4. Reduction of armaments to the level needed for domestic safety
5. Fair resolution of colonial claims that arose because of the war
6. Evacuation of Russia and restoration of its conquered territories
7. Preservation of Belgium's sovereignty
8. Restoration of France's territory, including Alsace-Lorraine
9. Redrawing Italy's borders according to nationalities
10. Divide up Austria-Hungary according to nationalities
11. Redraw the borders of the Balkan states according to nationalities
12. Self-determination for Turks and other nationalities under Turkish rule
13. Creation of an independent Polish nation
14. Creation of a League of Nations

Analyze Historical Sources
How do Wilson's ideas for foreign policy in the Fourteen Points reflect the democratic ideals expressed in the nation's founding documents?

Woodrow Wilson (1856–1924)

At the end of the war, President Wilson wanted the United States to become more involved in international affairs. He believed the nation had a moral duty to help maintain peace in the world. Wilson's sense of moral purpose had a lasting influence on American foreign policy.

Background
Few ethnic groups have been as successful in influencing foreign policy as were Polish Americans after World War I. The re-creation of Poland has been linked to the Wilson administration's interest in securing the Polish-American vote.

the interests of the colonial peoples as well as the interests of the imperialist powers. Wilson believed strongly in **self-determination**—the right of people to choose their own political status. He wanted groups that claimed distinct ethnic identities to be able to form their own nation-states or decide for themselves to what nations they would belong.

The final point called for the creation of an international organization. Its purpose would be to address diplomatic crises like those that had sparked the war. This **League of Nations** would provide a forum for nations to discuss and settle their differences without having to resort to war.

THE PARIS PEACE CONFERENCE Wilson planned to present his Fourteen Points to world leaders at a peace conference in Paris in January 1919. Leaders from 32 nations attended. They represented about three-quarters of the world's population. For example, delegates from Poland attended the conference seeking independence. Poland had been divided between Germany and Russia during the war. Also attending were representatives from several Central European Slavic groups.

Contrary to custom, the peace conference did not include the defeated Central powers. Nor did it include Russia, which was now under the control of a Communist government, or many of the smaller Allied nations. From the beginning, the negotiations were dominated by leaders of the four major Allied countries: the United States, Great Britain, France, and Italy. Together, these leaders became known as the "Big Four." Wilson was an idealist. He

(left to right) David Lloyd George, Georges Clemenceau, and Woodrow Wilson in Paris in 1919

Aims at the Paris Peace Conference

Wilson	• to create a League of Nations • to ensure Germany was not destroyed • to avoid blaming Germany for the war
Clemenceau	• to take revenge on and punish Germany • to reclaim Alsace-Lorraine for France • to avoid creation of the League of Nations • to gain reparations • to disband the German army and prevent future attacks
Lloyd George	• to achieve a "just" peace that would satisfy those who wanted to "make Germany pay" but leave Germany strong enough to trade • to retain land for Britain's empire • to protect Britain's naval supremacy

hoped that the other leaders would share his dream of restoring peace to Europe without punishing Germany too harshly.

Wilson was naive about the political aspects of securing a peace treaty. This was shown by his failure to understand the anger felt by the Allied leaders. The French premier, **Georges Clemenceau** (klĕm′ən-sō′), had lived through two German invasions of France. He was determined to prevent future invasions. **David Lloyd George**, the British prime minister, had just won reelection on the slogan "Make Germany Pay." The Italian prime minister, Vittorio Orlando, wanted control of Austrian-held territory.

Reading Check
Analyze Motives
Why did the Allies reject Wilson's plan?

These differences of opinion created tension within the Big Four. Eventually, Lloyd George persuaded Clemenceau to agree to the League of Nations and a more lenient peace treaty. Also, in order to get others to agree to establish the League of Nations, Wilson had to give up most of his Fourteen Points.

Debate over the Treaty of Versailles

On June 28, 1919, the Big Four and the leaders of the defeated nations gathered in the Hall of Mirrors of the Palace of Versailles (vər-sī′) to sign the peace treaty. They had suffered four years of devastating warfare. Everyone hoped that the treaty would create stability for a rebuilt Europe. Instead, anger held sway.

PROVISIONS OF THE TREATY The **Treaty of Versailles** established nine new nations—including Poland, Czechoslovakia, and Yugoslavia. It changed the boundaries of other nations. It carved areas out of the Ottoman Empire and gave them to France and Great Britain as mandates, or temporary colonies. Those two Allies were to administer their respective mandates until the areas were ready for self-rule and then independence.

The treaty barred Germany from maintaining an army, and it required Germany to return the region of Alsace-Lorraine to France. It also compelled Germany to pay **reparations**, or war damages, to the Allies in the amount of $33 billion.

THE TREATY'S WEAKNESSES This treatment of Germany weakened the ability of the Treaty of Versailles to provide a lasting peace in Europe. Several basic flaws in the treaty sowed the seeds of postwar international problems. These problems eventually would lead to the Second World War.

First, the treaty humiliated Germany. It contained a **war-guilt clause**. This clause forced Germany to admit sole responsibility for starting World War I and causing the resulting damage. German militarism had played a major role in igniting the war. However, other European nations had been guilty of provoking diplomatic crises before the war. Furthermore, there was no way Germany could pay the huge financial reparations. Germany was stripped of its colonial possessions in the Pacific, which might have helped it pay its reparations bill.

In addition, for three years the Russians had fought on the side of the Allies. Russia suffered higher casualties than any other nation. However,

Russia was excluded from the peace conference. As a result, it lost more territory than Germany did. The Union of Soviet Socialist Republics (or Soviet Union), as Russia was officially called after 1922, became determined to regain its former territory.

Finally, the treaty ignored the claims of colonized people for self-determination. One example was in Southeast Asia. There, the Vietnamese people were beginning to demand the same political rights enjoyed by people in Western nations.

OPPOSITION TO THE TREATY When Wilson returned to the United States, he faced strong opposition to the treaty. Some people, including Herbert Hoover, believed it was too harsh. Hoover noted, "The economic consequences alone will pull down all Europe and thus injure the United States."

POINT		COUNTERPOINT

"The League of Nations was the world's best hope for lasting peace."

President Wilson campaigned for the League of Nations. He explained that it was "necessary to meet the differing and unexpected contingencies" that could threaten world peace. Wilson believed that the League would create a forum where nations could talk through their disagreements. He also hoped it would provide collective security. He saw this as a way for nations to "respect and preserve as against external aggression the territorial integrity and existing political independence of all members of the League." Wilson believed the League could prevent devastating warfare.

Critics complained that membership in the League would limit American independence in international affairs. However, Wilson argued that League membership included "a moral, not a legal, obligation." Congress would be free to decide its own course of action. Wilson tried to assure Congress as well as the general public that the League was "not a straitjacket, but a vehicle of life." It was also "a definite guaranty . . . against the things that have just come near bringing the whole structure of civilization into ruin."

"The League of Nations posed a threat to U.S. self-determination."

Senator William Borah was one of the foremost critics of the Treaty of Versailles because he objected to U.S. membership in the League of Nations. Borah feared that membership in the League "would draw America away from her isolation and into the internal affairs and concerns of Europe" and involve the United States in foreign wars. "Once having surrendered and become a part of the European concerns," Borah wondered, "where, my friends, are you going to stop?"

Many opponents also feared that the League would nullify the Monroe Doctrine. They believed the League would limit "the right of our people to govern themselves free from all restraint, legal or moral, of foreign powers."

Wilson argued that the League of Nations would have no such power of restraint. However, Borah was not convinced. He responded to Wilson's argument by asking, "What will your League amount to if it does not contain powers that no one dreams of giving it?"

Critical Thinking

1. **Connect to History** Both supporters and opponents of the League hoped to preserve peace. How did each group propose to secure peace for the United States?

2. **Connect to Today** What are some contemporary arguments against United States participation in international organizations such as the United Nations or the World Court?

Others believed the treaty was a sell-out to imperialism. They thought it simply exchanged one set of colonial rulers for another.

Some ethnic groups in the United States objected to the treaty and tried to block its passage in the Senate. They objected to the new national boundaries established by the treaty. They argued that the new boundaries did not satisfy their particular demands for self-determination. For example, many Armenian Americans feared that the treaty left their homeland open to domination by the Soviet Union. Italian Americans were angry that the Italian city of Fiume was excluded from Italy's control. Irish Americans criticized the president for failing to consider Irish independence in the peace settlement. Syrian Americans, Greek Americans, and Lithuanian Americans also fought against ratification of the treaty.

The main domestic opposition, however, centered on the issue of the League of Nations. A few opponents believed that the League threatened the U.S. foreign policy of isolationism. Conservative senators, headed by **Henry Cabot Lodge**, were suspicious of the provision for joint economic and military action against aggression, even though it was voluntary. They wanted the constitutional right of Congress to declare war included in the treaty.

WILSON REFUSES TO COMPROMISE Wilson unwisely ignored the Republican majority in the Senate when he chose the members of the American delegation. If he had been more willing to accept a compromise on the League, it would have been more likely that the Senate would have approved the treaty. Wilson, however, was exhausted from his efforts at Versailles.

Despite ill health, Wilson set out in September 1919 on an 8,000-mile tour. He delivered 34 speeches in about 3 weeks, explaining why the United States should join the League of Nations. On October 2 Wilson suffered a stroke (a ruptured blood vessel to the brain). He lay partially paralyzed for more than two months, unable to even meet with his cabinet. His once-powerful voice was no more than a thick whisper.

The treaty came up for a vote in the Senate in November 1919. Senator Lodge introduced a number of amendments. The most important one

Major Provisions of the Treaty of Versailles

Military changes	The treaty limited the German army to 100,000 men, with no tanks or heavy artillery. It also limited the German navy to 15,000 men and banned Germany from having an air force.
Territory changes	The treaty required Germany to cede land to France, Denmark, Poland, Czechoslovakia, and Belgium. It also required Germany to surrender all colonies to the control of the League of Nations. Finally, Germany and Austria were prohibited from uniting.
War-guilt provisions	The treaty's war-guilt clause held Germany solely responsible for all losses and damages suffered by the Allies during the war. It required Germany to pay reparations of $33 billion.
League of Nations	The treaty initially did not permit Germany to join the League.

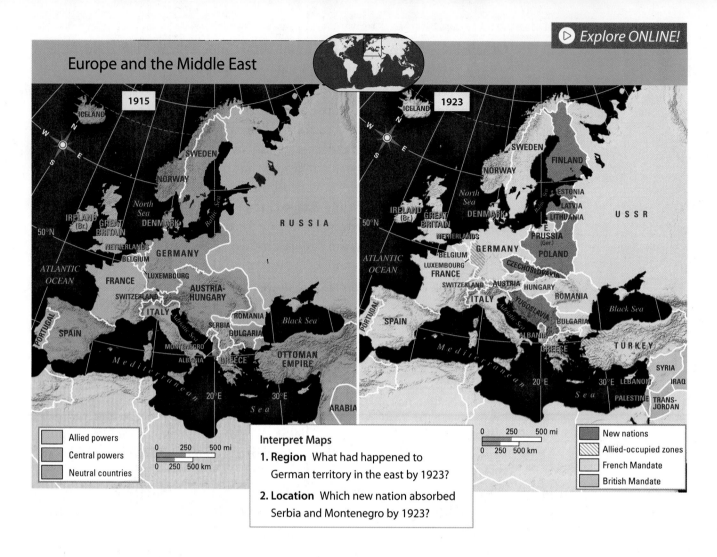

Europe and the Middle East

1915

1923

Allied powers
Central powers
Neutral countries

0 250 500 mi
0 250 500 km

0 250 500 mi
0 250 500 km

New nations
Allied-occupied zones
French Mandate
British Mandate

Interpret Maps

1. **Region** What had happened to German territory in the east by 1923?

2. **Location** Which new nation absorbed Serbia and Montenegro by 1923?

qualified the terms under which the United States would enter the League of Nations. It was feared that League membership would force the United States to make foreign policy in agreement with the League. The Senate rejected the amendments. It also failed to ratify the treaty.

Wilson refused to compromise. "I will not play for position," he proclaimed. "This is not a time for tactics. It is a time to stand square. I can stand defeat; I cannot stand retreat from conscientious duty." The treaty again came up for a vote in March 1920. The Senate again rejected the Lodge amendments. Again it failed to gather enough votes for ratification.

The United States finally signed a separate treaty with Germany in 1921, after Wilson was no longer president. The United States never joined the League of Nations. However, it had an unofficial observer at League meetings.

Reading Check
Make Inferences
Why were some people afraid of the treaty's influence over American foreign policy?

The Legacy of the War

When World War I ended, many Americans looked forward to a return of what Warren G. Harding called "normalcy." However, both the United States and the rest of the world had been utterly transformed by the war. World War I had devastated many European economies. The war had also revealed the military and industrial potential of the United States. The combination of these factors meant that the United States emerged from the war as a new world power. The war had strengthened the power of government in the United States. It had also accelerated social change, especially for African Americans and women. In addition, the propaganda campaign had provoked powerful fears and antagonisms that were left unchanneled when the war finally came to an end.

In Europe, the destruction and massive loss of life severely damaged social and political systems. In many countries, the war created political instability and violence that persisted for decades. During the war years, the first Communist state was established in Russia, while after the war, militant fascist organizations seized control in Italy, Spain, and Germany.

Americans began to call World War I "the war to end all wars," in the hope that humanity would never again fight such a war. Although the United States had returned mostly to a policy of isolationism, unresolved issues in Europe would eventually drag America into an even wider war. The Treaty of Versailles had settled nothing. The redrawn maps of Europe and European colonial possessions created a new set of problems. In addition, the reparations imposed on Germany had crippled its economy, and the war-guilt clause caused much anger and hostility there. In fact, some European nations longed to resume the fight, and the League of Nations did not have the power to stop them. The ominous shape of things to come emerged in the writings of an Austrian named Adolf Hitler, an angry veteran of World War I: "It cannot be that two million [Germans] should have fallen in vain. . . . No, we do not pardon, we demand—vengeance!" Two decades after the end of the Great War, Adolf Hitler's desire for vengeance would plunge the world into an even greater war, in which the United States would play a leading role

Vocabulary
fascist
characteristic of or relating to fascism, a system of totalitarian government

Reading Check
Analyze Effects
How did World War I transform the United States into a world power?

Lesson 4 Assessment

1. **Organize Information** Fill in a spider diagram with information about the provisions and weaknesses of the Treaty of Versailles and opposition to it.

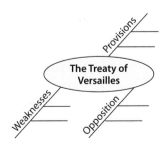

Do you think Congress should not have ratified the treaty?

2. **Key Terms and People** For each key term or person in the lesson, write a sentence explaining its significance.

3. **Predict** Predict how the Treaty of Versailles would affect international conflicts after World War I. Give reasons for your predictions.

   Think About:
   - what Germans thought of the war-guilt clause, reparations, and the loss of territory
   - the redrawn map of Europe
   - how the League of Nations affected international relations
   - the rise of authoritarian governments and ideologies in Europe following World War I

4. **Synthesize** What was Wilson's philosophy of foreign policy? How did he reflect it in the way that he dealt with Germany and the other Central powers?

5. **Summarize** Why did so many Americans oppose the Treaty of Versailles?

6. **Develop Historical Perspective**
   Why didn't the Treaty of Versailles lay the foundations for a lasting peace?

Module 7 Assessment

Key Terms and People

For each key term or person below, write a sentence explaining its connection to World War I.

1. nationalism
2. Zimmermann note
3. Selective Service Act
4. General John J. Pershing
5. trench warfare
6. armistice
7. Espionage and Sedition Acts
8. Great Migration
9. Fourteen Points
10. Treaty of Versailles

Main Ideas

Use your notes and the information in the module to answer the following questions.

World War I Begins

1. Where did Germany begin its war offensive, and what happened there?
2. Why did the war in Europe become a stalemate?
3. Describe some ways in which World War I threatened the lives of civilians on both sides of the Atlantic.
4. Why did the Allies reject President Wilson's "peace without victory" plan?
5. What were the main reasons for U.S. involvement in the war? How did events in Russia in 1917 lead the United States to enter the war?

The United States Joins the War

6. How did the United States mobilize a strong military during World War I?
7. What new weapons made fighting in World War I deadlier than fighting in previous wars?
8. How did American troops help the Allies break the stalemate with Germany?

The War at Home

9. Why did the U.S. government impose regulations on industrial and food production during the war? What was the impact of the regulation for the Allies?
10. How did World War I affect the economy of the United States?
11. What methods did the U.S. government use to finance and direct public support of the war?
12. What effect did the war have on the lives of recent immigrants in the United States?
13. What events during the war undermined civil liberties?

Wilson Fights for Peace

14. What were the goals of the Fourteen Points and the League of Nations? How did Wilson's goals for peace differ from those of the other Allies?
15. What were the major effects of the Treaty of Versailles?
16. How did Wilson's support for the League of Nations stand in the way of Senate support for the Treaty of Versailles?

Critical Thinking

1. **Analyze Causes** In a chart, provide causes for the listed effects of World War I.

Causes	Effects
	Russia's new government withdraws Russian army from the eastern front
	U.S. enters World War I
	German advance into France stopped
	Germany collapses
	U.S. economy becomes more productive

2. **Analyze Causes** Do you think that Germany's submarine warfare was an appropriate response to the British blockade?

3. **Make Inferences** How did the United States intend to "make the world safe for democracy" when most of the European countries on both sides of the war were monarchies?

4. **Evaluate** Was trench warfare effective as a military strategy in World War I? Explain.

5. **Analyze Issues** Do you think it was right that some people, such as Native Americans, willing to serve the nation in war were excluded from full citizenship? Explain why or why not.

6. **Evaluate** Why do you think General Pershing refused to put American troops into foreign units? Do you think his decision to train his troops in Europe rather than have them immediately join the Allies was wise? Explain.

7. **Predict** Could the Allies have won the war without the help of the United States? Explain why or why not.

8. **Draw Conclusions** Why do you think it was necessary for the government to set prices and production controls for food and fuel during the war?

9. **Form Opinions** Do you think that that government propaganda and positive stories in the media were needed to generate support for the war? Explain.

10. **Interpret Maps** Look at the maps of Europe before and after World War I in Lesson 4. Describe the changes in national boundaries after the Versailles peace settlement. How might the redrawn map of Europe lead to new conflict among European powers?

11. **Analyze Motives** Why did some special interest groups work to influence U.S. foreign policy and public opinion in World War I?

12. **Evaluate** Explain the significance of President Wilson's foreign policy decisions during and after World War I. Which principles do you think should guide American diplomacy: moral and legal ideals or national interest?

13. **Develop Historical Perspective** Between 1914 and 1920, Americans debated the role their country should have in world affairs. From the events of World War I, what might Americans have learned about intervention in the affairs of other nations?

Engage with History

Imagine you are a diplomat participating in the peace talks at the end of World War I. Decide whether you support or oppose the provisions of the Treaty of Versailles. As you determine your position, think of some of the reasons different nations had for supporting or opposing measures, such as creating the League of Nations, to prevent future wars. Then write a speech convincing the other participants to adopt your point of view. If you support the treaty, explain why. If you oppose it, offer an alternate version. Use persuasive language and clear examples.

Focus on Writing

Given its history of neutrality, was the United States justified in going to war against Germany and the other Central powers? Write an essay, arguing for or against American involvement in World War I. Use information from the module to support your argument.

Multimedia Activity

Use library and Internet resources to find out about other world conflicts in which the United States became involved. What were the United States' motives for getting involved in each of these wars? With a partner, write and record a short podcast in which you describe the different motives, and debate whether these motives would be valid today.

Dear home: LETTERS FROM WWI

When U.S. troops arrived in Europe in 1917 to fight in World War I, the war had been dragging on for nearly three years. The American soldiers suddenly found themselves in the midst of chaos. Each day, they faced the threats of machine-gun fire, poison gas, and aerial attacks. Still, the arrival of American reinforcements had sparked a new zeal among the Allies, who believed the new forces could finally turn the tide in their favor. The letters soldiers wrote to their families back home reveal the many emotions they felt on the battlefield: confusion about their surroundings, fear for their own safety, concern for friends and loved ones, and hope that the war would soon be over.

Explore World War I online through the eyes of the soldiers who fought in it. You can find a wealth of information, video clips, primary sources, activities, and more through your online textbook.

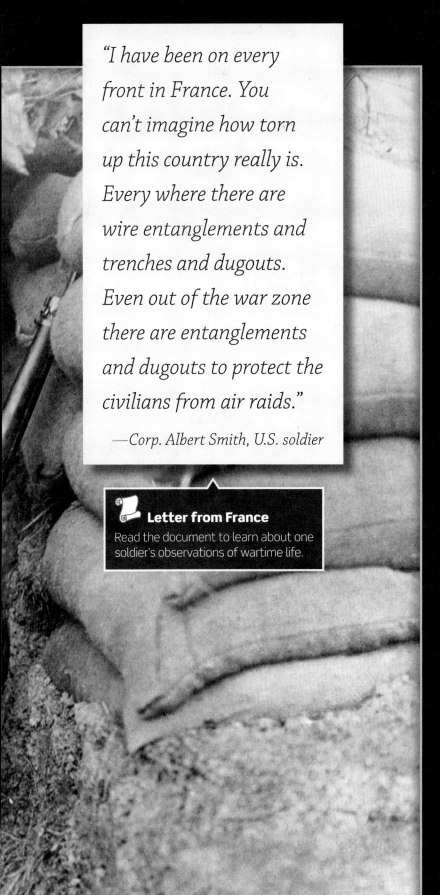

"*I have been on every front in France. You can't imagine how torn up this country really is. Every where there are wire entanglements and trenches and dugouts. Even out of the war zone there are entanglements and dugouts to protect the civilians from air raids.*"

—Corp. Albert Smith, U.S. soldier

Letter from France
Read the document to learn about one soldier's observations of wartime life.

Go online to view these and other **HISTORY**® resources.

Over There
Watch the video to learn about the experiences of American soldiers on the way to Europe and upon their arrival.

War on the Western Front
Watch the video to hear one soldier's vivid account of battle and its aftermath.

Surrender!
Watch the video to experience soldiers' reactions to the news that the war was finally over.

Module 8

The Roaring Twenties

★

Essential Question

Why did political, economic, and social tensions characterize the 1920s?

About the Photograph: Gertrude "Ma" Rainey was one of the earliest professional blues singers. She made over 100 recordings, including some with Louis Armstrong. Ma Rainey has been called "The Mother of the Blues."

▶ Explore ONLINE!

VIDEOS, including...
- Boom
- The Presidents: Warren G. Harding
- Henry Ford and the Model T
- The True Story of Sacco and Vanzetti
- America Goes Dry with Prohibition
- The Monkey Trial

 Document-Based Investigations

 Graphic Organizers

✓ Interactive Games

✓ Carousel: Women of the 1920s

✓ Image with Hotspots: Harlem in the 1920s

In this module you will learn about the challenges and changes that the nation faced after World War I. You will also discover the vibrant cultural life of the 1920s.

SS.912.A.1.4 Analyze how images, symbols, objects, cartoons, graphs, charts, maps, and artwork may be used to interpret the significance of time periods and events from the past. **SS.912.A.1.7** Describe various sociocultural aspects of American life including arts, artifacts, literature, education, and publications. **SS.912.A.3.7** Compare the experience of European immigrants in the east to that of Asian immigrants in the west. **SS.912.A.5.1** Discuss the economic outcomes of demobilization. **SS.912.A.5.2** Explain the causes of the public reaction associated with the Red Scare. **SS.912.A.5.3** Examine the impact of United States foreign economic policy during the 1920s. **SS.912.A.5.4** Evaluate how the economic boom during the Roaring Twenties changed consumers, businesses, manufacturing, and marketing practices. **SS.912.A.5.5** Describe efforts by the United States and other world powers to avoid future wars. **SS.912.A.5.6** Analyze the influence that Hollywood, the Harlem Renaissance, the Fundamentalist movement, and prohibition had in changing American society in the 1920s. **SS.912.A.5.7** Examine the freedom movements that advocated civil rights for African Americans, Latinos, Asians, and women. **SS.912.A.5.8** Compare the views of Booker T. Washington, W.E.B. DuBois, and Marcus Garvey relating to the African American experience. **SS.912.A.5.9** Explain why support for the Ku Klux Klan varied in the 1920s with respect to issues such as anti-immigration, anti-African American, anti-Catholic, anti-Jewish, anti-women, and anti-union ideas. **SS.912.A.5.10** Analyze support for and resistance to civil rights for women, African Americans, Native Americans, and other minorities. **SS.912.G.4.2** Use geographic terms and tools to analyze the push/pull factors contributing to human migration within and among places. **SS.912.G.4.3** Use geographic terms and tools to analyze the effects of migration both on the place of origin and destination, including border areas. **SS.912.H.1.1** Relate works in the arts of varying styles and genre according to the periods in which they were created. **SS.912.H.1.3** Relate works in the arts to various cultures. **SS.912.H.1.5** Examine artistic response to social issues and new ideas in various cultures.

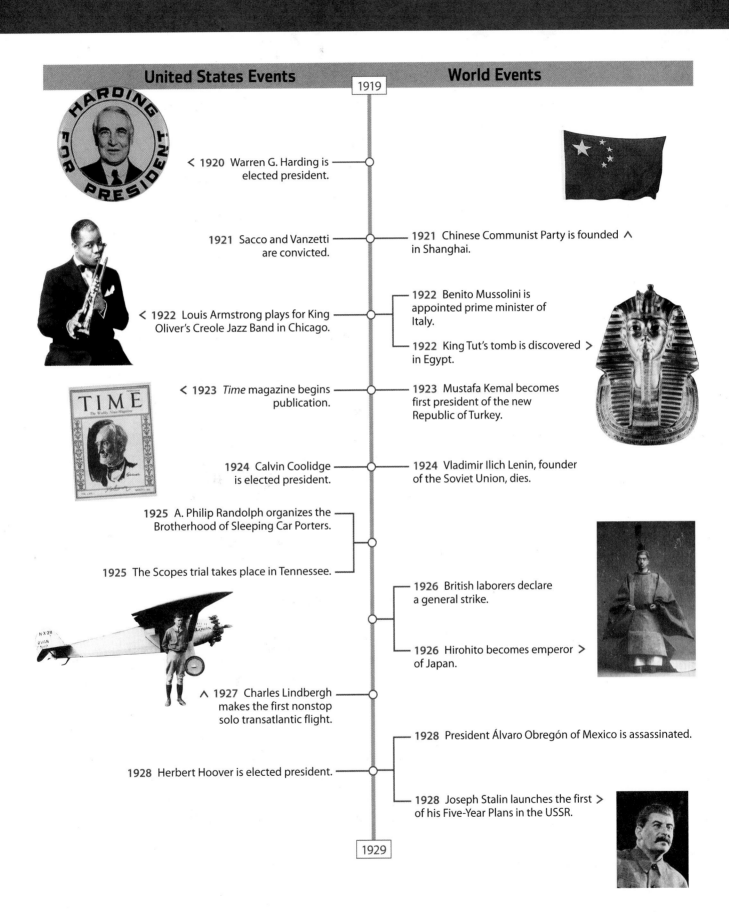

| United States Events | 1919 | World Events |

< 1920 Warren G. Harding is elected president.

1921 Sacco and Vanzetti are convicted.

1921 Chinese Communist Party is founded ∧ in Shanghai.

< 1922 Louis Armstrong plays for King Oliver's Creole Jazz Band in Chicago.

1922 Benito Mussolini is appointed prime minister of Italy.

1922 King Tut's tomb is discovered > in Egypt.

< 1923 *Time* magazine begins publication.

1923 Mustafa Kemal becomes first president of the new Republic of Turkey.

1924 Calvin Coolidge is elected president.

1924 Vladimir Ilich Lenin, founder of the Soviet Union, dies.

1925 A. Philip Randolph organizes the Brotherhood of Sleeping Car Porters.

1925 The Scopes trial takes place in Tennessee.

1926 British laborers declare a general strike.

1926 Hirohito becomes emperor > of Japan.

∧ 1927 Charles Lindbergh makes the first nonstop solo transatlantic flight.

1928 President Álvaro Obregón of Mexico is assassinated.

1928 Herbert Hoover is elected president.

1928 Joseph Stalin launches the first > of his Five-Year Plans in the USSR.

1929

The Business of America

The Big Idea

Although the U.S. government was rocked by scandal during the early 1920s, a business boom fueled a rise in America's standard of living.

Why It Matters Now

The government must guard against scandal and corruption to merit public trust. In addition, business, technological, and social developments of the 1920s launched the era of modern consumerism.

Key Terms and People

Warren G. Harding

Charles Evans Hughes

Fordney-McCumber Tariff

Ohio gang

Teapot Dome scandal

Albert B. Fall

Calvin Coolidge

urban sprawl

consumerism

installment plan

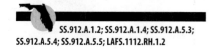

SS.912.A.1.2; SS.912.A.1.4; SS.912.A.5.3;
SS.912.A.5.4; SS.912.A.5.5; LAFS.1112.RH.1.2

One American's Story

Charles E. Sorensen emigrated from Denmark to the United States at the age of four. After working at several other jobs, he met Henry Ford at a Detroit foundry. Sorensen went to work for Ford as a patternmaker, turning Henry Ford's ideas into reality. Over the years, Sorensen would play an instrumental role in developing Ford's dream of building automobiles that almost anyone could afford to buy and maintain. Sorensen and Ford succeeded to a remarkable degree with the Model T, a carefully crafted product.

A Ford Model T

"Many of the world's greatest mechanical discoveries were accidents in the course of other experimentation. Not so Model T, which ushered in the motor transport age and set off a chain reaction of machine production now known as automation. All our experimentation at Ford in the early days was toward a fixed and, then, wildly fantastic goal."
—Charles E. Sorensen, from *My Forty Years with Ford*

The Model T and its successor, the Model A, transformed the United States. The automobile became the backbone of the American economy in the 1920s and remained such until the 1970s. It profoundly altered the country's landscape and society, but it was only one of several factors in the business boom of the 1920s.

Struggles for Peace

In 1920 the American people were weary with war and the zeal of the Progressive era. The postwar economy had faltered. Strikes and riots disrupted the cities. Voters wanted peace and quiet. The presidential election reflected those attitudes. Senator **Warren G. Harding**, the handsome Ohio Republican presidential candidate, promised "normalcy" if he were elected. Harding won a landslide victory. His tenure began with sincere peacekeeping efforts.

LEGISLATING PEACE After World War I, problems surfaced relating to arms control, war debts, and the reconstruction of war-torn countries. In 1921 President Harding invited several major powers to the Washington Naval Conference, also known as the Washington Disarmament Conference. Russia was left out because of its Communist government. At the conference, Secretary of State **Charles Evans Hughes** urged that no more warships be built for ten years. He suggested that the five major naval powers—the United States, Great Britain, Japan, France, and Italy—scrap many of their battleships, cruisers, and aircraft carriers.

Conference delegates cheered, wept, and threw their hats into the air. For the first time in history, powerful nations agreed to disarm. Later, in 1928, 15 countries signed the Kellogg-Briand Pact, which renounced war as a national policy. However, the pact was futile, as it provided no means of enforcement.

HIGH TARIFFS AND REPARATIONS New conflicts arose when it came time for Britain and France to pay back the $10 billion they had borrowed from America. They could do this in two ways: by selling goods to the United States or by collecting reparations from Germany. However, in 1922 America adopted the **Fordney-McCumber Tariff**, which raised taxes on some U.S. imports to 60 percent—the highest level ever. The tax protected U.S. businesses—especially in the chemical and metals industries—from foreign competition, but made it impossible for Britain and France to sell enough goods in the United States to repay debts.

The two countries looked to Germany, which was experiencing terrible inflation. When Germany defaulted on (failed to make) payment, French troops marched in. To avoid another war, American banker Charles G. Dawes was sent to negotiate loans. Through what came to be known as the Dawes Plan, American investors loaned Germany $2.5 billion to pay back Britain and France with annual payments on a fixed scale. Those countries then paid the United States. Thus, the United States actually arranged to be repaid with its own money.

The solution caused resentment all around. Britain and France considered the United States a miser for not paying a fair share of the costs of World War I. Further, the U.S. had benefited from the defeat of Germany, while Europeans had paid for the victory with millions of lives. At the same time, the United States considered Britain and France financially irresponsible.

Vocabulary
reparations payments demanded from a defeated enemy

Reading Check
Summarize How did the United States try to solve the political and financial issues that faced the country as the 1920s began?

Harding's Domestic Policies and Problems

On domestic issues, Harding favored a limited role for government in business affairs and in social reform.

Warren G. Harding, shown here in 1923, looked presidential, but he is considered one of the least successful presidents.

ECONOMIC POLICIES Harding believed the answer to the nation's postwar economic struggles could be found in his campaign slogan, "Less government in business and more business in government." To help achieve his pro-business goal, Harding sought to cut the federal budget and to reduce taxes on the wealthiest Americans. Harding and his advisers believed that it was the wealthy who started and expanded businesses. By taxing them less, the thinking went, business would grow and pull the nation out of hard times. These policies did contribute to a period of prosperity—but only for a time.

Some of Harding's policies were more progressive. He set up the Bureau of the Budget to help run the government more efficiently and urged U.S. Steel to abandon the 12-hour workday.

HARDING'S CABINET Harding appointed Charles Evans Hughes as secretary of state. Hughes later went on to become Chief Justice of the Supreme Court. The president made Herbert Hoover the secretary of commerce. Hoover had done a masterful job of handling food distribution and refugee problems during World War I. Andrew Mellon, one of the country's wealthiest men, became secretary of the treasury and set about drastically cutting taxes and reducing the national debt. However, the cabinet also included the so-called **Ohio gang**, the president's poker-playing cronies, who would soon cause a great deal of embarrassment.

SCANDAL PLAGUES HARDING The president's main problem was that he didn't understand many of the issues. He admitted as much to a secretary.

"John, I can't make a . . . thing out of this tax problem. I listen to one side and they seem right, and then . . . I talk to the other side and they seem just as right. . . . I know somewhere there is an economist who knows the truth, but I don't know where to find him and haven't the sense to know him and trust him when I find him. . . . What a job!"

—Warren G. Harding, quoted in *Only Yesterday*

Harding's discomfort with policy details contributed to his inability to see the criminal behavior going on right under his nose.

Harding's administration began to unravel as his corrupt friends engaged in graft. That is, they used their offices improperly to become wealthy. One example was Charles R. Forbes, the head of the Veterans Bureau. He was caught illegally selling government and hospital supplies to private companies. Colonel Thomas W. Miller, the head of the Office of Alien Property, was another corrupt official. He was caught taking a bribe.

The elephant, shaped like a teapot here, is the symbol of the Republican Party (also referred to as the Grand Old Party). The cartoonist implies that Republicans were responsible for the Teapot Dome scandal.

Reading Check
Make Inferences
How did the corruption of the Harding administration affect the country economically?

THE TEAPOT DOME SCANDAL The most spectacular example of corruption was the **Teapot Dome scandal**. The government had set aside oil-rich public lands at Teapot Dome, Wyoming, and Elk Hills, California, for use by the U.S. Navy. Secretary of the Interior **Albert B. Fall**, a close friend of various oil executives, managed to get the oil reserves transferred from the navy to the Interior Department. Then, Fall secretly leased the land to two private oil companies, including Henry Sinclair's Mammoth Oil Company at Teapot Dome. Although Fall claimed that these contracts were in the government's interest, he suddenly received more than $400,000 in "loans, bonds, and cash." He was later found guilty of bribery and became the first American to be convicted of a felony while holding a cabinet post.

In the summer of 1923, Harding declared, "I have no trouble with my enemies. . . . But my . . . friends, they're the ones that keep me walking the floor nights!" Shortly thereafter, on August 2, 1923, he died suddenly, probably from a heart attack or stroke.

Americans sincerely mourned their good-natured president. The crimes of the Harding administration were coming to light just as Vice-President Calvin Coolidge assumed the presidency. Coolidge, a respected man of integrity, helped to restore people's faith in their government and in the Republican Party. The next year, Coolidge was elected president.

American Industries Flourish

The new president, **Calvin Coolidge**, fit into the pro-business spirit of the 1920s very well. It was he who said, "the chief business of the American people is business. . . . The man who builds a factory builds a temple—the man who works there worships there." Both Coolidge and his Republican successor, Herbert Hoover, favored government policies that would keep taxes down and business profits up, and give businesses more available credit in order to expand. Their goal was to minimize government involvement in business and to allow private enterprise to flourish. This approach echoed the laissez faire economic policy of 19th-century industrialization—the idea that business should not be regulated.

For most of the 1920s, this tactic seemed to work. Coolidge's administration continued to place high tariffs on foreign imports, which helped American manufacturers. Reducing income taxes meant that people had more money in their pockets. Wages were rising, and so was productivity.

THE AUTO INDUSTRY AND INCREASED PRODUCTIVITY The auto industry was one of the biggest business successes of the 1920s. Henry Ford and his Model T led the way. To create his Model Ts, Ford used several methods to make production as efficient and cost-effective as possible. He used assembly-line manufacturing, increased pay for workers, and avoided changes to the car's design. Other industries learned from Ford. Manufacturers began using assembly-line techniques to make many types of products in large quantities and at lower costs. During the 1920s, productivity—a measure of output per unit such as labor—rose by about 45 percent. American workers were producing more in less time, which helped the growth of American manufacturers.

THE IMPACT OF THE AUTOMOBILE The automobile literally changed the American landscape. Its most visible effect was the construction of paved roads suitable for driving in all types of weather. One such road was the legendary Route 66, which provided a route for people trekking west from Chicago to California. Many people, however, settled in towns along the route.

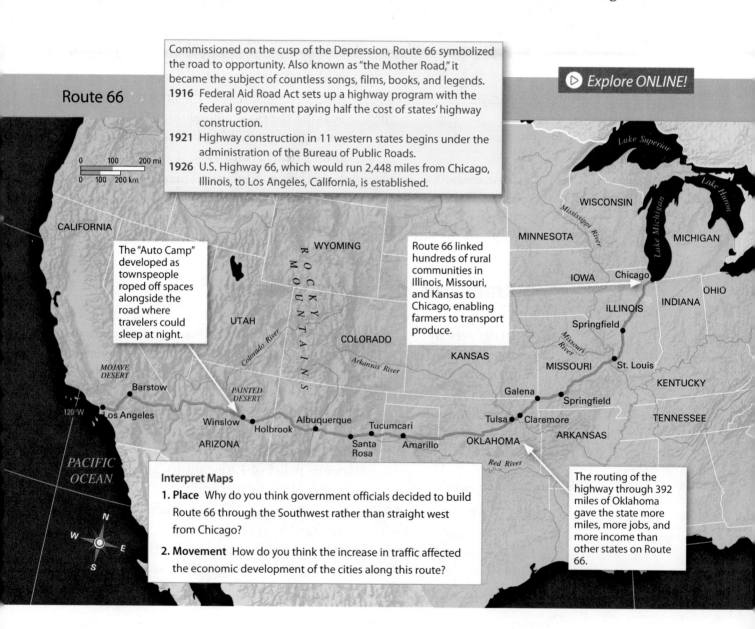

Route 66

Commissioned on the cusp of the Depression, Route 66 symbolized the road to opportunity. Also known as "the Mother Road," it became the subject of countless songs, films, books, and legends.

1916 Federal Aid Road Act sets up a highway program with the federal government paying half the cost of states' highway construction.

1921 Highway construction in 11 western states begins under the administration of the Bureau of Public Roads.

1926 U.S. Highway 66, which would run 2,448 miles from Chicago, Illinois, to Los Angeles, California, is established.

▶ Explore ONLINE!

The "Auto Camp" developed as townspeople roped off spaces alongside the road where travelers could sleep at night.

Route 66 linked hundreds of rural communities in Illinois, Missouri, and Kansas to Chicago, enabling farmers to transport produce.

The routing of the highway through 392 miles of Oklahoma gave the state more miles, more jobs, and more income than other states on Route 66.

Interpret Maps

1. **Place** Why do you think government officials decided to build Route 66 through the Southwest rather than straight west from Chicago?

2. **Movement** How do you think the increase in traffic affected the economic development of the cities along this route?

In addition to the changing landscape, architectural styles also changed, as new houses typically came equipped with a garage or carport and a driveway—and a smaller lawn as a result. The automobile also launched the rapid construction of gasoline stations, repair shops, public garages, motels, tourist camps, and shopping centers. The first automatic traffic signals began blinking in Detroit in the early 1920s. The Holland Tunnel, the first underwater tunnel designed specifically for motor vehicles, opened in 1927 to connect New York City and Jersey City, New Jersey.

The automobile liberated the isolated rural family, who could now travel to the city for shopping and entertainment. It also gave families the opportunity to vacation in new and faraway places. It allowed both women and young people to become more independent through increased mobility. It allowed workers to live miles from their jobs, resulting in **urban sprawl** as cities spread in all directions. The automobile industry also provided an economic base for such cities as Akron, Ohio, where several tire companies were headquartered, and Michigan cities Detroit, Dearborn, Flint, and Pontiac, where the cars were manufactured. The industry drew people to oil-producing states such as California and Texas. The automobile even became a status symbol—both for individual families and to the rest of the world. In their work *Middletown,* the social scientists Robert and Helen Lynd noted one woman's comment: "I'll go without food before I'll see us give up the car."

The auto industry symbolized the success of the free enterprise system and the Coolidge era. Nowhere else in the world could people with little money own their own automobile. By the late 1920s around 80 percent of all registered motor vehicles in the world were in the United States—about one automobile for every five people. The humorist Will Rogers remarked to Henry Ford, "It will take a hundred years to tell whether you helped us or hurt us, but you certainly didn't leave us where you found us."

Vocabulary
status symbol a possession believed to enhance the owner's social standing

---

BIOGRAPHY

Calvin Coolidge (1872–1933)

Stepping into office in 1923, the tightlipped Vermonter was respected for his solemnity and wisdom. Coolidge supported American business and favored what he called "a constructive economy."

Known for his strength of character, Coolidge forced the resignation of Attorney General Harry Daugherty and other high officials who had created scandal in office.

Shortly after Coolidge was elected, his son died of blood poisoning. Coolidge later wrote, "The power and the glory of the presidency went with him." When he decided not to seek reelection in 1928, Coolidge stumped the nation. Keeping in character, he said, "Goodbye, I have had a very enjoyable time in Washington."

Reading Check
Analyze Effects
How did the widespread use of new transportation options affect the country?

THE YOUNG AIRPLANE INDUSTRY Automobiles weren't the only form of transportation taking off. The airplane industry began as a mail-carrying service for the U.S. Post Office. Although the first flight in 1918 was a disaster, a number of successful flights soon established the airplane as a peacetime means of transportation. With the development of weather forecasting, planes began carrying radios and navigational instruments. Henry Ford made a trimotor airplane in 1926. Transatlantic flights by Charles Lindbergh and Amelia Earhart helped to promote cargo and commercial airlines. In 1927 the Lockheed Company produced a single-engine plane, the Vega. It was one of the most popular transport airplanes of the late 1920s. Founded in 1927, Pan American Airways inaugurated the first transatlantic passenger flights.

America's Standard of Living Soars

The 1920s were prosperous ones for the United States. It seemed like the American Dream was coming true. Americans owned around 40 percent of the world's wealth, and that wealth changed the way most Americans lived. The average annual income increased by more than 35 percent during the period—from $522 to $705. People found it easy to spend all that extra income and then some. **Consumerism**, or the acquisition of goods in ever-greater amounts, began to play a significant role in the American economy and culture.

ELECTRICAL CONVENIENCES Gasoline powered much of the economic boom of the 1920s, but the use of electricity also transformed the nation. American factories used electricity to run their machines. Also, the development of an alternating electrical current made it possible to distribute electric power efficiently over longer distances. Now electricity was no longer restricted to central cities but could be transmitted to suburbs. The number of electrified households grew, although most farms still lacked power.

The electrification of new areas of the country made it possible for people to use the latest home conveniences. By the end of the 1920s, more and more homes had electric irons, while well-to-do families used electric refrigerators, cooking ranges, vacuum

American consumers in the 1920s could purchase the latest household electrical appliances, such as a refrigerator, for as little as a dollar down and a dollar a week.

Goods and Prices, 1900 and 1928

1900		1928	
wringer and washboard	$ 5	washing machine	$150
brushes and brooms	$ 5	vacuum cleaner	$ 50
sewing machine (mechanical)	$25	sewing machine (electric)	$ 60

cleaners, and toasters. The new refrigerators' freezers might hold foods quick-frozen by a process developed by Clarence Birdseye. Homemakers could save time by shopping at the new self-service grocery stores that Clarence Saunders created.

The new appliances and food preparation options made the lives of housewives easier, freed them for other community and leisure activities, and coincided with a growing trend of women working outside the home.

THE DAWN OF MODERN ADVERTISING With new goods flooding the market, advertising agencies no longer just informed the public about products and prices. Now they hired psychologists to study how to appeal to people's desire for youthfulness, beauty, health, and wealth. Results were impressive. The slogan "Say it with flowers" doubled florists' business between 1912 and 1924. "Reach for a Lucky instead of a sweet" lured weight-conscious Americans to cigarettes and away from candy. Brand names became familiar from coast to coast, and luxury items now seemed like necessities.

One of those "necessities" was mouthwash. Listerine advertisements aimed to convince readers that without mouthwash a person ran the risk of having halitosis—bad breath—and that the results could be a disaster.

"She was a beautiful girl and talented too. She had the advantages of education and better clothes than most girls of her set. She possessed that culture and poise that travel brings. Yet in the one pursuit that stands foremost in the mind of every girl and woman—marriage—she was a failure."

—Listerine advertisement

Reading Check
Find Main Ideas
What were some popular laborsaving devices and concepts that changed lifestyles in the 1920s?

Businesspeople applied the power of advertising to other areas of American life. Across the land, they met for lunch with fellow members of such service organizations as Rotary, Kiwanis, and the Lions. As one observer noted, they sang songs, raised money for charities, and boosted the image of the businessman "as a builder, a doer of great things, yes, and a dreamer whose imagination was ever seeking out new ways of serving humanity." Many Americans idolized business during these prosperous times.

ANOTHER PERSPECTIVE

The Needy

While income rose for many Americans in the 1920s, it did not rise for everyone. Industries such as textile and steel manufacturing made very little profit. Mining and farming actually suffered losses. Farmers were deeply in debt because they had borrowed money to buy land and machinery so that they could produce more crops during World War I. When European agriculture bounced back after the war, the demand for U.S. crops fell, as did prices. Before long there were U.S. farm surpluses.

Many American farmers could not make their loan and mortgage payments. They lost their purchasing power, their equipment, and their farms. As one South Dakota state senator remarked, "There's a saying: 'Depressions are farm led and farm fed.'"

A Superficial Prosperity

During the 1920s most Americans believed prosperity would go on forever—the average factory worker was producing 50 percent more at the end of the decade than at its start. Hadn't national income grown from $64 billion in 1921 to $87 billion in 1929? Weren't most major corporations making fortunes? Wasn't the stock market reaching new heights?

PRODUCING GREAT QUANTITIES OF GOODS As the adoption of mass production techniques increased productivity, businesses expanded. There were numerous mergers of companies that manufactured automobiles, steel, and electrical equipment, as well as mergers of companies that provided public utilities. Chain stores sprouted, selling groceries, drugs, shoes, and clothes. Five-and-dime stores like Woolworth's also spread rapidly. Mail-order catalogs allowed Americans who lived far from big cities to buy the attractive new products. Congress passed a law that allowed national banks to open branch offices within cities where their main office was located.

As the number of businesses grew, however, so did the income gap between workers and managers. There were a number of other clouds in the blue sky of prosperity. The iron and railroad industries, among others, weren't very prosperous, and farms nationwide suffered losses—with new machinery, they were producing more food than was needed and this drove down food prices.

BUYING GOODS ON CREDIT In addition to advertising, industry provided another solution to the problem of luring consumers to purchase the mountain of goods produced each year: easy credit, or "a dollar down and a dollar forever." The **installment plan**, as it was called, enabled people to buy goods

Document-Based Investigation Historical Source

Coolidge and Big Business

This cartoon depicts Calvin Coolidge playing a saxophone labeled "Praise" while a woman representing "Big Business" dances and sings "Yes, Sir, He's My Baby."

Analyze Historical Sources

1. The dancing woman is a 1920s "flapper"— independent, confident, and assertive. In what ways was big business in the 1920s comparable to the flappers?

2. What do you think the cartoonist suggests about Coolidge's relationship with big business?

over an extended period, without having to put down much money at the time of purchase. Banks provided the money at low interest rates. Advertisers pushed the "installment plan" idea with such slogans as "You furnish the girl, we'll furnish the home" and "Enjoy while you pay."

Some economists and business owners worried that installment buying might be getting out of hand. They feared that the practice was really a sign of fundamental weaknesses behind a superficial economic prosperity. Still, most Americans focused their attention on the present. What could possibly go wrong with the nation's economy in the future? What little concern there was for the years ahead often took the form of speculation, or investing in risky ventures in the hope that prices would rise and big profits would result. Speculation would eventually spell financial disaster for many investors.

The decade of the 1920s had brought about many technological and economic changes. And yet the Coolidge era was built on paradox—the president stood for economy and a frugal way of life, but he was favored by a public who had thrown all care to the wind. Life definitely seemed easier and more enjoyable for hundreds of thousands of Americans. From the look of things, there was little warning of what was to come.

Reading Check
Make Inferences
How do you think the changes in spending will affect the economy?

Lesson 1 Assessment

1. **Organize Information** Create a web diagram and fill it in with events that illustrate the central idea.

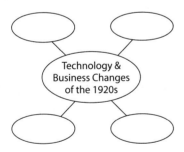

Technology & Business Changes of the 1920s

2. **Key Terms and People** For each key term or person in the lesson, write a sentence explaining its significance.

3. **Form Opinions** Do you agree with President Coolidge's statement: "The man who builds a factory builds a temple—the man who works there worships there"? Explain your answer.

   Think About:
   • the goals of business and of religion
   • the American idolization of business
   • the difference between workers and management

4. **Evaluate** How successful was Harding in fulfilling his campaign pledge of returning the country to "normalcy"? Support your opinion with specific examples.

5. **Analyze Effects** How do you think the postwar feelings in America influenced the election of 1920?

★ Postwar Issues

One American's Story

During the 1920s and 1930s, Irving Fajans, a department store sales clerk in New York City, tried to persuade his fellow workers to join the Department Store Employees Union. He described some of the techniques union organizers used.

The Big Idea

A desire for normality after the war and a fear of communism and "foreigners" led to postwar isolationism.

Why It Matters Now

Americans today continue to debate political isolationism and immigration policy.

Key Terms and People

xenophobia

nativism

isolationism

communism

anarchists

Sacco and Vanzetti

quota system

John L. Lewis

Irving Fajans organized department store workers in their efforts to gain better pay and working conditions during the 1920s.

"If you were caught distributing . . . union literature around the job you were instantly fired. We thought up ways of passing leaflets without the boss being able to pin anybody down. . . . We . . . swiped the key to the toilet paper dispensers in the washroom, took out the paper and substituted printed slips of just the right size! We got a lot of new members that way—It appealed to their sense of humor."

—Irving Fajans, quoted in *The Jewish Americans*

During the war, workers' rights had been suppressed. Then in 1919, workers began to cry out for fair pay and better working conditions. Tensions arose between labor and management, and a rash of labor strikes broke out across the country. The public, however, was not supportive of striking workers. Many citizens longed to get back to normal, peaceful living—they felt resentful of anyone who caused unrest.

SS.912.A.1.2; SS.912.A.1.4; SS.912.A.3.7; SS.912.A.5.1; SS.912.A.5.2; SS.912.A.5.9; SS.912.G.4.2; SS.912.G.4.3; LAFS.1112.RH.2.4; LAFS.1112.RH.4.10; MAFS.K12.MP.1.1; MAFS.K12.MP.5.1

Postwar Trends

World War I had left much of the American public exhausted. The debate over the League of Nations had deeply divided America. Further, the Progressive Era had caused numerous wrenching changes in American life. The economy, too, was in a difficult state of adjustment. Demobilized soldiers, those returning from the war, faced unemployment or took their old jobs away from women and minorities. Also, the cost of living had doubled. Farmers and factory workers suffered as wartime orders diminished.

POSTWAR FEARS Many Americans responded to the stressful conditions by becoming fearful of outsiders. Such unreasoned fear of things or people seen as foreign or strange is called **xenophobia**. A wave of **nativism**, or prejudice against foreign-born people, swept the nation. World War I had caused a wave of anti-German sentiment, which continued after the war's end. For example, some schools stopped teaching German language classes and some Americans of German heritage changed their names to be more English-sounding. Anti-Semitism, or the hatred of Jews, also increased during the 1920s, as immigration from Jewish communities in Eastern Europe surged. Also prevalent was a belief in **isolationism**, a policy of pulling away from involvement in world affairs. Isolationism was in contrast to internationalism, the engagement in global concerns that had begun to develop in the previous century.

A GLOBAL ECONOMY At the same time that isolationism dominated public opinion and government policy, however, the U.S. economy was becoming more international. American prosperity allowed loans to Europe, which helped pull those countries out of a post-war slump. U.S. factories exported manufactured goods. More efficient farming techniques increased agricultural production so much that during the early 1920s, American products were marketed to countries around the world. After European agriculture recovered, however, U.S. farmers suffered from overproduction and increased competition.

Reading Check
Summarize What challenges faced the United States after World War I ended?

Fear of Communism

One perceived threat to American life was the spread of **communism**, an economic and political system based on a single-party government ruled by a dictatorship. In order to equalize wealth and power, Communists would put an end to private property, substituting government ownership of factories, railroads, and other businesses.

THE RED SCARE The panic in the United States began in 1919, after revolutionaries in Russia overthrew the czarist regime. Vladimir I. Lenin and his followers, or Bolsheviks ("the majority"), established a new Communist state. Waving their symbolic red flag, Communists, or "Reds," cried out for a worldwide revolution that would abolish capitalism everywhere.

A Communist Party formed in the United States. Some 70,000 radicals joined, including some from the Industrial Workers of the World (IWW). When several dozen bombs were mailed to government and business leaders, the public grew fearful that the Communists were taking over. A "Red Scare" gripped the country. U.S. Attorney General A. Mitchell Palmer took the lead in trying to eradicate what many Americans saw as a real threat.

THE PALMER RAIDS In August 1919 Palmer appointed J. Edgar Hoover as his special assistant. Palmer, Hoover, and their agents hunted down suspected Communists and Socialists; officials did not distinguish between the two groups. Also targeted were **anarchists**—people who opposed any form of government. The government agents trampled people's civil rights, invading private homes and offices and jailing suspects without allowing them legal counsel. Hundreds of foreign-born radicals were deported without trials.

But Palmer's raids failed to turn up evidence of a revolutionary conspiracy—or even explosives. Many thought Palmer was just looking for a campaign issue to gain support for his presidential aspirations. Soon, the public decided that Palmer didn't know what he was talking about.

SACCO AND VANZETTI Although short-lived, the Red Scare fed people's suspicions of foreigners and immigrants. This nativist attitude led to ruined reputations and wrecked lives. The two most famous victims of this attitude were shoemaker Nicola Sacco and fish seller Bartolomeo Vanzetti. Both were Italian immigrants and anarchists; both had evaded the draft during World War I.

In May 1920 **Sacco and Vanzetti** were arrested and charged with the robbery and murder of a factory paymaster and his guard in South Braintree, Massachusetts. Witnesses had said the criminals appeared to be Italians. The accused asserted their innocence and provided alibis. In addition, the evidence against them was circumstantial, and the presiding judge made prejudicial remarks. Nevertheless, the jury found them guilty and sentenced them to death.

Background
On August 23, 1977, exactly 50 years after the executions, Massachusetts governor Michael Dukakis declared that Sacco and Vanzetti had not been given a fair trial.

Document-Based Investigation Historical Source

Palmer and the Red Scare
As fear of Communists spread, Palmer expressed the panic that many Americans felt.

> *"The blaze of revolution was sweeping over every American institution of law and order . . . eating its way into the homes of the American workman, its sharp tongues of revolutionary heat . . . licking the altars of the churches, leaping into the belfry of the school bell, crawling into the sacred corners of American homes, . . . burning up the foundations of society."*
>
> —A. Mitchell Palmer, from "The Case Against the Reds"

Analyze Historical Sources
1. What are some words and phrases that Palmer used to stir emotions?

2. Why do you think that Palmer doesn't provide any evidence of his claims?

Reading Check
Analyze Motives
What fears drove the Red Scare, the Palmer raids, and the Sacco and Vanzetti arrest?

Protests rang out in the United States, Europe, and Latin America. Many people thought Sacco and Vanzetti were mistreated because of their radical beliefs; others asserted it was because they were immigrants. The poet Edna St. Vincent Millay donated proceeds from her poem "Justice Denied in Massachusetts" to their defense. She personally appealed to Governor Alvan Fuller of Massachusetts for their lives. However, after reviewing the case and interviewing Vanzetti, the governor decided to let the executions go forward. The two men died in the electric chair on August 23, 1927.

In 1961 new ballistics tests showed that the pistol found on Sacco was in fact the one used to murder the guard. However, there was no proof that Sacco had actually pulled the trigger.

Immigration and Citizenship Issues

During the wave of nativist sentiment, "Keep America for Americans" became the prevailing attitude. Anti-immigrant attitudes had been growing in the United States ever since the 1880s, when new immigrants began arriving from southern and eastern Europe. Many of these immigrants were willing to work for low wages in industries such as coal mining, steel production, and textiles. But after World War I, the need for unskilled labor in the United States decreased. Nativists believed that because the United States now had fewer unskilled jobs available, fewer immigrants should be let into the country. Nativist feelings were fueled by the fact that some of the people involved in postwar labor disputes were immigrant anarchists and Socialists, who many Americans believed were actually Communists. Racist ideas like those expressed by Madison Grant, an anthropologist at the American Museum of Natural History in New York City, fed nativist attitudes.

> "The result of unlimited immigration is showing plainly in the rapid decline in the birth rate of native Americans . . . [who] will not bring children into the world to compete in the labor market with the Slovak, the Italian, the Syrian and the Jew. The native American is too proud to mix socially with them."
> —Madison Grant, quoted in *United States History: Ideas in Conflict*

Vocabulary
bigot a person who is intolerant of any creed, race, religion, or political belief that differs from his own

THE KLAN RISES AGAIN As a result of the Red Scare and anti-immigrant feelings, different groups of bigots used anti-communism as an excuse to harass any group unlike themselves. One such group was the Ku Klux Klan (KKK). The KKK was devoted to "100 percent Americanism." By 1924 KKK membership reached 4.5 million "white male persons, native-born gentile citizens."

The Klan also believed in keeping blacks "in their place." The Great Migration, the movement of African Americans to northern cities, had heightened racial tensions there. The KKK took advantage of that tension

In August 1925 nearly 60,000 Ku Klux Klan members marched along Pennsylvania Avenue in Washington, DC.

to increase its repression and violence against black Americans. Other Klan activities included destroying saloons, opposing unions, and driving Roman Catholics, Jews, and foreign-born people out of the country.

Support for Klan activities varied according to what members perceived as the biggest threats to their way of life. For example, in Birmingham, Alabama, an industrial city, Klan members used violence to keep African Americans from getting good jobs in the local steel mills and associated factories. Birmingham Klan leaders also suppressed unions. Another example of targeted Klan activities comes from the 1928 presidential election. New Yorker Al Smith, a Catholic, was the Democratic nominee. The Klan encouraged anti-Catholic prejudice, helping the Republicans win.

KKK members were paid to recruit new members into their world of secret rituals and racial violence. Though the Klan dominated state politics in many states, by the end of the decade its criminal activity led to a decrease in power.

THE QUOTA SYSTEM From 1919 to 1921 the number of immigrants had grown almost 600 percent—from 141,000 to 805,000 people. Congress, in response to nativist pressure, decided to limit immigration from certain countries, namely those in southern and eastern Europe. Although some Americans wanted to end immigration from those countries, a compromise was reached.

The Emergency Quota Act of 1921 set up a **quota system**. This system established the maximum number of people who could enter the United States from each foreign country. The goal of the quota system was to cut sharply European immigration to the United States. It achieved that goal.

As amended in 1924, the law limited immigration from each European nation to 2 percent of the number of its nationals living in the United States in 1890. This provision discriminated against people from eastern and southern Europe—mostly Roman Catholics and Jews—who had not started coming to the United States in large numbers until after 1890. Later, the base year was shifted to 1920. In 1927 the law reduced the total number of persons to be admitted in any one year to 150,000.

U.S. Patterns of Immigration, 1921–1929

The map and graph below show the change in immigration patterns resulting from the Emergency Quota Act, among other factors. Hundreds of thousands of people were affected, including people from Asia who were excluded from entering the U.S. due to the new quotas. For example, while the number of immigrants from Mexico rose from 30,758 in 1921 to 40,154 in 1929, the number of Italian immigrants dropped drastically from 222,260 in 1921 to 18,008 in 1929.

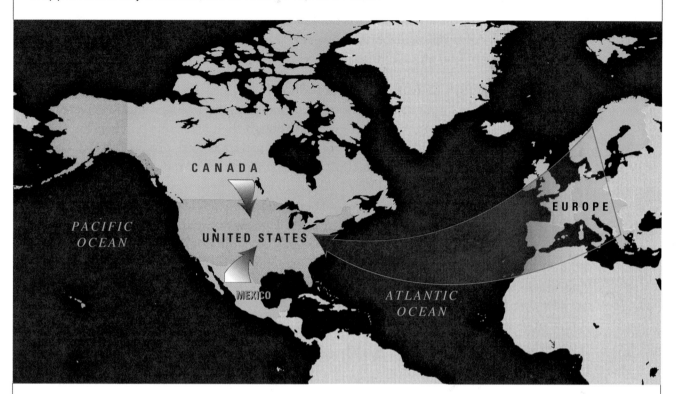

Immigration to the United States, 1921 and 1929

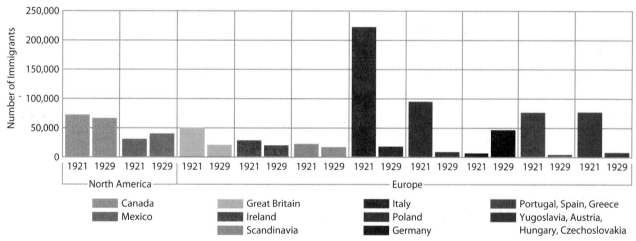

Source: *Historical Statistics of the United States, Colonial Times to 1970*

Interpret Graphs

1. Which geographical areas show the sharpest decline in immigration to the U.S. between 1921 and 1929? What are the only areas to register an increase in immigration to the U.S.?

2. How did the quota system affect where immigrants came from?

In addition, the law prohibited Japanese immigration, causing much ill will between the two nations. Japan—which had faithfully kept the Gentlemen's Agreement to limit immigration to the United States, negotiated by Theodore Roosevelt in 1907—expressed anger over the insult. President Calvin Coolidge, who signed the bill into law, was also unhappy with the exclusion of Japanese immigrants. He added a statement to the bill in which he expressed his disapproval.

The national origins quota system did not apply to immigrants from the Western Hemisphere, however. During the 1920s about a million Canadians and almost 500,000 Mexicans crossed the nation's borders.

CHANGES FOR NATIVE AMERICANS While laws and intimidation were limiting immigration for some people during the 1920s, conditions were finally improving for another group. Although their ancestors had lived on the land for centuries, thousands of Native Americans were not yet full U.S. citizens. Nonetheless, some 17,000 Native Americans had registered for military service during World War I. About 10,000 of them served in the armed forces. Partially in recognition of their service, President Coolidge signed the Indian Citizenship Act into law in 1924. The law granted citizenship to about 125,000 native people. However, the act did not include people born before the effective date of the 1924 act. Nor did it ensure voting rights. Loopholes allowed states to deny suffrage to Native Americans. Not until 1948 was the right extended to all. Native Americans' right to full self-determination would also be delayed for many more years.

Reading Check
Compare What challenges faced African Americans, Native Americans, and immigrant Europeans and Japanese who sought the rights of U.S. citizenship?

A Time of Labor Unrest

Another severe postwar conflict formed between labor and management. During the war, the government wouldn't allow workers to strike because nothing could interfere with the war effort. The American Federation of Labor (AFL) pledged to avoid strikes.

However, 1919 saw more than 3,000 strikes during which some 4 million workers walked off the job. Employers didn't want to give raises, nor did they want employees to join unions. Some employers, either out of a sincere belief or because they saw a way to keep wages down, attempted to show that union members were planning a revolution. Employers labeled striking workers as Communists. Newspapers screamed, "Plots to Establish Communism." Three strikes in particular grabbed public attention.

THE BOSTON POLICE STRIKE The Boston police had not been given a raise since the beginning of World War I. Among their many grievances was that they had been denied the right to unionize. When

Strikers included working women tailors who fought for improved working conditions.

representatives asked for a raise and were fired, the remaining policemen decided to strike. Massachusetts governor Calvin Coolidge called out the National Guard. He said, "There is no right to strike against the public safety by anybody, anywhere, any time." The strike ended, but members weren't allowed to return to work; new policemen were hired instead. People praised Coolidge for saving Boston, if not the nation, from communism and anarchy. In the 1920 election he became Warren G. Harding's vice-presidential running mate.

THE STEEL MILL STRIKE Workers in the steel mills wanted the right to negotiate for shorter working hours and a living wage. They also wanted union recognition and collective bargaining rights. In September 1919 the U.S. Steel Corporation refused to meet with union representatives. In response, over 300,000 workers walked off their jobs. Steel companies hired strikebreakers—employees who agreed to work during the strike—and used force. Striking workers were beaten by police, federal troops, and state militias. Then the companies instituted a propaganda campaign, linking the strikers to Communists. In October 1919 negotiations between labor and management produced a deadlock. President Woodrow Wilson made a written plea to the combative "negotiators."

> "At a time when the nations of the world are endeavoring to find a way of avoiding international war, are we to confess that there is no method to be found for carrying on industry except . . . the very method of war? . . . Are our industrial leaders and our industrial workers to live together without faith in each other?"
>
> —Woodrow Wilson, quoted in *Labor in Crisis*

The steel strike ended in January 1920. In 1923 a report on steel mills' harsh working conditions shocked the public. The steel companies agreed to an eight-hour workday, but the steelworkers remained without a union.

THE COAL MINERS' STRIKE Unionism was more successful in America's coalfields. In 1919 the United Mine Workers of America, organized since 1890, got a new leader—**John L. Lewis**. In protest of low wages and long workdays, Lewis called his union's members out on strike on November 1, 1919. Attorney General Palmer obtained a court order sending the miners back to work. Lewis then declared it over, but he quietly gave the word for it to continue. In defiance of the court order, the mines stayed closed another month. Then President Wilson appointed an arbitrator, or judge, to put an end to the dispute. The coal miners received a 27 percent wage increase, and John L. Lewis became a national hero. The miners, however, did not achieve a shorter workday and a five-day workweek until the 1930s.

LABOR MOVEMENT LOSES APPEAL In spite of limited gains, the 1920s hurt the labor movement badly. Over the decade, union membership dropped from more than 5 million to around 3.5 million. Membership declined for several reasons:

John Llewellyn Lewis (1880–1969)

John L. Lewis was born in the little mining town of Lucas, Iowa. His family had traditionally been concerned with labor rights and benefits.

Lewis grew up with a fierce determination to fight for what he believed companies owed their employees: decent working conditions and a fair salary. As he said years later, "I have pleaded your case not in the tones of a feeble mendicant [beggar] asking alms but in the thundering voice of the captain of a mighty host, demanding the rights to which free men are entitled."

- restrictive government policies had intimidated union advocates,
- much of the workforce consisted of immigrants willing to work in poor conditions,
- since immigrants spoke a multitude of languages, unions had difficulty organizing them,
- farmers who had migrated to cities to find factory jobs were `used to relying on themselves, and
- most unions excluded African Americans.

Reading Check
Compare How do the results of the Boston police strike and the steel mill strike compare?

By 1929 about 82,000 African Americans—or less than 1 percent of their population—held union memberships. By contrast, just over 3 percent of all whites were union members. However, African Americans joined some unions like the mine workers', longshoremen's, and railroad porters' unions. In 1925 A. Philip Randolph founded the Brotherhood of Sleeping Car Porters to help African Americans gain a fair wage.

Lesson 2 Assessment

1. Organize Information
In a cause-and-effect chart like the one shown, list examples of the aftereffects of World War I.

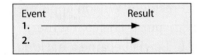

What event do you think was the most significant? Explain your choice.

2. Key Terms and People
For each key term or person in the lesson, write a sentence explaining its significance.

3. Evaluate
Do you think Americans were justified in their fear of radicals and foreigners in the decade following World War I? Explain your answer.
Think About:
- the goals of the leaders of the Russian Revolution
- the challenges facing the United States

4. Analyze Issues
In the various fights between management and union members, what did each side believe?

5. Draw Conclusions
What do you think the Sacco and Vanzetti case shows about America in the 1920s?

★
Changing Ways of Life

The Big Idea

Americans experienced cultural conflicts as customs and values changed in the 1920s.

Why It Matters Now

The way in which different groups react to change continues to cause conflict today.

Key Terms and People

Prohibition

speakeasy

bootlegger

fundamentalism

Clarence Darrow

Scopes trial

One American's Story

As the 1920s dawned, social reformers who hoped to ban alcohol—and the evils associated with it—rejoiced. The Eighteenth Amendment to the U.S. Constitution, banning the manufacture, sale, and transportation of alcohol, took effect in January 1920. Billy Sunday, an evangelist who preached against the evils of drinking, predicted a new age of virtue.

"The reign of tears is over! The slums will soon be only a memory. We will turn our prisons into factories and our jails into storehouses and corncribs. Men will walk upright now, women will smile and the children will laugh. Hell will be forever for rent!"
—Billy Sunday, quoted in *How Dry We Were: Prohibition Revisited*

1920s evangelist Billy Sunday

Sunday's dream was not to be realized in the 1920s, as the law proved unenforceable. The failure of Prohibition was a sign of cultural conflicts most evident in the nation's cities. Lured by jobs and by the challenge and freedom that the city represented, millions of people rode excitedly out of America's rural past and into its urban future.

SS.912.A.1.2; SS.912.A.5.6; MAFS.K12.MP.3.1

Rural and Urban Differences

America changed dramatically in the years before 1920, as was revealed in the 1920 census. According to figures that year, 51.2 percent of Americans lived in communities with populations of 2,500 to more than 1 million. Between 1922 and 1929, migration to the cities accelerated, with nearly 2 million people leaving farms and towns each year. "Cities were the place to be, not to get away from," said one historian. The agricultural world that millions of Americans left behind was largely unchanged from the 19th century. It was a world of small towns and farms bound together by conservative moral values and close social relationships. Yet small-town attitudes began to lose their hold on the American mind as the city rose to prominence.

Cars and pedestrians crowd the streets of New York City on Easter Sunday, 1920.

THE NEW URBAN SCENE At the beginning of the 1920s, New York, with a population of 5.6 million people, topped the list of big cities. Next came Chicago, with nearly 3 million, and Philadelphia, with nearly 2 million. Another 65 cities claimed populations of 100,000 or more, and they grew more crowded by the day. Life in these booming cities was far different from the slow-paced, intimate life in America's small towns. Chicago, for instance, was an industrial powerhouse. It was home to native-born whites and African Americans, immigrant Poles, Irish, Russians, Italians, Swedes, Arabs, French, and Chinese. Each day, an estimated 300,000 workers, 150,000 cars and buses, and 3,000 streetcars filled the pulsing downtown. At night, people crowded into ornate movie theaters and vaudeville houses offering live variety shows.

For small-town migrants, adapting to the urban environment demanded changes in thinking as well as in everyday living. The city was a world of competition and change. City dwellers read and argued about current scientific and social ideas. They judged one another by accomplishment more often than by background. City dwellers also tolerated drinking, gambling, and casual dating. These worldly behaviors were considered shocking and sinful in small towns.

For all its color and challenge, though, the city could be impersonal and frightening. Streets were filled with strangers, not friends and neighbors. Life was fast-paced, not leisurely.

> *"It is not for nothing that the predominating color of Chicago is orange. It is as if the city, in its taxicabs, in its shop fronts, in the wrappings of its parcels, chose the color of flame that goes with the smoky black of its factories. It is not for nothing that it has repelled the geometric street arrangement of New York and substituted . . . great ways with names that a stranger must learn if he can. . . . He is in a [crowded] city, and if he has business there, he tells himself, 'If I weaken I shan't last long.'"*
>
> —Walter L. George, from *Hail Columbia!*

In the city, lonely migrants from the country often ached for home. Throughout the 1920s Americans found themselves caught between rural and urban cultures. It was a tug that pitted what seemed to be a safe, small-town world of close ties, hard work, and strict morals against a big-city world of anonymous crowds, moneymakers, and pleasure-seekers. This tension between traditional, rural attitudes and modern, urban lifestyles was both a reflection of and a reaction to changes in American society during the 1920s. The conflict would be expressed in several ways.

THE PROHIBITION EXPERIMENT One vigorous clash between small-town and big-city Americans began in earnest in January 1920, when the Eighteenth Amendment went into effect. This amendment launched the era known as **Prohibition**, during which the manufacture, sale, and transportation of alcoholic beverages were legally prohibited.

Reformers had long considered liquor a prime cause of corruption. They thought that too much drinking led to crime, wife and child abuse, accidents on the job, and other serious social problems. Support for Prohibition came largely from the rural South and West, areas with large populations of native-born Protestants. The church-affiliated Anti-Saloon League had led the drive to pass the Prohibition amendment. The Woman's Christian Temperance Union, which considered drinking a sin, had helped push the measure through.

At first, saloons closed their doors, and arrests for drunkenness declined. But in the aftermath of World War I, many Americans were tired of making sacrifices; they wanted to enjoy life. Most immigrant groups did not consider drinking a sin but a natural part of socializing, and they resented government meddling.

Eventually, the government sealed Prohibition's fate when it failed to budget enough money to enforce the law. The Volstead Act established a Prohibition Bureau in the Treasury Department in 1919, but the agency was underfunded. The job of enforcement involved patrolling 18,700 miles of coastline as well as inland borders, tracking down illegal stills (equipment for distilling liquor), monitoring highways for truckloads of illegal alcohol, and overseeing all the industries that legally used alcohol to be sure none was siphoned off for illegal purposes. The task fell to approximately 1,500 poorly paid federal agents and local police. It was clearly an impossible job.

DIFFICULT DECISIONS

To Prohibit Alcohol or Not?

The question of whether to outlaw alcohol divided Americans. Many believed the government should make alcohol illegal to protect the public, while others believed it was a personal decision and not morally wrong.

1. Examine the pros and cons of each position. Which do you agree with? What other factors, if any, do you think would influence your position?

2. If you had been a legislator asked to vote for the Eighteenth Amendment, what would you have said? Explain.

3. What happens when the government legislates moral values? Give contemporary examples to support your answer.

A young woman demonstrates one of the means used to conceal alcohol—hiding it in containers strapped to one's legs.

SPEAKEASIES AND BOOTLEGGERS To obtain liquor illegally, drinkers went underground to hidden saloons and nightclubs known as **speakeasies**—so called because when inside, one spoke quietly, or "easily," to avoid detection. Speakeasies could be found everywhere—in penthouses, cellars, rooming houses, office buildings, tenements, hardware stores, and tearooms. To be admitted to a speakeasy, one had to present a card or use a password. Inside, one would find a mix of fashionable middle-class and upper-middle-class men and women.

Before long, people grew bolder in getting around the law. They learned to distill alcohol and built their own stills. Since alcohol was allowed for medicinal and religious purposes, prescriptions for alcohol and sales of sacramental wine (intended for church services) skyrocketed. People also bought liquor from **bootleggers** (named for a smuggler's practice of carrying liquor in the legs of boots). Bootleggers smuggled alcohol in from Canada, Cuba, and the West Indies. "The business of evading [the law] and making a mock of it has ceased to wear any aspects of crime and has become a sort of national sport," wrote the journalist H. L. Mencken.

ORGANIZED CRIME Prohibition had a devastating unintended consequence. Not only did Prohibition generate disrespect for the law, it also contributed to organized crime in nearly every major city. Chicago became notorious as the home of Al Capone, a gangster whose bootlegging empire netted over $60 million a year. Capone took control of the Chicago liquor business by killing off his competition. During the 1920s headlines reported 522 bloody gang killings and made the image of flashy Al Capone part of the folklore of the period.

Prohibition, 1920–1933

Causes	Effects
• Various religious groups thought drinking alcohol was sinful. • Reformers believed that the government should protect the public's health. • Reformers believed that alcohol led to crime, wife and child abuse, and accidents on the job. • During World War I, native-born Americans developed hostility to German-American brewers and toward other immigrant groups that used alcohol.	• Consumption of alcohol declined. • Disrespect for the law developed. • An increase in lawlessness, such as smuggling and bootlegging, was evident. • Criminals found a new source of income. • Organized crime grew.

Al Capone in Chicago

In 1940 the writer Herbert Asbury recalled the Capone era in Chicago:

> "The famous seven-ton armored car, with the pudgy gangster lolling on silken cushions in its darkened recesses, a big cigar in his fat face, and a $50,000 diamond ring blazing from his left hand, was one of the sights of the city; the average tourist felt that his trip to Chicago was a failure unless it included a view of Capone out for a spin. The mere whisper: 'Here comes Al,' was sufficient to stop traffic and to set thousands of curious citizens craning their necks along the curbing."
>
> —Herbert Asbury, from
> *Gem of the Prairie*

Analyze Historical Sources
1. How does Capone's reputation reflect attitudes toward Prohibition?
2. How does the image of Capone contribute to his reputation?

Reading Check
Contrast What are some ways that urban and rural ways of life differed?

By the mid-1920s only 19 percent of Americans supported Prohibition. The rest wanted the amendment changed or repealed. They believed that Prohibition caused worse effects than the initial problem. Rural Protestant Americans, however, defended a law that they felt strengthened moral values. The Eighteenth Amendment remained in force until 1933, when it was repealed by the Twenty-First Amendment.

Science and Religion Clash

Another bitter controversy highlighted the growing rift between traditional and modern ideas during the 1920s. This battle raged between fundamentalist religious groups and secular thinkers over the validity of certain scientific discoveries.

AMERICAN FUNDAMENTALISM The Protestant Christian movement grounded in a literal, or nonsymbolic, interpretation of the Bible was known as **fundamentalism**. Fundamentalists were skeptical of some scientific discoveries and theories; they argued that all important knowledge could be found in the Bible. They believed that the Bible was inspired by God, and that therefore its stories in all their details were true.

Their beliefs led fundamentalists to reject the theory of evolution advanced by Charles Darwin in the 19th century. This theory states that species of plants and animals descended from common ancestors. The implication they found most objectionable was that humans were related to apes. They pointed instead to the Bible's account of creation, in which God made the world and all life forms, including humans, in six days.

Fundamentalism expressed itself in several ways. In the South and West, preachers led religious revivals based on the authority of the Scriptures. One of the most powerful revivalists was Billy Sunday, a baseball player turned preacher who staged emotional meetings across the South. In Los Angeles, Aimee Semple McPherson used Hollywood showmanship to preach the word to homesick midwestern migrants and devoted followers of her radio broadcasts. In the 1920s fundamentalism gained followers who began to call for laws prohibiting the teaching of evolution.

THE SCOPES TRIAL In March 1925 Tennessee passed the nation's first law that made it a crime to teach evolution. Immediately, the American Civil Liberties Union (ACLU) promised to defend any teacher who would challenge the law. John T. Scopes, a young biology teacher in Dayton, Tennessee, accepted the challenge. In his biology class, Scopes read this passage from Civic Biology: "We have now learned that animal forms may be arranged so as to begin with the simple one-celled forms and culminate with a group which includes man himself." Scopes was promptly arrested, and his trial was set for July.

Vocabulary
culminate to come to completion; end

"*When Shall We Three Meet Again?*"

A 1925 newspaper cartoon portrays Bryan (left) and Darrow (right) at the close of the Scopes "monkey" trial on the teaching of evolution, so-called because of the theory of evolution that states humans are related to apes.

The ACLU hired **Clarence Darrow**, the most famous trial lawyer of the day, to defend Scopes. William Jennings Bryan, three-time Democratic candidate for president and a devout fundamentalist, served as a special prosecutor. There was no real question of guilt or innocence: Scopes was honest about his action. The **Scopes trial** was a fight over evolution and the role of science and religion in public schools and in American society.

The trial opened on July 10, 1925, and almost overnight became a national sensation. Darrow called on Bryan to testify as an expert on the Bible—the contest that everyone had been waiting for. To handle the throngs of Bryan supporters, Judge Raulston moved the court outside, to a platform built under the maple trees. There, before a crowd of several thousand people, Darrow relentlessly questioned Bryan about his beliefs. He asked Bryan if he agreed with Bishop James Ussher's 17th-century calculation that, according to the Bible, creation happened in 4004 BC. Had every living thing on earth appeared since that time? Did Bryan know that ancient civilizations had thrived before 4004 BC? Did he know the age of the earth? Bryan grew edgy but stuck to his guns. Finally, Darrow asked Bryan, "Do you think the earth was made in six days?" Bryan answered, "Not six days of 24 hours." People sitting on the lawn gasped.

Science and Social Change

Evolution was not the only scientific theory to make news during the 1920s. On November 23, 1924, the New York Times reported a major find by Edwin Hubble. The astronomer had discovered that blobs of light beyond the Milky Way were entire galaxies, not just clouds of gas. The announcement disturbed the notion that our galaxy is the only one in the universe. Implicit in the announcement was the possibility that other planets and living beings might exist. This was a shocking idea for the time.

A telescope now orbiting Earth bears Edwin Hubble's name. Because it operates beyond Earth's distorting atmosphere, the Hubble Space Telescope (HST) can record astoundingly detailed images of the sky. The HST's most remarkable images have proven that the universe contains hundreds of billions of galaxies. Just as we did in 1924, we who live on planet Earth continue to ask questions about humanity's place in the universe.

Reading Check
Analyze Issues
What was the conflict between fundamentalists and those who accepted evolution?

With this answer, Bryan admitted that the Bible might be interpreted in different ways. But in spite of this admission, Scopes was found guilty and fined $100. The Tennessee Supreme Court later changed the verdict based on a technicality, but the law outlawing the teaching of evolution remained in effect. To this day, teaching evolution remains controversial in some communities.

This clash over evolution, the Prohibition experiment, and the emerging urban scene all were evidence of the changes and conflicts occurring during the 1920s. During that period, women also experienced conflict as they redefined their roles and pursued new lifestyles.

Lesson 3 Assessment

1. **Organize Information**
   Create two cause-and-effect diagrams to show how government attempted to deal with (a) problems thought to stem from alcohol use and (b) the teaching of evolution.

   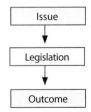

   Was the legislation effective? Explain.

2. **Key Terms and People**
   For each key term or person in the lesson, write a sentence explaining its significance.

3. **Analyze Issues**
   How might the overall atmosphere of the 1920s have contributed to the failure of Prohibition?

   Think About:
   • the growth of cities
   • the increase in immigration

4. **Analyze Causes**
   Why do you think organized crime spread so quickly through the cities during the 1920s? Explain your answer.

5. **Predict**
   How might the 1920s conflict between traditional and more modern values affect decades to come?

The Twenties Woman

SS.912.A.1.2; SS.912.A.5.6; SS.912.H.1.1;
LAFS.1112.RH.1.2

The Big Idea

American women pursued new lifestyles and assumed new jobs and different roles in society during the 1920s.

Why It Matters Now

Workplace opportunities and trends in family life are still major issues for women today.

Key Terms and People

flapper

double standard

One American's Story

Christine Frederick was an advertising consultant and efficiency expert. She applied her skills to encouraging women to buy the new appliances quickly becoming available. One of the glamorous new devices she praised was a washing machine.

A woman uses an electric washing machine, a time-saving appliance that was marketed in the 1920s

"No housekeeper today persists in roasting her Sunday dinner over a spit when she can buy an insulated oven, or in using a dirt-scattering corn broom when she can procure a dust-absorbing vacuum cleaner. So too, where is the housekeeper of this progressive year who will refuse to understand the new, slightly different, but still very simple principles which make machine washing a success?"

—Christine McGaffey Frederick, from "You and Your Laundry," 1922

As a businessperson and public figure, Frederick represented the new woman of the 1920s, who broke free of established roles. However, the arena in which she worked was the home, where women had traditionally remained. This contradiction reflects the conflict between modernity and convention that many women of the 1920s experienced.

Young Women Change the Rules

By the 1920s the experiences of World War I, the pull of cities, and changing attitudes had opened up a new world for many young Americans. These "wild young people," wrote John F. Carter Jr. in a 1920 issue of *Atlantic Monthly,* were experiencing a world unknown to their parents: "We have seen man at his lowest, woman at her lightest, in the terrible moral chaos of Europe. We have been forced to question, and in many cases to discard, the religion of our fathers. . . . We have been forced to live in an atmosphere of 'tomorrow we die,' and so, naturally, we drank and were merry." In the rebellious, pleasure-loving atmosphere of the twenties, many women began to assert their independence, reject the values of the 19th century, and demand the same freedoms as men.

THE FLAPPER During the twenties, a new ideal emerged for some women: the **flapper**. This was a liberated young woman who embraced the new fashions and urban attitudes of the day. Close-fitting felt hats, bright waistless dresses an inch above the knees, skin-toned silk stockings, sleek pumps, and strings of beads replaced the dark and prim ankle-length dresses, whalebone corsets, and petticoats of Victorian days. Young women clipped their long hair into boyish bobs and dyed it jet black.

Many young women became more assertive. In their bid for equal status with men, some began smoking cigarettes, drinking in public, and talking openly about sex. These same actions would have ruined their reputations not many years before. They danced the fox trot, camel walk, tango, Charleston, and shimmy with abandon.

Attitudes toward marriage changed as well. Many middle-class men and women began to view marriage as more of an equal partnership, although both agreed that housework and child-rearing remained a woman's job.

Flappers compete in a Charleston dance competition in 1926.

THE DOUBLE STANDARD Magazines, newspapers, and advertisements promoted the image of the flapper, and young people openly discussed courtship and relationships in ways that scandalized their elders. Although many young women donned the new outfits and ignored tradition, the flapper was more an image of rebellious youth than a widespread reality. It did not reflect the attitudes and values of many young people. During the 1920s, morals loosened only so far. Traditionalists in churches and schools protested the new casual dances and women's acceptance of smoking and drinking.

In the years before World War I, when men "courted" women, they pursued only women they intended to marry. In the 1920s, however, casual dating became increasingly accepted. Even so, a **double standard**—a set of principles granting greater sexual freedom to men than to women—required women to observe stricter standards of behavior than men did. As a result, many women were pulled back and forth between the old standards and the new.

Reading Check
Compare and Contrast How was the 1920s woman like and unlike women of today?

Women Shed Old Roles at Home and at Work

The fast-changing world of the 1920s produced new roles for women outside the home and new trends in family life. A booming industrial economy opened new work opportunities for women in offices, factories, stores, and professions. The same economy churned out time-saving appliances and products that reshaped the roles of housewives and mothers.

A young woman works as a typesetter in a publishing house in 1920.

NEW OPPORTUNITIES Women had worked successfully during the war. After the war, employers who believed that men had the responsibility to financially support their families often replaced female workers with men. Women continued to seek paid employment, but their opportunities changed. Many female college graduates turned to "women's professions" and became teachers, nurses, and librarians. Big businesses required extensive correspondence and recordkeeping. This created a huge demand for clerical workers such as typists, filing clerks, secretaries, stenographers, and office-machine operators. Others became clerks in stores or held jobs on assembly lines. A handful of women broke the old stereotypes by doing work once reserved for men, such as flying airplanes, driving taxis, and drilling oil wells.

More options for higher education also expanded women's roles in public life. Several women's colleges opened during the 1920s. Among them were Sarah Lawrence College and Scripps College, both established in 1926. In addition, new community or junior colleges made low-cost higher education available to more women with jobs or families.

By 1930, 10 million women were earning wages; however, few rose to managerial jobs, and wherever they worked, women earned less than men. Fearing competition for jobs, men argued that women were just temporary workers whose real job was at home. Between 1900 and 1930, the patterns of discrimination and inequality for women in the business world were established.

THE CHANGING FAMILY Widespread social and economic changes reshaped the family. The birthrate had been declining for several decades, and it dropped at a slightly faster rate in the 1920s. This decline was due in part to the wider availability of birth-control information. Margaret Sanger, who had opened the first birth-control clinic in the United States in 1916, founded the American Birth Control League in 1921 and fought for the legal rights of physicians to give birth-control information to their patients.

At the same time, social and technological innovations simplified household labor and family life. Stores overflowed with ready-made clothes, sliced bread, and canned foods. Public agencies provided services for the elderly, public health clinics served the sick, and workers' compensation assisted those who could no longer work. These innovations and institutions had the effect of freeing homemakers from some of their traditional family responsibilities. Many middle-class housewives, the main shoppers and money managers, focused their attention on their homes, husbands, children, and pastimes. "I consider time for reading clubs and my children more important than . . . careful housework and I just don't do it," said an Indiana woman.

Margaret Sanger was arrested at least eight times for her activities in support of birth control.

Document-Based Investigation Historical Source

Working-Class Women in the 1920s
Helen Wright, who worked for the Women's Bureau in Chicago, recorded the struggle of an Irish mother of two.

Analyze Historical Sources
How does the woman described in this account reflect the contradicting expectations women experienced during the 1920s?

"She worked in one of the meat-packing companies, pasting labels from 7 a.m. to 3:30 p.m. She had entered the eldest child at school but sent her to the nursery for lunch and after school. The youngest was in the nursery all day. She kept her house 'immaculately clean and in perfect order,' but to do so worked until eleven o'clock every night in the week and on Saturday night she worked until five o'clock in the morning. She described her schedule as follows: on Tuesday, Wednesday, Thursday, and Friday she cleaned one room each night; Saturday afternoon she finished the cleaning and put the house in order; Saturday night she washed; Sunday she baked; Monday night she ironed."
—Helen Wright, quoted in *Wage-Earning Women*

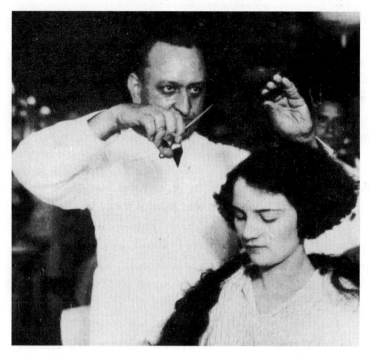

In the 1920s women began to bob their hair, cutting it much shorter than the long styles that had been fashionable for years.

As their spheres of activity and influence expanded, women experienced greater equality in marriage. Marriages were based increasingly on romantic love and companionship. Children were no longer thrown together with adults in factory work, farm labor, and apprenticeships. Instead, they spent most of their days at school and in organized activities with others their own age. At the same time, parents began to rely more heavily on manuals of childcare and the advice of experts.

Working-class and college-educated women quickly discovered the pressure of juggling work and family, but the strain on working-class women was more severe.

As women adjusted to changing roles, some also struggled with rebellious adolescents, who put an unprecedented strain on families. Teens in the 1920s studied and socialized with other teens and spent less time with their families. As peer pressure intensified, some adolescents resisted parental control, much as the flappers resisted societal control.

This theme of adolescent rebelliousness can be seen in much of the popular culture of the 1920s. The decade known as the Roaring Twenties was a celebration of youth culture—the way young people lived, their values, and their styles. Education and entertainment reflected the conflict between traditional attitudes and modern ways of thinking.

Reading Check Summarize What changes affected women and families in the 1920s?

Lesson 4 Assessment

1. Organize Information
Create a web diagram to record examples that illustrate how women's lives changed in the 1920s.

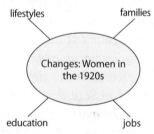

Write a paragraph explaining how you think women's lives changed most dramatically in the 1920s.

2. Key Terms and People
For each key term in the lesson, write a sentence explaining its significance.

3. Evaluate
During the 1920s, a double standard required women to observe stricter codes of behavior than men. Do you think that some women of this decade made real progress toward equality? Support your answer with examples.

Think About:
• the flapper's style and image
• changing views of marriage

4. Analyze Primary Sources
In 1920 veteran suffragist Anna Howard Shaw stated that equality in the workplace would be harder for women to achieve than the vote.

"You younger women will have a harder task than ours. You will want equality in business, and it will be even harder to get than the vote."

Why do you think Shaw held this belief? Support your answer with evidence from the text.

Education and Popular Culture

The Big Idea

The mass media, movies, and spectator sports played important roles in creating the popular culture of the 1920s—a culture that many artists and writers criticized.

Why It Matters Now

Much of today's popular culture can trace its roots to the popular culture of the 1920s.

Key Terms and People

Charles A. Lindbergh

George Gershwin

Irving Berlin

Georgia O'Keeffe

modernism

Sinclair Lewis

F. Scott Fitzgerald

Edna St. Vincent Millay

Ernest Hemingway

SS.912.A.1.2; SS.912.A.1.3; SS.912.A.1.4; SS.912.A.1.7; SS.912.A.5.6; SS.912.H.1.1; SS.912.H.1.5; LAFS.1112.RH.4.10; MAFS.K12.MP.1.1; MAFS.K12.MP.5.1

One American's Story

On September 22, 1927, approximately 50 million Americans sat listening to their radios as Graham McNamee, radio's most popular announcer, breathlessly called the boxing match between the former heavyweight champ Jack Dempsey and the current titleholder, Gene Tunney.

After punches flew for ten rounds, Tunney defeated the legendary Dempsey. So suspenseful was the brutal match that a number of radio listeners died of heart failure. The "fight of the century" was just one of a host of spectacles and events that transformed American popular culture in the 1920s.

By 1920 radio had morphed from a way to communicate wirelessly with ships at sea to an impactful form of mass communication. Before radio, people often had to wait days or even weeks to get news and information from newspapers. New radio stations broadcast news, sports, dramas, and comedies—providing entertainment and information to more than 3 million U.S. households by 1924. For the first time, people could experience sporting events, concerts, shows, and other performances in real time without physically attending.

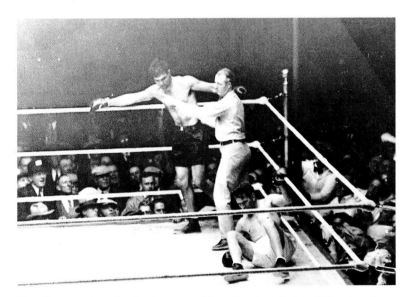

Gene Tunney, down for the "long count," went on to defeat Jack Dempsey in their epic 1927 battle.

Schools and the Mass Media Shape Culture

During the 1920s developments in education and mass media had a powerful impact on the nation.

SCHOOL ENROLLMENTS In 1914 approximately 1 million American students attended high school. By 1926 that number had risen to nearly 4 million, an increase sparked by prosperous times and higher educational standards for industry jobs.

Prior to the 1920s, high schools had catered to college-bound students. In contrast, high schools of the 1920s began offering a broad range of courses such as vocational training for those interested in industrial jobs.

The public schools met another challenge in the 1920s—teaching the children of new immigrant families. The years before World War I had seen the largest stream of immigrants in the nation's history—close to 1 million a year. Unlike the earlier English and Irish immigrants, many of the new immigrants spoke no English. By the 1920s their children filled city classrooms. Determined teachers met the challenge and developed a large pool of literate Americans.

Taxes to finance the schools increased as well. School costs doubled between 1913 and 1920, and then doubled again by 1926. The total cost of American education in the mid-1920s amounted to $2.7 billion a year.

EXPANDING NEWS COVERAGE Widespread education increased literacy in America, but it was the growing mass media that shaped a mass culture. Newspaper circulation rose. Imitating the sensational stories in the tabloids, newspaper writers and editors learned how to hook readers. By 1914 about 600 local newspapers had shut down and 230 had been swallowed up by huge national chains, giving readers more expansive coverage from the big

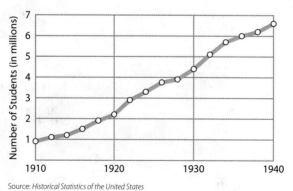

High School Enrollment, 1910–1940

Source: *Historical Statistics of the United States*

Interpret Graphs
What was the approximate increase in the number of high school students between 1920 and 1930?

cities. Mass-circulation magazines also flourished during the 1920s. Many of these magazines summarized the week's news, both foreign and domestic. By the end of the 1920s, ten American magazines—including *Reader's Digest* (founded in 1922) and *Time* (founded in 1923)—boasted a circulation of over 2 million each.

RADIO COMES OF AGE Although major magazines and newspapers reached big audiences, radio was the most powerful communications medium to emerge in the 1920s. Americans added terms such as "airwaves," "radio audience," and "tune in" to their everyday speech. By the end of the decade, the radio networks had created something new in the United States—the shared national experience of hearing the news as it happened. The wider world had opened up to Americans, who could hear the voice of their president or listen to the World Series live.

Reading Check
Analyze Effects
How did changes in education and mass media affect Americans' knowledge of world affairs?

Radio Broadcasts of the 1920s

Prior to the 1920s, radio broadcasts were used primarily for transmitting important messages and speeches regarding World War I. After the first commercial radio station—KDKA Pittsburgh—made its debut on the airwaves in 1920, the radio industry changed forever. Listeners tuned in for news, entertainment, and advertisements.

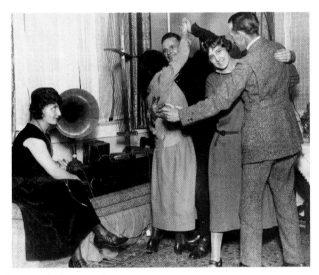

Radio dance parties were common in the 1920s.

By 1930, 40 percent of U.S. households had radios, like this 1927 Cosser three-valve Melody Maker.

In the 1920s radio was a formal affair. Announcers and musicians dressed in their finest attire, even without a live audience.

Although the media glorified sports heroes, the Golden Age of Sports reflected common aspirations. Athletes set new records, inspiring ordinary Americans. When poor, unknown athletes rose to national fame and fortune, they restored Americans' belief in the power of the individual to improve his or her life.

Gertrude Ederle

In 1926, at the age of 19, Gertrude Ederle became the first woman to swim the English Channel. Here, an assistant applies heavy grease to combat the cold Channel waters.

Babe Ruth

New York Yankees slugger Babe Ruth was the home run king during the 1920s. When the legendary star hit a record 60 home runs in 1927, Americans went wild.

Lou Gehrig

Dubbed the "Iron Horse" for his endurance, baseball star Lou Gehrig set several major league records. His life was cut short by amyotrophic lateral sclerosis (ALS), a condition now commonly called Lou Gehrig's disease.

Helen Wills

Helen Wills dominated women's tennis, winning the singles title at the U.S. Open seven times and the Wimbledon title eight times.

Andrew "Rube" Foster

Andrew "Rube" Foster was a celebrated pitcher and team manager. He made his greatest contribution to black baseball in 1920 when he founded the Negro National League.

Red Grange

During his college days, athlete Red Grange scored at least one touchdown in almost every game he played. His professional career helped legitimize the National Football League.

America Chases New Heroes and Old Dreams

During the 1920s many people had money and the free time to enjoy it. In 1929 Americans spent $4.5 billion on entertainment, much of it on ever-changing fads. Early in the decade, Americans engaged in new leisure pastimes such as working crossword puzzles and playing mahjong, a Chinese game with playing pieces that resemble dominoes. They also flooded athletic stadiums to see sports stars, who were glorified as superheroes by the mass media. In 1922 explorers opened the dazzling tomb of the Egyptian pharaoh Tutankhamen. Afterward, consumers mobbed stores for pharaoh-inspired accessories, jewelry, and furniture.

LINDBERGH'S FLIGHT America's most beloved hero of the time wasn't an athlete but a small-town pilot named **Charles A. Lindbergh**. He made the first nonstop solo flight across the Atlantic. A handsome, modest Minnesotan, Lindbergh decided to go after a $25,000 prize offered for the first nonstop solo transatlantic flight. On May 20, 1927, he took off near New York City in the *Spirit of St. Louis*. Lindbergh flew up the coast to Newfoundland and headed over the Atlantic. The weather was so bad, Lindbergh recalled, that "the average altitude for the whole . . . second 1,000 miles of the [Atlantic] flight was less than 100 feet." After 33 hours and 29 minutes, Lindbergh set down at Le Bourget airfield outside of Paris, France, amid beacons, searchlights, and mobs of enthusiastic people.

Paris threw a huge party. On his return to the United States, New York City showered Lindbergh with ticker tape, the president received him at the White House, and America made him its idol. In an age of sensationalism, excess, and crime, Lindbergh stood for the honesty and bravery the nation seemed to have lost. Lindbergh's accomplishment paved the way for others. In the next decade, Amelia Earhart was to undertake many brave aerial exploits.

Reading Check
Summarize
What were some of the ways Americans spent their leisure time in the 1920s?

Historic Flights

Charles Lindbergh established a record of 33 hours 29 minutes in his 3,614-mile nonstop solo flight across the Atlantic. He left New York City on May 20, 1927, and arrived in Paris, France, the following day.

On May 20, 1932, Amelia Earhart was the first woman to fly solo across the Atlantic. She completed the trip in a record time of about 15 hours from Newfoundland to Ireland.

Popular Culture Reflects New Attitudes

During the 1920s America's thirst for fun and entertainment seemed unquenchable. The decade's youth culture set the tone. Energetic dances such as the Charleston were all the rage. Bizarre fads caught the public's attention. One of the oddest was sitting on tiny platforms on top of flagpoles, for days at a time. Radically new styles of clothing captured the public's fancy. Young men who wanted to attract the glamorous flappers wore extremely baggy trousers and slicked down their hair. Public entertainment and the arts also underwent dramatic changes.

MOVIES, DRAMA, MUSIC, AND ART The leisure culture that developed during the 1920s stimulated the arts, including the newest art form, motion pictures. Movies became a national pastime, offering viewers a means of escape through romance and comedy. During the early years of the decade, all Hollywood movies were silent. Written dialogue and live music helped move the plot and enhance the mood. Then in 1927 the first major movie with sound, *The Jazz Singer*, was released. The plot followed a young Jewish man who rebels against his family heritage to become a stage star. Walt Disney's *Steamboat Willie*, the first animated film with sound, was released in 1928. By 1930 the new "talkies" had doubled movie attendance, with millions of Americans going to the movies every week. Other countries, too, quickly developed their own film industries, which brought popular culture to millions of eager customers. Not everyone approved of the new medium, however. Almost as soon as the first movies hit the screens, viewers who held

Edward Hopper's *Night Windows* (1928)

more traditional values declared some films "immoral" for their depictions of religious and sexual topics.

Both playwrights and composers of music broke away from the European traditions of the 1920s. Eugene O'Neill's plays, such as *The Hairy Ape*, forced Americans to reflect upon modern isolation, confusion, and family conflict. Jewish composer **George Gershwin** earned fame when he merged popular concert music with American jazz, thus creating a new sound that was identifiably American. *Rhapsody in Blue* and *An American in Paris* are among his most famous compositions. **Irving Berlin** was another important composer of the period. Berlin wrote 1,500 songs, some of which appeared in Broadway shows or Hollywood movies. He may be best remembered for the song "White Christmas," recordings of which have sold more than 100 million copies over the years.

Painters appealed to Americans by recording an America of dreams and the contrasting realities. Edward Hopper caught the loneliness of American life in his canvases of empty streets and solitary people. **Georgia O'Keeffe** produced intensely colored canvases that captured the grandeur of New Mexico. Other O'Keeffe paintings depicted flowers in extreme close-ups. Hopper and O'Keeffe were just two of the many artists whose works were representative of **modernism**. This artistic movement rejected traditional art as outdated and no longer meaningful in the new, industrialized, urban world.

WRITERS OF THE 1920s The 1920s also brought an outpouring of fresh and insightful writing, making it one of the richest eras in the country's literary history. In contrast to the merriment of popular entertainment, many works of the decade's writers revealed the tensions gnawing below the surface.

Sinclair Lewis was the first American to win a Nobel Prize in literature. He was among the era's most outspoken critics. In his novel *Babbitt,* Lewis used the main character of George F. Babbitt to ridicule Americans of the period.

Charlie Chaplin was one of the biggest stars of the early film era.

Document-Based Investigation Historical Source

A Businessman Changes His Suit

One of the defining novels of the 1920s, Sinclair Lewis's *Babbitt* is a blistering satire of American culture. Set in a fictional Midwestern city named Zenith, the novel pokes fun at the empty shallowness of the booster clubs and lodges where deals were made and social status was measured.

Analyze Historical Sources
For what was Sinclair Lewis ridiculing Americans?

"A sensational event was changing from the brown suit to the gray the contents of his pockets. He was earnest about these objects. They were of eternal importance, like baseball or the Republican Party. They included a fountain pen and a silver pencil . . . which belonged in the righthand upper vest pocket. Without them he would have felt naked. On his watch-chain were a gold penknife, silver cigar-cutter, seven keys . . . and incidentally a good watch . . . . Last, he stuck in his lapel the Boosters' Club button. With the conciseness of great art the button displayed two words: 'Boosters—Pep!'"

—Sinclair Lewis, from *Babbitt*

American Literature

The Lost Generation

F. Scott Fitzgerald's 1922 story titled "Winter Dreams" reflected the gloom behind the decade's glitter. The main character, Dexter Green, has achieved wealth and success but is crushed when his dream of a lifelong love is dashed. Life empty of meaning is his fate.

Winter Dreams

"The dream was gone. Something had been taken from him. . . . For the first time in years the tears were streaming down his face. But they were for himself now. . . . He wanted to care, and he could not care. For he had gone away and he could never go back any more. The gates were closed, the sun was gone down, and there was no beauty but the gray beauty of steel that withstands all time. Even the grief he could have borne was left behind in the country of illusion, of youth, of the richness of life, where his winter dreams had flourished.

'Long ago,' he said, 'long ago, there was something in me, but now that thing is gone. Now that thing is gone, that thing is gone. I cannot cry. I cannot care. That thing will come back no more.'"

—F. Scott Fitzgerald, from "Winter Dreams" (1922)

Analyze American Literature
Consider the date when Fitzgerald wrote this story. What recent global events might have affected his melancholy frame of mind?

It was **F. Scott Fitzgerald** who coined the term "Jazz Age" to describe the 1920s. In *This Side of Paradise* and *The Great Gatsby*, he revealed the negative side of the period's gaiety and freedom, portraying wealthy and attractive people leading imperiled lives in gilded surroundings.

In New York City, a brilliant group of writers routinely lunched together at the Algonquin Hotel's "Round Table." Among the best known of them was Dorothy Parker, a short-story writer, poet, and essayist. Parker was famous for her wisecracking wit, expressed in such lines as "I was the toast of two continents—Greenland and Australia." Many writers also met important issues head on. In *The Age of Innocence*, Edith Wharton dramatized the clash between traditional and modern values that had undermined high society 50 years earlier. Willa Cather celebrated the simple, dignified lives of people such as the immigrant farmers of Nebraska in *My Ántonia*. **Edna St. Vincent Millay** wrote poems celebrating youth and a life of independence and freedom from traditional constraints.

Several writers saw action in World War I, and their early books denounced war. John Dos Passos's novel *Three Soldiers* attacked war as a machine designed to crush human freedom. Later, he turned to social and political themes, using modern techniques to capture the mood of city life and the losses that came with success. **Ernest Hemingway**, wounded in World War I, became one of the country's most popular authors. In his novels *The Sun Also Rises* and *A Farewell to Arms*, Hemingway criticized the glorification of war. He also introduced a tough, simplified style of writing that set a new literary standard, using sentences a *Time* reporter compared to "round stones polished by rain and wind."

F. Scott Fitzgerald (1896–1940)

F. Scott Fitzgerald married vivacious Zelda Sayre in 1920 after his novel This Side of Paradise became an instant hit. He said of this time in his life: "Riding in a taxi one afternoon between very tall buildings under a mauve and rosy sky, I began to bawl because I had everything I wanted and knew I would never be so happy again."

Flush with money, the couple plunged into a wild social whirl and outspent their incomes. The years following were difficult. Zelda suffered from repeated mental breakdowns, and Scott's battle with alcoholism took its toll.

Vocabulary
expatriate a person who has taken up residence in a foreign country

Reading Check
Make Inferences
Why do you think both frivolous entertainment and serious fiction were popular during the 1920s?

Some writers such as Fitzgerald, Hemingway, and Dos Passos were so soured by American culture that they chose to settle in Europe, mainly in Paris. Socializing in the city's cafes, these expatriates formed a group that the writer Gertrude Stein called the Lost Generation—not vanished or misplaced, but aimless and disoriented. They joined other American writers already in Europe, such as poets Ezra Pound and T. S. Eliot, whose poem The Waste Land presented an agonized view of a society that seemed stripped of humanity.

During this rich literary era, vital developments were also taking place in African American society. Black Americans of the 1920s began to voice pride in their heritage, and black artists and writers revealed the richness of African American culture.

Lesson 5 Assessment

1. **Organize Information**
Create a timeline of key events relating to 1920s popular culture.

In a sentence or two, explain which of these events interests you the most and why.

2. **Key Terms and People**
For each key term or person in the lesson, write a sentence explaining its significance.

3. **Form Generalizations**
In what ways do you think the mass media and mass culture helped Americans create a sense of national community in the 1920s? Support your answer with details from the text.
Think About:
- the content and readership of newspapers and magazines
- popularity of sports events and Hollywood movies
- the scope of radio broadcasts

4. **Analyze Primary Sources**
How did some writers of the 1920s respond to social and political changes in the United States?

5. **Summarize**
In two or three sentences, summarize the effects of education and mass media on society in the 1920s.

The Harlem Renaissance

The Big Idea

African American ideas, politics, art, literature, and music flourished in Harlem and elsewhere in the United States.

Why It Matters Now

The Harlem Renaissance provided a foundation of African American intellectualism to which African American writers, artists, and musicians contribute today.

Key Terms and People

Zora Neale Hurston

National Association for the Advancement of Colored People (NAACP)

James Weldon Johnson

Marcus Garvey

Harlem Renaissance

Claude McKay

Langston Hughes

Paul Robeson

Louis Armstrong

Duke Ellington

Bessie Smith

One American's Story

When the spirited **Zora Neale Hurston** was a girl in Eatonville, Florida, in the early 1900s, she loved to read adventure stories and myths. The powerful tales struck a chord with the young, talented Hurston and made her yearn for a wider world.

"My soul was with the gods and my body in the village. People just would not act like gods. . . . Raking back yards and carrying out chamber-pots, were not the tasks of Thor. I wanted to be away from drabness and to stretch my limbs in some mighty struggle."

—Zora Neale Hurston, quoted in *The African American Encyclopedia*

Zora Neale Hurston

After spending time with a traveling theater company and attending Howard University, Hurston ended up in New York. She struggled to the top of African American literary society by hard work, flamboyance, and, above all, grit. "I have seen that the world is to the strong regardless of a little pigmentation more or less," Hurston wrote later. "I do not weep at [being Negro]—I am too busy sharpening my oyster knife." Hurston was on the move, like millions of others. And, like them, she went after the pearl in the oyster—the good life in America.

SS.912.A.1.2; SS.912.A.1.7; SS.912.A.5.6; SS.912.A.5.7; SS.912.A.5.8; SS.912.A.5.10; SS.912.G.1.2; SS.912.G.4.2; SS.912.G.4.3; SS.912.H.1.3; SS.912.H.1.5; LAFS.1112.RH.4.10

African American Voices in the 1920s

After World War I, Jim Crow laws continued to make life hard for African Americans in the South. Many black Americans looked north for more security, freedom, and opportunities.

During the 1920s African Americans set new goals for themselves as they moved north to the nation's cities. Their migration was an expression of their changing attitude toward themselves—an attitude perhaps best captured in a phrase first used around this time, "Black is beautiful."

THE MOVE NORTH Between 1910 and 1920 a movement known as the Great Migration took place. Hundreds of thousands of African Americans uprooted themselves from their homes in the South and moved north to the big cities in search of jobs. By the end of the decade, 5.2 million of the nation's 12 million African Americans—over 40 percent—lived in cities.

However, northern cities in general had not welcomed the massive influx of African Americans. Tensions had escalated in the years prior to 1920. In the summer of 1919, these tensions culminated in approximately 25 urban race riots. In addition, the concentration of African Americans in big cities would eventually lead to legal discrimination in mortgage lending practices.

AFRICAN AMERICAN GOALS The prosperity of the 1920s did not benefit all Americans equally. African Americans remained the targets of discrimination. Several new organizations sought to improve the lives of African Americans. One was the National Urban League. This organization tried to remove barriers to black employment. Founded in 1909 the **National Association for the Advancement of Colored People (NAACP)** urged African Americans to protest racial violence. W.E.B. DuBois, a founding member of the NAACP, led a parade of 10,000 African American men in New York City to protest such violence. The event, called the Silent Parade or the Silent Protest, failed to convince President Woodrow Wilson to improve protections for African Americans. Du Bois also used the NAACP's magazine, *The Crisis*, as a platform for leading a struggle for civil rights. *The Crisis* is still being published four times a year.

Under the leadership of **James Weldon Johnson**—poet, lawyer, and NAACP executive secretary—the organization fought for legislation to protect African American rights. It made antilynching laws one of its main priorities. In 1919, three antilynching bills were introduced in Congress, although none was passed. The NAACP continued its campaign through antilynching organizations that had been established in 1892 by Ida B. Wells. Gradually, the number of lynchings dropped. The NAACP represented the new, more militant voice of African Americans.

MARCUS GARVEY AND THE UNIA Although many African Americans found their voice in the NAACP, they still faced daily threats and discrimination. **Marcus Garvey**, an immigrant from Jamaica, believed that African Americans should build a separate society. His different, more radical message of black pride aroused the hopes of many.

James Weldon Johnson
(1871–1938)

James Weldon Johnson served the public in many ways. During Theodore Roosevelt's administration, Johnson was a U.S. consul in Venezuela and Nicaragua. He was a school principal, newspaper editor, and lawyer. Later in life, Johnson became a professor of creative literature and writing.

In the 1920s Johnson straddled the worlds of politics and art. He served as executive secretary of the NAACP, spearheading the fight against lynching. In addition, he wrote well-known works, such as God's Trombones, a series of sermonlike poems, and Black Manhattan, a look at black cultural life in New York City during the Roaring Twenties.

Vocabulary
oratory the art of public speaking

Reading Check
Compare and Contrast What did James Weldon Johnson and Marcus Garvey have in common? How were their efforts to change society different?

In 1914 Garvey founded the Universal Negro Improvement Association (UNIA). In 1918 he moved the UNIA to New York City and opened offices in urban ghettos in order to recruit followers. By the mid-1920s Garvey claimed he had a million followers. He appealed to African Americans with a combination of spellbinding oratory, mass meetings, parades, and a message of pride.

Garvey also lured followers with practical plans, especially his program to promote African American businesses. Further, Garvey encouraged his followers to return to Africa, a scheme sometimes called the "Back to Africa" movement. When they had arrived in Africa, the new arrivals were to throw off white colonial oppressors and build a mighty nation. These goals formed the basis of Black Nationalism—the idea that all black people are one and that they should put aside their differences to unite. Garvey's ideas struck a chord in many African Americans, as well as in Africans and people of African heritage in the Caribbean region.

Despite the appeal of Garvey's movement, support for it declined in the mid-1920s. At that time, he was convicted of mail fraud and jailed. Although the movement dwindled, Garvey left behind a powerful legacy of newly awakened black pride, economic independence, and reverence for Africa.

Document-Based Investigation Historical Source

Marcus Garvey on the Rights of African Americans

"In view of the fact that the black man of Africa has contributed as much to the world as the white man of Europe, and the brown man and yellow man of Asia, we of the Universal Negro Improvement Association demand that the white, yellow, and brown races give to the black man his place in the civilization of the world. We ask for nothing more than the rights of 400 million Negroes."
—Marcus Garvey, from a speech at Liberty Hall, New York City, 1922

Analyze Historical Sources
How do you think reaction to Garvey's speech might have varied among the audience members?

The Harlem Renaissance Flowers in New York

Many African Americans who migrated north moved to Harlem, a neighborhood on the upper west side of New York's Manhattan Island. In the 1920s Harlem became the world's largest black urban community. Residents came from the South, the West Indies, Cuba, Puerto Rico, and Haiti. James Weldon Johnson described Harlem as the capital of black America.

> *"Harlem is not merely a Negro colony or community, it is a city within a city, the greatest Negro city in the world. It is not a slum or a fringe, it is located in the heart of Manhattan and occupies one of the most beautiful . . . sections of the city. . . . It has its own churches, social and civic centers, shops, theaters, and other places of amusement. And it contains more Negroes to the square mile than any other spot on earth."*
>
> —James Weldon Johnson, from "Harlem: The Culture Capital"

Like many other urban neighborhoods, Harlem suffered from overcrowding, unemployment, and poverty. But its problems in the 1920s were eclipsed by a flowering of creativity called the **Harlem Renaissance**, a literary and artistic movement celebrating African American culture.

AFRICAN AMERICAN WRITERS Above all, the Harlem Renaissance was a literary movement led by well-educated, middle-class African Americans who expressed a new pride in the African American experience. They celebrated their heritage and wrote with defiance and poignancy about the trials of being black in a white world. W.E.B. DuBois and James Weldon Johnson helped these young talents along, as did Harvard-educated former Rhodes Scholar Alain Locke. In 1925 Locke published *The New Negro*. It was a landmark collection of literary works by many promising young African American writers.

Claude McKay, a novelist, poet, and Jamaican immigrant, was a major figure in the movement. His verses urged African Americans to resist prejudice and discrimination. His poems also expressed the pain of life in the black ghettos and the strain of being black in a world dominated by whites. Another gifted writer of the time was Jean Toomer. His experimental book *Cane* was a mix of poems and sketches about blacks in the North and the South. It was among the first full-length literary works of the Harlem Renaissance.

Missouri-born **Langston Hughes** was the movement's best-known poet. Many of Hughes's 1920s poems described the difficult lives of working-class African Americans. Hughes gained an international reputation for his work. His poems influenced generations of African American writers.

In many of her novels, stories, poems, and books of folklore, Zora Neale Hurston portrayed the lives of poor, unschooled blacks—in her words, "the greatest cultural wealth of the continent." Much of her work celebrated what she called the common person's art form—the simple folkways and values of people who had survived slavery through their ingenuity and strength.

Harlem in the 1920s

At the turn of the century, New York's Harlem neighborhood was overbuilt with new apartment houses. Enterprising African American realtors began buying and leasing property to other African Americans who were eager to move into the prosperous neighborhood. As the number of blacks in Harlem increased, many whites began moving out. Harlem quickly grew to become the center of black America and the birthplace of the political, social, and cultural movement known as the Harlem Renaissance.

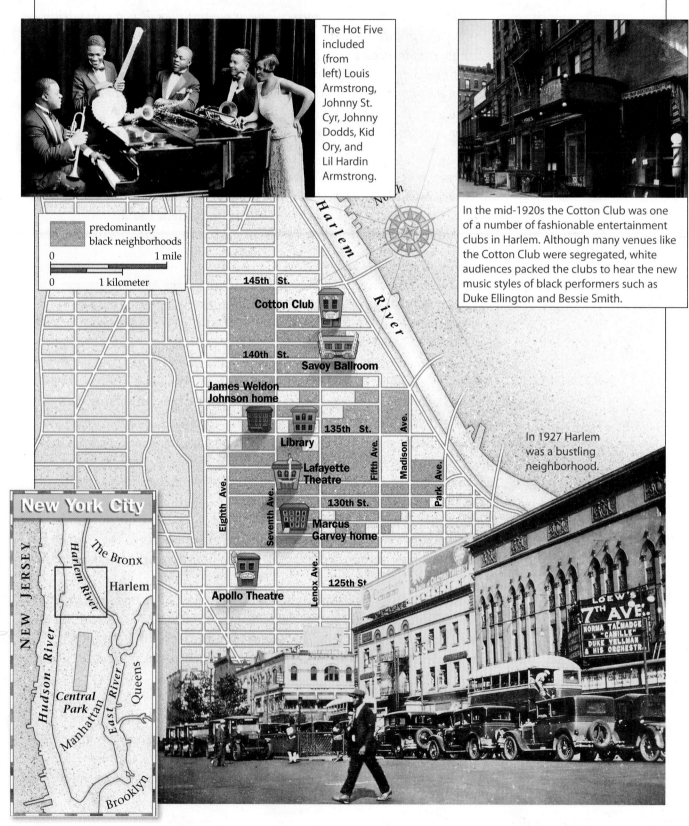

The Hot Five included (from left) Louis Armstrong, Johnny St. Cyr, Johnny Dodds, Kid Ory, and Lil Hardin Armstrong.

In the mid-1920s the Cotton Club was one of a number of fashionable entertainment clubs in Harlem. Although many venues like the Cotton Club were segregated, white audiences packed the clubs to hear the new music styles of black performers such as Duke Ellington and Bessie Smith.

predominantly black neighborhoods

0   1 mile

0   1 kilometer

North

Harlem River

145th St.

Cotton Club

140th St.

Savoy Ballroom

James Weldon Johnson home

135th St.

Fifth Ave.

Madison Ave.

Park Ave.

Library

Lafayette Theatre

130th St.

Eighth Ave.

Seventh Ave.

Marcus Garvey home

In 1927 Harlem was a bustling neighborhood.

Lenox Ave.

125th St

Apollo Theatre

New York City

NEW JERSEY

The Bronx

Harlem River

Harlem

Hudson River

East River

Central Park

Manhattan

Queens

Brooklyn

The Harlem Renaissance

A towering figure of the Harlem Renaissance, Langston Hughes often imbued his poetry with the rhythms of jazz and blues. He was a teenager when he wrote the following poem.

The Negro Speaks of Rivers

I've known rivers:
 I've known rivers ancient as the world
 and older than the flow of human blood
 in human veins.

My soul has grown deep like the rivers.

I bathed in the Euphrates when dawns were
 young.
I built my hut near the Congo and it lulled
 me to sleep.

I looked upon the Nile and raised the pyramids above it.
I heard the singing of the Mississippi when
 Abe Lincoln went down to New Orleans,
 and I've seen its muddy bosom turn all
 golden in the sunset.

I've known rivers;
Ancient, dusky rivers.

My soul has grown deep like the rivers

—Langston Hughes, "The Negro Speaks of Rivers," from *The Crisis* (1921)

Analyze American Literature
What does Hughes achieve by referring to the Euphrates, Congo, and Nile rivers?

AFRICAN AMERICAN PERFORMERS The spirit and talent of the Harlem Renaissance reached far beyond the world of African American writers and intellectuals. Some observers, including Langston Hughes, thought the movement was launched with *Shuffle Along*, a black musical comedy popular in 1921. "It gave just the proper push . . . to that Negro vogue of the '20s," he wrote. The show also spotlighted the talents of several black performers, including the singers Florence Mills, Josephine Baker, and Mabel Mercer.

During the 1920s African Americans in the performing arts won large followings. The tenor Roland Hayes rose to stardom as a concert singer. Actress and singer Ethel Waters debuted on Broadway in the musical *Africana*. **Paul Robeson**, the son of a one-time slave, became a major dramatic actor. His performance in Shakespeare's *Othello*, first in London and later in New York City, was widely acclaimed. Subsequently, Robeson struggled with the racism he experienced in the United States and the indignities inflicted upon him because of his support of the Soviet Union and the Communist Party. He took up residence abroad, living for a time in England and the Soviet Union.

AFRICAN AMERICANS AND JAZZ Jazz was born in the early 20th century in New Orleans. Musicians blended instrumental ragtime and vocal blues into an exuberant new sound. In 1918 Joe "King" Oliver and his Creole Jazz Band traveled north to Chicago, carrying jazz with them. In 1922 a young trumpet player named **Louis Armstrong** joined Oliver's group, which became known as the Creole Jazz Band. Armstrong's talent rocketed him to stardom in the jazz world.

Famous for his astounding sense of rhythm and his ability to improvise, Armstrong made personal expression a key part of jazz. After two years in Chicago, he joined Fletcher Henderson's band in 1924. At that time it was the most important big jazz band in New York City. Armstrong went on to become perhaps the most important and influential musician in the history of jazz.

Jazz quickly spread to such cities as Kansas City, Memphis, and New York City. It became the most popular music for dancing. In fact, the new musical style became so fashionable that the 1920s are often called the Jazz Age. Harlem pulsed to the sounds of jazz, which lured throngs of whites to the showy, exotic nightclubs there, including the famed Cotton Club. In the late 1920s **Edward Kennedy "Duke" Ellington**, a jazz pianist and composer, led his ten-piece orchestra at the Cotton Club. In a 1925 essay titled "The Negro Spirituals," Alain Locke seemed almost to predict the career of the talented Ellington.

> *"Up to the present, the resources of Negro music have been tentatively exploited in only one direction at a time—melodically here, rhythmically there, harmonically in a third direction. A genius that would organize its distinctive elements in a formal way would be the musical giant of his age."*
>
> —Alain Locke, quoted in *Afro-American Writing: An Anthology of Prose and Poetry*

Through the 1920s and 1930s, Ellington won renown as one of America's greatest composers. Among his most popular works were "Mood Indigo" and "Sophisticated Lady."

Cab Calloway, a talented drummer, saxophonist, and singer, formed another important jazz orchestra. It played at Harlem's Savoy Ballroom and the Cotton Club, alternating with Duke Ellington. Along with Louis Armstrong, Calloway popularized "scat," or improvised jazz singing using sounds instead of words.

Bessie Smith, a female blues singer, was probably the most outstanding vocalist of the decade. She recorded on black-oriented labels produced by

---

BIOGRAPHY

Duke Ellington (1899–1974)

Edward Kennedy "Duke" Ellington, one of the greatest composers of the 20th century, was largely a self-taught musician. He developed his skills by playing at family socials. He wrote his first song, "Soda Fountain Rag," at age 15 and started his first band at 22.

Ellington played at Harlem's glittering Cotton Club for five years. During that time he set a new standard, playing mainly his own stylish compositions. Through radio and the film short Black and Tan, the Duke Ellington Orchestra was able to reach nationwide audiences. Billy Strayhorn, Ellington's long-time arranger and collaborator, said, "Ellington plays the piano, but his real instrument is his band."

Josephine Baker found more fame abroad than in America. Born in Missouri, she made her name in Paris for her singing, dancing, and acting.

the major record companies. She achieved enormous popularity and in 1927 became the highest-paid black artist in the world. Her fame continued to the movie screen when she starred in a film based on her wildly popular song "Saint Louis Blues," composed by blues musician W. C. Handy.

Many of the jazz tunes were published as sheet music by companies on New York City's West 28th Street. The area came to be called Tin Pan Alley for the sound of conflicting tunes blasting from the street's businesses.

Some African American musical artists achieved great celebrity in Europe. The most popular was Josephine Baker, who lived in Paris and wowed French audiences with her singing, dancing, and comedy.

AFRICAN AMERICAN ARTISTS Painters and other artists also contributed their talents to the Harlem Renaissance. Sculptor Richmond Barthé's many works included a monument to Haitian hero Toussaint L'Ouverture and a portrait statue of Booker T. Washington. Aaron Douglas painted murals and illustrated books and magazines. Many of Palmer Hayden's paintings were inspired by African American folklore. James Van Der Zee used innovative techniques in his photographs of middle-class black New Yorkers. Many other names could be cited as prominent artists of the era.

ENDURING INFLUENCE The Harlem Renaissance put African Americans on the country's cultural stage. With their increased numbers in the big cities and their significant contributions to the arts, African Americans were inspired to take new pride in their achievements and importance. In addition, the Harlem Renaissance represented a portion of the great social and cultural changes that swept America in the 1920s. The period was characterized by economic prosperity, new ideas, changing values, and personal freedom, as well as important developments in the arts. Most of the social changes were lasting. The economic boom, however, was short-lived.

Reading Check
Form
Generalizations
How did writers, musicians, and artists of the Harlem Renaissance affect American culture and values?

Lesson 6 Assessment

1. **Organize Information**
   In a tree diagram, identify four areas of artistic achievement in the Harlem Renaissance. For each, name at least two outstanding African Americans.

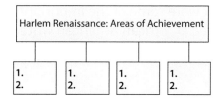

   Write a paragraph explaining the impact of these achievements.

2. **Key Terms and People**
   For each key term or person in the lesson, write a sentence explaining its significance.

3. **Analyze Causes**
   Speculate on why an African American renaissance flowered during the 1920s. Support your answer.
   Think About:
   • racial discrimination in the South
   • campaigns for equality in the North
   • Harlem's diverse cultures
   • the changing culture of all Americans

4. **Form Generalizations**
   How did popular culture in America change as a result of the Great Migration?

5. **Draw Conclusions**
   What did the Harlem Renaissance contribute to both black and general American culture?

Module 8 Assessment

Key Terms and People

For each key term or person below, write a sentence explaining its significance during the 1920s.

1. Teapot Dome scandal
2. Calvin Coolidge
3. Sacco and Vanzetti
4. quota system
5. speakeasy
6. Scopes trial
7. flapper
8. Georgia O'Keeffe
9. Marcus Garvey
10. Langston Hughes

Main Ideas

Use your notes and the information in the module to answer the following questions.

The Business of America

1. Why was Harding's promise to return America to "normalcy" popular with voters?
2. What economic ideas drove events during the Harding and Coolidge administrations?
3. How did government actions affect big business?
4. How did Henry Ford affect industry during the 1920s?
5. How did Americans' shopping habits change during the 1920s?

Postwar Issues

6. How did World War I affect the attitudes of many Americans?
7. What groups did the Ku Klux Klan target during the 1920s? How did its actions vary?
8. Describe the primary goal of the immigration quota system established in 1921.
9. What are some attacks on civil liberties that reflected a return to isolationism?
10. How did fears of various groups affect government actions?

Changing Ways of Life

11. Why was heavy funding needed to enforce the Volstead Act?
12. Explain the circumstances, outcome, and legacy of the Scopes trial. How was the Tennessee Supreme Court involved?

The Twenties Woman

13. In what ways did flappers rebel against the earlier styles and attitudes of the Victorian Age?
14. What key social, economic, educational, and technological changes of the 1920s affected women's marriages and family life?

Education and Popular Culture

15. How did high schools change in the 1920s?
16. Who were some of the popular culture heroes of the 1920s?
17. What are some 1920s fads that were part of youth culture?
18. Cite examples of the flaws of American society that some famous 1920s authors attacked in their writing.

The Harlem Renaissance

19. Where is Harlem? What distinction did it earn in the 1920s?
20. What roles did *The Crisis* and the Silent Protest play in African American history?
21. What do the growth of the NAACP and UNIA reveal about the African American experience in this period?
22. What did Marcus Garvey propose to African Americans?
23. What were some of the important themes treated by African American writers during the Harlem Renaissance?

CRITICAL THINKING

1. **Analyze Events** Create a cause-and-effect web, similar to the one shown below, in which you give several causes for the declining power of labor unions in the 1920s and give examples of the unions' decline.

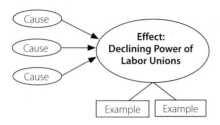

2. **Analyze Issues** Calvin Coolidge said, "After all, the chief business of the American people is business." What events and trends of the 1920s support Coolidge's statement?

3. **Compare and Contrast** Why can it be said that the Great Migration resulted in both positive and negative effects?

4. **Develop Historical Perspective** What were some ways in which the conflict between rural, traditional values and urban, modern values were expressed throughout the 1920s?

5. **Make Inferences** How might the popularity of radio during the 1920s have challenged traditional values?

6. **Evaluate** What were some of the events and trends that were a reflection of and a reaction to changes in American society of the 1920s?

7. **Predict** How do you think the Harlem Renaissance would affect American politics in the years after the 1920s?

Engage with History

Imagine that you are a young man or woman in the 1920s who has moved to New York City from a small Midwest farming town. How are your days and nights different from what they were like before? What employment and entertainment opportunities are available to you? What ideas conflict with what you learned in your rural community? What previously unknown dangers may threaten your thrilling new urban life? Are you living the "American Dream"? Write a letter to your family in which you describe not just the excitement, but also the conflicts and difficulties of your life in the big city. Conclude by saying if you want to stay or go back home, and why.

Focus on Writing

Imagine it is the 1920s. Write a persuasive letter to your member of Congress in support of or in opposition to a quota system for controlling immigration. In the first part of your letter, present the evidence that supports your position on immigration. In the second half of your letter, acknowledge the opposing viewpoint and provide a counterargument to address it.

Multimedia Activity

Use the Internet and other sources to research the impact of mass production and the widespread availability of automobiles on the American economy and society. Work with a group to produce a multimedia presentation on the topic. Incorporate video, maps, art, graphs, or similar formats into your presentation.

Henry Ford

Henry Ford was a brilliant inventor and industrialist and founder of the Ford Motor Company. He helped bring about a time of rapid growth and progress that forever changed how people worked and lived. Henry Ford grew up on his family's farm near Dearborn, Michigan. As a child, he disliked life on the farm. He found the clicks and whirs of machinery much more exciting. When Ford was 16, he went to nearby Detroit to work in a machine shop. From there, he turned his ideas for how to make affordable and well-built cars into one of the world's largest automobile companies.

Explore the amazing life and career of Henry Ford online. You can find a wealth of information, video clips, primary sources, activities, and more through your online textbook.

> "My 'gasoline buggy' was the first and for a long time the only automobile in Detroit. It was considered . . . a nuisance, for it made a racket and it scared horses."
>
> —Henry Ford

 My Life and Work
Read the document to learn more about Henry Ford's life and career in his own words.

Big Plans
Watch the video to learn more about Henry Ford's early career.

Taking the Low Road
Watch the video to explore Henry Ford's vision for his car company.

The Assembly Line
Watch the video to see how Henry Ford used the assembly line to produce cars more efficiently and cheaply.

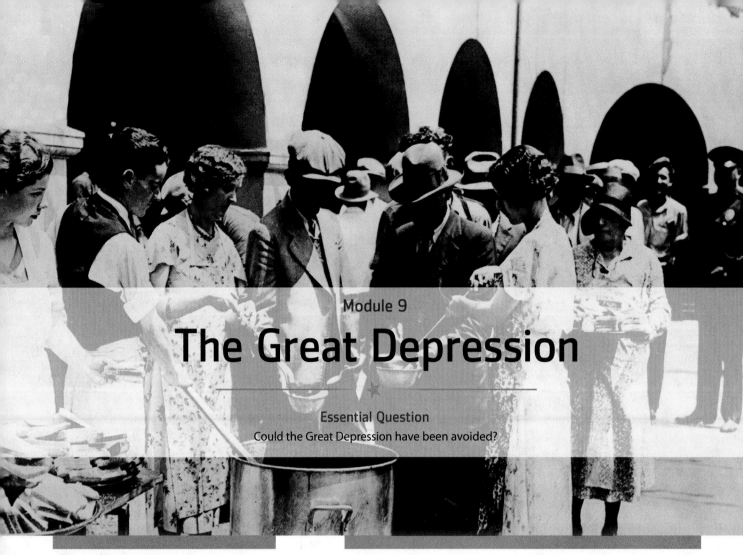

The Great Depression

Essential Question
Could the Great Depression have been avoided?

About the Photograph: This photo shows women serving soup and bread to unemployed men in an outdoor bread line. Such soup kitchens became common during the Great Depression.

 Explore ONLINE!

VIDEOS, including...
• The Depression Strikes

☑ Document-Based Investigations

☑ Graphic Organizers

☑ Interactive Games

☑ Image with Hotspots: Building Boulder Dam

☑ Difficult Decisions: Hoover and Direct Relief

In this module you will learn how weaknesses in the American economy helped bring about the Great Depression and how it affected millions of Americans.

SS.912.A.1.2 Utilize a variety of primary and secondary sources to identify author, historical significance, audience, and authenticity to understand a historical period. **SS.912.A.1.4** Analyze how images, symbols, objects, cartoons, graphs, charts, maps, and artwork may be used to interpret the significance of time periods and events from the past. **SS.912.A.5.11** Examine causes, course, and consequences of the Great Depression and the New Deal. **SS.912.A.5.12** Examine key events and people in Florida history as they relate to United States history. **SS.912.G.1.2** Use spatial perspective and appropriate geographic terms and tools, including the Six Essential Elements, as organizational schema to describe any given place. **SS.912.G.2.1** Identify the physical characteristics and the human characteristics that define and differentiate regions. **SS.912.G.4.2** Use geographic terms and tools to analyze the push/pull factors contributing to human migration within and among places. **SS.912.G.4.3** Use geographic terms and tools to analyze the effects of migration both on the place of origin and destination, including border areas. **LAFS.1112.RH.1.2** Determine the central ideas or information of a primary or secondary source; provide an accurate summary that makes clear the relationships among the key details and ideas. **LAFS.1112.RH.3.7** Integrate and evaluate multiple sources of information presented in diverse formats and media in order to address a question or solve a problem. **LAFS.1112.RH.4.10** By the end of grade 12, read and comprehend history/social studies texts in the grades 11–CCR text complexity band independently and proficiently. **MAFS.K12.MP.1.1** Make sense of problems and persevere in solving them. **MAFS.K12.MP.3.1** Construct viable arguments and critique the reasoning of others. **MAFS.K12.MP.5.1** Use appropriate tools strategically.

Timeline of Events 1928–1934

▶ *Explore ONLINE!*

United States Events		World Events

1928

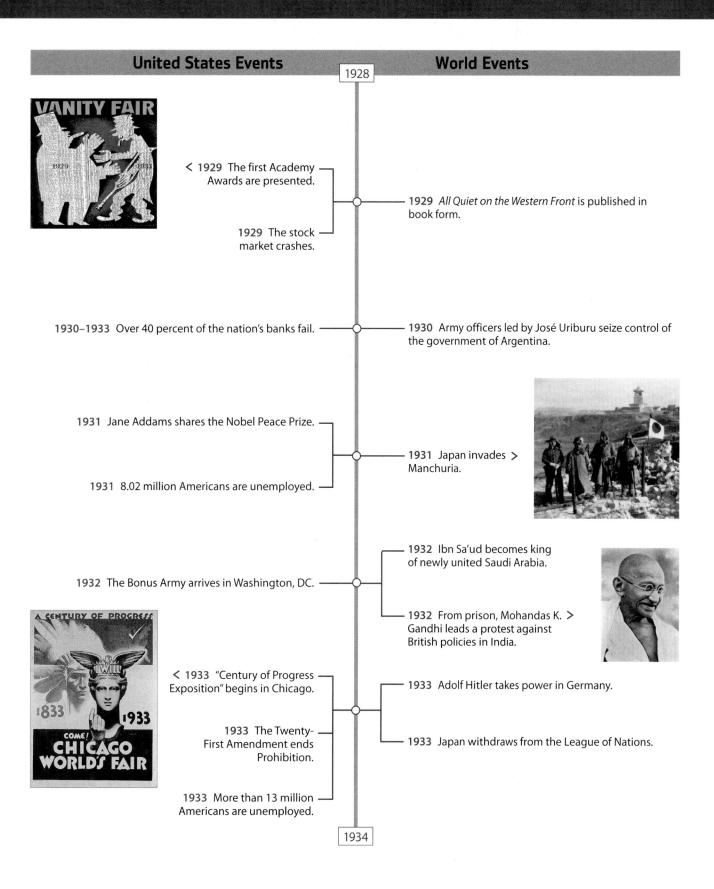

VANITY FAIR
1929 1933

< **1929** The first Academy Awards are presented.

1929 The stock market crashes.

1929 *All Quiet on the Western Front* is published in book form.

1930–1933 Over 40 percent of the nation's banks fail.

1930 Army officers led by José Uriburu seize control of the government of Argentina.

1931 Jane Addams shares the Nobel Peace Prize.

1931 8.02 million Americans are unemployed.

1931 Japan invades > Manchuria.

1932 The Bonus Army arrives in Washington, DC.

1932 Ibn Sa'ud becomes king of newly united Saudi Arabia.

1932 From prison, Mohandas K. > Gandhi leads a protest against British policies in India.

A CENTURY OF PROGRESS
1833 1933
COME!
CHICAGO WORLD'S FAIR

< **1933** "Century of Progress Exposition" begins in Chicago.

1933 The Twenty-First Amendment ends Prohibition.

1933 More than 13 million Americans are unemployed.

1933 Adolf Hitler takes power in Germany.

1933 Japan withdraws from the League of Nations.

1934

The Nation's Sick Economy

SS.912.A.1.2; SS.912.A.1.4; SS.912.A.5.11; SS.912.A.5.12; LAFS.1112.RH.3.7; MAFS.K12.MP.1.1; MAFS.K12.MP.3.1; MAFS.K12.MP.5.1

The Big Idea

As the prosperity of the 1920s ended, severe economic problems gripped the nation.

Why It Matters Now

The Great Depression has had lasting effects on how Americans view themselves and their government.

Key Terms and People

deflation

price supports

credit

Alfred E. Smith

Dow Jones Industrial Average

speculation

buying on margin

Black Tuesday

Great Depression

Hawley-Smoot Tariff Act

One American's Story

Gordon Parks, the well-known photographer, author, and filmmaker, was a 16-year-old high school student in the fall of 1929. He supported himself as a busboy at the exclusive Minnesota Club, where prosperous club members spoke confidently about the economy. Parks, too, looked forward to a bright future. Then came the stock market crash of October 1929. In his autobiography, Parks recalled his feelings at the time.

"I couldn't imagine such financial disaster touching my small world; it surely concerned only the rich. But by the first week of November . . . I was without a job. All that next week I searched for any kind of work that would prevent my leaving school. Again it was, 'We're firing, not hiring.' . . . I went to school and cleaned out my locker, knowing it was impossible to stay on. A piercing chill was in the air as I walked back to the rooming house."
—Gordon Parks, from *A Choice of Weapons*

Gordon Parks, shown here in 1968 discussing the movie version of his autobiographical novel, *The Learning Tree*

The crash of 1929, and the Depression that followed, dealt a crushing blow to the hopes and dreams of millions of Americans. The high-flying prosperity of the 1920s was over. Hard times had begun.

Economic Troubles on the Horizon

As the 1920s advanced, serious problems threatened economic prosperity. The federal government's laissez-faire economic policies played a part. During the decade, high tariffs had protected some businesses but hurt international trade and weakened European economies. Taxes on the richest Americans and on businesses had been reduced. As a result, government revenues dropped, and federal spending declined. Meanwhile, some businesses thrived, making a few people rich. But Americans with yearly incomes of more than $100,000 made up just 0.1 percent of the population. Many more Americans could not earn a decent living. Industries that had once been central to the American economy struggled. Farmers grew more crops and raised more livestock than they could sell at a profit. Both consumers and farmers were steadily going deeper into debt. As the decade ended, these slippages in the economy signaled the end of an era.

INDUSTRIES IN TROUBLE The superficial prosperity of the late 1920s masked weaknesses that would signal the onset of the Great Depression. Key basic industries, such as railroads, textiles, and steel, had barely made a profit. Railroads lost business to new forms of transportation—trucks, buses, and private automobiles, for instance. As these industries declined, they laid off workers or reduced their hours.

Mining and lumbering, which had expanded during wartime, were no longer in high demand. Coal mining was especially hard-hit, in part due to stiff competition from new forms of energy, including hydroelectric power, fuel oil, and natural gas. By the early 1930s these sources supplied more than half the energy that had once come from coal. Overproduction weakened even the boom industries of the 1920s—automobiles, construction, and consumer goods. As easy credit had allowed these businesses to expand, they had manufactured far more products than consumers could afford to buy.

One important economic indicator that declined during this time was housing starts—the number of new dwellings being built. Real estate prices were too high for too many people. When housing starts fall, so do jobs in many related industries, such as furniture manufacturing and lumbering. The situation was particularly evident in Florida, where expectations of big profits had driven real estate prices way up, but actual buyers were scarce.

FARMERS NEED A LIFT Perhaps agriculture suffered the most. During World War I, prices rose, and international demand for crops such as wheat and corn soared so the troops could be fed. Farmers had planted more and taken out loans for land and equipment. However, demand fell after the war, and crop prices declined by 40 percent or more. **Deflation**, or a decrease in the general price level of goods and services, took hold.

Farmers boosted production in the hopes of selling more crops, but this only dropped prices further. Between 1919 and 1921 annual farm income declined from $10 billion to just over $4 billion. Farmers who had gone into debt had difficulty paying off their loans. Many lost their farms when banks

Farm equipment is auctioned off in Hastings, Nebraska.

foreclosed and seized the property as payment for the debt. As farmers began to default on their loans, many rural banks began to fail. Auctions were held to recoup some of the banks' losses.

Congress tried to help out farmers with a piece of legislation called the McNary-Haugen bill. This called for federal **price supports** for key products such as wheat, corn, cotton, and tobacco. The government would buy surplus crops at guaranteed prices and sell them on the world market.

President Coolidge vetoed the bill twice. He commented, "Farmers have never made money. I don't believe we can do much about it."

CONSUMERS HAVE LESS MONEY TO SPEND As farmers' incomes fell, they bought fewer goods and services, but the problem was larger. By the late 1920s Americans were buying less—mainly because of rising prices, stagnant wages, unbalanced distribution of income, and overbuying on credit in the preceding years. Production had also expanded much faster than wages, resulting in an ever-widening gap between the rich and the poor.

LIVING ON CREDIT Although many Americans appeared to be prosperous during the 1920s, they were, in fact, living beyond their means. They often bought goods on **credit**—an arrangement in which consumers agreed to buy now and pay later for purchases. This was often in the form of an installment plan (usually in monthly payments) that included interest charges.

By making credit easily available, businesses encouraged Americans to pile up a large consumer debt. Many people then had trouble paying off what they owed on their purchases. Faced with debt, consumers cut back on spending.

UNEVEN DISTRIBUTION OF INCOME During the 1920s the rich got richer and the poor got poorer. Between 1920 and 1929, the income of the wealthiest 1 percent of the population rose by 75 percent, compared with a 9 percent increase for Americans as a whole.

More than 70 percent of the nation's families earned less than $2,500 per year, then considered the minimum amount needed for a decent standard of living. Even families earning twice that much could not afford many of the household items that manufacturers produced. Economists estimate that the average man or woman bought a new outfit of clothes only once a year. Scarcely half the homes in many cities had electric lights or a furnace for heat. Only one city home in ten had an electric refrigerator.

This unequal distribution of income meant that most Americans could not participate fully in the economic advances of the 1920s. Many people did not have the money to purchase the flood of goods that factories produced. The prosperity of the era rested on a fragile foundation.

Hoover Takes the Nation

Although economic disaster was around the corner, the election of 1928 took place in a mood of apparent national prosperity. This election pitted Republican candidate Herbert Hoover against Democrat **Alfred E. Smith**.

THE ELECTION OF 1928 Hoover, the secretary of commerce under Harding and Coolidge, was a mining engineer from Iowa who had never run for public office. Smith was a career politician who had served four terms as governor of New York. He was personable and enjoyed being in the limelight, unlike the quiet and reserved Hoover. Still, Hoover had one major advantage: he could point to years of prosperity under Republicans since 1920. In a famous campaign address, often called the "rugged individualism" speech, Hoover praised the postwar American spirit, comparing it to European systems.

> *"We were challenged with a peace-time choice between the American system of rugged individualism and a European philosophy of diametrically opposed doctrines—doctrines of paternalism and state socialism. The acceptance of these ideas would have meant the destruction of self-government through centralization of government. It would have meant the undermining of the individual initiative and enterprise through which our people have grown to unparalleled greatness."*
> —Herbert Hoover, from a campaign speech, October 22, 1928

For Hoover, the American system of government was the opposite of the governments in Europe. He believed that a focus on individual achievement—instead of a central government that controlled most aspects of the economy—made the United States great. According to Hoover, to shift away from this focus would destroy the nation. This confidence in the American spirit helped many believe him when he declared, "We in America are nearer to the final triumph over poverty than ever before."

It was an overwhelming victory for Hoover. The message was clear: most Americans were happy with Republican leadership.

Vocabulary
stock a share of
ownership in a
company

DREAMS OF RICHES IN THE STOCK MARKET By 1929 some economists had warned of weaknesses in the economy, but most Americans maintained the utmost confidence in the nation's economic health. In increaing numbers, those who could afford to invested in the stock market. The stock market had become the most visible symbol of a prosperous American economy. Then, as now, the **Dow Jones Industrial Average** was the most widely used barometer of the stock market's health. The Dow is a measure based on the stock prices of 30 representative large firms trading on the New York Stock Exchange.

Through most of the 1920s, stock prices rose steadily. The Dow had reached a high of 381 points, nearly 300 points higher than it had been five years earlier. Eager to take advantage of this "bull market"—a period of rising stock prices—Americans rushed to buy stocks and bonds. One observer wrote, "It seemed as if all economic law had been suspended and a new era opened up in which success and prosperity could be had without knowledge or industry." By 1929 about 4 million Americans—or 3 percent of the nation's population—owned stocks. Many of these investors were already wealthy, but others were average Americans who hoped to strike it rich.

NOW & THEN

New York Stock Exchange

In the 21st century, the New York Stock Exchange (NYSE) remains at its core what it has been since it opened its doors in 1792: the nation's premier marketplace for the buying and selling of stocks. The NYSE has undergone significant changes, however.

In the 1920s orders to buy or sell a stock arrived at brokers' telephone booths located around the edge of the trading floor. They were then carried or sent by pneumatic tube to where that stock would be traded. All trades were done by hand.

With the introduction of computer technology, the activities of the exchange are less and less centered on human interaction. A trade can now be completed electronically within milliseconds.

This capability has prompted some to insist that all future trading will be done via computers, thus eliminating the need for physical exchanges such as the New York Stock Exchange. On the other hand, some analysts see hazards in removing the human element from stock trades. Those critics cite the possibility that trade decisions can be made so quickly that mistakes cannot be controlled. Such mistakes could have devastating consequences.

The NYSE trading floor in 1914

The NYSE trading floor in 2000

However, the seeds of trouble were taking root. People were engaging in **speculation**—that is, they bought stocks and bonds on the chance of a quick profit, while ignoring the risks. Many began **buying on margin**—paying a small percentage of a stock's price as a down payment and borrowing the rest. With easy money available to investors, the unrestrained buying and selling fueled the market's upward spiral. The government did little to discourage such buying or to regulate the market. In reality, these rising prices did not reflect companies' worth. Worse, if the value of stocks declined, people who had bought on margin had no way to pay off the loans.

The trend of buying on margin troubled the governing board of the Federal Reserve System, known as the Fed. The Fed had been created in 1913 to serve as the nation's central bank, a role it continues to fill. The Fed sets monetary policy to promote economic growth. In the late 1920s the Fed decided to make it harder for brokers to offer margin loans to investors. Their strategy was partly successful, at least at first. Borrowing from banks decreased, but large corporations began providing brokers with the cash to make margin loans. As a result, the run-up of the stock market continued despite the Fed's shift in monetary policy.

Reading Check
Analyze Events
How did speculation and buying on margin cause stock prices to rise?

The Stock Market Crashes

In early September 1929 stock prices peaked and then fell. Confidence in the market started to waver, and some investors quickly sold their stocks and pulled out. On October 24 the market took a plunge. Panicked investors unloaded their shares. But the worst was yet to come.

On October 29—now known as **Black Tuesday**—the bottom fell out of the market and the nation's confidence. Shareholders frantically tried to sell before prices dropped even lower. The number of shares dumped onto the market that day was a record 16.4 million. Additional millions of shares could not find buyers. People who had bought stocks on credit were stuck with huge debts as the prices plummeted, while others lost most of their savings. By mid-November, investors had lost about $30 billion, an amount equal to how much America spent in World War I. The stock market bubble had finally burst. One eyewitness to these shocking events described the resulting situation.

"The Big Bull Market was dead. Billions of dollars' worth of profits—and paper profits—had disappeared. The grocer, the window cleaner, and the seamstress had lost their capital [savings]. In every town there were families which had suddenly dropped from showy affluence into debt. . . . With the Big Bull Market gone and prosperity going, Americans were soon to find themselves living in an altered world which called for new adjustments, new ideas, new habits of thought, and a new order of values."

—Frederick Lewis Allen, from *Only Yesterday*

Reading Check
Analyze Effects
How did Black Tuesday affect rich and middle-class investors?

Day of Wrath

After the apparent prosperity of the 1920s, few Americans were prepared for the devastating effects of the stock market crash. This cartoon by James N. Rosenberg, which shows Wall Street crumbling on October 29, 1929, is titled *Dies Irae*, Latin for "day of wrath." "Dies Irae" is also the title of a sequence in the Roman Catholic *Mass for the Dead* that describes the final judgment at the end of the world.

Analyze Historical Sources
Why do you think the cartoonist used the title *Dies Irae*?

Financial Collapse

The stock market crash signaled the beginning of the **Great Depression**— the period from 1929 through the 1930s in which the economy plummeted and unemployment skyrocketed. The crash alone did not cause the Great Depression, but it hastened the collapse of the economy and made the Depression more severe.

BANK AND BUSINESS FAILURES After the crash, many people panicked and withdrew their money from banks. But some couldn't get their money because the banks had no money, either. They had invested the cash in the stock market. In 1929, 600 banks closed. By 1933, 11,000 of the nation's 25,000 banks had failed. Because the government did not protect or insure bank accounts, millions of people lost their savings. The Federal Reserve System might have supplied more money to banks, but rules linking currency to gold reserves hampered those efforts. On the other hand, some Fed officials saw bank failures in a positive light—as a good way to get rid of bad managers.

The Great Depression hit other businesses along with banks. Between 1929 and 1932, the gross national product—the nation's total output of goods and services—was cut nearly in half, from $104 billion to $59 billion. Approximately 90,000 businesses went bankrupt. Among these failed enterprises were once-prosperous automobile and railroad companies.

The stock market crash affected business in another way, too. Prior to the crash, businesses had attracted a large amount of capital for investment in new machinery, new markets, and other ventures. With the crash, Americans lost confidence in business, and business, in turn, lost confidence in consumers. Businesses sharply reduced their investments, which cascaded into reducing their workforces.

Depression Indicators

Economic indicators are measures that signal trends in a nation's economy. During the Great Depression, several trends were apparent. Those indicated at the right are linked—the conditions of one can affect another. For instance, when banks fail **1**, some businesses may have to close down **2**, which can cause unemployment to rise **3**. Thus, people have less money and spending declines **4**.

1 Bank Failures

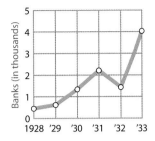

2 Business Failures

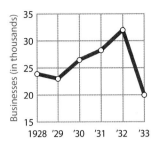

3 Unemployment

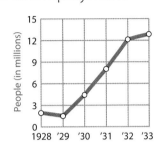

4 Income and Spending

Source: Historical Statistics of the United States

Interpret Graphs

1. In what year did the biggest jump in bank failures occur?

2. What measure on the graphs seems to indicate an improvement in the U.S. economy during the Depression? What might explain this?

This British election poster shows that the Great Depression was a global event.

As the economy plunged into a tailspin, millions of workers lost their jobs. Unemployment jumped from 3 percent (1.6 million workers) in 1929 to 25 percent (13 million workers) in 1933. One out of every four workers was out of a job. Those who kept their jobs faced pay cuts and reduced hours.

Not everyone fared so badly, of course. Before the crash, some speculators had sold off their stocks and made money. Joseph P. Kennedy, the father of future president John F. Kennedy, was one who did. Most, however, were not so lucky or shrewd.

WORLDWIDE SHOCK WAVES Due to a growth in international trade, many of the world's nations had become interdependent. However, when the U.S. economy failed, American investors withdrew their money from European markets. As a result, the United States was not the only country gripped by the Great Depression. Much of Europe, for example, had suffered throughout the 1920s. European countries trying to recover from the ravages of World War I faced high war debts, so their economies were already unstable. In addition, Germany had to pay war reparations—payments to compensate the Allies for the damages Germany had caused. The Great Depression compounded these problems by limiting America's ability to import European goods. This made it difficult to sell American farm products and manufactured goods abroad.

Eventually, countries all around the world were affected by the financial collapse as unemployment rates soared and prices plummeted. In Europe, Austria's largest bank failed. In Asia, both farmers and urban workers suffered as the value of exports fell by half between 1929 and 1931. In Latin America, a decrease in U.S. and European demand for their products—such as sugar, beef, and copper—caused prices to fall.

In 1930 Congress passed the **Hawley-Smoot Tariff Act**, which established the highest protective tariff in U.S. history. It was designed to protect American farmers and manufacturers from foreign competition. Yet it had the opposite effect. By reducing the flow of goods into the United States, the tariff prevented other countries from earning American currency to buy American goods. The tariff made unemployment worse in industries that could no longer export goods to Europe. Many countries retaliated by raising their own tariffs. Within a few years, world trade had fallen more than 40 percent.

CAUSES OF THE GREAT DEPRESSION Although historians and economists emphasize different causes of the Great Depression, most cite a common set of factors, among them:

- tariffs and war debt policies that reduced the foreign market for American goods
- a crisis in the farm sector
- the availability of easy credit
- an unequal distribution of income

These factors led to falling demand for consumer goods, even as newly mechanized factories produced more products. The federal government contributed to the crisis by keeping interest rates low, thereby allowing companies and individuals to borrow easily and build up large debts. Some of this borrowed money was used to buy the stocks that later led to the crash.

At first people found it hard to believe that economic disaster had struck. In November 1929 President Hoover encouraged Americans to remain confident about the economy. Yet, the most severe depression in American history was well on its way.

Reading Check
Summarize
How did the Great Depression affect the world economy?

Lesson 1 Assessment

1. **Organize Information** Use a web diagram to list the causes of the stock market crash. Add more causes to the diagram as necessary.

Which do you see as the most significant cause? Why?

2. **Key Terms and People** For each key term or person in the lesson, write a sentence explaining its significance.

3. **Make Inferences** How did the economic trends of the 1920s help cause the Great Depression?
   Think About:
   - what happened in industry
   - what happened in agriculture
   - what happened with consumers
   - what happened in real estate

4. **Draw Conclusions** Judging from the events of the late 1920s and early 1930s, what role do you think public confidence plays in the health of the economy? Explain.

Hardship and Suffering

The Big Idea

During the Great Depression, Americans did what they had to do to survive.

Why It Matters Now

Since the Great Depression, many Americans have been more cautious about saving, investing, and borrowing.

Key Terms and People

shantytown

soup kitchen

bread line

Dust Bowl

direct relief

One American's Story

Ann Marie Low lived on her parents' North Dakota farm when the stock market crashed and the Great Depression hit. Hard times were familiar to Ann's family. But the worst was yet to come.

In the early 1930s a ravenous drought hit the Great Plains, destroying crops and leaving the earth dry and cracked. Then came the deadly dust storms. On April 25, 1934, Ann wrote an account in her diary.

"[T]he air is just full of dirt coming, literally, for hundreds of miles. It sifts into everything. After we wash the dishes and put them away, so much dust sifts into the cupboards we must wash them again before the next meal. . . . Newspapers say the deaths of many babies and old people are attributed to breathing in so much dirt."
—Ann Marie Low, from *Dust Bowl Diary*

Ann Marie Low

The drought and winds lasted for more than seven years. The dust storms in Kansas, Colorado, New Mexico, Nebraska, the Dakotas, Oklahoma, and Texas were a great hardship—but only one of many—that Americans faced during the Great Depression.

SS.912.A.1.4; SS.912.A.5.11; SS.912.G.1.2; SS.912.G.2.1; SS.912.G.4.2; SS.912.G.4.3; LAFS.1112.RH.4.10

The Depression Devastates People's Lives

Statistics such as the unemployment rate tell only part of the story of the Great Depression. More important was the impact that it had on people's lives: the Depression brought hardship, homelessness, and hunger to millions.

THE DEPRESSION IN THE CITIES In cities across the country, people lost their jobs, were evicted from their homes, and ended up in the streets. Some slept in parks or sewer pipes, wrapping themselves in newspapers to fend off the cold.

Others built makeshift shacks out of scrap materials. Before long, numerous **shantytowns**—little towns consisting of shacks—sprang up. An observer recalled one such settlement in Oklahoma City: "Here were all these people living in old, rusted-out car bodies. . . . There were people living in shacks made of orange crates. One family with a whole lot of kids were living in a piano box. . . . People were living in whatever they could junk together." Hundreds of such settlements dotted the country. They were the only shelter available to hundreds of thousands of people who had lost their homes. Many Americans called these shantytowns "Hoovervilles," since they blamed President Hoover for the Depression.

Every day, the poor dug through garbage cans or begged. **Soup kitchens** offering free or low-cost food and **bread lines**, or lines of people waiting to receive food provided by charitable organizations or public agencies, became a common sight. Herman Shumlin, a Broadway theatrical producer, described the men he saw around him in New York City.

Background
Relief programs largely discriminated against African Americans. However, some black organizations, like the National Urban League, were able to give private help.

Unemployed people built shacks in a shantytown in New York City in 1932.

"Two or three blocks along Times Square, you'd see these men, silent, shuffling along in a line. Getting this handout of coffee and doughnuts, dealt out from great trucks. . . . I'd see that flat, opaque, expressionless look which spelled, for me, human disaster. Men . . . who had responsible positions. Who had lost their jobs, lost their homes, lost their families . . . They were destroyed men."

—Herman Shumlin, quoted in *Hard Times*

Conditions for African Americans and Latinos were especially difficult. Their unemployment rates were higher, and they were the lowest paid. They also dealt with increasing racial violence from unemployed whites. Twenty-four African Americans were lynched in 1933.

An African American View of the Great Depression

Although the suffering of the 1930s was severe for many people, it was especially grim for African Americans. Hard times were already a fact of life for many of them, as one African American man noted:

> *"The Negro was born in depression. It didn't mean too much to him, The Great American Depression. . . . The best he could be is a janitor or a porter or shoeshine boy. It only became official when it hit the white man."*

Nonetheless, the African American community was very hard hit by the Great Depression. In 1932 the unemployment rate among African Americans stood at over 50 percent, while the overall unemployment rate was approximately 25 percent.

Background
The most severe storms were called "black blizzards." They were said to have darkened the sky in New York City and Washington, DC.

Latinos—mainly Mexicans and Mexican Americans living in the Southwest—were also targets. Whites demanded that Latinos be deported, or expelled from the country, even though many had been born in America. By the late 1930s hundreds of thousands of people of Mexican descent relocated to Mexico. Some of them left voluntarily; others the federal government deported.

THE DEPRESSION IN RURAL AREAS Life in rural areas was hard, but it did have one advantage over city life: most farmers could grow food for their families. With falling prices and rising debt, though, thousands of farmers lost their land. Between 1929 and 1932, about 400,000 farms were lost through foreclosure—the process by which a mortgage holder takes back property if an occupant has not made payments. Many farmers turned to tenant farming and barely scraped out a living.

THE DUST BOWL Drought that began in the early 1930s wreaked havoc on the Great Plains. It was a disaster that developed gradually. Several years of good rain and mild winters had lulled farmers into thinking the land was suitable for intensive agriculture. They were soon proved wrong. During the 1920s farmers from Texas to North Dakota had used newly affordable tractors to break up the grasslands and plant millions of acres of new farmland. Deep plowing had removed the thick protective layer of prairie grasses. Farmers had then exhausted the land through overproduction of crops, and the grasslands became unsuitable for farming. When the rains stopped and winds began to blow in the early 1930s, little grass and few trees were left to hold down the soil. Wind scattered the topsoil, exposing sand and grit underneath. The dust traveled hundreds of miles. One windstorm in 1934 picked up millions of tons of dust from the plains and carried it to East Coast cities.

A farmer and his sons brave a dust storm in 1936.

The Dust Bowl, 1933–1936

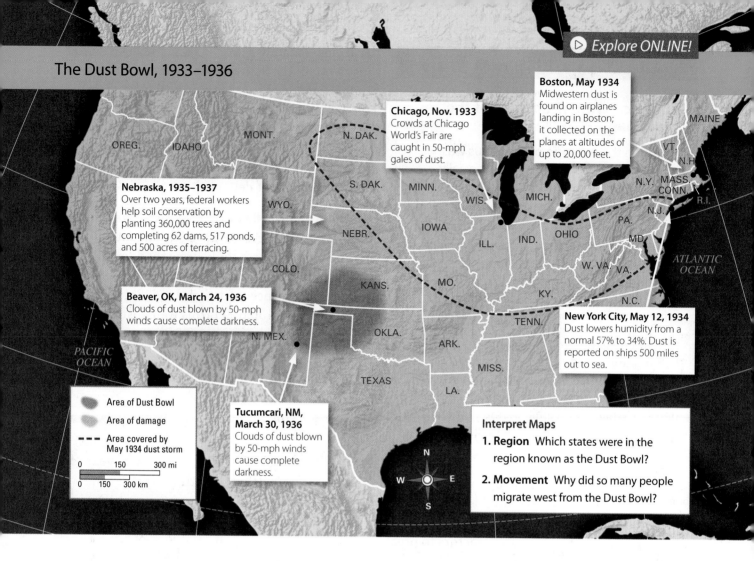

Explore ONLINE!

Boston, May 1934
Midwestern dust is found on airplanes landing in Boston; it collected on the planes at altitudes of up to 20,000 feet.

Chicago, Nov. 1933
Crowds at Chicago World's Fair are caught in 50-mph gales of dust.

Nebraska, 1935–1937
Over two years, federal workers help soil conservation by planting 360,000 trees and completing 62 dams, 517 ponds, and 500 acres of terracing.

Beaver, OK, March 24, 1936
Clouds of dust blown by 50-mph winds cause complete darkness.

New York City, May 12, 1934
Dust lowers humidity from a normal 57% to 34%. Dust is reported on ships 500 miles out to sea.

Tucumcari, NM, March 30, 1936
Clouds of dust blown by 50-mph winds cause complete darkness.

Area of Dust Bowl
Area of damage
- - - Area covered by May 1934 dust storm

0   150   300 mi
0   150   300 km

Interpret Maps
1. **Region** Which states were in the region known as the Dust Bowl?
2. **Movement** Why did so many people migrate west from the Dust Bowl?

The region that was the hardest hit, including parts of Kansas, Oklahoma, Texas, New Mexico, and Colorado, came to be known as the **Dust Bowl**. Plagued by dust storms and evictions, farmers had to decide whether to continue cultivating unproductive land or give up and move on. Thousands of farmers and sharecroppers decided to leave their land behind. They packed up their families and few belongings and headed west, following Route 66 to California, where they thought they would find jobs. Some of these migrants—known as Okies (a term that originally referred to Oklahomans but came to be used negatively for all migrants)—found work as farmhands. But others continued to wander in search of work. By the end of the 1930s, hundreds of thousands of farm families had migrated to California and other Pacific coast states.

Effects on the American Family

In the face of the suffering the Great Depression caused, the family stood as a source of strength for most Americans. Although some people feared that hard times would undermine moral values, those concerns were largely unfounded. In general, Americans believed in traditional values and emphasized the importance of family unity. At a time when money was tight, many

Reading Check
Summarize How did the Depression affect city dwellers, farmers, and minorities?

families entertained themselves by staying at home and playing board games, such as Monopoly®, which was invented in 1933, and listening to the radio. Nevertheless, the economic difficulties of the Great Depression put severe pressure on family life. Making ends meet was a daily struggle, and, in some cases, families broke apart under the strain.

MEN IN THE STREETS Failed industries meant unemployment for countless men. Many of them had difficulty coping with unemployment because they were accustomed to working and supporting their families. Every day, they would set out to walk the streets in search of jobs. As Frederick Lewis Allen noted in *Since Yesterday,* "Men who have been sturdy and self-respecting workers can take unemployment without flinching for a few weeks, a few months, even if they have to see their families suffer; but it is different after a year . . . two years . . . three years." Some men became so discouraged that they simply stopped trying. Some even abandoned their families.

Having left their families behind, some men hit the road. As many as 300,000 transients—or "hoboes" as they were called—wandered the country, hitching rides on railroad boxcars and sleeping under bridges. Over time these hoboes developed a hidden language to help them survive. They would mark houses or fences near railroad yards with symbols that revealed where they could get food, water, or a place to sleep. Some hoboes would occasionally turn up at homeless shelters in big cities.

During the early years of the Great Depression, there was no federal system of **direct relief**—cash payments or food the government provides to the poor. Some cities and charity services did offer help to those who needed it, but the benefits were meager. In New York City, for example, the weekly payment was just $2.39 per family. This was the most generous relief any city offered, but it was still well below the amount needed to feed a family.

WOMEN STRUGGLE TO SURVIVE Women worked hard to help their families survive adversity during the Great Depression. Many canned food and sewed clothes. They also carefully managed household budgets. Jeane Westin,

---

Document-Based Investigation Historical Source

The Hoboes
Novelist Thomas Wolfe described a group of hoboes in New York City.

Analyze Historical Sources
1. Why do you think the men that Wolfe described were so stunned by their poverty?

2. How might the despair of these men have affected those who witnessed their misery?

"*These were the wanderers from town to town, the riders of freight trains, the thumbers of rides on highways, the uprooted, unwanted male population of America. They . . . gathered in the big cities when winter came, hungry, defeated, empty, hopeless, restless . . . always on the move, looking everywhere for work, for the bare crumbs to support their miserable lives, and finding neither work nor crumbs.*"
—Thomas Wolfe, from *You Can't Go Home Again*

the author of Making Do: *How Women Survived the '30s*, recalled, "Those days you did everything to save a penny. . . . My next door neighbor and I used to shop together. You could get two pounds of hamburger for a quarter, so we'd buy two pounds and split it—then one week she'd pay the extra penny and the next week I'd pay."

Artist Ben Shahn photographed this Ozark sharecropper family in Arkansas during the 1930s.

Many women also worked outside the home, though they usually received less money than men did. As the Depression wore on, however, working women became the targets of enormous resentment. Many people believed that women, especially married women, had no right to work when there were men who were unemployed. In the early 1930s some cities refused to hire married women as schoolteachers.

Many Americans assumed that women were having an easier time than men during the Great Depression because few were seen begging or standing in bread lines. As a matter of fact, many women were starving to death in cold attics and rooming houses. As one writer pointed out, women were often too ashamed to reveal their hardship.

"I've lived in cities for many months, broke, without help, too timid to get in bread lines. I've known many women to live like this until they simply faint in the street. . . . A woman will shut herself up in a room until it is taken away from her, and eat a cracker a day and be as quiet as a mouse. . . . [She] will go for weeks verging on starvation, . . . going through the streets ashamed, sitting in libraries, parks, going for days without speaking to a living soul, shut up in the terror of her own misery."

—Meridel Le Seuer, from *America in the Twenties*

Background
Rickets is caused by a vitamin D deficiency and results in defective bone growth.

CHILDREN SUFFER HARDSHIPS Children also suffered during the 1930s. Poor diets and a lack of money for health care led to serious health problems. Milk consumption declined across the country, and clinics and hospitals reported a dramatic rise in malnutrition and diet-related diseases, such as rickets. At the same time, child-welfare programs were slashed as cities and states cut their budgets in the face of dwindling resources.

Falling tax revenues also caused school boards to shorten the school year and even close schools. By 1933 some 2,600 schools across the nation had shut down, leaving more than 300,000 students out of school. Thousands of children went to work instead; they often labored in crowded sweatshops under horrendous conditions.

Two young boys, ages 15 and 16, walk beside freight cars in the San Joaquin Valley.

Many teenagers looked for a way out of the suffering or to ease the pressure on their families. Eugene Williams, age 13, was one of the desperate teens. He said "If I leave my mother, it will mean one less mouth to feed." Eugene may have been one of the hundreds of thousands of teenage boys, and some girls, who hopped aboard America's freight trains to zigzag the country in search of work, adventure, and an escape from poverty. These "wild boys" came from every section of the United States, from every corner of society. They were the sons of poor farmers, out-of-work miners, and wealthy parents who had lost everything. "Hoover tourists," as they were called, were eager to tour America for free.

From the age of 11 until 17, George Phillips rode the rails, first catching local freights out of his hometown of Princeton, Missouri. "There is no feeling in the world like sitting in a side-door Pullman and watching the world go by, listening to the clickety-clack of the wheels, hearing that old steam whistle blowing for crossings and towns." While exciting, the road could also be deadly. Many riders were beaten or jailed by "bulls"—armed freight yard patrolmen. Often riders had to sleep standing up in a constant deafening rumble. Some were accidentally locked in ice cars for days on end. Others fell prey to murderous criminals. From 1929 to 1939, 24,647 trespassers were killed and 27,171 injured on railroad property.

SOCIAL AND PSYCHOLOGICAL EFFECTS The hardships of the Great Depression had a tremendous social and psychological impact. Some people were so demoralized by hard times that they lost their will to survive. Between 1928 and 1932, the suicide rate rose more than 30 percent. Three times as many people were admitted to state mental hospitals as in normal times.

The economic problems forced many Americans to accept compromises and make sacrifices that affected them for the rest of their lives. Adults

The label that someone wrote on this photo of jobless men seems to describe both their emotional state and the events that brought on their despair.

stopped going to the doctor or dentist because they couldn't afford it. Young people gave up their dreams of going to college. Others put off getting married, raising large families, or having children at all.

For many people, the stigma of poverty and of having to scrimp and save never disappeared completely. For some, achieving financial security became the primary focus in life. As one woman recalled, "Ever since I was twelve years old there was one major goal in my life . . . one thing . . . and that was to never be poor again."

During the Great Depression, many people showed great kindness to strangers who were down on their luck. People often gave food, clothing, and a place to stay to the needy. Families helped other families and shared resources and strengthened the bonds within their communities. In addition, many people developed habits of saving and thriftiness—habits they would need to see themselves through the dark days ahead as the nation and President Hoover struggled with the Great Depression. These habits shaped a whole generation of Americans.

Vocabulary
stigma a mark or indication of disgrace

Reading Check
Analyze Effects
How did the Great Depression affect men, women, and children?

Lesson 2 Assessment

1. **Organize Information** In a Venn diagram, list the effects that the Great Depression had on farmers and city dwellers. Find the differences and the similarities.

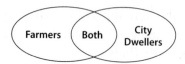

Which group do you think suffered less?

2. **Key Terms and People** For each key term in the lesson, write a sentence explaining its significance.

3. **Contrast** How was what happened to men during the Great Depression different from what happened to women? to children?

   Think About:
   • each group's role in their families
   • the changes each group had to make
   • what help was available to them

4. **Analyze Effects** How did Dust Bowl conditions in the Great Plains affect the entire country?

5. **Draw Conclusions** In what ways did the Great Depression affect people's outlook?

★
Hoover's Failed Policies

The Big Idea

President Hoover's conservative response to the Great Depression drew criticism from many Americans.

Why It Matters Now

Worsening conditions in the country caused the government to become more involved in the health and economic security of the people.

Key Terms and People

Herbert Hoover

Boulder Dam

Federal Home Loan Bank Act

Reconstruction Finance Corporation

Bonus Army

One American's Story

Oscar Ameringer was a newspaper editor in Oklahoma City during the Great Depression. In 1932 he traveled around the country collecting information on economic and social conditions. Testifying in unemployment hearings that same year, Ameringer described desperate people who were losing patience with the government. "Unless something is done for them and done soon you will have a revolution on hand." Ameringer told the following story.

A Depression-era family from Arkansas walks through Texas, looking for work in the cotton fields along the Rio Grande.

"The roads of the West and Southwest teem with hungry hitchhikers. . . . Between Clarksville and Russellville, Ark., I picked up a family. The woman was hugging a dead chicken under a ragged coat. When I asked her where she had procured the fowl, first she told me she had found it dead in the road, and then added in grim humor, 'They promised me a chicken in the pot, and now I got mine.'"

—Oscar Ameringer, quoted in *The American Spirit*

The woman was recalling President Hoover's empty 1928 campaign pledge: "A chicken in every pot and a car in every garage." Now many Americans were disillusioned. They demanded that the government help them.

SS.912.A.1.4; SS.912.A.5.11; LAFS.1112.RH.1.2; MAFS.K12.MP.3.1

Hoover Tries to Reassure the Nation

After the stock market crash of October 1929, President **Herbert Hoover** tried to reassure Americans that the nation's economy was on a sound footing. "Any lack of confidence in the economic future . . . is foolish," he declared. In his view, the important thing was for Americans to remain optimistic and to go about their business as usual. Most Americans believed depressions were a normal part of the business cycle. According to this theory, periods of rapid economic growth were naturally followed by periods of depression. The best course in a slump, many experts believed, was to do nothing and let the economy fix itself. Hoover took a slightly different position. He felt that government could play a limited role in helping to solve problems.

HOOVER'S PHILOSOPHY Herbert Hoover had been an engineer, and he put great faith in the power of reason. He was also a humanitarian, as he made clear in one of his last speeches as president.

> *"Our first objective must be to provide security from poverty and want. . . . We want to see a nation built of home owners and farm owners. We want to see their savings protected. We want to see them in steady jobs. We want to see more and more of them insured against death and accident, unemployment and old age. We want them all secure."*
>
> —Herbert Hoover, from "Challenge to Liberty," October 1936

Like many Americans of the time, Hoover believed that one of government's chief functions was to foster cooperation between competing groups and interests in society. If business and labor were in a conflict, for example, government should step in and help them find a solution that served their mutual interests. This cooperation must be voluntary rather than forced, he said. Hoover felt government's role was to encourage and facilitate cooperation, not to control it.

On the other hand, Americans also valued the "rugged individualism" that Hoover had praised during his campaign in 1928—the idea that people should succeed through their own efforts. They should take care of themselves and their families, rather than depend on the government to bail them out. Thus, Hoover opposed any form of federal welfare, or direct relief to the needy. He believed that handouts would weaken people's self-respect and "moral fiber." His answer to the needy was that individuals, charities, and local organizations should pitch in to help care for the less fortunate. The federal government should direct relief measures, but not through a vast federal bureaucracy. Such a bureaucracy, he said, would be too expensive and would stifle individual liberties.

However, when the Great Depression took hold, moral fiber wasn't what people were worried about. Hoover's response shocked and frustrated suffering Americans.

Herbert Hoover (1874–1964)

Born to a Quaker family in Iowa, Herbert Hoover was orphaned at an early age. His life was a rags-to-riches story. He worked his way through Stanford University and later made a fortune as a mining engineer and consultant in China, Australia, Europe, and Africa. During and after World War I, he coordinated U.S. relief efforts in Europe, earning a reputation for efficiency and humanitarian ideals.

As president, Hoover asserted, "Every time we find solutions outside of government, we have not only strengthened character, but we have preserved our sense of real government."

HOOVER TAKES CAUTIOUS STEPS Hoover's political philosophy caused him to take a cautious approach to the Depression. Soon after the stock market crash, he called together key business, banking, and labor leaders. He urged them to work together to find solutions to the nation's economic woes and to act in ways that would not make a bad situation worse. For example, he asked employers not to cut wages or lay off workers, and he asked labor leaders not to demand higher wages or go on strike. He also created a special organization to help private charities generate contributions for the poor.

None of these steps made much of a difference. A year after the crash, the economy was still shrinking, and unemployment was still rising. More companies went out of business, soup kitchens became a common sight, and general misery continued to grow. Shantytowns arose in every city, and hoboes continued to roam.

BOULDER DAM One project that Hoover approved did make a difference. Years earlier, when Hoover served as secretary of commerce, one of his earliest proposed initiatives was the construction of a dam on the Colorado River. Aiming to minimize federal intervention, Hoover proposed to finance the dam's construction by using profits from sales of the electric power that the dam would generate. He also helped to arrange an agreement on water rights among the seven states of the Colorado River basin—Arizona, California, Colorado, Nevada, New Mexico, Utah, and Wyoming.

By the time the massive project won congressional approval in 1928, as part of a $700 million public works program, Hoover had been elected to the White House. In the fall of 1929, nearly one year into his presidency, Hoover was finally able to authorize construction of **Boulder Dam** (later called Hoover Dam). At 726 feet high and 1,244 feet long, it would be the world's tallest dam and the second largest. In addition to providing electricity and flood control, the dam also provided a regular water supply, which enabled the growth of California's massive agricultural economy. Today, the dam also helps to provide water for cities such as Los Angeles and Las Vegas.

DEMOCRATS WIN IN 1930 CONGRESSIONAL ELECTIONS As the country's economic difficulties increased, the political tide turned against Hoover and the Republicans. In the 1930 congressional elections, the Democrats took advantage of anti-Hoover sentiments to win more seats in Congress. As a result of that election, the Republicans lost control of the House of Representatives and saw their majority in the Senate dwindle to one.

As Americans grew more and more frustrated by the Depression, they expressed their anger in a number of ways. Farmers stung by low crop prices burned their corn and wheat and dumped their milk on highways rather than sell it at a loss. Some farmers even declared a "farm holiday" and refused to work their fields. A number blocked roads to prevent food from getting to market, hoping that food shortages would raise prices. Some farmers also used force to prevent authorities from foreclosing on farms.

Americans expressed their dissatisfaction with Hoover and his policies by attaching his name to various symbols of the Depression. In addition to referring to shantytowns as "Hoovervilles," homeless people called the newspapers they wrapped themselves in "Hoover blankets." Empty pockets turned inside out were "Hoover flags." Many Americans who had hailed Hoover as a great humanitarian a few years earlier now saw him as a cold and heartless man. Despite public criticism, Hoover continued to hold firm to his principles. He refused to support direct relief or other forms of federal welfare. Many Americans were going hungry, and they blamed Hoover for their plight. Criticism of the president and his policies continued to grow. An anonymous ditty that skewered Hoover, Treasury Secretary Andrew W. Mellon, and powerful business interests was widely repeated.

Reading Check
Make Inferences
Why did people blame Hoover for the nation's difficulties?

"Mellon pulled the whistle
Hoover rang the bell
Wall Street gave the signal
And the country went to hell."

Document-Based Investigation Historical Source

Carrying the Weight of the Depression
In this cartoon, both farmers and President Hoover are carrying heavy loads. The caption plays on the two different meanings of the word credit.

Analyze Historical Sources
1. What does the farmer want from President Hoover? What does Hoover want from the farmer?

2. What does the cartoonist suggest that the farmers and Hoover should do?

Hoover Takes Action

As time went on and the Depression deepened, President Hoover gradually softened his position on government intervention in the economy and took a more activist approach to the nation's economic troubles.

HOOVER BACKS COOPERATIVES In Hoover's view, Boulder Dam was a model of how the federal government could encourage cooperation. His attempts to relieve the Depression involved negotiating agreements among private entities, again reflecting his belief in small government. For example, he backed the creation of the Federal Farm Board, an organization of farm cooperatives. The farm board was intended to raise crop prices by helping members buy crops and keep them off the market until prices rose.

In addition, Hoover tried to prop up the banking system by persuading the nation's largest banks to establish the National Credit Corporation. This organization loaned money to smaller banks to help them avoid bankruptcy.

DIRECT INTERVENTION By late 1931, however, many people could see that these measures had failed to turn the economy around. With a presidential election looming, Hoover appealed to Congress to pass a series of measures to reform banking, provide mortgage relief, and funnel more federal money into business investment. In 1932 Hoover signed into law the **Federal Home Loan Bank Act**, which lowered mortgage rates for homeowners and allowed farmers to refinance their farm loans and avoid foreclosure. It was not until Hoover's time in office was over that Congress passed the Glass-Steagall Banking Act, which separated investment from commercial banking and would, Congress hoped, prevent another crash.

The **Reconstruction Finance Corporation** (RFC) was Hoover's most ambitious economic measure, however, and was approved by Congress in January 1932. It authorized up to $2 billion for emergency financing for banks, life insurance companies, railroads, and other large businesses. Hoover believed that the money would trickle down to the average citizen through job growth and higher wages. Many critics questioned this approach; they argued that the program would benefit only corporations and that the poor still needed direct relief. Hungry people could not wait for the benefits to trickle down to their tables.

Vocabulary
refinance to provide new financing; to pay off a mortgage with a new mortgage obtained at a lower interest rate

DIFFICULT DECISIONS

Hoover and Federal Projects

On the one hand, President Hoover opposed federal welfare and intervention in the economy. On the other, he felt that government had a duty to help solve problems and ease suffering. The question was, What kind of assistance would be proper and effective?

1. Consider the pros and cons of Hoover's actions during the Depression. Did he do enough to try to end the Depression? Why or why not?

2. If you had been president during the Great Depression, what policies would you have supported? Explain the approach you would have taken.

In 1932 these veterans from Muncie, Indiana, decided to remain in the capital until their bonus was paid to them.

Reading Check
Evaluate What were some of the projects proposed by Hoover, and how effective were they?

In its first five months of operation, the RFC loaned more than $805 million to large corporations, but business failures continued. The RFC was an unprecedented example of federal involvement in a peacetime economy, but in the end it was too little, too late.

The Bonus Army Incident

In 1932 an incident further damaged Hoover's image and public morale. That spring, between 10,000 and 20,000 World War I veterans and their families arrived in Washington, DC, from various parts of the country. They called themselves the Bonus Expeditionary Force, or the **Bonus Army**.

THE PATMAN BILL DENIED Led by Walter Waters, an unemployed cannery worker from Oregon, the Bonus Army came to the nation's capital to support a bill under debate in Congress. The Patman Bill authorized the government to pay a bonus to World War I veterans who had not been compensated adequately for their wartime service. This bonus, which Congress had approved in 1924, was supposed to be paid out in 1945 in the form of cash and a life insurance policy. Congressman Wright Patman believed that the money—an average of $500 per soldier—should be paid immediately.

Hoover thought that the Bonus Marchers were "communists and persons with criminal records" rather than veterans. He opposed the legislation, but he respected the marchers' right to peaceful assembly. He even provided food and supplies so that they could erect a shantytown within sight of the Capitol. On June 17, however, the Senate voted down the Patman Bill. Hoover then called on the Bonus Army marchers to leave. Most did, but approximately 2,000, still hoping to meet with the president, refused to budge.

Not even this flag was safe from the violence of July 28, 1932.

HOOVER DISBANDS THE BONUS ARMY Nervous that the angry group could become violent, President Hoover decided that the Bonus Army should be disbanded. On July 28 a force of 1,000 soldiers under the command of General Douglas MacArthur and his aide, Major Dwight D. Eisenhower, came to roust the veterans. A government official watching from a nearby office recalled what happened next.

"The 12th infantry was in full battle dress. Each had a gas mask and his belt was full of tear gas bombs. . . . At orders, they brought their bayonets at thrust and moved in. The bayonets were used to jab people, to make them move. Soon, almost everybody disappeared from view, because tear gas bombs exploded. The entire block was covered by tear gas. Flames were coming up, where the soldiers had set fire to the buildings to drive these people out. . . . Through the whole afternoon, they took one camp after another."

—Everette McIntyre, quoted in *Hard Times*

In the course of the operation, the infantry gassed more than 1,000 people, including an 11-month-old baby, who died, and an 8-year-old boy, who was partially blinded. Two people were shot and many were injured. Most Americans were stunned and outraged when they heard about the treatment of the veterans.

Once again, President Hoover's image suffered, and now an election was nearing. In November, Hoover would face a formidable opponent, the Democratic candidate and popular New York governor Franklin Delano Roosevelt. When Roosevelt heard about the attack on the Bonus Army, he said to his friend Felix Frankfurter, "Well, Felix, this will elect me." The downturn in the economy and Hoover's inability to deal effectively with the Depression had sealed his political fate.

Reading Check
Summarize What did the Bonus Army want?

Lesson 3 Assessment

1. **Organize Information** In a cluster diagram, record what Hoover said and did in response to the Great Depression.

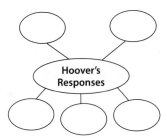

Which response was most helpful? Explain your choice.

2. **Key Terms and People** For each key term or person in the lesson, write a sentence explaining its significance.

3. **Analyze Issues** How did Hoover's belief in "rugged individualism" shape his policies during the Great Depression?

   Think About:
   • what his belief implies about his view of people
   • how that translates into the role of government
   • Hoover's policies

4. **Draw Conclusions** When Franklin D. Roosevelt heard about the attack on the Bonus Army, why was he so certain that he would defeat Hoover?

Module 9 Assessment

Key Terms and People

For each key term or person below, write a sentence explaining its significance to the beginning of the Great Depression.

1. credit
2. speculation
3. buying on margin
4. Black Tuesday
5. Dow Jones Industrial Average
6. Great Depression
7. Dust Bowl
8. direct relief
9. Herbert Hoover
10. Bonus Army

Main Ideas

Use your notes and the information in the module to answer the following questions.

The Nation's Sick Economy

1. What governmental ideas, policies, and actions of the 1920s set the stage for the Great Depression?
2. How did what happened to farmers during the 1920s foreshadow events of the Great Depression?
3. What argument was President Hoover making about government in the excerpt from the "rugged individualism" speech?
4. What were some of the effects of the stock market crash in October 1929?

Hardship and Suffering

5. How did many charitable organizations and public agencies help people during the Depression?

6. Why were shantytowns often called "Hoovervilles"?
7. What factors led to the Dust Bowl?
8. Why did minorities often experience an increase in discrimination during the Great Depression?
9. What pressures did the American family experience during the Depression?

Hoover's Failed Policies

10. How did Hoover's treatment of the Bonus Army affect his standing with the public?
11. How did Boulder Dam change places both nearby and far away?
12. In what ways did Hoover try to use the government to relieve the Depression?

Critical Thinking

1. **Categorize** In a chart, show how Hoover's attitudes and actions changed over the course of the Great Depression's early years. Include the reasons for the changes.

Herber Hoover's Philosophy

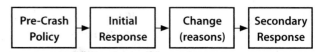

2. **Make Inferences** Do you think it would have been difficult for individuals to recover financially during the Depression without the entire economy recovering? Why or why not?
3. **Develop Historical Perspective** How do you think the Great Depression changed Americans' view of themselves and of the American Dream?

Engage with History

Suppose the year is 1935 and you are the head of your household. Write a letter to a relative overseas in which you describe your family's situation and how you have handled the crisis. Discuss the challenges created by the Great Depression and what you've learned as a result of enduring such hardships.

Focus on Writing

The Great Depression is not the only period of economic instability that the United States has experienced. Conduct research on other such periods, such as the Panic of 1837. In an expository essay, compare and contrast the chosen period to the Great Depression of the 1930s, paying particular attention to the causes and outcomes of the economic disruptions.

Multimedia Activity

Organize a small group into two subgroups. One subgroup should look at Internet and library resources for information on the physical causes of the Dust Bowl. Sources might include information from geographers and meteorologists. The other subgroup should examine first-person accounts of the Dust Bowl. With your findings, create a multimedia presentation about the causes of the Dust Bowl and its effects on Americans in both rural and urban areas. Include video, music, and personal narratives in your presentation.

Module 10

The New Deal

Essential Question

What should be the role of the government of the United States during economic crises?

About the Photograph: This photograph shows men at work on a project funded by the Civil Works Administration (CWA). President Franklin D. Roosevelt initated the CWA and similar programs to combat unemployment during the Great Depression.

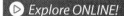 Explore ONLINE!

VIDEOS, including...
- FDR's New Deal
- FDR's First Inaugural Address
- FDR Delivers First Fireside Chat
- The Tennessee Valley Authority Act
- The National Recovery Administration
- Eleanor Roosevelt
- War of the Worlds

☑ Document-Based Investigations

☑ Graphic Organizers

☑ Interactive Games

☑ Video Carousel: Opponents of the New Deal

☑ Carousel: Art of the New Deal Era

In this module you will learn about the programs of the New Deal and the impact that these programs had on the nation.

SS.912.A.1.2 Utilize a variety of primary and secondary sources to identify author, historical significance, audience, and authenticity to understand a historical period. **SS.912.A.1.4** Analyze how images, symbols, objects, cartoons, graphs, charts, maps, and artwork may be used to interpret the significance of time periods and events from the past. **SS.912.A.1.6** Use case studies to explore social, political, legal, and economic relationships in history. **SS.912.A.1.7** Describe various sociocultural aspects of American life including arts, artifacts, literature, education, and publications. **SS.912.A.2.7** Review the Native American experience. **SS.912.A.5.7** Examine the freedom movements that advocated civil rights for African Americans, Latinos, Asians, and women. **SS.912.A.5.10** Analyze support for and resistance to civil rights for women, African Americans, Native Americans, and other minorities. **SS.912.A.5.11** Examine causes, course, and consequences of the Great Depression and the New Deal. **SS.912.A.5.12** Examine key events and people in Florida history as they relate to United States history. **SS.912.H.1.1** Relate works in the arts of varying styles and genre according to the periods in which they were created. **SS.912.H.1.3** Relate works in the arts to various cultures. **SS.912.H.1.5** Examine artistic response to social issues and new ideas in various cultures. **LAFS.1112.RH.1.1** Cite specific textual evidence to support analysis of primary and secondary sources, connecting insights gained from specific details to an understanding of the text as a whole. **LAFS.1112.RH.1.2** Determine the central ideas or information of a primary or secondary source; provide an accurate summary that makes clear the relationships among the key details and ideas. **LAFS.1112.RH.2.6** Evaluate authors' differing points of view on the same historical event or issue by assessing the authors' claims, reasoning, and evidence. **LAFS.1112.RH.4.10** By the end of grade 12, read and comprehend history/social studies texts in the grades 11–CCR text complexity band independently and proficiently.

Timeline of Events 1932–1941

 Explore ONLINE!

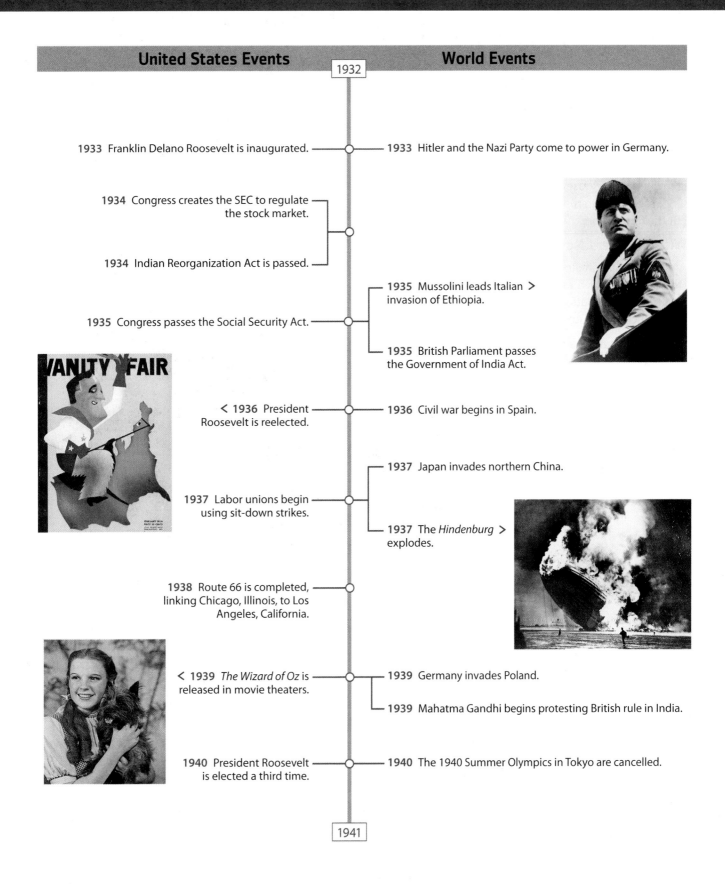

United States Events

1932

World Events

1933 Franklin Delano Roosevelt is inaugurated.

1933 Hitler and the Nazi Party come to power in Germany.

1934 Congress creates the SEC to regulate the stock market.

1934 Indian Reorganization Act is passed.

1935 Mussolini leads Italian > invasion of Ethiopia.

1935 Congress passes the Social Security Act.

1935 British Parliament passes the Government of India Act.

VANITY FAIR

< **1936** President Roosevelt is reelected.

1936 Civil war begins in Spain.

1937 Japan invades northern China.

1937 Labor unions begin using sit-down strikes.

1937 The *Hindenburg* > explodes.

1938 Route 66 is completed, linking Chicago, Illinois, to Los Angeles, California.

< **1939** *The Wizard of Oz* is released in movie theaters.

1939 Germany invades Poland.

1939 Mahatma Gandhi begins protesting British rule in India.

1940 President Roosevelt is elected a third time.

1940 The 1940 Summer Olympics in Tokyo are cancelled.

1941

The New Deal **439**

A New Deal Fights the Depression

The Big Idea

After becoming president, Franklin Delano Roosevelt used government programs to combat the Depression.

Why It Matters Now

Americans still benefit from New Deal programs, such as bank and stock market regulations and the Tennessee Valley Authority.

Key Terms and People

Franklin Delano Roosevelt

New Deal

Glass-Steagall Act

Federal Securities Act

Agricultural Adjustment Act (AAA)

Civilian Conservation Corps (CCC)

National Industrial Recovery Act (NIRA)

deficit spending

Huey Long

One American's Story

As the Depression dragged on, Keith Hufford had lost most hope of ever finding work. Then President Roosevelt began creating programs to employ young, able men like Hufford. Through one of these programs, the Civilian Conservation Corps (CCC), Hufford found work protecting Utah forests. Finally, he was able to help his family financially. He recalled how his CCC job gave him a new sense of purpose after unsuccessfully looking for work for so long.

CCC workers clear brush and plant seedlings in an Idaho forest.

"You must go through the actual experience before you can really understand the hopeless state of mind most of the prospective members of the CCC were in when we . . . tramped half-heartedly into the forests and fields to plant and cut trees, build dams, lime kilns, fire breaks and trails, control insect pests, tree diseases, and risk our lives . . . A great deal of credit must be given to the boys for . . . the enthusiasm and zest with which they attacked a new project, anxious to get it completed . . . and in the meantime, secure in their knowledge the folks "back home" had a small, but helpful income."

—Keith Hufford, quoted in "CCC in Utah"

President Roosevelt's programs raised the hopes of the American people. To many, it appeared as if the country had turned a corner. It was beginning to emerge from the nightmare of the Great Depression.

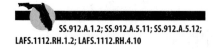

SS.912.A.1.2; SS.912.A.5.11; SS.912.A.5.12; LAFS.1112.RH.1.2; LAFS.1112.RH.4.10

Americans Get a New Deal

The 1932 presidential election showed that Americans were clearly ready for a change. The Depression had robbed people of work, food, and hope.

ELECTING FRANKLIN DELANO ROOSEVELT The Republicans renominated President Hoover. But they recognized he had little chance of winning. Too many Americans blamed Hoover for doing too little about the Depression. They wanted a new president. The Democrats pinned their hopes on **Franklin Delano Roosevelt**, known popularly as FDR. He was the two-term governor of New York and a distant cousin of former president Theodore Roosevelt.

As governor, FDR had proved an effective, reform-minded leader, working to combat unemployment and poverty. Unlike Hoover, Roosevelt possessed a "can-do" attitude and projected an air of friendliness and confidence. This attitude attracted voters.

Indeed, Roosevelt won an overwhelming victory. He captured nearly 23 million votes to Hoover's nearly 16 million. In the Senate, Democrats claimed a nearly two-thirds majority. In the House, they won almost three-fourths of the seats. It was their greatest victory since before the Civil War.

WAITING FOR ROOSEVELT TO TAKE OVER Four months would elapse between Roosevelt's victory in the November election and his inauguration as president in March 1933. The Twentieth Amendment, which moved presidential inaugurations to January, was not ratified until February 1933. It therefore did not apply to the 1932 election.

FDR was not idle during this waiting period, however. He worked with his team of carefully picked advisers—a select group of professors, lawyers, and journalists that came to be known as the "Brain Trust." Roosevelt began to formulate a set of policies for his new administration. This program, designed to alleviate the problems of the Great Depression, became known as the **New Deal**. The term originated in a campaign speech when Roosevelt had promised "a new deal for the American people." New Deal policies focused on three general goals: relief for the needy, economic recovery, and financial reform.

THE HUNDRED DAYS Roosevelt knew that for the New Deal to be able to improve the U.S. economy, he first needed to reestablish Americans' confidence. His inauguration speech in 1933 was one of his first steps to do so. He reminded Americans that their fears for their economic future were unfounded and concerned "only material things."

> *"This great Nation will endure as it has endured, will revive and will prosper. So, first of all, let me assert my firm belief that the only thing we have to fear is fear itself—nameless, unreasoning, unjustified terror which paralyzes needed efforts to convert retreat into advance."*
>
> —Franklin D. Roosevelt, from his first Inaugural Address, 1933

Franklin D. Roosevelt (1882–1945)

Born into an old, wealthy New York family, Franklin Delano Roosevelt entered politics as a state senator in 1910 and later became assistant secretary of the navy. In 1921 he was stricken with polio and became partially paralyzed from the waist down. He struggled to regain the use of his legs, and he eventually learned to stand with the help of leg braces.

Roosevelt became governor of New York in 1928, and because he "would not allow bodily disability to defeat his will," he went on to the White House in 1933. Always interested in people, Roosevelt gained greater compassion for others as a result of his own physical disability.

Eleanor Roosevelt (1884–1962)

A niece of Theodore Roosevelt and a distant cousin of her husband, Franklin, Eleanor Roosevelt lost her parents at an early age. She was raised by a strict grandmother.

As First Lady, she often urged the president to take stands on controversial issues and was even influential in his policymaking. A popular public speaker, Eleanor was particularly interested in child welfare, housing reform, and equal rights for women and minorities. In presenting a booklet on human rights to the United Nations in 1958, she said, "Where, after all, do human rights begin? . . . [In] the world of the individual person: the neighborhood . . . the school . . . the factory, farm or office where he works."

Immediately upon taking office, the Roosevelt administration launched a period of intense activity known as the Hundred Days, lasting from March 9 to June 16, 1933. During this period, Congress passed more than 15 major pieces of New Deal legislation. These laws, and others that followed, significantly expanded the federal government's role in the nation's economy and in citizens' lives. They also changed the relationship between the federal and state governments.

Roosevelt's first step as president was to reform banking and finance. By 1933 widespread bank failures had caused most Americans to lose faith in the banking system. On March 5, one day after taking office, Roosevelt declared a bank holiday and closed all banks to prevent further withdrawals. He persuaded Congress to pass the Emergency Banking Relief Act, which authorized the Treasury Department to inspect the country's banks. Those that were sound could reopen at once. Those that were insolvent—unable to pay their debts—would remain closed. Those that needed help could receive loans. This measure revived public confidence in banks, since customers now had greater faith that the open banks were in good financial shape.

AN IMPORTANT FIRESIDE CHAT On March 12, the day before the first banks were to reopen, President Roosevelt gave the first of his many fireside chats—radio talks about issues of public concern, explaining in clear, simple language his New Deal measures. These informal talks made Americans feel as if the president were talking directly to them. In his first chat, Roosevelt took time to calm Americans' fears about the bank crisis. He acknowledged that closing the banks had caused stress and hardship. But he reassured his listeners that the banks would reopen and the American financial system would return as strong as ever.

As Roosevelt explained, the banking crisis was caused in large part by panic. When too many people demanded their savings in cash, banks would fail. This was not because banks were weak but because even strong banks could not meet such heavy demands. Over the next few weeks, many Americans returned their savings to banks.

REGULATING BANKING AND FINANCE Congress took another step to reorganize the banking system by passing the **Glass-Steagall Act** of 1933. This act established the Federal Deposit Insurance Corporation (FDIC). The FDIC provided federal insurance for individual bank accounts of up to $5,000, reassuring millions of bank customers that their money was safe. It also required banks to act cautiously with their customers' money.

Congress and the president also worked to regulate the stock market, in which people had lost faith because of the crash of 1929. The **Federal Securities Act**, passed in May 1933, required corporations to provide complete information on all stock offerings and made them liable for any misrepresentations. In June 1934 Congress created the Securities and Exchange Commission (SEC) to regulate the stock market. One goal of this commission was to prevent people with inside information about companies from "rigging" the stock market for their own profit.

In addition, Roosevelt persuaded Congress to approve a bill allowing the manufacture and sale of some alcoholic beverages. The bill's main purpose was to raise government revenues by taxing alcohol. By the end of 1933, the Twenty-First Amendment had repealed prohibition altogether.

**Reading Check
Summarize** What were the three main categories of the programs and actions of Roosevelt's New Deal?

Document-Based Investigation Historical Source

First Fireside Chat

In the first of his popular radio broadcasts known as fireside chats, President Roosevelt encouraged Americans not to lose faith in the banking system. Understanding that the complexities of modern banking were a mystery to most people, he sought to explain the system in simple terms. At the same time, he stressed to his listeners the vital role of banks in maintaining the American way of life.

Analyze Historical Sources
According to Roosevelt, why is the money invested in banks important to the U.S. economy?

"When you deposit money in a bank the bank does not put the money into a safe deposit vault. It invests your money . . . to keep the wheels of industry and agriculture turning around. A comparatively small part of the money that you put into the bank is kept in currency—an amount which in normal times is wholly sufficient to cover the cash needs of the average citizen. . . . Some of our bankers had shown themselves either incompetent or dishonest in the handling of the people's funds. . . . And so it became the Government's job to straighten out this situation and do it as quickly as possible."

—Franklin D. Roosevelt, from a Fireside Chat, March 12, 1933

Helping the American People

While working on banking and financial matters, the Roosevelt administration also focused on other ways to stimulate economic recovery and to aid Americans.

RURAL ASSISTANCE Having suffered the double blow of the drought in the Dust Bowl and the national economic crisis, farmers were perhaps the hardest hit by the Depression. The government soon implemented several rural assistance programs to aid them. The **Agricultural Adjustment Act (AAA)** sought to raise crop prices by lowering production. The government achieved this goal by paying farmers to leave a certain amount of every acre of land unseeded. The theory was that reduced supply would boost prices. In some cases, crops were too far advanced for the acreage reduction to take effect. As a result, the government paid cotton growers $200 million to plow under 10 million acres of their crop. It also paid hog farmers to slaughter 6 million pigs. These subsidies upset many Americans, who protested the destruction of food when many people were going hungry. It did, however, help raise farm prices and put more money in farmers' pockets.

Several New Deal programs focused specifically on the impoverished Tennessee River Valley. The Tennessee Valley Authority (TVA), established on May 18, 1933, was particularly ambitious. The TVA renovated five existing dams and constructed 20 new ones, created thousands of jobs, and provided flood control, hydroelectric power, and other benefits to the region. The government also established the Cumberland Homesteads in eastern Tennessee. There, hundreds of poor families were resettled on small farms and worked in community-owned businesses. The community never attracted enough good-paying jobs, however, and the venture ultimately failed.

PROVIDING WORK PROJECTS The administration also established programs to provide relief through work projects and cash payments. One important program, the **Civilian Conservation Corps (CCC)**, put young men aged 18 to 25 to work. CCC members built roads, developed parks, planted trees, and helped in soil-erosion and flood-control projects. By the time the program ended in 1942, almost 3 million young men had passed through the CCC. The CCC paid a small wage, $30 a month, of which $25 was automatically sent home to the worker's family. It also supplied free food and uniforms and lodging in work camps. Many of the camps were located on the Great Plains, where, within a period of eight years, the men of the CCC planted more than 200 million trees. This tremendous

Vocabulary
subsidy financial assistance, such as that granted by a government to a private enterprise

THE GALLOPING SNAIL

This 1933 cartoon depicts Roosevelt spurring on a slow-moving Congress with his many reform policies.

Civilian Conservation Corps

- The CCC provided almost 3 million men aged 18–25 with work and wages between 1933 and 1942.

- The men lived in work camps under a strict regime. The majority of the camps were racially segregated.

- By 1938 the CCC had an 11 percent African American enrollment.

- Accomplishments of the CCC include planting over 3 billion trees, developing over 800 state parks, and building more than 46,000 bridges.

reforestation program was aimed at preventing another Dust Bowl. Another major CCC project took place in Florida, where CCC workers built the 100-mile Overseas Highway to link Miami and Key West. The new highway was needed to replace the railroad—destroyed in a 1935 hurricane—that once linked these tourist destinations.

The Public Works Administration (PWA) was created in June 1933 as part of the **National Industrial Recovery Act (NIRA)**. The PWA provided money to states to create jobs chiefly in the construction of schools and other community buildings. When these programs failed to make a sufficient dent in unemployment, President Roosevelt established the Civil Works Administration (CWA) in November 1933. It provided 4 million immediate jobs during the winter of 1933–1934. Some critics of the CWA claimed that the programs were "make-work" projects and a waste of money. However, the CWA built 40,000 schools and paid the salaries of more than 50,000 schoolteachers in America's rural areas. It also built more than half a million miles of roads.

PROMOTING FAIR PRACTICES The NIRA also sought to promote industrial growth by establishing codes of fair practice for individual industries. It created the National Recovery Administration (NRA), which set prices of many products and established standards. The aim of the NRA was to promote recovery by interrupting the trend of wage cuts, falling prices, and layoffs. Economist Gardiner C. Means attempted to justify the NRA by stating the goal of industrial planning.

> *"The National Recovery Administration [was] created in response to an overwhelming demand from many quarters that certain elements in the making of industrial policy . . . should no longer be left to the market place and the price mechanism but should be placed in the hands of administrative bodies."*
>
> —Gardiner C. Means, from "Industrial Prices and Their Relative Inflexibility"

The codes of fair practice had been drafted in joint meetings of businesses and representatives of workers and consumers. These codes limited production and established prices. Because businesses were given new concessions, workers made demands. Congress met their demands by passing a section of the NIRA guaranteeing workers' right to unionize and to bargain collectively.

Many businesses and politicians criticized the NRA. Some charged that the codes served large business interests. There were also charges of increasing code violations.

FOOD, CLOTHING, AND SHELTER A number of New Deal programs concerned housing and home mortgage problems. The Home Owners Loan Corporation (HOLC) provided government loans to homeowners who faced foreclosure because they couldn't make their loan payments. In addition, the 1934 National Housing Act created the Federal Housing Administration (FHA). This agency continues to furnish loans for home mortgages and repairs today.

Reading Check
Contrast How did the goals of the AAA, CCC, NIRA, and FERA differ?

Another program, the Federal Emergency Relief Administration (FERA), was funded with $500 million to provide direct relief for the needy. Half of the money was given to the states as direct grants-in-aid to help furnish food and clothing to the unemployed, the aged, and the ill. The rest was distributed to states to support work relief programs. For every $3 within the state program, FERA donated $1. Harry Hopkins, who headed this program, believed that, whereas money helped people buy food, it was meaningful work that enabled them to gain confidence and self-respect.

The New Deal Comes Under Attack

By the end of the Hundred Days, millions of Americans had benefited from the New Deal programs. The public's confidence in the nation's future had rebounded as well. The government's policy of **deficit spending**—spending more money than it receives in revenue—was stimulating economic recovery, despite putting the government deeply into debt. With more of their own money in their hands, consumers could buy goods and services and thus fuel economic growth.

Although President Roosevelt agreed to deficit spending, he did so reluctantly. He regarded it as a necessary evil to be used only at a time of great economic crisis. Nevertheless, the New Deal did not end the Depression, and opposition grew among some parts of the population.

Liberal critics worried that the New Deal would not go far enough to help the poor and to reform the nation's economic system. Conservative critics argued that Roosevelt's direct relief plan would cost the government too much. They also believed that he would use New Deal policies to control business and socialize the economy. Conservatives were particularly angered by laws such as the Agricultural Adjustment Act and the National Industrial Recovery Act, which they believed gave the federal government too much control over agriculture and industry. Many critics believed the New Deal would interfere with the workings of a free-market economy.

THAT COMPASS
DOESN'T POINT THE WAY
I WANT TO GO.
CHANGE IT.
NOW!

Roosevelt proposed a court reform bill that would essentially have allowed him to "pack" the Court with judges supportive of the New Deal. This political cartoon shows Roosevelt as a sea captain ordering a shocked Congress to change course.

THE SUPREME COURT REACTS By the mid-1930s conservative opposition to the New Deal had received a boost from two Supreme Court decisions. In 1935 the Court ruled the NIRA unconstitutional. It declared that the law upset the established system of checks and balances by giving legislative powers to the executive branch. Additionally, the Court said that the enforcement of industry codes within states went beyond the federal government's constitutional powers to regulate interstate commerce. The next year, the Supreme Court struck down the AAA on the grounds that agriculture is a local matter and should be regulated by the states rather than by the federal government.

President Roosevelt feared that further Court decisions might dismantle the New Deal. To prevent such a Court action, in February 1937 he asked Congress to enact a court reform bill. If passed, the bill would reorganize the federal judiciary and allow FDR to appoint six new Supreme Court justices. Most observers saw this bill as a clumsy effort to "pack" the Supreme Court with friendly justices. They also viewed it as a dangerous attempt to upset the constitutional balance of power. Some of the Supreme Court's rulings had been based on the belief that the executive branch had usurped too much legislative power. The court reform bill would further shift the relationship between the branches by allowing the executive to use legislation to interfere with judicial independence. As it turned out, the president got his way without reorganizing the judiciary. In 1937 an elderly justice retired, and Roosevelt appointed the liberal Hugo S. Black, shifting the balance of the Court. Rulings of the Court began to favor the New Deal. Over the next four years, because of further resignations, Roosevelt was able to appoint seven new justices.

THREE FIERY CRITICS In 1934 some of the strongest conservative opponents of the New Deal banded together to form an organization called the American Liberty League. The American Liberty League opposed New Deal measures that it believed violated respect for the rights of individuals and property. Three of the toughest critics the president faced, however, were three men who expressed views that appealed to poor Americans: Charles Coughlin, Dr. Francis Townsend, and Huey Long.

Every Sunday, Father Charles Coughlin, a Roman Catholic priest from a suburb of Detroit, broadcast radio sermons that combined economic, political, and religious ideas. Initially a supporter of the New Deal, Coughlin soon turned against Roosevelt. He favored a guaranteed annual income and the nationalization of banks. At the height of his popularity, Father Coughlin claimed a radio audience of as many as 40–45 million people, but his increasingly anti-Semitic (anti-Jewish) views eventually cost him support.

Vocabulary
nationalization
conversion
from private to
governmental
ownership

Another critic was Dr. Francis Townsend, a physician and health officer in Long Beach, California. He believed that Roosevelt wasn't doing enough to help the poor and elderly, so he devised a pension plan that would provide monthly benefits to the aged. The plan found strong backing among the elderly, thus undermining their support for Roosevelt.

Perhaps the most serious challenge to the New Deal came from Senator **Huey Long** of Louisiana. Like Coughlin, Long was an early supporter of the New Deal. But he, too, turned against Roosevelt. Eager to win the presidency for himself, Long proposed a nationwide social program called Share-Our-Wealth. Under the banner slogan "Every Man a King," he promised something for everyone.

> *"We owe debts in America today, public and private, amounting to $252 billion. That means that every child is born with a $2,000 debt tied around his neck. . . . We propose that children shall be born in a land of opportunity, guaranteed a home, food, clothes, and the other things that make for living, including the right to education."*
>
> —Huey Long, quoted in *Record,* 74 Congress, Session 1

Long's Share-Our-Wealth program was very popular. By 1935 he boasted of having perhaps as many as 27,000 Share-Our-Wealth clubs and 7.5 million members. That same year, however, at the height of his popularity, Long was assassinated by a lone gunman.

As the initial impetus of the New Deal began to wane, President Roosevelt started to look ahead. He knew that much more needed to be done to help the people and to solve the nation's economic problems.

Reading Check
Contrast How did liberal and conservative critics differ in their opposition to the New Deal?

Lesson 1 Assessment

1. **Organize Information** In a two-column chart, list problems that President Roosevelt confronted and how he tried to solve them.

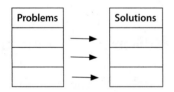

Problems		Solutions
	→	
	→	
	→	

Write a paragraph telling which solution had the greatest impact and why.

2. **Key Terms and People** For each key term or person in the lesson, write a sentence explaining its significance.

3. **Evaluate** Of the New Deal programs discussed in this lesson, which do you consider the most important? Explain your choice.

Think About:
• the type of assistance offered by each program
• the scope of each program
• the short-term and long-term impact of each program

4. **Draw Conclusions** Why do you think Roosevelt's first act as president was to try to restore confidence in the nation's banking system?

5. **Predict** How do you think the NIRA would affect interactions between labor unions and business?

6. **Analyze Issues** Why did some critics see Roosevelt's court reform bill as an attempt to upset the constitutional balance of power?

7. **Form Opinions** Do you think Roosevelt was wrong to try to "pack" the Supreme Court with those in favor of the New Deal? Explain your answer.

The Second New Deal

The Big Idea

The Second New Deal included new programs to extend federal aid and stimulate the nation's economy.

Why It Matters Now

Second New Deal programs continue to assist homebuyers, farmers, workers, and the elderly in the 2000s.

Key Terms and People

Eleanor Roosevelt

Works Progress Administration (WPA)

National Youth Administration (NYA)

Wagner Act

Social Security Act

SS.912.A.1.2; SS.912.A.1.4; SS.912.A.1.6; SS.912.A.1.7; SS.912.A.5.11; SS.912.H.1.1; SS.912.H.1.5; LAFS.1112.RH.1.2; LAFS.1112.RH.4.10

One American's Story

Dorothea Lange was a photographer who documented American life during the Great Depression and the New Deal. Lange spent considerable time getting to know her subjects—destitute migrant workers—before she and her assistant set up their cameras.

Dorothea Lange taking photographs on the Texas plains in 1934

"So often it's just sticking around and remaining there, not swooping in and swooping out in a cloud of dust. . . . We found our way in . . . not too far away from the people we were working with. . . . The people who are garrulous and wear their heart on their sleeve and tell you everything, that's one kind of person. But the fellow who's hiding behind a tree and hoping you don't see him, is the fellow that you'd better find out why."

—Dorothea Lange, quoted in *Restless Spirit: The Life and Work of Dorothea Lange*

Lange also believed that her distinct limp, the result of a childhood case of polio, worked to her advantage. Seeing that Lange, too, had suffered, people were kind to her and more at ease.

Federal agencies, such as the Farm Security Administration, which was established to alleviate rural poverty, funded much of Lange's work. Her photographs of migrant workers helped draw attention to the desperate conditions in rural America. They also helped underscore the need for direct relief.

The Second Hundred Days

By 1935 the Roosevelt administration was trying to build on the programs established during the Hundred Days. Although the economy had improved, the gains were not as great as the president had expected. Unemployment remained high despite government work programs. And production still lagged behind the levels of the 1920s.

Nevertheless, the New Deal was popular. And President Roosevelt launched a second burst of activity, often called the Second New Deal or the Second Hundred Days. During this phase, the president called on Congress to provide more extensive relief for both farmers and workers.

Eleanor Roosevelt visits a children's hospital in 1937.

First Lady **Eleanor Roosevelt**, a social reformer who combined her deep humanitarian impulses with great political skills, prodded her husband in this direction. Throughout FDR's first Hundred Days, Eleanor Roosevelt had used her influence in the Democratic National Committee to urge the administration to appoint women to government positions. In addition, she made sure that the New Deal included relief programs for women, as well as for men. She continued to focus on social issues during FDR's second term. She traveled the country, observing social conditions. She also reminded the president about the continuing suffering throughout the country. She lobbied for civil rights and workers' rights as well. Rexford Tugwell, one of the president's top advisers, later said of the First Lady's influence, "It would be impossible to say how often and to what extent American governmental processes have been turned in new directions because of her determination."

**Reading Check
Summarize** Why did Roosevelt launch the Second Hundred Days?

REELECTING FDR The Second New Deal was underway by the 1936 presidential election. The Republicans nominated Alfred Landon, the governor of Kansas, while the Democrats, of course, nominated President Roosevelt. The election resulted in an overwhelming victory for the Democrats, who won the presidency and large majorities in both houses. The election marked the first time that most African Americans had voted Democratic rather than Republican. It also marked the first time that labor unions gave united support to a presidential candidate. The 1936 election was a vote of confidence in FDR and the New Deal.

Helping Farmers

Farmers were still in crisis as Roosevelt won reelection. Many were still suffering from the environmental disaster in the Dust Bowl. In addition, two of every five farms in the United States were mortgaged, and many farmers had defaulted on their loans. Thousands of these farm owners became tenant farmers when they lost their land to the banks. Making the farmers' situation even harder was the fact that some owners of large farms were replacing workers with tractors and other automated farm machines. An official from a farmers' association in Oklahoma described the effect of automation on poor tenant farmers in his state:

"In Creek County . . . we have the record of one land-owner purchasing 3 tractors and forcing 31 of his 34 tenants and croppers from the land. Most of these families left the State when neither jobs nor relief could be secured. This is over 10 families per machine, 10 families who must quit their profession and seek employment in an unfriendly, industrialized farming section of Arizona or California. . . . Tractors produce crops cheaper. A small farmer who is unable to equip his farm with a tractor loses out and is driven from the land. The small independent farmer begins slipping down on the ladder of agriculture, slipping down toward becoming a migrant."

—Otis Nation, Director of the Oklahoma Tenant Farmers' Union, from testimony before Congress

Seeing their needs, the government once again turned its attention to struggling farmers and worked to find ways to protect the land from the devastating effects of soil erosion.

Document-Based Investigation Historical Source

"Migrant Mother" (1936), Dorothea Lange

In 1935 Roy Stryker hired photographer Dorothea Lange to work for the New Deal's Resettlement Administration, documenting the harsh living conditions of farmers. In February 1936 Lange visited a camp in Nipomo, California, where some 2,500 destitute pea pickers lived in tents or, like this mother of seven children, in lean-tos. Lange described her encounter with the woman. "I saw and approached the hungry and desperate mother, as if drawn by a magnet. . . . She said that they had been living on frozen vegetables from the surrounding fields, and birds that the children killed. She had just sold the tires from her car to buy food." One of Lange's photographs of the woman, titled "Migrant Mother," was published in the *San Francisco News* on March 10, 1936. The photograph became one of the most recognizable symbols of the Depression and perhaps the strongest argument in support of New Deal relief programs.

Analyze Historical Sources
Why do you think "Migrant Mother" was effective in persuading people to support FDR's relief programs?

Carl Mydans, a photographer hired by the FSA, captured a farmer working his land in Granger Homesteads, Iowa, in 1936.

FOCUSING ON FARMS When the Supreme Court struck down the AAA early in 1936, Congress passed another law to replace it: the Soil Conservation and Domestic Allotment Act. This act paid farmers for cutting production of soil-depleting crops. It also rewarded farmers for practicing good soil conservation methods. Two years later, in 1938, Congress approved a second Agricultural Adjustment Act that brought back many of the Dust Bowl recovery features of the first AAA. The second AAA did not include a processing tax to pay for farm subsidies, a provision of the first AAA that the Supreme Court had declared unconstitutional.

The Second New Deal also attempted to help tenant farmers, sharecroppers, migrant workers, and many other poor farmers. The Resettlement Administration, created by executive order in 1935, provided monetary loans to small farmers to buy land. In 1937 the agency was replaced by the Farm Security Administration (FSA). The FSA loaned more than $1 billion to help tenant farmers become landholders. It also established camps for migrant farm workers, who had traditionally lived in squalid housing.

The FSA hired photographers such as Dorothea Lange, Ben Shahn, Walker Evans, Arthur Rothstein, and Carl Mydans to take many pictures of rural towns and farms and their inhabitants. The agency used their photographs to create a pictorial record of the difficult situation in rural America.

Reading Check
Summarize What challenges did people in rural areas still face as Roosevelt started a second term?

Roosevelt Extends Relief

In addition to farmers, the Second New Deal assisted students, women, African Americans, and Native Americans. One of the largest programs was the **Works Progress Administration (WPA)**, headed by Harry Hopkins, the former chief of the Federal Emergency Relief Administration. The WPA set out to create as many jobs as possible as quickly as possible. Between 1935 and 1943 it spent $11 billion to give jobs to more than 8 million workers, most of them unskilled. These workers built 850 airports throughout the country,

WORLD'S HIGHEST STANDARD OF LIVING

There's no way like the American Way

This photograph by Margaret Bourke-White shows people waiting for food in a Kentucky bread line in 1937.

constructed or repaired 651,000 miles of roads and streets, and put up more than 125,000 public buildings. In addition, the WPA employed many professionals who wrote guides to cities, collected historical slave narratives, painted murals on the walls of schools and other public buildings, and performed in theater troupes around the country. At the urging of Eleanor Roosevelt, the WPA made special efforts to help women, minorities, and young people. Women workers in sewing groups made 300 million garments for the needy.

Although criticized by some as a make-work project, the WPA produced public works of lasting value to the nation. It also gave working people a sense of hope and purpose. As one man recalled, "It was really great. You worked, you got a paycheck and you had some dignity. Even when a man raked leaves, he got paid, he had some dignity."

Another program, the **National Youth Administration (NYA)**, was created specifically to provide education, jobs, counseling, and recreation for young people. The NYA provided student aid to high school, college, and graduate students. In exchange, students worked in part-time positions at their schools. One participant later described her experience.

> "I lugged . . . drafts and reams of paper home, night after night. . . . Sometimes I typed almost all night and had to deliver it to school the next morning. . . . This was a good program. It got necessary work done. It gave teenagers a chance to work for pay. Mine bought me clothes and shoes, school supplies, some movies and mad money. Candy bars, and big pickles out of a barrel. It gave my mother relief from my necessary demands for money."
> —Helen Farmer, quoted in *The Great Depression*

For graduates unable to find jobs, or youth who had dropped out of school, the NYA provided part-time jobs, such as working on highways, parks, and the grounds of public buildings.

Improving Labor and Other Reforms

In a speech to Congress in January 1935, the president declared, "When a man is convalescing from an illness, wisdom dictates not only cure of the symptoms but also removal of their cause." During the Second New Deal, Roosevelt, with the help of Congress, brought about important reforms in the areas of labor relations and economic security for retired workers.

Reading Check
Evaluate Do you think work programs like the WPA were a valid use of federal money? Why or why not?

IMPROVING LABOR CONDITIONS   In 1935 the Supreme Court declared the NIRA unconstitutional, citing that the federal government had violated legislative authority reserved for individual states. One of the first reforms of the Second New Deal was passage of the National Labor Relations Act. More commonly called the **Wagner Act**, after its sponsor, Senator Robert F. Wagner of New York, the act reestablished the NIRA provision of collective bargaining. The federal government again protected the right of workers to join unions and engage in collective bargaining with employers.

The Wagner Act also prohibited unfair labor practices such as threatening workers, firing union members, and interfering with union organizing. The act set up the National Labor Relations Board (NLRB) to hear testimony about unfair practices and to hold elections to find out if workers wanted union representation.

In 1938 Congress passed the Fair Labor Standards Act, which set maximum hours at 44 hours per week, decreasing to 40 hours after two years. It also set minimum wages at 25 cents an hour, increasing to 40 cents an hour by 1945. The exploitation of child workers, famously documented by photojournalist Lewis Hine at the turn of the century, was still a problem in many factories. Consequently, the act also set rules for the employment of workers under 16 and banned hazardous work for those under 18.

THE SOCIAL SECURITY ACT   One of the most important achievements of the New Deal was creating the Social Security system. Roosevelt had a vision for a comprehensive system of social provisions. He said,

> "I see no reason why every child, from the day he is born, shouldn't be a member of the social security system. When he begins to grow up, he should know he will have old-age benefits . . . If he is out of work, he gets a benefit. If he is sick or crippled, he gets a benefit . . . Everybody ought to be in on it—the farmer and his wife, and his family . . . cradle to the grave they ought to be in a social insurance system."
>
> —Franklin D. Roosevelt, quoted in *The Roosevelt I Knew*

With these goals in mind, the **Social Security Act**, passed in 1935, was created by a committee chaired by Secretary of Labor Frances Perkins. The act had three major parts:

- *Old-age insurance for retirees 65 or older and their spouses.* The insurance was a supplemental retirement plan. Half of the funds came from the worker and half from the employer. Although some groups were excluded from the system, it helped to make retirement comfortable for millions of people.
- *Unemployment compensation system.* The unemployment system was funded by a federal tax on employers. It was administered at the state level. The initial payments ranged from $15 to $18 per week.
- *Aid to families with dependent children and people with disabilities.* The aid was paid for by federal funds made available to the states.

New Deal Programs

EMPLOYMENT PROJECTS	PURPOSE
1933 Civilian Conservation Corps (CCC)	Provided jobs for single males on conservation projects.
1933 Federal Emergency Relief Administration (FERA)	Helped states to provide aid for the unemployed.
1933 Public Works Administration (PWA)	Created jobs on government projects.
1933 Civil Works Administration (CWA)	Provided work in federal jobs.
1935 Works Progress Administration (WPA)	Quickly created as many jobs as possible—from construction jobs to positions in symphony orchestras.
1935 National Youth Administration (NYA)	Provided job training for unemployed young people and part-time jobs for needy students.

BUSINESS ASSISTANCE AND REFORM	PURPOSE
1933 Emergency Banking Relief Act (EBRA)	Banks were inspected by Treasury Department and those that were stable could reopen.
1933 Federal Deposit Insurance Corporation (FDIC)	Protected bank deposits up to $5,000. (Today, accounts are protected up to $250,000.)
1933 National Recovery Administration (NRA)	Established codes of fair competition.
1934 Securities and Exchange Commission (SEC)	Supervised the stock market and eliminated dishonest practices.
1935 Banking Act of 1935	Created a seven-member board to regulate the nation's money supply and interest rates on loans.
1938 Federal Food, Drug, and Cosmetic Act (FFDCA)	Required manufacturers to list ingredients in foods, drugs, and cosmetic products.

FARM RELIEF AND RURAL DEVELOPMENT	PURPOSE
1933 Agricultural Adjustment Administration (AAA)	Aided farmers and regulated crop production.
1933 Tennessee Valley Authority (TVA)	Developed the resources of the Tennessee Valley.
1935 Rural Electrification Administration (REA)	Provided affordable electricity for isolated rural areas.

HOUSING	PURPOSE
1933 Home Owners Loan Corporation (HOLC)	Loaned money at low interest rates to homeowners who could not meet mortgage payments.
1934 Federal Housing Administration (FHA)	Insured loans for building and repairing homes.
1937 United States Housing Authority (USHA)	Provided federal loans for low-cost public housing.

LABOR RELATIONS	PURPOSE
1935 National Labor Relations Board (Wagner Act)	Defined unfair labor practices and established the National Labor Relations Board (NLRB) to settle disputes between employers and employees.
1938 Fair Labor Standards Act	Established a minimum hourly wage and a maximum number of hours in the workweek for the entire country. Set rules for the employment of workers under 16 and banned hazardous factory work for those under 18.

RETIREMENT	PURPOSE
1935 Social Security Administration	Provided a pension for retired workers and their spouses and aided people with disabilities.

In addition to electricity, many rural homes received running water through the REA.

In the end, because of political opposition and funding problems, the Social Security Act was not the total pension system or complete welfare system that Roosevelt envisioned. To avoid a huge tax hike, Roosevelt agreed to exclude certain workers, including farm workers and household workers, from the new program. Even so, it provided substantial benefits to millions of Americans.

EXPANDING AND REGULATING UTILITIES The Second New Deal also included laws to promote rural electrification and to regulate public utilities. In 1935 only 12.6 percent of American farms had electricity. Roosevelt established under executive order the Rural Electrification Administration (REA). The REA financed and worked with electrical cooperatives to bring electricity to isolated areas. By 1945, 48 percent of America's farms and rural homes had electricity. That figure rose to 90 percent by 1949.

The Public Utility Holding Company Act of 1935 took aim at financial corruption in the public utility industry. It outlawed the ownership of utilities by multiple holding companies—a practice known as the pyramiding of holding companies. Lobbyists for the holding companies fought the law fiercely, and it proved extremely difficult to enforce.

Reading Check
Draw Conclusions
Whom did Social Security help?

Lesson 2 Assessment

1. **Organize Information** Create a chart to show how groups such as farmers, the unemployed, youth, and retirees were helped by the programs of the Second New Deal.

Second New Deal	
Group	How Helped

Which group do you think benefited the most from the Second New Deal? Explain.

2. **Key Terms and People** For each key term or person in the lesson, write a sentence explaining its significance.

3. **Evaluate** Why might the Social Security Act be considered the most important achievement of the New Deal?

Think About:
• the types of relief needed in the 1930s
• alternatives to government assistance to the elderly, the unemployed, and people with disabilities
• the scope of the act and its impact on citizens today

4. **Draw Conclusions** Why might critics of the first New Deal have favored the Second New Deal?

5. **Form Generalizations** Why was the NIRA considered pro-labor?

6. **Analyze Primary Sources** Many WPA posters were created to promote New Deal programs—in this case, the Rural Electrification Administration. How does this poster's simplistic design convey the program's goal?

NLRB v. Jones and Laughlin Steel Corp. (1937)

ORIGINS OF THE CASE

In 1936 the Jones and Laughlin Steel Corporation was charged with intimidating union organizers and firing several union members. The National Labor Relations Board (NLRB) found the company guilty of "unfair labor practices" and ordered it to rehire the workers with back pay.

THE RULING

The Supreme Court ruled that Congress had the power to regulate labor relations and confirmed the authority of the NLRB.

LEGAL REASONING

In the 1935 National Labor Relations Act, or Wagner Act, Congress claimed that its authority to regulate labor relations came from the commerce clause of the Constitution. Jones and Laughlin Steel argued that its manufacturing business did not involve interstate commerce—it operated a plant and hired people locally.

The Court disagreed. Although production itself may occur within one state, it said, production is a part of the interstate "flow of commerce." If labor unrest at a steel mill would create "burdens and obstructions" to interstate commerce, then Congress has the power to prevent labor unrest at the steel mill.

The Court also explained that the act went "no further than to safeguard the right of employees to self-organization and to select representatives . . . for collective bargaining." Departing from earlier decisions, the Court affirmed that these are "fundamental" rights.

"Long ago we . . . said . . . that a single employee was helpless in dealing with an employer; that he was dependent . . . on his daily wage for the maintenance of himself and family; that, if the employer refused to pay him the wages that he thought fair, he was . . . unable to leave the employ and resist arbitrary and unfair treatment; that union was essential to give laborers opportunity to deal on an equality with their employer."

As a result, the Wagner Act was allowed to stand.

LEGAL SOURCES

LEGISLATION

U.S. Constitution, Article 1, Section 8 (Commerce Clause)

"The Congress shall have Power . . . To regulate Commerce with foreign Nations and among the several States."

National Labor Relations Act (1935)

"The term 'affecting commerce' means . . . tending to lead to a labor dispute burdening or obstructing commerce or the free flow of commerce."

"It shall be an unfair labor practice for an employer . . . to interfere with, restrain, or coerce employees in the exercise of the rights [to organize unions]."

RELATED CASES

Schechter *Poultry Corp.* v. *United States* (1935)

The Court struck down the National Industrial Recovery Act, a key piece of New Deal legislation.

Chief Justice Charles Evans Hughes

Choosing to work despite the strike, a storekeeper at the Jones and Laughlin Steel Corporation tries to pass through picket lines.

WHY IT MATTERED

The 1935 Wagner Act was one of the most important pieces of New Deal legislation. Conservative justices on the Supreme Court, however, thought New Deal legislation increased the power of the federal government beyond what the Constitution allowed. By the time the Jones and Laughlin case reached the Court in 1937, the Court had already struck down numerous New Deal laws. It appeared to many as if the Wagner Act was doomed.

In February 1937 Roosevelt announced a plan to appoint enough justices to build a Court majority in favor of the New Deal. Critics immediately accused Roosevelt of trying to pack the Supreme Court, thus crippling the Constitution's system of checks and balances.

Two months later, the Court delivered its opinion in *Jones and Laughlin* and at about the same time upheld other New Deal legislation as well. Most historians agree that the Court's switch was not a response to Roosevelt's "Court-packing" plan, which already seemed destined for failure. Nevertheless, the decision resolved a potential crisis.

HISTORICAL IMPACT

The protection that labor unions gained by the Wagner Act helped them to grow quickly. Union membership among non-farm workers grew from around 12 percent in 1930 to around 31 percent by 1950. This increase helped improve the economic standing of many working-class Americans in the years following World War II.

Most significantly, *Jones and Laughlin* greatly broadened Congress's power. Previously, neither the federal nor the state governments were thought to have sufficient power to control the large corporations and holding companies doing business in many states. Now, far beyond the power to regulate interstate commerce, Congress had the power to regulate anything "essential or appropriate" to that function. For example, federal laws barring discrimination in hotels and restaurants rest on the Court's allowing Congress to decide what is an "essential or appropriate" subject of regulation.

More recently, the Court has placed tighter limits on Congress's power to regulate interstate commerce. In *United States* v. *Lopez* (1995), the Court struck down a law that banned people from having handguns near a school. The Court said Congress was not justified in basing this law on its power to regulate interstate commerce.

Critical Thinking
1. **Connect to History** Lawyers for Jones and Laughlin said that the Wagner Act violated the Tenth Amendment. Chief Justice Hughes said that since the act fell within the scope of the commerce clause, the Tenth Amendment did not apply. Read the Tenth Amendment and then write a paragraph defending Hughes's position.

2. **Connect to Today** Do Internet research to read the opening sections of *United States* v. *Lopez*. There, Chief Justice Rehnquist offers a summary of the Court's interpretation of the commerce clause over the years. Summarize in your own words Rehnquist's description of the current meaning of the commerce clause.

New Deal, New Opportunities

The Big Idea

New Deal policies and actions affected various social and ethnic groups.

Why It Matters Now

The New Deal made a lasting impact on increasing the government's role in the struggle for equal rights.

Key Terms and People

Frances Perkins

Mary McLeod Bethune

John Collier

New Deal coalition

Congress of Industrial Organizations (CIO)

One American's Story

In 1939 African American singer Marian Anderson was invited to perform in Washington, DC. Despite being one of the most admired singers in the world and one of the top box office draws in the country, she was not allowed to perform at Constitution Hall because of her race. First Lady Eleanor Roosevelt and the NAACP arranged for Anderson to perform at the Lincoln Memorial on Easter Sunday. A crowd of nearly 75,000 people came to hear her sing. At the concert, Walter White, an official of the NAACP, noticed one girl in the crowd.

Marian Anderson sang from the steps of the Lincoln Memorial on April 9, 1939.

"Her hands were particularly noticeable as she thrust them forward and upward, trying desperately . . . to touch the singer. They were hands which despite their youth had known only the dreary work of manual labor. Tears streamed down the girl's dark face. Her hat was askew, but in her eyes flamed hope bordering on ecstasy. . . . If Marian Anderson could do it, the girl's eyes seemed to say, then I can, too."

—Walter White, quoted in
A Man Called White

The event became one of the most dramatic cultural events of the period. And it made Marian Anderson a symbol of progress for minorities in the United States. Her life reflected some of the difficulties African Americans and other minorities faced during the New Deal era. But Anderson's triumph gave many African Americans and other minorities, including the girl that Walter White witnessed, hope that they too would get a "new deal," instead of a "raw deal."

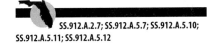

SS.912.A.2.7; SS.912.A.5.7; SS.912.A.5.10; SS.912.A.5.11; SS.912.A.5.12

Women Make Their Mark

In some ways, the New Deal represented an important opportunity for minorities and women; but what these groups gained was limited. Long-standing patterns of prejudice and discrimination continued to plague them and to prevent their full and equal participation in national life.

One of the most notable changes during the New Deal was the naming of several women to important government positions. **Frances Perkins** became America's first female cabinet member. As secretary of labor, she played a major role in creating the Social Security system and supervised labor legislation. President Roosevelt, encouraged by his wife Eleanor and seeking the support of women voters, also appointed two female diplomats and a female federal judge.

However, women continued to face discrimination in the workplace. Male workers believed that working women took jobs away from men. A Gallup poll taken in 1936 reported that 82 percent of Americans said that a wife should not work if her husband had a job. One journalist suggested a simple plan for solving unemployment: fire all the women currently working and replace them with men instead.

Additionally, New Deal laws yielded mixed results. The National Recovery Administration, for example, set wage codes, some of which set lower minimum wages for women. The Federal Emergency Relief Administration and the Civil Works Administration hired far fewer women than men, and the Civilian Conservation Corps hired only men.

In spite of these barriers, women continued their movement into the workplace. Although the overall percentage of women working for wages increased only slightly during the 1930s, the percentage of married women in the workplace grew from 11.7 percent in 1930 to 15.6 percent in 1940. In short, widespread criticism of working women did not halt the long-term trend of women working outside the home.

Reading Check
Summarize How did women fare in the New Deal work force?

– BIOGRAPHY

Frances Perkins (1882–1965)

As a student at Mount Holyoke College, Frances Perkins attended lectures that introduced her to social reform efforts. Her initial work in the settlement house movement sparked her interest in pursuing a career in the social service. After witnessing the Triangle Shirtwaist Factory fire in 1911, Perkins pledged to fight for labor reforms, especially those for women. A pioneer for labor and women's issues, she changed her name from Fannie to Frances, believing she would be taken more seriously in her work.

African American Activism

In the 1920s African Americans had gained more political influence during the Harlem Renaissance. They built upon their success in the 1930s, as well. One notable activist was A. Philip Randolph, who organized the country's first all-black trade union, the Brotherhood of Sleeping Car Porters. His work and that of others laid the groundwork for what would become the civil rights movement.

Mary McLeod Bethune, a close friend of Eleanor Roosevelt, was a strong supporter of the New Deal.

AFRICAN AMERICANS TAKE LEADERSHIP ROLES During the New Deal, Roosevelt appointed more than 100 African Americans to key positions in the government. **Mary McLeod Bethune**—an educator who dedicated herself to promoting opportunities for young African Americans—was one such appointee. Hired by the president to head the Division of Negro Affairs of the National Youth Administration, Bethune worked to ensure that the NYA hired African American administrators and provided job training and other benefits to minority students.

Bethune also helped organize a "Black Cabinet" of influential African Americans to advise the Roosevelt administration on racial issues. Among these figures were William H. Hastie and Robert C. Weaver, both appointees to Roosevelt's Department of the Interior. Never before had so many African Americans had a voice in the White House.

Eleanor Roosevelt played a key role in opening doors for African Americans in government. She invited African American leaders, including Walter White of the NAACP, for an unprecedented meeting at the White House to help end discrimination against African Americans in some New Deal programs. She also coordinated meetings between the president and the NAACP to discuss anti-lynching legislation.

THE PRESIDENT FAILS TO SUPPORT CIVIL RIGHTS Despite efforts to promote racial equality, Roosevelt was never committed to full civil rights for African Americans. He was afraid of upsetting white Democratic voters in the South, an important segment of his supporters. He refused to approve a federal anti-lynching law and an end to the poll tax, two key goals of the civil rights movement. Further, a number of New Deal agencies clearly discriminated against African Americans, including the NRA, the CCC, and the TVA. These programs gave lower wages to African Americans and favored whites.

African Americans recognized the need to fight for their rights and to improve conditions in areas that the New Deal ignored. In 1934 they helped organize the Southern Tenant Farmers Union, which sought to protect the rights of tenant farmers and sharecroppers, both white and black. In the North, the union created tenants' groups and launched campaigns to increase job opportunities.

Reading Check
Evaluate
Evaluate the actions and policies of the Roosevelt administration on civil rights.

In general, however, African Americans supported the Roosevelt administration and the New Deal, generally seeing them as their best hope for the future. As one man recalled, "Roosevelt touched the temper of the black community. You did not look upon him as being white, black, blue or green. He was President Roosevelt."

Mexican American Fortunes

Mexican Americans also tended to support the New Deal, even though they received even fewer benefits than African Americans did. Large numbers of Mexican Americans had come to the United States during the 1920s, settling mainly in the Southwest. Most found work laboring on farms, an occupation that was essentially unprotected by state and federal laws.

During the Depression, the need for farm labor decreased and farm wages fell to as little as nine cents an hour. Farm workers who tried to unionize often met with violence from employers and government authorities. The unemployment rate for Mexican Americans significantly increased during this time.

Reading Check
Identify Problems
Why was life
difficult for farm
laborers during the
Depression?

Although the CCC and WPA helped some Mexican Americans, these agencies also discriminated against them by disqualifying from their programs migrant workers who had no permanent address. Many of these workers decided to return to Mexico. But the United States government deported others. During the 1930s as many as 400,000 persons of Mexican descent, many of them U.S. citizens, were deported to Mexico. Those who remained in the United States lived in extreme poverty.

Native Americans Gain Support

Native Americans were another group that benefited from New Deal programs. In 1924 a law had granted Native Americans full citizenship. In 1933 President Roosevelt appointed **John Collier** as commissioner of Indian Affairs. Collier helped create the Indian Reorganization Act of 1934, which marked a complete change in government policy. After nearly 50 years of forcing Native Americans to assimilate, the government abandoned this approach and moved to grant Native Americans autonomy. It also helped to restore some reservation lands to tribal ownership. The act mandated changes in three areas.

- *economic*—Native American lands would belong to an entire tribe. This provision strengthened Native American land claims by prohibiting the government from taking over unclaimed reservation lands and selling them to people other than Native Americans.
- *cultural*—The number of boarding schools for Native American children was reduced, and children could now attend public school on the reservations.
- *political*—Tribes were given permission to elect tribal councils to govern their reservations.

Reading Check
Summarize What
changes occurred for
Native Americans as a
result of the New Deal?

Some Native Americans who valued their tribal traditions hailed the act as an important step forward. Other Native Americans who had become more "Americanized" as individual landowners under the previous Dawes Act objected, because they were tired of white people telling them what was good for them.

Reviving Organized Labor

Although New Deal policies had mixed results for minorities, these groups generally backed President Roosevelt. In fact, one of FDR's great achievements was to create the **New Deal coalition**—an alignment of diverse groups dedicated to supporting the Democratic Party. The coalition included southern whites, various urban groups, African Americans, and unionized industrial workers. As a result, Democrats dominated national politics throughout the 1930s and 1940s. The period also saw the growth of organized labor.

LABOR UNIONS FLOURISH As a result of the Wagner Act and other pro-labor legislation passed during the New Deal, union members enjoyed better working conditions and increased bargaining power. In their eyes, President Roosevelt was a "friend of labor." Labor unions donated money to Roosevelt's reelection campaigns. Union workers pledged him their votes.

Between 1933 and 1941, union membership grew from less than 3 million to more than 10 million. Unionization especially affected coal miners and workers in mass-production industries, such as the automobile, rubber, and

The Growing Labor Movement, 1933–1940

The Growth of Union Membership, 1930–1940

Source: *Historical Statistics of the United States*

UNION MEMBERSHIP SOARS
A Ben Shahn poster from the late 1930s boasted of the rise in union membership.

SIT-DOWN STRIKES
Union workers—such as these CIO strikers at the Fisher automobile plant in Flint, Michigan, in 1937—found the sit-down strike an extremely effective method for getting their demands met.

ROBERT F. WAGNER
A Democratic senator from New York (1927–1949), Robert F. Wagner was especially interested in workers' welfare. Wagner introduced the National Labor Relations Act in Congress in 1935.

electrical industries. It was in these industries, too, that a struggle for dominance within the labor movement began to develop.

The American Federation of Labor (AFL) had traditionally been restricted to the craft unions, such as carpenters and electricians. Most of the AFL leaders opposed industry-wide unions that represented all the workers in a given industry, such as automobile manufacturing.

Frustrated by this position, several key labor leaders, including John L. Lewis of the United Mine Workers of America and David Dubinsky of the International Ladies Garment Workers, formed the Committee for Industrial Organization to organize industrial unions. The committee rapidly signed up unskilled and semiskilled workers, and within two years it had won union recognition in both the steel and automobile industries. In 1938 the Committee for Industrial Organization was expelled from the AFL and changed its name to the **Congress of Industrial Organizations (CIO)**. This split lasted until 1955.

LABOR DISPUTES One of the main bargaining tactics of the labor movement in the 1930s was the sit-down strike. Instead of walking off their jobs, workers remained inside their plants. But they did not work. This prevented the factory owners from carrying on production with strikebreakers, or scabs. Some Americans disapproved of the sit-down strike, calling it a violation of private property. Nonetheless, it proved to be an effective bargaining tool.

Not all labor disputes in the 1930s were peaceful. Perhaps the most dramatic incident was the clash at the Republic Steel plant in Chicago on Memorial Day, 1937. Police attacked striking steelworkers outside the plant. One striker, an African American man, recalled the experience.

> *"I began to see people drop. There was a Mexican on my side, and he fell; and there was a black man on my side and he fell. Down I went. I crawled around in the grass and saw that people were getting beat. I'd never seen police beat women, not white women. I'd seen them beat black women, but this was the first time in my life I'd seen them beat white women—with sticks."*
>
> —Jesse Reese, quoted in *The Great Depression*

Chicago police attack strikers at what would become known as the Memorial Day Massacre (1937).

Ten people were killed and 84 wounded in this incident, which became known as the Memorial Day Massacre. Shortly afterward, the National Labor Relations Board stepped in and required the head of Republic Steel, Tom Girdler, to negotiate with the union. This and other actions helped labor gain strength during the 1930s.

FDR WINS IN 1936 Urban voters were another important component of the New Deal coalition. Support for the Democratic Party surged, especially in large northern cities, such as New York, Boston, Philadelphia, and Chicago. These and other cities had powerful city political organizations that provided services, such as jobs, in exchange for votes. In the 1936 election, President Roosevelt carried the nation's 12 largest cities.

Support for President Roosevelt came from various religious and ethnic groups—Roman Catholics, Jews, Italians, Irish, and Polish and other Slavic peoples—as well as from African Americans. His appeal to these groups was based on New Deal labor laws and work-relief programs, which aided the urban poor. The president also made direct and persuasive appeals to urban voters at election time. To reinforce his support, he also appointed many officials of urban-immigrant backgrounds, particularly Roman Catholics and Jews, to important government positions.

Women, African Americans, Mexican Americans, Native Americans, and workers from all walks of life were greatly affected by the New Deal. It also had a tremendous influence on American society and culture.

Reading Check
Analyze Causes
What factors contributed to labor's growth?

Lesson 3 Assessment

1. **Organize Information** Using a web diagram, note the effects of New Deal policies on American women, African Americans, Mexican Americans, Native Americans, unionized workers, and urban Americans.

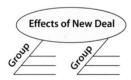

Write a paragraph explaining the effects of the New Deal on one of the groups.

2. **Key Terms and People** For each key term or person in the lesson, write a sentence explaining its significance.

3. **Synthesize** Why was the "Black Cabinet" important to the Roosevelt administration?

4. **Evaluate** How effective were unions in shaping political and economic policies? Do you think unions became too powerful? Explain.

5. **Analyze Motives** Why did urban voters support President Roosevelt?

6. **Summarize** What steps did women take toward equality during the 1930s?

Think About:
- hiring practices in federal programs
- women's opportunities in business and industry
- New Deal programs that protected the rights of women
- the role of women, such as Eleanor Roosevelt and Frances Perkins, in shaping New Deal policies

Culture in the 1930s

The Big Idea

Motion pictures, radio, art, and literature blossomed during the New Deal.

Why It Matters Now

The films, music, art, and literature of the 1930s still captivate today's public.

Key Terms and People

Gone with the Wind

Orson Welles

Richard Wright

Zora Neale Hurston

The Grapes of Wrath

One American's Story

Don Congdon, editor of the book *The Thirties: A Time to Remember*, was a high school student when the New Deal began. While many writers and artists in the 1930s produced works that reflected the important issues of the day, it was the movies and radio that most clearly captured the public imagination. Congdon remembers the role movies played at the time.

People line up to get into a movie theater during the Great Depression.

"Lots of us enjoyed our leisure at the movies. The experience of going was like an insidious [tempting] candy we could never get quite enough of; the visit to the dark theater was an escape from the drab realities of Depression living, and we were entranced by the never-ending variety of stories. Hollywood, like Scheherazade [the storyteller] in The Thousand and One Nights, *supplied more the next night, and the next night after that."*

—Don Congdon, quoted in *The Thirties: A Time to Remember*

During the Great Depression, movies provided a window on a different, more exciting world. Despite economic hardship, many people gladly paid the 25 cents it cost to go to the movies. Along with radio, motion pictures became an increasingly dominant feature of American life.

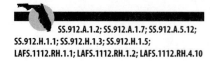

SS.912.A.1.2; SS.912.A.1.7; SS.912.A.5.12; SS.912.H.1.1; SS.912.H.1.3; SS.912.H.1.5; LAFS.1112.RH.1.1; LAFS.1112.RH.1.2; LAFS.1112.RH.4.10

The Lure of Motion Pictures and Radio

Although the 1930s were a difficult time for many Americans, it was a profitable and golden age for the motion picture and radio industries. By the late 1930s approximately 65 percent of the population attended the movies once a week. The nation boasted over 15,000 movie theaters. This was more than the number of banks and double the number of hotels. Sales of radios also greatly increased during the 1930s, from just over 13 million in 1930 to 28 million by 1940. Nearly 90 percent of American households owned a radio. More than ever before, people across the country and around the world shared cultural experiences through radio and motion pictures. Clearly, movies and radio had taken the world, especially Americans, by storm.

MOVIES ARE A HIT Wacky comedies, lavish musicals, love stories, and gangster films all vied for the attention of the movie-going public. Following the end of silent films and the rise of "talking" pictures, new stars such as Clark Gable, Marlene Dietrich, and James Cagney rose from Hollywood, the center of the film industry. These stars helped launch a new era of glamour and sophistication in Hollywood.

Clark Gable and Vivien Leigh starred in *Gone with the Wind,* a sweeping drama about life among southern plantation owners during the Civil War.

Some films made during the 1930s offered pure escape from the hard realities of the Depression. By presenting visions of wealth, romance, and good times, the movies made people forget their troubles. Perhaps the most famous film of the era, and one of the most popular of all time, was **Gone with the Wind** (1939). Another film, *Flying Down to Rio* (1933), was a light romantic comedy featuring Fred Astaire and Ginger Rogers. Astaire and Rogers went on to make many movies together, becoming America's favorite dance partners. Other notable movies of the era include *The Wizard of Oz* (1939) and *Snow White and the Seven Dwarfs* (1937), which showcased the dazzling and innovative animation of Walt Disney.

Comedies, such as *Monkey Business* (1931) and *Duck Soup* (1931) starring the zany Marx Brothers, became very popular. So did films that combined escapist appeal with more realistic plots and settings. Americans flocked to see gangster films that presented images of the dark, gritty streets and looming skyscrapers of urban America. These movies featured hard-bitten characters struggling to succeed in a harsh environment where they faced difficulties that Depression-era audiences could easily understand. Notable films in this genre include *Little Caesar* (1930) and *The Public Enemy* (1931).

Some commentators believed that several films, such as *Mr. Deeds Goes to Town* (1936) by director Frank Capra, presented the social and political accomplishments of the New Deal in a positive light. These films portrayed honest, kindhearted people winning out over those with greedy special interests. In much the same way, the New Deal seemed to represent the interests of average Americans.

The radio broadcast of *The War of the Worlds,* narrated by Orson Welles, demonstrated the power of radio in American society.

RADIO ENTERTAINS Even more than movies, radio embodied the democratic spirit of the times. Families typically spent several hours a day gathered together, listening to their favorite programs. It was no accident that President Roosevelt chose radio as the medium for his "fireside chats." It was the most direct means of access to the American people.

Like movies, radio programs offered a range of entertainment. In the evening, radio networks offered excellent dramas and variety programs. **Orson Welles**, an actor, director, producer, and writer, created one of the most renowned radio broadcasts of all time. On October 30, 1938, radio listeners heard news that Martians had invaded Earth. Panic set in as many Americans became convinced that the world was ending. Of course, the story wasn't true. It was Welles's radio drama based on H. G. Wells's novel *The War of the Worlds.* The broadcast revealed the power of radio at a time when Americans received fast-breaking news over the airwaves. Later, Welles directed movie classics such as *Citizen Kane* (1941) and *Touch of Evil* (1958). After making their reputation in radio, comedians Bob Hope, Jack Benny, and the duo Burns and Allen moved on to work in television and movies. Soap operas—so named because soap companies usually sponsored them—tended to play late morning to early afternoon for homemakers. Children's programs, such as *The Lone Ranger,* generally aired later in the afternoon, when children were home from school.

One of the first worldwide radio broadcasts described for listeners the horrific crash of the *Hindenburg,* a German zeppelin (rigid airship), in New Jersey on May 6, 1937. Such immediate news coverage became a staple in society.

Reading Check
Draw Conclusions
Why do you think movies were so popular during the Depression?

The Arts in Depression America

In contrast to many radio and movie productions of the 1930s, much of the art, music, and literature of the time was sober and serious. Despite grim artistic tones, however, much of this artistic work conveyed a more uplifting message. It often emphasized the strength of character and the democratic values of the American people.

A number of artists and writers embraced the spirit of social and political change the New Deal fostered. In fact, many received direct support through New Deal work programs. The government officials who headed these programs often believed that art played an important role in national life. Also, as Harry Hopkins, the head of the WPA, put it, "They've got to eat just like other people." Some people, however, objected that artists got WPA assistance. Art, they claimed, was not real work.

ARTISTS DECORATE AMERICA The Federal Art Project (FAP), a branch of the WPA, paid artists a living wage to produce public art. It also aimed to increase public appreciation of art and to promote positive images of

American Gothic *(1930), Grant Wood. Oil on beaver board, 30 11/16" x 25 11/16" (78 cm x 65.3 cm) unframed. The Art Institute of Chicago, Friends of American Art Collection [1930.934]. Photography © The Art Institute of Chicago/All rights reserved by the Estate of Nan Wood Graham/Licensed by VAGA, New York, NY*

American society. Project artists created posters, taught art in the schools, and painted murals on the walls of public buildings. These murals, inspired in part by the revolutionary work of Mexican muralists such as Diego Rivera, typically portrayed the dignity of ordinary Americans at work.

During the New Deal era, a number of American painters, such as Edward Hopper, Thomas Hart Benton, Jackson Pollock, and Iowa's Grant Wood, whose work includes the famous painting *American Gothic,* produced outstanding works of art.

The WPA's Federal Theater Project hired actors to perform plays. The project also hired artists to provide stage sets and props for theater productions that played around the country. It subsidized the work of important American playwrights, including Clifford Odets, whose play *Waiting for Lefty* (1935) dramatized the labor struggles of the 1930s.

WOODY GUTHRIE SINGS OF AMERICA Experiencing firsthand the tragedies of the Depression, singer and songwriter Woody Guthrie used music to capture the hardships of America. Along with tens of thousands of people from the Great Plains region, Guthrie was forced by the Dust Bowl to seek a better life elsewhere. He took the road west in search of brighter opportunities and wrote about his experiences in his songs. These "Dust Bowl Ballads" told

"For the Present We Are Busy"

Sculptor Beniamino Benvenuto Bufano received assistance through the Federal Art Project (FAP). The FAP paid for his studio space in San Francisco, as well as a salary for him and his assistants. In a report to Congress, he stressed the value of public art and the importance of supporting artists to make it.

Analyze Historical Sources
According to Bufano, how was the FAP benefiting society?

"Our art must become . . . big enough to belong to everybody, too big for anyone to put in his pocket and call his own. We ask no more than this, but if we are to do these things we must have help. We must have money for our granite, we must have tools for our metals. We must have men who have schooled themselves in the crafts to help us produce. Art, to have power, must have these things. . . . Movements like a government art project are not an accident; they come from great needs, the need of the artist to give something to the world as much as from his need to survive. . . . WPA/FAP has been the hope of the greatest cultural renaissance in recent times. For the present we have steel, stone, and tools. We have the spirit of great men and great cities to move us. We are busy."

—Beniamino Bufano, quoted in *Federal Support for the Visual Arts: The New Deal and Now*

of the devastation brought by the dust storms. The ballads also revealed the trials of the journey west and the challenges that migrant farm workers faced.

A likable and easy-going performer, Guthrie had his own radio show—first in Los Angeles and later in New York City. However, disagreements with management and Guthrie's desire to be on the move meant he rarely stayed at a job very long. When he was traveling, Guthrie wrote, often at the pace of a song a day. The hundreds of simple but honest songs Guthrie wrote about hard times and hope became popular around the country. Most notably, his song "This Land Is Your Land" would become a classic American folk song. Woody Guthrie had a major influence on the course of American folk music.

DIVERSE WRITERS DEPICT AMERICAN LIFE Many writers received support through yet another WPA program, the Federal Writers' Project. This project gave the future Pulitzer and Nobel Prize winner Saul Bellow his first writing job. It also helped **Richard Wright**, an African American author, complete his acclaimed novel *Native Son* (1940), about a young man trying to survive in a racist world. **Zora Neale Hurston** wrote a stirring novel with FWP assistance—*Their Eyes Were Watching God* (1937), about a young woman growing up in rural Florida.

John Steinbeck, one of this country's most famous authors, received assistance from the Federal Writers' Project. He was able to publish his epic novel *The Grapes of Wrath* (1939). The novel reveals the lives of Oklahomans who left the Dust Bowl and ended up in California, where their hardships continued. Before his success, however, Steinbeck had endured the difficulties of the Depression like most other writers.

Zora Neale Hurston

Writer John Steinbeck depicted the struggles of one tenant farmer and his family in his novel *The Grapes of Wrath*. The book was adapted into a film in 1940.

Other books and authors examined the difficulties of life during the 1930s. James T. Farrell's *Studs Lonigan* trilogy (1932–1935) provides a bleak picture of working-class life in an Irish neighborhood of Chicago. Jack Conroy's novel *The Disinherited* (1933) portrays the violence and poverty of the Missouri coalfields, where Conroy's own father and brother died in a mine disaster. Another best-selling novel of the time was Marjorie Kinnan Rawlings's *The Yearling,* which depicted the tough life of a family living in rural Florida.

Other writers found hope in the positive values of American culture. Writer James Agee and photographer Walker Evans collaborated on a book about Alabama sharecroppers, *Let Us Now Praise Famous Men* (1941). Though it deals with the difficult lives of poor farmers, it portrays the dignity and strength of character in the people it presents. Thornton Wilder's play *Our Town* (1938) captures the beauty of small-town life in New England. Although artists and writers recognized America's flaws, they contributed positively to the New Deal legacy. These intellectuals praised the virtues of American life and took pride in the country's traditions and accomplishments.

Reading Check
Analyze Issues How did the art and literature of the time reflect issues of the Depression?

Lesson 4 Assessment

1. **Organize Information** Create a web, filling in the names of those who contributed to each aspect of American culture in the 1930s.

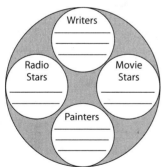

What contribution did each group make?

2. **Key Terms and People** For each key term or person in the lesson, write a sentence explaining its significance.

3. **Draw Conclusions** In your opinion, what were the main benefits of government support for art and literature in the 1930s? Support your response with details from the text.

   Think About:
   - the experiences of Americans in the Great Depression
   - the writers who got their start through the FWP
   - the subject matter of WPA murals and other New Deal–sponsored art
   - the benefits of art to society

4. **Make Inferences** What type of movies do you think might have been produced if the government had supported moviemaking as part of the New Deal? Use evidence from the module to support your response.

5. **Analyze Effects** How did the entertainment industry affect the economy?

6. **Analyze Causes** Why did the New Deal fund art projects?

The Impact of the New Deal

The Big Idea

The New Deal affected American society not only in the 1930s but also in the decades that followed.

Why It Matters Now

Americans still debate over how large a role government should play in American life.

Key Terms and People

Securities and Exchange Commission (SEC)

Federal Deposit Insurance Corporation (FDIC)

National Labor Relations Board (NLRB)

parity

Tennessee Valley Authority (TVA)

One American's Story

George Dobbin, a 67-year-old cotton-mill worker, staunchly supported Franklin Delano Roosevelt and his New Deal policies. In an interview, Dobbin explained his feelings about the president.

"I do think that Roosevelt is the biggest-hearted man we ever had in the White House. . . . It's the first time in my recollection that a President ever got up and said, 'I'm interested in and aim to do somethin' for the workin' man.' Just knowin' that for once . . . [there] was a man to stand up and speak for him, a man that could make what he felt so plain nobody could doubt he meant it, has made a lot of us feel a sight [lot] better even when [there] wasn't much to eat in our homes."

—George Dobbin, quoted in *These Are Our Lives*

A coal miner, Zeno Santinello, shakes hands with Franklin D. Roosevelt as he campaigns in Elm Grove, West Virginia, in 1932.

FDR was extremely popular among working-class Americans. Because of him, thousands of Americans like George Dobbin had gotten jobs, food, and money. The New Deal had given them hope and helped them to regain a sense of dignity. Far more important than FDR's personal popularity, however, was the impact of the policies he initiated.

SS.912.A.1.2; SS.912.A.1.4; SS.912.A.5.11; LAFS.1112.RH.2.6; MAFS.K12.MP.1.1; MAFS.K12.MP.3.1; MAFS.K12.MP.5.1

The End of the New Deal

The New Deal had helped reduce the suffering of Americans. Millions of people had received some form of help that ranged from direct relief to jobs that provided a steady paycheck. But Roosevelt's programs still did not end the Great Depression. During his second term, FDR hinted at plans to launch a Third New Deal. In his inaugural address, the president exclaimed, "I see millions of families trying to live on incomes so meager that the pall of family disaster hangs over them day by day. . . . I see one third of a nation ill-housed, ill-clad, ill-nourished."

However, the president did not favor deficit spending. And the federal government had already gone deeply into debt to provide jobs and aid to the American people. Although economic troubles still plagued the nation, President Roosevelt faced rising pressure from Congress to scale back New Deal programs. He cut back on spending, and as a result, industrial production dropped again. The number of unemployed increased from 7.7 million in 1937 to 10.4 million in 1938.

Meanwhile, President Roosevelt was becoming increasingly concerned with events in Europe, particularly Hitler's rise to power in Germany. The federal government was soon preparing for war and spending money producing guns, tanks, ships, airplanes, and other war supplies. In 1939 the deficit rose again, to $2.9 billion. This massive spending finally brought the nation out of the Great Depression. During World War II, the deficit reached a high of about $54.5 billion in 1943.

Reading Check
Analyze Events Why did industrial production drop and unemployment go up again in 1938?

Federal Deficit and Unemployment, 1933–1945

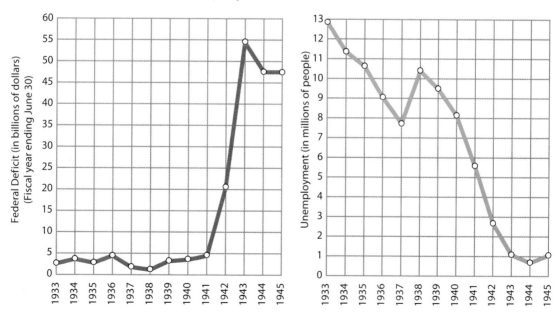

Interpret Graphs

1. What was the peak year of the deficit?

2. What relationship does there seem to be between deficit spending and unemployment? Why do you think this is so?

New Deal Programs Endure

The New Deal was effectively over by 1939, but its impact would last. New Deal economic and financial reforms, including the creation of the FDIC, the SEC, and Social Security, have helped to stabilize the nation's finances and economy. Although the nation still experiences economic downturns, known as recessions, people's savings are insured. They can also receive unemployment compensation if they lose their jobs.

BANKING AND FINANCE New Deal programs established new federal agencies in banking and finance. The **Securities and Exchange Commission (SEC)**, created in 1934, continues to monitor the stock market. The SEC also enforces laws regarding the sale of stocks and bonds. The **Federal Deposit Insurance Corporation (FDIC)**, created by the Glass-Steagall Act of 1933, has shored up the banking system. It reassures individual depositors that their savings are protected against loss in the event of a bank failure. Today, the Federal Deposit Insurance Corporation insures individual accounts in United States federal banks for up to $250,000.

PROTECTING WORKERS' RIGHTS Another area in which New Deal policies have had a lasting effect is the protection of workers' rights. New Deal legislation, such as the Wagner Act and the Fair Labor Standards Act, set standards for wages and hours, banned child labor, and ensured the right of workers to organize and to bargain collectively. Today, the **National Labor Relations Board (NLRB)**, created under the Wagner Act, continues to act as a mediator in labor disputes between unions and employers.

SOCIAL SECURITY One of the most important legacies of the New Deal has been that the federal government has assumed some responsibility for the social welfare of its citizens. Under President Roosevelt, the government created the Social Security system, designed to help a large number of needy Americans receive some assistance.

Document-Based Investigation Historical Source

A Monthly Check to You

When the Social Security system was established in 1935, the government distributed posters to familiarize Americans with the benefits of Social Security. This poster was printed in 1936 during the initial issuance of social security numbers at U.S. post offices.

Analyze Historical Sources
How does the Social Security poster illustrate how the federal government assumed some responsibility for the social welfare of citizens?

Social Security

Today, the Social Security system relies on mandatory contributions paid by workers—through payroll deductions—and by employers. The money is invested in a trust fund, from which retirement benefits are later paid. However, several problems have surfaced. For example, benefits have expanded. And Americans live longer than they did in 1935. Also, fewer workers are contributing to the system relative to the number of retirees eligible to receive benefits.

The long-range payment of benefits may be in jeopardy because of the large number of recipients. Continuing disagreement about how to address the costs has prevented legislative action.

Reading Check
Summarize Why was the Social Security system such an important part of the New Deal?

The Social Security Act provided an old-age insurance program and aid to people with disabilities and families with dependent children. It also included an unemployment compensation system run jointly by the federal government and the states. It has had a major impact on the lives of millions of Americans since its founding in 1935.

THE RURAL SCENE The New Deal also had an impact on agriculture. New Deal legislation set quotas on wheat production to control surpluses. Under the second Agricultural Adjustment Act, passed in 1938, the Commodity Credit Corporation made loans to farmers. The amount of a farmer's surplus crops and the **parity** price, a price intended to keep farmers' income steady, determined the value of a loan. Establishing agricultural price supports set a precedent of federal subsidies to farmers that continued into the 2000s. Other programs, such as rural electrification, helped to improve conditions in rural America.

THE ENVIRONMENT New Deal efforts have affected the environment, both positively and negatively. President Roosevelt was highly committed to conservation and promoted policies designed to protect the nation's natural resources. The Civilian Conservation Corps planted trees, created hiking trails, and built fire lookout towers. The Soil Conservation Service taught farmers how to conserve the soil through contour plowing, terracing, and crop rotation. Congress also passed the Taylor Grazing Act in 1934 to help reduce grazing on public lands. Such grazing had contributed to the erosion that brought about the dust storms of the 1930s. Some projects involved government-sponsored strip mining and coal burning, however, which caused air, land, and water pollution.

The **Tennessee Valley Authority (TVA)** put people to work building dams. These dams harnessed water power to generate electricity and helped prevent disastrous floods in the Tennessee Valley. The government also added to the national park system in the 1930s and established new wildlife refuges and wilderness areas. Great Smoky Mountains National Park, chartered in 1934, remains the most visited national park.

The Legacy of the New Deal

The reforms begun under the New Deal continue to influence American politics and society. The greatest impact of the New Deal is perhaps the extent to which it expanded the power of the federal government. By infusing the nation's economy with millions of dollars, creating federal jobs, attempting to regulate supply and demand, and increasing government involvement in settling labor and management disputes, New Deal reforms gave the government—and particularly the president—a more active role in shaping the economy. These changes also established the authority of the government to create agencies to regulate banking and investment activities. The increased federal oversight of the economy during the New Deal set a precedent for additional government involvement going forward.

The expansion during the New Deal also affected the relationship between the federal government and state governments. Federal officials attempted to involve the states in New Deal programs. Federal aid to the states increased from $217 million in 1932 to $2 billion in 1935. With these funds, state governments increased relief spending and provided new services. Some critics felt that the size of the government at both the federal and state levels got out of hand. They believed the expansion threatened the basic character of the nation. Supporters, on the other hand, believed this change was a welcome shift from the laissez-faire policies of the 1920s.

POINT		COUNTERPOINT

"The New Deal transformed the way American government works."

Supporters of the New Deal believe that it was successful. Many historians and journalists make this judgment by using the economic criterion of creating jobs. *The New Republic,* for example, argued that the shortcomings of the WPA "are insignificant beside the gigantic fact that it has given jobs and sustenance to a minimum of 1,400,000 and a maximum of 3,300,000 persons for five years."

Some historians stress that the New Deal was more than a temporary solution to a crisis. Professor A. A. Berle stated that, "human beings cannot indefinitely be sacrificed by millions to the operation of economic forces."

According to historian William E. Luechtenburg, "It is hard to think of another period in the whole history of the republic that was so fruitful or of a crisis that was met with as much imagination."

To Pulitzer Prize–winning historian Allan Nevins, the New Deal was a turning point in which the U.S. government assumed a greater responsibility for the economic welfare of its citizens.

"Many more problems have been created than solved by the New Deal."

Critics of the New Deal believe that it failed to reach its goals. Historian Barton J. Bernstein accepted the goals of the New Deal but declared that they were never met. To him, the New Deal "failed to raise the impoverished, it failed to redistribute income, [and] it failed to extend equality."

In Senator Robert A. Taft's opinion, "many more problems have been created than solved" by the New Deal. He maintained, "Whatever else has resulted from the great increase in government activity . . . it has certainly had the effect of checking private enterprise completely. This country was built up by the constant establishment of new business and the expansion of old businesses. . . . In the last six years this process has come to an end because of government regulation and the development of a tax system which penalizes hard work and success." Senator Taft claimed that "The government should gradually withdraw from the business of lending money and leave that function to private capital under proper regulation."

Critical Thinking

1. **Connect to History** How did the New Deal succeed? How did it fail? Write a paragraph that summarizes the main points.

2. **Connect to Today** Research the programs of the WPA and draft a proposal for a WPA-type program that would benefit your community today.

The New Deal angered those who believed that it took more of their money in taxes and curtailed their freedom through increased government regulations. Many conservatives think President Roosevelt's policies made the federal government too large and too powerful. They believe that the government stifled free enterprise and individual initiative. Liberal critics, in contrast, argue that President Roosevelt didn't do enough to socialize the economy and to eliminate social and economic inequalities. Supporters of the New Deal contend, however, that the president struck a reasonable balance between two extremes—unregulated capitalism and overregulated social-ism—and helped the country recover from its economic difficulties. One of Roosevelt's top advisers made this assessment of the president's goals.

"He had in mind a comprehensive welfare concept, infused with a stiff tincture of morality . . . He wanted all Americans to grow up healthy and vigorous and to be practically educated. He wanted business men to work within a set of understood rules. Beyond this he wanted people free to vote, to worship, to behave as they wished so long as a moral code was respected; and he wanted officials to behave as though office were a public trust."

—Rexford Tugwell, quoted in *Redeeming the Time*

Overall, the New Deal legacy has many dimensions. It brought hope and gratitude from some people for the benefits and protections they received. The New Deal changed the relationship between government and citizens as well as the expectations about what citizens expect from their government. Roosevelt's efforts to end the Great Depression also fueled one of the most fundamental and lasting debates about government in the nation's history. To this day, Americans disagree about the appropriate role and size of the federal government.

Reading Check
Summarize How did the New Deal expand the power of the federal government?

Lesson 5 Assessment

1. **Organize Information** In a cluster diagram, show long-term effects of the New Deal.

New Deal's Long-Term Effects

Which long-term benefit do you think has had the most impact? Why?

2. **Key Terms and People** For each key term in the lesson, write a sentence explaining its significance.

3. **Form Generalizations** Some critics have charged that the New Deal was antibusiness and anti–free enterprise. Explain why you agree or disagree with this charge.

   Think About:
   - the expanded role of the federal government and the growth of federal bureaucracy
   - the short-term effects on economic policies and capitalism
   - the long-term effects on economic policies and capitalism

4. **Summarize** What events marked the end of the New Deal?

5. **Evaluate** How successful do you think Franklin Roosevelt was as a president? How did his ability to effect change compare with some of his predecessors? Support your answer with details from the text.

6. **Analyze Effects** How did New Deal programs benefit and harm the environment?

The Tennessee Valley Authority

The Tennessee Valley Authority (TVA) is a federal agency that was established in 1933 to construct dams and power plants along the Tennessee River and its tributaries. The Tennessee River basin is one of the largest river basins in the United States, and people who live in this area have a number of common concerns. The TVA has helped the region in various ways: through flood and navigation control, the conservation of natural resources, and the generation of electric power, as well as through agricultural and industrial development.

The Tennessee Valley covers parts of seven states. Thus, the TVA became an enormous undertaking, eventually comprising dozens of major dams, each with associated power plants, recreational facilities, and navigation aids.

Like many dam projects, the TVA's plans were not without controversy, however. The government forced people to move from the land that would be flooded upstream from the dams. The displaced families usually received little resettlement help. Relocation was especially hard for the residents who were affected by the construction of Norris Dam and Dale Hollow Dam. These areas had been home to many families for generations. Their family members were buried there and had to be exhumed and reburied elsewhere. Also of concern for some was the destruction of important animal habitats. In addition, some power companies in the region claimed that the cheap energy offered by the TVA gave the government an unfair advantage.

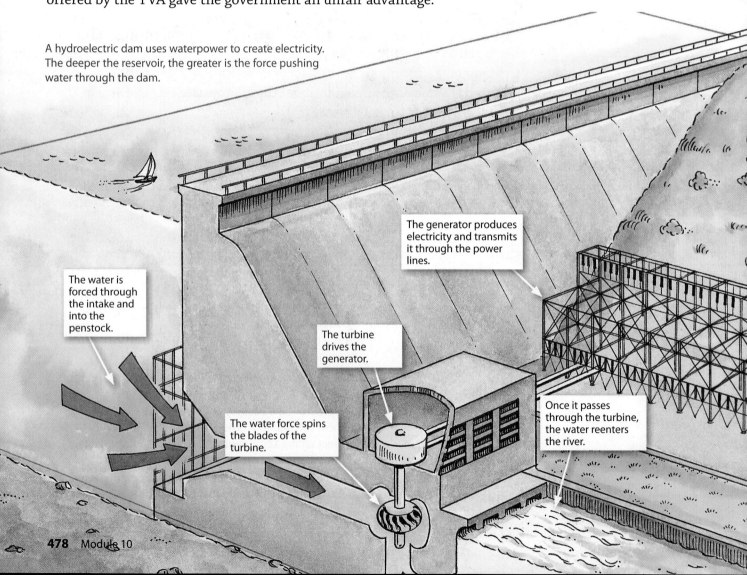

A hydroelectric dam uses waterpower to create electricity. The deeper the reservoir, the greater is the force pushing water through the dam.

The generator produces electricity and transmits it through the power lines.

The water is forced through the intake and into the penstock.

The turbine drives the generator.

The water force spins the blades of the turbine.

Once it passes through the turbine, the water reenters the river.

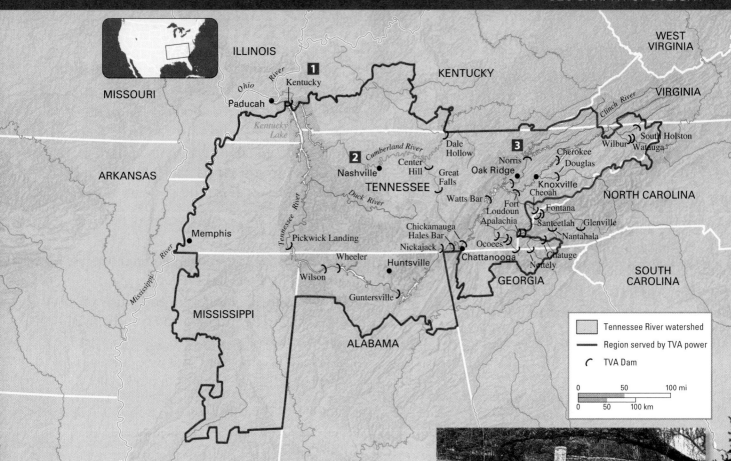

1 KENTUCKY DAM

Over a mile and a half long and 206 feet high, the Kentucky Dam created the 184-mile-long Kentucky Lake, a paradise for fishing.

2 THE CUMBERLAND RIVER

A similar series of dams, operated by the Corps of Engineers, is found on the Cumberland River. This system cooperates with the TVA.

3 NORRIS DAM

Located on the Clinch River, a tributary of the Tennessee River, the Norris Dam is named after Senator George W. Norris of Nebraska. Norris was a progressive leader who called for government involvement in the development of the power potential of the Tennessee River.

Before 1930 most homes in the area had no electricity. Women wash clothes outside this homestead near Andersonville, Tennessee, in 1933. Their estate was submerged when the Norris Dam filled.

Critical Thinking

1. **Analyze Distributions** Locate the dams on this map. Why do you think they might have been placed in these particular areas?

2. **Create a Model** Create a 3D model of a dam. Before you begin, pose a historical question your model will answer. Think about environmental changes caused by the construction of a dam.

Module 10 Assessment

Key Terms and People

For each key term or person below, write a sentence explaining its historical significance or contribution to the New Deal.

1. Franklin Delano Roosevelt
2. New Deal
3. Eleanor Roosevelt
4. Works Progress Administration (WPA)
5. National Youth Administration (NYA)
6. Social Security Act
7. Frances Perkins
8. Mary McLeod Bethune
9. Congress of Industrial Organizations (CIO)
10. Richard Wright

Main Ideas

Use your notes and the information in the module to answer the following questions.

A New Deal Fights the Depression

1. How did President Roosevelt change the role of the federal government during his first Hundred Days?
2. How did the public benefit from the Federal Securities Act?
3. Why did some people oppose the New Deal?
4. Why did conflict develop between the Supreme Court and other branches of government over aspects of the New Deal?

The Second New Deal

5. What were the key programs of the Second New Deal, and in what ways did they extend federal aid?
6. How did the Wagner Act help working people?
7. Why was the passage of the Social Security Act noteworthy? What compromises did Roosevelt ultimately make to his vision for a comprehensive Social Security system?

New Deal, New Opportunities

8. Summarize the impact the New Deal had on various ethnic groups.
9. Why did many urban voters support Roosevelt and the Democratic Party?
10. Which do you think was more important in labor's success: the passage of the Wagner Act or the success of the sit-down strikes? Explain.

Culture in the 1930s

11. What purpose did movies and radio serve during the Great Depression?
12. How did the literature, art, and music of the 1930s differ from the radio and movie productions of the time?
13. Explain how the New Deal programs supported artists and writers in the 1930s.

The Impact of the New Deal

14. List five New Deal agencies that are still in place today.
15. What benefits did the Tennessee Valley Authority provide? What negative impact did it have?
16. How did the New Deal affect the relationship between the states and the federal government?

Critical Thinking

1. **Categorize** Classify key New Deal programs as relief, recovery, or reform programs. In which area do you think the New Deal was most successful? Why?

New Deal Programs		
Relief	Recovery	Reform

2. **Analyze Effects** Which kind of New Deal program do you think was intended to have the most immediate effect: those for relief, recovery, or reform? Explain.

3. **Make Inferences** Why do you think that most of the relief programs of the New Deal no longer exist?

4. **Develop Historical Perspective** Of the New Deal programs that were discontinued, which ones might be of use to the nation today? Explain and support your opinion.

5. **Form Opinions** Do you think the federal programs from the 1930s that still exist today are necessary?

6. **Evaluate** How would you judge the value of work programs such as the CCC, CWA, and the TVA?

7. **Contrast** Explain the different criticisms of the New Deal. How did business leaders' reasons for opposing the New Deal differ from those of the American Liberty League?

8. **Form Generalizations** Do you think the expanded role of government as a result of the New Deal has been mostly positive or negative? Explain.

9. **Form Opinions** As a result of the New Deal, Americans began to look regularly to government for help. Do you think this is a good or bad trend?

10. **Develop Historical Perspective** The New Deal has often been referred to as a turning point in American history. Cite examples of political, economic, and social change that occurred as a result of the New Deal to explain why.

Engage with History

Imagine that you are a journalist during the Great Depression. Your editor has asked you to write a feature about photographer Dorothea Lange. Write an article that analyzes how Lange used her camera to depict the Great Depression. In the article, describe Lange's life and explain why she focused on the plight of sharecroppers and tenant farmers. Include some of Lange's images, and make sure to credit them properly.

Focus on Writing

Do you think President Roosevelt adequately addressed the needs of the ailing economy? Do you think his New Deal policies extended far enough to restore public confidence? How far do you think the government should go to try to improve the lives of citizens? Is it appropriate to use deficit spending to relieve suffering? Write an essay in which you support your opinions with examples.

Multimedia Activity

Organize into small groups. Use the Internet and other sources to research other economic recessions in U.S. history, including those in recent history. Learn about the scope of the recessions and how they compare to the Great Depression in the 1930s. Analyze how effective each president at the time was in addressing the social and economic problems associated with the recessions. Then create a website that compares and contrasts the policies and leadership abilities of these presidents in economic crises.

Module 11
World War II

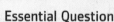

Essential Question
Why did the Allies win World War II?

About the Painting: This painting, *Dawn Patrol Launching* by Paul Sample, depicts an aircraft carrier. Carriers were used extensively in the Pacific Theater of World War II.

In this module you will learn about the events that led to the outbreak of World War II. You will also discover how political decisions, military campaigns, and home front sacrifices led to an Allied victory.

▶ Explore ONLINE!

HISTORY

VIDEOS, including...
- Digging In
- The Holocaust
- The Lend-Lease Act
- Black Soldiers in World War II
- Battle of the Bulge
- Battle of Midway
- Mourning FDR
- The Manhattan Project

✓ Document-Based Investigations

✓ Graphic Organizers

✓ Interactive Games

✓ Carousel: World War II Propaganda Posters

✓ Image with Hotspots: D-Day, June 6, 1944

SS.912.A.1.2 Utilize a variety of primary and secondary sources to identify author, historical significance, audience, and authenticity to understand a historical period. **SS.912.A.1.4** Analyze how images, symbols, objects, cartoons, graphs, charts, maps, and artwork may be used to interpret the significance of time periods and events from the past. **SS.912.A.1.6** Use case studies to explore social, political, legal, and economic relationships in history. **SS.912.A.1.7** Describe various sociocultural aspects of American life including arts, artifacts, literature, education, and publications. **SS.912.A.5.5** Describe efforts by the United States and other world powers to avoid future wars. **SS.912.A.6.1** Examine causes, course, and consequences of World War II on the United States and the world. **SS.912.A.6.2** Describe the United States response in the early years of World War II. **SS.912.A.6.3** Analyze the impact of the Holocaust during World War II on Jews as well as other groups. **SS.912.A.6.4** Examine efforts to expand or contract rights for various populations during World War II. **SS.912.A.6.5** Explain the impact of World War II on domestic government policy. **SS.912.A.6.6** Explain the impact of World War II on domestic government policy. **SS.912.A.6.7** Describe the attempts to promote international justice through the Nuremberg Trials. **SS.912.A.6.9** Describe the rationale for the formation of the United Nations, including the contribution of Mary McLeod Bethune. **SS.912.A.6.15** Examine key events and peoples in Florida history as they relate to United States history. **SS.912.G.1.2** Use spatial perspective and appropriate geographic terms and tools, including the Six Essential Elements, as organizational schema to describe any given place. **SS.912.G.2.1** Identify the physical characteristics and the human characteristics that define and differentiate regions. **SS.912.G.4.2** Use geographic terms and tools to analyze the push/pull factors contributing to human migration within and among places. **SS.912.G.4.3** Use geographic terms and tools to analyze the effects of migration both on the place of origin and destination, including border areas.

Timeline of Events 1930–1946   ▶ *Explore ONLINE!*

United States Events		World Events

1930

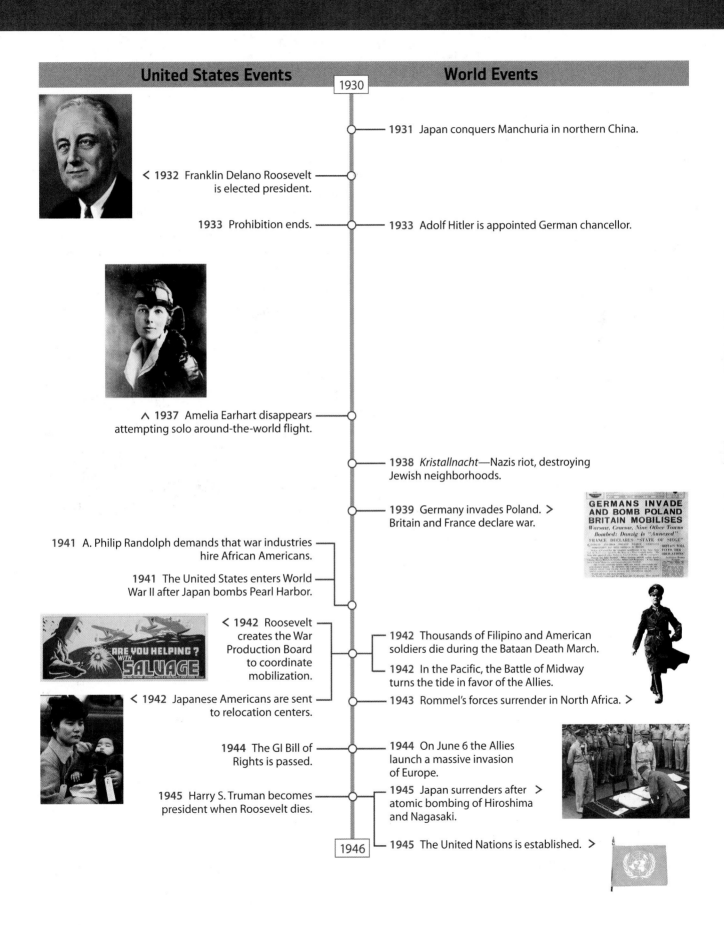

1931 Japan conquers Manchuria in northern China.

< **1932** Franklin Delano Roosevelt is elected president.

1933 Prohibition ends.

1933 Adolf Hitler is appointed German chancellor.

∧ **1937** Amelia Earhart disappears attempting solo around-the-world flight.

1938 *Kristallnacht*—Nazis riot, destroying Jewish neighborhoods.

1939 Germany invades Poland. > Britain and France declare war.

1941 A. Philip Randolph demands that war industries hire African Americans.

1941 The United States enters World War II after Japan bombs Pearl Harbor.

< **1942** Roosevelt creates the War Production Board to coordinate mobilization.

1942 Thousands of Filipino and American soldiers die during the Bataan Death March.

1942 In the Pacific, the Battle of Midway turns the tide in favor of the Allies.

< **1942** Japanese Americans are sent to relocation centers.

1943 Rommel's forces surrender in North Africa. >

1944 The GI Bill of Rights is passed.

1944 On June 6 the Allies launch a massive invasion of Europe.

1945 Harry S. Truman becomes president when Roosevelt dies.

1945 Japan surrenders after > atomic bombing of Hiroshima and Nagasaki.

1946

1945 The United Nations is established. >

GERMANS INVADE AND BOMB POLAND BRITAIN MOBILISES

★ War Breaks Out

The Big Idea
The rise of rulers with total power in Europe and Asia led to World War II.

Why It Matters Now
Dictators of the 1930s and 1940s changed the course of history when their actions started World War II, serving as a warning to be vigilant about totalitarian government.

Key Terms and People
Joseph Stalin
totalitarian
Benito Mussolini
fascism
Adolf Hitler
Nazism
Hideki Tojo
Neville Chamberlain
Winston Churchill
appeasement
nonaggression pact
blitzkrieg

One American's Story

Martha Gellhorn arrived in Madrid in 1937 to cover the brutal civil war that had broken out in Spain the year before. Hired as a special correspondent for *Collier's Weekly,* she had come with very little money and no special protection. On assignment there, she met the writer Ernest Hemingway, whom she later married. To Gellhorn, a young American writer, the Spanish Civil War was a deadly struggle between tyranny and democracy. For the people of Madrid, it was also a daily struggle for survival.

"You would be walking down a street, hearing only the city noises of streetcars and automobiles and people calling to one another, and suddenly, crushing it all out, would be the huge stony deep booming of a falling shell, at the corner. There was no place to run, because how did you know that the next shell would not be behind you, or ahead, or to the left or right?"
—Martha Gellhorn, from
The Face of War

Martha Gellhorn, one of the first women war correspondents, began her career during the Spanish Civil War.

Less than two decades after the end of World War I—"the war to end all wars"—fighting erupted again in Europe and in Asia. As Americans read about distant battles, they hoped the conflicts would remain on the other side of the world.

SS.912.A.1.2; SS.912.A.1.4; SS.912.A.6.1; SS.912.G.1.2; LAFS.1112.RH.4.10

Failures of the Treaty of Versailles

The Treaty of Versailles, which ended World War I, left many European nations dissatisfied. The treaty's war-guilt clause placed the blame for the war solely on Germany. The treaty also demanded that the Germans pay reparations, or payments for damages and expenses caused by the war. The amount demanded far exceeded what the German government could actually afford to pay.

Instead of securing a "just and secure peace," the Treaty of Versailles caused anger and resentment. Germans saw nothing fair in a treaty that blamed them for starting the war. Nor did they find security in a settlement that stripped them of their overseas colonies and border territories. The terms of the treaty did serious damage to the German economy. It forced Germany to give up control of some of its major industrial regions, which made the reparations payments even more challenging. These factors helped bring about a period of severe inflation, or rising prices. Prices increased at such an incredible rate that by 1923, German currency had simply ceased to have any meaningful value. These problems overwhelmed the Weimar Republic, the democratic government set up in Germany after World War I.

Italy was also unhappy with the treaty. The Italians had been on the winning side in the war. They had hoped to be rewarded with territory as part of the treaty. Instead, they were largely ignored during the peace talks. Similarly dissatisfied, the Soviets resented the carving up of parts of Russia.

The peace settlement had not fulfilled President Wilson's hope of a world "safe for democracy." New democratic governments that emerged in Europe after the war floundered. Without a democratic tradition, people turned to authoritarian leaders to solve their economic and social problems. The new democracies collapsed, and dictators were able to seize power. Some had great ambitions.

Reading Check
Analyze Causes
What factors contributed to the rise of authoritarian governments during this period?

Germany was expected to pay off huge debts while dealing with widespread poverty. By 1923 an inflating economy made a five-million German mark worth less than a penny. Here children build blocks with stacks of useless German marks.

The Spread of Totalitarianism

The seeds of new conflicts had been sown in World War I. For many nations, peace had brought not prosperity but revolution fueled by economic depression and struggle. The postwar years also brought the rise of powerful dictators driven by the belief in nationalism—loyalty to one's country above all else—and dreams of territorial expansion.

JOSEPH STALIN TRANSFORMS THE SOVIET UNION In Russia, hopes for democracy gave way to civil war, resulting in the establishment of a communist state, officially called the Soviet Union, in 1922. After V. I. Lenin died in 1924, **Joseph Stalin**, whose last name means "man of steel," took control of the country. Stalin focused on creating a model communist state. In doing so, he made both agricultural and industrial growth the prime economic goals of the Soviet Union. Stalin abolished all privately owned farms and replaced them with collectives—large government-owned farms, each worked by hundreds of families.

Stalin moved to transform the Soviet Union from a backward rural nation into a great industrial power. In 1928 the Soviet dictator outlined the first of several "five-year plans" for industrialization. All economic activity was placed under state management. By 1937 the Soviet Union had become the world's second-largest industrial power, surpassed in overall production only by the United States. The human costs of this transformation were enormous.

In his drive to purge, or eliminate, anyone who threatened his power, Stalin did not spare even his most faithful supporters. While the final toll will never be known, historians estimate that Stalin was responsible for the deaths of 8 million to 13 million people. Millions more died in famines caused by the restructuring of Soviet society.

By 1939 Stalin had firmly established a **totalitarian** government that tried to exert complete control over its citizens. In a totalitarian state, individuals have no rights, and the government suppresses all opposition.

THE RISE OF FASCISM IN ITALY While Stalin was consolidating his power in the Soviet Union, **Benito Mussolini** was establishing a totalitarian regime in Italy, where unemployment and inflation produced bitter strikes. Some of those strikes were led by Communists. Alarmed by these threats, the middle and upper classes demanded stronger leadership. Mussolini took advantage of this situation. A powerful speaker, Mussolini knew how to appeal to Italy's wounded national pride. He played on the fears of economic collapse and communism. "Italy wants peace, work, and calm. I will give these things with love if possible, with force if necessary," he said. In this way, he won the support of many discontented Italians.

By 1921 Mussolini had established the Fascist Party. **Fascism** (făsh´ĭz´əm) stressed nationalism and placed the interests of the state above those of individuals. To strengthen the nation, Fascists argued, power must rest with a single strong leader and a small group of devoted party members. (The Latin *fasces*—a bundle of rods tied around an ax handle—had been a symbol of unity and authority in ancient Rome.)

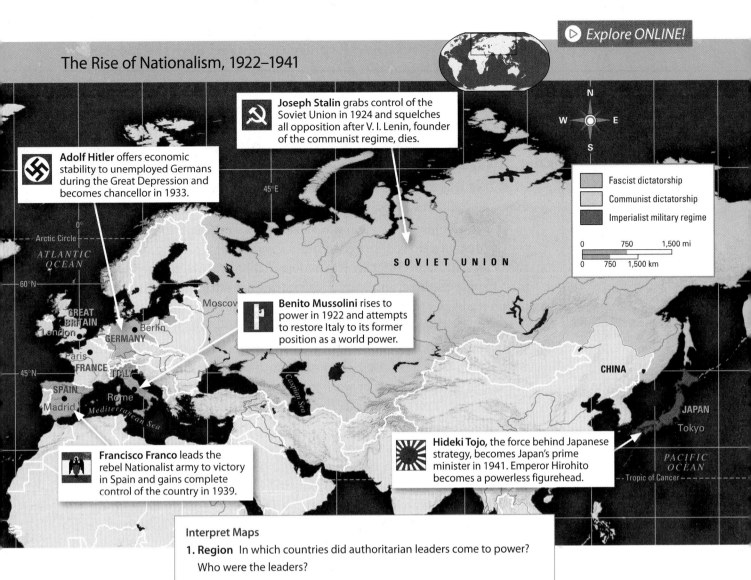

The Rise of Nationalism, 1922–1941

▶ Explore ONLINE!

Joseph Stalin grabs control of the Soviet Union in 1924 and squelches all opposition after V. I. Lenin, founder of the communist regime, dies.

Adolf Hitler offers economic stability to unemployed Germans during the Great Depression and becomes chancellor in 1933.

Benito Mussolini rises to power in 1922 and attempts to restore Italy to its former position as a world power.

Francisco Franco leads the rebel Nationalist army to victory in Spain and gains complete control of the country in 1939.

Hideki Tojo, the force behind Japanese strategy, becomes Japan's prime minister in 1941. Emperor Hirohito becomes a powerless figurehead.

Fascist dictatorship

Communist dictatorship

Imperialist military regime

| 0 | 750 | 1,500 mi |

| 0 | 750 | 1,500 km |

Interpret Maps

1. **Region** In which countries did authoritarian leaders come to power? Who were the leaders?

2. **Location** What geographic features might have led Japan to expand?

In October 1922 Mussolini marched on Rome with thousands of his followers, whose black uniforms gave them the name "Black Shirts." When important government officials, the army, and the police sided with the Fascists, the Italian king appointed Mussolini head of the government.

Calling himself *Il Duce,* or "the leader," Mussolini gradually extended Fascist control to every aspect of Italian life. Tourists marveled that *Il Duce* had even "made the trains run on time." Mussolini achieved this efficiency, however, by crushing all opposition and by making Italy a totalitarian state.

THE NAZIS TAKE OVER GERMANY In Germany, **Adolf Hitler** had followed a path to power similar to Mussolini's. At the end of World War I, Hitler had been a jobless soldier drifting around Germany. In 1919 he joined a struggling group called the National Socialist German Workers' Party, better known as the Nazi Party. Despite its name, this party had no ties to socialism.

Hitler proved to be such a powerful public speaker and organizer that he quickly became the party's leader. Calling himself *Der Führer*—"the Leader"—he promised to bring Germany out of chaos.

In his book *Mein Kampf* [My Struggle], Hitler set forth the basic beliefs of Nazism that became the plan of action for the Nazi Party. **Nazism** (nät′sĭz′əm), the German brand of fascism, was based on extreme nationalism. Hitler, who had been born in Austria, dreamed of uniting all German-speaking people in a great German empire.

Hitler also wanted to enforce racial "purification" at home. In his view, Germans—especially blue-eyed, blond-haired "Aryans"—formed a "master race" that was destined to rule the world. "Inferior races," such as Jews, Slavs, and all nonwhites, were deemed fit only to serve the Aryans.

A third element of Nazism was national expansion. Hitler believed that for Germany to thrive, it needed more *lebensraum,* or living space. One of the Nazis' aims, as Hitler wrote in *Mein Kampf,* was "to secure for the German people the land and soil to which they are entitled on this earth," even if this could be accomplished only by "the might of a victorious sword."

The Great Depression helped the Nazis come to power. Because of war debts and dependence on American loans and investments, Germany's economy was hit hard. By 1932 some 6 million Germans were unemployed. Many men who were out of work joined Hitler's private army, the "storm troopers" (or "Brown Shirts"). The German people were desperate and turned to Hitler as their last hope.

Background
According to Hitler there were three German empires: the Holy Roman Empire, the German Empire of 1871–1918, and the Third Reich.

By mid-1932, the Nazis had become the strongest political party in Germany. In January 1933 Hitler was appointed chancellor (prime minister). Once in power, Hitler quickly dismantled Germany's democratic Weimar Republic. In its place he established the *Third Reich,* or Third German Empire. According to Hitler, the Third Reich would be a "Thousand-Year Reich"—it would last for a thousand years.

The Faces of Totalitarianism

Fascist Italy	Nazi Germany	Communist Soviet Union
Benito Mussolini	Adolf Hitler	Joseph Stalin
• Extreme nationalism • Militaristic expansionism • Charismatic leader • Private property with strong government controls • Anticommunist	• Extreme nationalism and racism • Militaristic expansionism • Forceful leader • Private property with strong government controls • Anticommunist	• Planned to create a sound communist state and wait for world revolution • Forceful leader • Eventual rule by working class • State ownership of property

MILITARISTS GAIN CONTROL IN JAPAN Halfway around the world, Japan was another country torn by political and economic conflict. Among the problems facing Japan was the limited size of its territory. The islands of Japan were growing crowded. At the time, Japan's government was under civilian control. Many Japanese, however, were unhappy with their leaders. Dissatisfaction was especially high among members of the military who held strong nationalist beliefs.

In the early 1930s a group of military leaders used violence to take control of the imperial government of Japan. Like Hitler and Mussolini, these leaders believed in the need for a strong army to accomplish their country's goals, a philosophy known as militarism. Also like Hitler, they felt the need for more living space for a growing population. Many Japanese wanted to expand their territory and gain greater access to wealth and resources. This desire grew even stronger as a result of the worldwide economic depression of the 1930s.

CIVIL WAR BREAKS OUT IN SPAIN In 1936 a group of Spanish army officers led by General Francisco Franco rebelled against the Spanish republic. Revolts broke out all over Spain, and the Spanish Civil War began. The war aroused passions not only in Spain but also throughout the world. About 3,000 Americans formed the Abraham Lincoln Battalion and traveled to Spain to fight against Franco. "We knew, we just knew," recalled Martha Gellhorn, "that Spain was the place to stop fascism."

Such limited aid was not sufficient to stop the spread of fascism, however. The Western democracies remained neutral. Although the Soviet Union sent equipment and advisers, Hitler and Mussolini backed Franco's forces with troops, weapons, tanks, and fighter planes. The war forged a close relationship between the German and Italian dictators, who signed a formal alliance known as the Rome-Berlin Axis. After a loss of almost 500,000 lives, Franco's victory in 1939 established him as Spain's fascist dictator. Once again a totalitarian government ruled in Europe.

Reading Check
Summarize What are the characteristics of a totalitarian state?

Dictators Expand Their Territory

Having established their totalitarian regimes, many dictators sought to increase their territories, often through military action. Unfortunately the League of Nations, which had been established after World War I to prevent such aggressive acts, did little to thwart their efforts.

JAPAN'S AMBITIONS IN THE PACIFIC In 1931 the militarists in control of Japan's government began working in earnest to achieve their goals of growing Japan's territory and access to resources. Ignoring the protests of more moderate Japanese officials, they launched a surprise attack and seized control of the Chinese province of Manchuria. Within several months, Japanese troops controlled the entire province, a large region about twice the size of Texas that was rich in natural resources.

This action was a significant test of the power of the League of Nations. The League sent representatives to Manchuria to investigate the situation.

Their report condemned Japan, who in turn simply quit the League. Meanwhile, the success of the Manchurian invasion put the militarists firmly in control of Japan's government.

As Germany began to expand its territory in Europe, it opened new opportunities for Japanese expansionists. Already in control of Manchuria, in July 1937 **Hideki Tojo** (hē′d-kē tō′jō′), chief of staff of Japan's Kwantung Army, launched an invasion farther into China. As French, Dutch, and British colonies lay unprotected in Asia, Japanese leaders leaped at the opportunity to unite East Asia under Japanese control by seizing the colonial lands.

AGGRESSION IN EUROPE AND AFRICA The failure of the League of Nations to take action against Japan did not escape the notice of Europe's dictators. In 1933 Hitler pulled Germany out of the League of Nations. In 1935 he began a military buildup in violation of the Treaty of Versailles. A year later he sent troops into the Rhineland, a German region bordering France and Belgium that was demilitarized as a result of the Treaty of Versailles. The League did nothing to stop Hitler.

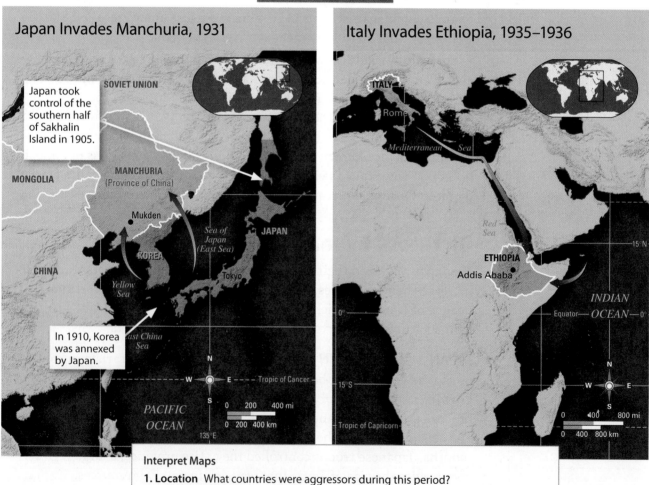

Explore ONLINE!

Interpret Maps

1. **Location** What countries were aggressors during this period?

2. **Movement** Notice the size and location of Italy and of Japan with respect to the country each invaded. What similarities do you see?

Meanwhile, Mussolini began building his new Roman Empire. His first target was Ethiopia, one of Africa's few remaining independent countries. By the fall of 1935, tens of thousands of Italian soldiers stood ready to advance on Ethiopia. The League of Nations reacted with brave talk of "collective resistance to all acts of unprovoked aggression."

When the invasion began, however, the League's response was an ineffective economic boycott—little more than a slap on Italy's wrist. By May 1936 Ethiopia had fallen. In desperation, Haile Selassie, the ousted Ethiopian emperor, appealed to the League for assistance. Nothing was done. "It is us today," he told them. "It will be you tomorrow."

AUSTRIA AND CZECHOSLOVAKIA FALL On November 5, 1937, Hitler met secretly with his top military advisers. He boldly declared that to grow and prosper Germany needed the land of its neighbors. His plan was to absorb Austria and Czechoslovakia into the Third Reich. When one of his advisors protested that annexing those countries could provoke war, Hitler replied, "'The German Question' can be solved only by means of force, and this is never without risk."

Austria was Hitler's first target. The Paris Peace Conference following World War I had created the relatively small nation of Austria out of what was left of the Austro-Hungarian Empire. The majority of Austria's 6 million people were Germans who favored unification with Germany. On March 12, 1938, German troops marched into Austria unopposed. A day later Germany announced that its *Anschluss,* or "union," with Austria was complete. The United States and the rest of the world did nothing.

Hitler then turned to Czechoslovakia. About 3 million German-speaking people lived in the western border regions of Czechoslovakia which were called the Sudetenland. The mountainous region formed Czechoslovakia's main defense against German attack. Hitler wanted to annex Czechoslovakia to provide more living space for Germany as well as to control its important natural resources.

Hitler charged that the Czechs were abusing the Sudeten Germans, and he began massing troops on the Czech border. The U.S. correspondent William Shirer, then stationed in Berlin, wrote in his diary: "The Nazi press [is] full of hysterical headlines. All lies. Some examples: 'Women and Children Mowed Down by Czech Armored Cars,' or 'Bloody Regime—New Czech Murders of Germans.'"

Early in the crisis, both France and Great Britain promised to protect Czechoslovakia. Then, just when war seemed inevitable, Hitler invited French premier Édouard Daladier and British prime minister **Neville Chamberlain** to meet with him in Munich. When they arrived, the führer declared that the annexation of the Sudetenland would be his "last territorial demand." In their eagerness to avoid war, Daladier and Chamberlain chose to believe him. On September 30, 1938, they signed the Munich Agreement, which turned the Sudetenland over to Germany without a single shot being fired. Chamberlain returned home and proclaimed: "My friends, there has come back from Germany peace with honor. I believe it is peace in our time."

Chamberlain's satisfaction was not shared by **Winston Churchill**, Chamberlain's political rival in Great Britain. In Churchill's view, by signing the

Germany, Italy, and Japan were a threat to the entire world. They believed they were superior and more powerful than other nations, especially democracies. This cartoon shows their obsession with global domination.

Munich Agreement, Daladier and Chamberlain had adopted a shameful policy of **appeasement**—or giving up principles to pacify an aggressor. As Churchill bluntly put it, "Britain and France had to choose between war and dishonor. They chose dishonor. They will have war." Nonetheless, the House of Commons approved Chamberlain's policy toward Germany and Churchill responded with a warning.

> "[W]e have passed an awful milestone in our history. . . . And do not suppose that this is the end. . . . This is only the First sip, the First foretaste of a bitter cup which will be proffered to us year by year unless, by a supreme recovery of moral health and martial vigor, we arise again and take our stand for freedom as in the olden time."
>
> —Winston Churchill, from a speech to the House of Commons, quoted in *The Gathering Storm*

Reading Check
Analyze Issues
What was appeasement, and why did Churchill oppose it so strongly?

The German Offensive

As Churchill had warned, Hitler was not finished expanding the Third Reich. As dawn broke on March 15, 1939, German troops poured into what remained of Czechoslovakia. At nightfall Hitler gloated, "Czechoslovakia has ceased to exist." After that, the German dictator turned his land-hungry gaze toward Germany's eastern neighbor, Poland.

THE SOVIET UNION DECLARES NEUTRALITY Like Czechoslovakia, Poland had a sizable German-speaking population. In the spring of 1939, Hitler began his familiar routine, charging that Germans in Poland were mistreated by the Poles and needed his protection. Some people thought that this time Hitler must have been bluffing. After all, an attack on Poland might bring

Germany into conflict with the Soviet Union, Poland's eastern neighbor. At the same time, such an attack would most likely provoke a declaration of war from France and Britain—both of whom had promised military aid to Poland. The result would be a two-front war. Fighting on two fronts had exhausted Germany in World War I. Surely, many thought, Hitler would not be foolish enough to repeat that mistake.

As tensions rose over Poland, Stalin surprised everyone when he signed a **nonaggression pact** with Hitler. Once bitter enemies, on August 23, 1939, fascist Germany and Communist Russia now committed never to attack each other. Germany and the Soviet Union also signed a second, secret pact, agreeing to divide Poland between them. With the danger of a two-front war eliminated, the fate of Poland was sealed.

***BLITZKRIEG* IN POLAND** As day broke on September 1, 1939, the German *Luftwaffe*, or German air force, roared over Poland, raining bombs on military bases, airfields, railroads, and cities. At the same time, German tanks raced across the Polish countryside, spreading terror and confusion. This invasion was the initial test of Germany's newest military strategy, the *blitzkrieg*, or lightning war. Blitzkrieg made use of advances in military technology—such as fast tanks that had been adapted to move quickly over rough terrain and more powerful aircraft that could travel over longer distances—to take the enemy by surprise and then quickly crush all opposition with overwhelming force. On September 3, two days following the terror in Poland, Britain and France declared war on Germany.

The blitzkrieg tactics worked perfectly. Major fighting was over in three weeks, long before France, Britain, and their allies could mount a defense. In the last week of fighting, the Soviet Union attacked Poland from the east, grabbing some of its territory. The portion Germany annexed in western Poland contained almost two-thirds of Poland's population. By the end of the month, Poland had ceased to exist—and World War II had begun.

A German tank unit moves through western Poland in 1939.

THE PHONY WAR For several months after the fall of Poland, French and British troops on the Maginot Line, a system of fortifications built along France's eastern border, sat staring into Germany, waiting for something to happen. On the Siegfried Line a few miles away German troops stared back. The blitzkrieg had given way to what the Germans called the *sitzkrieg* ("sitting war"), and what some newspapers referred to as the phony war.

After occupying eastern Poland, Stalin began annexing the Baltic states of Estonia, Latvia, and Lithuania. Late in 1939 Stalin sent his Soviet army into Finland. After three months of fighting, the outnumbered Finns surrendered.

Suddenly, on April 9, 1940, Hitler launched a surprise invasion of Denmark and Norway in order "to protect [those countries'] freedom and independence." But in truth, Hitler planned to build bases along the coasts to strike at Great Britain. Next, Hitler turned against the Netherlands, Belgium, and Luxembourg, which were overrun by the end of May. The phony war had ended.

THE FALL OF FRANCE France's Maginot Line proved to be ineffective; the German army threatened to bypass the line during its invasion of Belgium. Hitler's generals sent their tanks through the Ardennes, a region of wooded ravines in northeast France, thereby avoiding British and French troops who thought the Ardennes were impassable. The Germans continued to march toward Paris.

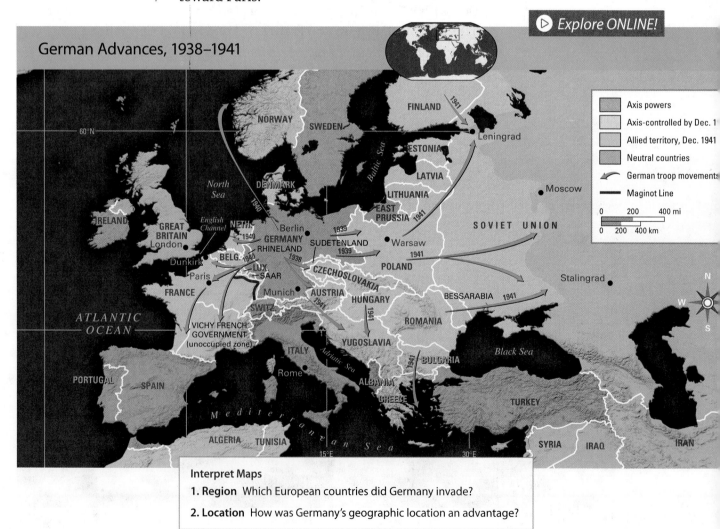

German Advances, 1938–1941

Explore ONLINE!

Legend:
- Axis powers
- Axis-controlled by Dec. 1
- Allied territory, Dec. 1941
- Neutral countries
- German troop movements
- Maginot Line

0   200   400 mi
0   200   400 km

Interpret Maps

1. **Region** Which European countries did Germany invade?

2. **Location** How was Germany's geographic location an advantage?

The German offensive trapped almost 400,000 British and French soldiers as they fled to the beaches of Dunkirk on the French side of the English Channel. In less than a week, a makeshift fleet of fishing trawlers, tug boats, river barges, and pleasure craft—more than 800 vessels in all—ferried about 330,000 British, French, and Belgian troops to safety across the Channel.

A few days later Italy entered the war on the side of Germany and invaded France from the south as the Germans closed in on Paris from the north. On June 22, 1940, at Compiègne, as William Shirer and the rest of the world watched, Hitler handed French officers his terms of surrender. Germans would occupy the northern part of France, and a Nazi-controlled puppet government, headed by Marshal Philippe Pétain, would be set up at Vichy in southern France.

After France fell, a French general named Charles de Gaulle fled to England, where he set up a government-in-exile. De Gaulle proclaimed defiantly, "France has lost a battle, but France has not lost the war."

THE BATTLE OF BRITAIN In the summer of 1940, the Germans began to assemble an invasion fleet along the French coast. Because its naval power could not compete with that of Britain, Germany also launched an air war at the same time. The Luftwaffe began making bombing runs over Britain. Its goal was to gain total control of the skies by destroying Britain's Royal Air Force (RAF). Hitler had 2,600 planes at his disposal. On a single day—August 15—approximately 2,000 German planes ranged over Britain. Bombers pounded London every night for two solid months.

The Battle of Britain raged on through the summer and fall. Night after night, German planes pounded British targets. At first the Luftwaffe concentrated on airfields and aircraft. Next it targeted cities.

The RAF fought back brilliantly. With the help of a new technological device called radar, British pilots accurately plotted the flight paths of German planes, even in darkness. On September 15, 1940 the RAF shot down

---

Document-Based Investigation Historical Source

The London Blitz
Londoner Len Jones was just 18 years old when bombs fell on his East End neighborhood.

> "[T]he suction and the compression from the high-explosive bombs just pushed you and pulled you, and the whole of the atmosphere was turbulating so hard that, after an explosion of a nearby bomb, you could actually feel your eyeballs being [almost] sucked out . . . and the suction was so vast, it ripped my shirt away, and ripped my trousers. Then I couldn't get my breath, the smoke was like acid and everything round me was black and yellow. And these bombers kept on and on, the whole road was moving, rising and falling . . . ."
>
> —Len Jones, quoted in *The Blitz: The British Under Attack*

Analyze Historical Sources
How do you think the Blitz might have affected civilian morale in London?

Winston Churchill (1874–1965)

Winston Churchill may have been Great Britain's greatest weapon in the fight against the Nazis during World War II. He had been active in British politics since 1900, but it was the growing danger posed by Germany in the 1930s that brought out his finest qualities as a leader and a speaker. He became prime minister of Great Britain in May 1940. In that role, he used his gift as a speaker to rouse and unite the British people, urging them to remain strong in their opposition to Nazi Germany. His refusal to consider surrender helped maintain Britain as a base from which the Allies could eventually attack Hitler's armies.

over 185 German planes; at the same time, they lost only 26 aircraft. Six weeks later Hitler called off the invasion of Britain indefinitely. "Never in the field of human conflict," said Churchill in praise of the RAF pilots, "was so much owed by so many to so few."

Still, German bombers continued to pound Britain's cities trying to disrupt production and break civilian morale. Even late in the war, when the Luftwaffe had been weakened and no longer had enough planes to send to Britain, the bombing continued. German scientists developed two types of rockets, the V-1 and the V-2, that could rain devastation on British cities from launch sites on the European mainland. At the same time, British pilots also bombed German cities. Civilians in both countries unrelentingly carried on.

Reading Check Summarize How did German blitzkrieg tactics rely on new military technology?

Lesson 1 Assessment

1. **Organize Information** Use a chart to record details about the goals and actions of each leader.

Leader	Goals	Actions
Stalin		
Mussolini		
Hitler		
Franco		
Tojo		

What were the consequences of the rise of fascism and other totalitarian governments during this period?

2. **Key Terms and People** For each key term or person in the lesson, write a sentence explaining its significance.

3. **Analyze Effects** How did the Treaty of Versailles sow the seeds of instability in Europe?

   Think About:

   • effects on Germany and the Soviet Union
   • effects of the treaty on national pride
   • the economic legacy of the war

4. **Form Generalizations** Why do you think Hitler found widespread support among the German people? Support your answer with details from the text.

5. **Evaluate** If you had been a member of the British House of Commons in 1938, would you have voted for or against the Munich Agreement? Support your decision.

6. **Draw Conclusions** Review Germany's aggressive actions between 1938 and 1945. At what point do you think Hitler concluded that he could take any territory without being stopped? Why?

7. **Analyze Issues** How did the development of new conventional weapons factor into Germany's blitzkrieg strategy and attacks on Britain? How did geographic factors affect the development of those weapons?

The Holocaust

The Big Idea

During the Holocaust, the Nazis systematically executed 6 million Jews and 5 million other "non-Aryans."

Why It Matters Now

After the atrocities of the Holocaust, agencies formed to publicize human rights. These agencies continue to fight for social justice in today's world.

Key Terms and People

Holocaust

Kristallnacht

genocide

ghetto

concentration camp

One American's Story

Gerda Weissmann was a carefree girl of 15 when, in September 1939, invading German troops shattered her world. Because the Weissmanns were Jews, they were forced to give up their home to a German family. In 1942 Gerda, her parents, and most of Poland's 3,000,000 Jews were sent to labor camps. Gerda recalls when members of Hitler's elite *Schutzstaffel,* or "security squadron" (SS), came to round up the Jews.

"We had to form a line and an SS man stood there with a little stick. I was holding hands with my mother and . . . he looked at me and said, 'How old?' And I said, 'eighteen,' and he sort of pushed me to one side and my mother to the other side. . . . And shortly thereafter, some trucks arrived . . . and we were loaded onto the trucks. I heard my mother's voice from very far off ask, 'Where to?' and I shouted back, 'I don't know.'"

—Gerda Weissmann Klein, quoted in the film *One Survivor Remembers*

Gerda Weissmann Klein

American lieutenant Kurt Klein liberated her from the Nazis in 1945. It was just one day before her 21st birthday. She weighed 68 pounds, and her hair had turned white. Of all her family and friends, she alone had survived the Nazis' campaign to exterminate Europe's Jews. Klein would later become Gerda's husband.

SS.912.A.1.2; SS.912.A.1.4; SS.912.A.6.1; SS.912.A.6.3; LAFS.1112.RH.2.6; LAFS.1112.RH.4.10; MAFS.K12.MP.1.1; MAFS.K12.MP.5.1

The Persecution Begins

On April 7, 1933, shortly after Hitler took power in Germany, he ordered all "non-Aryans" to be removed from government jobs. This order was one of the first moves in a campaign for racial purity. That campaign eventually led to the **Holocaust**, the systematic murder of 6 million Jews across Europe. The Nazis also murdered 5 million other people.

JEWS TARGETED Although Jews were not the only victims of the Holocaust, they were the main Nazi targets. Anti-Semitism, or hatred of the Jews, had a long history in parts of Europe. For decades many Germans had been looking for a scapegoat. They blamed the Jews as the cause of their failures.

Adolf Hitler rose to power in part by promising to return Germany to its former glory. Hitler found that a majority of Germans were willing to support his belief that Jews were responsible for Germany's economic problems and defeat in World War I. He also told the Germans that they came from a superior race, the Aryans, an idea that was found in German music and folktales. Hitler effectively used this notion to build support for his plans.

As the Nazis tightened their hold on Germany, their persecution of the Jews increased. In 1935 the Nuremberg Laws stripped Jews of their German citizenship, jobs, and property. Jews had to wear a bright yellow Star of David attached to their clothing to make it easier for the Nazis to identify them. Worse things were yet to come.

KRISTALLNACHT November 9–10, 1938 became known as *Kristallnacht* (krĭs'täl'nächt´), or "Night of Broken Glass." Nazi storm troopers attacked Jewish homes, businesses, and synagogues across Germany, Austria, and the recently occupied Sudetenland in Czechoslovakia. The Nazis claimed the attacks were a spontaneous reaction to the assassination of a Nazi official by a Jewish teenager. In fact, Nazi officials encouraged the violence.

On November 17, 1938, two passersby examine the shattered window of a Jewish-owned store in the aftermath of *Kristallnacht*.

During the rampage, thousands of Jewish businesses and places of worship were damaged or destroyed. An American who witnessed the violence wrote, "Jewish shop windows by the hundreds were systematically and wantonly smashed. . . . The main streets of the city were a positive litter of shattered plate glass." Around 100 Jews were killed, and hundreds more were injured. Some 30,000 Jews were arrested. Afterward, the Nazis blamed the Jews for the destruction and held them financially responsible. Jews were fined a total of 1 billion marks.

A FLOOD OF JEWISH REFUGEES Kristallnacht marked an increase in the Nazis' Jewish persecution and sent a clear message to those Jews still in Germany. Over 100,000 managed to leave in the months following the attacks. However, many had trouble finding countries that would accept them. Nazi laws had left many German Jews without money or property, and most countries were unwilling to take in poor immigrants. France already had 40,000 Jewish refugees and did not want more. The British worried about fueling anti-Semitism. They refused to admit more than 80,000 Jewish refugees. The British also controlled the Palestine Mandate, part of which later became Israel. They did allow 30,000 refugees to settle there. Late in 1938 Germany's foreign minister, Joachim von Ribbentrop, observed, "We all want to get rid of our Jews. The difficulty is that no country wishes to receive them."

Although the average Jew had little chance of reaching the United States, "persons of exceptional merit" were allowed in. Physicist Albert Einstein, author Thomas Mann, architect Walter Gropius, and theologian Paul Tillich were among 100,000 refugees the United States accepted.

Many Americans wanted the door closed. Americans were concerned that letting in more refugees during the Great Depression would deny jobs to U.S. citizens. They also thought it would threaten economic recovery. Among Americans, there was widespread anti-Semitism and fear that "enemy agents" would enter the country. President Roosevelt said that he sympathized with the Jews. But he also said that he would not "do anything which would conceivably hurt the future of present American citizens."

THE PLIGHT OF THE *ST. LOUIS* Official indifference to the situation of Germany's Jews was clear in the case of the ship *St. Louis*. This German ocean liner passed Miami, Florida, in 1939. Although 740 of the liner's 943 passengers had U.S. immigration papers, the Coast Guard followed the ship to prevent anyone from getting off in America. The ship was forced to return to Europe. "The cruise of the *St. Louis*," wrote the *New York Times*, "cries to high heaven of man's inhumanity to man." Passenger Liane Reif-Lehrer recalls her childhood experiences.

"My mother and brother and I were among the passengers who survived. . . . We were sent back to Europe and given haven in France, only to find the Nazis on our doorstep again a few months later."
—Liane Reif-Lehrer, quoted in *A History of US*

More than half of the passengers were later killed in the Holocaust.

Reading Check
Analyze Issues
What problems did German Jews face in Nazi Germany from 1935 to 1938?

Hitler's "Final Solution"

By 1939 only about a quarter million Jews remained in Germany. But other nations that Hitler occupied had millions more. Obsessed with a desire to rid Europe of its Jews, Hitler imposed what he called the "Final Solution"—a policy of **genocide**, the deliberate and systematic killing of an entire population.

THE CONDEMNED Hitler's Final Solution rested on the belief that Aryans were a superior people and that the strength and purity of this "master race" must be preserved. To accomplish this, the Nazis condemned the Jews to slavery and death. They did the same to other groups that they viewed as inferior or unworthy or as "enemies of the state."

After taking power in 1933, the Nazis had concentrated on silencing their political opponents: communists, socialists, liberals, and anyone else who spoke out against the government. Once the Nazis had eliminated these enemies, they turned against other groups in Germany. In addition to Jews, these groups included the following:

- *Gypsies*—whom the Nazis believed to be an "inferior race"
- *Freemasons*—whom the Nazis charged as supporters of the "Jewish conspiracy" to rule the world
- *Jehovah's Witnesses*—who refused to join the army or salute Hitler

The Nazis also targeted other Germans whom they found unfit to be part of the "master race." Such victims included homosexuals, the mentally deficient, the mentally ill, the physically disabled, and the incurably ill.

Hitler began implementing his Final Solution in Poland with special Nazi death squads. Hitler's elite Nazi "security squadrons" (or SS), rounded up Jewish men, women, children, and babies, and shot them on the spot.

FORCED RELOCATION Jews also were ordered into dismal, overcrowded **ghettos**, segregated Jewish areas in certain Polish cities. The Nazis sealed off the ghettos with barbed wire and stone walls. Those Jews who tried to leave were shot.

On May 9, 1945, inmates at the Ebensee concentration camp in Austria were liberated by U.S. soldiers.

Concentration Camp Uniforms

Prisoners were required to wear color-coded triangles on their uniforms. There were several categories of prisoners. They included communists, socialists, criminals, emigrants, Jehovah's Witnesses, and homosexuals. They also included Germans and other nationalities "shy of work." The categories show a variation among the rows. One row is for repeat offenders, and one is for prisoners assigned to punish other prisoners. The double triangles are for Jews. Letters on top of a patch indicate nationality.

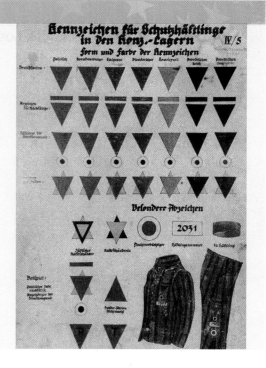

Analyze Historical Sources
Why do you think the Nazis established this color-coded system to identify prisoners in the concentration camps?

Life inside the ghetto was miserable. Food was scarce. Diseases spread quickly in the cramped conditions, and many Jews fell ill. The bodies of victims of the death squads piled up in the streets faster than they could be removed. Factories were built alongside ghettos where people were forced to work for German industry. In spite of the impossible living conditions, the Jews hung on. While some formed resistance movements inside the ghettos, others resisted by other means. They published and distributed underground newspapers. Secret schools were set up to educate Jewish children. Even theater and music groups continued to operate.

CONCENTRATION CAMPS Finally, Jews in communities not reached by the killing squads were dragged from their homes and herded onto trains or trucks for shipment to **concentration camps**, or labor camps. Families were often separated, sometimes—like the Weissmanns—forever.

Nazi concentration camps were originally set up to imprison political opponents and protesters. The camps were later turned over to the SS, who expanded the concentration camps and used them to warehouse other "undesirables." Life in the camps was a cycle of hunger, humiliation, and work that almost always ended in death.

The prisoners were crammed into crude wooden barracks that held up to a thousand people each. They shared their crowded quarters, as well as their meager meals, with hordes of rats and fleas. One survivor remembered such intense hunger "that if a bit of soup spilled over, prisoners would converge on the spot, dig their spoons into the mud and stuff the mess into their mouths." Inmates in the camps worked from dawn to dusk, seven days a week, until they collapsed. Those too weak to work were killed.

Reading Check
Find Main Ideas
What was Hitler's Final Solution?

Estimated Jewish Losses

	Pre-Holocaust Population	Number Killed	
		Low Estimate	High Estimate
Austria	191,000	50,000	65,500
Belgium	60,000	25,000	29,000
Bohemia/Moravia	92,000	77,000	78,300
Denmark	8,000	60	116
Estonia	4,600	1,500	2,000
France	260,000	75,000	77,000
Germany	566,000	135,000	142,000
Greece	73,000	59,000	67,000
Hungary	725,000	502,000	569,000
Italy	48,000	6,500	9,000
Latvia	95,000	70,000	72,000
Lithuania	155,000	130,000	143,000
Luxembourg	3,500	1,000	2,000
Netherlands	112,000	100,000	105,000
Norway	1,700	800	800
Poland	3,250,000	2,700,000	3,000,000
Romania	441,000	121,000	287,000
Slovakia	89,000	60,000	71,000
USSR	2,825,000	700,000	1,100,000
Yugoslavia	68,000	56,000	65,000
TOTALS	9,067,800	4,869,860	5,894,716

Source: Columbia Guide to the Holocaust

Interpret Charts
Approximately what percentage of the total Jewish population in Europe was killed during the Holocaust?

The Final Stage

The Final Solution reached its final stage in early 1942. Hitler called his top officials to a meeting held in Wannsee, a suburb near Berlin. There they agreed to a new phase of the mass murder of Jews. Nazis already were using mass slaughter and starvation. Now they would add murder by poison gas.

MASS EXTERMINATIONS Overwork, starvation, beatings, and bullets did not kill fast enough to satisfy the Nazis. The Germans built six death camps in Poland. The first, Chelmno, began operating in 1941—before the meeting at Wannsee. Each camp had several huge gas chambers. As many as 12,000 people a day could be killed in them.

Auschwitz was the largest of the death camps. When prisoners arrived there, they had to walk past several SS doctors. The doctors separated those strong enough to work from those who would die that day. Both groups had to leave all their belongings behind, supposedly to be returned to them later. Those assigned to die were taken to a room outside the gas chamber. They were told to undress for a shower and were even given pieces of soap. Finally, they were led into the chamber and poisoned with cyanide gas that came out of vents in the walls. Sometimes an orchestra of camp inmates played cheerful music during the killings. Those inmates had been temporarily spared from death because of their musical abilities.

Children taken from Eastern Europe and imprisoned in Auschwitz look out from behind the barbed-wire fence in July 1944.

At first the bodies were buried in huge pits. At Belzec, Rudolf Reder was part of a 500-man death brigade that worked all day, he said, "either at grave digging or emptying the gas chambers." But the decaying corpses gave off an odor that could be smelled for miles around. Worse yet, mass graves left evidence of the mass murder.

At some camps, Nazis tried to cover up the evidence of their slaughter. They installed huge crematoriums, or ovens, in which to burn the dead. At other camps, the bodies were simply thrown into a pit and set on fire.

Gassing was not the only method of extermination used in the camps. Prisoners were also shot, hanged, or injected with poison. Others died from horrible medical experiments done by camp doctors. Some of these victims were injected with deadly germs. The SS doctors wanted to study the effect of disease on different groups of people. Many more inmates were used to test methods of sterilization. Some Nazi doctors were interested in this as a possible way to improve the "master race."

THE GLOBAL RESPONSE In the United States, news of the Nazi violence against European Jews was not always noticeably reported. Anti-Jewish violence increased from 1939 to 1941. After that, some newspapers carried stories about German shooting operations in Poland and the Soviet Union. However, the victims' ethnic background was not always identified. Also, the fate of Europe's Jews was just one of many issues of concern to the United States. The war was the main focus of many countries' attention.

By 1942 the world began to become aware of the horrifying details of Hitler's Final Solution. That year, one escapee from a concentration camp, Jacob Grojanowski, published a report of his experiences in the camp. From Poland, the report made its way to London and then to other parts of Europe. Also in 1942, Gerhart Riegner, the head of a major Jewish organization in Switzerland, sent a report to the U.S. State Department about the atrocities occurring in Europe. Those who read these reports or heard them described on the radio were horrified by their contents. Leaders of the Allied nations publicly condemned the Nazis for their disgraceful actions.

The response to the Holocaust varied by nation and by individual. Some risked their own lives to save Jews from the Nazis. In 1942 King Christian X rejected the Nazis' demand to enforce the Nuremberg Laws against the Jews in German-occupied Denmark. Almost all of Denmark's Jews were rescued by being taken to Sweden in boats. Aristides de Sousa Mendes, a Portuguese diplomat stationed in France, defied his government's orders to deny entry to Jewish refugees. Instead he issued some 10,000 visas to Jews seeking to enter Portugal. The Swedish diplomat Raoul Wallenberg issued "protective passports" that allowed thousands of Hungarian Jews to escape the Nazi death camps. Even citizens of Germany lent a hand. And Sempo Sugihara, Japanese consul in Lithuania, helped over 6,000 Jews to escape the Nazis' clutches, an act that cost him his career.

The United States did not immediately take steps to protect Europe's Jewish population. Many observers have criticized that inaction. In part, the U.S. government was unsure how to arrange rescue operations in Europe. It was also unsure of what the outcome of those operations would be. It was not until January 1944 that President Roosevelt announced the creation of the War Refugee Board. The task of this organization was to rescue thousands of Jews in Hungary, Romania, and other parts of Europe. Those Jews might otherwise have fallen into the hands of the Nazis. In the spring of 1944, some Jewish organizations received detailed reports about the mass murders by gassing happening at Auschwitz. Those organizations proposed bombing the camp. The U.S. War Department refused, uncertain of the results. They

American Literature

The Holocaust

Elie Wiesel and his family were deported from Romania to Auschwitz in 1944. Only he and two older sisters survived the camps. His parents and younger sister perished. In 1960 his memoir was published in English as *Night*. Critics consider it to be one of the most significant literary works about the Holocaust.

Night

"Never shall I forget that night, the first night in camp, that turned my life into one long night seven times sealed. Never shall I forget that smoke. Never shall I forget the small faces of the children whose bodies I saw transformed into smoke under a silent sky. Never shall I forget those flames that consumed my faith forever. Never shall I forget the nocturnal silence that deprived me for all eternity of the desire to live. Never shall I forget those moments that murdered my God and my soul and turned my dreams to ashes. Never shall I forget those things, even were I condemned to live as long as God Himself. Never."

—Elie Wiesel, from *Night*.

ELIE WIESEL

Analyze American Literature

How does the personal testimony of survivors such as Wiesel help people understand the Holocaust?

explained that they were not able to carry out a bombing raid with enough accuracy. They also argued that the best way to help the Jews was to end the war as quickly as possible. The War Department believed its focus should be exclusively on military targets.

THE SURVIVORS An estimated six million Jews died in the death camps and in the Nazi massacres. But some miraculously escaped the worst of the Holocaust. Many had help from ordinary people who were appalled by the Nazis' treatment of Jews. Some Jews even managed to survive the horrors of the concentration camps.

In Gerda Weissmann Klein's view, survival depended as much on one's spirit as on getting enough to eat. "I do believe that if you were blessed with imagination, you could work through it," she wrote. "If, unfortunately, you were a person that faced reality, I think you didn't have much of a chance." Those who did come out of the camps alive were forever changed by what they had witnessed.

For survivor Elie Wiesel, who entered Auschwitz at the age of 15, the sun had set forever. Although he survived his ordeal, Wiesel's experiences in Auschwitz irrevocably altered his worldview. After his liberation in 1945, Wiesel moved to France where he studied and became a journalist. He first recorded memoirs of his time in Auschwitz in Yiddish in 1956. The work, which was published as *Night* in 1960, has become known as one of the great pieces of Holocaust literature. Wiesel became a noted lecturer about the Holocaust. His work condemning violence, hatred, and oppression brought him worldwide fame, and in 1986 he was awarded the Nobel Peace Prize.

Reading Check
Summarize How was news of the Holocaust reported in the United States?

Lesson 2 Assessment

1. **Organize Information** List at least four events that led to the Holocaust.

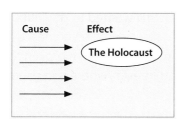

Write a paragraph explaining how significant you think the different events were in contributing to the Holocaust.

2. **Key Terms and People** For each key term in the lesson, write a sentence explaining its significance.

3. **Evaluate** Do you think that the United States was justified in not doing more to aid Holocaust victims, either by allowing more Jewish refugees to immigrate or by attempting rescue missions in Europe? Why or why not?

   Think About:
   - the views of isolationists in the United States
   - some Americans' prejudices and fears
   - the unknowns of a military response

4. **Develop Historical Perspective** Why do you think the Nazi system of systematic genocide was so brutally effective? Support your answer with details from the text.

5. **Analyze Motives** How might concentration camp doctors and guards have justified to themselves the death and suffering they caused other human beings?

6. **Analyze Events** How did word of the Holocaust spread beyond Germany, and how did people in other countries react to the news?

★ America Moves Toward War

The Big Idea
The United States hesitated to become involved in another global conflict. However, it did provide economic and military aid to help the Allies achieve victory.

Why It Matters Now
U.S. military capability became a key factor in World War II, and it has been a consideration in world affairs ever since.

Key Terms and People
Neutrality Acts

Axis powers

Selective Training and Service Act

Lend-Lease Act

Atlantic Charter

Allies

One American's Story

Two days after Hitler invaded Poland, President Roosevelt spoke to Americans about the outbreak of war in Europe. Roosevelt talked clearly about how the United States should be consistent in seeking peace for all people. He also announced a new proclamation declaring American neutrality.

"This nation will remain a neutral nation, but I cannot ask that every American remain neutral in thought as well. . . . Even a neutral cannot be asked to close his mind or his conscience. . . . I have said not once, but many times, that I have seen war and I hate war. . . . As long as it is my power to prevent, there will be no blackout of peace in the U.S."
—Franklin D. Roosevelt, from a radio speech, September 3, 1939

Franklin D. Roosevelt

Roosevelt knew that Americans still wanted to stay out of war. However, he also believed that there could be no peace in a world controlled by dictators. "When peace has been broken anywhere," he said, "the peace of all countries everywhere is in danger."

SS.912.A.1.2; SS.912.A.1.4; SS.912.A.5.5; SS.912.A.6.1; SS.912.A.6.2; LAFS.1112.RH.1.2; LAFS.1112.RH.4.10

Isolationism Amidst Conflict

Most Americans were alarmed by the international conflicts of the mid-1930s. But they believed that the United States should not get involved. Since World War I, the United States had kept a policy of isolationism. The nation's leaders avoided any action that would involve the United States in global affairs.

This cartoon imagines Woodrow Wilson, who led the United States through World War I, looking over Roosevelt's shoulder and wishing him luck maintaining U.S. neutrality.

THE ROOTS OF ISOLATIONISM Because of the horrors of World War I, many Americans were determined never to be involved in an international war again. In 1919 Congress refused to allow the United States to join the League of Nations. They feared that the league would control American foreign policy. They also feared that it would tie the country too closely to Europe.

After World War I, the United States made sure that it would not be pulled into war again. At the Washington Naval Conference of 1921, the United States and its allies signed a disarmament treaty. They also promised not to build any warships during the next decade. In 1928 the United States signed the Kellogg-Briand Pact. The treaty was signed by 62 countries. It stated that war would not be used "as an instrument of national policy." Yet it did not include a way to deal with countries that broke their pledge. Therefore, the Pact was only a small step toward peace.

AMERICANS CLING TO ISOLATIONISM In the early 1930s numerous books argued that greedy bankers and arms dealers had dragged the United States into World War I. Public outrage led a congressional committee to investigate these charges. North Dakota senator Gerald Nye chaired the committee. The Nye committee found that banks and manufacturers had made large profits during the war. Anger grew over these "merchants of death." Americans became even more determined to avoid war. Antiwar feeling was very strong. The Girl Scouts of America even changed the color of its uniforms to green. The original khaki was similar to the color used by the military.

News of Japan's invasion of Manchuria reached the United States in 1932. The U.S. government avoided getting involved. Secretary of State Henry Stimson's response was supported by President Hoover. Stimson notified the governments of both Japan and China that the United States would not recognize the conflict. The U.S. government would continue to consider Manchuria a part of China. The Hoover-Stimson note also insisted that Americans kept all their trade rights in China.

Americans' growing isolationism eventually affected President Roosevelt's foreign policy. When he first took office in 1933, Roosevelt reached out to other nations in several ways. He officially recognized the Soviet Union in 1933 and agreed to exchange ambassadors with Moscow. His Good Neighbor Policy continued the nonintervention policy in Latin America begun by Presidents Coolidge and Hoover. Roosevelt also withdrew armed forces stationed there. In 1934 Roosevelt pushed Congress to pass the Reciprocal Trade Agreement Act. It lowered trade barriers by giving the president the power to make trade agreements with other nations. It was aimed at reducing tariffs by as much as 50 percent.

Congress, however, disagreed with Roosevelt's efforts to involve the country in foreign affairs. In 1934 it passed the Johnson Debt Default Act, which prohibited any foreign aid loans to countries that had not paid back their World War I debts. Congress also passed a series of **Neutrality Acts** to keep the country out of future wars. The first two acts, passed in 1935 and 1937, outlawed arms sales or loans to nations at war. The third act was passed in 1939 in response to the fighting in Spain. This act prohibited arms sales and loans to nations engaged in civil wars.

NEUTRALITY BREAKS DOWN Even though Congress passed laws to keep the country neutral, Roosevelt found it impossible to remain neutral. When Japan launched a new attack on China in July 1937, Roosevelt found a way around the Neutrality Acts. Because Japan had not formally declared war against China, the president claimed there was no need to enforce the Neutrality Acts. The United States continued sending arms and supplies to China. A few months later Roosevelt spoke out strongly against isolationism in a speech delivered in Chicago. He called on peace-loving nations to "quarantine," or isolate, aggressor nations in order to stop the spread of war.

"The peace, the freedom, and the security of 90 percent of the population of the world is being jeopardized by the remaining 10 percent who are threatening a breakdown of all international order and law. Surely the 90 percent who want to live in peace under law and in accordance with moral standards that have received almost universal acceptance through the centuries, can and must find some way . . . to preserve peace."

—Franklin D. Roosevelt, from the "Quarantine Speech," October 5, 1937

Document-Based Investigation Historical Source

"The Only Way We Can Save Her"

During the late 1930s Americans watched events in Europe with growing alarm. Dictators were destroying democratic systems of government throughout Europe. They were dragging the continent into war. These political events divided American public opinion. Some Americans felt that the United States should help European democracies. However, isolationists—people who believed that the United States should not interfere in other nations' affairs—opposed getting involved in European disagreements.

Analyze Historical Sources

1. What does the kneeling figure fear will happen to America if Uncle Sam gets involved?

2. What U.S. policy does the cartoon support?

The Only Way We Can Save Her

" STAY OUT! STAY OUT FOR MY SAKE, AS WELL AS YOUR OWN!"

WAR MAD EUROPE

DEMOCRACY

AMERICA, THE LAST REFUGE OF DEMOCRACY

At last Roosevelt seemed ready to take a stand against aggression—

At last Roosevelt seemed ready to take a stand against aggression—until isolationist newspapers exploded in protest. They accused the president of leading the nation into war. Roosevelt backed off as a result of this criticism, but his speech did begin to shift the debate. For the moment the conflicts remained "over there."

Moving Away from Neutrality

As German tanks rolled across Poland, Roosevelt revised the Neutrality Act of 1935. At the same time, he began to prepare the nation for the struggle he feared lay just ahead.

CAUTIOUS STEPS In September 1939 Roosevelt persuaded Congress to pass a "cash-and-carry" provision. It allowed warring nations to buy U.S. arms as long as they paid cash and transported them in their own ships. Roosevelt argued that providing the arms would help France and Britain defeat Hitler and keep the United States out of the war. Isolationists attacked Roosevelt for his actions. However, after six weeks of heated debate, Congress passed the Neutrality Act of 1939, and a cash-and-carry policy went into effect.

THE AXIS THREAT The United States's cash-and-carry policy seemed like too little, too late. By summer 1940 France had fallen and Britain was under siege. Roosevelt worked to provide the British with "all aid short of war." By June he had sent Britain 500,000 rifles and 80,000 machine guns. In early September the United States traded 50 old destroyers for leases on British military bases in the Caribbean and Newfoundland. British prime minister Winston Churchill would later recall this move with affection as "a decidedly unneutral act."

On September 27 Americans were startled by the news that Germany, Italy, and Japan had signed a mutual defense treaty, the Tripartite Pact. The three nations became known as the **Axis powers**.

The Tripartite Pact was intended to keep the United States out of the war. Under the treaty each Axis nation agreed to defend the others in case of attack. This meant that if the United States declared war on any one of the Axis powers, it would have to fight a two-ocean war, in both the Atlantic and the Pacific.

BUILDING U.S. DEFENSES Meanwhile, Roosevelt asked Congress to increase spending for national defense. Despite years of U.S. isolationism, Nazi victories in 1940 changed U.S. thinking. Congress boosted defense spending. Congress also passed the nation's first peacetime military draft—the **Selective Training and Service Act**. Under this law 16 million men between the ages of 21 and 35 were registered. Of these, one million would be drafted for one year. They were allowed to serve only in the Western Hemisphere. Roosevelt drew the first draft numbers. He told a national radio audience, "This is a most solemn ceremony."

Reading Check
Analyze
Causes What factors contributed to Americans' growing isolationism after World War I?

ROOSEVELT RUNS FOR A THIRD TERM That same year, Roosevelt broke the tradition of a two-term presidency begun by George Washington. He decided to run for reelection. Roosevelt's Republican opponent was a public utilities executive named Wendell Willkie. He supported Roosevelt's policy of aiding Britain, which disappointed isolationists. At the same time, both Willkie and Roosevelt promised to keep the nation out of war. Because there was so little difference between the candidates, the majority of voters chose the one they knew better. Roosevelt was reelected with nearly 55 percent of the votes cast.

Not long after the election, President Roosevelt continued his drive to provide aid to the Allies in their fight against the Axis powers. He told his radio audience during a fireside chat that it would be impossible to negotiate a peace with Hitler. "No man can tame a tiger into a kitten by stroking it." He warned that if Britain fell, the Axis powers would be left unchallenged to conquer the world. At that point, he said, "all of us in all the Americas would be living at the point of a gun." To prevent such a situation, the United States had to help defeat the Axis threat. It had to become what Roosevelt called "the great arsenal of democracy."

THE LEND-LEASE PLAN By late 1940 Britain had no more cash to spend on arms. In addition, as a result of the Johnson Debt Default Act, Roosevelt was unable to lend money to Britain directly. Instead, he tried to help by suggesting a new plan that he called a lend-lease policy. Under this plan the president would lend or lease arms and other supplies to "any country whose defense was vital to the United States."

Roosevelt compared his plan to lending a garden hose to a neighbor whose house was on fire. He maintained that this was the only sensible thing to do to prevent the fire from spreading to your own property. Isolationists opposed the plan, but most Americans favored it. Congress passed the **Lend-Lease Act** in March 1941.

Britain was not the only nation to receive lend-lease aid. In June 1941 Hitler broke the agreement he had made in 1939 with Stalin not to go to war and invaded the Soviet Union. Acting on the principle that "the enemy of my enemy is my friend," Roosevelt worked to improve the diplomatic relationship between the United States and the Soviet Union. He began sending lend-lease supplies to the Soviets. Some Americans opposed providing aid to Stalin. However, Roosevelt agreed with Winston Churchill, who had said "if Hitler invaded Hell," the British would work with the devil himself. The cooperation among these three nations laid the groundwork for what Churchill would come to call the Grand Alliance.

As a result of policies such as the Lend-Lease Act, American industries began shifting to wartime production before the United States officially entered the war. Defense spending skyrocketed in 1940. Idle factories came back to life. They changed from making consumer goods to producing war supplies. A merry-go-round company began producing gun mounts, and a stove factory made lifeboats. A famous New York toy maker made compasses. A pinball-machine company made armor-piercing shells. This increase in production did what all of the programs of the

Vocabulary
lease to grant use or occupation of under the terms of a contract

Reading Check
Analyze Effects
What impact did the
outbreak of war in Europe
have on U.S. foreign and
defense policy?

New Deal could not do: it ended the Great Depression. With factories hiring again, the nation's unemployment level began shrinking rapidly. It fell by 400,000 in August 1940 and by another 500,000 in September. By the end of 1941, America was going back to work.

POINT	COUNTERPOINT

POINT

"The United States should not become involved in European wars."

Many Americans were still recovering from World War I and struggling with the Great Depression. They believed their country should remain neutral in the war in Europe.

Representative James F. O'Connor expressed the country's reservations. He asked, "Dare we set America up and commit her as the financial and military blood bank of the rest of the world?" O'Connor maintained that the United States could not "right every wrong" or "police [the] world."

The aviator Charles Lindbergh stated his hope that "the future of America . . . not be tied to these eternal wars in Europe." Lindbergh asserted that "Americans [should] fight anybody and everybody who attempts to interfere with our hemisphere." However, he also said, "Our safety does not lie in fighting European wars. It lies in our own internal strength, in the character of the American people and American institutions." Like many isolationists, Lindbergh believed that democracy would not be saved "by the forceful imposition of our ideals abroad, but by example of their successful operation at home."

COUNTERPOINT

"The United States must protect democracies throughout the world."

As the conflict in Europe deepened, interventionists embraced President Franklin D. Roosevelt's declaration that "when peace has been broken anywhere, peace of all countries everywhere is in danger." Roosevelt emphasized the global character of 20th-century commerce and communication by noting, "Every word that comes through the air, every ship that sails the sea, every battle that is fought does affect the American future."

Roosevelt and other political leaders also appealed to the nation's conscience. Secretary of State Cordell Hull noted that the world was "face to face . . . with an organized, ruthless, and implacable movement of steadily expanding conquest." Similarly, Undersecretary of State Sumner Welles called Hitler "a sinister and pitiless conqueror [who] has reduced more than half of Europe to abject serfdom."

After the war expanded into the Atlantic, Roosevelt stated, "It is time for all Americans . . . to stop being deluded by the romantic notion that the Americas can go on living happily and peacefully in a Nazi-dominated world." He added, "Let us not ask ourselves whether the Americas should begin to defend themselves after the first attack . . . or the twentieth attack. The time for active defense is now."

Critical Thinking

1. Connect to History Compare and contrast different perspectives about how the United States should have responded to the aggressive actions taken by other nations leading up to World War II. What arguments did supporters and opponents of isolationism present to make their cases? Write a paragraph presenting your findings.

2. Connect to Today After World War I, many Americans became isolationists. Do you recommend that the United States practice isolationism today? Why or why not?

FDR Plans for War

Although Roosevelt was popular, his foreign policy was under constant attack. Still, he recognized that American forces were seriously under-armed. Roosevelt took a number of actions to ensure that the U.S. military would be prepared for the war he was certain would come.

GERMAN WOLF PACKS Lend-lease aid was helping, but supply lines across the Atlantic Ocean had to be kept open to deliver goods to Britain and the Soviet Union. Hitler tried to prevent delivery of lend-lease shipments by sending out hundreds of German submarines, or U-boats, to attack supply ships.

From the spring through the fall of 1941, attacks by individual U-boats were replaced by the wolf pack attack. At night groups of up to 40 submarines patrolled areas in the North Atlantic where convoys could be expected. Wolf packs were successful in sinking as much as 350,000 tons of shipments in a single month. In June 1941 President Roosevelt granted the navy permission for U.S. warships to attack German U-boats in self-defense.

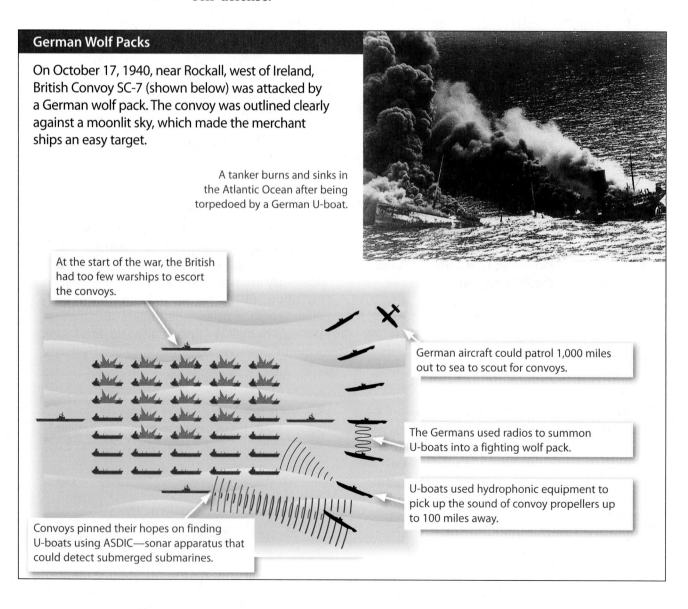

German Wolf Packs

On October 17, 1940, near Rockall, west of Ireland, British Convoy SC-7 (shown below) was attacked by a German wolf pack. The convoy was outlined clearly against a moonlit sky, which made the merchant ships an easy target.

A tanker burns and sinks in the Atlantic Ocean after being torpedoed by a German U-boat.

At the start of the war, the British had too few warships to escort the convoys.

German aircraft could patrol 1,000 miles out to sea to scout for convoys.

The Germans used radios to summon U-boats into a fighting wolf pack.

U-boats used hydrophonic equipment to pick up the sound of convoy propellers up to 100 miles away.

Convoys pinned their hopes on finding U-boats using ASDIC—sonar apparatus that could detect submerged submarines.

THE ATLANTIC CHARTER In August 1941 Roosevelt and Churchill met secretly at a summit aboard the battleship USS *Augusta*. Although Churchill hoped for a military commitment, he settled for a joint declaration of war goals called the **Atlantic Charter**. Both countries pledged collective security, disarmament, self-determination, economic cooperation, and freedom of the seas. Roosevelt told Churchill that he couldn't ask Congress for a declaration of war against Germany. But he said that he "would wage war" and do "everything" to "force an incident."

The Atlantic Charter became the basis of a new document called "A Declaration of the United Nations." Roosevelt suggested the term United Nations to express the common purpose of the **Allies**, those nations that fought the Axis powers. The declaration was signed on January 1, 1942, by 26 nations: Australia, Belgium, Canada, China, Costa Rica, Cuba, Czechoslovakia, the Dominican Republic, El Salvador, Great Britain, Greece, Guatemala, Haiti, Honduras, India, Luxembourg, the Netherlands, New Zealand, Nicaragua, Norway, Panama, Poland, South Africa, the Soviet Union, the United States, and Yugoslavia. By the end of the war, another 21 countries had added their signatures.

SHOOT ON SIGHT After a German submarine fired on the U.S. destroyer *Greer* in the Atlantic on September 4, 1941, Roosevelt ordered navy commanders to respond. "When you see a rattlesnake poised to strike," the president explained, "you crush him." Roosevelt ordered the navy to shoot the German submarines on sight.

Two weeks later the *Pink Star*, an American merchant ship, was sunk off Greenland. In mid-October a U-boat sank the U.S. destroyer *Kearny,* and 11 lives were lost.

Days later German U-boats torpedoed the U.S. destroyer *Reuben James,* killing more than 100 sailors. "America has been attacked," Roosevelt announced grimly. "The shooting has started. And history has recorded who fired the first shot." As the death toll mounted, the Senate repealed a ban against arming merchant ships. A formal declaration of a full-scale war seemed inevitable.

Reading Check
Summarize Why was the Atlantic Charter important?

Japan Attacks the United States

The United States was now involved in an undeclared naval war with Hitler. However, the attack that finally brought the United States into the war came from Japan. By the late fall of 1941, American leaders had become convinced that war between the United States and Japan was likely. The only remaining question was how and where the fighting would start.

ECONOMIC MOTIVATIONS By early 1941 the Japanese had already pushed eastward into Manchuria and other parts of China. They also set their sights on the European colonial possessions to the south. By 1941 the European powers were too busy fighting Hitler to block Japanese expansion. Only the United States and its Pacific islands remained in Japan's way.

The Japanese began a southward push in July 1941. They took over French military bases in Indochina (now Vietnam, Cambodia, and Laos). The United States protested this aggression by halting trade with Japan. One item that Japan could not live without was oil for its war machine. Japanese military leaders warned that a lack of oil could defeat Japan without its enemies ever striking a blow. The leaders declared that Japan must either persuade the United States to end its oil embargo or capture the oil fields in the Dutch East Indies. Any attack on the East Indies, though, would mean war.

PEACE TALKS ARE QUESTIONED Shortly after becoming the prime minister of Japan, Hideki Tojo met with emperor Hirohito. Tojo promised the emperor that the Japanese government would try to keep peace with the Americans. But on November 5, 1941, Tojo ordered the Japanese navy to prepare an attack on the United States.

The U.S. military had broken Japan's secret communication codes. It learned that Japan was preparing an attack. But it didn't know where the attack would happen. Late in November Roosevelt sent a "war warning" to military commanders in Hawaii, Guam, and the Philippines. If war could not be avoided, the warning said, "the United States desires that Japan commit the first overt act." And the nation waited.

After the embargo began, representatives of the two nations met to try to settle their growing differences. U.S. Secretary of State Cordell Hull held several meetings with the Japanese ambassador. The United States wanted Japan to pull out of China, but the Japanese refused. The peace talks went on until December 6, 1941, when Roosevelt received a decoded message. It instructed Japan's peace envoy to refuse all American peace proposals. "This means war," Roosevelt declared.

THE ATTACK ON PEARL HARBOR Early the next morning, a Japanese dive-bomber flew low over Pearl Harbor—the largest U.S. naval base in the Pacific. The bomber was followed by more than 180 Japanese warplanes from six aircraft carriers. Japanese bombs began falling on the base. A radio operator sent this message: "Air raid on Pearl Harbor. This is not a drill."

For an hour and a half, the Japanese planes attacked. The U.S. antiaircraft guns had little effect, and the planes hit target after target. By the time the last plane flew away around 9:30 a.m., there was widespread devastation. The Japanese goal had been to weaken U.S. naval power in the Pacific. They thought that this would keep the Americans from preventing Japanese expansion, and they were successful.

In less than two hours, the Japanese had killed 2,403 Americans and wounded 1,178 more. The surprise attack had sunk or damaged 21 ships, including 8 battleships—nearly the whole U.S. Pacific fleet. More than 300 aircraft were severely damaged or

At Pearl Harbor, American sailors are rescued by motorboat after the bombing of their battleships—the USS *West Virginia* and the USS *Tennessee*.

Japanese Aggression, 1931–1941

▶ Explore ONLINE!

MONGOLIA

SOVIET UNION

MANCHURIA (Province of China)

Peking

Sakhalin

Kamchatka

Kurile Islands

150°E

165°E

KOREA

JAPAN

Yellow R.

CHINA

Shanghai

Yangtze R.

PACIFIC OCEAN

Ryukyu Islands

Formosa

Tropic of Cancer

BURMA

Hong Kong

Mariana Islands

Wake Island

15°S

THAILAND

PHILIPPINES

FRENCH INDOCHINA

Guam

Hawaiian Islands (U.S.)

Caroline Islands

Marshall Islands

Pearl Harbor Invasion, December 7, 1941

MALAYA

Singapore

0°

DUTCH EAST INDIES

New Guinea

Solomon Islands

INDIAN OCEAN

150°E

165°E

AUSTRALIA

Pearl Harbor Invasion

First Attack, 7:55 A.M

Second Attack, 8:55 A.M

PACIFIC OCEAN

Fighters

Oahu

Fighters

Wheeler Air Force Base

Horizontal bombers

Torpedo bombers

Dive bombers

Dive bombers

21°30'N

Kaneohe Naval Air Station

Pearl Harbor Naval Base

Horizontal bombers

Honolulu

Pearl Harbor

158°W

0   8   16 mi

0   8   16 km

	Japanese Empire in 1931
	Areas under Japanese control, 1941
	Extent of Japanese control, 1941

0   600   1,200 mi

0   600   1,200 km

U.S. Ships at Pearl Harbor

Detroit

Phoenix

Raleigh

Solace

Utah

Nevada

Tangier

Curtiss

Tennessee

Arizona

Vestal

West Virginia

Ford Island

Maryland

Oklahoma

Neosho

California

San Francisco

New Orleans

Oglala

Honolulu

St. Louis

Helena

Pennsylvania

Shaw

Cassin

Downes

U.S. NAVAL STATION

Pearl Harbor

	Ships undamaged
	Ships damaged
	Ships sunk

0   .25   .5 mi

0   .25   .5 km

Interpret Maps

1. Region Which countries had Japan invaded by 1941?

2. Movement On the lower inset map notice the placement of the U.S. ships in Pearl Harbor. What might the navy have done differently to minimize damage from a surprise attack?

destroyed. This damage was greater than the U.S. Navy had suffered in all of World War I. By chance, three aircraft carriers at sea escaped the disaster. Their survival would be key to the war's outcome.

REACTION TO PEARL HARBOR In Washington, the mood ranged from outrage to panic. At the White House, Eleanor Roosevelt stood by as her husband received the news from Hawaii, "each report more terrible than the last." Beneath the president's calm, Eleanor could see how worried he was. "I never wanted to have to fight this war on two fronts," Roosevelt told his wife. "We haven't the Navy to fight in both the Atlantic and the Pacific . . . so we will have to build up the Navy and the Air Force and that will mean that we will have to take a good many defeats before we can have a victory."

The next day, President Roosevelt addressed Congress.

"Yesterday, December 7, 1941—a date which will live in infamy—the United States of America was suddenly and deliberately attacked by naval and air forces of the Empire of Japan."
—Franklin D. Roosevelt, from his address to Congress requesting a declaration of war, December 8, 1941

In his speech, Roosevelt asked for a declaration of war against Japan, which Congress quickly approved. Three days later both Germany and Italy declared war on the United States.

Terrible damage was done to Pearl Harbor. Great damage also was done to the cause of isolationism. After the surprise attack, many isolationists supported a strong American response. Isolationist senator Burton Wheeler proclaimed, "The only thing now to do is to lick the hell out of them."

Vocabulary
infamy evil fame or reputation

Reading Check
Draw Conclusions
Why was Japan's attack on Pearl Harbor so devastating?

Lesson 3 Assessment

1. **Organize Information**
   Use a graphic organizer to trace the events that led the United States from isolationism and neutrality toward full involvement in World War II.

   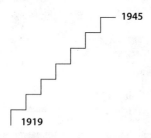

   1945

   1919

   Which of the events that you listed was most influential in bringing the United States into the war? Why?

2. **Key Terms and People**
   For each key term in the lesson, write a sentence explaining its significance.

3. **Evaluate**
   Do you think that the United States should have waited to be attacked before declaring war?
   Think About:
   - the ongoing negotiations between the United States and Japan
   - the influence of isolationists
   - the events at Pearl Harbor

4. **Analyze Issues**
   What steps did world powers take after World War I to avoid future wars? Why?

5. **Form Generalizations**
   Would powerful nations or weak nations be more likely to follow an isolationist policy? Explain.

6. **Draw Conclusions**
   Would you consider Roosevelt a strong president or a weak one? How did his leadership abilities compare to those of other presidents you have studied?

The War Effort on the Home Front

The Big Idea

Following the attack on Pearl Harbor, the United States mobilized for war.

Why It Matters Now

Changes on the home front reshaped American society as well as the economy.

Key Terms and People

George Marshall

Women's Auxiliary Army Corps (WAAC)

Office of Price Administration (OPA)

War Production Board (WPB)

rationing

Manhattan Project

A. Philip Randolph

James Farmer

Congress of Racial Equality (CORE)

internment

Japanese American Citizens League (JACL)

SS.912.A.1.2; SS.912.A.1.4; SS.912.A.1.6; SS.912.A.6.1; SS.912.A.6.4; SS.912.A.6.5; SS.912.A.6.15; SS.912.G.1.2; SS.912.G.2.1; LAFS.1112.RH.3.7; LAFS.1112.RH.4.10; LAFS.1112.WHST.3.7; MAFS.K12.MP.1.1; MAFS.K12.MP.5.1

One American's Story

As soldiers left home to fight in Europe and the Pacific, many American families were separated. This letter from Marine 1st Lt. Leonard Isacks expresses the emotions that many soldiers felt when thinking of their loved ones back home.

"My dear little boys:

I am writing to you today, just a week before Christmas eve, in the hope that you will get this little note at Christmas time. All of this coming week will be holidays, and I can just imagine the fun you will be having . . .

Leonard Isacks's wife and children

I won't be able to give you a Christmas present personally this year, but I do want you to know that I think of you all the time. . . . I know that you would like to give me a Xmas present too, so I will tell you what you can do, and this will be your Xmas present to me. Everyday ask Mummie if there are any errands that you can do for her, and when there are errands to run, say, 'sure Mummie' and give her a big smile; . . ."

—Leonard Isacks, from "Letter from Marine 1st Lt. Leonard Isacks"

As the United States began to mobilize for war, the Isacks family, like most Americans, had few illusions about what lay ahead. It would be a time filled with hard work, hope, sacrifice, and sorrow.

Americans Join the Military

The Japanese attacked Pearl Harbor expecting that after Americans experienced Japan's power, they would shrink from further conflict. The day after the raid, the *Japan Times* boasted that the United States was reduced to a third-rate power and was "trembling in her shoes." But if Americans were trembling, it was with rage, not fear. American patriotism drove citizens to incredible acts of bravery and sacrifice, on the battlefields of Europe and the Pacific as well as at home. Uniting under the battle cry "Remember Pearl Harbor!" they set out to prove Japan wrong.

SELECTIVE SERVICE AND THE GI After Pearl Harbor, patriotic young Americans jammed recruiting offices. "I wanted to be a hero, let's face it," admitted Roger Tuttrup. "I was havin' trouble in school. . . . The war'd been goin' on for two years. I didn't wanna miss it. . . . I was an American. I was seventeen."

Even the 5 million who volunteered for military service, however, were not enough to face the challenge of an all-out war on two fronts—Europe and the Pacific. The Selective Service System expanded the draft and eventually provided another 10 million soldiers to meet the armed forces' needs.

All of the Americans entering the armed forces needed training and housing. This required building hundreds of new military bases and training centers. In general, the military wanted to build new bases in rural areas where there was plenty of open land. A warm climate was also important. The military buildup changed many parts of the country. California became home to more military bases than any other state. In Florida, Camp Blanding had 55,000 soldiers and became the state's fourth-largest city almost overnight.

Volunteers and draftees reported to these and other military bases around the country. There they received eight weeks of basic training. In this short period, seasoned sergeants did their best to turn raw recruits into disciplined, battle-ready GIs. Army Chief of Staff General **George Marshall** was the leader of the armed forces mobilization effort. He ensured that American soldiers were well equipped and properly trained. Marshall also played an important role in developing the nation's military strategy.

According to Sergeant Debs Myers, however, there was much more to basic training than teaching a recruit how to stand at attention, march in step, handle a rifle, and follow orders.

> *"The civilian went before the Army doctors, took off his clothes, feeling silly; jigged, stooped, squatted, wet into a bottle; became a soldier. He learned how to sleep in the mud, tie a knot, kill a man. He learned the ache of loneliness, the ache of exhaustion, the kinship of misery. He learned that men make the same queasy noises in the morning, feel the same longings at night; that every man is alike and that each man is different."*
>
> —Sergeant Debs Myers, quoted in *The GI War: 1941–1945*

Background
The initials *GI* originally stood for "galvanized iron." They were later reinterpreted as "government issue," meaning uniforms and supplies. In time, the abbreviation came to stand for American soldiers.

EXPANDING THE MILITARY The military's workforce needs were so great that Marshall pushed for the formation of a **Women's Auxiliary Army Corps (WAAC)**. "There are innumerable duties now being performed by soldiers that can be done better by women," Marshall said in support of a bill to establish the Women's Auxiliary Army Corps. Under this bill, women volunteers would serve in noncombat positions.

Some members of Congress called the bill "the silliest piece of legislation" they had ever seen. Despite their opposition, the bill establishing the WAAC became law on May 15, 1942. The law gave the WAACs an official status and salary but few of the benefits that male soldiers received. Even so, thousands of patriotic women enlisted. They wanted to help the army win the war. In July 1943 the U.S. Army dropped the "auxiliary" status and gave members of the Women's Army Corps (WAC) full U.S. Army benefits. WACs worked as nurses, ambulance drivers, radio operators, electricians, and pilots. They performed nearly every duty not involving direct combat.

More than 1,000 women who had been trained as pilots before the war also signed up for duty. They formed the Women Airforce Service Pilots (WASP). WASPs flew noncombat missions. They transported supplies, moved aircraft between bases, and tested new planes. This freed male pilots for combat missions. Among the first women to sign up to be a WASP was Cornelia Fort. She was a civilian pilot who had witnessed the bombing of Pearl Harbor from the air.

RECRUITING AND DISCRIMINATION For many minority groups—especially African Americans, Native Americans, Mexican Americans, and Asian Americans—the war created new difficulties. They were restricted to racially segregated neighborhoods and reservations. They were denied basic citizenship rights. Some members of these groups questioned whether this was their war to fight. "Why die for democracy for some foreign country when we don't even have it here?" asked an editorial in an African American newspaper.

NOW & THEN

Women in the Military

A few weeks after the bill to establish the Women's Auxiliary Army Corps (WAAC) had become law, Oveta Culp Hobby (shown, far right), a Texas newspaper executive and the first director of the WAAC, put out a call for recruits. More than 13,000 women applied on the first day. In all, some 350,000 women served in this and other auxiliary branches during the war.

After the war, many expected the U.S. military to dismiss most of the women who had served. Instead, in 1948 President Truman signed the Women's Armed Services Integration Act. This law allowed women to serve as full members of the U.S. armed forces. Still, American women continued to serve in separate units. Not until 1978 were male and female forces integrated. In 2013 U.S. military leaders signed a directive to allow the more than 200,000 women who were serving in the active-duty military to fill front-line combat positions.

When one African American received his draft notice, he responded unhappily, "Just carve on my tombstone, 'Here lies a black man killed fighting a yellow man for the protection of a white man.'"

Some African Americans, however, saw the war effort as an opportunity to fight this discrimination. Across the country, African American newspapers supported the Double V Campaign. Government posters with the slogan "V For Victory" inspired the campaign. It encouraged African Americans to join together to support the war effort. Double V Clubs collected money and supplies. They sponsored patriotic events and met with local leaders to promote fairer hiring practices. Their hope was that African Americans could win two victories. One would be a victory over the country's enemies, and one would be over poor treatment at home. The nationalism that inspired these contributions also made many African Americans believe that their situation could improve.

DRAMATIC CONTRIBUTIONS Despite discrimination in the military, more than 300,000 Mexican Americans joined the armed forces. Mexican Americans in Los Angeles made up only a tenth of the city's population. However, they suffered a fifth of the city's wartime casualties.

About 1 million African Americans also served in the military. African American soldiers lived and worked in segregated units. They were limited mostly to noncombat roles. After much protest, African Americans did finally see combat beginning in April 1943.

Asian Americans also took part in the struggle. More than 13,000 Chinese Americans, or about one of every five adult males, joined the armed forces. In addition, 33,000 Japanese Americans put on uniforms. Of these, several thousand volunteered to serve as spies and interpreters in the Pacific war. "During battles," wrote an admiring officer, "they crawled up close enough to be able to hear [Japanese] officers' commands and to make verbal translations to our soldiers."

Some 25,000 Native Americans also enlisted in the armed services, including 800 women. The willingness of Native Americans to serve led *The Saturday Evening Post* to comment, "We would not need the Selective Service if all volunteered like Indians."

Reading Check
Contrast How did the American response to the raid on Pearl Harbor differ from Japanese expectations?

In March 1941 a group of African American men in New York City enlisted in the United States Army Air Corps. This was the first time the Army Air Corps accepted African Americans.

The Federal Government Manages the War Effort

The United States was much better prepared to enter World War II than it had been for World War I. Before the attack on Pearl Harbor, Roosevelt had recognized the importance of managing the war effort. He created a series of agencies to aid in this task. The Office of War Mobilization was created in 1943 to oversee the agencies and coordinate all wartime efforts.

This U.S. government poster created during the war advised Americans to conserve fuel.

WINNING AMERICAN SUPPORT American leaders understood that public support for the war effort was vital to its success. In June 1942 the government created the Office of War Information (OWI). This agency was responsible for spreading propaganda to influence the thoughts, feelings, and actions of the public in favor of the war effort.

The OWI produced dozens of posters and films during the war. Many of these encouraged a positive vision of the United States and stressed positive actions. For example, some encouraged men to join the armed forces and women to take jobs in war industries. Others encouraged those on the home front to save essential resources, such as gasoline and aluminum. The OWI also issued warnings to the public about the dangers they faced. Drawings of Nazi or Japanese soldiers threatening small children were meant to inspire fear in Americans—and the desire to take action against the Axis nations. Another technique was to show the harmful outcomes of improper actions, such as sharing sensitive military information.

Movies remained enormously popular during the war years. In the early 1940s some 85 million Americans went to the movies each week. As a result, the nation's film industry became a major producer of wartime propaganda. Movie studios churned out patriotic films that featured soldiers and workers on the home front. The OWI helped by reviewing movie scripts for the proper messages. Moviemakers also created informational films, such as Frank Capra's *Why We Fight* series. As the war dragged on, moviegoers grew tired of propaganda and war themes. Hollywood responded with musicals, romances, and other escapist fare. These were designed to take viewers away from the grim realities of war, if only for an hour or two.

ECONOMIC CONTROLS Due to their experiences in World War I, government officials knew that wartime inflation could threaten the American economy. Inflation is a general rise in the level of prices. When it occurs, each dollar that a person earns will buy fewer goods and services than it did before. As war production increased, fewer consumer products would be available. With demand increasing and supplies dropping, prices seemed likely to climb.

Roosevelt responded to this threat by creating the **Office of Price Administration (OPA)**. The OPA fought inflation by freezing prices on most goods. Congress also raised income tax rates and extended the tax to millions of people who had never paid it before. As a result, workers had less to spend. This reduced consumer demand on scarce goods. In addition, the government encouraged Americans to buy war bonds with their extra cash. As a result of these measures, inflation remained below 30 percent for the entire period of World War II. This was about half the inflation level during World War I.

These measures also helped fund the war effort. According to some estimates, preparations for World War II cost the U.S. government more than $300 billion. After restructuring the tax system, Congress created the withholding system of payroll deductions to collect income taxes. Employers

Children of all ages helped with wartime recycling. This 5-year-old boy pounded the pavement in New York City collecting aluminum.

withheld a percentage of their workers' pay from each paycheck. Then they sent the money directly to the U.S. treasury, supplying a steady flow of funds. The money that ordinary citizens invested in war bonds also helped pay for the war. It paid for shipping, aircraft, and other weaponry produced in American factories. By war's end, 85 million Americans had purchased war bonds, raising nearly $185 billion.

Besides controlling inflation and paying for the war effort, the government had to make sure that the armed forces and war industries received the resources they needed. The **War Production Board (WPB)** assumed that responsibility. The WPB decided which companies would change from peacetime to wartime production. It allocated raw materials to key industries. The WPB also organized drives to collect scrap iron, tin cans, paper, rags, and cooking fat to recycle into war goods. Across America, children searched attics, cellars, garages, vacant lots, and back alleys, looking for useful junk. During one five-month-long paper drive in Chicago, schoolchildren collected 36 million pounds of old paper. Their effort was equal to about 65 pounds per child.

CONSERVING FOOD AND OTHER GOODS Meeting the food needs of the military took top priority in the United States. One way to grow more food for Americans on the home front was to plant victory gardens. Americans prepared with a few simple tools, some seed and fertilizer, and a patriotic spirit. They farmed small plots of land to overcome food shortages. In small towns and large cities, any spare piece of land was likely to be used to grow food. Many victory gardens were small and humble, but the combined efforts of millions of Americans produced big results. In 1943 the nation's 20 million victory gardens yielded an astounding 8 million tons of produce.

However, victory gardens alone could not fulfill all of the nation's food needs. Some foods could not be grown in home gardens. There were shortages of other products as well. As a result, the OPA set up a system for **rationing**, or establishing fixed allotments of goods deemed essential for the military. Under this system, households received ration books with coupons to be used for buying such scarce goods. These included meat, shoes, sugar, coffee, and gasoline. Most Americans willingly accepted rationing as a personal contribution to the war effort. Inevitably, some cheated by hoarding scarce goods or purchasing them through the "black market." There, rationed items could be bought illegally without coupons at inflated prices. However, the penalties for breaking the rules could be severe.

Some materials were so vital to the war effort that even rationing was not enough to preserve the country's supply. To help fulfill the military's needs—and to keep civilians from suffering too much—scientists developed synthetic versions of some of these products. For example, rubber was necessary for making tires and other automotive parts. Nearly all of the world's rubber supply came from parts of Asia that had been conquered by Japan. American companies began to produce synthetic rubber for many of these uses. The synthetic fabric nylon was produced to replace silk in parachutes, protective gear, and other military applications.

MOBILIZATION OF SCIENTISTS In 1941 Roosevelt created the Office of Scientific Research and Development (OSRD) to bring scientists into the war effort. The OSRD stimulated improvements in semiconductor technology, which is vital for modern communications equipment. In turn, these advances led to the development of radar and sonar. These new technologies were used to locate submarines under water. Scientists with the OSRD also worked to improve weapons technology. For example, they developed new bombs and guided missiles. They also improved aircraft technology. The first combat jet aircraft were launched during World War II, although they were not actually used in fighting during the war.

The OSRD also supported research into lifesaving medications and techniques. For example, it pushed the development of "miracle drugs," such as penicillin. These drugs saved countless lives on and off the battlefield. It also funded research into new ways to isolate blood plasma—the liquid portion of blood—and transport both plasma and whole blood to where they were needed on the battlefield. The OSRD encouraged the use of pesticides like DDT to fight insects. As a result, U.S. soldiers were probably the first in history to be relatively free from body lice.

The most significant achievement of the OSRD, however, was the secret development of a new weapon, the atomic bomb. Interest in such a weapon began in 1939, after German scientists succeeded in splitting uranium atoms. That process released an enormous amount of energy. This news prompted physicist and German refugee Albert Einstein to write a letter to President Roosevelt. Einstein warned that the Germans could use their discovery to build a weapon of enormous destructive power.

Roosevelt responded by creating an Advisory Committee on Uranium to study the new discovery. In 1941 the committee reported that it would take from three to five years to build an atomic bomb. The OSRD hoped to shorten that time. It set up an intensive program in 1942 to develop a bomb as quickly as possible. Much of the early research was performed at Columbia University in Manhattan. As a result, the **Manhattan Project** became the code name for research work that was done across the country.

The Government Takes Control of the Economy, 1942–1945

Agencies and Laws	Actions and Results
Office of War Information (OWI)	• Spread propaganda to increase support for the war effort • Produced posters and films alerting Americans to the need for rationing and to potential dangers
Office of Price Administration (OPA)	• Fought inflation by freezing wages, prices, and rents • Rationed foods such as meat, butter, cheese, vegetables, sugar, and coffee
Department of the Treasury	• Issued war bonds to raise money for the war effort and to fight inflation
Revenue Act of 1942	• Raised the top personal-income tax rate to 88 percent • Added lower- and middle-income Americans to the income-tax rolls
War Production Board (WPB)	• Rationed fuel and materials vital to the war effort, such as gasoline, heating oil, metals, rubber, and plastics
Office of Scientific Research and Development (OSRD)	• Developed and improved military technology • Researched new medications and medical techniques • Established Manhattan Project to develop the atomic bomb
National War Labor Board (NWLB)	• Limited wage increases • Allowed negotiated benefits such as paid vacation, pensions, and medical insurance • Kept unions stable by forbidding workers to change unions
Smith-Connally Anti-Strike Act (1943)	• Limited the right to strike in industries crucial to the war effort • Gave the president power to take over striking plants
Fair Employment Practices Committee	• Prohibited job discrimination based on race or religion

Interpret Tables
1. Why did President Roosevelt create the OSRD, and what did it do?
2. What was the purpose of the Fair Employment Practices Committee?

TRANSPORTING GOODS All of the products made in American factories and saved by citizens had to be shipped to the soldiers overseas. Soldiers on both fronts needed weapons, food, medicines, and other supplies to be successful. Much of the responsibility for transporting goods to the war fronts fell to the U.S. merchant marine, a fleet of civilian merchant ships. More than 200,000 Americans served in the merchant marine during the war.

With battles raging on two fronts, transporting goods presented a huge challenge. Any goods transported to either Europe or the Pacific front had to cross an ocean patrolled by enemy ships, submarines, and planes. For safety, most merchant ships traveled in convoys. These groups were often escorted by warships. Even with such precautions, however, merchant shipping was dangerous. Dozens of ships were sunk, and tens of thousands of sailors were killed.

The nature of some products made them more challenging to ship. Many medicines and foods were perishable. They could not be shipped or stored without refrigeration, which often was not available. Fragile containers, such as glass jars, were difficult to transport without damage. However, American ingenuity provided solutions. Researchers developed methods to freeze-dry vital medical supplies, including penicillin and blood plasma. Dried supplies did not need refrigeration. They could also be transported in more durable containers, such as cans. Freeze-drying was also used later in the war to preserve food to ship to soldiers on both fronts.

Reading Check
Identify Problems
What basic problems were the OPA and WPB created to solve?

A Production Miracle

One of the most important and most challenging aspects of mobilization was the rapid industrial change from peacetime to wartime production. Following the outbreak of war, the federal government spent tens of billions of dollars on weapons and supplies. Roosevelt set the ambitious goal of building 60,000 new planes in 1942 and 125,000 more the next year. He asked for 120,000 tanks in the same period. To meet these goals, Roosevelt relied on government agencies to regulate industry. They determined what factories produced, what prices they charged, and how raw materials would be allocated. He also relied on the efforts of millions of Americans who went to work in the nation's factories, many for the first time.

The Production Miracle

Aircraft and Ship Production, 1940-45

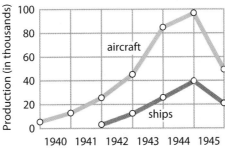

U.S. Budget Expenditure, 1941-45

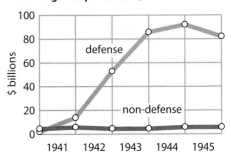

Source: *The Times Atlas of the Second World War*

Interpret Graphs
1. Study the first graph. In what year did aircraft and ship production reach their highest production levels?
2. How does the second graph help explain how this production miracle was possible?

THE INDUSTRIAL RESPONSE Early in February 1942, American newspapers reported the end of automobile production for private use. The last car to roll off an automaker's assembly line was a gray sedan with "victory trim,"—that is, without chrome-plated parts. Within weeks of the shutdown in production, the nation's automobile plants had been retooled. They began to produce tanks, planes, boats, and command cars. They were not alone. Across the nation, factories were quickly converted to war production. A maker of mechanical pencils produced bomb parts. A bedspread manufacturer made mosquito netting. A soft-drink company converted from filling bottles with liquid to filling shells with explosives.

Meanwhile, shipyards and defense plants expanded with dizzying speed. By the end of 1942, industrialist Henry J. Kaiser had built seven massive new shipyards that turned out Liberty ships (cargo carriers), tankers, troop transports, and "baby" aircraft carriers at an astonishing rate. Late that year Kaiser invited reporters to Way One in his Richmond, California, shipyard. They watched as his workers assembled *Hull 440,* a Liberty ship, in a record-breaking four days. Before the end of the fourth day, 25,000 amazed spectators watched as *Hull 440* slid into the water. How could such a ship be built so fast? Kaiser used prefabricated, or factory-made, parts that could be assembled quickly at his shipyards. Equally important were his workers, who worked at record speeds.

LABOR'S CONTRIBUTION When the war began, defense contractors warned the Selective Service System that the nation did not have enough workers to meet both its military and its industrial needs. They were wrong. A wave of patriotism swept through the country, binding Americans together against a common enemy. Some Americans expressed their patriotic feelings by enlisting in the armed forces. Others rushed to take jobs in factories to support the war effort. By 1944, despite the draft, nearly 18 million workers were laboring in war industries, three times as many as in 1941.

Liberty Ship Production

These images illustrate the progress of a Liberty ship at the Bethlehem-Fairfield Shipyards in Baltimore, Maryland, in the spring of 1943. From left to right, the construction is documented from Day 1 to Day 10 to Day 24, when the ship is complete and ready to launch.

Swept up in the national wave of patriotism, laborers threw themselves fully into the war effort. Individuals willingly worked long hours with few breaks. Labor unions pledged not to strike or take any other action that would slow down production. As the war dragged on and prices climbed, however, some workers grew frustrated. They called on union leaders to fight for higher wages. To head off a potential production slowdown, Roosevelt established the National War Labor Board (NWLB) in 1942. The board served as a mediator between labor and management to prevent strikes. It prevented protests about wages by setting limits on wage increases, which took the decision out of management's hands. To prevent union instability, which could affect production, it banned workers from quitting or changing unions while employed.

During the war, women took many jobs previously held by men. In this 1943 photo, a young woman is seen operating a hand drill in Nashville, Tennessee.

A lathe operator at the Consolidated Aircraft plant in Fort Worth, Texas, creates parts for transport planes.

NEW WORKERS Among those who committed to working in war industries were more than 6 million women who wanted to support their country. At first, war industries feared that most women lacked the necessary strength for factory work and were reluctant to hire them. But women proved that they could operate welding torches or riveting guns as well as men. After that, employers could not hire enough of them, especially since women earned only about 60 percent as much as men doing the same jobs. The character "Rosie the Riveter" was inspired by a popular song of the era. Her image was that of a strong woman hard at work in an arms factory. That image became an enduring symbol of these women and their contributions to the war.

Defense plants also hired more than 2 million minority workers during the war years. These included African Americans, Mexican Americans, Asian Americans, Native Americans, and others. Like women, minorities faced strong prejudice at first. Before the war, 75 percent of defense contractors simply refused to hire African Americans. Another 15 percent employed them only in menial jobs. Nationalism and a desire to contribute led African American workers to take these menial jobs. However, many were not happy about the situation. "Negroes will be considered only as janitors," declared the general manager of North American Aviation. "It is the company policy not to employ them as mechanics and aircraft workers."

Many of the new workers in America's factories had previously worked on farms, as had many soldiers. The departure of so many workers from American farms led to a severe shortage of agricultural laborers. Faced with the possibility of low harvests, the U.S. government responded. In 1942 it launched a program in which Mexican *braceros*, or hired hands, were invited

Women in the Workplace

After the bombing of Pearl Harbor many women, barred from serving in the military, took jobs to support the war effort. Among those women were Mary Cohen of New York City and her sister.

> *"We both wanted to get something to help the war effort. We saw an ad in the paper about working on aircraft on fighter planes. . . . We didn't realize how much stress that would be, but we were young, so it didn't bother us at that time. . . . It didn't matter as far as the money. We just wanted to get these planes out. It was a very patriotic feeling. It took its toll. I got sick once. I never even took time off. I just went in all the time."*
>
> —Mary Cohen, quoted in the Rosie the Riveter WWII Oral History Project

Analyze Historical Sources
How did the outbreak of war change the lives of Mary Cohen and women like her?

Reading Check
Form
Generalizations
How did women and minorities contribute to the wartime work force?

to the United States to work on farms. Hundreds of thousands of braceros entered the United States between 1942 and 1947. By the war's end, many braceros had also taken jobs in the railroad industry.

In theory, the bracero program guaranteed that all workers would receive fair pay and equal treatment under the law. In practice, however, many farm owners ignored these guidelines. Some shorted workers' paychecks or gave them inadequate tools for their work. In addition, many braceros entering the country were met with scorn and abuse from other farm workers and from supervisors.

Opportunity, Discrimination, and Adjustment

The war opened up many opportunities for women and minorities. At the same time, though, old prejudices and policies persisted, both in the military and at home. In addition, Americans of all ethnicities and backgrounds had to adjust to the absence of loved ones fighting abroad.

CONFRONTING LABOR ISSUES To protest discrimination both in the military and in industry, **A. Philip Randolph** organized a march on Washington. Randolph was president and founder of the Brotherhood of Sleeping Car Porters and the nation's most respected African American labor leader. He called on African Americans everywhere to come to the capital on July 1, 1941. They were to march under the banner "We Loyal Colored Americans Demand the Right to Work and Fight for Our Country."

President Roosevelt feared that the march might provoke white resentment or violence. He called Randolph to the White House and asked him to back

A. Philip Randolph in 1942

down. "I'm sorry Mr. President," the labor leader said, "the march cannot be called off." Roosevelt then asked, "How many people do you plan to bring?" Randolph replied, "One hundred thousand, Mr. President." Roosevelt was stunned. Even half that number of African American protesters would be far more than Washington—still a very segregated city—could feed, house, and transport.

In the end it was Roosevelt, not Randolph, who backed down. In return for Randolph's promise to cancel the march, the president issued an executive order creating the Fair Employment Practices Committee. It called on employers and labor unions "to provide for the full and equitable participation of all workers in defense industries, without discrimination because of race, creed, color, or national origin."

CIVIL RIGHTS PROTESTS African Americans made some progress on the home front. During the war, thousands of African Americans left the South. The majority moved to the Midwest where they could find better jobs. Between 1940 and 1944 the percentage of African Americans working in skilled or semiskilled jobs rose from 16 to 30 percent.

Wherever African Americans moved, however, discrimination presented tough hurdles. In 1942 civil rights leader **James Farmer** founded an interracial organization called the **Congress of Racial Equality (CORE)**. Its purpose was to confront urban segregation in the North. That same year, CORE staged its first sit-in at a segregated Chicago restaurant.

As African American migrants moved into already overcrowded cities, tensions rose. In 1943 a tidal wave of racial violence swept across the country. The worst conflict erupted in Detroit on a hot Sunday afternoon in June. It began as a disagreement between blacks and whites at a beach on the Detroit River. It grew into a riot when white sailors stationed nearby joined in. The fighting continued for three days. False rumors circulated that whites had murdered a black woman and her child and that black rioters had killed 17 whites. By the time President Roosevelt sent federal troops to restore order, 9 whites and 25 blacks lay dead or dying.

The violence of 1943 showed both black and white Americans just how serious racial tensions had become in the United States. By 1945 more than 400 committees had been established by American communities to improve race relations. Progress was slow, but African Americans were determined not to give up the gains they had made.

TENSION IN LOS ANGELES Mexican Americans also experienced prejudice during the war years. In the violent summer of 1943, Los Angeles exploded in anti-Mexican "zoot-suit" riots. The zoot suit was a style of dress adopted by Mexican American youths to symbolize their rebellion against tradition. It consisted of a long jacket and pleated pants. Broad-brimmed hats were often worn with the suits.

These Mexican Americans, involved in the 1943 Los Angeles riots, are seen here leaving jail to make court appearances.

The riots began when 11 sailors in Los Angeles reported that they had been attacked by zoot-suit-wearing Mexican Americans. This charge triggered violence involving thousands of servicemen and civilians. Mobs poured into Mexican neighborhoods and grabbed any zoot-suiters they could find. The attackers ripped off their victims' clothes and beat them senseless. The riots lasted almost a week and resulted in the beatings of hundreds of Mexican American youth and other minorities.

In spite of such unhappy experiences with racism, many Mexican Americans expressed hope that their sacrifices during wartime would lead to a better future.

> *"This war . . . is doing what we in our Mexican-American movement had planned to do in one generation. . . . It has shown those 'across the tracks' that we all share the same problems. It has shown them what the Mexican American will do, what responsibility he will take and what leadership qualities he will demonstrate. After this struggle, the status of the Mexican Americans will be different."*
>
> —Manuel de la Raza, quoted in *A Different Mirror: A History of Multicultural America*

HARDSHIPS FOR NATIVE AMERICANS Native Americans, too, faced discrimination during the war. Native Americans on the whole were among the most enthusiastic volunteers for military service. Although they risked their lives to defend American values, many states still prohibited them from voting. Even in states that did not bar Native Americans from voting outright, local policies prevented many from casting ballots.

During the war, the federal government reclaimed some reservation land for its own use. Some of this land was used to build or enlarge military bases or to create weapons-testing areas. Parts of two reservations in Arizona were designated as relocation camps, despite the objections of the residents. Huge tracts of Native American land were mined for valuable resources, including oil, gas, lead, and helium. During the war, these lands yielded more than $39 million worth of vital minerals. However, the Native American tribes on the lands received only $6 million in compensation.

SOCIAL ADJUSTMENTS Americans willingly put up with many hardships and managed without comforts during the war. For many, the hardest part was dealing with the absence of loved ones. Across the country, families with loved ones in the armed forces showed their sacrifice by displaying a flag with a blue star. If the service member was killed, the blue star was replaced with a gold one. Over the course of the war, more than 400,000 American service members were killed, leaving many grieving families behind.

Families adjusted to the changes brought on by war as best they could. With millions of fathers in the armed forces, mothers struggled to raise their children alone. Many young children got used to being left with neighbors or relatives or in child-care centers as more and more mothers went to work. Teenagers left at home without parents sometimes drifted into juvenile delinquency. And when fathers finally did come home, there was often a painful period of readjustment as family members got to know one another again.

The war helped create new families, too. Longtime sweethearts—as well as couples who barely knew each other—rushed to marry before the soldier or sailor was shipped overseas. In booming towns like Seattle, the number of marriage licenses issued went up by as much as 300 percent early in the war. A New Yorker observed in 1943, "On Fridays and Saturdays, the City Hall area is blurred with running soldiers, sailors, and girls hunting the license bureau, floral shops, ministers, blood-testing laboratories, and the Legal Aid Society."

Reading Check
Summarize Why did A. Philip Randolph propose a march on Washington, DC, and how did President Roosevelt respond?

Internment of Japanese Americans

While some minorities struggled with tension and discrimination, the war produced tragic result for others. After Pearl Harbor, government officials began to fear that people of German, Italian, and Japanese descent might resort to sabotage or other disloyal behavior in order to help the enemy. Italians and Germans who had immigrated to the United States but not yet completed the citizenship process were considered "enemy aliens." Many were forced to register with the government and carry identification cards. In addition, the government designated certain areas restricted from enemy aliens. Such restrictions on people's civil liberties placed a huge burden on those living or working in these areas. Thousands of Germans and Italians were placed in prison camps. But the worst treatment was reserved for the Japanese Americans.

Japanese Relocation Camps, 1942

On March 3, 1942, a Japanese American mother carries her sleeping daughter during their relocation to an internment camp.

Interpret Maps

1. **Location** In which states were the Japanese internment camps located in 1942?

2. **Place** Why do you think the majority of these camps were located in the West?

When the war began, 120,000 Japanese Americans lived in the United States, mostly on the West Coast. The sense of fear and uncertainty following Pearl Harbor caused a wave of prejudice against them. The surprise in Hawaii had stunned the nation. After the bombing, panic-stricken citizens feared that the Japanese would soon attack the United States. Frightened people believed false rumors that Japanese Americans were committing sabotage by mining coastal harbors and poisoning vegetables.

Early in 1942 the War Department called for the mass evacuation of all Japanese Americans from Hawaii. General Delos Emmons, the military governor of Hawaii, resisted the order because 37 percent of the people in Hawaii were Japanese Americans. To remove them would have destroyed the islands' economy and hindered U.S. military operations there. However, he was eventually forced to order the **internment**, or confinement, of 1,444 Japanese Americans, 1 percent of Hawaii's Japanese American population.

On February 19, 1942, President Roosevelt signed Executive Order 9066 requiring the removal of people of Japanese ancestry from California and parts of Washington, Oregon, and Arizona. Based on strong recommendations from the military, he justified this step as necessary for national security. In the following weeks, the army rounded up some 110,000 Japanese Americans. They were sent to ten hastily constructed remote "relocation centers," euphemisms for prison camps.

About two-thirds were Nisei, or Japanese people born in this country of parents who emigrated from Japan. Thousands of Nisei had already joined the armed forces. To Monica Itoi Sone, a Nisei teenager from Seattle, the evacuation to the Minidoka camp in Idaho seemed unbelievable.

"We couldn't believe that the government meant that the Japanese-Americans must go. . . . We were quite sure that our rights as American citizens would not be violated, and we would not be marched out of our homes on the same basis as enemy aliens."

—Monica Itoi Sone, from *Nisei Daughter*

No specific charges were ever filed against Japanese Americans, and no evidence of subversion was ever found. Faced with expulsion, terrified families were forced to sell their homes, businesses, and all their belongings for less than their true value.

Japanese Americans fought for justice, both in the courts and in Congress. The initial results were discouraging. In 1944 the Supreme Court decided, in *Korematsu* v. *United States*, that the government's policy of evacuating Japanese Americans to camps was justified under the Constitution on the basis of "military necessity." After the war, however, the **Japanese American Citizens League (JACL)** pushed the government to compensate those sent to the camps for their lost property. In 1965 Congress authorized the spending of $38 million for that purpose. This amount represented less than a tenth of Japanese Americans' actual losses.

The JACL did not give up its quest for justice. In 1978 it called for the payment of reparations, or restitution, to each individual that suffered internment. A decade later Congress passed, and President Ronald Reagan signed, a bill that promised $20,000 to every Japanese American sent to a relocation camp. When the checks were sent in 1990, a letter from President George Bush accompanied them, in which he stated, "We can never fully right the wrongs of the past. But we can take a clear stand for justice and recognize that serious injustices were done to Japanese Americans during World War II."

Reading Check
Analyze Motives
Why did President Roosevelt order the internment of Japanese Americans?

Lesson 4 Assessment

1. **Organize Information** Use a web diagram to record the ways that the war affected the lives of Americans on the home front.

Preparation for War, 1941–1942

2. **Key Terms and People** For each key term or person in the lesson, write a sentence explaining its significance.

3. **Analyze Issues** How did government agencies manage wartime mobilization?

Think About:
- the Office of War Information and the use of propaganda
- the Office of Price Administration and inflation
- the War Production Board and industrial mobilization

4. **Summarize** How did the scientific and technological advances made by American researchers during World War II meet wartime needs?

5. **Analyze Events** How did the U.S. government finance the country's involvement in World War II?

6. **Analyze Causes** Why did many women and minority Americans contribute to the war effort despite facing discrimination?

7. **Evaluate** Do you think the government's actions toward German, Italian, and Japanese Americans were justified on the basis of "military necessity" or a denial of civil rights? Explain your answer.

Korematsu v. United States (1944)

ORIGINS OF THE CASE

Following the Japanese attack on Pearl Harbor on December 7, 1941, U.S. military officials argued that Japanese Americans posed a threat to the nation's security. Based on recommendations from the military, President Franklin Roosevelt issued Executive Order 9066, which gave military officials the power to limit the civil rights of Japanese Americans. Military authorities began by setting a curfew for Japanese Americans. Later, they forced Japanese Americans from their homes and moved them into detention camps. Fred Korematsu was convicted of defying the military order to leave his home. At the urging of the American Civil Liberties Union (ACLU), Korematsu appealed that conviction.

THE RULING

The Court upheld Korematsu's conviction and argued that military necessity made internment constitutional.

LEGAL REASONING

Executive Order 9066 was clearly aimed at one group of people—Japanese Americans. Korematsu argued that this order was unconstitutional because it was based on race. Writing for the Court majority, Justice Hugo Black agreed "that all legal restrictions which curtail the civil rights of a single racial group are immediately suspect." However, in this case, he said, the restrictions were based on "a military imperative" and not "group punishment based on antagonism to those of Japanese origin." As such, Justice Black stated that the restrictions were constitutional.

"Compulsory exclusion of large groups, . . . except under circumstances of direct emergency and peril, is inconsistent with our basic governmental institutions. But when under conditions of modern warfare our shores are threatened by hostile forces, the power to protect must be commensurate with the threatened danger."

Justice Frank Murphy, however, dissented—he opposed the majority. He believed that military necessity was merely an excuse that could not conceal the racism at the heart of the restrictions.

"This exclusion . . . ought not to be approved. Such exclusion goes over 'the very brink of constitutional power' and falls into the ugly abyss of racism."

Two other justices also dissented, but Korematsu's conviction stood.

LEGAL SOURCES

LEGISLATION

U.S. Constitution, Fifth Amendment (1791)

"No person shall . . . be deprived of life, liberty, or property, without due process of law."

Executive Order 9066 (1942)

"I hereby authorize and direct the Secretary of War . . . to prescribe military areas in such places and of such extent as he . . . may determine, from which any or all persons may be excluded."

RELATED CASES

Hirabayashi v. United States (June 1943)

The Court upheld the conviction of a Japanese American man for breaking curfew. The Court argued that the curfew was within congressional and presidential authority.

Ex Parte Endo (December 1944)

The Court ruled that a Japanese American girl, whose loyalty had been clearly established, could not be held in an internment camp.

Internees did what they could to adjust to confinement in the camps. They established schools for their children, produced newspapers, planted gardens, and formed a variety of community groups. Inset: President Clinton presents Fred Korematsu with a Presidential Medal of Freedom during a ceremony at the White House on January 15, 1998.

WHY IT MATTERED

About 110,000 Japanese Americans were forced into internment camps, as shown above, during World War II. Many had to sell their businesses and homes at great loss. Thousands were forced to give up their possessions. In the internment camps, Japanese Americans lived in a prison-like setting under constant guard.

The Court ruled that these government actions did not violate people's rights because the restrictions were based on military necessity rather than on race. But the government treated German Americans and Italian Americans much differently. In those instances, the government identified potentially disloyal people but did not harass the people it believed to be loyal. By contrast, the government refused to make distinctions between loyal and potentially disloyal Japanese Americans.

HISTORICAL IMPACT

In the end, the internment of Japanese Americans became a national embarrassment. In 1976 President Gerald R. Ford repealed Executive Order 9066.

Similarly, the Court's decision in *Korematsu* became an embarrassing example of court-sanctioned racism often compared to the decisions on *Dred Scott* (1857) and *Plessy* v. *Ferguson* (1896). In the early 1980s a scholar conducting research obtained copies of government documents related to the *Hirabayashi* and *Korematsu* cases. The documents showed that the army had lied to the Court in the 1940s. Japanese Americans had not posed any security threat. Korematsu's conviction was overturned in 1984. Hirabayashi's conviction was overturned in 1986. In 1988 Congress passed a law ordering reparations payments to surviving Japanese Americans who had been detained in the camps.

Critical Thinking
1. **Connect to History** Do Internet research to locate the three dissenting opinions in *Korematsu* written by Justices Frank Murphy, Robert Jackson, and Owen Roberts. Read one of these opinions, and then write a summary that states its main idea. What constitutional principle, if any, does the opinion use?

2. **Connect to Today** The internment of Japanese Americans during World War II disrupted lives and ripped apart families. What do you think can be done today to address this terrible mistake? How can the government make amends?

The War for Europe and North Africa

One American's Story

The Big Idea

Allied forces, led by the United States and Great Britain, battled Axis powers for control of Europe and North Africa.

Why It Matters Now

During World War II, the United States assumed a leading role in world affairs that continues today.

Key Terms and People

Dwight D. Eisenhower

Omar Bradley

D-Day

George Patton

Battle of the Bulge

It was 1951, and John Patrick McGrath was just finishing his second year in drama school. For an acting class, his final exam was to be a performance of a death scene. McGrath knew his lines perfectly. But as he began the final farewell, he broke out in a sweat and bolted off the stage. Suddenly he had a flashback to a frozen meadow in Belgium during the Battle of the Bulge in 1945. Three German tanks were spraying his platoon with machine-gun fire.

"Only a few feet away, one of the men in my platoon falls. . . . He calls out to me. 'Don't leave me. Don't. . . .' The tanks advance, one straight for me. I grab my buddy by the wrist and pull him across the snow. . . . The tank nearest to us is on a track to run us down. . . . When the German tank is but 15 yards away, I grab my buddy by the

Private John P. McGrath carried this bullet-riddled letter in a pack that saved his life. In 1990 he visited Anzio, where members of his company were buried.

wrist and feign a lurch to my right. The tank follows the move. Then I lurch back to my left. The German tank clamors by, only inches away. . . . In their wake the meadow is strewn with casualties. I turn to tend my fallen comrade. He is dead."

—John Patrick McGrath, from *A Cue for Passion*

Like countless other soldiers, McGrath would never forget both the heroism and the horrors he witnessed while fighting to free Europe.

SS.912.A.1.2; SS.912.A.1.3; SS.912.A.1.4; SS.912.A.6.1; SS.912.G.1.2; SS.912.G.2.1; LAFS.1112.RH.1.2

The United States and Britain Join Forces

"Now that we are, as you say, 'in the same boat,'" British prime minister Winston Churchill wired President Roosevelt two days after the Pearl Harbor attack, "would it not be wise for us to have another conference. . . . and the sooner the better." As commander in chief of the U.S. military, it would fall to Roosevelt to direct the country's overall war strategy. He responded to Churchill's wire with an invitation to come to Washington at once. So began a remarkable alliance between the two nations.

WAR PLANS Prime Minister Churchill arrived at the White House on December 22, 1941, and spent the next three weeks working out war plans with President Roosevelt and his advisers. The strategy they developed was called Germany First. Believing that Germany and Italy posed a greater threat than Japan, Churchill convinced Roosevelt to strike first against Hitler. Once the Allies had gained an upper hand in Europe, they could pour more resources into the Pacific War.

By the end of their meeting, Roosevelt and Churchill had formed, in Churchill's words, "a very strong affection, which grew with our years of comradeship." When Churchill reached London, he found a message from the president waiting for him. "It is fun," Roosevelt wrote in the message, "to be in the same decade with you."

THE BATTLE OF THE ATLANTIC After the attack on Pearl Harbor, Hitler ordered submarine raids against ships along America's east coast. The German aim in the Battle of the Atlantic was to prevent food and war materials from reaching Great Britain and the Soviet Union. Britain depended on supplies from the sea. The 3,000-mile-long shipping lanes from North America were her lifeline. Hitler knew that if he cut that lifeline, Britain would be starved into submission.

The Allies responded by organizing their cargo ships into convoys. Convoys were groups of ships traveling together for mutual protection, as they had done in the First World War. However, for a long time, it looked as though Hitler might succeed in his mission. Early in the war, the Allies did not have enough vessels to form effective convoys. As a result, American ships proved to be easy targets for the Germans. In the first four months of 1942, the Germans sank 87 ships off the Atlantic shore. Seven months into the year, German wolf packs had destroyed a total of 681 Allied ships in the Atlantic. Something had to be done or the war at sea would be lost.

Gradually, the Allied situation began to improve. As U.S. industry shifted to wartime production, the United States launched a crash ship-building program. By early 1943, 140 Liberty ships were produced each month. Launchings of Allied ships began to outnumber sinkings. At the same time, U.S. aircraft production ramped up, with four times as many airplanes built in 1943 as were constructed in 1941.

A convoy of British and American ships rides at anchor in the harbor of Hvalfjord, Iceland.

As a result, convoys began to be escorted across the Atlantic accompanied by more destroyers equipped with sonar for detecting submarines underwater and by airplanes that used radar to spot U-boats on the ocean's surface. With this improved tracking and support, the Allies were able to find and destroy German U-boats faster than the Germans could build them. In late spring of 1943, Admiral Karl Doenitz, the commander of the German U-boat offensive, reported that his losses had "reached an unbearable height."

By mid-1943 the tide of the Battle of the Atlantic had turned. A happy Churchill reported to the House of Commons that June "was the best month [at sea] from every point of view we have ever known in the whole 46 months of the war."

The Eastern Front and the Mediterranean

By the winter of 1943, the Allies began to see victories on land as well as sea. The first great turning point came in the Battle of Stalingrad.

THE BATTLE OF STALINGRAD The Germans had been fighting in the Soviet Union since June 1941. In November 1941 the bitter cold had stopped them in their tracks outside the Soviet cities of Moscow and Leningrad. When spring came, the German tanks were ready to roll.

In the summer of 1942, the Germans took the offensive in the southern Soviet Union. Hitler hoped to capture Soviet oil fields in the Caucasus Mountains. He also wanted to wipe out Stalingrad, a major industrial center on the Volga River.

Reading Check
Find Main Ideas
Where did Churchill believe the Allies should focus their efforts and why?

The German army confidently approached Stalingrad in August 1942. "To reach the Volga and take Stalingrad is not so difficult for us," one German soldier wrote home. "Victory is not far away." The Luftwaffe—the German air force—prepared the way with nightly bombing raids over the city. Nearly every wooden building in Stalingrad was set on fire. The situation looked desperate. Soviet officers in Stalingrad recommended blowing up the city's factories and abandoning the city. A furious Stalin ordered them to defend his namesake city no matter what the cost.

For weeks the Germans pressed in on Stalingrad, conquering it house by house in brutal hand-to-hand combat. By the end of September, they controlled nine-tenths of the city—or what was left of it. Then another winter set in. The Soviets saw the cold as an opportunity to roll fresh tanks across the frozen landscape and begin a massive counterattack. The Soviet army closed around Stalingrad. This action trapped the Germans in and around the city and cut off their supplies. The Germans' situation was hopeless, but Hitler's orders came: "Stay and fight! I won't go back from the Volga."

The fighting continued as winter turned Stalingrad into a frozen wasteland. "We just lay in our holes and froze, knowing that 24 hours later and 48 hours later we should be shivering precisely as we were now," wrote a German soldier, Benno Zieser. "But there was now no hope whatsoever of relief, and that was the worst thing of all." The German commander surrendered on January 31, 1943. Two days later his starving troops also surrendered.

In defending Stalingrad, the Soviets lost a total of 1,100,000 soldiers—more than all American deaths during the entire war. Despite the staggering death toll, the Soviet victory marked a turning point in the war. From that point on, the Soviet army began to move westward toward Germany.

Document-Based Investigation Historical Source

Stalingrad Prisoners of War

Dazed, starved, and freezing, these German soldiers were taken prisoner after months of struggle. But they were the lucky ones. More than 230,000 of their comrades died in the Battle of Stalingrad.

Analyze Historical Sources
What does the photograph tell you about the conditions faced by the German soldiers at the Battle of Stalingrad? What details in the photograph support your conclusions?

THE NORTH AFRICAN FRONT While the Battle of Stalingrad raged, Stalin pressured Britain and America to open a "second front" in Western Europe. He argued that an invasion across the English Channel would force Hitler to divert troops from the Soviet front. Churchill and Roosevelt didn't think the Allies had enough troops to attempt an invasion on European soil. Instead, they launched Operation Torch, an invasion of Axis-controlled North Africa, commanded by American general **Dwight D. Eisenhower**.

The British and the Italians had begun a battle for North Africa in June 1940, shortly after the fall of France. Control of the territory was vital to the Allies because it would protect Mediterranean shipping lanes that provided the British with Middle Eastern oil via the Suez Canal. Without oil, Great Britain would not be able to defend itself, much less defeat the Axis.

In the early fighting, Italian forces tried to drive the British from their stronghold in Egypt and failed. The Italians were beaten badly and driven back. In early 1941 Hitler was forced to send troops, led by General Erwin Rommel, to support the Italians. The German forces fought a back-and-forth battle against the British for control of North Africa throughout 1941 and 1942. Rommel led brilliantly, earning the nickname Desert Fox. But the British ultimately gained the upper hand. They struck a major blow when they defeated the Germans at the Battle of El Alamein.

▶ *Explore ONLINE!*

World War II: Europe and North Africa, 1942–1944

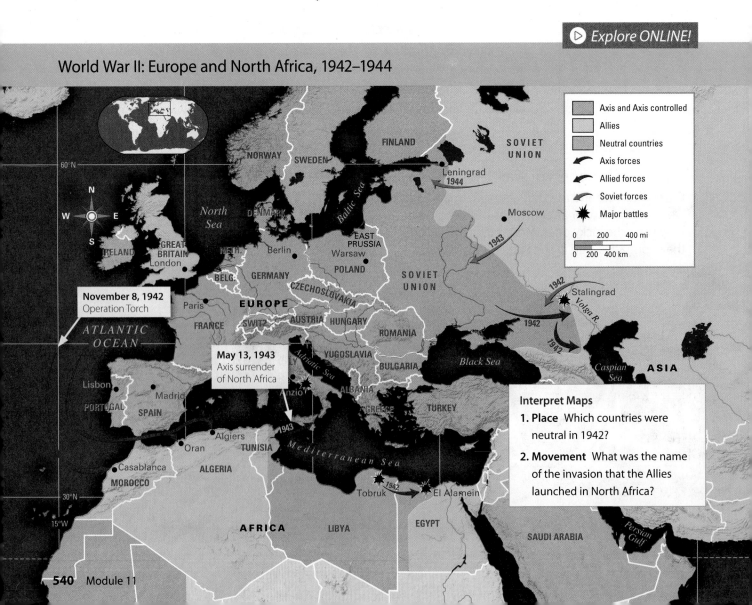

Interpret Maps

1. **Place** Which countries were neutral in 1942?

2. **Movement** What was the name of the invasion that the Allies launched in North Africa?

Operation Torch called for an Allied invasion of Morocco and Algeria. France had controlled these areas before the war. In November 1942 some 107,000 Allied troops, most of them Americans, landed in Casablanca, Oran, and Algiers in North Africa. From there they sped eastward, chasing Rommel's Afrika Korps. After months of heavy fighting, the last of the Afrika Korps surrendered in May 1943. British general Harold Alexander sent a message to Churchill: "All enemy resistance has ceased. We are masters of the North African shores."

Some 20,000 Americans were killed or wounded during the six months of fighting. However, as a result of the campaign in North Africa, American troops gained some much-needed combat experience. Their efforts toward the victory in North Africa proved that they could make a significant contribution to the war effort.

THE ITALIAN CAMPAIGN Even before the battle in North Africa was won, Roosevelt, Churchill, and their commanders met in Casablanca. At this meeting, the two leaders agreed to accept only the unconditional surrender of the Axis powers. That is, enemy nations would have to accept whatever terms of peace the Allies dictated. The two leaders also discussed where to attack next. The Americans argued for organizing a massive invasion fleet in Britain and launching it across the English Channel. Then Allied troops would move through France and into the heart of Germany. Churchill, however, thought it would be safer to first attack Italy.

The Italian campaign got off to a good start with the capture of Sicily in the summer of 1943. Stunned by their army's collapse in Sicily, the Italian government forced dictator Benito Mussolini to resign. On July 25, 1943, King Victor Emmanuel III summoned *Il Duce* (Italian for "the leader") to his palace. The king stripped Mussolini of power and had him arrested. "At this moment," the king told Mussolini, "you are the most hated man in Italy." Italians began celebrating the end of the war.

Their cheers were premature. Hitler was determined to stop the Allies in Italy rather than fight on German soil. One of the hardest battles the Allies encountered in Europe was fought less than 40 miles from Rome. This battle, "Bloody Anzio," lasted four months, until the end of May 1944. It left about 25,000 Allied and 30,000 Axis casualties. During the year after Anzio, German armies continued to put up strong resistance. The effort to free Italy did not succeed until 1945, when Germany itself was close to collapse.

HEROES IN COMBAT Among the brave men who fought in Italy were several units composed entirely of minority groups. The soldiers in these units sometimes had to deal with discrimination and poor treatment. Even so, their feelings of nationalism led them to risk their lives for their country.

The most celebrated of these minority units were the pilots of the all-black 99th Pursuit Squadron—the first squadron of Tuskegee Airmen. In Sicily the squadron registered its first victory against an enemy aircraft. Then it went on to more impressive strategic strikes against the German forces throughout Italy. The Tuskegee Airmen won two Distinguished Unit Citations (the military's highest commendation) for their outstanding aerial combat against the German Luftwaffe.

The 99th Pursuit Squadron was the first group of African American pilots trained at the Tuskegee Institute. In addition to the Presidential Unit citation, the highly decorated squadron earned over 100 Distinguished Flying Crosses, a Legion of Merit, and other commendations.

Reading Check
Summarize
Describe the contributions of minorities to the war effort.

Another African American unit to distinguish itself was the famous 92nd Infantry Division, nicknamed the Buffaloes. In just six months of fighting in Europe, the Buffaloes won 7 Legion of Merit awards, 65 Silver Stars, and 162 Bronze Stars for courage under fire.

Like African Americans, most Mexican Americans served in segregated units. Seventeen Mexican American soldiers were awarded the Congressional Medal of Honor. An all-Chicano unit—Company E of the 141st Regiment, 36th Division—became one of the most decorated of the war.

Japanese Americans also served in Italy and North Africa. At the urging of General Delos Emmons, the army created the 100th Battalion. It consisted of 1,300 Hawaiian Nisei. (The word *Nisei* refers to American citizens whose parents had emigrated from Japan.) The 100th saw brutal combat and became known as the Purple Heart Battalion. Later the 100th was merged into the all-Nisei 442nd Regimental Combat Team. It became the most decorated unit in U.S. history.

The Allies Gain Ground in Europe

Even as the Allies were battling for Italy in 1943, they had begun work on a dramatic plan to free Western Europe from the Nazis. In late 1943 Roosevelt, Churchill, and Stalin met in Tehran, Iran, to discuss the Allied strategy. The Tehran Conference had two major outcomes. The Soviet Union agreed to launch a major offensive against Germany from the east. At the same time, the other Allies planned to invade the Normandy region of France. This would force Germany to fight on two fronts. The Soviets had been asking Allied leaders to open a second front to help relieve the pressure on the Soviet army. The Allies eventually agreed to the Soviet request. Their delay, however, caused lingering resentment between Soviet and Western leaders.

D-DAY General Dwight D. Eisenhower was chosen to command the Allied invasion of Normandy, code-named Operation Overlord. He selected General **Omar Bradley** to lead the American forces participating in the mission. From this point on, Bradley commanded all U.S. ground troops invading Europe from the west.

Under Eisenhower's direction in England, the Allies gathered a massive force. It consisted of nearly 3 million British, American, and Canadian troops and mountains of military equipment and supplies. To keep their plans secret, the Allies set up a huge phantom army with its own headquarters and equipment. In radio messages they knew the Germans could read, Allied commanders sent orders to this make-believe army to attack the French port of Calais—150 miles away—where the English Channel is narrowest. As a result, Hitler ordered his generals to keep a large army at Calais.

The Allied invasion was originally set for June 5, but bad weather forced a delay. Based on a forecast for clearing skies, Eisenhower gave the go-ahead for **D-Day**—June 6, 1944, the first day of the invasion. Shortly after midnight, two American divisions—the 82nd and 101st Airborne divisions—and one British division parachuted down behind German lines. They were followed in the early morning hours by thousands upon thousands of seaborne soldiers. This was the largest land-sea-air operation in army history.

Background
American paratroopers on D-Day carried a simple signaling device to help them find one another in the dark. Each had a metal toy cricket to click. No German radio operators could intercept these messages.

– BIOGRAPHY

Dwight D. "Ike" Eisenhower (1890–1969)

When Army Chief of Staff General George Marshall chose modest Lieutenant General Dwight David Eisenhower to become the Supreme Commander of U.S. forces in Europe, he knew what he was doing. Eisenhower, or "Ike" as he was known, was a superb planner and possessed a keen mind for military tactics.

More important, Eisenhower had an uncommon ability to work with all kinds of people, even competitive and temperamental allies. After V-E Day a grateful Marshall wrote to Ike, saying, "You have been selfless in your actions, always sound and tolerant in your judgments and altogether admirable in the courage and wisdom of your military decisions.

You have made history, great history for the good of mankind." In 1953 Dwight D. Eisenhower became the 34th president of the United States.

Despite the massive air and sea bombardment by the Allies, German retaliation was brutal, particularly at Omaha Beach. "People were yelling, screaming, dying, running on the beach, equipment was flying everywhere, men were bleeding to death, crawling, lying everywhere, firing coming from all directions," soldier Felix Branham wrote of the scene there. "We dropped down behind anything that was the size of a golf ball."

THE ALLIES ADVANCE Despite heavy casualties, the Allies held the beachheads. The invasion of Normandy was a success. After seven days of fighting, the Allies held an 80-mile strip of France. Within a month they had landed a million troops, 567,000 tons of supplies, and 170,000 vehicles in France. On July 25, General Bradley unleashed massive air and land bombardment against the enemy at St. Lô. This attack opened a gap in the German line of

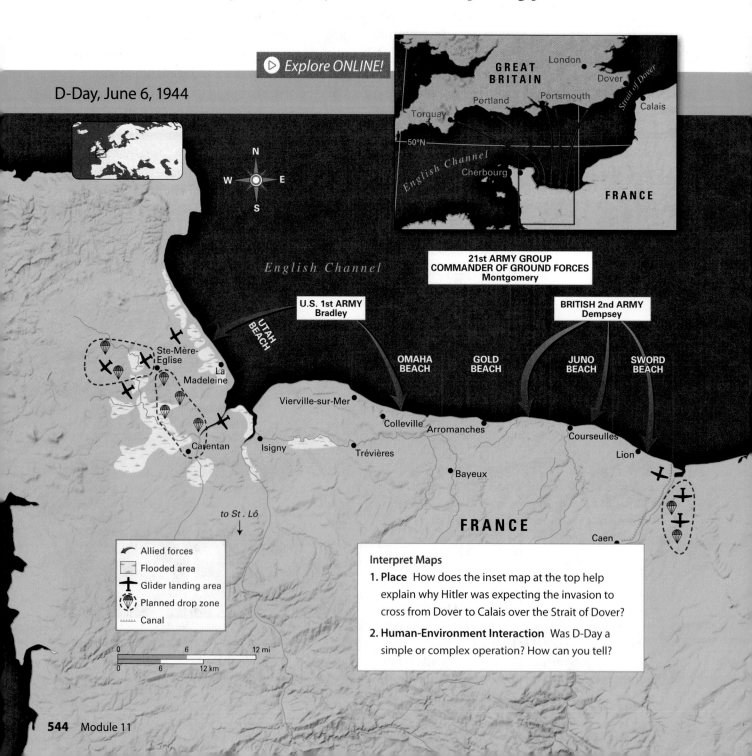

D-Day, June 6, 1944

Explore ONLINE!

GREAT BRITAIN

London

Dover

Strait of Dover

Portland

Portsmouth

Calais

Torquay

50°N

English Channel

Cherbourg

FRANCE

N W E S

English Channel

21st ARMY GROUP
COMMANDER OF GROUND FORCES
Montgomery

U.S. 1st ARMY
Bradley

BRITISH 2nd ARMY
Dempsey

UTAH BEACH

OMAHA BEACH

GOLD BEACH

JUNO BEACH

SWORD BEACH

Ste-Mère-Eglise

La Madeleine

Vierville-sur-Mer

Colleville

Arromanches

Courseulles

Lion

Carentan

Isigny

Trévières

Bayeux

Caen

to St. Lô

FRANCE

Allied forces

Flooded area

Glider landing area

Planned drop zone

Canal

0   6   12 mi
0   6   12 km

Interpret Maps

1. **Place** How does the inset map at the top help explain why Hitler was expecting the invasion to cross from Dover to Calais over the Strait of Dover?

2. **Human-Environment Interaction** Was D-Day a simple or complex operation? How can you tell?

defense through which General **George Patton** and his Third Army could advance. On August 23 Patton and the Third Army reached the Seine River south of Paris. Two days later French resistance forces and American troops liberated the French capital from four years of German occupation. Parisians were delirious with joy. Patton announced this joyous event to his commander in a message that read, "Dear Ike: Today I spat in the Seine."

By September 1944 the Allies had freed France, Belgium, and Luxembourg. This good news—and the American people's desire not to "change horses in midstream"—helped Franklin Roosevelt. He was elected to an unprecedented fourth term in November, along with his running mate, Senator Harry S. Truman.

THE BATTLE OF THE BULGE In October 1944 Americans captured their first German town, Aachen. Hitler responded with a desperate last-gasp offensive. He ordered his troops to break through the Allied lines and to recapture the Belgian port of Antwerp. The Führer hoped that this bold move would cut the enemy's supply lines and discourage the Allies.

On December 16, under cover of dense fog, eight German tank divisions broke through weak American defenses along an 80-mile front. Hitler hoped that a victory would split American and British forces. German tanks drove 60 miles into Allied territory. Their advance created a bulge in the lines that gave this desperate last-ditch offensive its name, the **Battle of the Bulge**. As the Germans moved westward, they captured 120 American GIs near Malmédy. Elite German troops—the SS troopers—herded the prisoners into a large field and mowed them down with machine guns and pistols.

The battle raged for a month. When it was over, the Germans had been pushed back and little seemed to have changed. But in fact, events had taken a decisive turn. The Germans had lost 120,000 troops, 600 tanks and assault guns, and 1,600 planes in the Battle of the Bulge. These were soldiers and weapons that they could not replace. From that point on, the Nazis could do little but retreat.

Vocabulary
elite a small and privileged group

Reading Check
Analyze Effects
How did the Battle of the Bulge signal the beginning of the end of World War II in Europe?

Lesson 5 Assessment

1. **Organize Information** Create a timeline of the major events influencing the fighting in Europe and North Africa.

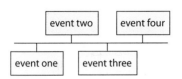

Write a paragraph indicating how any two of these events are related.

2. **Key Terms and People** For each key term or person in the lesson, write a sentence explaining its significance.

3. **Evaluate** Evaluate the military contributions of leaders during World War II.

   Think About:
   • Dwight Eisenhower
   • Omar Bradley
   • George Patton

4. **Draw Conclusions** Why did Stalin want the other Allied nations to open a second front? Why did Roosevelt and Churchill resist?

5. **Analyze Events** Why was the invasion of Normandy significant?

6. **Summarize** What were the results of the Casablanca and Tehran conferences?

The War in the Pacific

The Big Idea

After early defeats in the Pacific, the United States gained the upper hand and began to fight its way, island by island, to Japan.

Why It Matters Now

These battles in the Pacific convinced world leaders that a powerful weapon would be required to win the war.

Key Terms and People

Douglas MacArthur

Bataan Death March

Chester Nimitz

Battle of Midway

island hopping

kamikaze

One American's Story

The writer William Manchester left college after Pearl Harbor to join the marines. Manchester says that, as a child, his "horror of violence had been so deep-seated that I had been unable to trade punches with other boys." On a Pacific island, he would have to confront that horror the first time he killed a man in face-to-face combat. Manchester's target was a Japanese sniper firing on Manchester's buddies from a fisherman's shack.

American soldiers fighting on Leyte in the Philippine Islands in late 1944.

"My mouth was dry, my legs quaking, and my eyes out of focus. Then my vision cleared. I . . . kicked the door with my right foot, and leapt inside. . . . I . . . saw him as a blur to my right. . . . My first shot missed him, embedding itself in the straw wall, but the second caught him dead-on. . . . A wave of blood gushed from the wound. . . . He dipped a hand in it and listlessly smeared his cheek red. . . . Almost immediately a fly landed on his left eyeball. . . . A feeling of disgust and self-hatred clotted darkly in my throat, gagging me."

—William Manchester, from *Goodbye Darkness: A Memoir of the Pacific War*

The Pacific War was a savage conflict fought with raw courage. Few who took part in that fearsome struggle would return home unchanged.

SS.912.A.1.2; SS.912.A.1.4; SS.912.A.1.7; SS.912.A.6.1; SS.912.G.1.2

A Slow Start for the Allies

While the Allies agreed that the defeat of the Nazis was their first priority, the United States did not wait until V-E Day to move against Japan. Fortunately, the Japanese attack on Pearl Harbor in 1941 had missed the Pacific Fleet's submarines. Even more importantly, the attack had missed the fleet's aircraft carriers, which were out at sea at the time.

JAPANESE ADVANCES Still, the attack on Pearl Harbor had dealt a tremendous blow to the U.S. Pacific Fleet, one that would take months to overcome. Pearl Harbor also provided a major boost to Japanese pride and encouraged them to continue their assault on territory in Asia. The combination of these factors led to a quick string of Japanese victories unimpeded by U.S. forces.

In the first six months after Pearl Harbor, the Japanese conquered an empire that dwarfed Hitler's Third Reich. On the Asian mainland, Japanese troops overran Hong Kong, French Indochina, Malaya, Burma, Thailand, and much of China. The British had believed that the mighty fortress of Singapore, part of Malaya, would never fall to invaders. The Japanese captured it in just two weeks.

They also swept south and east across the Pacific, conquering the Dutch East Indies, Guam, Wake Island, the Solomon Islands, and countless other outposts in the ocean, including two islands in the Aleutian chain, which were part of Alaska. Their conquests gave them control of rich oil reserves, which were vital to their military plans, and also functioned as strategic bases for future operations.

The Allies were stunned by the rapid success of the Japanese military in the months following Pearl Harbor. They had underestimated the skill of Japanese soldiers, not realizing that they were so well trained. The Japanese military also had excellent equipment. For instance, Japanese fighter aircraft were as good as—or better than—anything the Allies could produce. Japanese ships and torpedoes were also of high quality. These factors gave the Japanese an important advantage early in the war.

THE PHILIPPINES Japan's attacks on Hong Kong, Singapore, the Dutch East Indies, and Burma were part of a larger offensive strategy with one other major target: the American-controlled islands of the Philippines. At the time of the Japanese invasion in December 1941, General **Douglas MacArthur** was in command of Allied forces on the islands. He led a small force of Americans plus a number of poorly trained and equipped Filipino soldiers, totaling roughly 80,000 troops. They were no match for the 200,000 Japanese invaders who came ashore in December 1941.

As the Japanese gained ground, MacArthur planned a retreat to the Bataan Peninsula. There he hoped to hold off the Japanese for as long as possible. Simply getting his troops into this defensive position took determined fighting and brilliant leadership. Once there, the soldiers found that food, medicine, and other supplies were terribly limited. MacArthur urged Allied officials to send ships to help relieve his starving, battle-worn troops. War planners, however, decided that such a move was too risky.

Douglas MacArthur
(1880–1964)

Douglas MacArthur was too arrogant and prickly to be considered a "regular guy" by his troops. But he was arguably the most brilliant Allied strategist of World War II. For every American soldier killed in his campaigns, the Japanese lost ten.

He was considered a real hero of the war, both by the military and by the prisoners on the Philippines, whom he freed. "MacArthur took more territory with less loss of life," observed journalist John Gunther, "than any military commander since Darius the Great [king of Persia, 522–486 BC]."

MacArthur and his forces fought on bravely. They held out against the invading Japanese troops for four months on the Bataan Peninsula. Hunger, disease, and bombardments killed 14,000 Allied troops and left 48,000 wounded. When American and Filipino forces found themselves with their backs to the wall on Bataan, President Roosevelt ordered MacArthur to leave. On March 11, 1942, MacArthur left the Philippines with his wife, his son, and his staff. As he left, he pledged to the many thousands of men who did not make it out, "I shall return." Less than a month later, about 10,000 American and 60,000 Filipino troops remaining on Bataan surrendered.

Although the fighting was over, the suffering of the soldiers had just begun. For five days and nights, the Japanese forced the captured soldiers through what came to be called the **Bataan Death March**. The prisoners had little food or water, and those who dropped out of line were beaten or shot. Thousands perished. Those who completed this terrible journey did not fare much better. In the Japanese prison camp, lack of food and medicine claimed hundreds more lives.

Reading Check
Analyze Causes
What factors contributed to Japan's series of rapid military victories following Pearl Harbor?

Fortunes Shift in the Pacific

The loss of the Philippines was a low point for the United States in the Pacific war. In the spring of 1942, however, the Allies began to turn the tide against the Japanese. In fact, just days after the surrender on Bataan, Americans finally got some good news.

DOOLITTLE'S RAID On April 18, 1942, Army Lieutenant Colonel James Doolittle led 16 bombers in a daring raid on Tokyo and several other Japanese cities. The next day, Americans awoke to headlines that read "Tokyo Bombed! Doolittle Do'od It." Doolittle's raid, as the event came to be known, did not do major damage to the Japanese targets, but it still had some significant effects. Pulling off a Pearl Harbor-style air raid over Japan lifted America's sunken spirits. At the same time, it dampened spirits in Japan.

BATTLE OF THE CORAL SEA Close on the heels of Doolittle's raid came another morale booster for the Allies. Since the beginning of the war, Allied forces in the Pacific, mainly Americans and Australians, had seen little success in slowing Japanese conquests. In May 1942, however, the Allies finally turned a corner. They succeeded in stopping the Japanese drive toward Australia in the five-day Battle of the Coral Sea. During this battle, the fighting was done by airplanes that took off from enormous aircraft carriers. Not a single shot was fired by surface ships. It was not a decisive win for the Allies. Both sides suffered losses and both, in fact, claimed victory. But it was a strategic triumph. For the first time since Pearl Harbor, a Japanese invasion had been stopped and turned back.

THE BATTLE OF MIDWAY Japanese leaders had been troubled by Doolittle's raid. They were determined to stop any future attacks on the Japanese mainland. To do so, they planned to lure the Americans into a large sea battle with the goal of destroying what remained of U.S. naval forces. The first step in their plan would be to attack Midway Island, a strategic island that lies northwest of Hawaii. The Japanese had a large advantage in the number of ships and carriers they could bring to the battle. However, the Americans had an advantage that Japan did not know about. Naval intelligence officers had broken the Japanese code and knew that Midway was to be their next target. They also knew the date of the planned attack and the direction from which the Japanese ships would approach. Here again the Allies succeeded in stopping the Japanese.

Admiral **Chester Nimitz**, the commander of American naval forces in the Pacific, moved to defend the island, carefully placing his forces based on his knowledge of the Japanese military's plans. On June 3, 1942, his scout planes found the Japanese fleet. The Americans sent torpedo planes and dive bombers to attack. The Japanese were caught with their planes still on the decks of their carriers. The results were devastating. By the end of the **Battle of Midway**, it was clear the Allies had won a tremendous victory. The Japanese had lost 4 aircraft carriers, a cruiser, and 250 planes. In the words of a Japanese official, at Midway the Americans had "avenged Pearl Harbor."

The Allies Go on the Offensive

The Battle of Midway was a turning point in the Pacific War. With the Japanese navy crippled, the Allies decided to take the fight to Japan.

GUADALCANAL The first step in the new Allied strategy was to win control of territory in the Solomon Islands. The Japanese had taken these islands in 1942, and an Allied presence there would help protect nearby Australia. A key goal in the Solomons was the capture of an island called Guadalcanal. The Japanese had nearly completed an airfield there, making it a tempting

Reading Check
Find Main Ideas
What was the significance of the Battle of the Coral Sea?

War in The Pacific and in Europe, 1941–1946

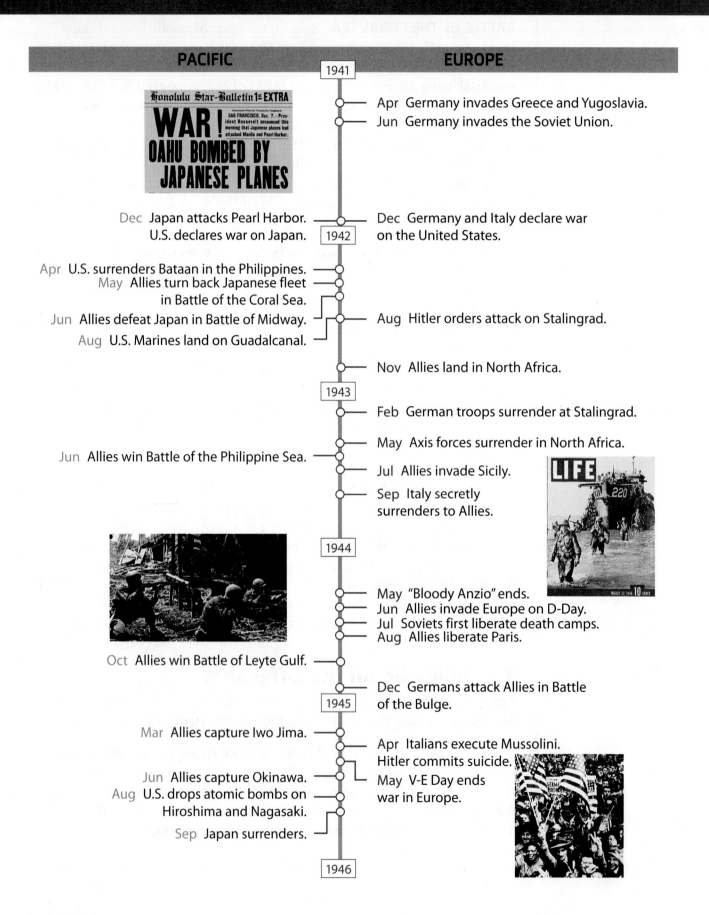

PACIFIC		EUROPE
	1941	
		Apr Germany invades Greece and Yugoslavia.
		Jun Germany invades the Soviet Union.
Dec Japan attacks Pearl Harbor. U.S. declares war on Japan.		Dec Germany and Italy declare war on the United States.
	1942	
Apr U.S. surrenders Bataan in the Philippines.		
May Allies turn back Japanese fleet in Battle of the Coral Sea.		
Jun Allies defeat Japan in Battle of Midway.		Aug Hitler orders attack on Stalingrad.
Aug U.S. Marines land on Guadalcanal.		
		Nov Allies land in North Africa.
	1943	
		Feb German troops surrender at Stalingrad.
Jun Allies win Battle of the Philippine Sea.		May Axis forces surrender in North Africa.
		Jul Allies invade Sicily.
		Sep Italy secretly surrenders to Allies.
	1944	
		May "Bloody Anzio" ends.
		Jun Allies invade Europe on D-Day.
		Jul Soviets first liberate death camps.
		Aug Allies liberate Paris.
Oct Allies win Battle of Leyte Gulf.		
		Dec Germans attack Allies in Battle of the Bulge.
	1945	
Mar Allies capture Iwo Jima.		
		Apr Italians execute Mussolini. Hitler commits suicide.
Jun Allies capture Okinawa.		May V-E Day ends war in Europe.
Aug U.S. drops atomic bombs on Hiroshima and Nagasaki.		
Sep Japan surrenders.		
	1946	

target. The rest of the island, however, offered little. It was covered by swamps and dense jungles, and daytime temperatures regularly reached into the 90s. It was a miserable place to fight.

The Allied offensive against Guadalcanal began in August 1942 when 19,000 troops stormed the island. The battle took place on land, at sea, and in the air. Each side won small victories until the Japanese finally abandoned Guadalcanal six months later. At the time, they called it the Island of Death. To war correspondent Ralph Martin and the troops who fought there, it was simply "hell."

"Hell was red furry spiders as big as your fist, giant lizards as long as your leg, leeches falling from trees to suck blood, armies of white ants with a bite of fire, scurrying scorpions inflaming any flesh they touched, enormous rats and bats everywhere, and rivers with waiting crocodiles. Hell was the sour, foul smell of the squishy jungle, humidity that rotted a body within hours, . . . stinking wet heat of dripping rain forests that sapped the strength of any man."

—Ralph G. Martin, from *The GI War*

THE ALLIES PRESS ON Guadalcanal marked Japan's first defeat on land, but not its last. However, the Japanese still controlled a number of heavily fortified islands throughout the Pacific. Attacking those islands would have been a costly and time-consuming endeavor. Instead, the Allies chose to bypass them in favor of strategically important but less-well-defended islands. Soon the Allies began "**island hopping.**" This method used a powerful combination of land, sea, and air forces to capture and secure islands while avoiding the heaviest concentrations of enemy forces. These captured islands would then become bases from which future military actions could be launched. Island by island they won territory back from the Japanese. With each island, Allied forces moved closer to Japan.

American diversity and ingenuity aided their progress. Hundreds of Native Americans of the Navajo nation worked as code talkers, translating messages into a coded version of their own language. The Navajo language was spoken only in the American Southwest and traditionally had no alphabet or other written symbols. This unwritten language was so complex that the Japanese never deciphered it, allowing quick and secure transmission of vital military information. Although the Navajo had no words for combat terms, they developed terms such as *chicken hawk* for *dive-bomber* and *war chief* for *commanding general*. Throughout the Pacific campaign—from Midway to Iwo Jima—the code talkers were considered indispensable to the war effort. They finally received national recognition in 1969.

Four hundred Navajo were recruited into the Marine Corps as code talkers. Their primary duty was transmitting telephone and radio messages.

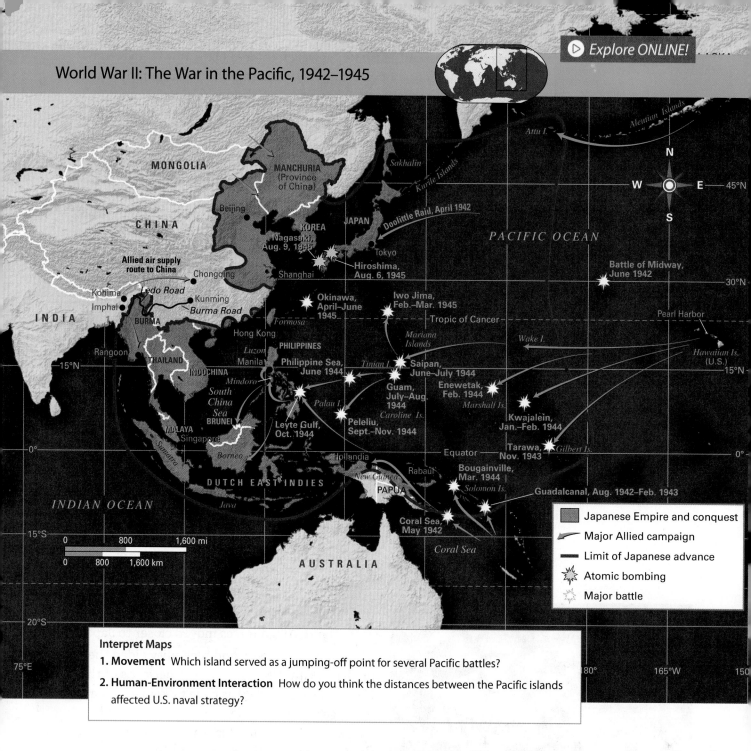

Explore ONLINE!

Legend:
- Japanese Empire and conquest
- Major Allied campaign
- Limit of Japanese advance
- Atomic bombing
- Major battle

Interpret Maps

1. **Movement** Which island served as a jumping-off point for several Pacific battles?

2. **Human-Environment Interaction** How do you think the distances between the Pacific islands affected U.S. naval strategy?

The Allies also began to take advantage of the United States' vast resources. The fighting in the Pacific was extremely costly, and both sides lost dozens of ships and thousands of aircraft. These were losses the Japanese were unable to replace. Busy American factories, though, produced planes and ships at a tremendous rate. At same time, gains in Europe allowed the Allies to send more troops and resources to the Pacific.

THE BATTLE OF LEYTE GULF The Americans continued leapfrogging across the Pacific toward Japan, and in October 1944 some 178,000 Allied troops and 738 ships converged on Leyte Island in the Philippines. General MacArthur, who had left the Philippines two years earlier, waded ashore and announced, "People of the Philippines: I have returned."

The Japanese threw their entire fleet into the Battle of Leyte Gulf. They also tested a new tactic, the **kamikaze** (kä′mĭ-kä′zē), or suicide-plane, attack in which Japanese pilots crashed their bomb-laden planes into Allied ships. (*Kamikaze* means "divine wind" and refers to a legendary typhoon that saved Japan in 1281 by destroying a Mongol invasion.) In the Philippines, 424 kamikaze pilots embarked on suicide missions, sinking 16 ships and damaging another 80.

Americans watched these terrifying attacks with "a strange mixture of respect and pity" according to Vice Admiral Charles Brown. "You have to admire the devotion to country demonstrated by those pilots," recalled Seaman George Marse. "Yet, when they were shot down, rescued and brought aboard our ship, we were surprised to find the pilots looked like ordinary, scared young men, not the wide-eyed fanatical 'devils' we imagined them to be."

Despite the damage done by the kamikazes, the Battle of Leyte Gulf was a disaster for Japan. In three days of battle, it lost 3 battleships, 4 aircraft carriers, 13 cruisers, and almost 500 planes. From then on the Imperial Navy played only a minor role in the defense of Japan.

IWO JIMA After retaking much of the Philippines and liberating the American prisoners of war there, the Allies turned to Iwo Jima, an island that writer William Manchester later described as "an ugly, smelly glob of cold

Historical Source

Raising the Flag on Iwo Jima

In February 1945 U.S. Marines captured Mount Suribachi, Iwo Jima's highest point, after four days of intense fighting. Although the battle raged on, troops were sent to place a flag at the top of the peak, large enough that it could be seen from across the island. Photographer Joe Rosenthal saw the flag raising, grabbed his camera, and snapped a hasty photo. It appeared the next morning on the front pages of American newspapers and has become an enduring symbol of World War II.

Analyze Historical Sources
What human qualities or events do you think Rosenthal's photograph symbolizes?

Japanese kamikaze pilots pose—smiling—just before taking off on the mission that would be their last.

lava squatting in a surly ocean." Iwo Jima (which means "sulfur island" in Japanese) was critical to the United States as a base from which heavily loaded bombers might reach Japan. It was also perhaps the most heavily defended spot on earth, with 20,700 Japanese troops entrenched in tunnels and caves. More than 6,000 marines died taking this desolate island, the greatest number in any battle in the Pacific to that point. Only 200 Japanese survived. Just one obstacle now stood between the Allies and a final assault on Japan—the island of Okinawa.

THE BATTLE FOR OKINAWA In April 1945 U.S. Marines invaded Okinawa. The Japanese unleashed more than 1,900 kamikaze attacks on the Allies during the Okinawa campaign. They sank 30 ships, damaged over 300 more, and killed almost 5,000 seamen.

Once ashore, the Allies faced even fiercer opposition than on Iwo Jima. By the time the fighting ended on June 21, 1945, more than 7,600 Americans had died. But the Japanese paid an even ghastlier price—110,000 lives—in defending Okinawa. This total included two generals who chose ritual suicide over the shame of surrender. A witness to this ceremony described their end: "A simultaneous shout and a flash of the sword . . . and both generals had nobly accomplished their last duty to their Emperor."

The Battle of Okinawa was a chilling foretaste of what the Allies imagined the invasion of Japan's home islands would be. Churchill predicted the cost would be a million American lives and half that number of British lives.

Reading Check
Draw Conclusions
Why was Okinawa a significant island in the war in the Pacific?

Lesson 6 Assessment

1. **Organize Information** Use a chart to describe the significance of key Allied military actions in the Pacific during World War II.

Military Action	Significance
1.	
2.	
3.	
4.	
5.	

Which military action was a turning point for the Allies?

2. **Key Terms and People** For each key term or person in the lesson, write a sentence explaining its significance.

3. **Evaluate** Evaluate the military contributions of leaders during World War II.

 Think About:
 • Douglas MacArthur
 • Chester Nimitz

4. **Predict** What was the Bataan Death March? How do you think it affected the Allied war effort?

5. **Develop Historical Perspective** Analyze the significance of the Battle of Midway as a turning point in the war in the Pacific.

6. **Draw Conclusions** How were the Allies able to gain ground against the Japanese in the Pacific?

The End of World War II

The Big Idea

While the Allies completed the defeat of the Axis Powers on the battlefield, Allied leaders were making plans for the postwar world.

Why It Matters Now

Wartime decisions affected global affairs for the next several decades.

Key Terms and People

V-E Day

Harry S. Truman

J. Robert Oppenheimer

Hiroshima

Nagasaki

United Nations (UN)

Nuremberg trials

GI Bill of Rights

SS.912.A.1.3; SS.912.A.6.1; SS.912.A.6.4; SS.912.A.6.6; SS.912.A.6.7; SS.912.A.6.9; SS.912.G.4.2; SS.912.G.4.3; MAFS.K12.MP.1.1; MAFS.K12.MP.5.1

One American's Story

Brigadier General Thomas F. Farrell served as second-in-command of the Manhattan Project. Early on the morning of July 16, 1945, Farrell and other key figures gathered at White Sands in the remote New Mexico desert to witness the first official test of the atomic bomb. Code-named "Trinity," the test would determine whether the bomb would work as a weapon. Farrell and the rest watched from several miles away as the bomb successfully exploded at 5:29 a.m.

Brigadier General Thomas F. Farrell

"The effects could well be called unprecedented, magnificent, beautiful, stupendous and terrifying. No man-made phenomenon of such tremendous power had ever occurred before. . . . The whole country was lighted by a searing light with the intensity many times that of the midday sun. It was golden, purple, violet, gray and blue. . . . Thirty seconds after the explosion came first, the air blast pressing hard against the people and things, to be followed almost immediately by the strong, sustained, awesome roar which warned of doomsday and made us feel that we puny things were blasphemous to dare tamper with the forces heretofore reserved to The Almighty."
—Thomas F. Farrell, from a memorandum for the Secretary of War, July 18, 1945

The test was a success. Scientists and military personnel cheered and danced in celebration. Finally, Farrell reflected, they had found a weapon that could end the war.

The Allies Liberate Europe

Even as Manhattan Project scientists were feverishly working to create a weapon to end it, war raged on. In both Europe and the Pacific, the tide had turned in the Allies' favor, but neither Germany nor Japan was beaten. Still, as the months passed, the Allies moved closer and closer to victory.

LIBERATION OF THE DEATH CAMPS In Europe, the Battle of the Bulge left Germany severely weakened. Allied troops pressed eastward into the German heartland, and the Soviet army pushed westward across Poland toward Berlin. Soviet troops were the first to come upon one of the Nazi death camps, in July 1944. As the Soviets drew near a camp called Majdanek in Poland, SS guards worked feverishly to bury and burn all evidence of their hideous crimes. But they ran out of time. When the Soviets entered Majdanek, they found a thousand starving prisoners barely alive, the world's largest crematorium, and a storehouse containing 800,000 shoes. "This is not a concentration camp," reported a stunned Soviet war correspondent, "it is a gigantic murder plant." The Americans who later liberated Nazi death camps in Germany were equally horrified.

"We started smelling a terrible odor and suddenly we were at the concentration camp at Landsberg. Forced the gate and faced hundreds of starving prisoners. . . . We saw emaciated men whose thighs were smaller than wrists, many had bones sticking out thru their skin. . . . Also we saw hundreds of burned and naked bodies. . . . That evening I wrote my wife that 'For the first time I truly realized the evil of Hitler and why this war had to be waged.'"

—Robert T. Johnson, quoted in *Voices: Letters from World War II*

MARCHING DEEPER INTO GERMANY As the Soviet army approached Germany from the east, Allied forces in the west were preparing to cross the Rhine River. The Rhine was the last physical obstacle between Germany and France, and Hitler was determined to stop the Allied advance there. He ordered his soldiers to destroy all bridges across the river and to hold defensive positions on its banks.

Despite the efforts of German troops, American forces were able to capture a railroad bridge over the Rhine at Remagen in March 1945. Allied forces poured across the Rhine into the heart of Germany. The forces that had sought to stop the Allies' passage suddenly found themselves surrounded. More than a quarter of a million German soldiers were captured, and tens of thousands more were killed.

With the Rhine crossed, there was little to stop the Allied advance through Germany. Allied planes roamed the skies freely, raining bombs down on German targets. Allied troops pushed toward Berlin from both sides, ready to end the war once and for all. Meanwhile, the leaders of the Allies were meeting half a continent away to debate Germany's postwar fate.

THE YALTA CONFERENCE

In January 1945 Franklin D. Roosevelt took the presidential oath of office for the fourth time. He had run in 1944 believing that he needed to see the nation through to victory. A majority of American voters had agreed. Shortly after his inauguration in February 1945, an ailing Roosevelt met with Churchill and Stalin at the Black Sea resort city of Yalta in the Soviet Union. Stalin graciously welcomed the president and the prime minister. The Big Three, as they were called, toasted the defeat of Germany that now seemed certain.

For eight grueling days, the three leaders discussed the fate of Germany and the postwar world. Stalin's country was devastated by German forces, and he favored a harsh approach. He wanted to keep Germany divided into occupation zones—areas controlled by Allied military forces—so that Germany would never again threaten the Soviet Union.

When Churchill strongly disagreed, Roosevelt acted as a mediator in an effort to maintain the Grand Alliance. He was prepared to make concessions to Stalin for two reasons. First, he hoped that the Soviet Union would stand by its commitments to join the war against Japan that was still waging in the Pacific. Stalin had thus far refused to send troops to the region. This had caused tension among the Allies. Second, Roosevelt wanted Stalin's support for a new world peacekeeping organization to be named the United Nations.

Winston Churchill, Franklin D. Roosevelt, and Joseph Stalin meet at the Yalta Conference.

The historic meeting at Yalta produced a series of compromises. To pacify Stalin, Roosevelt convinced Churchill to agree to a temporary division of Germany into four zones. There would be one zone each for the Americans, the British, the Soviets, and the French. Churchill and Roosevelt assumed that, in time, all the zones would be brought together in a reunited Germany. For his part, Stalin promised "free and unfettered elections" in Poland and other Soviet-occupied Eastern European countries.

Stalin also agreed to join in the war against Japan. That struggle was expected to continue for another year or more. All three leaders hoped that Soviet participation would hasten the war's end. In addition, Stalin agreed to participate in an international conference to take place in April in San Francisco. There, Roosevelt's dream of a United Nations (UN) would become a reality. Although Roosevelt had secured Stalin's agreement, the Yalta Conference had been tense. Friction between the Soviet Union and the other Allies was growing.

UNCONDITIONAL SURRENDER

By April 25, 1945, the Soviet army had stormed Berlin. As Soviet shells burst overhead, the city panicked. "Hordes of soldiers stationed in Berlin deserted and were shot on the spot or hanged from the nearest tree," wrote Claus Fuhrmann, a Berlin clerk. "On their chests they had placards reading, 'We betrayed the Führer.'"

New Yorkers celebrate V-E Day with a massive party that began in Times Square and went on for days at sites throughout the city.

In his underground headquarters in Berlin, Hitler prepared for the end. On April 29 he married Eva Braun, his longtime companion. The same day, he wrote out his last address to the German people. In it he blamed the Jews for starting the war and his generals for losing it. "I die with a happy heart aware of the immeasurable deeds of our soldiers at the front. I myself and my wife choose to die in order to escape the disgrace of . . . capitulation," he said. The next day Hitler shot himself while his new wife swallowed poison. In accordance with Hitler's orders, the two bodies were carried outside, soaked with gasoline, and burned.

A week later General Eisenhower accepted the unconditional surrender of the Third Reich. On May 8, 1945, the Allies proclaimed **V-E Day**—Victory in Europe Day. The war in Europe was finally over. Many celebrated throughout the United States and Europe. Many others, however, still had work to do to end the war in the Pacific.

TRUMAN BECOMES PRESIDENT President Roosevelt did not live to see V-E Day. On April 12, 1945, while posing for a portrait in Warm Springs, Georgia, the president had a stroke and died. Vice-President **Harry S. Truman** became the nation's 33rd president that same night.

Truman, previously a U.S. senator from Missouri, had been picked as Roosevelt's running mate in 1944. He had served as vice-president for just a few months before Roosevelt's death. During his term as vice-president, Truman had not been included in top policy decisions. He had not even known that the United States was developing an atomic bomb. Many Americans doubted Truman's ability to serve as president. But Truman was honest and had a willingness to make tough decisions. These were qualities that he would need desperately during his presidency.

Vocabulary
capitulation
surrender

Reading Check
Summarize What decisions did Roosevelt, Churchill, and Stalin make at the Yalta Conference?

The Atomic Bomb Ends the War in the Pacific

The taking of Iwo Jima and Okinawa opened the way for an invasion of Japan. However, Allied leaders knew that such an invasion would become a desperate struggle. Japan still had a huge army that would defend every inch of home-land. President Truman saw only one way to avoid an invasion of Japan. He decided to use a powerful new weapon that had been developed by scientists working on the Manhattan Project—the atomic bomb.

THE MANHATTAN PROJECT General Leslie Groves led the project, with research directed by American scientist **J. Robert Oppenheimer**. The development of the atomic bomb was the most ambitious scientific enter-prise in history. It was also a very costly enterprise, requiring more than $2 billion in government investment. There was also significant oppor-tunity cost involved with the project. Resources and personnel who could have been used in other war industries were instead employed in a highly theoretical undertaking. Over the life of the project, more than 600,000 Americans at sites across the country were involved in it.

Among the major sites were Oak Ridge, Tennessee, where the project was headquartered, and Los Alamos, New Mexico, where the actual bomb was built. Despite the number of people involved, though, the Manhattan Project was the best kept secret of the war. Few of the workers engaged in the project knew its ultimate purpose. The government and the mili-tary took every precaution to keep news of the bomb's development from reaching enemy ears.

The first test of the new bomb took place on the morning of July 16, 1945, in an empty expanse of desert near Alamogordo, New Mexico. A blinding flash, which was visible 180 miles away, was followed by a deafening roar as a tremen-dous shock wave rolled across the trembling desert. Otto Frisch, a scientist on the project, described the huge mushroom cloud that rose over the desert as "a red-hot elephant standing balanced on its trunk." The bomb worked!

WEIGHING THE OPTIONS President Truman now faced a difficult deci-sion. Should the Allies use the bomb to bring an end to the war? Many advisors to President Truman, including Secretary of War Henry Stimson, believed the bomb should be used to end the war and save American lives. Some scientists working on the bomb agreed—even more so as the casu-alty figures from Iwo Jima and Okinawa sank in. "Are we to go on shed-ding American blood when we have available a means to a steady victory?" they petitioned. "No! If we can save even a handful of American lives, then let us use this weapon—now!"

Diplomatic and political considerations also factored into the decision. Ten-sion and distrust were already developing between the Western Allies and the Soviets. At the Yalta Conference, Roosevelt had received Stalin's promise that the Soviet Union would enter the war in the Pacific. After the successful test of the atomic bomb, Secretary of State James F. Byrnes and other top advis-ers agreed that Soviet entry into the Pacific war should be reconsidered. As a result of the bomb, it was seen as no longer necessary. If it could be prevented, it would reduce Soviet influence in East Asia after the war. Additionally, some

Atom Bombs to Brain Scans

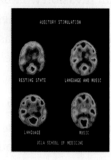

Faced with alarming rumors of work on a German atomic bomb, America mobilized some of the finest scientific minds in the world to create its own atomic bomb. The energy released by its nuclear reaction was enough to kill hundreds of thousands of people, as evidenced by the destruction of Hiroshima and Nagasaki.

But the resulting ability to harness the atom's energy also led to new technologies for diagnosing and treating human diseases. Today, the diagnostic techniques using radioisotopes instead of x-rays can allow imaging of both bones and soft tissues. For example, positron emission tomography (PET) is able to reveal the inner workings of the human brain. Another major use of radioisotopes as a diagnostic tool is in laboratory blood tests. Radiation is also used to treat a variety of cancers. One new field is Targeted Alpha Therapy (TAT), which uses alpha emissions to control cancers dispersed throughout the body.

American officials believed that a successful use of the atomic bomb would give the United States a powerful advantage over the Soviets in shaping the postwar world. Finally, some feared that if the bomb were not dropped, the project would be seen as a gigantic waste of money and wartime resources.

However, many of the scientists who had worked on the bomb had doubts about using it. So did some military leaders and civilian policymakers. Dr. Leo Szilard, a Hungarian-born physicist who had helped President Roosevelt launch the project and who had a major role in developing the bomb, was a key figure opposing its use. A petition drawn up by Szilard and signed by 70 other scientists argued that it would be immoral to drop an atomic bomb on Japan without fair warning. Many supported staging a demonstration of the bomb for Japanese leaders. They suggested exploding one on a deserted island near Japan to convince the Japanese to surrender. Others, such as Supreme Allied Commander General Dwight D. Eisenhower, argued that Japan had already been defeated and was on the verge of surrender. He maintained that "dropping the bomb was completely unnecessary" to save American lives.

Truman did not hesitate. In a journal entry, he acknowledged that the bomb "seems to be the most terrible thing ever discovered, but it can be made the most useful." Truman was committed to fulfilling Roosevelt's legacy. Throughout the war, Roosevelt's fundamental strategy had been to commit the vast industrial and technological resources of the United States to achieve total victory with the lowest cost in American lives. In Truman's estimation, the bomb was the way to achieve this goal. He believed it would bring about an end to the war in the Pacific without sacrificing lives in an Allied invasion.

On July 25, 1945, Truman ordered the military to make final plans for dropping two atomic bombs on Japanese targets. Meanwhile, he and other Allied leaders meeting at Potsdam, Germany, discussed plans for ending the war in the Pacific. A day after Truman's order to the military, the United States and the other Allies warned Japan that it faced "prompt and utter destruction" unless it surrendered at once. Japan refused. Truman later wrote, "The final decision of where and when to use the atomic bomb was up to me. Let there be no mistake about it. I regarded the bomb as a military weapon and never had any doubt that it should be used."

HIROSHIMA AND NAGASAKI On August 6 a B-29 bomber named *Enola Gay* released an atomic bomb, code-named Little Boy, over **Hiroshima**, an important Japanese military center. Forty-three seconds later, almost every building in the city collapsed into dust from the force of the blast. Hiroshima had ceased to exist. Still, Japan's leaders hesitated to surrender. Three days later a second bomb, code-named Fat Man, was dropped on **Nagasaki**, leveling half the city. By the end of the year, an estimated 200,000 people had died due to injuries and radiation poisoning caused by the atomic blasts. Shinji Mikamo was a teenager living less than a mile from the epicenter when the first bomb hit Hiroshima. He later told his daughter Akiko about the blast.

"In that instant, I felt a searing pain that spread through my entire body. It was as if a bucket of boiling water had been dumped over my whole body and scoured my skin.

At the same time, I was thrown into a pit of absolute darkness. What had happened? I couldn't see anything. I was in total shock. I could feel nothing at all."

—Shinji Mikamo, as recounted by Akiko Mikamo in *Rising from the Ashes*

Reading Check
Find Main Ideas
What were the main arguments for and against dropping the atomic bomb on Japan?

Emperor Hirohito was horrified by the destruction wrought by the bomb. "I cannot bear to see my innocent people suffer any longer," he told Japan's leaders tearfully. Then he ordered them to draw up papers "to end the war." On September 2, formal surrender ceremonies took place on the U.S. battleship *Missouri* in Tokyo Bay. "Today the guns are silent," General MacArthur said in a speech marking this historic moment. "The skies no longer rain death—the seas bear only commerce—men everywhere walk upright in the sunlight. The entire world is quietly at peace."

Hiroshima was in ruins following the atomic bomb blast on August 6, 1945.

The Challenges of Victory

With Japan's surrender, the Allies turned to the challenge of rebuilding war-torn nations in a changed world. The creation and use of the atomic bomb had brought the world into the nuclear age. No one had ever used such a destructive weapon before, and it was destined to change the nature of warfare. American leaders hoped it would give them leverage over the Soviet Union in the postwar world. However, they could not foresee that it would eventually prompt a massive arms race. The Soviet Union and other nations sought to build their own atomic weapons in an effort to feel secure and restore the balance of power. At the time, all they could see were the challenges of restoring order after a destructive war. Even before the last guns fell silent, Allied leaders were thinking about principles that would govern the postwar world.

THE UNITED NATIONS In the fall of 1943, Secretary of State Cordell Hull began working with other Allied leaders on a declaration of the intent to form an international organization based on the equality of nations. Details of the organization were discussed at several wartime conferences. At the Yalta Conference, Roosevelt, Churchill, and Stalin declared their intention to establish "a general international organization to maintain peace and security."

In the midst of war, hopes for world peace were high. The most visible symbol of these hopes was the **United Nations (UN)**. On April 25, 1945, the representatives of 50 nations met in San Francisco to establish this new peacekeeping body. President Truman appointed Mary McLeod Bethune to serve as the U.S. representative at the founding conference. She was the only woman of color in attendance. After two months of debate, on June 26, 1945, the delegates signed the charter establishing the UN. The UN officially came into being on October 24, 1945. On that day, China, France, Great Britain, the Soviet Union, the United States, and a number of other nations ratified the charter.

One of the UN's first actions was to commission a document declaring the fundamental equal rights of all human beings. This act was a sign of the international community's commitment to preventing the atrocities of World War II and the Holocaust from ever happening again. The Commission on Human Rights was made up of 18 men and women from a variety of political and cultural backgrounds. Eleanor Roosevelt chaired the committee responsible for drafting the declaration. The committee worked for two years, and in December 1948 the UN General Assembly adopted the Universal Declaration of Human Rights.

Although the UN had been founded as a union of many nations, it soon came to be dominated by two. The United States and the Soviet Union were the most powerful countries in the world following World War II, and they became the major players in UN affairs. In the years following the war, tensions arose between the two countries. Their conflicts crept into international debates. The UN was intended to promote peace, but it soon became a place in which the two superpowers competed. Both the United States and the Soviet Union used the UN as a forum to spread their influence over others.

Delegates of 50 nations gathered in San Francisco in 1945 to draft the United Nations charter.

THE POTSDAM CONFERENCE The tension between the United States and the Soviet Union had arisen even before World War II ended. In July 1945, just a month after the UN charter was signed, Allied leaders came together for the final wartime conference at Potsdam near Berlin. The countries that participated were the same ones that had been represented at Yalta in February. Stalin still represented the Soviet Union. Clement Attlee replaced Churchill as Britain's representative mid-conference, because Churchill's party lost a general election. And Harry Truman took Roosevelt's place.

At Yalta, Stalin had promised Roosevelt that he would allow free elections—that is, a vote by secret ballot in a multiparty system—in Poland and other parts of Eastern Europe that the Soviets occupied at the end of the war. By the time of the Potsdam Conference, however, it was clear that Stalin would not keep this promise. The Soviets prevented free elections in Poland and banned democratic parties. Stalin's refusal to allow free elections in Poland convinced Truman that U.S. and Soviet aims were deeply at odds. Truman's goal in demanding free elections was to spread democracy to nations that had been under Nazi rule. These disagreements would influence postwar relations.

Despite the conflict over Poland, most of the discussion at Potsdam dealt with the question of how to deal with Germany after the war. At the Yalta Conference, the Soviets had wanted to take reparations from Germany to help repay Soviet wartime losses. Now, at Potsdam, Truman objected to that. He feared that crippling reparations against Germany would eventually backfire, as they had after World War I. Those reparations nearly destroyed the German economy and paved the way for the growth of the Nazi Party.

After hard bargaining, the leaders at Potsdam reached a compromise. They confirmed the plan made at Yalta to divide Germany into four occupation zones. The zones would be administered by the United States, Great Britain, France, and the Soviet Union. It was agreed that each occupying country could independently take reparations from its own occupation zone. In addition, the German navy and merchant fleet were to be divided among the United States, Great Britain, and the Soviet Union.

Clement Attlee, Harry Truman, and Joseph Stalin at the Potsdam Conference

THE NUREMBERG WAR TRIALS

Besides geographic division, Germany had another price to pay for its part in the war. The discovery of Hitler's death camps led the Allies to put 24 surviving Nazi leaders on trial. They were charged with crimes against humanity, crimes against the peace, and war crimes. The trials were held in the southern German town of Nuremberg, between November 20, 1945 and October 1, 1946.

At the **Nuremberg trials**, the defendants included Hitler's most trusted party officials, government ministers, military leaders, and powerful industrialists. Each defendant at the Nuremberg trials was accused of one or more of the following crimes:

The Nuremberg trials began in November 1945. The last case concluded in April 1949.

- *Crimes Against the Peace*—Germany had planned and waged an aggressive war against other countries.
- *War Crimes*—The Germans had performed acts against the customs of warfare, such as the killing of hostages and prisoners. Such acts violated the Geneva Conventions. Those were a series of international agreements signed after World War I that protected the rights of prisoners. In addition, the Germans had stolen private property and destroyed towns and cities.
- *Crimes Against Humanity*—In the Holocaust, the Germans had attempted the murder, extermination, deportation, or enslavement of civilians.

In his opening argument, the chief prosecutor for the United States, Supreme Court Justice Robert Jackson, explained the significance of the event.

"The wrongs which we seek to condemn and punish have been so calculated, so malignant and so devastating, that civilization cannot tolerate their being ignored because it cannot survive their being repeated. . . . It is hard now to perceive in these miserable men . . . the power by which as Nazi leaders they once dominated much of the world and terrified most of it. Merely as individuals, their fate is of little consequence to the world. What makes this inquest significant is that these prisoners represent sinister influences that will lurk in the world long after their bodies have returned to dust. They are living symbols of racial hatreds, of terrorism and violence, and of the arrogance and cruelty of power. . . . Civilization can afford no compromise with the social forces which would gain renewed strength if we deal ambiguously or indecisively with the men in whom those forces now precariously survive."

—Robert Jackson, from the opening address to the Nuremberg War Crimes Trial

In the end, 12 of the 24 defendants were sentenced to death. Most of those remaining were sent to prison. In later trials of lesser leaders, nearly 200 more Nazis were found guilty of war crimes. Still, many people have argued that the trials did not go far enough in seeking out and punishing war criminals. Many Nazis who took part in the Holocaust did indeed go free.

Yet no matter how imperfect the trials might have been, they did establish an important principle. This was the idea that individuals are responsible for their own actions, even in times of war. Nazi executioners could not escape punishment by claiming that they were merely "following orders." The principle of individual responsibility was now part of international law.

THE OCCUPATION OF JAPAN Following its surrender, Japan was occupied by U.S. forces under the command of General Douglas MacArthur. In the early years of the occupation, more than 1,100 Japanese, from former prime minister Hideki Tojo to lowly prison guards, were arrested and put on trial. Seven, including Tojo, were sentenced to death. In the Philippines, in China, and in other Asian battlegrounds, additional Japanese officials were tried for atrocities against civilians or prisoners of war.

During the seven-year American occupation, MacArthur reshaped Japan's economy by introducing free-market practices that led to a remarkable economic recovery. MacArthur also worked to transform Japan's government. He called for a new constitution that would provide for woman suffrage and guarantee basic freedoms. Americans followed these changes with interest. The *New York Times* reported that "General MacArthur . . . has swept away an autocratic regime by a warrior god and installed in its place a democratic government presided over by a very human emperor and based on the will of the people as expressed in free elections." The Japanese apparently agreed. To this day, their constitution is known as the MacArthur Constitution.

Reading Check
Summarize Why was the United Nations formed, and who was involved in its formation?

Changes on the Home Front

Despite the devastation it caused in Europe and Japan, World War II was a time of opportunity for millions of Americans. Jobs abounded, and despite rationing and shortages, people had money to spend. At the end of World War II, the nation emerged as the world's dominant economic and military power.

The war years were good ones for working people. As defense industries boomed, unemployment fell to a low of 1.2 percent in 1944. Even with price and wage controls, average weekly pay (adjusted for inflation) rose 10 percent during the war. And although workers still protested long hours, overtime, and night shifts, they were able to save money for the future. Some workers invested up to half their paychecks in war bonds.

Farmers also prospered during the war. During the Depression years, farmers had battled dust storms and floods. But the early 1940s featured good weather for growing crops. Farmers benefited from improvements in farm machinery and fertilizers. They reaped the profits from rising crop prices. As a result, crop production increased by 50 percent, and farm income tripled. Before the war ended, many farmers could pay off their mortgages.

African American Migration, 1940–1950

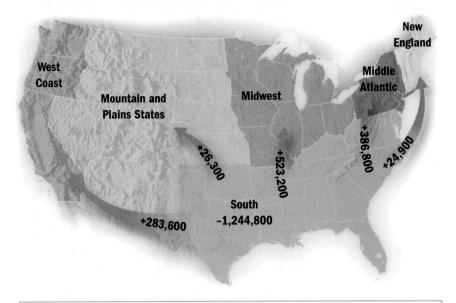

West Coast

Mountain and Plains States

Midwest

New England

Middle Atlantic

+26,300

+523,200

+386,800

+24,900

+283,600

South
−1,244,800

Interpret Maps

1. **Movement** To which geographic region did the greatest number of African Americans migrate?

2. **Movement** How did the wartime economy contribute to this mass migration?

The war gave women the chance to prove they could be just as productive as men. But their pay usually did not reflect their productivity.

Women also enjoyed employment gains during the war, although many lost their jobs when the war ended. Over 6 million women had entered the work force for the first time, boosting the percentage of women in the total work force to 35 percent. A third of those jobs were in defense plants, which offered women more challenging work and better pay than jobs traditionally associated with women, such as waitressing, clerking, and domestic service. With men away at war, many women also took advantage of openings in journalism and other professions. "The war really created opportunities for women," said Winona Espinosa, a wife and mother who became a riveter and bus driver during the war. "It was the first time we got a chance to show that we could do a lot of things that only men had done before." In the years that followed the war, many women fought to regain the rights they had enjoyed during the war. They wanted the same opportunities available to men, such as access to better jobs and education.

In addition to revamping the economy, the war triggered one of the greatest mass migrations in American history. Americans whose families had lived for decades in one place suddenly uprooted themselves to seek work elsewhere. Men and women left farms and small towns to take jobs in shipyards, steel mills, and aircraft plants across the country. More than a million

Attending Pennsylvania State College under the GI Bill of Rights, William Oskay Jr. paid $28 a month for the trailer home in which you see him working.

newcomers poured into California alone between 1941 and 1944. Across the country, towns with defense industries saw their populations double and even triple, sometimes almost overnight. Among the most eager migrants during the war were African Americans. Looking for new jobs and an escape from discrimination, hundreds of thousands of African Americans left the South for cities in the North and West.

The war also created new opportunities for the country's millions of new veterans. In 1944, to help ease the transition of returning servicemen to civilian life, Congress passed the Servicemen's Readjustment Act, better known as the **GI Bill of Rights**. This legislation provided education and training for veterans, paid for by the federal government. Just over half the returning soldiers, or about 7.8 million veterans, attended colleges and technical schools under the GI Bill. Among those who attended college under the GI Bill were many African Americans and members of other minority groups. For many, it was their first opportunity to receive higher education. The act also provided federal loan guarantees to veterans buying homes or farms or starting new businesses.

Reading Check
Analyze Causes
How did World War II alter the population distribution of the United States?

Lesson 7 Assessment

1. **Organize Information** Trace on a timeline the events leading up to the end of the war in Europe and in the Pacific and the beginning of planning for the postwar world.

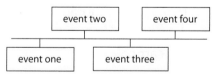

2. **Key Terms and People** For each key term or person in the lesson, write a sentence explaining its significance.

3. **Form Generalizations** What were the key diplomatic outcomes of World War II?

   Think About:
   • the decisions made at Yalta and Potsdam
   • the goals of the United Nations
   • the results of the Nuremberg trial
   • plans for after the war

4. **Draw Conclusions** What were the economic, diplomatic, and military consequences of developing the atomic bomb?

5. **Analyze Primary Sources** Review the quotation from Robert T. Johnson about liberating the death camps. Why was the liberation of concentration camps an important event in World War II?

6. **Analyze Causes** What led to the growth of the defense and agricultural industries during World War II?

7. **Predict** How do you think increased tension among Allied leaders would affect the postwar world?

Module 11 Assessment

Key Terms and People

For each term or person below, write a sentence explaining its significance during World War II.

1. fascism
2. Adolf Hitler
3. Winston Churchill
4. appeasement
5. Holocaust
6. rationing
7. Dwight D. Eisenhower
8. D-Day
9. Hiroshima
10. GI Bill of Rights

Main Ideas

Use your notes and the information in the module to answer the following questions.

War Breaks Out

1. What factors led to the rise of totalitarian governments, such as fascism and communism, in Europe?
2. Why did Japan invade Manchuria?
3. Why was the blitzkrieg effective?
4. How did the civil and political values of Nazi Germany and Imperial Japan differ from those of the United States?
5. How effective was the League of Nations in dealing with aggression among nations in the 1930s?

The Holocaust

6. How did the United States respond to Jewish refugees after Kristallnacht?
7. What groups did Nazis deem unfit to belong to the Aryan "master race"?
8. How did some Europeans show their resistance to Nazi persecution of the Jews?
9. How did the Holocaust affect Jews and other targeted groups living in territory controlled by the Nazis?

America Moves Toward War

10. How did isolationist policy shape U.S. foreign policy in the 1920s and 1930s? What were the consequences of U.S. isolationism?

11. Why did Roosevelt take one "unneutral" step after another to assist Britain and the Soviet Union in 1941?
12. How did the isolationist views of many Americans challenge Roosevelt's political leadership?
13. What factors led Japan to attack the United States at Pearl Harbor?
14. Why did the United States enter World War II?

The War Effort on the Home Front

15. What was the Double V Campaign?
16. What role did the media play in helping the country mobilize?
17. Why did the outbreak of World War II create a need for new military bases across the country?
18. What were the causes and consequences of racial tension in the 1940s?
19. How did the war affect families?

The War for Europe and North Africa

20. What role did Franklin Roosevelt play as commander in chief of the U.S. military?
21. How did the Allies win control of the Atlantic Ocean between 1941 and 1943?
22. What two key decisions determined the final outcome at Stalingrad?
23. What was the outcome of the North African and Italian campaigns?

The War in the Pacific

24. Briefly describe the strategy of island hopping during the war in the Pacific.
25. Why was the Battle of Leyte Gulf so crucial to the Allies?
26. What was significant about the Battle of Iwo Jima?

The End of World War II

27. Why did President Truman decide to use atomic weapons?

28. How are the Nuremberg trials an example of the humanitarian effects of World War II?

29. How did World War II expand access to education?

30. What issues did Allied leaders address at the Potsdam Conference, and what decisions did they make?

Critical Thinking

1. **Categorize** In a chart like the one shown below, explain the opportunities and obstacles that women and ethnic and racial minorities faced during World War II.

	Women	Minorities
Opportunities		
Obstacles		

2. **Draw Conclusions** How did the rise of dictatorships in Italy, Germany, and Japan and the aggression of those nations toward other countries lead to World War II?

3. **Interpret Maps** Look at the map "German Advances, 1938–1941" in Lesson 1. How might Poland's location have influenced the secret pact that Germany and the Soviet Union signed on August 23, 1939?

4. **Compare** How were the geography and events in the European and Pacific theaters of World War II similar? How were they different?

5. **Summarize** Explain the bravery and contributions of women and ethnic minorities in the armed forces during World War II, including the Tuskegee Airmen, the 442nd Regimental Combat Team, and the Navajo code talkers.

6. **Evaluate** Do you think the United States was justified in using atomic bombs against the Japanese? Write a paragraph explaining your response.

7. **Analyze Effects** Apply opportunity cost and trade-offs to evaluate the shift in economic resources from the production of domestic to military goods during World War II, and analyze the impact of the post-war shift back to domestic production.

8. **Make Inferences** How do you think World War II helped some Americans attain their vision of the American Dream?

9. **Analyze Effects** How did policies such as the Lend-Lease Act and other wartime changes affect the American economy?

10. **Evaluate** Evaluate the domestic and international leadership of Presidents Franklin D. Roosevelt and Harry S. Truman during World War II. Consider the U.S. domestic industry's rapid mobilization for the war effort and the nation's relationship with its allies.

Engage with History

Imagine that you are a journalist in 1955, working for a major magazine that is preparing an issue focusing on the ten-year anniversary of the end of World War II. Write an article in which you look back at the changes in American life brought about by involvement in the war. Discuss political and economic changes that resulted from the war as well as social changes that stemmed from issues on the home front.

Focus on Writing

Write an expository essay in which you explain the Holocaust as an instance of genocide. Include varying perspectives, such as those of victims, perpetrators, and observers.

Multimedia Activity

Conduct library or Internet research to learn more about some of the actions the U.S. government took between World Wars I and II to preserve its isolationist policy. Then investigate the events that drew the country into World War II. Consider the perspectives of people on both sides of the debate. Use your findings to draw a political cartoon that supports or opposes the U.S. policy of neutrality at the beginning of World War II. Write a caption to accompany your cartoon.

Memories of WORLD WAR II

A global conflict, World War II shaped the history of both the United States and the world. Americans contributed to the war effort in numerous ways. Many enlisted in the military and served in Africa, Europe, and the Pacific. Others contributed by working in factories to produce the massive amounts of ships, planes, guns, and other supplies necessary to win the war. In the process, these Americans left behind firsthand accounts of their experiences during the war, both at home and abroad. Explore some of the personal stories and recollections of World War II online. You can find a wealth of information, video clips, primary sources, activities, and more through your online textbook.

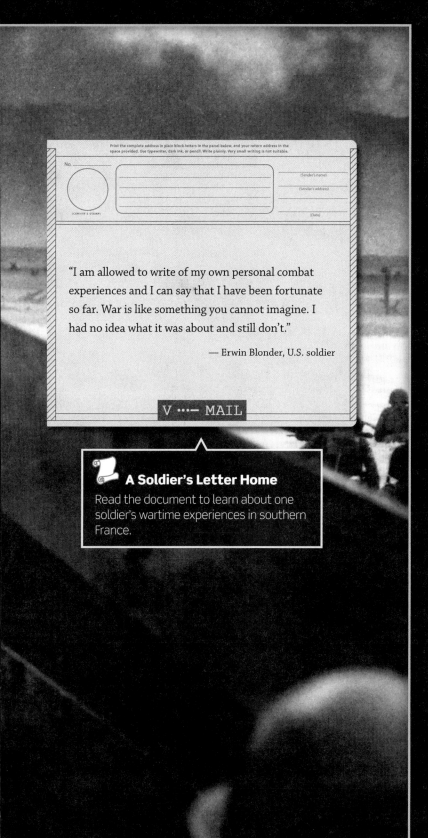

Print the complete address in plain block letters in the panel below, and your return address in the space provided. Use typewriter, dark ink, or pencil. Write plainly. Very small writing is not suitable.

No. _____

(Sender's name)

(Sender's address)

(CENSOR'S STAMP)

(Date)

"I am allowed to write of my own personal combat experiences and I can say that I have been fortunate so far. War is like something you cannot imagine. I had no idea what it was about and still don't."

— Erwin Blonder, U.S. soldier

V ···· – MAIL

A Soldier's Letter Home

Read the document to learn about one soldier's wartime experiences in southern France.

HISTORY

Go online to view these and other **HISTORY®** resources.

America Mobilizes for War

Watch the video to see how the United States mobilized its citizens for war and how society changed as a result.

Air War Over Germany

Watch the video to see how the P-51 Mustang helped the Allies win the air war over Germany.

The Pacific Islands

Watch the video to hear veterans describe their experiences fighting in the Pacific theater.

The Cold War

★

Essential Question
Did anyone win the Cold War?

About the Photograph: As anti-Communist feelings rose in America, Senator Joseph McCarthy became a national sensation. He charged that Communists had infiltrated many areas of American life. In this photograph, McCathy presents his claims to a U.S. Senate subcommittee.

In this module you will learn about the Cold War, a five-decade struggle for world influence between the United States and the Soviet Union.

Explore ONLINE!

HISTORY.

VIDEOS, including...
- Superpower
- The Firing of MacArthur
- Fear of Communism at Home
- The Arms Race
- U-2 Spy Plane Shot Down
- Bay of Pigs Declassified
- Cuban Missile Crisis

☑ Document-Based Investigations

☑ Graphic Organizers

☑ Interactive Games

☑ Causes and Effects of McCarthyism

☑ Image with Hotspots: The Moon Landing

SS.912.A.1.2 Utilize a variety of primary and secondary sources to identify author, historical significance, audience, and authenticity to understand a historical period. **SS.912.A.1.4** Analyze how images, symbols, objects, cartoons, graphs, charts, maps, and artwork may be used to interpret the significance of time periods and events from the past. **SS.912.A.1.7** Describe various sociocultural aspects of American life including arts, artifacts, literature, education, and publications. **SS.912.A.6.6** Explain the impact of World War II on domestic government policy. **SS.912.A.6.8** Analyze the effects of the Red Scare on domestic United States policy. **SS.912.A.6.9** Describe the rationale for the formation of the United Nations, including the contribution of Mary McLeod Bethune. **SS.912.A.6.10** Examine causes, course, and consequences of the early years of the Cold War. **SS.912.A.6.11** Examine the controversy surrounding the proliferation of nuclear technology in the United States and the world. **SS.912.A.6.12** Examine causes, course, and consequences of the Korean War. **SS.912.A.6.13** Analyze significant foreign policy events during the Truman, Eisenhower, Kennedy, Johnson, and Nixon administrations. **SS.912.A.6.15** Examine key events and peoples in Florida history as they relate to United States history. **SS.912.A.7.4** Evaluate the success of 1960s era presidents' foreign and domestic policies. **SS.912.G.1.2** Use spatial perspective and appropriate geographic terms and tools, including the Six Essential Elements, as organizational schema to describe any given place. **SS.912.G.1.3** Employ applicable units of measurement and scale to solve simple locational problems using maps and globes. **SS.912.G.2.1** Identify the physical characteristics and the human characteristics that define and differentiate regions. **SS.912.H.1.1** Relate works in the arts of varying styles and genre according to the periods in which they were created. **SS.912.H.1.5** Examine artistic response to social issues and new ideas in various cultures. **LAFS.1112.RH.2.4** Determine the meaning of words and phrases as they are used in a text, including analyzing how an author uses and refines the meaning of a key term over the course of a text.

Timeline of Events 1944–1992 ▶ *Explore ONLINE!*

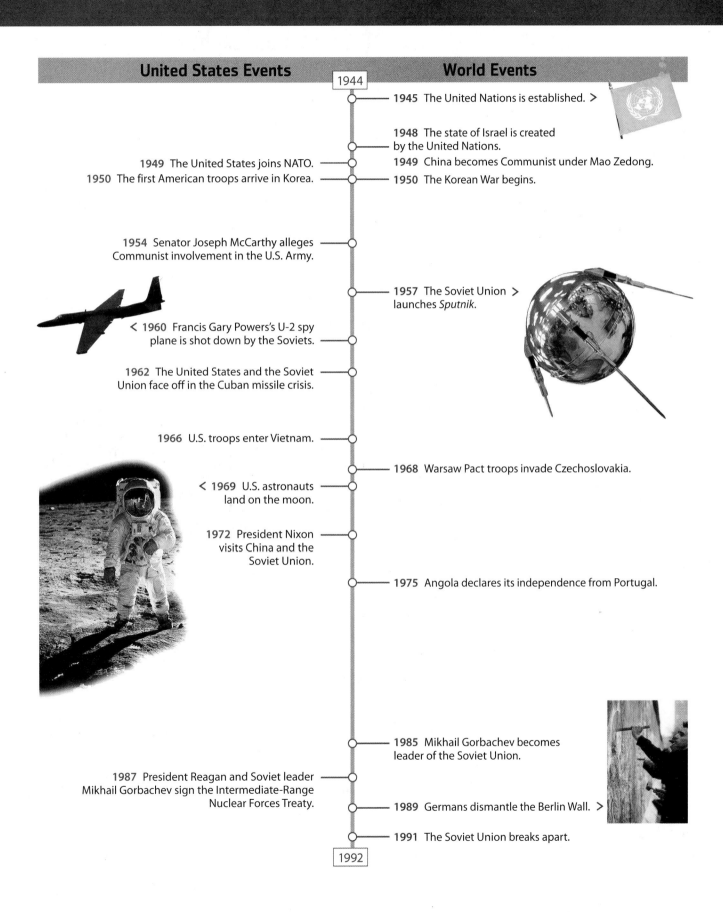

United States Events

1944

1949 The United States joins NATO.
1950 The first American troops arrive in Korea.

1954 Senator Joseph McCarthy alleges Communist involvement in the U.S. Army.

< 1960 Francis Gary Powers's U-2 spy plane is shot down by the Soviets.

1962 The United States and the Soviet Union face off in the Cuban missile crisis.

1966 U.S. troops enter Vietnam.

< 1969 U.S. astronauts land on the moon.

1972 President Nixon visits China and the Soviet Union.

1987 President Reagan and Soviet leader Mikhail Gorbachev sign the Intermediate-Range Nuclear Forces Treaty.

1992

World Events

1945 The United Nations is established. **>**

1948 The state of Israel is created by the United Nations.
1949 China becomes Communist under Mao Zedong.
1950 The Korean War begins.

1957 The Soviet Union **>** launches *Sputnik*.

1968 Warsaw Pact troops invade Czechoslovakia.

1975 Angola declares its independence from Portugal.

1985 Mikhail Gorbachev becomes leader of the Soviet Union.

1989 Germans dismantle the Berlin Wall. **>**

1991 The Soviet Union breaks apart.

The Origins of the Cold War

The Big Idea

The United States and the Soviet Union emerged from World War II as two "superpowers" with vastly different political and economic systems.

Why It Matters Now

After World War II, differences between the United States and the Soviet Union led to a Cold War that lasted almost to the 21st century.

Key Terms and People

Harry S. Truman

satellite nation

iron curtain

Cold War

containment

Central Intelligence Agency (CIA)

Truman Doctrine

Marshall Plan

Berlin airlift

North Atlantic Treaty Organization (NATO)

SS.912.A.1.2; SS.912.A.1.4; SS.912.A.6.6; SS.912.A.6.9; SS.912.A.6.10; SS.912.A.6.13; SS.912.G.2.1; LAFS.1112.RH.1.2; LAFS.1112.RH.4.10; MAFS.K12.MP.1.1; MAFS.K12.MP.5.1

One American's Story

Seventy miles south of Berlin, Joseph Polowsky and a patrol of American soldiers were scouting for signs of the Soviet army advancing from the east. As the soldiers neared the Elbe River, they saw lilacs in bloom. Polowsky later said the sight of the flowers filled them with joy.

Across the Elbe, the Americans spotted Soviet soldiers, who signaled for them to cross over. When the Americans reached the opposite bank, their joy turned to shock. They saw to their horror that the bank was covered with dead civilians, victims of bombing raids.

"Here we are, tremendously exhilarated, and there's a sea of dead. . . . [The platoon leader] was much moved. . . . He said, 'Joe, let's make a resolution with these Russians here and also the ones on the bank: this would be an important day in the lives of the two countries.' . . . It was a solemn moment. There were tears in the eyes of most of us. . . . We embraced. We swore never to forget."
—Joseph Polowsky, quoted in *The Good War*

American and Soviet soldiers meet at the Elbe River in Germany near the end of World War II. A 1996 postage stamp commemorates the historic meeting.

U.S. and Soviets link up at Elbe River, April 1945

The Soviet and U.S. soldiers believed that their encounter would serve as a symbol of peace. Unfortunately, such hopes were soon dashed. After World War II, the United States and the Soviet Union emerged as rival superpowers. Each was strong enough to greatly influence world events.

Former Allies Clash

At the end of World War II, many once-powerful countries in Europe were devastated militarily and economically. In the wake of this destruction, the United States and the Soviet Union emerged as the world's two leading nations. They were superpowers with the might and influence to shape world events. However, the two former allies had very different ambitions for the future. These differences created a climate of icy tension that plunged the two countries into a bitter rivalry.

POLITICAL AND ECONOMIC DIFFERENCES The U.S.-Soviet rivalry stemmed in large part from deep-rooted ideological differences. The two countries represented opposite ends of the political spectrum. In the American democratic system, the people voted to elect a president and a Congress from competing political parties. In the Soviet Union, the Communist Party had removed the czar by force. In his place, it had established a totalitarian government in which no opposing parties were allowed to exist. The Soviets were deeply resentful that the United States had not recognized their Communist government until 16 years after the revolution.

Economically, too, the countries were ideological opposites. Under Soviet communism, the state controlled all property and all economic activity. Individuals were expected to work only for the betterment of the country as a whole. In the American capitalist system, citizens and corporations drove almost all economic activity. Individuals had the right to work as they chose and to potentially become wealthy through their own efforts.

WARTIME TENSIONS Events during World War II widened the gap between the United States and the Soviet Union. The United States was furious that Joseph Stalin—the leader of the Soviet Union—had been an ally of Hitler for a time. Stalin had supported the Allies only after Hitler invaded the Soviet Union in June 1941. In return, Stalin resented the Western Allies' delay in attacking the Germans in Europe. Such an attack, he thought, would have drawn part of the German army away from the Soviet Union.

Relations worsened after Stalin learned that the United States had kept its development of the atomic bomb secret. This revelation came at one of a series of conferences held by the Allied leaders during the last year of World War II. The goal of the conferences was to promote cooperation among the Allies. Instead of cooperation, they resulted in increased tension between President **Harry S. Truman** and Stalin. The American nuclear secret was only the beginning of the growing problem.

Much of the new tension stemmed from Stalin's refusal to allow democracy in Poland and other parts of Eastern Europe. At the Yalta Conference in January 1945, Stalin had agreed to allow free elections after the war. By the time of the Potsdam Conference six months later, however, he had backed off from his promise. The Soviet government banned democratic parties in countries under its control and arrested non-Communist leaders. Truman had hoped to spread democracy into areas that had been under Nazi control. He viewed Stalin's actions as intolerable.

Harry S. Truman (1884–1972)

Harry S. Truman, the son of a Missouri livestock trader, did not seem destined for greatness. When he graduated from high school in 1901, he drifted from job to job. After World War I, he invested in a men's clothing store, but the business failed.

Discouraged by his business failure, Truman sought a career in politics. As a politician, his blunt and outspoken style won both loyal friends and bitter enemies. As president, his decisiveness and willingness to accept responsibility for his decisions ("The Buck Stops Here" read a sign on his desk) earned him respect that has grown over the years.

Joseph Stalin (1879–1953)

As a young revolutionary, Iosif Vissarionovich Dzhugashvili took the name *Stalin,* which means "man of steel" in Russian. His father was a failed shoemaker and an alcoholic. His mother helped support the family by washing clothes.

Stalin is credited with turning the Soviet Union into a world power but at a terrible cost to its citizens. He ruled with terror and brutality and saw enemies everywhere, even among friends and supporters. He subdued the population with the use of secret police and labor camps, and he is believed to have been responsible for the murder of millions of Soviets.

In addition to spreading political freedom, Truman also felt that the United States had a large economic stake in spreading democracy and free trade across the globe. U.S. industry boomed during the war, making the United States the economic leader of the world. To continue growing, American businesses wanted access to raw materials in Eastern Europe. They also wanted to be able to sell goods to Eastern European countries.

SOVIETS TIGHTEN THEIR GRIP ON EASTERN EUROPE Like the United States, the Soviet Union had emerged from the war as a nation of enormous economic and military strength. However, unlike the United States, the Soviet Union had suffered heavy devastation on its own soil. Soviet deaths from the war have been estimated at 20 million, half of them civilians. As a result, the Soviets felt justified in laying claim to Eastern Europe. By dominating this region, the Soviets felt they could stop future invasions from the west. Stalin installed Communist governments in Albania, Bulgaria, Czechoslovakia, Hungary, Romania, and Poland. These countries became known as **satellite nations**, countries dependent upon and dominated by the Soviets.

In a 1946 speech, Stalin announced that communism and capitalism were incompatible—and that another war was inevitable. Therefore, he said, the Soviet Union would concentrate on producing weapons rather than consumer goods. The United States interpreted this speech as a direct challenge.

As tensions mounted, Europe found itself divided into two political and economic regions. One was the mostly democratic and capitalist Western Europe. The other was Communist Eastern Europe. In March 1946 Winston Churchill traveled to the United States. He gave a speech that described the situation in Europe.

> "A shadow has fallen upon the scenes so lately lighted by the Allied victory. . . . From Stettin in the Baltic to Trieste in the Adriatic, an iron curtain has descended across the Continent. Behind that line lie all the capitals of the ancient states of Central and Eastern Europe . . . . All these famous cities and the populations around them lie in . . . the Soviet sphere, and all are subject in one form or another, not only to Soviet influence but to a very high and . . . increasing measure of control from Moscow."
>
> —Winston Churchill, from "Iron Curtain" speech in Fulton, Missouri, 1946

The phrase "**iron curtain**" came to stand for the division of Europe. When Stalin heard about the speech, he declared Churchill's words a "call to war."

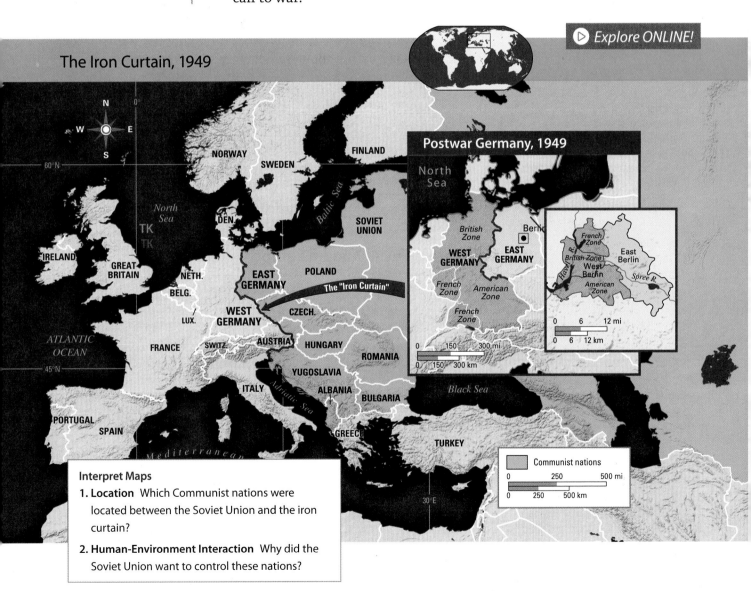

Explore ONLINE!

The Iron Curtain, 1949

Postwar Germany, 1949

Interpret Maps

1. **Location** Which Communist nations were located between the Soviet Union and the iron curtain?

2. **Human-Environment Interaction** Why did the Soviet Union want to control these nations?

CONFLICT IN THE UNITED NATIONS Wars like the one Stalin predicted were supposed to be prevented by the United Nations (UN). That organization had been established in the closing years of World War II to prevent conflict. In theory, the UN gave countries a forum in which to discuss and peacefully resolve disputes. In practice, however, the UN became another sort of battleground in which opposing nations could face off.

The unexpected tensions within the United Nations originated in part from its structure. The UN charter established a General Assembly, in which every member nation has a voice, and several councils. One of these councils, the Security Council, is charged with maintaining global peace and security. It was originally made up of 11 nations—later expanded to 15. Five of these nations have permanent membership. China, France, the Soviet Union, the United Kingdom, and the United States are the permanent members. Each has the power to veto the discussion of any issue brought before the council.

This veto power initially proved counterproductive to the Security Council's mission. The Soviet Union in particular used its veto to head off discussion on any issue that it felt could hinder the spread of communism or increase support for its opponents. By the end of 1947, the Soviets had blocked discussion of more than 20 issues brought before the council. The issues ranged from complaints about Soviet activity in Eastern Europe to applications from Western European countries to join the UN. No other member of the Security Council used a single veto during that period.

Over the next few decades, the veto stalemate continued in the UN. Although increasing tension between the United States and the Soviet Union threatened to lead to war in hotspots around the world, the UN was kept from intervening. UN assistance was limited largely to conflicts unrelated to U.S.-Soviet tension.

Reading Check
Analyze Causes
What caused the tension between the Soviet Union and the United States after the war?

U.S. Aims Versus Soviet Aims in Europe

The United States wanted to . . .	The Soviet Union wanted to . . .
• Create a new world order in which all nations had the right of self-determination	• Encourage communism in other countries as part of the worldwide struggle between workers and the wealthy
• Gain access to raw materials and markets for its industries	• Rebuild its war-ravaged economy using Eastern Europe's industrial equipment and raw materials
• Rebuild European governments to ensure stability and to create new markets for American goods	• Control Eastern Europe to balance U.S. influence in Western Europe
• Reunite Germany, believing that Europe would be more secure if Germany were productive	• Keep Germany divided and weak so that it would never again threaten the Soviet Union

Interpret Tables
1. Which aims involved economic growth of the United States?
2. Which Soviet aims involved self-protection?

New Foreign Policies

The conflicting U.S. and Soviet aims in Eastern Europe led to the **Cold War**. This was a conflict between the United States and the Soviet Union in which neither nation directly confronted the other on the battlefield. The Cold War would dominate global affairs—and U.S. foreign policy—from 1945 until the breakup of the Soviet Union in 1991.

UNITED STATES ESTABLISHES A POLICY OF CONTAINMENT Faced with the Soviet threat, American officials decided it was time, in Truman's words, to stop "babying the Soviets." This changed stance toward the Soviet Union required the development of a new foreign policy. In February 1946 George F. Kennan, an American diplomat in Moscow, proposed a policy he called **containment**. By containment, he meant taking measures to prevent any extension of Communist rule to other countries. In Kennan's plan, such measures would mostly include diplomatic outreach and financial assistance to countries to help them resist Soviet influence.

Under the containment policy, assistance generally first went to countries near existing Communist states, where Communist influence was likely to be strongest. As a result, Western Europe was the first region to receive U.S. aid. This was a result of fears that communism would creep into the area from Soviet-dominated Eastern Europe. Billions of dollars in loans and material assistance flowed across the Atlantic into Western Europe.

As time passed, however, the containment policy came to depend more on military intervention than on purely financial assistance. When the Soviet Union also began sending aid to its allies and exerting influence in various parts of the world, the United States reacted. American troops and funds went to Asia, Africa, Latin America, and elsewhere in hopes of keeping communism in check.

American and Soviet Uses of Force

	Number of Uses	
Location	United States 1946–1975	Soviet Union 1946–1979
Latin America	61	5
Western Europe	20	36
Eastern Europe	26	56
Middle East/North Africa	39	36
Sub-Saharan Africa/South Asia	11	15
Southeast/East Asia	61	42
Totals	**218**	**190**

Interpret Tables
Based on this table, how did proximity influence American and Soviet military activity?

The idea of containment began to guide the Truman administration's foreign policy. Naturally, this placed the United States directly in opposition to the Soviet Union on the world stage. Several times over the next few decades, the United States intervened in conflicts around the globe in support of those who sought to keep Communists out of their homelands. In addition, the country would pour billions of dollars of economic aid into building up and supporting democratic governments. All of these efforts were focused on stopping the advance of communism.

UNITED STATES CREATES AN INTELLIGENCE COMMUNITY Increasingly complex foreign relations during the Cold War required the United States to develop a more complex bureaucracy. In particular, the country needed more intelligence-gathering organizations. These organizations would collect information about Communist activity, both in Europe and at home. The core of this new bureaucracy was formed in 1947 when President Truman signed the National Security Act.

The 1947 act created two new intelligence agencies to help the president formulate the country's foreign policy and to prevent future surprises like the attack on Pearl Harbor. The National Security Council (NSC) was created as a coordinating agency. It sorted through reports and diplomatic dispatches to identify potential national security concerns. Its members included the president, vice-president, secretary of state, and others. They met regularly to address both immediate and long-term issues. The act also established the **Central Intelligence Agency (CIA)**. The CIA gathered intelligence from the military and the state department. It also performed covert, or secret, operations in foreign countries.

In addition to creating an intelligence community, the National Security Act reorganized the U.S. military. The goal was to streamline military decision making. Three existing departments—the War Department, Navy Department, and Department of the Air Force—were combined into the new Department of Defense. Each branch of the military still had its own secretary, but the new secretary of defense oversaw all of them.

Reading Check
Analyze Motives
What was Truman's goal in establishing the policy of containment and creating new intelligence agencies?

Efforts to Rebuild Europe

Truman's new containment policy was tested almost immediately in Europe. The heavy destruction caused by World War II had left much of the continent in financial ruin. Economic devastation led to political instability and talk of revolution in some countries. Truman and his advisers feared that these circumstances could lead to increased Soviet influence and the establishment of new Communist regimes.

THE TRUMAN DOCTRINE The United States first tried to contain Soviet influence in Greece and Turkey. For years, Britain had been financially supporting both nations' resistance to growing Communist influence in the region. However, Britain's economy had been badly hurt by the war. The formerly wealthy nation could no longer afford to give aid. It asked the United States to take over the responsibility.

President Truman accepted the challenge. On March 12, 1947, Truman asked Congress for $400 million in economic and military aid for Greece and Turkey. In his statement, he expressed what became known as the **Truman Doctrine**. He declared that the United States would be supporting people around the world who were fighting against outside forces trying to take over their governments. Congress agreed with Truman. It decided that the doctrine was essential to keep Soviet political and economic influence from spreading. Between 1947 and 1950, the United States sent $400 million in aid to Turkey and Greece. This greatly reduced the danger of Communist subjugation in those nations.

THE MARSHALL PLAN Like post-war Greece, Western Europe was in chaos. Most of its factories had been bombed or looted. Millions of people were living in refugee camps while European governments tried to figure out where to resettle them. To make matters worse, the winter of 1946–1947 was the bitterest in several centuries. The weather severely damaged crops and froze rivers, cutting off water transportation and causing a fuel shortage.

Vocabulary
subjugation
bringing under control

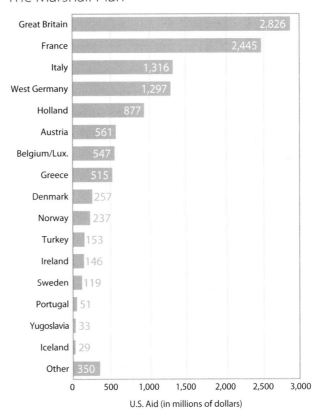

The Marshall Plan

Source: *Problemes Economiques*, No. 306

Interpret Graphs
1. Which two countries received the most aid?
2. Why do you think these countries received so much aid?

The Truman Doctrine

In a 1947 speech to Congress, President Truman announced a significant change in U.S. foreign policy. With isolation no longer feasible and communism posing a threat around the world, Truman explained why he supported taking action to contain Soviet influence.

> *"I believe that it must be the policy of the United States to support free peoples who are resisting attempted subjugation by armed minorities or by outside pressures.*
>
> *I believe that we must assist free peoples to work out their own destinies in their own way.*
>
> *I believe that our help should be primarily through economic and financial aid which is* essential to economic stability and orderly political processes. . . .
>
> *Collapse of free institutions and loss of independence would be disastrous not only for them but for the world. Discouragement and possibly failure would quickly be the lot of neighboring peoples striving to maintain their freedom and independence. . . ."*
>
> —Harry S. Truman, from a speech to a joint session of Congress, March 12, 1947

Analyze Historical Sources
How does Truman intend to help other countries resist Communist influence?

Background
The Marshall Plan also benefited America. U.S. farm and factory production increased to supply Europe with goods, and the wartime economic boom continued.

Reading Check
Summarize
What was the U.S. response to tensions with the Soviets in the late 1940s?

In June 1947 Secretary of State George Marshall proposed that the United States provide aid to all European nations that needed it. He said that this move was directed "not against any country or doctrine but against hunger, poverty, desperation, and chaos." The **Marshall Plan** revived European hopes. Over the next four years, 16 countries received some $13 billion in aid. Marshall's original plan even offered assistance to the Soviet Union and its allies. Stalin, however, refused to accept any assistance from the United States.

By 1952 Western Europe was flourishing, and the Communist Party had lost much of its appeal to voters. In addition, the economic aid had helped the United States build strong alliances with the nations of Western Europe. These alliances would prove valuable in the coming years as the struggle against communism continued.

Superpowers Struggle over Germany

As Europe began to get back on its feet, the United States and its allies clashed with the Soviet Union over the issue of German reunification. At the Potsdam Conference near the end of World War II, Allied leaders agreed to leave Germany divided into four zones occupied by the United States, Great Britain, and France in the west and the Soviet Union in the east. In 1948 Britain,

France, and the United States decided to combine their three zones into one nation. The western part of Berlin, which had been occupied by the French, British, and Americans, was surrounded by Soviet-occupied territory.

Although the three nations had a legal right to unify their zones, they had no written agreement with the Soviets guaranteeing free access to Berlin. Stalin saw this loophole as an opportunity. If he moved quickly, he might be able to take over the part of Berlin held by the three Western powers. In June 1948 Stalin closed all highway and rail routes into West Berlin. As a result, no food or fuel could reach that part of the city. The 2.1 million residents of the city had only enough food to last for approximately five weeks.

THE BERLIN AIRLIFT The resulting situation was dire. In an attempt to break the blockade, American and British officials started the **Berlin airlift** to fly food and supplies into West Berlin. For 327 days, planes took off and landed every few minutes, around the clock. In 277,000 flights, they brought in 2.3 million tons of supplies—everything from food, fuel, and medicine to Christmas presents that the planes' crews bought with their own money.

West Berlin survived because of the airlift. In addition, the mission to aid Berlin boosted American prestige around the world, while causing Soviet prestige to drop. By May 1949 the Soviet Union realized it was beaten and lifted the blockade.

In the same month, the western part of Germany officially became a new nation, the Federal Republic of Germany, also called West Germany. It included West Berlin. A few months later, from its occupation zone, the Soviet Union created the German Democratic Republic, called East Germany. It included East Berlin.

Beginning in June 1948 planes bringing tons of food and other supplies to West Berlin landed every few minutes.

This cartoon depicts the nations that signed the North Atlantic Pact, which created NATO in 1949. The nations, shown as hats, are arranged in a pyramid to show the bigger countries on the bottom supporting the smaller, weaker nations on top.

THE NATO ALLIANCE The Berlin blockade increased Western European fear of Soviet aggression. As a result, ten Western European nations—Belgium, Denmark, France, Great Britain, Iceland, Italy, Luxembourg, the Netherlands, Norway, and Portugal—joined with the United States and Canada on April 4, 1949, to form a defensive military alliance called the **North Atlantic Treaty Organization (NATO)**. The 12 members of NATO pledged military support to one another in case any member was attacked. By signing the North Atlantic Treaty, the United States also pledged to help the countries of Western Europe rebuild their defense capabilities. In the year following the creation of NATO, Congress authorized more than $1 billion to help restore European military power.

For the first time in its history, the United States had entered into a military alliance with other nations during peacetime. The Cold War had ended any hope of a return to U.S. isolationism. Greece and Turkey joined NATO in 1952, and West Germany joined in 1955. By then, NATO kept a standing military force of more than 500,000 troops as well as thousands of planes, tanks, and other equipment.

Reading Check
Analyze Effects
What were the effects of the Berlin airlift?

Lesson 1 Assessment

1. **Organize Information**
   Use a table to describe the U.S. actions and the Soviet actions that contributed most to the Cold War.

U.S. Actions	Soviet Actions

   Write a paragraph explaining which country was more responsible for increased tension and why you think so.

2. **Key Terms and People** For each key term or person in the lesson, write a sentence explaining its significance.

3. **Evaluate** People who had served as aides to President Franklin Roosevelt worried that Truman was not qualified to handle world leadership. Considering what you learned in this section, evaluate Truman as a world leader.

   Think About:
   - his behavior toward Stalin
   - his economic support of European nations
   - his support of West Berlin

4. **Make Inferences** Which of the two superpowers do you think was more successful in achieving its aims during the period 1945–1949? Support your answer by referring to historical events.

5. **Analyze Motives** What were Stalin's motives in supporting Communist governments in Eastern Europe?

6. **Summarize** What steps did the United States take to help rebuild Western Europe after the war?

The Cold War Heats Up

The Big Idea

After World War II, China became a Communist nation and Korea was split into a Communist north and a democratic south.

Why It Matters Now

Ongoing tensions with China and North Korea continue to involve the United States.

Key Terms and People

Chiang Kai-shek

Mao Zedong

Taiwan

38th parallel

Korean War

SS.912.A.1.3; SS.912.A.1.4; SS.912.A.6.10; SS.912.A.6.12; SS.912.A.6.13; SS.912.G.1.2

One American's Story

First Lieutenant Philip Day Jr. vividly remembers his first taste of battle in Korea. On the morning of July 5, 1950, Philip Day spotted a column of eight enemy tanks moving toward his company.

"I was with a 75-mm recoilless-rifle team. 'Let's see,' I shouted, 'if we can get one of those tanks.' We picked up the gun and moved it to where we could get a clean shot. I don't know if we were poorly trained, . . . but we set the gun on the forward slope of

American soldiers in Korea, November 1950

the hill. When we fired, the recoilless blast blew a hole in the hill which instantly covered us in mud and dirt. . . . When we were ready again, we moved the gun to a better position and began banging away. I swear we had some hits, but the tanks never slowed down. . . . In a little less than two hours, 30 North Korean tanks rolled through the position we were supposed to block as if we hadn't been there."

—Philip Day Jr., quoted in *The Korean War: Pusan to Chosin*

Only five years after World War II ended, the United States became embroiled in a war in Korea. The policy of containment had led the United States into battle to halt Communist expansion. In this conflict, however, the enemy was not the Soviet Union, but North Korea and China.

China Becomes a Communist Country

American involvement in Korea grew out of events that took place during World War II and the early years of the Cold War. For more than a decade before the war, Chinese Communists had struggled against the nationalist government of **Chiang Kai-shek** (chăng′ kī′shěk′). When the Japanese invaded China in 1937, though, the two sides temporarily interrupted their civil war and joined in the common cause against the invader. The Communists led the struggle in the north. The Nationalists under Chiang fought in the south. The United States supported Chiang.

CHINA UNDER CHIANG Many Americans were impressed by Chiang Kai-shek and admired the courage and determination that the Nationalists showed resisting the Japanese. However, U.S. officials who dealt with Chiang held a different view. They found his government inefficient and hopelessly corrupt. They noted that his policies actually weakened support for his own party. For example, the Nationalists collected a grain tax from farmers even during the famine of 1944. When city dwellers demonstrated against a 10,000 percent increase in the price of rice, Chiang's secret police opened fire on them.

In contrast, the Communists, led by **Mao Zedong** (mou′ dzŭ′dŏng′), gained strength throughout the country. In the areas they controlled, Communists worked to win peasant support. They encouraged peasants to learn to read, and they helped to improve food production. As a result, more and more recruits flocked to the Communists' Red Army. By 1945 much of northern China was under Communist control.

RENEWED CIVIL WAR As soon as the defeated Japanese left China at the end of World War II, cooperation between the Nationalists and the Communists ceased. Civil war erupted again between the two groups. In spite of the problems in the Nationalist regime, American policy favored the Nationalists because they opposed communism.

From 1944 to 1947 the United States played peacemaker between the two groups while still supporting the Nationalists. However, U.S. officials repeatedly failed to negotiate peace. Truman also refused to commit American soldiers to back up the Nationalists, although the United States did send $2 billion worth of military equipment and supplies.

The aid wasn't enough to save the Nationalists, whose weak military leadership and corrupt, abusive practices drove many peasants to the Communist side. In May 1949 Chiang and the remnants of his demoralized government fled to the island of **Taiwan**, which Westerners called Formosa. There, about 100 miles from the Chinese mainland, the United States helped set up a Nationalist government—the Republic of China. From 1949 through the 1960s, the United States poured millions of dollars of aid into the Taiwanese economy. However, Chiang had not attained his goal. After more than 20 years of struggle, the Communists ruled all of mainland China. They established a new government, the People's Republic of China, which the United States refused to accept as China's true government.

Nationalists Versus Communists, 1945

Chiang Kai-shek, Leader of the Nationalists	Mao Zedong, Leader of the Communists
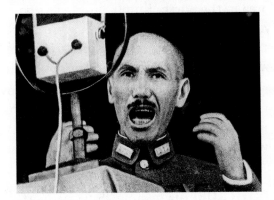	
• Ruled in southern and eastern China • Relied heavily on aid from United States • Struggled with inflation and a failing economy • Suffered from weak leadership and poor morale	• Ruled in northern China • Relied heavily on financial aid from Soviet Union • Attracted peasants with promises of land reform • Benefited from experienced guerrilla army and a highly motivated leadership

AMERICA REACTS TO THE COMMUNIST TAKEOVER The American public was stunned that China had become Communist. Containment had failed. In Congress, conservative Republicans and Democrats attacked the Truman administration for supplying only limited aid to Chiang. If containing communism was important in Europe, they asked, why was it not equally important in Asia?

The State Department replied by saying that what had happened in China was a result of internal forces. The United States had failed in its attempts to influence these forces, such as Chiang's inability to retain the support of his people. Trying to do more would only have started a war in Asia—a war that the United States wasn't prepared to fight.

Some conservatives in Congress rejected this argument as a lame excuse. They claimed that the American government was riddled with Communist agents. Like wildfire, American fear of communism began to burn out of control, and the flames were fanned even further by events in Korea the following year.

Reading Check
Analyze Causes
What factors led to the Communist takeover in China?

The Korean War

As part of its imperialist expansion, Japan had taken over Korea in 1910. During World War II, some 300,000 Japanese troops had occupied the Korean peninsula, and millions of Koreans were forced into military service or into hard labor. When the war ended in 1945, Japanese troops in northern Korea, north of the **38th parallel** (38° N latitude), surrendered to the Soviets. Japanese troops south of the parallel surrendered to the Americans. As in Germany, two nations developed, one Communist and one democratic.

South Korean president Syngman Rhee *(center, wearing a suit)* meets with U.S. General James Van Fleet in 1952.

TWO NATIONS In 1948 the Republic of Korea, usually called South Korea, was established in the zone that had been occupied by the United States. Its government, headed by Syngman Rhee, was based in Seoul, Korea's traditional capital. Simultaneously, the Communists formed the Democratic People's Republic of Korea in the north. Kim Il Sung led its government, which was based in Pyongyang. Both Kim and Rhee were devoted Nationalists who wanted to reunite the two halves of Korea. However, they strongly disagreed about how the unified country should be governed.

By 1949, under a UN agreement, both the United States and the Soviet Union had withdrawn their troops from Korea, although both nations left advisers in place. Negotiations intended to reunite the peninsula went nowhere, leaving the two new nations glaring at each other across the 38th parallel. Each government claimed the sole right to rule all of Korea.

NORTH KOREA ATTACKS SOUTH KOREA On June 25, 1950, North Korean forces swept across the 38th parallel in a surprise attack on South Korea. Supported by money and materials from the Soviet Union, the North Koreans intended to take control of all of Korea through one quick strike. The conflict that followed became known as the **Korean War**.

Within a few days, North Korean troops had penetrated deep into South Korea. South Korea called on the United Nations to stop the North Korean invasion. When the matter came to a vote in the UN Security Council, the Soviet Union was not there. The Soviets were boycotting the council in protest over the UN's decision to recognize the Nationalist government in Taiwan rather than Communist China. Thus, the Soviets could not veto the UN's plan of military action. In their absence, the United States pushed for intervention on behalf of South Korea. American leaders feared that allowing communism to spread in the south would pose a threat to the free world and its security. The vote passed.

On June 27, in a show of military strength, President Truman ordered troops stationed in Japan to support the South Koreans. He also sent an American fleet into the waters between Taiwan and China. According to the Constitution, however, the power to declare war lies with the legislative branch, and Congress never voted to declare war in Korea. Therefore, Truman's critics cried that he had overstepped his constitutional authority by sending troops to Asia. Truman countered that he was acting in response to a call for action by the United Nations, which he claimed lay within his powers as Commander in Chief. As a result, the United States was never officially at war in Korea, but instead was involved in a United Nations "police action."

In all, 16 nations sent some 520,000 troops to aid South Korea. Over 90 percent of these troops were American. South Korean troops numbered an additional 590,000. The combined forces were placed under the command of General Douglas MacArthur, former World War II hero in the Pacific.

ANOTHER PERSPECTIVE

India's Viewpoint

Nonaligned nations such as India were on neither side of the Cold War and had their own perspectives. In 1951 the prime minister of India, Jawaharlal Nehru, had this to say about the Korean War:

"This great struggle between the United States and Soviet Russia is hardly the proper role in this world for those great powers. . . . Their role should be to function in their own territories and not be a threat to others."

Reading Check
Analyze Events
How did Korea become a divided nation after World War II?

The United States Fights in Korea

At first, North Korea seemed unstoppable. Driving steadily south, its troops captured Seoul. After a month of bitter combat, the North Koreans had forced UN and South Korean troops into a small defensive zone around Pusan in the southeastern corner of the peninsula.

MACARTHUR'S COUNTERATTACK To stop the North Korean advance, MacArthur launched a counterattack with tanks, heavy artillery, and fresh troops from the United States. On September 15, 1950, his troops made a surprise amphibious landing behind enemy lines at Inchon, on Korea's west coast. Other troops moved north from Pusan. Trapped between the two attacking forces, about half of the North Korean troops surrendered; the rest fled back across the 38th parallel. MacArthur's plan had saved his army from almost certain defeat. His brilliant strategy and phenomenal success—both in Korea and in World War II—made him a hero to the American public.

The UN army chased the retreating North Korean troops across the 38th parallel into North Korea. In late November, UN troops approached the Yalu River, the border between North Korea and China. It seemed as if Korea was about to become a single country again.

THE CHINESE FIGHT BACK The Chinese, however, had other ideas. Communist China's foreign minister, Zhou Enlai, warned that his country would not stand idly by and "let the Americans come to the border"— meaning the Yalu River, the boundary between North Korea and China. In late November 1950, 300,000 Chinese troops joined the war on the side of North Korea. The Chinese wanted North Korea as a Communist buffer state to protect the northeastern region of Manchuria. They also felt threatened by the American fleet that lay off their coast. The fight between North Korea and South Korea had escalated into a war in which the main opponents were the Chinese Communists and the Americans.

Vocabulary
amphibious capable of traveling both on land and on water

American paratroopers comb through a village in North Korea on October 20, 1950, during the Korean War.

By sheer force of numbers, the Chinese quickly drove the UN troops southward. At some points along the battlefront, the Chinese outnumbered UN forces ten to one. By early January 1951 all UN and South Korean troops had been pushed out of North Korea. The Chinese advanced to the south, once again capturing the South Korean capital, Seoul. "We face an entirely new war," declared MacArthur.

For two years, the two sides fought bitterly to obtain strategic positions in the Korean hills, but neither side was able to make important advances. One officer remembered the standoff.

Beverly Scott

"Our trenches . . . were only about 20 meters in front of theirs. We were eyeball to eyeball. . . . We couldn't move at all in the daytime without getting shot at. Machine-gun fire would come in, grenades, small- arms fire, all from within spitting distance. It was like World War I. We lived in a maze of bunkers and deep trenches. . . . There were bodies strewn all over the place. Hundreds of bodies frozen in the snow."

—Beverly Scott, quoted in *No Bugles, No Drums: An Oral History of the Korean War*

Vocabulary
conspirator a person who takes part in secretly planning something unlawful

MACARTHUR RECOMMENDS ATTACKING CHINA To halt the bloody stalemate, in early 1951 MacArthur called for an extension of the war into China. Convinced that Korea was the place "where the Communist conspirators have elected to make their play for global conquest," MacArthur called for a blockade of the Chinese coast and the use of nuclear weapons. He also wanted to use Chiang Kai-shek's troops to invade southern China.

Truman rejected MacArthur's request. The president did not want the United States involved in a massive land war in Asia. He preferred to fight a limited war, focusing only on containing Communist forces, not destroying communism outright. Plus, the Soviet Union had a mutual-assistance pact with China. Attacking China could set off World War III. As General Omar N. Bradley, chairman of the Joint Chiefs of Staff, said, an all-out conflict with China would be "the wrong war, at the wrong place, at the wrong time, and with the wrong enemy."

Instead of attacking China, the UN and South Korean forces began to advance once more, using the U.S. Eighth Army, led by Matthew B. Ridgway, as a spearhead. By April 1951 Ridgway had retaken Seoul and had moved back up to the 38th parallel. The situation was just what it had been before the fighting began.

MACARTHUR VERSUS TRUMAN Not satisfied with the recapture of South Korea, MacArthur continued to urge the waging of a full-scale war against China. Certain that his views were correct, MacArthur tried to go over the president's head. He spoke and wrote privately to newspaper and magazine publishers and, especially, to Republican leaders.

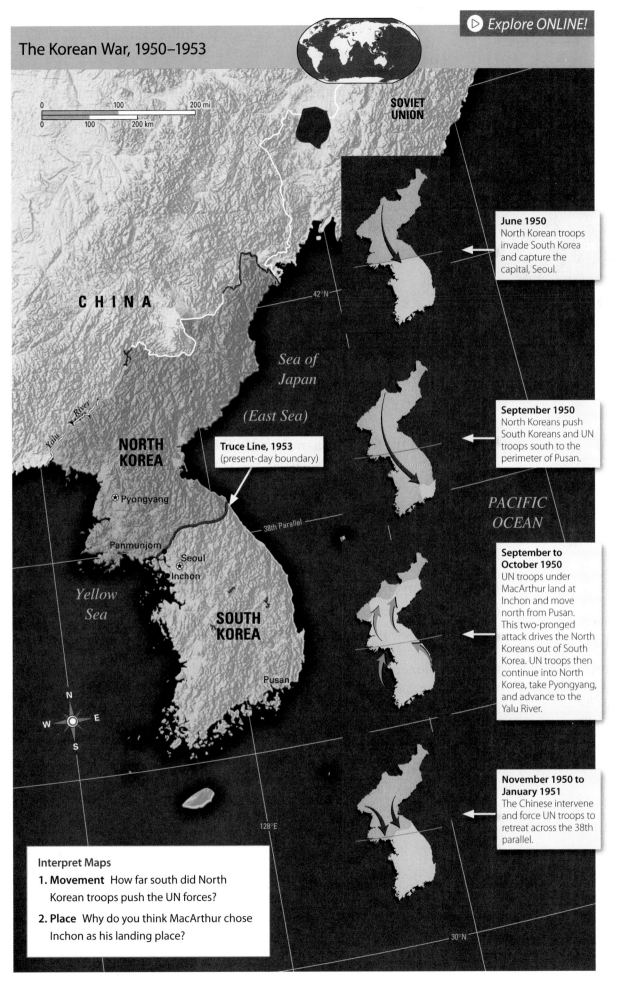

The Korean War, 1950–1953

Explore ONLINE!

SOVIET
UNION

0   100   200 mi
0   100   200 km

CHINA

Yalu River

Sea of
Japan

(East Sea)

42°N

NORTH
KOREA

Truce Line, 1953
(present-day boundary)

⊛ Pyongyang

Panmunjom

38th Parallel

Seoul

⊛ Inchon

Yellow
Sea

SOUTH
KOREA

Pusan

PACIFIC
OCEAN

128°E

30°N

N
W   E
S

June 1950
North Korean troops invade South Korea and capture the capital, Seoul.

September 1950
North Koreans push South Koreans and UN troops south to the perimeter of Pusan.

September to October 1950
UN troops under MacArthur land at Inchon and move north from Pusan. This two-pronged attack drives the North Koreans out of South Korea. UN troops then continue into North Korea, take Pyongyang, and advance to the Yalu River.

November 1950 to January 1951
The Chinese intervene and force UN troops to retreat across the 38th parallel.

Interpret Maps

1. **Movement** How far south did North Korean troops push the UN forces?

2. **Place** Why do you think MacArthur chose Inchon as his landing place?

General Douglas MacArthur and President Truman strongly disagreed about how best to proceed in the Korean War.

MacArthur's superiors informed him that he had no authority to make decisions of policy. Despite repeated warnings to follow orders, MacArthur continued to criticize the president. President Truman, who as president was Commander in Chief of the armed forces and thus MacArthur's boss, was just as stubborn as MacArthur. Truman refused to stand for this kind of behavior. He wanted to put together a settlement of the war and could no longer tolerate a military commander who was trying to sabotage his policy. On April 11, 1951, Truman made the shocking announcement that he had fired MacArthur.

Many Americans were outraged over their hero's downfall. A public opinion poll showed that 69 percent of the American public backed General MacArthur. When MacArthur returned to the United States, he gave an address to Congress, an honor usually awarded only to heads of government. New York City honored him with a ticker-tape parade. In his closing remarks to Congress, MacArthur said, "Old soldiers never die, they just fade away."

Throughout the fuss, Truman stayed in the background. After MacArthur's moment of public glory passed, the Truman administration began to make its case. Before a congressional committee investigating MacArthur's dismissal, a parade of witnesses argued the case for limiting the war. The committee agreed with them. As a result, public opinion swung around to the view that Truman had done the right thing. As a political figure, MacArthur did indeed fade away.

CONFLICT ENDS IN STALEMATE As the MacArthur controversy died down, the Soviet Union unexpectedly suggested a cease-fire on June 23, 1951. Truce talks began in July 1951. The opposing sides reached agreement on two points: the location of the cease-fire line at the existing battle line and the establishment of a demilitarized zone between the opposing sides. Negotiators spent another year wrangling over the exchange of prisoners. Finally, in July 1953 the two sides met in the town of Panmunjom and signed an armistice ending the war.

At best, the agreement was a stalemate. On the one hand, the North Korean invaders had been pushed back, and communism had been contained without the use of atomic weapons. On the other hand, Korea was still two nations rather than one.

On the home front, the war had affected the lives of ordinary Americans in many ways. It had cost 54,000 American lives and $67 billion in expenditures. The high cost of this unsuccessful war was one of many factors leading Americans to reject the Democratic Party in 1952 and to elect a Republican administration under World War II hero Dwight D. Eisenhower.

Vocabulary
demilitarize to ban military forces in an area or region

NOW & THEN

The Two Koreas

Korea was split into North Korea and South Korea at the end of World War II. Today, more than 60 years later, the peninsula is still divided. South Korea is booming economically, while North Korea, still Communist, struggles with severe food and energy shortages.

Periodically, discussions about reuniting the two countries resume. In 2000 South Korean president Kim Dae-jung, pictured here, won the Nobel Peace Prize for his efforts to improve ties with North Korea. The two nations met in North Korea for the first time since the nations were established in 1948. Although economic and political differences continue to keep the two countries apart, there is hope that one day Korea will become a united nation.

Reading Check
Compare
How did Truman and MacArthur differ over strategy in the Korean War?

In addition, the Korean War had long-lasting effects on U.S. foreign policy. The hostilities put further strain on already tense relations between the United States and China. After the Communist takeover and the Korean War, it seemed unlikely that the two countries would find any sort of diplomatic accord. At the same time, the repulsion of communism from South Korea convinced U.S. officials that containment was a workable foreign policy. As a result, the United States began to station more troops in Asia in efforts to prevent any further Communist advances. Many of those troops were stationed along the North Korea–South Korea border as a deterrent to further military action in that area. Increased anti-Communist sentiment also had repercussions at home, as government officials began a hunt for Americans who might be blamed for the Communist gains.

Lesson 2 Assessment

1. **Organize Information** Use a timeline to list the major events of the Korean War.

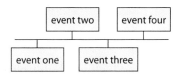

Choose two events and explain how one event led to the other.

2. **Key Terms and People** For each key term or person in the lesson, write a sentence explaining its significance.

3. **Analyze Events** Many Americans have questioned whether fighting the Korean War was worthwhile. What is your opinion? Why?

   Think About:
   • the loss of American lives
   • the fear of communism that enveloped the country at the time
   • the stalemate that ended the war

4. **Analyze Effects** What were the effects of the Korean War on U.S. foreign policy?

5. **Predict** What might have happened if MacArthur had convinced Truman to expand the fighting into China? How might today's world be different?

6. **Evaluate** At the end of China's civil war, the United States refused to accept the Communist People's Republic of China as China's true government. What were the advantages of such a policy? What were the disadvantages? Do you agree with this decision? Why or why not?

The Cold War **591**

The Cold War at Home

The Big Idea

During the late 1940s and early 1950s, fear of communism led to reckless charges against innocent citizens.

Why It Matters Now

Americans today remain vigilant about unfounded accusations.

Key Terms and People

House Un-American Activities Committee (HUAC)

Hollywood Ten

blacklist

Alger Hiss

Ethel and Julius Rosenberg

Joseph McCarthy

McCarthyism

One American's Story

Tony Kahn made the neighbors uncomfortable because they thought his father, Gordon Kahn, was a Communist. In 1947 Gordon Kahn was a successful screenwriter. However, when a congressional committee began to investigate Communists in Hollywood, Kahn was deemed unfit to hire. Later, in 1951, he was scheduled to testify before the committee himself.

To save himself, Gordon Kahn simply had to name others as Communists, but he refused. Rather than face the congressional committee, he fled to Mexico. Tony Kahn remembers how the Cold War hurt him and his family.

"The first time I was called a Communist, I was four years old. . . . I'll never forget the look in our neighbors' eyes when I walked by. I thought it was hate. I was too young to realize it was fear."
—Tony Kahn, from *The Cold War Comes Home*

Tony Kahn

The members of the Kahn family were among thousands of victims of the anti-Communist hysteria that gripped this country in the late 1940s and early 1950s. By the end of the period, no one was immune from accusations.

Fear of Communist Influence

In the early years of the Cold War, many Americans believed that there was good reason to be concerned about the security of the United States. The Soviet domination of Eastern Europe and the Communist takeover of China shocked the American public. These events fueled a fear that communism would spread around the world. In addition, at the height of World War II, about 80,000 Americans claimed membership in the Communist Party. Some people feared that the first loyalty of these American Communists was to the Soviet Union. Their fears led to a new Red Scare, an anti-Communist movement similar to the one that had gripped the United States after World War I.

LOYALTY REVIEW BOARD As U.S.-Soviet tensions increased after World War II, strongly anti-Communist Republicans began to accuse Truman of being soft on communism. They feared that Communists had infiltrated the federal government and held positions of authority. Consequently, in March 1947 President Truman issued an executive order setting up the Federal Employee Loyalty Program. This program included the Loyalty Review Board. Its purpose was to investigate government employees and to dismiss those who were found to be disloyal to the U.S. government. The Federal Bureau of Investigation (FBI), a national law enforcement agency, was responsible for the first round of screening. Under the leadership of director J. Edgar Hoover, the FBI conducted extensive background checks of all federal employees and applicants for federal jobs. Those found to have Communist ties were dismissed, although they could appeal their cases to the Loyalty Review Board. In addition, the U.S. attorney general drew up a list of 91 "subversive" organizations. Membership in any of these groups was grounds for suspicion.

From 1947 to 1951 government loyalty boards investigated 3.2 million employees and dismissed 212 as security risks. Another 2,900 resigned because they did not want to be investigated or felt that the investigation violated their constitutional rights. Individuals under investigation were not allowed to see the evidence against them.

THE HOUSE UN-AMERICAN ACTIVITIES COMMITTEE Other agencies investigated possible Communist influence, both inside and outside the U.S. government. The most famous such agency was the **House Un-American Activities Committee (HUAC)**. HUAC first made headlines in 1947, when it began to investigate Communist influence in the movie industry. The committee believed that Communists were sneaking propaganda into films. The committee pointed to the pro-Soviet films made during World War II when the Soviet Union had been an ally of the United States.

HUAC subpoenaed 43 witnesses from the Hollywood film industry in September 1947. Many of the witnesses were "friendly," supporting the accusation that Communists had infiltrated the film industry. For example, the movie star Gary Cooper said he had "turned down quite a few scripts because I thought they were tinged with Communistic ideas." However, when asked which scripts he meant, Cooper couldn't remember their titles.

Ten "unfriendly" witnesses were called to testify but refused. These men, known as the **Hollywood Ten**, decided not to cooperate with HUAC because they believed that the hearings were unconstitutional. They argued that the hearings violated their rights of freedom of speech and assembly and the right of accused persons to be fully informed of the nature of accusations against them. Because the Hollywood Ten refused to answer the committee's questions, they were sent to prison.

In response to the hearings, Hollywood executives instituted a **blacklist**. This was a list of people whom they condemned for having a Communist background. Approximately 500 actors, writers, producers, and directors were blacklisted. Their careers were ruined because they could no longer work. For example, in 1950 actor and singer Paul Robeson refused to sign an affidavit indicating whether he had ever been a member of the Communist Party. As a result, he was blacklisted and could not find work at home. In addition, the State Department revoked his passport for eight years. He was unable to travel abroad to perform. His income fell from $150,000 a year to $3,000 a year.

THE MCCARRAN ACT As Hollywood tried to rid itself of Communists, Congress decided that Truman's Loyalty Review Board did not go far enough in protecting the nation's security. In 1950 it passed the McCarran Internal Security Act. This act required all Communist organizations in the United States to register with the federal government. It also made it unlawful to plan any action that might lead to the establishment of a totalitarian dictatorship in the United States. Immigrants suspected of promoting communism or totalitarianism could be barred from entering the country or—if already living in the United States—deported. Truman vetoed the bill, saying, "In a free country, we punish men for the crimes they commit, but never for the opinions they have." But Congress enacted the law over Truman's veto.

Document-Based Investigation Historical Source

"It's OK—We're Hunting Communists"

The fear of Communist subversion affected the entire society. People were so suspicious that almost any unusual opinion might be labeled "un-American." The climate of suspicion was most severe in the years 1947–1954, but it lasted throughout the 1950s. Loyalty boards questioned federal employees about their memberships and the books they read.

"It's Okay—We're Hunting Communists"

A 1947 Herblock Cartoon, copyright by the Herb Block Foundation

Analyze Historical Sources
1. What organization does the car represent?

2. What does the cartoon imply about the methods of this organization?

THE VENONA PROJECT In 1943 the U.S. Army Signal Intelligence Service began the Venona Project. This organization was a predecessor of the National Security Agency (NSA). The project's goal was to decode messages sent by Soviet intelligence agencies. Analysts soon decoded enough to learn that Soviet spies had infiltrated all levels of the U.S. government.

The 3,000 decoded messages that make up the Venona Papers were declassified in 1995. They confirm that 349 U.S. residents had secret relationships with the Soviet Union. It is clear that these individuals delivered classified information to the Soviets. That information hindered U.S. efforts during the Cold War. The suspicions that HUAC and others had about Communist spies in the United States were in fact well founded. However, their extreme investigative methods and scare tactics intensified the fear and tension of the era.

Spy Cases Stun the Nation

Two spy cases added to the fear that was spreading across the country. One case involved a former State Department official named Alger Hiss.

ALGER HISS In 1948 a former Communist spy named Whittaker Chambers accused **Alger Hiss** of spying for the Soviet Union. To support his charges, Chambers produced microfilm of government documents. He claimed that the documents had been typed on Hiss's typewriter. Too many years had passed for government prosecutors to charge Hiss with espionage. However, a jury convicted him of perjury—lying about passing the documents—and sent him to jail. A young conservative Republican congressman named Richard Nixon gained fame for pursuing the charges against Hiss. Within four years of the highly publicized case, Nixon was elected vice-president.

Hiss claimed that he was innocent and that Chambers had forged the documents used against him. However, in the 1990s Soviet cables released by the National Security Agency seemed to prove Hiss's guilt.

Ethel and Julius Rosenberg were executed in June 1953 despite numerous pleas to spare their lives.

THE ROSENBERGS Another spy case rocked the nation even more than the Hiss case, in part due to international events. On September 3, 1949, Americans learned that the Soviet Union had exploded an atomic bomb. Most American experts had predicted that it would take the Soviets three to five more years to make the bomb. People began to wonder if Communist supporters in the United States had leaked the secret of the bomb.

This second spy case seemed to confirm that suspicion. In 1950 German-born physicist Klaus Fuchs admitted giving the Soviet Union information about America's atomic bomb. The information probably enabled Soviet scientists to develop their own atomic bomb years earlier than they would have otherwise.

Television: Making News

Some historians of popular culture believe that the early 1950s were the best years of television. Most programs were filmed live and had a fresh, unrehearsed look. Along with variety shows, early television presented some of the best serious drama of the age.

Since the 1950s, television has also become a major vehicle for reporting the news. Not only does television report the news, it also has increasingly helped shape it.

1954
In 1954 Communist-hunting senator Joseph McCarthy, in U.S. Senate hearings that were televised live, accused the U.S. Army of "coddling Communists." As many as 20 million Americans watched the combative senator malign people who had no chance to defend themselves.

1960
In the 1960 presidential election, a major factor in John Kennedy's victory over Richard Nixon was a series of four televised debates, the first televised presidential debates in history. An estimated 85 million to 120 million Americans watched one or more of the debates, which turned the tide in favor of Kennedy.

1967
By 1967 American support for the Vietnam War had plummeted as millions of TV viewers witnessed the horrors of war on the nightly news. Images of dead and wounded soldiers helped turn some against the war effort.

1974
The Watergate scandal that toppled Richard Nixon's presidency in 1974 played to a rapt TV audience. During the Senate hearings in 1973, the televised testimony of John Dean, the president's counsel, and other prominent government officials convinced two out of three Americans that the president had committed a crime.

2000
During the 2000 presidential election, the TV networks first projected that Al Gore would win Florida. Later, George W. Bush was declared the winner of Florida. This declaration led Al Gore to concede. Then, when the Florida vote became too close to call, Gore retracted his concession. That "election muddle" blurred even more the already unclear line between reporting the news and making it.

2011
With the rise of online communication in the 21st century, fewer Americans depend on television news broadcasts for information. When President Barack Obama appeared on television to announce the death of terrorist Osama bin Laden, the news had already been leaked and spread across the country via social media.

Ethel and Julius Rosenberg, minor activists in the American Communist Party, were implicated in the Fuchs case. The Rosenbergs were asked if they were Communists. They denied the charges against them and cited their Fifth Amendment right not to incriminate themselves. They claimed they were being persecuted both for being Jewish and for holding radical beliefs. The Rosenbergs were found guilty of espionage and sentenced to death. In pronouncing their sentence, Judge Irving Kaufman declared their crime "worse than murder." To him, they were directly responsible for one of the deadliest clashes of the Cold War.

> *"I believe your conduct in putting into the hands of the Russians the A-bomb years before our best scientists predicted Russia would perfect the bomb has already caused, in my opinion, the Communist aggression in Korea. . . ."*
>
> —Irving Kaufman, quoted in
> *The Unquiet Death of Julius and Ethel Rosenberg*

Reading Check
Analyze Causes
Why did the cases of Alger Hiss and the Rosenbergs heighten the anti-Communist mood of Americans?

People from all over the world appealed for clemency for the Rosenbergs. Many considered the evidence and the testimony too weak to justify the death sentence. The case was appealed to the U.S. Supreme Court, but the Court refused to overturn the conviction. Julius and Ethel Rosenberg died in the electric chair in June 1953, leaving behind two sons. They became the first U.S. civilians executed for espionage.

Senator Joseph McCarthy claimed to have evidence of Communist influence across the country.

Vocabulary
infiltration the act of penetrating a group or organization without being noticed for purposes such as spying

McCarthy Launches His "Witch Hunt"

The most famous anti-Communist activist was Senator **Joseph McCarthy**, a Republican from Wisconsin. During his first three years in the Senate, he had gained a reputation for being an ineffective legislator. By January 1950 he realized that he needed a winning issue in order to be reelected in 1952. Looking for such an issue, McCarthy charged that Communists were taking over the government.

MCCARTHY'S TACTICS Taking advantage of people's concerns about communism—especially after Mao's rise in China—McCarthy made one unsupported accusation after another. At various times, McCarthy claimed to have in his hands the names of 57, 81, and 205 Communists in the State Department. (He never actually produced a single name.) He also charged that the Democratic Party was guilty of "20 years of treason" for allowing Communist infiltration into the government.

McCarthy's style of attacking suspected Communists in the early 1950s became known as **McCarthyism**. (Since that time, *McCarthyism* has referred to the unfair tactic of accusing people of disloyalty without providing evidence.) When challenged, McCarthy simply launched more accusations. He was always careful to do his name-calling only in the Senate, though. There, he had legal immunity that protected him from being sued for slander.

However, McCarthyism's tactics quickly spread beyond the Senate. The fear they inspired also spread. Proof of a Communist Party connection was no longer required. The FBI and other investigators compiled lists of people who held questionable political views. Lists also included people who had refused to cooperate with their investigations. These investigations spread to other branches of the government, universities, labor unions, and private businesses. Americans feared that if they did not take action against the listed individuals, they might be labeled "soft on communism." As a result, thousands of Americans lost their jobs for political reasons.

The Republicans did little to stop the attacks of McCarthy and his allies. Republicans believed they would win the 1952 presidential election if the public saw them ridding the nation of Communists. But one group of six senators, led by Senator Margaret Chase Smith of Maine, did speak out.

"I speak as a Republican. I speak as a woman. I speak as a United States senator. I speak as an American. . . . I am not proud of the way in which the Senate has been made a publicity platform for irresponsible sensationalism. I am not proud of the reckless abandon in which unproved charges have been hurled from this side of the aisle."

—Margaret Chase Smith, from *Declaration of Conscience*

Few Americans shared Smith's willingness to denounce McCarthy, or her legal protections as a senator. Across the country, people hesitated to criticize McCarthy or any aspect of the government. People were afraid of being called Communists or Communist sympathizers. Americans were particularly cautious about speaking out against Cold War foreign policy. Such opposition could make one an easy target. McCarthyism had, in effect, made many American people wary of their own government.

Causes and Effects of McCarthyism

Causes	Effects
• Soviets successfully establish Communist regimes in Eastern Europe after World War II. • Soviets develop the atomic bomb more quickly than expected. • Korean War ends in a stalemate. • Republicans gain politically by accusing Truman and Democrats of being soft on communism.	• Millions of Americans are forced to take loyalty oaths and undergo loyalty investigations. • Activism by labor unions goes into decline. • Many people are afraid to speak out on public issues. • Anti-communism continues to drive U.S. foreign policy.

Interpret Tables
1. How did world events help lead to McCarthyism?
2. How did McCarthyism affect the behavior of individual Americans?

OTHER ANTI-COMMUNIST MEASURES Others besides Joseph McCarthy made it their mission to root communism out of American society. By 1953, 39 states had passed laws making it illegal to advocate the violent overthrow of the government, even though such laws clearly violated the constitutional right of free speech. Across the nation, cities and towns passed similar laws.

At times, the fear of communism seemed to have no limits. In Indiana, professional wrestlers had to take a loyalty oath. In experiments run by newspapers, pedestrians on the street refused to sign petitions that quoted the Declaration of Independence because they were afraid the ideas were Communist. The government investigated union leaders, librarians, newspaper reporters, and scientists. It seemed that no profession was safe from the hunt for Communists.

MCCARTHY'S DOWNFALL Finally, in 1954 McCarthy made accusations against the U.S. Army. This resulted in a nationally televised Senate investigation. The audience watched as McCarthy bullied witnesses. This behavior alienated the audience and cost him public support. The Senate criticized him for improper conduct that "tended to bring the Senate into dishonor and disrepute." Three years later, Joseph McCarthy, suffering from alcoholism, died a broken man.

Reading Check
Summarize What tactics did McCarthy use in his campaign against Communists?

Lesson 3 Assessment

1. **Organize Information** Use a web diagram to fill in events that illustrate the anti-Communist fear in the United States.

Anti-Communist fear gripped the country.

Which event had the greatest impact on the country?

2. **Key Terms and People** For each key term or person in the lesson, write a sentence explaining its significance.

3. **Form Opinions** If you had lived in this period and had been accused of being a Communist, what would you have done?

   Think About:

   • the Hollywood Ten, who refused to answer questions
   • the Rosenbergs, who pleaded the Fifth Amendment

4. **Analyze Motives** Choose one of the following roles: Harry Truman, a member of HUAC, Judge Irving Kaufman, or Joseph McCarthy. As the person you have chosen, explain your motivation for opposing communism.

5. **Analyze Primary Sources** What does this cartoon suggest about McCarthy's downfall?

"I Can't Do This To Me!" a 1954 Herblock Cartoon, copyright by the Herb Block Foundation.

Two Nations Live on the Edge

The Big Idea

During the 1950s the United States and the Soviet Union came to the brink of nuclear war.

Why It Matters Now

The Cold War continued into the following decades, affecting U.S. policies in Cuba, Central America, Southeast Asia, and the Middle East.

Key Terms and People

H-bomb

arms race

Dwight D. Eisenhower

massive retaliation

mutually assured destruction

John Foster Dulles

brinkmanship

Warsaw Pact

Eisenhower Doctrine

Nikita Khrushchev

Francis Gary Powers

U-2 incident

SS.912.A.1.2; SS.912.A.1.4; SS.912.A.1.7; SS.912.A.6.10; SS.912.A.6.11; SS.912.A.6.13; SS.912.G.1.2; SS.912.G.2.1; SS.912.H.1.1; SS.912.H.1.5; LAFS.1112.RH.4.10; MAFS.K12.MP.1.1; MAFS.K12.MP.5.1; MAFS.K12.MP.6.1

One American's Story

Writer Annie Dillard was one of thousands of children who grew up in the 1950s with the chilling knowledge that nuclear war could obliterate their world in an instant. Dillard recalls practicing what to do in case of a nuclear attack.

A father helps his daughter practice getting into a bomb shelter.

"At school we had air-raid drills. We took the drills seriously; surely Pittsburgh, which had the nation's steel, coke, and aluminum, would be the enemy's first target. . . . When the air-raid siren sounded, our teachers stopped talking and led us to the school basement. There the gym teachers lined us up against the cement walls and steel lockers, and showed us how to lean in and fold our arms over our heads. . . . The teachers stood in the middle of the room, not talking to each other. We tucked against the walls and lockers. . . . We folded our skinny arms over our heads, and raised to the enemy a clatter of gold scarab bracelets and gold bangle bracelets."

—Annie Dillard, from *An American Childhood*

The fear of nuclear attack was a direct result of the Cold War. After the Soviet Union developed its atomic bomb, the two superpowers began a competition for power that enormously increased both the number and the destructive capability of weapons.

Brinkmanship Rules U.S. Policy

Although air-raid drills were not common until the Eisenhower years (1953–1961), nuclear tensions had begun under Truman. When the Soviet Union exploded its first atomic bomb in 1949, President Truman had to make a terrible decision—whether to develop an even more horrifying weapon.

RACE FOR THE H-BOMB The scientists who developed the atomic bomb had suspected since 1942 that it was possible to create an even more destructive thermonuclear weapon—the hydrogen bomb, or **H-bomb**. They estimated that such a bomb would have the force of 1 million tons of TNT (67 times the power of the bomb dropped on Hiroshima). But they argued fiercely about the morality of creating such a destructive weapon.

Despite such concerns, the United States entered into a deadly race with the Soviet Union to see which country would be the first to produce an H-bomb. On November 1, 1952, the United States won the race when it exploded the first H-bomb. However, the American advantage lasted less than a year. In August 1953 the Soviets exploded their own thermonuclear weapon.

THE ARMS RACE With the Soviet development of the H-bomb, the two superpowers were once again technologically matched. Leaders on each side, however, feared that the other would gain an advantage. These fears led both countries to build enormous stockpiles of weapons. Any improvement or technological advance made by one country was soon matched by the other. Thus, the United States and the Soviet Union began an **arms race**—an international contest between countries seeking a military advantage over each other.

Although it began under Truman, the arms race reached new heights under President **Dwight D. Eisenhower**. Eisenhower's foreign policy was focused on keeping the lead in the arms race. This lead would allow for a strategy of **massive retaliation**. Eisenhower's goal was to discourage the Soviet Union from launching a nuclear offensive. Eisenhower did this by vowing to launch a devastating counterstrike to any attack, whether nuclear or not. Such a counterattack would be as damaging—or even more damaging—to the attacking nation as it was to the one attacked, thereby deterring anyone from attacking the United States.

By the mid- to late 1950s, the Soviet Union had increased its nuclear capabilities to match those of the United States. Both superpowers now had the ability to retaliate to any attack with nuclear force. This essentially guaranteed that any such attack would result in the total destruction of both parties. As a result, neither country was willing to consider a direct attack against its opponent. This policy of **mutually assured destruction** would form a cornerstone of American and Soviet nuclear policy for the next few decades.

Eisenhower's nuclear planning was supported and encouraged by his secretary of state, **John Foster Dulles**. Like many Americans, Dulles was staunchly anti-Communist. For him, the Cold War was a moral crusade against communism. Dulles proposed that the United States could prevent the spread of communism by promising to use all of its force, including nuclear weapons, against any aggressor nation.

Effects of the Arms Race

As the United States and the Soviet Union rushed to produce nuclear weapons, many civilians lived in fear of a catastrophic attack. Eisenhower's policies of retaliation and brinkmanship increased those fears. Across the country, civil defense agencies tried to prepare people for how to survive in the case of such an attack.

Analyze Historical Sources
How does this poster reflect Americans' increased fears of conflict with the Soviet Union?

The willingness of the United States under President Eisenhower to go to the edge of all-out war became known as **brinkmanship**. Under this policy, the United States trimmed its army and navy and expanded its air force (which would deliver the bombs) and its buildup of nuclear weapons. The Soviet Union did the same.

The threat of nuclear attack was unlike any the American people had ever faced. Even if only a few bombs reached their targets, millions of civilians would die. Schoolchildren like Annie Dillard practiced air-raid procedures. Some families built underground fallout shelters in their backyards. Fear of nuclear war became a constant in American life for the next 30 years.

THE MILITARY-INDUSTRIAL COMPLEX In addition to social changes, the arms race caused profound changes in the American economy. The production of so many weapons created tremendous growth for the companies that made them. In fact, some munitions companies grew so large that many Americans began to fear they would begin to dominate the economy.

Among those who feared the growing influence of these companies was President Eisenhower. Although he fully supported the beginning of the arms race, he had quickly grown concerned that defense spending had gotten out of hand. Before leaving office, Eisenhower warned against the dangers of what he called the "military-industrial complex." In his final speech as president, he warned Americans to beware its growing power.

"This conjunction of an immense military establishment and a large arms industry is new in the American experience. The total influence—economic, political, and even spiritual—is felt in every city, every statehouse, and every office of the federal government. We recognize the imperative need for this development. Yet we must not fail to comprehend its grave implications. . . . The potential for the disastrous rise of misplaced power exists and will persist."

—Dwight D. Eisenhower, from his Farewell Address, January 17, 1961

Reading Check
Analyze Causes
How did the United States and the Soviet Union start the arms race?

Despite Eisenhower's concerns, defense spending in the United States would continue to grow long after his administration ended.

The Cold War Spreads Around the World

As the nation shifted to a dependence on nuclear arms for defense, the Eisenhower administration began to depend heavily on the recently formed Central Intelligence Agency (CIA) for information. The CIA used spies to gather information abroad. The CIA also began to carry out covert, or secret, operations to weaken or overthrow governments unfriendly to the United States. Most of these governments had ties to communism.

COVERT ACTIONS IN THE MIDDLE EAST AND LATIN AMERICA One of the CIA's first covert actions took place in the Middle East. In 1951 Iran's prime minister, Mohammad Mossadegh, nationalized Iran's oil fields. That means that he placed the formerly private industries (mostly British-owned) under Iranian control. To protest, the British stopped buying Iranian oil. Fearing that economic trouble might lead Mossadegh to seek Soviet assistance, the CIA began to support anti-Mossadegh rebels. It wanted the pro-American shah of Iran, who had recently been forced to flee, to return to power. The plan worked. The shah returned. He turned over control of Iranian oil fields to Western companies.

In 1954 the CIA also took covert actions in Guatemala, a small Central American country just south of Mexico. Eisenhower believed that Guatemala's government had Communist sympathies because it had given more than 200,000 acres of American-owned land to peasants. In response, the CIA trained an army, which invaded Guatemala. The Guatemalan army refused to defend the president, and he resigned. The army's leader then became dictator of the country.

INTERVENTION IN AFRICA AND ASIA Even as the CIA was working behind the scenes in some parts of the world, the U.S. government was openly helping other nations fight against communism. Most of this assistance went to former European colonies in Africa and Asia. During the 1940s and 1950s, many colonies sought independence, either peacefully or through violent uprisings. American leaders feared that the governments of these newly independent nations would be receptive to Communist influence, especially if the Soviets promised them financial or military aid.

To prevent this possible expansion of communism, the United States offered its own aid to Africa and Asia. The government sent money, technical assistance, and sometimes military forces to such countries as Indonesia and Vietnam. This aid was intended to convince the new countries to form Western, democratic governments. Feeling trapped between rival powers, many of these new nations chose to remain unaligned with either the United States or the Soviet Union. They wanted no part of the Cold War.

Some Asian countries, on the other hand, were eager to align with the United States and its allies. In 1954 the governments of the Philippines, Thailand, and Pakistan joined with the United States, France, Great Britain, Australia, and New Zealand to form the Southeast Asia Treaty Organization (SEATO). This organization was dedicated to fighting the spread of

Background
From ancient times until 1935, Iran was known as Persia. Persia once ruled a great empire that stretched from the Mediterranean Sea to India's Indus River.

SEATO

COLLECTIVE SECURITY —
THE PATHWAY TO PEACE

communism in Southeast Asia. Although most of its members were not actually located in that region, they all had cultural or economic ties there. None wanted to see it fall under Soviet domination.

THE WARSAW PACT Despite the growing tension between the superpowers, U.S.-Soviet relations seemed to thaw following the death of Joseph Stalin in 1953. The Soviets recognized West Germany. They also concluded peace treaties with Austria and Japan.

However, tensions flared up again in 1955 when NATO leaders invited West Germany to join NATO. Soviet leaders saw this expansion of NATO as a threat and grew fearful. The existence of so powerful an alliance dedicated to containing communism threatened the very existence of the Soviet Union and its satellite nations. To counter this threat, the Soviets formed their own military alliance, known as the **Warsaw Pact**. The Warsaw Pact linked the Soviet Union with seven Eastern European countries. Together, these countries believed they would be able to withstand any NATO offensives.

Unlike NATO, which was governed jointly by a council of its member states, the Warsaw Pact was firmly under Soviet control. In addition to countering NATO threats, Soviet leaders used Warsaw Pact troops to crush internal rebellions. In June 1956, for example, Pact troops violently put down an anti-Communist protest in Poland, killing dozens of civilians.

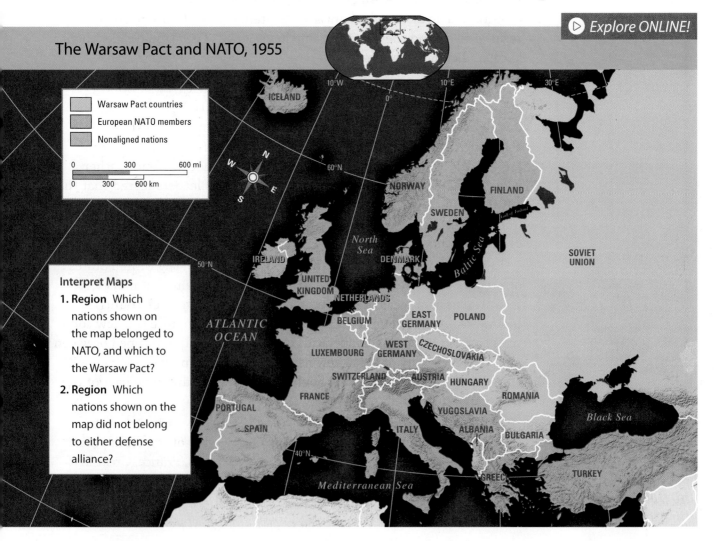

Explore ONLINE!

The Warsaw Pact and NATO, 1955

Warsaw Pact countries

European NATO members

Nonaligned nations

0   300   600 mi
0   300   600 km

Interpret Maps

1. **Region** Which nations shown on the map belonged to NATO, and which to the Warsaw Pact?

2. **Region** Which nations shown on the map did not belong to either defense alliance?

ICELAND

NORWAY   FINLAND

SWEDEN

North Sea   DENMARK

IRELAND

UNITED KINGDOM

NETHERLANDS

BELGIUM   EAST GERMANY   POLAND

ATLANTIC OCEAN

LUXEMBOURG   WEST GERMANY   CZECHOSLOVAKIA

SWITZERLAND   AUSTRIA   HUNGARY

FRANCE   ROMANIA

PORTUGAL   YUGOSLAVIA

SPAIN   ITALY   ALBANIA   BULGARIA

SOVIET UNION

Baltic Sea

Black Sea

Mediterranean Sea   GREECE   TURKEY

THE SUEZ WAR In 1955 Great Britain and the United States agreed to help Egypt finance construction of a dam at Aswan on the Nile River. However, Gamal Abdel Nasser, Egypt's head of government, tried to play the Soviets and the Americans against each other. He tried to improve relations with each one in order to get more aid. In 1956, after learning that Nasser was making deals with the Soviets, Secretary of State Dulles withdrew his offer of a loan. Angered, Nasser responded by nationalizing the Suez Canal, the Egyptian waterway that was owned by France and Great Britain. The French and the British were outraged.

Egyptian control of the canal also affected Israel, which had become independent following World War II. On May 14, 1948, the United Nations created the nation of Israel out of the Palestine Mandate. The Palestine Mandate was a territory in the Middle East created by the League of Nations after World War I. Placed under British control, the mandate was intended in part to eventually provide a home for Jews from around the world. Thousands of Jews had migrated there from Europe before and during World War II. Israel became the "promised land" they had been seeking since biblical times. The creation of Israel was one of the few issues upon which the United States and the Soviet Union agreed, as people around the world reacted to the horror that had happened to the Jews in the Holocaust. Arab nations in the region, however, considered the creation of Israel an invasion of their territory. Several launched raids and large-scale attacks on Israel. They were determined to reclaim what they considered their land. Although outnumbered, the Israelis defended their borders.

When he took control of the Suez Canal, Nasser refused to let ships bound for Israel pass through, even though the canal was supposed to be open to all nations. Great Britain, France, and Israel responded by sending troops. The three countries seized the Mediterranean end of the canal. Although the United States had supported the creation of Israel and remained a supporter, Eisenhower objected to the use of force to regain access to the canal. Soviet leaders also objected. With both superpowers in agreement, the UN quickly stepped in to stop the fighting. It persuaded Great Britain, France, and Israel to withdraw. However, it allowed Egypt to keep control of the canal.

Because of its support for Egypt in the Suez Crisis, the Soviet Union gained prestige in the Middle East. To counterbalance this development, President Eisenhower issued a warning in January 1957. This warning, known as the **Eisenhower Doctrine**, said that the United States would defend the Middle East against an attack by any Communist country. In March, Congress officially approved the doctrine.

THE HUNGARIAN UPRISING Even as fighting was raging in the Middle East, a revolt began in Hungary. Dominated by the Soviet Union since the end of World War II, the Hungarian people rose in revolt in 1956. They demanded the removal of the most oppressive leaders, to which Khrushchev agreed. The Hungarians formed a new government led by Imre Nagy (ēm'rĕ nŏd'yə), the most popular and liberal Hungarian Communist leader. A great supporter of reform, Nagy promised free elections. He also denounced the Warsaw Pact and demanded that all Soviet troops leave Hungary.

Crowds surround a captured Russian tank during the anti-Communist revolution in Hungary.

The Soviet response was swift and brutal. In November 1956 Soviet tanks rolled into Hungary and killed approximately 30,000 Hungarians. Armed with only pistols and bottles, thousands of Hungarian freedom fighters threw up barricades in the streets and fought the invaders to no avail. The Soviets overthrew the Nagy government and replaced it with pro-Soviet leaders. Nagy himself was executed. Some 200,000 Hungarians fled to the west.

Although the Truman Doctrine had promised to support free peoples who resisted communism, the United States did nothing to help Hungary break free of Soviet control. Many Hungarians were bitterly disappointed. The American policy of containment did not extend to driving the Soviet Union out of its satellites.

No help came to Hungary from the United Nations either. Although the UN passed one resolution after another condemning the Soviet Union, the Soviet veto in the Security Council stopped the UN from taking any action.

The Cold War Takes to the Skies

After Stalin's death in 1953, the Soviet Union had no well-defined way for one leader to succeed another. For the first few years, a group of leaders shared power. As time went by, however, one man did gain power. That man was **Nikita Khrushchev** (krōōsh′chĕf). Like Stalin, Khrushchev believed that communism would take over the world, but Khrushchev thought it could triumph peacefully. He favored a policy of peaceful coexistence, in which two powers would compete economically and scientifically.

THE SPACE RACE In the competition for international prestige, the Soviets leaped to an early lead in what came to be known as the space race. On October 4, 1957, they launched *Sputnik,* the world's first artificial satellite. *Sputnik* traveled around the earth at 18,000 miles per hour, circling the globe every 96 minutes. Its launch was a triumph of Soviet technology.

Reading Check
Summarize What steps did the United States take to try to contain communism in Asia, the Middle East, and Africa?

Science Fiction in the Cold War

Many science fiction writers draw on scientific and social trends to describe future events that might occur if those trends were to continue. In the 1950s those trends included nuclear proliferation, the space race, and the pervasive fear of Cold War dangers. In *The Martian Chronicles,* Ray Bradbury describes how earthlings who have colonized Mars watch helplessly as their former planet is destroyed by nuclear warfare.

The Martian Chronicles

They all came out and looked at the sky that night. They left their suppers or their washing up or their dressing for the show and they came out upon their now-not-quite-as-new porches and watched the green star of Earth there. It was a move without conscious effort; they all did it, to help them understand the news they had heard on the radio a moment before. There was Earth and there the coming war, and there hundreds of thousands of mothers or grandmothers or fathers or brothers or aunts or uncles or cousins. They stood on the porches and tried to believe in the existence of Earth, much as they had once tried to believe in the existence of Mars; it was a problem reversed. To all intents and purposes, Earth now was dead; they had been away from it for three or four years. Space was an anesthetic; seventy million miles of space numbed you, put memory to sleep, depopulated Earth, erased the past, and allowed these people here to go on with their work. But now, tonight, the dead were risen, Earth was reinhabited, memory awoke, a million names were spoken: What was so-and-so doing tonight on Earth? What about this one and that one? The people on the porches glanced sidewise at each other's faces.

RAY BRADBURY

At nine o'clock Earth seemed to explode, catch fire, and burn.

The people on the porches put up their hands as if to beat the fire out.

They waited.

—Ray Bradbury, from *The Martian Chronicles* (1950)

Analyze American Literature
How might readers' interpretations of Bradbury's writing today differ from readers' interpretations during the Cold War?

Americans were shocked at being beaten and promptly poured money into their own space program. U.S. scientists worked frantically to catch up to the Soviets. The first attempt at an American satellite launch was a humiliating failure, with the rocket toppling to the ground. However, on January 31, 1958, the United States successfully launched its first satellite.

U.S. Budget, 1950–2010

Percentage Spent on Defense

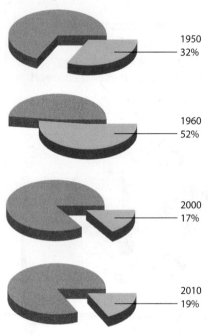

1950
32%

1960
52%

2000
17%

2010
19%

Source: *Historical Tables, Budget of the United States Government*

Interpret Graphs
1. By how much did the percentage of the federal budget for defense increase between 1950 and 1960?
2. Why do you think it increased that much?

A U-2 IS SHOT DOWN In July 1955 Eisenhower traveled to Geneva, Switzerland, to meet with Soviet leaders. There, Eisenhower put forth an "open skies" proposal. He suggested that the United States and the Soviet Union allow flights over each other's territory to guard against surprise nuclear attacks. Although the Soviet Union rejected this proposal, the world hailed the "spirit of Geneva" as a step toward peace.

Following the rejection of Eisenhower's "open skies" proposal, the CIA began making secret high-altitude flights over Soviet territory. The plane used for these missions was the U-2, which could fly at high altitudes without detection. As a U-2 passed over the Soviet Union, its infrared cameras took detailed photographs of troop movement and missile sites.

By 1960, however, many U.S. officials were nervous about the U-2 program for two reasons. First, the existence and purpose of the U-2 was an open secret among some members of the American press. Second, the Soviets had been aware of the flights since 1958, as U-2 pilot **Francis Gary Powers** explained.

"We . . . knew that the Russians were radar-tracking at least some of our flights. . . . We also knew that SAMs [surface-to-air missiles] were being fired at us, that some were uncomfortably close to our altitude. But we knew too that the Russians had a control problem in their guidance system. . . . We were concerned, but not greatly."

—Francis Gary Powers, from *Operation Overflight: The U-2 Spy Pilot Tells His Story for the First Time*

Finally, Eisenhower himself wanted the flights discontinued. He and Khrushchev were going to hold another summit conference on the arms race on May 15, 1960. "If one of these aircraft were lost when we were engaged in apparently sincere deliberations, it could . . . ruin my effectiveness," he told an aide. However, Dulles persuaded him to authorize one last flight.

That flight took place on May 1, and the pilot was Francis Gary Powers. Four hours after Powers entered Soviet airspace, a Soviet pilot, Igor Mentyukov, shot down his plane, and Powers was forced to parachute into Soviet-controlled territory. The United States issued a false story that a plane had disappeared while on a weather mission. Khrushchev announced that the U-2 had been brought down 1,300 miles inside the Soviet Union by a Soviet rocket and that Powers had been captured alive and had confessed his activities. The Soviets tried Powers for espionage and sentenced him to ten years in prison. After 17 months, however, he was returned to the United States in exchange for a Soviet spy.

Recognized as American in part by his military identification card (*above*), Francis Gary Powers was arrested as a spy. Following his release, Powers spoke at a Senate committee hearing (*right*).

RENEWED CONFRONTATION At first, Eisenhower denied that Powers had been spying. With his confession, however, Eisenhower finally had to admit it. Khrushchev demanded an apology for the flights and a promise to halt them. Eisenhower agreed to stop the U-2 flights, but he would not apologize.

Khrushchev angrily called off the summit. He also withdrew his invitation to Eisenhower to visit the Soviet Union. Because of the **U-2 incident**, the 1960s opened with tension between the two superpowers as great as ever. The few hopeful events of the 1950s—such as the rise of a Soviet government willing to work toward peace—had been eclipsed by aggression, competitiveness, and mutual suspicion. The Cold War would continue into the next decade, with an enormous effect on U.S. foreign policy.

Reading Check
Compare How were Joseph Stalin and Nikita Khrushchev alike, and how were they different?

Lesson 4 Assessment

1. **Organize Information** Use a table to list Cold War trouble spots in Iran, Guatemala, Egypt, and Hungary. For each, write a newspaper headline that summarizes the U.S. role and the outcome of the situation.

Trouble Spot	Headline

   Choose one headline and write a paragraph about that trouble spot.

2. **Key Terms and People** For each key term or person in the lesson, write a sentence explaining its significance.

3. **Predict** How might the Cold War have progressed if the U-2 incident had never occurred?

   Think About:
   - the mutual distrust between the Soviet Union and the United States
   - the outcome of the incident

4. **Draw Conclusions** How do you think opponents of the policy of brinkmanship reacted to the stockpiling of weapons during the arms race?

5. **Evaluate** Which of the two superpowers do you think contributed more to Cold War tensions during the 1950s?

6. **Form Generalizations** Should one nation have the right to remove another nation's leader from power? If so, when? If not, why?

Mounting Tensions in the Sixties

The Big Idea

The Kennedy administration faced some of the most dangerous Soviet confrontations in American history.

Why It Matters Now

America's response to Soviet threats developed the United States as a military superpower.

Key Terms and People

John F. Kennedy

flexible response

domino theory

Lyndon Baines Johnson

Fidel Castro

Berlin Wall

hot line

Limited Test Ban Treaty

Nuclear Non-Proliferation Treaty (NPT)

SS.912.A.1.2; SS.912.A.1.4; SS.912.A.6.11; SS.912.A.6.13; SS.912.A.6.15; SS.912.A.7.4; SS.912.G.1.3; LAFS.1112.RH.1.1; LAFS.1112.RH.1.2; LAFS.1112.RH.2.4; LAFS.1112.RH.4.10

One American's Story

On May 5, 1961, American astronaut Alan Shepard climbed into *Freedom 7,* a tiny capsule on top of a huge rocket booster. The capsule left the earth's atmosphere in a ball of fire and returned the same way, and Shepard became the first American to travel into space. Years later, he recalled his emotions when a naval crew fished him out of the Atlantic.

"Until the moment I stepped out of the flight deck . . . I hadn't realized the intensity of the emotions and feelings that so many people had for me, for the other astronauts, and for the whole manned space program. . . . I was very close to tears as I thought, it's no longer just our fight to get 'out there.' The struggle belongs to everyone in America. . . . From now on there was no turning back."

—Alan Shepard, from *Moon Shot: The Inside Story of America's Race to the Moon*

Astronaut Alan Shepard prepares to enter the space capsule for his *Mercury* flight.

Shepard's journey into orbit was more than just a demonstration of American ingenuity. It was another step in the continued Cold War struggles between the United States and the Soviet Union, which had launched a man into orbit a month earlier. As the 1960s dawned, the competition between the two nations continued to affect nearly every aspect of American life.

A New Military Policy

The improvements in the space program that sent Alan Shepard into orbit were strongly supported by President **John F. Kennedy**. Since taking office in 1961, Kennedy had focused on the Cold War. He thought the Eisenhower administration had not done enough about the Soviet threat. The Soviets, he concluded, were outpacing Americans in technological developments. They were also gaining the loyalties of economically less-developed third-world countries in Asia, Africa, and Latin America. He criticized the Republicans for allowing communism to develop in Cuba, at America's doorstep.

MILITARY STRATEGY REDEFINED Kennedy believed his most urgent task as president was to redefine the nation's nuclear strategy. The Eisenhower administration had relied on the policy of massive retaliation to discourage Soviet aggression and imperialism. However, threatening to use nuclear arms over a minor conflict was not a risk Kennedy wished to take. Instead, his team developed a policy of **flexible response**. Kennedy's secretary of defense, Robert McNamara, explained the policy.

> *"The Kennedy administration worried that [the] reliance on nuclear weapons gave us no way to respond to large non-nuclear attacks without committing suicide. . . . We decided to broaden the range of options by strengthening and modernizing the military's ability to fight a nonnuclear war."*
>
> —Robert S. McNamara, from *In Retrospect*

Kennedy increased defense spending to boost conventional, nonnuclear forces such as troops, ships, and artillery. He also created an elite branch of the army called the Special Forces, or Green Berets. In addition, he tripled the overall nuclear capabilities of the United States. These changes enabled the United States to fight limited wars around the world, while maintaining a balance of nuclear power with the Soviet Union. Kennedy hoped to reduce the risk of nuclear war. However, his administration found itself drawn into conflict in Vietnam that threatened to increase that risk.

CONTAINMENT IN VIETNAM The developing conflict in Vietnam had been continuing for more than a decade. In the 1940s Vietnam was a French colony. The people had declared their independence. For more than a decade, Vietnamese forces led by Ho Chi Minh battled the French. Presidents Truman and Eisenhower had supported the French with money and troops. By 1954, however, the French had surrendered and withdrawn from the region.

When Kennedy took office, Vietnam was divided. A Communist government headed by Ho Chi Minh held power in the north. Democratically elected president Ngo Dinh Diem governed the south. The Kennedy administration wanted to contain any further spread of communism in Southeast Asia. It supported Diem, pouring financial assistance into the region. It sent thousands of military advisers to train South Vietnamese troops.

Kennedy's foreign policy in Vietnam was based on the **domino theory**. President Eisenhower first expressed the domino theory. It proposed that one country falling to Communist influence would quickly lead to other countries in the same area falling as well. He feared that if South Vietnam became Communist, then the rest of Southeast Asia would be vulnerable. Kennedy was determined to stop that.

After Kennedy's death in 1963, his successor, **Lyndon Baines Johnson**, continued the policies he had begun. Like Kennedy, Johnson was determined to contain communism in Vietnam. During his term, however, the conflict in Vietnam escalated. Johnson sent tens of thousands of soldiers to Vietnam. When Johnson left office in 1969, the struggle against communism in Vietnam was still going on.

Reading Check
Summarize What was the goal of the doctrine of flexible response?`

Crises over Cuba

Another test of Kennedy's foreign policy came in Cuba, just 90 miles off the coast of Florida. About two weeks before Kennedy took office, on January 3, 1961, President Eisenhower had cut off diplomatic relations with Cuba because of a revolutionary leader named **Fidel Castro**. Castro openly declared himself a Communist and welcomed aid from the Soviet Union.

Vocabulary
guerrilla a soldier who travels in a small group, harassing and undermining the enemy

political repression government intimidation of those with different political views

THE CUBAN REVOLUTION Castro gained power with the promise of democracy. From 1956 to 1959 he led a guerrilla movement to overthrow dictator Fulgencio Batista. Castro won control in 1959. He later told reporters, "Revolutionaries are not born, they are made by poverty, inequality, and dictatorship." Castro then promised to eliminate these conditions from Cuba.

Although the United States was suspicious of Castro's intentions, it did recognize the new government. However, when Castro seized three American and British oil refineries, relations between the United States and Cuba worsened. Castro also broke up commercial farms into communes that would be worked by formerly landless peasants. American sugar companies controlled 75 percent of the cropland in Cuba. They appealed to the U.S. government for help. In response, Congress established trade barriers against Cuban sugar.

To put his reforms into action, Castro relied increasingly on Soviet aid. He also depended on using political repression on those who did not agree with him. Some Cubans were impressed by his charisma and his willingness to stand up to the United States. Others saw Castro as a tyrant who had replaced one dictatorship with another. About 10 percent of Cuba's population went into exile. Most went to the United States. By 1962 more than 200,000 Cubans had fled their homeland for new homes in the United States. The majority

Castro celebrates after gaining power in Cuba.

of these Cuban exiles settled in Florida, especially in and around the city of Miami. Many hoped that the political turmoil in Cuba would be resolved quickly so that they could return home. That did not happen, however, and most never went back.

THE BAY OF PIGS With Castro in power, American policymakers became alarmed by a Communist government so close to the United States. In March 1960 President Eisenhower gave the CIA permission to secretly train Cuban exiles for an invasion of Cuba. The CIA and the exiles hoped it would cause a mass uprising that would overthrow Castro.

Kennedy learned of the plan only nine days after his election. Although he had doubts about the operation, he approved it anyway. On the night of April 17, 1961, some 1,300 to 1,500 Cuban exiles supported by the U.S. military landed on the island's southern coast at Bahía de Cochinos, the Bay of Pigs. Nothing went as planned. An air strike had failed to knock out the Cuban air force, although the CIA reported that it had succeeded. A small advance group sent to distract Castro's forces never reached shore. When the main unit landed, it lacked American air support as it faced 25,000 Cuban troops backed up by Soviet tanks and jets. Some of the invading exiles were killed, others imprisoned.

Castro turned the failed invasion into a public relations victory. The Cuban media announced the defeat of "North American mercenaries." One United States commentator said that Americans "look like fools to our friends, rascals to our enemies, and incompetents to the rest." The disaster left Kennedy embarrassed. Publicly, he accepted blame for the failure. Privately, he asked, "How could that crowd at the CIA and the Pentagon be this wrong?"

Kennedy negotiated with Castro for the release of surviving commandos and paid a ransom of $53 million in food and medical supplies. In a speech in Miami, he promised exiles that they would one day return to a "free Havana." Kennedy warned that he would resist further Communist expansion in the Western Hemisphere. However, Castro defiantly welcomed further Soviet aid.

The Bay of Pigs mission was said to have blown up in Kennedy's face.

THE CUBAN MISSILE CRISIS Castro had a powerful ally in Moscow. Soviet premier Nikita Khrushchev promised to defend Cuba with Soviet arms. During the summer of 1962, the flow of Soviet weapons to Cuba increased greatly. These weapons included nuclear missiles. President Kennedy responded with a warning that America would not tolerate offensive nuclear weapons in Cuba. Then, on October 14, photographs taken by American U-2 planes revealed Soviet missile bases in Cuba. Some contained missiles ready to launch. They could reach U.S. cities in minutes.

On October 22 Kennedy spoke to an anxious nation. He told Americans about the Soviet missile sites in Cuba and his plans to remove them. He made it clear that any missile attack from Cuba would trigger an attack on the Soviet Union.

Cuban Missile Crisis, October 1962

Legend:
- Missile complex
- Possible missile path
- Range of quarantine
- U.S. military installation

0   200   400 mi
0   200   400 km

2,000 MILES (17 MINUTES)
1,500 MILES (15 MINUTES)
1,898 MILES
1,000 MILES (12 MINUTES)
1,554 MILES
1,432 MILES
1,259 MILES
837 MILES
1,020 MILES

Denver
Chicago
New York
Washington, DC
UNITED STATES
Atlanta
Houston
Havana
CUBA
Guantanamo

PACIFIC OCEAN
ATLANTIC OCEAN
Gulf of Mexico
Tropic of Cancer
Caribbean Sea

40°N
30°N
110°W
90°W
80°W

OCT. 24 Kennedy implements a naval "quarantine" of Cuba, blocking Soviet ships from reaching the island. A U.S. patrol plane flies over a Soviet freighter.

OCT. 28 Khrushchev announces plan to remove missiles from Cuba.

OCT. 14 U.S. spy planes reveal nuclear missile sites in Cuba.

MISSILE EQUIPMENT
MARIEL PORT FACILITY
4 NOVEMBER 1962

OCT. 22 Kennedy tells the nation of his intention to halt the missile buildup.

OCT. 25 Soviet ships approaching Cuba come to a halt.

Interpret Maps

1. **Movement** About how long would it have taken for a missile launched from Cuba to reach New York?

2. **Human-Environment Interaction** Why do you think it may have been important for Soviet missiles to reach the U.S. cities shown above?

For the next six days, the world faced the terrifying possibility of imminent nuclear war. Soviet ships in the Atlantic Ocean headed toward Cuba. They presumably were carrying more missiles. The U.S. Navy prepared to quarantine Cuba and prevent the ships from coming within 500 miles of it. In Florida, 100,000 troops waited. This was the largest invasion force ever assembled in the United States. C. Douglas Dillon was Kennedy's secretary of the treasury and a veteran of nuclear diplomacy. He recalled those tension-filled days of October.

"The only time I felt a fear of nuclear war or a use of nuclear weapons was on the very first day, when we'd decided that we had to do whatever was necessary to get the missiles out. There was always some background fear of what would eventually happen, and I think this is what was expressed when people said they feared they would never see another Saturday."

—C. Douglas Dillon, quoted in *On the Brink*

— BIOGRAPHY

John F. Kennedy (1917–1963)

John F. "Jack" Kennedy grew up in a politically powerful family that helped make his dreams possible. His parents instilled in him the drive to accomplish great things.

During World War II, he enlisted in the navy and was decorated for heroism. In 1946 he won his first seat in Congress from a Boston district where he had never lived. While a senator, he won a Pulitzer Prize for his book *Profiles in Courage*.

Although he radiated self-confidence, Kennedy suffered many ailments, including Addison's disease—a debilitating condition that he treated with daily injections of cortisone. "At least one half of the days that he spent on this earth were days of intense physical pain," recalled his younger brother Robert.

Nikita Khrushchev (1894–1971)

"No matter how humble a man's beginnings," boasted Nikita Khrushchev, "he achieves the stature of the office to which he is elected." Khrushchev, the son of a miner, became a Communist Party organizer in the 1920s. Within four years of Stalin's death in 1953, Khrushchev had consolidated his own political power in the Soviet Union.

During his regime, which ended in 1964, Khrushchev kept American nerves on edge with alternately conciliatory and aggressive behavior. During a 1959 trip to the United States, he met for friendly talks with President Eisenhower. The next year, in front of the UN General Assembly, he took off his shoe and angrily pounded it on a desk to protest the U-2 incident.

The first break in the crisis occurred when the Soviet ships stopped suddenly to avoid a confrontation at sea. Secretary of State Dean Rusk said, "We are eyeball to eyeball, and the other fellow just blinked." A few days later, Khrushchev offered to remove the missiles in return for an American pledge not to invade Cuba. The United States also secretly agreed to remove missiles from Turkey. The leaders agreed, and the crisis ended. "For a moment, the world had stood still," Robert Kennedy wrote years later, "and now it was going around again."

KENNEDY AND KHRUSHCHEV TAKE THE HEAT The crisis severely damaged Khrushchev's prestige in the Soviet Union and the world. Kennedy did not escape criticism, either. Some people criticized Kennedy for practicing brinkmanship. They thought that private talks might have resolved the crisis without the threat of nuclear war. Others believed he had passed up an ideal chance to invade Cuba and oust Castro. (It was learned in the 1990s that the CIA had underestimated the numbers of Soviet troops and nuclear weapons on the island.)

The effects of the crisis lasted long after the missiles had been removed. Many Cuban exiles blamed the Democrats for "losing Cuba" and switched their allegiance to the Republican Party. Kennedy had earlier made the same charge against the Republicans.

Meanwhile, Castro closed Cuba's doors to the exiles in November 1962. He banned all flights to and from Miami. Three years later, hundreds of thousands of people took advantage of an agreement that allowed Cubans to join relatives in the United States. By the time Castro sharply cut down on exit permits in 1973, the Cuban population in Miami had increased to about 300,000 people.

Reading Check
Analyze Causes
What led to the Cuban missile crisis?

U.S.-Soviet Tensions

One goal had guided Kennedy through the Cuban missile crisis. That goal was to prove to Khrushchev his determination to contain communism. All the while, Kennedy was thinking of their recent confrontation over Berlin. That confrontation had led to the construction of the **Berlin Wall**, a concrete wall topped with barbed wire that divided the city in two.

THE BERLIN CRISIS In 1961 Berlin was a city in great turmoil. In the 11 years since the Berlin Airlift, almost 3 million East Germans had fled into West Berlin because it was free from Communist rule. These refugees represented 20 percent of East Germany's population. They demonstrated the failure of that country's Communist government. Their departure also dangerously weakened East Germany's economy.

Khrushchev realized that this problem had to be solved. At a summit meeting in Vienna, Austria, in June 1961, he threatened to sign a treaty with East Germany. The treaty would enable that country to close all the access roads to West Berlin. Kennedy refused to give up U.S. access to West Berlin. Khrushchev furiously responded, "I want peace. But, if you want war, that is your problem."

After returning home, Kennedy spoke to the nation in a televised address. He said that Berlin was "the great testing place of Western courage and will." He pledged "We cannot and will not permit the Communists to drive us out of Berlin."

Kennedy's determination and America's superior nuclear striking power prevented Khrushchev from closing the air and land routes between West Berlin and West Germany. Instead, the Soviet premier surprised the world with a shocking decision. Just after midnight on August 13, 1961, East German troops began to unload concrete posts and rolls of barbed wire along the border. Within days, the Berlin Wall was erected, separating East Germany from West Germany. The wall isolated West Berlin from a hostile German Democratic Republic (GDR). Passing from East to West was almost impossible without the Communist government's permission.

During the 28 years the wall was standing, approximately 5,000 people succeeded in fleeing. Almost 200 people died in the attempt. Most were shot by the GDR border guards.

The construction of the Berlin Wall ended the Berlin crisis, but it heightened Cold War tensions. The wall and its armed guards successfully reduced the flow of East German refugees to a tiny trickle. This solved Khrushchev's main problem. At the same time, however, the wall became an ugly symbol of Communist oppression.

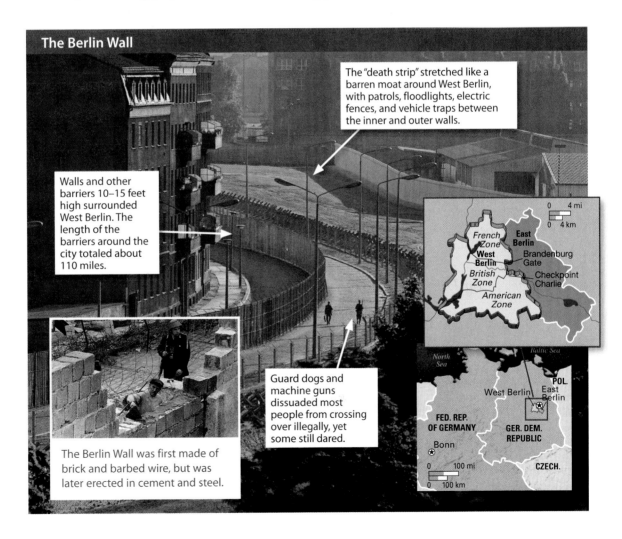

The Berlin Wall

The "death strip" stretched like a barren moat around West Berlin, with patrols, floodlights, electric fences, and vehicle traps between the inner and outer walls.

Walls and other barriers 10–15 feet high surrounded West Berlin. The length of the barriers around the city totaled about 110 miles.

Guard dogs and machine guns dissuaded most people from crossing over illegally, yet some still dared.

The Berlin Wall was first made of brick and barbed wire, but was later erected in cement and steel.

French Zone
East Berlin
West Berlin
Brandenburg Gate
British Zone
Checkpoint Charlie
American Zone

0   4 mi
0   4 km

North Sea
Baltic Sea
POL.
West Berlin
East Berlin
FED. REP. OF GERMANY
GER. DEM. REPUBLIC
Bonn
CZECH.

0   100 mi
0   100 km

EFFORTS TO EASE TENSIONS Showdowns like Cuba and Berlin made both Kennedy and Khrushchev aware of the seriousness of split-second decisions that separated peace from nuclear disaster. A rash decision or unfortunate hesitation could lead to global catastrophe.

Faced with this realization, Kennedy searched for ways to tone down his hardline position. In 1963 he announced that the two nations had established a **hot line** between the White House and the Kremlin. This dedicated phone enabled the leaders of the two countries to communicate immediately should another crisis arise. Later that year, the United States and the Soviet Union also agreed to a **Limited Test Ban Treaty**. The treaty banned nuclear testing in the atmosphere.

The Limited Test Ban Treaty was a good beginning to easing nuclear fears. However, both American and Soviet leaders believed more steps were necessary to prevent catastrophe. Over the next few years, more treaties were signed to limit nuclear activity. For example, a 1967 treaty banned the deployment of nuclear weapons in space and on the moon. This had been a common fear as the space race continued.

Document-Based Investigation Historical Source

Ich Bin ein Berliner

Two years after the construction of the Berlin Wall, President Kennedy traveled to West Berlin to renew his commitment to the city. In a famous speech, he praised the spirit of the city's people. He also declared the Berlin Wall a symbol of communism's weakness.

Reading from this note card during a speech in West Berlin, Kennedy proclaimed "Ich bin ein Berliner" ("I am a Berliner").

"There are many people who really don't understand, or say they don't, what is the great issue between the free world and the Communist world. Let them come to Berlin. There are some who say that communism is the wave of the future. Let them come to Berlin. And there are some who say in Europe and elsewhere we can work with the Communists. Let them come to Berlin. . . . When all are free, then we can look forward to that day when this city will be joined as one. . . . All free men, wherever they may live, are citizens of Berlin, and, therefore, as a free man, I take pride in the words 'Ich bin ein Berliner!"

—John F. Kennedy, from a speech in Berlin, June 26, 1963

Analyze Historical Sources

1. Why does Kennedy repeatedly call on people to visit Berlin?

2. What does Kennedy seek to accomplish by calling himself a Berliner?

During the 1950s and 1960s, the buildup of nuclear weapons led to worldwide fears.

Reading Check
Analyze Motives
What led Khrushchev to erect the Berlin Wall?

By the late 1960s the fear of nuclear catastrophe had spread around the world. The United States and the Soviet Union were no longer the only countries capable of launching nuclear attacks. The United Kingdom, France, and China had all successfully tested nuclear weapons by 1964. As the number of nuclear-capable countries increased, so did fears of global disaster. Some world leaders were concerned about the idea of nuclear weapons in the hands of developing nations, especially those not influenced by either side in the Cold War. Such nations would not be kept in check by Cold War rivalries. In addition, many were involved in bitter border disputes with their neighbors. These disputes could invite a preemptive attack.

To help reduce some of these fears, world leaders agreed to take steps to limit the spread of nuclear weapons. In 1968 representatives from more than 60 countries signed the **Nuclear Non-Proliferation Treaty (NPT)**. Signers included both the United States and the Soviet Union. Under this treaty, nuclear powers agreed not to sell or give nuclear weapons to any other country. Nonnuclear powers promised not to develop or acquire such weapons. The NPT did not completely end the spread of nuclear weapons. Some countries refused to sign it, and some of those, including India and Pakistan, eventually developed their own weapons. But the treaty was a significant step toward relieving some of the world's fears of total destruction.

The Space Race Continues

While American diplomats were trying to soothe hostilities with Soviet leaders, scientists were hard at work challenging Soviet technological advances. In the 1950s the Soviets had launched the first artificial satellite. Americans soon matched this feat. Then, on April 12, 1961, Soviet cosmonaut Yuri A. Gagarin became the first human in space. Kennedy saw this as a challenge. He grew determined to surpass the Soviets by sending a man to the moon.

In less than a month, the United States had also successfully launched a man into space: astronaut Alan Shepard. Later that year, a communications satellite called *Telstar* relayed live television pictures across the Atlantic Ocean from Maine to Europe. Meanwhile, America's National Aeronautics and Space Administration (NASA) had begun new construction projects. It built new launch facilities at Cape Canaveral, Florida, and a mission control center in Houston, Texas. America's pride and prestige were restored. Speaking before a crowd at Houston's Rice University, Kennedy expressed the spirit of "the space race."

"We choose to go to the moon in this decade and do the other things, not because they are easy, but because they are hard, because that goal will serve to organize and measure the best of our energies and skills, because that challenge is one that we are willing to accept, one we are unwilling to postpone, and one which we intend to win, and the others, too."

—John F. Kennedy, from his address on the nation's space effort, September 12, 1962

Seven years later, the United States would achieve its goal. However, Kennedy himself would not live to see it. Early on the morning of July 16, 1969, more than 5,000 dignitaries and reporters gathered at Cape Canaveral's Kennedy Space Center. They witnessed the beginning of the first flight to the moon. Nearly half a million more people flocked to the fields around the site, hoping to see the historic event. Following the successful launch, oversight of the mission shifted to Houston, Texas. Technicians there monitored the craft's progress.

Four days later on July 20, an excited nation sat glued to its televisions. Americans watched as U.S. astronaut Neil Armstrong climbed down the ladder of his lunar module and stepped onto the surface of the moon. "That's one small step for man," Armstrong said, "one giant leap for mankind." Americans swelled with pride as they watched the historic moon landing on their televisions. President Richard Nixon, who had taken office a few months earlier, spoke to the astronauts from the White House. He said, "For every American, this has to be the proudest day of our lives."

As a result of the space program, universities expanded their science programs. The huge federal funding for research and development gave rise to new industries and new technologies. Many could be used in business and industry and also in new consumer goods. Space- and defense-related industries sprang up in the southern and western states, which grew rapidly.

Reading Check
Analyze Causes
How did the Cold War help bring about the space race?

Lesson 5 Assessment

1. **Organize Information** Use a series of web diagrams to list two outcomes for each of these events: the Bay of Pigs invasion, the Cuban missile crisis, and construction of the Berlin Wall.

Which of these outcomes led directly to other events listed here or described in this lesson?

2. **Key Terms and People** For each key term or person in the lesson, write a sentence explaining its significance.

3. **Evaluate** How well do you think President Kennedy handled the Cuban missile crisis? Justify your opinion with specific examples from the text.

Think About:

• Kennedy's decision to impose a naval "quarantine" of Cuba

• the nuclear showdown between the superpowers

• Kennedy's decision not to invade Cuba

4. **Analyze Primary Sources** Examine the cartoon above of Kennedy *(left)* facing off with Khrushchev and Castro. What do you think the cartoonist was trying to convey?

5. **Draw Conclusions** What kind of political statement was made by the United States' support of West Berlin?

The End of the Cold War

The Big Idea

Changes in foreign policy beginning with the Nixon administration gradually led to an easing of U.S.-Soviet tensions and an end to the Cold War.

Why It Matters Now

The end of the Cold War led to more open political and economic ties between the United States and the Soviet Union, despite some continued differences.

Key Terms and People

Richard Nixon

Henry Kissinger

realpolitik

détente

SALT I Treaty

Gerald Ford

Jimmy Carter

Ronald Reagan

Mikhail Gorbachev

Strategic Defense Initiative

glasnost

perestroika

Intermediate-Range Nuclear Forces (INF) Treaty

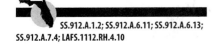

SS.912.A.1.2; SS.912.A.6.11; SS.912.A.6.13; SS.912.A.7.4; LAFS.1112.RH.4.10

One American's Story

Colin Powell did not start out in life with any special privileges. Born in Harlem and raised in the Bronx, he only tolerated school. Then, while attending the City College of New York, he joined the Reserve Officer Training Corps (ROTC). He got straight A's in ROTC, and so he decided to make the army his career.

Powell served in several Cold War hotspots, first in Vietnam and then in Korea and West Germany. He rose in rank to become a general; then President Reagan made him national security advisor. In this post, Powell noted that the Soviet Union was a factor in all the administration's foreign policy decisions.

General Colin Powell

"Our choosing sides in conflicts around the world was almost always decided on the basis of East–West competition. The new Soviet leader, Mikhail Gorbachev, however, was turning the old Cold War formulas on their head. . . . Ronald Reagan . . . had the vision and flexibility, lacking in many knee-jerk Cold Warriors, to recognize that Gorbachev was a new man in a new age offering new opportunities for peace."

— Colin Powell, from *My American Journey*

After nearly 50 years of tension between the United States and the Soviet Union, Powell was witnessing the end of the Cold War. Though U.S. foreign policy in the early 1980s was marked by intense hostility toward the Soviet Union, economic problems destroyed the Soviets' ability to continue the standoff.

Nixon's Foreign Policy Triumphs

Although the Cold War finally wound down in the late 1980s and early 1990s, tensions still ran high when **Richard Nixon** became president in 1969. Throughout his presidency, Nixon's foreign policy focused on soothing Cold War tension. His top priority was gaining an honorable peace in Vietnam. At the same time, he also made significant advances in America's relationships with China and the Soviet Union.

KISSINGER AND REALPOLITIK The architect of Nixon's foreign policy was his adviser for national security affairs, **Henry Kissinger**. Kissinger, who would later become Nixon's secretary of state, promoted a philosophy known as **realpolitik** (rā-äl'pō'lĭ-tēk'), from a German term meaning "political realism." According to realpolitik, foreign policy should be based solely on consideration of power, not ideals or moral principles.

Kissinger believed in evaluating a nation's power, not its philosophy or beliefs. If a country was weak, Kissinger argued, it was often more practical to ignore that country, even if it was Communist. This marked a departure from the former policy of containment, which refused to recognize the major Communist countries. On the other hand, Kissinger's philosophy called for the United States to confront powerful nations. In realpolitik, however, confrontation meant negotiation as well as military engagement.

Nixon shared Kissinger's belief in realpolitik. Together the two adopted a more flexible approach in dealing with Communist nations. They called their policy **détente**—a policy aimed at easing Cold War tensions. One of the most startling applications of détente came in early 1972 when Nixon—who had risen in politics as a strong anti-Communist—visited Communist China.

NIXON VISITS CHINA Since the Communist takeover of mainland China in 1949, the United States had not formally recognized the Chinese Communist government. In late 1971 Nixon decided to reverse that policy. He announced that he would visit China "to seek the normalization of relations between the two countries."

President Nixon tours the Great Wall as part of his visit to China in 1972.

Kissinger on Détente

Under President Richard Nixon and Secretary of State Henry Kissinger, the focus of U.S. foreign policy shifted from containment to détente. Kissinger offered a clear explanation of what this policy meant while visiting China in 1975.

Analyze Historical Sources
How does Kissinger's description of détente differ from earlier Cold War foreign policies?

"The differences between us are apparent. Our task is not to intensify those differences. Our task is to advance our relationship on the basis of our mutual interests. Such a relationship would strengthen each of us. It would threaten no one and it would contribute to the well-being of all peoples. . . . Each country must pursue a policy suitable to its own circumstances. . . . In this policy we will be guided by actions and realities and not rhetoric."

—Henry Kissinger, from a toast to Chinese officials, October 19, 1975

By going to China, Nixon was trying, in part, to take advantage of the decade-long rift between China and the Soviet Union. China had long criticized the Soviet Union as being too "soft" in its policies against the West. The two Communist superpowers officially broke ties in 1960. Nixon had thought about exploiting the broken relationship for several years. "We want to have the Chinese with us when we sit down and negotiate with the Russians," he told a reporter in 1968. Upon his arrival at the Beijing Airport in February 1972, Nixon recalls his meeting with Chinese premier Zhou Enlai.

"I knew that Zhou had been deeply insulted by Foster Dulles's refusal to shake hands with him at the Geneva Conference in 1954. When I reached the bottom step, therefore, I made a point of extending my hand as I walked toward him. When our hands met, one era ended and another began."

—Richard M. Nixon, from *The Memoirs of Richard Nixon*

Besides its enormous symbolic value, Nixon's visit also was a huge success with the American public. U.S. television crews flooded American living rooms with film clips of Nixon at the Great Wall of China, at the Imperial Palace, and even toasting top Communist leaders at state dinners.

Observers noted that Nixon's visit opened up diplomatic and economic relations with the Chinese and resulted in important agreements between China and the United States. The two nations agreed that neither would try to dominate the Pacific and that both would henceforth cooperate in settling disputes peacefully. They also agreed to participate in scientific and cultural exchanges. In addition, the United States recognized Taiwan as a part of mainland China and promised to eventually withdraw American forces from the island.

During the Cold War, the Soviet Union regularly displayed its military strength in parades. Shown here is an ICBM in a 1965 parade through Moscow's Red Square.

NIXON TRAVELS TO MOSCOW In May 1972, three months after visiting Beijing, President Nixon headed to Moscow. He was the first U.S. president ever to visit the Soviet Union. By the time he arrived for a summit meeting with Soviet premier Leonid Brezhnev, relations with the Soviet Union had already warmed. In 1971 the two nations reached an agreement about Berlin. The Soviets promised to guarantee Western nations free access to West Berlin and to respect the city's independence. In return, the Western allies agreed to officially recognize East Germany.

Like his visit to China, Nixon's trip to the Soviet Union received wide approval. Nixon and Brezhnev held a series of meetings called the Strategic Arms Limitation Talks. Then they signed the **SALT I Treaty**. This five-year agreement limited the number of intercontinental ballistic missiles (ICBMs) and submarine-launched missiles to 1972 levels. It appeared that Nixon's policy of détente was helping to slow the arms race.

The foreign policy triumphs with China and the Soviet Union helped reelect Nixon as president in 1972. So did the administration's announcement that peace "is at hand" in Vietnam. But peace in Vietnam proved elusive. The Nixon administration grappled with the war for nearly six more months before withdrawing troops and ending America's involvement in Vietnam.

COLD WAR HOTSPOTS UNDER NIXON While the attention of most Americans was focused on events in Asia, President Nixon also kept a wary eye on developments in South America and the Middle East.

In 1970 the people of Chile elected Marxist candidate Salvador Allende (ä-yĕn′dä) president. Allende's election alarmed Nixon and his advisers, who feared that he would introduce communism to Chile. To prevent such a development, the CIA began covert operations, secretly providing funding and training to opposition groups in Chile, including some units of the Chilean military. On September 11, 1973, the military rebelled, killing Allende and more than 3,000 others. General Augusto Pinochet (pĕ′nō-chĕt′), who was staunchly opposed to socialism, was named Chile's new president.

Also in 1973 Nixon sent military aid to Israel, which had been invaded by forces from Syria and Egypt. This was not the first time the United States had helped Israel defend against its neighbors. In the 1960s President Johnson had sold tanks and aircraft to the Israeli military to offset aid the Soviets had given to Israel's Arab neighbors. When war broke out between Israel and its neighbors in 1967, the United States did not actively take part. It did, however, attempt to negotiate a cease-fire. Johnson feared that continued hostilities in the region would force the Soviet Union to come to the aid of its Arab allies, potentially beginning a major world conflict.

Like Johnson had before, Nixon feared that Israeli conflict would lead to direct confrontation with the Soviets. Although the United States supplied massive amounts of military aid to Israel, U.S. officials also worked to broker a cease-fire between the warring nations. In what became known as "shuttle diplomacy," Secretary of State Kissinger traveled back and forth between Middle Eastern countries in an attempt to forge a peace agreement. His efforts eventually paid off. Israel signed a cease-fire with Egypt in January 1974. Four months later, it signed another with Syria.

Reading Check
Analyze Effects
How did Nixon's trip change the U.S. relationship with China?

Ford Confronts the Cold War

Nixon resigned as president in 1974 amid political scandal, making **Gerald Ford** president. Ford mostly continued on the path Nixon had begun, relying heavily on the assistance of Secretary of State Kissinger.

President Ford signs the Helsinki Accords, August 1, 1975.

CONTINUING NIXON'S FOREIGN POLICIES Following Kissinger's advice, Ford pushed ahead with Nixon's policy of negotiation with China and the Soviet Union. In November 1974 he met with Soviet premier Brezhnev. Less than a year later, he traveled to Helsinki, Finland, where 35 nations, including the Soviet Union, signed the Helsinki Accords—a series of agreements that promised greater cooperation between the nations of Eastern and Western Europe. The Helsinki Accords would be Ford's greatest presidential accomplishment.

ONGOING TURMOIL IN SOUTHEAST ASIA Like presidents before him, Ford encountered trouble in Southeast Asia. The 1973 cease-fire in Vietnam had broken down. Heavy fighting resumed, and Ford asked Congress for over $722 million to help South Vietnam. Congress refused. Without American financial help, South Vietnam surrendered to the North in 1975.

Also in 1975 the Communist government of Cambodia seized the U.S. merchant ship *Mayagüez* in the Gulf of Siam. President Ford responded with a massive show of military force. He ordered air strikes against Cambodia.

He also sent an elite team of U.S. Marines to rescue 39 crew members aboard the ship. The operation cost the lives of 41 U.S. troops. Most Americans applauded the action as evidence of the country's strength. However, critics argued that the mission had cost more lives than it had saved. They also argued that the president had acted without consulting Congress.

CRISIS IN AFRICA In late 1974 the Ford administration was faced with a new crisis far from Vietnam. American forces became involved in a civil war in Angola, a country in southern Africa. Newly independent from Portuguese control, Angola was nominally governed by three political organizations working together. Each organization wanted power for itself, however, and the country soon fell into civil war.

The struggle in Angola soon became an international affair. World superpowers took sides in the conflict, lending aid to opposing factions. The United States supported two of the three warring factions, while the Soviet Union and China backed the third. The Soviet-backed forces quickly drove their opponents from the capital. Ford requested additional funds to provide more aid to the Angola rebels, but Congress, unwilling to get involved in another foreign war so soon after Vietnam, refused. A Marxist government took control of the country.

Reading Check Summarize Why did American forces become involved in events in Cambodia and Angola?

The Angola crisis put a new strain on U.S.-Soviet relations during a period when the relationship between the two countries seemed to be thawing. The conflict in Angola, especially coming as it did on the heels of Vietnam, led many to believe détente would not be a successful strategy for dealing with the Soviet Union. Many began to call for a new foreign policy.

A New Direction Under Carter

Gerald Ford ran for reelection in 1976. He was defeated by Democrat **Jimmy Carter**. Carter was inexperienced in national politics and had no previous foreign policy experience. However, he did have a sincere devotion to human rights. This became the cornerstone of his actions as president. This devotion strained relations between Carter and Soviet leaders and necessitated changes in foreign policy.

THE COLLAPSE OF DÉTENTE When Jimmy Carter took office, détente had reached a high point. There was a relaxation of tensions between the world's superpowers. It had begun with President Nixon and continued with President Ford. U.S. officials had worked to ease relations with the Communist superpowers of China and the Soviet Union.

However, Carter's firm insistence on human rights led to a breakdown in relations with the Soviet Union. President Carter was unhappy about the Soviet Union's treatment of dissidents, or opponents of the government's policies. He delayed a second round of SALT negotiations. President Carter and Soviet premier Leonid Brezhnev finally met in June 1979 in Vienna, Austria. There they signed an agreement known as SALT II. The agreement did not reduce armaments. However, it did limit the number of strategic weapons and nuclear-missile launchers that each side could produce.

The SALT II agreement met sharp opposition in the Senate. Critics argued that it would put the United States at a military disadvantage. Then, in December 1979 the Soviets invaded the neighboring country of Afghanistan. This action struck a major blow to U.S.-Soviet relations.

THE SOVIET-AFGHAN WAR Afghanistan is an Islamic country along the southern border of the Soviet Union. It had been run by a Communist, pro-Soviet government for a number of years. However, a strong Muslim rebel group known as the *mujahideen* was intent on overthrowing the Afghan government. The Soviet Union feared a rebel victory in Afghanistan. It sent troops to Afghanistan in late 1979. The rebels used guerrilla tactics and their knowledge of the country's mountainous landscape. The Soviets had superior weaponry, but the rebels fought them to a stalemate.

When President Carter heard of the invasion, he activated the seldom-used White House-Kremlin hot line. He protested to Brezhnev that his actions posed a serious threat to world peace. As a result of the invasion, Carter withdrew his support for the SALT II agreement, and the treaty died.

Soviet military helicopters and tanks patrol in Afghanistan several years after the 1979 invasion.

Reading Check
Analyze Causes
What led to the collapse of détente with the Soviet Union?

Several days later, Carter outlined the American response to the Soviet invasion. He called the invasion a "gross interference in the internal affairs of Afghanistan." He said that the United States would block all exports of grain to the Soviet Union. In addition, the United States would boycott the 1980 Olympics, which were to be held in Moscow. Both the grain embargo and the Olympic boycott proved to be unpopular with the public. Many Americans felt that these actions punished Americans as much as they hurt the Soviets. They also argued that the government's response made both Carter and the country appear weak.

Reagan and the End of the Cold War

Carter served only one term as president. **Ronald Reagan** was elected in 1980 on a platform that included staunch opposition to communism. Yet as president, Reagan helped bring about the end of the Cold War. During his administration, Reagan developed a complex relationship with **Mikhail Gorbachev**. Gorbachev became the general secretary of the Communist Party in the Soviet Union in March 1985. Gorbachev's rise to power marked the beginning of a new era in the Soviet Union.

REAGAN AND COMMUNISM As president, Reagan rejected the policy of détente. He was not interested in accommodating communism. He wanted to utterly destroy it. In speeches, he referred to the Soviet Union as "the evil empire" and "the focus of evil in the modern world."

To support his anti-Soviet foreign policy, Reagan greatly increased the U.S. defense budget. In part, he hoped that any effort to match his spending would bankrupt the struggling Soviets. During his first term in office, the Pentagon's annual budget grew by almost 25 percent. Much of the new spending he authorized went toward new weapons systems. In 1981 Reagan announced plans to add thousands of nuclear warheads to the U.S. arsenal. He revived two discontinued weapons systems—the MX missile and the B-1 bomber.

In 1983 Reagan asked U.S. scientists to develop a special defense system to keep Americans safe from missiles. Officially called the **Strategic Defense Initiative**, or SDI, it quickly became known as Star Wars. With a projected price tag of trillions of dollars, SDI immediately met with opposition. Opponents, including many scientists, argued that the system would not work.

Reagan's hardline anti-Communist position and increased defense spending worsened U.S.-Soviet relations during his first term. For example, Soviet leaders saw SDI as an offensive weapon rather than a defensive one. They said that it would allow the United States to launch a nuclear strike without fear of retaliation. The Soviets ended arms control talks and boycotted the 1984 Olympic Games in Los Angeles. Reagan's policies also drew criticism from Americans. Hundreds of thousands of protesters marched in demonstrations. They called for a nuclear freeze, a halt in the production of nuclear weapons. Critics feared that Reagan's aggressive position could provoke a nuclear war.

However, Reagan's position also gained him support from some Americans and from like-minded world leaders. These included conservative British prime minister Margaret Thatcher and Polish-born Pope John Paul II. Like Reagan, they believed the Soviet Union was devoted to global conquest.

GORBACHEV INITIATES REFORM Within the Soviet Union, however, leaders were more focused on internal issues. When he took control in 1985, Gorbachev had inherited a host of problems. Many of them revolved around the Soviet economy, which was under a great amount of stress. Reagan added pressure by increasing U.S. defense spending. When the Soviets tried to keep up, their economy was pushed to the brink of collapse.

A skilled diplomat and politician, Gorbachev promoted a policy known as *glasnost* (Russian for "openness"). He allowed open criticism of the Soviet government and granted limited freedom of the press. In 1985 he outlined his plans for *perestroika*, a restructuring of Soviet society. He called for less government control of the economy and the introduction of some private enterprise. He also took steps toward establishing a democratic government.

IMPROVED U.S.-SOVIET RELATIONS Gorbachev recognized that better relations with the United States would allow the Soviets to reduce their military spending and reform their economy. Realizing that Gorbachev represented a dramatic change in Soviet leadership, Reagan was also willing to negotiate. Between 1985 and 1988 the two leaders met four times to discuss the future of relations between their countries.

President Reagan *(right)* and Gorbachev sign the INF Treaty, which includes the strictest nuclear arms verification system up to that time.

The most obvious sign of the changing U.S.-Soviet relationship was the signing of the **Intermediate-Range Nuclear Forces (INF) Treaty** on December 8, 1987. The treaty eliminated two classes of weapons systems in Europe. It allowed each nation to make on-site inspections of the other's military installations. More than 2,500 missiles were destroyed under the treaty.

THE COLLAPSE OF COMMUNIST REGIMES As the leader of the Soviet Union, Gorbachev encouraged the people of East Germany and Eastern Europe to go their own ways. People in some Eastern European nations had been calling for increased freedom even before Gorbachev rose to power. In Poland, for example, workers had begun calling for economic change. In 1980 some 17,000 workers in the Polish city of Gdansk had locked themselves in a factory to protest rising food prices. The workers were led by Lech Walesa (wä-lĕn'sə). They wanted the Soviet-backed Polish government to recognize their labor union, called Solidarity. The protest inspired thousands of other workers throughout Poland. They also went on strike. Eventually, the government gave in. It officially recognized Solidarity as a union. To the people of Poland, this recognition represented much more than an economic victory. It was a first step toward freedom from Communist control.

Once in power, Gorbachev reduced the number of Soviet troops in Eastern Europe. He allowed non-Communist parties to organize in satellite nations, such as East Germany and Poland and encouraged these nations to move toward democracy. During a speech at the Berlin Wall in 1987, President Reagan challenged Gorbachev to back up his reforms with decisive action.

"General Secretary Gorbachev, if you seek peace, if you seek prosperity for the Soviet Union and Eastern Europe, if you seek liberalization: Come here to this gate! Mr. Gorbachev, open this gate! Mr. Gorbachev, tear down this wall!"

—Ronald Reagan, speech at the Brandenburg Gate, June 12, 1987

In October 1989 East Germans startled the world by rejecting their Communist government. At a celebration of the 40th anniversary of East Germany, protesters began calling for more freedom. "Gorby, help us!," they chanted, seeking more of Gorbachev's reforms.

On November 9, 1989, in an effort to calm rising protests, East German officials threw open the gates of the Berlin Wall. This allowed free passage between the two parts of the city for the first time in 28 years. East German border guards stood by and watched as Berliners from both sides pounded away with hammers and other tools—or with their bare hands—at the despised wall. Television signals carried images of the jubilant Germans around the world. In early 1990 East Germany held its first free elections. On October 3 of that year, less than a year after the wall came down, the two German nations were united.

Other European nations also adopted democratic reforms. Czechoslovakia withdrew from the Soviet bloc. Hungary, Bulgaria, and Romania made successful transitions from communism. The United States sought to help these countries in their transition away from Communist governments, promoting the growth of multiparty governments and market economies. After East Germany, Poland, and Czechoslovakia left the Warsaw Pact in 1990, the alliance dissolved within a year.

Yugoslavia, however, collapsed. Four of its six republics seceded. Ethnic rivalries deteriorated into a brutal war among Muslims, Orthodox Serbs, and Roman Catholic Croats, who were dividing Yugoslavia, each claiming parts of it. Serbia backed Serb minorities who were stirring up civil unrest in Croatia and Bosnia. Although President Bush tried to convince the various parties to avoid bloodshed and resolve their issues democratically, he was unsuccessful. The former Yugoslavia became embroiled in a civil war that would last for many years.

A demonstrator pounds away on the Berlin Wall as East German border guards look on from above at the Brandenburg Gate, on November 11, 1989.

This magazine cover marking the end of the Soviet Union depicts Vladimir Lenin, the founder of Soviet communism.

Reading Check
Evaluate Which evidence in the text supports the viewpoint that Gorbachev was a skilled politician and diplomat?

THE SOVIET UNION DECLINES Gorbachev's introduction of democratic ideals led to a dramatic increase in nationalism on the part of the Soviet Union's non-Russian republics. In December 1991, 14 non-Russian republics declared their independence from the Soviet Union. Muscled aside by Russian reformers who thought he was working too slowly toward democracy, Gorbachev resigned as Soviet president on December 25. After 74 years, the Soviet Union dissolved.

A loose federation known as the Commonwealth of Independent States (CIS) took the place of the Soviet Union. In February 1992 President George H. W. Bush and Russian president Boris Yeltsin met at Camp David to discuss the future of Russia and its neighbors. On behalf of the United States, Bush promised to aid Russia in its transition to democracy, and he pledged more than $4 billion in economic aid to help the Russian economy. At the conclusion of the meeting, the two leaders issued a formal statement declaring an end to the Cold War that had plagued the two nations and divided the world since 1945. In January 1993, Yeltsin and Bush signed the START II pact, designed to cut both nations' nuclear arsenals by two-thirds.

Upon his return to Russia, Yeltsin ended price controls and increased private business ownership. The Russian parliament opposed Yeltsin's policies, even though a majority of voters supported them.

In December 1993 Russian voters installed a new parliament and approved a new constitution, parts of which resembled the U.S. Constitution. In 1996 Yeltsin won reelection as president of Russia.

Lesson 6 Assessment

1. **Organize Information** Use a table to identify steps taken by Ronald Reagan and Mikhail Gorbachev that helped end the Cold War.

Reagan	Gorbachev
•	•
•	•
•	•

Which leader do you think was more responsible for ending the conflict? Support your answer.

2. **Key Terms and People** For each key term or person in the lesson, write a sentence explaining its significance.

3. **Analyze Causes** What factors caused the end of the Cold War?
Think About:
- events in the Soviet Union
- events in Germany and Eastern Europe
- how leaders responded to these events

4. **Draw Conclusions** Why were Nixon's foreign policy achievements particularly important?

5. **Evaluate** Do you think the United States was justified in supporting military efforts in places like Chile and Angola? Support your answer with evidence from the text.

6. **Form Generalizations** Is it possible for an authoritarian government to make economic reforms without also making political reforms? Support your answer with details from the text.

Module 12 Assessment

Key Terms and People

For each key term or person below, write a sentence explaining its significance to the Cold War.

1. containment
2. Central Intelligence Agency (CIA)
3. North Atlantic Treaty Organization (NATO)
4. Mao Zedong
5. Korean War
6. McCarthyism
7. John Foster Dulles
8. brinkmanship
9. Nikita Khrushchev
10. U-2 incident

Main Ideas

Use your notes and the information in the module to answer the following questions.

The Origins of the Cold War

1. What were the goals of U.S. foreign policy in the early Cold War?
2. What did Stalin do to make President Truman distrust him?
3. Describe the Truman Doctrine and how America reacted to it.
4. What was the purpose of the NATO alliance?
5. What necessitated the Berlin airlift?

The Cold War Heats Up

6. What global events led to U.S. involvement in Korea?
7. What constitutional issue arose when Truman ordered troops to Korea?
8. What issue between General Douglas MacArthur and President Truman eventually cost MacArthur his job?
9. How did the involvement of Communist China affect the Korean War?

The Cold War at Home

10. What actions of Joseph McCarthy worsened the national hysteria about communism?

11. How did the Rosenberg case fuel anti-Communist feelings?
12. How did McCarthyism affect public views of the government?

Two Nations Live on the Edge

13. What was the strategy behind the arms race?
14. Why did the Soviet Union form the Warsaw Pact?
15. What were the results of the Suez War?
16. How did the nuclear arms race affect life in the United States in the 1950s?
17. What was the role of the CIA in the Cold War?

Mounting Tensions in the Sixties

18. How did relations between the United States and Cuba change after the Cuban Revolution?
19. What were the most significant results of the Cuban missile crisis?
20. What goal did presidents Kennedy and Johnson have in sending U.S. troops to Vietnam? Did they attain that goal?
21. What steps did Kennedy and Khrushchev take to relieve tensions between their countries?
22. How did the world react to the growth of nuclear-capable countries in the 1960s?

The End of the Cold War

23. What was the philosophy of realpolitik?
24. What effects did the Soviet invasion of Afghanistan have on the United States? What was the American response to the invasion?
25. What caused the downfall of the Soviet Union and the founding of the Commonwealth of Independent States?
26. What events signaled that the Cold War had come to an end?
27. How did arms talks affect relations between the United States and the Soviet Union?

Critical Thinking

1. **Analyze Causes** List at least two causes for each of these events and explain how they relate to the event: (a) the United States' adoption of a policy of containment, and (b) the beginning of the nuclear arms race between the United States and the Soviet Union.

2. **Contrast** How did foreign policy in the early Cold War represent a shift in foreign policy from the period before World War II?

3. **Interpret Maps** Look carefully at the "Iron Curtain" map in Lesson 1. How did the absence of a natural barrier on the western border of the Soviet Union affect post–World War II Soviet foreign policy? Explain your answer.

4. **Form Generalizations** What role did the United Nations play in the Cold War?

5. **Summarize** What were the effects of the Marshall Plan on Western Europe?

6. **Synthesize** How did the Cold War lead to an expansion of government bureaucracy in the United States?

7. **Analyze Effects** How did the space race affect U.S.-Soviet relations during the Cold War? What other effects did it have?

8. **Evaluate** Consider the U.S. presidents from Richard Nixon to Ronald Reagan. Who do you think was most effective in resolving Cold War tensions? Who do you think was least effective? Support your answer.

9. **Form Generalizations** How did the policy of containment shape U.S. foreign policy in the Cold War?

10. **Analyze Events** What role did the United States play in the creation of Israel, and how did it affect foreign policy?

Engage with History

Suppose your best friend has been accused of being a Communist. You have been called to serve as a character witness for him or her. Write a speech that you will present to the House Un-American Activities Committee (HUAC). In your speech, explain why you feel that your friend's constitutional rights are being violated.

Focus on Writing

In a brief essay, trace the development of U.S. foreign policy over the course of the Cold War. Note major changes in approaches taken to fighting communism by various presidents during the period, and explain how each president built upon or rejected the policies of his predecessors.

Multimedia Activity

In a small group, discuss American fears of nuclear holocaust during the Cold War. Consider factors that worried citizens, such as the stockpiling of nuclear weapons, civil defense strategies based on retaliation and mutually assured destruction, and the Soviet development of missiles and *Sputnik*. With your group, create a multimedia presentation that highlights American concerns and the decisions that caused them. In addition, identify strategies that Americans developed to deal with the possibility of nuclear war.

OCTOBER FURY:
THE CUBAN MISSILE CRISIS

The Cuban missile crisis was perhaps the most dangerous event of the Cold War period. For several days in October 1962, the United States and the Soviet Union stood on the brink of nuclear war. The crisis began when the Soviet Union sent weapons, including nuclear missiles, to Cuba. It deepened when the United States blockaded Cuba to prevent the Soviets from delivering more missiles. With Soviet ships sailing toward the blockade, a confrontation seemed inevitable. However, at the last moment, the Soviet ships turned back and war was averted.

Explore the development and resolution of the Cuban missile crisis online. You can find a wealth of information, video clips, primary sources, activities, and more through your online textbook.

HISTORY

Go online to view these and other **HISTORY**® resources.

Prelude to Crisis

Watch the video to learn about the buildup to the Cuban missile crisis.

🎥 **Getting Ready for War**

Watch the video to see how the missiles in Cuba created tension between the United States and the Soviet Union.

🎥 **Crisis Averted?**

Watch the video to see how the Cuban missile crisis brought the United States and the Soviet Union to the brink of nuclear war.

🎥 **Lessons Learned**

Watch the video to learn about the impact of the Cuban missile crisis.

Module 13
The Postwar Boom

★

Essential Question
Were the 1950s a time of prosperity for all Americans?

About the Painting: During the 1950s the economy boomed and many Americans enjoyed prosperity. However, while affluent suburban homeowners lounged in the privacy of their backyards, millions of other Americans lived in poverty.

In this module you will learn about the changes that took place in the United States after World War II.

▷ *Explore ONLINE!*

HISTORY

VIDEOS, including...

- Eisenhower Wins in a Landslide
- Desegregation of the Army
- Nixon's Checkers Speech
- Suburbia and the Baby Boom
- The Age of the Automobile
- The Rise of Television

☑ Document-Based Investigations

☑ Graphic Organizers

☑ Interactive Games

☑ Image with Hotspots: Building Levittown

☑ Carousel: Americans Hit the Road

SS.912.A.1.2 Utilize a variety of primary and secondary sources to identify author, historical significance, audience, and authenticity to understand a historical period. **SS.912.A.1.4** Analyze how images, symbols, objects, cartoons, graphs, charts, maps, and artwork may be used to interpret the significance of time periods and events from the past. **SS.912.A.1.7** Describe various sociocultural aspects of American life including arts, artifacts, literature, education, and publications. **SS.912.A.7.1** Identify causes for Post-World War II prosperity and its effects on American society. **SS.912.A.7.2** Compare the relative prosperity between different ethnic groups and social classes in the post-World War II period. **SS.912.A.7.3** Examine the changing status of women in the United States from post-World War II to present. **SS.912.G.2.1** Identify the physical characteristics and the human characteristics that define and differentiate regions. **SS.912.H.1.1** Relate works in the arts of varying styles and genre according to the periods in which they were created. **SS.912.H.1.3** Relate works in the arts to various cultures. **SS.912.H.1.5** Examine artistic response to social issues and new ideas in various cultures. **LAFS.1112.RH.1.1** Cite specific textual evidence to support analysis of primary and secondary sources, connecting insights gained from specific details to an understanding of the text as a whole. **LAFS.1112.RH.1.2** Determine the central ideas or information of a primary or secondary source; provide an accurate summary that makes clear the relationships among the key details and ideas. **LAFS.1112.RH.4.10** By the end of grade 12, read and comprehend history/social studies texts in the grades 11–CCR text complexity band independently and proficiently. **MAFS.K12.MP.1.1** Make sense of problems and persevere in solving them. **MAFS.K12.MP.5.1** Use appropriate tools strategically. **MAFS.K12.MP.6.1** Attend to precision.

Timeline of Events 1945–1961

▶ *Explore ONLINE!*

United States Events		World Events

1945

1946 Baby boom begins. ——○

< **1947** Jackie Robinson integrates ——○
major league baseball.

1948 Harry S. Truman is elected president. ——○

○—— **1949** Mao Zedong's Communist forces gain control of China.

< **1950s** Disc jockey Alan Freed ——○—— **1950** Korean War begins. >
is the first to use the term
"rock 'n' roll" on the air.

1952 Dwight D. Eisenhower is elected president. ——○

○—— **1953** Korean War cease-fire is signed.

1954 *Brown* v. *Board of Education of* ——○
Topeka outlaws school segregation.
                                          1954 USSR opens the first small nuclear power plant.

1956 Eisenhower is reelected. ——○—— **1956** Soviets crush uprising in Hungary.

○—— **1957** Soviets launch *Sputnik I.*

< **1958** NASA—National
Aeronautics and Space
Administration—is established. ——○

1959 Alaska and Hawaii become ——○—— **1959** Fidel Castro comes >
the 49th and 50th states.   to power in Cuba.

1960 John F. Kennedy is elected president. ——○

1961

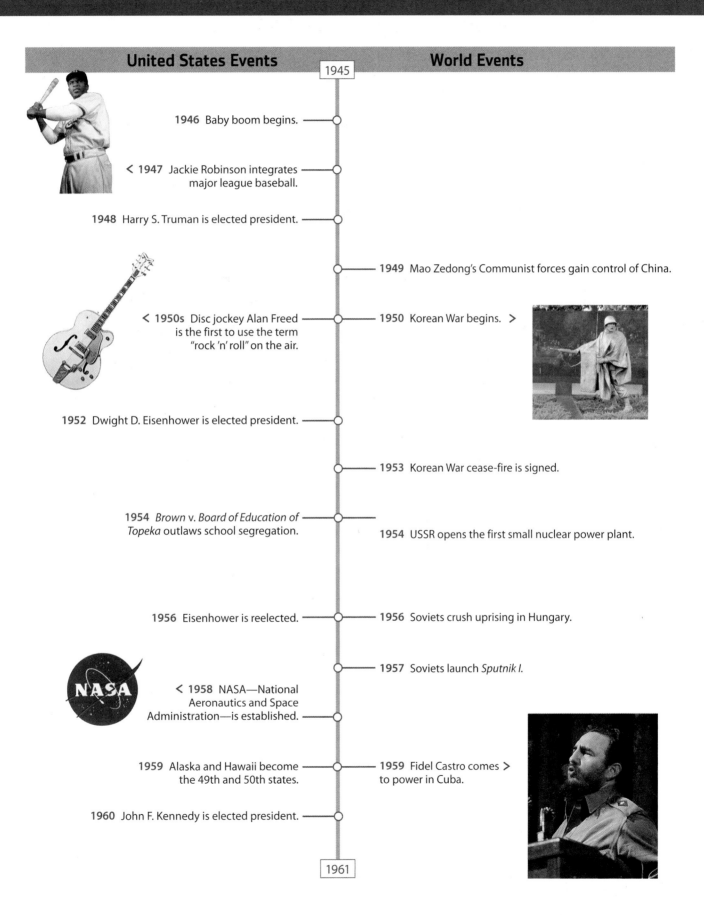

Postwar America

The Big Idea

The Truman and Eisenhower administrations led the nation to make social, economic, and political adjustments following World War II.

Why It Matters Now

In the years after World War II, the United States became the economic and military power that it still is today.

Key Terms and People

GI Bill of Rights

suburb

Harry S. Truman

Dixiecrat

Fair Deal

One American's Story

Sam Gordon had been married less than a year when he was shipped overseas in July 1943. As a sergeant in the United States Army, he fought in Belgium and France during World War II. Arriving back home in November 1945, Sam nervously anticipated a reunion with his family. A friend, Donald Katz, described Sam's reactions.

> "Sam bulled through the crowd and hailed a taxi. The cab motored north through the warm autumn day as he groped for feelings appropriate to being back home alive from a terrible war. . . . [He was] nearly panting under the weight of fear. . . . Back home alive . . . married to a girl I haven't seen since 1943 . . . father of a child I've never seen at all."
>
> —Donald Katz, from *Home Fires*

GIs returned home to their families after World War II with new hope but also with new problems.

Sam Gordon met his daughter, Susan, for the first time the day he returned home from the war, and he went to work the next morning. Like many other young couples, the Gordons began to put the nightmare of the war behind them and return to normality.

SS.912.A.1.3; SS.912.A.1.4; SS.912.A.7.1; SS.912.A.7.3; SS.912.G.2.1; MAFS.K12.MP.1.1; MAFS.K12.MP.5.1; MAFS.K12.MP.6.1

Readjustment and Recovery

By the summer of 1946, about 10 million men and women had been released from the armed forces. Veterans like Sam Gordon—along with the rest of American society—settled down to rebuild their lives.

THE IMPACT OF THE GI BILL During the war, patriotism was high. As veterans returned home, the federal government committed to help ease their return to civilian life. Congress passed the Servicemen's Readjustment Act, or the **GI Bill of Rights**, in 1944. In addition to encouraging veterans to get an education by paying part of their tuition, the GI Bill guaranteed them a year's worth of unemployment benefits while job hunting. It also offered low-interest, federally guaranteed loans. Millions of young families used these benefits to buy homes and farms or to establish businesses.

The suburbs were a mass phenomenon, even on moving day.

HOUSING CRISIS In 1945 and 1946 returning veterans faced a severe housing shortage. Many families lived in cramped apartments or moved in with relatives. In addition, the years after World War II saw a sharp increase in birth- rates. In response to the population growth and housing crisis, developers like William Levitt and Henry Kaiser used efficient, assembly-line methods to mass-produce houses. Levitt bragged that his company could build a house in 16 minutes. He offered homes in small residential communities surrounding cities, called **suburbs**, for less than $7,000.

Levitt's first postwar development—rows of standardized homes built on treeless lots—was located on New York's Long Island and named Levittown. These homes looked exactly alike, and certain zoning laws ensured that they would stay the same. Despite their rigid conformity, Americans loved the openness and small-town feel to the planned suburbs. With the help of the GI Bill, many veterans and their families moved in and cultivated a new lifestyle.

REDEFINING THE FAMILY Tension created by changes in men's and women's roles after the war contributed to a rising divorce rate. Traditionally, men were the breadwinners and heads of households, while women were expected to stay home and care for the family. During the war, however, about 8 million women, 75 percent of whom were married, entered the paid workforce. These women supported their families and made important household decisions. Many were reluctant to give up their newfound independence when their husbands returned. Although most women did leave their jobs, by 1950 more than a million war marriages had ended in divorce.

A Dynamic Economy

Home Ownership

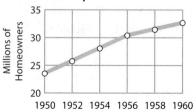

Automobile Registrations

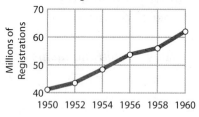

Median Family Income

Savings Accounts

Source: *Historical Statistics of the United States, Colonial Times to 1970*

Interpret Graphs

1. From 1950 to 1960, by what percentage did each of the economic indicators shown above increase?

2. Which years show the biggest increases for each of the graphs above?

Reading Check
Identify Problems
What problems did Americans face after World War II?

ECONOMIC READJUSTMENT After World War II, the United States converted from a wartime to a peacetime economy. The U.S. government immediately canceled war contracts totaling $35 billion, and more than a million defense workers were laid off. Unemployment increased as veterans joined laid-off defense workers in the search for jobs. The government vowed to tackle this problem. In February 1946 President Truman signed the Employment Act of 1946. This act stated that the government would do everything in its power to bring about full employment and a stable economy. At the peak of postwar unemployment in March 1946, nearly 3 million people were seeking work.

Rising unemployment was not the nation's only postwar economic problem, however. During the war, the Office of Price Administration (OPA) had halted inflation by imposing maximum prices on goods. When these controls ended on June 30, 1946, prices skyrocketed. In the next two weeks, the cost of consumer products soared 25 percent, double the increase of the previous three years. In some cities, consumers stood in long lines, hoping to buy scarce items such as sugar, coffee, and beans. Shortages caused prices to continue to rise for the next two years, until the supply of goods caught up with the demand.

While prices spiraled upward, many American workers also earned less than they had earned during the war. To halt runaway inflation and to help the nation convert to a peacetime economy, Congress eventually reestablished controls similar to the wartime controls on prices, wages, and rents.

REMARKABLE RECOVERY Most economists who had forecast a postwar depression were proved wrong because they had failed to consider consumers' pent-up accumulation of needs and wants. People had gone without many goods for so long that by the late 1940s, with more than $135 billion in savings from defense work, service pay, and investments in war bonds, Americans suddenly had money to spend. They snatched up everything from automobiles to houses. After a brief period of postwar economic readjustment, the American economy boomed. The demand for goods and services outstripped the supply and increased production, which created new jobs. Many Americans prospered in the 1950s in what economist John Kenneth Galbraith called "the affluent society."

The Cold War also contributed to economic growth. Concern over Soviet expansion kept American defense spending high and people employed. Foreign-aid programs like the Marshall Plan provided another boost to the American economy. By helping nations in Western Europe recover from the war, the United States created strong foreign markets for its exports.

Meeting Economic Challenges

Despite an impressive recovery, Americans faced a number of economic problems. Their lives had been in turmoil throughout the war, and a desire for stability made the country more conservative.

PRESIDENT TRUMAN'S INHERITANCE When **Harry S. Truman** suddenly became president after Franklin D. Roosevelt's death in 1945, he asked Roosevelt's widow, Eleanor, if there was anything he could do for her. She replied, "Is there anything we can do for you? For you are the one in trouble now." In many ways, President Truman was in trouble.

> *"I don't know whether you fellows ever had a load of hay fall on you, but when they told me yesterday what had happened [Roosevelt's death], I felt like the moon, the stars, and all the planets had fallen on me."*
>
> —Harry S. Truman, from a speech delivered April 13, 1945

Although he may have felt unprepared for the job, Truman was widely viewed as honorable, down-to-earth, and self-confident. Most important of all, he had the ability to make difficult decisions and to accept full responsibility for their consequences. As the plaque on his White House desk read, "The Buck Stops Here." Truman faced two huge challenges: dealing with the rising threat of communism and restoring the American economy to a strong footing after the war's end.

TRUMAN FACES STRIKES One economic problem that Truman had to address was strikes. During World War II, labor unions had agreed not to strike or seek pay raises. Conditions had not changed, however, after the war was over. Facing higher prices and lower wages, 4.5 million discontented workers, including steelworkers, coal miners, and railroad workers, went on strike in 1946 for better pay. Although he generally supported organized labor, Truman refused to let strikes cripple the nation. He threatened to draft the striking workers and to order them as soldiers to stay on the job. He authorized the federal government to seize the mines, and he threatened to take control of the railroads as well. Truman appeared before Congress and asked for the authority to draft the striking railroad workers into the army. Before he could finish his speech, the unions gave in.

"HAD ENOUGH?" Disgusted by shortages of goods, rising inflation, and labor strikes, Americans were ready for a change. The Republicans asked the public, "Had enough?" Voters gave their answer at the polls. In the 1946 congressional elections, the Republican Party won control of both the Senate and the House of Representatives for the first time since 1928. The new 80th Congress ignored Truman's domestic proposals. In 1947 Congress passed the Taft-Hartley Act over Truman's veto. This bill reduced the strength of organized labor and overturned many rights won by the unions under the New Deal.

Reading Check
Summarize What actions did President Truman take to avert labor strikes?

Social Unrest Persists

Problems arose not only in the economy but in the very fabric of society. After World War II, a wave of racial violence erupted in the South. Many African Americans, particularly those who had served in the armed forces during the war, demanded their rights as citizens.

TRUMAN SUPPORTS CIVIL RIGHTS Truman put his presidency on the line for civil rights. "I am asking for equality of opportunity for all human beings," he said, ". . . and if that ends up in my failure to be reelected, that failure will be in a good cause." In 1946 Truman created a President's Commission on Civil Rights. Following the group's recommendations, Truman asked Congress for several measures. These included a federal antilynching law, a ban on the poll tax as a voting requirement, and a permanent civil rights commission.

Congress refused to pass these measures, or a measure to integrate the armed forces. As a result, Truman himself took action. In July 1948 he issued an executive order for integration of the armed forces, calling for "equality of treatment and opportunity in the armed forces without regard to race, color, religion, or national origin." In addition, he ordered an end to discrimination in the hiring of government employees. The Supreme Court also ruled that the lower courts could not bar African Americans from residential neighborhoods. These actions represented the beginnings of a federal commitment to dealing with racial issues.

THE 1948 ELECTION Although many Americans blamed Truman for the nation's inflation and labor unrest, the Democrats nominated him for president in 1948. To protest Truman's emphasis on civil rights, a number of

Vocabulary
discrimination
treatment based on class or category rather than individual merit

---

— BIOGRAPHY —

Jackie Robinson (1919–1972)

Jackie Robinson took a brave step when he turned the Brooklyn Dodgers into an integrated baseball team in 1947. But he—and the country—had a long way to go.

Unhappy fans hurled insults at Robinson from the stands. Some players on opposing teams tried to hit him with pitches or to injure him with the spikes on their shoes. He even received death threats. He endured this with poise and restraint, saying, "Plenty of times, I wanted to haul off when somebody insulted me for the color of my skin but I had to hold myself. I knew I was kind of an experiment."

In 1949, Robinson was voted the National League's most valuable player. He later became the first African American to be inducted into the Baseball Hall of Fame.

Southern Democrats—who became known as **Dixiecrats**—formed the States' Rights Democratic Party. They nominated their own presidential candidate, Governor J. Strom Thurmond of South Carolina. Discontent reigned at the far left of the Democratic spectrum as well. The former vice-president Henry A. Wallace led his supporters out of mainstream Democratic ranks to form a more liberal Progressive Party.

As the election approached, opinion polls gave the Republican candidate, New York governor Thomas E. Dewey, a comfortable lead. Refusing to believe the polls, Truman poured his energy into the campaign. First, he called the Republican-dominated Congress into a special session. He challenged it to pass laws supporting such elements of the Democratic Party platform as public housing, federal aid to education, a higher minimum wage, and extended Social Security coverage. Not one of these laws was passed. Then he took his campaign to the people. He traveled from one end of the country to the other by train, speaking from the rear platform in a sweeping "whistlestop campaign." Day after day, people heard the president denounce the "do-nothing, 80th Congress."

STUNNING UPSET Truman's "Give 'em hell, Harry" campaign worked. He won the election in a close political upset. The Democrats gained control of Congress as well, even though they suffered losses in the South, which had been solidly Democratic since Reconstruction.

Truman surprised the newspapers by winning the 1948 election.

Presidential Election of 1948

* Tennessee—11 electoral votes for Truman,
1 electoral vote for Thurmond

Party	Candidate	Electoral Votes	Popular Votes
☐ Democratic	Harry S. Truman	303	24,179,000
☐ Republican	Thomas E. Dewey	189	21,991,000
☐ States' Rights	J. Strom Thurmond	39	1,176,000
Progressive	Henry A. Wallace	—	1,157,000

Interpret Maps

1. Place In which regions of the country did Truman carry states? Dewey? Thurmond?

2. Place Which regions showed the weakest support for Truman?

THE FAIR DEAL After his victory, Truman continued proposing an ambitious economic program. Truman's **Fair Deal**, an extension of Roosevelt's New Deal, included proposals for a nationwide system of compulsory health insurance and a crop-subsidy system to provide a steady income for farmers. These ideas were opposed by powerful business interests, including the American Medical Association and the Farm Bureau Federation, who worked against these proposals. In Congress, some Northern Democrats joined Dixiecrats and Republicans in defeating both measures.

In other instances, however, Truman's ideas prevailed. Congress raised the hourly minimum wage from 40 cents to 75 cents. They extended Social Security coverage to about 10 million more people and initiated flood control and irrigation projects. Congress passed the Employment Act in 1946, which recognized government's responsibility to help achieve full employment. Congress also provided financial support for cities to clear out slums and build 810,000 housing units for low-income families.

Overall, though, the Fair Deal had limited success in an increasingly conservative postwar political climate. Americans had become less enthusiastic about reform programs that would further expand the government. Most people, weary of the upheavals of recent years, just wanted peace, stability, and gradual prosperity.

Republicans Take the Middle Road

Despite these social and economic victories, Truman's approval rating sank to an all-time low of 23 percent in 1951. The stalemate in the Korean War and the rising tide of McCarthyism, which cast doubt on the loyalty of some federal employees, became overwhelming issues. Truman decided not to run for reelection in 1952. The year before, the states had ratified the Twenty-Second Amendment, which limited the number of times a president could be elected to two. Although Truman was specifically excluded from the amendment's limits, he felt he had served long enough. The Democrats nominated the intellectual and articulate governor Adlai Stevenson of Illinois to run against the Republican candidate, General Dwight D. Eisenhower, known popularly as "Ike."

I LIKE IKE! During the campaign, the Republicans accused the Democrats of "plunder at home and blunder abroad." To fan the anti-Communist hysteria that was sweeping over the country, Republicans raised the specter of the rise of communism in China and Eastern Europe. They also criticized the growing power of the federal government and the alleged bribery and corruption among Truman's political allies.

Eisenhower's campaign hit a snag, however, when newspapers accused his running mate, California senator Richard M. Nixon, of profiting from a secret slush fund set up by wealthy supporters. Nixon decided to reply to the charges. In an emotional speech to an audience of 58 million, now known as the "Checkers speech," he exhibited masterful use of a new medium—television. Nixon denied any wrongdoing, but he did admit to accepting one gift from a political supporter.

Reading Check
Summarize What were some of Truman's achievements as president?

Vocabulary
slush fund a fund often designated for corrupt practices, such as bribery

642 Module 13

"You know what it was? It was a little cocker spaniel dog in a crate, that he'd [the political supporter] sent all the way from Texas. Black and white spotted. And our little girl—Tricia, the six-year-old—named it Checkers. And you know the kids, like all kids, love the dog and I just want to say this right now, that regardless of what they say about it, we're going to keep it."

—Richard M. Nixon, from the "Checkers speech," September 23, 1952

Nixon's speech saved his place on the Republican ticket. In November 1952 Eisenhower won 55 percent of the popular vote and a majority of the Electoral College votes, while the Republicans narrowly captured Congress.

WALKING THE MIDDLE OF THE ROAD President Eisenhower's style of governing differed from that of the Democrats. His approach, which he called "dynamic conservatism," was also known as "Modern Republicanism." He called for government to be "conservative when it comes to money and liberal when it comes to human beings."

Eisenhower avoided many controversial issues. However, he could not completely sidestep a persistent domestic issue—civil rights—that gained national attention due to court rulings and acts of civil disobedience in the mid-1950s. The most significant judicial action occurred in 1954, when the Supreme Court ruled in *Brown* v. *Board of Education of Topeka* that public schools must be racially integrated. In a landmark act of civil disobedience a year later, a black seamstress named Rosa Parks refused to give up her seat on a bus to a white man. Her arrest sparked a boycott of the entire Montgomery, Alabama, bus system. The civil rights movement had entered a new era.

Although Eisenhower did not lead on civil rights issues, he did press hard for programs that would bring about a balanced budget and a cut in taxes. During his two terms, Eisenhower's administration raised the minimum wage, extended Social Security and unemployment benefits, increased funding for public housing, and backed the creation of interstate highways and the Department of Health, Education, and Welfare. His popularity soared, and he won reelection in 1956.

Reading Check
Identify Cause and Effect How did rising anti-communist feeling lead to Eisenhower's election and Republicans taking control of Congress?

Lesson 1 Assessment

1. **Organize Information** Create a timeline and record key events relating to postwar America.

Write a paragraph describing the effects of one of these events.

2. **Key Terms and People** For each key term or person in the lesson, write a sentence explaining its significance.

3. **Draw Conclusions** Do you think Eisenhower's actions reflected his philosophy of dynamic conservatism? Why or why not?

   Think About:
   - the definition of dynamic conservatism
   - Eisenhower's actions on civil rights policies
   - Eisenhower's accomplishments on other domestic issues

4. **Evaluate** Why do you think most Americans went along with Eisenhower's conservative approach to domestic policy?

5. **Contrast** How did Presidents Truman and Eisenhower differ regarding civil rights?

The American Dream in the Fifties

The Big Idea

During the 1950s the economy boomed and many Americans enjoyed material comfort.

Why It Matters Now

The "American dream," a notion that was largely shaped by the 1950s, is still pursued today.

Key Terms and People

conglomerate

franchise

baby boom

Dr. Jonas Salk

consumerism

planned obsolescence

SS.912.A.1.2; SS.912.A.1.4; SS.912.A.1.7; SS.912.A.7.1; SS.912.A.7.2; SS.912.A.7.3; LAFS.1112.RH.1.1; LAFS.1112.RH.1.2; MAFS.K12.MP.1.1; MAFS.K12.MP.5.1; MAFS.K12.MP.6.1

One American's Story

Settled into her brand new house near San Diego, California, Carol Freeman felt very fortunate. Her husband Mark had his own law practice, and when their first baby was born, she became a full-time homemaker. She was living the American dream. Yet Carol felt dissatisfied—as if there were "something wrong" with her because she was not happy.

"As dissatisfied as I was, and as restless, I remember so well this feeling [we] had at the time that the world was going to be your oyster. You were going to make money, your kids were going to go to good schools, everything was possible if you just did what you were supposed to do. The future was rosy. There was a tremendous feeling of optimism. . . . Much as I say it was hateful, it was also hopeful. It was an innocent time."

—Carol Freeman, quoted in *The Fifties: A Women's Oral History*

The dream woman of the 1950s was depicted in advertising and on TV as doing constant housework, but always with a smile.

After World War II ended, Americans turned their attention to their families and jobs. The economy prospered. New technologies and business ideas created fresh opportunities for many. By the end of the decade, Americans were enjoying the highest standard of living in the world. The American dream of a happy and successful life seemed within the reach of many people.

The Organization and the Organization Man

During the 1950s businesses expanded rapidly. Some 5,000 companies merged to form larger corporations. American factories were changing as well. Throughout the 1950s companies introduced machines that could perform industrial operations faster and more efficiently than human workers. This process of automation increased productivity, but it also reduced the amount of manufacturing jobs. As the number of blue-collar, or industrial, jobs decreased, professional and service jobs increased. Huge new corporations required a multitude of managers and clerical workers, positions referred to as white-collar jobs.

CONGLOMERATES Many white-collar workers performed their services in large corporations or government agencies. Some of these corporations continued expanding by forming **conglomerates**. (A conglomerate is a major corporation that includes a number of smaller companies in unrelated industries.) For example, one conglomerate, International Telephone and Telegraph (ITT), whose original business was communications, bought car-rental companies, insurance companies, and hotel and motel chains. Through this diversification, or investment in various areas of the economy, ITT tried to protect itself from declines in individual industries. Other huge parent companies included American Telephone and Telegraph, Xerox, and General Electric.

FRANCHISES In addition to diversifying, another strategy for business expansion—franchising—developed at this time. A **franchise** is a company that offers similar products or services in many locations. (*Franchise* is also used to refer to the right, sold to an individual, to do business using the parent company's name and the system that the parent company developed.)

NOW & THEN

Franchises

In the decades since Ray Kroc opened his first McDonald's restaurant, franchising has become all but a way of life in the United States.

Today, nearly 3,000 franchised companies operate over 500,000 businesses throughout the country. Officials estimate that franchises account for nearly one-third of all U.S. retail sales. American franchises today provide a wide array of goods and services, from car maintenance to tax services to hair care.

In an attempt to tap into the international market, hundreds of U.S. companies have established overseas franchises. The franchise with perhaps the greatest global reach is the one that started it all. In addition to its more than 13,000 U.S. franchises, McDonald's now operates over 18,600 franchises in dozens of countries around the world.

Fast-food restaurants developed some of the first and most successful franchises. McDonald's, for example, had its start at a small drive-in restaurant in San Bernardino, California. The McDonald brothers developed unusually efficient service, based on assembly-line methods. They simplified the menu, featured 15-cent hamburgers, and mechanized their kitchen.

Salesman Ray Kroc paid the McDonalds $2.7 million for the franchise rights to their hamburger drive-in. In April 1955 he opened his first McDonald's restaurant in Des Plaines, Illinois. There he further improved the assembly-line process and introduced the trademark arches that are now familiar all over the world.

> *"It requires a certain kind of mind to see the beauty in a hamburger bun. Yet is it any more unusual to find grace in the texture and softly curved silhouette of a bun than to reflect lovingly on the . . . arrangements and textures and colors in a butterfly's wings? . . . Not if you view the bun as an essential material in the art of serving a great many meals fast."*
>
> —Ray Kroc, quoted in *The Fifties*

SOCIAL CONFORMITY While franchises like McDonald's helped standardize what people ate, some American workers found themselves becoming standardized as well. Employees who were well paid and held secure jobs in thriving companies sometimes paid a price for economic advancement. The price was a loss of their individuality. In general, businesses did not want creative thinkers, rebels, or anyone who would rock the corporate boat.

The Organization Man is a book based on a classic 1956 study of suburban Park Forest, Illinois, and other communities. In it, William H. Whyte described how the new, large organizations created "company people." Companies would give personality tests to people applying for jobs to make sure they would "fit in" the corporate culture. Companies rewarded employees for teamwork, cooperation, and loyalty. These qualities contributed to the growth of conformity, which Whyte called "belongingness." Despite their success, a number of workers questioned whether pursuing the American dream exacted too high a price, as rigid conformity replaced individuality.

UNIONS Changes in the workplace also influenced organized labor. Boosted in part by the merger of the American Federation of Labor (AFL) and the Congress of Industrial Organizations (CIO) in 1955, union membership grew in the 1950s. To help workers improve their economic position, union leaders sought to cooperate with management. Many unions fought for and won guaranteed annual wages and cost-of-living adjustments—automatic pay raises linked to the rate of inflation.

The "organization man" had to step lively to keep up with the Joneses.

Reading Check
Analyze Effects
What effects did
the climate in many
corporations have on
some workers?

Union support weakened in the late 1950s when newspapers reported widespread corruption and linked many unions to organized crime. Congress attempted to crack down on union corruption. Carey Estes Kefauver, a senator from Tennessee, had already launched hearings earlier in the decade to investigate organized crime in the United States. These hearings were widely followed by the American public and led to the passage of new laws. The negative publicity hurt union membership, which declined steadily after 1957. During the next decade, Attorney General Robert Kennedy would continue to fight organized crime. Several union leaders, including Teamsters union president Jimmy Hoffa, would be sent to prison.

The Suburban Lifestyle

Achieving job security took a psychological toll on some Americans who resented having to repress their own personalities. However, it also enabled people to provide their families with the so-called good things in life. Most Americans worked in cities, but fewer and fewer of them lived there. New highways and the availability and affordability of automobiles and gasoline made commuting possible. By the early 1960s every large city in the United States was surrounded by suburbs. Of the 13 million new homes built in the 1950s, 85 percent were built in the suburbs. For many people, the suburbs embodied the American dream of an affordable single-family house, good schools, a safe, healthy environment for children, and congenial neighbors just like themselves.

American Birthrate, 1940–1970

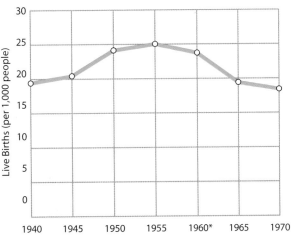

*First year for which figures include Alaska and Hawaii.
Source: *Historical Statistics of the United States, Colonial Times to 1970*

Some of the 40 million new Americans who were born during the baby boom

Interpret Graphs
1. What was the overall trend in the birthrate at the start of World War II, and after the war ended?
2. What was the difference in the birthrate between 1960 and 1970?

THE BABY BOOM As soldiers returned from World War II and settled into family life, they contributed to an unprecedented population explosion known as the **baby boom**. During the late 1940s and through the early 1960s, the birthrate (number of live births per 1,000 people) in the United States soared. At the height of the baby boom, in 1957, one American infant was born every seven seconds—a total of 4,308,000 that year. The result was the largest generation in the nation's history.

Many factors contributed to the size of the baby-boom generation. These included the reunion of husbands and wives after the war, decreasing marriage age, desirability of large families, confidence in continued economic prosperity, and advances in medicine.

ADVANCES IN MEDICINE AND CHILDCARE Among the medical advances that saved hundreds of thousands of children's lives was the discovery of drugs to fight and prevent childhood diseases, such as typhoid fever. Another breakthrough came when **Dr. Jonas Salk** developed a vaccine for the crippling disease poliomyelitis—polio. Polio was an infectious disease that often struck children. When polio hit, it spread quickly, and many of its victims died. Fear of the disease caused families to dramatically alter their daily lives during outbreaks, keeping children out of school for weeks at a time. After the development of the polio vaccine, children began receiving the shot and the number of polio cases plunged.

Many parents raised their children according to guidelines devised by pediatrician and author Dr. Benjamin Spock. His *Common Sense Book of Baby and Child Care*, published in 1946, sold nearly 10 million copies during the 1950s. In it, he advised parents not to spank or scold their children. He also encouraged families to hold meetings in which children could express themselves. He considered it so important for mothers to be at home with their children that he proposed having the government pay mothers to stay home.

— BIOGRAPHY —

Jonas Salk (1914–1995)

One of the most feared diseases in the 1950s was polio, the disease that had partially paralyzed President Franklin D. Roosevelt. Polio afflicted 58,000 American children in 1952. It killed some children and made others reliant on crutches, wheelchairs, or iron lungs (machines that helped people with paralyzed chest muscles to breathe).

In the early 1950s Dr. Jonas Salk developed an effective vaccine to prevent the disease. The government sponsored a free inoculation program for children. The vaccine was extremely effective.

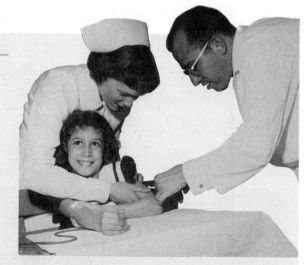

By 1974, thanks to Salk's vaccine and a new oral vaccine developed by Dr. Albert Sabin, only seven new polio cases were reported in the country.

The baby boom had a tremendous impact not only on childcare but on the American economy and the educational system as well. In 1958 toy sales alone reached $1.25 billion. During the decade, 10 million new students entered the elementary schools. The sharp increase in enrollment caused overcrowding and teacher shortages in many parts of the country. In California, a new school opened every seven days.

Competition with the Soviet Union caused many Americans to wonder if a decline in the nation's schools had enabled the Soviets to surpass the United States in technological achievements. In response to this concern, Congress passed the National Defense Education Act in 1958, which provided hundreds of millions of dollars for education in the United States. This legislation included funding for additional loans for college students. It also provided for improved science, math, and foreign language instruction in elementary and secondary schools.

WOMEN'S ROLES During the 1950s the role of homemaker and mother was glorified in popular magazines, movies, and TV programs such as *Father Knows Best* and *The Adventures of Ozzie and Harriet. Time* magazine described the homemaker as "the key figure in all suburbia, the thread that weaves between family and community—the keeper of the suburban dream." In contrast to the ideal portrayed in the media, however, some women, like Carol Freeman, who spoke of her discontentment, were not happy with their roles. They felt isolated, bored, and unfulfilled. According to one survey in the 1950s, more than one-fifth of suburban wives were dissatisfied with their lives. Betty Friedan, author of the groundbreaking 1963 book about women and society, *The Feminine Mystique*, described the problem.

> *"For the first time in their history, women are becoming aware of an identity crisis in their own lives, a crisis which . . . has grown worse with each succeeding generation. . . . I think this is the crisis of women growing up—a turning point from an immaturity that has been called femininity to full human identity."*
>
> —Betty Friedan, from *The Feminine Mystique*

The number of women working outside the home rose steadily during the decade. By 1960 almost 40 percent of mothers with children between ages 6 and 17 held paying jobs.

But having a job didn't necessarily contribute to a woman's happiness. A woman's career opportunities tended to be limited to fields such as nursing, teaching, and office support. These positions paid less than other professional and business positions did. Women also earned less than men for comparable work. Although increasing numbers of women attended four-year colleges, the percentage of women college students in the 1950s was smaller than the 1920s. Female students generally received little financial, academic, or psychological encouragement to pursue their goals. Revealingly, in a 1962 Gallup poll of 2,300 women, more than 90 percent hoped that their daughters would be better educated and would lead different lives than they had.

LEISURE IN THE FIFTIES Most Americans of the 1950s had more leisure time than ever before. Employees worked a 40-hour week and earned several weeks' vacation per year. Scientific advances led to more labor-saving devices. Washing machines, clothes dryers, dishwashers, and power lawn mowers allowed more time for leisure activities. *Fortune* magazine reported that, in 1953, Americans spent more than $30 billion on leisure goods and activities.

Americans also enjoyed a wide variety of recreational pursuits—both active and passive. Millions of people participated in such sports as fishing, bowling, hunting, boating, and golf. More fans than ever attended baseball, basketball, and football games. Others watched professional sports on television.

3-D comics and 3-D movies were two of the many fads that mesmerized the nation in the 1950s.

Americans also became avid readers. They devoured books about cooking, religion, do-it-yourself projects, and homemaking. They also read mysteries, romance novels, and fiction by popular writers such as Ernest Hemingway, John Steinbeck, Daphne du Maurier, and J. D. Salinger. Book sales doubled, due in part to a thriving paperback market. The circulation of popular magazines like *Reader's Digest* and *Sports Illustrated* steadily rose, from about 148 million to more than 190 million readers. Sales of comic books also reached a peak in the mid-1950s.

Document-Based Investigation Historical Source

"Little Boxes"

In a popular protest song, Malvina Reynolds sings about boxes lining a hillside. She is referring to the suburban housing developments that were planned and built in the 1950s. Ticky-tacky is the cheap, shoddy building material that was used to construct the homes. The song continues to say that the people who live in the boxes are also "all made out of ticky-tacky" and "all look just the same."

Analyze Historical Sources
What statement do you think this song is making about planned suburban neighborhoods?

"Little boxes on the hillside,
Little boxes made of ticky-tacky,
Little boxes on the hillside,
Little boxes all the same.
There's a pink one and a green one,
And a blue one and a yellow one,
And they're all made out of ticky-tacky,
And they all look just the same."
—Malvina Reynolds, from "Little Boxes"

Reading Check
Analyze Effects
How did the baby boom affect American life in the 1950s?

Suburban life during this time encouraged conformity. In addition to buying the same consumer items and reading the same publications, many suburban families participated in the same social activities as their neighbors. Adults joined Parent-Teacher Associations (PTAs) and religious organizations, while children took up scouting and sports. For uprooted Americans in the suburbs, participation in these shared social activities provided a sense of belonging. Television and other popular media reinforced the image of the sameness of suburban lives. Media helped to create the stereotype that all suburban Americans were alike regardless of where they lived and worked.

The Automobile Culture

During World War II the U.S. government had rationed gasoline and converted many automobile factories for wartime use. Postwar changes made cars appealing and, in some cases, necessary.

GROWING DEPENDENCE ON CARS After the war automobiles joined the list of products once again widely available for purchase. Also, an abundance of petroleum—the raw material from which gasoline is made—led to inexpensive, plentiful fuel for consumers. Easy credit terms and extensive advertising persuaded Americans to buy cars in record numbers. New car sales rose from 6.7 million in 1950 to 7.9 million in 1955. The number of private cars on the road jumped from 40 million in 1950 to over 60 million in 1960.

Suburban living made owning a car a necessity. Most of the new suburbs did not offer public transportation. People had to drive to their jobs in the cities. Also, many of the schools, stores, synagogues, churches, and doctors' and dentists' offices were not within walking distance of suburban homes.

Not just for transport, cars were marketed for fashion and fun. Car ads used words like "fresh" and "frisky."

The interstate highway system made travel much easier and faster.

THE INTERSTATE HIGHWAY SYSTEM The more cars there were, the more roads were needed. "Automania" spurred local and state governments to construct roads. These roads linked the major cities while connecting schools, shopping centers, and workplaces to residential suburbs, which were booming along with the population. In 1956 President Eisenhower signed the National Interstate and Defense Highways Act of 1956. The act was funded in 1957 and authorized the building of a nationwide highway network—41,000 miles of expressways. The new roads, in turn, encouraged the development of new suburbs farther from the cities.

Interstate highways also made high-speed, long-haul trucking possible, which contributed to a decline in the commercial use of railroads. Towns located along the new highways prospered, while towns situated along the older, smaller roads experienced hard times. The system of highways also helped unify and homogenize the nation. As John Keats observed in his 1958 book, *The Insolent Chariots,* "Our new roads, with their ancillaries, the motels, filling stations, and restaurants advertising Eats, have made it possible for you to drive from Brooklyn to Los Angeles without a change of diet, scenery, or culture."

With access to cars, affordable gas, and new highways, more and more Americans hit the road. They flocked to mountains, lakes, national parks, historic sites, and amusement parks for family vacations. Disneyland, which opened in California in July 1955, attracted 3 million visitors the next year.

MOBILITY TAKES ITS TOLL As the automobile industry boomed, it stimulated production and provided jobs in other areas, such as drive-in movies, restaurants, and shopping malls. Yet cars also created new problems for both society and the environment. Noise and exhaust polluted the air. Automobile accidents claimed more lives every year. Traffic jams raised people's stress levels. Heavy use damaged the roads. Because cars made it possible for Americans to live in suburbs, many upper-class and middle-class whites

Vocabulary
homogenize to make the same or similar

NOW & THEN

Southern California and the Automobile

No state has exemplified automania in the United States more than California. By the late 1990s Californians owned more cars, held more driver's licenses, and traveled more miles on their roads than the people of any other state. The center of this automobile culture is the metropolitan area of Los Angeles.

Contributing to the importance of the automobile is Southern California's suburban lifestyle. This dependence on cars has contributed to problems of air pollution and traffic jams. But, California is

addressing these problems. It is reviving public transportation systems and promoting the use of electric cars that produce no pollution.

Reading Check
Analyze Causes
Why did auto sales
surge in the 1950s?

left the crowded cities. Jobs and businesses eventually followed them to the suburbs. Public transportation declined. Poor people in the inner cities were often left without jobs and vital services. As a result, the economic gulf between suburban and urban dwellers and between the middle class and the poor widened.

Consumerism Unbound

By the mid-1950s nearly 60 percent of Americans were members of the middle class, about twice as many as before World War II. They wanted, and had the money to buy, increasing numbers of products. **Consumerism**, buying material goods, came to be equated with success.

NEW PRODUCTS One new product after another appeared in the market-place, as new technologies emerged and various industries responded to consumer demand. *Newsweek* magazine reported in 1956 that "hundreds of brand-new goods have become commonplace overnight." Consumers purchased electric household appliances—such as washing machines, clothes dryers, blenders, freezers, and dishwashers—in record numbers.

With more and more leisure time to fill, people invested in recreational items. They bought televisions, tape recorders, and the new hi-fi (high-fidelity) record players. They bought casual clothing to suit their suburban lifestyles as well as power lawn mowers, barbecue grills, swimming pools, and lawn decorations for their suburban homes.

PLANNED OBSOLESCENCE In addition to creating new products, manu-facturers began using a marketing strategy called **planned obsolescence**. In order to encourage consumers to purchase more goods, manufactur-ers purposely designed products to become obsolete. That is, products were designed to wear out or become outdated in a short period of time. Carmakers brought out new models every year, urging consumers to stay up-to-date. Because of planned obsolescence, Americans came to expect new and better products. They began to discard items that were sometimes barely used. Some observers commented that American culture was on its way to becoming a "throwaway society."

BUY NOW, PAY LATER Many consumers made their purchases on credit and therefore did not have to pay for them right away. The Diner's Club issued the first credit card in 1950, and the American Express card was introduced in 1958. These first cards were fairly exclusive, carrying a high fee which limited their use to middle-class people. In addition, people bought large items on the installment plan and made regular payments over a fixed time. Home mortgages (loans for buying a house) and automobile loans worked the same way. During the decade, the total private debt grew from $73 billion to $179 billion. Instead of sav-ing money, Americans were spending it, confident that prosperity would continue. As a result, consumer debt became a crucial engine driving the U.S. economy.

THE ADVERTISING AGE The advertising industry capitalized on this runaway consumerism by encouraging even more spending. Ads were everywhere—in newspapers and magazines, on radio and television, and on billboards along the highways. The ads prompted people to buy goods that ranged from cars to cereals to cigarettes. Advertisers spent about $6 billion in 1950. By 1955 the figure was up to $9 billion. Since most Americans had satisfied their basic needs, advertisers tried to convince them to buy things they really didn't need.

"On May 18, 1956, The New York Times printed a remarkable interview with a young man named Gerald Stahl, executive vice-president of the Package Designers Council. He stated: 'Psychiatrists say that people have so much to choose from that they want help—they will like the package that hypnotizes them into picking it.' He urged food packers to put more hypnosis into their package designing, so that the housewife will stick out her hand for it rather than one of many rivals.

Mr. Stahl has found that it takes the average woman exactly twenty seconds to cover an aisle in a supermarket if she doesn't tarry. So a good package design should hypnotize the woman like a flashlight waved in front of her eyes."

—Vance Packard, from *The Hidden Persuaders*

In the 1950s, advertisers made "keeping up with the Joneses" a way of life for consumers.

More and more, ad executives and designers turned to psychology to create new strategies for selling. Advertisers appealed to people's desire for status and "belongingness." They strived to associate their products with those values. For example, Cadillac ads appealed to the desire for status and mouthwash ads held the promise of social acceptance.

Television became a powerful new advertising tool. The first one-minute TV commercial was produced in 1941 at a cost of $9. In 1960 advertisers spent a total of $1.6 billion for television ads. By 2001 a 30-second commercial during the Super Bowl cost an advertiser $2.2 million. Television had become not only the medium for mass transmission of cultural values, but a symbol of popular culture itself.

Reading Check
Analyze Causes
How did manufacturers influence Americans to become a "throwaway society"?

Lesson 2 Assessment

1. **Organize Information** Use a graphic organizer to list examples of specific goals that characterized the American dream for suburbanites in the 1950s.

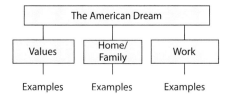

What do you think the most important goal was?

2. **Key Terms and People** For each key term or person in the lesson, write a sentence explaining its significance.

3. **Analyze Effects** In what ways do you think current environmental consciousness is related to the "throwaway society" of the 1950s? Support your answer.

   Think About:
   • the purchasing habits of 1950s consumers
   • the effects of planned obsolescence
   • today's emphasis on recycling

4. **Analyze Effects** Analyze how technological and scientific advancements impacted daily life for Americans in the 1950s. How did the daily lives of mothers and housekeepers change?

5. **Evaluate** Do you think that the life of a typical suburban homemaker during the 1950s was fulfilling or not? Support your answer.

6. **Analyze Primary Sources** This ad is typical of how the advertising industry portrayed housewives in the 1950s. What message about women is conveyed by this ad?

The Road to Suburbia

"Come out to Park Forest where small-town friendships grow—and you still live so close to a big city." Advertisements like this one for a scientifically planned Chicago suburb captured the lure of the suburbs for thousands of growing families in the 1950s. The publicity promised affordable housing, congenial neighbors, fresh air and open spaces, good schools, and easy access to urban jobs and culture. Good transportation was the lifeline of suburban growth a half century ago, and it continues to spur expansion today.

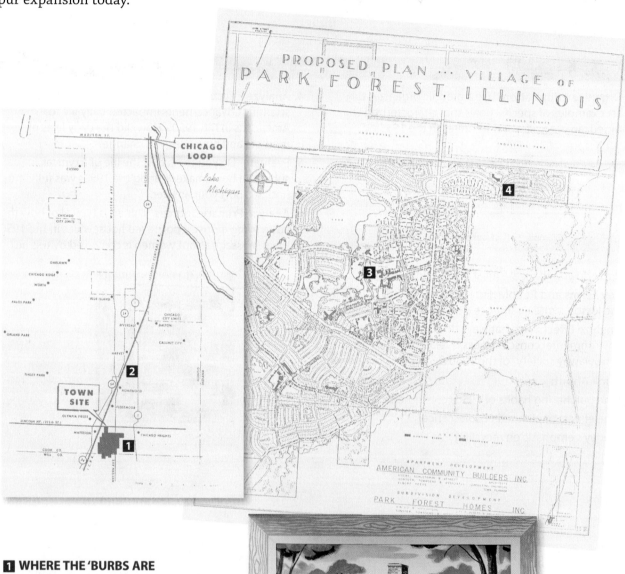

1 WHERE THE 'BURBS ARE
Park Forest was planned from its conception in 1945 to be a "complete community for middle-income families with children." The setting was rural— amidst cornfields and forest preserves about 30 miles south of Chicago. But it was convenient to commuter lines, like the Illinois Central (IC) Railroad, and to major roads, such as Western Avenue.

Chicagoland's COMPLETELY PLANNED *Suburb*

2 THE COMMUTER CRUSH

Men commuted to work on the IC railroad, while their wives usually stayed home to take care of the children, who thrived in Park Forest's safe, wholesome family environment.

3 SHOPPING CENTERS

Consumerism became a driving force in the 1950s, and Park Forest kept up with the trend. The central shopping center served the community well until the late 1960s. When Interstate 57 was constructed, a mammoth mall built just off the highway caused the original shopping area to decline. Park Forest is still struggling to revive its central shopping area.

4 SHARED PRIVACY

By 1952, development in Park Forest, Illinois had expanded to include both low-cost rental units and single-family homes. All the streets were curved to slow traffic, present a pleasing sweep of space, and give residents maximum privacy and space for yards.

Critical Thinking

1. **Analyze Effects** How did the availability of transportation influence the creation and ongoing development of Park Forest?

2. **Create a Database** Pose a historical question about a suburb near you. Collect statistics about changes in population, living patterns, income, and economic development in that suburb. Use those statistics to create a database that will help answer your questions.

★
Popular Culture

The Big Idea

Mainstream Americans, as well as the nation's subcultures, embraced new forms of entertainment during the 1950s.

Why It Matters Now

Television and rock 'n' roll, integral parts of the nation's culture today, emerged during the postwar era.

Key Terms and People

mass media

Federal Communications Commission (FCC)

beat movement

rock 'n' roll

jazz

One American's Story

H. B. Barnum was a 14-year-old saxophone player who later became a music producer. He was one of many teenagers in the 1950s drawn to a new style of music that featured hard-driving African American rhythm and blues. Barnum described the first time he saw the rhythm-and-blues performer Richard Wayne Penniman, better known as Little Richard.

Little Richard helped change rhythm and blues into a new musical genre—rock 'n' roll.

"He'd just burst onto the stage from anywhere, and you wouldn't be able to hear anything but the roar of the audience. . . . He'd be on the stage, he'd be off the stage, he'd be jumping and yelling, screaming, whipping the audience on. . . . Then when he finally did hit the piano and just went into di-di-di-di-di-di-di, you know, well nobody can do that as fast as Richard. It just took everybody by surprise."
—H. B. Barnum, quoted in *The Rise and Fall of Popular Music*

Born poor, Little Richard wore flashy clothes on stage, curled his hair, and shouted the lyrics to his songs. As one writer observed, "In two minutes [he] used as much energy as an all-night party." The music he and others performed became a prominent part of the American culture in the 1950s. It was a time when both mainstream America and those outside it embraced new and innovative forms of entertainment.

SS.912.A.1.2; SS.912.A.1.4; SS.912.A.1.7; SS.912.A.7.1; SS.912.H.1.1; SS.912.H.1.3; SS.912.H.1.5; LAFS.1112.RH.4.10; MAFS.K12.MP.1.1; MAFS.K12.MP.5.1

New Era of the Mass Media

Compared with other **mass media**—means of communication that reach large audiences—television developed with lightning speed. First widely available in 1948, television had reached 9 percent of American homes by 1950 and 55 percent of homes by 1954. In 1960 almost 90 percent—45 million—of American homes had television sets. Clearly, TV was the entertainment and information marvel of the postwar years.

THE RISE OF TELEVISION Early television sets were small boxes with round screens. Programming was meager, and broadcasts were in black and white. The first regular broadcasts, beginning in 1949, reached only a small part of the East Coast. It offered only two hours of programs per week. Post–World War II innovations such as microwave relays, which could transmit television waves over long distances, sent the television industry soaring. By 1956 the **Federal Communications Commission (FCC)** had allowed 500 new stations to broadcast. The FCC is the government agency that regulates and licenses television, telephone, telegraph, radio, and other communications industries.

This period of rapid expansion was the "golden age" of television entertainment. In the 1950s, entertainment often meant comedy. Milton Berle attracted huge audiences with *The Texaco Star Theater*. Lucille Ball and Desi Arnaz's early situation comedy, *I Love Lucy*, began its enormously popular run in 1951.

At the same time, veteran radio broadcaster Edward R. Murrow introduced two innovations. He introduced on-the-scene news reporting, with his program, *See It Now* (1951–1958), and interviewing, with *Person to Person* (1953–1960). Westerns, sports events, and original dramas shown on *Playhouse 90* and *Studio One* offered entertainment variety. Children's programs, such as *The Mickey Mouse Club* and *The Howdy Doody Show*, attracted many loyal young fans.

Glued to the Set

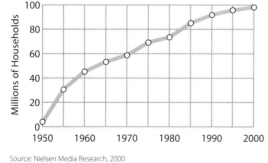

Households with TV Sets, 1950–2000

Source: Nielsen Media Research, 2000

Average Daily Hours of TV Viewing, 1950–2000

Source: Nielsen Media Research, 2007

Interpret Graphs

1. During which decade did the number of households with TV sets increase the most?
2. During what period did TV viewing decline?

American businesses took advantage of the opportunities offered by the new television industry. Advertising expenditures on TV, which were $170 million in 1950, reached nearly $2 billion in 1960.

Sales of *TV Guide*, introduced in 1953, quickly outpaced sales of other magazines. In 1954 the food industry introduced a new convenience item, the frozen TV dinner. These dinners were complete, ready-to-heat individual meals on disposable aluminum trays. TV dinners made it easy for people to eat without missing their favorite shows.

STEREOTYPES AND GUNSLINGERS Not everyone was thrilled with television, though. Critics objected to its effects on children and its stereotypical portrayal of women and minorities. Women did, in fact, appear in stereotypical roles, such as the ideal mothers of *Father Knows Best* and *The Adventures of Ozzie and Harriet*. Male characters outnumbered women characters three to one. The programs portrayed primarily white, middle-class suburban experiences. African Americans and Hispanic Americans rarely appeared in television programs.

Television in the 1950s portrayed an idealized white America. For the most part, it omitted references to poverty, diversity, and contemporary conflicts, such as the struggle of the civil rights movement against racial discrimination. Instead, it glorified the historical conflicts of the western frontier in hit shows such as *Gunsmoke* and *Have Gun Will Travel*. The level of violence in these popular shows led to ongoing concerns about the effect of television on children. In 1961 Federal Communications Commission chairman Newton Minow voiced this concern to the leaders of the television industry.

Popular comedy star Lucille Ball had to fight to have her real-life husband, Cuban-born Desi Arnaz, cast in the popular TV series *I Love Lucy*.

Vocabulary
stereotypical
conventional, formulaic, and oversimplified

"When television is bad, nothing is worse. I invite you to sit down in front of your television set when your station goes on the air . . . and keep your eyes glued to that set until the station signs off. I can assure you that you will observe a vast wasteland."
—Newton Minow, from a speech to the National Association of Broadcasters, Washington, DC, May 9, 1961

RADIO AND MOVIES Although TV turned out to be wildly popular, radio and movies survived. But instead of competing with television's mass market for drama and variety shows, radio stations turned to local programming of news, weather, music, and community issues. The strategy paid off. During the decade, radio advertising rose by 35 percent. The number of radio stations increased by 50 percent.

From the beginning, television cut into the profitable movie market. In 1948, 18,500 movie theaters had drawn nearly 90 million paid admissions per week. As more people stayed home to watch TV, the number of moviegoers

Actor James Dean, seen here in the movie *Giant,* had a self-confident indifference that made him the idol of teenagers. He died in a car accident at age 24.

decreased by nearly half. As early as 1951, producer David Selznick worried about Hollywood. "It'll never come back. It'll just keep on crumbling until finally the wind blows the last studio prop across the sands."

But Hollywood did not crumble and blow away. Instead, it capitalized on the advantages that movies still held over television—size, color, and stereophonic sound. Stereophonic sound, which surrounded the viewer, was introduced in 1952. By 1954 more than 50 percent of movies were in color. By contrast, color television, which became available that year, did not become widespread until the next decade. In 1953, 20th Century Fox introduced CinemaScope, which projected a wide-angle image on a broad screen. The industry also tried novelty features. Smell-O-Vision and Aroma-Rama piped smells into the theaters to coincide with events shown on the screen. Three-dimensional images, viewed through special glasses supplied by the theaters, appeared to leap into the audience.

Reading Check
Analyze Effects
How did the emergence of television affect American culture in the 1950s?

A Subculture Emerges

Although the mass media found a wide audience for their portrayals of mostly white popular culture, dissenting voices rang out throughout the 1950s. The messages of the beat movement in literature, and of rock 'n' roll in music, clashed with the tidy suburban view of life. This set the stage for the counterculture that would burst forth in the late 1960s.

THE BEAT MOVEMENT Centered in San Francisco, Los Angeles, and New York City's Greenwich Village, the **beat movement** expressed the social and literary nonconformity of artists, poets, and writers. The word *beat* originally meant "weary" but came to refer as well to a musical beat.

Followers of this movement, called beats or beatniks, lived nonconformist lives. They tended to shun regular work. They sought a higher consciousness through Zen Buddhism, music, and, sometimes, drugs.

The Beatniks

Jack Kerouac and other writers of the beat movement took the position of outsiders, writing about nonconformist lifestyles.

Analyze Historical Sources

Why do you think Kerouac's writing style appealed to teenagers and college students? How do you think it made them feel?

"They danced down the streets like dingledodies, and I shambled after as I've been doing all my life after people who interest me, because the only people for me are the mad ones, the ones who are mad to live, mad to talk, mad to be saved, desirous of everything at the same time, the ones that never yawn or say a commonplace thing, but burn, burn, burn like fabulous yellow roman candles exploding like spiders across the stars. . . ."
—Jack Kerouac, from *On the Road*

Many beat poets and writers believed in imposing as little structure as possible on their artistic works, which often had a free, open form. They read their poetry aloud in coffeehouses and other gathering places. Works that capture the essence of this era include Allen Ginsberg's long, free-verse poem, *Howl,* published in 1956, and Jack Kerouac's novel of the movement, *On the Road,* published in 1957. This novel describes a nomadic search across America for authentic experiences, people, and values.

Many mainstream Americans found this lifestyle less enchanting. *LOOK* magazine proclaimed, "There's nothing really new about the beat philosophy. It consists merely of the average American's value scale—turned inside out. The goals of the Beat are *not* watching TV, *not* wearing gray flannel, *not* owning a home in the suburbs, and especially—*not* working." Nonetheless, the beatnik attitudes, way of life, and literature attracted the attention of the media and fired the imaginations of many college students.

Reading Check
Analyze Causes
Why do you think many young Americans were attracted to the beat movement?

African Americans and Rock 'n' Roll

While beats expressed themselves in unstructured literature, musicians in the 1950s added electronic instruments to traditional blues music, creating rhythm and blues. In 1951 a Cleveland, Ohio, radio disc jockey named Alan Freed was among the first to play the music. This audience was mostly white, but the music usually was produced by African American musicians. Freed's listeners responded enthusiastically. Freed began promoting the new music that grew out of rhythm and blues and country and pop. He called the music **rock 'n' roll**, a name that has come to mean music that's both black and white—music that is American.

ROCK 'N' ROLL During the 1950s the teenage years began to be recognized as an important and unique developmental stage between childhood and adulthood. The booming postwar economy made it possible for teenagers to stay in school instead of working to help support their families and allowed their parents to give them generous allowances. In the early and mid-1950s, Little Richard, Chuck Berry, Bill Haley and His Comets, and especially Elvis Presley brought rock 'n' roll to a frantic pitch of popularity among the newly affluent teens who bought their records. The music's heavy rhythm, simple melodies, and lyrics captivated teenagers across the country. Lyrics featured love, cars, and the problems of being young.

Elvis Presley became the unofficial "King of Rock 'n' Roll." He first developed his musical style by singing in church and listening to gospel, country, and blues music on the radio in Memphis, Tennessee. When he was a young boy, his mother gave him a guitar. Years later he paid four dollars of his own money to record two songs in 1953. Sam Phillips, a rhythm-and-blues producer, ran Sun Studios in Memphis, where many early rock 'n' roll records were recorded. He discovered Presley and produced his first records. In 1955 Phillips sold Presley's contract to RCA for $35,000.

Presley's live appearances were immensely popular. Forty-five of his records sold over a million copies, including "Heartbreak Hotel," "Hound Dog," "All Shook Up," "Don't Be Cruel," and "Burning Love." *LOOK* magazine dismissed him as "a wild troubadour who wails rock 'n' roll tunes, flails erratically at a guitar, and wriggles like a peep-show dancer." However, Presley's rebellious style captivated young audiences. Girls screamed and fainted when he performed, and boys tried to imitate him.

Not surprisingly, many adults condemned rock 'n' roll. They believed that the new music would lead to teenage delinquency and immorality. In a few cities, rock 'n' roll concerts were banned. But despite this controversy, television and radio exposure helped bring rock 'n' roll into the mainstream. It became more acceptable by the end of the decade. Record sales, which were 189 million in 1950, grew with the popularity of rock 'n' roll, reaching 600 million in 1960.

Chuck Berry is known as much for his "duck walk" as he is for his electric guitar playing heard on hit records including "Johnny B. Goode" and "Maybellene."

Elvis Presley recorded "Hound Dog" in 1956, making it a popular hit.

Innovative American jazz trumpeter and composer Miles Davis is shown during a recording session in 1959. He continued to blaze musical trails throughout his career.

THE RACIAL GAP African American music had inspired the birth of rock 'n' roll. Many of the genre's greatest performers were—like Berry and Little Richard—African Americans. In other musical genres, singers Nat "King" Cole and Lena Horne, singer and actor Harry Belafonte, and many others paved the way for minority representation in the entertainment fields. Musicians like Miles Davis, Sonny Rollins, Charlie Parker, Dizzy Gillespie, and Thelonious Monk played a style of music characterized by the use of improvisation, called **jazz**. Earlier forms of jazz had evolved into a genre of music called swing, a fast, upbeat musical style that features big bands with strong rhythm sections. Swing music was widely popular before and during the war. Many of its stars were also African American, such as bandleaders Count Basie, Cab Calloway, and Duke Ellington. These artists entertained audiences of all races. Record studios such as Stax Records in Memphis, originally named Satellite Records, were beginning to put out R&B and southern soul records that appealed to white and black consumers alike.

But throughout the 1950s African American shows were mostly broadcast on separate stations. By 1954 there were 250 radio stations nationwide aimed specifically at African American listeners. African American stations were part of radio's attempt to counter the mass popularity of television by targeting specific audiences. These stations also served advertisers who wanted to reach a large African American audience. But it was the black listeners who appreciated the stations most. They had fewer television sets than whites and did not find themselves reflected in mainstream programming. Thulani Davis, a poet, journalist, and playwright, expressed the feelings of one listener about African American radio (or "race radio" as the character called it) in her novel *1959*.

> "Billie Holiday died and I turned twelve on the same hot July day. The saddest singing in the world was coming out of the radio, race radio that is, the radio of the race. The white stations were on the usual relentless rounds of Pat Boone, Teresa Brewer, and anybody else who couldn't sing but liked to cover songs that were once colored. . . . White radio was at least honest—they knew anybody in the South could tell Negro voices from white ones, and so they didn't play our stuff."

—Thulani Davis, *from 1959*

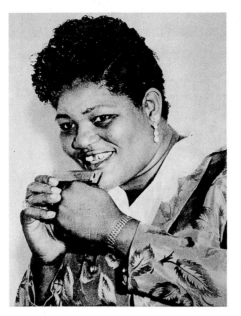

Willie Mae "Big Mama" Thornton is remembered as the first artist to record the song "Hound Dog."

Many African American artists influenced various forms of popular music in the 1950s. Styles such as rock 'n' roll, jazz, and rhythm and blues at first sold mostly to African Americans. As the sound became more popular, and saleable to white audiences, white singers "covered," or released their own versions, of these songs. The white singers made more money and gained more fame, while the African American singers failed to attract similar success.

Few examples highlight the influence African Americans had on rock 'n' roll more than the story of Willie Mae "Big Mama" Thornton. Her story also shows the lack of credit and compensation they received for their efforts.

In 1953 she recorded and released the song "Hound Dog" to little fanfare. She received a mere $500 in royalties. Only three years later, white artist Elvis Presley recorded his own version of the tune, which sold millions of records. Despite her contributions, Thornton reaped few rewards and struggled her entire career to make ends meet.

At the end of the 1950s, African Americans were still largely segregated from the dominant culture of white America. This ongoing segregation—and the racial tensions it fed—would become a powerful force for change in the turbulent 1960s.

Reading Check
Make Inferences
Based on Elvis Presley's song titles, what do you think were teenagers' concerns in the 1950s?

Lesson 3 Assessment

1. **Organize Information** Create a "Who's Who" chart of popular culture idols of the 1950s. Identify the art form and major achievements associated with each person.

Person	Art Form	Achievements

Why do you think they appealed to the young people of the 1950s?

2. **Key Terms and People** For each key term in the lesson, write a sentence explaining its significance.

3. **Compare and Contrast** In what ways were the rock 'n' roll musicians and the beat poets of the 1950s similar and different? Support your answer with details from the text.

Think About:
• the values the musicians and poets believed in
• people's reactions to the musicians, poets, and writers

4. **Evaluate** Do you agree with Newton Minow's statement that TV was "a vast wasteland"? Support your answer with details from the text.

5. **Analyze Effects** How did radio and television contribute to the success of rock 'n' roll?

The Other America

The Big Idea

Amidst the prosperity of the 1950s, millions of Americans lived in poverty.

Why It Matters Now

America today continues to experience a marked income gap between affluent and nonaffluent people.

Key Terms and People

urban renewal

termination policy

One American's Story

James Baldwin was born in New York City. He was the eldest of nine children and grew up in the poverty of the Harlem ghetto. As a novelist, essayist, and playwright, he eloquently portrayed the struggles of African Americans against racial injustice and discrimination. He wrote a letter to his young nephew to mark the 100th anniversary of emancipation. In his words, "the country is celebrating one hundred years of freedom one hundred years too soon."

James Baldwin

"[T]hese innocent and well-meaning people, your countrymen, have caused you to be born under conditions not very far removed from those described for us by Charles Dickens in the London of more than a hundred years ago. . . . This innocent country set you down in a ghetto in which, in fact, it intended that you should perish. . . . You were born where you were born and faced the future that you faced because you were black and for no other reason."
—James Baldwin, from *The Fire Next Time*

For many Americans, the 1950s were a time of unprecedented prosperity. But not everyone experienced this financial well-being. In the "other" America, about 40 million people lived in poverty, untouched by the economic boom.

SS.912.A.1.2; SS.912.A.1.4; SS.912.A.1.7; SS.912.A.7.2; LAFS.1112.RH.4.10

The Challenges of Poverty

Despite the portrait painted by popular culture, life in postwar America did not live up to the "American dream." In 1962 nearly one out of every four Americans was living below the poverty level. Many of these poor were elderly people, single women and their children, or members of minority groups, including African Americans, Hispanic Americans, and Native Americans. Rural residents, particularly farmers, represented the poorest segment of the American population.

FARMERS STRUGGLE Although farming productivity increased from 1950 to 1960, the income from farms actually shrank. As foreign countries recovered from World War II, they imported less food from the United States. The prices of agricultural products dropped dramatically.

At the same time, scientific advances led to new farm technology, such as gasoline-powered tractors and other large equipment. This allowed farm owners to operate with fewer workers. As a result, many of the poorest farm laborers, particularly migrant field hands, found fewer opportunities for employment. Many of these displaced workers flocked to U.S. cities in search of a better life. Between the end of World War II and 1960, nearly 5 million African Americans moved from the rural South to urban areas. However, most of the rural-to-urban migrants experienced little improvement in their economic status.

WHITE FLIGHT At the same time that the rural poor were migrating to the inner cities, another large segment of the population was also on the move. Millions of middle-class white Americans left the cities for the suburbs. They took with them precious economic resources and isolated themselves from other races and classes.

Document-Based Investigation Historical Source

Poverty in America

In 1962 Michael Harrington published *The Other America: Poverty in the United States*, revealing the realities of widespread poverty.

Analyze Historical Sources
How do you think middle-class, suburban Americans felt when reading Harrington's descriptions of the poor and their struggles?

> "The poor get sick more than anyone else in the society. . . . When they become sick, they are sick longer than any other group in the society. Because they are sick more often and longer than anyone else, they lose wages and work, and find it difficult to hold a steady job. And because of this, they cannot pay for good housing, for a nutritious diet, for doctors."
>
> —Michael Harrington, from *The Other America*

Income Gap in America
(Ratio of Black Male Earnings to White Male Earnings*)

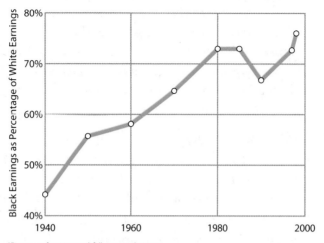

*Figures are for year round, full-time employment.

Source: *The First Measured Century*, Theodore Caplow, 2001

Interpret Graphs

1. What factors does the graph show from 1940 to 1980?
2. What factors affecting people's lives might contribute to the income gap?

The urban crisis prompted by the "white flight" had a direct impact on poor whites and nonwhites. The cities lost not only people and businesses. They also lost the taxes on the property residents had owned and the income taxes they had paid. City governments could no longer afford to properly maintain or improve schools, public transportation, and police and fire departments. The urban poor suffered.

THE INNER CITIES While poverty grew rapidly in the decaying inner cities, many suburban Americans remained unaware of it. Some even refused to believe that poverty could exist in the richest, most powerful nation on earth. Each year, the federal government calculates the minimum amount of income needed to survive—the poverty line. In 1959 the poverty line for a family of four was $2,973. In 2000 it was $17,601.

After living among the nation's poor across America, Michael Harrington published a shocking account that starkly illuminated the issue of poverty. In *The Other America: Poverty in the United States* (1962), he not only confirmed that widespread poverty existed but also exposed its brutal reality.

URBAN RENEWAL Most African Americans, Native Americans, and Hispanic Americans in the cities had to live in dirty, crowded slums. One proposed solution to the housing problem in inner cities was **urban renewal**. The Housing Act of 1949 was passed to provide "a decent home and a suitable living environment for every American family." This act called for tearing down rundown neighborhoods and constructing low-income housing. Later, the nation's leaders would create a new cabinet position, Housing and Urban Development (HUD), to aid in improving conditions in the inner city.

Reading Check
Analyze Effects
Why were attempts at urban renewal viewed as less than successful?

Dilapidated areas were razed, and parking lots, shopping centers, highways, parks, and factories were constructed on some of the cleared land. However, there was seldom enough new housing built to accommodate all the displaced people. For example, a *barrio* in Los Angeles was torn down to make way for Dodger Stadium. Poor people who were displaced from their homes simply moved from one ghetto to another. Some critics of urban renewal claimed that it had merely become urban *removal*.

Poverty Leads to Activism

Despite ongoing poverty, during the 1950s African Americans began to make significant strides toward the reduction of racial discrimination and segregation. Inspired by the African American civil rights movement, other minorities also began to develop a deeper political awareness and a voice. Mexican American activism gathered steam after veterans returned from World War II. A major change in government policy under Eisenhower's administration fueled Native American protest.

MEXICANS SEEK EMPLOYMENT Many Mexicans had become U.S. citizens during the 19th century, when the United States had annexed the Southwest after the war with Mexico. Large numbers of Mexicans had also crossed the border to work in the United States during and after World War I.

Background
In 1954 the United States launched a program designed to find and return undocumented immigrants to Mexico. Between 1953 and 1955, more than 2 million illegal Mexican immigrants were deported.

When the United States entered World War II, there was a shortage of agricultural laborers. This spurred the federal government to initiate a program in which Mexican *braceros*, or hired hands, were allowed into the United States to harvest crops. As a result of this program, hundreds of thousands of braceros came to the United States. When their employment was ended, the braceros were expected to return to Mexico. However, many of them remained in the United States illegally. In addition, hundreds of thousands of Mexicans entered the country illegally to escape poor economic conditions in Mexico.

In 1942 Mexican farmworkers on their way to California bid farewell to their families.

THE LONGORIA INCIDENT One of the more notorious instances of prejudice against Mexican Americans involved the burial of Felix Longoria. Longoria was a Mexican American World War II hero who had been killed in the Philippines. The only undertaker in his hometown in Texas refused to provide Longoria's family with funeral services.

In the wake of the Longoria incident, outraged Mexican Americans stepped up their efforts to stamp out discrimination. In 1948 several hundred Hispanic veterans formed the American G.I. Forum. They won national attention for their efforts when their Texas leader, Hector P. Garcia, accepted Senator Lyndon Johnson's offer that Longoria be buried at Arlington National Cemetery. The Forum also worked to win full access to military benefits for Hispanic veterans. Meanwhile, activist Ignacio Lopez founded the Unity League of California to register Mexican American voters and to promote candidates who would represent their interests.

NATIVE AMERICANS CONTINUE THEIR STRUGGLE Native Americans also continued to fight for their rights and identity. From the passage of the Dawes Act, in 1887, until 1934, the policy of the federal government toward Native Americans had been one of "Americanization" and assimilation. In 1924 the Snyder Act granted citizenship to all Native Americans, but they remained second-class citizens.

In 1934 the Indian Reorganization Act moved official policy away from assimilation and toward Native American autonomy. Its passage signaled a change in federal policy. In addition, because the government was reeling from the Great Depression, it wanted to stop subsidizing the Native Americans. Native Americans also took the initiative to improve their lives. In 1944 they established the National Congress of American Indians. The congress had two main goals: (1) to ensure for Native Americans the same civil rights that white Americans had, and (2) to enable Native Americans on reservations to retain their own customs.

Vocabulary
subsidizing
a government giving financial assistance to a person or group to support an undertaking regarded as being in the public interest

Native Americans like this man received job training from the Bureau of Indian Affairs to help them settle in urban areas.

During World War II over 65,000 Native Americans left their reservations for military service and war work. As a result, they became very aware of discrimination. When the war ended, Native Americans stopped receiving family allotments and wages. Outsiders also grabbed control of tribal lands, primarily to exploit their deposits of minerals, oil, and timber.

THE TERMINATION POLICY In 1953 the federal government announced that it would give up its responsibility for Native American tribes. This new approach was known as the **termination policy**. It eliminated federal economic support, discontinued the reservation system, and distributed tribal lands among individual Native Americans. In response to the termination policy, the Bureau of Indian Affairs began a voluntary relocation program to help Native Americans resettle in cities.

The termination policy was a dismal failure, however. The Bureau of Indian Affairs helped relocate 35,000 Native Americans to urban areas during the 1950s. Unfortunately, they were often unable to find jobs in their new locations because of poor training and racial prejudice. They were also left without access to medical care when federal programs were abolished. In 1963 the termination policy was abandoned.

Reading Check
Analyze Issues How did the Longoria incident motivate Mexican Americans to increase their political and social activism?

Lesson 4 Assessment

1. **Organize Information** Use a Venn diagram to record the common problems that African Americans, Mexican Americans, and Native Americans faced during the 1950s. Note how their goals and objectives are similar and how they are different.

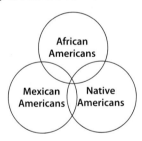

What do these problems illustrate about life in the 1950s?

2. **Key Terms and People** For each key term in the lesson, write a sentence explaining its significance.

3. **Evaluate** Do you think that urban renewal was an effective approach to the housing problem in inner cities? Why or why not?

   Think About:
   • the goals of the Housing Act of 1949
   • the claims made by some critics of urban renewal
   • the residents' best interests

4. **Analyze Issues** How did Native Americans work to increase their participation in the U.S. political process?

5. **Draw Conclusions** Which major population shift— "white flight," migration from Mexico, or relocation of Native Americans—do you think had the greatest impact on U.S. society? Why?

6. **Analyze Effects** What effect did scientific advances have on the United States and global economies?

Module 13 Assessment

Key Terms and People

For each term below, write a sentence explaining its historical significance in the 1950s.

1. suburb
2. Dixiecrat
3. Fair Deal
4. conglomerate
5. baby boom
6. consumerism
7. mass media
8. beat movement
9. rock 'n' roll
10. urban renewal

Main Ideas

Use your notes and the information in the module to answer the following questions.

Postwar America

1. How did the GI Bill of Rights help World War II veterans?
2. What factors contributed to the American postwar economic boom?
3. How did Truman use his executive power to advance civil rights?
4. What domestic and foreign issues concerned voters during the 1952 presidential election?

The American Dream in the Fifties

5. What shift in employment trends had occurred by the mid-1950s?
6. How were conglomerates and franchises alike and how were they different?
7. How did the membership and accomplishments of unions change during the 1950s?
8. How did life in the suburbs provide the model for the American dream?
9. What positive and negative effects did the mass availability of the automobile have on American life in the 1950s?

Popular Culture

10. How did radio and movies maintain their appeal in the 1950s?
11. Do you think the rise of television had a positive or a negative effect on Americans? Explain.
12. How did African American performers influence American popular culture in the 1950s?

The Other America

13. How did many major cities change in the 1950s?
14. What effect did white flight have on America's cities?
15. What obstacles to improving their lives did Native Americans face in the 1950s?

Critical Thinking

1. **Draw Conclusions** In a web like the one below, show the postwar technological advances you consider most influential.

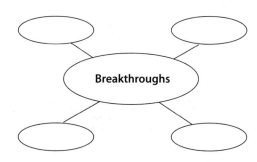

2. **Analyze Causes** During America's first two centuries, the national character was marked by individualism. Why do you think conformity became the norm in the 1950s? How did suburban living support conformity and stereotyping?
3. **Analyze Primary Sources** Do you agree or disagree with the following quotation from *Life* magazine about American culture in 1954: "Never before so much for so few"? Support your answer with evidence.

4. **Evaluate** After World War II, many Americans chased after their perception of the "American Dream." Which Americans had the most opportunities to attain this idealized way of living? What opportunities were given to veterans that might have helped them achieve this lifestyle? Did white-collar workers and blue-collars workers have the same opportunities? Explain your answers.

5. **Form Generalizations** How did women's roles and opportunities in the 1950s differ from women's roles today?

6. **Analyze Issues** How did television support and promote stereotyping?

7. **Draw Conclusions** In what ways did popular music and literature help bring about the subculture movement?

8. **Analyze Effects** In what ways did mass media impact the American economy?

9. **Evaluate** How effective were the economic policies the U.S. government put into place to fight inflation?

Engage with History

Suppose you are a beat poet who has been asked to write an original poem entitled *A Postwar American Dream*. Use information from the module and your knowledge of American history to support your poem. Remember to include a wide range of lifestyles in your poem.

Focus on Writing

In 1956 President Eisenhower signed the Interstate Highway Act that led to the construction of a nationwide highway network. Write a persuasive essay supporting the law. In the first part of your essay, clearly outline the benefits created by the law. Include information about the factors that led to the creation of suburbs and planned communities such as Levittown and how those factors were related to the need for new roads. In the second part of your essay, address the concerns of those who oppose the law.

Multimedia Activity

During the baby boom generation, there were many important advancements in science and technology that led to new inventions and new lifestyles for Americans. Write a blog post about a postwar technological change or invention, and explain how it changed American culture. For example, you could write about how the development of microwave relays led to the spread of television and explain the resulting changes to American life. Use the Internet to research a variety of primary and secondary sources to create your post, such as videos, photographs, maps, and first-person accounts.

An Era of Social Change

★

Essential Question

How are significant and lasting social changes created?

About the Photograph: Hippies gather in El Rito, New Mexico, at a Fourth of July parade in 1969.

In this module you will learn about how the Kennedy and Johnson administrations pushed for social reforms from within the government. You will also learn how citizens banded together to create movements that changed the social climate in the 1960s and 1970s.

▶ *Explore ONLINE!*

VIDEOS, including...
- Kennedy Elected
- JFK: A New Generation
- Assassination of John F. Kennedy
- LBJ's Management Style

✓ Document-Based Investigations

✓ Graphic Organizers

✓ Interactive Games

✓ Carousel: Kennedy Style

✓ Carousel: Pollution in the 1970s

SS.912.A.1.2 Utilize a variety of primary and secondary sources to identify author, historical significance, audience, and authenticity to understand a historical period. **SS.912.A.1.4** Analyze how images, symbols, objects, cartoons, graphs, charts, maps, and artwork may be used to interpret the significance of time periods and events from the past. **SS.912.A.1.7** Describe various sociocultural aspects of American life including arts, artifacts, literature, education, and publications. **SS.912.A.7.1** Identify causes for Post-World War II prosperity and its effects on American society. **SS.912.A.7.2** Compare the relative prosperity between different ethnic groups and social classes in the post-World War II period. **SS.912.A.7.3** Examine the changing status of women in the United States from post-World War II to present. **SS.912.G.2.1** Identify the physical characteristics and the human characteristics that define and differentiate regions. **SS.912.H.1.1** Relate works in the arts of varying styles and genre according to the periods in which they were created. **SS.912.H.1.3** Relate works in the arts to various cultures. **SS.912.H.1.5** Examine artistic response to social issues and new ideas in various cultures. **LAFS.1112.RH.1.1** Cite specific textual evidence to support analysis of primary and secondary sources, connecting insights gained from specific details to an understanding of the text as a whole. **LAFS.1112.RH.1.2** Determine the central ideas or information of a primary or secondary source; provide an accurate summary that makes clear the relationships among the key details and ideas. **LAFS.1112.RH.4.10** By the end of grade 12, read and comprehend history/social studies texts in the grades 11–CCR text complexity band independently and proficiently. **MAFS.K12.MP.1.1** Make sense of problems and persevere in solving them. **MAFS.K12.MP.5.1** Use appropriate tools strategically. **MAFS.K12.MP.6.1** Attend to precision.

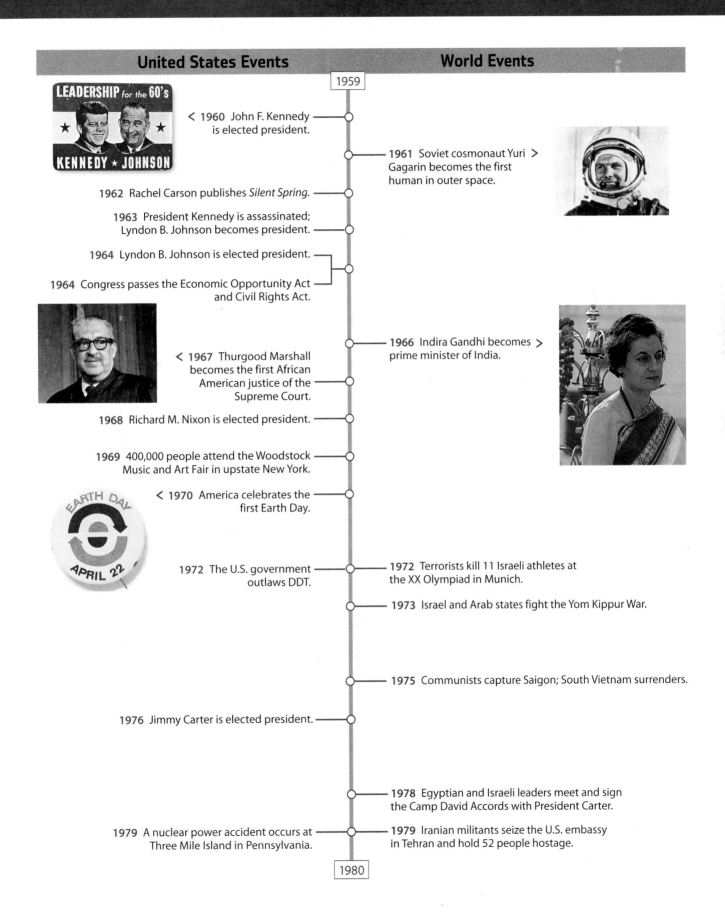

United States Events   **World Events**

1959

‹ 1960 John F. Kennedy is elected president.

1961 Soviet cosmonaut Yuri **›** Gagarin becomes the first human in outer space.

1962 Rachel Carson publishes *Silent Spring.*

1963 President Kennedy is assassinated; Lyndon B. Johnson becomes president.

1964 Lyndon B. Johnson is elected president.

1964 Congress passes the Economic Opportunity Act and Civil Rights Act.

1966 Indira Gandhi becomes **›** prime minister of India.

‹ 1967 Thurgood Marshall becomes the first African American justice of the Supreme Court.

1968 Richard M. Nixon is elected president.

1969 400,000 people attend the Woodstock Music and Art Fair in upstate New York.

‹ 1970 America celebrates the first Earth Day.

1972 The U.S. government outlaws DDT.

1972 Terrorists kill 11 Israeli athletes at the XX Olympiad in Munich.

1973 Israel and Arab states fight the Yom Kippur War.

1975 Communists capture Saigon; South Vietnam surrenders.

1976 Jimmy Carter is elected president.

1978 Egyptian and Israeli leaders meet and sign the Camp David Accords with President Carter.

1979 A nuclear power accident occurs at Three Mile Island in Pennsylvania.

1979 Iranian militants seize the U.S. embassy in Tehran and hold 52 people hostage.

1980

★ Kennedy and the New Frontier

The Big Idea

John F. Kennedy brought energy, initiative, and important new ideas to the presidency.

Why It Matters Now

Kennedy's programs and proposals addressed important social issues and laid groundwork for reforms that would make America a more innovative and progressive nation.

Key Terms and People

John F. Kennedy

New Frontier

mandate

Peace Corps

Alliance for Progress

Warren Commission

One American's Story

John F. Kennedy became the 35th president of the United States on a crisp and sparkling day in January 1961. Appearing without a coat in freezing weather, he issued a challenge to the American people. He said that the world was in "its hour of maximum danger," as Cold War tensions ran high. Rather than shrinking from the danger, the United States should confront the "iron tyranny" of communism.

"Let the word go forth from this time and place, to friend and foe alike, that the torch has been passed to a new generation of Americans, born in this century, tempered by war, disciplined by a hard and bitter peace, proud of our ancient heritage, and unwilling to witness or permit the slow undoing of those human rights to which this nation has always been committed. . . .

After taking the oath of office, President Kennedy delivers his inaugural address.

Let every nation know, whether it wishes us well or ill, that we shall pay any price, bear any burden, meet any hardship, support any friend, oppose any . . . foe, in order to assure . . . the survival and the success of liberty."

John F. Kennedy, from his Inaugural Address, January 20, 1961

SS.912.A.7.4; SS.912.A.7.12

The Election of 1960

In 1960, as President Eisenhower's second term drew to a close, a mood of restlessness arose among voters. The economy was in a recession. The USSR's launch of *Sputnik I* in 1957 and its development of long-range missiles had sparked fears that the American military was falling behind that of the Soviets. Further setbacks including the U-2 incident and the alignment of Cuba with the Soviet Union had Americans questioning whether the United States was losing the Cold War.

The Democratic nominee for president, Massachusetts senator John Kennedy, promised active leadership "to get America moving again." His Republican opponent, Vice-President Richard M. Nixon, hoped to win by riding on the coattails of Eisenhower's popularity. Both candidates had similar positions on policy issues. Two factors helped put Kennedy over the top: television and the civil rights issue.

THE TELEVISED DEBATE AFFECTS VOTES Kennedy had a well-organized campaign and the backing of his wealthy family. He was also handsome and charismatic. Yet many felt that, at 43, he was too inexperienced. If elected, he would be the second-youngest president in the nation's history.

Americans also worried that having a Roman Catholic in the White House would lead either to influence of the pope on American policies or to closer ties between church and state. Kennedy was able to allay worries by discussing the issue openly.

One event in the fall determined the course of the election. This event showed how the spread of mass media would impact politics for years to

Vocabulary
charismatic
possessing personal
charm that attracts
devoted followers

John F. Kennedy *(right)* appeared confident and at ease during a televised debate with his opponent, Richard M. Nixon.

come. Kennedy and Nixon took part in the first televised debate between presidential candidates. On September 26, 1960, some 70 million TV viewers watched the two articulate and knowledgeable candidates debating issues. Nixon, an expert on foreign policy, had agreed to the forum in hopes of exposing Kennedy's inexperience. However, Kennedy had been coached by television producers. He looked and spoke better than Nixon. Kennedy also had a tan from campaigning in Southern California and looked rested and fit. According to some sources, Nixon was running a high fever the night of the debate. He looked pale, ill, and tired in his gray suit. Radio listeners thought Nixon narrowly won the debate, but those watching on television gave Kennedy the edge.

Kennedy's success in the debate launched a new era in American politics: the television age. As journalist Russell Baker, who covered the Nixon campaign, said, "That night, image replaced the printed word as the natural language of politics." Nixon and Kennedy's debate was the first of four televised debates between the candidates for president. The debates brought the candidates into America's living room in a brand new way. The candidate could appeal directly to the voters. Scenes of the candidates' presentations could be repeated indefinitely, adding to the public's exposure to the candidates' views. As a result, television began to undercut the value of a party structure in drumming up support for a candidate. Running a political campaign now demanded tapping into the power of television to gain an advantage.

KENNEDY AND CIVIL RIGHTS A second major event of the campaign took place in October. Police in Atlanta, Georgia, arrested the Reverend Martin Luther King Jr. and 33 other African American demonstrators for sitting at a segregated lunch counter. Although the other demonstrators were released, King was sentenced to months of hard labor. Officially his offense was a minor traffic violation. The Eisenhower administration refused to intervene, and Nixon took no public position.

When Kennedy heard of the arrest and sentencing, he telephoned King's wife, Coretta Scott King, to express his sympathy. Meanwhile, Robert Kennedy, his brother and campaign manager, persuaded the judge who had sentenced King to release the civil rights leader on bail, pending appeal. News of the incident captured the immediate attention of the African American community. African American votes would help Kennedy carry key states in the Midwest and South.

The Camelot Years

The election in November 1960 was the closest since 1884. Kennedy won by fewer than 119,000 votes. His inauguration set the tone for a new era at the White House: one of grace, elegance, and wit. On the podium sat over 100 writers, artists, and scientists that the Kennedys had invited. Included was opera singer Marian Anderson, who had once been barred from singing at Constitution Hall because she was African American. Kennedy's inspiring speech called for hope, commitment, and sacrifice. "And so, my fellow

Kennedy campaign poster, 1960

Reading Check
Analyze Effects
What effect do you think the televised debate had on American politics?

Americans," he proclaimed, "ask not what your country can do for you—ask what you can do for your country."

THE KENNEDY MYSTIQUE During his term, the president and his beautiful young wife, Jacqueline, invited many artists and celebrities to the White House. In addition, Kennedy often appeared on television. The press loved his charm and wit and helped to bolster his image.

Critics of Kennedy's presidency argued that his smooth style lacked substance. But the new First Family fascinated the public. For example, after learning that JFK could read 1,600 words a minute, thousands of people enrolled in speed-reading courses. The First Lady, too, captivated the nation with her eye for fashion and culture. It seemed the nation could not get enough of the First Family. Newspapers and magazines filled their pages with pictures and stories about the president's young daughter, Caroline, and his infant son, John.

THE BEST AND THE BRIGHTEST With JFK's youthful glamour and his talented advisers, the Kennedy White House reminded many of a modern-day Camelot, the mythical court of King Arthur. Kennedy surrounded himself with a team that one journalist called "the best and the brightest." They included McGeorge Bundy, a Harvard University dean, as national security advisor; Robert McNamara, president of Ford Motor Company, as secretary of defense; and Dean Rusk, president of the Rockefeller Foundation, as secretary of state. Of all the advisers who comprised Kennedy's inner circle, he relied most heavily on his 35-year-old brother, Robert, whom he appointed attorney general.

Background
The fictional King Arthur was based on a real fifth- or sixth-century Celt. In literature, Arthur's romantic world is marked by chivalry and magic.

Reading Check
Draw Conclusions
What factors help explain the public's fascination with the Kennedys?

President and Mrs. Kennedy enjoy time with their children, Caroline and John Jr., while vacationing in Hyannis Port, Massachusetts.

The Promise of Progress

Kennedy had often promoted his plans for changing the nation in his campaign speeches. Once in office, he set out to transform his broad vision of progress into what he called the **New Frontier**. "We stand today on the edge of a New Frontier," Kennedy had announced upon accepting the nomination for president. He called on Americans to be "new pioneers" and explore "uncharted areas of science and space, . . . unconquered pockets of ignorance and prejudice, unanswered questions of poverty and surplus."

EARLY CHALLENGES Kennedy had difficulty turning his vision into reality, however. As part of his New Frontier plans, he offered Congress proposals to provide medical care for the aged, rebuild blighted urban areas, and improve education, but he couldn't gather enough votes. The makeup of Congress reflected the American public's mood. Kennedy faced the same conservative coalition that had blocked President Truman's Fair Deal.

In his efforts to push his domestic reform measures through Congress, Kennedy showed little skill. Since he had been elected by the slimmest of margins, he lacked a popular **mandate**—a clear indication that voters approved of his plans. As a result, he often tried to play it safe politically. Nevertheless, Kennedy did persuade Congress to enact measures to boost the economy, build the national defense, provide international aid, and fund a massive space program. He also succeeded in making significant improvements to education through measures such as increasing funding to school libraries, allocating special funds to teach children with specialized needs, and expanding opportunities for vocational training.

STIMULATING THE ECONOMY One domestic problem the Kennedy team tackled was the economy. By 1960 America was in a recession. A recession is, in a general sense, a moderate slowdown of the economy marked by increased unemployment and reduced personal consumption. In 1961 the nation's jobless rate climbed from just under 6 percent to nearly 7 percent, one of the highest levels since World War II. Personal consumption of several major items declined that year. People worried about job security and, as a result, spent less money.

During the campaign, Kennedy had criticized the Eisenhower administration for failing to stimulate growth. The American economy, he said, was lagging behind those of other Western democracies and the Soviet Union. Kennedy's advisers pushed for the use of deficit spending, which had been the basis for Roosevelt's New Deal. They said that stimulating economic growth depended on increased government spending and lower taxes, even if it meant that the government spent more than it took in.

Accordingly, the proposals Kennedy sent to Congress in 1961 called for increased spending. The Department of Defense received a nearly 20 percent budget increase for new nuclear missiles and nuclear submarines, as well as for an expansion of the armed services. Congress also approved a package that increased the minimum wage to $1.25 an hour, extended unemployment insurance, and provided assistance to cities with high unemployment.

A Peace Corps volunteer gives a ride to a Nigerian girl.

ADDRESSING POVERTY ABROAD One of the first campaign promises Kennedy fulfilled was the creation of the **Peace Corps**. It was a program of volunteer assistance to the developing nations of Asia, Africa, and Latin America. Critics in the United States called the program "Kennedy's Kiddie Korps" because many volunteers were just out of college. Some foreign observers questioned whether Americans could understand other cultures.

Despite these reservations, the Peace Corps became a huge success. It succeeded in its goal of increasing good-will toward the United States throughout the world. People of all ages and backgrounds signed up to work as agricultural advisers, teachers, or health aides or to do whatever work the host country needed. By 1968 more than 35,000 volunteers had served in 60 nations around the world.

Today, the mission of the organization remains the same: to promote world peace and friendship. However, the role of the Peace Corps has evolved along with the changing world. Volunteers now bring along cutting-edge technology to tackle the modern challenges facing the countries they serve. Many volunteers serve as teachers and health workers, but there is now a wider variety of volunteer opportunities to address a broader span of global issues, such as gender equality and climate change. In 2014 policy changes allowed volunteers to choose specific countries and missions for the first time, causing a surge in applications.

A second foreign aid program, the **Alliance for Progress**, offered economic and technical assistance to Latin American countries. Between 1961 and 1969, the United States invested almost $12 billion in Latin America, in part to deter these countries from picking up Fidel Castro's revolutionary ideas. While the money brought some development to the region, it didn't bring fundamental reforms.

CONFRONTING DOMESTIC PROBLEMS Although progress was being made internationally, many Americans suffered at home. Poverty continued to be a serious issue. The number of poor shocked many Americans. A number of Americans also faced racial discrimination and segregation.

Gradually, the fight against segregation took hold. Throughout the South, demonstrators raised their voices in what would become some of the most controversial civil rights battles of the 1960s. Kennedy had not pushed aggressively for legislation on the issues of poverty and civil rights, although he effected changes by executive action. For example, Kennedy's administration introduced affirmative action policies to place more African Americans in federal jobs and banned discriminatory hiring practices by government contractors. However, now he felt that it was time to take further actions to live up to his campaign promises.

In 1963 Kennedy began to focus more closely on the issues at home. He called for a "national assault on the causes of poverty." He also confronted discrimination, ordering Robert Kennedy's Justice Department to investigate racial injustices in the South. Finally, he presented Congress with a sweeping civil rights bill and a proposal to cut taxes by over $10 billion.

Reading Check
Make Inferences
In what directions did President Kennedy seem to be taking his administration in 1963?

Tragedy in Dallas

In the fall of 1963, public opinion polls showed that Kennedy was losing popularity because of his advocacy of civil rights. Yet most Americans still supported their beloved president. No one could foresee the terrible national tragedy just ahead.

FOUR DAYS IN NOVEMBER On the sunny morning of November 22, 1963, *Air Force One*, the presidential aircraft, landed in Dallas, Texas. President and Mrs. Kennedy had come to Texas to mend political fences with members of the state's Democratic Party. Kennedy had expected a cool reception from the conservative state. Instead, he basked in warm waves of applause from crowds that lined the streets of downtown Dallas.

Jacqueline and her husband sat in the back seat of an open-air limousine. In front of them sat Texas governor John Connally and his wife, Nellie. As the car approached a state building known as the Texas School Book Depository, Nellie Connally turned to Kennedy and said, "You can't say that Dallas isn't friendly to you today." A few seconds later, rifle shots rang out, and Kennedy was shot in the head. His car raced to a nearby hospital, where doctors frantically tried to revive him, but it was too late. President Kennedy was dead.

As the tragic news spread through America's schools, offices, and homes, people reacted with disbelief. Questions were on everyone's lips: Who had killed the president, and why? What would happen next?

During the next four days, television became "the window of the world." A photograph of a somber Lyndon Johnson taking the oath of office aboard the presidential airplane was broadcast. Soon, audiences watched as Dallas police charged Lee Harvey Oswald with the murder. His palm print had been found on the rifle used to kill John F. Kennedy.

The 24-year-old ex-Marine had a suspicious past. After receiving a dishonorable discharge, Oswald had briefly lived in the Soviet Union, and he supported Castro. On Sunday, November 24, millions watched live television coverage of Oswald being transferred from the

John Kennedy Jr. salutes his father's casket as it is prepared for the trip to Arlington National Cemetery. His uncles Edward Kennedy and Attorney General Robert Kennedy, his mother, and his sister look on.

Dallas Police Department to the county jail. Then Jack Ruby, a Dallas nightclub owner with ties to organized crime, broke through the crowd and shot and killed Oswald.

The next day, all work stopped for Kennedy's funeral as America mourned its fallen leader. The assassination and televised funeral became a historic event. Americans who were alive then can still recall what they were doing when they first heard about the shooting of their president.

UNANSWERED QUESTIONS The bizarre chain of events made some people wonder if Oswald was part of a conspiracy. In 1963 the **Warren Commission** investigated and concluded that Oswald had shot the president while acting on his own. Later, in 1979, a reinvestigation concluded that Oswald was part of a conspiracy. Investigators also said that two persons may have fired at the president. Numerous other people have made investigations. Their explanations have ranged from a plot by anti-Castro Cubans, to a Communist-sponsored attack, to a conspiracy by the CIA.

What Americans did learn from the Kennedy assassination was that their system of government is remarkably sturdy. A crisis that would have crippled a dictatorship did not prevent a smooth transition to the presidency of Lyndon Johnson. Some worried that the assassination would have a negative impact on the progress being made on civil rights legislation, but Johnson vowed to continue the work that Kennedy had begun.

In a speech to Congress, Johnson expressed his hope that "from the brutal loss of our leader we will derive not weakness but strength." Right away, he began to push for the passage of the civil rights legislation that had been stalled in Congress. Johnson wanted to do more than follow in Kennedy's footsteps, however. He had ambitious plans of his own. As president, Johnson would be a strong leader, using his considerable political talents to achieve greater legislative success than Kennedy.

Vocabulary
conspiracy an agreement by two or more persons to take illegal political action

Reading Check
Contrast How did the Warren Commission's findings differ from other theories?

Lesson 1 Assessment

1. **Organize Information** Use a web diagram to list the programs of the New Frontier.

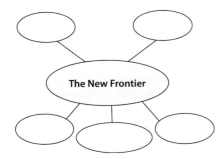

The New Frontier

Which do you think was most successful? Why?

2. **Key Terms and People** For each term or person in the lesson, write a sentence explaining its significance.

3. **Evaluate** Do you think President Kennedy was a successful leader and successful civil rights advocate? Explain your viewpoint.

 Think About:
 • the reasons for his popularity
 • the goals he expressed
 • his foreign policy
 • his legislative record

4. **Make Inferences** Why do you think Kennedy lost popularity for supporting civil rights?

5. **Draw Conclusions** Why did the fate of President Kennedy affect people so deeply?

The Movement of Migrant Workers

The nation's 2 million farm workers are responsible for harvesting much of the fruit and vegetables that families eat each day. Most fieldworkers on United States farms remain in one place most of the year. Others are migrant workers, who move with their entire family from one region to the next as the growing seasons change. Nationally, migrant workers make up some 50 percent of hired farm workers, depending on the season and other factors.

As the map shows, there were three major streams of migrant worker movements in the 1960s: the Pacific Coast, the Midwest, and the Atlantic Coast streams. While these paths may have changed slightly since then, the movement of migrant workers into nearly every region of the nation continues today.

THE PACIFIC COAST
The Pacific Coast region's moderate climate allows for year-round harvesting. Most of California's migrant farm workers work on large fruit farms for much of the year. About 65,000 workers make their way up to Washington each year to pick cherries, apples, and other crops.

THE MIDWEST
Workers along the Midwest and East Coast streams, where crops are smaller, must keep moving in order to find work. These workers picking strawberries in Michigan will soon move on. For example, one family may travel to Ohio for the tomato harvest and then return to Michigan to pick apples before heading back to Texas for the winter months.

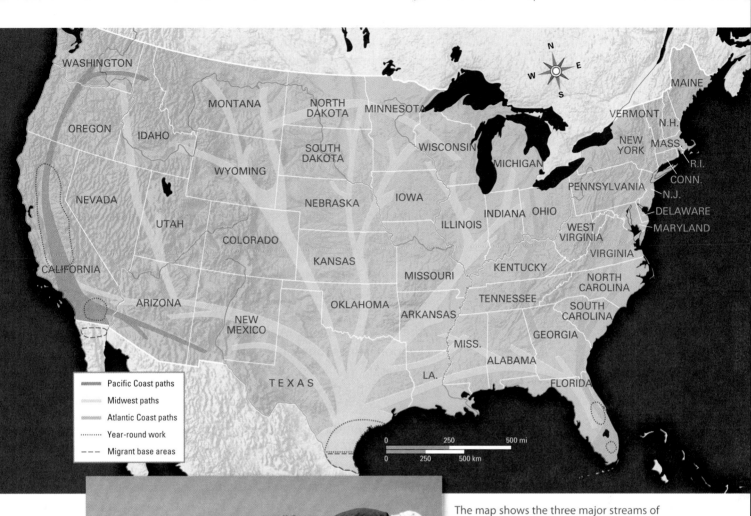

The map shows the three major streams of migrant worker movements in the 1960s.

Map Legend:
- Pacific Coast paths
- Midwest paths
- Atlantic Coast paths
- Year-round work
- Migrant base areas

0   250   500 mi
0   250   500 km

THE ATLANTIC COAST

While some workers along the Atlantic Coast stream remain in Florida, others travel as far north as New Hampshire and New York, like the workers shown here harvesting onions. There, they work from March through September. Due to the winters, migrant workers in most of the Midwest and Atlantic regions can find work for only six months out of the year.

Critical Thinking

1. **Analyze Patterns** Retrace the movement of migrant workers in the three regions. Why do you think migrant workers have to keep moving?

2. **Create a Database** Pose a historical question about the relationship between crops and planting seasons. For example, what types of crops are harvested in Michigan during the fall? Then research and create a database that answers this and other such questions.

Johnson and the Great Society

The Big Idea

The demand for reform helped create a new awareness of social problems, especially on matters of civil rights and the effects of poverty.

Why It Matters Now

Reforms made in the 1960s have had a lasting effect on the American justice system by increasing the rights of minorities.

Key Terms and People

Lyndon Baines Johnson

Economic Opportunity Act

Great Society

Medicare

Medicaid

Immigration Act of 1965

Warren Court

reapportionment

SS.912.A.1.2; SS.912.A.1.4; SS.912.A.1.6; SS.912.A.7.4; SS.912.A.7.8; SS.912.A.7.12; SS.912.A.7.13; SS.912.A.7.16; HE.912.C.2.4; LAFS.1112.RH.4.10

One American's Story

In 1966 family finances forced Larry Alfred to drop out of high school in Mobile, Alabama. He turned to the Job Corps, a federal program that trained young people from poor backgrounds. He learned to operate construction equipment, but his dream was to help people. On the advice of his Job Corps counselor, he joined VISTA (Volunteers in Service to America). VISTA was often called the "domestic Peace Corps."

Both the Job Corps and VISTA sprang into being in 1964, when President **Lyndon Baines Johnson** signed the Economic Opportunity Act. This law was the main offensive of Johnson's "war on poverty" and a cornerstone of the Great Society.

VISTA assigned Alfred to work with a community of poor farm laborers in Robstown, Texas, near the Mexican border. There he found a number of children with mental and physical disabilities who had no special assistance, education, or training. So he established the

VISTA volunteers worked in a variety of capacities. This woman is teaching art to young pupils.

Robstown Association for Retarded People. He started a parents education program, sought state funds, and created a rehabilitation center. At age 20, Larry Alfred was a high school dropout, Job Corps graduate, VISTA volunteer, and, in Robstown, an authority on people with disabilities. Alfred embodied Johnson's Great Society in two ways. Its programs helped him turn his life around, and he made a difference in people's lives.

LBJ's Path to Power

By the time Lyndon B. Johnson, or LBJ, as he was called, succeeded to the presidency, his ambition and drive had become legendary. In explaining his frenetic energy, Johnson once remarked, "That's the way I've been all my life. My daddy used to wake me up at dawn and shake my leg and say, 'Lyndon, every boy in town's got an hour's head start on you.'"

FROM THE TEXAS HILLS TO CAPITOL HILL A fourth-generation Texan, Johnson grew up in the dry Texas Hill Country of Blanco County. The Johnsons never knew great wealth, but they also never missed a meal.

LBJ entered politics in 1937 when he won a special election to fill a vacant seat in the U.S. House of Representatives. Johnson styled himself as a "New Dealer" and spokesperson for the small ranchers and struggling farmers of his district. He caught the eye of President Franklin Roosevelt, who took Johnson under his wing. Roosevelt helped him secure key committee assignments in Congress and steer much-needed electrification and water projects to his Texas district. Johnson, in turn, idolized FDR and imitated his leadership style.

Once in the House, Johnson eagerly eyed a seat in the Senate. In 1948, after an exhausting, bitterly fought campaign, he won the Democratic primary election for the Senate by a margin of only 87 votes out of 988,000.

A MASTER POLITICIAN Johnson proved himself a master of party politics and behind-the-scenes maneuvering. After just one term as a senator, he rose to the position of Senate majority leader in 1955. People called his legendary ability to win over reporters and persuade senators to support his bills the "LBJ treatment."

Johnson's deft handling of Congress led to the passage of the Civil Rights Act of 1957. This act was a voting rights measure—the first civil rights legislation since Reconstruction. By 1960 Johnson had more influence in Washington, DC, than any other Democrat. His knack for achieving legislative results had captured John F. Kennedy's attention, too, during Kennedy's run

---

Lyndon B. Johnson (1908–1973)

LBJ received his teaching degree from Southwest Texas State Teachers College in 1930. To finance his own education, Johnson took a year off from college to work at a Mexican American school in Cotulla, Texas. He later taught public speaking and debate at the Sam Houston High School in Houston. At age 26 he became the state director of the National Youth Administration, a New Deal agency.

As president, Johnson pushed hard for the passage of the Elementary and Secondary Education Act. In 1965 he signed the act at the one-room schoolhouse near Stonewall, Texas, where his own education had begun. Johnson later wrote,

"My education had begun with what I learned in that schoolroom. Now what I had learned and experienced since that time had brought me back to fulfill a dream."

Reading Check
Analyze Motives
Why did Kennedy choose Johnson to be his running mate?

for the White House. To Kennedy, Johnson's congressional connections and his Southern Protestant background compensated for his own drawbacks as a candidate. He asked Johnson to be his running mate. Johnson's presence on the ticket helped Kennedy win key states in the South, especially Texas, which went Democratic by just a few thousand votes.

Johnson's Domestic Agenda

In the wake of Kennedy's assassination, President Johnson addressed a joint session of Congress. It was the fifth day of his administration. "All I have I would have given gladly not to be standing here today," he began. Kennedy had inspired Americans to begin to solve national and world problems. Johnson urged Congress to pass the civil rights and tax-cut bills that Kennedy had sent to Capitol Hill. He asserted that the passage of these bills would be the best way to honor the memory of the fallen president.

CONTINUING KENNEDY'S PROGRAMS In February 1964 Congress passed a tax reduction of over $10 billion into law. As the Democrats had hoped, the tax cut spurred economic growth. People spent more, which meant profits for businesses. This in turn increased tax revenues and lowered the federal budget deficit from $6 billion in 1964 to $4 billion in 1966.

Then in July, Johnson pushed the Civil Rights Act of 1964 through Congress. He persuaded southern senators to stop blocking its passage. It prohibited discrimination based on race, religion, national origin, and sex and granted the federal government new powers to enforce its provisions.

THE WAR ON POVERTY Following these successes, LBJ pressed on with his own agenda—to alleviate poverty. Early in 1964 he had declared "unconditional war on poverty in America." He proposed sweeping legislation designed to help Americans "on the outskirts of hope."

In August 1964 Congress enacted the **Economic Opportunity Act** (EOA). They approved nearly $1 billion for youth programs, antipoverty measures, small-business loans, and job training. The EOA legislation created
- the Job Corps Youth Training Program,
- VISTA (Volunteers in Service to America),
- Head Start, an education program for underprivileged preschoolers, and
- the Community Action Program, which encouraged poor people to participate in public-works programs.

THE 1964 ELECTION In 1964 the Republicans nominated conservative senator Barry Goldwater to oppose Johnson. Goldwater believed the federal government had no business trying to right social and economic wrongs such as poverty and discrimination. He attacked such long-established federal programs as Social Security, which he wanted to make voluntary. He also attacked the Tennessee Valley Authority, which he wanted to sell.

In 1964 most American people were in tune with Johnson. They believed that government could and should help solve the nation's problems. Moreover, Goldwater had frightened many Americans by suggesting that he might use

Campaign buttons like this one capitalized on the nation's growing liberal democratic sentiments.

nuclear weapons on Cuba and North Vietnam. Johnson's campaign capitalized on this fear. It produced a chilling television commercial in which a picture of a little girl counting the petals on a daisy dissolved into a mushroom cloud created by an atomic bomb. Goldwater advocated intervention in Vietnam. Johnson assured the American people that sending U.S. troops there "would offer no solution at all to the real problem of Vietnam."

Reading Check
Identify Problems
What problems in American society did the Economic Opportunity Act seek to address?

LBJ won the election by a landslide. He won 61 percent of the popular vote and 486 electoral votes, while Senator Goldwater won only 52. The Democrats also increased their majority in Congress. For the first time since 1938, a Democratic president did not need the votes of conservative Southern Democrats in order to get laws passed. Now Johnson could launch his reform program in earnest.

Building the Great Society

In May 1964 Johnson had summed up his vision for America in a phrase: the **Great Society**. In a speech at the University of Michigan, Johnson outlined a legislative program that would end poverty and racial injustice. But, he told an enthusiastic crowd, that was "just the beginning."

A PLAN FOR CHANGE Like his idol FDR, LBJ wanted to change America. And like the New Deal, the policies of the Great Society would expand existing programs and create new government programs designed to improve social welfare. The New Deal addressed the greatest needs of the Great Depression—relief for the needy, economic recovery, and financial reform. The policies and programs of the Great Society also strove to address the ongoing problem of poverty and the related needs of health care, education, and housing for low-income families and the elderly. It also addressed

Document-Based Investigation Historical Source

The Great Society Speech
Speaking at the University of Michigan, President Johnson told an enthusiastic crowd that he envisioned a legislative program that would create not only a higher standard of living and equal opportunity but also promote a richer quality of life for all.

> "The Great Society is a place where every child can find knowledge to enrich his mind and to enlarge his talents. It is a place where leisure is a welcome chance to build and reflect, not a feared cause of boredom and restlessness. It is a place where the city of man serves not only the needs of the body and the demands of commerce but the desire for beauty and the hunger for community. It is a place where man can renew contact with nature. It is a place which honors creation for its own sake and for what it adds to the understanding of the race."
>
> —Lyndon B. Johnson, from "The Great Society," May 22, 1964

Analyze Historical Sources
How did President Johnson use language to inspire Americans to share his vision?

These preschoolers in a Head Start classroom are among the millions of Americans whose daily lives have been affected by Great Society programs.

other social issues of the 1960s, including civil rights, immigration reform, environmental concerns, and protection for consumers. By the time Johnson left the White House in 1969, Congress had passed 206 of his measures. The president personally led the battle to get most of them passed.

EDUCATION During 1965 and 1966, the LBJ administration introduced a flurry of bills to Congress. Johnson considered education "the key which can unlock the door to the Great Society." The Elementary and Secondary Education Act of 1965 provided more than $1 billion in federal aid. It helped public and parochial schools purchase textbooks and new library materials. This was the first major federal aid package for education in the nation's history.

HEALTH CARE LBJ and Congress changed Social Security by establishing Medicare and Medicaid. **Medicare** provided hospital insurance and low-cost medical insurance for almost every American age 65 or older. **Medicaid** extended health insurance to welfare recipients.

HOUSING Congress also made several important decisions that shifted the nation's political power from rural to urban areas. These decisions included appropriating money to build some 240,000 units of low-rent public housing and help low- and moderate-income families pay for better private housing. It

---

NOW & THEN

Medicare on the Line

When President Johnson signed the Medicare bill in 1965, only half of the nation's elderly had health insurance. Today, thanks largely to Medicare, nearly all persons 65 years or older have medical coverage.

Over the years, federal spending on Medicare has steadily increased. Today it accounts for about 12 percent of all federal outlays. Experts have debated whether Medicare can be sustained as people live longer, health care costs increase, and the baby boomer generation reaches retirement age. Though most Americans are not in favor of cutbacks to Medicare, efforts have been made in the last few years to cut the growth in spending.

included urban renewal and slum rebuilding for select cities and establishing the Department of Housing and Urban Development (HUD). It also included naming Robert Weaver, the first African American cabinet member in American history, as Secretary of HUD.

IMMIGRATION The Great Society also brought profound changes to the nation's immigration laws. The Immigration Act of 1924 and the National Origins Act of 1924 had established immigration quotas. These quotas discriminated strongly against people from outside Western Europe. The act set a quota of about 150,000 people annually. It discriminated against southern and eastern Europeans and barred Asians completely. Ending the quotas based on nationality, the **Immigration Act of 1965** opened the door for many non-European immigrants to settle in the United States. This led to a sharp increase in immigration from Asia, Africa, and Latin America. The new immigrants brought their languages, cultures, and traditions with them, slowly and permanently changing the demographic makeup of the United States. The increase in immigration since 1965 has been a constant topic of political debate in the United States, leading to subsequent reform laws in the 1980s and 1990s. The greatest amount of political concern during those decades was focused on illegal immigration, which many felt was encouraged by lax policies.

THE ENVIRONMENT In 1962, *Silent Spring,* a book by Rachel Carson, had exposed a hidden danger: the effects of pesticides on the environment. Carson's book and the public's outcry resulted in the Water Quality Act of 1965, which required states to clean up rivers. Johnson also ordered the government to search out the worst chemical polluters. "There is no excuse . . . for chemical companies and oil refineries using our major rivers as pipelines for toxic wastes." Such words and actions helped trigger the environmental movement in the United States.

CONSUMER PROTECTION Consumer advocates also made headway. They convinced Congress to pass major safety laws, including a truth-in-packaging law that set standards for labeling consumer goods. Ralph Nader, a young lawyer, wrote a book, *Unsafe at Any Speed.* Nader's book sharply criticized the U.S. automobile industry for ignoring safety concerns. His testimony helped persuade Congress to establish safety standards for automobiles and tires. Precautions extended to food, too. Congress passed the Wholesome Meat Act of 1967. "Americans can feel a little safer now in their homes, on the road, at the supermarket, and in the department store," said Johnson.

Reading Check
Analyze Effects
How did the Immigration Act of 1965 change the nation's immigration system?

Reforms of the Warren Court

The wave of liberal reform that characterized the Great Society also swept through the Supreme Court of the 1960s. Beginning with the 1954 landmark decision *Brown* v. *Board of Education,* which ruled school segregation unconstitutional, the Court under Chief Justice Earl Warren took an activist stance on the leading issues of the day.

Great Society Programs, 1964–1967

POVERTY

1964 Tax Reduction Act cut corporate and individual taxes to stimulate growth.

1964 Economic Opportunity Act created Job Corps, VISTA, Head Start, and other programs to fight the "war on poverty."

1965 Medicare Act established Medicare and Medicaid programs.

1965 Appalachian Regional Development Act targeted aid for highways, health centers, and resource development in that economically depressed area.

CITIES

1965 Omnibus Housing Act provided money for low-income housing.

1965 Department of Housing and Urban Development was formed to administer federal housing programs.

1966 Demonstration Cities and Metropolitan Area Redevelopment Act funded slum rebuilding, mass transit, and other improvements for selected "model cities."

EDUCATION

1965 Elementary and Secondary Education Act directed money to schools for textbooks, library materials, and special education.

1965 Higher Education Act funded scholarships and low-interest loans for college students.

1965 National Foundation on the Arts and the Humanities was created to financially assist painters, musicians, actors, and other artists.

1967 Corporation for Public Broadcasting was formed to fund educational TV and radio broadcasting.

DISCRIMINATION

1964 Civil Rights Act outlawed discrimination in public accommodations, housing, and jobs; increased federal power to prosecute civil rights abuses.

1964 Twenty-Fourth Amendment abolished the poll tax in federal elections.

1965 Voting Rights Act ended the practice of requiring voters to pass literacy tests and permitted the federal government to monitor voter registration.

1965 Immigration Act ended national-origins quotas established in 1924.

ENVIRONMENT

1965 Wilderness Preservation Act set aside over 9 million acres for national forest lands.

1965 Water Quality Act required states to clean up their rivers.

1965 Clean Air Act Amendment directed the federal government to establish emission standards for new motor vehicles.

1967 Air Quality Act set federal air pollution guidelines and extended federal enforcement power.

CONSUMER ADVOCACY

1966 Truth in Packaging Act set standards for labeling consumer products.

1966 National Traffic and Motor Vehicle Safety Act set federal safety standards for the auto and tire industries.

1966 Highway Safety Act required states to set up highway safety programs.

1966 Department of Transportation was created to deal with national air, rail, and highway transportation.

Interpret Tables
What did the Great Society programs indicate about the federal government's changing role?

Chief Justice Earl Warren

Several major Court decisions in the 1960s affected American society. The **Warren Court** banned prayer in public schools and declared state-required loyalty oaths unconstitutional. It limited the power of communities to censor books and films. It said that free speech included the wearing of black arm-bands to school by antiwar students. Furthermore, the Court brought about change in federal and state reapportionment and the criminal justice system.

CONGRESSIONAL REAPPORTIONMENT In a key series of decisions, the Warren Court addressed the issue of **reapportionment**. Reapportionment is the way in which states redraw election districts based on the changing number of people in them. By 1960 about 80 percent of Americans lived in cities and suburbs. However, many states had failed to change their congressional districts to reflect this development. Instead, rural districts might have fewer than 200,000 people, while some urban districts had more than 600,000. Thus, the voters in rural areas had more representation—and also more power—than those in urban areas.

Baker v. *Carr* (1962) was the first of several decisions that established the principle of "one person, one vote." The Court asserted that the federal courts had the right to tell states to reapportion—redivide—their districts for more equal representation. In later decisions, the Court ruled that congressional district boundaries should be redrawn so that districts would be equal in population. In *Reynolds* v. *Sims* (1964), the Court extended the principle of "one person, one vote" to state legislative districts. These decisions led to a shift of political power throughout the nation from rural to urban areas.

RIGHTS OF THE ACCUSED Other Warren Court decisions greatly expanded the rights of people accused of crimes. In *Mapp* v. *Ohio* (1961), the Court ruled that evidence seized illegally could not be used in state courts. This is called the exclusionary rule. In *Gideon* v. *Wainwright* (1963), the justices required criminal courts to provide free legal counsel to those who could not afford it. In *Escobedo* v. *Illinois* (1964), the justices ruled that an accused person has a right to have a lawyer present during police questioning. In 1966 the Court went one step further in *Miranda* v. *Arizona*. It ruled that all suspects must be read their rights before questioning. (See Historic Decisions of the Supreme Court: *Miranda* v. *Arizona*.) In *Katz* v. *United States* (1967), the Court established the constitutional "right to privacy." It set parameters around what constituted a legal search, stating that the Fourth Amendment guarantees the right to privacy when a person has "reasonable expectation of privacy."

These rulings had a significant impact on the legal court system and greatly divided public opinion. Liberals praised the decisions. They argued that they placed necessary limits on police power and protected the right of all citizens to a fair trial. Conservatives, however, bitterly criticized the Court. They claimed that *Mapp* and *Miranda* benefited criminal suspects and severely limited the power of the police to investigate crimes. During the late 1960s and 1970s, Republican candidates for office seized on the "crime issue." They portrayed liberals and Democrats as being soft on crime and citing the decisions of the Warren Court as major obstacles to fighting crime.

Reading Check
Contrast What were the differing reactions to the Warren Court decisions on the rights of the accused?

"The Great Society succeeded in prompting far-reaching social change."

Defenders of the Great Society contend that it bettered the lives of millions of Americans. Historian John Morton Blum notes, "The Great Society initiated policies that by 1985 had profound consequences: Blacks now voted at about the same rate as whites, and nearly 6,000 blacks held public offices; almost every elderly citizen had medical insurance, and the aged were no poorer than Americans as a whole; a large majority of small children attended preschool programs."

Attorney Margaret Burnham argues that the civil rights gains alone justify the Great Society: "For tens of thousands of human beings . . . giving promise of a better life was significant. . . . What the Great Society affirmed was the responsibility of the federal government to take measures necessary to bring into the social and economic mainstream any segment of the people [who had been] historically excluded."

"Failures of the Great Society prove that government-sponsored programs do not work."

The major attack on the Great Society is that it created "big government": an oversized bureaucracy, too many regulations, waste and fraud, and rising budget deficits. As journalist David Alpern writes, this comes from the notion that government could solve all the nation's problems: "The Great Society created unwieldy new mechanisms like the Office of Economic Opportunity and began 'throwing dollars at problems. . . .' Spawned in the process were vast new constituencies of government bureaucrats and beneficiaries whose political clout made it difficult to kill programs off."

Conservatives say the Great Society's social welfare programs created a culture of dependency. Economist Paul Craig Roberts argues that "The Great Society . . . reflected our lack of confidence in the institutions of a free society. We came to the view that it is government spending and not business innovation that creates jobs and that it is society's fault if anyone is poor."

Critical Thinking

1. **Connect to History** What was the impact of the Great Society programs? Do you think the Great Society was a success or a failure? Explain.

2. **Connect to Today** Research the most pressing problems in your own neighborhood or precinct. Then propose a social program you think would address at least one of those problems while avoiding the pitfalls of the Great Society programs.

Impact of the Great Society

The Great Society and the Warren Court changed the United States. People disagree on whether these changes left the nation better or worse. However, most agree that no one president in the post–World War II era extended the power and reach of the federal government more than Lyndon Johnson. The optimism of the Johnson presidency fueled an activist era in all three branches of government, for at least the first few years.

The "war on poverty" did help. The number of poor people fell from 21 percent of the population in 1962 to 11 percent in 1973. However, many of Johnson's proposals, though well intended, were hastily conceived and proved difficult to accomplish.

As this cartoon points out, President Johnson had much to deal with at home and abroad. This autographed copy was presented to President Johnson by the cartoonist.

" SUNRISE....ALL THE FOREIGN TROUBLE MAKERS GOIN' TO SLEEP AN' ALL THE DOMESTIC ONES WAKIN' UP "

Johnson's massive tax cut spurred the economy, but there were also economic compromises. Funding the Great Society contributed to a growing budget deficit—a problem that continued for decades. The new programs also greatly expanded the size of the government. Questions about government finances, as well as debates over the effectiveness of these programs and the role of the federal government, left a number of people disillusioned. Some members of Congress expressed concern over the rapid pace of reform. They argued over whether the federal government should play such a large role in matters of social welfare. A conservative backlash began to take shape as a new group of Republican leaders rose to power. In 1966, for example, a conservative Hollywood actor named Ronald Reagan swept to victory in the race for governor of California over the Democratic incumbent.

Thousands of miles away, the increase of Communist forces in Vietnam also began to overshadow the goals of the Great Society. The fear of communism was deeply rooted in the minds of Americans from the Cold War era. Four years after initiating the Great Society, Johnson, a peace candidate in 1964, would be labeled a "hawk"—a supporter of one of the most divisive wars in recent U.S. history.

Reading Check
Identify Problems
What events and problems may have affected the success of the Great Society?

Lesson 2 Assessment

1. **Organize Information** List four or more Great Society programs and Warren Court rulings.

Great Society Programs	Warren Court Rulings
1.	1.
2.	2.
3.	3.
4.	4.

Choose one item and describe its lasting effects.

2. **Key Terms and People** For each term or person in the lesson, write a sentence explaining its significance.

3. **Evaluate** Explain how Lyndon Johnson's personal and political experiences might have influenced his actions as president.

   Think About:
   • his family's background and education
   • his relationship with Franklin Roosevelt
   • his powers of persuasion

4. **Analyze Primary Sources** Look at the political cartoon illustrating LBJ at sunrise. What do you think the artist was trying to convey about the Johnson administration?

Miranda v. Arizona (1966)

ORIGINS OF THE CASE

In 1963 Ernesto Miranda was arrested at his home in Phoenix, Arizona, on charges of kidnapping and rape. After two hours of questioning by police, he signed a confession and was later convicted, largely based on the confession. Miranda appealed. He claimed that his confession was invalid because it was coerced and because the police never advised him of his right to an attorney or his right to avoid self-incrimination.

THE RULING

The Court overturned Miranda's conviction, holding that the police must inform criminal suspects of their legal rights at the time of arrest and may not interrogate suspects who invoke their rights.

LEGAL REASONING

Chief Justice Earl Warren wrote the majority opinion in *Miranda* v. *Arizona*. He based his argument on the Fifth Amendment, which guarantees that an accused person cannot be forced "to be a witness against himself" or herself. Warren stressed that when suspects are interrogated in police custody, the situation is "inherently intimidating." Such a situation, he argued, undermines any evidence it produces because "no statement obtained from the defendant [while in custody] can truly be the product of his free choice."

For this reason, the Court majority found that Miranda's confession could not be used as evidence. In the opinion, Chief Justice Warren responded to the argument that police officials might find this requirement difficult to meet.

"Not only does the use of the third degree [harassment or torture used to obtain a confession] involve a flagrant violation of law by the officers of the law, but it involves also the dangers of false confessions, and it tends to make police and prosecutors less zealous in the search for objective evidence."

Ernesto Miranda *(at right)* converses with attorney John J. Flynn in February 1967.

LEGAL SOURCES

U.S. CONSTITUTION

U.S. CONSTITUTION, FIFTH AMENDMENT (1791)

"No person . . . shall be compelled in any criminal case to be a witness against himself, nor be deprived of life, liberty, or property, without due process of law."

RELATED CASES

***Mapp* v. *Ohio* (1961)**

The Court ruled that prosecutors may not use evidence obtained in illegal searches (exclusionary rule).

***Gideon* v. *Wainwright* (1963)**

The Court said that a defendant accused of a felony has the right to an attorney, which the government must supply if the defendant cannot afford one.

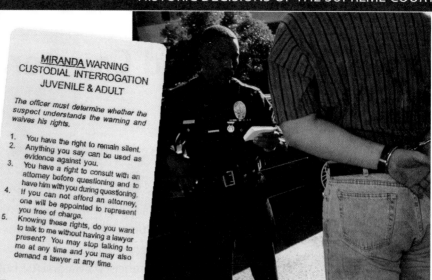

(right) This card is carried by police officers in order to read suspects their rights. *(far right)* An officer reads a suspect his rights.

MIRANDA WARNING
CUSTODIAL INTERROGATION
JUVENILE & ADULT

The officer must determine whether the suspect understands the warning and waives his rights.

1. You have the right to remain silent.
2. Anything you say can be used as evidence against you.
3. You have a right to consult with an attorney before questioning and to have him with you during questioning.
4. If you can not afford an attorney, one will be appointed to represent you free of charge.
5. Knowing these rights, do you want to talk to me without having a lawyer present? You may stop talking to me at any time and you may also demand a lawyer at any time.

WHY IT MATTERED

Miranda was one of four key criminal justice cases decided by the Warren Court (see Related Cases). In each case, the decision reflected the Chief Justice's strong belief that all persons deserve to be treated with respect by their government. In *Miranda*, the Court directed police to inform every suspect of his or her rights at the time of arrest and even gave the police detailed instructions about what to say.

The rights of accused people need to be protected in order to ensure that innocent people are not punished. These protections also ensure that authorities will not harass people for political reasons. This often happened to civil rights activists in the South in the 1950s and 1960s, for example.

Critics of the Warren Court claimed that *Miranda* would lead to more crime because it would become more difficult to convict criminals. Police departments, however, adapted. They placed the list of suspects' rights mentioned in *Miranda* on cards for police officers to read to suspects. The statement of these rights became known as the *Miranda* warning.

As for the defendant, Ernesto Miranda, he was retried and convicted on the basis of other evidence.

HISTORICAL IMPACT

The *Miranda* decision was highly controversial. Critics complained that the opinion would protect the rights of criminals at the expense of public safety.

Since *Miranda*, the Court has continued to try to strike a balance between public safety and the rights of the accused. Several cases in the 1970s and 1980s softened the *Miranda* ruling. They gave law enforcement officers more power to gather evidence without informing accused people of their rights. Even so, conservatives still hoped to overturn the *Miranda* decision.

In 2000, however, the Supreme Court affirmed *Miranda* by a 7–2 majority in *Dickerson* v. *United States*. Writing for the majority, Chief Justice William Rehnquist argued, "There is no such justification here for overruling *Miranda*. *Miranda* has become embedded in routine police practice to the point where warnings have become part of our national culture."

Critical Thinking

1. **Connect to History** Critics charged that *Miranda* incorrectly used the Fifth Amendment. The right to avoid self-incrimination, they said, should only apply to trials, not to police questioning. Do you agree or disagree? Why?

2. **Connect to Today** Do Internet research to locate laws and other Court decisions related to *Mapp* and *Miranda*. Then, prepare a debate on whether courts should or should not set a guilty person free if the government broke the law in establishing that person's guilt.

Culture and Counterculture

The Big Idea
The ideals and lifestyle of the counterculture challenged the traditional views of Americans.

Why It Matters Now
The music, art, and politics of the counterculture have left enduring marks on American society.

Key Terms and People
counterculture

Haight-Ashbury

the Beatles

Woodstock

One American's Story

In 1966 Alex Forman left his conventional life in mainstream America and headed to San Francisco. Arriving there with little else but a guitar, he joined thousands of others who were determined to live in a more peaceful and carefree environment. He recalled his early days in San Francisco's Haight-Ashbury district, the hub of hippie life.

Members of the counterculture relax in a California park

"It was like paradise there. Everybody was in love with life and in love with their fellow human beings to the point where they were just sharing in incredible ways with everybody. Taking people in off the street and letting them stay in their homes. . . . You could walk down almost any street in Haight-Ashbury where I was living, and someone would smile at you and just go, 'Hey, it's beautiful, isn't it?' . . . It was a very special time."
—Alex Forman, quoted in *From Camelot to Kent State*

Forman was part of the **counterculture**—a movement made up mostly of white, middle-class college youths who had grown disillusioned with the war in Vietnam and injustices in America during the 1960s. Instead of challenging the system, they turned their backs on traditional America. They tried to establish a whole new society based on peace and love. Although their heyday was short-lived, their legacy remains.

SS.912.A.1.2; SS.912.A.1.7; SS.912.A.7.9; SS.912.A.7.12; SS.912.H.1.1; SS.912.H.1.3; SS.912.H.1.5

The Counterculture

In the late 1960s historian Theodore Roszak deemed these idealistic youths the counterculture. It was a culture, he said, so different from the mainstream "that it scarcely looks to many as a culture at all, but takes on the alarming appearance of a barbarian intrusion." The attitude of these youths was so different from their parents that it led to a generation gap. The older generation had a difficult time understanding or sympathizing with the young people's beliefs, ideas, and attitudes.

"TUNE IN, TURN ON, DROP OUT" Members of the counterculture, known as hippies, shared some of the beliefs of the New Left movement. Specifically, they felt that American society—and its materialism, technology, and war—had grown hollow. Influenced by the art, music, and literature of the beat movement of the 1950s, hippies embraced the idea of nonconformity. They followed the credo of Harvard psychology professor and counterculture philosopher Timothy Leary: "Tune in, turn on, drop out." Throughout the middle and late 1960s, tens of thousands of idealistic youths left school, work, or home. They left to create what they hoped would be an idyllic community of peace, love, and harmony.

HIPPIE CULTURE The hippie era was sometimes known as the Age of Aquarius. It was marked by rock 'n' roll music, outrageous clothing, sexual license, and illegal drugs—in particular, marijuana and a new hallucinogenic drug called LSD, or acid. Timothy Leary, an early experimenter with the drug, promoted the use of LSD as a "mindexpanding" aid for self-awareness. Hippies also turned to Eastern religions such as Zen Buddhism. This religion professed that one could attain enlightenment through meditation rather than the reading of scriptures.

A prominent symbol of the counterculture movement was bright colors.

Hippies donned ragged jeans, tie-dyed T-shirts, military garments, love beads, and Native American ornaments. Thousands grew their hair out, despite the fact that their more conservative elders saw this as an act of disrespect. Signs across the country said, "Make America beautiful—give a hippie a haircut."

Hippies also rejected conventional home life. Many joined communes, renouncing private property to live communally. By the mid-1960s, **Haight-Ashbury** in San Francisco was known as the hippie capital, mainly because California did not outlaw hallucinogenic drugs until 1966.

DECLINE OF THE MOVEMENT After only a few years, the counterculture's peace and harmony gave way to violence and disillusionment. The urban communes eventually turned seedy and dangerous. Alex Forman recalled, "There were ripoffs, violence . . . people living on the street with no place to stay." Having dispensed with society's conventions and rules, the hippies had to rely on each other. Many discovered that the philosophy of "do your own thing" did not provide enough guidance for how to live. "We were together at the level of peace and love," said one disillusioned hippie. "We fell apart over who would cook and wash dishes and pay the bills." By 1970 many had fallen victim to the drugs they used, experiencing drug addiction and mental breakdowns. Rock singer Janis Joplin and legendary guitarist Jimi Hendrix both died of drug overdoses in 1970.

As the mystique of the 1960s wore off, thousands of hippies lined up at government offices to collect welfare and food stamps. They were dependent on the very society they had once rejected. Illegal drug use also rose significantly during the 1960s, particularly among college students. In response to this troubling increase, the government passed a series of laws, beginning with the Narcotic Addict Rehabilitation Act of 1966. With this law, the government tried to shift its focus from criminal penalties to rehabilitation and treatment for drug addicts.

A Changing Culture

In a declaration of their individuality and desire for more freedom, counterculture youth embraced a variety of new ideas in art and music. These ideas became the catalyst that helped fuel the counterculture movement. And unlike many aspects of the counterculture, they also left a more lasting imprint on the world.

ART The counterculture's rebellious style left its mark on the art world. The 1960s saw the rise of pop art (popular art). Pop artists, led by Andy Warhol, attempted to bring art into the mainstream. Pop art was characterized by bright, simple, commercial-looking images often depicting everyday life. For instance, Warhol became famous for his bright silk-screen portraits of soup cans, Marilyn Monroe, and other icons of mass culture. These images were repeated to look mass-produced and impersonal. It was a criticism of the times implying that individual freedoms had been lost to a more conventional, "cookie-cutter" lifestyle.

Reading Check
Analyze Causes
What events and other factors hastened the decline of the counterculture movement?

Andy Warhol created this image of movie actress and popular icon Marilyn Monroe.

The Beatles, shown here in 1967, influenced fashion with their long hair and psychedelic clothing.

ROCK MUSIC During the 1960s the counterculture movement embraced rock 'n' roll as its loud and biting anthem of protest. The music was an offshoot of African American rhythm and blues music that had captivated so many teenagers during the 1950s.

The band that, perhaps more than any other, helped propel rock music into mainstream America was **the Beatles**. The British band, made up of four youths from working-class Liverpool, England, arrived in America in 1964. They immediately took the country by storm. By the time the Beatles broke up in 1970, the four "lads" had inspired a countless number of other bands and had won over millions of Americans to rock 'n' roll.

One example of rock 'n' roll's popularity occurred in August 1969 on a farm in upstate New York. More than 400,000 showed up for a music festival called "Woodstock Music and Art Fair," commonly known as **Woodstock**. Despite the huge crowd, the festival was peaceful and well organized. Woodstock represented, as one songwriter put it, "the '60s movement of peace and love and some higher cultural cause." Over four days, the most popular bands and musicians performed, including Jimi Hendrix, Janis Joplin, Joe Cocker, Joan Baez, the Grateful Dead, and Jefferson Airplane. Woodstock was more than just a rock concert. It was a celebration of an era and became a defining experience for a whole generation.

PROTEST SONGS In the midst of the turbulent climate of the sixties, hippies and other activists also used music as a vehicle for political expression. In bus terminals, in the streets, and on the White House lawn, thousands united in song. They expressed their rejection of mainstream society, their demand for civil rights, and their outrage over the Vietnam War. Musicians like Bob Dylan stirred up antiwar sentiment in songs like "The Times They Are A-Changin'," while Joan Baez and Pete Seeger popularized the great African American spiritual "We Shall Overcome," which became the anthem of the civil rights movement.

CHANGING ATTITUDES While the counterculture movement faded, its casual "do your own thing" philosophy left its mark. American attitudes toward sexual behavior became more casual and permissive, leading to what became known as the sexual revolution. During the 1960s and 1970s, mass culture—including TV, books, magazines, music, and movies—began to address subjects that had once been prohibited, particularly sexual behavior and explicit violence.

Bob Dylan's Music

Although Bob Dylan did not claim to be a spokesperson for his generation, millions of Americans felt his songs perfectly expressed their frustrations, fears, and hopes. In 1999 *Time* magazine included Dylan in its "Time 100: The Most Important People of the Century."

"Come senators, congressmen
Please heed the call
Don't stand in the doorway
Don't block up the hall
For he that gets hurt
Will be he who has stalled
There's a battle outside
And it is ragin'.
It'll soon shake your windows
And rattle your walls
For the times they are a-changin'."

—Bob Dylan, from "The Times They Are A-Changin'," 1962

Analyze Historical Sources
How might listeners of different ages and cultures have responded to these lyrics?

Reading Check
Make Inferences
What did rock 'n' roll symbolize for American youth?

While some hailed the increasing permissiveness as liberating, others attacked it as a sign of moral decay. For millions of Americans, the new tolerance was merely an uncivilized lack of respect for established social norms. Eventually, the counterculture movement would lead a great many Americans to more liberal attitudes about dress and appearance, lifestyle, and social behavior. In the short run, though, it produced largely the opposite effect.

The Conservative Response

In the late 1960s many believed that the country was losing its sense of right and wrong. Increasingly, conservative voices began to express people's anger. At the 1968 Republican convention in Miami, candidate Richard M. Nixon expressed that anger.

"As we look at America we see cities enveloped in smoke and flame. We hear sirens in the night. . . . We see Americans hating each other . . . at home. . . . Did we come all this way for this? . . . die in Normandy and Korea and in Valley Forge for this?"

—Richard Nixon, from a speech at Republican convention, 1968

CONSERVATIVES ATTACK THE COUNTERCULTURE Nixon was not the only conservative voice expressing alarm. FBI director J. Edgar Hoover issued a warning that "revolutionary terrorism" was a threat on campuses and in cities. Other conservative critics warned that campus rebels posed a danger

In contrast to the 1968 Democratic convention in Chicago, the Republican convention was orderly and united—particularly in the delegates' opposition to the counterculture.

to traditional values and threatened to plunge American society into anarchy. Conservatives also attacked the counterculture for what they saw as its decadent values. In the view of psychiatrist Bruno Bettelheim, student rebels and members of the counterculture had been pampered in childhood. As young adults, they did not have the ability for delayed gratification. According to some conservative commentators, the counterculture had abandoned rational thought in favor of the senses and uninhibited self-expression.

The angry response of mainstream Americans caused a profound change in the political landscape of the United States. By the end of the 1960s, conservatives were presenting their own solutions on such issues as lawlessness and crime, the size of the federal government, and welfare. This growing conservative movement would propel Nixon into the White House—and set the nation on a more conservative course.

Reading Check
Form Generalizations
Why were conservatives angry about the counterculture?

Lesson 3 Assessment

1. **Organize Information** Use a tree diagram to list examples that illustrate the beliefs, lifestyle, and impact on society of the 1960s counterculture.

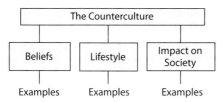

Which example do you think had the biggest impact on society? Why?

2. **Key Terms and People** For each term or person in the lesson, write a sentence explaining its significance.

3. **Develop Historical Perspective** A stereotype is a generalization made about a group. What stereotype do you think hippies might have formed about mainstream Americans? What stereotype do you think mainstream Americans might have formed about hippies? Why?

   Think About:
   • Alex Forman's comments in "One American's Story"
   • hippies' values and lifestyle
   • mainstream Americans' values and lifestyle

4. **Make Inferences** In your opinion, why didn't the hippies succeed?

5. **Analyze Issues** What role did the counterculture and antiwar movement play in helping Richard Nixon win the presidency?

★ Environmental Activism

The Big Idea

During the 1960s and 1970s, Americans strengthened their efforts to address the nation's environmental problems.

Why It Matters Now

The nation today continues to struggle to balance environmental concerns with industrial growth.

Key Terms and People

Rachel Carson

Earth Day

environmentalist

Environmental Protection Agency (EPA)

Three Mile Island

One American's Story

In 1972 Lois Gibbs and her family moved to Niagara Falls, New York. Underneath this quiet town, however, was a disaster in the making. In the 1890s the Love Canal had been built to provide hydroelectric power for the Niagara Falls area. Chemical companies were dumping hazardous waste into the canal. In 1953 bulldozers filled in the canal. Shortly thereafter, a school and rows of homes were built nearby.

In 1977, when Lois Gibbs's son fell sick, she decided to investigate. She eventually uncovered the existence of the toxic waste and mobilized the community to demand government action.

In 1980 President Carter authorized funds for many Niagara Falls families to move to safety. Years later, Lois Gibbs wrote a book detailing her efforts.

Lois Gibbs

"I want to tell you our story— my story—because I believe that ordinary citizens—using the tools of dignity, self-respect, common sense, and perseverance—can influence solutions to important problems in our society. . . . In solving any difficult problem, you have to be prepared to fight long and hard, some-times at great personal cost; but it can be done. It must be done if we are to survive . . . at all."
—Lois Gibbs, from *Love Canal: My Story*

Lois Gibbs's concerns about environmental hazards were shared by many Americans in the 1970s. Through the energy crisis, Americans learned that their natural resources were limited. They could no longer take the environment for granted. Americans—from grassroots organizations to the government—began to focus on conservation of the environment and new forms of energy.

SS.912.A.1.4; SS.912.A.7.9; SS.912.A.7.12; HE.912.C.2.4; LAFS.1112.RH.1.2

The Roots of Environmentalism

The widespread realization that pollution and overconsumption were damaging the environment began in the 1960s. One book in particular had awakened America's concerns about the environment and helped lay the groundwork for the activism of the early seventies.

RACHEL CARSON AND SILENT SPRING In 1962 **Rachel Carson**, a marine biologist, published a book entitled *Silent Spring*. In it, she warned against the growing use of pesticides—chemicals used to kill insects and rodents. Pesticides first came into widespread use in the 1940s. In 1939 Paul Muller developed a pesticide called DDT. This chemical could kill a wide range of pests and seemed to be relatively harmless to humans and other mammals. With DDT, malaria—a disease spread by mosquitoes—was able to be brought under control. Farmers were able to increase crop production. In addition, DDT was easy to apply and cheap to produce. At the time, it seemed like a miracle substance.

Carson disagreed. In her book, she argued that pesticides poisoned the very food they were intended to protect and as a result killed many birds and fish. Carson cautioned that America faced a "silent spring," in which birds killed off by pesticides would no longer fill the air with song. She added that of all the weapons used in "man's war against nature," pesticides were some of the most harmful.

> *"These sprays, dusts, and aerosols . . . have the power to kill every insect, the 'good' and the 'bad,' to still the song of birds and the leaping of fish in the streams, to coat the leaves with a deadly film, and to linger on in soil—all this though the intended target may be only a few weeds or insects. Can anyone believe it is possible to lay down such a barrage of poisons on the surface of the earth without making it unfit for all life?"*

—Rachel Carson, from *Silent Spring*

— BIOGRAPHY

Rachel Carson (1907–1964)

Marine biologist Rachel Carson was born far from the sea, in the small town of Springdale, Pennsylvania.

Carson was a sickly child who often had to remain at home, where her mother tutored her. Throughout her youth and into her college years, Carson was a studious, but quiet and aloof, person.

Carson entered college intent on becoming a writer. During her sophomore year, she took a biology class to fulfill her science requirement. She quickly fell in love with the study of nature. By the next year, Carson switched her major from English to zoology—the study of animals.

Within six months of its publication, *Silent Spring* sold nearly half a million copies. Many chemical companies called the book inaccurate and threatened legal action. However, for a majority of Americans, Carson's book was an early warning about the danger that human activity posed to the environment. Shortly after the book's publication, President Kennedy established an advisory committee to investigate the situation.

With Rachel Carson's prodding, the nation slowly began to focus more on environmental issues. Carson would not live to see the U.S. government outlaw DDT in 1972. However, her work helped many Americans realize that their everyday behavior, as well as the nation's industrial growth, had a damaging effect on the environment.

Environmental Concerns in the 1970s

During the 1970s the administrations of Richard Nixon and Jimmy Carter confronted such environmental issues as conservation, pollution, and the growth of nuclear energy.

THE FIRST EARTH DAY The United States ushered in the 1970s with the first **Earth Day** celebration. It was a fitting celebration for a decade in which the nation would actively address its environmental issues. On that day, April 22, 1970, nearly every community in the nation and more than 10,000 schools and 2,000 colleges hosted some type of environmental-awareness activity. Activities spotlighted problems such as pollution, the growth of toxic waste, and the earth's dwindling resources. The Earth Day celebration continues today. Each year on April 22, millions of people around the world gather to heighten public awareness of environmental problems.

THE GOVERNMENT TAKES ACTION Although President Nixon was not considered an **environmentalist**, or someone who takes an active role in the protection of the environment, he recognized the nation's growing concern about the environment. In an effort to "make our peace with nature," President Nixon set out on a course that led to the passage of several landmark measures. In 1970 he consolidated 15 existing federal pollution programs into one—the **Environmental Protection Agency (EPA)**. The new agency was given the power to set and enforce pollution standards, to conduct environmental research, and to assist state and local governments in pollution

A flag celebrating the first Earth Day in 1970

Reading Check
Analyze Effects
What effects did Rachel Carson's book have on the nation as a whole?

Vocabulary
toxic capable of causing injury or death, especially by chemical means; poisonous

control. Today, the EPA remains the federal government's main instrument for dealing with environmental issues.

Some 35 environmental laws took effect during the decade. These laws addressed every aspect of conservation and cleanup—from protecting endangered animals to regulating auto emissions. One important and complex environmental problem was how to control air pollution. In 1970 Nixon signed a new Clean Air Act that added several amendments to the Clean Air Act of 1963. The new act established new programs that regulated toxic air pollutants and required the best available technology to be used to help control all new major sources of air pollution. It also required a 90 percent reduction of emissions from new cars by 1975. The new act gave the EPA the authority to set air standards. It also increased the authority of the government to enforce regulations.

Following the 1970 Clean Air Act, Congress passed the Endangered Species Act. It was signed into law in 1973 to "halt and reverse the trend toward species extinction, whatever the cost." The act provides for the protection and recovery of fish, wildlife, and plants that are endangered or threatened. The act makes it illegal to possess, sell, or transport those species. It also protects and conserves the ecosystems that these species depend on to survive. Congress also passed laws that limited pesticide use and curbed strip mining. Strip mining is the practice of mining for ore and coal by digging gaping holes in the land.

The government also pushed to strengthen laws protecting all the "waters of the United States." In 1972 the Clean Water Act was passed by the United States Congress, after being vetoed by President Nixon. It gave the EPA the power to improve the nation's water quality through the regulation of cities and industries. It made it illegal to dump chemicals or other pollutants into U.S. waters. It also provided money to build water treatment plants to help cities control sewage.

Document-Based Investigation Historical Source

Clean Air Poster

President Nixon created the EPA in 1970 by signing the National Environmental Policy Act (NEPA). A major element of the NEPA is the requirement that an environmental impact statement (EIS) be prepared for all major federal actions that might significantly affect the environment.

Analyze Historical Sources

1. What does the poster claim regarding the power of the federal government?

2. What does the poster imply about the role of governmental regulations?

BALANCING PROGRESS AND CONSERVATION IN ALASKA During the 1970s the federal government took steps to ensure the continued well-being of Alaska. It is the largest state in the nation and one of its most ecologically sensitive.

The discovery of oil there in 1968, and the subsequent construction of a massive pipeline to transport it, created many new jobs and greatly increased state revenues. However, the influx of new development also raised concerns about Alaska's wildlife, as well as the rights of its native peoples. In 1971 Nixon signed the Alaska Native Claims Settlement Act. This act turned over millions of acres of land to the state's native tribes for conservation and tribal use. In 1978 President Carter enhanced this conservation effort by setting aside an additional 56 million acres in Alaska as national monuments. In 1980 Congress added another 104 million acres as protected areas.

THE DEBATE OVER NUCLEAR ENERGY As the 1970s came to a close, Americans became acutely aware of the dangers that nuclear power plants posed to both humans and the environment. During the 1970s America realized the drawbacks to its heavy dependence on foreign oil for energy. Nuclear power seemed to many to be an attractive alternative.

Opponents of nuclear energy warned the public against the industry's growth. They contended that nuclear plants, and the wastes they produced, were potentially dangerous to humans and their environment.

THREE MILE ISLAND In the early hours of March 28, 1979, the concerns of nuclear energy opponents were validated. That morning, one of the nuclear reactors at a plant on **Three Mile Island** near Harrisburg, Pennsylvania, malfunctioned. The reactor overheated after its cooling system failed. Fear quickly arose that radiation might escape and spread over the region. Two days later, low-level radiation actually did escape from the crippled reactor. Officials evacuated some residents, while others fled on their own. One homemaker who lived near the plant recalled her desperate attempt to find safety.

Background
In 2010 President Obama established a commission to develop a long-term plan for the management of used nuclear fuel. This plan, he said, would include not only ideas on disposal but also ways to reprocess and recycle this waste.

"On Friday, a very frightening thing occurred in our area. A state policeman went door-to-door telling residents to stay indoors, close all windows, and turn all air conditioners off. I was alone, as were many other homemakers, and my thoughts were focused on how long I would remain a prisoner in my own home.... Suddenly, I was scared, real scared. I decided to get out of there, while I could. I ran to the car not knowing if I should breathe the air or not, and I threw the suitcases in the trunk and was on my way within one hour. If anything dreadful happened, I thought that I'd at least be with my girls. Although it was very hot in the car, I didn't trust myself to turn the air conditioner on. It felt good as my tense muscles relaxed the farther I drove."

—an anonymous homemaker, quoted in *Accident at Three Mile Island: The Human Dimensions*

The Accident at Three Mile Island

A series of human and mechanical errors that caused the partial meltdown of the reactor core brought the Three Mile Island nuclear power plant to the brink of disaster. The accident at Three Mile Island caused widespread concern about nuclear power throughout the American public.

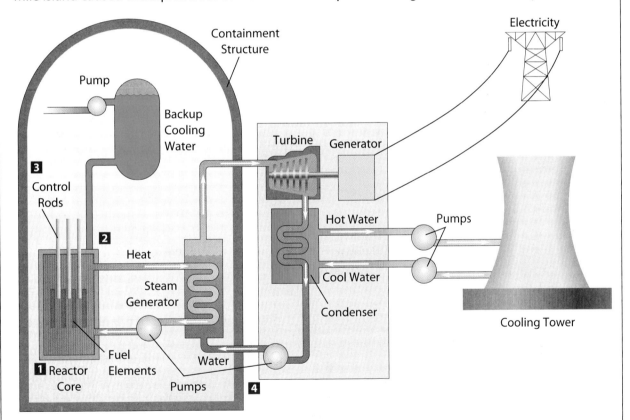

REACTOR MELTDOWN

1 The radioactive reactor core generates heat as its atoms split during a controlled chain reaction.

2 An inoperative valve releases thousands of gallons of coolant from the reactor core.

3 Half of the 36,816 exposed fuel rods melt in temperatures above 5,000 degrees.

4 The melted material burns through the lining of the reactor chamber and spills to the floor of the containment structure.

In the late 1970s and early 1980s, Hollywood made a number of films reflecting Americans' concerns about the relatively new field of nuclear energy and alerting the public to the need for regulation. In 1979's thriller *The China Syndrome*, starring Jane Fonda and Jack Lemmon, a television reporter exposes cover-ups at a nuclear plant.

In all, more than 100,000 residents were evacuated from the surrounding area. On April 9 the Nuclear Regulatory Commission, the federal agency that monitors the nuclear power industry, announced that the immediate danger was over.

The events at Three Mile Island rekindled the debate over nuclear power. Supporters of nuclear power pointed out that no one had been killed or seriously injured. Opponents countered by saying that chance alone had averted a tragedy. They demanded that the government call a halt to the construction of new power plants and gradually shut down existing nuclear facilities.

While the government did not do away with nuclear power, federal officials did recognize nuclear energy's potential danger to both humans and the environment. As a result of the accident at Three Mile Island, the Nuclear Regulatory Commission strengthened its safety standards and improved its inspection procedures.

LOVE CANAL Another environmental disaster was uncovered at Love Canal in New York. There, long-buried chemicals left behind by a chemical company began seeping up through the ground. Exposure to the chemicals was linked to the high rates of birth defects in the community. To solve the problem, the state of New York bought the homes of some 200 residents. The government then began the costly task of cleaning up the mess. Experts warned that there were likely many more toxic waste sites like Love Canal around the country.

Reading Check
Summarize
What were the environmental actions taken during the Nixon administration?

A Continuing Movement

In the years since the first Earth Day, environmental issues have gained increasing attention and support, but also some opposition. Government, industry, and environmentalists must work together. They must find a balance between environmental protection and economic interests.

PRIVATE CONSERVATION GROUPS As concerns about pollution and the depletion of nonrenewable resources grew, so did membership in private, nonprofit organizations dedicated to the preservation of wilderness and endangered species. Many of these groups lobbied government for protective legislation. Some filed lawsuits to block projects such as road or dam construction or logging that would threaten habitats. The Environmental Defense Fund (today Environmental Defense) brought lawsuits that led to the bans on DDT and on leaded gasoline.

Radical groups also emerged. Greenpeace was formed by a group of individuals who wanted to stop nuclear testing on an island in Alaska that was home to endangered species of sea otters, eagles, and other wildlife. The group became known for its antinuclear stance and for its members' willingness to take direct action to stop activities that threatened the environment. Members of Greenpeace risked their lives at sea to escort whales and protect them from commercial hunters. Later in the decade, an even more radical group called Environmental Life Force began to use explosives in their fight against the use of pesticides. The group disbanded in 1978 after its leader, John Hanna, was arrested for attaching bombs to seven crop-duster planes at an airport in California.

ECONOMIC CONCERNS The environmental movement has also faced a struggle to balance environmental concerns with jobs and progress. As the environmental movement gained popular support, opponents also made their voices heard. In Tennessee, for example, a federal dam project was halted because it threatened a species of fish. Local developers took out ads asking residents to "tell the government that the size of your wallet is more important than some two-inch-long minnow." When confronted with environmental concerns, one unemployed steelworker spoke for others. He remarked, "Why worry about the long run, when you're out of work right now."

Reading Check
Contrast
How are the goals of supporters and opponents of the environmental movement different?

Lesson 4 Assessment

1. **Organize Information** Draw a web diagram, filling in events that illustrate the main idea "Concern for the environment grew in the United States."

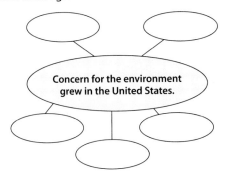

Concern for the environment grew in the United States.

2. **Key Terms and People** For each term or person in the lesson, write a sentence explaining its significance.

3. **Analyze Causes** How much should the United States rely on nuclear power as a source of energy? Explain your view.

   Think About:
   • the safety of nuclear power
   • the alternatives to nuclear power
   • U.S. energy demands

4. **Analyze Effects** In what ways has the environmental movement influenced the federal government?

Module 14 Assessment

Key Terms and People

For each term or person below, write a sentence explaining its connection to social change in the United States during the 1960s and 1970s.

1. John F. Kennedy
2. New Frontier
3. Warren Court
4. Lyndon Baines Johnson
5. Great Society
6. Economic Opportunity Act
7. counterculture
8. Environmental Protection Agency (EPA)
9. Rachel Carson
10. Woodstock

Main Ideas

Use your notes and the information in the module to answer the following questions.

Kennedy and the New Frontier

1. Explain the factors that led to Kennedy's victory over Nixon in the 1960 presidential campaign.
2. What was Kennedy's New Frontier? Why did he have trouble getting his New Frontier legislation through Congress?
3. What two international aid programs were launched during the Kennedy administration?
4. How did Kennedy's assassination affect the public?
5. What was the political impact of Kennedy's assassination?

Johnson and the Great Society

6. Describe ways that Great Society programs addressed the problem of poverty.
7. How did the courts increase the political power of people in urban areas?

8. How did the Warren Court decisions expand the rights of those accused of crimes?
9. What economic compromise was made in order to fund the Great Society programs?

Culture and Counterculture

10. What was the counterculture movement a reaction to?
11. Briefly explain the role Timothy Leary played in the counterculture movement.
12. How did the rise of the counterculture lead to a generation gap?
13. How did drug use in the counterculture movement lead to new laws and a change in government policy?
14. What unintended impact did the counterculture have on many mainstream Americans?

Environmental Activism

15. What factors increased Americans' concerns about environmental issues during the 1960s and 1970s?
16. What actions did private nonprofit groups take to influence the government?
17. What was the impact of the Three Mile Island incident?
18. What environmental disaster was discovered at Love Canal?

Critical Thinking

1. **Categorize** Use a Venn diagram to show the major legislative programs of the New Frontier and the Great Society.

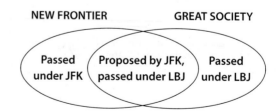

NEW FRONTIER   GREAT SOCIETY

Passed under JFK | Proposed by JFK, passed under LBJ | Passed under LBJ

2. **Form Generalizations** John F. Kennedy said, "[M]y fellow Americans, ask not what your country can do for you—ask what you can do for your country." Do you agree with his view about the relationship between individuals and the country? Explain your opinion.

3. **Evaluate** Do you think the Great Society met the goal of helping people make their lives better for themselves and their children? What were the compromises that resulted? Explain.

4. **Analyze Effects** What were the social and political effects of the increase in immigration following the Immigration Act of 1965?

5. **Analyze Causes** How did new music and art act as a catalyst for the counterculture movement?

6. **Analyze Primary Sources** Reread the song lyrics of Bob Dylan's "The Times They Are A-Changin.'" How do you think this song captured the main message of the counterculture movement?

7. **Synthesize** Explain the effect mass media had on American politics during the 1960s and 1970s. Note several examples of how television, music, art, and literature influenced the government during these decades.

8. **Compare** How were the counterculture movement and the environmental movement similar in terms of impact on society?

9. **Summarize** Explain the actions the government took in the 1970s to confront environmental issues.

Engage with History

Write a job description for "U.S. President." Include sections on "Responsibilities" and "Requirements" that list necessary traits and experience.

Think About:

- Kennedy's and Johnson's (and Nixon's) background and style
- the role of the media
- challenges each leader faced and how he dealt with them
- the American public's tastes and preferences
- the influence that groups, individuals, and social movements have on the government

Focus on Writing

Imagine that the year is 1964. President Johnson has introduced a series of programs as a part of his vision for a Great Society. Write a persuasive letter to your congressional representative telling him or her to either support or oppose the new programs.

Multimedia Activity

Use the Internet to research examples of 1960s or 1970s culture, such as songs, paintings, posters, clothing, cars, and so on. Prepare an electronic museum exhibit of several artifacts that display a trend or theme discussed in the module. Write captions for the artifacts explaining their historical context and relating them to your chosen theme.

Module 15

Civil Rights

★

Essential Question

Why should all Americans have equal rights and opportunities?

About the Photograph: Civil Rights activists lead the 1965 voting rights march from Selma to Montgomery, Alabama.

In this module you will learn how African Americans fought for equal rights and how their struggle inspired Hispanic Americans, Native Americans, women, and other groups to lead their own movements to seek equality and fair treatment.

▷ *Explore ONLINE!*

HISTORY

VIDEOS, including...
- Civil Rights Act of 1964
- Freedom March

✓ Document-Based Investigations

✓ Graphic Organizers

✓ Interactive Games

✓ Image Compare: Public School Segregation

✓ Carousel: March on Washington

SS.912.A.1.2 Utilize a variety of primary and secondary sources to identify author, historical significance, audience, and authenticity to understand a historical period. **SS.912.A.1.3** Utilize timelines to identify the time sequence of historical data. **SS.912.A.1.4** Analyze how images, symbols, objects, cartoons, graphs, charts, maps, and artwork may be used to interpret the significance of time periods and events from the past. **SS.912.A.1.6** Use case studies to explore social, political, legal, and economic relationships in history. **SS.912.A.2.7** Review the Native American experience. **SS.912.A.7.3** Examine the changing status of women in the United States from post-World War II to present. **SS.912.A.7.5** Compare nonviolent and violent approaches utilized by groups to achieve civil rights. **SS.912.A.7.6** Assess key figures and organizations in shaping the Civil Rights Movement and Black Power Movement. **SS.912.A.7.7** Assess the building of coalitions between African Americans, whites, and other groups in achieving integration and equal rights. **SS.912.A.7.8** Analyze significant Supreme Court decisions relating to integration, busing, affirmative action, the rights of the accused, and reproductive rights. **SS.912.A.7.9** Examine the similarities of social movements of the 1960s and 1970s. **SS.912.A.7.16** Examine changes in immigration policy and attitudes toward immigration since 1950. **LAFS.1112.SL.2.4** Present information, findings, and supporting evidence, conveying a clear and distinct perspective, such that listeners can follow the line of reasoning, alternative or opposing perspectives are addressed, and the organization, development, substance, and style are appropriate to purpose, audience, and a range of formal and informal tasks. **LAFS.1112.WHST.3.8** Gather relevant information from multiple authoritative print and digital sources, using advanced searches effectively; assess the strengths and limitations of each source in terms of the specific task, purpose, and audience; integrate information into the text selectively to maintain the flow of ideas, avoiding plagiarism and overreliance on any one source and following a standard format for citation.

Timeline of Events 1953–2010

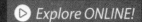 Explore ONLINE!

United States Events		World Events

1953

1954 *Brown* v. *Board of Education* decision orders the desegregation of public schools.

< **1955** Montgomery bus boycott begins.

1957 The African nation of > Ghana wins independence.

1962 César Chávez and Dolores Huerta found the National Farm Workers Association.

1962 South African civil rights leader > Nelson Mandela is imprisoned.

1966 National Organization for Women (NOW) is formed.

1968 Martin Luther King Jr. is assassinated.

1970 Political party La Raza Unida is formed.

1972 Earthquake kills 10,000 in Nicaragua.

< **1973** Native Americans stage a protest at Wounded Knee, South Dakota.

1975 The Vietnam War comes to an end.

1977 Stephen Biko, an anti-apartheid activist in South Africa, dies while in police custody.

1979 Margaret Thatcher becomes the first woman prime minister of Great Britain.

< **1981** Sandra Day O'Connor becomes the first woman appointed to the Supreme Court.

1982 Equal Rights Amendment fails to win ratification.

1989 The Chinese government kills student protesters in Tiananmen Square.

∧ **1995** The "Million Man March" is held in Washington, DC.

1994 In South Africa's first all-race election, Nelson Mandela is elected president.

1997 Madeleine Albright is the first woman to become secretary of state.

2005 Iraqis choose new leaders in a democratic election.

< **2008** Barack Obama is elected 44th president.

2009 Congress passes the Lilly Ledbetter Fair Pay Act.

2010

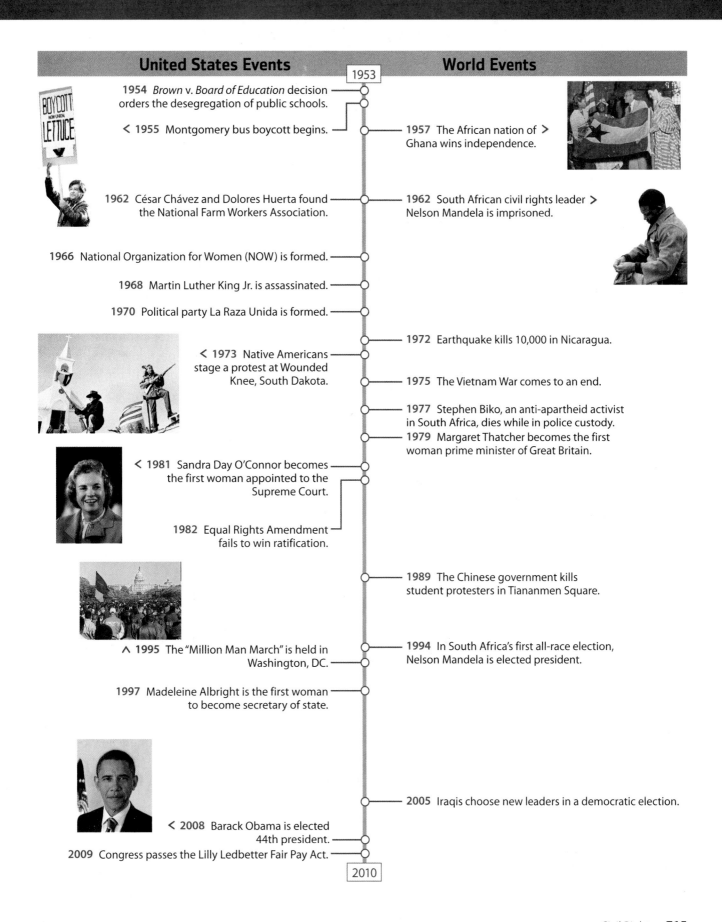

Taking on Segregation

The Big Idea

Activism and a series of Supreme Court decisions advanced equal rights for African Americans in the 1950s and 1960s.

Why It Matters Now

Landmark Supreme Court decisions beginning in 1954 have guaranteed civil rights for Americans today.

Key Terms and People

Thurgood Marshall

Brown v. *Board of Education of Topeka*

Rosa Parks

Martin Luther King Jr.

Southern Christian Leadership Conference (SCLC)

Student Nonviolent Coordinating Committee (SNCC)

sit-in

SS.912.A.1.2; SS.912.A.1.4; SS.912.A.1.6; SS.912.A.1.7; SS.912.A.7.5; SS.912.A.7.6; SS.912.A.7.7; SS.912.A.7.8; SS.912.G.2.1; LAFS.1112.RH.1.2; LAFS.1112.SL.2.4; LAFS.1112.WHST.3.7; LAFS.1112.WHST.3.8

One American's Story

Jo Ann Gibson Robinson drew back in self-defense as the white bus driver raised his hand as if to strike her. "Get up from there!" he shouted. Robinson, laden with Christmas packages, had forgotten the rules and sat down in the front of the bus, which was reserved for whites.

Humiliating incidents were not new to the African Americans who rode the segregated buses of Montgomery, Alabama, in the mid-1950s. The bus company required them to pay at the front and then exit and reboard at the rear. "I felt like a dog," Robinson later said. A professor at the all-black Alabama State College, Robinson was also president of the Women's Political Council, a group of professional African American women determined to increase black political power.

"We had members in every elementary, junior high, and senior high school, and in federal, state, and local jobs. Wherever there were more than ten blacks employed, we had a member there. We were prepared to the point that we knew that in a matter of hours, we could corral the whole city."
—Jo Ann Gibson Robinson, quoted in *Voices of Freedom: An Oral History of the Civil Rights Movement*

Jo Ann Gibson Robinson

On December 1, 1955, police arrested an African American woman for refusing to give up her seat on a bus. Robinson promptly sent out a call for all African Americans to boycott Montgomery buses.

The Segregation System

Segregated buses might never have rolled through the streets of Montgomery if the Civil Rights Act of 1875 had remained in force. This act outlawed segregation in public facilities. It decreed that "all persons . . . shall be entitled to the full and equal enjoyment of the accommodations . . . of inns, public conveyances on land or water, theaters, and other places of public amusement." In 1883, however, the all-white Supreme Court declared the act unconstitutional.

PLESSY* v. *FERGUSON During the 1890s a number of other court decisions and state laws severely limited African American rights. In 1890 Louisiana passed a law requiring railroads to provide "equal but separate accommodations for the white and colored races." In the *Plessy* v. *Ferguson* case of 1896, the Supreme Court ruled that this "separate but equal" law did not violate the Fourteenth Amendment, which guarantees all Americans equal treatment under the law.

Passengers wait at a bus station in Durham, North Carolina, in 1940.

Armed with the *Plessy* decision, states throughout the nation, but especially in the South, passed what were known as Jim Crow laws, aimed at separating the races. These laws forbade marriage between blacks and whites. They also established many other restrictions on social and religious contact between the races. There were separate schools as well as separate streetcars, waiting rooms, railroad coaches, elevators, witness stands, and public restrooms. The facilities provided for blacks were always inferior to those for whites. Nearly every day, African Americans faced humiliating signs that read: "Colored Water"; "No Blacks Allowed"; "Whites Only!"

SEGREGATION CONTINUES INTO THE 20TH CENTURY After the Civil War, some African Americans tried to escape southern racism by moving north. This migration of southern African Americans sped up greatly during World War I. It accelerated again after World War II, as many African American sharecroppers abandoned farms for the promise of industrial jobs in northern cities. However, they discovered racial prejudice and segregation there, too. Most could find housing only in all-black neighborhoods. Many white workers also resented the competition for jobs. This sometimes led to violence.

A DEVELOPING CIVIL RIGHTS MOVEMENT In many ways, the events of World War II set the stage for the civil rights movement. First, the demand for soldiers in the early 1940s created a shortage of white male laborers. That labor shortage opened new job opportunities for African Americans, Latinos, and white women.

Second, during the war, civil rights organizations actively campaigned for African American voting rights and challenged Jim Crow laws. In response to protests, President Roosevelt issued a presidential directive. The directive prohibited racial discrimination by federal agencies and all companies that were engaged in war work. The groundwork was laid for more organized campaigns to end segregation throughout the United States.

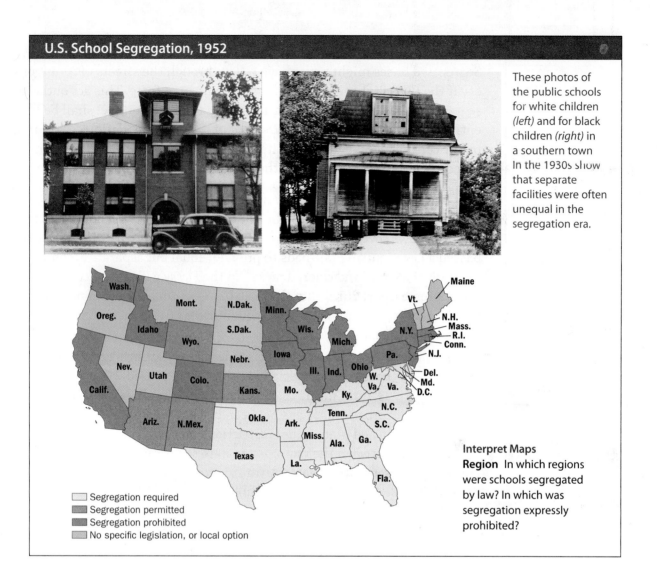

U.S. School Segregation, 1952

These photos of the public schools for white children *(left)* and for black children *(right)* in a southern town In the 1930s show that separate facilities were often unequal in the segregation era.

Segregation required
Segregation permitted
Segregation prohibited
No specific legislation, or local option

Interpret Maps
Region In which regions were schools segregated by law? In which was segregation expressly prohibited?

Third, nearly one million African Americans served in the armed forces, which needed so many fighting men that they had to end their discriminatory policies. Such policies had previously kept African Americans from serving in fighting units. Many African American soldiers returned from the war determined to fight for their own freedom now that they had helped defeat fascist and racist regimes overseas. However, black veterans who had risked their lives to serve their country returned home to face discrimination, which inevitably led to clashes.

One major event occurred in February of 1946 in Columbia, Tennessee. U.S. Navy veteran James Stephenson was arrested and charged with intent to commit murder after he fought with a white store clerk over the way the clerk treated his mother. This led to violence between the police and the black citizens and veterans in the town. State highway patrol officers were called in and raided the black section of town without warrants. They shot up buildings, stole money and other goods, and confiscated every gun they found. They also arrested over 100 blacks without providing legal counsel or granting bail. A few days later, two black men were killed while in police custody. The "Columbia Race Riots," as this incident came to be known, made national headlines. It is regarded as a key event leading up to the civil rights movement.

Reading Check
Find Main Ideas
How did events during World War II lay the groundwork for African Americans to fight for civil rights in the 1950s?

Challenging Segregation in Court

The desegregation campaign was led largely by the NAACP, which had fought to end segregation since 1909. One influential figure in this campaign was Charles Hamilton Houston, a brilliant Howard University law professor who served as chief legal counsel for the NAACP from 1934 to 1938.

THE NAACP LEGAL STRATEGY In deciding the NAACP's legal strategy, Houston focused on the inequality between the separate schools that many states provided. At that time, the nation spent ten times as much money educating a white child as an African American child. Thus, Houston focused the organization's limited resources on challenging the most glaring inequalities of segregated public education.

In 1938 Houston placed a team of his best law students under the direction of **Thurgood Marshall**. Over the next 23 years, Marshall and his NAACP lawyers would win 29 out of 32 cases argued before the Supreme Court.

Several of the cases became legal milestones, each chipping away at the segregation platform of *Plessy* v. *Ferguson.* In the 1946 case *Morgan* v. *Virginia,* the Supreme Court declared segregated seating on interstate buses unconstitutional. In 1950 the high court ruled in *Sweatt* v. *Painter* that state law schools must admit black applicants, even if separate black schools exist.

BROWN* v. *BOARD OF EDUCATION Marshall's most stunning victory came on May 17, 1954, in the case known as ***Brown* v. *Board of Education of Topeka.*** In this case, the father of eight-year-old Linda Brown had charged the board of education of Topeka, Kansas, with violating Linda's rights by denying her admission to an all-white elementary school four blocks from her house. The nearest all-black elementary school was 21 blocks away.

Reading Check
Make Inferences
How did the *Brown* decision affect schools outside of Topeka?

In a landmark verdict, the Supreme Court unanimously ruled that segregated schools violated the Fourteenth Amendment's Equal Protection Clause. Chief Justice Earl Warren wrote that, "[I]n the field of public education, the doctrine of separate but equal has no place." The *Brown* decision was relevant for some 12 million schoolchildren in 21 states.

– BIOGRAPHY

Thurgood Marshall (1908–1993)

Thurgood Marshall dedicated his life to fighting racism. His father had labored as a steward at an all-white country club, his mother as a teacher at an all-black school. Marshall himself was denied admission to the University of Maryland Law School because of his race.

In 1961 President John F. Kennedy nominated Marshall to the U.S. Court of Appeals. Lyndon Johnson picked Marshall for U.S. solicitor general in 1965 and two years later named him as the first African American Supreme Court justice. In that role he remained a strong advocate of civil rights until he retired in 1991.

After Marshall died in 1993, a copy of the *Brown* v. *Board of Education* decision was placed beside his casket. On it, an admirer wrote: "You shall always be remembered."

Reaction to the *Brown* Decision

Official reaction to the ruling was mixed. In Kansas and Oklahoma, state officials said they expected segregation to end with little trouble. In Texas, the governor warned that plans might "take years" to work out. He actively prevented desegregation by calling in the Texas Rangers. In Mississippi and Georgia, officials vowed total resistance. Governor Herman Talmadge of Georgia said "The people of Georgia will not comply with the decision of the court. . . . We're going to do whatever is necessary in Georgia to keep white children in white schools and colored children in colored schools."

RESISTANCE TO SCHOOL DESEGREGATION Within a year, more than 500 school districts had desegregated their classrooms. In Baltimore, St. Louis, and Washington, DC, black and white students sat side by side for the first time in history. However, in many areas where African Americans were a majority, whites resisted desegregation. Groups calling themselves White Citizens' Councils used economic pressure as a weapon, calling for boycotts of businesses and individuals who supported desegregation. These "councils" were made up of prominent community members who expressed their racism with pride. Some white supremacists felt that even stronger action should be taken to stop desegregation. In some places, the Ku Klux Klan (KKK) reappeared. The KKK had been the most widespread white supremacist group during the late 1860s, with a resurgence in the 1920s. In the 1950s and 1960s, the KKK claimed responsibility for hundreds of violent attacks against African Americans and white supporters of civil rights.

In 1955 the Supreme Court handed down a second ruling, known as *Brown II,* that ordered school desegregation implemented "with all deliberate speed." Still, southern states resisted. Three years later, the Court acted again to uphold and enforce the law, stating in *Cooper* v. *Aaron* that school districts had to follow desegregation laws and could no longer delay taking action to integrate.

Initially President Eisenhower refused to enforce compliance. "The fellow who tries to tell me that you can do these things by force is just plain nuts," he said. Events in Little Rock, Arkansas, would soon force Eisenhower to go against his personal beliefs.

CRISIS IN LITTLE ROCK In 1948 Arkansas had become the first southern state to admit African Americans to state universities without being required by a court order. By the 1950s some scout troops and labor unions in Arkansas had quietly ended their Jim Crow practices. Little Rock citizens had elected two men to the school board who publicly backed desegregation. And the school superintendent, Virgil Blossom, began planning for desegregation soon after *Brown.*

However, Governor Orval Faubus publicly supported segregation. In September 1957 he ordered the National Guard to turn away the "Little Rock Nine"—nine African American students who had volunteered to integrate Little Rock's Central High School as the first step in Blossom's plan. A federal judge ordered Faubus to let the students into school.

As white students jeer her and members of the Arkansas National Guard look on, Elizabeth Eckford enters Little Rock Central High School in 1957.

NAACP members called eight of the students and arranged to drive them to school. They could not reach the ninth student, Elizabeth Eckford, who did not have a phone, and she set out alone. Outside Central High, Eckford faced an abusive crowd. Terrified, the 15-year-old made it to a bus stop, where two friendly whites stayed with her.

The crisis in Little Rock forced Eisenhower to act. He placed the Arkansas National Guard under federal control. He also ordered 1,000 paratroopers into Little Rock. The nation watched the televised coverage of the event. Under the watch of soldiers, the nine African American teenagers attended class.

But even these soldiers could not protect the students from troublemakers who confronted them in stairways, in the halls, and in the cafeteria. Throughout the year, African American students were regularly harassed by other students. At the end of the year, Faubus shut down Central High rather than let integration continue.

CIVIL RIGHTS ACT OF 1957 On September 9, 1957, Congress passed the Civil Rights Act of 1957, the first civil rights law since Reconstruction. Shepherded by Senator Lyndon B. Johnson of Texas, the law gave the attorney general greater power over school desegregation. It also gave the federal government jurisdiction, or authority, over violations of African American voting rights.

The act passed despite fierce opposition from some members of Congress. Almost a decade earlier, a group of politicians who staunchly supported segregation broke away from the Democrats to form the States' Rights Democratic Party, more commonly called the Dixiecrats. They nominated Strom Thurmond, then the governor of South Carolina, to represent them in the 1948 presidential election. Although the party disbanded after losing the election, the term *Dixiecrat* continued to be used for southern politicians who opposed desegregation and other civil liberties for African Americans. Dixiecrat Thurmond, elected into the Senate in 1954, unsuccessfully attempted to block the bill by filibuster, speaking for 24 hours and 18 minutes straight.

Reading Check
Analyze Causes
Why weren't schools in all regions desegregated immediately after the *Brown II* decision?

The Montgomery Bus Boycott

The face-to-face confrontation at Central High School was not the only showdown over segregation in the mid-1950s. Impatient with the slow pace of change in the courts, African American activists had begun taking direct action to win the rights the Fourteenth and Fifteenth Amendments to the Constitution promised them. Among those on the frontline of change was Jo Ann Gibson Robinson.

Rosa Parks (1913–2005)

Long before December 1955, Rosa Parks had protested segregation through everyday acts. She refused to use drinking fountains labeled "Colored Only." When possible, she shunned segregated elevators and climbed stairs instead.

Parks joined the Montgomery chapter of the NAACP in 1943 and became the organization's secretary. A turning point came for her in the summer of 1955, when she attended a workshop designed to promote integration by giving the students the experience of interracial living.

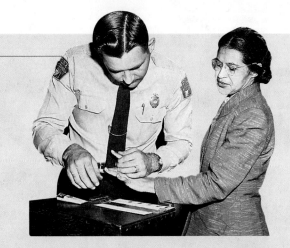

Returning to Montgomery, Parks was even more determined to fight segregation. As it happened, her act of protest against injustice on the buses inspired a whole community to join her cause.

BOYCOTTING SEGREGATION Four days after the *Brown* decision in May 1954, Robinson wrote a letter to the mayor of Montgomery, Alabama. In it she asked that bus drivers no longer be allowed to force riders in the "colored" section to yield their seats to whites. The mayor refused. Little did he know that in less than a year another African American woman from Alabama would be at the center of this controversy, and that her name and her words would far outlast segregation.

On December 1, 1955, **Rosa Parks**, a seamstress and an NAACP officer, took a seat in the front row of the "colored" section of a Montgomery bus. As the bus filled, the driver ordered Parks and three other African American passengers to empty the row they were occupying so that a white man could sit down without having to sit next to an African American. "It was time for someone to stand up—or in my case, sit down," recalled Parks. "I refused to move."

As Parks stared out the window, the bus driver said, "If you don't stand up, I'm going to call the police and have you arrested." The soft-spoken Parks replied, "You may do that."

News of Parks's arrest spread rapidly. Jo Ann Gibson Robinson and NAACP leader E. D. Nixon suggested a one-day bus boycott. The majority of bus passengers were black, and about 90 percent of them participated in the boycott. This level of success led leaders of the African American community, including many ministers, to extend the boycott. They formed the Montgomery Improvement Association to coordinate efforts and elected the pastor of the Dexter Avenue Baptist Church, 26-year-old **Martin Luther King Jr.**, to lead the group. An ordained minister since 1948, King had just earned a PhD in theology from Boston University.

WALKING FOR JUSTICE On the night of December 5, 1955, Dr. King addressed an estimated crowd of between 5,000 and 15,000 people, calling for justice. King's passionate and eloquent speech brought people to their feet and filled the audience with a sense of mission. African Americans filed a lawsuit and for 381 days—over a year—refused to ride the buses in Montgomery. In most cases they had to find other means of transportation by organizing carpools or walking long distances. Support came from within the black community—workers donated one-fifth of their weekly salaries—as well as from outside groups like the NAACP, the United Auto Workers, Montgomery's Jewish community, and sympathetic white southerners. The boycotters remained nonviolent even after a bomb ripped apart King's home (no one was injured). Finally, in 1956 the Supreme Court outlawed bus segregation.

Reading Check
Synthesize Why was Rosa Parks's action on December 1, 1955, significant?

The Movement Spreads

The Montgomery bus boycott proved to the world that the African American community could unite and organize a successful protest movement. It also proved the power of nonviolent resistance, the peaceful refusal to obey unjust laws. Despite threats to his life and family, King urged his followers to remain calm and not to give in to the hatred shown to them.

CHANGING THE WORLD WITH SOUL FORCE King called his brand of nonviolent resistance "soul force." He based his ideas on the teachings of several people. From the teachings of Jesus, he learned to love one's enemies. From writer Henry David Thoreau he took the concept of civil disobedience—the refusal to obey an unjust law. From labor organizer A. Philip Randolph he learned to organize massive demonstrations. From Mohandas Gandhi, the leader who helped India throw off British rule, he learned to resist oppression without violence. King predicted that demonstrators would experience consequences for their protest but would eventually win over the hearts and minds of their opponents through their willingness to suffer.

King held steadfast to his philosophy, even when a wave of racial violence swept through the South after the *Brown* decision. The violence included the

— BIOGRAPHY

Martin Luther King Jr. (1929–1968)

Born Michael Luther King Jr., King had to adjust to a new name in 1934. In that year, his father— Rev. Michael King Sr.—returned home from a trip to Europe, where he had toured the site where Martin Luther had begun the Protestant Reformation. Upon his return, the elder King changed his and his son's names to Martin.

Like Luther, the younger King became a reformer. In 1964 he won the Nobel Peace Prize. Yet there was a side of King unknown to most people— his inner battle to overcome his hatred of the white bigots. As a youth, he had once vowed "to hate all white people." As leader of the

civil rights movement, King said the freedom of all Americans was limited by the effects of segregation and bigotry.

1955 murder of Emmett Till—a 14-year-old African American boy who had allegedly flirted with a white woman. There were also shootings and beatings, some fatal, of civil rights workers.

FROM THE GRASSROOTS UP After the bus boycott ended, King joined with ministers and civil rights leaders to found the **Southern Christian Leadership Conference (SCLC)** in 1957. Its purpose was "to carry on nonviolent crusades against the evils of second-class citizenship." Using African American churches as a base, the SCLC planned to stage protests and demonstrations throughout the South. The leaders hoped to build a movement from the grassroots up and to win the support of ordinary African Americans of all ages. King, president of the SCLC, used the power of his voice and ideas to fuel the movement's momentum.

The nuts and bolts of organizing the SCLC was handled by its first director, Ella Baker, the granddaughter of slaves. While with the NAACP, Baker had served as national field secretary, traveling over 16,000 miles throughout the South. From 1957 to 1960, Baker used her contacts to set up branches of the SCLC in southern cities. In April 1960, Baker helped students at Shaw University, an African American university in Raleigh, North Carolina, organize a national protest group, the **Student Nonviolent Coordinating Committee**, or **SNCC**, pronounced "snick" for short.

It had been six years since the *Brown* decision, and many college students viewed the pace of change as too slow. Although these students risked a great deal—losing college scholarships, being expelled from college, being physically harmed—they were determined to challenge the system. SNCC hoped to harness the energy of these student protesters. It would soon create one of the most important student activist movements in the nation's history.

DEMONSTRATING FOR FREEDOM Although SNCC adopted King's ideas in part, its members had ideas of their own. Many people called for a more confrontational strategy and set out to reshape the civil rights movement.

Document-Based Investigation Historical Source

Sit-Ins

Sit-in demonstrators, such as these at a Jackson, Mississippi, lunch counter in 1963, faced intimidation and humiliation from white segregationists.

Analyze Historical Sources

1. What does this photograph tell you about how many whites in the South felt about equal rights for African Americans?

2. What can you tell about the protesters sitting at the counter?

The founders of SNCC had models to build on. In 1942 in Chicago, the Congress of Racial Equality (CORE) had staged the first **sit-ins**, sometimes called sit-downs. During these sit-ins, African American protesters sat down at segregated lunch counters and refused to leave until they were served. Like boycotts, this tactic brought attention to the movement while applying economic pressure—sit-ins blocked business at the stores. In February 1960 African American students from North Carolina's Agricultural and Technical College staged a sit-in at a whites-only lunch counter at a Woolworth's store in Greensboro. This time, television crews brought coverage of the protest into homes throughout the United States. There was no denying the ugly face of racism. Day after day, news reporters captured the scenes of whites beating, jeering at, and pouring food over students who refused to strike back. The coverage sparked many other sit-ins across the South. In Nashville, Tennessee, for example, James Lawson and Diane Nash led a series of sit-ins from February 13 to May 10, 1960, targeting several downtown businesses.

In response to such protests, store managers called in the police, raised the price of food, and removed counter seats. But the movement continued and spread to the North. There, students formed picket lines around national chain stores that maintained segregated lunch counters in the South.

By late 1960 students had descended on and desegregated lunch counters in some 48 cities in 11 states. To help the many sit-ins, supporters of all races boycotted and picketed the targeted businesses. They endured arrests, beatings, suspension from college, and tear gas and fire hoses, but the army of nonviolent students refused to back down. "My mother has always told me that I'm equal to other people," said Ezell Blair Jr., one of the students who led the first SNCC sit-in in 1960.

Coalitions between groups like SNCC, the SCLC, CORE, and the NAACP would prove crucial in the fight to end segregation. For the rest of the 1960s, many Americans banded together to convince the rest of the country that blacks and whites deserved equal treatment.

Reading Check
Analyze Effects
How did the SCLC help in the fight to achieve civil rights?

Lesson 1 Assessment

1. **Organize Information** Fill in a spider diagram with examples of tactics, organizations, leaders, and Supreme Court decisions of the civil rights movement up to 1960.

2. **Key Terms and People** For each key term or person in the lesson, write a sentence explaining its significance.

3. **Evaluate** Do you think the nonviolence used by civil rights activists was a good tactic? Explain.
   Think About:
   • the Montgomery bus boycott
   • television coverage of events
   • sit-ins

4. **Contrast** How did the tactics of the student protesters from SNCC differ from those of the boycotters in Montgomery?

5. **Draw Conclusions** After the *Brown* v. *Board of Education of Topeka* ruling, what do you think was the most significant event of the civil rights movement prior to 1960? Why?

Brown v. Board of Education of Topeka (1954)

ORIGINS OF THE CASE

In the early 1950s the school system of Topeka, Kansas, like southern elementary school systems, operated separate schools for "the two races"—blacks and whites. Reverend Oliver Brown protested that this was unfair to his eight-year-old daughter, Linda. Although the Browns lived near a "white" school, Linda was forced to take a long bus ride to her "black" school across town.

THE RULING

The Court ruled that segregated public schools were "inherently" unequal and therefore unconstitutional.

Linda Brown's name headed a list of five school desegregation cases heard by the Supreme Court.

LEGAL REASONING

While the correctness of the *Brown* ruling seems obvious today, some justices had difficulty agreeing to it. One reason was the force of legal precedent. Normally, judges follow a policy of *stare decisis*, "let the decision stand." The *Plessy* v. *Ferguson* decision endorsing segregation had stood for over 50 years. It clearly stated that "separate but equal" facilities did not violate the Fourteenth Amendment.

Thurgood Marshall, the NAACP lawyer who argued *Brown*, spent years laying the groundwork to chip away at Jim Crow— the local laws that required segregated facilities. Marshall had recently won two Supreme Court decisions in 1950 (*McLaurin* and *Sweatt*; see Legal Sources) that challenged segregation at graduate schools. Then in 1952 the Supreme Court agreed to hear the Browns' case. The Court deliberated for two years, deciding how to interpret the Fourteenth Amendment.

In the end, Chief Justice Earl Warren carefully sidestepped *Plessy*, claiming that segregated schools were not and never could be equal. On Monday, May 17, 1954, Warren read the unanimous decision:

"Does segregation of children in public schools . . . deprive the children of . . . equal educational opportunities? We believe that it does. . . . To separate them . . . solely because of their race generates a feeling of inferiority . . . that may affect their hearts and minds in a way unlikely ever to be undone."

—Brown v. Board of Education of Topeka

LEGAL SOURCES

U.S. CONSTITUTION

Fourteenth Amendment, Equal Protection Clause (1868)

"No state shall . . . deny to any person within its jurisdiction the equal protection of the laws."

RELATED CASES

Plessy v. Ferguson (1896)
- Upheld Louisiana's laws requiring that train passengers be segregated by race.
- Established the doctrine of "separate but equal."

McLaurin v. Oklahoma State (1950)

Ruled that Oklahoma State University violated the Constitution by keeping its one "Negro" student in the back of the class and the cafeteria.

Sweatt v. Painter (1950)

Required the University of Texas to admit an African American student to its previously all-white law school.

Thurgood Marshall was appointed the first African American Supreme Court justice by President Johnson in 1967.

WHY IT MATTERED

The Court's decision in *Brown* had an immediate impact on pending rulings. In a series of cases after *Brown,* the Supreme Court prohibited segregation in housing, at public beaches, at recreation facilities, and in restaurants. Later decisions extended equal access to other groups, including women and resident aliens.

The decision encountered fierce resistance, however. It awakened the old battle cry of states' rights. Directly following *Brown,* some members of Congress circulated the "Southern Manifesto," claiming the right of the states to ignore the ruling. In taking a stand on a social issue, they said, the Court had taken a step away from simply interpreting legal precedents. Critics charged that the Warren Court had acted as legislators and even as sociologists.

The *Brown* case strengthened the civil rights movement, however, and paved the way for the end of Jim Crow. The NAACP had fought and won the legal battle and had gained prestige and momentum. Americans got the strong message that the federal government now took civil rights seriously.

HISTORICAL IMPACT

Three of the parties involved in *Brown*—Delaware, Kansas, and the District of Columbia—began to integrate schools in 1954. Topeka County informed the Court that 123 black students were already attending formerly all-white schools. Even so, the Supreme Court was well aware that its decision would be difficult to enforce. In a follow-up ruling, *Brown II* (1955), the Court required that integration take place with "all deliberate speed." To some, this meant quickly. Others interpreted *deliberate* to mean slowly.

Only two southern states even began to integrate classrooms in 1954; Texas and Arkansas opened one and two districts, respectively. By 1960 less than 1 percent of the South's students attended integrated schools. Many school districts were ordered to use aggressive means to achieve racial balance. Courts spent decades supervising forced busing, a practice that often pitted community against community.

Still, despite the resistance and the practical difficulties of implementation, *Brown* stands today as a watershed, the single point at which breaking the "color barrier" officially became a federal priority.

Critical Thinking

1. **Connect to History** Legal precedents are set not only by rulings but also by dissenting opinions, in which justices explain why they disagree with the majority. Justice John Marshall Harlan was the one dissenting voice in *Plessy v. Ferguson.* Do Internet research to read his opinion and comment on how it might apply to *Brown.*

2. **Connect to Today** Do Internet research to learn about the Supreme Court's changing opinions on civil rights. Compile a chart or timeline to present the facts—date, plaintiff, defendant, major issue, and outcome—of several major cases. Then give an oral presentation explaining the Supreme Court's role in civil rights.

The Triumphs of a Crusade

The Big Idea

Civil rights activists broke through racial barriers. Their activism prompted landmark legislation.

Why It Matters Now

Activism pushed the federal government to end segregation and ensure voting rights for African Americans.

Key Terms and People

freedom riders

James Meredith

Civil Rights Act of 1964

Freedom Summer

Fannie Lou Hamer

Voting Rights Act of 1965

One American's Story

In 1961 James Peck, a white civil rights activist, joined other CORE members on a historic bus trip across the South. The two-bus trip would test the Supreme Court decisions banning segregated seating on interstate bus routes and segregated facilities in bus terminals. Peck and other **freedom riders** expected a violent reaction. They hoped that this would convince the Kennedy administration to enforce the law. The violence was not long in coming.

At the Alabama state line, white racists got on Bus One carrying chains, brass knuckles, and pistols. They brutally beat African American riders and white activists who tried to intervene. Still the riders managed to go on. Then on May 4, 1961—Mother's Day—the bus pulled into the Birmingham bus terminal. James Peck saw a hostile mob waiting, some holding iron bars.

"I looked at them and then I looked at Charles Person, who had been designated as my team mate. . . . When I looked at him, he responded by saying simply, 'Let's go.' As we entered the white waiting room, . . . we were grabbed bodily and pushed toward the alleyway . . . and out of sight of onlookers in the waiting room, six of them started swinging at me with fists and pipes. Five others attacked Person a few feet ahead."
—James Peck, from *Freedom Ride*

Three days after being beaten unconscious in Birmingham, freedom rider James Peck demonstrates in New York City to pressure national bus companies to support desegregation.

The ride of Bus One had ended, but Bus Two continued southward on a journey that would shock the Kennedy administration into action.

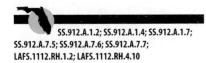

SS.912.A.1.2; SS.912.A.1.4; SS.912.A.1.7;
SS.912.A.7.5; SS.912.A.7.6; SS.912.A.7.7;
LAFS.1112.RH.1.2; LAFS.1112.RH.4.10

Riding for Freedom

In Anniston, Alabama, about 200 angry whites attacked Bus Two. The mob followed the activists out of town. When one of the tires blew, they smashed a window and tossed in a firebomb. The freedom riders spilled out just before the bus exploded.

NEW VOLUNTEERS The bus companies refused to carry the CORE freedom riders any farther. Even though the determined volunteers did not want to give up, they ended their ride. However, CORE director James Farmer and SNCC leader Diane Nash announced that a group of SNCC volunteers in Nashville were ready to pick up where the others had left off. Knowing they risked death, some riders made out their wills or wrote farewell letters.

When the new band of freedom riders rode into Birmingham, policemen pulled them from the bus, beat them, and drove them into Tennessee. Defiantly, they returned to the Birmingham bus terminal. Their bus driver, however, feared for his life and refused to transport them. In protest, they occupied the whites-only waiting room at the terminal for 18 hours until a solution was reached. After an angry phone call from U.S. Attorney General Robert Kennedy, bus company officials convinced the driver to proceed. The riders set out for Montgomery on May 20.

ARRIVAL OF FEDERAL MARSHALS Although Alabama officials had promised Kennedy that the riders would be protected, a mob of whites—many carrying bats and lead pipes—fell upon the riders when they arrived in Montgomery. John Doer, a Justice Department official on the scene, called

In May 1961 a mob firebombed this bus of freedom riders outside Anniston, Alabama, and attacked passengers as they tried to escape.

the attorney general to report what was happening. "A bunch of men led by a guy with a bleeding face are beating [the passengers]. There are no cops. It's terrible. There's not a cop in sight. People are yelling. 'Get 'em, get 'em.' It's awful."

The violence provoked exactly the response the freedom riders wanted. Newspapers throughout the nation and abroad denounced the beatings.

President Kennedy arranged to give the freedom riders direct support. The Justice Department sent 400 U.S. marshals to protect the riders on the last part of their journey to Jackson, Mississippi. In addition, the attorney general and the Interstate Commerce Commission banned segregation in all interstate travel facilities, including waiting rooms, restrooms, and lunch counters.

Reading Check
Analyze Issues
What did the freedom riders hope to achieve?

Standing Firm

With the integration of interstate travel facilities underway, some civil rights workers turned their attention to integrating some southern schools and pushing the movement into additional southern towns. At each turn they encountered opposition and often violence.

INTEGRATING OLE MISS In September 1962 Air Force veteran **James Meredith** won a federal court case that allowed him to enroll in the all-white University of Mississippi, nicknamed Ole Miss. But when Meredith arrived on campus, he faced Governor Ross Barnett, who refused to let him register as a student.

President Kennedy ordered federal marshals to escort Meredith to the registrar's office. Barnett responded with a heated radio appeal: "I call on every Mississippian to keep his faith and courage. We will never surrender." The broadcast turned out white demonstrators by the thousands.

On the night of September 30, riots broke out on campus, resulting in two deaths. It took thousands of soldiers, 200 arrests, and 15 hours to stop the rioters. In the months that followed, federal officials accompanied Meredith to class and protected his parents from nightriders who shot up their house.

HEADING INTO BIRMINGHAM The trouble continued in Alabama. Birmingham, a city known for its strict enforcement of total segregation in public life, also had a reputation for racial violence, including 18 bombings from 1957 to 1963. Reverend Fred Shuttlesworth, head of the Alabama Christian Movement for Human Rights and secretary of the SCLC, decided something had to be done. Believing Birmingham the ideal place to test the power of nonviolence, Shuttlesworth invited Martin Luther King Jr. and the SCLC to help desegregate the city. On April 3, 1963, King flew into Birmingham to hold a planning meeting with members of the African American community. He told them that to be successful in Birmingham, one of the most segregated cities in the United States, they would have to work together.

After days of demonstrations led by Shuttlesworth and others, King and a small band of marchers were finally arrested during a demonstration on Good Friday, April 12. The next day, a group of local white clergy took out a

News photos and television coverage of police dogs in Birmingham attacking African Americans shocked the nation.

full-page ad in the city's newspaper. They attacked King's actions as unwise and argued that he was pushing too fast. In his jail cell, King rejected these charges with an eloquent response that gained fame as "Letter from a Birmingham Jail." King expressed the difficulty of waiting for change in the face of vicious, hateful treatment.

On April 20 King posted bail and began planning more demonstrations. On May 2 more than a thousand African American children marched in Birmingham. Police commissioner Eugene "Bull" Connor's men arrested 959 of them. On May 3 a second "children's crusade" came face to face with a helmeted police force. Police swept the marchers off their feet with high-pressure fire hoses, set attack dogs on them, and clubbed those who fell. TV cameras captured all of it, and millions of viewers heard the children screaming. Several commenters noted that the media coverage of police dogs and fire hoses did much to advance the cause of civil rights among Americans who previously had been undecided on the issue.

Continued protests, an economic boycott, and negative media coverage finally convinced Birmingham officials to end segregation. This stunning civil rights victory inspired African Americans across the nation. It also convinced President Kennedy that only a new civil rights act could end racial violence and satisfy the demands of African Americans—and many whites— for racial justice.

KENNEDY TAKES A STAND Another confrontation occurred on the campus of the University of Alabama. A federal judge had ordered the university to admit Vivian Malone and James Hood, two black students. On June 11, 1963, President Kennedy sent National Guard troops to escort the students and ensure the court's orders were carried out. Alabama governor George C. Wallace stood in front of the enrollment building to try to stop Malone and Hood from going inside. Aware of the resistance they might meet, the National Guard soldiers were prepared to physically lift and remove the governor if necessary. The action was not needed. After making a short speech about states' rights, Wallace let the black students pass.

That evening, Kennedy asked the nation: "Are we to say to the world—and much more importantly, to each other—that this is the land of the free, except for the Negroes?" He demanded that Congress pass a civil rights bill.

A tragic event just hours after Kennedy's speech highlighted the racial tension in much of the South. Shortly after midnight, a sniper murdered Medgar Evers in front of his home in Jackson, Mississippi. Evers was a World War II veteran, the NAACP field secretary in Mississippi, and one of the movement's most effective leaders. His killing shocked many Americans. Police soon arrested a white supremacist, Byron de la Beckwith, but he was released after two trials resulted in hung juries. His release brought a new militancy to African Americans. Many demanded, "Freedom now!"

Background
Beckwith was finally convicted in 1994, after the case was reopened based on new evidence.

Reading Check
Analyze Causes
What events led to desegregation in Birmingham?

Document-Based Investigation Historical Source

Capturing the Movement

Born in Memphis in 1922, photographer Ernest Withers believed that if the struggle for equality could be shown to people, things would change. Armed with only a camera, he braved violent crowds to capture the heated racism during the Montgomery bus boycott, the desegregation of Central High in Little Rock, and the 1968 Memphis sanitation workers strike, shown in this photograph, led by Martin Luther King Jr. The night before the Memphis march, Withers helped make some of the signs he photographed.

Analyze Historical Sources

What do the signs tell you about African Americans' struggle for civil rights?

What kind of treatment do you suppose these men had experienced? Why do you think so?

Marching to Washington

The civil rights bill that President Kennedy sent to Congress guaranteed equal access to all public accommodations and gave the U.S. attorney general the power to file school desegregation suits. With this bill, Kennedy hoped to take the important first steps to ending racial discrimination. To persuade Congress to pass the bill, two veteran organizers—labor leader A. Philip Randolph and Bayard Rustin of the SCLC—summoned Americans to a march on Washington, DC.

THE DREAM OF EQUALITY On August 28, 1963, more than 250,000 people—including about 75,000 whites—converged on the nation's capital. They assembled on the grassy lawn of the Washington Monument and marched to the Lincoln Memorial. There, people listened to speakers demand the immediate passage of the civil rights bill.

When Dr. Martin Luther King Jr. appeared, the crowd exploded in applause. In his now famous speech, "I Have a Dream," he appealed for peace and racial harmony. This speech, like King's other writings, brought national attention to the movement and to the progress that still needed to be made.

"I have a dream that one day this nation will rise up, live out the true meaning of its creed: 'We hold these truths to be self-evident, that all men are created equal.' . . . I have a dream that my four little children will one day live in a nation where they will not be judged by the color of their skin but by the content of their character. . . . I have a dream that one day in Alabama, . . . one day right there in Alabama little black boys and black girls will be able to join hands with little white boys and white girls as sisters and brothers."

—Martin Luther King Jr., from "I Have a Dream"

MORE VIOLENCE Two weeks after King's historic speech, on September 15, 1963, violence once again struck Birmingham. In what came to be known as the Birmingham Church Bombing, a bomb exploded at the 16th Street Baptist Church, killing four girls—11-year-old Denise McNair and three 14-year-olds—Cynthia Wesley, Carole Robertson, and Addie Mae Collins. Two more African Americans died in the unrest that followed.

Two months later, an assassin shot and killed John F. Kennedy. His successor, President Lyndon B. Johnson, pledged to carry on Kennedy's work. On July 2, 1964, Johnson signed the **Civil Rights Act of 1964**, which prohibited discrimination because of race, religion, national origin, and gender. It gave all citizens the right to enter and use public accommodations such as washrooms, restaurants, and theaters.

Title VI of the act specifically addressed all agencies and institutions that receive federal funding, stating, "No person in the United States shall, on the ground of race, color, or national origin, be excluded from participation in, be denied the benefits of, or be subjected to discrimination under any program

Civil Rights Acts of the 1950s and 1960s

CIVIL RIGHTS ACT OF 1957	• Established federal Commission on Civil Rights • Established a Civil Rights Division in the Justice Department to enforce civil rights laws • Enlarged federal power to protect voting rights
CIVIL RIGHTS ACT OF 1964	• Banned most discrimination in employment and in public accommodations • Enlarged federal power to protect voting rights and speed up school desegregation • Established Equal Employment Opportunity Commission to ensure fair treatment in employment
VOTING RIGHTS ACT OF 1965	• Eliminated voter literacy tests • Enabled federal examiners to register voters
CIVIL RIGHTS ACT OF 1968	• Prohibited discrimination in the sale or rental of most housing • Strengthened antilynching laws • Made it a crime to harm civil rights workers

Interpret Tables
Which law do you think benefited the most people? Explain your choice.

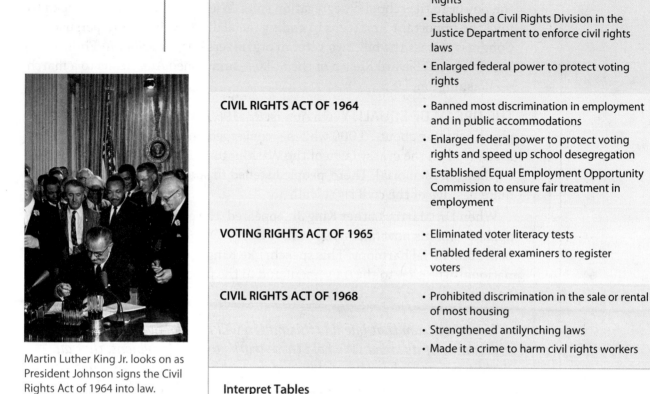

Martin Luther King Jr. looks on as President Johnson signs the Civil Rights Act of 1964 into law.

Reading Check
Analyze Events
Why did civil rights organizers ask their supporters to march on Washington?

or activity receiving Federal financial assistance." This ensured rights for all citizens to use public, federally funded facilities such as parks and libraries. It also protected against discrimination at public schools and universities. Title VII of the act prohibited employment discrimination on the basis of race, color, religion, sex, or national origin. It created the Equal Employment Opportunity Commission (EEOC) to investigate and resolve charges of workplace discrimination.

Like other civil rights laws, the Civil Rights Act of 1964 faced resistance from staunch opponents, especially in the South. Some private business owners looked for loopholes in the act. Later that year, the law was tested and upheld when it appeared in a case before the Supreme Court. In *Heart of Atlanta Hotel, Inc.* v. *United States,* the Supreme Court ruled that even private businesses like hotels and restaurants could not legally discriminate by claiming they had the right to choose their customers. This landmark ruling made it clear that businesses had no legal right to refuse to serve blacks. The act and the actions of the Supreme Court to uphold it gave a strong legal backbone to the fight against discrimination in public places.

Fighting for Voting Rights

Meanwhile, the right of all African Americans to vote remained elusive. In 1964 CORE and SNCC workers in the South began working together to register as many African Americans as they could to vote. They hoped their campaign would receive national publicity, which would in turn influence Congress to pass a voting rights act. Focused in Mississippi, the project became known as **Freedom Summer**.

FREEDOM SUMMER To fortify the project, civil rights groups recruited college students and trained them in nonviolent resistance. Thousands of student volunteers—mostly white, about one-third female—went into Mississippi to help register voters. For some, the job proved deadly. In June 1964, three civil rights workers disappeared in Neshoba County, Mississippi. Investigators later learned that Klansmen and local police had murdered the men, two of whom were white. Through the summer, the racial beatings and murders continued, along with the burning of businesses, homes, and churches.

A NEW POLITICAL PARTY African Americans needed a voice in the political arena if sweeping change was to occur. In order to gain a seat in Mississippi's all-white Democratic Party, SNCC organized the Mississippi Freedom Democratic Party (MFDP). **Fannie Lou Hamer**, the daughter of Mississippi sharecroppers, would be their voice at the 1964 Democratic National Convention. In a televised speech that shocked the convention and viewers nationwide, Hamer described how civil rights activists had experienced violence and injustice. She also described how she was jailed after attending a voter registration workshop in 1963 and how police forced other prisoners to beat her.

> *"The first [prisoner] began to beat [me], and I was beat by the first until he was exhausted. . . . The second [prisoner] began to beat. . . . I began to scream and one white man got up and began to beat me in my head and tell me to 'hush.' . . . All of this on account we want to register, to become first-class citizens, and if the Freedom Democratic Party is not seated now, I question America."*
>
> —Fannie Lou Hamer, quoted in
> *The Civil Rights Movement: An Eyewitness History*

In response to Hamer's speech, telegrams and telephone calls poured in to the convention in support of seating the MFDP delegates. President Johnson feared losing the southern white vote if the Democrats sided with the MFDP, so his administration pressured civil rights leaders to convince the MFDP to accept a compromise. The Democrats would give 2 of Mississippi's 68 seats to the MFDP, with a promise to ban discrimination at the 1968 convention.

When Hamer learned of the compromise, she said, "We didn't come all this way for no two seats." The MFDP and supporters in SNCC felt that the leaders had betrayed them.

In the summer of 1964, college students volunteered to go to Mississippi to help register that state's African American voters.

THE SELMA CAMPAIGN At the start of 1965, the SCLC conducted a major voting rights campaign in Selma, Alabama, where SNCC had been working for two years to register voters. By the end of 1965, more than 2,000 African Americans had been arrested in SCLC demonstrations. After a demonstrator named Jimmy Lee Jackson was shot and killed, King responded by announcing a 50-mile protest march from Selma to Montgomery, the state capital. On March 7, 1965, about 600 protesters set out for Montgomery.

That night, mayhem broke out. Once again, television cameras captured the scene. The rest of the nation watched in horror as police swung whips and clubs, and clouds of tear gas swirled around fallen marchers. Demonstrators poured into Selma by the hundreds. Ten days later, President Johnson presented Congress with a new voting rights act and asked for its swift passage.

On March 21, about 3,000 marchers again set out for Montgomery, this time with federal protection. Soon the number grew to an army of 25,000.

EXTENDING VOTING RIGHTS That summer, Congress finally passed Johnson's **Voting Rights Act of 1965**. The act eliminated the so-called literacy tests that had disqualified many voters. It also stated that federal examiners could enroll voters who had been denied suffrage by local officials. In Selma, the proportion of African Americans registered to vote rose from 10 percent in 1964 to 60 percent in 1968. Overall, the percentage of registered African American voters in the South tripled.

THE TWENTY-FOURTH AMENDMENT Another step toward ensuring voting rights for African Americans occurred on January 24, 1964, when South Dakota became the 38th state to ratify the Twenty-Fourth Amendment to the Constitution. The key clause in the amendment reads: "The right of citizens of the United States to vote in any primary or other election . . . shall not be denied or abridged by the United States or any State by reason of failure to pay any poll tax or other tax."

Poll taxes were often used to keep poor African Americans from voting. Although most states had already abolished their poll taxes by 1964, five southern states—Alabama, Arkansas, Mississippi, Texas, and Virginia—still had such laws on the books. By making these laws unconstitutional, the Twenty-Fourth Amendment gave the vote to millions who had been disqualified because of poverty.

Together, the Twenty-Fourth Amendment and the Voting Rights Act marked a major civil rights victory. These significant policy changes abolished many of the barriers that had prevented African Americans from exercising their constitutionally protected right to vote. However, some felt that the law did not go far enough. Centuries of discrimination had produced social and economic inequalities. Anger over these inequalities led to a series of violent disturbances in the cities of the North.

Reading Check
Compare In what ways was the civil rights campaign in Selma similar to the one in Birmingham?

Lesson 2 Assessment

1. **Organize Information** Use a graphic organizer to list the steps that African Americans took to desegregate buses and schools from 1962 to 1965.

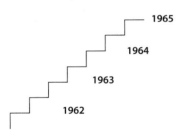

1965
1964
1963
1962

2. **Key Terms and People** For each key term or person in the lesson, write a sentence explaining its significance.

3. **Analyze Issues** What assumptions and beliefs do you think guided the fierce opposition to the civil rights movement in the South? Support your answer with evidence from the text.

Think About:

• the social and political structure of the South
• Mississippi governor Ross Barnett's comment during his radio address
• the actions of police and some white southerners

4. **Analyze Primary Sources** Just after the Civil Rights Act of 1964 was passed, white Alabama governor George Wallace said,

"It is ironical that this event occurs as we approach the celebration of Independence Day. On that day we won our freedom. On this day we have largely lost it."

What do you think Wallace meant by his statement?

5. **Develop Historical Perspective** Explain the significance of Martin Luther King Jr.'s "Letter from a Birmingham Jail" and "I Have a Dream" speech.

Challenges and Changes in the Movement

The Big Idea

Disagreements among civil rights groups and the rise of black nationalism created a violent period in the fight for civil rights.

Why It Matters Now

From the fight for equality came a resurgence of racial pride for African Americans, a legacy that influences today's generations.

Key Terms and People

de facto segregation

de jure segregation

Malcolm X

Nation of Islam

Stokely Carmichael

Black Power

Black Panthers

Kerner Commission

Civil Rights Act of 1968

affirmative action

SS.912.A.1.2; SS.912.A.7.5; SS.912.A.7.6; LAFS.1112.RH.4.10

One American's Story

Alice Walker, the prize-winning novelist, became aware of the civil rights movement in 1960, when she was 16. Her mother had recently scraped together enough money to purchase a television.

Alice Walker during an interview in New York's Central Park in August 1970

"Like a good omen for the future, the face of Dr. Martin Luther King Jr. was the first black face I saw on our new television screen. And, as in a fairy tale, my soul was stirred by the meaning for me of his mission—at the time he was being rather ignominiously dumped into a police van for having led a protest march in Alabama—and I fell in love with the sober and determined face of the Movement."
—Alice Walker, from *In Search of Our Mothers' Gardens*

The next year, Walker attended the all-black Spelman College. In 1963 she took part in the March on Washington. She then traveled to Africa to discover her spiritual roots. After returning home in 1964, she worked on voter registration, taught African American history and writing, and wrote poetry and fiction.

Walker's interest in her heritage was part of a growing trend among African Americans in the mid-1960s. But millions of African Americans were still living in poverty. Angry and frustrated over the difficulty in finding jobs and decent housing, some participated in riots that broke out between 1964 and 1966.

African Americans Seek Greater Equality

In the early 1960s civil rights groups were united in their calls for a new-found pride in black identity. They were also committed to changing the social and economic structures that kept people in a life of poverty. However, by 1965 the leading civil rights groups began to drift apart. Some younger leaders felt that the older leaders had made too many compromises. New leaders emerged as the movement turned its attention to the North, where African Americans faced not legal segregation but deeply entrenched and oppressive racial prejudice. State and city governments did not act to address these problems.

NORTHERN SEGREGATION The problem facing African Americans in the North was **de facto segregation**—segregation not supported by laws but continued in practice. De facto segregation can be harder to fight than **de jure** (dē jŏŏr′ē) **segregation**, or segregation by law, because eliminating it requires changing people's attitudes rather than repealing laws. Activists in the mid-1960s would find it much more difficult to convince whites to share economic and social power with African Americans than to convince them to share lunch counters and bus seats. Just as many southern state governments had resisted ending de jure segregation, local and state governments in all regions often turned a blind eye toward the problems of de facto segregation and economic inequality.

De facto segregation intensified after African Americans migrated to northern cities during and after World War II. This began a "white flight," in which great numbers of whites moved out of the cities to the nearby suburbs. By the mid-1960s most urban African Americans lived in decaying slums, paying rent to landlords who didn't comply with housing and health ordinances. The schools for African American children deteriorated along with their neighborhoods. Unemployment rates were more than twice as high as those among whites.

In addition, many blacks were angry at the sometimes brutal treatment they received from the mostly white police forces in their communities. In 1966 King spearheaded a campaign in Chicago to end de facto segregation and create an "open city." On July 10 he led about 30,000 African Americans in a march on City Hall. In late July, when King led demonstrators through a Chicago neighborhood, angry whites threw rocks and bottles. On August 5 hostile whites stoned King as he led 600 marchers. King left Chicago without accomplishing what he wanted, yet pledging to return.

URBAN VIOLENCE ERUPTS In the mid-1960s racial clashes spread like wildfire. In New York City in July 1964, an encounter between white police and African American teenagers ended in the death of a 15-year-old student. This event sparked a six-day race riot in central Harlem. On August 11, 1965, only five days after President Johnson signed the Voting Rights Act into law, one of the worst race riots in the nation's history raged through the streets of Watts, a predominantly African American neighborhood in Los Angeles. Thirty-four people were killed. Hundreds of millions of dollars' worth of property was destroyed. The next year, 1966, saw even more racial disturbances. And in 1967 alone, riots and violent clashes swept through more than 100 cities.

One of the largest and most notorious riots of 1967 occurred in Detroit. On July 23 police raided an illegal after-hours saloon in one of Detroit's largest African American neighborhoods. The arrest of over 80 occupants of the saloon caused a crowd to gather. Eventually, tensions simmered over, and the crowd became violent. The violence continued for five days, causing the deaths of 43 people and millions of dollars' worth of property damage. Some of the effects of the civil unrest lasted for several years.

The African American rage baffled many whites. "Why would blacks turn to violence after winning so many victories in the South?" they wondered. Some realized that what African Americans wanted and needed was equal opportunity in jobs, housing, and education. Advances in civil rights were happening too slowly. And African Americans were frustrated.

Even before the riots in 1964, President Johnson had announced his War on Poverty, a program to help poor Americans. But the flow of money needed for Johnson's Great Society was soon redirected to fund the war in Vietnam.

Reading Check
Analyze Causes
What were some of the causes of urban rioting in the 1960s?

New Leaders Voice Discontent

The anger that sent rioters into the streets stemmed in part from African American leaders who urged their followers to take complete control of their communities, livelihoods, and culture. One such leader, **Malcolm X**, declared to a Harlem audience that they were under no obligation to white society.

AFRICAN AMERICAN SOLIDARITY Malcolm X, born Malcolm Little, went to jail at age 20 for burglary. While in prison, he studied the teachings of Elijah Muhammad, the head of the **Nation of Islam**, or the Black Muslims. Malcolm changed his name to Malcolm X (dropping what he called his "slave name") and, after his release from prison in 1952, became an Islamic minister. As he gained a following, the brilliant thinker and engaging speaker

— BIOGRAPHY —

Malcolm X (1925–1965)

Malcolm X's early life left him alienated from white society. White racists allegedly killed his father. His mother had an emotional collapse, leaving Malcolm and his siblings in the care of the state. At the end of eighth grade, Malcolm quit school. He was later jailed for criminal behavior. In 1946, while in prison, Malcolm joined the Nation of Islam. He developed a philosophy of black superiority and separatism from whites.

In the later years of his life, he urged African Americans to identify with Africa. He also urged them to work with world organizations and even progressive whites to attain equality. Although silenced by gunmen, Malcolm X is a continuing inspiration for many Americans.

openly preached Elijah Muhammad's views that whites were the cause of the black condition and that blacks should separate from white society. He also advocated armed self-defense.

The press gave Malcolm X a great deal of publicity because his controversial statements made dramatic news stories. This had two effects. First, his call for armed self-defense frightened most whites and many moderate African Americans. Second, all of the attention Malcolm received awakened resentment in some other members of the Nation of Islam.

BALLOTS OR BULLETS? In March 1964 Malcolm broke with Elijah Muhammad over differences in strategy and doctrine. He then formed another Muslim organization. One month later, he made a pilgrimage to Mecca, Saudi Arabia, a trip required of followers of orthodox Islam. In Mecca, he learned that orthodox Islam preached racial equality, and he worshiped alongside people from many countries. Malcolm wrote of his encounter with Muslims of different races and nationalities, including those who appeared white. When he returned to the United States, his attitude toward whites had changed radically. He explained his new slogan, "Ballots or bullets," to a follower that if they didn't try to use the political system (ballots), they would be forced to resort to violence (bullets). He said he preferred to try to change the system through ballots first.

Because of his split with the Black Muslims, Malcolm believed his life might be in danger. On February 21, 1965, while giving a speech in Harlem, the 39-year-old Malcolm X was shot and killed.

BLACK POWER In early June 1966, tensions that had been building between SNCC and the other civil rights groups finally erupted in Mississippi. Here, James Meredith, the man who had integrated the University of Mississippi, set out on a 225-mile "walk against fear." Meredith planned to walk all the way from the Tennessee border to Jackson. However, he was shot by a white racist and was too injured to continue.

Martin Luther King Jr. of the SCLC, Floyd McKissick of CORE, and **Stokely Carmichael** of SNCC decided to lead their followers in a march to

Document-Based Investigation Historical Source

Black Power

Stokely Carmichael was arrested in Greenwood, Mississippi, during the march to complete Meredith's walk. When he showed up at a rally later, his face swollen from a beating, he electrified the crowd.

> *"This is the twenty-seventh time I have been arrested—and I ain't going to jail no more! The only way we're gonna stop them white men from whippin' us is to take over. We been saying freedom for six years—and we ain't got nothin'. What we gonna start now is BLACK POWER."*
>
> —Stokely Carmichael, quoted in *The Civil Rights Movement: An Eyewitness History*

Analyze Historical Sources
Why do you think Carmichael's message appealed to many African Americans?

finish what Meredith had started. But it soon became apparent that SNCC and CORE members were quite militant, as they began to shout slogans similar to those of the black separatists who had followed Malcolm X. When King tried to rally the marchers with the refrain of "We Shall Overcome," many SNCC workers—bitter over the violence they'd suffered during Freedom Summer—began singing, "We shall overrun."

Black Power, Carmichael said, was a "call for black people to begin to define their own goals . . . [and] to lead their own organizations." King urged him to stop using the phrase. He believed it would provoke African Americans to violence and antagonize whites. Carmichael refused to compromise. He urged SNCC to stop recruiting whites and to focus on developing African American pride.

BLACK PANTHERS Later that year, another development demonstrated the growing radicalism of some segments of the African American community. In Oakland, California, in October 1966, Huey Newton and Bobby Seale founded a political party known as the **Black Panthers** to fight police brutality in the ghetto. The party advocated self-sufficiency for African American communities, as well as full employment and decent housing. Members maintained that African Americans should be exempt from military service because an unfair number of black youths had been drafted to serve in Vietnam.

Dressed in black leather jackets, black berets, and sunglasses, the Panthers preached self-defense. They also sold copies of the writings of Mao Zedong, leader of the Chinese Communist revolution. Several shootouts occurred between the Panthers and police. And the FBI conducted numerous investigations of group members (sometimes using illegal tactics). Even so, many of the Panthers' activities—the establishment of daycare centers, free breakfast programs, free medical clinics, assistance to the homeless, and other services—won support in the ghettos.

Though the Black Panthers remained active throughout the 1970s, the group eventually fell apart. Many black Americans objected to the group's militant tactics. Some Panther leaders tried to shift the group's focus to more traditional politics, but the Black Panthers had essentially broken up by the early 1980s.

King Is Assassinated

Martin Luther King Jr. objected to the Black Power movement. He believed that preaching violence could only end in grief. King was planning to lead a Poor People's March on Washington, DC. However, this time the people would have to march without him.

Dr. King seemed to sense that death was near. On April 3, 1968, he addressed a crowd in Memphis, where he had gone to support the city's striking garbage workers. He predicted that he might not be with his people at the end of their journey to full civil rights. But he told them that he was unafraid, that he knew they would achieve their goals. The next day, as King stood on his hotel balcony, James Earl Ray thrust a high-powered rifle out of a window and squeezed the trigger. King crumpled to the floor.

The slogan "Black Power" became the battle cry of militant civil rights activists.

Reading Check
Make Inferences
Why was the public reaction to the Black Panthers mixed?

The night King died, Robert F. Kennedy was campaigning for the Democratic presidential nomination. Fearful that King's death would spark riots, Kennedy's advisers told him to cancel his appearance in an African American neighborhood in Indianapolis. However, Kennedy attended anyway, making an impassioned plea for nonviolence.

> *"For those of you who are black—considering the evidence . . . that there were white people who were responsible—you can be filled with bitterness, with hatred, and a desire for revenge. We can move in that direction as a country, in great polarization—black people amongst black, white people amongst white, filled with hatred toward one another.*
>
> *Or we can make an effort, as Martin Luther King did, to understand and comprehend, and to replace that violence, that stain of bloodshed that has spread across our land, with an effort to understand [with] compassion and love."*
>
> —Robert F. Kennedy, from "A Eulogy for Dr. Martin Luther King Jr."

Despite Kennedy's plea, rage over King's death led to the worst urban rioting in U.S. history. Over 100 cities exploded in flames. The hardest-hit cities included Baltimore, Chicago, Kansas City, and Washington, DC. Then, in June 1968 Robert Kennedy himself was assassinated.

King's assassination caused social turmoil and marked a turning point in the fight for civil rights. The Poor People's Campaign continued. But without King's eloquence and leadership, it failed to clearly express its goals and ended in disaster. The SCLC and its role in the movement declined.

The Movement Continues

On March 1, 1968, the **Kerner Commission**, which President Johnson had appointed to study the causes of urban violence, issued its 200,000-word report. In it, the panel named one main cause: white racism. Said the report: "This is our basic conclusion: Our nation is moving toward two societies, one black, one white—separate and unequal." The report called for the nation to create new jobs, construct new housing, and end de facto segregation in order to wipe out the destructive ghetto environment. However, the Johnson administration ignored many of the recommendations because of white opposition to such sweeping changes. So what had the civil rights movement accomplished?

CIVIL RIGHTS GAINS The civil rights movement ended de jure segregation by bringing about legal protection for the civil rights of all Americans. Congress passed the most important civil rights legislation since Reconstruction, including the **Civil Rights Act of 1968**, which ended discrimination in housing. After school segregation ended, the numbers of African Americans who finished high school and who went to college increased significantly. This in turn led to better jobs and business opportunities.

Vocabulary
polarization
separation into
opposite camps

Reading Check
Analyze Causes
Why do you think
so many African
Americans failed
to heed Robert
Kennedy's plea for
moderation after
Martin Luther King
was assassinated?

Another accomplishment of the civil rights movement was to give African Americans greater pride in their racial identity. Many African Americans adopted African-influenced styles and proudly displayed symbols of African history and culture. College students demanded new Black Studies programs so they could study African American history and literature. In the entertainment world, the "color bar" was lowered. African Americans began to appear more frequently in movies and on television shows and commercials.

In addition, African Americans made substantial political gains. By 1970 an estimated two-thirds of eligible African Americans were registered to vote. A significant increase in African American elected officials resulted.

The movement also inspired other groups to seek more rights, including women, Hispanic Americans, and Native Americans. Asian Americans led a "yellow power" movement in the 60s and 70s, focusing on ending discrimination and promoting the inclusion of ethnic studies in college curriculums.

UNFINISHED WORK The civil rights movement was successful in changing many discriminatory laws. Yet as the 1960s turned to the 1970s, the challenges for the movement changed. The issues it confronted—housing and job discrimination, educational inequality, poverty, and racism—involved the difficult task of changing people's attitudes and behavior. Some of the proposed solutions, such as more tax monies spent in the inner cities and the forced busing of schoolchildren, angered some whites, who resisted further changes. Public support for the civil rights movement declined because the urban riots and the Black Panthers frightened some whites.

American Literature

Alex Haley

In 1964 American author Alex Haley collaborated with Malcolm X to publish *Autobiography of Malcolm X*, giving Americans new access to the civil rights leader's thoughts and philosophies. In 1976 Haley published *Roots: The Saga of an American Family*. Haley said he began writing *Roots* after listening to his grandmother talk about the family's history. The novel told the story of Kunta Kinte, captured in Africa and sold into slavery in the United States, and followed the lives of Kunta's descendants through the 19th and 20th centuries. The saga earned Haley numerous accolades, including a Pulitzer Prize.

Roots: The Saga of an American Family

"The first time he had taken the massa to one of these "high-falutin' to-dos," as Bell called them, Kunta had been all but overwhelmed by conflicting emotions: awe, indignation, envy, contempt, fascination, revulsion—but most of all a deep loneliness and melancholy from which it took him almost a week to recover. He couldn't believe that such incredible wealth actually existed, that people really lived that way. It took him a long time, and a great many more parties, to realize that they *didn't* live that way, that it was all strangely unreal, a kind of beautiful dream the white folks were having, a lie they were telling themselves: that goodness can come from badness, that it's possible to be civilized with one another without treating as human beings those whose blood, sweat, and mother's milk made possible the life of privilege they led."

—Alex Haley, from *Roots: The Saga of an American Family*

Analyze American Literature
What is the "beautiful dream" to which Kunta alludes in the passage?

Shirley Chisholm (1924–2005)

African American women such as Shirley Chisholm exemplified the advances won in the civil rights movement. In 1968 Chisholm became the first African American woman in the United States House of Representatives.

In the mid-1960s Chisholm served in the New York state assembly, representing a district in New York City. While there, she supported programs to establish public daycare centers and provide unemployment insurance to domestic workers.

In 1972 Chisholm gained national prominence by running for the Democratic presidential nomination. Despite the fact that she never won more than 10 percent of the vote in the primaries, she controlled 152 delegates at the Democratic convention in Miami.

Vocabulary
quota requirement that a certain number of positions are filled by minorities

Reading Check
Synthesize
What were some accomplishments of the civil rights movement?

To help equalize education and job opportunities, the government in the 1960s began to promote **affirmative action**. Affirmative-action programs involve making special efforts to hire or enroll groups that have suffered discrimination. This was seen as one way to improve educational and economic opportunities for minorities. Many colleges and almost all companies that do business with the federal government adopted such programs. But in the late 1970s, some people began to criticize affirmative-action programs as "reverse discrimination" that set minority hiring or enrollment quotas and deprived whites of opportunities. The scope of affirmative action would continue to narrow in the 1980s in response to these concerns. The fate of affirmative action is still to be decided.

Today, African Americans and whites interact in ways that could have only been imagined before the civil rights movement. In many respects, Dr. King's dream has been realized—yet much remains to be done.

Lesson 3 Assessment

1. **Organize Information** Create a timeline of key events of the civil rights movement.

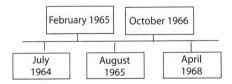

February 1965   October 1966

July 1964   August 1965   April 1968

In your opinion, which event was most significant? Why?

2. **Key Terms and People** For each key term or person in the lesson, write a sentence explaining its significance.

3. **Analyze Issues** What factors contributed to the outbreak of violence in the fight for civil rights?
   Think About:
   • different leaders' approach to civil rights issues
   • living conditions in urban areas
   • de facto and de jure segregation

4. **Compare and Contrast** Compare and contrast the beliefs and civil rights strategies of Malcolm X and Martin Luther King Jr. Whose strategies do you think were more effective? Explain and support your response.

Hispanic and Native Americans Seek Equality

The Big Idea

Hispanic Americans and Native Americans confronted injustices in the 1960s.

Why It Matters Now

Campaigns for civil rights and economic justice won better representation and opportunity for Hispanic Americans and Native Americans.

Key Terms and People

César Chávez

United Farm Workers Organizing Committee

Rodolfo "Corky" Gonzales

La Raza Unida

American Indian Movement (AIM)

One American's Story

Jessie Lopez de la Cruz's life changed one night in 1962, when **César Chávez** came to her home. Chávez, a Mexican American farm worker, was trying to organize a union for California's mostly Spanish-speaking farm workers. Chávez said, "The women have to be involved. They're the ones working out in the fields with their husbands." Soon Jessie was in the fields, talking to farm workers about the union.

> "*Wherever I went to speak I told them about . . . how we had no benefits, no minimum wage, nothing out in the fields—no restrooms, nothing. . . . I said, 'Well! Do you think we should be putting up with this in this modern age? . . . We can stand up! We can talk back! . . . This country is very rich, and we want a share of the money those growers make [off] our sweat and our work by exploiting us and our children!'*"
>
> —Jessie Lopez de la Cruz, quoted in *Moving the Mountain: Women Working for Social Change*

Carrying signs that say "Strike" *(huelga)*, Mexican American farm workers protest poor working conditions.

The efforts of Jessie Lopez de la Cruz were just part of a larger rights movement during the turbulent and revolutionary 1960s. As African Americans were fighting for civil rights, Hispanic Americans and Native Americans rose up to assert their own rights and improve their lives.

SS.912.A.1.2; SS.912.A.1.3; SS.912.A.1.6; SS.912.A.2.7; SS.912.A.7.5; SS.912.A.7.9; SS.912.A.7.16; LAFS.1112.RH.1.2; LAFS.1112.RH.4.10

The Hispanic American Presence Grows

Hispanic Americans, or Americans of Latin American or Spanish descent, are a large and diverse group. During the 1960s the Hispanic American population in the United States grew from 3 million to more than 9 million. Today, the Hispanic American population includes people from several different areas, primarily Mexico, Puerto Rico, Cuba, the Dominican Republic, Central America, and South America. Each of these groups has its own history, its own pattern of settlement in the United States, and its own set of economic, social, cultural, and political concerns.

Mexican Americans, the largest Hispanic American group, have lived mostly in the Southwest and California. This group includes descendants of the nearly 100,000 Mexicans who had lived in territories Mexico ceded to the United States in 1848. Another million or so Mexicans came to the United States in the 1910s, following Mexico's revolution. Still others came as braceros, or temporary laborers, during the 1940s and 1950s. In the 1960s close to half a million Mexicans immigrated, most in search of better-paying jobs.

Puerto Ricans began immigrating to the United States after the U.S. occupation of Puerto Rico in 1898. As of 1960 almost 900,000 Puerto Ricans were living in the continental United States, many on New York City's West Side.

Large Cuban communities also formed in New York City , Miami, and New Jersey. This is because hundreds of thousands of Cubans, many of whom were academics and professionals, fled to the United States in 1959 to escape Fidel Castro's Communist rule. In addition, tens of thousands of Salvadorans, Guatemalans, Nicaraguans, and Colombians immigrated to the United States after the 1960s to escape civil war and chronic poverty.

Wherever they had settled, during the 1960s many Hispanic Americans encountered ethnic prejudice and discrimination in jobs and housing. Most lived in segregated *barrios,* or Spanish-speaking neighborhoods. The Hispanic American jobless rate was nearly 50 percent higher than that of whites. So too, was the percentage of Hispanic American families living in poverty.

Reading Check
Identify Problems
What problems did different groups of Hispanic American immigrants share?

Hispanic Americans Fight for Change

As the presence of Hispanic Americans in the United States grew, so too did their demand for greater representation and better treatment. During the 1960s Hispanic Americans demanded not only equal opportunity but also a respect for their culture and heritage.

THE FARM WORKER MOVEMENT As Jessie Lopez de la Cruz explained, thousands of people working on California's fruit and vegetable farms did backbreaking work for little pay and few benefits. César Chávez believed that farm workers had to unionize. Their strength would come from bargaining as a group.

César Chávez (1927–1993)

César Chávez spoke from experience when he said, "Many things in farm labor are terrible."

As a teenager, Chávez moved with his family from farm to farm, picking such crops as grapes, apricots, and olives. "The worst crop was the olives," Chávez recalled. "The olives are so small you can never fill the bucket."

The seeds of protest grew early in Chávez. As a teenager, he once went to see a movie, only to find that the theater was segregated. Whites sat on one side of the aisle. Mexicans sat on the other side. "I really hadn't thought much about what

I was going to do, but I had to do something," Chávez recalled. The future union leader sat down in the whites-only section. He stayed there until the police arrived and arrested him.

In 1962 Chávez and Dolores Huerta established the National Farm Workers Association. Four years later, this group merged with a Filipino agricultural union (also founded by Huerta) to form the **United Farm Workers Organizing Committee** (UFWOC). Chávez and his fellow organizers insisted that California's large fruit and vegetable companies accept their union as the bargaining agent for the farm workers.

In 1965, when California's grape growers refused to recognize the union, Chávez launched a nationwide boycott of the companies' grapes. Chávez, like Martin Luther King Jr., believed in using nonviolence to reach his goal. The union sent farm workers across the country to convince supermarkets and shoppers not to buy California grapes. Chávez then went on a three-week fast in which he lost 35 pounds. He ended his fast by attending Mass with Senator Robert F. Kennedy.

The boycott ultimately proved successful. As Chávez later declared, "To us, the boycott of grapes was the most near-perfect of nonviolent struggles." By 1969 the boycott had even spread beyond the United States to Great Britain. As people in other European nations also considered joining the boycott, the grape growers faced so much economic pressure that they gave in. In 1970 Huerta negotiated a contract between the grape growers and the UFWOC. Union workers would finally be guaranteed higher wages and other benefits long denied them.

CULTURAL PRIDE The activities of the California farm workers helped to inspire other Hispanic American "brown power" movements across the country. In New York, Puerto Ricans began to demand that schools offer Spanish-speaking children classes taught in their own language as well as programs about their culture. In 1968 Congress enacted the Bilingual Education Act, which provided funds for schools to develop bilingual and cultural heritage programs for non-English-speaking children.

Some young Mexican Americans began to embrace a form of cultural nationalism similar to the Black Power movement. They called themselves Chicanos or Chicanas—a shortened version of *Mexicanos*. The name conveyed their ethnic pride and commitment to political activism. In earlier generations, the term *Chicano* had carried a negative connotation. Now Chicanos adopted the name proudly.

One leading figure in the Chicano movement was **Rodolfo "Corky" Gonzales**. In 1966 he founded the Crusade for Justice, a group that promoted Mexican American nationalism. Operating out of an old church, the group provided legal aid, a theater for increasing cultural awareness, a Spanish-language newspaper, and other community services. It also ran a school that offered children free bilingual classes and lessons in Chicano culture. The ultimate goal of the Crusade for Justice was to build a unified Chicano community that was empowered to determine its own future.

In the late 1960s the Brown Berets emerged as one of the most militant organizations in the Chicano movement. Founded by working-class Chicano students in 1967 under the leadership of David Sanchez, the Brown Berets began their activism by protesting police brutality in East Los Angeles. Soon the group began to focus on education. They fought for bilingual education, better school conditions, Chicano studies, and more Chicano teachers. In 1968 the Brown Berets organized walkouts in East Los Angeles high schools. About 15,000 Chicano students walked out of class. Their demands included smaller classes, more Chicano teachers and administrators, and programs to reduce the high Hispanic American dropout rate. Militant Mexican American students also won the establishment of Chicano studies programs at colleges and universities.

Document-Based Investigation Historical Source

Labor Unions

César Chávez firmly believed that unionization was the best way to improve working conditions and wages.

Analyze Historical Sources
What role does Chávez hope that the government will play in labor relations?

"The need is for amendments that will make strong, effective labor unions realistically possible in agriculture. I say 'realistically possible' because laws cannot deliver a good union any more than laws can bring an end to poverty. Only people can do that through hard work, sacrifice and dedicated effort. . . . Our cause, our strike and our international boycott are all founded upon the deep conviction that the form of collective self-help which is unionization holds far more hope for the farm worker than any other single approach, . . . The best insurance against strikes and boycotts lies not in repressive legislation, but in strong unions that will satisfy the farmworker's hunger for decency and dignity and self-respect. Unionization cannot make progress in the face of hostile employer attitudes unless it receives effective governmental support."

—César Chávez, from a speech before the Senate Subcommittee on Labor, April 16, 1969

Background
Before 1960, 32
Hispanics had been
elected to Congress,
beginning with
Joseph Hernandez
in 1822.

La Raza Unida button

Reading Check
Compare and
Contrast How
was the Chicano
movement similar
to the Black Power
movement?

Vocabulary
homogeneous
uniform or similar
throughout

POLITICAL POWER Hispanic Americans also began organizing politically during the 1960s. Some worked within the two-party system. For example, the Mexican American Political Association (MAPA) helped elect Los Angeles politician Edward Roybal to the House of Representatives. During the 1960s, eight Hispanic Americans served in the House, and one Hispanic senator was elected—Joseph Montoya of New Mexico.

Others, like Texan José Angel Gutiérrez, sought to create an independent Hispanic American political movement. In 1970 he established **La Raza Unida** (The People United, also known as RUP). The party campaigned for bilingual education, improved public services, education for children of migrant workers, and an end to job discrimination. In 1970 RUP candidates were elected to offices in several Texas cities with large Chicano populations. The party moved to the state level in 1972, backing Ramsey Muñiz for governor and supporting many Chicano candidates for other offices. Although Muñiz did not win his race, La Raza Unida successfully changed the landscape of Texas politics.

The RUP expanded into Colorado and other parts of the Southwest. In New Mexico, Arizona, and California, it registered some 10,000 new voters. The party ran Hispanic American candidates in five states and won races for mayor, as well as other local positions on school boards and city councils. In the late 1970s, disagreements among the RUP leaders caused the party to fall apart. However, for almost a decade, it symbolized growing Chicano power.

While the RUP sought change by running for political office, other Hispanic Americans were more confrontational. In 1963, one-time evangelical preacher Reies Tijerina founded the Alianza Federal de Mercedes (Federal Alliance of Land Grants). Tijerina wanted to reclaim land taken from Mexican landholders in the 1800s. He and his followers raided the Rio Arriba County Courthouse in Tierra Amarilla, New Mexico, to force authorities to recognize the plight of New Mexican small farmers. They were later arrested.

Native Americans Struggle for Equality

Native Americans are sometimes viewed as one homogeneous group, despite the hundreds of distinct Native American tribes and nations in the United States. One thing these diverse peoples have shared is a mostly bleak existence and a lack of autonomy, or ability to control and govern their own lives. Through the years, many Native Americans have clung to their heritage, refusing to assimilate, or blend, into mainstream society. Native American nationalist Vine Deloria Jr. expressed the view that mainstream society was nothing more than "ice cream bars and heart trouble and . . . getting up at six o'clock in the morning to mow your lawn in the suburbs."

NATIVE AMERICANS SEEK GREATER AUTONOMY Despite their cultural diversity, Native Americans as a group have been the poorest of Americans and have suffered from the highest unemployment rate. They have also been more likely than any other group to suffer from tuberculosis and alcoholism.

Although the Native American population rose during the 1960s, the death rate among Native American infants was nearly twice the national average. Life expectancy was several years less than for other Americans.

In 1954 the Eisenhower administration enacted a "termination" policy to deal with these problems. But it did not respect Native American culture. Native Americans were relocated from isolated reservations into mainstream urban American life. The plan failed miserably. Most who moved to the cities remained desperately poor.

In 1961 representatives from 61 Native American groups met in Chicago and drafted the Declaration of Indian Purpose. The declaration stressed the determination of Native Americans to "choose our own way of life." It also called for an end to the termination program in favor of new policies designed to create economic opportunities for Native Americans on their reservations. In 1968 President Lyndon Johnson established the National Council on Indian Opportunity to "ensure that programs reflect the needs and desires of the Indian people."

AIM leader Dennis Banks speaks at the foot of Mount Rushmore in South Dakota during a 1970s rally.

VOICES OF PROTEST Many young Native Americans were dissatisfied with the slow pace of reform. Their discontent fueled the growth of the **American Indian Movement (AIM)**, an often militant Native American rights organization. AIM began in 1968 largely as a self-defense group against police brutality. It soon branched out to include protecting the rights of large Native American populations in northern and western states.

For some, this new activism meant demanding that Native American lands, burial grounds, and fishing and timber rights be restored. Others wanted a new respect for their culture. Mary Crow Dog, a Lakota Sioux, described AIM's impact.

"My first encounter with AIM was at a pow-wow held in 1971. . . . One man, a Chippewa, stood up and made a speech. I had never heard anybody talk like that. He spoke about genocide and sovereignty, about tribal leaders selling out. . . . He had himself wrapped up in an upside-down American flag, telling us that every star in this flag represented a state stolen from the Indians. . . . Some people wept. An old man turned to me and said, 'These are the words I always wanted to speak, but had kept shut up within me.'"
—Mary Crow Dog, quoted in *Lakota Women*

CONFRONTING THE GOVERNMENT In its early years, AIM, as well as other groups, actively—and sometimes violently—confronted the government. In 1972 AIM leader Russell Means organized the "Trail of Broken Treaties" march in Washington, DC, to protest the U.S. government's treaty violations throughout history. Native Americans from across the country joined the march. They sought the restoration of 110 million acres of land. They also pushed for the abolition of the Bureau of Indian Affairs (BIA), which many believed was corrupt. The marchers temporarily occupied the BIA building, destroyed records, and caused $2 million in property damage.

Ben Nighthorse Campbell
(1933–)

Whereas many Native Americans rejected assimilation, Ben Nighthorse Campbell chose to work within the system to improve the lives of Native Americans. Campbell's father was a North Cheyenne, and his great-grandfather, Black Horse, fought in the 1876 Battle of the Little Bighorn— in which the Cheyenne and the Sioux defeated Lieutenant Colonel George Custer.

In 1992 Campbell was elected to the U.S. Senate from Colorado. Not since 1929 had a Native American been elected to the Senate. Campbell stated that while he served the entire nation, the

needs of Native Americans would always remain a priority. He retired from the Senate in 2004.

A year later, AIM led nearly 200 Sioux to the tiny village of Wounded Knee, South Dakota, where the U.S. cavalry had massacred a Sioux village in 1890. In protest against both tribal leadership and federal policies, the Sioux seized the town, taking hostages. After tense negotiations with the FBI and a shootout that left two Native Americans dead and others wounded, the confrontation ended with a government promise to reexamine Native American treaty rights.

NATIVE AMERICAN VICTORIES In 1924 the Snyder Act had granted full U.S. citizenship to Native Americans born in the United States. However, despite the right of U.S. citizens to vote guaranteed by the Fifteenth Amendment, many states restricted Native American voting rights. It took lawsuits from Native Americans eager to exercise their rights to change the situation.

In 1947 Frank Harrison, a Native American from Maricopa County in Arizona, challenged these restrictions. In the end, the Arizona supreme court ruled unanimously in Harrison's favor, striking down a provision in the state constitution. Soon after, the other states followed Arizona's lead.

In 1962 the last challenge to Native American voting rights was brought in New Mexico when a non-Native American candidate lost an election. He challenged the result, claiming that Native Americans should not have been allowed to vote. However, the state supreme court, which reaffirmed that all Native Americans were U.S. citizens, quickly struck down this challenge. In 1965 the Voting Rights Act, which further strengthened protections for Native Americans and other minorities, finally settled the issue of Native American voting rights.

Congress and the federal courts made additional reforms on behalf of Native Americans in the 1970s. In 1972 Congress passed the Indian Education Act. In 1975 it passed the Indian Self-Determination and Education Assistance Act. These laws gave tribes greater control over their own affairs and over their children's education.

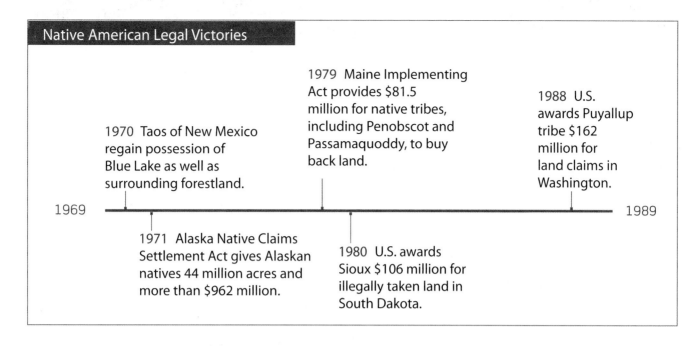

Native American Legal Victories

1969

1970 Taos of New Mexico regain possession of Blue Lake as well as surrounding forestland.

1971 Alaska Native Claims Settlement Act gives Alaskan natives 44 million acres and more than $962 million.

1979 Maine Implementing Act provides $81.5 million for native tribes, including Penobscot and Passamaquoddy, to buy back land.

1980 U.S. awards Sioux $106 million for illegally taken land in South Dakota.

1988 U.S. awards Puyallup tribe $162 million for land claims in Washington.

1989

Armed with copies of old land treaties that the U.S. government had broken, Native Americans went to federal court and regained some of their land. In 1970 the Taos of New Mexico regained possession of their sacred Blue Lake, as well as a portion of its surrounding forestland. Land claims by natives of Alaska resulted in the Alaska Native Claims Settlement Act of 1971. This act gave more than 40 million acres to native peoples and paid out more than $962 million in cash. Throughout the 1970s and 1980s, Native Americans won settlements that provided legal recognition of their tribal lands as well as financial compensation.

While the 1960s and the early 1970s saw a wave of activism from the nation's minority groups, another group of Americans also pushed for changes. Women, while not a minority group, were in many ways treated like second-class citizens, and many joined together to demand equal treatment in society.

Reading Check
Summarize What tactics did AIM use in its attempts to gain reforms?

Lesson 4 Assessment

1. **Organize Information** Create a Venn diagram to show the broad similarities between the issues faced by Hispanic Americans and Native Americans during the 1960s, as well as the unique concerns of the two groups.

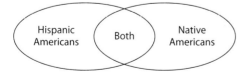

Which group do you think had more to gain by fighting for what they wanted?

2. **Key Terms and People** For each key term or person in the lesson, write a sentence explaining its significance.

3. **Evaluate** How would you judge whether an activist organization was effective? List criteria you would use, and justify your criteria.

   Think About:
   • UFWOC, MAPA, and La Raza Unida
   • AIM
   • the leaders and activities of these organizations

4. **Analyze Effects** In what ways did the Hispanic American campaign for economic and social equality affect non-Hispanic Americans?

5. **Analyze Primary Sources** Vine Deloria Jr. said,

   "When you get far enough away from the reservation, you can see it's the urban man who has no identity."

   What do you think he meant by this?

Reynolds v. Sims (1964)

ORIGINS OF THE CASE

In 1901 seats in the Alabama state legislature were apportioned, or assigned to districts, based on population. By the early 1960s each Alabama county still had the same number of representatives as it did in 1901, even though the populations of the counties had changed. A group of voters sued to make representation proportional to the changed populations. When the suit succeeded, state legislators who were threatened with losing their seats appealed to the Supreme Court.

THE RULING

The Supreme Court upheld the principle of "one person, one vote" and ruled that the equal protection clause required representation in state legislatures to be based on population.

LEGAL REASONING

Prior to *Reynolds,* the Court had already applied the "one person, one vote" principle to federal congressional elections (see Legal Sources). In *Reynolds,* Chief Justice Earl Warren extended this principle to state legislatures. He argued that when representation does not reflect population, some people's votes are worth more than others'.

"The fundamental principle of representative government in this country is one of equal representation for equal numbers of people, without regard to . . . place of residence within a State. Legislators represent people, not trees or acres. Legislators are elected by voters, not farms or cities or economic interests."

Warren concluded that Alabama's apportionment scheme discriminated against people because of where they live.

For these reasons, the Court ruled that any acceptable apportionment plan must provide an equal number of legislative seats for equally populated areas. A plan that does not is unconstitutional because it denies some voters the equal protection of the laws.

LEGAL SOURCES

U.S. CONSTITUTION

U.S. Constitution, Fourteenth Amendment (1868)

"No state shall . . . deprive any person of life, liberty, or property, without due process of law; nor deny to any person within its jurisdiction the equal protection of the laws."

RELATED CASES

Baker v. Carr (1962)

The Court decided that federal courts could settle issues of apportionment. Previously, federal courts had refused to address such issues on the grounds that they were political issues.

Gray v. Sanders (1963)

The Court ruled that states must follow the principle of "one person, one vote" in primary elections.

Wesberry v. Sanders (1964)

The Court applied the "one person, one vote" rule to congressional districts.

Chief Justice Warren *(front, center)* and members of the 1964 Supreme Court

WHY IT MATTERED

The voters who initiated the suit against Alabama's apportionment were part of America's tremendous urban growth in the 20th century. During and after World War II, tens of thousands of Americans—including large numbers of African Americans—moved from rural areas to cities and suburbs. Voters in Alabama's more urban areas found that they were underrepresented. Likewise, before *Reynolds*, urban residents as a whole paid far more in taxes than they received in benefits. A great deal was at stake.

The "one person, one vote" principle increased the influence of urban residents by forcing legislatures to create new election districts in the cities to reflect their large populations. As more legislators representing urban and suburban needs were elected, they were able to change funding formulas, funneling more money into their districts. In addition, minorities, immigrants, and professionals, who tend to make up a large proportion of urban populations, gained better representation.

On the other hand, the power of farmers was eroded as election districts in rural areas were combined and incumbents had to campaign against each other for a single seat.

HISTORICAL IMPACT

The Warren Court's reapportionment decisions in *Baker* v. *Carr, Gray* v. *Sanders, Wesberry* v. *Sanders,* and *Reynolds* were a revolution in U.S. politics. The lawsuit that culminated in the *Reynolds* decision was also part of a broader movement in the 1960s to protect voting rights. Largely because of the Voting Rights Act of 1965, voter registration among African Americans in Mississippi, for instance, climbed from 6.7 percent to 59.8 percent. Viewed together, the combination of increased protection of voting rights and acceptance of the "one person, one vote" principle brought the United States several steps closer to fulfilling its democratic ideals.

In the 1990s the Court revisited reapportionment. A 1982 act of Congress had required states to create districts with "minority majorities" in order to increase the number of nonwhite representatives. As a result, following the 1990 census, a record number of African Americans were elected to Congress. But opponents contended that defining districts by race violated equal protection and "one person, one vote." In a series of decisions, the Court agreed and abolished minority districting.

These two apportionment maps show Alabama's 35 state senatorial districts in 1901 *(left)* and 1973 *(right)*. The 1973 map shows how the districts were redrawn after the *Reynolds* decision, based on the 1970 census. Notice how the 1973 map reflects the growth of Alabama cities.

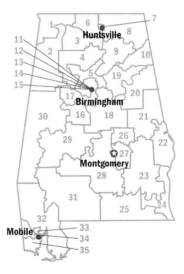

Critical Thinking

1. **Connect to History** Use Internet resources to research minority redistricting decisions such as *Shaw* v. *Hunt* (1996). Write a summary of the rulings and how they have affected elections.

2. **Connect to Today** Obtain a map of the state legislative districts in your state. Then compare the map created following the 2010 census with the map based on the 1990 census. Study the differences in the size and location of the districts. Write a paragraph explaining which regions of the state gained representatives and which lost representatives.

Women Fight for Equality

SS.912.A.1.4; SS.912.A.1.7; SS.912.A.7.3; SS.912.A.7.5; SS.912.A.7.8; SS.912.A.7.9

The Big Idea

Through protests and marches, women confronted social and economic barriers in American society.

Why It Matters Now

The rise of the women's movement during the 1960s advanced women's place in the work force and in society.

Key Terms and People

Betty Friedan

feminism

National Organization for Women (NOW)

Gloria Steinem

Equal Rights Amendment (ERA)

Phyllis Schlafly

One American's Story

During the 1950s writer **Betty Friedan** seemed to be living the American dream. She had a loving husband, healthy children, and a house in the suburbs. According to the experts—doctors, psychologists, and women's magazines—that was all a woman needed to be fulfilled. Why, then, wasn't she happy? In 1957, after conducting a survey of her Smith College classmates 15 years after graduation, she found she was not alone. Friedan eventually wrote a book, *The Feminine Mystique,* in which she addressed this "problem that has no name."

Betty Friedan, November 1967

"The problem lay buried, unspoken. . . . It was a strange stirring, a sense of dissatisfaction, a yearning that women suffered in the middle of the twentieth century in the United States. Each suburban wife struggled with it alone. As she made the beds, shopped for groceries, matched slipcover material, ate peanut butter sandwiches with her children, chauffeured Cub Scouts and Brownies, lay beside her husband at night—she was afraid to ask even of herself the silent question—'Is this all?'"

—Betty Friedan, from *The Feminine Mystique*

During the 1960s women answered Friedan's question with a resounding "no." In increasing numbers, they joined the nation's African Americans, Hispanic Americans, Native Americans, and Asian Americans in the fight for greater civil rights and equality in society.

A New Women's Movement Arises

The theory behind the women's movement of the 1960s was **feminism**, the belief that women should have economic, political, and social equality with men. Feminist beliefs had gained momentum during the mid-1800s and in 1920 won women the right to vote. While the women's movement declined after this achievement, it reawakened during the 1960s, spurred by the political activism of the times.

This photograph, taken in 1966, shows the typical office roles at the time—women working as data processors, supervised by male managers.

WOMEN IN THE WORKPLACE In 1950 only one out of three women worked for wages. By 1960 that number had increased to about 40 percent. A scientific development in 1960 helped even more women enter the workplace—the birth control pill was approved for contraceptive use. This gave women new choices. Women who wanted to avoid pregnancy or postpone having children in order to start a career now had that freedom. By 1963 nearly one-third of American workers were women.

Still, during this time, certain jobs were considered "men's work" and women were shut out. The jobs available to women— mostly clerical work, domestic service, retail sales, social work, teaching, and nursing—paid poorly.

The country largely ignored this discrimination until President Kennedy appointed the Presidential Commission on the Status of Women in 1961. In 1963 the commission reported that women were paid far less than men, even when doing the same jobs. Furthermore, women were seldom promoted to management positions, regardless of their education, experience, and ability. The Equal Pay Act was signed into law in 1963 as part of Kennedy's New Frontier program, requiring employers to pay men and women equal salaries for the same work. Still, these newly publicized facts awakened many women to their unequal status in society.

WOMEN AND ACTIVISM Ironically, many women felt the sting of discrimination when they became involved in the civil rights and antiwar movements—movements that toted the ideological banner of protecting people's rights. This was not the first time this situation occurred. Women such as Elizabeth Cady Stanton and Susan B. Anthony had been active in the abolitionist movement. When they tried to assert women's rights, they were rejected by the male leaders of the abolitionist movement.

Within some organizations, such as SNCC and SDS, men led most of the activities, while women were assigned lesser roles. When women protested this arrangement, the men usually brushed them aside. They were told that there were more important issues to discuss than "women's liberation."

Such experiences led some women to organize small groups to discuss their concerns. During these discussions, or "consciousness-raising" sessions, women shared their lives with each other and discovered that their experiences were not unique. Rather, they reflected a much larger pattern of sexism, or discrimination based on gender. Author Robin Morgan delineated this pattern.

"It makes you very sensitive—raw, even, this consciousness. Everything, from the verbal assault on the street, to a 'well-meant' sexist joke your husband tells, to the lower pay you get at work (for doing the same job a man would be paid more for), to television commercials, to rock-song lyrics, to the pink or blue blanket they put on your infant in the hospital nursery, to speeches by male 'revolutionaries' that reek of male supremacy—everything seems to barrage your aching brain. . . . You begin to see how all-pervasive a thing is sexism."

—Robin Morgan, quoted in *Sisterhood Is Powerful: An Anthology of Writings from the Women's Liberation Movement*

Reading Check
Analyze Effects
What effects did the civil rights and the antiwar movements have on many women?

THE WOMEN'S MOVEMENT EMERGES *The Feminine Mystique*, which captured the very discontent that many women were feeling, quickly became a best seller. Housewives who were part of the major population shift from cities to the suburbs in the 1950s were asking themselves the same questions as Friedan. Her book helped to galvanize women across the country. By the late 1960s women were working together for change. "This is not a movement one 'joins,'" observed Robin Morgan. "The Women's Liberation Movement exists where three or four friends or neighbors decide to meet regularly . . . on the welfare lines, in the supermarket, the factory, the convent, the farm, the maternity ward."

The Movement Experiences Gains and Losses

As the women's movement grew, it achieved remarkable and enduring political and social gains for women. Along the way, however, it also suffered setbacks, most notably in its attempt to ensure women's equality in the Constitution.

THE CREATION OF NOW The women's movement gained strength with the passage of the Civil Rights Act of 1964, which prohibited discrimination based on race, religion, national origin, and gender. Title VII of the act, which focused on employment discrimination, created the Equal Employment Opportunity Commission (EEOC) to handle discrimination claims. By 1966, however, some women argued that the EEOC didn't adequately address women's grievances. That year, 28 women, including Betty Friedan, created the **National Organization for Women (NOW)** to pursue women's goals. "The time has come," the founders of NOW declared, "to confront with concrete action the conditions which now prevent women from enjoying the equality of opportunity . . . which is their right as individual Americans and as human beings."

NOW members pushed for the creation of childcare facilities that would enable mothers to pursue jobs and education. NOW also pressured the EEOC to enforce more vigorously the ban on gender discrimination in hiring. The

Gloria Steinem (1934–)

Gloria Steinem became one of the more prominent figures of the women's movement after she and several other women founded *Ms.* magazine in 1972. The magazine soon became a major voice of the women's movement. Steinem said that she decided to start the feminist magazine after editors in the mainstream media continually rejected her stories about the women's movement:

"Editors who had assumed I had some valuable biological insight into food, male movie stars, and textured stockings now questioned whether I or other women writers were biologically capable of writing objectively about feminism. That was the beginning."

organization's efforts prompted the EEOC to declare sex-segregated job ads illegal and to issue guidelines to employers, stating that they could no longer refuse to hire women for traditionally male jobs.

A DIVERSE MOVEMENT In its first three years, NOW's ranks swelled to 175,000 members. A number of other women's groups sprang up around the country, too. In 1968 a militant group known as the New York Radical Women staged a well-publicized demonstration at the annual Miss America Pageant. The women threw bras, girdles, wigs, and other "women's garbage" into a "Freedom Trash Can." They then crowned a sheep "Miss America." Around this time, **Gloria Steinem**, a journalist, political activist, and ardent supporter of the women's liberation movement, made her voice heard on the subjects of feminism and equality. Steinem's grandmother had served as president of the Ohio Woman Suffrage Association from 1908 to 1911; Steinem had inherited her passion and conviction. In 1971 Steinem helped found the National Women's Political Caucus, a moderate group that encouraged women to seek political office.

LEGAL AND SOCIAL GAINS As the women's movement progressed, women began to question all sorts of gender-based distinctions. People protested that a woman's physical appearance was often considered a job qualification. Girls' exclusion from sports such as baseball and football came into question. Some women began using the title Ms., instead of the standard Miss or Mrs., and refused to adopt their husband's last name upon marriage.

Numerous legal changes paralleled these changes in attitude. In 1972 Congress expanded the powers of the EEOC and gave working parents a tax break for childcare expenses. That same year, Congress passed Title IX, a ban on gender discrimination in "any education program or activity receiving federal financial assistance," as part of the Higher Education Act.

Ms. Magazine

In 1972 Gloria Steinem and other women created a new women's magazine, *Ms.*, designed to treat contemporary issues from a feminist perspective. On the cover of this 1972 issue of *Ms.*, the woman shown has eight arms and is holding a different object in each hand.

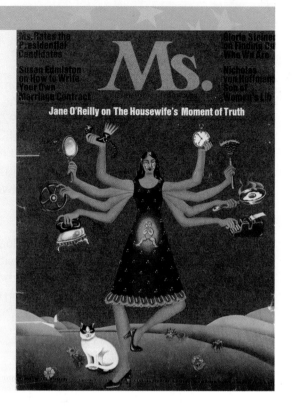

Analyze Historical Sources

1. What do you think these objects symbolize in terms of women's roles?

2. What do you think this drawing says about women in the 1960s? Explain.

Title IX had a tremendous effect on women's access to higher education. All-male colleges opened their doors to women, and more and more female students began to enroll in colleges and universities in the years to follow. By 1979 women outnumbered men on college campuses. Today, women make up about 57 percent of the total college population.

Athletics, especially at the collegiate level, also felt the impact of Title IX. Prior to the 1970s, funding for women's athletics was almost nonexistent. Female athletes didn't begin receiving athletic scholarships until 1973. As a result of Title IX, female participation in intercollegiate sports increased. In 1972 approximately 21 percent of all college athletes were female, and that percentage climbed to almost 43 percent by 2012. This also affected interest in participation in high school athletics, and female participation in high school sports rose from 294,000 in 1971 to nearly 3 million in 2006.

Gains in equality were also made in the U.S. military. Although Truman signed the Women's Armed Forces Integration Act in 1948, allowing women to serve as full members of the armed services, women were not allowed to serve in certain roles or to serve in the same units as men. These restrictions began to change in the 1970s. Pilot training in the army and the navy opened to women in 1972, and the Air Force began training female pilots in 1976. West Point military academy accepted its first group of female cadets in 1976. In 1977 women in the army began training in the same basic training units as men, and in 1979 the military's enlistment qualifications changed to be the same for men and women. However, women were barred from combat units until 2013.

ROE* v. *WADE One of the more controversial positions that NOW and other feminist groups supported was a woman's right to have an abortion. In 1973 the Supreme Court ruled in *Roe* v. *Wade* that women do have the right to choose an abortion during the first three months of pregnancy. Some thought the ruling might "bring to an end the emotional and divi-
- sive public argument. . . ." However, the decision sparked a debate that continues to this day.

Supporters argued that women could not achieve equality until they could control when or whether to have children. Supporters also believed that legal abortion was necessary to protect a woman's health. They argued that many women would otherwise resort to inept, "back-alley" practitioners who often botched the procedure, endangering the life of the patient.

Many people opposed the decision because of religious or moral beliefs that all life, including that of a fetus, was sacred and should be protected. Other opponents of the ruling argued that the Court's assumption of a right to privacy strayed too far from the original intent of the Fourteenth Amendment of the Constitution.

THE EQUAL RIGHTS AMENDMENT (ERA) In what seemed at first to be another triumph for the women's movement, Congress passed the **Equal Rights Amendment (ERA)** in 1972. The amendment then needed ratification by 38 states to become part of the Constitution. First introduced to Congress in 1923, the ERA would guarantee that both men and women would enjoy the same rights and protections under the law. It was, many supporters said, a matter of "simple justice."

The amendment scared many people, and a Stop-ERA campaign was launched in 1972. Conservative **Phyllis Schlafly**, along with conservative religious groups, political organizations, and many antifeminists, felt that the ERA would lead to "a parade of horribles," such as the drafting of

Phyllis Schlafly in 1977

women, the end of laws protecting homemakers, the end of a husband's responsibility to provide for his family, and same-sex marriages. Schlafly said that radical feminists "hate men, marriage, and children" and were oppressed "only in their distorted minds." However, supporters of the ERA argued that women's rights were compromised without the protection of the amendment.

"The U.S. Constitution is not the place for symbols or slogans, it is not the proper device to alleviate psychological problems of personal inferiority. Symbols and slogans belong on bumper strips—not in the Constitution. It would be a tragic mistake for our nation to succumb to the tirades and demands of a few women who are seeking a constitutional cure for their personal problems."

—Phyllis Schlafly, quoted in *The Equal Rights Amendment: The History and the Movement*

THE NEW RIGHT EMERGES In order to combat the ERA and the pro-abortion supporters, conservatives built what they called a new "pro-family" movement. In the 1970s this coalition—which focused on social, cultural, and moral problems—came to be known as the New Right. The New Right and the women's movement debated family-centered issues such as whether the government should pay for daycare, which the New Right opposed. Throughout the 1970s the New Right built grassroots support for social conservatism. It would later play a key role in the election of Ronald Reagan to the presidency in 1980.

The New Right and the women's movement clashed most dramatically over the ERA. By 1977 it had won approval from 35 of the 38 states needed for ratification, but the New Right gained strength. By June 1982—the deadline for ratification—not enough states had approved the amendment. The ERA went down in defeat.

Reading Check
Form
Generalizations
What gains did the women's movement make by the early 1970s?

Lesson 5 Assessment

1. **Organize Information** Create a timeline of key events relating to the women's movement.

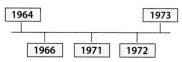

Explain which event you think best demonstrates progressive reform.

2. **Key Terms and People** For each key term or person in the lesson, write a sentence explaining its significance.

3. **Draw Conclusions** What if the Equal Rights Amendment had been ratified? Speculate on how women's lives might have been different. Use reasons to support your answer.

   Think About:
   - rights addressed by the amendment
   - legal support that the amendment might have provided
   - possible reactions from groups opposing the amendment

4. **Analyze Effects** What were the successes and failures of the women's movement in the 1960s and 1970s?

The Struggle Continues

The Big Idea

In the decades that followed the civil rights and equal rights movements, groups and individuals continued to pursue equal rights for all Americans.

Why It Matters Now

Issues involving equal rights and equal opportunities continue to challenge American society.

Key Terms and People

Barack Obama

L. Douglas Wilder

Colin Powell

Condoleezza Rice

Sonia Sotomayor

Madeleine Albright

pay equity

Stonewall riots

Americans with Disabilities Act

One American's Story

In 2008 President **Barack Obama** was elected the 44th president of the United States of America, becoming the first African American to hold the office. In 2013, during his second term in office, the country celebrated the 50th anniversary of the March on Washington. From the steps of the Lincoln Memorial, Obama praised the courage of those who fought for equal rights. He pointed to the progress made and victories won. But he also acknowledged that the work started by civil rights pioneers should not be considered complete.

"The arc of the moral universe may bend towards justice, but it doesn't bend on its own. To secure the gains this country has made requires constant vigilance, not complacency. Whether by challenging those who erect new barriers to the vote, or ensuring that the scales of justice work equally for all, and the criminal justice system is not simply a pipeline from underfunded schools to overcrowded jails, it requires vigilance. And we'll suffer the occasional setback. But we will win these fights."

—Barack Obama, from a speech commemorating the March on Washington, August 28, 2013

At the Let Freedom Ring ceremony, President Obama marks the 50th anniversary of the March on Washington.

As the United States entered the 21st century, many groups of Americans were working toward recognition and protection of their civil rights. For some, the struggle had begun decades before. For others, the process had only recently begun.

SS.912.A.1.2; SS.912.A.1.4; SS.912.A.2.7; SS.912.A.7.3; SS.912.A.7.5; SS.912.A.7.6; SS.912.A.7.7; SS.912.A.7.8; SS.912.A.7.16; LAFS.1112.RH.4.10; MAFS.K12.MP.1.1; MAFS.K12.MP.5.1; MAFS.K12.MP.6.1

The Fight for Rights Continues

During the height of the civil rights movements of the 1960s and 1970s, African Americans, Hispanic Americans, Native Americans, and others had made tremendous strides. All had moved toward gaining full equality under the law. However, they had not yet fully achieved their goals. In the decades that followed, members of these and other groups continued their crusade, often in the face of lingering opposition.

AFRICAN AMERICANS African Americans made striking political gains during the 1980s. By the mid-1980s African American mayors governed many cities, including Los Angeles, Detroit, Chicago, Atlanta, New Orleans, Philadelphia, and Washington, DC. Hundreds of communities in both the North and the South had elected African Americans to serve as sheriffs, school board members, state legislators, and members of Congress. The Reverend Jesse Jackson ran for the Democratic presidential nomination in 1984 and 1988, winning a few state primaries. In 1990 **L. Douglas Wilder** of Virginia became the nation's first African American governor since Reconstruction. He was the first African American in U.S. history to be elected—not appointed—to the position. The number of African Americans holding elected office grew from fewer than 100 in 1965 to more than 7,000 in 1992. Since the early 1990s, several African Americans have held key positions in the federal government. Both **Colin Powell** and **Condoleezza Rice** served as secretary of state under President George W. Bush. In 2008 Barack Obama made history as the first African American to be elected president. In doing so, he inspired countless Americans of all ethnicities and backgrounds to believe that they could achieve their dreams.

Jesse Jackson campaigns for the Democratic presidential nomination in 1984.

Despite these great political gains, African Americans on the whole have not fared as well economically since the 1980s. While middle-class African Americans often held professional and managerial positions, the poor faced an uncertain future of diminishing opportunities. In 1989 the newly conservative Supreme Court handed down a series of decisions that continued to change the nation's course on economic equality. In the case of *Richmond* v. *J. A. Croson Company,* for example, the Court further limited the scope of affirmative action, policies that had been designed to correct the effects of discrimination against minority groups or women. The Court found that claims of past discrimination were not enough to justify the racial quotas that the city of Richmond, Virginia, had put into effect for granting city contracts and other business. Other Court decisions outlawed contracts set aside for

Affirmative Action

Affirmative action refers to the effort to provide education and employment opportunities for historically disadvantaged groups, such as women and racial and ethnic minorities. The federal government first instituted affirmative action policies under the Civil Rights Act of 1964.

Presidents Reagan and Bush actively opposed affirmative action and racial quotas. Today, the future of affirmative action is uncertain. In 2001 President Bush expressed support for equal opportunity. But civil rights groups denounced his first attorney general, John Ashcroft, in part because of his anti-affirmative action record. Several state governments have acted to ban affirmative action practices, actions that the Supreme Court has upheld. In 2003 the Supreme Court protected the University of Michigan's race-conscious admissions policy. But in 2007 initiative campaigns to prohibit affirmative action were active in several states. In 2013 and 2014 Supreme Court decisions reversed the earlier Michigan decision and effectively banned racial considerations in university admissions.

minority businesses. Sylvester Monroe, an African American correspondent for *Newsweek* magazine, commented on the way in which some African Americans saw the backlash against affirmative action.

"There's a finite pie and everybody wants his piece. Everybody is afraid of losing his piece of the pie. That's what the fight against affirmative action is all about. People feel threatened. As for blacks, they're passé. They're not in any more. Nobody wants to talk about race."

—Sylvester Monroe, quoted in *The Great Divide*

The 1980s and 1990s also witnessed a reversal in the trend toward school integration. As whites moved out of many cities into the suburbs, the remaining urban populations were largely African American. As a result, by 1996–1997, 28 percent of blacks in the South and 50 percent of blacks in the Northeast were attending schools with fewer than 10 percent whites. Still, African Americans have made tremendous gains in education since the civil rights movement. While a high percentage of African American students once dropped out of high school, today the percentage finishing high school is only a few points lower for African Americans than for white Americans. Still, some negative trends in education have potentially far-reaching consequences. Although more African Americans attend college today than in the 1960s, the percentage of these students who graduate is only about half of that of white Americans. This disparity contributes to a substantial income and employment gap between African Americans and whites. This has had a significant impact on black children, about 30 percent of whom live in poverty.

Although incidents of racial violence are not as common in the United States as they once were, they still occur. One such riot began in Los Angeles in 1992 after white police officers beat a black motorist, Rodney King. More than 50 people were killed in the rioting, which destroyed more than $1 billion worth of property. More recently, the 2014 shooting of a young black man in Ferguson, Missouri, led to several days of protesting, looting, and violence.

Changes in Poverty and Education

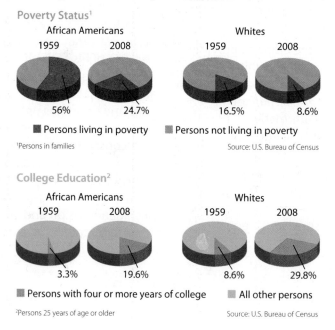

Poverty Status[1]

African Americans

1959 — 56%

2008 — 24.7%

Whites

1959 — 16.5%

2008 — 8.6%

■ Persons living in poverty   ■ Persons not living in poverty

[1]Persons in families

Source: U.S. Bureau of Census

College Education[2]

African Americans

1959 — 3.3%

2008 — 19.6%

Whites

1959 — 8.6%

2008 — 29.8%

■ Persons with four or more years of college   ■ All other persons

[2]Persons 25 years of age or older

Source: U.S. Bureau of Census

Interpret Graphs

1. Did the economic situation for African Americans get better or worse between 1959 and 2008?

2. About how much greater was the percentage of whites completing four or more years of college in 1959 than the percentage of African Americans?

Faced with continued challenges, many African American leaders are working to improve conditions for black Americans. Such organizations as the National Urban League strive to empower African Americans through leadership and education programs. African Americans are also working to improve education, health care, and the criminal justice system. At the ceremony celebrating the 50th anniversary of Dr. King's March on Washington, civil rights leaders named three areas that they believe still need to be addressed. These include the gap between rich and poor, efforts to restrict voters' access to the polls, and discrimination in the criminal justice system. Martin Luther King III, the son of Dr. King, has said that more work needs to be done to achieve his father's vision of a country free of racial prejudice.

Today's civil rights workers hope to bring about as much progress as was made a half-century ago. They are taking up the cause of justice and equality with new tools. They use the Internet and social media to spread their message. Technology has allowed them to register student voters electronically and file online petitions in response to key issues.

GAINS FOR HISPANIC AMERICANS During the 1980s Hispanic Americans became the fastest-growing minority in the United States. By 1990 they constituted almost 9 percent of the population. And demographers estimated that Hispanic Americans would soon outnumber African Americans as the nation's largest minority group. About two out of three Hispanic Americans were Mexican Americans, who lived mostly in the Southwest. A Puerto Rican

Vocabulary
demographer a person who studies the characteristics of human population, such as growth, density, and distribution

community thrived in the Northeast, and a Cuban population was concentrated in Florida. Like African Americans, Hispanic Americans gained political power during the 1980s. Toney Anaya became governor of New Mexico, while Robert Martinez became governor of Florida. In August 1988 President Reagan appointed Lauro Cavazos as secretary of education. In 1990 President Bush named Dr. Antonia Coello Novello to the post of surgeon general. In 2009 **Sonia Sotomayor** became the first Hispanic justice to serve on the U.S. Supreme Court.

Many Hispanic Americans worked to preserve their cultures within the United States. For example, they supported bilingual education. They feared that abandoning Spanish would weaken their distinctive culture. In the words of Daniel Villanueva, a television executive, "We want to be here, but without losing our language and our culture. They are a richness, a treasure that we don't care to lose." The Bilingual Education Act of 1968 and the 1975 amendment to the Voting Rights Act enabled Spanish speakers to attend school and vote in their own language. But by the mid-1980s, opposition to bilingualism was rising. Critics argued that it slowed the rate at which Spanish-speaking people entered mainstream American life. They also feared that the nation would become split between English speakers and Spanish speakers.

By the 1990s some Americans had grown concerned about the rapid growth of the Hispanic population in the United States. Many of their concerns stemmed from the number of Latin American immigrants who entered the United States illegally in search of jobs. These undocumented workers, opponents claim, take jobs from U.S. citizens and cost the government millions of dollars each year. To combat this issue, many Americans began calling for better border security, particularly between the United States and Mexico. Some states took action as well. For example, in 2010 Arizona passed a law that enhanced state and local police authority to enforce federal immigration laws. Unfortunately, the protest against illegal immigration affected many Hispanic American citizens as well. Even some Hispanic Americans whose families had been living in the United States for hundreds of years faced increased discrimination.

In 2004 some anti-immigrant activists began organizing along the U.S.–Mexico border. Groups who supported immigrant rights held rallies to counter those activists. In 2006 Latin American immigrants and their supporters began holding demonstrations across the country in support of immigrant rights. They also protested the growing hostility toward undocumented workers. In May 2006 some Hispanic immigrants took part in an event called A Day Without Immigrants. For one day they boycotted work, school, and shopping areas to remind people of the importance of immigrants to the U.S. economy.

In the discussion of Hispanic civil rights, immigration reform remains one of the most important and most polarizing issues. The president and leaders from both parties in Congress continue to debate the issue. But it has been difficult to reach agreement among all the different groups involved. Meanwhile, advocacy organizations such as the League of United Latin American Citizens (LULAC) continue to work for equal rights and equal opportunities for Hispanic Americans.

NATIVE AMERICANS SPEAK OUT Native Americans also became more self-conscious of their dignity and more demanding of their rights. In the 1970s they organized schools to teach young Native Americans about their past. They also began to fight for the return of ancestral lands wrongfully taken from them.

During the 1980s the Reagan administration slashed federal aid to Native Americans for health, education, and other services. Driven to find new sources of revenue, many Native Americans campaigned for the right to build gambling casinos on their land as a way to bring in money. After the Supreme Court ruled in favor of Native Americans, many tribes opened Las Vegas-style casinos, which provided additional funding for the tribes that operated them. Nonetheless, gambling casinos have not solved the long-term problems faced by Native Americans, although the new wealth has helped improve conditions to some extent.

One issue still facing many Native American groups is a lack of federal recognition. Currently, the Bureau of Indian Affairs, a division of the Department of the Interior, recognizes more than 560 distinct Native American groups. This recognition entitles the groups to receive funding and special protections from the government. Federal recognition also grants the right to establish self-government. Hundreds more groups from all around the country have petitioned the government for federal recognition and are still awaiting determination of their status.

AN EXPANDING ASIAN AMERICAN POPULATION Since 1980 Asian Americans have been among the fastest growing minorities in the United States. By 1982 Asian Americans constituted 3.25 percent of the U.S. population. By 2011 that number had grown to 5.8 percent, a population of more than 18.2 million people. The Asian American population today includes immigrants and the descendants of immigrants from nearly every country in Asia.

Unlike some other minority groups, Asian Americans did not conduct their own extensive civil rights movement. However, they did benefit from many of the gains made during the movements of the 1960s and 1970s. For example, the same law that ended the ban on interracial marriage for African Americans also allowed Asian Americans to marry whomever they chose. The Voting Rights Act of 1965 protected the voting rights of Asian Americans in addition to those of other groups. Also, the Immigration and Nationality Act of 1965 lifted quotas on the number of immigrants allowed into the United States from Asian countries.

Before the 1980s few people thought of themselves as Asian American. Instead, they considered themselves members of individual nationalities: Chinese American, Indian American, and so on. However, a terrible crime in 1982 helped create a sense of Asian American community nationwide. In that year, white autoworkers killed a Chinese American man in Detroit. Upset by the success of the Japanese auto industry and its effects on American companies, the workers attacked the man, whom they wrongly assumed had Japanese ancestry. News of the killing spread through the country, shocking people of all Asian backgrounds. As a result of this terrible incident, people of various backgrounds came together to protest discrimination against Asian Americans.

Some Asian Americans have also been the targets of violence because of their religion. After the terrorist attacks of September 11, 2001, several Sikhs—mostly people of South Asian descent—and Sikh temples were attacked. In most cases, the Sikhs were mistaken for Muslims by people who knew little about the religion. The attacks were part of a wave of violence and discrimination against Muslims (and those perceived as Muslims) and Arab Americans by people who held all Muslims responsible for the 2001 attacks.

Despite incidents of discrimination, Asian Americans have largely thrived economically and socially. For example, 2006 statistics indicate that 49 percent of all Asian Americans over the age of 25 have college degrees, a much higher percentage than the 28.6 percent of white Americans with college educations. Partially because of this educational success, the median income for Asian American families was about $16,000 higher than the median for other American households. In addition, Asian Americans generally have low crime rates, low school dropout rates, and low divorce rates. For these reasons, Asian Americans have sometimes been called a "model minority."

Reading Check
Analyze Issues
What political gains did African Americans make during the 1980s?

However, many Asian Americans dispute the model minority label, arguing that it hides the real issues they face. The Asian American community is not without its challenges. Although poverty rates are low among Americans with Chinese or Japanese ancestry, those with Southeast Asian backgrounds have experienced above average poverty rates. In addition, some Southeast Asian immigrant groups, especially Hmong and Cambodian Americans, generally have lower education levels than other immigrants. But these issues are frequently overlooked by those who see only Asian American successes.

The Equal Rights Struggle

The failure of the Equal Rights Amendment in 1982 was a setback for the women's rights movement. That failure, however, was not the end of the movement. Since the 1980s women have continued to campaign to improve their political and economic situations.

POLITICAL GAINS With the failure of the Equal Rights Amendment, women's organizations began to concentrate on electing women to public office. More women candidates began to run for office, including offices at the highest levels of government. By 1983 women held 13.5 percent of elected state offices as well as 24 seats in the U.S. Congress. In 1984 the Democrats chose Geraldine Ferraro as their vice-presidential candidate. She had spoken of the necessity for women to continue working for equal opportunities in American society.

As this poster shows, women have made significant political strides by being elected to the U.S. Congress.

"It is not just those of us who have reached the top who are fighting this daily battle. It is a fight in which all of us—rich and poor, career and home oriented, young and old—participate, simply because we are women."

—Geraldine Ferraro, quoted in *Vital Speeches of the Day*

In the November 1992 election, the number of women in the House of Representatives increased to 47, and the number of female senators tripled—from two to six. By 2009 those numbers had risen to 73 women in the House and 17 in the Senate. In 2007 Nancy Pelosi of California became the first female Speaker of the House. Several women had also served in key cabinet positions. Among them was **Madeleine Albright**, the first female secretary of state, appointed by President Bill Clinton in 1997. Four women—Sandra Day O'Connor, Ruth Bader Ginsburg, Sonia Sotomayor, and Elena Kagan—have sat on the Supreme Court. Nevertheless, women remained underrepresented in political affairs.

INEQUALITY In 1961 President John F. Kennedy had named a commission to study the status of women in the workplace. Its report revealed that employers paid women less than men for equal work. The report also said that women were rarely promoted to top positions in their fields.

Several factors contributed to what some called the "feminization of poverty." By the early 2000s about 60 percent of the nation's women worked outside the home, making up 47 percent of the American work force. Yet women earned only about 75 cents for every dollar men earned. Female college graduates earned only slightly more than male high school graduates. Also, about 31 percent of female heads of households lived in poverty. Among African American women, the poverty rate was even higher. New trends in divorce settlements aggravated the situation. Because of no-fault divorce, fewer women won alimony payments, and the courts rarely enforced the meager child support payments they awarded.

To close the income gap that left so many women poor, women's organizations and unions proposed a system of **pay equity**. Jobs would be rated on the basis of the amount of education they required, the amount of physical strength needed to perform them, and the number of people that an employee supervised. Instead of relying on traditional pay scales, employers would establish pay rates that reflected each job's requirements. By 1989, 20 states had begun adjusting government jobs to offer pay equity for jobs of comparable worth. In 2009 Congress passed the Lilly Ledbetter Fair Pay Act. The new law amended Title VII of the Civil Rights Act of 1964, which prohibited discrimination in hiring. The new act provided federal protection against pay discrimination as well.

Women also fought for improvements in the workplace. Since many working women headed single-parent households or had children under the age of six, they pressed for family benefits. Government and corporate benefit packages began to include maternity leaves, flexible hours and workweeks, job sharing, and work-at-home arrangements. Individual firms launched some of these changes, while others required government intervention. Yet the Reagan administration sharply cut the budget for federally-funded daycare and other similar programs.

Women have made great strides in recent decades. In 2002 they filled half of all jobs in managerial and professional specialty areas. Women have also been entering new fields, including construction work and equipment repair. The increase in the number of women in managerial and other professional jobs has helped change and shape American culture.

Despite these positive signs, the key issues of unequal pay and unequal representation remain. Women are still making less than their male counterparts—averaging only 77 cents for every dollar men earn.

In the nation's most top-level jobs, men continue to vastly outnumber women. As of 2007 women headed only ten Fortune 500 companies. Very few women who became corporate officers held line positions, jobs with profit-and-loss responsibility. In 2005 women held only 10.6 percent of line positions.

Reading Check
Summarize What steps did women take to help them move forward after the ERA failed to pass?

Civil Rights for All

Civil rights and equality are not issues only for racial or ethnic minorities and women. Since the 1960s, members of various groups in the United States have worked to secure the protection of their rights under state and federal law.

LGBT RIGHTS Among the groups that fought for civil rights was the lesbian, gay, bisexual, and transgender, or LGBT, community. In the 1940s LGBT Americans were banned from working for the federal government or serving in the military. Members of the community were also frequent targets of discrimination and police harassment. In 1969 New York City police officers raided the Stonewall Inn, a popular LGBT gathering spot. Angry patrons clashed with the police. And the confrontation sparked several days of riots in the neighborhood of Greenwich Village. The **Stonewall riots** are credited as the beginning of the LGBT rights movement.

During the 1970s and 1980s, members of the LGBT community began to fight openly for civil rights. Direct action groups sprang up throughout the country, calling for an end to antigay discrimination. Some people condemned this activism but were unable to slow the pace of change. By the early 1990s, several states and more than 100 local communities had outlawed such discrimination. In 1994 the U.S. government implemented the "Don't Ask,

A LGBT rights march in Washington, DC, October 1987

Don't Tell" policy. While openly LGBT individuals were still banned from serving in the military, the new policy forbade military officials from asking about an individual's orientation.

The LGBT rights movement in the United States has made great strides toward equal rights and opportunities in recent years. For instance, after years of protesting the U.S. military's policies regarding gay soldiers, the "Don't Ask, Don't Tell" policy was repealed in September 2011. For the first time, military service was open to LGBT individuals.

One major area of focus for LGBT activists and many other American citizens has been obtaining and protecting legal rights for same-sex couples who want to get married. LGBT rights activists and groups such as Marriage Equality USA used education, outreach, and media campaigns to advocate for the legalization of same-sex marriage in the United States. Although 37 states and the District of Columbia had legalized same-sex marriage by mid-2015, several states passed laws banning same-sex unions. On June 26, 2015, the Supreme Court issued a ruling stating that it is illegal for states to ban same-sex marriage, effectively making same-sex marriages legal everywhere in the United States.

RIGHTS FOR AMERICANS WITH DISABILITIES Another group that has had to campaign for protection of their rights are Americans with disabilities, a group that includes more than 56.7 million people. The term *disability* covers a wide range of conditions, including physical disabilities; chronic health impairments; mental illness; and visual, hearing, or speech impairments. Disabilities vary in severity.

In addition to dealing with health issues, many Americans with disabilities have had to deal with prejudice and discrimination, especially in employment. A common challenge facing Americans with disabilities is the stereotypical belief that disabilities limit their ability to perform productive work. As a result, people with disabilities have historically had trouble finding meaningful, well-paid jobs.

For decades, disability rights activists have struggled to gain the civil rights granted to other groups. Over the years, their efforts have resulted in legislation to protect many rights. The Education for All Handicapped Children Act of 1975, for example, guaranteed access to educational facilities and learning opportunities for children with disabilities. The Fair Housing Amendments Act, passed in 1988, protected persons with disabilities from discrimination in housing.

The most significant legislation protecting the rights of people with disabilities was the **Americans with Disabilities Act** (ADA), signed by President George H. W. Bush in 1990. The ADA addresses the rights of people with disabilities in four main areas: employment, public services, public accommodations, and telecommunications. The act outlawed all discrimination against people with disabilities. It required state and local government programs, public transportation vehicles, and businesses that serve the public to be made accessible to Americans with disabilities.

The ADA has improved opportunities for people with disabilities, but their struggle is not yet over. Finding rewarding work is still a challenge for many.

Americans with Disabilities Act

On July 26, 1990, President George H. W. Bush signed the Americans with Disabilities Act into law. He spoke to the crowd gathered on the White House lawn about the importance of the act and the new freedoms it would provide.

"With today's signing of the landmark Americans [with] Disabilities Act, every man, woman, and child with a disability can now pass through once-closed doors into a bright new era of equality, independence, and freedom. . . . I remember clearly how many years of dedicated commitment have gone into making this historic new civil rights act a reality. It's been the work of a true coalition, a strong and inspiring coalition of people who have shared both a dream and a passionate determination to make that dream come true . . . a joining of Democrats and Republicans, of the legislative and the executive branches, of Federal and State agencies, of public officials and private citizens, of people with disabilities and without.

This act . . . will ensure that people with disabilities are given the basic guarantees for which they have worked so long and so hard: independence, freedom of choice, control of their lives, the opportunity to blend fully and equally into the rich mosaic of the American mainstream. Legally, it will provide our disabled community with a powerful expansion of protections. . . . It will guarantee fair and just access to the fruits of American life which we all must be able to enjoy."

—George H. W. Bush, from a speech on July 26, 1990

Analyze Historical Sources
Explain why it takes a coalition such as the groups President Bush lists to create a new civil rights law.

STUDENTS' CIVIL RIGHTS In an age of social media, many questions have arisen about students' rights to expression and free speech. In recent years, students have been punished or suspended for comments made about classes, teachers, or other students online.

The debate about students' rights goes back several decades. In the 1960s, two key Supreme Court decisions set precedents for determining what freedoms students enjoyed. The first, *Engel* v. *Vitale* (1962), ruled that students could not be required to participate in school-sponsored prayer. The case stemmed from a challenge to a New York state law that required public schools to open each day with a nondenominational prayer. Although students could opt out of participating in this prayer, a group of parents filed suit, claiming that the law violated the First Amendment protection of freedom of religion. In the end, the Supreme Court agreed, and the law was struck down.

The Supreme Court reaffirmed students' First Amendment protections again in *Tinker* v. *Des Moines Independent Community School District* (1969). After a group of students was expelled for wearing black armbands in protest of the Vietnam War, they sued the school district, claiming their right to

Supreme Court Rulings on Student Rights

Case	Decision
Engel v. *Vitale* (1962)	Students cannot be allowed to participate in religious displays at school, even if the displays are nondenominational.
Tinker v. *Des Moines* (1969)	Students retain the right to free expression at school. Freedom of expression extends to symbolic speech as well as actual words.
New Jersey v. *T.L.O.* (1985)	Student lockers can be searched, as long as school officials have reasonable suspicion of wrongdoing.
Hazelwood School District v. *Kuhlmeier* (1988)	The contents of student newspapers can be limited with a valid educational reason for doing so.

free speech had been restricted. The Supreme Court agreed. Ruling that First Amendment protection extends not only to spoken words but also to "symbolic speech," or actions, the Court established the right of public school students to express political opinions at school.

In the years since the *Tinker* decision, the Supreme Court has clarified students' right of expression. In 1986 the Court ruled that disruptive or indecent speech was not protected. *Hazelwood School District* v. *Kuhlmeier* (1988) determined that student newspapers did not enjoy the same level of First Amendment protection as professional journalism. Schools could restrict the contents of student newspapers if there were a compelling educational reason for doing so. Furthermore, in 2007, the Court determined that schools could, within limits, restrict student speech at school-sponsored events.

Personal privacy has also been a key civil rights concern for students. Court decisions have determined that students have the right to privacy at school, but within limits. For example, the 1985 case *New Jersey* v. *T.L.O.* ruled that student lockers could be searched, but only if the school had a reasonable suspicion of wrongdoing. Random locker searches, however, violated student rights. In 1995 the Court ruled that students could not refuse to take drug tests mandated for participation in school athletics programs. Because the programs were optional, the Court ruled, the drug tests were not a violation of privacy. More recent cases have addressed the issue of students' online activity and whether schools have the right to monitor activity that takes place away from school grounds. Supporters of such monitoring say they are working to protect school and student security. Opponents compare the monitoring to illegal searches of student backpacks or possessions. As online activity increases, such debates will likely become more common.

THE RIGHTS OF NEW IMMIGRANTS As debates over immigration have heated up in recent years, some groups have begun campaigns to protect the civil rights of recent arrivals to the country. Over the last few decades, debates in Congress and state legislatures have addressed the issue.

Pro-immigration supporters take part in a rally held by the League of United Latin American Citizens (LULAC) in Dallas, Texas.

In 1980 Congress passed the Refugee Act, which made it easier for immigrants fleeing political turmoil or violence to settle in the country. The act supported English language education, promoted economic self-sufficiency, and banned gender discrimination in these programs. By the mid-1990s, however, the government had imposed new restrictions on immigration. The Immigration Reform and Control Act of 1986, for example, required that all immigrants seeking jobs prove their immigration status. In addition, the act increased the number of border patrols along the U.S.–Mexico border.

New laws passed in 1996 further limited the civil rights of immigrants. The new laws created a mandatory detention policy for immigrants with prior criminal records, even if their offenses were old or minor. Even immigrants with misdemeanor offenses faced potentially harsh punishments—and possibly deportation. More recently, some states have passed laws that allow officials to question anyone suspected of being in the country illegally, requiring them to present papers on demand. Civil rights advocates point to this requirement as a violation of immigrants' rights as Americans.

In recent years, immigration rights advocates have called for reform to American immigration policy. They want to streamline the path to permanent residency, making it easier for new Americans to find work and begin the path to citizenship. They also want an overhaul of the 1996 laws to impose less stringent punishments. Furthermore, they want to make it easier for recent immigrants to reunite with their families. With immigration a sensitive issue, however, the debate over reform is likely to last many years.

Reading Check
Form Generalizations
How has the federal government worked to protect the rights of students and Americans with disabilities?

Lesson 6 Assessment

1. **Organize Information** Use a chart to identify the civil rights challenges various groups in the United States face today and the steps that each group has made to address those challenges.

Group	Challenges	Solutions
LGBT community		
Americans with disabilities		
Students		
New immigrants		

2. **Key Terms and People** For each key term or person in the lesson, write a sentence explaining its significance.

3. **Analyze Effects** To what extent have civil rights movements been effective in creating political, economic, and social equality in the United States?

   Think About:
   • the gains made by various racial and ethnic minorities since 1980
   • women's struggle for equality
   • civil rights movements among other groups

4. **Evaluate** How is today's civil rights movement different from how it was in the past? How is it similar?

5. **Compare and Contrast** How have civil rights efforts among Asian Americans been different from those of other groups? How have they been similar?

Module 15 Assessment

Key Terms and People

For each key term or person below, write a sentence explaining its connection to the pursuit of civil rights and the fight for equality in the United States.

1. *Brown* v. *Board of Education*
2. Rosa Parks
3. freedom riders
4. Civil Rights Act of 1964
5. de facto segregation
6. Malcolm X
7. César Chávez
8. American Indian Movement (AIM)
9. Equal Rights Amendment (ERA)
10. Americans with Disabilities Act

Main Ideas

Use your notes and the information in the module to answer the following questions.

Taking on Segregation

1. What were Jim Crow laws and how were they applied?
2. What was the role of Martin Luther King Jr. within the civil rights movement?
3. How did White Citizens' Councils use boycotts as a weapon?
4. What is the connection between Dixiecrats and the Civil Rights Act of 1957?
5. What was the Montgomery bus boycott?

The Triumphs of a Crusade

6. What was the significance of the federal court case won by James Meredith in 1962?
7. Cite three examples of violence committed against African Americans and civil rights activists between 1962 and 1964.
8. Why did civil rights groups work together to organize Freedom Summer?
9. Why did young people in SNCC and the MFDP feel betrayed by some civil rights leaders?

Challenges and Changes in the Movement

10. How did the compromises of civil rights leaders lead to the rise of the Black Power movement?
11. How were civil rights problems in northern cities similar to those in the South?
12. What were some of the key beliefs Malcolm X advocated?
13. Why did some urge Stokely Carmichael to stop using the slogan "Black Power"?
14. Describe the social turmoil after the assassination of Martin Luther King Jr.

Hispanic and Native Americans Seek Equality

15. What strategies did both César Chávez and the UFWOC use to achieve their goals? How did they successfully apply these tactics?
16. Describe the Chicano movement and explain its main goals.
17. What were the demands of the American Indian Movement (AIM) organizers who staged "The Trail of Broken Treaties" march on Washington in 1972?
18. Explain the successes and failures of the American Indian Movement (AIM) in the pursuit of civil rights and equal opportunities.

Women Fight for Equality

19. Name three changes that members of the National Organization of Women (NOW) advocated.
20. What was the Supreme Court's decision in the *Roe* v. *Wade* case?
21. What prompted women to establish NOW?
22. What concerns motivated those who opposed the ERA?

The Struggle Continues

23. What progress and obstacles did different minority groups experience in the 1980s and 1990s?
24. What were some gains that women achieved in the 1980s and 1990s?

25. What problems did Native Americans face in the 1980s?

26. How did the cases *New Jersey* v. *T.L.O.* and *Hazelwood School District* v. *Kuhlmeier* limit student rights?

Critical Thinking

1. Draw Conclusions On your own paper, draw a cluster diagram and fill it in with four events from the civil rights movement that were broadcast on nationwide television and that you find the most compelling.

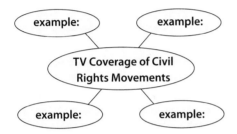

How do you think television coverage of these events affected American politics?

2. Develop Historical Perspective Would you characterize the civil rights struggle as a unified or disunified movement? Explain.

3. Draw Conclusions Why were national government actions needed to ensure civil rights for African Americans? Analyze the response of state governments and city officials, citing the actions of Orval Faubus, George Wallace, and Bull Connor as examples.

4. Evaluate Was Title VII effective in promoting civil liberties and equal opportunities? Explain.

5. Contrast Explain the difference between de jure and de facto segregation. How did state governments and state government officials confront each type of segregation?

6. Evaluate What were the main successes of La Raza Unida?

7. Analyze Effects How effective was Title IX in promoting civil liberties and equal opportunities for women? Explain.

8. Develop Historical Perspective Consider the organizations that Hispanic Americans, Native Americans, and women formed during the 1960s. Which do you think was the most influential? Why?

9. Form Opinions How do you think increasing numbers of women in managerial and other professional roles help shape American culture? Explain your answer.

10. Evaluate Have women met their goals of equality in the workplace and politics? Explain.

Engage with History

Create a script in which five characters—an African American activist, a Hispanic American activist, a Native American activist, a member of the women's movement, and a politician who wants to preserve the status quo—debate the following question: How much can a society change?

Focus on Writing

Write a persuasive essay explaining why civil rights for all people are necessary. Base your arguments on historical examples, democratic values, and constitutional principles. You may wish to support your arguments by listing the benefits that civil rights provide for all citizens.

Collaborative Learning

Working in a group, use library or Internet sources to find the full texts of Martin Luther King's March on Washington speech, the Declaration of Independence, the Seneca Falls Resolution, and the Gettysburg Address. Have one member of the group read King's speech aloud. Discuss the main points and ideas King expresses. Then take turns reading the other texts aloud. After each text is read, discuss how the ideas expressed are similar or different than the ideas presented in King's speech. Create a chart to list at least two differences and two similarities for each text.

Module 16

The Vietnam War

★

Essential Question
Should the United States have gotten involved in the conflict in Vietnam?

About the Photograph: This photograph shows U.S. troops on patrol with helicopter support in Vietnam in 1965.

In this module you will learn how the United States used its military to stop the spread of communism in Southeast Asia. You will also examine how the Vietnam War ultimately brought down a president and bitterly divided the nation.

▷ *Explore ONLINE!*

VIDEOS, including...

- America Is Drawn into the Vietnam Conflict
- Congress Passes the Tonkin Gulf Resolution
- Operation Rolling Thunder
- Search-and-Destroy Missions
- Cambodia
- Coming Home

 Document-Based Investigations

 Graphic Organizers

Interactive Games

 Image with Hotspots: Tunnels of the Vietcong

Carousel: Jungle Warfare

SS.912.A.1.2 Utilize a variety of primary and secondary sources to identify author, historical significance, audience, and authenticity to understand a historical period. **SS.912.A.1.4** Analyze how images, symbols, objects, cartoons, graphs, charts, maps, and artwork may be used to interpret the significance of time periods and events from the past. **SS.912.A.1.7** Describe various sociocultural aspects of American life including arts, artifacts, literature, education, and publications. **SS.912.A.6.13** Analyze significant foreign policy events during the Truman, Eisenhower, Kennedy, Johnson, and Nixon administrations. **SS.912.A.6.14** Analyze causes, course, and consequences of the Vietnam War. **SS.912.A.6.15** Examine key events and peoples in Florida history as they relate to United States history. **SS.912.A.7.4** Evaluate the success of 1960s era presidents' foreign and domestic policies. **SS.912.A.7.9** Examine the similarities of social movements of the 1960s and 1970s. **SS.912.A.7.10** Analyze the significance of Vietnam and Watergate on the government and people of the United States. **SS.912.H.1.1** Relate works in the arts of varying styles and genre according to the periods in which they were created. **SS.912.H.1.5** Examine artistic response to social issues and new ideas in various cultures. **LAFS.1112.RH.1.2** Determine the central ideas or information of a primary or secondary source; provide an accurate summary that makes clear the relationships among the key details and ideas. **LAFS.1112.RH.4.10** By the end of grade 12, read and comprehend history/social studies texts in the grades 11–CCR text complexity band independently and proficiently. **MAFS.K12.MP.1.1** Make sense of problems and persevere in solving them. **MAFS.K12.MP.3.1** Construct viable arguments and critique the reasoning of others. **MAFS.K12.MP.5.1** Use appropriate tools strategically.

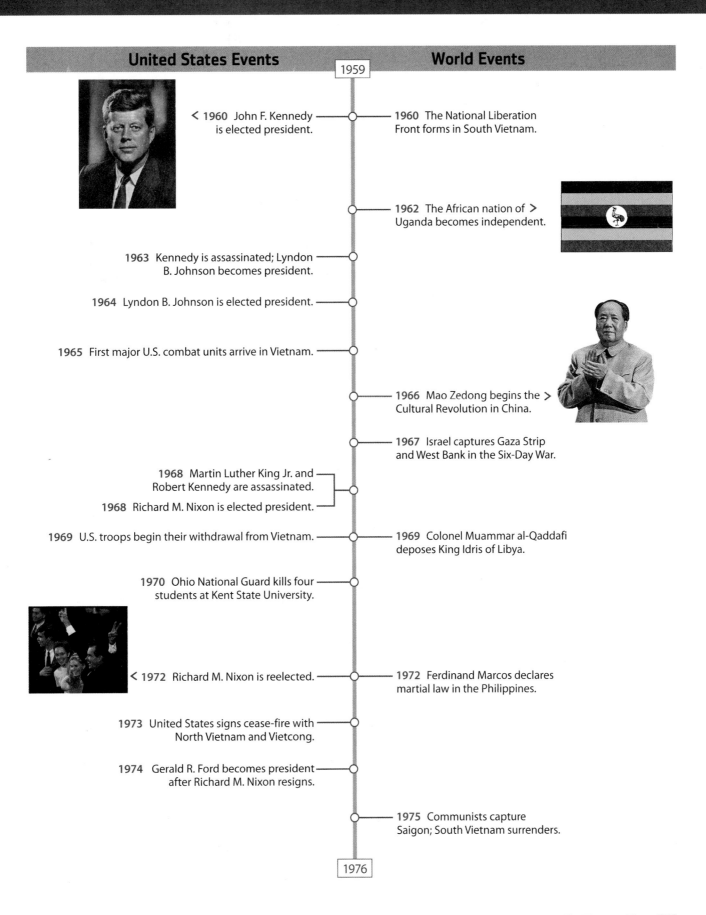

| United States Events | 1959 | World Events |

< 1960 John F. Kennedy is elected president.

1960 The National Liberation Front forms in South Vietnam.

1962 The African nation of **>** Uganda becomes independent.

1963 Kennedy is assassinated; Lyndon B. Johnson becomes president.

1964 Lyndon B. Johnson is elected president.

1965 First major U.S. combat units arrive in Vietnam.

1966 Mao Zedong begins the **>** Cultural Revolution in China.

1967 Israel captures Gaza Strip and West Bank in the Six-Day War.

1968 Martin Luther King Jr. and Robert Kennedy are assassinated.

1968 Richard M. Nixon is elected president.

1969 U.S. troops begin their withdrawal from Vietnam.

1969 Colonel Muammar al-Qaddafi deposes King Idris of Libya.

1970 Ohio National Guard kills four students at Kent State University.

< 1972 Richard M. Nixon is reelected.

1972 Ferdinand Marcos declares martial law in the Philippines.

1973 United States signs cease-fire with North Vietnam and Vietcong.

1974 Gerald R. Ford becomes president after Richard M. Nixon resigns.

1975 Communists capture Saigon; South Vietnam surrenders.

1976

Moving Toward Conflict

The Big Idea

To stop the spread of communism in Southeast Asia, the United States used its military to support South Vietnam.

Why It Matters Now

The United States' support role in Vietnam began what would become a long and controversial war.

Key Terms and People

Ho Chi Minh

Vietminh

domino theory

Dien Bien Phu

Geneva Accords

Ngo Dinh Diem

Vietcong

Ho Chi Minh Trail

Tonkin Gulf Resolution

One American's Story

On the morning of September 26, 1945, Lieutenant Colonel A. Peter Dewey was on his way to the Saigon airport in Vietnam. Only 28, Dewey served in the Office of Strategic Services, the chief intelligence-gathering body of the U.S. military and forerunner of the Central Intelligence Agency. Dewey was sent to assess what was becoming an explosive situation in Vietnam, a Southeast Asian country that had recently been freed from Japanese rule.

Lieutenant Colonel A. Peter Dewey

Before World War II, France had ruled Vietnam and the surrounding countries. Now it sought—with British aid—to regain control of the region. The Vietnamese had resisted Japanese occupation. Now they were preparing to fight the French. Dewey saw nothing but disaster in France's plan. "Cochinchina [southern Vietnam] is burning," he reported, "the French and British are finished here, and we [the United States] ought to clear out of Southeast Asia." On his way to the airport, Dewey encountered a roadblock staffed by Vietnamese soldiers and shouted at them in French. Presumably mistaking him for a French soldier, the guards shot him in the head. Thus, A. Peter Dewey, whose body was never recovered, was the first American to die in Vietnam.

Unfortunately, Dewey would not be the last. As Vietnam's independence effort came under Communist influence, the United States grew increasingly concerned about the small country's future. Eventually, America would fight a war to halt the spread of communism in Vietnam. The war would claim the lives of almost 60,000 Americans and more than 2 million Vietnamese. It also would divide the American nation as no other event since the Civil War.

SS.912.A.1.4; SS.912.A.6.13; SS.912.A.6.14; SS.912.A.7.4

America Supports France in Vietnam

America's involvement in Vietnam began in 1950, during the French Indochina War, the name given to France's attempt to reestablish its rule in Vietnam after World War II. Seeking to strengthen its ties with France and to help fight the spread of communism, the United States provided the French with massive economic and military support.

FRENCH RULE IN VIETNAM From the late 1800s until World War II, France ruled most of Indochina. This included Vietnam, Laos, and Cambodia. French colonists, who built plantations on peasant land and extracted rice and rubber for their own profit, encountered growing unrest among the Vietnamese peasants. French rulers reacted harshly by restricting freedom of speech and assembly and by jailing many Vietnamese nationalists. These measures failed to curb all dissent, and opposition continued to grow.

Many of the nationalists came to believe that a Communist revolution was a way for Vietnam to gain freedom from foreign leaders. The Indochinese Communist Party, founded in 1930, staged a number of revolts under the leadership of **Ho Chi Minh**. Although the French condemned Ho Chi Minh to death for his rebellious activity, he fled Vietnam and orchestrated Vietnam's growing independence movement from exile in the Soviet Union and later from China.

In 1940 the Japanese took control of Vietnam. The next year, Ho Chi Minh returned home and helped form the **Vietminh**, an organization whose goal it was to win Vietnam's independence from foreign rule. When the Allied defeat of Japan in August 1945 forced the Japanese to leave Vietnam, that goal suddenly seemed a reality. On September 2, 1945, Ho Chi Minh stood in the middle of a huge crowd in the northern city of Hanoi and declared Vietnam an independent nation.

Vocabulary
peasant a member of the class of agricultural laborers

– BIOGRAPHY –

Ho Chi Minh (1890–1969)

Born Nguyen Tat Thanh to a poor Vietnamese family, Ho Chi Minh (which means "He Who Enlightens") found work as a cook on a French steamship. This allowed him to visit such cities as Boston and New York.

Although he was a Communist, Ho Chi Minh preferred the United States to the Soviet Union as an ally. He even based the phrasing of the Vietnamese Declaration of Independence on the U.S. Declaration of Independence. But his admiration for the United States eventually turned to disappointment. In enforcing its containment policy, the United States chose to support France rather than his nationalist movement.

The Communist ruler's name lived on after his death in 1969. In 1975 the North Vietnamese Army conquered South Vietnam and changed the name of the South's capital from Saigon to Ho Chi Minh City.

FRANCE BATTLES THE VIETMINH France, however, had no intention of relinquishing its former colony. French troops moved back into Vietnam by the end of 1945, eventually regaining control of the cities and the country's southern half. Ho Chi Minh vowed to fight from the North to liberate the South from French control. "If ever the tiger pauses," Ho had said, referring to the Vietminh, "the elephant [France] will impale him on his mighty tusks. But the tiger will not pause, and the elephant will die of exhaustion and loss of blood."

The struggle against communism shaped Truman's perspective regarding the situation in Indochina. The policy of containment, which held that the United States should attempt to prevent the spread of communism to other nations, shaped the foreign relations of his administration. Truman decided to support France, a key ally in the effort to block Communist expansion in Europe, rather than the Vietminh—many of whom were themselves Communists. Events in Asia soon revealed the extent of Communist expansion. The Communist army of Mao Zedong seized China in 1949. The next year, Communist North Korea invaded South Korea. These events strengthened the U.S. commitment to contain communism in Southeast Asia.

In 1950 the United States entered the Vietnam struggle—despite A. Peter Dewey's warnings. That year, President Truman sent nearly $15 million in economic aid to France. Over the next four years, the United States paid for much of France's war. America pumped nearly $1 billion into the effort to defeat a man it had once supported. Ironically, during World War II, the United States had forged an alliance with Ho Chi Minh, supplying him with aid to resist the Japanese. But by 1950 the United States had come to view its one-time ally as a Communist aggressor.

THE VIETMINH DRIVE OUT THE FRENCH Upon entering the White House in 1953, President Eisenhower continued the policy of supplying aid to the French war effort. By this time, the United States had settled for a stalemate with the Communists in Korea. This only stiffened America's resolve to halt the spread of communism elsewhere. During a news conference in 1954, Eisenhower explained the **domino theory**, which had its roots in the containment policy. He warned that if Vietnam fell to communism, other Southeast Asian countries would soon follow, just like dominoes toppling. "You have a row of dominoes set up," the president said. "You knock over the first one, and what will happen to the last one is the certainty that it will go over very quickly."

Despite massive U.S. aid, however, the French could not retake Vietnam. They were forced to surrender in May 1954, when the Vietminh overran the French outpost at **Dien Bien Phu**, in northwestern Vietnam.

From May through July 1954, the countries of France, Great Britain, the Soviet Union, the United States, China, Laos, and Cambodia met in Geneva, Switzerland, with the Vietminh and with South Vietnam's anti-Communist nationalists to hammer out a peace agreement. The **Geneva Accords** temporarily divided Vietnam along the 17th parallel. The Communists and their leader, Ho Chi Minh, controlled North Vietnam from the capital of Hanoi. The anti-Communist nationalists controlled South Vietnam from the capital and southern port city of Saigon. An election to unify the country was called for in 1956.

Reading Check
Synthesize How and why did the United States support France's Vietnam War efforts?

The Vietcong saw the United States and South Vietnam as oppressors. This propaganda poster reads, "Vietnam will surely be victorious and America will surely be defeated."

Background
The Buddhist religion is based on the teachings of Siddhartha Gautama, also known as Shakyamuni. The Indian mystic believed that spiritual enlightenment could be obtained through right conduct, meditation, and wisdom.

The United States Steps In

In the wake of France's retreat, the United States took a more active role in halting the spread of communism in Vietnam. Wading deeper into the country's affairs, the Eisenhower and Kennedy administrations provided economic and military aid to South Vietnam's non-Communist regime.

DIEM CANCELS ELECTIONS Although he directed a brutal and repressive regime, Ho Chi Minh won popular support in the North by breaking up large estates and redistributing land to peasants. Moreover, his years of fighting the Japanese and French had made him a national hero. Recognizing Ho Chi Minh's widespread popularity, South Vietnam's president, **Ngo Dinh Diem** (ngō′ dĭn′ dē-ĕm′), a strong anti-Communist, refused to take part in the countrywide election of 1956. The United States also sensed that a countrywide election might spell victory for Ho Chi Minh and supported canceling elections. The Eisenhower administration promised military aid and training to Diem in return for a stable reform government in the South.

Diem, however, failed to hold up his end of the bargain. He ushered in a corrupt government that suppressed opposition of any kind and offered little or no land distribution to peasants. In addition, Diem, who was a devout Catholic, angered the country's majority Buddhist population by restricting Buddhist practices.

By 1957 a Communist opposition group in the South, known as the **Vietcong**, had begun attacks on the Diem government. Group members assassinated thousands of South Vietnamese government officials. Although the political arm of the group would later be called the National Liberation Front (NLF), the United States continued to refer to the fighters as the Vietcong.

Ho Chi Minh supported the group. In 1959 he began supplying arms to the Vietcong via a network of paths along the borders of Vietnam, Laos, and Cambodia that became known as the **Ho Chi Minh Trail**. As the fighters stepped up their surprise attacks, or guerrilla tactics, South Vietnam grew more unstable. The Eisenhower administration took little action, however, deciding to "sink or swim with Ngo Dinh Diem."

KENNEDY AND VIETNAM The Kennedy administration, which entered the White House in 1961, also chose initially to "swim" with Diem. Wary of accusations that Democrats were "soft" on communism, President Kennedy increased financial aid to Diem's teetering regime. He also sent thousands of military advisers to help train South Vietnamese troops. By the end of 1963, 16,000 U.S. military personnel were in South Vietnam.

Meanwhile, Diem's popularity plummeted because of ongoing corruption and his failure to respond to calls for land reform. To combat the growing Vietcong presence in the South's countryside, the Diem administration initiated the strategic hamlet program. This meant moving all villagers to protected areas. Many Vietnamese deeply resented being moved from their home villages where they had lived for generations and where ancestors were buried.

Explore ONLINE!

CHINA

Red River

NORTH VIETNAM

Dien Bien Phu

Hanoi

Haiphong

LAOS

Gulf of Tonkin

BURMA

Vientiane

Mekong River

THAILAND

17th Parallel

Hue

Da Nang

My Lai

15°N

Bangkok

CAMBODIA

Ho Chi Minh Trail

SOUTH VIETNAM

Phnom Penh

Cam Ranh Bay

Saigon

Gulf of Thailand

South China Sea

105°E

N
W E
S

0 — 150 — 300 mi
0 — 150 — 300 km

After parachuting into the mountains north of Dien Bien Phu, South Vietnamese troops await orders from French officers in 1953.

Rivers serve as places to work, bathe, and wash clothing.

The swampy terrain of South Vietnam made for difficult and dangerous fighting. This 1961 photograph shows South Vietnamese Army troops in combat operations against Vietcong.

Interpret Maps

1. **Movement** Through which countries did the Ho Chi Minh Trail pass?

2. **Location** How might North Vietnam's location have enabled it to get aid from its ally, China?

Vocabulary
coup a sudden
appropriation of
leadership; a takeover

Reading Check
Analyze Motives
Why did the United
States not support the
Geneva Accords?

Diem also intensified his attack on Buddhism. Fed up with continuing Buddhist demonstrations, the South Vietnamese ruler imprisoned and killed hundreds of Buddhist clerics. He also destroyed their temples. To protest these actions, several Buddhist monks and nuns publicly burned themselves to death. Horrified, American officials urged Diem to stop the persecutions. But Diem refused.

It had become clear that for South Vietnam to remain stable, Diem would have to go. On November 1, 1963, a U.S.-supported military coup toppled Diem's regime. Against Kennedy's wishes, Diem was assassinated. A few weeks later, Kennedy, too, fell to an assassin's bullet. The United States presidency—along with the growing crisis in Vietnam—now belonged to Lyndon B. Johnson.

President Johnson Expands the Conflict

Shortly before his death, Kennedy had announced his intent to withdraw U.S. forces from South Vietnam. "In the final analysis, it's their war," he declared. Whether Kennedy would have withdrawn from Vietnam remains a matter of debate. However, Lyndon Johnson escalated the nation's role in Vietnam. He eventually began what would become one of America's longest wars.

THE SOUTH GROWS MORE UNSTABLE Diem's death brought more chaos to South Vietnam. A string of military leaders attempted to lead the country. But each regime was more unstable and inefficient than Diem's had been. Meanwhile, the Vietcong's influence in the countryside steadily grew.

President Johnson believed that a Communist takeover of South Vietnam would be disastrous. Johnson, like Kennedy, was particularly sensitive to being perceived as "soft" on communism. "If I . . . let the communists take over South Vietnam," Johnson said, "then . . . my nation would be seen as an appeaser and we would . . . find it impossible to accomplish anything . . . anywhere on the entire globe."

THE TONKIN GULF RESOLUTION On August 2, 1964, a North Vietnamese patrol boat fired a torpedo at an American destroyer, the USS *Maddox*. The ship was patrolling in the Gulf of Tonkin off the North Vietnamese coast. The torpedo missed its target, but the *Maddox* returned fire and inflicted heavy damage on the patrol boat.

Two days later, the *Maddox* and another destroyer were again off the North Vietnamese coast. In spite of bad weather that could affect visibility, the crew reported enemy torpedoes. The American destroyers began firing. The crew of the *Maddox* later declared, however, that they had neither seen nor heard hostile gunfire.

The alleged attack on the U.S. ships prompted President Johnson to launch bombing strikes on North Vietnam. He asked Congress for powers to take "all necessary measures to repel any armed attack against the forces of the United States and to prevent further aggression." Congress approved Johnson's request, with only two senators voting against it, and adopted the **Tonkin Gulf Resolution** on August 7. While not a declaration of war, the resolution granted Johnson broad military powers in Vietnam. Some felt it altered the U.S. Constitution's system of checks and balances by allowing the executive branch to wage war without a formal declaration of war from the legislative branch.

Johnson did not tell Congress or the American people that the United States had been leading secret raids against North Vietnam. The *Maddox* had been in the Gulf of Tonkin to collect information for these raids. Furthermore, Johnson had prepared the resolution months beforehand. He was only waiting for the chance to push it through Congress.

In February 1965 President Johnson used his newly granted powers. In response to a Vietcong attack that killed eight Americans, Johnson unleashed "Operation Rolling Thunder." This was the first sustained bombing of North Vietnam. In March of that year, the first American combat troops began arriving in South Vietnam. By June more than 50,000 U.S. soldiers were battling the Vietcong. The Vietnam War had become Americanized.

Reading Check
Summarize What authority did the Tonkin Gulf Resolution give to President Johnson?

Lesson 1 Assessment

1. **Organize Information** In a table, cite the Vietnam policy for each of the following presidents: Truman, Eisenhower, Kennedy, and Johnson.

President	Vietnam Policy

Choose one of the four presidents, explain his policies in Vietnam, and evaluate the extent to which he achieved his goals.

2. **Key Terms and People** For each key term or person in the lesson, write a sentence explaining its significance.

3. **Evaluate** Do you think Congress was justified in passing the Tonkin Gulf Resolution? Use details from the text to support your response.

   Think About:
   - the questionable report of torpedo attacks on two U.S. destroyers
   - the powers that the resolution would give the president and how that action could affect the constitutional system of checks and balances
   - the fact that the resolution was not a declaration of war

4. **Evaluate** How was the Vietnam conflict seen as a Cold War struggle?

5. **Form Opinions** Do you think the Geneva Accords eased American concerns about a domino effect in Southeast Asia? Why or why not?

6. **Analyze Motives** Do you believe that Eisenhower's decision to send U.S. troops to Vietnam was wise? Why or why not?

U.S. Involvement and Escalation

One American's Story

Drafted at the age of 21, Tim O'Brien was sent to Vietnam in August 1968. He later wrote several novels based on his experiences there. In one book, O'Brien described the nerve-racking experience of walking through the fields and jungles of Vietnam, many of which were filled with land mines and booby traps.

U.S. soldiers faced treacherous jungles and rivers in Vietnam.

"You look ahead a few paces and wonder what your legs will resemble if there is more to the earth in that spot than silicates and nitrogen. Will the pain be unbearable? Will you scream and fall silent? Will you be afraid to look at your own body, afraid of the sight of your own red flesh and white bone? . . . It is not easy to fight this sort of self-defeating fear, but you try. You decide to be ultra-careful—the hard-nosed realistic approach. You try to second-guess the mine. Should you put your foot to that flat rock or the clump of weeds to its rear? Paddy dike or water? . . . You trace the footprints of the men to your front. You give up when he curses you for following too closely; better one man dead than two."

—Tim O'Brien, quoted in *A Life in a Year: The American Infantryman in Vietnam 1965–1972*

Deadly traps were just some of the obstacles that U.S. troops faced. As the infiltration of American ground troops into Vietnam failed to bring about a quick victory, a mostly supportive U.S. population began to question its government's war policy.

The Big Idea

The United States sent troops to fight in Vietnam, but the war quickly turned into a stalemate.

Why It Matters Now

Since Vietnam, Americans are more aware of the positive and negative effects of using U.S. troops in foreign conflicts.

Key Terms and People

Robert McNamara

Dean Rusk

William Westmoreland

Army of the Republic of Vietnam (ARVN)

napalm

Agent Orange

search-and-destroy mission

credibility gap

SS.912.A.1.2; SS.912.A.1.4; SS.912.A.1.7; SS.912.A.6.13; SS.912.A.6.14; SS.912.A.7.4; SS.912.H.1.1; SS.912.H.1.5; LAFS.1112.RH.1.2; LAFS.1112.RH.4.10

Johnson Increases U.S. Involvement

Much of the nation supported Lyndon Johnson's determination to contain communism in Vietnam. In the years following 1965, President Johnson began sending large numbers of American troops to fight alongside the South Vietnamese.

Lyndon B. Johnson celebrates his victory in the 1964 presidential election.

STRONG SUPPORT FOR CONTAINMENT Even after Congress had approved the Tonkin Gulf Resolution, President Johnson opposed sending U.S. ground troops to Vietnam. Johnson's victory in the 1964 presidential election was due in part to charges that his Republican opponent, Barry Goldwater, was an anti-Communist who might push the United States into war with the Soviet Union. In contrast to Goldwater's heated, war-like language, Johnson's speeches were more moderate, yet he spoke determinedly about containing communism. He declared he was "not about to send American boys 9 or 10,000 miles away from home to do what Asian boys ought to be doing for themselves."

However, in March 1965 that is precisely what the president did. Working closely with his foreign-policy advisers, particularly Secretary of Defense **Robert McNamara** and Secretary of State **Dean Rusk**, President Johnson began dispatching tens of thousands of U.S. soldiers to fight in Vietnam. Some Americans viewed Johnson's decision as contradictory to his position during the presidential campaign. However, most were of the opinion that the president was protecting national security by following an established and popular policy of confronting communism anywhere in the world. Congress, as well as the American public, strongly supported Johnson's strategy. A 1965 poll showed that 61 percent of Americans supported the U.S. policy in Vietnam, while only 24 percent opposed.

There were dissenters within the Johnson administration, too. In October 1964 Undersecretary of State George Ball had argued against escalation, warning that "once on the tiger's back, we cannot be sure of picking the place to dismount." However, the president's closest advisers strongly urged escalation, believing the defeat of communism in Vietnam to be of vital importance to the future of America and the world. Dean Rusk stressed this view in a 1965 memo to President Johnson.

> *"The integrity of the U.S. commitment is the principal pillar of peace throughout the world. If that commitment becomes unreliable, the communist world would draw conclusions that would lead to our ruin and* almost certainly to a catastrophic war. *So long as the South Vietnamese are prepared to fight for themselves, we cannot abandon them without disaster to peace and to our interests throughout the world."*
>
> —Dean Rusk, quoted in *In Retrospect*

William Westmoreland
(1914–2005)

General Westmoreland retired from the military in 1972, but even in retirement, he could not escape the Vietnam War.

In 1982 CBS-TV aired a documentary entitled *The Uncounted Enemy: A Vietnam Deception*. The report, viewed by millions, asserted that Westmoreland and the Pentagon had deceived the U.S. government about the enemy's size and strength during 1967 and 1968 to make it appear that U.S. forces were winning the war.

Westmoreland, claiming he was the victim of "distorted, false, and specious information . . . derived

by sinister deception," filed a $120 million libel suit against CBS. The suit was eventually settled, with both parties issuing statements pledging mutual respect. CBS, however, stood by its story.

THE TROOP BUILDUP ACCELERATES By the end of 1965, the U.S. government had sent more than 180,000 Americans to Vietnam. The American commander in South Vietnam, General **William Westmoreland**, continued to request more troops. Westmoreland, a West Point graduate who had served in World War II and Korea, was less than impressed with the fighting ability of the South Vietnamese Army, or the **Army of the Republic of Vietnam (ARVN)**. The ARVN "cannot stand up to this pressure without substantial U.S. combat support on the ground," the general reported. "The only possible response is the aggressive deployment of U.S. troops." Throughout the early years of the war, the Johnson administration complied with Westmoreland's requests for additional forces; by 1967 the number of U.S. troops in Vietnam had climbed to about 500,000.

Reading Check
Contrast What differing opinions did Johnson's advisers have about Vietnam?

Fighting in the Jungle

The United States entered the war in Vietnam believing that its superior weaponry would lead it to victory over the Vietcong. However, the jungle terrain and the enemy's guerrilla tactics quickly turned the war into a frustrating stalemate.

AN ELUSIVE ENEMY Because the Vietcong lacked the high-powered weaponry of the American forces, they used hit-and-run and ambush tactics, as well as a keen knowledge of the jungle terrain, to their advantage. Moving secretly in and out of the general population, the Vietcong destroyed the notion of a traditional frontline by attacking U.S. troops in both the cities and the countryside. Because some of the enemy lived amidst the civilian population, it was difficult for U.S. troops to discern friend from foe. A woman selling soft drinks to U.S. soldiers might be a Vietcong spy. A boy standing on the corner might be ready to throw a grenade.

Adding to the Vietcong's elusiveness was a network of elaborate tunnels that allowed them to withstand airstrikes and to launch surprise attacks and then disappear quickly. Connecting villages throughout the countryside, the tunnels became home to many guerrilla fighters. "The more the Americans tried to drive us away from our land, the more we burrowed into it," recalled Nguyen Quoc, a major in the Vietcong army.

In addition, the terrain was laced with countless booby traps and land mines. Because the exact location of the Vietcong was often unknown, U.S. troops laid land mines throughout the jungle. The Vietcong also laid their own traps and disassembled and reused U.S. mines. American soldiers marching through South Vietnam's jungles and rice paddies not only dealt with sweltering heat and leeches but also had to be cautious of every step. In a 1969 letter to his sister, Specialist Fourth Class Salvador Gonzalez described the tragic result from an unexploded U.S. bomb that the North Vietnamese Army had rigged.

> "Two days ago 4 guys got killed and about 15 wounded from the first platoon. Our platoon was 200 yards away on top of a hill. One guy was from Floral Park [in New York City]. He had five days left to go [before being sent home]. He was standing on a 250-lb. bomb that a plane had dropped and didn't explode. So the NVA [North Vietnamese Army] wired it up. Well, all they found was a piece of his wallet."
>
> —Salvador Gonzalez, quoted in *Dear America: Letters Home from Vietnam*

A FRUSTRATING WAR OF ATTRITION Westmoreland's strategy for defeating the Vietcong was to destroy their morale through a war of attrition, or the gradual wearing down of the enemy by continuous harassment. Introducing the concept of the body count, or the tracking of Vietcong killed in battle, the general believed that as the number of Vietcong dead rose, the guerrillas would inevitably surrender.

However, the Vietcong had no intention of quitting their fight. Despite the growing number of casualties and the relentless pounding from U.S. bombers, the Vietcong—who received supplies from China and the Soviet Union—remained defiant. Defense Secretary McNamara confessed his frustration to a reporter in 1966: "If I had thought they would take this punishment and fight this well, . . . I would have thought differently at the start."

General Westmoreland would say later that the United States never lost a battle in Vietnam. Whether or not the general's words were true, they underscored the degree to which America misunderstood its foe. The United States viewed the war strictly as a military struggle; the Vietcong saw it as a battle for their very existence, and they were ready to pay any price for victory.

THE BATTLE FOR "HEARTS AND MINDS" Another key part of the American strategy was to keep the Vietcong from winning the support of South Vietnam's rural population. Edward G. Lansdale, who helped found the fighting unit known as the U.S. Army Special Forces, or Green Berets, stressed the

War or Peace?

This photograph of a U.S. soldier wearing symbols of both war and peace illustrates how many U.S. soldiers struggled with their role in Vietnam. They were required to serve, but many wanted peace, not war.

Analyze Historical Sources

1. What symbols of war and peace is the soldier wearing?

2. How does the photograph reflect Americans' feelings about the war in Vietnam?

plan's importance. "Just remember this. Communist guerrillas hide among the people. If you win the people over to your side, the communist guerrillas have no place to hide."

The campaign to win the "hearts and minds" of the South Vietnamese villagers proved more difficult than imagined. For instance, in their attempt to expose Vietcong tunnels and hideouts, U.S. planes dropped **napalm**, a gasoline-based bomb that set fire to the jungle. They also sprayed **Agent Orange**, a leaf-killing toxic chemical. The saturation use of these weapons often wounded civilians and left villages and their surroundings in ruins. Years later, many would blame Agent Orange for cancers suffered by Vietnamese civilians and American veterans.

U.S. soldiers conducted **search-and-destroy missions**, uprooting civilians with suspected ties to the Vietcong, killing their livestock, and burning villages. Many villagers fled into the cities or refugee camps, creating by 1967 more than 3 million refugees in the South. The irony of the strategy was summed up in February 1968 by a U.S. major whose forces had just leveled the town of Ben Tre: "We had to destroy the town in order to save it."

SINKING MORALE The frustrations of guerrilla warfare, the brutal jungle conditions, and the failure to make substantial headway against the enemy took their toll on the U.S. troops' morale. Philip Caputo, a marine lieutenant in Vietnam who later wrote several books about the war, summarized the soldiers' growing disillusionment: "When we marched into the rice paddies . . . we carried, along with our packs and rifles, the implicit convictions that the Vietcong could be quickly beaten. We kept the packs and rifles; the convictions, we lost."

As the war continued, American morale dropped steadily. Many soldiers turned to alcohol, marijuana, and other drugs. Low morale even led a few soldiers to murder their officers. Morale worsened during the later years of the war when soldiers realized they were fighting even as their government was negotiating a withdrawal.

Another obstacle was the continuing corruption and instability of the South Vietnamese government. Nguyen Cao Ky, a flamboyant air marshal, led the government from 1965 to 1967. Ky ignored U.S. pleas to retire in favor of an elected civilian government. Mass demonstrations began, and by May 1966 Buddhist monks and nuns were once again burning themselves in protest against the South Vietnamese government. South Vietnam was fighting a civil war within a civil war, leaving U.S. officials confused and angry.

FULFILLING A DUTY Most American soldiers, however, firmly believed in their cause—to halt the spread of communism. They took patriotic pride in fulfilling their duty, just as their fathers had done in World War II.

Most American soldiers fought courageously. Particularly heroic were the thousands of soldiers who endured years of torture and confinement as prisoners of war. In 1966 navy pilot Gerald Coffee's plane was shot down over North Vietnam. Coffee spent the next seven years—until he was released in 1973 as part of a cease-fire agreement—struggling to stay alive in an enemy prison camp.

> *"My clothes were filthy and ragged. . . . With no boots, my socks—which I'd been able to salvage—were barely recognizable. . . . Only a few threads around my toes kept them spread over my feet; some protection, at least, as I shivered through the cold nights curled up tightly on my morguelike slab. . . . My conditions and predicament were so foreign to me, so stifling, so overwhelming. I'd never been so hungry, so grimy, and in such pain."*
>
> —Gerald Coffee, quoted in *Beyond Survival*

Reading Check
Make Inferences In what way did the United States underestimate the Vietcong?

The Early War at Home

The Johnson administration thought the war would end quickly. As it dragged on, support began to waver, and Johnson's domestic programs began to unravel.

THE GREAT SOCIETY SUFFERS As the number of U.S. troops in Vietnam continued to mount, the war grew more costly, and the nation's economy began to suffer. The inflation rate, which was less than 2 percent through most of the early 1960s, more than tripled to 5.5 percent by 1969. In August 1967 President Johnson asked for a tax increase to help fund the war and to keep inflation in check. Congressional conservatives agreed but only after demanding and receiving a $6 billion reduction in funding for Great Society programs. Vietnam was slowly claiming an early casualty: Johnson's grand vision of domestic reform.

THE LIVING-ROOM WAR Through the media, specifically television, Vietnam became America's first "living-room war." During previous wars, the military had imposed tight restrictions on the press. In Vietnam, however, reporters and television crews often accompanied soldiers on patrol. The combat footage that appeared nightly on the news in millions of homes showed stark pictures that seemed to contradict the administration's optimistic war scenario.

Quoting body-count statistics that showed large numbers of Communists dying in battle, General Westmoreland continually reported that a Vietcong surrender was imminent. Defense Secretary McNamara backed up the general, saying that he could see "the light at the end of the tunnel."

The repeated television images of Americans in body bags told a different story, though. While Communists may have been dying, so too were

American Literature

Literature of the Vietnam War

The Vietnam War, which left a deep impression on America's soldiers and citizens alike, has produced its share of literature. In contrast to the tales of pride and glory that came out of previous wars, much of this literature expresses disillusionment and doubt. In the short story "How to Tell a True War Story" from *The Things They Carried*, Vietnam veteran Tim O'Brien reflects on the difficulty of telling the truth about the horror of war.

TIM O'BRIEN

How to Tell a True War Story

In any war story, but especially a true one, it's difficult to separate what happened from what seemed to happen. What seems to happen becomes its own happening and has to be told that way. The angles of vision are skewed. When a booby trap explodes, you close your eyes and duck and float outside yourself. When a guy dies, like Curt Lemon, you look away and then look back for a moment and then look away again. The pictures get jumbled; you tend to miss a lot. And then afterward, when you go to tell about it, there is always that surreal seemingness, which makes the story seem untrue, but which in fact represents the hard and exact truth as it seemed.

In many cases a true war story cannot be believed. If you believe it, be skeptical. It's a question of credibility. Often the crazy stuff is true and the normal stuff isn't, because the normal stuff is necessary to make you believe the truly incredible craziness.

In other cases you can't even tell a true war story. Sometimes it's just beyond telling.

—Tim O'Brien, from "How to Tell a True War Story"
in *The Things They Carried* (1990)

Analyze American Literature
Why does O'Brien feel it is difficult to accurately describe the experiences of war?

Americans— more than 16,000 between 1961 and 1967. Some critics charged that a **credibility gap** was growing between what the Johnson administration reported and what was really happening.

One critic was Senator J. William Fulbright, chairman of the powerful Senate Foreign Relations Committee. Fulbright, a former Johnson ally, charged the president with a "lack of candor" in portraying the war effort. In early 1966 the senator conducted a series of televised committee hearings in which he asked members of the Johnson administration to defend their Vietnam policies. The Fulbright hearings delivered few major revelations, but they did contribute to the growing doubts about the war. One woman appeared to capture the mood of Middle America when she told an interviewer, "I want to get out, but I don't want to give in."

By 1967 Americans were evenly split over supporting and opposing the war. However, a small force outside of mainstream America, mainly from the ranks of the nation's youth, already had begun actively protesting the war. Their voices would grow louder and capture the attention of the entire nation.

Reading Check
Analyze Effects
How and why did public opinion about the conflict in Vietnam change?

Lesson 2 Assessment

1. **Organize Information** Use a table to record key military tactics and weapons of the Vietcong and Americans.

	Vietcong	Americans
Tactics		
Weapons		

Which weapons and tactics do you think were most successful? Explain.

2. **Key Terms and People** For each key term or person in the lesson, write a sentence explaining its significance.

3. **Form Generalizations** What were the effects of the nightly TV coverage of the Vietnam War? How might Americans' opinions about the war been different had there been no television reporting? Support your answer with examples from the text.

   Think About:
   • the impact of television images of Americans in body bags
   • the Johnson administration's credibility gap

4. **Draw Conclusions** Why did Americans fail to win the "hearts and minds" of the Vietnamese?

5. **Contrast** In a paragraph, contrast the morale of the U.S. troops with that of the Vietcong. Use evidence from the text to support your response.

6. **Analyze Effects** What effect did the Vietnam War have on President Johnson's domestic agenda?

★
A Nation Divided

The Big Idea

Opponents of the government's war policy were pitted against those who supported it.

Why It Matters Now

The painful process of healing a divided nation continues today.

Key Terms and People

draft

New Left

Students for a Democratic Society (SDS)

Free Speech Movement (FSM)

dove

hawk

One American's Story

In 1969 Stephan Gubar, 22, was called for possible military service in Vietnam. Because he was a conscientious objector (CO), or someone who opposed war on the basis of religious or moral beliefs, he was granted 1-A-O status. While he would not be forced to carry a weapon, he still qualified for noncombatant military duty. As did many other conscientious objectors, Gubar received special training as a medic. He described the memorable day his training ended.

"The thing that stands out most was . . . being really scared, being in formation and listening to the names and assignments being called. . . . Even though I could hear that every time a CO's name came up, the orders were cut for Vietnam, I still thought there was a possibility I might not go. Then, when they called my name and said 'Vietnam,' . . . I went to a phone and I called my wife. It was a tremendous shock."

Stephan Gubar

—Stephan Gubar, quoted in *Days of Decision*

While many Americans proudly went off to war, some found ways to avoid the draft, and others simply refused to go. They opposed the war for a variety of reasons. Many believed that the U.S. military had no business fighting in Vietnam's civil war. Some said that the oppressive South Vietnamese regime was no better than the Communist regime it was fighting. Others argued that the United States could not police the entire globe and that war was draining American strength in other important parts of the world. Still others saw war simply as morally unjust.

SS.912.A.1.2; SS.912.A.1.4; SS.912.A.6.14; SS.912.A.7.9; SS.912.H.1.5; LAFS.1112.RH.1.2; LAFS.1112.RH.4.10; MAFS.K12.MP.3.1; MAFS.K12.MP.5.1

The Working Class Goes to War

The idea of fighting a war in a faraway place for what they believed was a questionable cause prompted a number of young Americans to resist going to Vietnam.

A "MANIPULATABLE" DRAFT Most soldiers who fought in Vietnam were called into combat under the country's Selective Service System, or **draft**, which had been established during World War I. Under this system, all males had to register with their local draft boards when they turned 18. All registrants were screened, and unless they were excluded—such as for medical reasons—in the event of war, men between the ages of 18 and 26 would be called into military service.

As Americans' doubts about the war grew, thousands of men attempted to find ways around the draft. One man characterized it as a "very manipulatable system." Some men sought out sympathetic doctors to grant medical exemptions. Others changed residences in order to stand before a more lenient draft board. Some Americans even joined the National Guard or Coast Guard, which often secured a deferment from service in Vietnam.

One of the most common ways to avoid the draft was to receive a college deferment, by which a young man enrolled in a university could put off his military service. Because university students during the 1960s tended to be white and financially well-off, many of the men who fought in Vietnam were lower-class whites or minorities who were less privileged economically. With almost 80 percent of American soldiers coming from lower economic levels, Vietnam was a working-class war.

AFRICAN AMERICANS IN VIETNAM Large numbers of African Americans traditionally enlisted in the military. For this reason, a high percentage of soldiers in combat positions were African American during the war's early years, when the fighting was done by volunteers. Therefore, the casualty rates

U.S. Military Personnel in Vietnam*

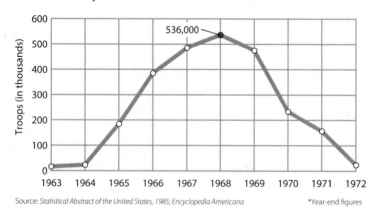

Source: *Statistical Abstract of the United States, 1985; Encyclopedia Americana*   *Year-end figures

Interpret Graphs
What years signaled a rapid increase in the deployment of U.S. troops?

Despite racial tensions, black and white soldiers fought side by side in Vietnam.

Two U.S. nurses rest at Cam Ranh Bay, the major entry point in South Vietnam for American supplies and troops.

of black soldiers at first were disproportionately high. During the first several years of the war, blacks accounted for more than 20 percent of American combat deaths despite representing only about 10 percent of the U.S. population. Some civil rights activists, including Martin Luther King Jr., lashed out against the "cruel irony" of American blacks dying for a country that still treated them as second-class citizens. The Defense Department took steps to correct that imbalance by instituting a draft lottery system in 1969.

In spite of the changes to the draft system, racial tensions ran high in many platoons. In some cases, the hostility led to violence. The racism that gripped many military units was yet another factor that led to low troop morale in Vietnam.

WOMEN JOIN THE RANKS While the U.S. military in the 1960s did not allow females to serve in combat, 10,000 women served in Vietnam—most of them as military nurses. Thousands more volunteered their services in Vietnam to the American Red Cross and the United Service Organizations (USO), which delivered hospitality and entertainment to the troops.

As the military marched off to Vietnam to fight against communist guerrillas, some of the men at home, as well as many women, waged a battle of their own. Tensions flared across the country as many of the nation's youths began to voice their opposition to the war.

Reading Check
Summarize How were U.S. forces mobilized for the war?

The Roots of Opposition

Even before 1965, students were becoming more active socially and politically. Throughout the 1960s young people participated in the civil rights struggle, while others pursued public service. This spirit of social change expressed itself in antiwar activism, too. As America became more involved in the war in Vietnam, college students across the country became a powerful and vocal group of protesters.

THE NEW LEFT The growing youth movement of the 1960s became known as the **New Left**. The movement was "new" in relation to the "old left" of the 1930s. The old left had generally tried to move the nation toward socialism, and, in some cases, communism. Although the New Left did not advocate socialism, the movement's followers did demand sweeping changes in American society.

Voicing these demands was one of the better-known New Left organizations, **Students for a Democratic Society (SDS)**, founded in 1960 by Tom Hayden and Al Haber. The group charged that corporations and large government institutions had taken over America. The SDS called for a restoration of "participatory democracy" and greater individual freedom.

In 1964 the **Free Speech Movement (FSM)** gained prominence at the University of California at Berkeley. The FSM grew out of a clash between students and administrators over free speech on campus. Led by Mario Savio, a philosophy student, the FSM focused its criticism on what it called the American "machine," the nation's faceless and powerful business and government institutions.

CAMPUS ACTIVISM Across the country, the ideas of the FSM and SDS quickly spread to college campuses. Students focused mainly on campus issues, such as dress codes, curfews, and dormitory regulations, as well as mandatory Reserve Officer Training Corps (ROTC) programs. At Fairleigh Dickinson University in New Jersey, students marched merely as "an expression of general student discontent."

Reading Check
Make Inferences
What concerns about American democratic society did the New Left voice?

With the onset of the Vietnam War, students across the country found a galvanizing issue and joined together in protest. By the mid-1960s, many youths believed the nation to be in need of fundamental change.

The Protest Movement Emerges

Throughout the spring of 1965, groups at a number of colleges began to host "teach-ins" to protest the war. At the University of Michigan, where only a year before President Johnson had announced his sweeping Great Society program, teachers and students now assailed his war policy. "This is no longer a casual form of campus spring fever," journalist James Reston noted about the growing demonstrations. As the war continued, the protests grew and divided the country.

Protestors march down Fifth Avenue in New York City to demonstrate against the Vietnam War in October 1965.

THE MOVEMENT GROWS In April 1965 SDS helped organize a march on Washington, DC, by some 20,000 protesters. By November of that year, a protest rally in Washington drew more than 30,000. Then, in February 1966 the Johnson administration changed deferments for college students. The government now required students to be in good academic standing in order to be granted a deferment. Campuses around the country erupted in protest. SDS called for civil disobedience at Selective Service centers and openly counseled students to flee to Canada or Sweden. By the end of 1969, SDS had chapters on nearly 400 campuses.

The antiwar movement grew beyond college campuses. Small numbers of returning veterans began to protest the war. Folk singers such as Pete Seeger, Joan Baez, Phil Ochs, and the trio Peter, Paul, and Mary used music as a popular protest vehicle. The number one song in September 1965 was "Eve of Destruction." In this song, vocalist Barry McGuire stressed the ironic fact that young men could be drafted at age 18 but had to be 21 to vote. Another popular antiwar song of the time was "I-Feel-Like-I'm-Fixin'-to-Die Rag" by Country Joe and the Fish. Written by bandleader Joe McDonald, a Vietnam veteran, this song sarcastically encouraged young men, politicians, businesses, and even parents to give their whole-hearted support to the war.

Not every Vietnam-era pop song about war was an antiwar song, however. At the top of the charts for five weeks in 1966 was "The Ballad of the Green Berets" by Staff Sergeant Barry Sadler of the U.S. Army Special Forces, known as the Green Berets:

Fighting soldiers from the sky,
Fearless men who jump and die,
Men who mean just what they say,
The brave men of the Green Beret.

The recording sold over a million copies in its first two weeks of release. It was *Billboard* magazine's song of the year.

FROM PROTEST TO RESISTANCE By 1967 the antiwar movement had intensified, with no sign of slowing down. "We were having no effect on U.S. policy," recalled one protest leader, "so we thought we had to up the ante." In the spring of 1967, nearly half a million protesters of all ages gathered in New York City's Central Park. Shouting "Burn cards, not people!" and "Hell, no, we won't go!" hundreds tossed their draft cards into a bonfire. A woman from New Jersey told a reporter, "So many of us are frustrated. We want to criticize this war because we think it's wrong, but we want to do it in the framework of loyalty."

Others were more radical in their view. David Harris, who would spend 20 months in jail for refusing to serve in Vietnam, explained his motives.

"Theoretically, I can accept the notion that there are circumstances in which you have to kill people. I could not accept the notion that Vietnam was one of those circumstances. And to me that left the option of either sitting by and watching what was an enormous injustice . . . or [finding] some way to commit myself against it. And the position that I felt comfortable with in committing myself against it was total non-cooperation—I was not going to be part of the machine."

—David Harris, quoted in *The War Within*

DIFFICULT DECISIONS

Resist the Draft or Serve Your Country?

As the fighting in Vietnam intensified, young men of draft age who opposed the war found themselves considering one of two options: register with the draft board and risk heading off to war, or find a way to avoid military service. Ways to avoid service included medical and educational deferments. But a great many men did not qualify for these. The choices that remained, such as fleeing the country, going to jail, or giving in and joining the ranks, came with a high price. Once a decision was made, there was no turning back.

1. Imagine you oppose the war and are called to serve in Vietnam. What decision would you make? Would you feel guilty if you avoided the draft? If you chose to serve, how would you view those who did not serve your country?

2. Do you think more young men would have been willing to serve had this been a different war? Explain.

Draft resistance continued from 1967 until President Nixon phased out the draft in the early 1970s. During these years, the U.S. government accused more than 200,000 men of draft offenses and imprisoned nearly 4,000 draft resisters. (Although some were imprisoned for four or five years, most won parole after 6 to 12 months.) Throughout these years, about 10,000 Americans fled, many to Canada.

In October 1967 a demonstration at Washington's Lincoln Memorial drew about 75,000 protesters. After listening to speeches, approximately 30,000 demonstrators locked arms for a march on the Pentagon in order "to disrupt the center of the American war machine," as one organizer explained. As hundreds of protesters broke past the military police and mounted the Pentagon steps, they were met by tear gas and clubs. About 1,500 demonstrators were injured and at least 700 arrested.

WAR DIVIDES THE NATION By 1967 it was clear that Americans were divided regarding the war. Those who strongly opposed the war and believed the United States should withdraw were known as **doves**. Feeling just as strongly that America should unleash much of its greater military force to win the war were the **hawks**.

Despite the visibility of the antiwar protesters, a majority of Americans in 1967 remained committed to the war. Others, while less certain about the proper U.S. role in Vietnam, were shocked to see protesters publicly criticize a war in which Americans were fighting and dying. A poll taken in December 1967 showed that 70 percent of Americans believed the war protests were "acts of disloyalty." A firefighter who lost his son in Vietnam articulated the bitter feelings a number of Americans felt toward the anti-war movement.

Document-Based Investigation Historical Source

Johnson Remains Determined

President Johnson faced criticism on both sides of the war debate. Doves criticized him for not withdrawing from Vietnam. Hawks accused him of not increasing military power rapidly enough. Johnson was dismissive of both groups and their motives. He defended his policy of slow escalation.

"We made our statement to the world of what we would do if we had Communist aggression in that part of the world in 1954. . . . We said we would stand with those people in the face of common danger. . . . Every country that I know in that area that is familiar with what is happening thinks it is absolutely essential that Uncle Sam keep his word and stay there until we can find an honorable peace. . . .

There has always been confusion, frustration, and difference of opinion in this country when there is a war going on. . . . We are going to have these differences. No one likes war. All people love peace. But you can't have freedom without defending it."

—Lyndon B. Johnson, from a press conference, November 17, 1967

Analyze Historical Sources

What are Johnson's justifications for continuing his policy of escalating U.S. involvement in Vietnam?

"I'm bitter. . . . It's people like us who give up our sons for the country. . . . The college types, the professors, they go to Washington and tell the government what to do. . . . But their sons, they don't end up in the swamps over there, in Vietnam. No sir. They're deferred, because they're in school. Or they get sent to safe places. . . . What bothers me about the peace crowd is that you can tell from their attitude, the way they look and what they say, that they don't really love this country."

—A firefighter, quoted in *Working-Class War*

Responding to antiwar posters, Americans who supported the government's Vietnam policy developed their own slogans: "Support our men in Vietnam" and "America—love it or leave it."

TURMOIL IN THE JOHNSON ADMINISTRATION Despite the division that engulfed the country during the early years of the war, President Johnson continued his policy of slow escalation. By the end of 1967, Johnson's approach—and the continuing stalemate—had begun to create turmoil within his own administration. In November, Defense Secretary Robert McNamara, a key architect of U.S. escalation in Vietnam, quietly announced he was resigning to become head of the World Bank. "It didn't add up," McNamara recalled later. "What I was trying to find out was how . . . the war went on year after year when we stopped the infiltration [from North Vietnam] or shrunk it and when we had a very high body count and so on. It just didn't make sense."

As it happened, McNamara's resignation came on the threshold of the most tumultuous year of the sixties. In 1968 the war—and Johnson's presidency—would take a drastic turn for the worse.

Reading Check
Summarize For what reasons did the protesters oppose the Vietnam War?

Lesson 3 Assessment

1. **Organize Information** Use a tree diagram to record examples of student organizations, issues, and demonstrations of the New Left.

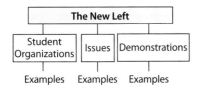

2. **Key Terms and People** For each key term in the lesson, write a sentence explaining its significance.

3. **Develop Historical Perspective** Would you have allied yourself with the hawks or with the doves? Give reasons that support your position.

   Think About:
   • the U.S. government's goals for fighting in Vietnam
   • the concerns of the antiwar movement

4. **Synthesize** Why did civil rights leaders call African Americans' fighting in Vietnam an "irony"?

5. **Evaluate** Do you agree that antiwar protests were "acts of disloyalty"? Why or why not?

6. **Analyze Primary Sources** This antiwar poster is a parody of recruiting posters from World War I. Why might the artist have chosen Uncle Sam to express the antiwar message? Compare the impact of this image to the traditional portrayal of Uncle Sam.

★
1968: A Tumultuous Year

The Big Idea

An enemy attack in Vietnam, two assassinations, and a chaotic political convention made 1968 an explosive year.

Why It Matters Now

Disturbing events in 1968 accentuated the nation's divisions, which are still healing in the 21st century.

Key Terms and People

Tet offensive

Clark Clifford

Robert Kennedy

Eugene McCarthy

Hubert Humphrey

George Wallace

One American's Story

On June 5, 1968, John Lewis, the first chairman of the Student Non-violent Coordinating Committee, fell to the floor and wept. Robert F. Kennedy, a leading Democratic candidate for president, had just been fatally shot. Two months earlier, when Martin Luther King Jr. had fallen victim to an assassin's bullet, Lewis had told himself he still had Kennedy. And now they both were gone. Lewis, who later became a congressman from Georgia, recalled the lasting impact of these assassinations.

"There are people today who are afraid, in a sense, to hope or to have hope again, because of what happened in . . . 1968. Something was taken from us. The type of leadership that we had in a sense invested in, that we had helped to make and to nourish, was taken from us. . . . Something died in all of us with those assassinations."
—John Lewis, quoted in *From Camelot to Kent State*

John Lewis

These violent deaths were but two of the traumatic events that rocked the nation in 1968. From a shocking setback in Vietnam to a chaotic Democratic National Convention in Chicago, the events of 1968 made it the most tumultuous year of a turbulent decade.

SS.912.A.1.4; SS.912.A.6.13; SS.912.A.6.14; SS.912.A.7.4; MAFS.K12.MP.1.1; MAFS.K12.MP.5.1

The Tet Offensive Turns the War

The year 1968 began with a daring surprise attack by the Vietcong on numerous cities in South Vietnam. The simultaneous strikes, while ending in military defeat for the Communist guerrillas, stunned the American public. Many people with moderate views began to turn against the war.

A SURPRISE ATTACK January 30 was the Vietnamese equivalent of New Year's Eve, the beginning of the lunar new year festivities known in Vietnam as Tet.

Throughout that day in 1968, villagers—taking advantage of a week-long truce proclaimed for Tet—streamed into cities across South Vietnam to celebrate their new year. At the same time, many funerals were being held for war victims. Accompanying the funerals were the traditional firecrackers, flutes, and, of course, coffins.

The coffins, however, contained weapons, and many of the villagers were Vietcong agents. That night, the Vietcong launched an overwhelming attack on over 100 towns and cities in South Vietnam, as well as 12 U.S. air bases. The fighting was especially fierce in Saigon and the former capital of Hue. The Vietcong even attacked the U.S. embassy in Saigon, killing five Americans. The **Tet offensive** continued for about a month before U.S. and South Vietnamese forces regained control of the cities.

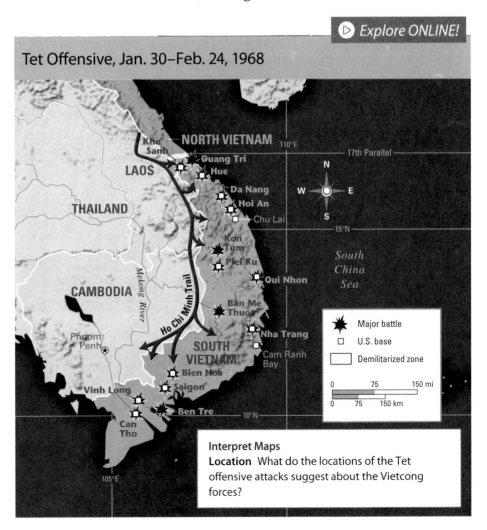

⊳ *Explore ONLINE!*

Tet Offensive, Jan. 30–Feb. 24, 1968

Interpret Maps
Location What do the locations of the Tet offensive attacks suggest about the Vietcong forces?

General Westmoreland declared the attacks an overwhelming defeat for the Vietcong, whose "well-laid plans went afoul." From a purely military standpoint, Westmoreland was right. The Vietcong lost about 32,000 soldiers during the month-long battle. The American and ARVN forces lost little more than 3,000.

TET CHANGES PUBLIC OPINION From a psychological—and political—standpoint, Westmoreland's claim could not have been more wrong. The Tet offensive greatly shook the American public, which had been told repeatedly and had come to believe that the enemy was close to defeat and that the United States would stop the spread of communism in Southeast Asia. Now the Pentagon's continued reports of favorable body counts—or massive Vietcong casualties—rang hollow. Daily, Americans saw the shocking images of attacks by an enemy that seemed to be everywhere.

In a matter of weeks, the Tet offensive changed millions of minds about the war. Despite the years of antiwar protest, a poll taken just before Tet showed that only 28 percent of Americans called themselves doves, while 56 percent claimed to be hawks. After Tet, both sides tallied 40 percent. The mainstream media, which had reported the war in a skeptical but generally balanced way, now openly criticized the war. One of the nation's most respected journalists, Walter Cronkite, told his viewers that it now seemed "more certain than ever that the bloody experience of Vietnam is to end in a stalemate."

Minds were also changing at the White House. To fill the defense secretary position left vacant by Robert McNamara's resignation, Johnson picked **Clark Clifford**, a friend and supporter of the president's Vietnam policy. However, after settling in and studying the situation, Clifford concluded that the war was unwinnable. "We seem to have a sinkhole," Clifford said. "We put in more—they match it. I see more and more fighting with more and more casualties on the U.S. side and no end in sight to the action."

Changing Opinions About the War

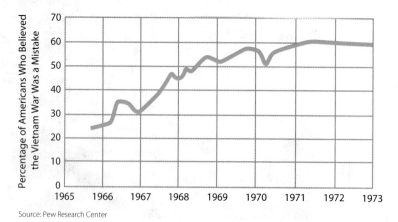

Source: Pew Research Center

Interpret Graphs
Between what two years did public opinion of the war change the most?

Following the Tet offensive, Johnson's popularity plummeted. In public opinion polls taken at the end of February 1968, nearly 60 percent of Americans disapproved of his handling of the war. Nearly half of the country now felt it had been a mistake to send American troops to Vietnam.

War weariness eventually set in, and 1968 was the watershed year. Johnson recognized the change, too. Upon learning of Cronkite's pessimistic analysis of the war, the president lamented, "If I've lost Walter, then it's over. I've lost Mr. Average Citizen."

Days of Loss and Rage

The growing division over Vietnam led to a shocking political development in the spring of 1968, a season in which Americans also endured two assassinations, a series of urban riots, and a surge in college campus protests.

JOHNSON WITHDRAWS Well before the Tet offensive, an antiwar coalition within the Democratic Party had sought a Democratic candidate to challenge Johnson in the 1968 primary elections. **Robert Kennedy**, John F. Kennedy's brother and a senator from New York, decided not to run, citing party loyalty. However, in November 1967, Minnesota senator **Eugene McCarthy** answered the group's call. He declared that he would run against Johnson on a platform to end the war in Vietnam. In the New Hampshire Democratic primary in March 1968, the little-known senator captured 42 percent of the vote. While Johnson won the primary with 48 percent of the vote, the slim margin of victory was viewed as a defeat for the president. Influenced by Johnson's perceived weakness at the polls, Robert Kennedy declared his candidacy for president. The Democratic Party had become a house divided.

In a televised address on March 31, 1968, Johnson announced a dramatic change in his Vietnam policy—the United States would seek negotiations to end the war. In the meantime, the policy of U.S. escalation would end. The bombing would eventually cease, and steps would be taken to ensure that the South Vietnamese played a larger role in the war.

The president paused and then ended his speech with a statement that shocked the nation. Declaring that he did not want the presidency to become "involved in the partisan divisions that are developing in this political year," Lyndon Johnson announced, "Accordingly, I shall not seek, and I will not accept, the nomination of my party for another term as your president." The president was stepping down from national politics. His grand plan for domestic reform was done in by a costly and divisive war. "That . . . war," Johnson later admitted, "killed the lady I really loved—the Great Society."

Reading Check
Analyze Issues Why did American support for the war change after the Tet offensive?

The Vietnam War and the divisiveness it caused took its toll on President Johnson.

VIOLENCE AND PROTEST GRIP THE NATION The Democrats—as well as the nation—were in for more shock in 1968. On April 4, America was rocked by the assassination of Martin Luther King Jr. in Memphis, Tennessee. In the weeks that followed, violence ripped through more than 100 U.S. cities as enraged followers of the slain civil rights leader burned buildings and destroyed neighborhoods.

Just two months later, a bullet cut down yet another popular national figure. Robert Kennedy had become a strong candidate in the Democratic primary, drawing support from minorities and urban Democratic voters. On June 4, Kennedy won the crucial California primary. Just after midnight of June 5, he gave a victory speech at a Los Angeles hotel. On his way out, he passed through the hotel's kitchen, where a young Palestinian immigrant, Sirhan Sirhan, was hiding with a gun. Sirhan, who later said he was angered by Kennedy's support of Israel, fatally shot the senator.

Jack Newfield, a speechwriter for Kennedy, described the anguish he and many Americans felt over the loss of two of the nation's leaders.

> "Things were not really getting better . . . we shall not overcome. . . . We had already glimpsed the most compassionate leaders our nation could produce, and they had all been assassinated. And from this time forward, things would get worse: Our best political leaders were part of memory now, not hope."
>
> —Jack Newfield, quoted in *Nineteen Sixty-Eight*

Meanwhile, students at the nation's college campuses continued to stage protests. During the first six months of 1968, almost 40,000 students on more than 100 campuses took part in more than 200 major demonstrations. Many of the demonstrations continued to target U.S. involvement in the Vietnam War. But students also clashed with university officials over campus and social issues. A massive student protest at Columbia University in New York City held the nation's attention for a week in April. There, students protested the university's policies and its relationship to the community where it was located. Protesters took over several buildings, but police eventually restored order and arrested nearly 900 protesters.

Recalling the violence and turmoil that plagued the nation in 1968, the journalist and historian Garry Wills wrote, "There was a sense everywhere . . . that things were giving way. That [people] had not only lost control of [their] history, but might never regain it."

A Turbulent Race for President

The chaos and violence of 1968 climaxed in August, when thousands of antiwar demonstrators converged on the city of Chicago to protest at the Democratic National Convention. The convention, which featured a bloody riot between protesters and police, fractured the Democratic Party and thus helped a nearly forgotten Republican win the White House.

Reading Check
Analyze Issues
Why was 1968 characterized as a year of "lost control" in America?

TURMOIL IN CHICAGO With Lyndon Johnson stepping down and Robert Kennedy gone, the 1968 Democratic presidential primary race pitted Eugene McCarthy against **Hubert Humphrey**, Johnson's vice-president. McCarthy, while still popular with the nation's antiwar segment, had little chance of defeating Humphrey, a loyal party man who had President Johnson's support. During the last week of August, the Democrats gathered at their convention in Chicago, supposedly to choose a candidate. In reality, Humphrey's nomination had already been determined. Many antiwar activists were upset by this decision.

As the delegates arrived in Chicago, so, too, did nearly 10,000 protesters. Led by men such as SDS veteran Tom Hayden, many demonstrators sought to pressure the Democrats into adopting an antiwar platform. Others came to voice their displeasure with Humphrey's nomination. Still others, known as Yippies (members of the Youth International Party), had come hoping to provoke violence that might discredit the Democratic Party. Chicago's mayor, Richard J. Daley, was determined to keep the protesters under control. With memories of the nationwide riots after King's death still fresh, Daley mobilized 12,000 Chicago police officers and over 5,000 National Guard. "As long as I am mayor," Daley vowed, "there will be law and order."

Order, however, soon collapsed. On August 28, as delegates cast votes for Humphrey, protesters were gathering in a downtown park to march on the convention. With television cameras focused on them, police moved into the crowd. Officers sprayed the protesters with Mace and beat them with nightsticks. Many protesters tried to flee, while others retaliated, pelting the riot-helmeted police with rocks and bottles. "The whole world is watching!" protesters shouted, as police attacked demonstrators and bystanders alike.

The rioting soon spilled out of the park and into the downtown streets. One nearby hotel, observed a *New York Times* reporter, became a makeshift aid station.

Vocabulary
platform a formal declaration of the principles on which a political party makes its appeal to the public

Chicago police attempt to disperse antiwar demonstrators at the 1968 Democratic convention.

> *"Demonstrators, reporters, McCarthy workers, doctors, all began to stagger into the [hotel] lobby, blood streaming from face and head wounds. The lobby smelled from tear gas, and stink bombs dropped by the Yippies. A few people began to direct the wounded to a makeshift hospital on the fifteenth floor, the McCarthy staff headquarters."*
> —J. Anthony Lukas, quoted in *Decade of Shocks*

Disorder of a different kind reigned inside the convention hall, where delegates bitterly debated an antiwar plank in the party platform. When word of the riot filtered into the hall, delegates angrily shouted at Mayor Daley, who was present as a delegate. Daley returned their shouts. The whole world was indeed watching—on their televisions. The images of the Democrats as a party of disorder became etched in the minds of millions of Americans.

NIXON TRIUMPHS One beneficiary of this turmoil was Republican presidential candidate Richard M. Nixon. By 1968 Nixon had achieved one of the greatest political comebacks in American politics. After his loss to Kennedy

Election of 1968

Party	Candidate	Electoral votes	Popular votes
Republican	Richard M. Nixon	301	31,785,480
Democratic	Hubert H. Humphrey	191	31,275,166
American Independent	George C. Wallace	46	9,906,473

Not shown:
3 Alaska
4 Hawaii
3 District of Columbia

Interpret Charts
1. In what region did Wallace carry states?
2. By how many electoral votes did Nixon defeat Humphrey?

Reading Check
Summarize How did the election of 1968 illustrate divisions in American society?

in the presidential race of 1960, Nixon tasted defeat again in 1962 when he ran for governor of California. His political career all but dead, Nixon joined a New York law firm. But he never strayed far from politics. In 1966 Nixon campaigned for Republican candidates in congressional elections, helping them to win back 47 House seats and 3 Senate seats from Democrats. In 1968 Nixon announced his candidacy for president and won the party's nomination.

During the presidential race, Nixon campaigned on a promise to restore law and order. This promise appealed to many middle-class Americans tired of years of riots and protests. He also promised, in vague but appealing terms, to end the war in Vietnam. Nixon's candidacy was helped by the entry of former Alabama governor **George Wallace** into the race as a third-party candidate. Wallace, a Democrat running on the American Independent Party ticket, was a longtime champion of school segregation and states' rights. Labeled the "white backlash" candidate, Wallace captured five southern states. In addition, he attracted a surprisingly high number of northern white working-class voters disgusted with inner-city riots and antiwar protests.

In the end, Nixon defeated Humphrey and inherited the quagmire in Vietnam. He eventually would end America's involvement in Vietnam, but not before his war policies created even more protest and further uproar within the country.

Lesson 4 Assessment

1. **Organize Information** Create a timeline of major events that occurred in 1968.

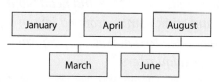

Which event do you think was most significant? Explain.

2. **Key Terms and People** For each key term or person in the lesson, write a sentence explaining its significance.

3. **Analyze Events** Why do you think the Tet offensive turned so many Americans against the war? Do you agree that the Tet offensive was a turning point in the war? Why or why not?

Think About:
- what American leaders had told the public about the war prior to Tet
- how public opinion changed after the Tet offensive

4. **Make Inferences** What do you think President Johnson meant when he said "If I've lost Walter [Cronkite], then it's over. I've lost Mr. Average Citizen"? Explain.

5. **Synthesize** What advice would you have given President Johnson about how to proceed with the war in 1968? Why?

The End of the War and Its Legacy

The Big Idea
President Nixon instituted his Vietnamization policy, and the long war finally came to an end.

Why It Matters Now
Since Vietnam, the United States considers more carefully the risks to its own interests before intervening in foreign affairs.

Key Terms and People
Richard Nixon

Henry Kissinger

Vietnamization

silent majority

My Lai

Kent State University

Pentagon Papers

War Powers Act

SS.912.A.1.2; SS.912.A.1.4; SS.912.A.6.13; SS.912.A.6.14; SS.912.A.6.15; SS.912.A.7.4; SS.912.A.7.10; MAFS.K12.MP.1.1; MAFS.K12.MP.5.1

One American's Story

Alfred S. Bradford served in Vietnam from September 1968 to August 1969. A member of the 25th Infantry Division, he was awarded several medals, including the Purple Heart, given to soldiers wounded in battle. One day, Bradford's eight-year-old daughter, Elizabeth, inquired about his experience in Vietnam. "Daddy, why did you do it?" she asked. Bradford recalled what he had told himself.

A U.S. soldier sits near Quang Tri, Vietnam, during a break in the fighting.

"Vietnam was my generation's adventure. I wanted to be part of that adventure and I believed that it was my duty as an American, both to serve my country and particularly not to stand by while someone else risked his life in my place. I do not regret my decision to go, but I learned in Vietnam not to confuse America with the politicians elected to administer America, even when they claim they are speaking for America, and I learned that I have a duty to myself and to my country to exercise my own judgment based upon my own conscience."
—Alfred S. Bradford, quoted in *Some Even Volunteered*

The legacy of the war was profound; it dramatically affected the way Americans viewed their government and the world. Richard Nixon had promised in 1968 to end the war, but it would take nearly five more years—and over 20,000 more American deaths—to end the nation's involvement in Vietnam.

President Nixon and Vietnamization

In the summer of 1969, newly elected president **Richard Nixon** announced the first U.S. troop withdrawals from Vietnam. "We have to get rid of the nightmares we inherited," Nixon later told reporters. "One of the nightmares is war without end." However, even as Nixon pulled out the troops, he continued the war against North Vietnam. This was a policy that some critics would charge prolonged the "war without end" for several more bloody years.

THE PULLOUT BEGINS As President Nixon settled into the White House in January 1969, negotiations to end the war in Vietnam were going nowhere. There were a number of complex issues to be resolved, and each party had different priorities. The United States and South Vietnam insisted that all North Vietnamese forces withdraw from the South. The Americans also wanted the government of Nguyen Van Thieu, then South Vietnam's ruler, to remain in power. The North Vietnamese and Vietcong demanded that U.S. troops withdraw from South Vietnam. The Communists also wanted the Thieu government to step aside for a coalition government that would include the Vietcong.

In the midst of the stalled negotiations, President Nixon conferred with National Security Advisor **Henry Kissinger** on a plan to end America's involvement in Vietnam. Kissinger, a German emigrant who had earned three degrees from Harvard, was an expert on international relations. Their plan, known as **Vietnamization**, called for the gradual withdrawal of U.S. troops in order for the South Vietnamese to take on a more active combat role in the war. By August 1969 the first 25,000 U.S. troops had returned home from Vietnam. Over the next three years, the number of American troops in Vietnam dropped from more than 500,000 to less than 25,000.

Total U.S. Bomb Tonnage

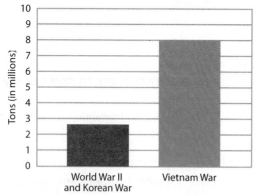

Source: *Vietnam War Almanac*

U.S. Aerial Bomb Tonnage, 1965–1971

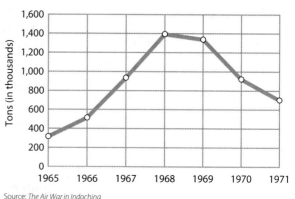

Source: *The Air War in Indochina*

Interpret Graphs

1. Examine the line graph. How did the Vietnam conflict change over time?

2. Based on the bar graph, what type of war would you say was fought in Vietnam?

"PEACE WITH HONOR"   Part of Nixon and Kissinger's Vietnamization policy was aimed at establishing what the president called a "peace with honor." Nixon intended to maintain U.S. dignity in the face of its withdrawal from war. A further goal was to preserve U.S. clout at the negotiation table. Nixon still demanded that the South Vietnamese government remain intact. With this objective—and even as the pull-out had begun—Nixon secretly ordered a massive bombing campaign against supply routes and bases in North Vietnam. The president also ordered that bombs be dropped on the neighboring countries of Laos and Cambodia, which held a number of Vietcong sanctuaries. Nixon told his aide H. R. Haldeman that he wanted the enemy to believe he was capable of anything.

"I call it the madman theory, Bob. . . . I want the North Vietnamese to believe I've reached the point where I might do anything to stop the war. We'll just slip the word to them that 'for God's sake, you know Nixon is obsessed about Communists. We can't restrain him when he's angry—and he has his hand on the nuclear button'—and Ho Chi Minh himself will be in Paris in two days begging for peace."

—Richard M. Nixon, quoted in *The Price of Power*

Reading Check
Synthesize What was the impact of Vietnamization on the United States?

Trouble Continues on the Home Front

While many average Americans did support the president, the events of the war continued to divide the country. Antiwar activists opposed Nixon's plan for Vietnamization because it did not immediately end the war. Yet Nixon was convinced that he had the firm backing of what he called the **silent majority**—moderate, mainstream Americans who he believed disapproved of antiwar protesters and quietly supported the U.S. efforts in Vietnam. Seeking to win support for his war policies, President Nixon spoke to the nation on November 3, 1969, urging Americans to help him uphold the nation's responsibilities to defend and spread democracy.

"Let historians not record that when America was the most powerful nation in the world we passed on the other side of the road and allowed the last hopes for peace and freedom of millions of people to be suffocated by the forces of totalitarianism.

And so tonight—to you, the great silent majority of my fellow Americans—I ask for your support. . . . Let us be united for peace. Let us also be united against defeat. Because let us understand: North Vietnam cannot defeat or humiliate the United States. Only Americans can do that."

—Richard M. Nixon, from "Address to the Nation on the War in Vietnam," November 3, 1969

THE MY LAI MASSACRE In November 1969 Americans learned of a shocking event. That month, *New York Times* correspondent Seymour Hersh reported that on March 16, 1968, a U.S. platoon under the command of Lieutenant William Calley Jr. had massacred innocent civilians in the small village of **My Lai** (mē′ lī′) in northern South Vietnam. Calley was searching for Vietcong rebels. Finding no sign of the enemy, the troops rounded up the villagers and shot more than 200 Vietnamese—mostly women, children, and elderly men. "We all huddled them up," recalled 22-year-old Private Paul Meadlo. "I poured about four clips into the group. . . . The mothers was hugging their children. . . . Well, we kept right on firing."

The troops insisted that they were not responsible for the shootings because they were only following Lieutenant Calley's orders. When asked what his directive had been, one soldier answered, "Kill anything that breathed." Twenty-five army officers were charged with some degree of responsibility. But only Calley was convicted and imprisoned.

President Nixon points to a map of Cambodia during a televised speech on April 30, 1970. His television appearances shaped public opinions about the war.

INVADING CAMBODIA AND LAOS Despite the shock over My Lai, the country's mood by 1970 seemed to be less explosive. American troops were on their way home. It appeared that the war was finally winding down.

On April 30, 1970, President Nixon announced that U.S. troops had invaded Cambodia to clear out North Vietnamese and Vietcong supply centers. The president defended his action: "If when the chips are down, the world's most powerful nation acts like a pitiful, helpless giant, the forces of totalitarianism and anarchy will threaten free nations . . . throughout the world." The following year, the United States attacked Communist supply routes in Laos. The campaign did not disrupt North Vietnamese operations, but it destroyed some ARVN military units.

News of the events in Cambodia and Laos triggered more student protests. In what became the first general student strike in the nation's history, more than 1.5 million students closed down some 1,200 campuses. The president of Columbia University called the month that followed the Cambodian invasion "the most disastrous month of May in the history of . . . higher education."

VIOLENCE ON CAMPUS Disaster struck hardest at **Kent State University** in Ohio, where a massive student protest led to the burning of the ROTC building. In response to the unrest, the local mayor called in the National Guard. On May 4, 1970, the Guards fired live ammunition into a crowd of campus protesters who were hurling rocks at them. The gunfire wounded nine people and killed four. Two of the victims had not even participated in the rally.

Ten days later, similar violence rocked the mostly all-black college of Jackson State in Mississippi. National Guardsmen there confronted a group of antiwar demonstrators and fired on the crowd after several bottles were thrown. In the hail of bullets, 12 students were wounded and 2 were killed, both innocent bystanders.

Kent State Shooting

Photographer John Filo was a senior at Kent State University when antiwar demonstrations rocked the campus. When the National Guard began firing at student protesters, Filo began shooting pictures, narrowly escaping a bullet himself. As he continued to document the horrific scene, a girl running to the side of a fallen student caught his eye. Just as she dropped to her knees and screamed, Filo snapped a photograph that would later win the Pulitzer Prize and become one of the most memorable images of the decade.

Analyze Historical Sources

1. What do you think is the most striking element of this photograph? Explain.

2. Why do you think this photograph remains a symbol of the Vietnam War era today?

In a sign that America still remained sharply divided about the war, the country hotly debated the campus shootings. Polls indicated that many Americans supported the National Guard. Respondents claimed that the students "got what they were asking for." The weeks following the campus turmoil brought new attention to a group known as "hardhats," construction workers and other blue-collar Americans who supported the U.S. government's war policies. In May 1970 nearly 100,000 members of the Building and Construction Trades Council of New York held a rally outside city hall to support the government.

THE PENTAGON PAPERS Nixon lost significant political support when he invaded Vietnam's neighbors. By first bombing and then invading Cambodia without even notifying Congress, the president stirred anger on Capitol Hill. On December 31, 1970, Congress repealed the Tonkin Gulf Resolution. This resolution had given the president near independence in conducting policy in Vietnam.

Support for the war eroded even further when in June 1971 former Defense Department worker Daniel Ellsberg leaked a 7,000-page document that became known as the **Pentagon Papers**. Written for Defense Secretary Robert McNamara in 1967–1968, the Pentagon Papers revealed among other things that the government had drawn up plans for entering the war even as President Lyndon Johnson promised that he would not send American troops to Vietnam. Furthermore, the papers showed that there was never any plan to end the war as long as the North Vietnamese persisted.

The Nixon administration tried unsuccessfully to block the publication of the papers, citing national security concerns. They even charged Ellsberg with felony acts of revealing national security secrets. Murray Gurfein, a U.S. District Court judge, expressed his thoughts about the case.

"The security of the Nation is not at the ramparts alone. Security also lies in the value of our free institutions. A cantankerous press, an obstinate press, an ubiquitous press, must be suffered by those in authority in order to preserve the even greater values of freedom of expression and the right of the people to know. These are troubled times. There is no greater safety valve for discontent and cynicism about the affairs of government than freedom of expression in any form."
—Murray Gurfein, from *United States v. New York Times Company*, 1971

In the end, the Supreme Court ruled that the press had a constitutional right to publish the classified information. For many Americans, the Pentagon Papers confirmed their belief that the government had not been honest about its war intentions. This led many to question the United States' policy of supporting any and all anticommunist governments. The document, while not particularly damaging to the Nixon administration, supported what opponents of the war had been saying.

Reading Check
Analyze Issues How did the campus shootings demonstrate the continued divisions within the country?

The Long War Ends

In March 1972 the North Vietnamese launched their largest attack on South Vietnam since the Tet offensive in 1968. President Nixon responded by ordering a massive bombing campaign against North Vietnamese cities. He also ordered that mines be laid in Haiphong harbor, the North's largest harbor. Soviet and Chinese ships used the harbor to supply North Vietnam. The Communists "have never been bombed like they are going to be bombed this time," Nixon vowed. The bombings halted the North Vietnamese attack, but the grueling stalemate continued. It was after this that the Nixon administration took steps to finally end America's involvement in Vietnam.

"PEACE IS AT HAND" By the middle of 1972, the country's growing social division and the looming presidential election prompted the Nixon administration to change its negotiating policy. Polls showed that more than 60 percent of Americans in 1971 thought that the United States should withdraw all troops from Vietnam by the end of the year.

Henry Kissinger, the president's adviser for national security affairs, served as Nixon's top negotiator in Vietnam. Since 1969, Kissinger had been meeting privately with North Vietnam's chief negotiator, Le Duc Tho. Eventually, Kissinger dropped his insistence that North Vietnam withdraw all its troops from the South before the complete withdrawal of American troops. On October 26, 1972, days before the presidential election, Kissinger announced, "Peace is at hand."

Henry Kissinger (1923–)

Henry Kissinger, who helped negotiate America's withdrawal from Vietnam and who later would help forge historic new relations with China and the Soviet Union, held a deep interest in the concept of power. "You know," he once noted, "most of these world leaders, you wouldn't want to know socially. Mostly they are intellectual mediocrities. The thing that is interesting about them is . . . their power."

At first, Kissinger seemed an unlikely candidate to work for Richard Nixon. Kissinger declared, "That man Nixon is not fit to be president." However, the two became trusted colleagues.

THE FINAL PUSH President Nixon won reelection. But the promised peace proved to be elusive. The Thieu regime, alarmed at the prospect of North Vietnamese troops stationed in South Vietnam, rejected Kissinger's plan. Talks broke off on December 16. Two days later, the president unleashed a ferocious bombing campaign against Hanoi and Haiphong, the two largest cities in North Vietnam. In what became known as the "Christmas bombings," U.S. planes dropped 100,000 bombs over the course of 11 straight days. The bombers paused only on Christmas Day.

At this point, calls to end the war resounded from the halls of Congress as well as from Beijing and Moscow. Everyone, it seemed, had finally grown weary of the war. The warring parties returned to the peace table. On January 27, 1973, the United States signed an "Agreement on Ending the War and Restoring Peace in Vietnam." Under the agreement, North Vietnamese troops would remain in South Vietnam. However, Nixon promised to respond "with full force" to any violation of the peace agreement. On March 29, 1973, the last group of U.S. combat troops left for home. For America, the Vietnam War had ended.

THE FALL OF SAIGON The war itself, however, raged on. Within months of the United States' departure, the cease-fire agreement between North and South Vietnam collapsed. In March 1975, after several years of fighting, the North Vietnamese launched a full-scale invasion against the South. Thieu appealed to the United States for help. America provided economic aid but refused to send troops. Soon thereafter, President Gerald Ford—who assumed the presidency after the Watergate scandal forced President Nixon to resign—gave a speech in which he captured the nation's attitude toward the war:

> "America can regain its sense of pride that existed before Vietnam. But it cannot be achieved by refighting a war that is finished as far as America is concerned."
>
> —Gerald Ford, from a speech at Tulane University, April 23, 1975

Reading Check
Summarize Explain what led to the agreement to end the war in Vietnam.

On April 30, 1975, North Vietnamese tanks rolled into Saigon and captured the city. Soon after, South Vietnam surrendered to North Vietnam.

The War Leaves a Painful Legacy

The Vietnam War exacted a terrible price from its participants. In all, 58,000 Americans were killed and some 303,000 were wounded. North and South Vietnamese deaths topped 2 million. In addition, the war left Southeast Asia highly unstable. This led to further war in Cambodia. In America, a divided nation attempted to come to grips with an unsuccessful war. In the end, the conflict in Vietnam left many Americans with a more cautious outlook on foreign affairs and a more cynical attitude toward their government.

AMERICAN VETERANS COPE BACK HOME While families welcomed home their sons and daughters, the nation as a whole extended a cold hand to its returning Vietnam veterans. There were no brass bands, no victory parades, no cheering crowds. Instead, many veterans faced indifference or even hostility from an America still torn and bitter about the war. Lily Jean Lee Adams, who served as an army nurse in Vietnam, recalled arriving in America in 1970 while still in uniform.

> *"In the bus terminal, people were staring at me and giving me dirty looks. I expected the people to smile, like, 'Wow, she was in Vietnam, doing something for her country—wonderful.' I felt like I had walked into another country, not my country. So I went into the ladies' room and changed."*
>
> —Lily Jean Lee Adams, quoted in *A Piece of My Heart*

Many Vietnam veterans readjusted successfully to civilian life. However, about 15 percent of the 3.3 million soldiers who served developed

Lieutenant Colonel Robert Stirm, a returning POW, receives a warm welcome from his family in 1973. The longest-held Vietnam POW was Lieutenant Everett Alvarez Jr. of California. He was imprisoned for more than eight years.

Each year, over 2 million people visit the Vietnam Veterans Memorial. Many leave remembrances that are collected nightly by park rangers and stored in a museum. Inscribed on the memorial are over 58,000 names of Americans who died in the war or were then still listed as missing in action.

post-traumatic stress disorder. Some had recurring nightmares about their war experiences. Many others suffered from severe headaches and memory lapses. Other veterans became highly apathetic or began abusing drugs or alcohol. Several thousand even committed suicide.

In an effort to honor the men and women who served in Vietnam, the U.S. government commissioned the Vietnam Veterans Memorial in Washington, DC. In 1981 the planners of the memorial held a competition to determine the memorial's design. Maya Ying Lin, a 21-year-old architecture student of Chinese descent, submitted the winning design. It consisted of two long, black granite walls on which are etched the names of the men and women who died or are missing in action. "I didn't want a static object that people would just look at," Lin said of her design, "but something they could relate to as on a journey, or passage, that would bring each to his own conclusions." Many Vietnam veterans, as well as their loved ones, have found visiting the memorial a deeply moving, even healing, experience.

FURTHER TURMOIL IN SOUTHEAST ASIA The end of the Vietnam War ushered in a new period of violence and chaos in Southeast Asia. In unifying Vietnam, the victorious Communists initially held out a conciliatory hand to the South Vietnamese. "You have nothing to fear," declared Colonel Bui Tin of the North Vietnamese Army.

However, the Communists soon imprisoned more than 400,000 South Vietnamese in harsh "reeducation," or labor, camps. As the Communists imposed their rule throughout the land, nearly 1.5 million people fled Vietnam. They included citizens who had supported the U.S. war effort, as well as business owners, whom the Communists expelled when they began nationalizing the country's business sector.

Also fleeing the country was a large group of poor Vietnamese, known as boat people because they left on anything from freighters to barges to rowboats. Their efforts to reach safety across the South China Sea often met with tragedy. Nearly 50,000 perished on the high seas due to exposure, drowning, illness, or piracy.

The people of Cambodia also suffered greatly after the war. The U.S. invasion of Cambodia had unleashed a brutal civil war in which a radical Communist group known as the Khmer Rouge, led by Pol Pot, seized power in 1975. In an effort to transform the country into a peasant society, the Khmer Rouge executed professionals and anyone with an education or foreign ties. During its reign of terror, the Khmer Rouge is believed to have killed at least 1 million Cambodians.

THE LEGACY OF VIETNAM Even after it ended, the Vietnam War remained a subject of great controversy for Americans. Many hawks continued to insist that the war could have been won if the United States had employed more military power. They also blamed the antiwar movement at home for destroying American morale. Doves countered that the North Vietnamese had displayed incredible resiliency and that an increase in U.S. military force would have resulted only in a continuing stalemate. In addition, doves argued that an unrestrained war against North Vietnam might have prompted a military reaction from China or the Soviet Union. As it was, the Vietnam War served as a proxy war. China and the Soviet Union provided money and weapons to the North Vietnamese. The United States directly supported the South Vietnamese. As such, it did not improve relations between the United States and China or the Soviet Union. But the war did serve as a replacement for full-scale conflict among these global rivals, preventing an escalation of hostility.

The war resulted in several major U.S. policy changes. First, the government abolished the draft, which had stirred so much antiwar sentiment. Also, the war was the impetus for the ratification of the Twenty-Sixth Amendment in 1971, which extended voting rights to Americans 18 years or older. During the war, young people had protested the unfairness of being drafted and sent to war without being allowed to vote.

After the war, the country also took steps to curb the president's war-making powers. Many thought both Johnson and Nixon had exceeded their constitutional powers by waging an undeclared war. So in November 1973 Congress passed the **War Powers Act**. It stipulated that a president must inform Congress within 48 hours of sending forces into a hostile area without a declaration of war. In addition, the troops may remain there no longer than 90

NOW & THEN

U.S. Recognition of Vietnam

In July 1995, more than 20 years after the Vietnam War ended, the United States extended full diplomatic relations to Vietnam. In announcing the resumption of ties with Vietnam, President Bill Clinton declared, "Let this moment . . . be a time to heal and a time to build." Demonstrating how the war still divides Americans, the president's decision drew both praise and criticism from members of Congress and veterans' groups.

In an ironic twist, Clinton nominated as ambassador to Vietnam a former prisoner of war from the Vietnam War, Douglas Peterson, a member of the U.S. House of Representatives from Florida. Peterson, an air force pilot, was shot down over North Vietnam in 1966 and spent six and a half years in a Hanoi prison.

days unless Congress approves the president's actions or declares war. Since its passage, the resolution's constitutionality has been the subject of debate. Some observers believe that it misinterprets the intention of the founders in granting Congress the power to declare war, taking too much power from the executive branch. Others feel it simply serves to clarify the separation of powers between the executive and legislative branches that the founders intended all along.

In a broader sense, the Vietnam War has significantly altered America's views on foreign policy. In what has been labeled the Vietnam syndrome, Americans now pause and consider possible risks to their own interests before deciding whether to intervene in the affairs of other nations. In part because of Vietnam, potential U.S. involvement in a foreign war comes under intense scrutiny today. Recent presidents have been pressured to present a case for a compelling national interest before sending U.S. forces to hostile overseas situations.

Finally, the war contributed to an overall cynicism among Americans about their government and political leaders that persists today. Americans grew suspicious of a government that could provide as much misleading information or conceal as many activities as the Johnson and Nixon administrations had done. Coupled with the Watergate scandal of the mid-1970s, the war diminished the optimism and faith in government that Americans felt during the Eisenhower and Kennedy years.

Reading Check
Contrast Contrast the two viewpoints regarding the legacy of the Vietnam War.

Lesson 5 Assessment

1. **Organize Information** In a web diagram, list the effects of the Vietnam War on America.

Vietnam War's Effect on America

Choose one effect to further explain in a paragraph.

2. **Key Terms and People** For each key term or person in the lesson, write a sentence explaining its significance.

3. **Analyze Effects** In your opinion, what was the main effect of the U.S. government's deception about its policies and military conduct in Vietnam? Support your answer with evidence from the text.

Think About:

• the contents of the Pentagon Papers
• Nixon's secrecy in authorizing military maneuvers

4. **Analyze Primary Sources** In his appeal to the "silent majority," what did President Nixon mean when he said that only Americans could "defeat or humiliate the United States"?

5. **Make Inferences** How would you account for the cold homecoming American soldiers received when they returned from Vietnam? Support your answer with reasons.

6. **Synthesize** In the end, do you think the United States' withdrawal from Vietnam was a victory for the United States or a defeat? Explain your answer.

Module 16 Assessment

Key Terms and People

For each key term or person below, write a sentence explaining its connection to the Vietnam War years.

1. Ho Chi Minh
2. Ngo Dinh Diem
3. Vietcong
4. William Westmoreland
5. napalm
6. Tet offensive
7. Robert Kennedy
8. Henry Kissinger
9. Vietnamization
10. Pentagon Papers

Main Ideas

Use your notes and the information in the module to answer the following questions.

Moving Toward Conflict

1. What was President Eisenhower's explanation of the domino theory?
2. What were the terms of the 1954 Geneva Accords? What was the purpose of the proposed 1956 elections?
3. How did the Tonkin Gulf Resolution lead to greater U.S. involvement in Vietnam?

U.S. Involvement and Escalation

4. Why did so much of the American public and many in the Johnson administration support U.S. escalation in Vietnam?
5. How was the Vietnam War different from previous wars for U.S. soldiers?
6. Why did the war begin to lose support at home? What contributed to the sinking morale of the U.S. troops?

A Nation Divided

7. What race-related problems existed for African American soldiers who served in the Vietnam War?

8. What issues surrounding the war divided the nation? How did the hawks and doves demonstrate these differences of opinion?

1968: A Tumultuous Year

9. What circumstances set the stage for President Johnson's public announcement that he would not seek another term as president?
10. What acts of violence occurred in the United States during 1968 that dramatically altered the mood of the country?
11. How did the Tet offensive differ from previous fighting in Vietnam? How did it cause many Americans to doubt that the United States would soon win the war?

The End of the War and Its Legacy

12. Briefly describe the military conflict in Vietnam soon after the last U.S. combat troops departed in 1973.
13. How well did Nixon's "Madman Theory" and Vietnamization strategy work? Explain.
14. Describe how and why the War Powers Act changed presidential power.
15. List the immediate effects and the more lasting legacies of America's involvement in the Vietnam War.

Critical Thinking

1. **Analyze Effects** Create a cause-and-effect diagram for each of these congressional measures: **a.** Tonkin Gulf Resolution (1964), **b.** repeal of the Tonkin Gulf Resolution (1970), **c.** War Powers Act (1973).

2. **Evaluate** Was the domino theory a good basis for American policy? Explain.
3. **Synthesize** In what ways was America's support of the Diem government a conflict of interests? Cite examples to support your answer.

4. **Analyze Motives** Do you think the United States was justified in supporting Ngo Dinh Diem over Ho Chi Minh? Why or why not?

5. **Draw Conclusions** Why do you think so many young Americans became so vocal in their condemnation of the Vietnam War?

6. **Develop Historical Perspective** Do you think the antiwar movement had a significant effect on American opinion toward the war? How were the goals of the antiwar protesters similar to those of other activists in the 1960s, such as those who worked for civil rights for women, African Americans, Hispanic Americans, and Native Americans?

7. **Analyze Events** Do you believe, as did General Westmoreland, that the Tet offensive was a defeat for the Communists?

8. **Compare** How did public support of the U.S. government and military during the Vietnam War compare with that of other conflicts?

9. **Analyze Effects** Of the lasting legacies of the Vietnam War, which do you think had the greatest impact on U.S. government? On the American people? Explain.

Engage with History

Recall the issues that you explored at the beginning of the module. Then write a paragraph that describes the domestic revolution in the United States during the Vietnam War years from the perspective of a group on the home front. Use evidence from the module to evaluate how the war impacted that group. In your paragraph, consider the impact of the antiwar movement, the draft, and the media.

Focus on Writing

Imagine you are a television news journalist. Write a script for a brief news report on the events of the Tet offensive or on the Democratic National Convention. Be sure to explain the significance of the event and to present multiple perspectives on it.

Multimedia Activity

Organize two teams to debate the United States' involvement in Vietnam. One team should argue for the side of the hawks, and the other team should argue on behalf of the doves. Use the Internet and other sources to research the arguments put forth by both sides, as well as how hawks and doves affected the political development of the nation. Then debate the issue before the class.

Module 17

Transitions and Conservatism

★

Essential Question

What was the defining moment of the 1970s through the 1990s in the United States?

About the Photograph: Richard Nixon leaves the White House after resigning as president on Friday, August 9, 1974.

In this module you will learn about an era of conservative policies during the 1970s, 1980s, and early 1990s with the Nixon, Ford, Reagan, and Bush administrations. You will also study the liberal policies of the Carter presidency.

▶ Explore ONLINE!

HISTORY

VIDEOS, including...

- Nixon and Watergate
- Richard Nixon: Impeachment
- Nixon's Farewell Speech
- Computers
- Jimmy Carter
- The Great Communicator
- Tiananmen Square

✓ Document-Based Investigations

✓ Graphic Organizers

✓ Interactive Games

✓ Carousel: The Inner Circle

✓ Image with Text Slider: Goals of the Conservative Movement

SS.912.A.1.2 Utilize a variety of primary and secondary sources to identify author, historical significance, audience, and authenticity to understand a historical period. **SS.912.A.1.4** Analyze how images, symbols, objects, cartoons, graphs, charts, maps, and artwork may be used to interpret the significance of time periods and events from the past. **SS.912.A.1.6** Use case studies to explore social, political, legal, and economic relationships in history. **SS.912.A.1.7** Describe various sociocultural aspects of American life including arts, artifacts, literature, education, and publications. **SS.912.A.2.4** Distinguish the freedoms guaranteed to African Americans and other groups with the 13th, 14th, and 15th Amendments to the Constitution. **SS.912.A.7.4** Evaluate the success of 1960s era presidents' foreign and domestic policies. **SS.912.A.7.8** Analyze significant Supreme Court decisions relating to integration, busing, affirmative action, the rights of the accused, and reproductive rights. **SS.912.A.7.10** Analyze the significance of Vietnam and Watergate on the government and people of the United States. **SS.912.A.7.11** Analyze the foreign policy of the United States as it relates to Africa, Asia, the Caribbean, Latin America, and the Middle East. **SS.912.A.7.12** Analyze political, economic, and social concerns that emerged at the end of the 20th century and into the 21st century. **SS.912.A.7.17** Examine key events and key people in Florida history as they relate to United States history. **SS.912.G.2.1** Identify the physical characteristics and the human characteristics that define and differentiate regions. **HE.912.C.2.4** Evaluate how public health policies and government regulations can influence health promotion and disease prevention. **LAFS.1112.RH.1.3** Evaluate various explanations for actions or events and determine which explanation best accords with textual evidence, acknowledging where the text leaves matters uncertain. **LAFS.1112.WHST.3.9** Draw evidence from informational texts to support analysis, reflection, and research.

Timeline of Events 1967–1992

▶ *Explore ONLINE!*

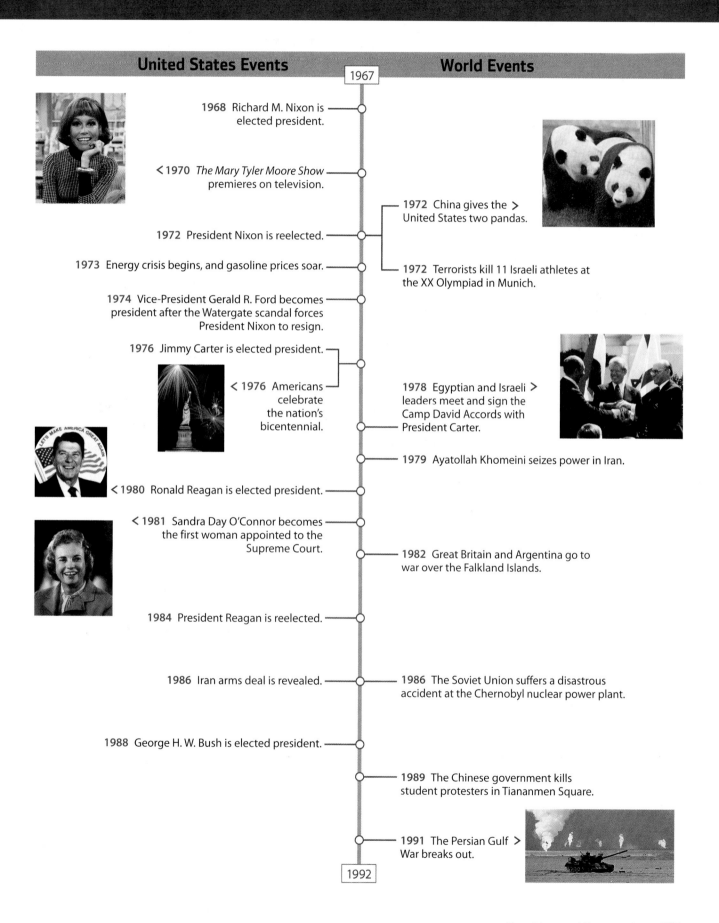

United States Events | World Events

1967

1968 Richard M. Nixon is elected president.

< **1970** *The Mary Tyler Moore Show* premieres on television.

1972 China gives the > United States two pandas.

1972 President Nixon is reelected.

1973 Energy crisis begins, and gasoline prices soar.

1972 Terrorists kill 11 Israeli athletes at the XX Olympiad in Munich.

1974 Vice-President Gerald R. Ford becomes president after the Watergate scandal forces President Nixon to resign.

1976 Jimmy Carter is elected president.

< **1976** Americans celebrate the nation's bicentennial.

1978 Egyptian and Israeli > leaders meet and sign the Camp David Accords with President Carter.

1979 Ayatollah Khomeini seizes power in Iran.

< **1980** Ronald Reagan is elected president.

< **1981** Sandra Day O'Connor becomes the first woman appointed to the Supreme Court.

1982 Great Britain and Argentina go to war over the Falkland Islands.

1984 President Reagan is reelected.

1986 Iran arms deal is revealed.

1986 The Soviet Union suffers a disastrous accident at the Chernobyl nuclear power plant.

1988 George H. W. Bush is elected president.

1989 The Chinese government kills student protesters in Tiananmen Square.

1991 The Persian Gulf > War breaks out.

1992

The Nixon Administration

The Big Idea

President Richard M. Nixon tried to steer the country in a conservative direction and away from federal control.

Why It Matters Now

American leaders of the early 1970s laid the foundations for the broad conservative base that exists today.

Key Terms and People

Richard M. Nixon

New Federalism

revenue sharing

Family Assistance Plan (FAP)

Southern Strategy

stagflation

OPEC (Organization of the Petroleum Exporting Countries)

One American's Story

In November 1968 **Richard M. Nixon** had just been elected president of the United States. He chose Henry Kissinger to be his special adviser on foreign affairs. In 1972, as the United States struggled to achieve an acceptable peace in Vietnam, Kissinger reflected on his relationship with Nixon.

President Nixon *(right)* confers with Henry Kissinger.

> "I . . . am not at all so sure I could have done what I've done with him with another president. . . . I don't know many leaders who would entrust to their aide the task of negotiating with the North Vietnamese, informing only a tiny group of people of the initiative."
>
> —Henry Kissinger, quoted in *The New Republic,* December 16, 1972

Nixon and Kissinger ended America's involvement in Vietnam, but as the war wound down, the nation seemed to enter an era of limits. The economic prosperity that had followed World War II was ending. President Nixon wanted to limit the federal government to reduce its power and to reverse some of Johnson's liberal policies. At the same time, he would seek to restore America's prestige and influence on the world stage—prestige that had been hit hard by the Vietnam experience.

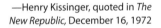

SS.912.A.1.2; SS.912.A.1.4; SS.912.A.7.4; SS.912.A.7.8; LAFS.1112.RH.1.2

Nixon's New Conservatism

President Richard M. Nixon entered office in 1969 determined to turn America in a more conservative direction. Toward that end, he tried to instill a sense of order into a nation still divided over the continuing Vietnam War.

NEW FEDERALISM One of the main items on President Nixon's agenda was to reduce the size and influence of the federal government. Nixon believed that Lyndon Johnson's Great Society programs had promoted greater federal involvement with social problems. He thought that this involvement had given the federal government too much responsibility. Nixon's plan, known as **New Federalism**, was to distribute a portion of federal power to state and local governments.

To implement this program, Nixon proposed a plan to give more financial freedom to local governments. Normally, the federal government told state and local governments how to spend their federal money. Under **revenue sharing**, state and local governments could spend their federal dollars however they saw fit within certain limitations. In 1972 the revenue-sharing bill, known as the State and Local Fiscal Assistance Act, became law.

In 1971 Nixon appointed the famous African American singer Sammy Davis Jr. to his National Advisory Council on Economic Opportunity.

WELFARE REFORM Nixon was not as successful, however, in his attempt to overhaul welfare. He believed welfare had grown unwieldy and inefficient. In 1969 the president advocated the so-called **Family Assistance Plan (FAP)**. Under the FAP, every family of four with no outside income would receive a basic federal payment. This payment would be $1,600 a year, with a provision to earn up to $4,000 a year in supplemental income. Unemployed participants would have to take job training and accept any reasonable work offered them. However, this requirement did not apply to mothers of preschool children.

Nixon presented the plan in conservative terms—as a program that would reduce the supervisory role of the federal government. It would also make welfare recipients responsible for their own lives. The House approved the plan in 1970. However, when the bill reached the Senate, lawmakers from both parties attacked it. Liberal legislators considered the minimum payments too low and the work requirement too strict. Conservatives objected to the guaranteed income. The bill went down in defeat.

NEW FEDERALISM WEARS TWO FACES Nixon's New Federalism enhanced several key federal programs as it dismantled others. Nixon needed to win support for his New Federalism program from a Democrat-controlled Congress, so he supported a number of congressional measures. As a result, federal spending increased for some social programs. Without fanfare, the Nixon administration increased Social Security, Medicare, and Medicaid payments. It also made food stamps more accessible.

However, the president also worked to dismantle some of the nation's social programs. Throughout his term, Nixon tried unsuccessfully to eliminate the Job Corps program that provided job training for the unemployed. In 1970 he vetoed a bill to provide additional funding for Housing and Urban Development. Nixon also turned to a little-used presidential practice called impoundment to deal with laws that he opposed. Nixon impounded, or

"Domestic Life"

Pulitzer Prize–winning cartoonist Paul Szep frequently used Nixon as the subject of his cartoons. Although President Nixon focused his domestic policy on dismantling a number of Great Society social programs, his chief interest was foreign policy.

Analyze Historical Sources

1. What does the cartoonist suggest about Nixon by showing him leaving with his bags packed?

2. Whom do the children represent in this cartoon?

withheld, necessary funds for programs. This delayed their implementation. By 1973 it was believed that Nixon had impounded almost $15 billion, affecting more than 100 federal programs. They included programs for health, housing, and education.

The federal courts eventually ordered the release of the impounded funds. They ruled that presidential impoundment was unconstitutional. Only Congress had the authority to decide how federal funds should be spent. Nixon did use his presidential authority to abolish the Office of Economic Opportunity. It had been a cornerstone of Johnson's antipoverty program.

LAW AND ORDER POLITICS As President Nixon fought with both houses of Congress, he also battled the more liberal elements of society, including the antiwar movement. Nixon had been elected in 1968 on a dual promise. He had pledged to end the war in Vietnam and mend the divisiveness within America that the war had created. Throughout his first term, Nixon aggressively moved to fulfill both pledges. The president de-escalated America's involvement in Vietnam and oversaw peace negotiations with North Vietnam. At the same time, he began the "law and order" policies that he had promised his "silent majority." Those were middle-class Americans who wanted order restored to a country plagued by urban riots and antiwar demonstrations.

To accomplish this, Nixon used the full resources of his office—sometimes illegally. Nixon and members of his staff ordered wiretaps of many left-wing individuals and the Democratic Party offices at the Watergate office building in Washington, DC. The CIA also investigated and compiled documents on thousands of American dissidents, people who objected to the government's policies. The administration even used the Internal Revenue Service to audit the tax returns of antiwar and civil rights activists. Nixon began building a personal "enemies list" of prominent Americans whom the administration would harass.

Reading Check
Analyze Issues In what ways did Nixon both strengthen and weaken federal programs?

Nixon also enlisted the help of his combative vice-president, Spiro T. Agnew, to denounce the opposition. The vice-president confronted the antiwar protesters. Then he turned his scorn on those who controlled the media. He viewed them as liberal cheerleaders for the antiwar movement. Agnew was known for his colorful quotes. He lashed out at the media and liberals as "an effete [weak] corps of impudent snobs" and "nattering nabobs of negativism."

Nixon's Southern Strategy

Even as President Nixon worked to steer the country along a more conservative course, he had his eyes on the 1972 presidential election. Nixon had won a slim majority in 1968—less than one percent of the popular vote. As president, he began working to create a new conservative coalition to build on his support. In one approach, known as the **Southern Strategy**, Nixon tried to attract southern conservative Democrats. He appealed to their unhappiness with federal desegregation policies and a liberal Supreme Court. He also promised to name a southerner to the Supreme Court.

A NEW SOUTH Since Reconstruction, the South had been a Democratic stronghold. But by 1968 many white southern Democrats had grown disillusioned with their party. In their eyes, the party—champion of the Great Society and civil rights—had grown too liberal. This conservative backlash first surfaced in the 1968 election. That year, thousands of southern Democrats supported former Alabama governor George Wallace, a conservative segregationist running as an independent. As a result, Wallace carried five southern states and captured 13 percent of the popular vote.

– BIOGRAPHY

Richard M. Nixon (1913–1994)

The hurdles that Richard Nixon overcame to win the presidency in 1968 included his loss in the 1960 presidential race and a 1962 defeat in the race for governor of California.

Nixon faced many obstacles from the start. As a boy, he rose every day at 4 a.m. to help in his father's grocery store. Nixon also worked as a janitor, a bean picker, and a barker at an amusement park.

The Nixon family suffered great tragedy when one of Nixon's brothers died from meningitis and another from tuberculosis.

None of these traumatic experiences, however, dulled the future president's ambition. Nixon

finished third in his law class at Duke University. After serving in World War II, he launched his political career.

After winning a seat in Congress in 1946, Nixon announced, "I had to win. That's the thing you don't understand. The important thing is to win."

Nixon wanted to win over the Wallace voters and other discontented Democrats. The president and his fellow Republicans hoped not only to keep the White House but also to recapture a majority in Congress.

NIXON SLOWS INTEGRATION To attract white voters in the South, President Nixon decided on a policy of slowing the country's desegregation efforts. In September 1969, less than a year after being elected president, Nixon made clear his views on civil rights. "There are those who want instant integration and those who want segregation forever. I believe we need to have a middle course between those two extremes," he said.

Throughout his first term, President Nixon worked to reverse several civil rights policies. In 1969 he ordered the Department of Health, Education, and Welfare (HEW) to delay desegregation plans for school districts in South Carolina and Mississippi. Nixon's actions violated the Supreme Court's second *Brown* v. *Board of Education* ruling. It called for the desegregation of schools "with all deliberate speed." In response to an NAACP suit, the high court ordered Nixon to follow the second *Brown* ruling. The president did so reluctantly. By 1972 nearly 90 percent of children in the South attended desegregated schools—up from about 20 percent in 1969.

In a further attempt to chip away at civil rights advances, Nixon opposed the extension of the Voting Rights Act of 1965. The act had added nearly 1 million African Americans to the voting rolls. Despite the president's opposition, Congress voted to extend the act.

CONTROVERSY OVER BUSING President Nixon then attempted to stop yet another civil rights initiative—the integration of schools through busing. In 1971 the Supreme Court ruled in *Swann* v. *Charlotte-Mecklenburg Board of Education* that school districts may bus students to other schools to end the pattern of all-black or all-white educational institutions. White students and parents in cities such as Boston and Detroit angrily protested busing. One South Boston mother spoke for other white northerners, many of whom still struggled with the integration process.

"I'm not against any individual child. I am not a racist, no matter what those high-and-mighty suburban liberals with their picket signs say. I just won't have my children bused to some . . . slum school, and I don't want children from god knows where coming over here."

—A South Boston mother, quoted in
The School Busing Controversy, 1970–75

Nixon also opposed integration through busing, and he spoke on national television to urge Congress to halt the practice. While busing continued in some cities, Nixon had made his position clear to the country—and to the South.

A demonstrator in Boston protests court-ordered school busing during the early 1970s.

Reading Check
Summarize What was Nixon's Southern Strategy, and how did he implement it?

A BATTLE OVER THE SUPREME COURT During the 1968 campaign, Nixon had criticized the Warren Court for being too liberal. Once in the White House, Nixon suddenly found himself with an opportunity to change the direction of the Court. During Nixon's first term, four justices, including Chief Justice Earl Warren, retired. President Nixon quickly moved to put a more conservative face on the Court. In 1969 the Senate approved Nixon's Chief Justice appointee, U.S. Court of Appeals judge Warren Burger.

Eventually, Nixon placed on the bench three more justices, who tilted the Court in a more conservative direction. However, the newly shaped Court did not always take the conservative route—for example, it handed down the 1971 ruling in favor of racially integrating schools through busing.

Confronting a Stagnant Economy

One of the more pressing issues facing Richard Nixon was a troubled economy. Between 1967 and 1973 the United States faced high inflation and high unemployment—a situation economists called **stagflation**.

THE CAUSES OF STAGFLATION The economic problems of the late 1960s and early 1970s had several causes. Chief among them was high inflation—a result of Lyndon Johnson's policy to fund the war and social programs through deficit spending. Also, increased competition in international trade and a flood of new workers, including women and baby boomers, led to stagflation. Another cause of the nation's economic woes was its growing dependency on foreign oil. In 1970 the United States got just over one-fifth of its oil from foreign sources. By 1973 that figure had risen to about one-third.

During the 1960s America received much of its foreign-sourced petroleum from oil-producing countries in the Middle East. Many of these countries belonged to **OPEC (Organization of the Petroleum Exporting Countries)**,

Dependent on foreign oil, Americans in 1979 wait in line for gas during the oil embargo.

Vocabulary
cartel a bloc of
independent business
organizations that
controls a service or
business

a cartel established to coordinate members' petroleum policies. During the 1960s OPEC gradually raised oil prices. Then, in 1973 Egypt and Syria started the Yom Kippur War against Israel. When the United States sent massive military aid to Israel, its longtime ally, Arab oil-producing nations responded by cutting off all oil sales to the United States. This oil embargo exposed a major challenge for U.S. foreign policy—balancing support for Israel, while maintaining friendly ties with oil-producing Arab nations in the region. The embargo and fuel shortages that followed led to long lines at gas stations, which fed the public's frustration with the economy. When OPEC resumed selling oil to the United States in 1974, the price had quadrupled. This sharp rise in oil prices only worsened the problem of inflation.

NIXON BATTLES STAGFLATION President Nixon took several steps to combat stagflation, but none met with much success. To reverse deficit spending, Nixon attempted to raise taxes and cut the budget. Congress, however, refused to go along with this plan. In another effort to slow inflation, Nixon tried to reduce the amount of money in circulation by urging that interest rates be raised. This measure did little except drive the country into a mild recession, or an overall slowdown of the economy.

In August 1971 the president turned to price and wage controls to stop inflation. He froze workers' wages as well as businesses' prices and fees for 90 days. Inflation eased for a short time, but the recession continued.

Reading Check
Analyze Causes
What factors brought
on the country's
economic problems
in the late 1960s and
early 1970s?

Lesson 1 Assessment

1. **Organize Information** In a two-column chart, list the policies of Richard Nixon that promoted change and those that slowed it down.

Promoted Change	Slowed Change
Policies	Policies

In what ways do you think Nixon was most conservative? In what ways was he least conservative? Explain.

2. **Key Terms and People** For each key term or person in the lesson, write a sentence explaining its significance.

3. **Draw Conclusions** In what ways was President Nixon's New Federalism a reaction to President Johnson's Great Society?

   Think About:
   • the growth of government influence under Johnson
   • Nixon's attempts to dismantle social programs
   • Nixon's use of impoundment

4. **Analyze Effects** What were the effects of the Arab OPEC oil embargo on the United States?

5. **Analyze Motives** Why did Nixon employ his Southern Strategy for the 1972 election?

Watergate: Nixon's Downfall

The Big Idea

President Richard Nixon's involvement in the Watergate scandal forced him to resign from office.

Why It Matters Now

The Watergate scandal raised questions of public trust that still affect how the public and media skeptically view politicians.

Key Terms and People

impeachment

Watergate

H. R. Haldeman

John Ehrlichman

John Mitchell

Committee to Reelect the President

John Sirica

Saturday Night Massacre

One American's Story

On July 25, 1974, Representative Barbara Jordan of Texas, a member of the House Judiciary Committee, along with the other committee members, considered whether to recommend that President Nixon be impeached for "high crimes and misdemeanors." Addressing the room, Jordan cited the Constitution in urging her fellow committee members to investigate whether impeachment was appropriate.

U.S. representative Barbara Jordan, 1974

"'We the people'—it is a very eloquent beginning. But when the Constitution of the United States was completed . . . I was not included in that 'We the people' . . . But through the process of amendment, interpretation, and court decision, I have finally been included in 'We the people.' . . . Today . . . [my] faith in the Constitution is whole. It is complete. It is total. I am not going to sit here and be an idle spectator in the diminution, the subversion, the destruction of the Constitution. . . . Has the President committed offenses . . . which the Constitution will not tolerate?"

—Barbara Jordan, quoted in *Notable Black American Women*

The committee eventually voted to recommend the **impeachment** of Richard Nixon for his role in the Watergate scandal. However, before Congress could take further action against him, the president resigned. Nixon's resignation was the first by a U.S. president.

SS.912.A.1.2; SS.912.A.1.4; SS.912.A.7.10; LAFS.1112.RH.1.2

President Nixon and His White House

The **Watergate** scandal centered on the Nixon administration's attempt to cover up a burglary of the Democratic National Committee (DNC) headquarters at the Watergate office and apartment complex in Washington, DC. However, the Watergate story began long before the actual burglary. Many historians believe that Watergate truly began with the personalities of Richard Nixon and his advisers, and with the changing role of the presidency.

AN IMPERIAL PRESIDENCY When Richard Nixon took office, the executive branch—as a result of the Great Depression, World War II, and the Cold War—had become the most powerful branch of government. In his book *The Imperial Presidency,* historian Arthur Schlesinger Jr. argued that by the time Richard Nixon became president, the executive branch had taken on an air of imperial, or supreme, authority.

President Nixon settled easily into this imperial role. He believed, as he told a reporter in 1980, that "a president must not be one of the crowd. . . . People . . . don't want him to be down there saying, 'Look, I'm the same as you.'" Nixon expanded the power of the presidency with little thought to constitutional checks and balances, as when he impounded funds for federal programs that he opposed, or when he ordered troops to invade Cambodia without congressional approval. The Constitution divides war powers between the president, who is Commander In Chief of the armed forces, and Congress, which makes declarations of war.

THE PRESIDENT'S MEN As he distanced himself from Congress, Nixon confided in a small and fiercely loyal group of advisers. They included **H. R. Haldeman**, White House chief of staff; **John Ehrlichman**, chief domestic adviser; and **John Mitchell**, Nixon's former attorney general. These men had played key roles in Nixon's 1968 election victory, and they now helped the president direct White House policy.

These men also shared President Nixon's desire for secrecy and the consolidation of power. Critics charged that these men, through their personalities and their attitude toward the presidency, developed a sense that they were above the law. This sense would, in turn, prompt President Nixon and his advisers to cover up their role in Watergate and fuel the coming scandal.

Reading Check
Summarize
What is meant by "imperial presidency"?

The Inner Circle

H. R. Haldeman
Chief of Staff

John Ehrlichman
Chief Domestic Adviser

John N. Mitchell
Attorney General

John W. Dean III
Presidential Counsel

The Drive Toward Reelection

Throughout his political career, Richard Nixon lived with the overwhelming fear of losing elections. By the end of the 1972 reelection campaign, Nixon's campaign team sought advantages by any means possible, including an attempt to steal information from the DNC headquarters.

A BUNGLED BURGLARY At 2:30 a.m., June 17, 1972, a guard at the Watergate complex in Washington, DC, caught five men breaking into the campaign headquarters of the DNC. The burglars planned to photograph documents outlining Democratic Party strategy and to place wiretaps, or "bugs," on the office telephones. The press soon discovered that the group's leader, James McCord, was a former CIA agent. He was also a security coordinator for a group known as the **Committee to Reelect the President** (CRP). John Mitchell, who had resigned as attorney general to run Nixon's reelection campaign, was the CRP's director.

Just three days after the burglary, H. R. Haldeman noted in his diary Nixon's near obsession with how to respond to the break-in.

> *"The P[resident] was concerned about what our counterattack is. . . .*
> *He raised it again several times during the day, and it obviously is*
> *bothering him. . . . He called at home tonight, saying that he wanted*
> *to change the plan for his press conference and have it on Thursday*
> *instead of tomorrow, so that it won't look like he's reacting to the*
> *Democratic break-in thing."*
>
> — H. R. Haldeman, from *The Haldeman Diaries*

THE COVER-UP The cover-up quickly began. Workers shredded all incriminating documents in Haldeman's office. The White House, with President Nixon's consent, asked the CIA to urge the FBI to stop its investigations into the burglary on the grounds of national security. In addition, the CRP passed

The inside source who helped Bob Woodward *(top)* and Carl Bernstein *(bottom)* did so on the condition that he remain anonymous. Not until 2005 did W. Mark Felt identify himself publicly as their source. At the time of Watergate, he had been the deputy director of the FBI.

nearly $450,000 to the Watergate burglars to buy their silence after they were indicted in September 1972.

Throughout the 1972 campaign, the Watergate burglary generated little interest among the American public and media. Only the *Washington Post* and two of its reporters, Bob Woodward and Carl Bernstein, kept on the story. As the two men dug deeper into the Watergate break-in, a mysterious inside source helped them uncover the scandal. In a series of articles, the reporters uncovered information that linked numerous members of the administration to the burglary. The White House denied each new *Post* allegation. Upon learning of an upcoming story that tied him to the burglars, John Mitchell told Bernstein, "That's the most sickening thing I ever heard."

The firm White House response to the charges, and its promises of imminent peace in Vietnam, proved effective in the short term. In November, Nixon was reelected by a landslide over liberal Democrat George S. McGovern. But Nixon's popular support was soon to unravel.

Reading Check
Analyze Motives
Why would the Nixon campaign team take such a risky action as breaking into the opposition's headquarters?

The Cover-Up Unravels

In January 1973 the trial of the Watergate burglars began. The trial's presiding judge, **John Sirica**, made clear his belief that the men had not acted alone. On March 20, a few days before the burglars were scheduled to be sentenced, James McCord sent a letter to Sirica, in which he indicated that he had lied under oath. He also hinted that powerful members of the Nixon administration had been involved in the break-in.

THE SENATE INVESTIGATES WATERGATE McCord's revelation of possible White House involvement in the burglary aroused public interest in Watergate. President Nixon moved quickly to stem the growing concern. On April 30, 1973, Nixon dismissed White House counsel John Dean and announced the resignations of Haldeman, Ehrlichman, and Attorney General Richard Kleindienst, who had recently replaced John Mitchell following Mitchell's resignation. The president then went on television and denied any attempt at a cover-up. He announced that he was appointing a new attorney general, Elliot Richardson, and was authorizing him to appoint a special prosecutor to investigate Watergate. "There can be no whitewash at the White House," Nixon said.

The president's reassurances, however, came too late. In May 1973 the Senate began its own investigation of Watergate. A special committee, chaired by Senator Samuel James Ervin of North Carolina, began to call administration officials to give testimony. Throughout the summer, millions of Americans sat attentively by their televisions as the "president's men" testified one after another.

John Dean's testimony at the Watergate hearings stunned the nation.

STARTLING TESTIMONY John Dean delivered the first bomb. In late June, during more than 30 hours of testimony, Dean provided a startling answer to Senator Howard Baker's repeated question, "What did the president know and when did he know it?" The former White House counsel declared that

The White House Tapes

During the Watergate hearings, a bombshell exploded when it was revealed that President Nixon secretly tape-recorded all conversations in the Oval Office. Although Nixon hoped the tapes would one day help historians document the triumphs of his presidency, they were used to confirm his guilt.

Analyze Historical Sources

1. What does this cartoon imply about privacy during President Nixon's term in office?

2. What building has been transformed into a giant tape recorder?

President Nixon had been deeply involved in the cover-up. Dean referred to one meeting in which he and the president, along with several advisers, discussed strategies for continuing the deceit.

The White House strongly denied Dean's charges. The hearings had suddenly reached an impasse as the committee attempted to sort out who was telling the truth. The answer came in July from an unlikely source: presidential aide Alexander Butterfield. Butterfield stunned the committee when he revealed that Nixon had taped virtually all of his presidential conversations. Butterfield later claimed that the taping system was installed "to help Nixon write his memoirs." However, for the Senate committee, the tapes were the key to revealing what Nixon knew and when he knew it.

THE SATURDAY NIGHT MASSACRE A year-long battle for the "Nixon tapes" followed. Archibald Cox, the special prosecutor whom Elliot Richardson had appointed to investigate the case, took the president to court in October 1973 to obtain the tapes. Nixon refused and ordered Attorney General Richardson to fire Cox. In what became known as the **Saturday Night Massacre**, Richardson refused the order and resigned. The deputy attorney general also refused the order, and he was fired. Solicitor General Robert Bork finally fired Cox. However, Cox's replacement, Leon Jaworski, proved equally determined to get the tapes. Several months after the "massacre," the House Judiciary Committee began examining the possibility of an impeachment hearing.

The entire White House appeared to be under siege. Just days before the Saturday Night Massacre, Vice-President Spiro Agnew had resigned after it was revealed that he had accepted bribes from engineering firms while governor of Maryland. Agnew pleaded *nolo contendere* (no contest) to the charge. Acting under the Twenty-Fifth Amendment, Nixon nominated the House minority leader, Gerald R. Ford, as his new vice-president. Congress quickly confirmed the nomination.

Reading Check
Draw Conclusions
What was significant about the revelation that Nixon taped his conversations?

The Fall of a President

In March 1974 a grand jury indicted seven presidential aides on charges of conspiracy, obstruction of justice, and perjury. The investigation was closing in on the president of the United States.

Background
Although historians sued for access to thousands of hours of tapes, it was not until some 21 years later, in 1996, that an agreement was made for over 3,700 hours of tape to be made public.

NIXON RELEASES THE TAPES In the spring of 1974, President Nixon told a television audience that he was releasing 1,254 pages of edited transcripts of White House conversations about Watergate. Nixon's offering failed to satisfy investigators, who demanded the unedited tapes. Nixon refused, and the case—*United States* v. *Nixon*—went before the Supreme Court. On July 24, 1974, the high court ruled unanimously that the president must surrender the tapes. The Court rejected Nixon's argument that doing so would violate national security. Evidence involving possible criminal activity could not be withheld, even by a president. President Nixon maintained that he had done nothing wrong. At a press conference in November 1973, he had proclaimed defiantly, "I am not a crook."

THE PRESIDENT RESIGNS Even without holding the original tapes, the House Judiciary Committee determined that there was enough evidence to impeach Richard Nixon. On July 27, the committee approved three articles of impeachment, charging the president with obstruction of justice, abuse of power, and contempt of Congress for refusing to obey a congressional subpoena to release the tapes.

On August 5, Nixon released the tapes. They contained many gaps, and one tape revealed a disturbing eighteen-and-a-half-minute gap. According to the White House, Rose Mary Woods, President Nixon's secretary, accidentally erased part of a conversation between H. R. Haldeman and Nixon. More importantly, a tape dated June 23, 1972—six days after the Watergate break-in—that contained a conversation between Nixon and Haldeman, disclosed

With wife, Pat, looking on, Richard Nixon bids farewell to his staff on his final day as president. Nixon's resignation letter was addressed to the secretary of state, Henry Kissinger.

the evidence investigators needed. Not only had the president known about the role of members of his administration in the burglary, he had agreed to the plan to obstruct the FBI's investigation.

The evidence now seemed overwhelming. On August 8, 1974, before the full House vote on the articles of impeachment began, President Nixon announced his resignation from office. Defiant as always, Nixon admitted no guilt. He merely said that some of his judgments "were wrong." The next day, Nixon and his wife, Pat, returned home to California. A short time later, Gerald Ford was sworn in as the 38th president of the United States.

THE EFFECTS OF WATERGATE The effects of Watergate have endured long after Nixon's resignation. Eventually, 25 members of the Nixon administration were convicted and served prison terms for crimes connected to Watergate. Along with the divisive war in Vietnam, Watergate produced a deep disillusionment with the "imperial" presidency. In the years following Vietnam and Watergate, the American public and the media developed a general cynicism about public officials that still exists today. Watergate remains the scandal and investigative story against which all others are measured.

Reading Check
Analyze Effects
What were the results of the Watergate scandal?

Lesson 2 Assessment

1. **Organize Information** Use a timeline to trace the events of the Watergate scandal.

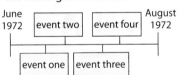

Which event made Nixon's downfall certain?

2. **Key Terms and People** For each key term or person in the lesson, write a sentence explaining its significance.

3. **Predict** If Nixon had admitted to and apologized for the Watergate break-in, how might subsequent events have been different? Explain.

   Think About:
   • the extent of the cover-up
   • the impact of the cover-up
   • Nixon's public image

4. **Analyze Events** How did the Watergate scandal create a constitutional crisis?

5. **Evaluate** Do you think that Nixon would have been forced to resign if the tapes had not existed? Explain your answer.

The Ford and Carter Years

The Big Idea
The Ford and Carter administrations attempted to remedy the nation's worst economic crisis in decades.

Why It Matters Now
Maintaining a stable national economy has remained a top priority for every president since Ford and Carter.

Key Terms and People
Gerald R. Ford

Jimmy Carter

National Energy Act

human rights

Camp David Accords

Ayatollah Ruhollah Khomeini

SS.912.A.1.2; SS.912.A.1.4; SS.912.A.1.6; SS.912.A.2.4; SS.912.A.7.8; SS.912.A.7.11; SS.912.A.7.17; LAFS.1112.RH.1.1; LAFS.1112.RH.1.2; LAFS.1112.RH.1.3; LAFS.1112.RH.4.10; LAFS.1112.WHST.3.7; LAFS.1112.WHST.3.9; MAFS.K12.MP.1.1; MAFS.K12.MP.3.1; MAFS.K12.MP.5.1

One American's Story

Barely a month after Richard Nixon had resigned amid the Watergate scandal, President **Gerald R. Ford** granted Nixon a full pardon. Ford explained his concern that a long, drawn-out trial would only increase the strain on the nation.

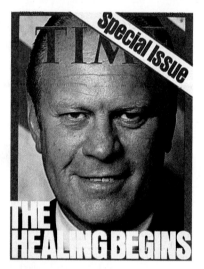

TIME gave extensive coverage to the Nixon pardon.

"During this long period of delay and potential litigation, ugly passions would again be aroused. And our people would again be polarized in their opinions. And the credibility of our free institutions of government would again be challenged at home and abroad. . . . My conscience tells me that only I, as President, have the constitutional power to firmly shut and seal this book. My conscience tells me it is my duty, not merely to proclaim domestic tranquility but to use every means that I have to insure it. . . . 'Now, therefore, I, Gerald R. Ford, President of the United States, . . . do grant a full, free, and absolute pardon unto Richard Nixon. . . .'"

—Gerald R. Ford, from remarks on Proclamation 4311, September 8, 1974

For many, though, Ford's actions contributed to feelings of anger and disillusionment with the presidency in the aftermath of the Watergate scandal. During the 1970s presidents Gerald Ford and Jimmy Carter sought to restore America's faith in its leaders. At the same time, both men had to focus much of their attention on battling the nation's worsening economic situation.

Ford Travels a Rough Road

Upon taking office, Gerald R. Ford urged Americans to put the Watergate scandal behind them. "Our long national nightmare is over," he declared. The nation's nightmarish economy persisted, however, and Ford's policies offered little relief.

"A FORD, NOT A LINCOLN" Gerald Ford seemed to many to be a likable and honest man. Upon becoming vice-president after Spiro Agnew's resignation, Ford candidly admitted his limitations. "I'm a Ford, not a Lincoln," he remarked. However, Ford's pardon of Nixon became the topic of fierce debate, and in the end would have a profound impact on Ford's political future. Many Americans admitted to voting against Ford in the 1976 election because of his pardon of Richard Nixon. Early on, Ford would also face major economic challenges that would make his presidency an uphill battle from the start.

FORD TRIES TO "WHIP" INFLATION By the time Ford took office, America's economy had gone from bad to worse. Both inflation and unemployment continued to rise. After the massive OPEC oil-price increases in 1973, gasoline and heating oil costs had soared, pushing inflation from 6 percent to over 10 percent by the end of 1974. Ford responded with a program of massive citizen action, called "Whip Inflation Now" or WIN. The president called on Americans to cut back on their use of oil and gas and to take other energy-saving measures.

In the absence of incentives, though, the plan fell flat. Ford then tried to curb inflation through a "tight money" policy. He cut government spending and encouraged the Federal Reserve Board to restrict credit through higher interest rates. These actions triggered the worst economic recession in 40 years.

Ford, like many of his fellow Republicans, was a fiscal conservative. He believed that deficit spending, or spending that added to the government's debt, was bad for the health of the economy. Facing a dire economic situation, though, Ford had little choice. He could approve spending increases and cut taxes or see the economy slip further into recession. Sacrificing his principles, Ford approved a stimulus package of spending increases and tax cuts in 1975. By the next year, unemployment had fallen from 9 to 7 percent and inflation had decreased from 12 to 5 percent. Although the economy had not fully recovered, Ford confidently declared that it was "headed in the right direction."

DIFFICULT DECISIONS

To Pardon President Nixon or Not?

President Ford's pardon of Richard Nixon outraged many Americans. But President Ford argued that the pardon was in the country's best interest. He believed that a Watergate trial, which could take years to complete, would keep the anger over the incident fresh in everyone's minds and keep the nation divided. Ford called the pardon decision "the most difficult of my life, by far."

In 2001, after more than 25 years, Ford received the John F. Kennedy Profiles in Courage Award for his courageous decision in the face of public opposition.

1. How might the country have been affected if a former United States president had gone on trial for possible criminal wrongdoing?

2. If you had been in President Ford's position, would you have pardoned Richard Nixon? Why or why not?

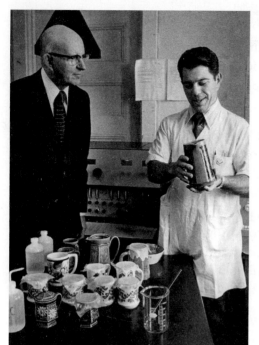

Two FDA scientists test pottery to make sure that it is safe for consumers.

FORD PUSHES FOR A STREAMLINED GOVERNMENT As Ford implemented his economic programs, he continually battled a Democratic Congress intent on pushing its own agenda. During his two years as president, Ford vetoed more than 50 pieces of legislation. In addition to cutting government spending, Ford wanted to curb government regulation. By the mid-1970s there were more than 90 federal agencies regulating different industries, which had developed over several decades of government. Such agencies included the Food and Drug Administration, established in 1931 to oversee the safety and quality of drugs, medical devices, and the nation's food supply, and the Occupational Health and Safety Administration, which had been formed in 1970 to ensure safe and healthful working conditions for American workers. Ford recognized the need for some government regulation. For example, he established the Nuclear Regulatory Commission (NRC) in 1974. Until the creation of the NRC, the Atomic Energy Commission (AEC) had been tasked with both regulating and promoting nuclear energy, a clear conflict of interest. The purpose of the NRC was to separate these two functions and take over regulation of the nuclear energy industry. However, Ford thought that government regulation had become so unwieldy that it was hurting the economy.

> "A necessary condition of a healthy economy is freedom from the petty tyranny of massive government regulation. We are wasting literally millions of working hours costing billions of taxpayers' and consumers' dollars because of bureaucratic redtape. . . . [W]e badly need reforms in . . . key areas in our economy: the airlines, trucking, railroads, and financial institutions. I have submitted concrete plans . . . not to help this or that industry, but to foster competition and to bring prices down for the consumer."
>
> —Gerald R. Ford, from State of the Union Address, January 19, 1976

Through reform of government regulation, the Ford administration hoped to bring down prices by increasing competition, making the public aware of the costs of regulation, making the regulation process more efficient, and replacing some regulation with antitrust enforcement. Upon winning the White House, the Carter administration embraced Ford's ideas of responsible and efficient regulation. President Carter even established the Regulatory Analysis Review Group to oversee a formal process for reviewing the economic impact of proposed government regulation.

Carter Enters the White House

Gerald Ford won the Republican nomination for president in 1976 after fending off a powerful conservative challenge from former California governor Ronald Reagan. Because the Republicans seemed divided over Ford's leadership, the Democrats confidently eyed the White House. "We could run an aardvark this year and win," predicted one Democratic leader. The

Reading Check
Make Inferences
Why was Ford's call for voluntary actions to help the economy unsuccessful?

Democratic nominee was indeed a surprise: a nationally unknown peanut farmer and former governor of Georgia, **Jimmy Carter**.

MR. CARTER GOES TO WASHINGTON During the post–Watergate era, cynicism toward the Washington establishment ran high. The soft-spoken, personable man from Plains, Georgia, promised to restore integrity to the nation's highest office, "I will never tell a lie to the American people."

Throughout the presidential campaign, Carter and Ford squared off over the key issues of inflation, energy, and unemployment. On Election Day, Jimmy Carter won by a narrow margin, claiming 40.8 million popular votes to Ford's 39.1 million.

From the very beginning, the new First Family brought a down-to-earth style to Washington. After settling into office, Carter stayed in touch with the people by holding Roosevelt-like "fireside chats" on radio and television.

Carter failed to reach out to Congress in a similar way, refusing to play the "insider" game of dealmaking. Relying mainly on a team of advisers from Georgia, Carter even alienated congressional Democrats. Both parties on Capitol Hill often joined to sink the president's budget proposals, as well as his major policy reforms of tax and welfare programs.

CARTER CONFRONTS THE ENERGY CRISIS Carter considered the energy crisis the most important issue facing the nation. A large part of the problem, the president believed, was America's reliance on imported oil.

Carter presented Congress with more than 100 proposals on energy conservation and development. Representatives from oil- and gas-producing states fiercely resisted some of the proposals. Automobile manufacturers also lobbied against gas-rationing provisions. "It was impossible for me to imagine the bloody legislative battles we would have to win," Carter later wrote.

Vocabulary
lobby to attempt to influence legislators to support a particular viewpoint

– BIOGRAPHY

Jimmy Carter (1924–)

James Earl Carter Jr. was born into relative prosperity. His father, Earl Carter, was a disciplinarian who tried to instill a sense of hard work and responsibility in his son.

To earn money for himself, Carter undertook a variety of jobs selling peanuts, running a hamburger and hot dog stand, collecting newspapers and selling them to fish markets, and selling scrap iron.

Before entering politics, Carter joined the navy, where he excelled in electronics and naval tactics. In 1952 he joined a select group of officers who helped develop the world's first nuclear submarines. The group's commander was Captain Hyman G. Rickover. Carter later wrote that Rickover "had a profound effect on my life—perhaps more than anyone except my own parents. . . . He expected the maximum from us, but he always contributed more."

Energy Crisis

On April 18, 1977, during a fireside chat, Carter urged his fellow Americans to cut their consumption of oil and gas.

"The energy crisis . . . is a problem . . . likely to get progressively worse through the rest of this century. . . . Our decision about energy will test the character of the American people. . . . This difficult effort will be the 'moral equivalent of war,' except that we will be uniting our efforts to build and not to destroy."

—Jimmy Carter, from *Keeping Faith*

Analyze Historical Sources
What do you think Carter means by comparing the energy crisis to war?

Out of the battle came the **National Energy Act**. The act placed a tax on gas-guzzling cars, removed price controls on oil and natural gas produced in the United States, and extended tax credits for the development of alternative energy. With the help of the act, as well as voluntary conservation measures, U.S. dependence on foreign oil had eased slightly by 1979.

THE ECONOMIC CRISIS WORSENS Unfortunately, these energy-saving measures could do little to combat a sudden new economic crisis. In the summer of 1979, renewed violence in the Middle East produced a second major fuel shortage in the United States. To make matters worse, OPEC announced another major price increase. In 1979 inflation soared from 7.6 percent to 11.3 percent.

Faced with increasing pressure to act, Carter attempted an array of measures, none of which worked. Carter's scatter-shot approach convinced many people that he had no economic policy at all. Carter fueled this feeling of uncertainty by delivering his now-famous "malaise" speech, in which he complained of a "crisis of spirit" that had struck "at the very heart and soul of our national will." Carter's address made many Americans feel that their president had given up.

By 1980 inflation had climbed to nearly 14 percent, the highest rate since 1947. The standard of living in the United States slipped from first place to fifth place in the world. Carter's popularity slipped along with it. This economic downswing—and Carter's inability to solve it during an election year—was one key factor in sending Ronald Reagan to the White House.

A CHANGING ECONOMY Many of the economic problems Jimmy Carter struggled with resulted from long-term trends in the economy. Since the 1950s the rise of automation and foreign competition had reduced the number of manufacturing jobs. At the same time, the service sector of the economy expanded rapidly. This sector includes industries such as communications, transportation, and retail trade.

Unemployment and Inflation, 1970–1980

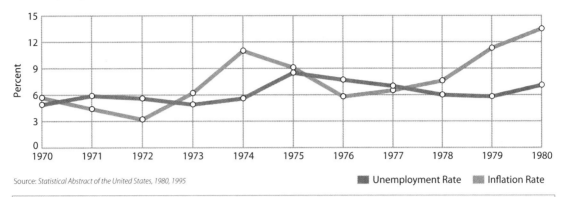

Source: *Statistical Abstract of the United States, 1980, 1995*

■ Unemployment Rate   ■ Inflation Rate

Interpret Graphs
1. What trends did the economy experience during the Carter years?
2. Which year of the Carter administration saw the greatest stagflation (inflation plus unemployment)?

The rise of the service sector and the decline of manufacturing jobs meant big changes for some American workers. Workers left out of manufacturing jobs faced an increasingly complex job market. Many of the higher-paying service jobs required more education or specialized skills than did manufacturing jobs. The lower-skilled service jobs usually did not pay well.

Growing overseas competition during the 1970s caused further change in America's economy. The booming economies of West Germany and countries on the Pacific Rim (such as Japan, Taiwan, and Korea) cut into many U.S. markets. Many of the nation's primary industries—iron and steel, rubber, clothing, automobiles—had to cut back production, lay off workers, and even close plants. Especially hard hit were the automotive industries of the Northeast. There, high energy costs, foreign competition, and computerized production led companies to eliminate tens of thousands of jobs.

Andrew Young stands outside the United Nations in New York City, in 1997.

CARTER AND CIVIL RIGHTS Although Carter felt frustrated by the country's economic woes, he took special pride in his civil rights record. His administration included more African Americans and women than any before it. In 1977 the president appointed civil rights leader Andrew Young as U.S. ambassador to the United Nations. Young was the first African American to hold that post. To the judicial branch alone, Carter appointed 28 African Americans, 29 women (including 6 African Americans), and 14 Latinos.

However, President Carter fell short of what many civil rights groups had expected in terms of legislation. Critics claimed that Carter—preoccupied with battles over energy and the economy—failed to give civil rights his full attention. Meanwhile, the courts began to turn

Reading Check
Analyze Causes
What factors played a significant role in Carter's election?

against affirmative action. In 1978, in the case of *Regents of the University of California* v. *Bakke,* the Supreme Court decided that the affirmative action policies of the university's medical school were unconstitutional. The decision made it more difficult for organizations to establish effective affirmative action programs.

Cultural Shifts in the 1970s

In the 1970s Americans began to confront lingering social issues through television and other media. The decade also produced a great leap in computer technology.

TELEVISION REFLECTS AMERICAN LIFE Television programming in the 1970s began to more closely reflect the realities of life in the United States. Hit shows like *All in the Family* confronted relevant social issues, such as racial and economic divisions in American society. For the first time, African Americans and other minorities appeared as main characters on television.

A Mirror to American Society

Chico and the Man was the first series set in a Mexican American barrio, East Los Angeles.

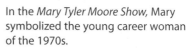

In the *Mary Tyler Moore Show,* Mary symbolized the young career woman of the 1970s.

All in the Family was the most popular series of the 1970s.

For example, the show *Chico and the Man* was the first series with a Mexican American lead character. Young, single, working women, like the character Mary Richards on the *Mary Tyler Moore Show*, were also portrayed for the first time. In addition, the newly established Public Broadcasting System began showing many issue-oriented programs and expanding educational programming for children.

THE COMPUTER AGE BEGINS In addition to innovations in television programming, the 1970s saw significant advances in computer technology. One of the first computers was developed by the U.S. military for use during World War II. It cost $500,000 to build, weighed 30 tons, and occupied 2,000 square feet of space. Through the 1940s and 1950s, engineers continued to develop new parts that would make computers smaller and more powerful.

The greatest technological leap, however, occurred in 1971 when an engineer named Ted Hoff developed one of the first microprocessors. This tiny "chip" that measured less than one inch had the same computing power as the hulking early computers. By 1974 there were personal computers that people could buy and build in their homes. In 1975 Paul Allen and Bill Gates formed Microsoft, developing new software that would make computers much easier to use for the average consumer. In 1977 Apple, founded by Steve Jobs and Steve Wozniak, would be the next to make a major breakthrough. That year, they introduced the Apple II computer, which had a keyboard, color screen, and data storage. Soon, more companies would join the marketplace, helping to make computers smaller, cheaper, and more powerful.

Reading Check
Analyze Causes
What great leap in technology made personal computers possible?

A Human Rights Foreign Policy

Jimmy Carter rejected the philosophy of realpolitik—the pragmatic policy of negotiating with powerful nations despite their behavior—and strived for a foreign policy committed to human rights.

EFFORTS FOR HUMAN RIGHTS Jimmy Carter, like Woodrow Wilson, sought to use moral principles as a guide for U.S. foreign policy. He believed that the United States needed to commit itself to promoting **human rights**—such as the freedoms and liberties listed in the Declaration of Independence and the Bill of Rights—throughout the world.

Putting his principles into practice, President Carter cut off military aid to Argentina and Brazil. These countries had good relations with the United States, but they had imprisoned or tortured thousands of their own citizens. Carter followed up this action by establishing a Bureau of Human Rights in the State Department.

Carter's philosophy was not without its critics. Supporters of the containment policy felt that the president's policy undercut allies such as Nicaragua, a dictatorial but anti-Communist country. Others argued that by supporting dictators in South Korea and the Philippines, Carter was acting inconsistently. In 1977 Carter's policies drew further criticism when his administration announced that it planned to give up ownership of the Panama Canal.

TRANSFER OF THE PANAMA CANAL Since 1914, when the United States obtained full ownership over the Panama Canal, Panamanians had resented having their nation split in half by a foreign power. In 1977 the two nations agreed to two treaties, one of which turned over control of the Panama Canal to Panama on December 31, 1999.

In 1978 the U.S. Senate, which had to ratify each treaty, approved the agreements by a vote of 68 to 32—one more vote than the required two-thirds. Public opinion was also divided. In the end, the treaties did improve relationships between the United States and Latin America.

THE MARIEL BOATLIFT The Carter administration had always had an open-door policy for Cuban refugees seeking asylum in the United States. In 1980, however, this policy would be put to the ultimate test. On April 20 of that year, Cuban dictator Fidel Castro announced that the port of Mariel would be open to any Cuban citizen wishing to leave the country. Over the next few months, about 125,000 Cuban refugees crowded onto boats bound for the coast of Florida, only 90 miles away. When it was later learned that the Castro government had released criminals to join the refugees, public opinion turned against the Carter administration.

Reading Check
Identify Problems
What problems did critics have with Carter's foreign-policy philosophy?

Triumph and Crisis in the Middle East

Through long gasoline lines and high energy costs, Americans became all too aware of the troubles in the Middle East. Since its inception in 1948, Israel had been in conflict with its Arab neighbors, many of whom refused to recognize the country's right to exist. In that region of ethnic, religious, and economic conflict, Jimmy Carter achieved one of his greatest diplomatic triumphs—and suffered his most tragic defeat.

NOW & THEN

Arab-Israeli Tension

Following the Camp David Accords in 1978, tensions between Israel and its Arab neighbors still ran high. The United States and other Western nations continued to help negotiate a series of peace agreements, including the Oslo Accords in 1993 and the Israel-Jordan Peace Treaty in 1994.

In 2003 the United States, Russia, the European Union, and the United Nations laid out a "roadmap for peace." The cornerstone of this proposal was a two-state solution, in which an independent Palestinian (Arab) state would be carved out of Israel. After some early progress, talks were halted on the "roadmap" in 2006. In 2007 President George W. Bush was able to bring Israeli leaders together with Palestinian leaders and the leaders of more than a dozen Arab countries to resume talks on the "roadmap."

Despite making significant progress, the talks broke down in 2008. In 2009 and 2013 the two sides agreed to resume talks, but both times they could not reach an agreement. By 2014 talks on the "roadmap" had ceased once again. Although the United States remains committed to negotiating a peaceful solution, the search for a lasting peace continues.

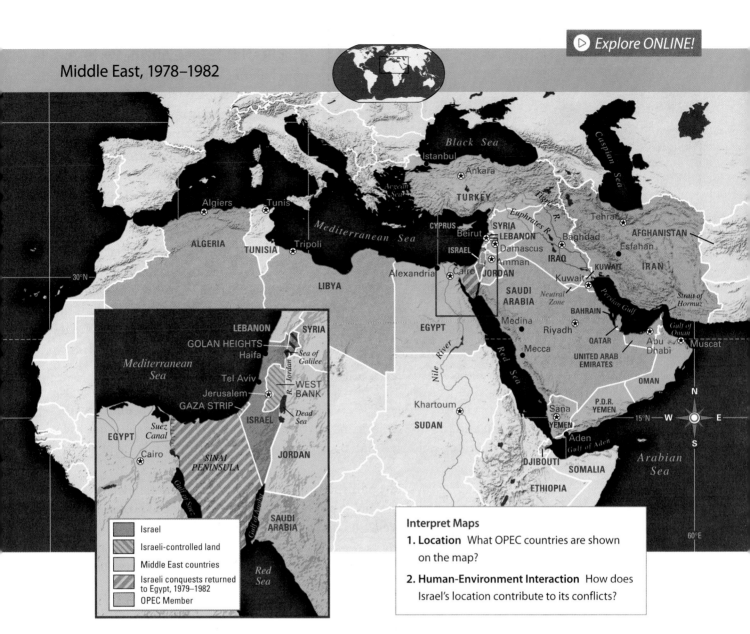

Explore ONLINE!

Key:
- Israel
- Israeli-controlled land
- Middle East countries
- Israeli conquests returned to Egypt, 1979–1982
- OPEC Member

Interpret Maps

1. **Location** What OPEC countries are shown on the map?

2. **Human-Environment Interaction** How does Israel's location contribute to its conflicts?

THE CAMP DAVID ACCORDS Through negotiation and arm-twisting, Carter helped forge peace between long-time enemies Israel and Egypt. In 1977 Egyptian president Anwar el-Sadat and Israeli prime minister Menachem Begin met in Jerusalem to discuss an overall peace between the two nations. In the summer of 1978, Carter seized on the peace initiative. When the peace talks stalled, he invited Sadat and Begin to Camp David, the presidential retreat in Maryland.

After 12 days of intense negotiations, the three leaders reached an agreement that became known as the **Camp David Accords**. Under this first signed peace agreement with an Arab country, Israel agreed to withdraw from the Sinai Peninsula, which it had captured from Egypt during the Six-Day War in 1967. Egypt, in turn, formally recognized Israel's right to exist.

Joking at the hard work ahead, Carter wrote playfully in his diary, "I resolved to do everything possible to get out of the negotiating business!" Little did the president know that his next Middle East negotiation would be his most painful.

U.S. hostages were blindfolded and paraded through the streets of Tehran.

THE IRAN HOSTAGE CRISIS By 1979 the shah of Iran, an ally of the United States, was in deep trouble. Many Iranians resented his regime's widespread corruption and dictatorial tactics.

In January 1979 revolution broke out. Rebels, led by the Muslim religious leader **Ayatollah Ruhollah Khomeini**, overthrew the shah and established a religious state that was based on strict obedience to the Qur'an, the sacred book of Islam. Carter had supported the shah until the very end. In October 1979 the president allowed the shah to enter the United States for cancer treatment, though he had already fled Iran in January 1979.

The act infuriated the revolutionaries of Iran. On November 4, 1979, armed students seized the U.S. embassy in Tehran and took 52 Americans hostage. The militants demanded that the United States send the shah back to Iran in return for the release of the hostages.

Carter refused, and a painful year-long standoff followed, in which the United States continued quiet but intense efforts to free the hostages. The captives were finally released on January 20, 1981, shortly after the new president, Ronald Reagan, was sworn in. Despite the hostages' release after 444 days in captivity, the crisis in Iran seemed to underscore the limits of American power and influence during the 1970s.

Reading Check
Summarize Why were the Camp David Accords considered such a huge diplomatic achievement?

Lesson 3 Assessment

1. **Organize Information** Create a timeline and record the major events of the Ford and Carter administrations.

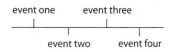

Which two events do you think were the most important? Why?

2. **Key Terms and People** For each key term or person in the lesson, write a sentence explaining its significance.

3. **Analyze Issues** Do you agree with President Carter that human rights concerns should steer U.S. foreign policy? Why or why not?

   Think About:
   - the responsibility of promoting human rights
   - the loss of good relations with certain countries
   - manipulation by other governments

4. **Evaluate** Do you think that Ford made a good decision in pardoning Nixon? Explain why or why not.

5. **Compare** How were the actions taken by presidents Ford and Carter to address the country's economic downturn similar? How did they differ?

Regents of the University of California v. Bakke (1978)

ORIGINS OF THE CASE

In 1973 Allan Bakke applied to the University of California at Davis Medical School. The school had a quota-based affirmative-action plan that reserved 16 out of 100 spots for racial minorities. Bakke, a white male, was not admitted to the school despite his competitive test scores and grades. Bakke sued for admission, arguing that he had been discriminated against on the basis of race. The California Supreme Court agreed with Bakke, but the school appealed the case.

THE RULING

The Court ruled that racial quotas were unconstitutional, but that schools could still consider race as a factor in admissions.

LEGAL REASONING

The Court was closely divided on whether affirmative-action plans were constitutional. Two different sets of justices formed 5–4 majorities on two different issues in *Bakke*.

Five justices agreed the quota was unfair to Bakke. They based their argument on the equal protection clause of the Fourteenth Amendment. Justice Lewis Powell, writing for the majority, explained their reasoning.

"The guarantee of equal protection cannot mean one thing when applied to one individual and something else when applied to a person of another color. If both are not accorded the same protection, then it is not equal."

The four justices who joined Powell in this part of the decision said race should *never* play a part in admissions decisions. Powell and the other four justices disagreed. These five justices formed a separate majority, arguing that "the attainment of a diverse student body . . . is a constitutionally permissible goal for an institution of higher education." In other words, schools could have affirmative-action plans that consider race as *one* factor in admission decisions in order to achieve a diverse student body.

Allan Bakke receives his degree in medicine from the medical school at U.C. Davis on June 4, 1982.

LEGAL SOURCES

LEGISLATION

U.S. Constitution, Fourteenth Amendment (1868)

"No state shall . . . deprive any person of life, liberty, or property, without due process of law; nor deny to any person within its jurisdiction the equal protection of the laws."

RELATED CASES

United Steelworkers of America v. Weber (1979)

The Court said a business could have a short-term program for training minority workers as a way of fixing the results of past discrimination.

Adarand Constructors v. Peña (1995)

The Court struck down a federal law to set aside 10 percent of highway construction funds for minority-owned businesses. The Court also said that affirmative-action programs must be focused to achieve a compelling government interest.

On October 8, 1977, protesters march in support of affirmative action at a park in Oakland, California.

WHY IT MATTERED

Many people have faced discrimination in America. The struggle of African Americans for civil rights in the 1950s and 1960s succeeded in overturning Jim Crow segregation. Even so, social inequality persisted for African Americans, as well as women and other minority groups. In 1965 President Lyndon Johnson explained why more proactive measures needed to be taken to end inequality.

"You do not take a person who for years has been hobbled by chains and . . . bring him up to the starting line of a race and then say, 'you are free to compete with all the others' and still justly believe that you have been completely fair."

As a result, Johnson urged companies to begin to take "affirmative action" to hire and promote African Americans, helping them to overcome generations of inequality. Critics quickly opposed affirmative-action plans as unfair to white people and merely a replacement of one form of racial discrimination with another.

University admissions policies became a focus of the debate over affirmative action. The Court's ruling in *Bakke* allowed race to be used as one factor in admissions decisions. Schools could consider a prospective student's race, but they could not use quotas or use race as the *only* factor for admission.

HISTORICAL IMPACT

Since *Bakke,* the Court has ruled on affirmative action several times, usually limiting affirmative-action plans. For example, in *Adarand Constructors* v. *Peña* (1995), the Court struck down a federal law to set aside "not less than 10 percent" of highway construction funds for businesses owned by "socially and economically disadvantaged individuals." The Court said that affirmative-action programs must be narrowly focused to achieve a "compelling government interest."

On cases regarding school affirmative-action plans, the courts have not created clear guidelines. The Supreme Court refused to hear an appeal of a 1996 lower court ruling that outlawed any consideration of race for admission to the University of Texas law school. Yet in the 2003 decision in *Grutter* v. *Bollinger,* the Court protected a University of Michigan law school admissions policy that required the admissions committee to consider the diversity of its student body. The Court reaffirmed the *Bakke* view that "student body diversity is a compelling state interest."

Since the *Grutter* decision, several states have passed laws or constitutional amendments requiring race-blind admissions—effectively barring affirmative action. These laws were passed by ballot initiative, reflecting a popular view that sees affirmative action as "reverse discrimination."

Critical Thinking

1. **Connect to History** Research articles about *Bakke* in the library or on the Internet. Read the articles, and write a paragraph for each one explaining the writer's point of view on the case. Conclude by telling which article gives the best discussion of the case. Cite examples to support your choice.

2. **Connect to Today** Do Internet research to learn about Proposition 209, California's 1996 law banning affirmative action at state universities. Prepare arguments for an in-class debate about whether the law will have a positive or negative long-term effect.

A Conservative Movement Emerges

The Big Idea

Conservatism reached a high point with the election in 1980 of President Ronald Reagan and Vice-President George Bush.

Why It Matters Now

In the early 21st century, conservative views strongly influenced both major political parties.

Key Terms and People

entitlement program

New Right

affirmative action

reverse discrimination

conservative coalition

Moral Majority

Ronald Reagan

Geraldine Ferraro

George H. W. Bush

One American's Story

Peggy Noonan grew up with a strong sense of social and political justice. After college, she went to work for CBS. Over the years, Noonan's political views became increasingly conservative. She eventually won a job as a speechwriter for Ronald Reagan, whose commitment to his conservative values moved her deeply. Noonan recalled that her response to Reagan was not unusual.

Peggy Noonan

"The young people who came to Washington for the Reagan revolution came to make things better. . . . They looked at where freedom was and . . . where freedom wasn't and what that did, and they wanted to help the guerrilla fighters who were trying to overthrow the Communist regimes that had been imposed on them. . . . The thing the young conservatives were always talking about, . . . was freedom, freedom:

> we'll free up more of your money,
> we'll free up more of the world,
> freedom freedom freedom—

It was the drumbeat that held a disparate group together, the rhythm that kept a fractious, not-made-in-heaven alliance in one piece."

— Peggy Noonan, from *What I Saw at the Revolution: A Political Life in the Reagan Era*

Like other supporters, Noonan agreed with the slogan that was the heart of Reagan's political creed: "Government is not the solution to our problem. Government is the problem."

SS.912.A.1.2; SS.912.A.7.12

The Conservative Movement Builds

Ever since Senator Barry Goldwater of Arizona had run for president in 1964, conservatives had argued that state governments, businesses, and individuals needed more freedom from the heavy hand of Washington, DC. By 1980 government spending on **entitlement programs**—programs that provide guaranteed benefits to particular groups—was nearly $300 billion annually. The costs together with stories of fraudulently obtained benefits caused resentment among many taxpayers.

In addition, some people had become frustrated with the government's civil rights policies. Congress had passed the Civil Rights Act of 1964 in an effort to eliminate racial discrimination. Over the years, however, judicial decisions and government regulations had broadened the reach of the act. A growing number of Americans viewed with skepticism what had begun as a movement toward equal opportunity. Although many people had rejected separate schools for blacks and whites as unfair and unequal, few people wanted to bus their children long distances to achieve a fixed ratio of black and white students.

Several high school students in New York hold a prayer meeting in 1973.

THE NEW RIGHT As the 1970s progressed, right wing grassroots groups across the country emerged to support and promote single issues that reflected their key interests. These people became known as the **New Right**. The New Right focused its energy on controversial social issues. These included opposing abortion, blocking the Equal Rights Amendment, and evading court-ordered busing. It also called for a return to school prayer, which the Supreme Court had outlawed in 1962.

Many in the New Right criticized **affirmative action**. Affirmative action required employers and educational institutions to give special consideration to women, African Americans, and other minority groups, even though these people were not necessarily better qualified. Many conservatives saw affirmative action as a form of **reverse discrimination**. They believed it favored one group over another on the basis of race or gender. To members of the New Right, liberal positions on affirmative action and other issues represented an assault on traditional values.

THE CONSERVATIVE COALITION Beginning in the mid-1960s, the conservative movement in the United States grew in strength. Eventually, conservative groups formed the **conservative coalition**—an alliance of business leaders, middle-class voters, disaffected Democrats, and fundamentalist Christian groups.

Conservative intellectuals argued the cause of the conservative coalition in newspapers such as *The Wall Street Journal* and magazines such as the *National Review,* founded in 1955 by conservative William F. Buckley Jr. Conservative think tanks, such as the American Enterprise Institute and the Heritage Foundation, were founded to develop conservative policies and principles that would appeal to the majority of voters.

Goals of the Conservative Movement

- Shrink the size of the federal government and reduce spending
- Promote family values and patriotic ideals
- Stimulate business by reducing government regulations and lowering taxes
- Strengthen the national defense

Reading Check
Analyze Issues
What was the agenda of the New Right?

THE MORAL MAJORITY Religion, especially evangelical Christianity, played a key role in the growing strength of the conservative coalition. The 1970s had brought a huge religious revival, especially among fundamentalist sects. Each week, millions of Americans watched evangelist preachers on television or listened to them on the radio. Two of the most influential televangelists were Jerry Falwell and Pat Robertson. Falwell formed an organization called the **Moral Majority**. The Moral Majority consisted mostly of evangelical and fundamentalist Christians who interpreted the Bible literally and believed in absolute standards of right and wrong. They condemned liberal attitudes and behaviors and argued for a restoration of traditional moral values. Jerry Falwell became the spokesperson for the Moral Majority.

As individual conservative groups formed networks, they created a movement dedicated to bringing back what they saw as traditional "family values." They hoped their ideas would help reduce the nation's high divorce rate and lower the number of out-of-wedlock births. They also wanted to encourage individual responsibility and generally revitalize the prosperity and patriotism of earlier times.

Conservatives Win Political Power

In 1976 **Ronald Reagan** lost the Republican nomination to the incumbent, Gerald Ford, in a very closely contested race. Four years later in a series of hard-fought primaries, Reagan won the 1980 nomination and chose George H. W. Bush as his running mate. Reagan and Bush ran against the incumbent president and vice-president, Jimmy Carter and Walter Mondale, who were nominated again by the Democrats despite their low standing in the polls.

Document-Based Investigation Historical Source

Moral Majority

The Moral Majority worked toward their political goals by using direct-mail campaigns to reach voters and by raising money to support candidates. In 1980 Reverend Jerry Falwell wrote a book in which he explained the motivations behind the actions of the Moral Majority.

> *"Our nation's internal problems are the direct result of her spiritual condition. . . . Right living must be reestablished as an American way of life. . . . Now is the time to begin calling America back to God, back to the Bible, back to morality."*
>
> —Jerry Falwell, from *Listen, America!*

Analyze Historical Sources
How did Falwell propose that the country fix its social problems?

REAGAN'S QUALIFICATIONS Originally a New Deal Democrat, Ronald Reagan had become a conservative Republican during the 1950s. He claimed that he had not left the Democratic Party but rather that the party had left him. As a spokesman for General Electric, he toured the country making speeches in favor of free enterprise and against big government. In 1964 he campaigned hard for Barry Goldwater, the Republican candidate for president. His speech supporting Goldwater in October 1964 made Reagan a serious candidate for public office. In 1966 Reagan was elected governor of California. He was reelected in 1970.

THE 1980 PRESIDENTIAL ELECTION In 1980 Reagan ran on a number of key issues. Supreme Court decisions on abortion, pornography, the teaching of evolution, and prayer in public schools all concerned conservative voters. And they rallied to Reagan. The prolonged Iranian hostage crisis and the weak economy under Carter, particularly the high rate of inflation, also helped Reagan.

Thanks in part to his acting career and his long experience in the public eye, Reagan was an extremely effective candidate. In contrast to Carter, who often seemed stiff and nervous, Reagan was relaxed, charming, and affable. He loved making quips: "A recession is when your neighbor loses his job. A depression is when you lose yours. And recovery is when Jimmy Carter loses his." Reagan's long-standing skill at simplifying issues and presenting clear-cut answers led his supporters to call him the Great Communicator. Also, his commitment to military and economic strength appealed to many Americans.

On October 28, 1980, Jimmy Carter and Ronald Reagan participated in the election's only presidential debate. This debate only helped to solidify the differences between the two candidates in voters' minds. Reagan attacked Carter's record as president and his handling of the energy crisis and international terrorism. Carter countered by claiming Reagan was too conservative for America, warning of cuts to social programs like Medicare.

Only 52.6 percent of American voters went to the polls in 1980. Reagan won the election by a narrow majority. He got 44 million votes, or 51 percent of the total. His support, however, was spread throughout the country, so that he carried 44 states and won 489 electoral votes. Republicans also gained control of the Senate for the first time since 1954. As Reagan assumed the presidency, many people were buoyed by his genial smile and his assertion that it was "morning again in America."

Presidential Election of 1980

Party	Candidate	Electoral Votes	Popular Votes
Republican	Ronald Reagan	489	43,904,153
Democratic	Jimmy Carter	49	35,483,883
Independent	John Anderson		5,720,060

Not shown:
3 Alaska
4 Hawaii
3 District of Columbia

Interpret Maps

1. **Location** Which states and/or district voted for Jimmy Carter in 1980?

2. **Region** Which region of the country—North, South, East, or West—voted exclusively for Ronald Reagan?

Ronald Reagan (1911–2004)

Ronald Wilson Reagan was born in 1911 in Tampico, Illinois. He grew up in Dixon, Illinois, graduated from nearby Eureka College, and then worked as a sports announcer in Iowa. In 1937 Reagan moved to Hollywood and became a movie actor, eventually making more than 50 films. As president of the Screen Actors Guild, he worked actively to remove alleged Communist influences from the movie industry.

Reagan had the ability to express his ideas in simple and clear language that the average voter could understand. When he proposed a

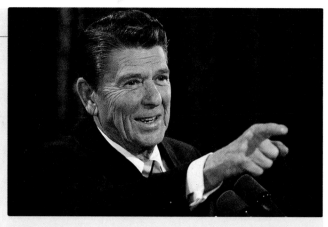

10 percent cut in government spending on social programs, he stated, "We can lecture our children about extravagance until we run out of voice and breath. Or we can cure their extravagance by simply reducing their allowance."

Reading Check
Analyze Causes
What factors led
to Reagan's victory
in 1980?

Now, conservatives had elected one of their own—a true believer in less government, lower taxes, and traditional values. After he was elected, Reagan worked to translate the conservative agenda into public policy. He used his charisma and the disillusionment of the public, fueled by scandal and years of ineffective government, to restore Americans' faith in the presidency and start a "Reagan revolution."

Conservative Victories in 1984 and 1988

It was clear by 1984 that the Reagan revolution had forged a large coalition of conservative voters who highly approved of his policies. These voters included the following:

- *businesspeople*—who wanted to deregulate the economy
- *southerners*—who welcomed the limits on federal power
- *westerners*—who resented federal controls on mining and grazing
- *Reagan Democrats*—who agreed with Reagan on limiting federal government and thought that the Democratic Party had drifted too far to the left

THE 1984 PRESIDENTIAL ELECTION In 1984 Reagan and Bush won the Republican nominations for reelection without challenge. Walter Mondale, who had been vice-president under President Carter, won the Democratic Party's nomination and chose Representative **Geraldine Ferraro** of New York as his running mate. Ferraro became the first woman on a major party's presidential ticket.

In 1984 the economy was strong. Reagan and Bush won by a landslide, carrying every state but Mondale's home state of Minnesota and the District of Columbia.

Geraldine Ferraro speaks at the 1984 Democratic convention.

George Bush announces his presidential candidacy at a rally in 1987.

THE 1988 PRESIDENTIAL ELECTION In 1988 a majority of Americans were economically comfortable. And they attributed their comfort to Reagan and Bush. When Michael Dukakis, the Democratic governor of Massachusetts, ran for the presidency in 1988 against **George H. W. Bush**, Reagan's vice-president, most voters saw little reason for change.

George Bush simply built on President Reagan's legacy by promising, "Read my lips: no new taxes" in his acceptance speech at the Republican Convention. He stressed his commitment to the conservative ideas of the Moral Majority. Though Bush asserted that he wanted a "kinder, gentler nation," his campaign sponsored a number of negative "attack ads." He told audiences that Dukakis was an ultraliberal whose views were outside the mainstream of American values, suggesting that Dukakis was soft on crime and unpatriotic.

Some commentators believed that the negative ads contributed to the lowest voter turnout in 64 years. Only half of the eligible voters went to the polls. George Bush won 426 electoral votes. His victory was viewed, as Reagan's had been, as a mandate for conservative social and political policies.

Reading Check
Analyze Causes
What factors contributed to Reagan's victory in 1984 and Bush's victory in 1988?

Lesson 4 Assessment

1. **Organize Information** Use a cluster diagram to record the issues that conservatives strongly endorsed.

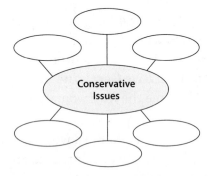

Conservative Issues

Choose one issue and explain in a paragraph the conservative position on that issue.

2. **Key Terms and People** For each key term or person in the lesson, write a sentence explaining its significance.

3. **Analyze Effects** What role did the Moral Majority play in the conservative movement of the 1970s and early 1980s?

4. **Evaluate** What personal qualities in Ronald Reagan helped him to win election as president in 1980?

5. **Analyze Motives** How did the leaders of the conservative movement of the 1980s want to change government?

   Think About:
   - the difference between the conservative view of government and the liberal view
   - the groups that made up the conservative coalition
   - conservatives' attitudes toward existing government programs

Reagan and Bush Confront Domestic Concerns

One American's Story

The Big Idea

Presidents Reagan and Bush pursued a conservative agenda. It included tax cuts, budget cuts, and increased defense spending, during an era of serious social problems.

Why It Matters Now

The conservative views of Reagan and Bush created policies and priorities that affect government spending and budgeting today.

Key Terms and People

Reaganomics

supply-side economics

Sandra Day O'Connor

deregulation

Environmental Protection Agency (EPA)

AIDS (acquired immune deficiency syndrome)

Throughout the 1980 presidential campaign and in the early days of his administration, President Reagan emphasized the perilous state of the economy during the Carter administration. In a speech to the nation on February 5, 1981—his first televised speech from the White House—Reagan announced his new economic program. He called for a reduction in income tax rates for individuals. He also called for a big reduction in government spending.

"I'm speaking to you tonight to give you a report on the state of our nation's economy. I regret to say that we're in the worst economic mess since the Great Depression. . . . It's time to recognize that we've come to a turning point. We're threatened with an economic calamity of tremendous proportions, and the old business-as-usual treatment can't save us. Together, we must chart a different course."

President Ronald Reagan

—Ronald Reagan, from a televised speech to the nation, February 5, 1981

President Reagan would deal with these problems by consistently stressing a sweeping package of new economic policies. These economic policies, dubbed "**Reaganomics**," consisted of three parts: (1) budget cuts, (2) tax cuts, and (3) increased defense spending.

SS.912.A.1.2; SS.912.A.1.4; SS.912.A.1.7; SS.912.A.7.12; SS.912.A.7.17; HE.912.C.2.4; MAFS.K12.MP.3.1; MAFS.K12.MP.6.1

"Reaganomics" Takes Over

As soon as Reagan took office, he worked to reduce the size and influence of the federal government. He thought these reductions would encourage private investment. Because people were anxious about the economy, they were open to new approaches to taxes and the federal budget.

BUDGET CUTS Reagan's strategy for downsizing the federal government included deep cuts in government spending on social programs. Yet his cuts did not affect all segments of the population equally. Entitlement programs that benefited the middle class, such as Social Security, Medicare, and veterans' pensions, remained intact. On the other hand, Congress slashed by 10 percent the budget for programs that benefited other groups. These programs included urban mass transit, food stamps, welfare benefits, job training, Medicaid, school lunches, and student loans. At the same time, Reagan authorized increases in military spending that more than offset cuts in social programs, adding to the deficit. In order to compete with the Soviet Union in the arms race, between 1981 and 1984 the Defense Department budget almost doubled.

TAX CUTS "Reaganomics" rested heavily upon **supply-side economics**. This theory held that if people paid fewer taxes, they would save more money. Banks could then loan that money to businesses. Businesses, in turn, could invest the money in resources to improve productivity. Then the supply of goods would increase, which would drive down prices. Reagan based his ideas for supply-side economics on the work of economists such as George Gilder and Arthur Laffer.

Ronald Reagan's budget director, David Stockman, used supply-side economics to draft the Economic Recovery Tax Act of 1981. At Reagan's urging, Congress lowered income taxes and business taxes by about 25 percent over a three-year period. The largest tax cuts went to those with the highest incomes. As Reagan decried in his first inaugural address, "those who . . . work are denied a fair return for their labor by a tax system which penalizes successful achievement." Administration officials defended the plan. They claimed that as prosperity returned, the extra income acquired by wealthy investors and large corporations would trickle down to the middle class and even the poor in the form of wages. Despite Reagan's "trickle-down" theory, the wealthy gained the most from these tax cuts. In the 1980s the rich got richer as poverty deepened for many others.

RECESSION AND RECOVERY While Reagan was charting a new course for the American economy, the economy itself was sinking into recession. Lasting from July 1981 until November 1982, it was the most severe recession since the Great Depression. However, early in 1983 an economic upturn began as consumers went on a spending spree. Tax cuts, a decline in interest rates, and lower inflation bolstered their confidence in the economy. The stock market surged. Unemployment declined. And the gross national product went up by almost 10 percent. The stock market boom lasted until 1987, when the market crashed, losing 508 points in one day. This fall was

Deficit Spending

During Reagan's first term, federal spending far outstripped federal revenue and created a huge budget deficit. In this cartoon, Reagan (with budget director David Stockman sitting beside him on the "Inflation" stagecoach) sees something that "shouldn't be there."

Analyze Historical Sources

1. What is the meaning of the wheel flying off the stagecoach?

2. Whom do the passengers inside the stagecoach represent?

due in large part to automated and computerized buying and selling systems. However, the market recovered and then continued its upward climb.

SAVINGS AND LOAN CRISIS Economic downturns in the late 1970s and early 1980s also had disastrous effects on the Savings and Loan (S&L) industry. S&Ls were small community banks that made mortgage loans. In 1980 there were about 4,000 S&Ls with about $600 billion in assets. By the early 1980s high interest rates and high inflation caused many of their mortgage investments to lose value. When the S&Ls could not attract enough depositors to offset these losses, the government loosened regulations. This allowed S&Ls more freedom to attract new depositors, but this only made the problem worse. By 1989 more than 1,000 S&Ls were forced to close. The Savings and Loan crisis of the 1980s cost the government, and the taxpayers, more than $120 billion.

THE NATIONAL DEBT CLIMBS Beneath the surface of recovery lay problems that continued to plague the economy. Tax cuts had helped the rich. At the same time, social welfare cuts had hurt the poor. Loose regulations played a significant part in the Savings and Loan crisis, leaving the government and taxpayers responsible for paying to clean up the mess. Despite large reductions in parts of the budget, federal spending still outstripped federal revenue. Budget deficits were growing. Even though Reagan backed away from supply-side economics in 1982 and imposed new taxes, they were not enough to balance the budget. By the end of his first term, the national debt had almost doubled.

Reading Check
Summarize
What are the main ideas of supply-side economics?

Reagan's Policy Goals

After setting his economic policies in motion, President Reagan turned his attention to social and political goals. The conservative coalition had identified two areas that they believed needed change. Their focus was on the Supreme Court and on government regulation policies.

Anita Hill and Clarence Thomas testify before the Senate Judiciary Committee in October 1991.

JUDICIAL POWER SHIFTS TO THE RIGHT One of the most important ways in which Reagan accomplished his conservative goals was through his appointments to the Supreme Court. Reagan nominated **Sandra Day O'Connor**, Antonin Scalia, and Anthony M. Kennedy to fill seats left by retiring justices. O'Connor was the first woman to be appointed to the Court. He also nominated Justice William Rehnquist, the most conservative justice on the Court at the time, to the position of Chief Justice.

When George Bush won the presidency, he followed Reagan's lead. Bush made the Court even more conservative by replacing retiring justice William Brennan with David H. Souter and nominating Clarence Thomas to take the place of Thurgood Marshall. However, controversy exploded when law professor Anita Hill testified that Thomas had sexually harassed her when she worked for him in the 1980s. During several days of televised Senate hearings, committee members questioned Thomas, Hill, and witnesses for each side. Thomas eventually won approval by a final vote of 52 to 48.

The Reagan and Bush appointments ended the liberal control over the Supreme Court that had begun under Franklin Roosevelt. These appointments became increasingly significant as the Court revisited constitutional issues related to such topics as discrimination, abortion, and affirmative action. In 1989 the Court, in a series of rulings, restricted a woman's right to an abortion. The Court also imposed new restrictions on civil rights laws that had been designed to protect the rights of women and minorities. During the 1990–1991 session, the Court narrowed the rights of arrested persons.

DEREGULATION OF THE ECONOMY Reagan achieved one of his most important objectives—reducing the size and power of the federal government. He did so in part by cutting federal entitlement programs but also through **deregulation**, the cutting back of federal regulation of industry. He removed price controls on oil and eliminated federal health and safety inspections for nursing homes. He deregulated the airline industry (allowing airlines to abandon unprofitable air routes) and the savings and loan industry. One of the positive results of this deregulation was that it increased competition and often resulted in lower prices for consumers.

In a further effort at deregulation, President Reagan cut the budget of the **Environmental Protection Agency (EPA)**. The EPA had been established in 1970 to fight pollution and conserve natural resources. He ignored pleas from Canada to reduce acid rain. He also appointed opponents of the regulations to enforce them. For example, James Watt, Reagan's secretary of the interior, sold millions of acres of public land to private developers—often at bargain prices. He opened the continental shelf to oil and gas drilling, which many people thought posed environmental risks. Watt also encouraged timber cutting in national forests and eased restrictions on coal mining.

Reading Check
Analyze Motives
How did Reagan achieve some of the social and political goals of the conservative movement?

Social Concerns

During the 1980s, both in the cities and in rural and suburban areas, local governments strove to deal with crises in health, education, and safety. Americans directed their attention to issues such as AIDS, drug abuse, abortion, and education.

HEALTH ISSUES One of the most troubling health issues during the 1980s was **AIDS (acquired immune deficiency syndrome)**. Possibly beginning as early as the 1960s, AIDS spread rapidly throughout the world. Caused by a virus that destroys the immune system, AIDS weakens the body so that it is prone to infections and normally rare cancers.

AIDS is transmitted through bodily fluids. And most of the early victims of the disease were either homosexual men or intravenous drug users who shared needles. However, many people also contracted AIDS through contaminated blood transfusions. And children acquired it by being born to infected mothers. As the 1980s progressed, increasing numbers of heterosexuals began contracting AIDS. As the epidemic grew, so did concern over prevention and cure.

NOW & THEN

AIDS Epidemic

Since 1985 the development of new AIDS medications has made great advances in treating patients and helping to slow the spread of the disease. Unfortunately, though, the drugs have remained expensive, making it difficult for many patients in poorer countries to receive treatment.

In 2003 President George W. Bush announced a plan to fight the AIDS epidemic in one of the hardest-hit regions—sub-Saharan Africa.

The President's Emergency Plan for AIDS Relief (PEPFAR) pledged an initial $15 billion to provide treatment for those infected. By 2008 the number of Africans receiving treatment increased from 50,000 to more than 2 million. These treatments helped prevent an estimated 12 million new infections. Between 2005 and 2011 the number of deaths from AIDS in sub-Saharan Africa decreased by 32 percent, from 1.8 million to 1.2 million per year.

The AIDS quilt was displayed on the National Mall in Washington, DC, in 1987. Each panel honors a person who died of AIDS.

ABORTION Many Americans were concerned about abortion. Abortion had been legal in the United States since 1973, when the Supreme Court ruled in *Roe* v. *Wade* that a woman's right to privacy protected first-trimester abortions. Abortion opponents quickly organized under the pro-life banner. They argued that human life begins at conception and that no woman has the right to terminate a human life by her individual decision. Abortion proponents described themselves as pro-choice. They argued that reproductive choices were personal health-care matters. They also noted that many women had died from abortions performed by unskilled people in unsterile settings before the procedure was legalized.

In July 1989 the Supreme Court ruled in *Webster* v. *Reproductive Health Care Services* that states had the right to impose new restrictions on abortion. As a result, abortion restrictions varied from state to state.

DRUG ABUSE Battles over abortion rights sometimes competed for public attention with concerns about rising drug abuse. A few people argued that drugs should be legalized to reduce the power of gangs who made a living selling illegal drugs. Others called for treatment facilities to treat addictions. The Reagan administration launched a war on drugs. It also supported moves to prosecute users as well as dealers. First Lady Nancy Reagan toured the country with an antidrug campaign that admonished students to "Just say no!" to drugs.

EDUCATION Education became another issue that stirred people's concerns. In 1983 a federal commission issued a report on education titled *A Nation at Risk.* The report revealed that American students lagged behind students in most other industrialized nations. In addition, the report stated that 23 million Americans were unable to follow an instruction manual or to fill out a job application.

The commission's findings touched off a debate about the quality of education. The commission recommended more homework, longer school days, and an extended school year. It also promoted increased pay and merit raises for teachers, as well as a greater emphasis on basic subjects such as English, math, science, social studies, and computer science.

A young boy offers clothes to a homeless man in Philadelphia, 1983.

THE URBAN CRISIS The crisis in education was closely connected to the crisis in the cities. Many undereducated students lived in cities such as Baltimore, Chicago, Detroit, Philadelphia, and Washington, DC. During the 1970s the United States had become increasingly suburbanized. More and more white families responded to the lure of new homes, big lawns, shopping malls, and well-equipped schools outside the cities. Businesses moved, too, taking jobs and tax revenue with them.

Poor people and racial minorities were often left in cities burdened by high unemployment rates, crumbling infrastructures, inadequate funds for sanitation and health services, deteriorating schools, and growing social problems. By 1992 thousands of people were homeless, including many families with children. Cities were increasingly divided into wealthy neighborhoods and poverty-stricken areas.

The crew of the space shuttle *Challenger*

Reading Check
Contrast What are the two viewpoints on legalized abortion?

HIGH COSTS OF SPACE EXPLORATION By the mid-1970s public interest in the space program waned as lofty goals gave way to routine missions. Beginning in 1981 NASA hoped to revive interest in space flight through the space shuttle program. That year, the space shuttle *Columbia* became the first reusable spaceship. NASA thought that a fleet of reusable spaceships, like *Columbia,* could help reduce costs and make space travel more routine. In 1983 NASA accomplished two more firsts. In June of that year, Sally Ride became the first American woman in space. In August, Guion S. Bluford became the first African American astronaut in space. Public interest in the new shuttle program seemed to be on the rise.

In 1986 NASA was set to complete yet another first. Christa McAuliffe was selected to become the first teacher and first civilian in space as a member of the *Challenger* crew. Tragically, the space shuttle *Challenger* never completed its mission to deploy a communications satellite. Shortly after takeoff, the shuttle exploded, killing McAuliffe and the other six crew members. The investigation that followed determined that a rubber O-ring on the solid rocket booster failed, causing the explosion. NASA suspended all space shuttle flights for more than two years, while they redesigned parts of the shuttle. Although shuttle flights resumed in 1988, with space shuttle *Discovery,* NASA's reputation never fully recovered from the *Challenger* disaster.

Bush's Domestic Policies

Many of the domestic issues that lingered through the 1980s fell to President Bush to try to resolve. In his inaugural address on January 20, 1989, Bush noted many of the problems American cities faced—homelessness, drug addiction, and crime. He pledged to support the efforts of community organizations and volunteers in cities across the country, calling them "a thousand points of light . . . that are spread like stars throughout the nation, doing good." His initial promises, though, often fell short.

DIFFICULT DECISIONS

Sending Money Into Space

Under the Reagan administration, the government shifted the emphasis of the space program from scientific to military and commercial applications. The space shuttle *Challenger* explosion caused a reexamination of ventures into space. NASA's budget had grown from about $3 billion in 1975 to about $7 billion in 1983. While this figure was still less that 1 percent of the total federal budget, many people began to question the value of the space program. Some thought that the money spent on space might be better spent on the country's growing social needs.

1. Should the federal government spend money on space exploration when so many American citizens require basic assistance?

2. If you were a legislator being asked to vote in favor of funding space exploration today, how would you vote? Why?

The federal deficit, now at $2.8 trillion, had tripled since 1980. During his campaign, Bush had also promised that he would not enact new taxes. This meant that there was no money in the federal budget to fund major domestic programs to address many of the social issues the country faced. Despite these financial constraints, President Bush was able to announce a new education initiative, "America 2000." He argued that choice was the salvation of American schools. And he recommended allowing parents to use public funds to send their children to the schools of their choice, whether public, private, or religious.

President Bush also signed two important pieces of legislation—the Americans with Disabilities Act (ADA) and the Clean Air Act Amendments. The ADA made it illegal to discriminate against individuals with disabilities in employment, transportation, and public buildings. Bush hoped that the amendments to the Clean Air Act of 1963 would bring government and business into a partnership to find innovative ways to reduce pollution and clean up the environment.

Although Bush had impressive foreign policy successes, his modest domestic achievements tarnished his image. Throughout his presidency, rising deficits and a recession that began in 1990 and lasted through most of 1992 hurt him. Forced to raise taxes despite his campaign pledge, Bush's approval rating had dropped to 49 percent by 1992. The weak economy and the tax hike doomed his reelection campaign, and 12 years of Republican leadership came to an end.

Reading Check
Analyze Causes
Why was President Bush unable to enact any major domestic programs?

Lesson 5 Assessment

1. **Organize Information** Use a chart to list some of the social problems of the Reagan and Bush years and how the government responded to them.

Social Problems	Government Responses

Choose one issue and write other responses the government might have made.

2. **Key Terms and People** For each key term or person in the lesson, write a sentence explaining its significance.

3. **Predict** How might improvements in the educational system help solve other social problems?

Think About:
- the impact education might have on health-related problems
- the impact that education might have on urban problems
- the impact that education might have on unemployment

4. **Analyze Motives** Why did President Reagan and President Bush think it was important to appoint conservative justices to the Supreme Court?

5. **Form Generalizations** Why might a widening gap between the richest and poorest citizens of a country be a cause for concern about that country's future?

From Rust Belt to Sun Belt

In the 1970s many Americans left the Midwest and Northeast regions, which came to be called the *Rust Belt* because many of their aging factories had been closed. These people moved to the South and Southwest, which became known as the *Sun Belt* due to their warm climate. In the postwar decades, the Sun Belt experienced an increase in job opportunities that attracted many new residents. These states typically had a lower cost of living, as well. And, with the widespread availability of air conditioning, living in these states became more practical than it had once been.

AMERICANS ON THE MOVE, 1970s

Between 1970 and 1975 the population center of the United States, which had generally moved westward for 17 decades, suddenly moved southward as well. The arrows show the net number of Americans who migrated and their patterns of migration in the early 1970s. The West gained 311,000 from the Northeast plus 472,000 from the Midwest region, for a total of 783,000 people. However, it also lost 75,000 people to the South. During the 1980s and 1990s the southward and westward shift continued.

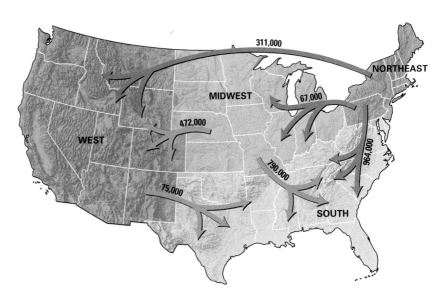

Source: Bernard L. Weinstein and Robert E. Firestine, *Regional Growth and Decline in the United States (1978)*

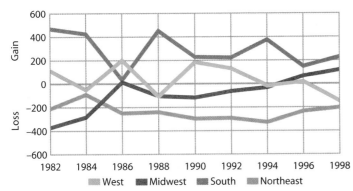

Regional Internal Migration, 1982–1998

Source: U.S. Census Bureau

REGIONAL EXCHANGES

As a geographical term, *region* is used to designate an area with common features or characteristics that set it apart from its surroundings. Between 1982 and 1998 internal migrations in the U.S. saw more people moving from Rust Belt states to Sun Belt states. Beginning in the early 1970s, the nation also saw a reverse migration of African Americans from the Midwest and Northeast back to the South. From 2005 to 2010, the South saw an average annual increase of about 66,000 African Americans per year due to migration. When the economic factors that pulled African Americans north began to wane, the Sun Belt's growing economy and climate enticed many to move south once again.

SHIFTS IN POLITICAL POWER

Between 1990 and 2000 our country's population grew by a record 32.7 million people to 281.4 million. For the first time in the 20th century, all 50 states gained people between census years. However, as people migrate internally from state to state, and from region to region, they gradually transform the balance of political and economic power in the nation. Each census in recent times has recorded how certain states have gained population and others have lost population. If the gains or losses are large enough, a state's representation in the U.S. House of Representatives will increase or decrease commensurately.

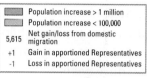

	Population increase > 1 million
	Population increase < 100,000
5,615	Net gain/loss from domestic migration
+1	Gain in apportioned Representatives
-1	Loss in apportioned Representatives

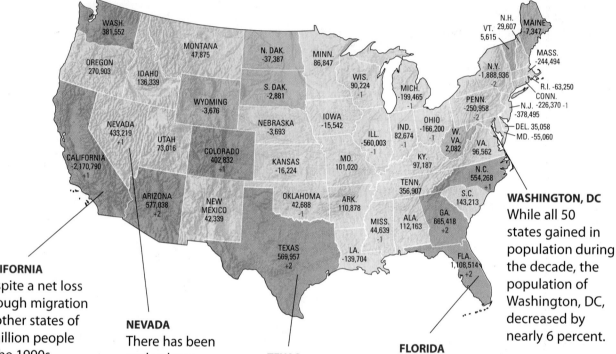

CALIFORNIA
Despite a net loss through migration to other states of 2 million people in the 1990s, international immigrants and in-state births gave California the greatest net increase in population among the 50 states.

NEVADA
There has been such a large influx of people since 1945 that building houses for newcomers has become a major industry in Nevada.

TEXAS
During the 1990s Texas eclipsed New York to become the nation's second-most-populous state behind California. Sixty percent of the Texas increase has been driven by Hispanic growth.

FLORIDA
During the 1990s Florida's population increased 23.5 percent, making it the nation's fourth-largest state. With so many new residents, Florida gained two additional House seats, bringing its congressional delegation to 25.

WASHINGTON, DC
While all 50 states gained in population during the decade, the population of Washington, DC, decreased by nearly 6 percent.

Critical Thinking

1. **Analyze Distributions** Which states lost the most people between 1990 and 2000? Which states gained the most people?

2. **Create a Graph** Choose one of the most populous states, and then pose a historical question about population in that state. Create a graph or graphs that show various aspects of population for the state you have chosen. Be sure that the graph(s) help answer the question you posed. Then display the graph(s) and the question in the classroom.

Foreign Policy Under Reagan and Bush

The Big Idea

New pressures, including the breakup of the Soviet Union in 1991 and the new role of the U.S. as the world's only superpower, affected foreign policy under Reagan and Bush.

Why It Matters Now

The United States continues to provide substantial economic, diplomatic, and military support to nations around the world.

Key Terms and People

apartheid

Tiananmen Square

Sandinistas

Contras

Operation Desert Storm

One American's Story

It was fitting that George H. W. Bush, former head of America's Cold War spy agency, the CIA, was the president who would preside over the end of the Cold War. Elected in 1988, President Bush soon confronted the fall of the Berlin Wall and the dissolution of the Soviet Union. The United States emerged from this period of massive global upheaval as the world's lone superpower. And the Bush administration became the first to be tasked with trying to define America's new role in the world.

President George H. W. Bush

"The end of the cold war has been a victory for all humanity. . . . Europe has become whole and free, and America's leadership was instrumental in making it possible. . . . For generations, America has led the struggle to preserve and extend the blessings of liberty. And today, in a rapidly changing world, American leadership is indispensable. Americans know that leadership brings burdens and sacrifices. But we also know why the hopes of humanity turn to us. We are Americans; we have a unique responsibility to do the hard work of freedom. And when we do, freedom works."

—George H. W. Bush, from State of the Union address, January 29, 1991

The end of the Cold War was just one of the foreign policy challenges the Reagan and Bush administrations faced. During their time in office, both presidents also had to confront issues in other parts of the world.

SS.912.A.1.4; SS.912.A.7.11; SS.912.A.7.12; LAFS.1112.WHST.3.7; LAFS.1112.WHST.3.9

Foreign Policy in Africa and Asia

As the leaders of a global superpower, U.S. presidents have often had to choose whether or not to become involved in regional conflicts. They have also had to weigh a number of factors, including U.S. national security, to determine the degree of involvement, either diplomatically or militarily. Presidents Reagan and Bush both had important decisions to make about trouble spots in Africa and Asia.

APARTHEID IN SOUTH AFRICA President Reagan took a noninterventionist position in confronting the South African government over **apartheid**. For decades, apartheid ("apartness") had mandated racial segregation throughout South African society. Under apartheid, the minority white population enjoyed great privileges. Meanwhile, the government forcibly relocated millions of people categorized as nonwhite to desolate frontier lands. Nonwhites were banned from decent jobs, schools, and housing. They could not own land, vote, or travel freely.

South African President F. W. de Klerk (*left*) oversaw the peaceful end of apartheid. In 1994 Nelson Mandela (*right*) succeeded him as president.

American companies and investments in the resource-rich country helped keep the white regime in power. Starting in the 1970s, anti-apartheid groups urged nations to divest, or withdraw investments, from South Africa.

Reagan preferred a policy of "constructive engagement." He wanted to maintain business ties, while offering incentives for reform and engaging in diplomacy with the government. Critics charged that the policy enriched a corrupt, white minority regime.

In 1986 Congress overrode a Reagan veto to pass the Comprehensive Anti-Apartheid Act, which imposed trade limits and sanctions. The Bush administration supported these sanctions and worked with South African president F. W. De Klerk to peacefully end apartheid. With a new constitution and democratic elections in South Africa in 1994, apartheid officially ended.

COMMUNISM CONTINUES IN CHINA Even before reforms began to unravel the Soviet Union, economic reform had begun in China. Early in the 1980s, the Chinese Communist government loosened its grip on business and eliminated some price controls. Students in China began to demand freedom of speech and a greater voice in government.

In April 1989, university students in China held marches that quickly grew into large demonstrations in Beijing's **Tiananmen** (tyän'än'měn') **Square** and on the streets of other cities. In Tiananmen Square, Chinese students constructed a version of the Statue of Liberty meant to symbolize their struggle for democracy.

China's premier, Li Peng, eventually ordered the military to crush the protesters. China's armed forces stormed into Tiananmen Square, slaughtering unarmed students. The world's democratic countries watched these events in horror on television. The collapse of the pro-democracy movement left the future in China uncertain. As one student leader said, "The government has won the battle here today. But they have lost the people's hearts."

A Chinese protester defies the tanks in Tiananmen Square in 1989.

Reading Check
Compare How was President Bush's foreign policy toward China similar to that of President Reagan's toward South Africa?

The United States and other nations condemned the actions of China's government and even imposed economic sanctions. Critics, however, felt that the actions of the Bush administration were not stern enough. When it was learned that U.S. officials had met with the Chinese government to ease tensions, critics accused the Bush administration of placing a higher value on economic concerns than human rights.

Central American and Caribbean Policy

Cold War considerations during the Reagan and Bush administrations continued to influence affairs in Central America and the Caribbean. There, the United States still opposed left-leaning and socialist governments in favor of governments friendly to the United States.

NICARAGUA The United States had a presence in Nicaragua ever since 1912, when President Taft sent U.S. Marines to protect American investments there. The marines left in 1933, but only after helping the dictator Anastasio Somoza come to power.

The Somoza family ruled Nicaragua for 42 years. To maintain control of its business empire, the family manipulated elections and assassinated their political rivals. Many people believed that only a revolution would end the Somoza dictatorship.

Between 1977 and 1979 Nicaragua was engulfed in a civil war between Somoza's national guard and the *Sandinistas,* rebels who took their name from a rebel leader named Sandino who had been killed in 1934. When Sandinista rebels toppled the dictatorship of Somoza's son in 1979, President Carter recognized the new regime and sent it $83 million in economic aid. The Soviet Union and Cuba sent aid as well.

In 1981, however, President Reagan charged that Nicaragua was a Soviet outpost that was exporting revolution to other Central American countries. Reagan cut all aid to the Sandinista government. He then threw his support to guerrilla forces known as the *Contras* because they were against the Sandinistas. By 1983 the Contra army had grown to nearly 10,000 men. And American CIA officials had stationed themselves to direct operations—without congressional approval. In response, Congress passed the Boland Amendment, banning military aid to the Contras for two years. However, Reagan's administration still found ways to negotiate aid to the Contras.

On February 25, 1990, Nicaraguan president Daniel Ortega held free elections. Violeta de Chamorro, a Contra supporter, was elected the nation's new president. Chamorro's coalition was united only in opposition to the Sandinistas. It was too weak and divided to solve Nicaragua's ongoing problems.

GRENADA On the tiny Caribbean island of Grenada, the United States used direct military force to accomplish its aims. After noting that the island was developing ties to Communist Cuba, President Reagan sent approximately

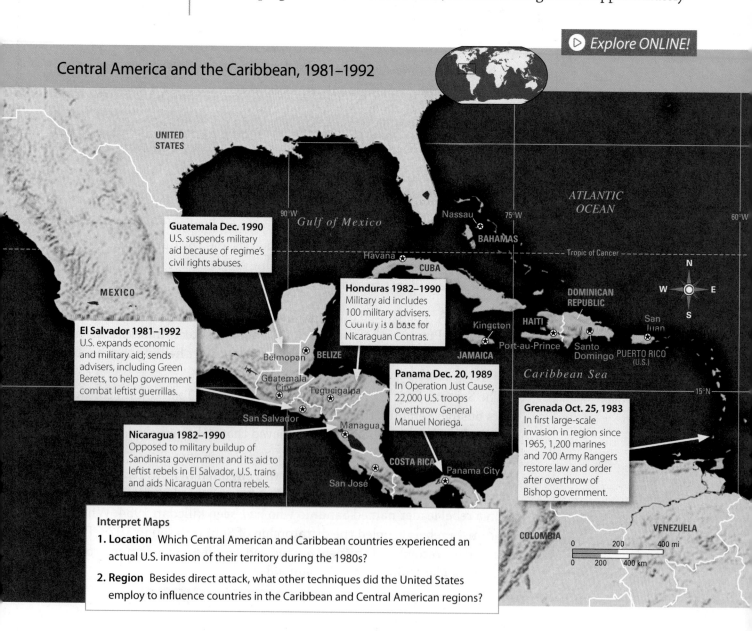

Explore ONLINE!

Central America and the Caribbean, 1981–1992

Guatemala Dec. 1990
U.S. suspends military aid because of regime's civil rights abuses.

Honduras 1982–1990
Military aid includes 100 military advisers. Country is a base for Nicaraguan Contras.

El Salvador 1981–1992
U.S. expands economic and military aid; sends advisers, including Green Berets, to help government combat leftist guerrillas.

Panama Dec. 20, 1989
In Operation Just Cause, 22,000 U.S. troops overthrow General Manuel Noriega.

Nicaragua 1982–1990
Opposed to military buildup of Sandinista government and its aid to leftist rebels in El Salvador, U.S. trains and aids Nicaraguan Contra rebels.

Grenada Oct. 25, 1983
In first large-scale invasion in region since 1965, 1,200 marines and 700 Army Rangers restore law and order after overthrow of Bishop government.

Interpret Maps

1. **Location** Which Central American and Caribbean countries experienced an actual U.S. invasion of their territory during the 1980s?

2. **Region** Besides direct attack, what other techniques did the United States employ to influence countries in the Caribbean and Central American regions?

2,000 troops to the island in 1983. There, they overthrew the pro-Cuban government, which was replaced by one friendlier to the United States. Eighteen American soldiers died in the attack. But Reagan declared that the invasion had been necessary to defend U.S. security.

PANAMA Six years later, in 1989, President Bush sent more than 20,000 soldiers and marines into Panama. Their goal was to overthrow and arrest General Manuel Antonio Noriega on charges of drug trafficking. Noriega had been receiving money since 1960 from the CIA. But he was also involved in the international drug trade. After a Miami grand jury indicted him, Noriega was taken by force by the American military and flown to Miami to stand trial. In April 1992 Noriega was convicted and sentenced to 40 years in prison. Many Latin American governments deplored the "Yankee imperialism" of the action. However, many Americans—and Panamanians—were pleased by the removal of a military dictator who supported drug smuggling.

Middle East Trouble Spots

Results favorable to U.S. interests were more difficult to obtain in the Middle East. Negotiating conflicts between ever-shifting governments drew the United States into conflict, scandal, and its first major war since Vietnam.

TRAGEDY IN LEBANON President Reagan believed that American interests required stability in the Middle East. For years, civil war had ripped apart the Mediterranean coastal country of Lebanon. Muslim and Christian factions battled for control of the country. Various groups, including the Palestinian Liberation Organization (PLO), used Lebanon as a base for attacks against Israel to the south. In 1982 Israel invaded and occupied southern Lebanon to expel the PLO and try to form a new reliably friendly government. The invasion threatened to turn Lebanon's civil war into a general Middle East war.

In 1983 an international peacekeeping force, including some 800 U.S. Marines, arrived in Lebanon's capital, Beirut. On October 23 a suicide bomber drove a truck filled with explosives into the marine barracks in Beirut. The blast leveled the building, killing 241 sleeping soldiers inside. This tragedy was one of the first suicide terrorist attacks against the United States.

THE IRAN-CONTRA SCANDAL In 1983 terrorist groups loyal to Iran took a number of Americans hostage in Lebanon. Reagan denounced Iran and urged U.S. allies not to sell arms to Iran for its war against Iraq. In 1985 he declared that "America will never make concessions to terrorists." Therefore,

Reading Check
Contrast
Between 1980 and 1992 how did U.S. policies regarding Central America differ from those regarding China?

President Reagan's message to television audiences about selling arms to Iran differed greatly from what was going on behind the scenes.

Americans were shocked to learn in 1986 that President Reagan had approved the sale of arms to Iran. In exchange for those sales, Iran promised to win the release of seven American hostages held in Lebanon by pro-Iranian terrorists. What's more, members of Reagan's staff sent part of the profits from those illegal arms sales to the Contras in Nicaragua—in direct violation of the Boland Amendment. President Reagan held a press conference to explain what had happened.

> "I am deeply troubled that the implementation of a policy aimed at resolving a truly tragic situation in the Middle East has resulted in such controversy. As I've stated previously, I believe our policy goals toward Iran were well founded."
>
> —Ronald Reagan, from a press conference, November 25, 1986

In the summer of 1987, special committees of both houses of Congress conducted a dramatic inquiry into the Iran-Contra affair during a month of joint televised hearings. Among those testifying was Lieutenant Colonel Oliver North, a member of the National Security Council staff who played a key role in providing aid to the Contras. North appeared in military uniform adorned with service ribbons and badges. In defending his actions, North talked about patriotism and love of country. He asserted that he thought he was carrying out the president's wishes and that the end of helping the Contras justified almost any means.

After a congressional investigation, Special Prosecutor Lawrence E. Walsh, early in 1988, indicted various members of the Reagan administration who were involved in the scandal. Oliver North was found guilty of aiding the cover-up. He was fined and sentenced to perform community service. (His conviction was later overturned because he testified under a grant of limited immunity.) On Christmas Eve of 1992, President Bush pardoned a number of Reagan officials.

THE PERSIAN GULF WAR Regardless of the scandal surrounding the Iran-Contra affair, conflict with Iraq (which was Iran's long-standing enemy) and its leader, Saddam Hussein, soon eclipsed U.S. problems with Iran. During the 1980s Iran and Iraq had fought a prolonged war, and Hussein found himself with enormous war debts to pay. Several times, Hussein had claimed that the oil-rich nation of Kuwait was really part of Iraq. On August 2, 1990, Iraqi troops invaded Kuwait. The Iraqi invaders looted Kuwait. Then they headed toward Saudi Arabia and its oil fields. If Iraq conquered

– BIOGRAPHY ———————

H. Norman Schwarzkopf
(1934–2012)

In 1988 Norman Schwarzkopf, shown above, became commander in chief of forces in Asia and Africa. During the Persian Gulf War, more than 540,000 men and women served under the command of "Stormin' Norman." Schwarzkopf said of Saddam Hussein that he was "neither a strategist, nor is he schooled in the operational art, nor is he a tactician, nor is he a general, nor is he a soldier. Other than that, he is a great military man."

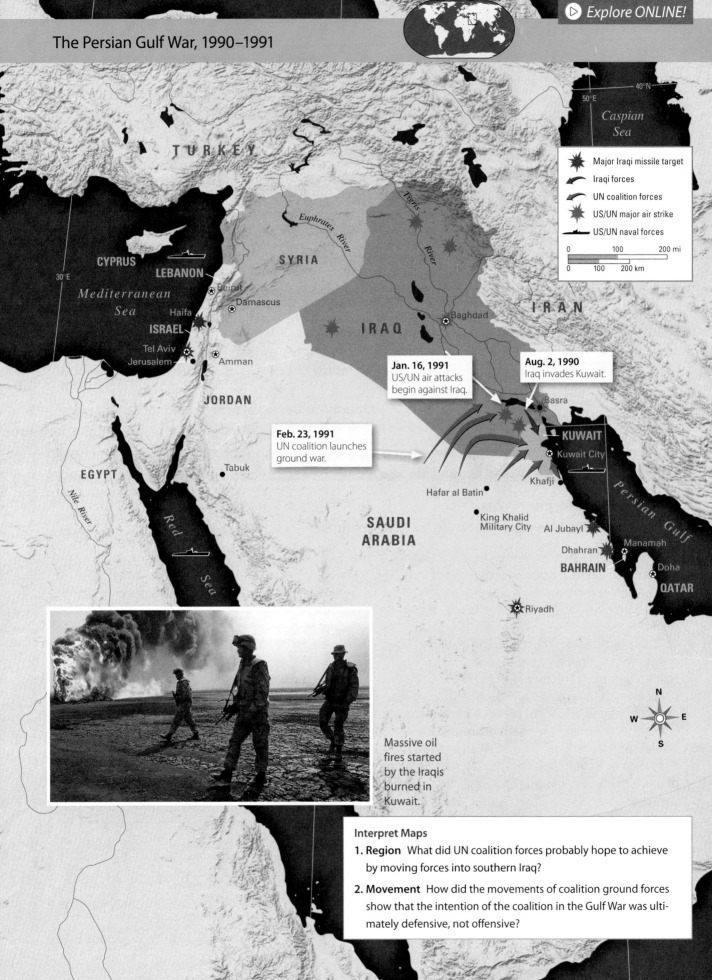

Explore ONLINE!

Caspian Sea

⬡ Major Iraqi missile target
↜ Iraqi forces
↜ UN coalition forces
✳ US/UN major air strike
⬓ US/UN naval forces

| 0 | 100 | 200 mi |
| 0 | 100 | 200 km |

TURKEY

CYPRUS

LEBANON

Mediterranean Sea

⊛ Beirut
• Damascus
Haifa

ISRAEL

Tel Aviv
Jerusalem
⊛ Amman

JORDAN

SYRIA

Euphrates River

Tigris River

IRAQ

⊛ Baghdad

IRAN

Jan. 16, 1991
US/UN air attacks begin against Iraq.

Aug. 2, 1990
Iraq invades Kuwait.

Basra

Feb. 23, 1991
UN coalition launches ground war.

EGYPT

Nile River

Red Sea

• Tabuk

SAUDI ARABIA

• Hafar al Batin

• King Khalid Military City

KUWAIT

⊛ Kuwait City

Khafji

Al Jubayl
Dhahran
⊛ Manamah

BAHRAIN

Doha
⊛ QATAR

Persian Gulf

⬡ Riyadh

Massive oil fires started by the Iraqis burned in Kuwait.

N
W   E
S

Interpret Maps

1. **Region** What did UN coalition forces probably hope to achieve by moving forces into southern Iraq?

2. **Movement** How did the movements of coalition ground forces show that the intention of the coalition in the Gulf War was ultimately defensive, not offensive?

Women served along with men in the military during the Gulf War.

Saudi Arabia as well as Kuwait, it would control one-half of the world's known oil reserves, which would severely threaten U.S. oil supplies.

For several months, President Bush and Secretary of State James Baker organized an international coalition against Iraqi aggression. They also sought the approval of the U.S. Congress, which would need to authorize any use of force against Iraq. According to the U.S. Constitution, only Congress has the power to declare war. With the support of Congress and the UN, President Bush launched **Operation Desert Storm** to liberate Kuwait from

POINT	COUNTERPOINT
"The United States must occasionally intervene militarily in regional conflicts."	*"The United States should not intervene militarily in regional conflicts."*
Proponents of U.S. military intervention abroad agreed with General Norman Schwarzkopf that "as the only remaining superpower, we have an awesome responsibility . . . to the rest of the world."	A foreign-policy analyst at the Cato Institute, Barbara Conry, stated that "intervention in regional wars is a distraction and a drain on resources." What's more, she argued, "it does not work." Recalling the presence of American troops in Lebanon, Conry argued that intervention not only jeopardized American soldiers, it often obstructed what it sought to achieve.
"The United States must take the lead in promoting democracy," urged Morton H. Halperin, former director of the ACLU (American Civil Liberties Union). "To say 'Let the UN do it' is a cop-out," stated adviser Robert G. Neumann.	
Political scientist Jane Sharp expressed a similar sentiment. She asked, "Can any nation that has taken no action [in Bosnia] to stop the Serbian practice of ethnic cleansing continue to call itself civilized?"	"The internal freedom of a political community can be achieved only by members of that community," agreed Professor Stephen R. Shalom. He added that "using [military action] encourages quick fix solutions that ignore the underlying sources of conflict."

Critical Thinking

1. **Connect to History** With at least one partner, research the events leading up to U.S. involvement in one of these countries: Lebanon, Grenada, Panama, or Kuwait. Then negotiate to resolve the conflict.

2. **Connect to Today** What do you think are the strongest arguments for and against military intervention in regional conflicts?

Iraqi control. On January 16, 1991, the United States and its allies staged a massive air assault and bombarded Iraq. On February 23 they launched a successful ground offensive from Saudi Arabia. On February 28, 1991, President Bush announced a cease-fire. Operation Desert Storm was over. Kuwait was liberated.

Millions of Americans turned out for the victory parades that greeted returning soldiers. After the debacle in Vietnam, they were thrilled the war was over, with fewer than 400 casualties among UN coalition forces. (However, there were subsequent reports that Gulf War veterans were suffering from disabilities caused by chemicals used in the war.) By contrast, Iraq had suffered an estimated 100,000 military and civilian deaths. During the embargo that followed, many Iraqi children died from outbreaks of cholera, typhoid, enteritis, and other diseases.

Reading Check
Draw Conclusions
What issue led to the conflict in the Middle East?

Lesson 6 Assessment

1. **Organize Information** Use a chart to explain U.S. foreign policy toward world regions.

Region	Foreign Policy
Africa and Asia	
Central America and the	
Middle East	

Write a paragraph in which you describe a trouble spot in one of these regions.

2. **Key Terms and People** For each key term in the lesson, write a sentence explaining its significance.

3. **Form Generalizations** What factors do you think determined whether or not the United States intervened militarily in other nations?

4. **Analyze Events** Over several months, the Bush administration used diplomacy to organize international support and the support of Congress for Operation Desert Storm. Why do you think they took these extra steps before invading Iraq?

Think About:

- the powers granted to Congress by the Constitution
- the costs of fighting a foreign war
- the economic importance of the region

Module 17 Assessment

Key Terms and People

For each key term or person below, write a sentence explaining its significance to the presidential administrations of the 1970s and 1980s.

1. stagflation
2. Watergate
3. Jimmy Carter
4. Camp David Accords
5. Moral Majority
6. Ronald Reagan
7. supply-side economics
8. Geraldine Ferraro
9. AIDS
10. Operation Desert Storm

Main Ideas

Use your notes and the information in the module to answer the following questions.

The Nixon Administration

1. In what ways did President Nixon attempt to reform the federal government?
2. How did President Nixon and the U.S. Supreme Court clash on school segregation?
3. Why had many Democratic voters in the South become potential Republican supporters by 1968?
4. Why did President Nixon oppose the extension of the Voting Rights Act?
5. How did Nixon try to combat stagflation?

Watergate: Nixon's Downfall

6. In what ways did the participants in Watergate attempt to cover up the scandal?
7. What role did the media play in the Watergate Scandal?
8. What events led to the Saturday Night Massacre?

The Ford and Carter Years

9. What were Gerald Ford's greatest successes as president?

10. Why did the Ford administration want to reform government regulation?
11. How did President Carter attempt to solve the energy crisis?
12. What factors played a role in America's economic stagnation?
13. How did the changing economy under Carter affect unemployment?

A Conservative Movement Emerges

14. What caused the conservative revolution of the early 1980s?
15. What were the main concerns of the Moral Majority?
16. What factors led to Ronald Reagan's victory in 1980?

Reagan and Bush Confront Domestic Concerns

17. What principles formed the basis of "Reaganomics"?
18. What were some of the effects of "Reaganomics"?
19. How were the domestic policies of the Nixon and Reagan administrations similar?
20. What is deregulation, and how did it affect certain industries in the 1980s?
21. What problems in education emerged during the 1980s?

Foreign Policy Under Reagan and Bush

22. How did the Bush administration respond to the events in Beijing's Tiananmen Square?
23. Why did the United States send troops to Panama in 1989?
24. Why did Israel become involved in the civil war in Lebanon?
25. Summarize the U.S. response to Iraq's invasion of Kuwait.

Critical Thinking

1. **Evaluate** In a chart, identify one major development for each issue listed that occurred between 1968 and 1980. Indicate whether you think the impact of the development was positive (+) or negative (–).

Issue	Development	Impact
Economic conditions		
Democratic government		
Efficient energy use		
Environmental protection		

2. **Analyze Events** Between 1972 and 1974 Americans were absorbed by the fall of President Nixon in the Watergate scandal. What might Americans have learned about the role of the executive branch? Explain.

3. **Synthesize** President Carter took special pride in his civil rights record. How did Carter's foreign policy mirror his domestic policy?

4. **Analyze Motives** In 1977 the Carter administration successfully negotiated the Camp David Accords. How might a peace agreement between Egypt and Israel affect the U.S. economy?

5. **Analyze Effects** Think about the short-term and long-term effects of Reaganomics. Do you think that Reaganomics was good or bad for the economy?

6. **Evaluate** Review the goals of the conservative movement and the actions of the federal government under presidents Reagan and Bush. Evaluate how well the goals had been achieved by the end of Bush's term.

7. **Compare and Contrast** In 1964 President Lyndon Johnson unveiled his domestic agenda—the Great Society. Compare and contrast the political philosophies of President Ronald Reagan with those of President Lyndon Johnson.

8. **Interpret Maps** Look at the map of Central America and the Caribbean, 1981–1992, in Lesson 6. Between 1982 and 1992, the United States intervened in Latin America many times. How might the presence of a Communist government on the island of Cuba have influenced U.S. actions?

9. **Form Opinions** Do you think the actions of the Reagan administration during the Iran-Contra affair were justified? Explain.

10. **Analyze Effects** What were the positive and negative effects of the Gulf War?

Engage with History

Imagine that you are working as a speechwriter for Ronald Reagan in 1980. Develop a campaign slogan, and then write a speech that contains your slogan and explains why Americans should vote for Reagan. Present your speech to the class.

Focus on Writing

Imagine that you are a journalist in the 1980s. Choose the social concern of the period that you believe to be the most significant domestic issue facing the United States. Write a newspaper editorial in which you persuade others that your issue is the most important and outline your approach for solving it. Use descriptive examples and vivid language to convince your audience to support your perspective.

Multimedia Activity

Do library or Internet research to find out more about Saddam Hussein's rise to power in Iraq. Write and record a short podcast describing the tactics that Hussein used to become dictator and how his policies affected the people of Iraq.

Module 18

Into a New Millennium

★

Essential Question

What issue or development has most affected the United States since the beginning of the 21st century?

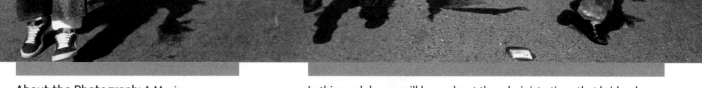

About the Photograph: A Mexican American dance troupe performs in a local parade.

In this module you will learn about the administrations that bridged the end of the 20th century and the beginning of the 21st. You will also examine how technology and changing demographics have shaped modern American culture.

▶ *Explore ONLINE!*

HISTORY

VIDEOS, including...
- Millennium
- I-Witness to 9/11
- Becoming a Candidate
- History and Development of Computers

☑ Document-Based Investigations

☑ Graphic Organizers

☑ Interactive Games

☑ Carousel: September 11, 2001

☑ Image with Hotspots: The International Space Station

SS.912.A.1.2 Utilize a variety of primary and secondary sources to identify author, historical significance, audience, and authenticity to understand a historical period. **SS.912.A.1.4** Analyze how images, symbols, objects, cartoons, graphs, charts, maps, and artwork may be used to interpret the significance of time periods and events from the past. **SS.912.A.1.6** Use case studies to explore social, political, legal, and economic relationships in history. **SS.912.A.1.7** Describe various sociocultural aspects of American life including arts, artifacts, literature, education, and publications. **SS.912.A.2.7** Review the Native American experience. **SS.912.A.7.12** Analyze political, economic, and social concerns that emerged at the end of the 20th century and into the 21st century. **SS.912.A.7.14** Review the role of the United States as a participant in the global economy. **SS.912.A.7.15** Analyze the effects of foreign and domestic terrorism on the American people. **SS.912.A.7.16** Examine changes in immigration policy and attitudes toward immigration since 1950. **SS.912.A.7.17** Examine key events and key people in Florida history as they relate to United States history. **SS.912.G.2.1** Identify the physical characteristics and the human characteristics that define and differentiate regions. **SS.912.G.4.2** Use geographic terms and tools to analyze the push/pull factors contributing to human migration within and among places. **SS.912.G.4.3** Use geographic terms and tools to analyze the effects of migration both on the place of origin and destination, including border areas. **SS.912.H.1.5** Examine artistic response to social issues and new ideas in various cultures. **SS.912.H.3.1** Analyze the effects of transportation, trade, communication, science, and technology on the preservation and diffusion of culture. **HE.912.C.2.4** Evaluate how public health policies and government regulations can influence health promotion and disease prevention. **LAFS.1112.WHST.3.9** Draw evidence from informational texts to support analysis, reflection, and research.

Timeline of Events 1991–2015 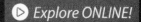 ▶ Explore ONLINE!

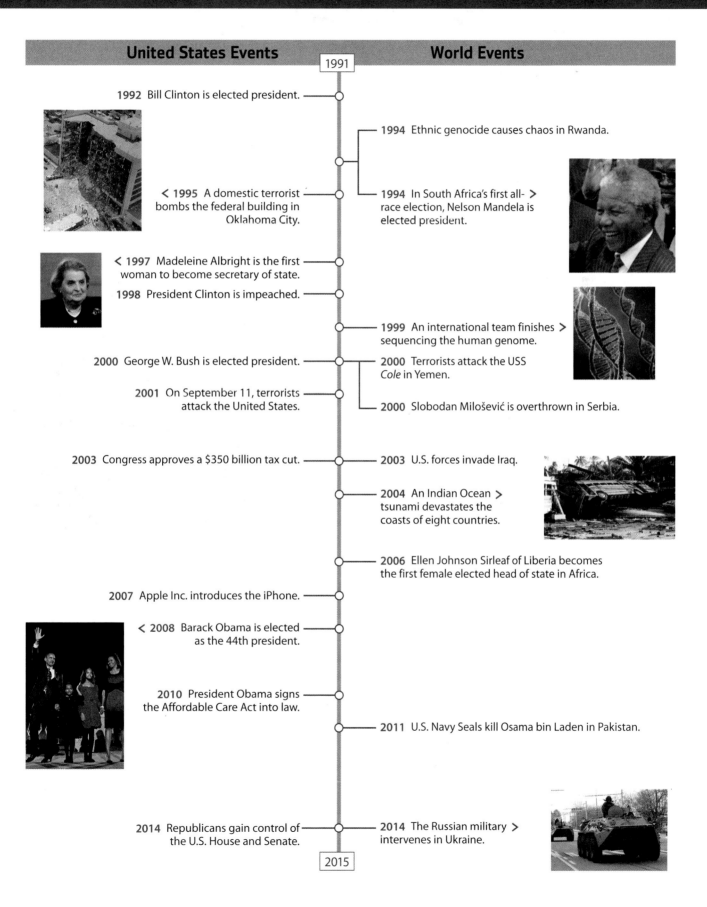

United States Events

1991

1992 Bill Clinton is elected president.

< 1995 A domestic terrorist bombs the federal building in Oklahoma City.

< 1997 Madeleine Albright is the first woman to become secretary of state.

1998 President Clinton is impeached.

2000 George W. Bush is elected president.

2001 On September 11, terrorists attack the United States.

2003 Congress approves a $350 billion tax cut.

2007 Apple Inc. introduces the iPhone.

< 2008 Barack Obama is elected as the 44th president.

2010 President Obama signs the Affordable Care Act into law.

2014 Republicans gain control of the U.S. House and Senate.

2015

World Events

1994 Ethnic genocide causes chaos in Rwanda.

1994 In South Africa's first all- **>** race election, Nelson Mandela is elected president.

1999 An international team finishes **>** sequencing the human genome.

2000 Terrorists attack the USS *Cole* in Yemen.

2000 Slobodan Milošević is overthrown in Serbia.

2003 U.S. forces invade Iraq.

2004 An Indian Ocean **>** tsunami devastates the coasts of eight countries.

2006 Ellen Johnson Sirleaf of Liberia becomes the first female elected head of state in Africa.

2011 U.S. Navy Seals kill Osama bin Laden in Pakistan.

2014 The Russian military **>** intervenes in Ukraine.

The Clinton Years

The Big Idea
Bill Clinton led the Democratic Party in a new direction, while Republican influence increased and the economy changed.

Why It Matters Now
Democrats and Republicans need to find a way to work together and unite a divided nation and improve the economy.

Key Terms and People
William Jefferson Clinton

H. Ross Perot

Hillary Rodham Clinton

Newt Gingrich

Contract with America

service sector

downsize

Bill Gates

Steve Jobs

Michael Dell

North American Free Trade Agreement (NAFTA)

outsourcing

SS.912.A.1.2; SS.912.A.1.4; SS.912.A.7.12; SS.912.A.7.14; SS.912.A.7.15

One American's Story

On January 20, 1993, **William Jefferson Clinton** was inaugurated as the 42nd president of the United States. Clinton entered the presidency at a time when America was at a turning point. A severe economic recession had made many Americans uneasy about the future. They looked to Clinton to lead a government that would be more responsive to the people.

"We must do what America does best: offer more opportunity to all and demand more responsibility from all. It is time to break the bad habit of expecting something for nothing from our Government or from each other. Let us all take more responsibility not only for ourselves and our families but for our communities and our country.

Bill Clinton delivers his inaugural address.

To renew America, we must revitalize our democracy."
—William Jefferson Clinton, from his First Inaugural Address, January 20, 1993

Clinton's speech recalled the one given by another president as he took office. In 1961 John F. Kennedy called on each American to "ask not what your country can do for you—ask what you can do for your country." Clinton had admired Kennedy since he was a teenager, and he drew inspiration from this historic message in his own inaugural address in an effort to galvanize the nation to confront the challenges it faced.

Clinton Wins the Presidency

Governor William Jefferson Clinton of Arkansas became the first member of the baby-boom generation to win the presidency. He captured the White House at the age of 46. He attracted support by vowing to strengthen the nation's weak economy and to lead the Democratic Party in a more moderate direction.

THE ELECTION OF 1992 After the U.S. victory in the Persian Gulf War in 1991, Republican president George H. W. Bush's popularity had climbed to an 89 percent approval rating. Shortly after the war ended, however, the nation found itself in the grip of a recession. In early 1992, Bush's approval rating nose-dived to 40 percent. In his run for reelection, President Bush could not convince the public that he had a clear strategy for ending the recession and creating jobs.

Throughout the presidential race, Bill Clinton campaigned as the candidate who would lead the nation out of its economic crisis. So did a third-party candidate—Texas billionaire **H. Ross Perot**. Perot targeted the soaring federal budget deficit as the nation's most serious problem. A budget deficit occurs when the federal government borrows money to meet all its spending commitments. "It's time," Perot declared in his usual blunt style, "to take out the trash and clean up the barn."

Election Day results, however, demonstrated that Clinton's center-of-the-road strategy had the widest appeal. Though Clinton won, he captured only 43 percent of the popular vote. Bush received 38 percent, while Perot managed an impressive 19 percent.

A "NEW" DEMOCRAT Bill Clinton won the presidency in part by promising to move away from traditional Democratic policies. He also emphasized the need to move people off welfare and called for growth in private business as a means to economic progress.

In office, Clinton worked to move the Democratic Party toward the political center by embracing both liberal and conservative programs. According to an ally, Clinton hoped "to modernize liberalism so it could sell again." By doing so, he sought to create a "new" and more inclusive Democratic Party.

KEY REFORMS Clinton had pledged to create a plan to guarantee affordable health care for all Americans. He especially wanted to help the millions of Americans who lacked medical insurance. Once in office, Clinton appointed First Lady **Hillary Rodham Clinton**, a skilled lawyer and child-welfare advocate, to head the team creating the plan. The president presented the health care reform bill to Congress in September 1993.

Congress debated the plan for a year. Intense lobbying by the health insurance industry and Republican attacks on the plan for promoting "big government" sealed its doom. In the end, Congress never even voted on the bill.

Another legislative effort had a more successful outcome. The Brady Handgun Violence Prevention Act was named for White House press secretary James Brady, who was shot during the attempted assassination of President Reagan in 1981. The Brady Law required that firearm buyers wait five days before completing the purchase. After 1998 gun buyers would have to undergo a background check when making a purchase from a licensed dealer. The bill also prohibited certain persons, such as those convicted of a domestic violence crime, from owning firearms. President Clinton signed the bill into law in 1993. By 2009 the law had blocked almost 2 million firearm purchases.

Clinton and the congressional Republicans cooperated to reform the welfare system. In 1996 a bill was proposed to place limits on how long people could receive benefits. The bill was called the Personal Responsibility and Work Opportunity Act. Its goal was often characterized as "welfare-to-work." The bill also put an end to a 61-year federal guarantee of welfare. It instead gave states "block grants"—set amounts of federal money they could spend on welfare or for other social concerns.

Although liberal Democrats feared the effects of eliminating the federal safety net for the poor, the president backed the bill. Over the next few years, states moved millions of people from welfare to jobs. Because of the strong economy, the transition was more successful than some had predicted.

A BALANCED BUDGET President Clinton had another success in his efforts to reduce the federal budget deficit. Clinton and the Republican-controlled Congress agreed in 1997 on legislation to balance the federal budget by the year 2002. The bill cut spending by billions of dollars, lowered taxes to win Republican support, and included programs aimed at helping children and improving health care.

A year later, Clinton announced that—for the first time in nearly 30 years—the federal budget had a surplus. That is, the government took in more money than it spent. Surpluses were used, in part, to pay down the nation's debt, which had soared to around $5.5 trillion.

Perhaps the most effective tool in generating a surplus was the booming economy. About the time Clinton took office, the economy rebounded. Unemployment fell and the stock market soared to new heights. As a result, the government's tax revenues rose. Fewer people received public aid. These factors helped slash the federal debt.

Reading Check
Analyze Issues
What were two ways Clinton showed his intention of being a "new Democrat"?

— BIOGRAPHY —————————————————————————————

William Jefferson Clinton (1946–)

Bill Clinton was born in Hope, Arkansas, at the beginning of the baby boom. Although he might have become a professional musician, Clinton decided on a political career when he was about 16 years old. He earned a degree in international affairs at Georgetown University. Clinton also studied on a Rhodes Scholarship in England, where he organized protests against the Vietnam War. After graduating from Yale Law School, Clinton returned to his home state. He taught at the University of Arkansas School of Law and dived into politics. He became the state's attorney general in 1977 and then governor of Arkansas in 1979 at the age of 32.

Clinton's Foreign Policy

Conflicts and confused alliances grew in the wake of the Cold War. The question of U.S. intervention overseas and the globalization of the economy presented the United States with a host of new challenges.

Vocabulary
globalization to make worldwide in scope or application

RELATIONS WITH FORMER COLD WAR FOES Maintaining strong relations with Russia and China became major goals for the Clinton administration. Throughout the 1990s, the United States and Russia cooperated on economic and arms-control issues. Still, Russia criticized U.S. intervention in Yugoslavia, where a bloody civil war raged. Meanwhile, U.S. officials protested against Russian attacks on rebels in the Russian region of Chechnya.

U.S. relations with China were strained as well. Clinton had stressed that he would lean on China to grant its citizens more democratic rights. As president, however, he put greater emphasis on increasing trade with the Asian giant. Despite concerns that Chinese spies had stolen U.S. defense secrets, Clinton supported a bill—passed in 2000—granting China permanent trade rights.

TROOPS ABROAD With the Cold War over, the United States turned more of its attention to regional conflicts. President Clinton proved willing to use troops to end conflicts overseas. In 1991 military leaders in Haiti forced the elected president from office. Thousands of refugees fled the military leaders' harsh rule. In 1994 President Clinton dispatched American troops to Haiti, and the military rulers were forced to step down.

Other interventions occurred in the Balkan Peninsula. In 1991 Yugoslavia broke apart into five nations. In Bosnia and Herzegovina, one of the new states, some Serb militias under Slobodan Milosevic began "ethnic cleansing," killing or expelling from their homes people of certain ethnic groups. A horrific phase of the conflict occurred in Sarajevo, the Bosnian capital. Troops intent on creating a new Serbian state besieged the city and bombed it intermittently for about four years. These attacks killed more than 5,000 civilians. To defend the people from such human rights abuses, in 1995 the United States helped negotiate a peace agreement in Bosnia. Clinton sent U.S. troops to join NATO troops to help ensure the deal. About three years later, Serb forces attacked ethnic Albanians in the Serb province of Kosovo. The United States and its NATO allies launched air strikes against Serbian targets in 1999, forcing the Serbs to back down. American troops followed up by participating in an international peace-keeping force. In both Bosnia and Kosovo, the administration promised early withdrawal. However, the U.S. troops stayed longer than had been intended, drawing criticism of Clinton's policies.

Two African countries also descended into chaos during Clinton's tenure. A disastrous famine and civil war in Somalia had prompted President George H. W. Bush to send humanitarian aid and peace-keeping troops to that nation. During President Clinton's first year in office, U.S. troops came under fire there and were caught behind enemy lines. Several were killed, and many others were wounded. The American public was horrified to see Somali rebels drag the bodies of two servicemen through the streets. The events in Somalia were a factor in the U.S. reluctance to intercede when an ethnic genocide consumed Rwanda in 1994. The Hutus, the dominant ethnic group, massacred between 500,000 and 1 million Tutsis and other people. Although the international community knew of the slaughter, little was done until the worst was over. President Clinton later called not interceding in Rwanda to defend human rights his worst foreign policy failure.

PROGRESS IN THE MIDDLE EAST President Clinton worked hard to calm the Israeli-Palestinian conflict. Negotiations led to a declaration of peace between Israeli prime minister Yitzhak Rabin and Palestine Liberation Army leader Yasser Arafat. The Oslo Accords, signed in 1993 at the White House, gave the Palestinians limited self-government in Gaza and the Israeli-occupied West Bank. The following year, Clinton helped convince Israel and Jordan to end their hostilities. Further negotiations that Clinton supported, however, did little to solve the region's ongoing conflict.

Reading Check
Analyze Effects
Which of the involvements in foreign conflicts were generally seen as successful? Not successful?

Vocabulary
partisan devoted to or biased in support of a party, group, or cause

Partisan Politics and Impeachment

While Clinton and Congress worked together on deficit reduction and welfare reform, relations in Washington became increasingly partisan. In the midst of political wrangling, a scandal rocked the White House. Bill Clinton became the second president in U.S. history to be impeached.

REPUBLICANS TAKE CONTROL OF CONGRESS In mid-1994, after the failure of President Clinton's health care plan and recurring questions regarding his leadership, Republican congressman **Newt Gingrich** began to turn voters' dissatisfaction with Clinton into support for Republicans. He drafted a document called the **Contract with America**—ten items Republicans promised to enact if they won control of Congress. Parts of the document were inspired by President Ronald Reagan's 1985 State of the Union Address. The "contract" included congressional term limits, a balanced-budget amendment, tax cuts, tougher crime laws, and welfare reform. The Republicans' return to controlling Congress can be said to be a revival of the "Reagan revolution" that began with Reagan's popularity in the 1980s.

In the November 1994 election, the Republicans handed the Democrats a humiliating defeat. Voters gave Republicans control of both houses of Congress for the first time since 1954. Chosen as the new Speaker of the House, Newt Gingrich was jubilant.

> *"I will never forget mounting the rostrum . . . for the first time. . . . The whole scene gave me a wonderful sense of the romance of America and the magic by which Americans share power and accept changes in government."*
>
> —Newt Gingrich, from *To Renew America*

President Clinton and the Republican-controlled Congress clashed. Clinton opposed Republican budgets that slowed spending on entitlements such as Social Security and Medicaid. Clinton and Congress refused to compromise, and no budget was passed. As a result, the federal government shut

These Americans protested the impeachment. Many Democrats claimed that prosecuting President Clinton was "pure partisanship."

down for almost a week in November 1995 and again for several weeks in the next two months. The President and Congress did eventually work together to pass welfare reform.

THE 1996 REELECTION The budget standoff helped Clinton, as did the strong economy and passage of the welfare reform law of 1996, which suggested an improved working relationship with Congress. As a result, voters reelected Clinton in November 1996. With 49 percent of the popular vote, he outpolled the Republican nominee, U.S. Senator Bob Dole, and the Reform Party candidate, H. Ross Perot. Still, the Republicans maintained control of the House and Senate. Both President Clinton and Republican leaders pledged to work more cooperatively. Soon, however, the president faced his most severe problem yet.

CLINTON IMPEACHED President Clinton was accused of improperly using money from a land deal with the Whitewater Development Company to fund his 1984 gubernatorial reelection campaign. In addition, Clinton allegedly had lied under oath about having an improper relationship with a White House intern. In 1998 Clinton admitted that he had an improper relationship with the young woman, but he denied lying about the incident under oath or attempting to obstruct the investigation.

Reading Check
Analyze Causes
What factors contributed most to Clinton's reelection?

In December 1998 the House of Representatives approved two articles of impeachment, charging the president with perjury and obstruction of justice. Clinton became only the second president—and the first in 130 years—to face a trial in the Senate. At the trial a month later, the Senate fell short of the 67 votes—a two-thirds majority—required to convict him. Clinton remained in office and apologized for his actions.

The Economy During the Clinton Years

Americans heard a great deal of good news about the economy during the 1990s. Millions of new jobs were created between 1993 and 1999. In fact, by the fall of 2000, the unemployment rate had fallen to the lowest it had been since 1970. But not all the changes in the economy were positive.

MORE SERVICE, LESS SECURITY Chief among the far-reaching changes in the workplace of the 1990s was the explosive growth of jobs that occurred in the **service sector**, the part of the economy that provides services to consumers. Examples of jobs in the service sector include teachers, medical professionals, lawyers, engineers, store clerks, and waitstaff.

Low-paying jobs, such as in retail sales and fast food, grew most rapidly. These positions, often part-time or temporary, offered limited benefits. Many corporations, rather than invest in salaries and benefits for full-time staff, hired temporary workers, or temps. Corporations also began to **downsize**— trim payrolls to streamline operations and increase profits. Manpower, Inc., a temporary services agency, became the largest U.S. employer, earning $2 billion in 1993 when 640,000 Americans cashed its paychecks.

The nation's shift to a service economy came at the expense of America's traditional workplaces. Manufacturing, which surpassed farming mid-century as the largest job sector, experienced a sharp decline. In 1992, for example, 140,000 steelworkers did the same work that 240,000 had accomplished only 10 years earlier.

The decline in industrial jobs contributed to a drop in union membership. In the 1990s and early 2000s, unions had trouble organizing. Union membership became a source of conflict between many employers and their employees. High-tech and professional workers felt no need for unions, while low-wage service employees feared losing their jobs in a strike. Some workers saw their incomes decline. The increased use of computer-driven robots to make manufactured goods eliminated many jobs that had been filled by union members, but it also spurred a vibrant high-tech economy.

HIGH-TECH INDUSTRIES In the late 1990s entrepreneurs turned innovative ideas about computer technology into huge personal fortunes, hoping to follow in the footsteps of **Bill Gates**, the decade's most celebrated entrepreneur. Gates founded the software company Microsoft. Another important high-tech entrepreneur of the time was **Steve Jobs**, who began Apple Inc. and revolutionized personal computers. **Michael Dell** made his fortune by selling computers directly to customers, ignoring the more typical retail method.

Many new businesses accompanied the explosive growth of the Internet late in the decade. Those with advanced training and specialized technical skills or a sense of entrepreneurial risk-taking saw their salaries rise. The

Robots increased production in America's automotive factories but cost many workers their jobs.

NASDAQ (National Association of Securities Dealers Automated Quotation System), a technology-dominated stock index on Wall Street, rose dramatically as enthusiasm grew for high-tech businesses. These businesses were known as dotcoms, a nickname derived from their addresses on the World Wide Web, which often ended in ".com." The dotcoms expanded rapidly and attracted young talent and, at times, excessive investment for such untested companies.

Thousands of smaller businesses were quick to anticipate the changes that the Internet would bring. Suddenly, companies could work directly with consumers or with other companies. Many predicted that the price of doing business would fall markedly and that overall worldwide productivity would jump dramatically. The expansion of new business was termed "The New Economy."

However, the positive economic outlook fueled by "The New Economy" was short-lived. By 2000, the dotcom "bubble" had burst. Only 38 percent of online retailing made a profit. As a result, many dotcoms went out of business. This decline had many causes. Entrepreneurs often provided inadequate advertising for their e-companies. Also, many dotcoms had hard-to-use websites that confused customers. The unsuccessful dotcoms caused many investors to stop putting money in Internet businesses.

INTERNATIONAL TRADE AND COMPETITION Trade had a global focus during President Clinton's tenure. Seeing flourishing trade as essential to U.S. prosperity and to world economic and political stability, President Clinton championed the **North American Free Trade Agreement (NAFTA)**. This legislation would bring Mexico into the free trade zone that the United States and Canada already had formed. Supporters said NAFTA would strengthen all three economies and create more American jobs. Opponents insisted that NAFTA would transfer American jobs to Mexico, where wages were lower, and harm the environment because of Mexico's weaker antipollution laws. Congress rejected these arguments, and the treaty was ratified by all three countries' legislatures in 1993. Once the treaty took effect, on January 1, 1994, trade with Mexico increased.

In the past, the United States had engaged in protectionism to support domestic businesses. In contrast, the new global economy of the 1990s stood firmly for free trade. In 1994, in response to increasing international economic competition among trading blocs, the United States joined many other nations in adopting a new version of the General Agreement on Tariffs and Trade (GATT). The new treaty lowered trade barriers, such as tariffs, and established the World Trade Organization (WTO) to resolve trade disputes. The WTO is an organization that promotes trade and economic development. As President Clinton announced at the 1994 meeting of the Group of Seven (the world's seven leading economic powers, which later became the Group of Eight when Russia joined in 1996), "[T]rade as much as troops will increasingly define the ties that bind nations in the twenty-first century."

Free trade and the global economy had their critics, however. In late 1999 the WTO met in Seattle. Demonstrators protested that the WTO made decisions with little public input and that these decisions harmed poorer countries, the environment, and American manufacturing workers.

Vocabulary
protectionism the practice of protecting domestic producers by hindering or limiting the importation of foreign goods and services

Outsourcing
Economic globalization created both problems and opportunities. Outsourcing was one unfortunate result.

Analyze Historical Sources
How does this cartoon illustrate changes in employment patterns?

"The last step says to dismantle the whole thing and ship all the jobs overseas."

Another criticism of international trade agreements came from American workers worried that they would lose their jobs to countries that produced the same goods as the United States but at a lower cost, a practice often called **outsourcing**. Their fears turned out to be well founded. In the 1990s U.S. businesses frequently moved their operations to less economically advanced countries, such as Mexico, where wages were lower. After the passage of NAFTA, more than 100,000 low-wage jobs were lost in U.S. manufacturing industries such as apparel, auto parts, and electronics. Also, competition with foreign companies helped U.S. companies maintain low wages and decrease benefits.

With the increase of global trade, many U.S. businesses transformed into multinational corporations, or large corporations with branches in several countries. Multinational corporations are beneficial in that they provide new jobs, goods, and services around the world and spread technological advances. However, by building factories in countries with lax governmental regulations, some multinational corporations are able to use harmful environmental and labor policies, leading to pollution and unsafe working conditions.

Reading Check
Summarize What are some of the economic changes that occurred during the 1990s?

Crime and Terrorism in the 1990s

The improved economy—along with larger police forces—combined to lower crime rates in the 1990s. However, fears were raised by acts of violence and terrorism that occurred both within the country's borders and in other nations. Several attacks were particularly disturbing, although they were not the only incidents.

TERRORISM ON THE HOME FRONT In 1993 Islamic terrorists exploded bombs in the World Trade Center in New York City to protest U.S. support for Israel. This event was an early expression of politicized Islam. The incident was followed by a 1995 blast that destroyed a nine-story federal office building in Oklahoma City, killing 168 children, women, and men. Timothy McVeigh, an American veteran of the Gulf War and antigovernment radical, was found guilty in the Oklahoma bombing. He was executed in 2001, the first use of the federal death penalty in 38 years. Another domestic terrorist,

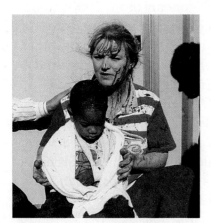

Injured victims after the April 1995 bombing of the Alfred P. Murrah Federal Building in Oklahoma City, Oklahoma.

Ted Kaczynski, often called the Unabomber, was arrested and jailed for several crimes in 1996. Over many years, Kaczynski had detonated numerous homemade bombs to protest modern technology and industrialization. He killed three people and injured 23 others. Also in 1996, a park near the Summer Olympics in Atlanta was rocked by a deadly bomb planted by antigay, antiabortion terrorist Eric Rudolph. He set off more bombs before being caught in 2003 and imprisoned.

A shocking crime occurred in April 1999 at Columbine High School in Colorado. Two students killed 12 classmates and a teacher and wounded 23 others, then shot themselves. Americans were appalled at copycat crimes that began to occur. Some called for tougher gun control, while others argued that exposure to violent imagery in the media should be curtailed.

ATTACKS ABROAD American citizens also came under attack in other countries. Various militant Islamic groups were blamed. In June 1996 in Dhahran, Saudi Arabia, a bomb exploded near the Khobar Towers, a building where U.S. Air Force personnel were staying. Almost 500 people of various nationalities were injured, while 19 U.S. service members were killed. Anonymous communications indicated the attackers' goal was to get U.S. troops out of Saudi Arabia. Iran and Hezbollah, a militant organization based in Lebanon, were determined to be responsible.

Then, in 1998, two U.S. embassies in East Africa came under attack. One was in Dar es Salaam, Tanzania, where explosives killed 10 people. At about the same time, a blast at the embassy in Nairobi, Kenya, cost more than 200 lives. Many more people, mostly local residents, suffered serious wounds. The attacks were linked to a group called Egyptian Islamic Jihad. Motivation for the attack was unclear. In response to the attacks, President Clinton ordered cruise missile strikes on targets in Afghanistan and Sudan believed to be connected to the bombers.

In October 2000 a suicide bomber attacked a U.S. Navy destroyer, the USS *Cole,* while it was in the harbor of Aden, Yemen. There were 56 casualties among the personnel on board. The terrorist organization al-Qaeda claimed responsibility for the slaughter, but a U.S. judge ruled that the government of Sudan was responsible for inciting the attack.

Reading Check
Analyze Effects
How do you think the American public responded to the terrorist attacks described?

Lesson 1 Assessment

1. **Organize Information** Create a timeline of President Clinton's major actions during his two terms.

2. **Key Terms and People** For each key term or person in the lesson, write a sentence explaining its significance.

3. **Analyze Causes** How did the end of the Cold War and the decline of communism affect the global power structure and Clinton's foreign policy?

   Think About:
   • changes in Eastern Europe
   • the fall of the Soviet Union
   • increasing trade with communist China

4. **Analyze Motives** What were the reasons behind some of the terrorist attacks during the Clinton administration?

5. **Compare and Contrast** What are some examples of when President Clinton and Congress conflicted and when they cooperated?

★
The Bush Administration

The Big Idea

Acts of terrorism, a troubled war, and a faltering economy dominated the millennium's first decade.

Why It Matters Now

Both domestic issues and foreign conflicts that began during the 2000s still simmer and require resolution.

Key Terms and People

Al Gore

George W. Bush

Osama bin Laden

al-Qaeda

Taliban

USA PATRIOT Act

weapons of mass destruction (WMD)

Sarbanes-Oxley Act

Great Recession

housing bubble

Troubled Asset Relief Program (TARP)

SS.912.A.1.2; SS.912.A.1.6; SS.912.A.7.12; SS.912.A.7.15; SS.912.A.7.17; LAFS.1112.WHST.3.7; LAFS.1112.WHST.3.9; LAFS.1112.RH.4.10

One American's Story

Terrorist attacks on the United States shocked the world on September 11, 2001. Americans, united in grief and anger, looked to their president for assurance that the perpetrators would be brought to justice. President Bush took action against the attackers and their protectors in Afghanistan. In an October speech, he promised the nation that the terrorists would find no rest.

President George W. Bush addresses the nation about U.S. military operations against terrorist forces in Afghanistan.

"On my orders, the United States military has begun strikes against al-Qaeda terrorist training camps and military installations of the Taliban regime in Afghanistan. These carefully targeted actions are designed to disrupt the use of Afghanistan as a terrorist base of operations, and to attack the military capability of the Taliban regimes. . . . Initially, the terrorists may burrow deeper into caves and other entrenched hiding places. Our military action is also designed to clear the way for sustained, comprehensive and relentless operations to drive them out and bring them to justice."

—George W. Bush, from his Address to the Nation, October 7, 2001

Thus began U.S. efforts to punish those guilty of the most devastating terrorist attack in U.S. history. Those efforts would dominate George W. Bush's years in the White House as goals became less clear and fighting dragged on. President Bush's tenure began with controversy.

The Race for the White House

In the 2000 presidential race, the Democrats chose Vice-President **Al Gore** to succeed Bill Clinton. The Republicans nominated **George W. Bush**, governor of Texas and the son of the former president. Ralph Nader, a long-time consumer advocate, ran for the Green Party. Nader's party championed environmental causes and promoted an overall liberal agenda. Throughout the campaign, debates focused on military intervention on foreign soil, health care, the environment, affirmative action, and similar topics.

On the eve of the election, polls showed that the race would be tight. In fact, the election proved one of the closest in U.S. history. The Electoral College played a major role in the long, drawn-out decision process.

Al Gore

ELECTION NIGHT CONFUSION As election night unfolded, Al Gore appeared to take the lead. The television networks projected that he would win Florida, Pennsylvania, and Michigan. These states were rich in Electoral College votes that would ultimately decide the winner of the race. Then, in a stunning turn of events, the TV networks recanted their original projection about Gore's victory in Florida. The networks proclaimed the state "too close to call." All eyes turned to Florida, a "swing state"—one where neither candidate had a clear lead. Although George W. Bush's brother Jeb, also a Republican, was the governor and enjoyed wide support, retirees who had moved from the Northeast, as well as the state's growing Hispanic population, provided many Democratic votes. Florida's 25 electoral votes were at stake, but no one knew to whom they would be awarded.

The election vote count ground on past midnight. At 2:00 a.m., the networks predicted Bush the winner of Florida—and the presidency. However, as the final votes in Florida rolled in, Bush's lead shrank. The state again became too close to call. By the next day, Al Gore had won the popular vote by more than 500,000 votes out of 105 million cast across the nation. Meanwhile, George Bush's razor-thin victory in Florida triggered an automatic recount.

FROM FLORIDA TO THE COURTS Soon, lawyers and spokespersons went to Florida to try to secure victory. The recount of the state's ballots gave Bush a win by just over 500 votes. But the battle for the presidency did not end there. The Gore campaign requested manual recounts in four mostly Democratic counties. Bush representatives expressed their opposition. James A. Baker III, former secretary of state and leader of the Bush team in Florida, argued that such recounts would raise the possibility of political mischief.

Manual recounting began, but the results from several recounts were unclear. Republican Florida secretary of state Katherine Harris stepped in and declared Bush the winner of the state's electoral votes. A long court fight followed. The battle ultimately reached the Supreme Court in a case titled *Bush v. Gore*. On December 12, the Court voted 5 to 4 to stop the recounts, thus awarding the Florida electoral votes and the presidency to Bush. The justices argued that manual recounts lacked uniform standards and, therefore, violated equal protection for voters. The Court's decision did not put an end to accusations of wrongdoing, however.

Reading Check
Analyze Issues
How did the election of 2000 highlight both the weaknesses and the strengths of America's election process?

September 11 and the Aftermath

George W. Bush was inaugurated as the 43rd president of the United States on January 20, 2001. His vice-president was Dick Cheney, a former congressman and secretary of defense for President George H. W. Bush. The secretary of state was Colin Powell, the first African American to fill that office. An important member of the Bush team was his national security advisor, political science scholar Condoleezza Rice. Rice would later become secretary of state, the first African American woman to hold the office. Before the new administration could accomplish much, however, the nation was struck by a terrorist attack that shocked the world.

A DAY OF DISASTERS Although American embassies and military targets abroad were subject to sporadic and deadly terrorist attacks during the 1990s, the country was not prepared for the devastating attacks that took place on its own soil the morning of September 11, 2001.

Nineteen Arab terrorists hijacked four commercial jets and used them as missiles in an attempt to destroy predetermined targets. In a coordinated effort, two of the planes struck the twin towers of the World Trade Center in New York City, one crashing just minutes after the other. The jets blew up on impact. Explosions and raging fire severely weakened the towers. Within two hours after the attacks, both skyscrapers had crumbled to the ground. The tallest buildings of New York City's skyline, the symbolic center of American finance, had been leveled. About an hour later, a third plane tore into the Pentagon building, the U.S. military headquarters outside Washington, DC. Air travel ceased almost immediately. Across the nation, planes in the air were ordered to land. During the evacuation of the White House and the New York City financial district, a fourth hijacked plane crashed near Pittsburgh, Pennsylvania. Onboard that plane, passengers had fought the hijackers. As a result of their courage, the plane went down before hitting its presumed target, either the White House or the U.S. Capitol.

About 3,000 people were killed in the attacks—the most destructive acts of terrorism in modern history. These included all the crew and passengers on all four planes, workers and visitors in the World Trade Center and the Pentagon, and hundreds of rescue workers.

RESCUE AND RECOVERY Amidst the brutal destruction at the World Trade Center, the courage, selflessness, and noble actions of New York City's firefighters, police officers, and rescue workers stood as a testament to the human spirit. Many of the first firefighters at the scene disappeared into the burning buildings to help those inside and never came out again. Entire squads were lost. Rescuers worked around the clock trying to find survivors in the wreckage. They had to contend with shifting rubble and smoky, ash-filled air. Medical workers from the area rushed to staff the city's trauma centers. But after the first wave of injured were rescued, there were few survivors to treat, only bodies to recover.

A flood of volunteers assisted rescue workers. From around the country, people sent generous donations of blood, food, and money to New York City.

A view across the Brooklyn Bridge shows the devastating impact of two jets used by terrorists as missiles to destroy the World Trade Center.

After the first few days, however, the work at "ground zero," the World Trade Center disaster site, shifted to recovering bodies and removing the massive amount of debris. The destroyed twin towers accounted for an estimated 2 billion pounds of rubble.

PURSUING THE ATTACKERS After conducting a massive investigation, the U.S. government determined that **Osama bin Laden**, a Saudi Arabian millionaire, had directed the terrorists responsible for the September 11 attacks. The terrorists were part of the **al-Qaeda** network, a global, militant Islamist organization. The home base for al-Qaeda was Afghanistan, ruled by a strict fundamentalist Islamic regime called the **Taliban**. The Taliban supported the terrorist group. In return, bin Laden provided fighters to the Taliban.

The United States, led by President George W. Bush, built an international coalition, or alliance, to fight terrorism and the al-Qaeda network. After the Taliban refused to turn over bin Laden, coalition forces led by the United States began military action in Afghanistan. In October 2001 the United States launched Operation Enduring Freedom. The military began bombing Taliban air defenses, airfields, and command centers, as well as al-Qaeda training camps. Within two months, U.S. forces and fighters from the Northern Alliance, a coalition of anti-Taliban Afghan troops, drove the Taliban from power. Osama bin Laden, however, remained at large.

Direct elections were held for the first time in Afghanistan in October 2004. The Afghan people chose interim president Hamid Karzai as their first democratically elected president. Although Afghanistan still faced many problems, the elections were seen as a positive move toward resolving them.

ANTITERRORIST MEASURES The attacks of September 11 altered the way Americans looked at life. For the first time, many Americans became afraid that terrorism could happen in their own country at any time. The political landscape also changed dramatically. Patriotism surged to an all-time high. The Bush administration, now with the overwhelming support of Congress and the American people, shifted its energy and attention to combating the threat of terrorism.

To give the government the power to conduct search and surveillance of suspected terrorists, the **USA PATRIOT Act** was signed into law on October 26, 2001. (The letters in the name stand for Uniting and Strengthening America by Providing Appropriate Tools Required to Intercept and Obstruct Terrorism.) This law allowed the government to:

- detain foreigners suspected of terrorism for seven days without charging them with a crime. In some cases, prisoners were held indefinitely.
- tap all phones used by suspects and monitor their email and Internet use.
- make search warrants valid across states.
- order U.S. banks to investigate sources of large foreign accounts.
- prosecute terrorist crimes without any time restrictions or limitations.

People who opposed the law claimed that it violated the First, Fourth, Fifth, Sixth, and Seventh Amendments to the U.S. Constitution. In 2005 it was revealed that President Bush had ordered the National Security Agency (NSA) to spy on American citizens' international telephone calls and emails without obtaining warrants.

Shortly after passage of the USA PATRIOT Act, Bush created the Department of Homeland Security, a government body set up to coordinate national efforts to combat terrorism. It was initially headed by former Pennsylvania governor Tom Ridge. This executive department was designed to analyze threats; guard the nation's borders, seaports, and airports; and coordinate the country's response to attacks. To help share information about the risk of terrorist attacks with the American people, the department created the Homeland Security Advisory System. This system used a set of "Threat Conditions" to advise the public about the level of terrorist threats. It also provided guidelines for response during a period of heightened alert.

The Department of Homeland Security also searched for terrorists in the United States. The government soon discovered that the al-Qaeda network had used "sleepers" to carry out its terrorist attacks. Sleepers are agents who enter a country and blend into a community. When called upon, the sleepers secretly prepare for and commit terrorist acts. An intensive search began for any al-Qaeda terrorists, including sleepers that remained in the United States. U.S. officials detained and questioned Arabs and other Muslims who behaved suspiciously or violated immigration regulations.

Due to the use of airplanes to carry out the September 11 attacks, aviation security was a key focus of antiterrorist measures. National Guard troops began patrolling airports, and sky marshals were assigned to airplanes. In addition, the Federal Aviation Administration (FAA) had bars installed on cockpit doors to prevent hijackers from entering cockpits.

In November 2001 President Bush signed into law the Aviation and Transportation Security Act. This law made airport security the responsibility of the federal government. Previously, individual airports had been responsible for their own security. Because of this new law, an agency called the Transportation Security Administration (TSA) was created to inspect airline passengers, baggage, and cargo, as well as noncitizens training to be pilots. The TSA is also responsible for safety on railroads, buses, and mass transit systems. Security operations at airports created several major concerns, including long delays and possible invasion of passengers' privacy.

Other countries, too, took steps to prevent further terrorist attacks. Many passed antiterror legislation, froze bank accounts suspected of al-Qaeda ties, and arrested suspected terrorists. Assessing the success of such measures is difficult, however.

Reading Check
Analyze Events
How did the Bush administration respond to the events of 9/11?

Bush's Foreign Policy

Antiterror efforts marked the early years of the Bush presidency. Those efforts would soon become more complex. The Bush administration claimed that Iraq's leader, Saddam Hussein, supported the al-Qaeda terrorists who had carried out the September 11 attacks. That allegation was one reason why the administration took further action in the Middle East.

THE WAR AGAINST IRAQ BEGINS In 2003 Bush expanded the war on terrorism to Iraq. Following the Persian Gulf War, Iraq had agreed to UN demands to stop the production of biological, chemical, and nuclear weapons, called **weapons of mass destruction (WMD)**. However, throughout the 1990s Iraqi president Saddam Hussein cooperated only partly with UN arms inspectors. He eventually barred them from entering his country.

Document-Based Investigation Historical Source

Knowns and Unknowns
Whether or not Iraq still controlled WMD became a hot topic, including at a news briefing where Secretary of Defense Donald Rumsfeld described the difficulty of learning the truth.

Analyze Historical Sources
Why do you think Rumsfeld's comments were both criticized and praised? With which stance do you agree, and why?

"Reports that say that something hasn't happened are always interesting to me, because as we know, there are known knowns; there are things we know we know. We also know there are known unknowns; that is to say we know there are some things we do not know. But there are also unknown unknowns—the ones we don't know we don't know. And if one looks throughout the history of our country and other free countries, it is the latter category that tend to be the difficult ones."

—Donald Rumsfeld, from a Department of Defense hearing, February 2002

After the September 11 attacks, Bush alleged that Hussein was supporting terrorists and might supply them with WMD. Bush called for renewed arms inspections in Iraq. The inspectors determined that Iraq had not resumed its WMD programs, but Hussein had again not cooperated fully with the inspection process.

The United States and Great Britain ended diplomacy with Iraq and invaded in March 2003. Within a month, Iraq's forces were defeated. In May President Bush declared the end of major military operations in Iraq. The president's popularity increased with the conflict's initial success. U.S. forces captured Saddam Hussein in December 2003. The former dictator was later tried and executed by the Iraqi government.

THE WAR CONTINUES U.S. forces then began an intensive search for WMD in Iraq. No traces of nuclear, chemical, or biological weaponry were found. This caused many Americans to question the war's original goal. Critics who accused the administration of invading Iraq to secure the country's vast oil reserves became more vocal. Some critics feared that war would inspire more terrorism, not reduce it. In contrast, many supporters of the war maintained that toppling Saddam Hussein was reason enough to invade, even though no link between him and al-Qaeda could be found.

Meanwhile, the situation in Iraq deteriorated. Various Iraqi groups fought each other. Some observers believed that Iraq was headed for a civil war. They feared it would become a breeding ground for more terrorism. The war was also costing hundreds of billions of dollars, and the number of soldiers killed in action was mounting. In September 2004 the toll passed 1,000. (The number of deaths would rise, to 4,491 between 2003 and 2015.) The tally of Iraqi deaths varied widely, but most reliable sources counted almost 200,000, the majority of whom were civilians. As Americans watched the war unfold on the evening news, its popularity dropped. So too did the president's approval rating.

POLICIES FOR IRAN AND ISRAEL President Bush also faced other challenges in the Middle East. For many years, Americans had worried that Iran's repressive and unstable Islamist government would acquire nuclear weapons.

In Baghdad, Iraqis pull down a statue of Saddam Hussein after the dictator's regime is overthrown.

During Bush's tenure, the UN Security Council passed a resolution requiring Iran to stop enriching uranium—a step crucial to building nuclear weapons—and promising to impose sanctions if Iran persisted in doing so. The resolution was seen as a success for Bush's foreign policy.

Bush addressed the Israeli-Palestinian conflict, too. He called for a separate Palestinian state to be established. Along with Russia, the European Union, and the United Nations, he called for a "road map" to settle the region's long-standing struggle. The plan required compromises on both sides. Neither side gave in on crucial points, however, so the plan was never put into practice.

ADDITIONAL CONTROVERSIES In 2002 President Bush established a prison at Guantanamo Bay Naval Base, in Cuba. The prison housed people who had been detained during antiterror actions. The Bush administration alleged that the Guantanamo prisoners did not qualify for basic protections under the Geneva Conventions—documents that define the rights of wartime prisoners. The U.S. Supreme Court later disagreed. Allegations of inmate mistreatment and torture have plagued the prison. Subsequent efforts to close it have not succeeded.

Stories of another prison made headlines in 2003. Investigations showed that U.S. personnel abused and even tortured detainees in Iraq's Abu Ghraib (ä´ bōō grĕb) prison. Photos of grinning American soldiers leashing prisoners like animals, beating them while handcuffed, and forcing them into humiliating, painful positions disgusted many Americans. Although the U.S. Department of Defense disciplined several of the abusive guards, the scandal tarnished the public image of the administration's war on terror. Outrage over Abu Ghraib further eroded America's image in the region—already dismal, due to the widespread fighting and many Iraqi civilian deaths.

Reading Check
Form Generalizations
How were WMD connected to the start of war in Iraq?

Bush's Domestic Goals

During his first months as president, Bush began to advance his political agenda. His actions followed a basically conservative viewpoint.

DOMESTIC ISSUES President Bush established education reform as a key accomplishment. He signed into law a plan titled No Child Left Behind (NCLB). This plan called for mandatory testing of basic skills at select grade levels. Students would be tested on their achievement of standards developed by each state. The law also required that schools' test scores improve at a defined rate. A school judged to be inadequate would be subject to various corrective actions. Under NCLB, parents could transfer their children out of schools that had not made the required progress.

Bush took pro-business stances on several issues. For example, he supported opening the Arctic National Wildlife Refuge to oil drilling. His Clear Skies Initiative promised to cut emissions of mercury and other pollutants. But critics said that it would actually allow polluters, such as power plants, to make environmental problems worse. On global climate change, Bush acknowledged that the threat was real, but refrained from blaming human

George W. Bush (1946–

George W. Bush was born into a family steeped in politics. His father, George H. W. Bush, was the 41st president of the United States (1989–1993). However, George W. Bush did not immediately follow in his father's political footsteps. In 1975 he started an oil company in Midland, Texas. For a time, he also was part owner of the Texas Rangers baseball team.

Eventually, Bush was elected governor of Texas in 1994. Six years later, he became the 43rd president of the United States. He won reelection in 2004.

Reading Check
Analyze Effects
How did President Bush's administration affect tax policy and education?

activity as the cause. However, Bush did propose increased funding for research into renewable energy sources.

Social Security was of particular interest to President Bush. He supported partial privatization of Social Security. That is, Bush favored allowing an individual to assume responsibility for investing part of his or her Social Security payments in a different pension plan. The proposal was not approved.

On social issues, President Bush also upheld conservative views. He promoted efforts to limit access to abortion and supported capital punishment. He received bipartisan support, however, for signing the Amber Alert bill into law. This law created a nationwide system for alerting the public about child abductions.

THE 2004 ELECTION Although the Bush administration received much initial support for the war on terrorism, many Americans came to question the decision to invade Iraq. They were dismayed by the failure to find WMD there. But despite deep divisions among the American people, President Bush was reelected in 2004.

During Bush's second term, discontent about the war grew. At the same time, controversies arose over warrantless spying on American citizens and allegations that the administration allowed torture of terrorist suspects. The Bush administration was also criticized over a delayed and ineffective response to Hurricane Katrina in 2005. In the 2006 midterm elections, Democrats regained control of both the House and the Senate.

Confronting Economic Problems

A flurry of economic issues plagued the Bush years. At the beginning of his tenure, the country enjoyed a national surplus. By the end of his presidency, the surplus had reversed into a large deficit. The wars in Afghanistan and Iraq had driven military spending to new heights. The continued threat of terrorism also had a negative effect on the economy, which by 2003 was sagging. That year, Congress passed and Bush signed into law a $350 billion tax cut. Bush claimed the cut would help the economy and create jobs. Democrats in Congress opposed the tax cut, saying it would mostly benefit the rich and would not promote job creation. The Democrats were overruled, however, because the Republican Party had regained control of the Senate in the 2002 midterm elections.

CORPORATE SCANDALS In 2001 and 2002 the U.S. economy was hard hit by corporate scandals. Enron, an energy company, was charged with using illegal accounting practices. The company declared bankruptcy, and several of its top officials were convicted of federal crimes. WorldCom, a telecommunications corporation, filed what was then the largest bankruptcy claim in U.S. history. WorldCom had to pay billions of dollars in penalties and restitution to investors. Congress responded to the scandals by passing the **Sarbanes-Oxley Act**. This act established a regulatory board to oversee the accounting industry and its involvement with corporations. Damage had been done, however, as some investors began to lose faith in corporations.

CAUSES OF THE GREAT RECESSION Toward the end of 2007, the country was entering a financial crisis. Questionable decisions by several major banking firms caused them to collapse, creating a ripple effect throughout the banking industry. A general economic slowdown resulted. By 2008 observers were saying the economy had entered a **Great Recession**, a severe decline in economic activity. In fact, the economy suffered its worst decline since the Great Depression of the 1930s. And like the Great Depression, other countries also faced big problems. Although economists debate the details regarding the recession's origins, some basic causes stand out:
  • government failure to regulate financial institutions
  • risk-taking by financial firms
  • mortgage loans to people who could not afford them
  • excessive borrowing by individuals and companies

Risky moves had become commonplace, especially for investment banks that operated without much government oversight. Some of these institutions, including Lehman Brothers, Morgan Stanley, and Goldman Sachs, faced bankruptcy when they could not fulfill their obligations. Their problems spread to regular banks.

For the previous two decades, U.S. government policies had encouraged home ownership, but without proper safeguards. Alan Greenspan, chairman of the Federal Reserve System, approved low mortgage interest rates. A boom in housing construction resulted, as more and more Americans could take out mortgage loans. Many families borrowed money to buy homes that were overpriced. Widespread overpricing of residential real estate was called the **housing bubble**. Moreover, financial institutions had made mortgage loans to families who did not earn enough income to pay back the money. High private debt became a problem for countless American families. At the end of 2007, the average household debt was 127 percent. That is, an average family that earned $50,000 per year was $63,500 in debt.

THE U.S. ECONOMY IN RECESSION For countless people, attaining the American Dream suddenly seemed impossible. As unstable financial institutions failed, even financially secure banks cut back on lending. As a result, businesses found it difficult to get the credit they needed to invest in new inventory or pay their employees, much less hire new ones. Unemployment rose from 5 percent to 10 percent by late 2009. The number of Americans without jobs went from about 7 million to 15 million. In general, incomes fell.

A Lehman Brothers worker is surrounded by photographers on the day that the investment bank declared bankruptcy.

Younger workers suffered higher rates of unemployment. In 2008 about 14 percent of workers aged 16 to 24 did not have jobs.

Housing prices dropped about 30 percent. When the housing bubble burst and home prices fell, many homeowners owed more on their mortgages than their houses were worth on the market. If they had lost their jobs, these people could neither make their mortgage payments nor sell their homes. Their situation was called being "underwater." Banks foreclosed on the homes of thousands of Americans who could not make their mortgage payments. That is, the banks took back the houses so they could be resold, and the residents had to find new places to live. During 2007 alone, nearly 1.3 million properties were threatened with foreclosure.

Stock prices also dropped, by about 57 percent. As a result, pensions and savings lost billions in value. Retirees saw their savings dwindle. While stock values dropped, the U.S. national debt rose from 66 percent of gross domestic product (GDP) to over 103 percent.

President Bush tried to limit the damage. In October 2008 he signed the **Troubled Asset Relief Program (TARP)**, which would authorize $700 billion to stabilize the U.S. banking and automobile industries. (The amount was later reduced to $475 billion.) Some critics called the act a "bailout" funded by taxpayers. Supporters said the action was essential to keep the U.S. banking system from crashing completely.

The Great Recession had begun just when Americans were looking toward the next presidential election. Concerns about the war in Iraq and the fragile economy would dominate the 2008 campaign.

Reading Check Summarize How did the nation's economy change during the Bush years?

Lesson 2 Assessment

1. **Organize Information** Create a chart that describes the causes and results of the economic problems of the Bush years.

Causes of Economic Problems	Results of Economic Problems

2. **Key Terms and People** For each key term or person in the lesson, write a sentence explaining its significance.

3. **Form Opinions** Do you think President Bush's decision to invade Iraq was justified? Explain why or why not.

   Think About:
   - arms inspections in Iraq
   - fear created by the September 11 attacks
   - the search for WMD

4. **Evaluate** Why do some people think the USA PATRIOT Act is unconstitutional?

5. **Predict** Do you think the actions taken by the United States and other countries to prevent terrorism will be effective? Why or why not?

Kelo v. City of New London (2005)

ORIGINS OF THE CASE

In 1998 a private company proposed building a research facility on a large piece of unused land in New London, Connecticut. Hoping the new facility would revive the surrounding area's economy, the city planned to use its power of eminent domain to give nearby land to a private developer. The developer intended to tear down the private homes that were occupying the land in order to build a hotel, restaurants, shops, offices, and private high-rise apartments. The city believed these projects qualified as public use, but local homeowners including Susette Kelo disagreed and took the matter to the courts.

THE RULING

The Supreme Court ruled that the planned development of the land qualified as a public use because it was intended to improve the city's poor economy.

LEGAL REASONING

The Fifth Amendment's Takings Clause gives the government the right of eminent domain, the power to take private property for public use. The question in *Kelo* v. *City of New London* was whether the economic benefits of a private development constitute public use under the Fifth Amendment. Justice John Paul Stevens, writing for the 5–4 majority, ruled:

"For more than a century, our public use jurisprudence has wisely eschewed [avoided] rigid formulas and intrusive scrutiny in favor of affording legislatures broad latitude in determining what public needs justify the use of the takings power."

According to the Court, the Fifth Amendment did not require a literal definition of public use; the "broader and more natural interpretation of public use as 'public purpose'" was sufficient. In her dissenting opinion, Justice Sandra Day O'Connor argued that the decision blurred the distinction between private and public use of property.

"Under the banner of economic development, all private property is now vulnerable to being taken and transferred to another private owner, so long as it might be upgraded—i.e., given to an owner who will use it in a way that the legislature deems more beneficial to the public—in the process."

LEGAL SOURCES

U.S. CONSTITUTION

U.S. Constitution, Fifth Amendment (1791)

"[N]or shall private property be taken for public use, without just compensation."

U.S. Constitution, Fourteenth Amendment (1868)

"[N]or shall any state deprive any person of life, liberty, or property, without due process of law. . . ."

RELATED CASES

Berman v. Parker (1954)

The Court interpreted the Takings Clause of the Fifth Amendment, determining that private property can be taken for a "public purpose" with just compensation.

Hawaii Housing Authority v. Midkiff (1984)

The Court held that the power of eminent domain allowed a state to take property from an oligopoly for distribution to a wider population of private residents.

WHY IT MATTERED

The Fifth Amendment protects an individual's right to own private property. This protection is one of the principles upon which our economic system is based. However, the same amendment also gives government the right to take private property for public use, with just compensation. This right allows government officials to force property owners to sell their land to the government at what is determined to be a fair price. In many instances, the government's use of eminent domain is beneficial for communities and the individuals and industries that live and operate there. For example, for years the right has been used to create public roads or railroad tracks that improve transportation and make trade more efficient, benefiting the community as a whole. By expanding the definition of public use to include ventures by private developers, *Kelo* has also expanded the circumstances under which local governments can seize private property. This decision has the potential to broaden the impact of governmental actions on individuals, industries, and communities with respect to Fifth Amendment property rights. Some observers worried that the *Kelo* decision would allow governments to take actions that would benefit some at the expense of the others.

HISTORICAL IMPACT

The *Kelo* decision has served as something of a cautionary tale. Many Americans worried that the ruling gave local government too much power to abuse its right of eminent domain. In response, 43 state legislatures and 8 state supreme courts have taken measures to restrict the use of eminent domain and strengthen property rights protections. In June 2013 the House Judiciary Committee approved the Private Property Rights Protection Act, which would prohibit governments that receive federal funds from using eminent domain to transfer private property from one owner to another for economic development. The legislation is a direct response to the *Kelo* ruling. In New London, the company whose research facility prompted the development has announced plans to leave the area, and the condemned and bulldozed neighborhood where Susette Kelo once lived remains vacant.

Susette Kelo outside her New London home

Critical Thinking

1. **Connect to History** Do research to find another example of a government exercising its right of eminent domain. Explain how the government's actions in that instance affected individuals, industries, and the community.

2. **Connect to Today** Do you think the government's right of eminent domain always serves the public good? What impact does such an action have on Fifth Amendment property rights? Explain your opinion, as well as any circumstances under which your perspective might change.

Obama's Presidency

The Big Idea

President Barack Obama changed domestic and foreign policies, but the Democratic Party lost power in Congress as U.S. politics became increasingly partisan.

Why It Matters Now

Increased tensions in the federal government hinder leaders' efforts to solve domestic and foreign problems.

Key Terms and People

Barack H. Obama

Joe Biden

John McCain

Sarah Palin

American Recovery and Reinvestment Act (ARRA)

Patient Protection and Affordable Care Act (PPACA)

Benghazi

tea party

One American's Story

The U.S. economy plunged into a recession, starting in 2007. As Americans lost their jobs and the value of their homes dropped, many of them blamed the Republican administration of George W. Bush. One result was the election of **Barack H. Obama,** the country's first African American president. He faced the difficult task of repairing the economy. A particularly knotty problem was dealing with big banks, some of which had knowingly taken risks at the consumers' expense by trading in troubled loans, often called assets. A few months after the election, Senator Barbara Boxer, a California Democrat, addressed the issue during a congressional hearing.

"Our President faces very hard choices when it comes to straightening out this mess. But the American people want him to try and try he is.

If we can get these bad assets off the hands of these banks and get them lending again, we basically save the financial system. If we don't save the finan-

Senator Barbara Boxer

cial system, we are going to have to take it over. This President does not want to do that and I do not want to do that and I do not think most Americans want that. So he is doing what it takes."

—Barbara Boxer, from the Congressional Record— Senate, Vol. 155, Pt. 7, March 25, 2009

A highly contentious campaign season preceded Obama's election.

SS.912.A.1.4; SS.912.A.7.12

The 2008 Election

The war in Iraq and a deteriorating economy contributed to President Bush's unpopularity, which dampened Republican chances in the next election. The Democratic Party hoped to regain the presidency in 2008. Their nominee was Barack Obama, a young U.S. senator from Illinois and the son of a white mother and African father. Senator Obama placed a challenge before American voters when he accepted the nomination at the Democratic convention.

> "America, we cannot turn back . . . not with so much work to be done; not with so many children to educate, and so many veterans to care for; not with an economy to fix, and cities to rebuild, and farms to save; not with so many families to protect and so many lives to mend. America, we cannot turn back. We cannot walk alone."
>
> —Barack H. Obama, from his acceptance speech at the Democratic National Convention, August 28, 2008

Obama's running mate was **Joe Biden**, a long-time senator from Delaware. Running on the Republican ticket was Senator **John McCain** of Arizona, a hero of the Vietnam War. His running mate was **Sarah Palin**, the governor of Alaska. McCain was widely seen as a moderate Republican, but Palin appealed to more conservative Republicans. Throughout the campaign, speeches and debates focused on both the economy and foreign policy. The Obama-Biden ticket won a clear victory.

During the 2008 election, the Democratic Party also increased its majority in the U.S. House of Representatives. Helping to set the congressional agenda as Speaker of the House was California Democrat Nancy Pelosi, the first woman to hold that position.

Reading Check
Summarize
What two factors were most significant in Obama's victory in the 2008 election?

Obama's Domestic Agenda

Shortly before the 2008 election, President Bush had signed the Troubled Asset Relief Program (TARP). The law authorized the U.S. secretary of the Treasury to spend up to $700 billion to buy problematic assets from banks and to send cash directly to banks in danger of failure. The so-called "bailout" for the banks came under criticism prior to Obama's inauguration and remained controversial throughout his tenure.

STIMULATING THE ECONOMY Upon taking office, Obama pushed through his own economic stimulus package to combat the recession. In 2009 he signed the **American Recovery and Reinvestment Act (ARRA)**, which distributed over $8 billion in funds to individuals in the form of tax credits and through programs such as Medicaid, food stamps, and unemployment benefits. Among the provisions were credits for college tuition and home

"Government intervention in the economy was necessary to prevent disaster."

The U.S. government committed more than $700 billion to fighting the effects of the recession that began in 2008. Supporters of government action say that this bailout was necessary to prevent the worst financial disaster since the Great Depression.

Although the crisis had been created by banks and investment firms, its effects would be felt far and wide. The bailout was intended to prevent an economic collapse that would damage the livelihood of the average American. As President Bush said to the American people in a 2008 radio address, "The rescue effort we're negotiating is not aimed at Wall Street; it is aimed at your street."

Much of the bailout money went to prop up failing banks. Supporters noted that the nature of the American financial system made government intervention necessary. Banks—especially the largest banks—had grown so intertwined that the failure of one would have catastrophic results on others. If one of the largest banks, those deemed "too big to fail," collapsed, it could take the whole economy with it, they argued. President Obama explained, "As a result, the failure of one firm threatened the viability of many others. We were facing one of the largest financial crises in history, and those responsible for oversight were caught off guard and without the authority to act."

"Government interference weakens the economy and rewards bad management."

Criticism of the government's intervention came from both sides of the political divide. Some opponents of the financial bailout feared that the government's measures would weaken the economy in the long run. By helping large banks recover—an action that Republican Speaker of the House John Boehner called "giving special perks to those who have acted irresponsibly"— the government would encourage businesses and financial institutions to take reckless risks with the assumption that the government would keep them from collapsing.

Phil Angelides, a Democrat and the chairman of the Financial Crisis Inquiry Commission, spoke for many Americans who were disgusted by the bank bailout. He compared saving big banks to throwing "flotation devices to major financial firms while most of America took on water." Angelides didn't like having only two choices— bailing out the banks or watching the American economy fail completely. "Many Americans believe that reckless financial institutions and greedy executives made appalling bets and came away not just unpunished but with a windfall of cheap capital that made them even more profitable. They remain justifiably angry that top executives pocketed big bonuses with taxpayer money. And they rightly worry that the largest surviving financial institutions are not just too big but now too big and too few to fail."

Critical Thinking

1. **Connect to History** How does the bank bailout compare to actions taken by the federal government during the New Deal?

2. **Connect to Today** Do you think any banks are "too big to fail"? Should the government let weak financial institutions go bankrupt, if doing so could severely hurt the economy?

improvements to increase energy efficiency. ARRA also affected the private sector through grants and loans for government contracts awarded to American businesses. As part of the ARRA, about 98 percent of Americans got a tax cut. Federal taxes were at their lowest level in 60 years. Some state and local taxes increased, however.

In 2010 Obama signed the Dodd-Frank Wall Street Reform and Consumer Protection Act. The act was written to regulate financial institutions more effectively, to protect consumers and investors, and, in essence, prevent another financial crisis. The Troubled Asset Relief Program, begun under President Bush, also continued.

Several economic studies agree that the government's stimulus efforts added jobs, increased GDP, and reduced unemployment. The recession officially ended in June 2009, though unease about the economy continued. At about the same time, Obama created the Financial Crisis Inquiry Commission to investigate the causes of the recession. The commission also examined the bank bailout.

Barack H. Obama (1961–)

Born in Honolulu, Hawaii, Obama spent part of his childhood in Indonesia, the home of his stepfather. He attended high school in Hawaii.

Obama graduated from Columbia University with a degree in political science and a specialty in international relations. Later, Obama earned a degree from Harvard Law School. After working as an attorney, Obama taught constitutional law at the University of Chicago Law School. Chicago was also where Obama worked as a community organizer, helping set up job training and other programs.

In 1996 Obama was elected to the Illinois Senate. In July 2004 Obama came to national attention when he delivered the keynote speech at the 2004 Democratic National Convention. Later that year, he was elected to represent Illinois in the U.S. Senate, having won 70 percent of the vote.

HEALTH CARE For some time, policymakers had been worried about the number of people without health insurance. Uninsured patients overburden the emergency rooms of hospitals required to accept all patients. In addition, uninsured patients often fail to seek medical attention in a timely manner. Then financial disaster can result when serious illness or injury strikes. This problem was extensive; in 2008 some 17.4 percent of nonelderly Americans did not have health insurance. About 8 million of the uninsured were children.

In 2008 Obama had made health care reform one of his major campaign issues. In 2010 President Obama signed the **Patient Protection and Affordable Care Act (PPACA)** into law. The act, often called Obamacare, extended the Children's Health Insurance Program (CHIP), a program that provides health coverage to children of low-income families. It also tackled the issue of uninsured adults, partly by offering incentives to states to increase their Medicaid programs, which fund health care for low-income patients.

One part of the PPACA allows young people to stay on their parents' insurance plans until the age of 26. In addition, patients cannot be denied coverage for having a preexisting health condition. The law extends private insurance coverage through individual mandates—that is, requiring individuals to get some level of health coverage or risk a fine. Federal subsidies are available to help some low-income people buy insurance.

On October 1, 2013, uninsured Americans began purchasing health insurance plans that had been set up in accordance with the Affordable Care Act. The computerized sign-up system was troubled by glitches, but by March 2015 some 16.4 million people had acquired health insurance under the PPACA. The rate of uninsured Americans dropped below 12 percent.

The PPACA remains controversial. Some Americans feel that the government does not have the right to require health insurance. Other critics say the law does not go far enough in guaranteeing health care for all. When the act was challenged as being unconstitutional, the U.S. Supreme Court disagreed, and the law remained in effect. Since its passage, the Republican-controlled Congress has voted to repeal the act almost 60 times.

ENVIRONMENTAL ISSUES One of Obama's first acts was to require that the Department of Transportation establish higher fuel efficiency standards. He also pushed for more use of renewable energy sources and for stricter limits on businesses that produce high levels of carbon pollution. A major controversy arose when Congress approved an oil pipeline, called the Keystone XL. This pipeline would run from western Canada, where surface mines dig out thick, oil-saturated sand, to the Gulf of Mexico. Environmentalists criticized the project for encouraging the use of a heavily polluting type of oil and for the risk of leaks. Congress approved the project, but Obama vetoed it. Congress was unable to override the veto. On many issues, Republicans have supported pro-business plans, while Democrats have criticized those proposals as hurting the environment. The Keystone XL Pipeline bill followed that same pattern.

The Keystone XL Pipeline Debate

Democratic Position	Republican Position
The pipeline would create only 5,000 to 6,000 temporary jobs and far fewer permanent jobs.	The pipeline would create from 9,000 to 20,000 good jobs.
The pipeline crosses areas that are environmentally sensitive, and oil spills would be disastrous.	The pipeline would be similar to others that have operated safely and will include new safety features.
Building the pipeline would encourage surface mining of tar sands, harming Canada's environment.	Surface tar sand mines affect only a small percentage of Canada's vast forest land.
Tar sands yield oil that must be cleaned by using the energy of more fossil fuels.	U.S. coal-fired plants produce more pollutants.
Most of the oil would be shipped to other countries.	Building the pipeline would reduce U.S. dependency on foreign oil.

Interpret Tables
Why do you think there is such a wide difference between the job figures shown in the table?

Reading Check
Find Main Ideas
What are some basic assumptions about government power that inspired the PPACA?

OTHER DOMESTIC POLICIES Shortly after taking office, President Obama issued several executive orders. One banned torture and other coercive methods for questioning suspects. The first bill that he signed, the Lilly Ledbetter Fair Pay Act of 2009, gave women who felt they had been treated unfairly on the job a longer time within which to file a sexual discrimination complaint. He also raised the tax on cigarettes and lifted restrictions on federal funding of embryonic stem cell research.

Foreign Policy Challenges

When Obama took office in 2009, the war in Iraq was still going on. He made it clear that he intended to bring the combat forces home. That goal was fulfilled in December 2011. In meetings with Iraqi leaders, Obama stressed the need for more inclusive government.

AFGHANISTAN Obama still faced the issue of what to do in Afghanistan. He sent in several thousand additional troops—a so-called surge, begun by President Bush. U.S. troops again confronted the Taliban, which had regained influence. Fierce fighting continued, with wins balanced by losses. A heavy civilian death toll, traumatic injuries to American soldiers, and suicide bombers kept the war in the headlines.

A lingering problem in the region was the failure to eliminate Osama bin Laden, the al-Qaeda leader who had orchestrated the September 11 terrorist attacks. During a presidential debate in 2008, Obama stated that killing bin Laden would be his highest national security priority. In early May 2011 he accomplished that objective. A coordinated operation of the Central Intelligence Agency (CIA), an airborne division of the U.S. Army, and U.S. Navy Seals tracked down bin Laden in Pakistan and killed him. Although 90 percent of the American public supported the raid, some critics objected that bin Laden had been unarmed. Soon after bin Laden's death, Obama announced that he would start withdrawing troops from Afghanistan.

President Obama and his staff watch the progress of the military operation against Osama bin Laden.

CONFLICTS AROUND THE GLOBE Like his predecessors, Obama faced disputes—diplomatic, economic, and military—around the world. Issues in the Middle East were not limited to Iraq. Relations between the Obama administration and Israel's government became strained in 2010 when Israel announced that it would build 1,600 new homes in a disputed area of Jerusalem, and Obama objected. On the other hand, Obama increased U.S. funding for Israel's military.

Countries of North Africa presented additional challenges. Egypt, for example, became unstable in 2010–2011, when pro-democracy demonstrators demanded that Hosni Mubarak, the long-time president of an oppressive regime, step down. Obama and several European leaders added their voices to that request. Mubarak eventually did leave office, and the Egyptians elected a new leader. The country remains very tense, however.

A violent episode took place in **Benghazi**, Libya, in the midst of a civil war between supporters and foes of dictator Muammar Gaddafi. The events became a crisis for the Obama administration. On September 11, 2012, Islamic militants attacked the U.S. diplomatic compound in Benghazi. Ambassador J. Christopher Stevens was killed, along with another U.S. State Department employee. A second attack nearby killed two CIA contractors and injured ten other people. Shocked, Americans questioned whether the State Department had provided ample security and wondered what had caused the attacks. Was it because an anti-Muslim video had suddenly enraged a crowd? Or was it a premeditated raid? Months after the violence, Secretary of State Hillary Clinton faced those and other questions during a Senate hearing.

"With all due respect, the fact is, we had four dead Americans! Was it because of a protest or was it because of guys out for a walk one night and decided they'd go kill some Americans? What difference—at this point, what difference does it make?"

—Hillary Clinton, from a Senate hearing, January 23, 2013

An extensive investigation later showed that the events in Benghazi were a combination of planned and spontaneous attacks. Although the government had earlier stated that al-Qaeda was not responsible, subsequent investigation showed that a local al-Qaeda affiliate was indeed connected to the violence.

Many other hot spots demanded attention. Among them was North Korea, which threatened to restart armed conflict with South Korea. Relations between Russia and the United States remained tense. In Pakistan, Obama increased attacks by unmanned aerial vehicles called drones—a program begun by President Bush.

Throughout his presidency, Obama won both praise and criticism for his foreign policy. Some conservatives accused him of being too hesitant to wield U.S. power abroad. On the other end of the political spectrum were liberals who criticized him for continuing too many of his predecessor's foreign policies, especially in Iraq.

Reading Check
Make Inferences
What kept President Obama from removing all troops from Afghanistan immediately?

Reelection and Stalemate

Although Obama's efforts to improve the economy had met with some success, many Americans were unhappy with continued high levels of unemployment. This discontent allowed Republicans to gain a majority of seats in the U.S. House of Representatives during the 2010 midterm elections. As a result, Obama met with resistance as he tried to pursue his agenda.

A GROWING DIVIDE During the 2008 election, observers noted growing partisanship in politics. That is, opponents were less willing to compromise, personal attacks became more common, and more people embraced extreme views. Many noted that politics had become more polarized, meaning that people were more likely to be on clearly opposite sides of issues. Talk-radio programs, unsubstantiated Internet rumors, and cable news shows on both ends of the political spectrum were blamed. Some political scientists point to modern gerrymandering as a cause. They say that drawing voting districts to concentrate like-minded voters leads to elected representatives holding more radical positions than the general public. Scholars have also noted that over the last few decades, Americans more often surround themselves with like-minded people—not just on the regional or state level, but even in terms of cities and neighborhoods. Former president Bill Clinton has lamented this tendency in several speeches. "Some of us are going to have to cross the street, folks," he said.

This tea party demonstrator carries a sign that associates President Obama with the hammer and sickle, a symbol of the Communist party, and distorts his photo to make him appear ghoulish.

Increased partisanship over the role of government in American life found expression in the rise of a libertarian, conservative movement called the **tea party**. The loosely organized group took its name from the Boston Tea Party of 1773. Among the group's goals are lowering taxes, reducing government spending on programs such as health care, and lowering the national debt and the budget deficit. On social issues, a large majority of tea party supporters are against abortion, gay marriage, and gun control. Most identify themselves as Christians and vote Republican. Supporters of the tea party mostly see the U.S. Constitution as a conservative document and advocate strict constitutional interpretation in government policy. Although the movement is decentralized, polls have found that between 10 percent and 30 percent of Americans identify with the tea party's goals. It is often described a grassroots movement, but as with many other political parties, various corporate interests have also provided substantial financial support.

THE 2012 AND 2014 ELECTIONS The 2012 presidential election pitted President Obama and Vice-President Joe Biden against Mitt Romney, a former governor of Massachusetts, and Paul Ryan, a U.S. congressman from Wisconsin. Questions posed during the televised Obama-Romney debates were far-ranging. Examples include questions to Romney about how he differed from George W. Bush and what he would do about immigrants trying to gain permanent residency. Obama faced questions on the Benghazi disaster, pay inequality for women, and what he had done to reduce access to assault weapons, among others.

The Obama-Biden ticket won both the popular and electoral votes. Obama carried states in the far West, the upper Midwest, and the Northeast. All the Deep South states went to Romney, except for Florida. In general, Obama did well in big and mid-sized cities, while Romney earned majorities in suburbs, small towns, and rural areas.

In 2014 power in the U.S. Congress underwent a shakeup. The House of Representatives was already dominated by Republicans. In 2014 Democrats also lost control of the Senate.

SECOND-TERM POLICIES AND THE 2016 ELECTION During his second term in office, President Obama tried to solve lingering foreign policy dilemmas. He also began a dramatic move that changed decades of foreign policy—normalizing diplomatic relations with Cuba. Obama took steps to lift the trade embargo against Cuba, which had been in place since 1961. He and Raul Castro, Cuba's Communist leader, agreed to establish embassies in each other's countries. Restrictions on travel to Cuba were also eased. While some felt these changes would be more effective in bringing democracy to Cuba than the old policy of isolation, others saw them as giving in to a Communist regime. Others criticized President Obama for acting without congressional approval.

Iran was another focus of President Obama's concerns. In 2015, Obama coordinated with several key countries to begin negotiations that would relieve sanctions against Iran in exchange for significant restrictions on its nuclear program and increased inspections of its nuclear facilities. Israel's president, Benjamin Netanyahu, angrily called for the proposal's rejection. Several critics agreed with his indignation and claimed that Obama was anti-Israel. Nonetheless, in April 2015 all parties involved announced that they had reached a basic framework for further talks.

As President Obama's second-term entered its final year, campaigns for the 2016 presidential election intensified. Businessman and Republican candidate Donald Trump became the first person with no political or military experience to be elected president. Trump defeated Democratic candidate Hillary Clinton, who was the first woman to become the presidential nominee of a major U.S. political party.

Reading Check
Analyze Causes
Why did President Obama have difficulty advancing his goals during his second term?

Lesson 3 Assessment

1. **Organize Information** Create a timeline of President Obama's major actions while in office.

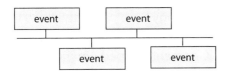

2. **Key Terms and People** For each key term or person in the lesson, write a sentence explaining its significance.

3. **Analyze Issues** What role should the government play in regulating economic institutions?
   Think About:
   • the need for financial stability
   • the possibility of political influence
   • the American tradition of free enterprise

4. **Summarize** What were the main issues in the presidential election of 2008?

5. **Predict** How do you think the PPACA will affect health care for your generation?

Technology Shapes Life

The Big Idea

Advances in technology have increased not only the pace but also the comfort and health of many Americans' daily lives.

Why It Matters Now

Providing access to the new technology and regulating its use are two challenges facing 21st-century America.

Key Terms and People

Internet

telecommute

geographic information system (GIS)

Telecommunications Act of 1996

intellectual property

genetic engineering

One American's Story

The crowds stood four-deep cheering for 12-year-old Rudy Garcia-Tolson as he captured a national record for his age group at the 2000 San Diego half-marathon. Despite the loss of his legs, Rudy competes in sports. He won gold medals in swimming at the 2004 and 2008 Paralympic Games, plus silver in 2012.

For years, Rudy was confined to a wheelchair, due to a genetic condition. After undergoing a double amputation, he was fitted with carbon fiber prostheses—artificial replacements for missing body parts. These lightweight, strong, and durable new legs now make many things possible for Rudy.

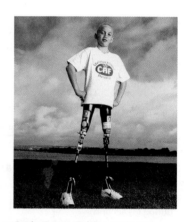

Rudy Garcia-Tolson, 2001

"I told them to cut my legs off. I saw pictures of people running with prosthetic legs. I didn't want to stay in a wheelchair. . . . My legs won't stop me. Nothing stops me. . . . I like to show kids that there's no limitations—kids or challenged people or adults, there's no limitations to what a person can do. . . . My motto is, if you have a brave heart, that's a powerful weapon."
—Rudy Garcia-Tolson, quoted in *Press-Enterprise*, January 1, 2000

Advances in medical technology have permitted Rudy to live a more fully active life. Throughout the 20th century and into the 21st, technological developments helped Americans become more active in many ways.

SS.912.A.1.2; SS.912.A.1.4; SS.912.A.7.12; SS.912.A.7.14; SS.912.H.1.5; SS.912.H.3.1; HE.912.C.2.4; LAFS.1112.RH.1.2

The Communications Revolution

In the 1940s, when computers first came into use, they took up huge rooms. The machines required elaborate air-conditioning systems to keep them from overheating. Today, the smartphone in your pocket can perform more tasks than one of those old room-sized computers. High-tech devices have also become affordable. The development of inexpensive personal computers has made it possible for ordinary families to use the latest technology.

ENTERING THE INFORMATION AGE In the 1960s the Department of Defense began to network its computers in order to protect its ability to launch nuclear missiles. Then, in the late 1980s the National Science Foundation created its own network, NSFNET, and allowed anyone to access it. However, only a small group of computer-science graduates and professors used the system.

A digital revolution soon took place, though. Thousands of industries across the country began using computers to run their businesses. Millions of Americans bought personal computers for their homes. With so many computers suddenly in use, NSFNET steadily grew into the large and crowded **Internet**. The Internet is an international network linking computers and allowing almost instant transmittal of text, images, and sound. The 1990s enjoyed explosive growth of the Internet. By 2014 some 3 billion of the world's people, or about 43.6 percent of world population, were using it. However, the majority of users were from the world's richest countries.

BUSINESS AND MARKETPLACE APPLICATIONS The late 20th-century advances in computers and communications have had an impact on American society and business comparable to the industrial developments of the late 1800s. Many observers credit computer technology with driving the astonishing economic growth that the United States experienced during the 1990s. With computers allowing employees in nearly every field to perform their jobs more quickly and easily, worker productivity and output increased. This was a major reason for the decade-long boom.

Computer-based management techniques have also allowed many businesses to streamline. For instance, some manufacturers have implemented just-in-time (JIT) systems. In these systems, they bring in only as many raw materials as are needed to produce the goods their customers demand. Such efficiencies allow them to use their resources elsewhere.

New and emerging technologies have also allowed companies and organizations to connect with branch offices, suppliers, or customers in other countries. Because of cell phones, the Internet, wireless connectivity, and overnight shipping, some employees can more readily **telecommute**. This allows them to work from a location of their choice instead of going to an office every day. Email and video conferences erase the thousands of miles that can separate coworkers. The increased business activity may stimulate economic development in both locations. In addition, the communication can enhance understanding between cultures.

Some businesses and governments use **geographic information system (GIS)** technology to improve efficiency and plan more effectively. A GIS is a computer system designed to collect and analyze many kinds of spatial or geographical data. For example, the state of Montana developed a GIS to keep track of land ownership, along with numerous details. A power company that needs to set up new power lines can easily track ownership and costs along the proposed route. Or, a local government can be alerted when a site that may be polluted with toxins changes hands. The government can step in quickly to test the site and remove the toxins.

The desire to capitalize on these innovations for profit drove several companies to enter the marketplace with technology products developed for personal use. As a result, consumers now clamor for the most current technology. This includes smartphones, laptop computers and tablets, and other personal electronic devices.

EVERYDAY USES Computer technology not only has improved how Americans work, but also has dramatically altered how they live. Millions of citizens now buy everything from flowers to books to stocks online. Every year, Americans spend tens of billions of dollars in electronic transactions, also known as e-commerce.

While Americans once spoke over the telephone or wrote letters for communication across distances, they now use their smartphones differently. Many people spend several hours a day sending instant messages—"texting"—or on social networking sites. Computers have also affected the way Americans learn. Now, most public school classrooms have Internet access. A growing number of universities offer classes and even complete degree programs over the Internet. Computer technology has, therefore, made education possible for anyone who can connect to the Internet. This is true wherever people live around the world.

Computer users can also download a vast number of applications, or "apps," for their mobile devices—tablets and smartphones. By 2015 almost 3 million apps were available from the various "app stores." Such apps allow users to perform a remarkable array of functions. Examples range from showing how to save a heart attack victim's life to checking a watermelon's ripeness. A new class of entrepreneurs has made fortunes by developing popular apps.

Document-Based Investigation Historical Source

"Vacation, 2000"

By the end of the 20th century, millions of Americans owned any number of personal communication devices. People were able to speak to or correspond with each other instantaneously almost anytime, almost anywhere.

Analyze Historical Sources
What does the cartoon suggest about Americans and their communication devices? Do you agree or disagree with the cartoonist's message? Explain your opinion.

VACATION, 2000

LEGISLATING TECHNOLOGY In the 1980s the government was slow to recognize the implications of the new communications technology. In 1994, however, the Federal Communications Commission (FCC) began to auction the valuable rights to airwaves. That year, the FCC collected over $9 billion. Then, with the rapid growth in the communications industry, the federal government took several steps to ensure that consumers received the best service. Congress passed the **Telecommunications Act of 1996**. This law removed barriers that had previously prevented one type of communications company from starting up or buying another related one. While it increased competition in the industry, the law also paved the way for major media mergers. For example, Capital Cities/ABC Inc. joined the Walt Disney Company. But industry watchdogs noted that this reflected the trend toward concentrating media influence in the hands of a few powerful conglomerates.

Computers and other technology are now commonplace tools used in classrooms to enhance students' learning.

The passage of the Telecommunications Act won applause from the communications industry. The law received only mixed reviews from the public. Consumer activists worried that the law would fail to ensure equal access to new technologies for rural residents and poor people. Civil rights advocates contended that the Communications Decency Act (part of the Telecommunications Act) restricted free speech. This is because it barred the transmission of "indecent" materials to minors via the Internet. Since the early 2000s the issue of network neutrality has created considerable controversy. In 2015 supporters of net neutrality applauded the FCC's ruling that prevented service providers or the government from restricting access to, or content delivered on, the Internet.

Another way that technology intersects with the law is in protecting the rights of content creators. Since the Internet developed, protecting **intellectual property** rights, a legal term that refers to creations of the mind, has become more difficult. With so much data available in cyberspace, it is easy for computer users to avoid giving proper credit—or payment—to those who created the material. The Internet has made copyright infringement, often called piracy, common. Musicians have gone to court to keep their unreleased songs from playing on the Internet. Writers may find their words attributed to others online or used in ways that were never intended. Balancing the need to protect intellectual property rights against freedom of information is a difficult task that will not be settled soon.

CHALLENGES FOR TODAY AND THE FUTURE For all the benefits and opportunities it has brought, computer technology has also created its own challenges. While it has become indispensable to many as a source of useful information, the Internet has also become a center for the dissemination of pornographic and anonymous hate material. In addition, the wide use of digital networks has also led to the growth of "cybercrime." Computer vandals, known as hackers, engage in many criminal activities. This includes the theft of Social Security numbers along with other vital personal information and the disabling of entire computer systems. The Federal Bureau of Investigation estimates that cybercrime costs Americans more than $10 billion a year. What concerns officials even more is the growing possibility of "cyberterrorism." This term refers to hackers stealing or altering vital military information such as nuclear missile codes.

Meanwhile, many Americans worry about the "digital divide." This is the notion that computer technology still remains out of reach for many of the nation's poor. Families unable to buy computers risk falling even further behind in a country where computer skills have become a necessity. Some communities are investing funds to help close the gap. Meanwhile, libraries, schools, and senior centers across the country provide free Internet access.

Over-reliance on digital devices can even become a problem for human relationships. Some observers worry that people spend so much time on social media or texting that they have forgotten—or never even learned—how to communicate face-to-face. At least one university has developed a seminar to help students with their interpersonal skills. Students in the New York University class had to pair off and talk, without using their phones, for six minutes. At the conclusion of the workshop, some of the students agreed that the encounter had been difficult. Facebook, they said, was easier.

Another example of overuse of digital gadgets is the tendency by some users to use their phones to film whatever they see, no matter how inappropriate. This practice has led to bystanders filming crimes such as assaults instead of helping the victim or calling police. On the other hand, the news is full of arrests and convictions based on people filming crimes as they happen.

The digital revolution shows no sign of slowing. The technology that has so transformed the nation will continue to present new opportunities. However, trying to predict just what those opportunities might be is pointless. After all, the technical marvels we take for granted today were once the fantasies only of comic book artists and science fiction writers.

Reading Check
Compare and Contrast What are some positive and negative results of the communication revolution?

Scientific Advances Enrich Lives

Developments that revolutionized robotics, space exploration, and medicine matched the exciting growth in the telecommunications industry. The world witnessed marvels that for many of the baby boom generation echoed science fiction. Moreover, new discoveries are made so often that describing any one of them as the "latest" is risky.

SIMULATION, ROBOTICS, AND MACHINE INTELLIGENCE Visual imaging and artificial intelligence (a computer's ability to perform activities that require intelligence) were combined to provide applications in industry, medicine, and education. For example, virtual reality began with the flight simulators used to train military and commercial pilots. Soon, with a headset that holds tiny video screens and earphones, and with a data glove that translates hand movements to a computer screen, users could navigate a "virtual landscape." Doctors have used virtual reality to take a computerized tour of a patient's throat and lungs to check for medical problems. Surgeons have performed long-distance surgery through telepresence systems. These systems include gloves, computers, and robotic elements specially wired so that a doctor can operate on a patient hundreds of miles away. Architects and engineers have used virtual reality to create visual, rather than physical, models of buildings, cars, and other designs. Modeling also affected the nightly newscast. Using supercomputers and improved satellite data, meteorologists could offer extended weather forecasts that reached the accuracy of one-day forecasts of 1980.

As technology became more sophisticated, computers increased in capability. In 1997 IBM's supercomputer Deep Blue defeated champion Garry Kasparov in a chess match. Computational linguists steadily improved natural language understanding in computers. This fine-tuned the accuracy of voice recognition systems.

Robots grew more humanlike as engineers equipped them with high-capacity chips simulating brain function. By the early 2000s robots had the ability to walk on two legs, interact with people, and learn taught behaviors. They could also express artificial feelings with facial gestures.

SPACE EXPLORATION Astronomers and engineers have expanded our view of the universe. In 1997 NASA's *Pathfinder* and its rover *Sojourner* transmitted the first live pictures of the surface of Mars. Several rovers have been sent to Mars since then to gather data on the planet's environmental and geological history. In July 2015 the spacecraft *New Horizons* flew past Pluto and sent back detailed information about the dwarf planet and its moons.

Shuttle missions, meanwhile, concentrated on scientific research and assembly, transport, and repair of orbiting objects. This paved the way for possible human missions to Mars and other space travel. NASA concentrated on working with other nations to build the *International Space Station (ISS).* The *ISS* promised to offer scientists a zero-gravity laboratory for research in medicine, space mechanics and architecture, and long-term living in space.

A shuttle crew in 1993 aboard the *Endeavor* repaired the Hubble Space Telescope, which returns dazzling intergalactic views. In late 1995 astronomers discovered the first planet outside our own solar system. By 2015 about 2,000 such "exoplanets" had been confirmed. On July 21, 2011, the *Atlantis* crew completed the final mission of NASA's 30-year shuttle program. However, U.S. space exploration goes on. In August 2011 NASA launched the probe *Juno,* for arrival at Jupiter in 2016. Also, American astronauts will continue to spend time on the *ISS.* But they will rely on Russian spacecraft to transport them.

Background
The *International Space Station* was established by joining and expanding upon the Russian station *Mir* and the American Spacelab.

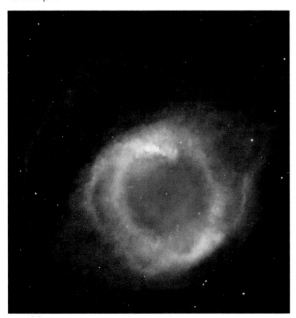

A view of the celestial body known as the Helix Nebula taken by the Hubble Space Telescope.

BIOTECHNOLOGY Profound insights into the book of life came from the field of biotechnology. The Human Genome Project and Celera, a private company in molecular biology, simultaneously announced in 2000 that they had mapped nearly all of the genes in the human body only a decade after the research began. Cooperation via the Internet and access to computerized databases by multiple research groups vastly accelerated the scientists' ability to identify and order over 3 billion chemical "letters" of the genetic code of DNA. Molecular biologists hoped that this genetic map would offer the key to treating many inherited diseases and diagnosing congenital disabilities.

DNA had been in the spotlight before the breakthrough announcement. In legal proceedings, prosecutors relied on DNA evidence to help prove the guilt of defendants who may have left behind a single hair at a crime scene. Others, wrongly imprisoned, were released when genetic analysis proved their innocence. By 2015 DNA testing had exonerated more than 300 people.

Different opinions arose over some of the new advances. Some speculated that technological progress outpaced social evolution and society's ability to grapple with the consequences. In 1997 Scottish researchers cloned Dolly the sheep from one cell of an adult sheep. Many wondered whether human cloning was next. Advances such as these sparked heated debates among scientists, ethicists, religious leaders, and politicians. Developments in gene therapy and testing embryos for genetic defects created similar controversies.

Researchers work at the Beijing Genomics Institute at Shenzhen in southern China.

The use of **genetic engineering**—the artificial changing of the molecular biology of organisms' cells to alter an organism—also aroused public concern. Food products that have been altered in this way are called genetically modified (GM) foods. Monsanto, a multinational corporation, was among the first companies to modify a plant cell's genetic code. Scientists in the late 1990s modified corn and rice to provide resistance to pests and increase nutritional value. Since then, many other crops have been modified. The U.S. Food and Drug Administration (FDA) holds that GM foods are safe and that they require no extra labeling. Many scientists agree. Others say that the long-term results of eating GM foods are not yet known.

Genetic engineering also raises legal issues. Firms can patent genes used for medical and research applications, using the principle of invention and property. They can also patent genetically modified seeds and require that farmers purchase seeds directly from the company every year. This prevents farmers from keeping seeds from their own crops for replanting. Disputes over use of GM crops have resulted in hundreds of court cases.

Progress in the pharmaceutical industry has raised an ethical question. Drug manufacturers take out patents on their formulas, which limits competition and drives up income. The drug companies want longer-lasting patents to protect their investment in researching and testing new medications. Critics say that the patents protect mainly the most profitable drugs but do not spur innovation. Industry defenders say that only by extending patents can drug makers afford to bring new lifesaving medications to market.

MEDICAL PROGRESS People suffering from some diseases benefited from remarkable medical advances. Cancer survival rates improved dramatically. For certain types of the disease, a cancer diagnosis is no longer a death sentence. Improved diagnostic methods, gene therapy, and genetically engineered antibodies make improved survival rates possible.

One therapy that offers great promise is the use of stem cells, which can differentiate into different types of cells. Chemotherapy to treat cancer often destroys healthy cells along with the cancerous ones. Injected stem cells can replace the cells lost during treatment. Stem cells can also help kill cancer cells themselves. The use of stem cells is controversial, however. Stem cells taken from embryos, such as those removed during abortion, are particularly useful for therapies. But removing the stem cells destroys the embryo. President George W. Bush fought to outlaw any use of embryonic stem cells. President Obama loosened restrictions slightly.

Improvements in tracking the spread of HIV—the virus that causes AIDS—through the body made researchers better prepared to find a cure. AIDS patients were treated with combination therapies. Public health officials addressed risky behaviors to control the spread of HIV. Deaths from AIDS have dropped. More people are still living long after a positive diagnosis.

Improved technology for making medical diagnoses offered new hope as well. Magnetic resonance imaging (MRI), for example, produces cross-sectional images of any part of the body. Advances that will make the MRI procedure ten times faster will also make MRI more widely available and cheaper to use. Medical researchers look ahead to using fleets of tiny "nanosensors" one-thousandth the width of a human hair to find tumors. Researchers also hope to someday deploy "nanobots" to repair tissues and even genes. Robotics and medical science have combined in a particularly remarkable field—3D bioprinting. This process places living cells in a structure that is built up by a 3D printer, layer after layer. With this method, technicians can build new tissues for repairing organs such as kidneys, livers, and hearts.

Another medical procedure grabbed headlines in 2007. That year, Dr. Laurent Lantieri, a French plastic surgeon, led a team that performed the first successful transplant of a face from a donor to a patient. The patient was a man whose face had been disfigured by tumors. Since then, more patients whose faces had been ruined by disease or accidents have undergone the grueling surgery. They awakened with not just new faces, but new lives.

Reading Check
Summarize How has technology affected health care?

Lesson 4 Assessment

1. **Organize Information** On a chart, list four of the technological changes described in this lesson, and explain how each change has affected your life.

Technological Change	Effect on Me
1.	
2.	
3.	
4.	

2. **Key Terms and People** For each key term in the lesson, write a sentence explaining its significance.

3. **Analyze Issues** Why are some technological, medical, and pharmaceutical advances controversial?

4. **Predict** How do you think technology will affect the global workforce and entrepreneurship in the future?

5. **Make Inferences** Explain how government, business, and consumers relate to genetically modified food crops.

Think About:
- legal and regulatory issues related to GM foods
- corporate involvement
- product safety

The Changing Face of America

The Big Idea

As the 20th century ended and the 21st began, the demographics of the U.S. population changed.

Why It Matters Now

Americans of all locations, backgrounds, and stages in life share common goals: the desire for equal rights and economic opportunity.

Key Terms and People

urban flight

gentrification

Proposition 187

One American's Story

Any effort to describe someone as a "typical American" is bound to be inadequate, as people move from cities to suburbs and back to the cities, arrive from other countries, and live longer than in years past. Our perceptions often do not keep pace with the changes. Doris Roberts, star of the TV show *Everybody Loves Raymond* and winner of five Emmy Awards, expressed her frustration with age discrimination at a hearing before a Senate Special Committee on Aging.

Doris Roberts

"[S]ociety considers me discardable. My peers and I are portrayed as dependent, helpless, unproductive and demanding rather than deserving. In reality, the majority of seniors are self-sufficient middle-class consumers with more assets than most young people and the time and talent to offer society. . . .

Age discrimination negates the value of wisdom and experience, robs us of our dignity and denies us the chance to continue to grow, to flourish, and to become all that we are capable of being. We all know that medical advances have changed the length and the quality of our lives today, but we have not, however, changed our attitudes about aging or addressed the disabling myths that disempower us."
—Doris Roberts, from a hearing before the Special Committee on Aging, United States Senate, 107th Congress, September 4, 2002

Issues related to youth and age are among several that are changing the country's demographic portrait.

SS.912.A.1.4; SS.912.A.1.7; SS.912.A.2.7; SS.912.A.7.12; SS.912.A.7.16; SS.912.G.2.1; SS.912.G.4.2; SS.912.G.4.3; MAFS.K12.MP.1.1; MAFS.K12.MP.5.1; MAFS.K12.MP.6.1

Urban Challenges

One of the most significant sociocultural changes in American history has been the movement of Americans from the cities to the suburbs. The years after World War II through the 1980s saw a widespread pattern of **urban flight**. This was the process in which Americans left the cities and moved to the suburbs. At mid-century, the population of cities exceeded that of suburbs. By 1970 the ratio became even.

CHANGES IN CITIES AND SUBURBS Several factors contributed to the movement of Americans out of the cities. Because of the continued movement of job-seekers into cities in the 1950s and 1960s, many urban neighborhoods became overcrowded. Overcrowding, in turn, contributed to such problems as increasing crime rates and decaying housing.

During the 1970s and early 1980s, city dwellers who could afford to do so moved to the suburbs for more space, privacy, security, and better schools. As middle-class Americans left cities for the suburbs, the economic base of many urban neighborhoods declined, and suburbs grew wealthy. Following the well-educated labor force, more industries relocated to suburban areas in the 1990s. In addition, many downtown districts fell into disrepair. Suburban shoppers abandoned city stores for suburban shopping malls. The economic base that provided tax money and supported city services in large cities such as New York, Detroit, and Philadelphia continued to shrink as people and jobs moved outward. According to the 1990 census, the 31 most impoverished communities in the United States were in cities.

By the mid-1990s, however, as the property values in the nation's inner cities declined, many people returned to live there. In a process known as **gentrification**, they purchased and rehabilitated deteriorating urban property. Old industrial sites and neighborhoods convenient to downtown became popular. These areas especially attracted young, single adults who preferred

Williamsburg is a neighborhood in Brooklyn, New York, where gentrification has taken place in recent years.

the excitement of city life and the uniqueness of urban neighborhoods to the more uniform suburban environments. The new arrivals often displaced lower-income people who could not afford to pay the higher property taxes that resulted from new development. Gentrification has become a contentious issue in urban politics.

Smaller cities and towns have had less of a problem with gentrification. But they did face deteriorating central business districts, as big national retailers built giant stores on the towns' outskirts. To revitalize their downtown cores, more than 2,000 cities and towns developed "main street" programs that offered incentives for revitalizing old buildings. These programs had positive economic and social effects. They created jobs, both during the rehabilitation process and when new businesses moved into the buildings. New businesses brought in new customers and clients, making urban cores safer and livelier. People moved downtown to live, also. Property tax revenues increased, making more money available for schools and other needs.

SUBURBAN LIVING Many suburbanites continued to commute to city jobs during the 1990s and early 2000s. Increasing numbers of workers began to telecommute, or use new communications technology to work from their homes. Another notable trend was the movement of minority populations to the suburbs. Nationwide, by the early 2000s, more Latinos, Asians, and African Americans lived in the suburbs than lived in the core cities.

Suburban growth led to intense competition between suburbs and cities, and among the suburbs themselves, for business and industry. Since low-rise suburban homes yielded low tax revenues, tax-hungry suburbs offered tax incentives for companies to locate within their borders. These incentives resulted in lower tax revenues for local governments. This means that less money was available for schools, libraries, and police departments. Consequently, taxes were often increased to fund these community services. Higher taxes were also needed to build the additional roads and other infrastructure necessary to support the new businesses.

Many suburbanites have reacted against the sameness that can afflict housing developments. To make suburbs more attractive, some town councils have required that developers include a certain amount of park acreage or hiking trails in their plans.

CITIES AND NATURAL DISASTERS Urban areas also face challenges due to natural disasters, such as extreme weather. In August 2005 New Orleans experienced widespread flooding as a result of both physical and human geographic factors. Hurricane Katrina—a massive storm with sustained winds of 125 miles per hour—made landfall along the coast of the Gulf of Mexico. During its course, the storm devastated parts of Alabama, Mississippi, and Louisiana. Much of the city of New Orleans lies below sea level, and levees are used to hold back surrounding waters. The city flooded when the levees failed in the aftermath of the hurricane. The human suffering due to the storm and subsequent flooding was immense. Nonprofit organizations rushed to help, as did the governments of neighboring states, which welcomed thousands of people driven out by the storm. Responses to the disaster were widely covered in the media. State leaders including Governor Rick Perry of Texas received

Vocabulary
infrastructure the basic facilities, services, and installations needed for the functioning of a community or society

praise for making state resources available. However, some felt the national response to the disaster was too slow and did not provide enough assistance.

Despite their location, northern cities are not safe from hurricanes. In October 2012 Hurricane Sandy devastated the entire eastern seaboard. New Jersey and New York were particularly hard hit. A storm surge flooded New York City's streets, trains, tunnels, and subways. The city fell into chaos. Deaths totaled more than 115. The cost estimate was $65 billion, a total exceeded only by Katrina.

Blizzards and earthquakes can also be devastating to cities. Such disasters can drain city coffers for years afterward, do irreparable damage to the environment, overburden local governments, create new political alliances, ruin property values, and affect population distribution. In the case of Katrina, for example, the destructive storm displaced more than 1 million people from the Gulf Coast region.

Reading Check
Analyze Causes
Why has a population shift back to cities happened in recent years?

The Aging of America

The U.S. Census Bureau documents that in 2010, Americans were older than ever before. The median age was 37.2—almost two years older than in 2000. In 2010 there were 40.3 million people who were 65 years old and older. This was an increase of 5.3 million people over the 2000 census. The percentage of older Americans also increased, from 12.4 percent of the population in 2000 to 13 percent in 2010.

Behind the rising median age lie several broad trends. The country's birthrate has slowed slightly. The huge baby boom generation has entered retirement age. Also, the number of seniors has increased as Americans live longer, thanks to advances in medical care and healthier lifestyles. The number of

The Graying of America, 1990–2030

Year	Number of Americans 65 and older*	Percentage of U.S. population
1990	31,081	12.4
2000	34,837	12.7
2010	40,229	13.0
2020	54,804**	16.1**
2030	72,092**	19.3**

*numbers in thousands
**projected totals
Source: U.S. Census Bureau

Interpret Tables
1. Between what years is America's elderly population expected to grow the most?
2. By roughly what percentage is America's elderly population expected to increase between 1990 and 2030?

people over 85 has increased at a faster rate than any other segment of the population, to 5.7 million in the year 2008. In 2010 more than 53,300 people had reached the age of 100. This was an increase of almost 3,000 from the 2000 census.

The graying of America has placed new demands on the country's programs that provide care for the elderly. These programs accounted for only 6 percent of the national budget in 1955. By 2015 these programs consumed more than one-third of the national budget. The major programs that provide care for elderly and disabled people are Medicare and Social Security. Medicare, which pays medical expenses for senior citizens, began in 1965. At that time, most Americans had lower life expectancies. By 2015 the costs of this program exceeded $492 billion.

Social Security, which pays benefits to retired Americans, was designed to rely on continued funding from a vast number of younger workers who would contribute taxes to support a small number of retired workers. That system worked well when younger workers far outnumbered retirees and when most workers didn't live long after retirement.

In 1996 it took Social Security contributions from three workers to support every retiree. By 2030, however, with an increase in the number of elderly persons and an expected decline in the birthrate, there will be only two workers' contributions available to support each senior citizen. What to do about Social Security has been an issue in recent presidential elections. If the government does not restructure the system, Social Security will eventually have to pay out more money than it will take in. Some analysts have suggested that the system could be reformed by raising deductions for workers, taxing the benefits paid to wealthier Americans, and raising the age at which retirees can collect benefits.

Reading Check
Predict What are the factors that will force an eventual restructuring of Social Security?

Immigration and Population

In addition to becoming increasingly suburban and elderly, the population of the United States has also been transformed by immigration. Between 1970 and 2010 the country's population swelled from 204 million to more than 309 million. Immigration accounted for much of that growth. Americans have long debated the effects of immigration on the country's character.

A CHANGING IMMIGRANT POPULATION The most recent immigrants to the United States differ from immigrants of earlier years. The large numbers of immigrants who entered the country before and just after 1900 came from Europe. In contrast, more than 30 percent of immigrants since the 1960s have come from Asia. About 50 percent arrived from the Western Hemisphere, primarily Mexico.

Conditions in Mexico and Central America are a major "push" factor in why so many people have risked coming to the United States. In Mexico, for example, during three months in 1994–1995, the Mexican peso devalued by 73 percent. The devaluation made the Mexican economy decline. As a result, almost a million Mexicans lost their jobs. Many of the unemployed people

Change in U.S. Immigration, 2000–2011

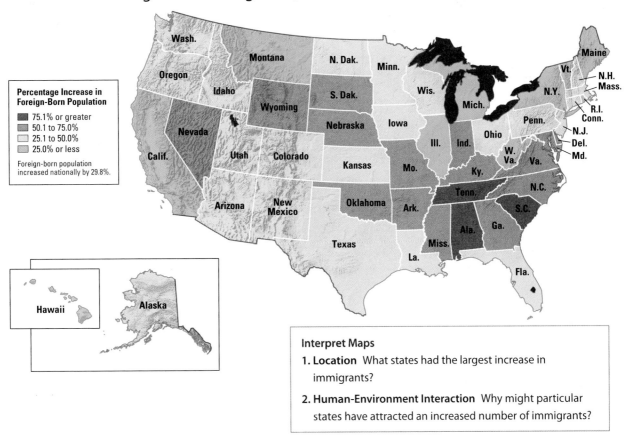

Percentage Increase in Foreign-Born Population

- ■ 75.1% or greater
- ■ 50.1 to 75.0%
- □ 25.1 to 50.0%
- ▨ 25.0% or less

Foreign-born population increased nationally by 29.8%.

Interpret Maps

1. **Location** What states had the largest increase in immigrants?

2. **Human-Environment Interaction** Why might particular states have attracted an increased number of immigrants?

headed north in search of jobs in the United States. In Central America, civil wars and drug gang violence have uprooted thousands of people, who then fled north to seek safety.

This search for a better opportunity continued throughout the 1990s. Thousands of legal and illegal immigrants arrived each day. To help those persons seeking more opportunity in America, a temporary guest worker program for those immigrants residing illegally in the United States was proposed several times in the early 2000s. But Congress has approved no such plan.

Census Bureau data indicated that patterns of immigration are changing the country's ethnic and racial makeup. By 2001, for example, California had become a "majority-minority" state. Asian Americans, Latinos, African Americans, and Native Americans make up more than half its population. By 2010 three other states—Hawaii, New Mexico, and Texas—had also become majority-minority states. Arizona, Florida, Georgia, Louisiana, Maryland, Mississippi, Nevada, New Jersey, and New York were close. In those states, the percentage of non-Hispanic white residents was below 60 percent. The United States as a whole is projected to become majority-minority by 2044.

DEBATES OVER IMMIGRATION POLICY The presence of such a large number of immigrants has also added to the continuing debate over U.S. immigration policies. Many Americans believe that the country can't absorb more immigrants. By the early 1990s an estimated 3.2 million illegal immigrants from Mexico, El Salvador, Guatemala, and Haiti had made their way

Lowe Shee Miu of Oakland, California, stands in front of a monument commemorating Chinese immigrants at Angel Island—the Ellis Island of the West.

to the United States. Many illegal immigrants also arrived from Canada, Poland, China, and Ireland. They took jobs as farm workers and domestic servants—jobs that many Americans turned down. They often received the minimum wage or less and no benefits. By 2013 perhaps 11.4 million illegal immigrants resided in the United States. Estimates vary widely, however, according to the source.

Hostility toward illegal immigration has increased in certain states, such as California and Arizona. In 1994 California passed **Proposition 187**, which cut all education and nonemergency health benefits to illegal immigrants. By March 1998 Proposition 187 was ruled unconstitutional. In 2010 Arizona passed a law that enhanced state and local police authority to enforce federal immigration laws. These efforts to control immigration inspired political participation among Hispanic voters, who saw themselves as targets.

As more immigrants make their way to the United States and the nation's ethnic composition changes, debates about immigration—particularly illegal immigration—will continue. Both the federal government and state governments grapple with the issue. Those who favor tighter restrictions argue that immigrants take desired jobs. Others, however, point to America's historical diversity and the new ideas and energy that immigrants bring. They also point out that some key industries, such as building construction, depend heavily on undocumented workers. Although various proposals had been suggested, by 2015 the U.S. Congress still had not passed a comprehensive plan for addressing immigration.

Background

The U.S. Census has asked a race question on every census since the first survey in 1790. Since 1890 the categories and definitions have changed with nearly every census.

NATIVE AMERICANS CONTINUE LEGAL BATTLES As the nation debated its immigrant policies, the ancestors of America's original inhabitants continued to struggle. The end of the 20th century found most members of this minority enduring extremely difficult lives. In 2007 about 25 percent of Native Americans lived below the poverty line. This was more than two times the poverty rate for white Americans. Furthermore, Native Americans endured suicide rates and alcoholism rates that were considerably higher than that of the general population.

In the face of such hardships, Native Americans strived to improve their condition. Throughout the 1990s dozens of tribes attained greater economic independence by establishing casinos. Although controversial for promoting gambling, reservation gaming was a thriving $27 billion-a-year industry by 2008. This income provided Native Americans with much-needed money for jobs, education, social services, and infrastructure.

Over the past decades, Native Americans have used the courts to attain greater recognition of their tribal ancestry and land rights. In 1999, for example, the U.S. Supreme Court ruled that the Chippewa Indians of Minnesota retained fishing and hunting rights on some 13 million acres of land that were guaranteed to them in an 1837 treaty. Across the nation, a number of other tribes have had similar land rights affirmed.

A NEW AMERICAN PORTRAIT Even though immigration remains a contentious issue and Native Americans still face hurdles, there is no denying that ours is a multicultural nation. Art, beliefs, literature, food, dance, festivals, music, customs—all have responded to the shifts in American society. Mexican food is almost as common as hamburgers. Mandarin Chinese classes appear in elementary school curriculums. Countries from Mali to Iceland influence American rock bands. A nationally known advice columnist wishes her Muslim readers "Happy Eid al-Fitr." This holiday ends the Islamic holy month of Ramadan. Jews invite non-Jews to share a Passover Seder and learn about the meal's ancient traditions. People of all faiths can be found throwing brightly colored powder on each other during Holi, originally a Hindu festival. Artists weave their heritage into their work. Classical composers adapt melodies, lyrics, and rhythms from their own ethnic backgrounds or those of others. Theater companies produce bilingual plays. Examples of multicultural influence on contemporary American society abound.

As the 21st century has progressed, there have been struggles to reconcile the many different cultures and belief systems that make up the United States. For example, in recent years, many loyal, peace-loving Muslims have found themselves vilified as terrorists. Sikhs have been attacked because their mode of dress sets them apart. Still, immigrants continue to come to the United States in pursuit of the American Dream. The newcomers bring a work ethic, innovation, and dedication to the ideals on which the United States was founded and make lasting contributions to help build the country.

Reading Check
Compare How are current arguments against immigration similar to those used in the past?

Lesson 5 Assessment

1. **Organize Information** Demography is the study of statistics about human populations. Use a table to summarize the demographic changes occurring in the United States.

Demographic Changes	
Urban distribution	
Age	
Ethnic and racial makeup	

2. **Key Terms and People** For each key term in the lesson, write a sentence explaining its significance.

3. **Predict** As urban problems become more common in the suburbs, how might the residents of suburbs respond? Base your answer on existing behavior patterns.

   Think About:
   • the spread of suburbs farther and farther from the city
   • the new ability to telecommute
   • the tax problems that suburbs face

4. **Compare and Contrast** How was the immigration that occurred in the 1990s and early 2000s similar to and different from earlier waves of immigration? How does the treatment of Muslim Americans compare to the treatment of other groups in the past?

5. **Analyze Effects** How have recent immigration and migration patterns in the United States affected social, economic, and political issues?

Module 18 Assessment

Key Terms And People

For each key term or person below, write a sentence explaining its significance.

1. William Jefferson Clinton
2. Contract with America
3. North American Free Trade Agreement (NAFTA)
4. George W. Bush
5. Osama bin Laden
6. weapons of mass destruction (WMD)
7. housing bubble
8. Barack Obama
9. Patient Protection and Affordable Care Act (PPACA)
10. genetic engineering
11. intellectual property
12. gentrification

Main Ideas

Use your notes and the information in the module to answer the following questions.

The Clinton Years

1. Which parts of the economy grew during the 1990s, and which declined?
2. How and why did the role of labor unions change as the economy changed?
3. What happened following the investigation of President Clinton?
4. How did the United States respond to acts of terrorism that occurred both at home and abroad during the Clinton years?

The Bush Administration

5. What role did the Electoral College play in the 2000 election?
6. What happened on September 11, 2001?
7. Why was the invasion of Iraq controversial? How did the war proceed?
8. How did support for the administration vary over the eight years Bush was president?
9. How did President Bush try to limit the damage of the country's economic problems?

Obama's Presidency

10. How did the American Recovery and Reinvestment Act (ARRA) stabilize the economy?
11. Why did environmentalists criticize the Keystone XL Pipeline project?
12. What are two examples of Obama continuing a foreign policy begun by President Bush?
13. What impact did President Obama have on foreign policies related to Cuba and Iran?

Technology Shapes Life

14. What are some ways technology has affected American businesses and individuals?
15. How is technology transforming access to education worldwide?
16. What did the Hubble Space Telescope discover in late 1995?
17. What change has occurred in recent years with AIDS and cancer survival rates?

The Changing Face of America

18. How has urban flight changed cities and suburbs?
19. How can natural disasters affect cities?
20. What special problems have struck the downtown areas of small cities and towns, and what solutions have been attempted?
21. Why did so many Mexican immigrants come to the United States in 1994–1995?
22. How has government addressed the issue of increasing minority populations?

Critical Thinking

1. **Sequence** Create a timeline of important events from the 2000 election.

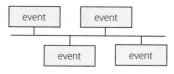

Which event do you think was the turning point? Explain.

2. **Evaluate** Do you think President Bush's domestic and foreign policy responses after the September 11 attacks were appropriate? Why or why not?

3. **Compare and Contrast** How did the domestic policies of presidents Clinton, Bush, and Obama differ? How did their foreign policies compare?

4. **Analyze Causes** How have interactions in the Middle East affected the image of the United States in the region?

5. **Analyze Issues** How far should the government go in protecting the public from terrorism and other threats, while guarding the privacy rights of the individual?

6. **Analyze Effects** How has the American workforce changed in recent years? What effects have the changes had on society?

7. **Synthesize** What are some issues discussed in this module that involve relationships between U.S. domestic and foreign policies?

8. **Develop Historical Perspective** What role did diplomacy play in developing peaceful relations with other nations and developing alliances and global agreements during the Clinton, Bush, and Obama presidencies?

9. **Identify Problems** Why is increased partisanship in government a problem? Is there anything you can do to improve communication and compromise between political opponents?

10. **Predict** What kinds of technological advancements might change American life during the 21st century?

11. **Form Opinions** Do you think you and your peers are too dependent on electronic gadgets? Why or why not?

12. **Evaluate** Assess the merit and effectiveness of recent legislation in addressing the citizenship status of individuals and groups in the United States.

Engage with History

Imagine that you are either an entrepreneur in a computer field or a researcher in biotechnology or pharmaceuticals. You have developed a remarkable new method, product, or medication. Before you can bring it to the global market, however, you need to investigate government regulations that relate to intellectual property rights, patents, personal privacy, and other ethical issues. Think of a process or product that you feel would be useful and research how the government would address its suitability for distribution.

Focus on Writing

Write an expository essay in which you describe the career and accomplishment of a woman or member of a minority group who achieved prominence during the administrations of President Clinton, Bush, or Obama. Examples include Madeleine Albright, Colin Powell, Alberto González, Condoleezza Rice, Hillary Clinton, Nancy Pelosi, Eric Holder, and Loretta Lynch.

Multimedia Activity

Organize the class into groups. Each group should conduct research on interventions by the U.S. military in various regions during the tenure of President Clinton, Bush, or Obama. Regions might include Eastern Europe, North Africa, sub-Saharan Africa, the Middle East, or South Asia (including Afghanistan and Pakistan). Groups should analyze the purposes and effects of the intervention and include the context of the Cold War, international peacekeeping efforts, and responses to terrorism, where appropriate. Present your findings to the class using video, text, and other formats.

Module 19

The United States in the 21st Century

★

Essential Question

What role should the United States play in global affairs?

About the Photograph: The port at Seattle, Washington, is an essential link in U.S. trade with Asian countries.

In this module you will learn about recent changes in U.S. political, social, environmental, and economic culture. You will also be challenged to look toward the future and consider ways that the country can effectively meet the issues that confront us all.

▷ Explore ONLINE!

HISTORY

VIDEOS, including...
- The Faces of America
- The Gun Effect
- A World Without Bees
- Return of the Pirates

☑ Document-Based Investigations

☑ Graphic Organizers

☑ Interactive Games

☑ Interactive Map: U.S. Diplomatic Issues Around the World, 2015

☑ Image with Hotspots: How Fracking Works

SS.912.A.1.2 Utilize a variety of primary and secondary sources to identify author, historical significance, audience, and authenticity to understand a historical period. **SS.912.A.1.3** Utilize timelines to identify the time sequence of historical data. **SS.912.A.1.4** Analyze how images, symbols, objects, cartoons, graphs, charts, maps, and artwork may be used to interpret the significance of time periods and events from the past. **SS.912.A.1.6** Use case studies to explore social, political, legal, and economic relationships in history. **SS.912.A.1.7** Describe various sociocultural aspects of American life including arts, artifacts, literature, education, and publications. **SS.912.A.7.12** Analyze political, economic, and social concerns that emerged at the end of the 20th century and into the 21st century. **SS.912.A.7.14** Review the role of the United States as a participant in the global economy. **SS.912.A.7.15** Analyze the effects of foreign and domestic terrorism on the American people. **SS.912.A.7.17** Examine key events and key people in Florida history as they relate to United States history. **SS.912.G.1.2** Use spatial perspective and appropriate geographic terms and tools, including the Six Essential Elements, as organizational schema to describe any given place. **SS.912.G.2.1** Identify the physical characteristics and the human characteristics that define and differentiate regions. **SS.912.H.1.5** Examine artistic response to social issues and new ideas in various cultures. **SS.912.H.3.1** Analyze the effects of transportation, trade, communication, science, and technology on the preservation and diffusion of culture. **LAFS.1112.RH.1.2** Determine the central ideas or information of a primary or secondary source; provide an accurate summary that makes clear the relationships among the key details and ideas. **LAFS.1112.RH.3.8** Evaluate an author's premises, claims, and evidence by corroborating or challenging them with other information. **LAFS.1112.RH.4.10** By the end of grade 12, read and comprehend history/social studies texts in the grades 11–CCR text complexity band independently and proficiently. **MAFS.K12.MP.1.1** Make sense of problems and persevere in solving them. **MAFS.K12.MP.5.1** Use appropriate tools strategically.

Timeline of Events 1999–2016

▶ *Explore ONLINE!*

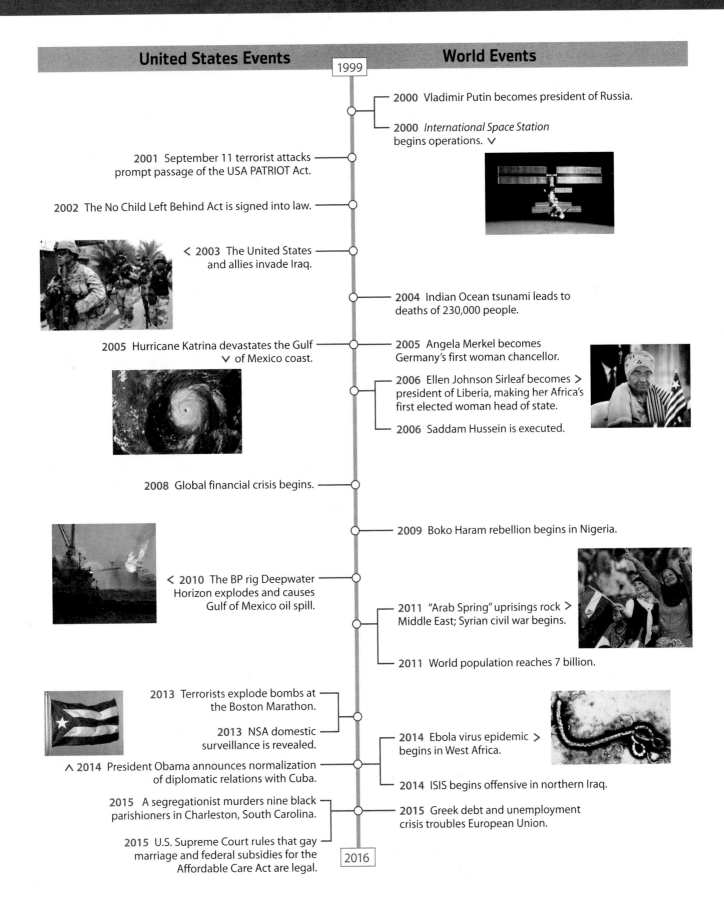

United States Events

1999

2001 September 11 terrorist attacks prompt passage of the USA PATRIOT Act.

2002 The No Child Left Behind Act is signed into law.

< **2003** The United States and allies invade Iraq.

2005 Hurricane Katrina devastates the Gulf ∨ of Mexico coast.

2008 Global financial crisis begins.

< **2010** The BP rig Deepwater Horizon explodes and causes Gulf of Mexico oil spill.

2013 Terrorists explode bombs at the Boston Marathon.

2013 NSA domestic surveillance is revealed.

∧ **2014** President Obama announces normalization of diplomatic relations with Cuba.

2015 A segregationist murders nine black parishioners in Charleston, South Carolina.

2015 U.S. Supreme Court rules that gay marriage and federal subsidies for the Affordable Care Act are legal.

2016

World Events

2000 Vladimir Putin becomes president of Russia.

2000 *International Space Station* begins operations. ∨

2004 Indian Ocean tsunami leads to deaths of 230,000 people.

2005 Angela Merkel becomes Germany's first woman chancellor.

2006 Ellen Johnson Sirleaf becomes > president of Liberia, making her Africa's first elected woman head of state.

2006 Saddam Hussein is executed.

2009 Boko Haram rebellion begins in Nigeria.

2011 "Arab Spring" uprisings rock > Middle East; Syrian civil war begins.

2011 World population reaches 7 billion.

2014 Ebola virus epidemic > begins in West Africa.

2014 ISIS begins offensive in northern Iraq.

2015 Greek debt and unemployment crisis troubles European Union.

National Security and Public Safety

The Big Idea

The U.S. government strives to safeguard the public while preserving individual liberties.

Why It Matters Now

As digital technology becomes more pervasive and new threats arise, American citizens must share the responsibility for protecting themselves and the country.

Key Terms and People

drone

National Security Agency (NSA)

racial profiling

human trafficking

One American's Story

Kate Martin was concerned that the need for national security be balanced by protecting individual liberties. An expert in national security topics, she has taught at George Washington University Law School. She also served as general counsel to the National Security Archive, a nongovernmental organization. Martin has often used the courts to fight for open government. As Director of the Center for National Security Studies, Martin testified during the Forum on National Security and the Constitution held in response to the September 11 terrorist attacks.

Kate Martin testifies before a congressional committee.

"While some have cast the terrible situation we find ourselves in today as one in which we must decide what liberties we are willing to sacrifice for an increased measure of safety, I do not believe that is an accurate or helpful analysis. Before asking what trade-offs are constitutional, we must ask what gain in security is accomplished by restrictions on civil liberties."

—Kate Martin, from testimony before the Committee of the Judiciary, House of Representatives, January 24, 2002

New tensions and modern technology increase the difficulty of keeping Americans both safe and free.

SS.912.A.1.2; SS.912.A.7.12; SS.912.A.7.15;
LAFS.1112.RH.4.10; MAFS.K12.MP.1.1; MAFS.K12.MP.5.1

Terrorism and Security

The FBI describes terrorism as violent acts intended to intimidate or coerce a civilian population; to influence the policy of a government by intimidation or coercion; or to affect the conduct of a government by mass destruction, assassination, or kidnapping. Terrorist acts have targeted Americans on foreign soil and in the United States.

The most deadly act of terrorism occurred on September 11, 2001. More than 3,000 people perished in New York City; Washington, DC; and rural Pennsylvania. In response to these threats, President George W. Bush created the Office of Homeland Security to protect the country from further attacks. The U.S. Congress approved the USA PATRIOT Act. This act gave the government broad powers to monitor Americans' communications and activities. Critics complained that the law posed a threat to basic freedoms. To address these concerns, Congress agreed to let some provisions of the law expire gradually. Since then, certain provisions have been extended repeatedly.

FOREIGN SOURCES OF TERRORISM Ever since the September 11 attacks, Americans have been alert to terrorist threats from abroad, especially from the Middle East. Modern air transportation makes it easier for people from other countries to bring violence to the United States. However, radicals can inspire violence in others without regard for national borders by posting hate-filled videos, manifestos, and recruitment appeals on websites and social media. But not all Internet sources of terrorist ideas come from other countries. Some U.S. citizens have also turned to electronic media to foment terrorism. One such citizen was Anwar al-Awlaki, who was born in New Mexico but was influenced by radical Middle Eastern Islamists. Al-Awlaki's writings and videos were found on the computer owned by Muhammad Youssef Abdulazeez, a Kuwaiti-born man who had been raised in the United States. Abdulazeez shot and killed four service members at military installations in Chattanooga, Tennessee, on July 16, 2015. Police officers ended the attack by killing Abdulazeez.

Radical Islamist rhetoric available on the Internet also helped inspire a horrific terrorist act that occurred on April 15, 2013, in Boston, Massachusetts. Brothers Tamerlan and Dzhokhar Tsarnaev, who had immigrated as

An airport security official inspects a traveler's shoe at a security checkpoint.

Radicals and the Internet

Security officials are facing new challenges in their efforts to keep Americans safe. During a U.S. Senate hearing, the witnesses were asked what keeps them awake at night. Following is FBI Director Robert Mueller's response.

> *"[I]t is the radicalization of individuals on the Internet, who develop the desire and the will to undertake attacks. They're finding it very difficult to find co-conspirators, others that would join in. But then again, the Internet can facilitate that kind of a meeting/coming together for an attack. And it is the lone wolves that we are principally concerned about."*
>
> —Robert Mueller, from testimony before the U.S. Senate Select Committee on Intelligence, March 12, 2013

Analyze Historical Sources
How does the Internet affect the spread of radical ideas?

children from Russia and Kyrgyzstan, detonated bombs along the route of the Boston Marathon. (Dzhokhar was a U.S. citizen, but Tamerlan was not.) Their goal was vengeance for U.S. wars in Muslim countries. Three people were killed, and more than 260 were injured. Tamerlan was killed during the search for those responsible. Dzhokhar was arrested, tried, and sentenced to death. Just as the September 11 attacks prompted admiration for the emergency workers who risked their lives to save others, Americans were moved by the courage of Boston victims. Some who had lost limbs in the bombing were determined not just to walk again, but to run in upcoming marathons. The phrase "Boston Strong" declared Bostonians' resolve to go about their daily lives.

DOMESTIC TERRORISM Some terrorist acts on U.S. soil grow from domestic disputes. Americans have committed crimes to intimidate civilians or influence government policy related to a range of issues. For instance, some activists have sabotaged facilities where commercial products were tested on animals. Those events primarily affected property.

Some terrorists choose to attack human targets. Various white supremacist groups have used beatings and murder to intimidate people they find objectionable. Examples of these groups include Aryan Nations, Stormfront, and the Ku Klux Klan. These groups and many others that mimic them share several basic beliefs, although with different emphases. Among those beliefs are the superiority of white people, anti-Semitism, veneration of the Confederacy, opposition to the federal government, and a militant Christian point of view. Antigay, anti-immigrant, anti-Muslim, anti–gun control, and neo-Nazi attitudes are also common in many of these groups. One incident inspired by these attitudes occurred in August 2012 at a Sikh temple in Oak Creek, Wisconsin. A white supremacist with ties to neo-Nazi groups fatally shot six people before killing himself. All of the shooter's victims were members of the Sikh faith.

The Southern Poverty Law Center maintains a list of organizations it designates as active hate groups. Hate groups are those that have "beliefs or practices that attack or malign an entire class of people, typically for their immutable [unchangeable] characteristics." In 2014 the SPLC counted 784 such organizations. Some black separatist organizations also appear on the list. Groups on the list do not necessarily advocate violence, although critics accuse them of inspiring others to commit violent acts. Like foreigners who urge violence, these domestic groups often use their websites and social media to spread their message and recruit followers.

Extremists who commit acts of violence and are not affiliated with any particular group are another threat. One such person was Joseph Stack. He flew his single-engine plane into an Austin, Texas, building that housed an Internal Revenue Service (IRS) field office in 2010. Stack's suicide note expressed his anger toward the IRS. One IRS employee was killed, and 13 other people were injured in the attack. In June 2015 Dylann Storm Roof shot and killed nine African Americans in a historic Charleston, South Carolina, church. According to several sources, he wanted to start a race war. Roof indicated on a social media site that he had found inspiration for his white supremacist views on the Internet. Investigations, however, have not found him to be affiliated with any particular group.

Both foreign and domestic terrorism can threaten the security and safety of the American public. However, many Americans refuse to succumb to fear.

Reading Check
Identify Problems
Which do you think pose more danger to the American public—foreign or domestic terrorists?

Vocabulary
surveillance close observation of an individual, group, or location

Surveillance and Privacy

While militants of all varieties use the Internet and social media to spread their views and recruit new members, intelligence agencies and law enforcement use technology to track their activities. Ordinary citizens, too, are subject to surveillance by high-tech mechanisms that were unimaginable just a few years ago.

TECHNOLOGY AND SECURITY Several technological innovations make such surveillance possible. Closed-circuit television (CCTV) records what goes on in areas where crimes are more likely, such as airports, banks, casinos, and convenience stores. The popularity of CCTV increased after the September 11 attacks. Some Americans don't like knowing that their innocent, day-to-day activities can be recorded. Other people are reassured by the cameras. They feel that CCTV can help deter crime or help solve crimes that do happen.

Drones, also known as unmanned aerial vehicles, are aircraft operated by pilots on the ground. Because drones can carry cameras, they have a range of uses. Drones can be used for movie-making, detecting forest fires, or inspecting power lines. Law enforcement can also use them for surveillance. Police departments may fly drones to keep an eye on crowded public events from above. The Department of Homeland Security flies drones along the Rio Grande to find immigrants crossing illegally from Mexico into Texas. Not all Americans are comfortable with this new technology. For example, residents

In the photo on the left, a closed-circuit TV camera provides security personnel with a wide view of a New York City street. In the photo on the right, a French surveillance official pilots a drone.

of Seattle, Washington, objected so strongly to their police force using drones that the city's mayor scrapped the plan.

Another surveillance tool may be in your pocket or backpack—the camera on your smartphone. In 2015 an estimated 64 percent of American adults owned a smartphone, up from 35 percent just four years earlier. Most people use them for ordinary tasks. Some people use their phones inappropriately, however, by taking photos or video of others without the subjects' knowledge. Using the stolen images for blackmail or other illegal purposes is a crime that law enforcement now must fight. Surveillance by camera phone can also solve crimes, however. In public places, suspicious activity attracts the attention—and cameras—of bystanders. There is even an app that allows the person filming a crime as it happens to send the video directly to the police.

KEEPING TABS ON AMERICANS Americans may be taking thousands of pictures of each other—legally or illegally—but the federal government can access a great deal more information on U.S. citizens. The **National Security Agency (NSA)** is an intelligence-gathering organization within the U.S. government. It was founded in 1952 during the Cold War. Although originally a highly secret department, more of the NSA's activities have come to light in recent decades. Investigations showed that the NSA has a history of monitoring civilian communications it considers suspect. More recently, the threat of terrorism increased the NSA's interception or monitoring of electronic communications.

Beginning in June 2013 the media exposed the extent of those actions, shocking many Americans. A series of top secret internal NSA documents revealed that the agency routinely collected telephone information on millions of people worldwide. Many of these people were never suspected of criminal activities. The documents also showed the web that connected the NSA, foreign intelligence agencies, and big telecommunications companies.

Edward Snowden, a contractor for the NSA, admitted that he was responsible for downloading the classified documents and making them available to journalists. Snowden maintained that he examined the documents carefully before sharing them to ensure that doing so was in the public interest. Some Americans called Snowden a heroic whistleblower for revealing government wrongdoing. Others said he was a traitor for endangering national security. The media also came under fire for sensationalizing the documents' revelations. While Snowden was in Hong Kong, the U.S. Department of Justice charged him with two counts of espionage and theft of government property. Since then, Snowden has not returned to the United States. As of 2015 he was living in Russia.

The NSA was in the headlines again in May and June of 2015. A federal appeals court ruled that the USA PATRIOT Act does not allow the program that the agency uses to gather millions of phone records. Since the act was not written to be permanent, the provisions that allowed bulk collection of data expired at the end of May. Senator Rand Paul of Kentucky, a libertarian popular with the tea party, halted the USA PATRIOT Act's extension in Congress. Some liberals agreed with Paul. However, early in June Congress passed a new bill that eliminated the NSA's bulk phone-records collection program. Instead, phone records would stay in the hands of phone companies. Other aspects of the government's surveillance program remained intact.

Many Americans feel conflicted about such surveillance activities. The NSA and other government agencies can indeed uncover vital information that leads to saving lives and property. The cost can be high, though, as individual rights and privacy may erode. Modern technology provides those hoping to do harm new outlets for their message. It also offers governments new methods for gathering information on criminal intentions. As a result, Americans will continue to struggle with the need to balance national security and individual rights. The tension between national security and civil liberties is not a new one, however. Benjamin Franklin offered his opinion on the topic long ago, when he said, "Those who would give up essential Liberty, to purchase a little temporary Safety, deserve neither Liberty nor Safety."

Reading Check
Analyze Effects
How has modern technology affected surveillance?

Crime and Public Safety

Although sensational acts of violence grab headlines, violent crime has actually decreased in the United States since the early 1990s. Certain issues related to crime and law enforcement reflect changes in society, however, and require a close look.

INCARCERATION AND DRUG LAWS One way that Americans have sought to battle crime is by putting more people in prison. The federal government and many states have "three strikes" laws on the books. Under these laws, any person found guilty of two previous crimes receives a stiff sentence of 20 to 30 years after conviction for a third. While many applaud this get-tough policy, others claim that it suffers from a serious problem: racial bias. African Americans represent just 12 percent of the U.S. population and about

U.S. Incarcerated Population

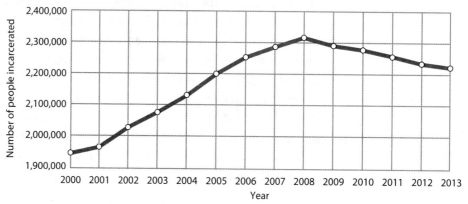

Source: U.S. Department of Justice, Bureau of Justice Statistics, *Correctional Populations in the United States, 2013*

Interpret Graphs
What trend does the graph show for the last five years listed?

13 percent of those who reported using illegal drugs on a monthly basis. Yet three-fourths of all prison sentences for possession of drugs involve African Americans.

The number of incarcerated Americans is huge—some 2.3 million people in jail or prison. Of all the world's countries, the United States jails the largest percentage of its people. Advocates of severe sentences say that incarceration deters people from committing crimes by warning them of the consequences. Critics of the U.S. prison situation say that incarceration just turns many nonviolent offenders into hardened criminals. They also point out that a large percentage of inmates are serving time for nonviolent drug offenses. In 2011 drug sentences accounted for almost half of the inmates in U.S. jails and prisons.

The issue of incarceration for drug crimes is one factor in the loosening of laws against the use of marijuana. Use for medical reasons was legal in about half of the U.S. states by 2015. Even laws against recreational use are changing. In 2012 the state of Colorado legalized the personal, private use of marijuana by adults. Alaska, Oregon, Washington, and the District of Columbia loosened their marijuana laws not long after. Proposals for legalization are active in several other states.

LAW ENFORCEMENT UNDER SCRUTINY Just as laws are changing, law enforcement is also transforming. Police forces are concentrating on community outreach. Digital technology has given police new tools for locating offenders and solving crimes. However, some police have been accused of inappropriate responses to public disturbances. Sometimes digital technology, in the form of a bystander's smartphone or a reporter's video, records those events.

In August 2014 the spotlight of public attention shone harshly on Ferguson, Missouri, a suburb of St. Louis. A young African American man, Michael Brown, robbed a convenience store. In a later confrontation, a police officer shot and killed Brown, although he was unarmed. The Ferguson community erupted in protests, both peaceful and violent. Many media reports labeled the police response to those protests as racist and overly militarized. Another case, in New York City, also caused outrage. During the arrest of Eric Garner, an unarmed black man, police used a controversial hold while Garner protested that he couldn't breathe. Garner died soon after. A third incident, this one in Baltimore, Maryland, involved Freddie Gray, whose neck and spine were injured while he was in police custody. After Gray died, charges were filed against the officers involved in the incident.

These events renewed scrutiny of how police relate to minorities, particularly young, urban, African American men. Civil rights advocates have presented case after case of what they characterize as racial profiling by law enforcement. **Racial profiling** is the act of suspecting or targeting a person simply on the basis of his or her race or ethnic background. These advocates also say that police are more apt to shoot or kill black and Hispanic suspects than whites. A study of police records and media reports by the *Washington Post* revealed that, just in the first five months of 2015, U.S. police killed 399 people. Most of the victims were armed, but 45 had no weapon. Although about half of the 399 victims were white, two-thirds of the unarmed victims were black or Hispanic. Some readers labeled the report as biased against police. Others said that police brutality statistics are actually underreported. In response to this increased focus on law enforcement, many police departments now require that their officers wear body cameras so that the circumstances of police actions are recorded.

GUNS AND AMERICAN SOCIETY Another issue that commands daily headlines is gun violence. The statistics are alarming. In 2013 alone, more than 11,200 people were killed by gunfire. In 2014 gunfire killed almost 3,000 children and teenagers. Sales of firearms, including automatic weapons, have soared. Efforts to expand gun-owners' rights have also increased. Several states have passed "open carry" laws. These laws allow gun owners to carry their weapons outside their clothing while in public. Details of these laws vary from state to state.

At the center of the gun-control issue lies a long-standing constitutional debate. The Second Amendment to the Constitution states: "A well-regulated militia, being necessary to the security of a free state, the right of the people to keep and bear arms shall not be infringed." The National Rifle Association (NRA) is an organization that supports gun ownership. It argues that gun-control laws violate this right to bear arms. Others contend that the amendment was not intended to guarantee a right to personal weapons. Rather, its purpose is to protect the states' right to maintain military units, such as National Guard forces. However, the U.S. Supreme Court has ruled that individuals do have the right to own firearms.

There may be no topic in American society that is more contentious than gun control. Besides the Second Amendment issue, gun-rights backers maintain that owning weapons enables them to protect themselves, their families, and their property. Gun control supporters cite the large number of accidental shootings, often the result of irresponsible gun ownership, in addition to

Gun Ownership Rates of Selected Countries

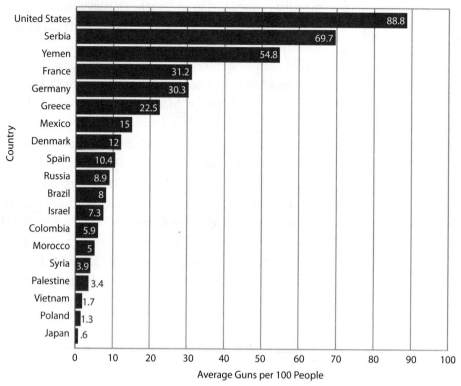

Source: United Nations Office on Drugs and Crime; Small Arms Survey, 2007

Interpret Graphs
1. Based on the graph, how does gun ownership in the United States compare to other countries?
2. How do the European countries represented on the graph compare to the two South American countries shown?

the large number of intentional firearm deaths. Those who want stricter gun laws also accuse the NRA of encouraging gun ownership while taking large sums of money from gun manufacturers.

HUMAN TRAFFICKING One crime that has recently drawn U.S. media attention is the practice known as **human trafficking**, in which people are brought into the United States against their will and in violation of the law. This cruel trade traps people—mostly women and children—into working for little or no money, with no hope of freedom from their captors. According to the U.S. Justice Department, more than 17,000 people are trafficked into the United States every year. The number may be higher, though, because finding and prosecuting the perpetrators is difficult. If the victims are afraid of punishment or deportation, some of them even side with their oppressors.

Poverty is a root cause of human trafficking. Some parents sell their children to traffickers. They do so hoping that their children will have a better life in the United States, not knowing that they will be abused. Adults desperate for work are lured into the trade with promises of employment, only

Many American teenagers who run away from home become victims of human traffickers. The National Runaway Switchboard helps teens break free from their captors. In this photo, switchboard personnel take calls from runaways in the Chicago area.

to find that the "jobs" are brutal physical labor or forced prostitution. The regions from which most trafficked persons come are South Asia, Southeast Asia, and Central America. Not all of the victims of human trafficking are foreigners, though. Some U.S. citizens are also trapped in the trade. Runaway teenagers are particularly vulnerable to being forced into sexual slavery.

States with several ports of entry and large immigrant populations are the main destinations. As a result, California, Texas, and Florida have had to focus law enforcement efforts on traffickers. Both the federal and state governments have passed laws to stop human trafficking and to bring the offenders to justice. Nonprofit organizations also seek to end the trade and help the victims. Unfortunately, human trafficking in the United States will probably continue for some time. Economic globalization plays a part in its survival. As global trade increases, so does the demand for cheap labor. The need for labor in turn encourages illegal immigration and a framework for trafficking. In addition, modern communication technology allows traffickers to operate on a worldwide scale.

Reading Check
Summarize
What are some recent developments affecting law enforcement?

Lesson 1 Assessment

1. **Organize Information** Create a web to show how modern technology affects national security and public safety. Add more branches as necessary.

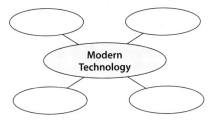

Modern Technology

2. **Key Terms and People** For each key term in the lesson, write a sentence explaining its significance.

3. **Evaluate** Why might some perceive Edward Snowden as heroic while others might view him as a traitor?
   Think About:
   - the need for national security
   - the right to privacy
   - Americans' right to know about government actions

4. **Analyze Causes** What is the connection between terrorism and the USA PATRIOT Act?

5. **Draw Conclusions** Do you think that actions taken to address the causes of continuing urban tensions and violence have been effective? Why or why not?

Foreign Policy

The Big Idea

In order to keep the peace whenever possible and safeguard U.S. interests, policymakers engage in a range of relationships with other countries.

Why It Matters Now

Relationships between our country and others can affect us directly, so we need to stay vigilant in our efforts to keep those relationships peaceful.

Key Terms and People

national interest

Vladimir Putin

ISIS

Boko Haram

One American's Story

Marco Rubio, a U.S. senator from Florida, is a Miami native of Cuban American descent. Throughout his political career he has been a staunch advocate for a strong national defense. Rubio has served as a member of the Senate Intelligence Committee and as co-chair of the Senate National Security Working Group. In a speech to the Concerned Veterans for America, Rubio compared the global situation during the period of the Barbary Wars to today's world. The Barbary Wars was a series of conflicts during the early 1800s when the United States fought pirates off the coast of North Africa.

Senator Marco Rubio

"America was dealt a hard lesson through this affair: we must be prepared for threats wherever they arise, because our nation is never isolated from the world. Tremors in global affairs can fracture the foundations of our domestic economy. This was true then, when our connection to the world was limited to a slow procession of merchant ships. It is even truer today. . . . Never before have our people and our economy been so connected to the world. What happens across the planet can have a greater impact on your family than what happens down the street."

—Marco Rubio, from a speech to Concerned Veterans for America, September 17, 2014

The complex web that connects the world's countries does indeed present new challenges for U.S. foreign policy.

SS.912.A.1.2; SS.912.A.1.4; SS.912.A.7.12; SS.912.A.7.15; SS.912.A.7.17; LAFS.1112.RH.1.2; LAFS.1112.RH.4.10; MAFS.K12.MP.1.1; MAFS.K12.MP.5.1

The United States as a World Leader

After World War II, much of Europe and East Asia was in shambles. Two major powers remained to face off in the coming decades—the Soviet Union and the United States. With the disintegration of the Soviet Union, the United States became the world's most powerful country. Much of the world still looks to the United States as a beacon of freedom, prosperity, and hope. However, some people in other regions resent the country's power and influence.

POLITICAL, MILITARY, AND ECONOMIC BENEFITS Although altruistic intentions can influence U.S. foreign policy, **national interest** is the guiding force in determining our relationships with other countries. National interest refers to a country's goals and ambitions. To further its interests, the U.S. government maintains complex diplomatic relations around the world. It also spends vast amounts of money on foreign aid for various purposes.

Some national interests are political. One political goal of U.S. foreign policy is to support the growth of democracy in new and developing countries. While fighting communism was an important priority throughout the Cold War, the focus has shifted with the development of regional conflicts. People in some other countries have seen their personal freedoms limited by their own governments. For example, during the so-called Arab Spring of 2010–2012, citizens of several middle eastern and north African countries rose up against their oppressive governments in mass demonstrations. Many Americans cheered the uprisings. In a speech at the U.S. Department of State, President Obama praised the demonstrators for their courage in demanding reforms. Extremists also crush dreams of freedom by committing violent acts against people of their own country. The U.S. government uses diplomacy to confront those forces also. One example is the promise that President Obama made to the newly elected, pro-democracy president of Nigeria. He promised to provide information-gathering expertise that will help in the fight against radical Islamists plaguing that country.

Military strength is also a major concern of U.S. policymakers. In the wake of the September 11 attacks and other dangers, halting the efforts of terrorists and preventing other threats to homeland security have become key goals of U.S. military policy. In 2015 the budget for the U.S. Department of Defense was about $575 billion—approximately 20 percent of the entire federal budget. Those dollars fund personnel, personnel benefits, weapons, other equipment, fuel, construction, and building maintenance, among various specialized programs. The United States also provides many countries with sophisticated weapons to keep military strength in balance. Much of the military's budget goes toward bases, research establishments, air fields, and other facilities in foreign countries, such as Germany, Italy, Japan, Kuwait, South Korea, and the United Kingdom. Germany alone hosts 37 U.S. Army installations. This military presence reminds neighboring powers that the United States will defend its interests and those of the host countries against aggression. Military installations in other countries may also assist the host countries in their efforts to reduce internal conflicts.

Officials who guide U.S. foreign policy also try to maintain the country's economic advantages. They often enter into agreements and treaties that stimulate global trade. In addition, the U.S. Department of Commerce has employees in more than 80 countries who work to protect American commercial interests. The International Trade Administration is an office within the Department of Commerce. It provides information to help Americans do business overseas, ensures that Americans have access to international markets, and safeguards U.S. businesses from unfair competition.

WORKING WITH INTERNATIONAL ORGANIZATIONS In the 21st century, the United States is widely involved in world affairs. Many of those interactions occur in the context of international organizations.

Since the creation of the United Nations (UN) in 1945, the United States has been a key member of that organization. As one of the victors of World War II, it is a permanent member of the UN Security Council. Despite its important role, U.S.-UN relations have often been strained. As a global organization, the UN tries to protect the interests of all nations. As a result, its efforts can sometimes run counter to American interests. The United States also owes dues money to the UN. Estimates range from several hundred million dollars to more than a billion. Opinions about the UN vary among Americans. Although many Americans support the UN, some want the United States to withdraw completely. Others want to change the organization to bring it into closer alignment with U.S. foreign policy.

The UN General Assembly In session

The United Nations continues to embrace ambitious goals. In 2000 about 150 world leaders gathered in New York City for a Millennium Summit. The topic was the role of the United Nations in the 21st century. Following the summit, policymakers wrote eight Millennium Development Goals to achieve by the year 2015. The goals aimed to solve a range of human misfortunes, including poverty, hunger, and disease.

Some countries have made dramatic progress toward fulfilling these goals. For example, in 2015 the UN reported that the world's hungry had dropped to 795 million people from more than a billion. In China alone, 170 million fewer people live in poverty than did before the summit.

United Nations Millennium Development Goals

1. to eradicate extreme poverty and hunger
2. to achieve universal primary education
3. to promote gender equality
4. to reduce child mortality
5. to improve maternal health
6. to combat HIV/AIDS, malaria, and other diseases
7. to ensure environmental sustainability
8. to develop a global partnership for development

The North Atlantic Treaty Organization (NATO) is another organization important to U.S. foreign affairs. Founded in 1949, NATO's original purpose was to unite Western Europe and the United States in a military alliance against the Soviet Union and its Eastern European allies. The Soviet Union's decline changed the organization's mission. Some former members of the Soviet bloc have even joined NATO. Recently, various hot spots have demanded NATO's attention and occasional military intervention. One was in Bosnia and Herzegovina. U.S. forces operated under NATO's command to end violence toward civilians. Attacks on civilians in nearby Kosovo also drew NATO's intervention. Although the worst violence ended in 1999, NATO deployed peacekeeping forces to the region. After the September 11 attacks on the United States, NATO members assisted in antiterrorist measures in the Middle East. In 2009 NATO sent warships to protect the shipping lanes in the western Indian Ocean. Pirates based in Somalia were hijacking ships and holding them for ransom. Two years later NATO intervened in the civil war raging in Libya.

Some U.S. officials have expressed frustration that other NATO members seem reluctant to take on as much financial and military responsibility as the United States does during NATO actions. Before he retired in 2011, Secretary of Defense Robert M. Gates rebuked some of America's NATO allies in a stinging speech.

> *"The blunt reality is that there will be dwindling appetite and patience in the U.S. Congress, and in the American body politic writ large, to expend increasingly precious funds on behalf of nations that are apparently unwilling to devote the necessary resources . . . to be serious and capable partners in their own defense."*
>
> —Robert M. Gates, from a speech before the NATO Council, June 10, 2011

As new problems arise or old hostilities calm, the United States will have to manage evolving relationships with the UN, NATO, and the member nations of those and other international organizations.

HUMANITARIAN AID The United States often steps in to provide humanitarian aid when people in other nations suffer. Humanitarian aid comes from private sources, nonprofit organizations, and governments. The United States sends tons of food, fresh water, medical supplies, temporary shelter, and other items to people in need. Along with supplies go doctors, nurses, scientists, and many other aid workers. These aid workers respond to natural disasters,

Responding to the devastating 2010 earthquake in Haiti, a U.S. military helicopter delivers needed food and other supplies.

such as floods or earthquakes, and man-made disasters, mainly refugee crises and other effects of war. Many crises are the result of natural disasters combined with human calamities.

The main U.S. government division responsible for providing humanitarian aid is the United States Agency for International Development (USAID). Created in 1961 by President John F. Kennedy, the agency's mission is to "partner to end extreme poverty and to promote resilient, democratic societies while advancing our security and prosperity." Promoting economic prosperity, improving global health, furthering education, and helping people recover from conflicts are among USAID's specific goals. One percent of the federal budget goes to USAID.

Global health care is among the agency's many targets. USAID reports that in 2013, 6.3 million of the world's children died before they turned five years old. Malnutrition, cholera, tuberculosis, and other conditions still kill millions of people every year. However, great strides have been made in some areas. For example, although malaria, a disease spread by mosquitoes, still claims thousands of victims annually, the World Health Organization reports that deaths from the illness have fallen. Preventive measures, such as the widespread use of mosquito nets treated with insecticide, have proven highly effective. USAID has supported these measures.

Another aid effort that has seen success is the President's Emerging Plan for AIDS Relief. This effort was designed to stop the spread of HIV/AIDS and to help the people already infected with the disease. Started by President George W. Bush, the program provides education on prevention and makes medication available to many patients. One 2009 study determined that the program had saved a million lives in Africa. Critics of the program, however, say it places too much emphasis on sexual abstinence. In addition, some detractors say the program does not take a realistic view of intravenous drug use as a means of spreading infection.

U.S. Foreign Assistance Planned, 2016

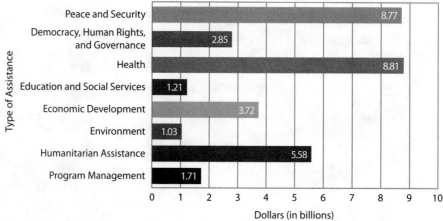

Source: USAID Foreign Assistance Dashboard

Interpret Charts
What U.S. foreign assistance priorities does the chart show for 2016?

As long as there are global problems, the United States will continue to provide humanitarian aid. Many people are particularly concerned about the possible impact of global climate change. If many of the predictions related to global climate change prove true, rising sea levels, wildly fluctuating temperatures, and more severe weather events will take an especially heavy toll on the world's most vulnerable people. Political conflicts will be worsened by dwindling supplies of food and water. Humanitarian aid organizations will be called upon to do even more to alleviate suffering.

HUMAN RIGHTS The United States also intercedes when other countries violate their citizens' human rights. Although definitions of the term "human rights" vary, most agree that everyone has certain fundamental rights, no matter who they are or where they live. Common among the definitions are the right to life; freedom from torture; freedom from slavery; the right to a fair trial; and freedom of speech, thought, conscience, religion, and movement. Some definitions add the right to education or gender equality. The Department of State's Bureau of Democracy, Human Rights, and Labor is the government agency that leads U.S. efforts to promote human rights around the world. Among the tools that U.S. policymakers use to fulfill those goals are foreign aid money, media exposure, and, when necessary, economic penalties.

The United States has an uneven history when it comes to promoting human rights abroad. Often America calls on repressive governments to end their human rights abuses. For example, during the 1980s, the U.S. government expressed disapproval of South Africa's racist apartheid government by passing travel restrictions to that country. Major U.S. universities also withdrew their investments in South Africa. The Department of State continually pressures China to account for the victims of the government's violent suppression of the 1989 demonstrations in Beijing's Tiananmen Square. Conversely, the U.S. government supports, under certain circumstances, some regimes with questionable human rights records. One example is Saudi Arabia, where the ruling royal family squelches opposition, demands religious uniformity, and severely restricts women's freedom. However, Saudi Arabia controls immense oil reserves. Moreover, it has been called a stabilizing force in the Middle East. For these reasons, among others, the country's poor human rights record does not severely affect its status as a U.S. ally.

Regional Policies

The Department of State is responsible for U.S. international relations. It has a difficult job trying to keep the peace, protect U.S. international business interests, and further global cooperation. U.S. foreign policies differ from region to region and from country to country.

WESTERN HEMISPHERE On our own continent, the United States has a close ally in Canada. Our two countries share the world's longest international border. A common language and a shared British heritage contribute

Reading Check
Analyze Causes
Why does the United States spend large sums of money on foreign aid?

to friendly relations. Each country is the other's greatest trading partner. Cross-border tourism is lively for both countries. Canada occasionally objects to U.S. actions, however. Notable examples include Canadians' negative views of the Iraq War and some of the actions taken by the United States to combat terrorism.

U.S. relationships with Mexico and some Central American countries are complicated by two main issues. The issues are the drug trade and the large number of immigrants who enter the United States illegally. Complaints that the Latin American countries don't do enough to restrict the drug trade and its violence are met with the argument that if U.S. users didn't want the drugs, the trade would end. In a similar vein is the contention that if U.S. employers would not hire undocumented workers, fewer Latin Americans would risk the trip north to reach the United States. Disagreements notwithstanding, economic connections remain strong.

In the Caribbean region, a major change in diplomatic relations between the United States and Cuba's Communist government is underway. Official relations broke in 1961, when Cuba was under the influence of the Soviet Union. Then in 2015 President Barack Obama and Cuban President Raúl Castro announced that their countries would reestablish diplomatic relations. Embassies reopened in Washington, DC, and Havana, and some travel and trade restrictions were lifted.

Farther south, U.S. connections to the countries of South America have fluctuated over the years. Many of those nations have experienced dramatic changes in their own governments. Relations with Brazil, the continent's largest country, have gone through phases. They cooled over recent allegations of U.S. surveillance programs but were soon repaired. The United States has especially warm relations with Argentina, partly because Argentina's navy assisted in the 1991 Gulf War. Chile is a close ally since its people returned the country to democracy after a long dictatorship. In contrast, relations with Venezuela have been rocky for many years. They worsened when the United States protested the Venezuelan government's violent treatment of peaceful protesters.

EUROPE AND RUSSIA Many ties bind the United States and the countries of Europe. A majority of Americans trace at least part of their heritage to a European country. In general, Europeans enjoy individual liberties and have a high standard of living. Trade between the United States and the region is brisk, as is tourism. But with the formation of the European Union (EU), the European countries gained more clout in dealing with the United States. Disagreements are not uncommon. For example, the EU restricts the importation of genetically modified foods, which angers U.S. agricultural businesses. Another example relates to the death penalty. All EU members have abolished the practice, while the United States has not. As a result, EU member countries will not extradite a criminal suspect to the United States unless a guarantee is made that the death penalty will not be imposed upon conviction.

In eastern Europe and Asia is Russia, where the diplomatic situation is more critical. Following the disintegration of the Soviet Union in 1991, relations with Russia eased. Many of the Russian people hoped, along with

Americans, that their country would become truly democratic. Those hopes dimmed with the rise to power of **Vladimir Putin**, a former agent of the KGB, the Soviet Union's spy agency. Since 1999 Putin has held one of the country's two top offices. In 2012 he was elected to his third term as president. Putin has imprisoned potential rivals, suppressed dissent, and stifled democratic reforms. As a result, Russia's relations with the United States chilled.

An especially volatile crisis began in early 2014. The people of Ukraine, formerly part of the Soviet Union, demanded governmental reforms and a closer connection to the European Union. Within weeks, Putin sent Russian troops into Ukraine's Crimean Peninsula, where ethnic Russians were in the majority. Crimea voted to join with Russia, and Russia annexed the region. Western leaders, including President Obama, called the referendum illegal and corrupted by Russian military pressure. Unrest continued to spread in eastern Ukraine. Russian troops moved freely among the Russian-speaking populace. In response to Russia's intervention, the United States, the European Union, and several other countries approved sanctions against Russia. An example of the sanctions is a ban against doing business with Russian banks, energy companies, and defense industries. Relations with Russia remain very tense.

EAST ASIA The giant power in East Asia is, of course, the People's Republic of China. Its connection to the United States has evolved. Although relations with China froze in 1949, President Nixon's trip to China in 1972 helped relations begin to thaw. As China's economy becomes more market oriented, the United States has engaged with China more actively. The country's Communist government continues to violate basic human rights, however, so U.S. policy toward China remains cautious.

At times China flexes its muscle, and the rest of the world has to take notice. For example, in 2009 China began to claim control over the Spratly Islands, a chain of tiny islands in the South China Sea. However, several other countries in the region claim control of the islands. The region is strategically sensitive, as some $5 trillion in ship-borne trade crosses the sea each year. In addition, each of the claimants would like the rights to fishing off the islands' shores. China has built artificial islands in the area, an action that many countries protest. In 2015 satellite imagery showed that China was building an airfield on a reef within the Spratly group. The Chinese navy warned the U.S. military to stay away. The region will, no doubt, draw global attention for some time to come.

China has grown in economic strength. Today, the East Asian giant is a commercial powerhouse. In 2010 China became the world's largest exporter. Since then, China surpassed the United States when its economy ranked as the largest in the world. China also holds more of the U.S. public debt, some $1.26 trillion, than any other entity. The United States also has a huge trade deficit with China. That is, we buy much more from the Chinese than they buy from us. However, what these facts do not reveal is that the average American is much richer than the average Chinese person. Low wages, harsh working conditions, and limited personal freedoms are still the norm for millions of Chinese citizens.

China is not the only East Asian country with which the United States has complex relations. U.S. forces are still stationed in South Korea. They are there mainly to protect our democratic ally from its militarily strong Communist neighbor, North Korea. Most South Koreans are strongly pro-America. In general, the Japanese people also think highly of the United States, and the two countries have strong diplomatic and economic ties. Some Japanese, however, resent the presence of U.S. military forces stationed within Japan's borders.

In Southeast Asia, diplomatic relations between the United States and Communist Vietnam have been normalized. The country is a popular tourist destination. Indonesia, with the world's fourth-largest population, is on good terms with the United States, with which it has strong economic and strategic ties. Causing concern, though, is a violent Islamist terrorist group, Jemaah Islamiyah. This group originated in Indonesia but has cells in other Asian countries.

SOUTH ASIA The largest countries of South Asia are India and Pakistan. India is the world's most populous democracy. Many American businesses rely on its high-tech industries. As a growing economic force, India also balances the growing power of China. Relations between India and the United States, as a result, are generally quite warm.

Relations with Pakistan, however, are worse. After many years of good relations, they soured when the United States accused Pakistan of protecting Taliban fighters who crossed the border from Afghanistan. The CIA had

Document-Based Investigation Historical Source

An East Asian Threat
Kim Jong Un rules North Korea as a militaristic dictatorship. The people there have few freedoms, and many struggle to survive. Yet North Korea—also known as the DPRK, or Democratic People's Republic of Korea—has a huge and powerful military program, as described by the CIA.

"After decades of economic mismanagement and resource misallocation [misuse], the DPRK since the mid-1990s has relied heavily on international aid to feed its population. The DPRK began to ease restrictions to allow semi-private markets, starting in 2002, but then sought to roll back the scale of economic reforms in 2005 and 2009. North Korea's history of regional military provocations; proliferation of military-related items; long-range missile development; WMD programs including tests of nuclear devices in 2006, 2009, and 2013; and massive conventional armed forces are of major concern to the international community. The regime in 2013 announced a new policy calling for the simultaneous development of the North's nuclear weapons program and its economy."

—Central Intelligence Agency, from *The World Factbook, 2015*

Analyze Historical Sources
What special problems does North Korea present for U.S. diplomacy?

suspected that Pakistani officials knew Osama bin Laden was hiding in their country when he was killed in 2011. Even with these issues, the United States sends much economic and military aid to Pakistan.

MIDDLE EAST For years, U.S. policy in the Middle East has been troubled by wars, terrorism, and mutual lack of trust. The situation is complicated by U.S. dependence on foreign oil, much of it imported from the region. Several Middle Eastern countries present particularly dangerous situations, both for the people who live there and for people in other countries.

Since the start of the Syrian refugee crisis, the United States has given $4.5 billion in humanitarian assistance. Shown here are hundreds of Syrian refugees leaving Budapest, Hungary.

In Syria, a civil war began in 2011 between the ruling party loyal to President Bashar al-Assad and those who wanted to end his brutal rule. Since then, the country has fallen into constant warfare, with various factions getting encouragement from outside interests. It has been a deadly conflict. By April 2015 an estimate put the death toll at 310,000 people. Millions of Syrians have been displaced, either fleeing to nearby countries or becoming refugees within their own country.

From this chaos rose a new and frightening terrorist enemy, the Islamic State of Iraq and Syria, often abbreviated as **ISIS**. This radical group's goal is to establish a strict new Islamic state ruled by religious authorities. ISIS has taken over large tracts of territory in both Iraq and Syria. ISIS uses publicized beheadings, mass executions, kidnappings, rape, and enslavement to intimidate local people. In its efforts to destroy anything they consider a threat to their religious beliefs, ISIS militants have also demolished ancient monuments built by pre-Islamic or non-Islamic cultures. Many Muslims have criticized ISIS severely, as have Western governments. Yet ISIS has been remarkably successful in recruiting fighters—some 20,000 from other countries by 2015. Even some women have been lured to its ranks by its very active Internet and social media presence. Observers are worried that ISIS will take more territory and spread its violent message even farther, inspiring others to take up its terrorist cause.

Vocabulary
sectarian based on religious differences

Iraq, too, remains in turmoil after the war that began there in 2003 and the subsequent withdrawal of U.S. troops. Sectarian violence has disrupted the economy and driven countless civilians from their homes. ISIS has taken over land in northern Iraq, spreading more fear and death. The U.S. Department of State supports the Iraqi government's efforts to fight ISIS and stabilize the country, but distrust of the West remains widespread.

The United States does not maintain formal diplomatic relations with Iran. Connections with that country broke when the U.S.-supported shah was overthrown in 1979 and an Islamic theocracy took over. The United States imposed an embargo on Iranian trade in 1995. Most Americans view Iran unfavorably. In contrast, Iranians have a generally positive view of the American people, although not of the U.S. government. Iranian sentiments may become more positive, however, if the Joint Comprehensive Plan of Action takes effect and is successful. The 2015 agreement among Iran, the United States, and other major Western powers requires Iran to reduce its nuclear program dramatically in exchange for the easing of punitive sanctions.

The United States does have some firm allies in the Middle East. Although Israel and the United States occasionally disagree over the Israeli-Palestinian conflict, the two countries remain connected economically, diplomatically, and militarily. In fact, U.S. military aid to Israel totaled $3.9 billion in 2014. Israelis in general have a positive view of the United States. Turkey, the only NATO member in the Middle East, is another major ally, though Turkey protested the U.S. invasion of Iraq in 2003. The influence of Islamist factions in the government could also complicate U.S. diplomatic relations with Turkey.

AFRICA In Africa a cultural divide separates the northern from the sub-Saharan countries. Islamic culture dominates the countries of North Africa, including the large, important nations of Libya and Egypt. Both countries experienced upheavals in recent years. Demonstrations by hundreds of thousands of Egyptians brought down the longtime president. Since then, Islamists, the military, and secularists have jockeyed for power. Relations between Egypt and the United States remain peaceful but guarded. Egyptian distrust of the United States is widespread. A 2014 poll showed that 85 percent of Egyptians viewed the United States unfavorably. Libya presents a very different situation. In 2011 the United States helped rebels oust leader Muammar Gaddafi, who had sponsored terrorist acts. A majority of Libyans approved of U.S. assistance. Relations between Libya and the United States remain friendly and cooperative.

Islam also influences some areas of West Africa, where a new threat has developed. A terrorist group known as **Boko Haram** is centered in Nigeria

Angered by Boko Haram's kidnapping of 276 schoolgirls in 2014, Nigerians marched to demand the girls' return.

but is also active in bordering countries. The name is usually translated as "Western education is forbidden." Boko Haram is allied with ISIS. Like ISIS, it seeks to establish an Islamic state under strict religious law. Boko Haram uses kidnapping as a major tactic. In April 2014 Boko Haram fighters kidnapped 276 primarily Christian schoolgirls. The Boko Haram leader admitted to kidnapping the girls and selling them into sexual slavery. He claimed that doing so was in line with his religion and that the girls should have been married and at home, not in school. Reports of the girls' fate included rape and murder. The United States sent assistance to search for the girls.

Relations between the United States and other countries in sub-Saharan Africa are generally good. U.S. connections with South Africa have been shaky at times. For example, the U.S. government refused to support South Africa's racist apartheid policy, but relations have improved dramatically. Now the countries have close economic and diplomatic ties. Kenya is another good friend in the sub-Saharan region. U.S. aid to Kenya includes help with fighting disease, improving human rights, and opposing terrorism. A 2012 poll reported that 69 percent of Kenyans view U.S. influence as a good thing.

Reading Check
Compare and Contrast What are some countries or regions where interactions have created a positive image of the American people? a negative image?

Lesson 2 Assessment

1. **Organize Information** Create a table to describe a major issue that negatively affects U.S. foreign policy toward the listed country or region.

Mexico	
Europe	
Russia	
China	
Pakistan	
Iraq	
Iran	

2. **Key Terms and People** For each key term or person in the lesson, write a sentence explaining its significance.

3. **Evaluate** What are some factors that contribute to U.S. foreign policy decisions?

   Think About:
   - strategic locations
   - economic competition
   - military concerns
   - dependence on foreign oil

4. **Form Opinions** Should the United States be stricter about other countries' human rights abuses? Why or why not?

5. **Make Inferences** What do you think are the most effective methods for developing peaceful relations, alliances, and global agreements with other nations?

★
Poverty and Social Concerns

The Big Idea

Although the United States is often called the richest country in the world, poverty grips millions of Americans, and the middle class is shrinking.

Why It Matters Now

A thriving middle class is essential to continuing the American way of life.

Key Terms and People

minimum wage

income gap

Citizens United v. *Federal Election Commission*

political action committee (PAC)

One American's Story

In 2014 the U.S. Department of Agriculture published interviews with some of the people who receive public assistance through the Supplemental Nutrition Assistance Program (SNAP), sometimes called food stamps. Among the interview topics were the recipients' circumstances and how they coped with their situations. The man quoted below explained how important Social Security payments were for his elderly mother and aunt. He also talked about how essential the network of friends and family was to his own survival. Many low-income Americans, however, have no such network and must depend on the government to fill their basic needs.

"I went to my aunt. I asked her for help, cause like my mom, she gets her Social Security . . . so—she helps when she can. She also knows—like she'll try to find people in the neighborhood to give me odd jobs to try to help me earn it myself. . . . I'll just mow their lawns, wash their cars. If . . . they'll say, 'We need some help to clean the basement,' I'll do that. It doesn't matter. I'm just trying to do something."

A man looking for work reads job postings.

—Male respondent, 30 years old, quoted in *Examining the Growth of the Zero-Income SNAP Caseload,* Vol. II

This young man is one of the many "working poor" who are desperate for any kind of job. If they do find work, the wages are often not enough for self-sufficiency.

SS.912.A.1.3; SS.912.A.1.4; SS.912.A.7.12; MAFS.K12.MP.1.1; MAFS.K12.MP.5.1

Poverty in America

Many societies have strict rules, perhaps unwritten or unacknowledged, about social class. In those societies, one's family ties, religion, and occupation can determine a person's social status. The United States does not have a hierarchy of that sort. A person of remarkable ability can still rise from nothing to achieve wealth and fame. American social class is, instead, defined primarily by one's wealth or lack thereof. Our country's riches are the wonder and envy of millions of the world's people, but beneath the glitter lies a chronic problem—poverty.

For 2015 the poverty threshold for a family of four was an annual income of $24,250. Poverty has hit children particularly hard. Nearly half of the Americans needing food stamps are children. More than half of U.S. school kids qualify for a free or reduced-price lunch. One of five children in the United States lives in a family with income below the official poverty level.

SOME CAUSES OF POVERTY Experts agree that there are many causes of poverty. Illness, natural disasters, and economic downturns can cause people to struggle. Lack of skills keeps many welfare recipients from finding or keeping jobs. Many observers insist that these people need not just skills training, but also training in work habits.

Another factor that keeps people in poverty is limited access to child care. Parents may eke out a living combining paid work with some outside support, such as food stamps. But a parent that leaves the welfare system and takes a full-time minimum-wage job would see his or her income decline by having to pay for quality child care.

For millions of Americans, the U.S. public education system has failed to provide the tools necessary for climbing out of poverty. Anne Lewis, an education writer, points out that "three-fourths of all welfare/food stamp recipients perform at the lowest levels of literacy." In turn, she notes, low levels of literacy generally lead to low employment rates and lower wages.

Another factor contributing to poverty has been discrimination against racial minorities. Statistics highlight how much more prevalent poverty is among minorities. In 2010 the poverty rate among non-Hispanic whites was 9.9 percent. Among Hispanics and African Americans it was 26.6 percent and 27.4 percent, respectively.

EMPLOYMENT, UNEMPLOYMENT, AND HOMELESSNESS It may be tempting to think that if only poor people could get jobs, then poverty would end. The truth, though, is that many adults who live below the poverty line do work. In fact, 2012 census data show that 23 percent of people in poverty spend 27 weeks or more in a year either working or looking for work. Known as the working poor, these Americans hold low-wage jobs with few benefits and almost never any health insurance.

Some analysts say that in order for low-income workers to advance, the **minimum wage** should be raised. The minimum wage is the lowest wage that employers can legally pay their workers. In 2009 the federal government set a minimum wage of $7.25 per hour. In 2014 Congress debated a bill raising

In many American cities, homeless men and women stand on street corners offering work in exchange for a meal. Others simply ask for a handout.

the federal minimum wage to $10.10 over two years, but the bill did not pass. Most states also have minimum wage laws. Several states have approved increases above the federal minimum that will go into effect in coming years. Individual cities, too, have approved higher minimums. Los Angeles residents, for example, voted to raise the minimum wage to $15 an hour by 2020.

Polls indicate that a majority of Americans favor raising the minimum wage. Many economists agree, saying that purchasing power has not kept pace with inflation. Proponents—more Democrats than Republicans—argue that an increase would boost buying power. This, in turn, would have a ripple effect across the economy, creating more jobs. Opponents claim that raising the minimum wage would kill jobs, hurt small businesses, and benefit only teenagers. However, most states actually saw job growth after recently raising their wage minimums. In addition, two-thirds of minimum-wage workers are employed by large corporations—many in the leisure and hospitality industries. About half of the low-wage earners are over 25 years old.

Perhaps the most visible sign of poverty in America is the many poor people who are homeless. During the 1980s, cuts in welfare and food stamp benefits brought the problem of homelessness to national attention. In addition, a move to close large mental health facilities resulted in many people with mental illness having nowhere to live but the streets. According to the National Alliance to End Homelessness (NAEH), about 750,000 Americans are without shelter on any given night. To illustrate the problem, consider Jim, a 55-year-old painter by trade, who retreats each night to a Boston homeless shelter. He spends his days doing any work he can find, but it's never enough to provide him with a roof over his head. Too many of the jobs available, he says, "pay only the minimum wage or a bit higher, and they cannot cover the rent and other bills." Jim never imagined he would find himself homeless. "I never thought it could happen to me," he says. In addition to homeless adults like Jim, more than 250,000 children are homeless.

Many experts say that the lack of housing is simply a symptom of larger problems. These include unemployment, low-wage jobs, and high housing costs. In many cases, personal problems such as substance abuse or mental illness contribute to chronic homelessness.

THE WIDENING INCOME GAP A troubling aspect of 21st-century social issues is the growing **income gap** between America's rich and poor. That is, the rich are getting richer, the poor are getting poorer, and the middle class is shrinking as a percentage of the population. Of all the democracies in the developed world, U.S. income inequality, or income gap, is surpassed only by Chile's. The income gap has been growing in the last several decades. To state the difference in dollar amounts, if income distribution today were the same as it was in the late 1970s, the average family would be making an additional $11,000 or so more per year.

Economists and politicians have listed various causes of the widening income gap.

- Tax policies have changed in recent decades to favor the rich.
- Difficulty affording health care, child care, and higher education keeps people of lower incomes from getting better jobs.

Income Growth of American Households, 1979–2011

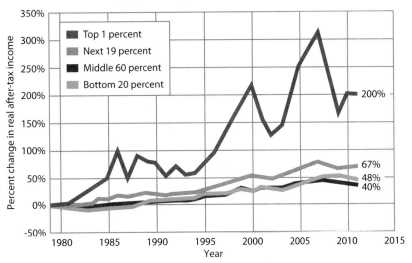

American Households (by percentage of wealth)

Sources: Congressional Budget Office; Center on Budget and Policy Priorities

Interpret Graphs

1. Which group's income has increased by 200 percent since 1979?

2. What percentage of American households experienced only a 40 percent increase?

- The decline of labor unions has led to lower incomes and less political influence for blue-collar workers.
- The global economy puts low-wage American workers in competition with workers in other countries.
- High technology has put many employees in traditional manufacturing fields out of work but rewards tech innovators with extremely high pay.
- Corporate CEOs receive huge salaries that are hundreds of times larger than their lowest-paid employees' salaries. Competition among businesses keeps those salaries high.

Listing the possible causes of income inequality, however, is easier than solving the problem. Why is income inequality an issue? Slower economic growth, general economic instability, high levels of personal debt, and fewer opportunities to advance one's own economic condition all result from income inequality. This also has implications for U.S. democracy. Income inequality can lead to distrust in government in general and, consequently, less interest in participating in government. It is not just the poor and middle class that see the income gap as a problem. A recent study showed that even 47 percent of American millionaires saw income inequality as a major concern. Wealthy individuals, however, spend a smaller percentage of their incomes than those who make less money. As a result, less money flows through the system. Financial manager William H. Gross pointed out that both the rich and the poor will suffer if the situation continues. He commented, "If Main Street is unemployed and undercompensated [underpaid], capital can only travel so far down Prosperity Road."

Reading Check
Summarize Why is the widening income gap a problem?

Money and Influence

As many Americans struggle financially, their situation contrasts with the vast sums of money spent on political campaigns. During the presidential election of 2012, each candidate—Barack Obama and Mitt Romney—raised and spent a billion dollars. Although small, individual donations counted for part of that sum, multi-million dollar contributions played a major role. Statewide campaigns also pull in millions of dollars. Even candidates in local races may seek huge donations from supporters. Observers may wonder what donors hope to receive from winning candidates in return for their money. Today, special interests representing viewpoints all along the political spectrum continue to seek and gain influence.

Citizens United **v.** *Federal Election Commission*, a 2010 Supreme Court case, affected campaign spending by organizations. Citizens United is a conservative nonprofit organization. During the 2008 presidential campaign season, the organization wanted to show a film critical of Hillary Clinton on national TV. A previous court ruling declared that the Federal Election Commission (FEC) had the right to prohibit the broadcasting of political films made or sold by corporations. After reviewing that case, the Supreme Court ruled in favor of Citizens United. The court said that the First Amendment could not restrict political expenditures by nonprofit corporations. For-profit corporations, labor unions, and other associations have also been freed from the previous restrictions by the decision. The court's ruling meant that organizations could spend money to advocate for candidates of their choice through methods such as TV ads. Corporations were still prohibited from donating directly to candidates. In his dissent to the majority opinion, Justice Stevens took a grim view of how the *Citizens United* ruling could affect future elections.

> *"A democracy cannot function effectively when its constituent members believe laws are being bought and sold."*
>
> —John Paul Stevens, from his opinion in
> *Citizens United* v. *Federal Election Commission*, 2010

The *Citizens United* ruling influenced another development related to the role of money in politics—the growth of the **political action committee (PAC)**. A PAC is an organization that merges campaign contributions from members. It uses the merged funds to campaign for or against candidates or legislation. Businesses, labor unions, or groups that stand for a certain issue can all sponsor PACs. The amount of money that a PAC can collect from donors and contribute directly to federal campaigns is limited by law. However, PACs can spend as much money as they want if they campaign on their own. For example, a PAC organized to fight a proposed environmental regulation can fund a TV ad about the damage such a rule could do to the economy. However, the PAC cannot contribute huge sums to the senatorial candidate fighting the regulation.

In a 2010 ruling, the FEC allowed the expansion of PACs. As a result, so-called Super PACs can collect unlimited amounts of money from

Another deteriorating bridge...

haves

have nots

ED FISCHER

The phrase "the haves and the have nots" is often used to informally describe the gap between the rich and the poor.

corporations, unions, and individuals. They can also spend unlimited amounts on ads for or against candidates. Super PACs are not allowed to coordinate directly with candidates' campaign staffs, however. Nor can Super PACs contribute directly to candidates. Still, the power of Super PACs to influence public opinion can be immense. Groups on both ends of the political spectrum have formed Super PACs. Many conservative Super PACs fund probusiness causes. Liberal Super PACs support prochoice, conservation, arts, and labor activists.

The Role of Government

To varying degrees, the U.S. government has always taken on some responsibility for the welfare of its people. Subsistence programs—those that provide just the necessities of life—are often controversial.

ARGUMENTS FOR AND AGAINST During the Great Depression, President Franklin D. Roosevelt, a Democrat, pushed through New Deal programs to create jobs for the unemployed. Many Republicans argued that the costly programs would increase the size of government and the country's debt. They feared a larger central government would rob people of their freedoms. Years later, President Lyndon Johnson proposed Great Society programs to eliminate poverty and racism. Republican objections echoed some of the same arguments used earlier against Roosevelt's New Deal.

With each new administration, leaders across the political spectrum propose and enact different approaches to public services to alleviate poverty, fund health care, and offer financial support for retirees. Some leaders advocate for government to play an expanded role in people's lives. They create government programs that redistribute income to provide benefits.

Reading Check
Analyze Causes
How did the *Citizens United* decision affect political campaigns?

Others believe that government should take a more limited approach, to keep people from becoming dependent on the government. This stance emphasizes allowing state and local programs to solve problems, often with the support of nongovernmental agencies.

GOVERNMENT PROGRAMS Ever since the New Deal, the federal government's main arm for providing basic needs to citizens has been the Social Security Administration. Funds for the agency come from a tax paid by almost all working Americans. The agency supports several programs. The main one is Social Security, which pays retirees monthly. Medicare funds health care for Americans with disabilities and those over the age of 65. Medicaid helps low-income Americans afford quality health care. There is also a health insurance program for children and temporary assistance to families in need. Payments to retirees form the largest Social Security Administration expenditure. Because retired people are now living longer, the ratio of contributions to Social Security to expenditures is shrinking. At some point, the system must be reformed to ensure that in coming years retirees will still receive benefits.

Medicare is also in danger of running out of funds, due to some of the same issues that threaten Social Security. By some estimates, Medicare's hospital insurance fund could run out of money before 2030. While rising numbers of elderly drive up the cost of Medicare, the revenues targeted to pay for it are not keeping pace. As the population ages, fewer people will work and pay the taxes that fund Medicare. In addition, elderly people tend to have higher medical costs. What is to be done? Among the proposals are placing more restrictions on Medicare benefits, raising the age of eligibility, or increasing the share to be paid by the elderly.

U. S. Government and Poverty

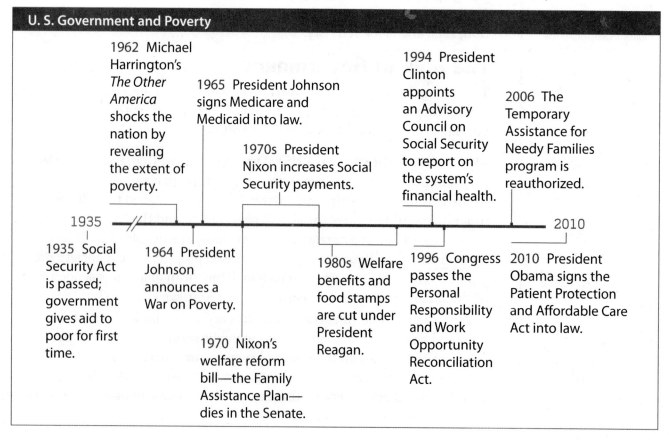

1962 Michael Harrington's *The Other America* shocks the nation by revealing the extent of poverty.

1965 President Johnson signs Medicare and Medicaid into law.

1970s President Nixon increases Social Security payments.

1994 President Clinton appoints an Advisory Council on Social Security to report on the system's financial health.

2006 The Temporary Assistance for Needy Families program is reauthorized.

1935 Social Security Act is passed; government gives aid to poor for first time.

1964 President Johnson announces a War on Poverty.

1970 Nixon's welfare reform bill—the Family Assistance Plan—dies in the Senate.

1980s Welfare benefits and food stamps are cut under President Reagan.

1996 Congress passes the Personal Responsibility and Work Opportunity Reconciliation Act.

2010 President Obama signs the Patient Protection and Affordable Care Act into law.

Citizens in favor of protecting Social Security rally on the grounds of the U.S. Capitol.

Reading Check
Analyze Problems
What basic challenge regarding Social Security and Medicare must be solved?

The Patient Protection and Affordable Care Act is the most recent major federal effort to improve Americans' health care. Signed into law by President Obama in 2010, the act's primary goal was to increase the accessibility and affordability of health insurance. By March 2015 the number of uninsured Americans had dropped by 11.4 million people.

As the federal government struggles to provide a safety net for its most vulnerable citizens, cities and states sometimes take the lead in solving at least some symptoms of poverty. Several cities are attacking homelessness in particular, some with remarkable success. One example is New Orleans, which settled more than 200 homeless veterans in permanent homes a year ahead of its 2015 goal. The idea of "Housing First" in Utah is about finding apartments where the previously homeless can live permanently, no strings attached. This has helped the state decrease it homeless population by 91 percent. Several other governments are taking the same approach.

Lesson 3 Assessment

1. **Organize Information** Create an idea web to identify the causes of the growing income gap in the United States. Add more ovals as needed.

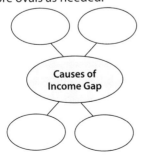

2. **Key Terms and People** For each key term in the lesson, write a sentence explaining its significance.

3. **Evaluate** Why is simply getting and holding a job not a sure way to end poverty for an individual?

   Think About:
   - access to child care
   - the minimum wage
   - skills needed for advancement

4. **Predict** What role do you think PACs and Super PACs will play in future elections? Explain.

5. **Form Opinions** What role do you think the federal government should have in solving social issues such as poverty? Support your opinion.

6. **Form Generalizations** Do you think the U.S. government has been effective in addressing Americans' welfare and limiting poverty? Why or why not?

Conservation and the Environment

The Big Idea

Although rich in natural resources, the American environment is being stressed by various factors.

Why It Matters Now

If we fail to protect our environment for the enjoyment, health, security, and prosperity of later generations, the country's future is bleak.

Key Terms and People

global climate change

fracking

biodiversity

One American's Story

Brenda Dardar Robichaux was principal chief of the 17,000-member United Houma Nation. For generations, this Native American group has made their living on the coastal lands of southeastern Louisiana. After watching the oil and seafood industries encroach on their land and water, Robichaux was further dismayed when she saw the damage done by the April 2010 explosion of a BP oil well in the Gulf of Mexico. The disaster took several lives and leaked millions of gallons of oil into the gulf waters and onto the shore.

"We have seen small canals turn into large bayous; we have watched hundreds of acres of wetlands wash away; we have seen freshwater bayous turn into saltwater. . . .When the oil spill happened, I was hopeful that all the attention it was bringing might finally wake people up. I was optimistic. I was thinking if we're ever going to get vision for coastal restoration off the ground, now is the time. But I don't see that happening. . . . Louisiana is paying a grave price for what the rest of the country is enjoying. . . ."

Oil from the 2010 disaster fouled this Gulf of Mexico beach.

—Brenda Dardar Robichaux, quoted in *Deep Water: The Gulf Oil Disaster and the Future of Offshore Drilling*

In 1989 the tanker *Exxon Valdez* spilled millions of gallons of crude oil into Alaska's Prince William Sound. Since then, it has become apparent that oil spills are just one of many threats to our environment.

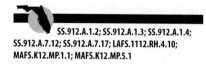

SS.912.A.1.2; SS.912.A.1.3; SS.912.A.1.4; SS.912.A.7.12; SS.912.A.7.17; LAFS.1112.RH.4.10; MAFS.K12.MP.1.1; MAFS.K12.MP.5.1

The American Environment

Perception is a significant factor in evaluating our nation's environmental condition and future. We look at the world through the lens of our own history, hopes, fears, needs, and wants. For example, someone from an industrial city might see the Alaskan wilderness as a haven that should remain untouched forever. A lumber company executive, in contrast, might look out over the same landscape and see profits, jobs, and progress. Hunters, oil industry workers, biologists, and real estate developers all might perceive the Alaskan backcountry differently. Meanwhile, the Yupik, Aleut, Tlingit, Haida, and other Native Americans whose ancestors came to the area thousands of years ago may see changes in the environment in yet another way. Balancing all these viewpoints is essential to our country's future.

Business is deeply tied to resource development. As the world's population grows, so do the demands for housing materials, food, and other commodities. Increased population growth causes strain on the environment as people and businesses compete for and deplete resources. As businesses use resources to meet demands, ecosystems are altered. Increased demand for natural resources continues to drive the debate between environmentalists and industrialists. The discussion is about how to use resources effectively while also safeguarding our air, land, water, forests, and wildlife.

THE STATE OF OUR ENVIRONMENT The United States is blessed with a large array of natural resources and beautiful vistas. Numerous creeks, rivers, and lakes shimmer across the landscape. In much of the country, one can take deep breaths of clean air. Tourists from densely populated countries marvel at our wide-open spaces and vast forests.

Valuable though they are, our natural resources are not distributed evenly. Farmers in one county may grow their crops in rich, deep soil. A farmer a few miles away struggles with thin, rocky dirt. Rivers in one part of the country may flood after heavy rainfall as rivers in other areas go dry. People do not always settle where resources match their needs, and some cities struggle

Hikers enjoying Arches National Park in eastern Utah

to keep water flowing from the taps. Conflicts can arise because of unequal resource distribution. For example, during periods of drought, rice farmers in southeast Texas clash with cities upstream over the amount of Colorado River water released by the river authority.

Our environment is fragile and under threat. As the population expands, our water supply shrinks. Making the water situation worse are regional droughts that have killed crops, livestock, and millions of trees. The air quality of some cities, such as Los Angeles, can be so poor that it damages hearts and lungs. Industrial pollutants can seep into the water and the land. One such event happened in January 2014. Some 10,000 gallons of a harmful chemical used in coal mining spilled into the Elk River, polluting the water supply of Charleston, West Virginia.

Other threats to the environment and its inhabitants include illegal logging on protected lands, which hurts our forests. A coal-mining technique known as mountain-top removal slices tons of rock and soil off the tops of mountains. The resultant debris damages surrounding environments. Many native animal species suffer from habitat loss, pollutants, and over-hunting. Plant life faces problems, too. Invasive species choke out native plants. People who live in the American South, for instance, know that kudzu can overwhelm forests. Invasive animal species are also causing havoc. One such species is the Burmese python. Thousands of these snakes have devastated the native mammal and bird populations of the Everglades.

LAW AND THE ENVIRONMENT The federal government has responded to environmental threats. Lawmakers have enacted legislation and created federal agencies connected to conservation and resource management. Business interests often argue that these agencies overstep their authority and unfairly limit access to the resources needed to support the growing population. Individuals, too, sometimes protest that their property rights are violated when legislation affects their land. Property owners may also protest when the federal government legally attempts to take over land. In the late 1800s the Supreme Court ruled that the federal government can take land for purposes that serve the public good. That process is called eminent domain. However, the Fifth Amendment to the U.S. Constitution requires that the owner receive appropriate compensation. Two examples of places where eminent domain has been used for environmental conservation are Florida's Everglades National Park and New Mexico's Valles Caldera National Preserve.

The U.S. government took steps in the 1800s toward conservation of our natural environment. The issue again became a focus of legislation in the 1960s and 1970s. President Lyndon Johnson signed one of the first major modern environmental laws, the Clean Air Act of 1963. This law established a program to control air pollution. The act has been amended many times since then to expand its scope. In 1970 President Richard Nixon created the Environmental Protection Agency (EPA) to address environmental issues surrounding pollution. The agency was charged with strengthening and enforcing laws that govern water and air quality. It also monitors the creation and emissions of toxic substances. In 1972 Congress passed the Clean Water Act, the main federal law addressing water pollution.

In addition to protecting the air and water, Congress has passed laws to protect plants and animals. In 1966 Congress passed the Endangered Species Preservation Act. Its purpose was to list threatened species as endangered and to protect their habitats to prevent their extinction. In 1973 Congress passed the Endangered Species Act. This act expanded protections for threatened and endangered wildlife. These acts have been instrumental in saving species once on the brink of extinction, including bald eagles, wolves, and the California condor. Congress has continued to amend this act as specific needs for conservation have grown and changed.

Many states have enacted their own environmental reforms. California, for instance, has some of the nation's strictest air-pollution control laws. They have helped to provide the Golden State with much cleaner air. Individual cities, too, pass ordinances to protect the environment. For example, dozens of cities have banned single-use plastic bags to control litter and reduce landfill waste. Nonprofit groups such as the Nature Conservancy and local land trusts have also been instrumental in improving the environment. These groups and others have raised money to purchase forest and watershed lands and keep them pristine. In Texas, for example, when the original owner of Fossil Rim Wildlife Ranch, a sanctuary for endangered species, faced financial ruin, the animals' fates were in question. Other conservationists stepped in to save the sanctuary. Now the Fossil Rim Wildlife Center shelters about 50 animal species.

Opinions about the reach of environmental laws can become heated. An Oregon logger provides an example. Bill Haire hung an ornament on the mirror of his truck—a tiny owl with an arrow through its head. Haire was angry about the federal government's decision to declare millions of acres of forest off limits to loggers in order to protect the spotted owl. "If it comes down to my family or that bird," said Haire, "that bird's going to suffer." The battle between loggers and environmentalists over the fate of the spotted owl is just one example of the nation's ongoing struggle to balance conservation with industrial progress.

Reading Check
Analyze Causes
Why might laws and rules about environmental issues be a source of conflict?

Populations of wolves and California condors have increased after strenuous efforts by conservationists to save these species from extinction.

History of Conservation in the United States

1903	President Theodore Roosevelt establishes the first federal wildlife refuge.
1933	President Franklin Roosevelt creates the Civilian Conservation Corps.
1962	Rachel Carson publishes *Silent Spring*.
1968	President Johnson signs the National Wild and Scenic River Act.
1970	President Nixon establishes the Environmental Protection Agency. Congress passes a new Clean Air Act.
1972	Congress overrides President Nixon's veto of the Clean Water Act.
1973	Congress passes the Endangered Species Act.
1976	Congress passes the Resource Conservation and Recovery Act.
1990	Congress amends the Clean Air Act to address new environmental problems, including acid rain and ozone depletion.
2005	The Kyoto Protocol, which commits countries to reduce greenhouse gas emissions, takes effect.
2010	The BP oil spill in the Gulf of Mexico sparks protests.
2014	A chemical spill pollutes the Elk River in West Virginia. Removal of dams on the Elwha River in Washington is completed.
2015	Pope Francis calls for global action to fight climate change.

Interpret Tables
Do you think real progress is being made in protecting the environment? Why or why not?

Challenges for Today and Tomorrow

As the U.S. population and economy continue to grow in the 21st century, so do environmental challenges. Increased needs for energy and productive land have required that Americans find ways to balance the desire for growth with the need for conservation.

A GLOBAL CONCERN The use of fossil fuels—oil, natural gas, and coal—is a basic issue. Fossil fuels drive our vehicles, factories, and offices. They cool and heat our buildings and create the electricity that operates appliances and electronic devices in our homes. Industries that depend on fossil fuels employ many thousands of Americans. As a result, the use of fossil fuels has become a central feature of 21st-century American society. Unfortunately, fossil fuels also cause problems.

Most scientists agree that the carbon dioxide, methane, and nitrous oxide released by burning fossil fuels are building up in the atmosphere. Without these gases, heat would escape into space, leaving Earth very cold. The gasses occur naturally in the atmosphere, but the burning of fossil fuels and other human activities add to their level. The gasses build up, trapping more and more heat, and the planet's average temperature increases. This so-called greenhouse effect has led to global warming and **global climate change**. The climate change is characterized by high temperatures and extreme weather

U.S. Greenhouse Gas Emissions by Source, 2013

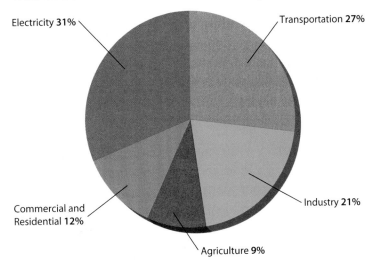

Electricity **31%**

Transportation **27%**

Industry **21%**

Agriculture **9%**

Commercial and Residential **12%**

Source: EPA, U.S. Greenhouse Inventory Report: 1990–2013

Interpret Graphs
What two sources accounted for almost 60 percent of U.S. greenhouse gas emissions in 2013?

events, such as droughts and floods. By reducing these greenhouse gasses, the negative effects of climate change may be offset or reduced. Differing opinions about climate change, including whether or not humans are causing it, have made it difficult to reach a consensus on what should be done. Meanwhile, there are signs that global climate change is affecting our planet. Average temperatures have risen and extreme weather events are occurring more often. Many glaciers and ice shelves are shrinking, and sea levels have risen.

A DRILLING ISSUE As people continue to consume non-renewable fossil fuels for their energy needs, they try to find additional sources of these fuels. One method for obtaining fossil fuels has generated controversy. Hydraulic fracturing, or **fracking** as it is often called, is a drilling process for extracting oil and natural gas. Pressurized liquid made of water, sand, and chemicals break up the rock. This process allows drillers to reach and extract oil and gas deposits that were not easily accessible before. However, the environmental impact of fracking is hotly debated. That a single fracked well requires millions of gallons of water over its lifetime is a primary concern. In some regions, farmers and well drillers must compete for limited water resources. Groundwater can become polluted by the chemicals injected into the well. Methane, which contributes to the greenhouse effect, can escape from fracked wells. Some fracked wells have exploded, throwing harmful chemicals onto the surrounding land.

Fracking has also been associated with an increase in earthquakes in areas where they were very rare or had never before been detected. Most of the scientific evidence indicates that the first stage of fracking is not to blame. However, when wastewater from fracked wells is injected back into the ground, the instability may lead to a quake. Additional research may clarify the role of fracking in earthquakes.

As fracking becomes more common, controversies over its use generate more media coverage. Environmentalists' opinions clash with those of oil and gas industry representatives. Even in the 1980s, though, EPA scientists were warning that fracking could pollute groundwater. Some EPA employees reported later that Reagan administration officials downplayed the hazard. Public scrutiny will probably increase as extracting oil and gas becomes more difficult.

BIODIVERSITY AND BEES Not all of our country's environmental challenges are related to fossil fuels. Another issue is the increasing lack of **biodiversity**—the entirety of a region's genes, species, and ecosystems. One example of a biodiverse ecosystem is a forest with many different kinds of trees and other plants, along with various microbe, insect, reptile, amphibian, and mammal species. Ecosystems that have biodiversity are generally healthier, can withstand stress better, and can recover more quickly from disruptions. Biodiversity of food crops is particularly vital. As certain agricultural plant species and varieties have been bred for qualities such as providing high yields, other qualities, such as disease resistance, have been lost. This situation could become critical if disease wiped out a key crop. Scientists recommend that U.S. agriculture include more biodiversity so that other plant varieties can fill gaps left by damaged crops.

The decline of the honeybee population is another puzzling environmental issue that may affect our food supply. By some accounts we have lost 40 percent of the bee colonies in the country. Honeybees are critical to the pollination of dozens of food crops, the value of which totals some $30 billion. It is feared that many staple crops, from apples to onions to tomatoes, may be lost if bee populations continue to decline.

Some scientists theorize that bees are suffering due to loss of habitat and food supply. In previous centuries, the United States had vast wild meadowlands. Wildflowers and bees were numerous. As the United States grew, farmers fenced and cultivated the prairies to plant crops. The loss of uncultivated

An Oregon State University bee researcher collects a sample of bees. Analysis of bee blood will help scientists determine the effects of pesticides on bees' immune systems.

Reading Check
Analyze Effects Of the environmental effects described, which do you think is the most problematic?

meadows to agriculture or suburban development means fewer wildflowers, which means less food for bees. Other theories regarding the honeybee decline include disease, inherited disorders, harsh weather, and parasites. In addition, the long-term effect of pesticides on bees is uncertain. The Obama administration created the Pollinator Task Force to research this problem in hopes of a solution. The group proposed ways to restore habitat. They also suggested additional investigation into the effects of pesticides and investment in further research and education.

Some Changes for the Better

Despite these problems, there are many ways in which the American environment is improving. Advances in research, coupled with the speed and reach of communications, have enabled people to be far more aware of environmental issues than they once were. Americans recycle millions of tons of trash every year, which saves energy and limited resources. Alternative energy sources, including solar and wind energy, are becoming more common. Many harmful pesticides and industrial chemicals have been banned. These are but a few examples that show progress in Americans' efforts to improve the environment.

One area where public awareness has led to change is our wetlands, which include swamps and marshes. Scientific studies show that wetlands are valuable resources because they shelter myriad aquatic and bird species,

Alternative-Fuel Vehicles

Carl Bielenberg of Calais, Vermont, holds a container of seeds of the jatropha plant. He runs his compact car on vegetable oil that is made from the seed.

A solar-powered car built by high school students from Saginaw, Michigan, makes its way through busy traffic.

Looking Back, Looking Forward

Journalist Elizabeth Kolbert reviewed the times in Earth's history when vast numbers of species were wiped out. She sees human beings as the cause of the next cataclysm. Yet she also sees hope.

Analyze Historical Sources
What gives Elizabeth Kolbert hope for America's future?

> *"Certainly humans can be destructive and shortsighted; they can also be forward-thinking and altruistic. Time and time again, people have demonstrated that they care about what Rachel Carson called "the problem of sharing our earth with other creatures," and that they're willing to make sacrifices on those creatures' behalf. . . . John Muir wrote about the damage being done in the mountains of California, and this led to the creation of Yosemite National Park. Silent Spring exposed the dangers posed by synthetic pesticides, and within a decade, most use of DDT had been prohibited. (The fact that there are still bald eagles in the U.S.—indeed the numbers are growing—is one of the many happy consequences of this development.)"*
> —Elizabeth Kolbert, from *The Sixth Extinction: An Unnatural History*

help control pollution, and limit damage done by floods. Agriculture and development, however, have claimed more than half of the wetlands that the country had 200 years ago. Some federal laws are aimed at reversing the trend. For example, the Food, Agriculture, Conservation, and Trade Act of 1990 includes a program that provides funds for converting croplands back to wetlands. Most states oversee wetlands conservation in some way. Private individuals and organizations, such as Ducks Unlimited and the Nature Conservancy, have also been instrumental in saving wetlands. As a result of these private efforts, more than 12 million acres of wetlands have been saved.

Another positive change is occurring on some American rivers. As the country grew, engineers built dams across countless waterways. The dams have produced many benefits. The benefits include hydroelectric power, flood control, and reservoirs for reliable water supplies. Dams and the reservoirs they create have also had negative effects. They can interrupt fish migration and their spawning patterns, overwhelm entire ecosystems, and displace people. In response to these problems, some dams are being removed and the rivers returned to a more natural condition. To date, the largest such project removed dams on the Elwha River in Washington state. After the demolition of two dams, native salmon and trout are migrating up the river again. The return of these species has had a positive cascading effect on other aspects of the local environment. For example, the fishes' return provided food for other species, such as wolves and bald eagles.

To reduce air pollution and dependence on foreign oil, Americans are buying more energy-efficient vehicles. In addition, the Environmental Protection Agency requires that certain gas mileage and emission standards be met by

Community efforts cleaned up the junkyard that used to occupy this area in northeastern Ohio. Now Cuyahoga Valley National Park allows visitors to experience a wetland and the wide range of plants and animals it supports.

carmakers. Once rare, hybrid vehicles that capture otherwise unused energy, leading to improved mileage and lower emissions, are becoming more common. Entrepreneurs in transportation, such as Elon Musk at Tesla Motors, are building fully electric cars that produce no tailpipe emissions. Depending on what kind of fuel is used to generate the electricity for the car's battery, electric cars can also cut down on oil consumption. Even cars powered by solar energy or vegetable oil are making headlines.

Gardens and green spaces are also receiving more attention. Community gardens, where residents can rent space to raise fruits and vegetables, are thriving. Boston, Massachusetts, alone has about 190 community gardens. Children are learning about both nutrition and the role of plants in the environment by growing vegetables on school grounds. Cities are requiring that developers set aside a certain amount of parkland as part of their building projects. A surprising place for new green spaces is on abandoned freeways and railroads. New York City's High Line Park is a ribbon of parkland more than a mile long on what was once an elevated section of a railroad line. Philadelphia residents want to turn the Reading Viaduct, also an abandoned railway, into a park that would bring greenery and recreation facilities to densely populated neighborhoods. These green spaces also scrub pollutants from the air and generate oxygen.

Reading Check
Draw Conclusions
What is one conclusion you can draw from the description of these projects?

Lesson 4 Assessment

1. **Organize Information** Create an idea web to identify some ways that governments, nonprofit organizations, and property owners may respond to threats to the environment.

2. **Key Terms and People** For each key term in the lesson, write a sentence explaining its significance.

3. **Analyze Effects** What are two effects of population growth and distribution on the physical environment?
   Think About:
   • energy use
   • supply and demand of natural resources

4. **Evaluate** How can individual decisions and business actions affect the environment?

5. **Analyze Issues** Is it possible for political leaders to address issues of conservation and balance economic progress at the same time? Support your answer.

★ Education

The Big Idea

Because resources are limited and American society is extremely diverse, educational institutions struggle to teach all of America's children and young people.

Why It Matters Now

A nation's success depends to a large extent on an educated populace.

Key Terms and People

flipped classroom

school vouchers

Individuals with Disabilities Education Act (IDEA)

One American's Story

Education has long been important to Michelle Obama. While a student at Princeton University, she ran a day care center and helped with after-school tutoring. She finished college and went on to earn a law degree at Harvard University. Her education allowed her to pursue a career as an attorney, as an administrator for the city of Chicago, and later as a community outreach worker. As first lady, Obama advocated for military families, healthy eating habits, the arts, physical activity, and education in general. In 2013 she gave a talk to students in Washington, DC, emphasizing the need for post-secondary education.

"[W]hen the year 2020 rolls around, nearly two-thirds of all jobs in this country are going to require some form of training beyond high school. That means whether it's a vocational program, community college, a four-year university, you all are going to

First Lady Michelle Obama at a gathering with Texas students

need some form of higher education in order to build the kind of lives that you want for yourselves, good careers, to be able to provide for your family."

—Michelle Obama, from remarks at Bell Multicultural High School, November 12, 2013

Achieving an education that fulfills those goals can be a challenge for many of America's youth.

SS.912.A.1.2; SS.912.A.1.4; SS.912.A.1.7; SS.912.A.7.12; LAFS.1112.RH.3.8; LAFS.1112.RH.4.10; MAFS.K12.MP.1.1; MAFS.K12.MP.5.1

The Changing Classroom

Teachers and administrators have seen many educational innovations come and go over the years. The digital revolution, however, has thoroughly transformed education. These changes are occurring around the world but are most evident in schools of developed countries. For example, students in the Australian Outback no longer have to depend on the radio for their lessons. Instead, they can submit homework and receive rapid feedback via the Internet.

In the United States, most classrooms now provide Internet access. Students are as likely to read assignments on electronic tablets or smart phones as they are to read from a printed book. Interactivity has also transformed classwork. As students complete assignments on digital devices, they get immediate feedback on their progress. Teachers can easily track the work of individual students or entire classes. For these reasons and others, e-learning has become standard in many U.S. schools. E-learning is the use of electronic technology in education. However, some school districts still prefer printed books and traditional teaching methods. They have determined that those approaches are best for their students.

E-learning is an important component of a recent innovation that may further transform conventional teaching methods. The **flipped classroom** is a strategy that reverses the traditional approach of delivering instructional content. With a flipped approach, content is delivered outside of the classroom, often online. Class time is reserved for research, group collaboration, discussion, individualized instruction, or other forms of active learning. The flipped classroom has raised test scores, graduation rates, and college attendance figures in some schools. However, critics note that students from poor families may not have ready access to the technology needed for the online lessons. Also, many students lack the self-direction that the flipped classroom demands. Teachers, too, may balk at the extra preparation time that online delivery of content might require.

Reading Check
Summarize What are two ways that American classrooms are changing?

E-learning is now standard in many U.S. classrooms.

Challenges for Education

The English colonies' first public school was established in 1635. Ever since, American educators have faced difficulties in their efforts to teach basic knowledge and skills to the country's children. Many of those issues, including how education should be funded, how to reach all students, and how best to teach them, remain with us today and will for the foreseeable future.

The amount of tax money available can affect the equipment and supplies available to students. This science lab, in a well-funded district, provides students with what they need to succeed. Districts that receive less revenue in property taxes may struggle to update their facilities and resources.

FUNDING PRIMARY AND SECONDARY EDUCATION In most states public school funding relies on local property taxes. Those taxes are paid on the value of real estate in a town or city. When schools are funded primarily by property taxes, however, schools in poorer areas receive less money than those in wealthier communities. The properties in poorer areas are assessed at lower rates. The disparity in funding between rich and poor districts varies across the country. According to the National Center for Education Statistics, the state of Pennsylvania has the widest difference in funding between low- and high-income schools. A study reports that Pennsylvania's poor districts receive 33 percent less state and local funding that their richest districts. Court cases have raised legal challenges to unequal school funding in more than 20 states.

School districts where property taxes don't produce high revenues are more likely to cut back on art, music, and other coursework. These subjects are sometimes viewed as less essential than math, reading, and science. Poor districts may also have higher student-to-teacher ratios; outdated facilities; or fewer support personnel, such as nurses. The impact of spending disparities is debatable, however. Some graduates from schools in low-income districts go on to excel at top universities. Also, attendance at a well-funded school is no guarantee of high achievement.

Although more than 90 percent of American children attend public schools, others attend private secular or religious schools or receive instruction at home. Most parents whose children pay tuition for private schools also pay the property taxes that help fund public schools. Some of these parents feel they should receive funding from the state to ease the load. These parents and their supporters back **school vouchers**. Vouchers are subsidies given directly to parents for tuition at any school, public or private. Proponents of the voucher system say that it increases competition among schools and gives low-performing schools an incentive to improve. Supporters cite studies that show public schools improved when nearby private schools were eligible to accept voucher students. On the other side of the argument, opponents say that the voucher system deprives public schools of much-needed funds. They also point out that private schools can pick and choose their pupils, skewing their statistics to the positive. Public schools must accept all students, including those with special needs or troubled histories. Opponents also claim that the voucher system is an attempt to fund religious schools at taxpayers' expense. Thus it violates the separation of church and state.

TEACHING ALL OF AMERICA'S KIDS Family income can be a powerful factor in a student's success. Although economic status is not a sure indicator, it is more likely that low-income students have untreated medical problems and less quiet time for completing assignments at home. These students may also have fewer opportunities for cultural enrichment activities, such as music lessons or museum visits. Federal data show that just over half of all students in U.S. public schools qualify for free or reduced-price lunches. This is the gauge that schools use to measure students' economic level. The percentage climbed from 38 percent in 2000 to 51 percent in 2013. The figures on low-income students differ from state to state. For the 2012–2013 school year in Mississippi, the number was 71 percent of all public school students. New Hampshire had the lowest figure, at 27 percent. Some states, such as California, are placing renewed emphasis on increasing funding to poor districts. The federal government is also focusing on supporting low-income students.

Economic is just one of many ways that student populations differ. Students in U.S. schools also come from dozens of different ethnic backgrounds. This diversity is apparent in public school enrollments. The percentage of public school students who participate in programs for English language learners (ELL) has been increasing steadily. In the 2002–2003 school year, the national figure was 8.7 percent ELL students. By 2011–2012 it was 9.1 percent. The figures for 2011–2012 vary widely by state. In California, more than 23 percent of the students qualified for ELL instruction. In contrast, West Virginia's ELL students totaled only 0.7 percent of the school population. For those districts with high percentages of ELL students, additional resources are needed for their education. Resources such as specially trained teachers, modified materials, and teacher's aids can put a strain on budgets.

Jessica Riley, a hearing-impaired volunteer teacher, helps a hearing-impaired second grader with his reading.

Public schools also face the challenge of educating students with special needs, including emotional, psychological, developmental, and physical needs. The **Individuals with Disabilities Education Act (IDEA)** requires that students with a disability are provided with a Free Appropriate Public Education (FAPE) that is tailored to their individual needs. Those needs may be for physical accommodations or extra instruction delivered in nontraditional ways. Students might also need psychological counseling or other specialized approaches.

Although educating all these varied populations can be costly in terms of funds and human resources, the benefits spread far beyond the students themselves. ELL students become more able to participate fully in American society, which requires fluency in English. Students whose special needs have been filled become more self-sufficient. This lessens their need for public support. If those special needs were for encouragement to explore unique skills or talents, we may all profit from the inventions, discoveries, or artistic achievements that result.

LEARNING AND TESTING In the winter of 2001, Paul Vallas, former head of the Chicago public school system, received some discouraging news. A three-year study found "little significant change" in the city's ailing public high schools. This was despite six years of intense reform efforts. "The issue is that the problem is tougher than we thought it was," the head of the study reported, "and we have to find more intense ways of improving what we've been doing." In response to the study, Vallas echoed those sentiments. "We still have a long way to go," he said.

Chicago's plight is far from unique. Across the country, many administrators review their graduation statistics with dismay. But proposals for improving American education have been touted for decades. Some people say that discipline is the problem. Others fault teachers' unions for failing to oust bad teachers. One can find many lists of what schools should do to improve performance. Suggestions range from more interdisciplinary study to longer school days to allowing more time to make up missed assignments. Many reforms involve standardized testing—either more tests or fewer.

In 2002 President Bush signed into law his education program, No Child Left Behind (NCLB). A cornerstone of the program was using results from national annual reading and math assessments to hold schools accountable for student performance. Schools that failed to show enough yearly progress could lose students to other schools, be forced to change staff, or even be closed. A few years after NCLB's passage, the National Assessment of Education Progress (NAEP) reported that achievement on state reading and math tests was rising. Critics found fault with the NAEP findings, however. They contended that positive aspects of the data were emphasized while negative

Document-Based Investigation Historical Source

Evaluating American Education

In a speech introducing his Race to the Top program, President Obama reviewed some of the problems facing the American educational system.

"In an economy where knowledge is the most valuable commodity a person and a country have to offer, the best jobs will go to the best educated—whether they live in the United States or India or China. In a world where countries that out-educate us today will out-compete us tomorrow, the future belongs to the nation that best educates its people. . . . But we also know that today, our education system is falling short. . . . The United States, a country that has always led the way in innovation, is now being outpaced in math and science education. African American, Latino students are lagging behind white classmates in one subject after another—an achievement gap that, by one estimate, costs us hundreds of billions of dollars in wages that will not be earned, jobs that will not be done, and purchases that will not be made. And most employers raise doubts about the qualifications of future employees, rating high school graduates' basic skills as only 'fair' or 'poor.'"

—Barack Obama, from a speech at the U.S. Department of Education, July 24, 2009

Analyze Historical Sources

Do you think President Obama's assessment is accurate? Why or why not?

elements were downplayed. NCLB itself has also drawn criticism. Among the problems cited is the claim that schools neglect subjects other than reading and math. Also, testing special education students along with at-level students unfairly distorted results. Other critics have complained that Congress has never funded the act to the level that would produce the hoped-for results. Many ideas for refining NCLB have been proposed. In 2009 President Obama proposed his own education plan, called Race to the Top (RTT). The plan focuses on rewarding schools for progress rather than punishing them for failure. RTT has earned its own share of criticism from both ends of the political spectrum. Some conservatives, for example, object to the federal government's close involvement in the program.

THE COST OF HIGHER EDUCATION The cost of attending a college or university has soared. Between 2001–2002 and 2011–2012, prices for undergraduate tuition, room, and board at public institutions rose 40 percent. The cost increase at private nonprofit institutions was close behind, at 28 percent. Increases in tuition and required fees account for most of the change.

Analysts have different views of why college tuition has risen so rapidly. Some contend that state legislatures have not allocated funds to public universities at the rate they once did. Others dispute that charge, saying that legislatures have actually increased their funding levels. The technology demands of some disciplines may also contribute to the problem. High-tech fields including engineering, computer science, and medicine require that students and faculty have access to the latest groundbreaking devices, equipment, and software to learn and conduct research. Some analysts say the problem lies with the universities. Some schools have expanded their nonteaching staffs, have embarked on ambitious building projects, or have tried to out-bid each other by offering high salaries to the most prestigious professors.

Average U.S. College Costs Since 1974

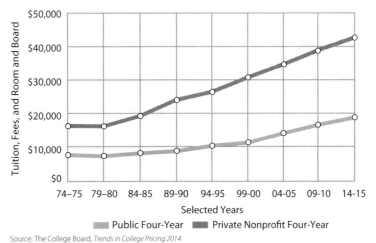

Source: The College Board, *Trends in College Pricing 2014*

Interpret Graphs
In what five-year span did the cost for public institutions show the largest increase?

The increased cost of higher education makes it difficult for many students of moderate means to finance their education. Even with part-time jobs and scholarships, most students take out loans to help pay for their education. In fact, some two-thirds of students earning bachelor's degrees have borrowed money to attend college. The amount of money that U.S. students owe collectively is immense. By 2012 it exceeded $1 trillion.

The fear of incurring debt can keep many students from even attempting a college degree. Many observers feel that if the United States wants to have an educated workforce, policymakers should focus on finding ways to make higher education affordable again. They should also provide relief to those already shouldering heavy debts. One officeholder intent on relieving student debt is Elizabeth Warren, a U.S. senator from Massachusetts. Senator Warren has proposed that loans to new student borrowers incur only 0.75 percent interest instead of the current 3.4 percent rate. Warren is proposing the same rate that banks pay to borrow money from the federal government.

Reading Check
Identify Problems
What are some issues facing students today?

Lesson 5 Assessment

1. **Organize Information** Create a table to describe some factors that are affecting U.S. education in the 21st century.

technology	
funding	
standardized testing	
vouchers	

2. **Key Terms and People** For each key term in the lesson, write a sentence explaining its significance.

3. **Analyze Effects** Some of America's children and young people may not get the public education they need and deserve. What challenges face students in various circumstances?

   Think About:
   • students without access to high technology
   • English language learners
   • students with special needs
   • college students of moderate means

4. **Analyze Causes** How is worldwide access to education and educational practices changing?

Globalization and Cultural Diffusion

The Big Idea

Modern communication and transportation technologies have created an international economic and cultural community.

Why It Matters Now

To be good citizens of the world, Americans must learn to enhance the positive and reduce the negative aspects of globalization.

Key Terms and People

globalization

free trade

comparative advantage

Kyoto Protocol

cultural diffusion

popular culture

One American's Story

Thomas Friedman is an American economist, journalist, and author. After earning a master's degree in Middle Eastern studies, Friedman went to Lebanon and Israel to report on conflicts there. Since then, Friedman has traveled to many other regions and written about his experiences. He has won a Pulitzer Prize three times. In his book *The World Is Flat,* Friedman proposes that the historical and geographic factors that once separated countries are becoming irrelevant. Even so, people and places can still maintain their uniqueness. In the quote that follows, he reflects on the role of technology in that process.

Thomas Friedman

"Uploading makes possible 'the globalization of the local.' The fact that so many people worldwide now have the tools to create and upload their own content—their own news reports, their own opinions, their own music, their own videos, their own photos, their own software, their own encyclopedias, their own dictionaries—is a very powerful force for the preservation and enhancement of cultural autonomy and particularity."

—Thomas Friedman, from *The World Is Flat*

It is indeed a different world than was imaginable just a few years ago.

SS.912.A.1.4; SS.912.A.1.6; SS.912.A.7.12; SS.912.A.7.14; SS.912.G.1.2; SS.912.G.2.1; SS.912.H.3.1

The Global Economic Community

In previous centuries, the United States went through periods when economic isolationism was a popular sentiment. In the 21st century, isolationism is no longer an option. Instead, expanded and improved transportation, communication, and technology systems mean that internationalism is the way of the world for the distribution of goods, services, and ideas. These forces are summarized by the word **globalization**. Globalization can be defined as the process of international integration resulting from the interchange of worldviews, products, ideas, and other aspects of culture. Globalization has opened up traditional marketplaces for acquiring raw materials. Businesses can choose more diverse geographic locations to source the different aspects of production and distribution. Stronger transportation systems and instantaneous communication systems allow access to these goods more quickly and economically. Many barriers that existed in the past have been removed. Modern global communications networks also enable entrepreneurs to reach out to funding sources and markets not available before.

With each change come costs as well as benefits. Some Americans are concerned that multinational corporations operating in a global context crowd out smaller businesses. Another concern is job loss as domestic companies move their factories and hire workers abroad to take advantage of lower wages and costs. In contrast, others feel globalization creates jobs as new international markets increase exports, and new workers are needed to create products.

TECHNOLOGY AND GLOBAL TRADE A key driver of economic globalization is the technology revolution. The industries related to computerization—from chip manufacturing to web design—are themselves big players in the global marketplace. Few industries have not been transformed by the products and services these industries produce.

Computers have changed not just industries but also the lives of individual workers. Technology has given people access to far more information than ever before. This access has improved productivity in many industries. Workers share information through computer networks. Laptops and cell phones have enabled increasing numbers of people to work at home or in multiple locations. Communication and technology advances allow many large companies to outsource various tasks such as support services. For example, a company in Florida may outsource customer technology support to telephone operators in India.

A KEY TO THE SUCCESS OF FREE TRADE Globalization is inextricably linked to free trade. **Free trade** is the policy in international markets in which governments do not restrict imports or exports. Many economists believe that a key to the success of free trade is a concept known as comparative advantage.

Globalization connects economies and cultures around the world.

Comparative advantage is the idea that a nation will specialize in what it can produce at a lower opportunity cost, or trade-off, than any other nation. Examining a possible trade situation involving China and Australia provides an example. Both countries produce iron ore and steel. Suppose that every week, Australia produces 5,000 tons of iron ore. From that iron ore, 1,000 tons of steel are produced. In the same period of time, and with the same amount of labor, China produces 2,700 tons of iron ore and 900 tons of steel. Australia's production ratio of steel is 1:5. In other words, Australia's opportunity cost for one ton of steel is five tons of iron ore. China's production ratio of steel to iron ore is 1:3. Its opportunity cost for one ton of steel is three tons of iron ore. So, in the production of steel, China has a comparative advantage. Australia would benefit by trading for Chinese steel. If the two nations establish a trade ratio of 1:4, both countries win. China trades one ton of its steel for four tons of iron ore. China now gets four tons of iron ore, instead of three, for a ton of steel. Also, one ton of steel now costs Australia only four tons of iron ore, when before it cost five.

PARTNERS AND COMPETITORS Globalization does not mean that international trade is without conflict. Competition for resources, trade routes, and markets is fierce. To improve their chances of economic success, countries form trading blocs, or alliances. These alliances reduce trade barriers, such as tariffs, among their members. To promote economic growth, the United States is allied with Canada and Mexico in the North American Free Trade Agreement (NAFTA). The United States is also a member of the Asia-Pacific Economic Cooperation (APEC), the Group of Eight (G8), and the World Trade Organization (WTO).

Among the United States' economic competitors is the Organization of the Petroleum Exporting Countries (OPEC). Except for members Ecuador and Venezuela, all OPEC countries are in Africa or the Middle East. Saudi Arabia controls about one-third of OPEC's total oil reserves and takes a leading role in the organization. OPEC exerts a great deal of control over the supply of oil and oil prices on world markets. Oil availability and prices can, in turn, affect prices of other products that depend on oil. For example, if OPEC allows the price of oil to rise dramatically, the price of fuel for farm machinery also rises. As a result, the price of wheat may increase. In recent decades, however, OPEC lost some of its influence as the United States increased domestic oil production. In fact, a 2014 analysis reported that since 2008, U.S. oil imports from OPEC nations have declined by 50 percent.

Members of another competitive trade alliance, the European Union (EU), are also among the strongest political allies of the United States. The EU consists of 28 member countries; several other countries are candidates for membership. Citizens of EU countries can move freely among the member nations, as can goods, services, and economic capital. A majority of the member countries use the same currency, the euro. The member countries work as a single economic unit in trade negotiations instead of competing against each other. As a result of this cooperation, the EU has become an immensely powerful trading bloc. In fact, according to some measures, in 2014 the EU had the largest economy in the world.

Reading Check
Summarize What are three factors that have increased economic globalization?

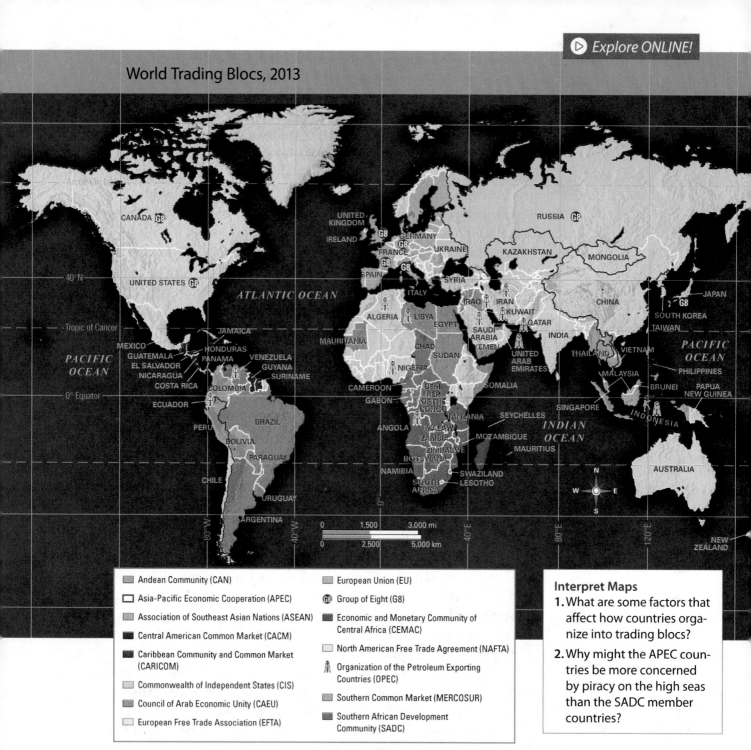

World Trading Blocs, 2013

Legend:

- Andean Community (CAN)
- Asia-Pacific Economic Cooperation (APEC)
- Association of Southeast Asian Nations (ASEAN)
- Central American Common Market (CACM)
- Caribbean Community and Common Market (CARICOM)
- Commonwealth of Independent States (CIS)
- Council of Arab Economic Unity (CAEU)
- European Free Trade Association (EFTA)
- European Union (EU)
- G8 Group of Eight (G8)
- Economic and Monetary Community of Central Africa (CEMAC)
- North American Free Trade Agreement (NAFTA)
- Organization of the Petroleum Exporting Countries (OPEC)
- Southern Common Market (MERCOSUR)
- Southern African Development Community (SADC)

Interpret Maps

1. What are some factors that affect how countries organize into trading blocs?
2. Why might the APEC countries be more concerned by piracy on the high seas than the SADC member countries?

Challenges of Globalization

Like most other changes that affect millions of people, globalization has its benefits and costs. Foremost among the costs are negative impacts on some workers and on the environment.

LABOR ISSUES Globalization has been largely beneficial to the countries that participate in free trade. Countries such as India and Bangladesh, once mired in poverty, have grown their economies. However, the effect on individual workers is not necessarily positive. Many of the new jobs made possible by economic globalization pay low wages and do not offer long-term, stable employment. Working conditions are often hazardous, hot, and crowded.

Some factory owners employ child workers in conditions similar to slavery. For example, children in Pakistan and India have been forced to sew soccer balls, to be sold on the international market, for 10 to 12 hours a day. Some of the children were chained to their workstations. International businesses that subcontract work to local employers are particularly at risk of profiting from such exploitative conditions, whether or not they are aware of them. When such abuses are publicized in international media, consumers may be challenged to examine their buying habits.

Economic globalization also affects workers in the United States. Even before it became as common as it is today, some opponents of globalization suggested that it would negatively affect the United States. For example, third-party candidate Ross Perot sounded an alarm during the 1992 presidential election. He warned that American jobs would be lost if NAFTA were approved. As trade barriers came down, many U.S. jobs were indeed lost to other countries where wages are lower. In particular, the number of U.S. factory jobs has declined. Union membership has declined along with the number of manufacturing jobs. However, many American businesses have also seen growth and success due to globalization.

ENVIRONMENTAL CONCERNS Just as many other countries allow poor working conditions and low wages, some may also have lax environmental regulations. As manufacturing increases in these countries, so do pollution and threats to the environment. Such problems have led some world leaders to propose aggressive plans to protect the air and water.

Document-Based Investigation Historical Source

Evaluating Globalization

Joseph Stiglitz has been the chief economist for the World Bank and chair of President Clinton's Council of Economic Advisers. He has studied the issues resulting from globalization, including resulting environmental damage and the impact on many poor workers. In the quote below, Stiglitz addresses the question of how to solve these dilemmas.

"To some, there is an easy answer: Abandon globalization. That is neither feasible nor desirable. . . . [G]lobalization has also brought huge benefits—East Asia's success was based on globalization, especially on the opportunities for trade, and increased access to markets and technology. Globalization has brought better health, as well as an active global civil society fighting for more democracy and greater social justice. The problem is not with globalization, but with how it has been managed. Part of the problem lies with the international economic institutions . . . which help set the rules of the game. They have done so in ways that, all too often, have served the interests of the more advanced industrialized countries—and particular interests within those countries— rather than those of the developing world."

—Joseph E. Stiglitz, from
Globalization and Its Discontents

Analyze Historical Sources
What responsibility does the American public have for making globalization a force that helps rich and poor alike?

Students in Beijing, China, show their support for the Kyoto Protocol.

The most significant of these proposals is the **Kyoto Protocol**, an international treaty that seeks to reduce emissions of greenhouse gases. The agreement is connected to the United Nations Framework Convention on Climate Change. The Kyoto Protocol was adopted in Kyoto, Japan, in December 1997. It went into effect in February 2005. Under the Protocol, countries' emissions of greenhouse gases have to be recorded and revealed in annual reports.

Many Americans who see global warming as affected by human activity feel that the Kyoto Protocol is a necessary step in the right direction. Some critics of the Protocol do not like the idea of American industries being monitored by an international organization. Other critics complain that the Protocol doesn't come down hard enough on fast-developing countries such as China and India. The United States is a signatory, or signer, of the treaty, but so far has declined to ratify it. This failure to ratify the Protocol is seen by some Americans as evidence that the fossil fuel industries wield too much power in the U.S. government.

A follow-up to the Kyoto treaty is the Copenhagen Accord, an international treaty that calls for a continuation of the Kyoto Protocol. It also encourages a strengthening of worldwide efforts to combat climate change. Like the Kyoto Protocol, the Accord stresses that dramatic cuts in greenhouse gas emissions are necessary to slow the effects of climate change. The Accord set an initial deadline of January 31, 2010, for countries to submit their goals for reducing emissions. The goal is to significantly reduce emissions by 2020. In the United States, support for the Accord is divided along similar lines as support for the Kyoto Protocol.

ETHICAL ISSUES IN INTERNATIONAL BUSINESS Multinational companies must deal with issues that arise from doing business in countries where laws and accepted practices are very different from those in the United States. Companies that do business on a global scale must confront several ethical questions—those that deal with right and wrong. They must decide how those issues affect their public image as much as their bottom line.

Parent companies that subcontract some tasks to local managers are particularly susceptible to using questionable practices, perhaps without their knowledge. Subcontractors whose employees work in sweatshop conditions without protection from hazardous chemicals may not be breaking any local laws. However, buyers may refuse to purchase the company's products when they hit U.S. shelves.

Some big companies hire workers in countries with poor human rights records. One can argue that giving people work is a way to improve that country's conditions from within. An opposing argument was used against U.S. companies that operated in South Africa during the apartheid era. Some argue that investment by foreign companies helps support repressive governments by boosting their economies.

Corruption is another situation that can trip up international businesses. In some countries, gifts to people who can help "seal the deal" are common and accepted. For example, in the 1970s a prominent U.S. aircraft manufacturer paid Japanese agents and government officials $12.5 million to secure sales of their jets to a leading airline. The company was operating on the assumption that such bribes were an accepted way of doing business in Japan. That assumption was woefully wrong, however. The scandal outraged the Japanese public. Those who had taken the bribes suffered for doing so.

Environmental issues overlap with ethical questions when a country's environmental laws are much weaker than U.S. regulations. A corrupt government may ignore environmental damage to keep from disrupting a profitable business. One example comes from Nigeria, where an oil multinational was criticized for polluting the air and water. Criticism also pointed to the failure to invest profits back into the impoverished communities from where the oil was extracted. In addition, the company was accused of conspiring with Nigeria's police force to put down demonstrations against widespread pollution. The resulting violence took the lives of dozens of Nigerian villagers. People who manage or invest in companies in situations like this must grapple with the extent of their responsibility.

Reading Check
Analyze Effects
How have lax labor and environmental laws affected people in some developing countries?

Congress has passed several laws aimed at ending such abuses. However, effective enforcement requires more cooperation in the countries where they occur.

Diffusion on a Global Scale

Just as globalization has affected economies as countries interact through business, it has also affected international politics. Ideas about justice and democracy can spread around the world by means of blogs and social media. Technology makes these outlets powerful forces in the hands of discontented people whose governments try to limit dissent. A 2011 rebellion in Egypt, for example, depended on the Internet to organize activities. It was also the means to tell the world what was going on.

Globalization also affects cultures. In our global marketplace, citizens interact more frequently with one another. This interaction influences beliefs, behaviors, and actions. The result is **cultural diffusion**, which describes the way cultural practices spread from one community to another. It is also how cultures borrow traits such as beliefs, ideas, and material objects from one another. With increased contact comes increased diffusion. In today's world of instantaneous communication, cultural diffusion is constant.

Cultural diffusion is not a new concept. People of various cultures have interacted with each other for centuries as people have traveled and traded around the world. The United States has always drawn merchants, immigrants, and tourists from other lands. In the process, people have brought and shared their foods, languages, traditions, and values. So today you can find Ethiopian, Chinese, Brazilian, and French restaurants in the United States. Likewise, American fast-food restaurants can be found from Australia to Zambia. For example, McDonald's has restaurants in more than 100 countries, and Starbucks has coffee shops in over 65 countries.

SHARING CULTURE Popular culture is a collection of ideas, attitudes, and images that are part of a mainstream culture heavily influenced by and spread through the media. Pop culture can include movies, television, music, fashion, and even values that are current in a particular culture.

Women from around the world have come to Senegal, on Africa's west coast, to learn traditional dances. Modern telecommunications make advertising such opportunities possible.

Technology has made the spread of pop culture more dramatic. In the 1920s new media such as radio and movies were able to reach a growing share of the nation's population. Increasingly, people all across the country were sharing the same information and enjoying the same pastimes, creating a shared culture. Today, the Internet, movies, and television are the driving forces spreading popular culture on a global scale. People around the world can hear the same news and listen to the same music. They can hear the same advertisements and buy the same products. Movies are made, seen, and distributed around the world. This provides viewers the opportunity to experience different cultures and to have a shared global experience. Not only can individuals receive the information, but they can help create and share it as well.

Thanks to these new technologies, American pop culture has spread like wildfire. Young people around the world listen to American music, watch American movies, and adopt American fashion fads. However, just as advances in communication, trade, transportation, and technology can spread cultural features around the world and make them more similar, those forces can also help maintain traditional cultures. A teacher of ancient dances can use social media to recruit more students, who will then keep the traditions alive. Shared videos of folkloric musical performances bring in new fans who want to learn the music for themselves. Global trade networks can introduce new buyers to the handicrafts of artisans who once had limited access to markets. This access encourages them to continue practicing their time-honored skills.

AN EXAMPLE OF CULTURAL DIFFUSION To look at how cultural diffusion can permeate the global market, examine the spread of hip-hop. Originating in New York City in the 1970s, hip-hop culture usually includes rap music, deejaying, graffiti painting, and hip-hop dancing.

Hip-hop quickly took hold of popular American culture in New York City and spread throughout the country. Globalization allowed hip-hop culture to spread even farther. Youth around the world identified with the themes and styles. American movies such as *Wild Style* introduced people as far away as

THE GLOBAL SPREAD OF HIP-HOP

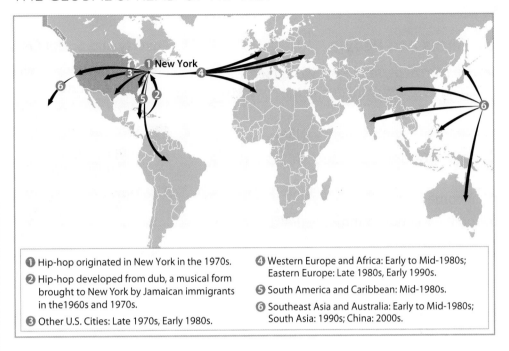

① Hip-hop originated in New York in the 1970s.

② Hip-hop developed from dub, a musical form brought to New York by Jamaican immigrants in the1960s and 1970s.

③ Other U.S. Cities: Late 1970s, Early 1980s.

④ Western Europe and Africa: Early to Mid-1980s; Eastern Europe: Late 1980s, Early 1990s.

⑤ South America and Caribbean: Mid-1980s.

⑥ Southeast Asia and Australia: Early to Mid-1980s; South Asia: 1990s; China: 2000s.

Japan to the new style of dance and music in the 1980s. In the 1990s global media companies saw an opportunity and began marketing hip-hop–related items to other countries. These included music, movies, clothing, and dance. Soon, the hip-hop culture had become popular on six continents.

As hip-hop spread, youth combined elements of American hip-hop culture with their own traditions. For example, in Japan, hip-hop fashion incorporated the Japanese language and symbols representing samurai. Lyrics often referred to Japanese food and other cultural elements.

Today, hip-hop is still popular, and the Internet draws the hip-hop community even more closely together. A website focusing on hip-hop allows people from around the world to share their thoughts about current trends or to sell hip-hop–related goods and services. Video-sharing websites, blogs, and social media remove any international barriers in the hip-hop community.

Reading Check
Analyze Causes
Why is cultural diffusion likely to increase?

Lesson 6 Assessment

1. **Organize Information** Create a graphic organizer to describe some benefits and costs of globalization.

Costs	Benefits

2. **Key Terms and People** For each key term in the lesson, write a sentence explaining its significance.

3. **Predict** How do you think technology will affect globalization in the future?

   Think About:
   • the global workforce
   • entrepreneurship
   • computer network security

4. **Analyze Issues** What responsibility do you think the government has in addressing issues, such as worker exploitation and air pollution, that arise from globalization?

5. **Develop Historical Perspective** How has the European Union's role in global economics evolved?

Module 19 Assessment

Key Terms and People

For each term or person below, write a sentence explaining its significance during the early 21st century.

1. National Security Agency (NSA)
2. racial profiling
3. ISIS
4. income gap
5. political action committee (PAC)
6. fracking
7. school vouchers
8. Kyoto Protocol
9. globalization
10. popular culture

Main Ideas

Use your notes and the information in the module to answer the following questions.

National Security and Public Safety

1. How has terrorism affected government policies?
2. Why do you think the USA PATRIOT Act has been renewed continually?
3. Why is there tension between protecting both individual liberty and national security?

Foreign Policy

4. In general terms, what are the UN's Millennium Development Goals trying to achieve?
5. How have concerns about homeland security affected U.S. foreign policy?
6. What impact have the UN and NATO had in recent years? How has their relationship with the United States changed over time?
7. Why might the United States try to maintain good relations with China?
8. What role has the United States played in international health care issues, including HIV/AIDS? Why are those efforts controversial?

Poverty and Social Concerns

9. What usually determines social class in the United States?
10. What are some causes of poverty?
11. What are some criticisms of federal subsistence programs? Where do the two main political parties usually stand on the issues?
12. How does a widening income gap affect individuals and society?

Conservation and the Environment

13. How does perception affect how people see environmental issues? What is the result?
14. What are some positive and negative events affecting American rivers?
15. Why do fossil fuels incite conflict?
16. How are advances in transportation helping the environment?

Education

17. Why might the flipped classroom not be suitable for all students or teachers?
18. What is the basic problem with using property taxes to fund public education?

Globalization and Cultural Diffusion

19. Which countries or organizations are usually U.S. trade partners? competitors?
20. What are some ethical issues that international companies face?
21. How can globalization both diminish and preserve traditional cultures?

Critical Thinking

1. **Categorize** Use a graphic organizer to draw conclusions about the economic, political, and social impacts of new and emerging technologies on individuals and countries.

	Individuals	Countries
Economic		
Political		
Social		

2. **Evaluate** Can the average citizen assess the effectiveness of U.S. actions to prevent terrorism? Why or why not?

3. **Analyze Causes** How has terrorism affected Americans' way of life?

4. **Draw Conclusions** Do you think the government has been effective in balancing the rights of the individual against the need for national security? Why or why not?

5. **Synthesize** How might political, military, and economic interests combine or conflict to affect U.S. diplomatic relationships?

6. **Analyze Issues** What are some ways that modern media affect public policy?

7. **Predict** Why might access to water and food continue to cause conflicts?

8. **Analyze Causes** How has U.S. dependence on foreign oil affected foreign policy?

9. **Analyze Effects** Has social legislation been effective in ending poverty? Explain.

10. **Compare** Why might nonprofits sometimes be more effective in protecting the environment than the federal government?

11. **Evaluate** How can decisions and actions by governments and businesses affect the environment?

Engage with History

Imagine that you are the president's chief economic advisor. He or she has asked you for your thoughts on solving the widening income gap. What advice will you provide? Consider how various public policies affect poverty in the United States and the arguments for and against them. Will you advise the more conservative, usually Republican, view or the more liberal, usually Democratic, approach? How do those views compare and contrast? Compile the major points you would make to the president in an essay or multimedia presentation.

Focus on Writing

Compose a persuasive essay on an issue related to 21st-century policies. Narrow your topic to a specific aspect of the general subject. Incorporate local or regional examples or applications to illustrate your point. Justify your position with a reasoned argument based upon historical antecedents and precedents and core democratic values or constitutional principles.

Multimedia Activity

The U.S. government has earned praise and criticism for policies and actions to support countries struggling for various reasons. The class should be organized into five groups. Each group should research a different topic: how U.S. government actions have supported the democratic growth of developing nations; U.S. attempts to support economic growth, also in developing countries; examples of the U.S. government providing humanitarian assistance during natural disasters; U.S. humanitarian aid to countries in other times of crisis; and U.S. efforts to support human rights. All groups should conduct research on their topics and evaluate the effectiveness of U.S. actions. You should also examine how other nations viewed U.S. efforts. Then work with other groups to examine situations when democratic and economic growth, natural and human-made disasters, and other crises intersected or overlapped. Each group should create a multimedia presentation to share your work with the class.

References

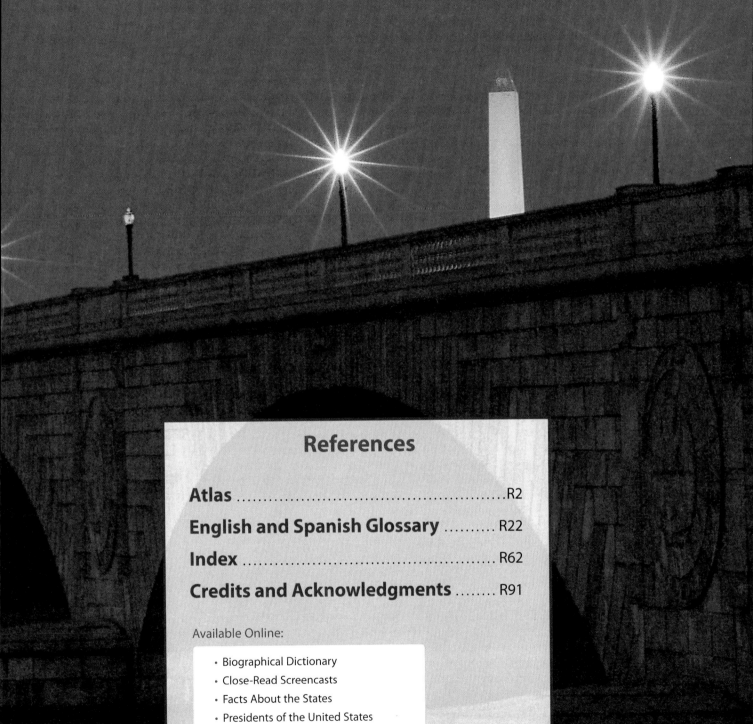

References

Available Online:

- Biographical Dictionary
- Close-Read Screencasts
- Facts About the States
- Presidents of the United States
- Economics Handbook
- Geography and Map Skills Handbook
- Skillbuilder Handbook

Strait of
Juan de Fuca

Puget
Sound

Franklin D.
Roosevelt Lake

45°N

● Seattle
★ Olympia ● Tacoma
● Spokane

WASHINGTON

Pend
Oreille

Flathead
Lake

● Great Falls

Helena ★ **MONTANA**

Fort Peck
Lake

Missouri River

NORTH DAKOTA

Lake
Sakakawea

★ Bismarck

● Portland

Columbia River

★ Salem

● Eugene

OREGON

Goose
Lake

Shasta
Lake

Cape
Mendocino

IDAHO

★ Boise

● Sun Valley

Snake
River

Yellowstone
Lake

Billings ●

Yellowstone River

WYOMING

Lake
Oahe

SOUTH DAKOTA

★ Pierre

● Rapid City

40°N

Sacramento River

Pyramid
Lake

● Reno
★ Carson City
Lake Tahoe

NEVADA

● Pocatello

Ogden ●
★ Salt Lake City
● Provo

Great
Salt
Lake

Utah
Lake

Green River

Cheyenne
★

NEBRASKA

Platte River

Berkeley
Oakland ★ Sacramento
San Francisco ●
San Francisco Bay
● San Jose

San Joaquin River

Monterey
Bay

● Fresno

CALIFORNIA

35°N

UTAH

Lake
Powell

● Boulder
Vail ● ★ Denver
Aspen ● Colorado
Springs ●

COLORADO

● Pueblo

Arkansas River

KANSAS

● Las
Vegas

Lake
Mead

Colorado River

● Flagstaff

Taos ●
Santa Fe ★

● Albuquerque

OKLAHOMA

Canadian River

Oklahoma City

Santa Barbara ●
Ventura ●
Long ●
Beach ●
San Diego ●

Channel
Islands

● Los
Angeles
● Riverside
● Palm Springs
● Anaheim
Santa Ana ●

Salton
Sea

ARIZONA

Phoenix ★

Gila River

● Casa Grande

NEW MEXICO

● Amarillo

Lawto

PACIFIC

OCEAN

Gulf of
California

● Tucson

● Las Cruces

● El Paso

● Lubbock

● Midland
● Odessa

Brazos River

● Abilene

Pecos River

Fort Wor

TEXAS

Colorado River

30°N

To understand the relative locations of Alaska and
Hawaii, as well as the vast distances separating them
from the rest of the United States, see the world map.

Austin ★

● San Antonio

Rio Grande

Amistad
Reservoir

Kauai

Niihau

Oahu

HAWAII

22°N

155°W

ARCTIC OCEAN

Honolulu ★

**PACIFIC
OCEAN**

Molokai

Lanai

Maui

Kahoolawe

RUSSIA

Bering
Strait

Arctic Circle

● Nome

Yukon River

CANADA

Corpus Christi

● Laredo

Padre
Island

0	75	150 mi

0	75	150 km

Projection: Mercator

Hilo ●
Hawaii

19°N

Bering Sea

St. Lawrence
Island

St. Matthew
Island

Nunivak
Island

● Fairbanks

ALASKA

MEXICO

170°E

55°N

50°N

Attu Island

**PACIFIC
OCEAN**

180°

ALEUTIAN
ISLANDS

0	250	500 mi

0	250	500 km

Projection: Albers Equal Area

● Anchorage
● Valdez

Gulf of Alaska

Kodiak Island

● Skagway

★ Juneau

Alexander
Archipelago

55°N

CANADA

MINNESOTA
Duluth
Superior
Marquette
Sault Ste. Marie
MICHIGAN

Lake Superior

WISCONSIN
Green Bay
Madison
Milwaukee
Grand Rapids
Saginaw
Lansing
Detroit
Ann Arbor

Lake Michigan
Lake Huron

Minneapolis
St. Paul
Minnesota River
Mississippi River

IOWA
Cedar Rapids
Davenport
Des Moines
Rockford
Chicago
Gary
South Bend
Fort Wayne
Peoria
Springfield
Indianapolis

ILLINOIS
INDIANA
Illinois River

MISSOURI
Kansas City
Kansas City
St. Louis
East St. Louis
Jefferson City
Lake of the Ozarks
Springfield

OHIO
Columbus
Dayton
Cincinnati
Cleveland
Youngstown
Akron
Toledo

Lake Erie

Louisville
Evansville
Frankfort
Lexington
KENTUCKY
Ohio River
Lake Barkley

WEST VIRGINIA
Charleston

PENNSYLVANIA
Allentown
Harrisburg
Pittsburgh
Philadelphia
Susquehanna River

NEW YORK
Rochester
Syracuse
Albany
Buffalo
Lake Ontario

MAINE
Augusta
Portland
Burlington
Montpelier
VT
NH
Concord
Manchester
Boston
Worcester
Providence
MA
Springfield
Hartford
CT
RI
Bridgeport
New Haven
Yonkers
Jersey City
Newark
New York City
Trenton
Camden
NJ
Atlantic City
DE
Dover
Baltimore
MD
Annapolis
Washington, DC
Delaware Bay
Chesapeake Bay
Long Island Sound
Long Island
Cape Cod

St. Lawrence River
Lake Champlain
Hudson R.
Connecticut R.

VIRGINIA
Richmond
Newport News
Norfolk
Virginia Beach

ATLANTIC OCEAN

TENNESSEE
Nashville
Knoxville
Chattanooga
Memphis
Kentucky Lake
Kentucky River
Mississippi River

NORTH CAROLINA
Greensboro
Durham
Raleigh
Winston-Salem
Asheville
Charlotte
Cape Hatteras

ARKANSAS
Little Rock
Pine Bluff
Fayetteville
Tulsa

SOUTH CAROLINA
Greenville
Columbia
Charleston
Savannah River

MISSISSIPPI
Vicksburg
Jackson
Meridian

ALABAMA
Huntsville
Birmingham
Montgomery

GEORGIA
Atlanta
Macon
Columbus
Savannah
Sea Islands
Chattahoochee R.

LOUISIANA
Shreveport
Baton Rouge
New Orleans
Biloxi
Mobile
Pensacola
Beaumont
Houston
Galveston
Red River
Toledo Bend Reservoir
Chandeleur Islands

Tallahassee
Jacksonville
Gainesville
FLORIDA
Orlando
Tampa
St. Petersburg
Lake Okeechobee
Fort Myers
Fort Lauderdale
Miami
Cape Canaveral
Cape Sable
Florida Keys
Straits of Florida

Gulf of Mexico

BAHAMAS

40°N
35°N
25°N
70°W
75°W
80°W
85°W
90°W
95°W

N W E S

⊛ National capital
★ State capitals
• Other cities

0 100 200 mi
0 100 200 km

Projection: Albers Equal Area

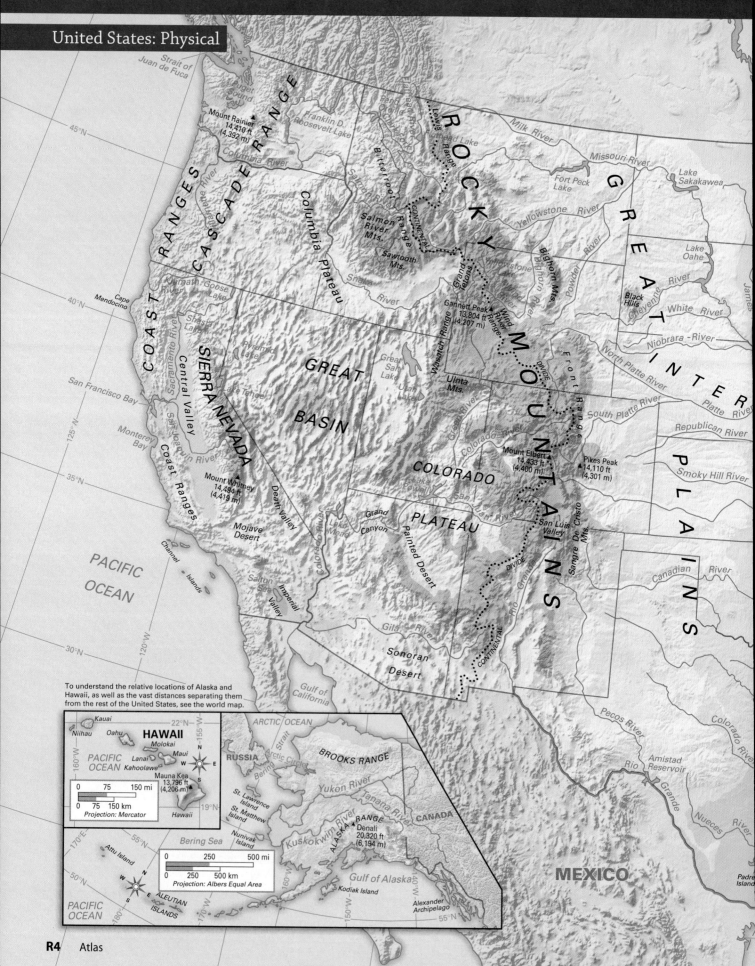

Strait of Juan de Fuca

45°N

Puget Sound

Mount Rainier
14,410 ft
(4,392 m)

Columbia River

Franklin D. Roosevelt Lake

Pend

COAST RANGES

CASCADE RANGE

Willamette River

Columbia Plateau

Bitterroot Range

Salmon River Mts.

Sawtooth Mts.

Snake River

ROCKY

Lewis Range

CONTINENTAL

Flathead Lake

Milk River

Missouri River

Fort Peck Lake

Yellowstone River

Lake Sakakawea

GREAT

Klamath 'Goose River Lake

40°N

Cape Mendocino

Shasta Lake

SIERRA NEVADA

Pyramid Lake

Lake Tahoe

Central Valley

Sacramento River

San Joaquin River

125°W

San Francisco Bay

Monterey Bay

35°N

GREAT

BASIN

Great Salt Lake

Utah Lake

Grand Tetons

Gannett Peak
13,804 ft
(4,207 m)

Wasatch Range

Uinta Mts.

Green River

Yellowstone Lake

Bighorn Mts.

Wind River Range

Powder River

DIVIDE

Front Range

Yellowstone River

MOUNTAINS

Bighorn River

North Platte River

Black Hills

Cheyenne River

Lake Oahe

White River

James River

Niobrara River

INTER

Platte River

Republican River

Lake Powell

Mount Whitney
14,494 ft
(4,419 m)

Death Valley

Mojave Desert

Lake Mead

Grand Canyon

Colorado River

Painted Desert

COLORADO

PLATEAU

San Juan River

Colorado River

Mount Elbert
14,433 ft
(4,400 m)

San Luis Valley

Sangre De Cristo Mts.

Pikes Peak
14,110 ft
(4,301 m)

South Platte River

Arkansas River

Smoky Hill River

30°N

PACIFIC

OCEAN

Channel Islands

Salton Sea

Imperial Valley

Gila River

Sonoran Desert

Gulf of California

Rio Grande

DIVIDE

CONTINENTAL

Canadian River

PLAINS

Pecos River

Colorado River

MEXICO

To understand the relative locations of Alaska and Hawaii, as well as the vast distances separating them from the rest of the United States, see the world map.

Kauai

Niihau

Oahu

HAWAII

Molokai

Maui

Lanai

Kahoolawe

PACIFIC
OCEAN

22°N

155°W

N
W E
S

Mauna Kea
13,796 ft
(4,206 m)

Hawaii

19°N

0   75   150 mi

0   75   150 km

Projection: Mercator

ARCTIC OCEAN

Arctic Circle

RUSSIA

Bering Strait

BROOKS RANGE

Yukon River

Tanana River

CANADA

St. Lawrence Island

St. Matthew Island

Nunivak Island

Kuskokwim River

ALASKA RANGE

Denali
20,320 ft
(6,194 m)

170°E

Attu Island

Bering Sea

55°N

50°N

N
W E
S

ALEUTIAN ISLANDS

180°

PACIFIC
OCEAN

0   250   500 mi

0   250   500 km

Projection: Albers Equal Area

Gulf of Alaska

Kodiak Island

Alexander Archipelago

55°N

Amistad Reservoir

Rio Grande

Nueces River

Padre Island

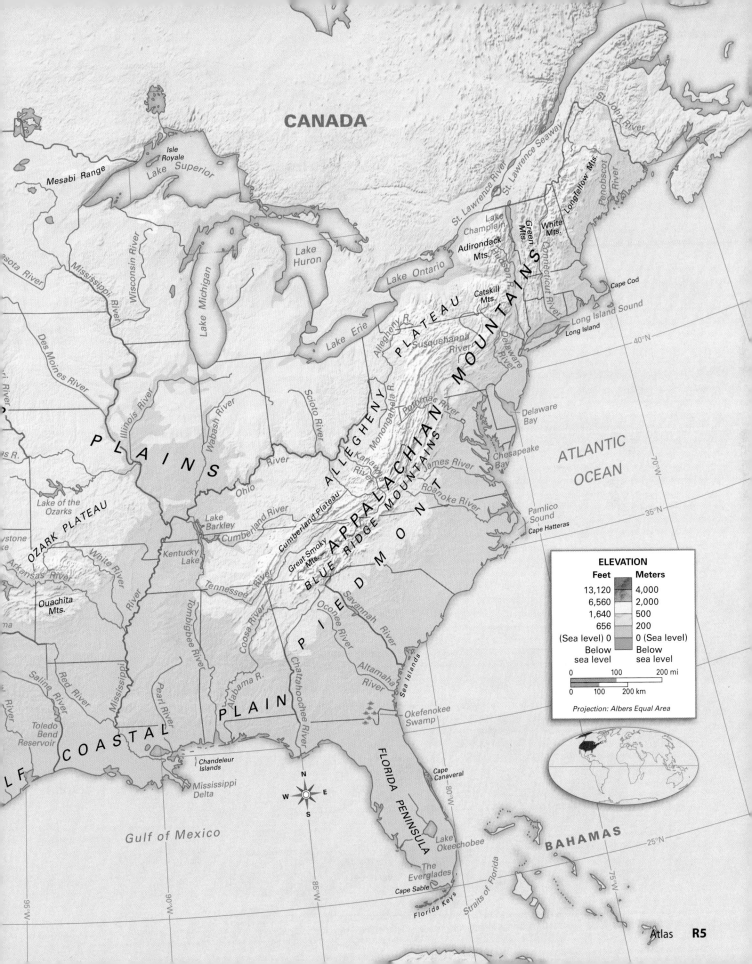

CANADA

Mesabi Range
Isle Royale
Lake Superior

Lake Huron
Lake Michigan
Lake Ontario
Lake Erie

St. Lawrence Seaway
St. Lawrence River
Lake Champlain
Adirondack Mts.
Catskill Mts.

Green Mts.
White Mts.
Longfellow Mts.
Penobscot River
St. John River

Cape Cod
Long Island Sound
Long Island

Hudson River
Connecticut River

Minnesota River
Mississippi River
Wisconsin River

P L A I N S

Des Moines River
Illinois River
Wabash River
Scioto River
Ohio River

Allegheny R.
Monongahela R.
Potomac River
Kanawha River
James River
Roanoke River

ALLEGHENY PLATEAU

Susquehanna River

APPALACHIAN MOUNTAINS

Delaware River
Delaware Bay
Chesapeake Bay

Pamlico Sound
Cape Hatteras

ATLANTIC OCEAN

40°N

70°W

35°N

ri R.
Missouri R.

Lake of the Ozarks
OZARK PLATEAU

Arkansas River
White River
Ouachita Mts.

Yellowstone
Lake

Lake Barkley
Kentucky Lake
Tennessee River
Cumberland River

Great Smoky Mts.
Cumberland Plateau
BLUE RIDGE MOUNTAINS

P I E D M O N T

Oconee River
Savannah River
Altamaha River
Sea Islands

Saline River
Red River
Mississippi River
Pearl River
Tombigbee River
Alabama R.
Coosa River
Chattahoochee River

Toledo Bend Reservoir

GULF COASTAL PLAIN

Chandeleur Islands
Mississippi Delta

Okefenokee Swamp

Cape Canaveral

FLORIDA PENINSULA

Lake Okeechobee

The Everglades
Cape Sable
Florida Keys
Straits of Florida

Gulf of Mexico

BAHAMAS

80°W
85°W
90°W
95°W
75°W

25°N

ELEVATION

Feet	Meters
13,120	4,000
6,560	2,000
1,640	500
656	200
(Sea level) 0	0 (Sea level)
Below sea level	Below sea level

0   100   200 mi
0   100   200 km

Projection: Albers Equal Area

N W E S

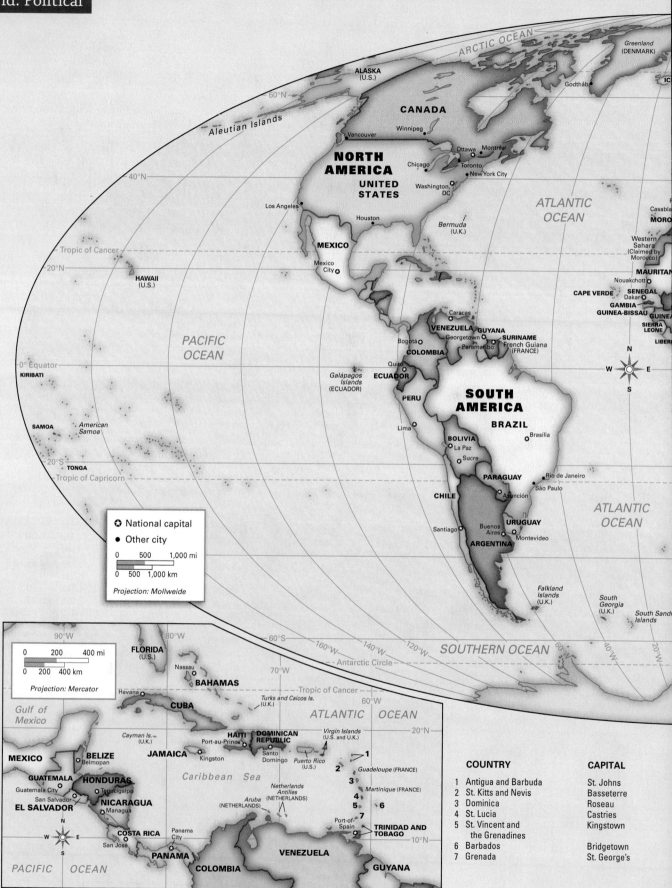

ARCTIC OCEAN

Greenland
(DENMARK)

ALASKA
(U.S.)

60°N

CANADA

IC

Godthåb

Aleutian Islands

Vancouver Winnipeg

NORTH
AMERICA

Ottawa Montréal

Chicago

Toronto

40°N

UNITED
STATES

New York City

Washington,
DC

ATLANTIC
OCEAN

Los Angeles

Houston

Bermuda
(U.K.)

Casabla

MORO

Tropic of Cancer

MEXICO

Western
Sahara
(Claimed by
Morocco)

20°N

HAWAII
(U.S.)

Mexico
City

MAURITAN

Nouakchott

CAPE VERDE

SENEGAL

Dakar

GAMBIA

Caracas

GUINEA-BISSAU

GUINEA

PACIFIC
OCEAN

VENEZUELA GUYANA

SURINAME

SIERRA
LEONE

Bogotá

Georgetown

Paramaribo

French Guiana
(FRANCE)

LIBER

0° Equator

KIRIBATI

COLOMBIA

Quito

N

Galápagos
Islands
(ECUADOR)

ECUADOR

W   E

PERU

SOUTH
AMERICA

S

SAMOA

American
Samoa

Lima

BRAZIL

Brasília

BOLIVIA

20°S

TONGA

La Paz

Sucre

Tropic of Capricorn

PARAGUAY

Rio de Janeiro

São Paulo

ATLANTIC
OCEAN

CHILE

Asunción

- ⊕ National capital

- ● Other city

URUGUAY

Santiago

0   500   1,000 mi

0   500 1,000 km

Buenos
Aires

Montevideo

ARGENTINA

Projection: Mollweide

60°S

Falkland
Islands
(U.K.)

South
Georgia
(U.K.)

160°W

140°W

120°W

SOUTHERN OCEAN

South Sandw
Islands

Antarctic Circle

70°W

Tropic of Cancer

60°W

0   200   400 mi

FLORIDA
(U.S.)

80°W

90°W

Nassau

0   200 400 km

Projection: Mercator

BAHAMAS

ATLANTIC OCEAN

20°N

Havana

Turks and Caicos Is.
(U.K.)

Gulf of
Mexico

CUBA

Cayman Is.
(U.K.)

HAITI

Virgin Islands
(U.S. and U.K.)

MEXICO

BELIZE

JAMAICA

Port-au-Prince

DOMINICAN
REPUBLIC

1

Belmopan

Kingston

Santo
Domingo

Puerto Rico
(U.S.)

Guadeloupe (FRANCE)

GUATEMALA

HONDURAS

Caribbean Sea

2

3

Martinique (FRANCE)

Guatemala City

Tegucigalpa

Netherlands
Antilles
(NETHERLANDS)

4

6

San Salvador

NICARAGUA

EL SALVADOR

Managua

Aruba
(NETHERLANDS)

5

7

Port-of-
Spain

COSTA RICA

Panama
City

San Jose

TRINIDAD AND
TOBAGO

PANAMA

N

W   E

VENEZUELA

10°N

S

PACIFIC   OCEAN

COLOMBIA

GUYANA

COUNTRY	CAPITAL
1 Antigua and Barbuda	St. Johns
2 St. Kitts and Nevis	Basseterre
3 Dominica	Roseau
4 St. Lucia	Castries
5 St. Vincent and the Grenadines	Kingstown
6 Barbados	Bridgetown
7 Grenada	St. George's

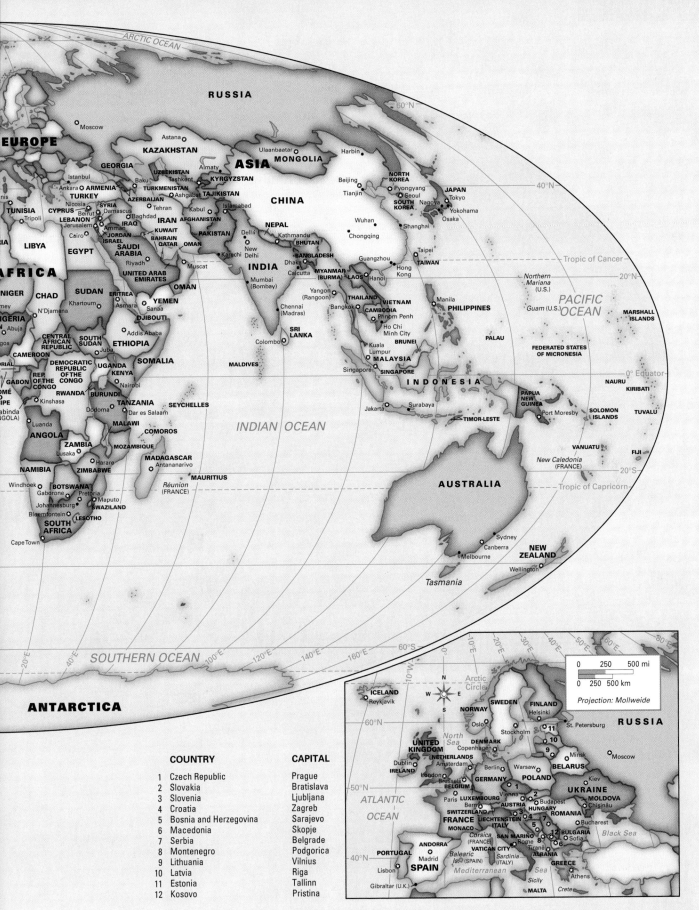

	COUNTRY	CAPITAL
1	Czech Republic	Prague
2	Slovakia	Bratislava
3	Slovenia	Ljubljana
4	Croatia	Zagreb
5	Bosnia and Herzegovina	Sarajevo
6	Macedonia	Skopje
7	Serbia	Belgrade
8	Montenegro	Podgorica
9	Lithuania	Vilnius
10	Latvia	Riga
11	Estonia	Tallinn
12	Kosovo	Pristina

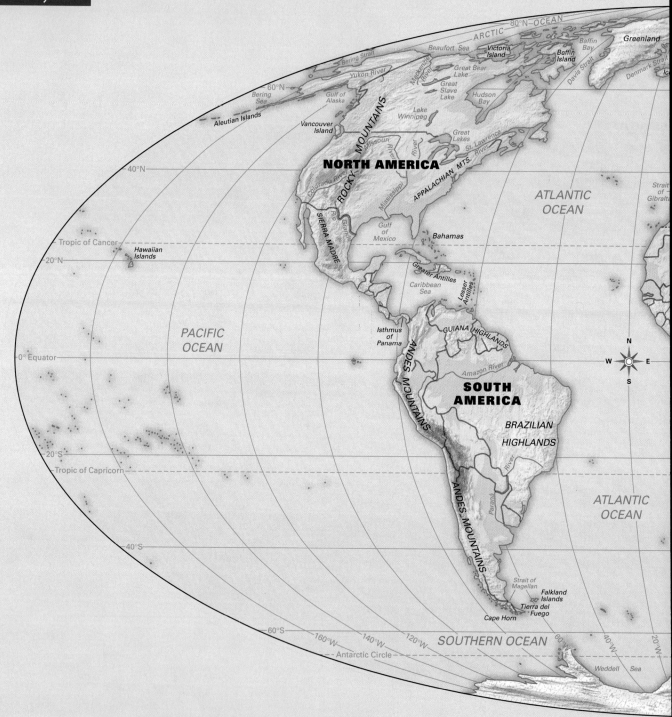

ARCTIC 80°N OCEAN
Beaufort Sea
Victoria Island
Baffin Island
Baffin Bay
Greenland
Bering Strait
Yukon River
Mackenzie River
Great Bear Lake
Davis Strait
Denmark Strait
Ic
60°N
Bering Sea
Gulf of Alaska
Great Slave Lake
Hudson Bay
Aleutian Islands
Vancouver Island
ROCKY MOUNTAINS
Missouri River
Lake Winnipeg
Great Lakes
St. Lawrence River
40°N
NORTH AMERICA
Colorado River
Mississippi River
APPALACHIAN MTS.
ATLANTIC OCEAN
Strait of Gibralt
SIERRA MADRE
Rio Grande
Gulf of Mexico
Bahamas
Tropic of Cancer
20°N
Hawaiian Islands
Greater Antilles
Caribbean Sea
Lesser Antilles
PACIFIC OCEAN
Isthmus of Panama
GUIANA HIGHLANDS
N
W E
S
0° Equator
ANDES MOUNTAINS
Amazon River
SOUTH AMERICA
BRAZILIAN HIGHLANDS
20°S
River
Tropic of Capricorn
ANDES MOUNTAINS
Paraná
ATLANTIC OCEAN
40°S
Strait of Magellan
Falkland Islands
Tierra del Fuego
Cape Horn
60°S
160°W 140°W 120°W
SOUTHERN OCEAN
60° 40°W 20°W
Antarctic Circle
Weddell Sea

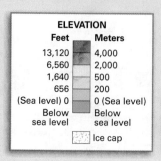

ELEVATION

Feet	Meters
13,120	4,000
6,560	2,000
1,640	500
656	200
(Sea level) 0	0 (Sea level)
Below sea level	Below sea level

Ice cap

0   1,000   2,000 mi

0   1,000   2,000 km

Projection: Mollweide

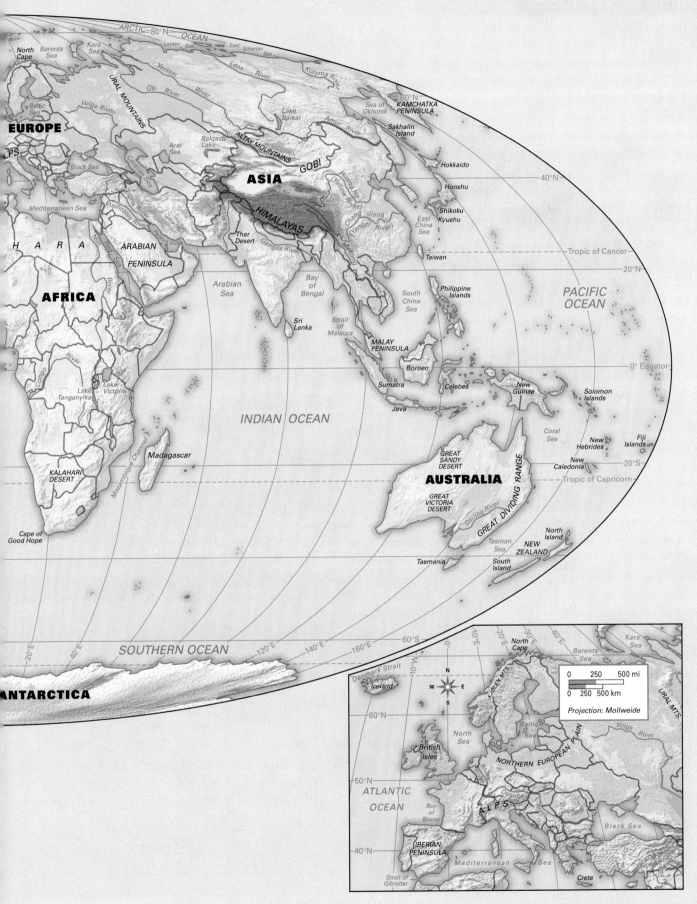

ARCTIC 80°N OCEAN

North Cape
Barents Sea
Kara Sea
Laptev Sea
East Siberian Sea

EUROPE

Baltic Sea
Volga River
URAL MOUNTAINS
Ob River
Yenisei River
Lena River
Kolyma River

Sea of Okhotsk
60°N
KAMCHATKA PENINSULA

ALPS

Black Sea
Aral Sea
Balqash Lake
ALTAY MOUNTAINS
Lake Baikal
Amur River
Sakhalin Island

Caspian Sea

ASIA
GOBI

Hokkaido

40°N

Mediterranean Sea
Tigris River
Euphrates River
Persian Gulf

ARABIAN PENINSULA

Thar Desert
Indus River
Huang He (Yellow River)
HIMALAYAS
Chang Jiang (Yangzi) River
Mekong River

Honshu
Shikoku
Kyushu
East China Sea

SAHARA

Niger River

AFRICA

Arabian Sea
Ganges River
Bay of Bengal

Taiwan
Tropic of Cancer
20°N

Congo River

Lake Tanganyika
Lake Victoria

Sri Lanka
Strait of Malacca

South China Sea

Philippine Islands

PACIFIC OCEAN

MALAY PENINSULA
Borneo

Sumatra
Celebes
Java

0° Equator

New Guinea
Solomon Islands

INDIAN OCEAN

Madagascar
Mozambique Channel

Coral Sea

New Hebrides

Fiji Islands

New Caledonia

20°S

KALAHARI DESERT

GREAT SANDY DESERT

AUSTRALIA
GREAT VICTORIA DESERT

Darling River
GREAT DIVIDING RANGE
Tropic of Capricorn

North Island

Cape of Good Hope

Tasman Sea
NEW ZEALAND

20°E
40°E
SOUTHERN OCEAN
120°E
140°E
160°E
60°S

Tasmania
South Island

ANTARCTICA

Inset map

20°E
10°E
North Cape
30°E
40°E
Kara Sea
Barents Sea

Denmark Strait
10°W
N
W E
S
Iceland
Baltic Sea
KJOLEN MTS.
URAL MTS.
Volga River

60°N

British Isles
North Sea
NORTHERN EUROPEAN PLAIN

0 250 500 mi
0 250 500 km

Projection: Mollweide

50°N
ATLANTIC OCEAN
Bay of Biscay
Rhine
Danube
ALPS
Black Sea

40°N
IBERIAN PENINSULA
Mediterranean Sea
Crete

Strait of Gibraltar

ASIA

ARCTIC OCEAN

EUROPE

+ North Pole

160°E

170°E

180°

170°W

160°W

150°W

140°W

130°W

120°W

110°W

100°W

90°W

80°W

70°N

80°N

Arctic Circle

ICELAND

Greenland
(DENMARK)

Denmark Strait

St.
Lawrence
Island

Point
Barrow

Nunivak
Island

Bering
Sea

Beaufort
Sea

Banks
Island

Queen
Elizabeth
Islands

Ellesmere Island

Baffin
Bay

ALASKA
(U.S.)

Anchorage

Kodiak
Island

Gulf of
Alaska

Victoria
Island

Great
Bear
Lake

Baffin Island

Davis Strait

Cape
Farewell

Juneau

Alexander
Archipelago

Great
Slave Lake

Southampton
Island
Coats
Island
Mansel
Island

Hudson Strait

Labrador
Sea

Queen
Charlotte
Islands

PACIFIC
OCEAN

Vancouver
Island

Edmonton

CANADA

Hudson
Bay

Vancouver

Calgary

Lake
Winnipeg

Anticosti
Island

Newfoundland

Seattle

Winnipeg

Lake
Superior

Prince
Edward
Island

Gulf of
St. Lawrence

Cape
Breton
Island

Gt. Pierre and
Miquelon (FRANCE)

Portland

Minneapolis

Lake
Michigan

Lake
Huron

Québec

Montréal

Milwaukee

Detroit

Ottawa

Toronto

Lake
Ontario

Lake Erie

Boston

Cape Cod

Salt Lake
City

Chicago

Cleveland

Columbus

New York City

ATLANTIC
OCEAN

San Francisco

San
Jose

Great
Salt
Lake

Denver

Indianapolis

St. Louis

Philadelphia

Baltimore

Washington, DC

Kansas City

Norfolk

UNITED STATES

Los Angeles
San Diego
Tijuana

Phoenix

Memphis

N
W   E
S

Atlanta

Birmingham

Jacksonville

Bermuda
(U.K.)

Dallas

Austin

San
Antonio

Houston

New Orleans

Gulf of California

Monterrey

Gulf of
Mexico

Florida
Keys

Miami

BAHAMAS

Nassau

Turks and Caicos
Islands (U.K.)

Puerto Rico (U.S.)

ST. KITTS & NEVIS

ANTIGUA &
BARBUDA

MEXICO

Havana

Straits of
Florida

CUBA

DOMINICAN
REPUBLIC

San
Juan

Guadeloupe
(FRANCE)

DOMINICA

Guadalajara

Mexico
City

Puebla

Mérida

Cayman Is.
(U.K.)

Kingston

Port-au-
Prince

HAITI

Santo
Domingo

Virgin Is.
(U.S., U.K.)

Martinique (FRANCE)

BARBADOS

ST. LUCIA

Belmopan

JAMAICA

ST. VINCENT AND
THE GRENADINES

Netherlands
Antilles
(NETHERLANDS)

GRENADA

BELIZE

Caribbean Sea

GUATEMALA

HONDURAS

Tegucigalpa

Aruba (NETHERLANDS)

TRINIDAD AND TOBAGO

Guatemala City

NICARAGUA

San Salvador

Managua

Panama
Canal

EL SALVADOR

San José

Panama City

COSTA
RICA

PANAMA

SOUTH
AMERICA

Tropic of Cancer

Equator

10°W

0°

10°E

20°W

30°W

40°W

50°W

60°N

50°N

40°N

30°N

20°N

10°N

0°

North Pole

⊛ National capital
• Other city

0   300   600 mi
0   300   600 km

Projection: Azimuthal Equal-Area

North America: Physical

ARCTIC OCEAN

North Pole

POLAR ICE PACK

ASIA

EUROPE

Bering Strait

St. Lawrence Island

Bering Sea

Nunivak Island

Beaufort Sea

Queen Elizabeth Islands

Ellesmere Island

Greenland

Denmark Strait

Banks Island

Baffin Bay

BROOKS RANGE

Yukon River

ALASKA RANGE

Denali 20,320 ft (6,194 m)

YUKON PLATEAU

Victoria Island

Baffin Island

Cape Farewell

Davis Strait

Kodiak Island

Gulf of Alaska

Mackenzie River

Great Bear Lake

Alexander Archipelago

Queen Charlotte Islands

ROCKY

Peace River

Great Slave Lake

Lake Athabasca

Southampton Island

Hudson Strait

Labrador Sea

PACIFIC OCEAN

Vancouver Island

Mount Rainier 14,410 ft (4,392 m)

CASCADE RANGE

COAST RANGE

Fraser River

Athabasca River

CANADIAN

Coats Island

Mansel Island

Hudson Bay

SHIELD

Anticosti Island

Newfoundland

Cape Mendocino

Columbia River

MOUNTAINS

Saskatchewan River

Nelson River

Lake Winnipeg

Prince Edward Island

Gulf of St. Lawrence

Cape Breton Island

St. Lawrence River

Snake River

SIERRA NEVADA

CENTRAL VALLEY

GREAT BASIN

DEATH VALLEY

Mount Whitney 14,494 ft (4,419 m)

Great Salt Lake

COLORADO PLATEAU

GREAT PLAINS

BLACK HILLS

Missouri River

Platte River

Lake Superior

Lake Michigan

Lake Huron

Lake Erie

Lake Ontario

APPALACHIAN MOUNTAINS

Cape Cod

Long Island

ATLANTIC OCEAN

Colorado River

INTERIOR PLAINS

Mississippi River

Ohio River

Arkansas River

OZARK PLATEAU

Cumberland R.

Tennessee River

PIEDMONT

ATLANTIC COASTAL PLAIN

Cape Hatteras

Bermuda

Guadalupe Island

BAJA CALIFORNIA

Gulf of California

SIERRA MADRE OCCIDENTAL

Red River

Brazos River

Rio Grande

GULF COASTAL PLAIN

SIERRA MADRE ORIENTAL

FLORIDA PENINSULA

Cape Canaveral

Tropic of Cancer

Gulf of Mexico

Florida Keys

Straits of Florida

Bahamas

Cuba

Popocatépetl 17,887 ft (5,452 m)

YUCATÁN PENINSULA

Greater Antilles

Jamaica

Hispaniola

Puerto Rico

Lesser Antilles

Caribbean Sea

Trinidad

SIERRA MADRE DEL SUR

CENTRAL AMERICA

Lake Nicaragua

ISTHMUS OF PANAMA

Equator

SOUTH AMERICA

Arctic Circle

ELEVATION

Feet	Meters
13,120	4,000
6,560	2,000
1,640	500
656	200
(Sea level) 0	0 (Sea level)
Below sea level	Below sea level

Ice cap

0   300   600 mi

0   300   600 km

Projection: Azimuthal Equal Area

CENTRAL
AMERICA

Caribbean Sea

Barranquilla
Cartagena

Caracas ✪

VENEZUELA

Georgetown ✪
Paramaribo

ATLANTIC
OCEAN

Medellín ●

Bogotá ✪

GUYANA

Cayenne

COLOMBIA

Cali ●

SURINAME

French
Guiana
(FRANCE)

*Malpelo
Island*
(COLOMBIA)

Quito ✪
ECUADOR

0° Equator

0° Equator

Guayaquil ●

Belém ●

*Galápagos
Islands*
(ECUADOR)

PERU

Trujillo ●

BRAZIL

Recife ●

PACIFIC
OCEAN

Callao ●✪ Lima

*Lake
Titicaca*

Salvador ●

Arequipa ●

✪ La Paz

Brasília ✪

*Lake
Poopó*

BOLIVIA

✪ Sucre

Belo Horizonte ●

PARAGUAY

São Paulo ●

Rio de Janeiro ●

Tropic of Capricorn

Asunción ✪

Curitiba ●

*Tropic of
Capricorn*

*San Ambrosio
Island*
(CHILE)

San Félix Island
(CHILE)

Pôrto Alegre ●

CHILE

Córdoba ●

*Juan Fernández
Islands*
(CHILE)

Rosario ●

URUGUAY

Valparaíso ✪
Santiago

Buenos Aires ✪

✪ Montevideo

ATLANTIC
OCEAN

ARGENTINA

| ✪ | National capital |
| ● | Other city |

0   250   500 mi

0   250   500 km

Projection: Azimuthal Equal-Area

*Strait of
Magellan*

*Falkland
Islands* (U.K.)

*Tierra del
Fuego*

*South Georgia
Island*
(U.K.)

ELEVATION

Feet	Meters
13,120	4,000
6,560	2,000
1,640	500
656	200
(Sea level) 0	0 (Sea level)
Below sea level	Below sea level

0 250 500 mi
0 250 500 km

Projection: Azimuthal Equal Area

Europe: Political

ASIA

URAL MOUNTAINS

RUSSIA

Nizhny Novgorod

Moscow

Barents Sea

White Sea

SOUTHWEST ASIA

Caspian Sea

Black Sea

St. Petersburg

FINLAND

Helsinki

Gulf of Bothnia

ESTONIA
Tallinn

LATVIA
Riga

LITHUANIA
Vilnius

RUSSIA

BELARUS
Minsk

Kiev
UKRAINE

MOLDOVA
Chişinău

ROMANIA
Bucharest

BULGARIA
Sofia

Rhodes

Crete

Aegean Sea

Athens

GREECE

SWEDEN

Stockholm

Göteborg

Baltic Sea

POLAND
Warsaw

Kraków

SLOVAKIA
Bratislava

HUNGARY
Budapest

SERBIA
Belgrade

KOSOVO
Pristina

MACEDONIA
Skopje

ALBANIA
Tirana

Podgorica
MONTENEGRO

NORWAY

Oslo

Bergen

DENMARK
Copenhagen

Hamburg

Berlin

Dresden

CZECH REPUBLIC
Prague

Vienna
AUSTRIA

SLOVENIA
Ljubljana

CROATIA
Zagreb

BOSNIA AND HERZEGOVINA
Sarajevo

San Marino
SAN MARINO

ITALY
Rome

VATICAN CITY

Naples

Sicily

MALTA
Valletta

ARCTIC OCEAN

North Cape

Arctic Circle

GERMANY

Cologne
Bonn

Munich

LUXEMBOURG
Luxembourg

SWITZERLAND
Bern

LIECHTENSTEIN
Vaduz

Lake Geneva

Milan

MONACO
Monaco

Corsica (FRANCE)

Sardinia (ITALY)

Adriatic Sea

Mediterranean Sea

North Sea

THE NETHERLANDS
Amsterdam

BELGIUM
Brussels

Paris

FRANCE

Lyon

Marseille

PYRENEES

ANDORRA
Andorra la Vella

Barcelona

Balearic Islands (SPAIN)

Shetland Islands

Faeroe Islands (DENMARK)

UNITED KINGDOM

SCOTLAND
Edinburgh

NORTHERN IRELAND
Belfast

IRELAND
Dublin

WALES

ENGLAND
Liverpool
London

British Isles

English Channel

Channel Islands (U.K.)

Bay of Biscay

SPAIN
Madrid

Valencia

Seville

Gibraltar (U.K.)

Strait of Gibraltar

PORTUGAL
Lisbon

ICELAND
Reykjavik

ATLANTIC OCEAN

AFRICA

70°N

60°N

50°N

40°N

Arctic Circle

20°W

10°W

0°

10°E

20°E

30°E

N
W E
S

○ National capital
● Other city

0   150   300 mi
0   150   300 km

Projection: Azimuthal Equal-Area

Europe: Physical

ASIA

URAL MOUNTAINS

Pechora River

Kama River

Ural River

Volga River

Caspian Sea

Mt. Elbrus 18,510 ft (5,642 m)

CAUCASUS MTS.

SOUTHWEST ASIA

EUROPEAN PLAIN

NORTHERN

Don River

Sea of Azov

CRIMEAN PENINSULA

Black Sea

Dnipro

Rybinsk Reservoir

Dvina River

Lake Onega

Lake Ladoga

White Sea

KOLA PENINSULA

Barents Sea

North Cape

70°N

50°E

40°E

30°E

20°E

10°E

0°

ARCTIC OCEAN

KJØLEN MOUNTAINS

Norwegian Sea

Gulf of Bothnia

Gulf of Finland

PLAINS

Daugava R.

BALTIC

Baltic Sea

Vistula River

Oder River

Elba River

Lake Vänern

Lake Vättern

Kattegat

Skagerrak

North Sea

ATLANTIC OCEAN

Arctic Circle

Iceland

Faeroe Islands

Shetland Islands

Orkney Islands

Hebrides

British Isles

Irish Sea

PENNINES

Thames River

English Channel

Seine River

Loire River

Garonne River

Bay of Biscay

Cape Finisterre

Rhine River

Mont Blanc 15,781 ft (4,810 m)

Lake Geneva

Rhône River

A L P S

APENNINES

Tiber River

PYRENEES

Ebro River

IBERIAN PENINSULA

Douro River

Tagus River

Guadiana River

Guadalquivir River

Strait of Gibraltar

AFRICA

Danube River

Nistru River

CARPATHIAN MTS.

TRANSYLVANIAN ALPS

Danube

Sava River

DINARIC ALPS

Adriatic Sea

Corsica

Sardinia

Balearic Islands

Tyrrhenian Sea

Sicily

Malta

Mediterranean Sea

BALKAN PENINSULA

Sea of Marmara

Aegean Sea

Rhodes

Crete

N E S W

ELEVATION

Feet	Meters
13,120	4,000
6,560	2,000
1,640	500
656	200
(Sea level) 0	0 (Sea level)
Below sea level	Below sea level

Ice cap

300 mi
150
0

300 km
150
0

Projection: Azimuthal Equal Area

10°W

20°W

70°N

60°N

50°N

40°N

30°N

10°W

20°W

Projection: Two-Point Equidistant

National capitals
Other cities

750 mi
375
0

750 km
375
0

PACIFIC OCEAN

Equator

New Guinea

AUSTRALIA

Arafura Sea

TIMOR-LESTE

Dili

PHILIPPINES

Manila

Celebes Sea

INDONESIA

Java Sea   Ujung Pandang

Surabaya

Jakarta

Bandung

Medan

BRUNEI

Bandar Seri Begawan

MALAYSIA

Kuala Lumpur

SINGAPORE

Singapore

South China Sea

Hainan (CHINA)

VIETNAM

Ho Chi Minh City

Gulf of Thailand

CAMBODIA

Phnom Penh

LAOS

Vientiane

THAILAND

Bangkok

Macao

Hong Kong

Guangzhou

Chongqing

Chengdu

Wuhan

Nanjing

CHINA

Beijing

Yellow Sea

Qingdao

Dalian

Fushun

Harbin

Shanghai

East China Sea

Ryukyu Islands (JAPAN)

Taipei

TAIWAN

Tropic of Cancer

Nagasaki

Hiroshima

Pusan

Osaka

Kyoto

JAPAN

Yokohama

Tokyo

Sapporo

Sakhalin Island

Kuril Islands (RUSSIA)

Vladivostok

SOUTH KOREA

Seoul

NORTH KOREA

Pyongyang

Aleutian Islands

Bering Sea

Sea of Okhotsk

Yakutsk

Lake Baykal

Irkutsk

Ulaanbaatar

MONGOLIA

RUSSIA

Novosibirsk

Omsk

URAL MOUNTAINS

Yekaterinburg

Chelyabinsk

Astana

KAZAKHSTAN

Lake Balkhash

Aral Sea

Almaty

Bishkek

KYRGYZSTAN

Tashkent

UZBEKISTAN

TAJIKISTAN

Dushanbe

Ashgabat

TURKMENISTAN

Kabul

AFGHANISTAN

Islamabad

PAKISTAN

Lahore

Karachi

Delhi

New Delhi

Jaipur

Ahmadabad

Mumbai (Bombay)

Lakshadweep Islands (INDIA)

Arabian Sea

INDIA

Bangalore

Chennai (Madras)

Bay of Bengal

Kolkata (Calcutta)

NEPAL

Kathmandu

BHUTAN

Thimphu

BANGLADESH

Dhaka

MYANMAR (BURMA)

Mandalay

Yangon (Rangoon)

Andaman Islands (INDIA)

Andaman Sea

Nicobar Islands (INDIA)

SRI LANKA

Colombo

MALDIVES

Male

INDIAN OCEAN

Moscow

EUROPE

RUSSIA

Black Sea

Istanbul

Ankara

Izmir

TURKEY

GEORGIA

Tbilisi

ARMENIA

Yerevan

AZERBAIJAN

Baku

Caspian Sea

Tehran

IRAN

Shiraz

Mosul

Baghdad

IRAQ

Basra

KUWAIT

Kuwait City

Damascus

SYRIA

LEBANON

Beirut

CYPRUS

Nicosia

ISRAEL

Tel Aviv

Jerusalem

Amman

JORDAN

Mecca

Jidda

Red Sea

SAUDI ARABIA

Riyadh

BAHRAIN

Manama

QATAR

Doha

UNITED ARAB EMIRATES

Abu Dhabi

Persian Gulf

OMAN

Masqat (Muscat)

YEMEN

Sanaa

Gulf of Aden

Socotra (YEMEN)

AFRICA

Mediterranean Sea

Barents Sea

Kara Sea

North Pole

Arctic Circle

Asia: Physical

ELEVATION

Feet	Meters
13,120	4,000
6,560	2,000
1,640	500
656	200
0 (Sea level)	0 (Sea level)
Below sea level	Below sea level

Ice cap

Projection: Two-Point Equidistant

0   375   750 mi
0   375   750 km

PACIFIC OCEAN

AUSTRALIA

Maoke Mountains

New Guinea

Arafura Sea

Banda Sea

Molucca B.

Celebes Sea

Celebes

Java Sea

Borneo

Bangka

Java

Sumatra

Mentawai Islands

Philippines

Mindanao

Luzon

Luzon Strait

Hainan

South China Sea

Taiwan

Okinawa

Ryukyu Islands

East China Sea

Tropic of Cancer

Bohea Hills

Yellow Sea

North China Plain

Sea of Japan (East Sea)

Hokkaido

Honshu

Shikoku

Kyushu

Korea Strait

Aleutian Islands

KAMCHATKA PENINSULA

Bering Sea

CENTRAL RANGE

Sakhalin Island

Kuril Islands

Sea of Okhotsk

KOLYMA MTS.

CHERSKY RANGE

STANOVOY MOUNTAINS

Amur River

GREATER KHINGAN RANGE

VERKHOYANSKY RANGE

Aldan River

Lena River

YABLONOVY RANGE

Shilka River

MONGOLIAN PLATEAU

G O B I

QIN LING

(Yellow River)

Huang He

Xi River

Hong Kong

INDOCHINA PENINSULA

Gulf of Tonkin

Mekong River

Chao Phraya River

MALAY PENINSULA

Gulf of Thailand

Andaman Sea

Nicobar Islands

Andaman Islands

Wrangel Island

New Siberian Islands

North Land

TAYMYR PENINSULA

CENTRAL SIBERIAN PLATEAU

S I B E R I A

Lower Tunguska River

Angara River

Yenisey River

SAYAN MOUNTAINS

ALTAY MOUNTAINS

KUNLUN MOUNTAINS

PLATEAU OF TIBET

Mount Everest 29,035 ft (8,850 m)

Brahmaputra River

H I M A L A Y A S

Nu River

Chang (Yangtze) River

Salween River

Bay of Bengal

Andaman Islands

Sri Lanka

North Pole

Franz Josef Land

Novaya Zemlya

Kara Sea

Laptev Sea

Ob River

Irtysh River

WEST SIBERIAN PLAIN

KAZAKH UPLANDS

Balqash Lake

TIAN SHAN

TARIM BASIN

TAKLIMAKAN DESERT

HINDU KUSH

Indus River

Sutlej River

Ganges River

INDO-GANGETIC PLAIN

THAR DESERT

DECCAN PLATEAU

Godavari River

EASTERN GHATS

WESTERN GHATS

Barents Sea

URAL MOUNTAINS

Ishim River

Tobol River

Syr Darya

TURAN LOWLAND

KYZYL KUM

Amu Darya

KARA KUM

Aral Sea

USTIURT PLATEAU

Caspian Sea

GREAT SALT DESERT

ZAGROS MTS.

Persian Gulf

Gulf of Oman

Arabian Sea

Lakshadweep Islands

Maldives

INDIAN OCEAN

EUROPE

Black Sea

Bosporus

CAUCASUS MTS.

Mount Ararat 16,945 ft (5,165 m)

ANATOLIAN PLATEAU

Cyprus

Mediterranean Sea

Tigris River

Euphrates River

SYRIAN DESERT

AN-NAFUD

SINAI PENINSULA

Red Sea

RUB' AL-KHALI

Socotra Island

Gulf of Aden

AFRICA

Equator

Africa: Political

EUROPE

SOUTHWEST ASIA

Mediterranean Sea

Strait of Gibraltar

Azores (PORTUGAL)

Madeira (PORTUGAL)

Canary Islands (SPAIN)

MOROCCO

Casablanca Rabat

Algiers Tunis

TUNISIA

Tripoli

Alexandria

Giza Cairo

El Aaiún

WESTERN SAHARA (Claimed by Morocco)

Tropic of Cancer

ALGERIA

LIBYA

EGYPT

Red Sea

CAPE VERDE

Praia

MAURITANIA

Nouakchott

MALI

NIGER

CHAD

SUDAN

Khartoum

ERITREA

Asmara

Gulf of Aden

SENEGAL

Dakar

GAMBIA

Banjul

Bamako

Niamey

N'Djamena

Lake Chad

DJIBOUTI

Djibouti

GUINEA-BISSAU

Bissau

BURKINA FASO

Ouagadougou

NIGERIA

Abuja

ETHIOPIA

Addis Ababa

GUINEA

Conakry

Freetown

CÔTE D'IVOIRE

BENIN

TOGO

GHANA

Yamoussoukro

Lomé

Lagos

CENTRAL AFRICAN REPUBLIC

SOUTH SUDAN

SOMALIA

SIERRA LEONE

Monrovia

Abidjan

Accra

Porto-Novo

Bangui

Juba

LIBERIA

Gulf of Guinea

Malabo

CAMEROON

Yaoundé

UGANDA

Kampala

KENYA

Mogadishu

EQUATORIAL GUINEA

SÃO TOMÉ AND PRÍNCIPE

São Tomé

REPUBLIC OF THE CONGO

Libreville

GABON

Kisangani

RWANDA

Kigali

Nairobi

0° Equator

INDIAN OCEAN

Victoria

SEYCHELLES

Brazzaville

Kinshasa

DEMOCRATIC REPUBLIC OF THE CONGO

Bujumbura

BURUNDI

Lake Victoria

Mombasa

Pemba

TANZANIA

Dodoma

Zanzibar

Dar es Salaam

Lake Tanganyika

CABINDA (ANGOLA)

ATLANTIC OCEAN

Luanda

Lubumbashi

Lake Malawi (Nyasa)

COMOROS

Moroni

St. Helena (U.K.)

ANGOLA

ZAMBIA

Lusaka

MALAWI

Lilongwe

MOZAMBIQUE

Antananarivo

MAURITIUS

MADAGASCAR

Port Louis

Harare

ZIMBABWE

Bulawayo

Réunion (FRANCE)

Tropic of Capricorn

NAMIBIA

Windhoek

BOTSWANA

Gaborone

Pretoria

Maputo

Mbabane

SWAZILAND

Johannesburg

Bloemfontein

Maseru

LESOTHO

SOUTH AFRICA

Cape Town

☆ National capital

• Other city

0   250   500 mi

0   250   500 km

Projection: Azimuthal Equal-Area

EUROPE

SOUTHWEST ASIA

Azores

Madeira Islands

Strait of Gibraltar

ATLAS MOUNTAINS

Mediterranean Sea

Gulf of Sidra

Suez Canal

QATTARA DEPRESSION

Canary Islands

Cape Blanc

Tropic of Cancer

SAHARA

AHAGGAR MOUNTAINS

EL DJOUF

AIR MTS

TIBESTI MOUNTAINS

LIBYAN DESERT

Nile River

Lake Nasser

NUBIAN DESERT

Red Sea

Cape Verde Islands

Senegal R.

Niger River

SAHEL

SUDAN

CHAD BASIN

Lake Chad

Blue Nile

White Nile

Lake Tana

Gulf of Aden

Cape Verde

White Volta R.

Black Volta R.

FOUTA DJALLON

Benue River

Lake Volta

ADAMAWA MTS.

SUDAN BASIN

ETHIOPIAN HIGHLANDS

HORN OF AFRICA

SOMALI PENINSULA

Cape Palmas

Gulf of Guinea

Ubangi River

Congo River

RIFT VALLEY

Lake Turkana

Mount Kenya 17,058 ft (5,199 m)

Cape Lopez

CONGO BASIN

Lake Albert

Lake Edward

Lake Victoria

Lake Kivu

WESTERN RIFT VALLEY

EASTERN RIFT VALLEY

Mount Kilimanjaro 19,340 ft (5,895 m)

INDIAN OCEAN

0° Equator

Kasai River

MITUMBA MOUNTAINS

SERENGETI PLAIN

MASAI STEPPE

Zanzibar

Seychelles

Lake Tanganyika

Ascension

ATLANTIC OCEAN

Cuanza River

Lake Mweru

Lake Rukwa

Lake Malawi (Nyasa)

Cape Delgado

Comoro Islands

Lake Kariba

Zambezi River

Mozambique Channel

Madagascar

Mauritius

Okavango Delta

Victoria Falls

Réunion

NAMIB DESERT

KALAHARI BASIN

KALAHARI DESERT

Limpopo River

Tropic of Capricorn

Orange River

Vaal River

GREAT KARROO

DRAKENSBERG MOUNTAINS

Cape of Good Hope

ELEVATION

Feet	Meters
13,120	4,000
6,560	2,000
1,640	500
656	200
(Sea level) 0	0 (Sea level)
Below sea level	Below sea level

0   250   500 mi
0   250   500 km

Projection: Azimuthal Equal-Area

The Pacific: Political

NORTH AMERICA

ASIA

NORTH PACIFIC OCEAN

SOUTH PACIFIC OCEAN

INDIAN OCEAN

Philippine Sea

South China Sea

Coral Sea

Arafura Sea

Timor Sea

Tasman Sea

Tropic of Cancer

Tropic of Capricorn

0° Equator

International Date Line

30°N
15°N
15°S
30°S
45°S

180°
165°W
150°W
135°W
120°W
165°E
150°E
135°E
120°E

MICRONESIA
MELANESIA
POLYNESIA

Hawaiian Islands
Hawaii (U.S.)

Midway Island (U.S.)

Johnston Island (U.S.)

Kingman Reef (U.S.)
Palmyra Island (U.S.)
Washington Island
Fanning Island

Jarvis I. (U.S.)

Howland I. (U.S.)
Baker I. (U.S.)

Starbuck Island

KIRIBATI
Phoenix Islands

McKean I.
Gardner I.

Manihiki Island

Cook Islands (NEW ZEALAND)
Rarotonga Island

Marquesas Islands (FRANCE)

Tuamotu Archipelago (FRANCE)

French Polynesia

Society Islands (FRANCE)
Papeete
Tahiti (FRANCE)

Tubuai Islands (FRANCE)

Rapa Island (FRANCE)

Pitcairn (U.K.)
Pitcairn Island

Ducie Island

Easter Island (CHILE)

Tokelau (N.Z.)
American Samoa
Pago Pago

SAMOA
Apia

Niue (N.Z.)

TONGA
Nuku'alofa

Wallis & Futuna (FR.)

TUVALU
Funafuti

FIJI
Suva

MARSHALL ISLANDS
Kwajalein Island
Eniwetok I.
Majuro

Wake Island (U.S.)

Tarawa
Gilbert Islands

NAURU

SOLOMON ISLANDS
Honiara
Guadalcanal I.

VANUATU
Espíritu Santo
Malekula I.
Port Vila

New Caledonia (FRANCE)
Noumea

Loyalty Islands (FRANCE)

Norfolk Island (AUSTRALIA)

Kermadec Islands (N.Z.)

Chatham Islands (N.Z.)

NEW ZEALAND
North Island
Auckland
Wellington
South Island
Christchurch

Bounty Islands (N.Z.)

Auckland Islands (NEW ZEALAND)

FEDERATED STATES OF MICRONESIA
Palikir
Truk Is.

Northern Marianas (U.S.)

Bonin Islands (JAPAN)
Volcano Islands (JAPAN)

Guam (U.S.)
Agana

PALAU
Melekeok

PAPUA NEW GUINEA
Port Moresby
Bismarck Archipelago
New Guinea

AUSTRALIA
Brisbane
Sydney
Canberra
Melbourne
Adelaide
Hobart
Perth
Darwin

Christmas Island (AUSTRALIA)

Legend
✪ National capital
● Other city

1,000 mi
1,000 km
500
0

Projection: Azimuthal Equal-Area

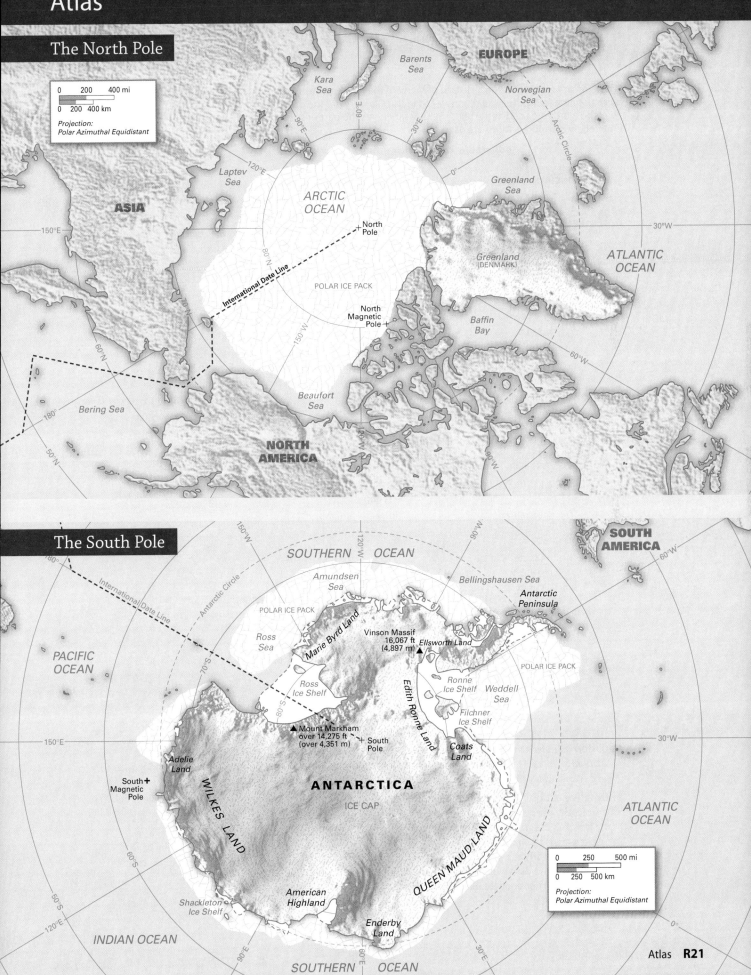

Atlas

The North Pole

0 200 400 mi
0 200 400 km

Projection:
Polar Azimuthal Equidistant

EUROPE

Barents Sea

Kara Sea

Norwegian Sea

60°E

90°E

30°E

Arctic Circle

Laptev Sea

ARCTIC OCEAN

+ North Pole

Greenland Sea

30°W

120°E

ASIA

80°N

POLAR ICE PACK

Greenland (DENMARK)

ATLANTIC OCEAN

150°E

International Date Line

North Magnetic Pole +

150°W

Baffin Bay

60°N

60°W

180°

Bering Sea

Beaufort Sea

90°W

50°N

NORTH AMERICA

The South Pole

SOUTH AMERICA

180°

SOUTHERN   OCEAN

120°W

90°W

60°W

International Date Line

150°W

Antarctic Circle

Amundsen Sea

Bellingshausen Sea

Antarctic Peninsula

POLAR ICE PACK

PACIFIC OCEAN

Ross Sea

70°S

Marie Byrd Land

▲ Vinson Massif 16,067 ft (4,897 m)

Ellsworth Land

POLAR ICE PACK

30°W

80°S

Ross Ice Shelf

Ronne Ice Shelf

Weddell Sea

150°E

▲ Mount Markham over 14,275 ft (over 4,351 m)

+ South Pole

Edith Ronne Land

Filchner Ice Shelf

Adelie Land

South + Magnetic Pole

WILKES LAND

ANTARCTICA

ICE CAP

Coats Land

ATLANTIC OCEAN

60°S

QUEEN MAUD LAND

30°W

Shackleton Ice Shelf

American Highland

50°S

0 250 500 mi
0 250 500 km

Projection:
Polar Azimuthal Equidistant

120°E

Enderby Land

INDIAN OCEAN

90°E

SOUTHERN   OCEAN

60°E

30°E

0°

English and Spanish Glossary

The Glossary is an alphabetical listing of many of the key terms from the modules, along with their meanings. The definitions listed in the Glossary are the ones that apply to the way the words are used in the text. The Glossary gives the part of speech of each word. The following abbreviations are used:

adj. = **adjective**   *n.* = **noun**   *v.* = **verb**

PRONUNCIATION KEY

Symbol	Examples	Symbol	Examples	Symbol	Examples
ă	at, gas	m	man, seem	v	van, save
ā	ape, day	n	night, mitten	w	web, twice
ä	father, barn	ng	sing, anger	y	yard, lawyer
âr	fair, dare	ŏ	odd, not	z	zoo, reason
b	bell, table	ō	open, road, grow	zh	treasure, garage
ch	chin, lunch	ô	awful, bought, horse	ə	awake, even, pencil,
d	dig, bored	oi	coin, boy		pilot, focus
ĕ	egg, ten	o͞o	look, full		
ē	evil, see, meal	o͞o ē	root, glue, through	ər	perform, letter
f	fall, laugh, phrase	ou	out, cow		
g	gold, big	p	pig, cap	**Sounds in Foreign Words**	
h	hit, inhale	r	rose, star	KH	*German* ich, auch;
hw	white, everywhere	s	sit, face		*Scottish* loch
ĭ	inch, fit	sh	she, mash	N	*French* entre, bon, fin
ī	idle, my, tried	t	tap, hopped	œ	*French* feu, coeur;
îr	dear, here	th	thing, with		*German* schön
j	jar, gem, badge	*th*	then, other	ü	*French* utile, rue;
k	keep, cat, luck	ŭ	up, nut		*German* grün
l	load, rattle	ûr	fur, earn, bird, worm		

STRESS MARKS

′ This mark indicates that the preceding syllable receives the primary stress. For example, in the world *lineage,* the first syllable is stressed: [lĭn′ē-ĭj].

ˊ This mark is used only in words in which more than one syllable is stressed. It indicates that the preceding syllable is stressed, but somewhat more weakly than the syllable receiving the primary stress. In the word *consumerism,* for example, the second syllable receives the primary stress, and the fourth syllable receives a weaker stress: [kən-so͞o′mə-rĭzˊəm].

Adapted from *The American Heritage Dictionary of the English Language, Fourth Edition;* Copyright © 2000 by Houghton Mifflin Company. Used with the permission of Houghton Mifflin Company.

A

abolition *n.* movement to end slavery. (p. 76)
 abolición *s.* movimiento para acabar con la esclavitud. (pág. 76)

affirmative action *n.* a policy that seeks to correct the effects of past discrimination by favoring the groups who were previously disadvantaged. (pp. 745, 852)
 acción afirmativa *s.* medidas para corregir los efectos de la discriminación anterior; favorecen a grupos que estaban en desventaja. (pág. 745, 852)

Agent Orange *n.* a toxic leaf-killing chemical sprayed by U.S. planes in Vietnam to expose Vietcong hideouts. (p. 791)
 Agente Naranja *s.* químico tóxico exfoliante que fumigaron las tropas estadounidenses en Vietnam para poner al descubierto refugios del Vietcong. (pág. 791)

Agricultural Adjustment Act (AAA) *n.* a law enacted in 1933 to raise crop prices by paying farmers to leave a certain amount of their land unplanted, thus lowering production. (p. 444)

Ley de Ajustes Agrícolas *s.* ley de 1933 que elevó el precio de las cosechas al pagarle a los granjeros para que no cultivaran cierta porción de sus tierras, reduciendo así la producción. (pág. 444)

AIDS (acquired immune deficiency syndrome) *n.* a disease caused by a virus that weakens the immune system, making the body prone to infections and otherwise rare forms of cancer. (p. 861)
SIDA (síndrome de inmunodeficiencia adquirida) *s.* enfermedad causada por un virus que debilita el sistema inmunológico y hace que el cuerpo sea vulnerable a infecciones y formas poco comunes de cáncer. (pág. 861)

Alliance for Progress *n.* a U.S. foreign-aid program of the 1960s, providing economic and technical assistance to Latin American countries. (p. 681)
Alianza para el Progreso *s.* programa de los sesenta para ofrecer ayuda económica a los países latinoamericanos. (pág. 681)

Allies *n.* **1.** in World War I, the group of nations—originally consisting of Great Britain, France, and Russia and later joined by the United States, Italy, and others—that opposed the Central powers. (p. 315). **2.** in World War II, the group of nations—including Great Britain, the Soviet Union, and the United States— that opposed the Axis powers. (p. 513)
Aliados *s.* **1.** en la Primera Guerra Mundial, naciones aliadas en un tratado contra Alemania y las otras Potencias Centrales; originalmente Gran Bretaña, Francia y Rusia; más adelante se unieron Estados Unidos, Japón, Italia y otros. (pág. 315). **2.** en la Segunda Guerra Mundial, naciones asociadas contra el Eje, en particular Gran Bretaña, la Unión Soviética y Estados Unidos. (pág. 513)

Al-Qaeda [ăl-kā′də] *n.* a global militant Islamist organization. (p. 893)
Al-Qaeda *s.* organización mundial islámica combativa. (pág. 893)

American Expeditionary Force (AEF) *n.* the U.S. forces, led by General John Pershing, who fought with the Allies in Europe during World War I. (p. 330)

Fuerza Americana de Expediciones *s.* fuerzas dirigidas por el general John Pershing, quien luchó con los Aliados en Europa durante la Primera Guerra Mundial. (pág. 330)

American Federation of Labor (AFL) *n.* an alliance of trade and craft unions, formed in 1886. (p. 178)
Federación Norteamericana del Trabajo *s.* sindicato de trabajadores calificados creado en 1886 y dirigido por Samuel Gompers. (pág. 178)

American Indian Movement (AIM) *n.* a frequently militant organization that was formed in 1968 to work for Native American rights. (p. 751)
Movimiento Indígena Americano *s.* organización con frecuencia militante creada en 1968 con el fin de luchar por los derechos de los amerindios. (pág. 751)

Americanization movement *n.* education program designed to help immigrants assimilate to American culture. (p. 197)
movimiento de americanización *s.* programa educativo ideado para facilitar la asimilación de los inmigrantes a la cultura estadounidense. (pág. 197)

American Recovery and Reinvestment Act (ARRA) *n.* an act signed by President Barack Obama in 2009 that distributed over $8 billion in funds to individuals and through various programs. (p. 904)
Ley de Reinversión y Recuperación de los Estados Unidos *s.* ley firmada por el presidente Barack Obama en 2009 por la que se distribuyeron más de 8 mil millones de dólares en fondos a personas y a través de diversos programas. (pág. 904)

Americans with Disabilities Act (ADA) *n.* a law signed by George H. W. Bush in 1990 that ruled all discrimination against people with disabilities illegal. (p. 772)
Ley de Estadounidenses con Discapacidades *s.* ley firmada por George H. W. Bush en 1990 por la que se declaró ilegal todo tipo de discriminación a personas con discapacidades. (pág. 772)

anarchist *n.* a person who opposes all forms of government. (p. 372)
anarquista *s.* persona que se opone a toda forma de gobierno. (pág. 372)

English and Spanish Glossary

Angel Island *n.* an island in the San Francisco Bay that was an entry point for many Asian immigrants to the United States beginning in 1910. (p. 192)
   isla Angel *s.* isla en la bahía de San Francisco que fue el punto de ingreso para muchos immigrantes asiáticos a partir de 1910. (pág. 192)

Antifederalist *n.* an opponent of a strong central government. (p. 32)
   antifederalista *s.* oponente de la Constitución y de un gobierno central fuerte. (pág. 32)

Apartheid [ə-pärt′hīt′] *n.* the South African government's official policy of legalized racial segregation throughout society. (p. 868)
   Apartheid *s.* política oficial del gobierno de Sudáfrica de segregación racial legalizada para todos los ámbitos de la sociedad. (pág. 868)

appeasement *n.* the granting of concessions to a hostile power in order to keep the peace. (p. 492)
   apaciguamiento *s.* política de ceder a las demandas de una potencia hostil con el fin de mantener la paz. (pág. 492)

Appomattox [ăp′ə-măt′əks] **Court House** *n.* town near Appomattox, Virginia, where Lee surrendered to Grant on April 9, 1865, thus ending the Civil War. (37°N 79°W). (p. 101)
   Appomattox Court House *s.* pueblo cerca de Appomattox, Virginia, donde Lee se rindió a Grant el 9 de abril de 1865. (37°N 79°O). (pág. 101)

arms race *n.* competition between nations to gain an advantage in weapons. (p. 601)
   carrera armamentista *s.* competencia entre las naciones para obtener ventaja respecto de los armamentos. (pág. 601)

Army of the Republic of Vietnam (ARVN) *n.* the southern Vietnamese soldiers with whom U.S. troops fought against communism and forces in the North during the Vietnam War. (p. 789)
   Ejército de la República de Vietnam *s.* soldados del sur de Vietnam que lucharon junto a soldados estadounidenses contra el comunismo y las fuerzas del norte de Vietnam durante la Guerra de Vietnam. (pág. 789)

Ashcan school *n.* a group of early 20th-century American artists who often painted realistic pictures of city life—such as tenements and homeless people—thus earning them their name. (p. 220)
   Ashcan school *s.* grupo de artistas estadounidenses de principios del siglo XX que a menudo pintaban escenas realistas de la vida urbana —como arrabales y gente sin hogar— ganándose así el nombre de la escuela del basurero. (pág. 220)

assimilation *n.* a minority group's adoption of the beliefs and way of life of the dominant culture. (p. 121)
   asimilación *s.* adopción, por parte de un grupo minoritario, de las creencias y estilo de vida de la cultura dominante. (pág. 121)

Atlantic Charter *n.* a 1941 declaration of principles in which the United States and Great Britain set forth their goals in opposing the Axis powers. (p. 513)
   Carta del Atlántico *s.* declaración de principios de 1941 en que Estados Unidos y Gran Bretaña establecieron sus objetivos contra las Potencias del Eje. (pág. 513)

Axis [ăk′sĭs] **powers** *n.* the group of nations—including Germany, Italy, and Japan—that opposed the Allies in World War II. (p. 509)
   Potencias del Eje *s.* países unidos contra los Aliados en la Segunda Guerra Mundial, que incluyeron a Alemania, Italia y Japón. (pág. 509)

B

baby boom *n.* the sharp increase in the U.S. birthrate following World War II. (p. 648)
   baby boom *s.* marcado aumento en el índice de natalidad en Estados Unidos después de la Segunda Guerra Mundial. (pág. 648)

balance of power *n.* a system in which each nation or alliance has equal strength. (p. 316)
   equilibrio de poder *s.* sistema en el que cada nación o alianza tiene igual poder. (pág. 316)

Bataan [bə-tăn′] **Death March** *n.* a forced march of American and Filipino soldiers captured by the Japanese along the Bataan Peninsula during World War II. (p. 548)

Marcha de la Muerte de Bataán *s.* marcha forzada de soldados estadounidenses y filipinos capturados por los japoneses a lo largo de la península de Bataán durante la Segunda Guerra Mundial. (pág. 548)

Battle of the Bulge *n.* a month-long battle of World War II, in which the Allies succeeded in turning back the last major German offensive of the war. (p. 548)
Batalla del Bolsón *s.* batalla de un mes de duración en la Segunda Guerra Mundial durante la cual los Aliados rompieron la última gran ofensiva alemana de la guerra. (pág. 545)

Battle of Midway *n.* a World War II battle that took place in early June 1942. The Allies decimated the Japanese fleet at Midway, an island lying northwest of Hawaii. The Allies then took the offensive in the Pacific and began to move closer to Japan. (p. 549)
Batalla de Midway *s.* batalla de la Segunda Guerra Mundial que ocurrió a principios de junio en 1942. Los Aliados redujeron la flotilla japonesa en Midway, una isla al noreste de Hawái. A partir de esta batalla los Aliados tomaron la ofensiva y comenzaron a moverse a Japón. (pág. 549)

Battle of Wounded Knee *n.* the massacre by U.S. soldiers of 300 unarmed Native Americans at Wounded Knee Creek, South Dakota, in 1890. (p. 124)
Batalla de Wounded Knee *s.* massacre de 300 indígenas desarmados en Wounded Knee Creek, South Dakota, en 1890. (pág. 124)

Beatles, the [bēt′lz] *n.* a British band that had an enormous influence on popular music in the 1960s. (p. 701)
Beatles, the *s.* conjunto inglés que tuvo gran influencia en la música popular en los años 60. (pág. 701)

beat movement *n.* a social and artistic movement of the 1950s, stressing unrestrained literary self-expression and nonconformity with the mainstream culture. (p. 661)
movimiento beat *s.* movimiento social y literario de los años 50 que enfatizó la expresión literaria sin reglas y la disconformidad. (pág. 661)

Benghazi [bĕn-gä′zē] *n.* a city in Libya where Islamic militants attacked a United States diplomatic compound on September 11, 2012. (p. 909)
Bengasi *s.* ciudad de Libia donde militantes islámicos atacaron el consulado estadounidense el 11 de septiembre de 2012. (pág. 909)

Berlin airlift *n.* a 327-day operation in which U.S. and British planes flew food and supplies into West Berlin after the Soviets blockaded the city in 1948. (p. 581)
puente aéreo de Berlín *s.* operación de 327 días de duración, en la que aviones estadounidenses y británicos llevaron alimentos y provisiones a Berlín Occidental después de que la Unión Soviética bloqueó la ciudad en 1948. (pág. 581)

Berlin Wall *n.* a concrete wall that separated East Berlin and West Berlin from 1961 to 1989, built by the Communist East German government to prevent its citizens from fleeing to the West. (p. 616)
Muro de Berlín *s.* muro de concreto que separó Berlín Oriental y Occidental de 1961 a 1989; construido por Alemania Oriental para impedir que sus ciudadanos se escaparan al occidente. (pág. 616)

Bessemer [bĕs′ə-mər] **process** *n.* a cheap and efficient process for making steel, developed around 1850. (p. 155)
método Bessemer *s.* técnica más eficiente y barata de fabricar acero, desarrollada hacia 1850. (pág. 155)

Bill of Rights *n.* the first ten amendments to the U.S. Constitution, added in 1791 and consisting of a formal list of citizens' rights and freedoms. (p. 32)
Carta de Derechos *s.* primeras diez enmiendas a la Constitución que identifican los derechos de los ciudadanos; se adoptaron en 1791. (pág. 32)

bimetallism [bī-mĕt′l-ĭz′əm] *n.* the use of both gold and silver as a basis for a national monetary system. (p. 147)
bimetalismo *s.* sistema monetario nacional que utiliza el oro y la plata para respaldar la moneda. (pág. 147)

English and Spanish Glossary

biodiversity *n.* the entirety of a region's genes, species, and ecosystems. (p. 968)
biodiversidad *s.* la totalidad de los genes, las especies y los ecosistemas de una región. (pág. 968)

black codes *n.* the discriminatory laws passed throughout the post-Civil War South which severely restricted African Americans' lives, prohibiting such activities as traveling without permits, carrying weapons, serving on juries, testifying against whites, and marrying whites. (p. 106)
códigos negros *s.* leyes discriminatorias aprobadas en el Sur después de la Guerra Civil, las cuales restringían severamente la vida de los afroamericanos, prohibiéndoles actividades como viajar sin permiso, llevar armas, participar como jurado, testificar contra los blancos y casarse con blancos. (pág. 106)

blacklist *n.* a list of about 500 actors, writers, producers, and directors who were not allowed to work on Hollywood films because of their alleged Communist connections. (p. 594)
lista negra *s.* lista de unos 500 actores, escritores, productores y directores a quienes no se permitía trabajar en películas de Hollywood debido a sus supuestos vínculos comunistas. (pág. 594)

Black Panthers *n.* a militant African American political organization formed in 1966 by Huey Newton and Bobby Seale to fight police brutality and to provide services in the ghetto. (p. 742)
Panteras Negras *s.* organización política afroamericana militante formada por Huey Newton y Bobby Seale en 1966 para luchar contra la violencia de la policía y suministrar servicios en el ghetto. (pág. 742)

Black Power *n.* a slogan used by Stokely Carmichael in the 1960s that encouraged African American pride and political and social leadership. (p. 742)
Poder Negro *s.* consigna usada por Stokely Carmichael en los años 60, que pedía poder político y social para los afroamericanos. (pág. 742)

Black Tuesday *n.* a name given to October 29, 1929, when stock prices fell sharply. (p. 417)

Martes Negro *s.* octubre 29 de 1929, día en que los precios de las acciones bajaron drásticamente. (pág. 417)

blitzkrieg [blĭts′krēg′] *n.* from the German word meaning "lightning war," a sudden, massive attack with combined air and ground forces, intended to achieve a quick victory. (p. 493)
blitzkrieg *s.* proveniente de la palabra alemana que significa "guerra relámpago". Repentina ofensiva de fuerzas aéreas y terrestres a gran escala con el fin de obtener una victoria rápida. (pág. 493)

Boko Haram [bō′kō hä-räm′] *n.* a terrorist group centered in Nigeria that seeks to establish an Islamic state under strict religious law. (p. 952)
Boko Haram *s.* grupo terrorista con base en Nigeria que busca establecer un estado islámico bajo estrictas leyes religiosas. (pág. 952)

bonanza farm *n.* an enormous farm on which a single crop is grown. (p. 142)
granja de bonanza *s.* extensa granja dedicada a un solo cultivo. (pág. 142)

Bonus Army *n.* a group of World War I veterans and their families who marched on Washington, DC, in 1932 to demand the immediate payment of a bonus they had been promised for military service. (p. 434)
Bonus Army *s.* grupo de veteranos de la Primera Guerra Mundial que marcharon en Washington, DC, en 1932 para exigir bonos prometidos a cambio de su servicio militar. (pág. 434)

bootlegger *n.* a person who smuggled alcoholic beverages into the United States during Prohibition. (p. 382)
bootlegger *s.* persona que contrabandeaba bebidas alcohólicas durante la época de Prohibición. (pág. 382)

Boston Tea Party *n.* the dumping of 18,000 pounds of tea into Boston harbor by colonists in 1773 to protest the Tea Act. (p. 17)
Motín del Té de Boston *s.* protesta en 1773 contra el impuesto británico sobre el té; los colonos arrojaron 18,000 libras de té al puerto de Boston. (pág. 17)

Boulder [bōl′dər] **Dam** *n.* a dam on the Colorado River—now called Hoover Dam—that was built during the Great Depression as part of a public-works program intended to stimulate business and provide jobs. (p. 431)
Presa de Boulder *s.* presa del río Colorado construida durante la Depresión con fondos federales para estimular la economía; ahora llamada Presa Hoover. (pág. 431)

Boxer Rebellion *n.* a 1900 rebellion in which members of a Chinese secret society sought to free their country from Western influence. (p. 298)
Rebelión de los Boxer *s.* rebelión encabezada en 1900 por los Boxer, sociedad secreta de China, para detener la difusión de la influencia occidental. (pág. 298)

bread line *n.* a line of people waiting for free food. (p. 422)
cola para comer *s.* fila de personas que esperan comida gratis. (pág. 422)

brinkmanship [brĭngk′mən-shĭp′] *n.* the practice of threatening an enemy with massive military retaliation for any aggression. (p. 602)
brinkmanship *s.* práctica de amenazar al enemigo con represalias militares extremas ante cualquier agresión. (pág. 602)

Brown* v. *Board of Education of Topeka *n.* a 1954 case in which the Supreme Court ruled that "separate but equal" education for black and white students was unconstitutional. (p. 719)
Brown* v. *Board of Education of Topeka *s.* decisión de la Suprema Corte en 1954 que declaró que la segregación de estudiantes negros y blancos era inconstitucional. (pág. 719)

Bull Moose Party *n.* a name given to the Progressive Party, formed to support Theodore Roosevelt's candidacy for the presidency in 1912. (p. 267)
Partido Bull Moose *s.* apodo del Partido Progresista, bajo el que Theodore Roosevelt aspiró, sin éxito, a la presidencia en 1912. (pág. 267)

buying on margin *n.* the purchasing of stocks by paying only a small percentage of the price and borrowing the rest. (p. 417)
compra con margen *s.* compra de acciones en la que se paga sólo una porción del valor de la acción al vendedor o corredor de bolsa, y se presta el resto. (pág. 417)

C

cabinet *n.* the group of department heads who serve as the president's chief advisers. (p. 33)
gabinete *s.* jefes de departamentos que son asesores directos del presidente. (pág. 33)

Camp David Accords *n.* historic agreements between Israel and Egypt, reached in negotiations at Camp David in 1978. (p. 847)
Acuerdos de Camp David *s.* acuerdos de paz históricos entre Israel y Egipto, nego ciados en Camp David, Maryland, en 1978. (pág. 847)

carpetbagger [kär′pĭt-băg′ər] *n.* a northerner who moved to the South after the Civil War. (p. 107)
carpetbagger *s.* norteños que se trasladaron al Sur después de la Guerra Civil. (pág. 107)

Central Intelligence Agency (CIA) *n.* U.S. agency created to gather secret information about foreign governments. (p. 578)
Agencia Central de Inteligencia *s.* agencia gubernamental establecida para espiar y realizer operaciones secretas en países extranjeros. (pág. 578)

Central powers *n.* the group of nations—led by Germany, Austria-Hungary, and the Ottoman Empire—that opposed the Allies in World War I. (p. 316)
Potencias Centrales *s.* en la Primera Guerra Mundial, el grupo de naciones—Alemania, Austro-Hungría y el imperio otomano—que se opuso a los Aliados. (pág. 316)

Chinese Exclusion Act *n.* a law, enacted in 1882, that prohibited all Chinese except students, teachers, merchants, tourists, and government officials from entering the United States. (p. 195)
Ley de Exclusión de Chinos *s.* ley de 1882 que prohibía la inmigración de ciudadanos chinos, con la excepción de estudiantes, maestros, comerciantes, turistas y funcionarios gubernamentales. (pág. 195)

Chisholm [chĭz′əm] **Trail** *n.* the major cattle route from San Antonio, Texas, through Oklahoma to Kansas. (p. 130)
Sendero Chisholm *s.* la ruta principal de Ganado que iba desde San Antonio, Texas, por Oklahoma hasta Kansas. (pág. 130)

Citizens United v. Federal Election Commission *n.* a 2010 U.S. Supreme Court case that decreed that the First Amendment could not restrict political expenditures by nonprofit corporations. (p. 958)
Ciudadanos Unidos contra *Comisión de Elecciones Federales* *s.* caso del año 2010 de la Corte Suprema de los Estados Unidos por el que se dispuso que la Primera Enmienda no podía limitar los desembolsos políticos por parte de organizaciones sin fines de lucro. (pág. 958)

Civilian Conservation Corps (CCC) *n.* an agency, established as part of the New Deal, that put young unemployed men to work building roads, developing parks, planting trees, and helping in erosion-control and flood-control projects. (p. 444)
Cuerpo Civil de Conservación *s.* agencia establecida como parte del New Deal con el fin de ocupar a jóvenes desempleados en trabajos como la construcción de carreteras y el cuidado de parques nacionales y ayudar en situaciones de emergencia. (pág. 444)

Civil Rights Act of 1964 *n.* a law that banned discrimination on the basis of race, sex, national origin, or religion in public places and most workplaces. (p. 733)
Ley de Derechos Civiles de 1964 *s.* ley que prohíbe la discriminación en lugares públicos, en la educación y en los empleos por cuestión de raza, color, sexo, nacionalidad o religión. (pág. 733)

Civil Rights Act of 1968 *n.* a law that banned discrimination in housing. (p. 743)
Ley de Derechos Civiles de 1968 *s.* ley que prohíbe la discriminación en la vivienda. (pág. 743)

civil service *n.* the nonmilitary branches of government administration. (p. 207)
servicio civil *s.* cualquier servicio gubernamental en el que se obtiene un cargo mediante exámenes públicos. (pág. 207)

Clayton Antitrust Act *n.* a law, enacted in 1914, that made certain monopolistic business practices illegal and protected the rights of labor unions and farm organizations. (p. 270)

Ley Antitrust Clayton *s.* ley de 1914 que declaraba ilegales ciertas prácticas empresariales injustas y protegía el derecho de los sindicatos y organizaciones agrícolas. (pág. 270)

Cold War *n.* the state of hostility, without direct military conflict, that developed between the United States and the Soviet Union after World War II. (p. 577)
Guerra Fría *s.* estado de hostilidad, sin llegar a conflictos armados, entre Estados Unidos y la Unión Soviética tras la Segunda Guerra Mundial. (pág. 577)

collective bargaining *n.* negotiation between employers and an organized group of employees on conditions of employment, such as wages or hours. (p. 178)
negociación colectiva *s.* negociación entre empleadores y un grupo organizado de empleados sobre las condiciones de trabajo, como el salario o las horas de trabajo. (pág. 178)

Committee on Public Information *n.* the nation's first propaganda agency, formed by President Wilson to influence public opinion to maximize support for the United States' involvement in World War I. (p. 339)
Comité de Información Pública *s.* primera agencia de propaganda de la nación, creada por el presidente Wilson para influenciar la opinión pública y maximizar el apoyo a la participación de los Estados Unidos en la Primera Guerra Mundial. (pág. 339)

Committee to Reelect the President *n.* an organization formed to run President Nixon's 1972 reelection campaign, which was linked to the break-in at the Democratic National Committee headquarters that set off the Watergate scandal. (p. 833)
Comité de Reelección del Presidente *s.* grupo que dirigió la campaña para la reelección del presidente Nixon en 1972, cuya conexión con el allanamiento de la Sede Nacional del Partido Demócrata hizo estallar el escándalo Watergate. (pág. 833)

Common Sense *n.* a pamphlet by Thomas Paine, published in 1776, that called for separation of the colonies from Britain. (p. 19)
Sentido común *s.* folleto escrito en 1776 por Thomas Paine que exhortaba la separación de las colonias británicas. (pág. 19)

communism *n.* an economic and political system based on one-party government and state ownership of property. (p. 371)
comunismo *s.* sistema económico y político basado en un gobierno de un solo partido y en la propiedad estatal. (pág. 371)

comparative advantage *n.* the idea that a nation will specialize in what it can produce at a lower opportunity cost, or trade-off, than any other nation. (p. 981)
ventaja comparativa *s.* concepto de que una nación tiende a especializarse en lo que puede producir a un costo de oportunidad menor, o trade-off, que cualquier otra nación. (pág. 981)

Comstock Lode [kŏm′stŏk′ lōd] *n.* Nevada gold and silver mine discovered by Henry Comstock in 1859. (p. 126)
veta de Comstock *s.* mina de oro y plata descubierta en Nevada por Henry Comstock en 1859. (pág. 126)

concentration camp *n.* a prison camp operated by Nazi Germany in which Jews and other groups considered to be enemies of Adolf Hitler were starved while doing slave labor or were murdered. (p. 501)
campo de concentración *s.* cam pa mento de presos operado por la Alemania nazi para judíos y otros grupos que consideraba enemigos de Adolfo Hitler; a los presos los mataban o los hacían morir de hambre y a causa de trabajos forzados. (pág. 501)

Confederacy [kən-fĕd′ər-ə-sē] *n.* the Confederate States of America, a confederation formed in 1861 by the southern states after their secession from the Union. (p. 89)
Estados Confederados de América *s.* confederación formada en 1861 por los estados del Sur después de que se separaron de la unión. (pág. 89)

conglomerate *n.* a major corporation that owns a number of smaller companies in unrelated businesses. (p. 645)
conglomerado *s.* corporación grande que posee compañías más pequeñas dedicadas a negocios diversos. (pág. 645)

Congress of Industrial Organizations (CIO) *n.* a labor organization composed of industrial unions founded in 1938, it merged with the AFL in 1955. (p. 464)
Congreso de Organizaciones Industriales *s.* organización sindical expulsada de la Federación Norteamericana del Trabajo en 1938. (pág. 464)

Congress of Racial Equality (CORE) *n.* an interracial group founded in 1942 by James Farmer to work against segregation in northern cities. (p. 529)
Congreso de Igualdad Racial *s.* grupo interracial, fundado por James Farmer en 1942, que luchaba contra la segregación en ciudades del Norte. (pág. 529)

conscientious objector *n.* a person who refuses, on moral grounds, to participate in warfare. (p. 334)
objetor de conciencia *s.* persona que se opone a toda guerra por principio de conciencia. (pág. 334)

conscription *n.* the drafting of citizens for military service. (p. 98)
conscripción *s.* servicio military obligatorio de ciertos miembros de la población. (pág. 98)

conservation *n.* the planned management of natural resources, involving the protection of some wilderness areas and the development of others for the common good. (p. 262)
conservación *s.* práctica de preservar algunas zonas naturales y desarrollar otras por el bien común. (pág. 262)

conservative coalition *n.* an alliance formed in the mid-1960s of right-wing groups opposed to big government. (p. 852)
coalición conservadora *s.* alianza de grupos de ultraderecha opuestos a la ingerencia del gobierno formada a mediados de los años sesenta. (pág. 852)

consumerism [kən-soo′mə-rĭz′əm] *n.* a preoccupation with the purchasing of material goods or acquiring goods in ever-greater amounts. (pp. 366, 653)
consumismo *s.* inquietud respecto de la compra de bienes materiales o adquisición de bienes en cantidades cada vez mayores. (pág. 366, 653)

containment *n.* the blocking of another nation's attempts to spread its influence—especially the efforts of the United States to block the spread of Soviet influence during the late 1940s and early 1950s. (p. 577)

English and Spanish Glossary

contención *s.* política estadounidense de formar alianzas con países más pequeños y débiles con el fin de bloquear la expansión de la infuencia soviética tras la Segunda Guerra Mundial. (pág. 577)

Contract with America *n.* a document that was drafted by Representative Newt Gingrich and signed by more than 300 Republican candidates in 1994, setting forth the Republicans' conservative legislative agenda. (p. 884)

Contrato con América *s.* document elaborado por el representante Newt Gingrich y firmado por 300 candidatos republicanos el 27 de septiembre de 1994, que presentaba sus planes legislativos conservadores. (pág. 884)

Contras [kŏn′trəz] *n.* Nicaraguan rebels who received assistance from the Reagan administration in their efforts to overthrow the Sandinista government in the 1980s. (p. 870)

la contra *s.* fuerzas anticomunistas nicaragüenses que recibieron asistencia de la administración Reagan para derrocar al gobierno sandinista de Nicaragua. (pág. 870)

convoy system *n.* the protection of merchant ships from U-boat—German submarine—attacks by having the ships travel in large groups escorted by warships. (p. 329)

flotilla de escolta *s.* medio de proteger los buques mercantes del ataque de submarinos alemanes al hacer que viajaran con una escorta de destructores. (pág. 329)

counterculture *n.* the culture of the young people who rejected mainstream American society in the 1960s, seeking to create an alternative society based on peace, love, and individual freedom. (p. 698)

contracultura *s.* cultura de la juventud de los años 60 que rechazaba la sociedad tradicional y buscaba paz, amor y libertad individual. (pág. 698)

credibility gap *n.* a public distrust of statements made by the government. (p. 794)

falta de credibilidad *s.* desconfianza del public en las declaraciones oficiales del gobierno. (pág. 794)

credit *n.* an arrangement in which a buyer pays later for a purchase, often on an installment plan with interest charges. (p. 414)

crédito *s.* acuerdo en el que se compran artículos en el presente para ser pagados en el futuro mediante un plan de cuotas con intereses. (pág. 414)

Crédit Mobilier [krĕd′ĭt mōbēl′yər] *n.* a construction company formed in 1864 by owners of the Union Pacific Railroad, who used it to fraudulently skim off railroad profits for themselves. (p. 165)

Crédit Mobilier *s.* compañía constructora formada en 1864 por los dueños de la Union Pacific Railroad; quienes la usaron ilegalmente para obtener ganancias. (pág. 165)

cultural diffusion *n.* the way cultural practices spread from one community to another and how cultures borrow traits such as beliefs, ideas, and material objects from one another. (p. 985)

difusión cultural *s.* manera en que las prácticas culturales se extienden de una comunidad a otra y cómo las culturas toman prestadas entre sí características como creencias, ideas y objetos materiales. (pág. 985)

D

Dawes [dôz] **Act** *n.* a law, enacted in 1887, that was intended to "Americanize" Native Americans by distributing reservation land to individual owners. (p. 123)

Ley Dawes *s.* ley aprobada por el Congreso en 1887 para "americanizar" a los indígenas distribuyendo a individuos la tierra de las reservaciones. (pág. 123)

D-Day *n.* a name given to June 6, 1944—the day on which the Allies launched an invasion of the European mainland during World War II. (p. 543)

Día D *s.* junio 6 de 1944, día en que los Aliados emprendieron una invasión por tierra, mar y aire contra el Eje. (pág. 543)

debt peonage [dĕt′pē′ə-nĭj] *n.* a system in which workers are bound in servitude until their debts are paid. (p. 247)

deuda por peonaje *s.* sistema de servidumbre en el que una persona es obligada a trabajar para pagar una deuda. (pág. 247)

de facto [dǐ fǎk′tō] **segregation** *n.* racial separation established by practice and custom, not by law. (p. 739)
segregación de facto *s.* segregación racial impuesta por la práctica y la costumbre más que por las leyes. (pág. 739)

deficit spending *n.* a government's spending of more money than it receives in revenue. (p. 446)
gasto deficitario *s.* práctica por parte de un gobierno de gastar más de lo que recibe por concepto de rentas públicas. (pág. 446)

deflation *n.* a decrease in the general price level of goods and services. (p. 413)
deflación *s.* disminución en el nivel general de precios de bienes y servicios. (pág. 413)

de jure [dē jŏŏr′ē] **segregation** *n.* racial separation established by law. (p. 739)
segregación de jure *s.* segregación racial impuesta por la ley. (pág. 739)

deregulation *n.* the cutting back of federal regulation of industry. (p. 860)
liberalización *s.* acción de limitar el alcance de la regulación federal sobre la industria. (pág. 860)

détente [dā-tänt′] *n.* the flexible policy, involving a willingness to negotiate and an easing of tensions, that was adopted by President Richard Nixon and his adviser Henry Kissinger in their dealings with Communist nations. (p. 622)
distensión *s.* política flexible con la intención de negociar y disminuir tensiones; fue adoptada por Richard Nixon y su consejero Henry Kissinger para tratar con países comunistas. (pág. 622)

Dien Bien Phu *n.* site of a battle between the French and the Vietminh in 1954; the French lost the battle and control of Vietnam. (p. 802)
Dien Bien Phu *s.* sitio de una batalla entre los franceses y el Viet Minh en 1954; los franceses perdieron la batalla y el control de Vietnam. (pág. 802)

direct relief *n.* the giving of money or food by the government directly to needy people. (p. 425)
ayuda directa *s.* alimentos o dinero que el gobierno da directamente a los necesitados. (pág. 425)

Dixiecrat [dǐk′sē-krăt′] *n.* one of the southern delegates who, to protest President Truman's civil rights policy, walked out of the 1948 Democratic National Convention and formed the States' Rights Democratic Party. (p. 641)
Dixiecrat *s.* delegado sureño que se retiró de la convención del Partido Demócrata en 1948 para protestar la plataforma del presidente Truman sobre derechos civiles y formó un grupo denominado States' Rights Democratic Party. (pág. 641)

dollar diplomacy *n.* the U.S. policy of using the nation's economic power to exert influence over other countries. (p. 305)
diplomacia del dólar *s.* política de usar el poder económico o la influencia económica de Estados Unidos para alcanzar sus objetivos de política exterior en otros países. (pág. 305)

domino theory *n.* the idea that if a nation falls under Communist control, nearby nations will also fall under Communist control. (pp. 612, 782)
teoría del dominó *s.* teoría que supone que si una nación se vuelve comunista, las naciones vecinas inevitablemente se volverán comunistas también. (pág. 612, 782)

double standard *n.* a set of principles granting greater sexual freedom to men than to women. (p. 388)
doble moral *s.* conjunto de principios que permite mayor libertad sexual al hombre que a la mujer. (pág. 388)

dove *n.* a person who opposed the Vietnam War and believed that the United States should withdraw from it. (p. 800)
paloma *s.* persona que se oponía a la Guerra de Vietnam y creía que Estados Unidos debía retirarse. (pág. 800)

Dow Jones Industrial Average *n.* a measure based on the prices of the stocks of 30 large companies, widely used as a barometer of the stock market's health. (p. 416)
Promedio Industrial Dow Jones *s.* medida que computa el valor de las acciones de 30 compañías grandes; se usa como barómetro de los mercados bursátiles. (pág. 416)

downsize *v.* to dismiss numbers of permanent employees in an attempt to make operations more efficient and save money. (p. 886)

English and Spanish Glossary

recortar *v.* despedir trabajadores de una organización con el fin de hacer las operaciones más eficientes y ahorrar dinero. (pág. 886)

draft *n.* required enrollment in the armed services. (p. 796)
reclutamiento *s.* requisito de matrícula en las fuerzas armadas. (pág. 796)

drone *n.* an unmanned aerial vehicle, or an aircraft operated by pilots on the ground. (p. 935)
drone *s.* vehículo aéreo no tripulado, o aeronave operada por pilotos desde tierra. (pág. 935)

Dust Bowl *n.* the region, including Texas, Oklahoma, Kansas, Colorado, and New Mexico, that was made worthless for farming by drought and dust storms during the 1930s. (p. 424)
Dust Bowl *s.* región que incluye Texas, Oklahoma, Kansas, Colorado y New Mexico que quedó inservible para la agricultura debido a la sequía y a las tormentas de arena durante los años 30. (pág. 424)

E

Earth Day *n.* a day set aside for environmental education, celebrated annually on April 22. (p. 706)
Día de la Tierra *s.* día dedicado a la educación ambiental que desde 1970 se celebra el 22 de abril de cada año. (pág. 706)

Economic Opportunity Act *n.* a law, enacted in 1964, that provided funds for youth programs, antipoverty measures, small-business loans, and job training. (p. 688)
Ley de Oportunidades Económicas *s.* ley promulgada en 1964, que adjudicó fondos a programas para la juventud, medidas para combatir la pobreza, préstamos para pequeños negocios y capacitación laboral. (pág. 688)

Eisenhower Doctrine *n.* a U.S. commitment to defend the Middle East against attack by any Communist country, announced by President Dwight D. Eisenhower in 1957. (p. 605)
Doctrina Eisenhower *s.* advertencia del presidente Eisenhower en 1957 de que Estados Unidos defendería el Oriente Medio contra el ataque de cualquier país comunista. (pág. 605)

Ellis Island *n.* an island in New York harbor that was the chief immigration station in the United States from 1892 to 1924. (p. 191)
Isla Ellis *s.* isla en el puerto de Nueva York que fue la principal estación de inmigración de los Estados Unidos desde 1892 hasta 1924. (pág. 191)

Emancipation Proclamation *n.* an executive order issued by Abraham Lincoln on January 1, 1863, freeing the slaves in all regions behind Confederate lines. (p. 97)
Proclama de Emancipación *s.* orden ejecutiva de Abraham Lincoln el 1º de enero de 1863 que abolía la esclavitud en los estados confederados. (pág. 97)

encomienda [ĕng-kô-myĕn′dä] *n.* a system in which Spanish authorities granted colonial landlords the service of Native Americans as forced laborers. (p. 6)
encomienda *s.* institución colonial de España en las Américas que repartía indígenas a los conquistadores para hacer trabajos forzados. (pág. 6)

Enlightenment *n.* an 18th-century intellectual movement that emphasized the use of reason and the scientific method as means of obtaining knowledge. (p. 11)
Ilustración *s.* movimiento intelectual del siglo 18 que enfatizaba la razón y los métodos científicos para obtener conocimientos. (pág. 11)

entitlement program *n.* a government program—such as Social Security, Medicare, or Medicaid—that guarantees and provides benefits to a specific group. (p. 852)
programa de subvención *s.* programa gubernamental, como Social Security, Medicare y Medicaid, que brinda beneficios a grupos específicos. (pág. 852)

entrepreneur *n.* a person who organizes, operates, and assumes the risk for a business venture. (p. 72)
empresario *s.* persona que organiza, opera y assume todo el riesgo de una ventura de negocios. (pág. 72)

environmentalist *n.* a person who works to protect the environment from destruction and pollution. (p. 706)

ambientalista *s.* persona que procura proteger el medio ambiente de la destrucción y de la contaminación. (pág. 706)

Environmental Protection Agency (EPA) *n.* a federal agency established in 1970 for the regulation of water and air pollution, toxic waste, pesticides, and radiation. (pp. 706, 860)
Agencia de Protección Ambiental *s.* agencia federal establecida en 1970 para la regulación de la contaminación del agua y el aire, los desperdicios tóxicos, los pesticidas y la radiación. (pág. 706, 860)

Equal Rights Amendment (ERA) *n.* a proposed and failed amendment to the U.S. Constitution that would have prohibited any government discrimination on the basis of sex. (p. 761)
Enmienda de Igualdad de Derechos *s.* enmienda propuesta pero rechazada que hubiese prohibido la discriminación del gobierno en razón del sexo de una persona. (pág. 761)

Espionage and Sedition Acts *n.* two laws, enacted in 1917 and 1918, that imposed harsh penalties on anyone interfering with or speaking against U.S. participation in World War I. (p. 341)
Leyes de Espionaje y Sedición *s.* dos leyes aprobadas en 1917 y 1918, que castigaban fuertemente a quienes criticaran o bloquearan la participación de Estados Unidos en la Primera Guerra Mundial. (pág. 341)

exoduster [ĕk′sə-dŭs′tər] *n.* an African American who migrated from the South to Kansas in the post-Reconstruction years. (p. 137)
exoduster *s.* afroamericano que emigró del Sur a Kansas después de la Reconstrucción. (pág. 137)

F

Fair Deal *n.* President Harry S. Truman's economic program—an extension of Franklin Roosevelt's New Deal—which included measures to increase the minimum wage, to extend social security coverage, and to provide housing for low-income families. (p. 642)
Fair Deal *s.* plan económico del presidente Truman que expandió El New Deal de Roosevelt; aumentó el salario mínimo, amplió El seguro social y le dio vivienda a familias de bajos recursos, entre otras medidas. (pág. 642)

Family Assistance Plan (FAP) *n.* a welfare-reform proposal, approved by the House of Representatives in 1970 but defeated in the Senate, that would have guaranteed an income to welfare recipients who agreed to undergo job training and to accept work. (p. 825)
Plan de Asistencia Familiar *s.* propuesta de reforma a los programas de beneficencia, aprobada por la Cámara de Representantes en 1970 pero rechazada por el Senado, que garantizaba un ingreso a los beneficiarios de ayuda pública que aceptaran capacitarse y emplearse en un oficio. (pág. 825)

Farmers' Alliances *n.* groups of farmers, or those in sympathy with farming issues, who sent lecturers from town to town to educate people about agricultural and rural issues. (p. 146)
Alianzas de granjeros *s.* grupos de granjeros o simpatizantes de éstos, que enviaban a oradores a viajar de pueblo a pueblo para educar a la gente sobre cuestiones agrarias y rurales. (pág. 146)

fascism [făsh′ĭz′əm] *n.* a political philosophy that advocates a strong, centralized, nationalistic government headed by a powerful dictator. (p. 486)
fascismo *s.* filosofía política que propone un gobierno fuerte, centralizado, nacionalista, caracteri zado por una rígida dictadura unipartidista. (pág. 486)

Federal Communications Commission (FCC) *n.* an agency that regulates U.S. communications industries, including radio and television broadcasting. (p. 659)
Comisión Federal de Comunicaciones *s.* agencia del gobierno que regula la industria de comunicaciones en EE.UU., incluso la transmission de radio y televisión. (pág. 659)

Federal Deposit Insurance Corporation (FDIC) *n.* an agency created in 1933 to insure individuals' bank accounts, protecting people against losses due to bank failures. (p. 474)
Corporación Federal de Seguros de Depósitos *s.* agencia creada en 1933 para garantizar depósitos bancarios individuales cuando un banco quiebra. (pág. 474)

Federal Home Loan Bank Act *n.* a law, enacted in 1931, that lowered home mortgage rates and allowed farmers to refinance their loans and avoid foreclosure. (p. 433)

English and Spanish Glossary

Ley Federal para Préstamos de Vivienda *s.* ley aprobada en 1931 que redujo las cuotas hipotecarias y permitió a los agricultores refinanciar sus préstamos para prevenir juicios hipotecarios. (pág. 433)

Federalists *n.* supporters of the Constitution and of a strong national government. (p. 32)
federalistas *s.* partidarios de la Constitución y de un gobierno nacional fuerte. (pág. 32)

Federal Reserve System *n.* a national banking system, established in 1913, that controls the U.S. money supply and the availability of credit in the country. (p. 272)
Sistema de la Reserva Federal *s.* sistema bancario nacional establecido por Woodrow Wilson en 1913 que controla el dinero circulante del país. (pág. 272)

Federal Securities Act *n.* a law, enacted in 1933, that required corporations to provide complete, accurate information on all stock offerings. (p. 443)
Ley Federal de Valores *s.* ley de 1933 que obliga a las corporaciones a suministrar información completa y fidedigna sobre sus ofertas de acciones. (pág. 443)

Federal Trade Commission (FTC) *n.* a federal agency established in 1914 to investigate and stop unfair business practices. (p. 270)
Comisión Federal de Comercio *s.* agencia federal establecida en 1914 para inves tiger y parar prácticas empresariales injustas. (pág. 270)

feminism *n.* the belief that women should have economic, political, and social equality with men. (p. 757)
feminismo *s.* creencia de que la mujer debe tener igualdad económica, política y social con respecto al hombre. (pág. 757)

Fifteenth Amendment *n.* an amendment to the U.S. Constitution, adopted in 1870, that prohibits the denial of voting rights to people because of their race or color or because they have previously been slaves. (p. 107)
Enmienda 15 *s.* enmienda a la Constitución, adoptada en 1870, que establece que a nadie puede negársele el derecho al voto por motivos de raza, color o por haber sido esclavo. (pág. 107)

flapper *n.* one of the free-thinking young women who embraced the new fashions and urban attitudes of the 1920s. (p. 387)
flapper *s.* jovencita típica de los años 20 que actuaba y se vestía de manera atrevida y nada convencional. (pág. 387)

flexible response *n.* a policy, developed during the Kennedy administration, that involved preparing for a variety of military responses to international crises rather than focusing on the use of nuclear weapons. (p. 611)
respuesta flexible *s.* doctrina, desarrollada durante la administración Kennedy, de prepararse para una variedad de respuestas militares, en vez de concentrarse en las armas nucleares. (pág. 611)

flipped classroom *n.* an educational strategy that reverses the traditional approach to teaching by delivering instructional content outside of the classroom and reserving class time for various forms of active learning. (p. 973)
aula invertida *s.* estrategia de educación en la que se invierte el enfoque tradicional de la enseñanza al entregar el contenido educativo fuera del salón de clases y reservar el tiempo de clase para diversas formas de aprendizaje activo. (pág. 973)

Foraker [fôr′ə-kər] **Act** *n.* legislation passed by Congress in 1900, in which the U.S. ended military rule in Puerto Rico and set up a civil government. (p. 294)
Ley Foraker *s.* legislación que el Congreso aprobó en 1900 para acabar con el gobierno militar en Puerto Rico y autorizar un gobierno civil. (pág. 294)

Fordney-McCumber Tariff [fôrd′nē mə-kŭm′bər tăr′ĭf] *n.* a set of regulations, enacted by Congress in 1922, that raised taxes on imports to record levels in order to protect American businesses against foreign competition. (p. 361)
Arancel Fordney-McCumber *s.* serie de reglas, aprobada por el Congreso en 1922, que elevó a niveles sin precedentes los impuestos a las importaciones en 1922 para proteger las compañías estadounidenses de la competencia extranjera. (pág. 361)

Fourteen Points *n.* the principles making up President Woodrow Wilson's plan for world peace following World War I. (p. 349)
los catorce puntos *s.* plan del presidente Wilson en pro de la paz mundial tras la Primera Guerra Mundial. (pág. 349)

Fourteenth Amendment *n.* an amendment to the U.S. Constitution, adopted in 1868, that makes all persons born or naturalized in the United States—including former slaves—citizens of the country and guarantees equal protection of the laws. (p. 106)
Enmienda 14 *s.* enmienda a la constitución adoptada en 1868 que hace ciudadano a toda persona nacida o naturalizada en Estados Unidos, incluso a antiguos esclavos, y garantiza igualdad de protección bajo la ley. (pág. 106)

fracking *n.* a drilling process for extracting oil and natural gas in which rock is broken up by a pressurized liquid made of water, sand, and chemicals. (p. 967)
fractura hidráulica *s.* procedimiento de perforación para extraer petróleo y gas natural en el que la roca se quiebra inyectando a presión líquido compuesto por agua, arena y productos químicos. (pág. 967)

franchise *n.* a business that has bought the right to use a parent company's name and methods, thus becoming one of a number of similar businesses in various locations. (p. 645)
franquicia *s.* forma de negocio en la que individuos compran el derecho a usar el nombre y los métodos de una compañía matriz, con lo que la compañía se multiplica. (pág. 645)

Freedmen's Bureau *n.* a federal agency set up to help former slaves after the Civil War. (p. 106)
Oficina de libertos *s.* agencia federal formada después de la Guerra Civil para ayudar a personas que habían sido esclavos antes. (pág. 106)

freedom rider *n.* one of the civil rights activists who rode buses through the South in the early 1960s to challenge segregation. (p. 728)
freedom rider *s.* activista de derechos civiles que viajó en autobús a través del Sur a comienzos de los años 60 para protestar contra la segregación. (pág. 728)

Freedom Summer *n.* a 1964 project to register African American voters in Mississippi. (p. 735)

Freedom Summer *s.* campaña de registro de votantes afroamericanos en el verano de 1964 en Mississippi. (pág. 735)

Free Speech Movement *n.* an antiestablishment New Left organization that originated in a 1964 clash between students and administrators at the University of California at Berkeley. (p. 798)
Movimiento de Libre Expresión *s.* movimiento activista de los años 60 que surgió a raíz de un enfrentamiento entre los estudiantes y la administración de la Universidad de California en Berkeley en 1964. (pág. 798)

free trade *n.* the policy in international markets in which governments do not restrict imports or exports. (p. 980)
libre comercio *s.* política en mercados internacionales en la que los gobiernos no restringen las importaciones ni las exportaciones. (pág. 980)

French and Indian War *n.* a conflict in North America, lasting from 1754 to 1763, that was a part of a worldwide struggle between France and Britain and that ended with the defeat of France and the transfer of French Canada to Britain. (p. 13)
Guerra contra Franceses e Indígenas *s.* guerra librada en Norteamérica (1754–1763) como parte de un conflicto mundial entre Francia y Gran Bretaña; finalizó con la derrota de Francia y el traspaso del Canadá francés a Gran Bretaña. (pág. 13)

Fundamentalism *n.* a Protestant religious movement grounded in the belief that all the stories and details in the Bible are literally true. (p. 383)
fundamentalismo *s.* movimiento religioso protestante basado en la interpretación textual, o palabra por palabra, de las escrituras. (pág. 383)

G

genetic engineering *n.* the alteration of the molecular biology of organisms' cells in order to create new varieties of bacteria, plants, and animals. (p. 918)
ingeniería genética *s.* alteración de la biología molecular de las células de un organismo para crear nuevas variedades de bacterias, plantas o animales. (pág. 918)

English and Spanish Glossary

Geneva Accords [jə-nĕ′və ə-kôrdz′] *n.* a 1954 peace agreement that divided Vietnam into Communist-controlled North Vietnam and non-Communist South Vietnam until unification elections could be held in 1956. (p. 782)
  Acuerdos de Ginebra *s.* plan de paz de Indochina en 1954 en el que Vietnam fue dividido temporalmente en Vietnam del Norte y Vietnam del Sur, mientras se celebraban las elecciones de 1956. (pág. 782)

genocide *n.* the deliberate and systematic extermination of a particular racial, national, or religious group. (p. 500)
  genocidio *s.* exterminio deliberado y sistemático de un grupo de personas por su raza, nacionalidad o religión. (pág. 500)

Gentlemen's Agreement *n.* a 1907–1908 agreement between the U.S. and Japanese governments to limit Japanese immigration to the United States. (p. 195)
  Acuerdo de Caballeros *s.* acuerdo concertado durante 1907 y 1908, mediante el cual el gobierno de Japón limitaron la inmigración a Estados Unidos. (pág. 195)

gentrification *n.* the process of restoring deteriorated urban property by middle-class people, which often results in the displacement of lower-income residents. (p. 921)
  aburguesamiento *s.* restauración de propiedades urbanas por personas de la clase media que a menudo resulta en la pérdida de vivienda para personas de medios escasos. (pág. 921)

geographic information system (GIS) *n.* a computer system designed to collect and analyze many kinds of spatial or geographical data. (p. 913)
  sistema de información geográfica *s.* sistema informático diseñado para recopilar y analizar gran cantidad de tipos de datos espaciales o geográficos. (pág. 913)

Gettysburg *n.* the Pennsylvania location of the most decisive battle of the Civil War, fought July 1–3, 1863. (p. 100)
  Gettysburg *s.* sitio de Pennsylvania donde tuvo lugar la batalla más decisiva de la Guerra de Secesión, del 1 al 3 de julio de 1863. (pág. 100)

ghetto *n.* a city neighborhood in which a certain minority group is pressured or forced to live. (p. 500)
  ghetto *s.* tipo de vecindario urbano donde cierto grupo minoritario es obligado o forzado a vivir. (pág. 500)

GI Bill of Rights *n.* a name given to the Servicemen's Readjustment Act, a 1944 law that provided financial and educational benefits for World War II veterans. (pp. 567, 637)
  Carta de Derechos de los Veteranos *s.* nombre dado a la Ley de Reajuste de Militares de 1944, que ofrecía beneficios financieros y educativos a los veteranos de la Segunda Guerra Mundial. (pág. 567, 637)

glasnost [gläs′nəst] *n.* the open discussion of social problems that was permitted in the Soviet Union in the 1980s. (p. 628)
  glasnost *s.* la discusión abierta de problemas sociales que se dio en la Unión Soviética durante los años 80. (pág. 628)

Glass-Steagall [glăs′stē′gəl] **Act** *n.* the 1933 law that established the Federal Deposit Insurance Corporation to protect individuals' bank accounts. (p. 443)
  Ley Bancaria Glass-Steagall *s.* ley de 1933 que aseguró los depósitos bancarios mediante la Corporación Federal de Seguros de Depósitos. (pág. 443)

global climate change *n.* the condition caused by global warming, characterized by high temperatures and extreme weather events. (p. 966)
  cambio climático global *s.* estado causado por el calentamiento global, que se caracteriza por altas temperaturas y sucesos climáticos extremos. (pág. 966)

globalization *n.* the process of international integration resulting from the interchange of world views, products, ideas, and other aspects of culture. (p. 980)
  globalización *s.* proceso de integración internacional que resulta del intercambio de puntos de vista, productos, ideas y otros aspectos de la cultura a nivel mundial. (pág. 980)

gold standard *n.* a monetary system in which the basic unit of currency is defined in terms of a set amount of gold. (p. 147)

patrón de oro *s.* sistema monetario en el cual la unidad básica de moneda se define en relación a una cantidad fija de oro. (pág. 147)

Gone with the Wind *n.* a 1939 movie dealing with the life of southern plantation owners during the Civil War—one of the most popular films of all time. (p. 467)
Lo que el viento se llevó *s.* película de 1939 sobre la vida de los dueños de plantaciones del Sur durante la Guerra Civil; una de las más populares de todos los tiempos. (pág. 467)

graft *n.* the illegal use of political influence for personal gain. (p. 206)
corrupción *s.* uso ilegal de un cargo político con el fin de ganancia personal. (pág. 206)

grandfather clause *n.* a provision that exempts certain people from a law on the basis of previously existing circumstances—especially a clause formerly in some southern states' constitutions that exempted whites from the strict voting requirements used to keep African Americans from the polls. (p. 243)
cláusula del abuelo *s.* estipulación que exime
de cumplir una ley a ciertas personas por circunstancias previas; específicamente, cláusula de la constitución de algunos estados sureños que eximía a los blancos de los estrictos equisitos que impedían que los afroamericanos votaran. (pág. 243)

Grange [grānj] *n.* the Patrons of Husbandry—a social and educational organization through which farmers attempted to combat the power of the railroads in the late 19th century. (p. 146)
la Granja *s.* The Patrons of Husbandry—organización de granjeros que intentaron, a partir de la década de 1870, combatir el poder de los ferrocarriles. (pág. 146)

Grapes of Wrath, The *n.* a novel by John Steinbeck, published in 1939, that deals with a family of Oklahomans who leave the Dust Bowl for California. (p. 470)
Las uvas de la ira *s.* novela de John Steinbeck, publicada en 1939, sobre una familia de Oklahoma que se va de la región del Dust Bowl a California. (pág. 470)

Great Awakening *n.* a revival of religious feeling in the American colonies during the 1730s and 1740s. (p. 11)

Gran Despertar *s.* serie de grandes asambleas religiosas en las décadas de 1730 y 1750. (pág. 11)

Great Depression *n.* a period, lasting from 1929 to 1940, in which the U.S. economy was in severe decline and millions of Americans were unemployed. (p. 418)
Gran Depresión *s.* período de 1929 a 1940 en el que la economía estadounidense quebró y millones quedaron sin empleo. (pág. 418)

Great Migration *n.* the large-scale movement of African Americans from the South to northern cities in the early 20th century. (p. 341)
Gran Migración *s.* movimiento de cientos de miles de afroamericanos sureños a ciudades del Norte a principios del siglo 20. (pág. 341)

Great Plains *n.* the vast grassland that extends through the central portion of North America, from Texas northward to Canada, east of the Rocky Mountains. (p. 117)
Grandes Praderas *s.* vasta pradera que se extiende a través de Norteamérica, de Texas a Canadá en dirección norte y hacia el este de las Montañas Rocosas. (pág. 117)

Great Recession *n.* a severe decline in U.S. economic activity that began in late 2007. (p. 899)
Gran Recesión *s.* grave descenso de la actividad económica de los Estados Unidos que comenzó a fines de 2007. (pág. 899)

Great Society *n.* President Lyndon B. Johnson's program to reduce poverty and racial injustice and to promote a better quality of life in the United States. (p. 689)
Gran Sociedad *s.* ambicioso programa legislative del presidente Lyndon B. Johnson para reducir la pobreza y la injusticia racial, y mejorar el nivel de vida. (pág. 689)

H

Haight-Ashbury [hāt′ăsh′bĕr-ē] *n.* a San Francisco district that became the "capital" of the hippie counterculture during the 1960s. (p. 700)
Haight-Ashbury *s.* distrito de San Francisco, "capital" de la contracultura hippie durante los años 60. (pág. 700)

English and Spanish Glossary

hard rock mining *n.* mining that requires cutting deep shafts in solid rock to extract the ore. (p. 127)
minería de roca dura *s.* explotación minera en la que es necesario hacer huecos profundos en la roca sólida para extraer el mineral. (pág. 127)

Harlem Renaissance *n.* a flowering of African American artistic creativity during the 1920s, centered in the Harlem community of New York City. (p. 403)
Renacimiento de Harlem *s.* período de sobresaliente creatividad afroamericana durante los años 20 y 30, en la zona de Harlem en la ciudad de Nueva York. (pág. 403)

hawk *n.* a person who supported U.S. involvement in the Vietnam War and believed that the United States should use increased military force to win it. (p. 800)
halcón *s.* persona que respaldaba la Guerra de Vietnam y creía que Estados Unidos debía incrementar su fuerza military para ganarla. (pág. 800)

Hawley-Smoot Tariff [hôlē smoot'tăr'ĭf] **Act** *n.* a law, enacted in 1930, that established the highest protective tariff in U.S. history, worsening the Depression in America and abroad. (p. 420)
Ley de Aranceles Hawley-Smoot *s.* ley de 1930 que estableció los más altos aranceles proteccionistas en la historia estadounidense, afectando negativamente el comercio internacional y empeorando le depresión mundial y doméstica. (pág. 420)

H-bomb *n.* the hydrogen bomb—a thermonuclear weapon much more powerful than the atomic bomb. (p. 601)
bomba de hidrógeno *s.* bomba de hidrógeno, o termonuclear, mucho más poderosa que la bomba atómica. (pág. 601)

Hiroshima [hĭr'ə-shē'mə] *n.* a Japanese city and important military center that was destroyed by the first atomic bomb used in World War II. (p. 560)
Hiroshima *s.* ciudad japonesa e importante centro militar que fue destruido por la primera bomba atómica usada en la Segunda Guerra Mundial. (pág. 560)

Ho Chi Minh [hō'chē'mĭn'] **Trail** *n.* a network of paths used by North Vietnam to transport supplies to the Vietcong in South Vietnam. (p. 783)
Sendero de Ho Chi Minh *s.* red de caminos por la que Vietnam del Norte abastecía al Vietcong en Vietnam del Sur. (pág. 783)

Hollywood Ten *n.* ten witnesses from the film industry who refused to cooperate with the HUAC's investigation of Communist influence in Hollywood. (p. 594)
los Diez de Hollywood *s.* diez testigos de la industria cinematográfica que se negaron a cooperar con la investigación de influencia comunista en Hollywood. (pág. 594)

Holocaust [hŏl'ə-kôst'] *n.* the systematic murder—or genocide—of Jews and other groups in Europe by the Nazis before and during World War II. (p. 498)
Holocausto *s.* asesinato sistemático o genocidio de judíos y de otros grupos en Europa por los nazis antes y durante la Segunda Guerra Mundial. (pág. 498)

Homestead [hōm'stĕd'] **Act** *n.* a U.S. law enacted in 1862, that provided 160 acres in the West to any citizen or intended citizen who was head of household and would cultivate the land for five years; a law whose passage led to record numbers of U.S. settlers claiming private property which previously had been reserved by treaty and by tradition for Native American nomadic dwelling and use; the same law strengthened in 1889 to encourage individuals to exercise their private property rights and develop homesteads out of the vast government lands. (p. 137)
Ley de la Heredad *s.* ley aprobada en 1862 que otorgaba 160 acres de tierra en el Oeste a cualquier ciudadano or ciudadano futuro que fuera cabeza de familia y que cultivara la tierra por cinco años; ley cuya aprobación llevó a un gran número de colonos estadounidenses a reclamar como propiedad privada tierra que había sido reservada por tratados y tradiciones para la vivienda de indígenas americanos; la misma ley, reforzada en 1889, dio incentivas para que los individuos ejercieran su derecho de propiedad privada y desarrollaran viviendas. (pág. 137)

horizontal integration *n.* the merging of companies that make similar products. (p. 171)
integración horizontal *s.* proceso mediante el cual compañías que fabrican productos similares se unen y reducen la competencia. (pág. 171)

hot line *n.* a communication link established in 1963 to allow the leaders of the United States and the Soviet Union to contact each other in times of crisis. (p. 618)
línea de emergencia *s.* línea directa de comunicación establecida en 1963 para que los líderes de Estados Unidos y la Unión Soviética pudieran hablarse durante una crisis. (pág. 618)

House Un-American Activities Committee (HUAC) *n.* a congressional committee created in 1938 that investigated Communist influence inside and outside the U.S. government in the years following World War II. (p. 593)
Comité de la Cámara de Representantes sobre Actividades Antiamericanas *s.* comité del Congreso creado en 1938 que investigó la influencia comunista dentro y fuera del gobierno durante los años que siguieron la Segunda Guerra Mundial. (pág. 593)

housing bubble *n.* widespread overpricing of residential real estate. (p. 899)
burbuja inmobiliaria *s.* sobreprecio generalizado de bienes inmuebles residenciales. (pág. 899)

human rights *n.* the rights and freedoms, such as those named in the Declaration of Independence and the Bill of Rights, to which all people are entitled. (p. 845)
derechos humanos *s.* derechos y libertades considerados básicos, como los que establece la Declaración de Independencia y la Carta de Derechos. (pág. 845)

human trafficking *n.* the act of bringing people into a different country against their will and in violation of the law. (p. 940)
trata de personas *s.* el acto de llevar personas a otro país contra su voluntad y violando la ley. (pág. 940)

hydraulic mining *n.* method of mining that uses water under high pressure to blast away gravel and dirt to expose the mineral underneath. (p. 127)

minería hidráulica *s.* método de explotación minera que utiliza aqua con alta presión para hacer volar la grava y la tierra, y así exponer el mineral que se oculta debajo. (pág. 127)

I

Immigration Act of 1965 *n.* a law that increased the number of immigrants allowed to settle in the United States. (p. 691)
Ley de Inmigración de 1965 *s.* ley que abrió las puertas a más inmigrantes. (pág. 691)

impeachment *n.* the process of accusing a public official of wrongdoing. (p. 831)
acusación *s.* proceso por el cual se acusa a un funcionario público de delitos. (pág. 831)

imperialism *n.* the policy of extending a nation's authority over other countries by economic, political, or military means. (p. 281)
imperialismo *s.* política de controlar países por medios económicos, políticos o militares. (pág. 281)

income gap *n.* income inequality. (p. 956)
brecha de ingresos *s.* desigualdad de ingresos. (pág. 956)

income tax *n.* a tax on earnings. (p. 98)
impuesto sobre la renta *s.* impuesto que retiene un porcentaje específico de ingresos. (pág. 98)

Individuals with Disabilities Education Act (IDEA) *n.* an act that requires that students with a disability are provided with a Free Appropriate Public Education (FAPE) that is tailored to their individual needs. (p. 975)
Ley de Educación para Personas con Discapacidades *s.* ley que requiere que a los estudiantes con una discapacidad se les provea Educación Pública Adecuada y Gratuita (FAPE, por su sigla en inglés) adaptada a sus necesidades individuales. (pág. 975)

Industrial Workers of the World (IWW) *n.* a labor organization for unskilled workers, formed by a group of radical unionists and socialists in 1905. (p. 179)
Industrial Workers of the World *s.* sindicato de trabajadores de mano de obra no calificada creado en 1905. (pág. 179)

English and Spanish Glossary

initiative *n.* a procedure by which a legislative measure can be originated by the people rather than by lawmakers. (p. 236)
iniciativa *s.* reforma gubernamental que permite a los ciudadanos presentar proyectos de ley en el Congreso o en cuerpos legislativos estatales. (pág. 236)

installment plan *n.* an arrangement in which a purchaser pays over an extended time, without having to put down much money at the time of purchase. (p. 368)
pago a plazos *s.* práctica de comprar a crédito mediante pagos regulares durante determinado período de tiempo. (pág. 368)

intellectual property *n.* a legal term describing creations of the mind. (p. 915)
propiedad intelectual *s.* término jurídico que describe creaciones de la mente. (pág. 915)

Intermediate-Range Nuclear Forces (INF) Treaty *n.* a 1987 agreement between the United States and the Soviet Union that eliminated some weapons systems and allowed for on-site inspection of military installations. (p. 629)
Tratado sobre Fuerzas Nucleares Intermedias *s.* tratado entre Estados Unidos y la Unión Soviética firmado en 1987, que eliminó algunas armas y permitió la inspección directa de emplazamientos de misiles. (pág. 629)

Internet *n.* a worldwide network, originally developed by the U.S. Department of Defense, that links computers and allows almost immediate communication of texts, pictures, and sounds. (p. 913)
Internet *s.* red mundial, originalmente diseñada por el Departamento de Defensa, que une computadores y permite una comunicación casi instantánea de textos, ilustraciones y sonidos. (pág. 913)

internment *n.* confinement or a restriction in movement, especially under wartime conditions. (p. 532)
confinamiento *s.* restricción de movimiento, en especial durante condiciones de guerra. (pág. 532)

Interstate Commerce Act *n.* a law, enacted in 1887, that reestablished the federal government's right to supervise railroad activities and created a five-member Interstate Commerce Commission to do so. (p. 167)

Ley de Comercio Interestatal *s.* ley de 1887 que restablecía el derecho del gobierno federal a supervisar los ferrocarriles; creó una Comisión de Comercio Interestatal de cinco miembros. (pág. 167)

iron curtain *n.* a phrase used by Winston Churchill in 1946 to describe an imaginary line that separated Communist countries in the Soviet bloc of Eastern Europe from countries in Western Europe. (p. 575)
cortina de hierro *s.* frase usada por Winston Churchill en 1946 para describir una línea imaginaria que separaba los países comunistas que estaban en la parte soviética al este de Europa de los países en Europa occidental. (pág. 575)

ISIS *n.* the Islamic State of Iraq and Syria, a terrorist group that seeks to establish a strict Islamic state ruled by religious authorities. (p. 951)
ISIS *s.* Estado Islámico de Irak y Siria, grupo terrorista que busca establecer un estado islámico estricto gobernado por autoridades religiosas. (pág. 951)

island hopping *n.* the Allied strategy in the Pacific theater during World War II of capturing and securing selected islands and using them as bases to advance closer to Japan while avoiding the heaviest concentrations of enemy forces (p. 551)
estrategia de island hopping *s.* estrategia de los Aliados en el teatro de operaciones del Pacífico durante la Segunda Guerra Mundial que consistía en capturar y asegurarse islas seleccionadas y usarlas como base para avanzar más cerca de Japón al tiempo que se evitaban las concentraciones más fuertes de las fuerzas enemigas. (pág. 551)

isolationism *n.* opposition to political and economic entanglements with other countries. (p. 371)
aislacionismo *s.* política que se opone a participar en conflictos políticos y económicos con otros países. (pág. 371)

J

Jamestown *n.* the first permanent English Colony in North America, founded in Virgina in 1607. (p. 7)

Jamestown *s.* primera colonia inglesa permanente en América del Norte, fundada en Virginia en 1607. (pág. 7)

Japanese American Citizens League (JACL) *n.* an organization that pushed the U.S. government to compensate Japanese Americans for property they had lost when they were interned during World War II. (p. 533)
Sociedad de Ciudadanos Americano-Japoneses *s.* organización que presionó al gobierno a compensar a los estadounidenses de origen japonés por las propiedades que perdieron al ser internados durante la Segunda Guerra Mundial. (pág. 533)

jazz *n.* a style of music characterized by the use of improvisation. (p. 664)
jazz *s.* estilo de música caracterizado por la improvisación. (pág. 664)

Jim Crow laws *n.* laws enacted by southern state and local governments to separate white and black people in public and private facilities. (p. 243)
leyes Jim Crow *s.* leyes impuestas por los gobiernos estatales y municipales del Sur con el fin de separar a blancos y afroamericanos en instalaciones públicas y privadas. (pág. 243)

joint-stock company *n.* a business in which investors pool their wealth for a common purpose. (p. 6)
sociedad de capitales *s.* institución empresarial tipo corporación en la que inversionistas unen riquezas con un fin común; se usa ron para financiar la exploración de las Américas. (pág. 6)

Jungle, The *n.* a novel by Upton Sinclair, published in 1906, that portrays the dangerous and unhealthy conditions prevalent in the meatpacking industry at that time. (p. 256)
La jungla *s.* novela publicada en 1906 por el periodista Upton Sinclair que denunciaba la insalubri dad de la industria de carne en aquella época; llevó a reformas nacionales. (pág. 256)

K

kamikaze [kä′mĭ-kä′zē] *adj.* involving or engaging in the deliberate crashing of a bomb-filled airplane into a military target. (p. 553)

kamikaze *adj.* que estrellaba deliberadamente un avión bombardero contra un blanco militar. (pág. 553)

Kent State University *n.* an Ohio university where National Guardsmen opened fire on students protesting the Vietnam War on May 4, 1970, wounding nine and killing four. (p. 812)
Universidad Estatal de Kent *s.* universidad de Ohio donde guardias militares abrieron fuego contra estudiantes durante una protesta contra la Guerra de Vietnam el 4 de mayo de 1970, hiriendo a nueve de ellos y matando a cuatro. (pág. 812)

Kerner [kûr′nər] **Commission** *n.* a group that was appointed by President Johnson to study the causes of urban violence and that recommended the elimination of de facto segregation in American society. (p. 743)
Comisión Kerner *s.* grupo designado por el presidente Lyndon B. Johnson para estudiar las causas de la violencia urbana; recomendó eliminar la segregación de facto en la sociedad estadounidense. (pág. 743)

Korean War *n.* a conflict between North Korea and South Korea, lasting from 1950 to 1953, in which the United States, along with other UN countries, fought on the side of the South Koreans and China fought on the side of the North Koreans. (p. 586)
Guerra de Corea *s.* guerra de 1950 a 1953 entre Corea del Norte y Corea del Sur; China respaldó a Corea del Norte y las tropas de las Naciones Unidas, integradas en su mayoría por soldados estadounidenses, apoyaron a Corea del Sur. (pág. 586)

Kristallnacht [krĭs′täl′nächt′] *n.* "night of broken glass," a name given to the night of November 9, 1938, when gangs of Nazi storm troopers attacked Jewish homes, businesses, and synagogues in Germany. (p. 498)
Kristallnacht *s.* "noche del cristal quebrado," noviembre 9 de 1938, noche en que milicianos nazis atacaron viviendas, negocios y sinagogas judías en Alemania. (pág. 498)

Ku Klux Klan [kōō′ klŭks klăn′] **(KKK)** *n.* a secret organization that used terrorist tactics in an attempt to restore white supremacy in southern states after the Civil War. (p. 110)

English and Spanish Glossary

Ku Klux Klan *s.* sociedad secreta de hombres blancos en los estados sureños después de la Guerra Civil que de sa tó terror para restaurar la supremacía blanca. (pág. 110)

Kyoto Protocol *n.* an international treaty designed to reduce emissions of greenhouse gases. (p. 984)
Protocolo de Kyoto *s.* tratado internacional diseñado para reducir las emisiones de gases de efecto invernadero. (pág. 984)

L

laissez-faire [lĕs´ā fâr´] *n.* in French, meaning "to let do"; a form of capitalism that allows companies to conduct business without intervention by the government. (p. 170)
laissez-faire *s.* expresión francesa que significa "dejar hacer"; forma de capitalismo que permite a las empresas hacer negocios sin intervención del gobierno. (pág. 170)

La Raza Unida [lä rä´sä ōō-nē´dä] *n.* a Latino political organization founded in 1970 by José Angel Gutiérrez. (p. 750)
La Raza Unida *s.* organización política latina establecida en 1970 por José Ángel Gutiérrez. (pág. 750)

League of Nations *n.* an association of nations established in 1920 to promote international cooperation and peace. (p. 350)
Liga de las Naciones *s.* organización internacional establecida en 1920 para pro mover la cooperación y la paz internacional. (pág. 350)

Lend-Lease Act *n.* a law, passed in 1941, that allowed the United States to ship arms and other supplies, without immediate payment, to nations fighting the Axis powers. (p. 510)
Ley de Préstamo y Alquiler *s.* ley aprobada en 1941, que autorizó al gobierno a mandar armas y otros productos, sin pago inmediato, a las naciones que luchaban contra el Eje. (pág. 510)

Limited Test Ban Treaty *n.* the 1963 treaty in which the United States and the Soviet Union agreed not to conduct nuclear weapons tests in the atmosphere. (p. 618)
Tratado de Limitación de Pruebas Nucleares *s.* tratado de 1963 en que Estados Unidos y la Unión Soviética acordaron no realizar pruebas de armas nucleares en la atmósfera. (pág. 618)

long drive *n.* the moving of cattle over trails to a shipping center. (p. 131)
arreo de ganado *s.* proceso mediante el cual los vaqueros llevaban por tierra ganado hacia el mercado. (pág. 131)

longhorn *n.* a breed of sturdy, long-horned cattle brought by the Spanish to Mexico and suited to the dry conditions of the Southwest. (p. 129)
longhorn *s.* resistente raza de ganado vacuno de cuernos largos llevada por los españoles a México, muy apta para las condiciones de esa región. (pág. 129)

Louisiana Purchase *n.* the 1803 purchase by the United States of France's Louisiana Territory—extending from the Mississippi River to the Rocky Mountains—for $15 million. (p. 36)
Compra de Louisiana *s.* compra de terrenos a Francia por 15 millones de dólares en 1803 de las tierras desde el río Mississippi hasta las montañas Rocosas. (pág. 36)

Loyalists *n.* colonists who supported the British government during the American Revolution. (p. 20)
realistas *s.* colonos que apoyaban al gobierno británico durante la Revolución Norteamericana. (pág. 20)

Lusitania [lōō´sĭ-ta´nē-ə] *n.* a British passenger ship that was sunk by a German U-boat on May 7, 1915. (p. 322)
Lusitania *s.* barco británico de pasajeros que se hundió cerca de costas irlandesas el 7 de mayo de 1915, tras ser atacado por un submarino alemán. (pág. 322)

M

mandate *n.* the authority to act that an elected official receives from the voters who elected him or her. (p. 680)
mandato *s.* conquista de una porción sufi cientemente grande del voto, que indica que un líder elegido tiene apoyo popular para sus programas. (pág. 680)

Manhattan Project *n.* the U.S. program to develop an atomic bomb for use in World War II. (p. 523)
Proyecto Manhattan *s.* programa estadounidense que se inició en 1942 con el fin de diseñar una bomba atómica para la Segunda Guerra Mundial. (pág. 523)

manifest destiny *n.* the 19th-century belief that the United States would inevitably expand westward to the Pacific Ocean and into Mexican territory. (p. 81)
destino manifiesto *s.* término usado en la década de 1840 para describir la creencia de que Estados Unidos estaba inexorablemente destinado a adquirir más territorio, especialmente mediante su expansión hacia el oeste. (pág. 81)

Marshall Plan *n.* the program, proposed by Secretary of State George Marshall in 1947, under which the United States supplied economic aid to European nations to help them rebuild after World War II. (p. 580)
Plan Marshall *s.* plan formulado por el Secretario de Estado George Marshall en 1947, me diante el que se ofreció ayuda a países europeos con el fin de reparar los daños de la Segunda Guerra Mundial. (pág. 580)

mass media *n.* the means of communication—such as television, newspapers, and radio—that reach large audiences. (p. 659)
medios informativos *s.* medios de comunicación—tales como televisión, prensa y radio—que llegan a grandes audiencias. (pág. 659)

mass transit *n.* transportation systems designed to move large numbers of people along fixed routes. (p. 200)
transporte público *s.* sistemas de transporte diseñados para llevar grandes números de personas por rutas fijas. (pág. 200)

massive retaliation *n.* a Cold War military strategy intended to discourage a nuclear attack by committing to launch a devastating counterstrike to any attack. (p. 629)
represalia masiva *s.* una estrategia militar de la Guerra Fría con la intención de desalentar un ataque nuclear, comprometiéndose a poner en marcha un contraataque devastador para cualquier ataque. (pág. 629)

McCarthyism [mə-kär′thē-ĭz′əm] *n.* the attacks, often unsubstantiated, by Senator Joseph McCarthy and others on people suspected of being Communists in the early 1950s. (p. 597)
macartismo *s.* ataques, a menudo sin respaldo, del senador Joseph McCarthy y otros contra presuntos comunistas en los años 50. (pág. 597)

Meat Inspection Act *n.* a law, enacted in 1906, that established strict cleanliness requirements for meatpackers and created a federal meat-inspection program. (p. 259)
Ley de Inspección de la Carne *s.* ley de 1906 que establecía estrictos requisitos sanitarios en las empacadoras de carne, así como un programa federal de inspección de carnes. (pág. 259)

Medicaid [məd′ĭ-kād′] *n.* a program, established in 1965, that provides health insurance for people on welfare. (p. 690)
Medicaid *s.* programa federal que se inició en 1965 para brindar atención médica a las personas que reciben ayuda pública. (pág. 690)

Medicare [məd′ĭ-kâr′] *n.* a federal program, established in 1965, that provides hospital insurance and low-cost medical insurance to Americans aged 65 and over. (p. 690)
Medicare *s.* programa federal que se inició en 1965 para brindar seguros médicos y de hospitalización a bajo costo a los mayors de 65 años. (pág. 690)

melting pot *n.* a mixture of people from different cultures and races who blend together by abandoning their native languages and cultures. (p. 194)
crisol de culturas *s.* mezcla de personas de diferentes culturas y razas que se amalgaman y abandonan su idioma y cultura natal. (pág. 194)

mercantilism [mûr′kən-tē-lĭz′əm] *n.* an economic system in which nations seek to increase their wealth and power by obtaining large amounts of gold and silver and by establishing a favorable balance of trade. (p. 8)
mercantilismo *s.* sistema económico en que un país aumenta su riqueza y poder al incrementar su posesión de oro y plata, y al exportar más productos de los que importa. (pág. 8)

English and Spanish Glossary

militarism *n.* the policy of building up armed forces in aggressive preparedness for war and their use as a tool of diplomacy. (p. 315)
militarismo *s.* política de mantener una sólida organización militar como preparación agresiva para la guerra y su empleo como herramienta diplomática. (pág. 315)

minimum wage *n.* the lowest wage that employers can legally pay their workers. (p. 955)
salario mínimo *s.* salario más bajo que los empleadores pueden pagar legalmente a sus trabajadores. (pág. 955)

Missouri Compromise *n.* a series of agreements passed by Congress in 1820–1821 to maintain the balance of power between slave states and free states. (p. 38)
Acuerdo de Missouri *s.* serie de acuerdos aprobados por el Congreso en 1820–1821 para mantener un equilibrio seccional entre los estados esclavistas y los estados libres. (pág. 38)

modernism *n.* a 20th-century artistic movement that contended that traditional art was outdated and no longer meaningful in the new, industrialized, urban world. (p. 397)
modernismo *s.* movimiento artístico del siglo XX que sostenía que el arte tradicional estaba pasado de moda y ya no era significativo en el nuevo mundo industrializado y urbano. (pág. 397)

monopoly *n.* having complete control in the marketplace, without any outside competition. (p. 173)
monopolio *s.* que tiene completo control en el mercado, sin ninguna competencia externa. (pág. 173)

Moral Majority *n.* a political alliance of religious groups, consisting mainly of evangelical and fundamentalist Christians, that was active in the 1970s and 1980s, condemning liberal attitudes and behavior and raising money for conservative candidates. (p. 853)
Mayoría Moral *s.* coalición política de organizaciones religiosas conservadoras en los años 70 y 80 que recaudó dinero para respaldar agendas y candidatos conservadores, y condenó actitudes y comportamientos liberales. (pág. 853)

Morrill [môr′əl] **Acts** *n.* laws enacted in 1862 and 1890 to help create agricultural colleges by giving federal land to states. (p. 141)
Leyes Morrill *s.* leyes aprobadas en 1862 y 1890 que otorgaban tierras federales a los estados para financiar universidades agrícolas. (pág. 141)

muckraker [mŭk′rāk′r] *n.* one of the magazine journalists who exposed the corrupt side of business and public life in the early 1900s. (p. 231)
muckraker *s.* uno de los reporteros de revistas que desenmascaraban el lado corrupto de las empresas y de la vida pública a principios del siglo 20. (pág. 231)

Munn v. Illinois *n.* an 1877 case in which the Supreme Court upheld states' regulation of railroads for the benefit of farmers and consumers, thus establishing the right of government to regulate private industry to serve the public interest. (p. 167)
Munn v. Illinois *s.* caso de la Suprema Corte en 1877; estableció el derecho del gobierno federal a regular la industria privada en beneficio del interés público. (pág. 167)

mutually assured destruction *n.* a Cold War policy to respond to any attack with nuclear force, resulting in the total destruction of both parties. (p. 629)
destrucción mutua asegurada *s.* política de la Guerra Fría para responder a cualquier ataque con fuerza nuclear, lo que resulta en la destrucción total de las dos partes. (pág. 629)

My Lai [mē′lī′] *n.* a village in northern South Vietnam where more than 200 unarmed civilians, including women and children, were massacred by U.S. troops in May 1968. (p. 812)
My Lai *s.* pueblo del norte de Vietnam del Sur, donde más de 200 civiles desarmados, incluso mujeres y niños, fueron masacrados por las tropas de EE.UU. en mayo de 1968. (pág. 812)

N

NAACP *n.* the National Association for the Advancement of Colored People—an organization founded in 1909 to promote full racial equality. (p. 263, 401)
NAACP *s.* National Association for the Advancement of Colored People (Asociación Nacional para el Avance de la Gente de Color), organización fundada en 1909 y dedicada a la igualdad racial. (pág. 263, 401)

NACW *n.* the National Association of Colored Women—a social service organization founded in 1896. (p. 254)
NACW *s.* National Association of Colored Women (Asociación Nacional de Mujeres de Color), organización de servicio social fundada en 1896. (pág. 254)

Nagasaki *n.* a Japanese city destroyed by the second atomic bomb used in World War II. (p. 561)
Nagasaki *s.* ciudad japonesa destruida por la segunda bomba atómica usada en la Segunda Guerra Mundial. (pág. 561)

napalm *n.* a gasoline-based substance used in bombs that U.S. planes dropped in Vietnam in order to burn away jungle and expose Vietcong hideouts. (p. 791)
napalm *s.* sustancia incendiaria de gasolina que lanzaban los aviones estadounidenses en Vietnam, con el fin de incendiar la selva y revelar los escondites del Vietcong. (pág. 791)

National Energy Act *n.* a law, enacted during the Carter administration, that established a tax on "gas-guzzling" automobiles, removed price controls on U.S. oil and natural gas, and provided tax credits for the development of alternative energy sources. (p. 842)
Ley Nacional de Energía *s.* ley promulgada durante la administración Carter para aliviar la crisis energética; aplicó impuestos a los autos que usan gasolina de manera ineficiente y suspendió el control de precios del petróleo y el gas natural estadounidenses. (pág. 842)

National Industrial Recovery Act (NIRA) *n.* a law enacted in 1933 to establish codes of fair practice for industries and to promote industrial growth. (p. 445)
Ley Nacional de Recuperación Industrial *s.* ley aprobada en 1933 que establecía agencias para supervisar industrias y suministrar empleos. (pág. 445)

national interest *n.* a country's goals and ambitions. (p. 943)
interés nacional *s.* las metas y ambiciones de un país. (pág. 943)

National Labor Relations Board (NLRB) *n.* an agency created in 1935 to prevent unfair labor practices and to mediate disputes between workers and management. (p. 474)

Junta Nacional de Relaciones Laborales *s.* agencia creada en 1935 con el fin de prevenir prácticas laborales injustas y mediar en disputas laborales. (pág. 474)

National Organization for Women (NOW) *n.* an organization founded in 1966 to pursue feminist goals, such as better childcare facilities, improved educational opportunities, and an end to job discrimination. (p. 758)
Organización Nacional de la Mujer *s.* organización fundada en 1966 con el fin de impulsar metas feministas, tales como mejores guarderías,bmayores oportunidades educativas y el fin de la discriminaciónblaboral. (pág. 758)

National Security Agency (NSA) *n.* an intelligence-gathering organization within the U.S. government. (p. 936)
Agencia de Seguridad Nacional *s.* organización de recopilación de información de inteligencia dentro del gobierno de los EE. UU. (pág. 936)

National Youth Administration *n.* an agency that provided young Americans with aid and employment during the Great Depression. (p. 453)
Administración Nacional de Recursos para la Juventud *s.* programa que suministraba ayuda y empleos a jóvenes durante la Depresión. (pág. 453)

Nation of Islam [ĭs-läm′] *n.* a religious group, popularly known as the Black Muslims, founded by Elijah Muhammad to promote black separatism and the Islamic religion. (p. 740)
Nación del Islam *s.* grupo religioso, popularmente conocido como musulmanes negros, fundado por Elijah Muhammad para promover el separatismo negro y la religión islámica. (pág. 740)

NAWSA *n.* the National American Woman Suffrage Association—an organization founded in 1890 to gain voting rights for women. (p. 254)
NAWSA *s.* National American Woman Suffrage Association (Asociación Nacional Americana del Sufragio Femenino), creada en 1890 para obtener derechos electorales para la mujer. (pág. 254)

English and Spanish Glossary

Nazism [nät′sĭz′əm] *n.* the political philosophy—based on extreme nationalism, racism, and militaristic expansionism—that Adolf Hitler put into practice in Germany from 1933 to 1945. (p. 488)
nazismo *s.* movimiento político basado en un extreme nacionalismo, racismo y expansionismo militar; instituido en Alemania como sistema de gobierno por Adolfo Hitler en 1933. (pág. 488)

Neutrality Acts *n.* a series of laws enacted in 1935 and 1936 to prevent U.S. arms sales and loans to nations at war. (p. 508)
Leyes de Neutralidad *s.* serie de leyes aprobadas por el Congreso en 1935 y 1936 que prohibieron la venta y el alquiler de armas a naciones en guerra. (pág. 508)

New Deal *n.* President Franklin Roosevelt's program to alleviate the problems of the Great Depression, focusing on relief for the needy, economic recovery, and financial reform. (p. 441)
New Deal *s.* medidas económicas y políticas adoptadas por el presidente Franklin Roosevelt en los años 30 para promover recuperación económica, ayuda a los necesitados y reforma financiera. (pág. 441)

New Deal Coalition *n.* an alliance of diverse groups—including southern whites, African Americans, and unionized workers—who supported the policies of the Democratic Party in the 1930s and 1940s. (p. 463)
Coalición del New Deal *s.* alianza temporal de distintos grupos, tales como blancos sureños, afroamericanos y sindicalistas, que apoyaban al Partido Demócrata en los años 30 y 40. (pág. 463)

New Federalism *n.* President Richard Nixon's program to turn over part of the federal government's power to state and local governments. (p. 825)
Nuevo Federalismo *s.* programa del president Richard Nixon para distribuir una porción del poder del gobierno federal a gobiernos estatales y locales. (pág. 825)

New Frontier *n.* President John F. Kennedy's legislative program, which included proposals to provide medical care for the elderly, to rebuild blighted urban areas, to aid education, to bolster the national defense, to increase international aid, and to expand the space program. (p. 680)

Nueva Frontera *s.* agenda legislativa del president John F. Kennedy; tenía medidas de atención médica para ancianos, renovación urbana y apoyo a la educación, que fueron rechazadas por el Congreso, así como medidas que sí se aprobaron de defensa nacional, ayuda internacional y programas espaciales. (pág. 680)

New Left *n.* a youth-dominated political movement of the 1960s, embodied in such organizations as Students for a Democratic Society and the Free Speech Movement. (p. 797)
Nueva Izquierda *s.* movimiento político juvenil de los años 60 con organizaciones como Students for a Democratic Society (Estudiantes por una Sociedad Democrática) y el Free Speech Movement (Movimiento de Libre Expresión). (pág. 797)

New Right *n.* a late-20th-century alliance of conservative special interest groups concerned with cultural, social, and moral issues. (p. 852)
Nueva Derecha *s.* alianza política de grupos conservadores de fines del siglo 20, con énfasis en asuntos culturales, sociales y morales. (pág. 852)

Niagara Movement *n.* founded by W.E.B. Du Bois in 1905 to promote the education of African Americans in the liberal arts. (p. 241)
Movimiento Niágara *s.* fundado en 1905 por W.E.B. Du Bois para promover la enseñanza de humanidades entre los afroamericanos. (pág. 241)

Nineteenth Amendment *n.* an amendment to the U.S. Constitution, adopted in 1920, that gives women the right to vote. (p. 273)
Enmienda 19 *s.* enmienda a la Constitución adoptada en 1920 que le otorga a la mujer el derecho de votar. (pág. 273)

"no man's land" *n.* an unoccupied region between opposing armies. (p. 319)
tierra de nadie *s.* en la Primera Guerra Mundial, extensión baldía de tierra entre trincheras de ejércitos enemigos. (pág. 319)

nonaggression pact *n.* an agreement in which two nations promise not to go to war with each other. (p. 493)
pacto de no agresión *s.* acuerdo entre dos naciones de no luchar entre sí. (pág. 493)

**North American Free Trade Agreement
(NAFTA)** *n.* a 1993 treaty that lowered tariffs
and brought Mexico into the free trade zone
established by the United States and Canada.
(p. 887)
Tratado de Libre Comercio, TLC *s.* tratado
de 1993 que redujo aranceles e incorporó a
México en la zona de libre comercio ya vigente
entre Estados Unidos y Canadá. (pág. 887)

North Atlantic Treaty Organization (NATO) *n.*
a defensive military alliance formed in 1949 by
ten Western European countries, the United
States, and Canada. (p. 582)
**Organización del Tratado del Atlántico
Norte** *s.* alianza militar defensiva formada
en 1949 por diez países de Europa del oeste,
Estados Unidos y Canadá. (pág. 582)

Nuclear Non-Proliferation Treaty (NPT) *n.*
treaty signed in 1968 under which nuclear
powers agreed not to sell or give nuclear
weapons to any other country and nonnuclear
powers promised not to develop or acquire
such weapons. (p. 619)
Tratado de No Proliferación Nuclear *s.*
tratado firmado en 1968 por el que las
potencias nucleares acordaron no vender
ni dar armas nucleares a ningún otro país y
las potencias no nucleares prometieron no
desarrollar ni adquirir dichas armas. (pág. 619)

nullification *n.* a state's refusal to recognize
an act of Congress that it considers
unconstitutional. (p. 35)
anulación *s.* rechazo de un estado a reconocer
cualquier ley del Congreso que considere
inconstitucional. (pág. 35)

Nuremberg trials *n.* the court proceedings held
in Nuremberg, Germany, after World War II, in
which Nazi leaders were tried for war crimes.
(p. 564)
juicios de Nuremberg *s.* juicios
llevados a cabo en Nuremberg, Alemania,
inmediatamente después de la Segunda Guerra
Mundial, a líderes nazis por sus crímenes de
guerra. (pág. 564)

O

Office of Price Administration (OPA) *n.* an
agency established by Congress to control
inflation during World War II. (p. 522)

Oficina de Administración de Precios *s.*
agencia establecida por el Congreso durante
la Segunda Guerra Mundial con facultad para
combatir la inflación al congelar los precios de
la mayoría de los artículos. (pág. 522)

Ohio gang *n.* a group of close friends and
political supporters whom President Warren G.
Harding appointed to his cabinet. (p. 362)
pandilla de Ohio *s.* amigos y partidarios
políticos del presidente Warren G. Harding, a
quienes éste nombró a su gabinete. (pág. 362)

**OPEC (Organization of the Petroleum
Exporting Countries)** *n.* an economic
association of oil-producing nations that is
able to set oil prices. (p. 829)
**OPEP (Organización de Países
Exportadores de Petróleo** *s.* alianza
económica para ejercer influencia sobre los
precios del petróleo. (pág. 829)

Open Door notes *n.* messages sent by Secretary
of State John Hay in 1899 to Germany, Russia,
Great Britain, France, Italy, and Japan, asking
the countries not to interfere with U.S. trading
rights in China. (p. 297)
notas de Puertas Abiertas *s.* notas que el
Secretario de Estado John Hay envió a Gran
Bretaña, Francia, Alemania, Italia, Japón y
Rusia, instándolos a no interponerse entre
el comercio de Estados Unidos y China.
(pág. 297)

Operation Desert Storm *n.* a 1991 military
operation in which UN forces, led by the
United States, drove Iraqi invaders from
Kuwait. (p. 874)
Operación Tormenta del Desierto *s.*
operación militar en la que fuerzas de las
Naciones Unidas, encabezadas por Estados
Unidos, liberaron a Kuwait y derrotaron al
ejército iraquí. (pág. 874)

outsourcing *n.* the process of producing goods
in countries other than the United States,
where costs are typically lower. (p. 888)
tercerización *s.* proceso de producción de
bienes en países distintos de los Estados
Unidos, donde los costos son típicamente más
bajos. (pág. 888)

P

Panama Canal *n.* an artificial waterway cut through the Isthmus of Panama to provide a shortcut between the Atlantic and Pacific oceans, opened in 1914. (p. 301)
canal de Panamá *s.* canal artificial construido a través del istmo de Panamá para abrir paso entre los océanos Atlántico y Pacífico; se abrió en 1914. (pág. 301)

parity *n.* a government-supported level for the prices of agricultural products, intended to keep farmers' incomes steady. (p. 475)
paridad *s.* regulación de precios de ciertos productos agrícolas, apoyada por el gobierno, con el fin de mantener estables los ingresos agrícolas. (pág. 475)

Patient Protection and Affordable Care Act (PPACA) *n.* an act signed in 2010 by President Barack Obama that extended access to private insurance coverage through individual mandates; often called Obamacare. (p. 906)
Ley de Protección del Paciente y Cuidados de la Salud Accesibles *s.* ley firmada en 2010 por el presidente Barack Obama que extendió el acceso a la cobertura de seguros privados mediante mandatos individuales; usualmente denominada ObamaCare. (pág. 906)

Patriots *n.* colonists who supported American independence from Britain. (p. 20)
patriotas *s.* colonos que apoyaban la independencia norteamericana de Gran Bretaña. (pág. 20)

patronage [pă′trə-nĭj] *n.* an officeholder's power to appoint people—usually those who have helped him or her get elected—to positions in government. (p. 207)
clientelismo *s.* sistema de otorgar empleos a personas que ayudan a la elección de un candidato. (pág. 207)

pay equity *n.* the basing of an employee's salary on the requirements of his or her job rather than on the traditional pay scales that have frequently provided women with smaller incomes than men. (p. 770)
equidad salarial *s.* sistema que basa el salario de un empleado en los requisitos del trabajo y no en escalas salariales tradicionales, que normalmente pagan menos a la mujer. (pág. 770)

Payne-Aldrich Tariff *n.* a set of tax regulations, enacted by Congress in 1909, that failed to significantly reduce tariffs on manufactured goods. (p. 265)
Arancel Payne-Aldrich *s.* serie de reglamentos de impuestos, aprobados por el Congreso en 1909, que no logró reducir mucho los aranceles de productos manufacturados. (pág. 265)

Peace Corps *n.* an agency established in 1961 to provide volunteer assistance to developing nations in Asia, Africa, and Latin America. (p. 681)
Cuerpo de Paz *s.* programa fundado en 1961 bajo iniciativa del presidente Kennedy, que envía voluntarios a las naciones en desarrollo de Asia, África y Latinoamérica para ayudar en escuelas, clínicas y otros proyectos. (pág. 681)

Pearl Harbor *n.* a United States naval base built in Hawaii in 1887 that became a coaling station for refueling American ships. (p. 284)
Pearl Harbor *s.* base naval de los Estados Unidos construida en Hawái en 1887 que se convirtió en una estación de reabastecimiento para embarcaciones estadounidenses. (pág. 284)

Pendleton Civil Service Act *n.* a law, enacted in 1883, that established a bipartisan civil service commission to make appointments to government jobs by means of the merit system. (p. 208)
Ley Pendleton *s.* ley de 1883 que autorizaba nombrar empleados del servicio civil por mérito. (pág. 208)

Pentagon Papers *n.* a 7,000-page document—leaked to the press in 1971 by the former Defense Department worker Daniel Ellsberg—revealing that the U.S. government had not been honest about its intentions in the Vietnam War. (p. 813)
Documentos del Pentágono *s.* documento de 7,000 páginas que dejó filtrar a la prensa en 1971 el antiguo funcionario del Departamento de Defensa Daniel Ellsberg, donde se revela que el gobierno mintió sobre sus planes en la Guerre de Vietnam. (pág. 813)

perestroika [pĕr′ĭ-stroi′kə] *n.* the restructuring of the economy and the government instituted in the Soviet Union in the 1980s. (p. 628)
perestroika *s.* palabra rusa para designar la reestructuración económica y burocrática de la Unión Soviética que ocurrió en los años 80. (pág. 628)

placer [plăs′ər] **mining** *n.* searching for gold by using pans or other devices to wash gold nuggets out of loose rock (p. 126)
minería con bandeja *s.* manera de buscar el oro con bandejas u otros utensilios que con la ayuda del agua separan las pepitas de oro de las piedras sueltas. (pág. 126)

planned obsolescence *n.* the designing of products to wear out or to become outdated quickly, so that people will feel a need to replace their possessions frequently. (p. 653)
obsolencia planeada *s.* diseño de artículos que se desgastan o pasan de moda muy pronto, para crear la necesidad de remplazarlos con frecuencia. (pág. 653)

Platt Amendment *n.* a series of provisions that, in 1901, the United States insisted Cuba add to its new constitution, commanding Cuba to stay out of debt and giving the United States the right to intervene in the country and the right to buy or lease Cuban land for naval and fueling stations. (p. 295)
Enmienda Platt *s.* serie de medidas implantadas por Estados Unidos en 1901, las cuales debieron ser incluidas por Cuba en su nueva constitución para quedar libre de su deuda y por las que Estados Unidos obtenía el derecho a intervenir en el país y a comprar o alquilar el territorio cubano para establecer estaciones navales y de combustible. (pág. 295)

Plessy v. Ferguson *n.* an 1896 case in which the Supreme Court ruled that separation of the races in public accommodations was legal, thus establishing the "separate but equal" doctrine. (p. 244)
Plessy v. Ferguson *s.* caso de 1896 en que la Suprema Corte declaró legal la separación de razas en instalaciones públicas y estableció la doctrina de "separados aunque iguales". (pág. 244)

political action committee (PAC) *n.* an organization that merges campaign contributions from members and uses the funds to campaign for or against candidates or legislation. (p. 958)
comité de acción política *s.* organización que recauda aportes de parte de miembros y usa los fondos para hacer campaña a favor o en contra de candidatos o leyes. (pág. 958)

political machine *n.* an organized group that controls a political party in a city and offers services to voters and businesses in exchange for political and financial support. (p. 205)
maquinaria política *s.* grupo organizado que controla un partido político en una ciudad y ofrece servicios a los votantes y negocios a cambio de apoyo político y financiero. (pág. 205)

poll tax *n.* an annual tax that formerly had to be paid in some southern states by anyone wishing to vote. (p. 243)
impuesto para votar *s.* impuesto anual que los ciudadanos debían pagar en algunos estados sureños para poder votar. (pág. 243)

popular culture *n.* a collection of ideas, attitudes, and images that are part of a mainstream culture, heavily influenced by and spread through the media. (p. 986)
cultura popular *s.* grupo de ideas, actitudes e imágenes que son parte de una cultura prevaleciente, fuertemente influenciada y difundida por los medios. (pág. 986)

popular sovereignty *n.* a system in which the residents vote to decide an issue. (p. 85)
soberanía popular *s.* sistema en el cual los ciudadanos votan para decidir sobre un tema. (pág. 85)

Populism *n.* a late-19th-century political movement demanding that people have a greater voice in government and seeking to advance the interests of farmers and laborers. (p. 146)
populismo *s.* movimiento político de finales del siglo 19 que exigía la voz popular en el gobierno y que representaba los intereses de los granjeros y promovía una reforma del sistema monetario. (pág. 146)

pragmatism *n.* a school of philosophical thought developed in the United States in the late 19th century that aimed to reconcile the tensions between science and morality and religion. (p. 220)
pragmatismo *s.* escuela de pensamiento filosófico desarrollada en los Estados Unidos a fines del siglo XIX que aspiraba a conciliar las tensiones entre ciencia, moral y religión. (pág. 220)

price support *n.* the maintenance of a price at a certain level through government intervention. (p. 414)
apoyo de precios *s.* apoyo de los precios de ciertos artículos al valor del mercado o por encima, algunas veces mediante la compra de excedentes por parte del gobierno. (pág. 414)

progressive movement *n.* an early-20th-century reform movement seeking to return control of the government to the people, to restore economic opportunities, and to correct injustices in American life. (p. 229)
movimiento progresista *s.* movimiento reformista de comienzos del siglo 20 cuyos objetivos eran mejorar el bienestar social, promover la moralidad, incrementar la justicia económica y devolver a la ciudadanía el control del gobierno. (pág. 229)

prohibition *n.* the banning of the manufacture, sale, and possession of alcoholic beverages. (p. 230)
prohibición *s.* prohibición de bebidas alcohólicas. (pág. 230)

Prohibition *n.* the period from 1920 to 1933 during which the Eighteenth Amendment forbidding the manufacture and sale of alcohol was in force in the United States. (p. 381)
Ley Seca *s.* período entre 1920 y 1933 durante el cual, por medio de la decimoctava enmienda, se prohibió la producción y la venta de alcohol en Estados Unidos. (pág. 381)

propaganda *n.* a kind of biased communication designed to influence people's thoughts and actions. (p. 339)
propaganda *s.* comunicación prejuiciada diseñada para influir los pensamientos y actos de la gente. (pág. 339)

Proposition 187 *n.* a bill passed in California in 1994 that ended all education and nonemergency health benefits to illegal immigrants. (p. 926)
Propuesta 187 *s.* proyecto de ley aprobado en California en 1994, el cual canceló todos los beneficios educativos y de salud que no fueran emergencias a los inmigrantes ilegales. (pág. 926)

protectorate *n.* a country whose affairs are partially controlled by a stronger power. (p. 295)

protectorado *s.* nación cuyo gobierno y asuntos son controlados por una potencia más fuerte. (pág. 295)

Pure Food and Drug Act *n.* a law enacted in 1906 to halt the sale of contaminated foods and drugs and to ensure truth in labeling. (p. 260)
Ley de Pureza de Alimentos y Drogas *s.* ley de 1906 que paró la venta de alimentos y drogas contaminadas y demandó etiquetas fidedignas. (pág. 260)

Q

quota system *n.* a system that sets limits on how many immigrants from various countries a nation will admit each year. (p. 374)
sistema de cuotas *s.* sistema que limita el número de inmigrantes de varios países que pueden ser admitidos a Estados Unidos cada año. (pág. 374)

R

racial profiling *n.* the act of suspecting or targeting a person simply on the basis of his or her race or ethnic background. (p. 939)
evaluación por perfil racial *s.* acto de sospechar de una persona o catalogarla basándose simplemente en su raza u origen étnico. (pág. 939)

Radical Republican *n.* one of the congressional Republicans who, after the Civil War, wanted to destroy the political power of former slaveholders and to give African Americans full citizenship and the right to vote. (p. 105)
republicano radical *s.* uno de los republicanos del Congreso después de la Guerra Civil que querían destruir el poder político de los antiguos dueños de esclavos y darles a los afroamericanos total ciudadanía y derecho a votar. (pág. 105)

rationing *n.* a restriction of people's right to buy unlimited amounts of particular foods and other goods, often implemented during wartime to ensure adequate supplies for the military. (p. 522)

racionamiento *s.* medida tomada durante tiempos de guerra para limitar la cantidad de ciertos alimentos y otros productos que cada persona puede comprar. (pág. 522)

Reaganomics [rā´gə-nŏm´ĭks] *n.* the economic policies of President Ronald Reagan, which were focused on budget cuts and the granting of large tax cuts in order to increase private investment. (p. 857)
reaganomía *s.* nombre dado a la política económica del presidente Reagan, que abogaba por recortes presupuestarios y por una gran reducción en los impuestos con el fin de incrementar la inversión privada. (pág. 857)

realpolitik [rā-äl´pō´lĭ-tēk´] *n.* a foreign policy advocated by Henry Kissinger in the Nixon administration, based on consideration of a nation's power rather than its ideals or moral principles. (p. 622)
realpolitik *s.* enfoque de política exterior, identificado con Henry Kissinger y Richard Nixon, que propone hacer lo que resulte realista y práctico en lugar de seguir una política al pie de la letra. (pág. 622)

reapportionment *n.* the redrawing of election districts to reflect changes in population. (p. 693)
nueva repartición *s.* redistribución de distritos electorales cuando cambia el número de personas en un distrito. (pág. 693)

recall [rĭ-kôl´] *n.* a procedure for removing a public official from office by a vote of the people. (p. 236)
destitución *s.* reforma gubernamental que permite a los votantes deponer a funcionarios públicos elegidos. (pág. 236)

Reconstruction *n.* the period of rebuilding that followed the Civil War, during which the defeated Confederate states were readmitted to the Union. (p. 105)
Reconstrucción *s.* período de reconstrucción después de la Guerra Civil y readmisión a la Unión de los estados de la Confederación que habían sido derrotados; de 1865 a 1877. (pág. 105)

Reconstruction Finance Corporation (RFC) *n.* an agency established in 1932 to provide emergency financing to banks, life insurance companies, railroads, and other large businesses. (p. 433)
Corporación Financiera de la Reconstrucción *s.* organización establecida en 1932 para dar financiación de emergencia a bancos, aseguradoras de vida, compañías ferroviarias y otras empresas grandes. (pág. 433)

referendum *n.* a procedure by which a proposed legislative measure can be submitted to a vote of the people. (p. 236)
referendo *s.* procedimiento que permite someter al voto popular propuestas legislativas. (pág. 236)

reparations *n.* the compensation paid by a defeated nation for the damage or injury it inflicted during a war. (p. 351)
reparación *s.* compensación que paga una nación derrotada en una guerra por las pérdidas económicas del vencedor o por crímenes cometidos contra individuos. (pág. 351)

revenue sharing *n.* the distribution of federal money to state and local governments with few or no restrictions on how it is spent. (p. 825)
distribución de rentas *s.* plan puesto en práctica en 1972 que faculta a los gobiernos estatales y locales a invertir el dinero federal a su conveniencia. (pág. 825)

reverse discrimination *n.* an unfair treatment of members of a majority group—for example, white men—resulting from efforts to correct discrimination against members of other groups. (p. 852)
discriminación a la inversa *s.* tratamiento injusto de los miembros de un grupo mayoritario, típicamente hombres blancos, como resultado de los esfuerzos por remediar la discriminación contra otros grupos. (pág. 852)

rock 'n' roll *n.* a form of American popular music that evolved in the 1950s out of rhythm and blues, country, jazz, gospel, and pop; the American musical form characterized by heavy rhythms and simple melodies, which has spread worldwide having significant impacts on social dancing, clothing fashions, and expressions of protest. (p. 662)

English and Spanish Glossary

rock 'n' roll *s.* forma de música popular estadounidense que evolucionó a finales de los 40 y durante los 50, a partir del rhythm and blues, el country, el jazz, el gospel y el pop; forma musical estadounidense caracterizada por ritmos fuertes y melodías simples, la cual se ha expandido por todo el mundo y ha tenido impactos significativos en el baile social, la moda de la vestimenta y las expresiones de protesta. (pág. 662)

Roosevelt Corollary *n.* an extension of the Monroe Doctrine, announced by President Theodore Roosevelt in 1904, under which the United States claimed the right to protect its economic interests by means of military intervention in the affairs of Western Hemisphere nations. (p. 304)
Corolario de Roosevelt *s.* declaración de 1904 del presidente Theodore Roosevelt en que advertía que Estados Unidos intervendría militarmente en los asuntos de cualquier nación del Hemisferio Occidental para proteger sus intereses económicos si fuera necesario. (pág. 304)

Rough Riders *n.* a volunteer cavalry regiment, commanded by Leonard Wood and Theodore Roosevelt, that served in the Spanish-American War. (p. 290)
Rough Riders *s.* regimiento de caballería voluntario comandado por Leonard Wood y Theodore Roosevelt en la Guerra Española-Norteamericana-Cubana. (pág. 290)

rural free delivery (RFD) *n.* the free government delivery of mail and packages to homes in rural areas, begun in 1896. (p. 223)
correo rural gratuito *s.* entrega gubernamental gratis de correo y paquetes a zonas rurales; se inició en 1896. (pág. 223)

S

SALT I Treaty *n.* a five-year agreement between the United States and the Soviet Union, signed in 1972, that limited the nations' numbers of intercontinental ballistic missiles and submarine-launched missiles. (p. 624)

Tratado Salt I *s.* acuerdo de cinco años entre Estados Unidos y la Unión Soviética que surgió de las Conversaciones sobre Limitación de Armas Estratégicas de 1972; limitó el número de misiles balísticos intercontinentales y de misiles de submarinos. (pág. 624)

Sandinista [săn´dĭ-nēs´tə] *n.* a member of a leftist rebel group that overthrew the Nicaraguan government in 1979. (p. 869)
Sandinista *s.* un miembro de un grupo rebelde izquierdista que derrocaron al gobierno nicaragüense en 1979; el president Reagan, quien respaldaba a la contra anticomunista, se les opuso. (pág. 869)

San Juan [săn wän´] **Hill** *n.* the site of a key victory by the American infantry during the 1898 conflict in Cuba with Spain. (p. 290)
Colina de San Juan *s.* sitio de una victoria clave de la infantería estadounidense durante el conflicto de 1898 en Cuba con España. (pág. 290)

Sarbanes-Oxley Act *n.* a 2002 act that established a regulatory board to oversee the accounting industry and its involvement with corporations. (p. 899)
Ley Sarbanes-Oxley *s.* ley de 2002 por la que se estableció una junta reguladora para supervisar la industria contable y su relación con las empresas. (pág. 899)

satellite nation *n.* a country that is dominated politically and economically by another nation. (p. 574)
nación satélite *s.* país dominado política y económicamente por otro. (pág. 574)

Saturday Night Massacre *n.* a name given to the resignation of the U.S. attorney general and the firing of his deputy in October 1973, after they refused to carry out President Nixon's order to fire the special prosecutor investigating the Watergate affair. (p. 835)
Masacre de Sábado en la Noche *s.* nombre dado a la renuncia del procurador general y al despido de su comisionado el 20 de octubre de 1973, después de haberse negado a acatar la orden del presidente Nixon de despedir al fiscal especial en el caso Watergate. (pág. 835)

scalawag [skăl´ə-wăg´] *n.* a white southerner who joined the Republican Party after the Civil War. (p. 108)

scalawag *s.* término despectivo para referirse a los sureños blancos que se unieron al Partido Republicano y apoyaron la Reconstrucción después de la Guerra Civil. (pág. 108)

school voucher *n.* a subsidy given directly to parents for school tuition. (p. 974)
cheque escolar *s.* subsidio dado directamente a los padres para pagar la matrícula escolar. (pág. 974)

scientific management *n.* the application of scientific principles to increase efficiency in the workplace. (p. 231)
administración científica *s.* aplicación de principios científicos para simplificar y facilitar las tareas laborales. (pág. 231)

Scopes trial *n.* a sensational 1925 court case in which the biology teacher John T. Scopes was tried for challenging a Tennessee law that outlawed the teaching of evolution. (p. 384)
juicio de Scopes *s.* sensacional juicio de 1925 en el que el maestro de biología John T. Scopes fue juzgado por desafiar una ley de Tennessee que prohibía la enseñanza de la evolución. (pág. 384)

search-and-destroy mission *n.* a U.S. military raid on a South Vietnamese village, intended to root out villagers with ties to the Vietcong but often resulting in the destruction of the village and the displacement of its inhabitants. (p. 791)
misión de búsqueda y destrucción *s.* ataque militar estadounidense a aldeas de Vietnam del Sur con el fin de erradicar al Vietcong, que solía resultar en la destrucción de la aldea y el desplazamiento de sus habitantes. (pág. 791)

sectionalism *n.* the placing of the interests of one's own region ahead of the interests of the nation as a whole. (p. 35)
regionalismo *s.* preocupación por los intereses de una región por encima de los de la nación como un todo. (pág. 35)

Securities and Exchange Commission (SEC) *n.* an agency, created in 1934, that monitors the stock market and enforces laws regulating the sale of stocks and bonds. (p. 474)
Comisión de Valores y Cambios *s.* agencia creada en 1934 para controlar el mercado bursátil y hacer cumplir las leyes que rigen la venta de acciones y bonos. (pág. 474)

segregation *n.* the separation of people on the basis of race. (p. 243)
segregación *s.* separación de la gente según su raza. (pág. 243)

Selective Service Act *n.* a law, enacted in 1917, that required men to register for military service. (p. 327)
Ley de Servicio Selectivo *s.* ley aprobada por el Congreso en mayo de 1917 que ordena que todos los hombres se inscriban para el servicio militar obligatorio. (pág. 327)

Selective Training and Service Act *n.* a U.S. law passed in 1940 that enacted the nation's first peacetime military draft. (p. 509)
Ley de Entrenamiento y Servicio Selectivo *s.* ley de los Estados Unidos aprobada en 1940 por la que se dispuso el primer reclutamiento militar de la nación en tiempos de paz. (pág. 509)

self-determination *n.* the right of people to choose their own political status. (p. 350)
autodeterminación *s.* derecho de las personas de elegir su propio estatuto político. (pág. 350)

Seneca Falls [sən′ĭ-kə fôlz′] **Convention** *n.* a women's rights convention held in Seneca Falls, New York, in 1848. (p. 78)
convención de Seneca Falls *s.* convención de derechos femeninos celebrada en 1848 en Seneca Falls, Nueva York. (pág. 78)

service sector *n.* the part of the economy that provides consumers with services rather than goods. (p. 885)
sector de servicios *s.* renglón de la economía que ofrece servicios en vez de productos. (pág. 885)

settlement house *n.* a community center providing assistance to residents—particularly immigrants—in a slum neighborhood. (p. 202)
casa de beneficencia *s.* centro comunitario en un barrio pobre que ayudaba a los residentes, particularmente a los inmigrantes. (pág. 202)

Seventeenth Amendment *n.* an amendment to the U.S. Constitution, adopted in 1913, that provides for the election of U.S. senators by the people rather than by state legislatures. (p. 236)
Enmienda 17 *s.* enmienda a la Constitución adoptada en 1913; dispone que los senadores federales sean elegidos por los votantes y no por cuerpos legislativos estatales. (pág. 236)

English and Spanish Glossary

shantytown [shăn′tē-toun′] *n.* a neighborhood in which people live in makeshift shacks. (p. 422)

tugurio *s.* vecindario en donde la gente vivía en chozas temporales. (pág. 422)

sharecropping *n.* a system in which landowners give farm workers land, seed, and tools in return for a part of the crops they raise. (p. 110)

aparcería *s.* sistema en el cual se da a los agricultores tierra, semillas, herramientas y alimentos para vivir, así como una parte de la cosecha, por cultivar la tierra. (pág. 110)

Sherman Antitrust Act *n.* a law, enacted in 1890, that was intended to prevent the creation of monopolies by making it illegal to establish trusts that interfered with free trade. (p. 174)

Ley Antitrust Sherman *s.* ley contra los monopolios de 1890 que declaró ilegal la formación de consorcios que obstruyeran el libre comercio. (pág. 174)

silent majority *n.* a name given by President Richard Nixon to the moderate, mainstream Americans who quietly supported his Vietnam War policies. (p. 811)

mayoría silenciosa *s.* nombre dado por el presidente Richard Nixon a los estadounidenses moderados que apoyaban silenciosamente su involucramiento en la Guerra de Vietnam. (pág. 811)

sit-in *n.* a form of demonstration used by African Americans to protest discrimination, in which the protesters sit down in a segregated business and refuse to leave until they are served. (p. 725)

sit-in *s.* forma de protesta en la que afroamericanos ingresaban a un lugar segregado, tal como el mostrador de un restaurante, y se negaban a salir hasta que se les sirviera. (pág. 725)

Social Darwinism *n.* an economic and social philosophy—supposedly based on the biologist Charles Darwin's theory of evolution by natural selection—holding that a system of unrestrained competition will ensure the survival of the fittest. (p. 170)

darvinismo social *s.* conjunto de creencias políticas y económicas basadas en la teoría del biólogo Charles Darwin sobre la selección natural o supervivencia del más apto; favorecía una competencia libre, no regulada, y creía que los individuos o grupos triunfaban porque eran genéticamente superiores. (pág. 170)

Social Gospel movement *n.* a 19th-century reform movement based on the belief that Christians have a responsibility to help improve working conditions and alleviate poverty. (p. 201)

movimiento del Evangelio Social *s.* movimiento de reforma del siglo 19 basado en la noción de que los cristianos tenían la responsabilidad social de mejorar las condiciones laborales y aliviar la pobreza urbana. (pág. 201)

social mobility *n.* the ability of families or individuals to move into a higher social class. (p. 203)

movilidad social *s.* capacidad de las familias o los individuos de pasar a una clase social más alta. (pág. 203)

Social Security Act *n.* a law enacted in 1935 to provide aid to retirees, the unemployed, people with disabilities, and families with dependent children. (p. 454)

Ley de Seguro Social *s.* ley aprobada en 1935 para ayudar a los jubilados, desempleados, incapacitados y familias con niños dependientes. (pág. 454)

social stratification *n.* the organization of people into social classes by wealth. (p. 199)

estratificación social *s.* organización de las personas en clases sociales según la riqueza. (pág. 199)

soddy [sŏd′ē] *n.* a home built of blocks of turf. (p. 140)

choza de tepe *s.* casa provisional hecha de césped, muy común en las llanuras, donde la madera era escasa. (pág. 140)

soup kitchen *n.* a place where free or low-cost food is served to the needy. (p. 422)

comedor de beneficencia *s.* lugar donde se sirven alimentos gratis o a bajo costo a los necesitados, muy común durante la Depresión. (pág. 422)

Southern Christian Leadership Conference (SCLC) *n.* an organization formed in 1957 by Dr. Martin Luther King Jr. and other leaders to work for civil rights through nonviolent means. (p. 724)
Conferencia de Líderes Cristianos del Sur *s.* organización formada en 1957 por el doctor Martin Luther King Jr. y otros líderes para promover los derechos civiles sin violencia. (pág. 724)

Southern Strategy *n.* President Nixon's attempt to attract the support of southern conservative Democrats who were unhappy with federal desegregation policies and the liberal Supreme Court. (p. 827)
estrategia sureña *s.* estrategia del president Nixon de apelar a los demócratas conservadores sureños que estaban descontentos con la integración y con una Suprema Corte liberal. (pág. 827)

speakeasy *n.* a place where alcoholic drinks were sold and consumed illegally during Prohibition. (p. 382)
speakeasy *s.* lugar donde se vendían bebidas alcohólicas ilegalmente, como ocurrió durante la Prohibición. (pág. 382)

speculation *n.* an involvement in risky business transactions in an effort to make a quick or large profit. (p. 417)
especulación *s.* transacciones de alto riesgo con el fin de obtener ganancias rápidas o grandes. (pág. 417)

Square Deal *n.* President Theodore Roosevelt's program of progressive reforms designed to protect the common people against big business. (p. 257)
Square Deal *s.* programa de reformas progresistas del president Theodore Roosevelt para proteger a la gente común y corriente de las grandes empresas. (pág. 257)

stagflation [stăg-flā′shən] *n.* an economic condition marked by both inflation and high unemployment. (p. 829)
estanflación *s.* situación económica en la que hay niveles altos de inflación y desempleo simultáneamente. (pág. 829)

Stamp Act *n.* a 1765 law in which Parliament established the first direct taxation of goods and services within the British colonies in North America. (p. 16)
Ley del Timbre *s.* primer impuesto directo aplicado en 1765 por Gran Bretaña a una variedad de artículos y servicios, tales como documentos legales y periódicos. (pág. 16)

Stonewall riots *n.* the riots that occurred in Greenwich Village in 1969 after a police raid of the Stonewall Inn, a popular LGBT gathering spot in New York City. (p. 771)
disturbios de Stonewall *s.* disturbios que ocurrieron en Greenwich Village en 1969 después de una redada policial en el pub Stonewall Inn, lugar popular de encuentro de la comunidad LGBT en la ciudad de Nueva York. (pág. 771)

Strategic Defense Initiative (SDI) *n.* a proposed defense system—popularly known as Star Wars—intended to protect the United States against missile attacks. (p. 628)
Iniciativa para la Defensa Estratégica *s.* sistema de defensa propuesto en los años 80, popularmente conocido como la Guerra de las Galaxias, cuyo fin era proteger a Estados Unidos de ataques de misiles. (pág. 628)

strike *n.* a work stoppage intended to force an employer to respond to demands. (p. 74)
huelga *s.* interrupción del trabajo para presionar a un patrono a responder a ciertas demandas. (pág. 74)

Student Nonviolent Coordinating Committee (SNCC) *n.* an organization formed in 1960 to coordinate sit-ins and other protests and to give young blacks a larger role in the civil rights movement. (p. 724)
Comité Coordinador de Estudiantes no Violentos *s.* organización fundada en 1960, conocida como SNCC, para coordinar sit-ins y otras protestas, y para darles a los jóvenes negros mayor participación en el movimiento de derechos civiles. (pág. 724)

Students for a Democratic Society (SDS) *n.* an antiestablishment New Left group, founded in 1960, that called for greater individual freedom and responsibility. (p. 798)

English and Spanish Glossary

Estudiantes por una Sociedad Democrática *s.* grupo activista de los años 60, conocido como SDS, que urgía una mayor libertad y responsabilidad individual. (pág. 798)

suburb *n.* a residential town or community near a city. (p. 637)
    suburbio *s.* pueblo o comunidad residencial cerca de una ciudad. (pág. 637)

suffrage *n.* the right to vote. (p. 254)
    sufragio *s.* derecho a votar. (pág. 254)

Sugar Act *n.* a trade law enacted by Parliament in 1764 in an attempt to reduce smuggling in the British colonies in North America. (p. 16)
    Ley del Azúcar *s.* ley británica de 1764 que aplicó un impuesto comercial a la melaza, el azúcar y otras importaciones para reducir el contrabando en las colonias. (pág. 16)

supply-side economics *n.* the idea that a reduction of tax rates will lead to increases in jobs, savings, and investments, and therefore to an increase in government revenue. (p. 858)
    economía de oferta *s.* teoría económica, que sostiene que recortar los impuestos de los ricos beneficia a todos pues aumenta empleos, ahorros e inversiones. (pág. 858)

Sussex pledge *n.* a promise by Germany in World War I not to sink merchant vessels "without warning and without saving human lives." (p. 322)
    promesa de Sussex *s.* promesa de Alemania en la Primera Guerra Mundial de no hundir barcos mercantes "sin advertencia y sin salvar vidas humanas". (pág. 322)

T

Taiwan [tī'wän'] *n.* the island about 100 miles from the Chinese mainland where the United States helped set up a Nationalist government in 1949. (p. 584)
    Taiwán *s.* isla ubicada aproximadamente a 100 millas de la China Continental donde los Estados Unidos ayudaron a establecer un gobierno nacionalista en 1949. (pág. 584)

Taliban [tăl'ə-băn'] *n.* a strict fundamentalist Islamic regime based in Afghanistan. (p. 893)
    Talibán *s.* régimen islámico fundamentalista estricto con base en Afganistán. (pág. 893)

tea party *n.* a libertarian, conservative movement that began in the United States in 2009. (p. 910)
    tea party *s.* movimiento libertario y conservador que comenzó en los Estados Unidos en 2009. (pág. 910)

Teapot Dome scandal *n.* Secretary of the Interior Albert B. Fall's secret leasing of oil-rich public land to private companies in return for money and land. (p. 363)
    escándalo de Teapot Dome *s.* escándalo generado cuando Albert Fall, Secretario del Interior del president Warren G. Harding, concedió en secreto valiosas reservas de petróleo en Wyoming y California a compañías privadas a cambio de dinero y tierras. (pág. 363)

Telecommunications Act of 1996 *n.* a law enacted in 1996 to remove barriers that had previously prevented communications companies from engaging in more than one type of communications business. (p. 915)
    Ley de Telecomunicaciones *s.* ley de 1996 que retiró las barreras que impedían que un tipo de compañía de comunicaciones ingresara a otro tipo de negocio en el mismo campo. (pág. 915)

telecommute *v.* to work at home for a company located elsewhere, by using such communications technologies as computers, the Internet, and fax machines. (p. 913)
    telecommute *v.* trabajar desde la casa para una compañía ubicada en otra parte, mediante la nueva tecnología de comunicaciones, como computadoras, Internet y máquinas de fax. (pág. 913)

tenement *n.* a multifamily urban dwelling, usually overcrowded and unsanitary. (p. 199)
    casa de pisos *s.* vivienda urbana de varias familias, usualmente sobrepoblada y poco sanitaria. (pág. 199)

Tennessee Valley Authority (TVA) *n.* a federal corporation established in 1933 to construct dams and power plants in the Tennessee Valley region to generate electricity as well as to prevent floods. (p. 475)
    Autoridad del Valle de Tennessee *s.* corporación federal creada en 1933 para construer presas y centrales eléctricas en la región del valle de Tennessee con el objeto de generar electricidad así como prevenir inundaciones. (pág. 475)

termination policy *n.* the U.S. government's plan, announced in 1953, to give up responsibility for Native American tribes by eliminating federal economic support, discontinuing the reservation system, and redistributing tribal lands. (p. 671)
política de terminación *s.* programa del gobierno federal en 1953 de cesar su responsa bilidad hacia las naciones amerindias y eliminar el apoyo económico federal, suspender el sistema de reservaciones y redistribuir las tierras tribales. (pág. 671)

Tet [tĕt'] **offensive** *n.* a massive surprise attack by the Vietcong on South Vietnamese towns and cities early in 1968. (p. 803)
ofensiva de Tet *s.* sorpresivo ataque masivo del Vietcong a pueblos y ciudades de Vietnam del Sur a comienzos de 1968; la batalla, de un mes de duración, convenció a muchos estadounidenses de que no era posible ganar la guerra. (pág. 803)

Thirteenth Amendment *n.* an amendment to the U.S. Constitution, adopted in 1865, that has abolished slavery and involuntary servitude. (p. 103)
Enmienda 13 *s.* enmienda a la Constitución, ratificada en 1865, que ha abolido la esclavitud y la servidumbre involuntaria. (pág. 103)

38th parallel *n.* the line of latitude that divides North and South Korea. (p. 585)
paralelo 38 la línea de latitude que divide a Corea del Norte de Corea del Sur. (pág. 585)

Three Mile Island *n.* an island in southeast Pennsylvania and the site of a major nuclear accident on March 28, 1979, when a partial meltdown released radioactive material, forcing the evacuation of thousands of nearby residents. (p. 708)
Three Mile Island *s.* isla en el sudeste de Pennsylvania y lugar de un gran accidente nuclear el 28 de marzo de 1979, cuando un colapso parcial liberó material radiactivo, lo cual forzó la evacuación de miles de residentes cercanos. (pág. 708)

Tiananmen [tyän'än'mĕn'] **Square** *n.* the site of 1989 demonstrations in Beijing, China, in which Chinese students demanded freedom of speech and a greater voice in government. (p. 868)

plaza Tiananmen *s.* lugar de protestas estudiantiles en 1989 en Beijing, China, por la falta de libertades democráticas, donde el gobierno atacó a los estudiantes. (pág. 868)

Tonkin Gulf [tŏn'kĭn gŭlf'] **Resolution** *n.* a resolution adopted by Congress in 1964, giving the president broad powers to wage war in Vietnam. (p. 786)
Resolución del Golfo de Tonkin *s.* resolución aprobada por el Congreso en 1964 que le otorgaba al presidente Johnson amplios poderes para la Guerra de Vietnam. (pág. 786)

totalitarian *adj.* characteristic of a political system in which the government exercises complete control over its citizens' lives. (p. 486)
totalitario *adj.* característico de un sistema politico en que el gobierno ejerce completo control sobre la vida de los ciudadanos. (pág. 486)

Trail of Tears [tîrz] *n.* the marches in which the Cherokee people were forcibly removed from Georgia to the Indian Territory in 1838–1840, with thousands of the Cherokee dying on the way. (p. 39)
Sendero de las Lágrimas *s.* marcha obligada del pueblo cherokee desde Georgia hasta el Territorio Indio entre 1838 y 1840, durante la cual murieron miles de ellos. (pág. 39)

transcontinental railroad *n.* a railroad line linking the Atlantic and Pacific coasts of the United States, completed in 1869. (p. 163)
ferrocarril transcontinental *s.* línea férrea finalizada en 1869 que unía la costa Atlántica y la costa Pacífica. (pág. 163)

Treaty of Guadalupe Hidalgo [gwäd'l-ōōp' hĭ-däl'gō] *n.* the 1848 treaty ending the U.S. war with Mexico, in which Mexico ceded California and New Mexico to the United States. (p. 84)
Tratado de Guadalupe Hidalgo *s.* tratado de 1848 que puso fin a la guerra entre Estados Unidos y México, mediante el cual Estados Unidos obtuvo enormes tierras en el Oeste y el Suroeste. (pág. 84)

Treaty of Paris (1783) *n.* the treaty that ended the Revolutionary War, confirming the independence of the United States and setting the boundaries of the new nation. (p. 24)

English and Spanish Glossary

Tratado de París *s.* tratado que puso fin a la Guerra Revolucionaria Norteamericana y estableció las fronteras de la nueva nación. (pág. 24)

Treaty of Paris (1898) *n.* the treaty ending the Spanish-American War, in which Spain freed Cuba, turned over the islands of Guam and Puerto Rico to the United States, and sold the Philippines to the United States for $20 million. (p. 291)

Tratado de París *s.* tratado el cual puso fin a la guerra entre España y Estados Unidos. Por medio de este tratado España liberó a Cuba, cedió las islas de Guam y Puerto Rico a Estados Unidos y vendió las Filipinas a este país por 20 millones de dólares. (pág. 291)

Treaty of Versailles [vər-sī′] *n.* the 1919 peace treaty at the end of World War I which established new nations, borders, and war reparations. (p. 351)

Tratado de Versalles *s.* tratado de paz firmado en 1919 al finalizar la Primera Guerra Mundial, el cual establecía nuevas naciones, fronteras y reparaciones de guerra. (pág. 351)

trench warfare *n.* military operations in which the opposing forces attack and counterattack from systems of fortified ditches rather than on an open battlefield. (p. 319)

guerra de trincheras *s.* guerra en que los combatientes atacan desde un sistema de zanjas fortificadas y no en un campo abierto de batalla. (pág. 319)

triangular trade *n.* the transatlantic system of trade in which goods and people, including slaves, were exchanged between Africa, England, Europe, the West Indies, and the colonies in North America. (p. 10)

triángulo comercial de esclavos *s.* sistema transatlántico de comercio en el cual la mercancía, incluidos los esclavos, se intercambiaba entre África, Inglaterra, Europa, las Indias Occidentales y las colonias de Norteamérica. (pág. 10)

Troubled Asset Relief Program (TARP) *n.* an act signed in 2008 by President George W. Bush that authorized $700 billion (later reduced) to stabilize the U.S. banking and automobile industries. (p. 900)

Programa de Alivio de Activos en Problemas *s.* ley firmada en 2008 por el presidente George W. Bush por la que se autorizaron 700 mil millones de dólares (monto después reducido) para estabilizar las industrias bancaria y automotriz de los Estados Unidos. (pág. 900)

Truman Doctrine *n.* a U.S. policy, announced by President Harry S. Truman in 1947, of providing economic and military aid to free nations threatened by internal or external opponents. (p. 579)

Doctrina Truman *s.* declaración del presidente Truman en 1947, que establecía que Estados Unidos debía dar apoyo económico y militar para liberar a naciones amenazadas por fuerzas internas o externas. (pág. 579)

trust *n.* a business organization in which competing companies are under the control of a single group of trustees. (p. 172)

trust *s.* organización de empresas en la que empresas competidoras están bajo el control de un solo grupo de administradores. (pág. 172)

Tuskegee [tŭs-kē′gē] **Normal and Industrial Institute** *n.* founded in 1881, and led by Booker T. Washington, to equip African Americans with teaching diplomas and useful skills in the trades and agriculture. (p. 241)

Instituto Normal e Industrial Tuskegee *s.* fundado en 1881 y dirigido por Booker T. Washington para otorgar diplomas de magisterio y enseñar destrezas comerciales y agrícolas a los afroamericanos. (pág. 241)

U

Underground Railroad *n.* a system of routes along which runaway slaves were helped to escape to Canada or to safe areas in the free states. (p. 86)

Ferrocarril Subterráneo *s.* red secreta de personas que ayudaban a los esclavos fugitivos a escapar a lo largo de diversas rutas hacia Canadá o hacia zonas seguras en los estados libres. (pág. 86)

United Farm Workers Organizing Committee (UFWOC) *n.* a labor union formed in 1966 to seek higher wages and better working conditions for Mexican American farm workers in California. (p. 748)
Comité Organizador de Trabajadores Agrícolas Unidos *s.* sindicato establecido en 1966 por César Chávez para mejorar los salarios y las condiciones laborales de los trabajadores agrícolas. (pág. 748)

United Nations (UN) *n.* an international peacekeeping organization to which most nations in the world belong, founded in 1945 to promote world peace, security, and economic development. (p. 562)
Naciones Unidas *s.* organización internacional promotora de la paz a la que pertenecen la mayoría de naciones, fundada en 1945 para fomentar la paz, la seguridad y el desarrollo económico del mundo. (pág. 562)

urban flight *n.* a migration of people from cities to the surrounding suburbs. (p. 921)
huida urbana *s.* migración de las ciudades a los suburbios aledaños. (pág. 921)

urbanization *n.* the growth of cities. (p. 197)
urbanización *s.* movimiento de personas a una ciudad. (pág. 197)

urban renewal *n.* the tearing down and replacing of buildings in rundown inner-city neighborhoods. (p. 668)
renovación urbana *s.* práctica que se inició con la Ley Nacional de Vivienda de 1949, de remplazar vecindarios urbanos decaídos por viviendas nuevas para gente de bajos recursos. (pág. 668)

urban sprawl *n.* the unplanned and uncontrolled spreading of cities into surrounding regions. (p. 365)
explosión urbana *s.* expansión desordenada y desmedida de las ciudades a las áreas contiguas. (pág. 365)

USA PATRIOT Act *n.* an act signed by President George W. Bush in 2001 that gave government the power to conduct search and surveillance of suspected terrorists. (p. 894)
Ley Patriota de los Estados Unidos *s.* ley firmada por el presidente George W. Bush en 2001 por la que se daba al gobierno el poder de investigar y vigilar a personas consideradas presuntos terroristas. (pág. 894)

USS *Maine* *n.* a U.S. warship that mysteriously exploded and sank in the harbor of Havana, Cuba, on February 15, 1898. (p. 288)
USS *Maine* *s.* buque de guerra estadounidense que explotó y naufragó misteriosamente el 15 de febrero de 1898 en el Puerto de La Habana, Cuba. (pág. 288)

U-2 incident *n.* the downing of a U.S. spy plane and capture of its pilot by the Soviet Union in 1960. (p. 609)
incidente del U-2 *s.* derribo en 1960 de un avión espía estadounidense U-2 en suelo soviético; complicó las conversaciones de paz entre Estados Unidos y la Unión Soviética. (pág. 609)

V

Valley Forge *n.* the site in Pennsylvania where the Continental army spent the winter of 1777–1778 under extremely harsh conditions. (p. 22)
Valley Forge *s.* sitio de Pennsylvania donde el Ejército Continental pasó el invierno de 1777–1778 bajo condiciones extremadamente duras. (pág. 22)

V-E Day *n.* a name given to May 8, 1945, "Victory in Europe Day" on which General Eisenhower's acceptance of the unconditional surrender of Nazi Germany marked the end of World War II in Europe. (p. 558)
Día V-E *s.* mayo 8 de 1945, día de la victoria europea, cuando el general Eisenhower aceptó la rendición incondicional de Alemania; puso fin a la Segunda Guerra Mundial en Europa. (pág. 558)

vertical integration *n.* a company's taking over its suppliers and distributors and transportation systems to gain total control over the quality and cost of its product. (p. 171)
integración vertical *s.* proceso mediante el cual una compañía se adueña de sus proveedores y distribuidores así como de los sistemas de transporte, con lo que obtiene control total sobre la calidad y el costo de su producción. (pág. 171)

Vietcong [vē-ĕt′kŏng′] *n.* the South Vietnamese Communists who, with North Vietnamese support, fought against the government of South Vietnam in the Vietnam War. (p. 783)

English and Spanish Glossary

Vietcong *s.* rebeldes comunistas de Vietnam del Sur apoyados por Vietnam del Norte a partir de 1959. (pág. 783)

Vietminh [vĕ-ĕt′mĭn′] *n.* an organization of Vietnamese Communists and other nationalist groups that between 1946 and 1954 fought for Vietnamese independence from the French. (p. 781)
Vietmin *s.* organización de comunistas vietnamitas y otros grupos nacionalistas que luchó contra los franceses por la independencia de Vietnam de 1946 a 1954. (pág. 781)

Vietnamization [vĕ-ĕt′nə-mĭ-zā′shən] *n.* President Nixon's strategy for ending U.S. involvement in the Vietnam War, involving the gradual withdrawal of U.S. troops and their replacement with South Vietnamese forces. (p. 810)
vietnamización *s.* plan del presidente Nixon de retiro gradual de las tropas estadounidenses de Vietnam y su remplazo por el ejército vietnamita. (pág. 810)

Voting Rights Act of 1965 *n.* a law that made it easier for African Americans to register to vote by eliminating discriminatory literacy tests and authorizing federal examiners to enroll voters denied at the local level. (p. 736)
Ley de Derechos Electorales de 1965 *s.* ley para facilitarles a los afroamericanos inscribirse para votar; eliminó las pruebas discriminatorias de lectura y escritura, y autorizó a los examinadores federales inscribir votantes rechazados a nivel local. (pág. 736)

W

Wagner Act *n.* a law—also known as the National Labor Relations Act—enacted in 1935 to protect workers' rights after the Supreme Court declared the National Industrial Recovery Act unconstitutional. (p. 454)
Ley Wagner *s.* ley—también conocida como Ley Nacional de Relaciones Laborales—promulgada en 1935 para proteger los derechos de los trabajadores después de que la Corte Suprema consideró que la Ley Nacional de Recuperación Industrial (NIRA) era inconstitucional. (pág. 454)

war-guilt clause *n.* a provision in the Treaty of Versailles by which Germany acknowledged that it alone was responsible for World War I. (p. 351)
cláusula de culpabilidad *s.* cláusula del Tratado de Versalles que obligaba a Alemania a reconocer que había sido totalmente responsable por la Primera Guerra Mundial. (pág. 351)

War Industries Board (WIB) *n.* an agency established during World War I to increase efficiency and discourage waste in war-related industries. (p. 337)
Junta de Industrias Bélicas *s.* junta establecida en 1917 que animaba a las compañías a usar técnicas de producción en masa para mejorar la eficiencia durante la Primera Guerra Mundial. (pág. 337)

War Powers Act (WPA) *n.* a law enacted in 1973, limiting a president's right to send troops into battle without consulting Congress. (p. 818)
Ley de Poderes de Guerra *s.* ley aprobada en 1973 tras la Guerra de Vietnam que limitaba el derecho de un presidente a enviar tropas a combatir sin consultar con el Congreso. (pág. 818)

War Production Board (WPB) *n.* an agency established during World War II to coordinate the production of military supplies by U.S. industries. (p. 522)
Junta de Producción Bélica *s.* agencia establecida durante la Segunda Guerra Mundial para coordinar la producción de suministros militares por la industria nacional. (pág. 522)

Warren Commission *n.* a group, headed by Chief Justice Earl Warren, that investigated the assassination of President Kennedy and concluded that Lee Harvey Oswald alone was responsible for it. (p. 683)
Comisión Warren *s.* grupo encabezado por Earl Warren, presidente de la Suprema Corte, que realizó la investigación oficial del asesinato del presidente Kennedy y concluyó que Lee Harvey Oswald había actuado por su cuenta. (pág. 683)

Warren Court *n.* the Supreme Court during the period when Earl Warren was Chief Justice, noted for its activism in the areas of civil rights and free speech. (p. 693)

la Corte Warren *s.* la Suprema Corte de la que fue presidente Earl Warren, que se destacó por sus actividades en torno a los derechos civiles y la libre expresión. (pág. 693)

Warsaw [wôr′sô′] **Pact** *n.* a military alliance formed in 1955 by the Soviet Union and its Eastern European satellites. (p. 604)
Pacto de Varsovia *s.* alianza militar formada en 1955 por la Unión Soviética y las naciones satélite de Europa del este. (pág. 604)

Watergate *n.* a scandal arising from the Nixon administration's attempt to cover up its involvement in the 1972 break-in at the Democratic National Committee headquarters in the Watergate apartment complex. (p. 832)
Watergate *s.* serie de escándalos en que el presidente Nixon trató de encubrir la participación de su comité de reelección en el allanamiento de la sede del Partido Demócrata en los apartamentos Watergate en 1972. (pág. 832)

weapons of mass destruction (WMD) *n.* biological, chemical, and nuclear weapons. (p. 895)
armas de destrucción masiva *s.* armas biológicas, químicas y nucleares. (pág. 895)

Women's Auxiliary Army Corps (WAAC) *n.* U.S. army unit created during World War II to enable women to serve in noncombat positions. (p. 519)
Unidad Auxiliar de Mujeres *s.* unidad del Ejército de EE.UU. creada durante la Segunda Guerra Mundial para permitir que las mujeres colaboraran en puestos que no fueran de combate. (pág. 519)

Woodstock *n.* a free music festival that attracted more than 400,000 young people to a farm in upstate New York in August 1969. (p. 701)
Woodstock *s.* festival gratuito de música que atrajo a más de 400,000 jóvenes a una granja del estado de Nueva York en agosto de 1969. (pág. 701)

Works Progress Administration (WPA) *n.* an agency, established as part of the Second New Deal, that provided the unemployed with jobs in construction, garment making, teaching, the arts, and other fields. (p. 452)
Administración para el Progreso de Obras *s.* agencia gubernamental del New Deal que empleó a personal desocupado en construcción de escuelas y hospitales, reparación de carreteras, enseñanza, escritura y artes. (pág. 452)

X

xenophobia [zĕn′ə-fō′bē-ə] *n.* an unreasoned fear of things or people seen as foreign or strange. (p. 371)
xenofobia *s.* miedo infundado a cosas o personas consideradas desconocidas o extrañas. (pág. 371)

Y

yellow journalism *n.* the use of sensationalized and exaggerated reporting by newspapers or magazines to attract readers. (p. 288)
prensa amarillista *s.* uso de métodos sensacionalistas en periódicos o revistas para atraer o influenciar lectores. (pág. 288)

Yorktown *n.* the site where the British army formally surrendered on October 19, 1781, ending the American Revolution. (p. 23)
Yorktown *s.* sitio donde el ejército británico formalmente se rindió el 19 de octubre de 1781, lo cual dio fin a la Guerra de Independencia de los Estados Unidos. (pág. 23)

Z

Zimmermann note *n.* a message sent in 1917 by the German foreign minister to the German ambassador in Mexico, proposing a German-Mexican alliance and promising to help Mexico regain Texas, New Mexico, and Arizona if the United States entered World War I. (p. 324)
nota Zimmermann *s.* mensaje enviado por el canciller alemán en 1917 al canciller mexicano en el que prometía a México los estados de Texas, New Mexico y Arizona si se aliaba a Alemania en contra de Estados Unidos en la Primera Guerra Mundial. (pág. 324)

Index

Index

Index

Index

Text Acknowledgments

Module 1

"The Search for the First Americans" from *National Geographic* by Thomas Canby. Text copyright © 1979 by National Geographic Creative. Reprinted by permission of National Geographic Creative.

Module 2

Excerpt from *We Pointed Them North: Recollections of a Cowpuncher* by Teddy Abbott. Text copyright © 1991 by Teddy Abbott. Reprinted by permission of the University of Oklahoma Press.

Module 9

Excerpts from "A. Everette McIntyre" and "Herman Sumlin," from *Hard Times* by Studs Terkel. Text copyright © 1970. Reprinted by permission of Donadio & Olson, Inc.

Module 10

Excerpt from "Remarks" by Rexford Tugwell from *Roosevelt Day Dinner Journal*. Text copyright © 1963 by Rexford Tugwell. Reprinted by permission of George Washington University Press.

Module 11

Excerpt from "One Survivor Remembers" by Gerda Weissmann Klein. Text copyright © Gerda Weissmann Klein. Reprinted by permission of Gerda Weissman Klein.

Excerpt from "Letter From Marine 1st Lt. Leonard Isacks" by Leonard Isacks. Text copyright © by Leonard Isacks. Reprinted by permission of the National World WWII Museum.

Excerpt from "A Cue for Passion" by John Patrick McGrath. Text copyright © 1994 by John Patrick McGrath. Reprinted by permission of the Estate of John Patrick McGrath.

Excerpt from "Interview With Mary Cohen" conducted by David Dunham from *Rosie the Riveter WWII Home Front Oral History Project*. Copyright © 2011 by David Dunham. Reprinted by permission of the Bancroft Library.

Excerpt from "Speech to the House of Commons" in *The Gathering Storm* by Winston S. Churchill. Text copyright © 1940 by Winston Churchill. Reprinted by permission of Curtis Brown Ltd., London, on behalf of the Estate of Sir Winston Churchill.

Excerpt from *Night* by Elie Wiesel. Text copyright © 1972, 1985 by Elie Wiesel. English translation copyright © 2006 by Marion Wiesel. Originally published as *La Nuit* by Les Editions de Minuit. Text copyright © 1958 by Les Editions de Minuit. Reprinted by permission of Farrar Straus and Giroux, George Borchardt, Inc. for Les Editions Minuit and Recorded Books.

Module 12

Excerpt from "The Sinews of Peace" speech by Winston Churchill, delivered March 5, 1946, at Westminster College. Text copyright © 1946 by Winston Churchill.

Reprinted by permission of Curtis Brown Ltd., London, on behalf of the Estate of Sir Winston Churchill.

Excerpt from *The Martian Chronicles* by Ray Bradbury. Text copyright 1950, renewed © 1977 by Ray Bradbury. Reprinted by permission of Don Congdon Associates, Inc.

Module 13

Excerpt from "Little Boxes," words and music by Malvina Reynolds. Text copyright © 1962, renewed © 1990 by Schroder Music Co (ASCAP). Reprinted by permission of Schroder Music. All rights reserved.

Module 14

Excerpt from "The Times They Are A-Changin'" by Bob Dylan. Text copyright © 1962 by Bob Dylan. Reprinted by permission of Special Rider Music, Inc.

Module 15

Excerpt from "I Have a Dream" by Martin Luther King, Jr. Text copyright © 1963 by Martin Luther King, Jr.; copyright renewed © 1991 by Coretta Scott King. Reprinted by permission of The Heirs to the Estate of Martin Luther King, Jr., c/o Writers House, Inc. as agent for the proprietor.

Excerpt from "Who Will Fight for the Worth of Women's Work?" by Geraldine Ferraro from *Vital Speeches of the Day*, Vol. 49, issue 3. Text copyright © November 15, 1982, by Geraldine Ferraro. Reprinted by permission of ICM on behalf of Geraldine Ferraro.

Module 16

Excerpt from "How to Tell a True War Story" from *The Things They Carried* by Tim O'Brien. Text copyright © 1990 by Tim O'Brien. Reprinted by permission of Houghton Mifflin Harcourt Publishing Company.

Excerpt from "The Ballad of the Green Berets" by Barry Sadler and Robin Moore. Text copyright © by Barry Sadler and Robin Moore. Reprinted by permission Eastaboga Entertainment Inc.

Module 17

Excerpt from "Kissinger: An Interview with Oriana Fallaci" from *The New Republic*. Text copyright © December 16, 1972, by Oriana Fallaci. Reprinted by permission of PARS International on behalf of the author.

"Americans on the Move, 1970s" (retitled from "Migration Patterns: Where Americans Are Going") from *Regional Growth and Decline in the United States* by Bernard L. Weinstein and Robert E. Firestine. Text copyright © 1978 by Bernard L. Weinstein, Harold T. Gross, and John Rees. Reprinted by permission of Dr. Bernard Weinstein.

Module 18

Excerpt from "Pres. Clinton Recommends the Big Sort," from The Daily Yonder. Text copyright © 2008 by The Daily Yonder. Reprinted by permission of The Daily Yonder.

Excerpt from "Rudy Garcia-Tolson" by Jacquie Paul from *Press-Enterprise* January 1, 2000. Text copyright © 2000 by Press-Enterprise. Reprinted by permission of Press-Enterprise, Inc.

Module 19

"Hate Map" from www.splcenter.org/hate-map by The Southern Poverty Law Center. Text copyright © 2015 by The Southern Poverty Law Center. Reproduced by permission of The Southern Poverty Law Center.

"Six Pac(k)in'" by William H. Gross. Text copyright © October, 2011 by PIMCO. Reprinted by permission of PIMCO.

Art and Photography Credits

Unless otherwise indicated below, all video reference screens are © 2010 A&E Television Networks, LLC. All rights reserved.

Maps: Altas maps by Houghton Mifflin Harcourt; maps on pages 548, 556, 982 by Maps.com. Unless otherwise indicated, all other maps, locators, and globe locators by GeoNova LLC.

Cover: *Lincoln Memorial* Dan Huntley Photography/Getty Images; *paper texture* Tolga Tezcan/Getty Images

Table of Contents: *Union soldiers* Library of Congress Prints and Photographs Division, Washington, DC [LC-USZC6-48]; *suffragists* © Corbis; *Civil Works Administration* Franklin D. Roosevelt Library, Hyde Park, New York; *Selma march* © Ivan Massar/Black Star; *robots in auto factory* © Monty Rakusen/Getty Images; *Arlington Memorial bridge and Lincoln Memorial* © Corbis.

Module 1: *Arrival of Henry Hudson* The Granger Collection, New York; Gutenberg and press Library of Congress Prints & Photographs Division, Washington, D.C (LC-USZ62-65195); *Portrait of a Man, said to be Christopher Columbus* (born about 1446, died 1506), (1519), Sebastiano del Piombo. Oil on canvas, 42" x 34 3/4". The Metropolitan Museum of Art, gift of J. Pierpont Morgan, 1900 (00.18.2). Photograph copyright ©1979 The Metropolitan Museum of Art; Liberty Bell ©Leif Skoogfors/Corbis; Louisiana Purchase ©Bettmann/Corbis; Irish Potato Famine, Elizabeth Cady Stanton The Granger Collection, New York; American flag ©Izzy Schwartz/Photodisc/Getty Images; Philadelphia *SE Prospect of the City of Philadelphia* (Detail) (1720), Peter Cooper, The Library Company of Philadelphia; *Portrait of a Man, said to be Christopher Columbus* (born about 1446, died 1506), (1519), Sebastiano del Piombo. Oil on canvas, 42" x 34 3/4". The Metropolitan Museum of Art, gift of J. Pierpont Morgan, 1900 (00.18.2). Photograph copyright ©1979 The Metropolitan Museum of Art; Benjamin Franklin, Jonathan Edwards, Battle at Fort Duquesne The Granger Collection, New York; American flag ©Izzy Schwartz/Photodisc/Getty Images;

Washington Crossing the Delaware (Detail) (1851), Emanuel Gottlieb Leutze. Photograph ©Bettmann/Corbis; Crispus Attucks Patrick Faricy/Houghton Mifflin Harcourt; tar and feathering cartoon, George Washington portrait The Granger Collection, New York; *Molly Pitcher at the Battle of Monmouth* (1854), Dennis Malone Carter. Oil on canvas, 42" x 56". Gift of Herbert P. Whitlock, 1913. Courtesy of Fraunces Tavern Museum, New York City; signatures National Archives and Records Administration (NARA); American flag ©Izzy Schwartz/Photodisc/Getty Images; Bill of Rights ©Bettmann/Corbis; John Dickinson James Barton Longacre, after Charles Wilson Peale. Sepia watercolor on artist board 11 5/8" x 8 7/8" (29.5 x 20 cm). National Portrait Gallery, Smithsonian Institution/Art Resource, New York; young John Adams ©Bettmann/Corbis; Thomas Jefferson Main Street Studios/EPCO, "The Oval Office Collection"/Houghton Mifflin Harcourt; Sequoyah, Trail of Tears (detail) The Granger Collection, New York; aerial of farmland ©David R. Frazier/Stone/Getty Images; township map Township VII, Range XIV, Ohio Company (1787), Rufus Putnam. Clements Library, University of Michigan; Constitution The Granger Collection, New York; one hundred dollar bill photo by Houghton Mifflin Harcourt; American flag ©Izzy Schwartz/Photodisc/Getty Images; *Erie Canal at Little Falls, New York* (1884) by William Rickarby Miller. Collection of The New-York Historical Society; Slater Mill The first cotton mill in America, established by Samuel Slater on the Blackstone River at Pawtucket, Rhode Island (ca.1790), American School. Oil on canvas. Smithsonian Institution, Washington DC/The Bridgeman Art Library; telegraph National Museum of American History, Smithsonian Institution, Electrical Collections (74-2491); telephone ©Robertstock.com; Marconi radio ©Bettmann/Corbis; television ©Bettmann/Corbis; computers ©Charles E. Rotkin/Corbis; laptop computer photo by Houghton Mifflin Harcourt; Frederick Douglass ©Hulton Archive/Getty Images; slave quarters Collection of The New-York Historical Society; Sojourner Truth The Granger Collection, New York; American flag ©Izzy Schwartz/Photodisc/Getty Images; wagons heading west The Granger Collection, New York; settlers with Conestoga wagons Library of Congress Prints and Photographs Division, Washington, D.C. [LC-USZC4-4580]; covered wagon interior National Archives and Records Administration (NARA); Navajo man Edward S. Curtis (ca. 1904). Library of Congress Prints and Photographs Division [LC-USZ62-97089]; Navajo woman Edward S. Curtis (ca. 1904). Library of Congress Prints and Photographs Division [LC-USZ62-103498]; *John Brown Going to His Hanging* (1942), Horrace Pippin. Oil on canvas, 24 1/8" x 30 1/4". Courtesy of the Museum of American

Art of the Pennsylvania Academy of the Fine Arts, Philadelphia, Pennsylvania. John Lambert Fund [1943.11]; Fort Boise Idaho State Historical Society. Photo number 1254-D-1; Blue Mountains ©MPI/Getty Images; Chief Looking Glass National Anthropological Archives, Smithsonian Institution (2953-A); Roger Taney ©Bettmann/Corbis; Dred Scott Engraving of Dred Scott in Frank Leslie's Illustrated Newspaper, June 27, 1857. Library of Congress Prints and Photographs Division, Washington, D.C. [LC-USZ62-79305]; American flag ©Izzy Schwartz/Photodisc/Getty Images; Battle of Gettysburg ©Stock Montage/Hulton Archive/Getty Images; *Mary Boykin Chesnut* (1856), Samuel S. Osgood. Oil on canvas adhered to masonite, 48" x 30". Private collection/Art Resource, New York; wounded Union soldiers Photograph by Matthew Brady. The Granger Collection, New York; *Surrender at Appomattox* ©Tom Lovell/National Geographic Image Collection; amputee soldier The Granger Collection, New York; American flag ©Izzy Schwartz/Photodisc/Getty Images; ruins in the south ©MPI/Hulton Archive/Getty Images; Andrew Johnson Culver Pictures; building ruins ©Corbis; carpetbagger cartoon The Granger Collection, New York; Hiram Revels *The First Colored Senators and Representatives in the 41st and 42nd Congress of the United States.* Lithograph, 1872, by Currier & Ives. The Granger Collection, New York.

Module 2: *American flag* © Izzy Schwartz/Photodisc/Getty Images; *Texas Longhorns* Buffalo Bill Historical Center, Cody, Wyoming (7.69); *Blackfoot Indians* © Bettmann/Corbis; *Red Cloud* The Granger Collection, New York; *Grover Cleveland* © MPI/Hulton Archive/Getty Images; *Suez Canal* © Hulton-Deutsch Collection/Corbis; *France takes over Indochina* © Bettmann/Corbis; *William Jennings Bryan* © Blank Archives/Hulton Archive/Getty Images; *Zitkala-Ša* Courtesy of Harold Lee Library, Brigham Young University; *Yankton Sioux coup stick* The Detroit Institute of Arts. Founders Society Purchase with funds from Flint Ink Corporation; *Sitting Bull* The Granger Collection, New York; *Colonel Custer* The Granger Collection, New York; *Buffalo grazing* © BGSmith/Shutterstock; *Buffalo skull* © Steven Fuller/Animals Animals; *spoon from Buffalo horn* © North Wind/Nancy Carter/North Wind Picture Archives; *hide scraper* © Peabody Essex Museum, Salem, Massachusetts, USA/Bridgeman Art Library (New York); *buffalo hide* © Buffalo Bill Historical Center/The Art Archive at Art Resource; *two Nez Perce men* © Don Ryan/AP Images; *miners climbing* Library of Congress Prints & Photographs Division, Washington, DC (LC-USZ62-41760); *sluicing for gold* University of Washington Libraries, Special Collections [Hegg 1312]; *Mark Twain* The Granger Collection, New York; *The Stampede* (1908), Frederic Remington.

Oil on canvas, 27" x 40." From the collection of the Gilcrease Museum, Tulsa, Oklahoma; *Klondike gold rush* Library of Congress Prints & Photographs Division, Washington, DC (LC-USZ62-37810); *Dyea Trail* Library of Congress Prints & Photographs Division, Washington, DC (LC-USZ62-57311); *Pioneer Woman* (1909), Harvey Dunn. Oil on canvas, 24 1/4" h x 30 1/4" w. Hazel L. Meyer Memorial Library, De Smet, South Dakota; *Poster for Settlers* The Granger Collection, New York; *freed slaves* Library of Congress Prints and Photographs Division, Washington, DC; *sod house in Nebraska* Library of Congress Prints & Photographs Division, Washington, DC (Digital ID: nbhips 10028); *barbed wire* The Granger Collection, New York; *reaper* North Wind Pictures; *steel flow* The Granger Collection, New York; *windmill* North Wind Pictures; *prairie landscape* © Dave Reede/All Canada Photos/Corbis; *Mary Elizabeth Lease* © Corbis; *Plight of Farmers political cartoon* Culver Pictures; *William Jennings Bryan cartoon* The Granger Collection, New York; *William Jennings Bryan* © Corbis.

Module 3: *American flag* © Izzy Schwartz/Photodisc/Getty Images; *locomotive* The Granger Collection, New York; *Sierra Nevada Railroad* Library of Congress Prints & Photographs Division; *Chinese immigrants* Underwood Photo Archives; *light bulb* National Museum of American History, Smithsonian Institution, Electrical Collections (791641); *Haymarket riot, Olympic Games* The Granger Collection, New York; *Pattillo Higgins* Reproduced from "Prospectus: The True History of the Beaumont Oil Fields" by Pattillo Higgins. 1902 Pattillo Higgins. Courtesy of the estate of Pattillo Higgins; *Thomas Edison with a Light Bulb* The Granger Collection, New York; *woman with typewriter* © Bettmann/Corbis; *rural Cleveland, map of Cleveland, Standard Oil Refinery* The Atlas of Cuyahoga County, Ohio, Titus, Simmons and Titus, The Western Reserve Historical Society, Cleveland, Ohio; *Cuyahoga River on fire* © Bettmann/Corbis; *town of Pullman* Historic Pullman Foundation Archives; *train in snow* The Granger Collection, New York; *railroad cartoon* The Granger Collection, New York; *Andrew Carnegie* The Granger Collection, New York; *Risen from the Ranks* The Granger Collection, New York; *John D. Rockefeller* © Bettmann/Corbis; *Rockefeller cartoon* Horace Taylor, January 22, 1900, edition of *Verdict.* Library of Congress Prints and Photographs Division, Washington, DC [LC-USZ62-61409]; *Samuel Gompers* Library of Congress Prints & Photographs Division, Washington, DC [LC-USZ62-61896]; *Boy carrying homework from NY Sweatshop* (1912) Lewis Wickes Hine. Gelatin silver print, 16.7 x 11.7 cm. Gift of the Photo League, New York. GEH NEG 3748/Courtesy of George Eastman House; *IWW protest* © Bettmann/Corbis; *Eugene V. Debs* Eugene Debs Collection/Tamiment

Institute Library, New York University; *Mother Jones* The Granger Collection, New York; *Triangle Shirtwaist Company fire* © Underwood & Underwood/Corbis.

Module 4: *American flag* © Izzy Schwartz/Photodisc/Getty Images; *Statue of Liberty* © Fotolia; *New York City, 1905* The Granger Collection, New York; *Rutherford B. Hayes* © Bettmann/Corbis; *Barnum & Bailey Circus* The Granger Collection, New York; *campaign button* © Bettmann/Corbis; *Model T* © Three Lions/Hulton Archive/Getty Images; *Mexican Revolution* © Charles & Josette Lenars/Corbis; *Chinese Family* © Corbis; *approaching the Statue of Liberty* The Granger Collection, New York; *immigrants arriving at Ellis Island* Culver Pictures; *mental competency test* New York Academy of Medicine Library; *mob attacking Chinese immigrants* © Bettmann/Corbis; *NYC tenement* Jacob Riis (ca. 1890). The Granger Collection, New York; *dead horse* Library of Congress Prints and Photographs Division [LC-D4-13645]; *Jane Addams* University of Illinois at Chicago Library, The Jane Addams Memorial Collection (JAMC494); *NYC apartment building, 1889* The Granger Collection, New York; *political boss cartoon* © Bettmann/Corbis; *Boss Tweed* The Granger Collection, New York; *Tammany Tiger cartoon* The Granger Collection, New York; *Rutherford B. Hayes* The Granger Collection, New York; *James A. Garfield* The Granger Collection, New York; *Chester A. Arthur* The Granger Collection, New York; *Brooklyn Bridge* Library of Congress Prints and Photographs Division; *Flatiron Building* Library of Congress Prints and Photographs Division [LCD401-14278]; *Chicago Civic Center* The Granger Collection, New York; *airplane cylinder* John Batchelor/Print Solutions; *Wright flight* Brown Brothers; *Kodak camera* © Eastman Kodak Company; *Coney Island* Culver Pictures; *bicycling* Houghton Mifflin Harcourt; *Negro League* National Baseball Hall of Fame Library, Cooperstown, New York; *The Champion Single Sculls* (Max Schmitt in a Single Scull), (1871), Thomas Eakins. Oil on canvas, 32 1/4" x 46 1/4". The Metropolitan Museum of Art, Purchase, The Alfred N. Punnett Endowment Fund and George D. Pratt Gift, 1934 (34.92). Photograph © 1974 The Metropolitan Museum of Art; *dime novels* The Granger Collection, New York; *catalog shopping* Courtesy of Sears Roebuck and Company; *new journalism cartoon* Houghton Mifflin Harcourt; *Bill "Bojangles" Robinson* © Underwood & Underwood/Corbis; *circus poster* The Granger Collection, New York; *Ellis Island* Illustration by Nick Rotundo/Bizzy Productions, Inc.; *screen captures (all)* © 2010 A&E Television Networks, LLC. All rights reserved.

Module 5: *American flag* © Izzy Schwartz/Photodisc/Getty Images; *women's rally* © Bettmann/Corbis; *Suffrage parade* © Bettmann/Corbis; *Ida B. Wells* The

Granger Collection, New York; *Eiffel Tower* © Michael Maslin Historic Photographs/Corbis; *W.E.B. Du Bois* © Bettmann/Corbis; *WWI plane* Ian Bellinger/Fotolibra; *Gandhi* © Peter Ruhe/Gandhiserve Foundation; *votes for women poster* The Granger Collection, New York; *Marie Curie* © Hulton Archive/Getty Images; *Theodore Roosevelt* The Granger Collection, New York; *mill workers* © Bettmann/Corbis; *Florence Kelley* © Bettmann/Corbis; *Ford factory* © Bettmann/Corbis; *spindle boys* © Lewis Hine/Corbis; *cartoon* © American Stock/Hulton Archive/Getty Images; *Ida M. Tarbell* The Granger Collection, New York; *Lincoln Steffens* The Granger Collection, New York; *The Butchers* (1917), Joesph Pennell. Chicago History Museum (Negative number CHi-4109); *classroom* Culver Pictures; *Ida B. Wells* The Granger Collection, New York; *Rex Theatre* © Marion Post Wolcott/Library of Congress/Getty Images; *railroad workers* Sacramento Archives and Museum Collection Center; *John Marshall Harlan* The Granger Collection, New York; *drinking fountains* © Elliott Erwitt/Magnum Photos; *Rosa Parks* © Reuters/Corbis; *Susette la Flesche* The Granger Collection, New York; *telephone operators* © Bettmann/Corbis; *suffragists* © Corbis; *Susan B. Anthony* © Bettmann/Corbis; *Upton Sinclair* © Bettmann/Corbis; *Lion-Tamer cartoon* © Bettmann/Corbis; *meat inspection* © Bettmann/Corbis; *W.E.B. Du Bois* © C. M. Battey/Hulton Archive/Getty Images; *Gifford Pinchot* The Granger Collection, New York; *William Howard Taft* © Bettmann/Corbis; *Taft portrait* The Granger Collection, New York; *Carrie Chapman Catt* © Bettmann/Corbis; *Frank Lloyd Wright house* © Peter Cook/VIEW/Corbis; *Victorian house* © Michael T. Sedam/Corbis.

Module 6: *American flag* © Izzy Schwartz/Photodisc/Getty Images; *Great White Fleet* Library of Congress Prints and Photographs Division [LC-USZC4-5232]; *Rough Riders* © Corbis; *Queen Liliuokalani* The Granger Collection, NYC; *Marie Curie* © Hulton Archive/Getty Images; *Panama Canal* © Underwood & Underwood/Corbis; *WWI poster* © Corbis; *U.S.S. Maine* © Bettmann/Corbis; *Boxer Rebellion* © The Trustees of the British Museum; *Zapatistas Marching - Led by Emiliano Zapata and Pancho Villa during the Mexican Revolution of 1911* (1931), Jose Clemente Orozco. Oil on canvas, 45" x 55" (114.3 x 139.7 cm). Private Collection/SOMAAP, Mexico/The Bridgeman Art Library/Artists Rights Society (ARS), New York. Multimedia product associated with this text program and its contents are protected under copyright law. Any theatrical, televised, or public display or performance, including transmission of any image over a network, excepting a local area network, is prohibited by law, as is the preparation of any derivative work, including the extraction in whole or in part, of any images without the permission of ARS. Reproduction, includ-

ing downloading of artist works is prohibited by copyright laws and international conventions without the express written permission of Artists Rights Society (ARS), New York; *Queen Lil* © Bettmann/Corbis; *Admiral Mahan* Culver Pictures; *Great White Fleet* The Granger Collection, New York; *Cuban rebels* © Bettmann/Corbis; *Jose Marti* The Granger Collection, New York; *Uncle Sam lithograph* © Bettmann/Corbis; *Luis Munoz Rivera* Puerto Rican Cultural Institute/Library of Congress Prints and Photographs Division; *Puerto Rico* © AFP/Getty Images; *Uncle Sam restaurant cartoon* The Granger Collection, New York; *Panama Canal workers* © Bettmann/Corbis; *Theodore Roosevelt* The Granger Collection, New York; *The New Diplomacy* The Granger Collection, New York; *cargo vessel* © Will & Deni McIntyre/Stone/Getty Images; *New York City* © The Mariners' Museum/Corbis; *U.S.S. Arizona in Panama Canal* Library of Congress Prints & Photographs Division, Washington, DC [LC-USZ62-98338].

Module 7: *American flag* © Izzy Schwartz/Photodisc/Getty Images; *Sopwith Triplane* Ian Bellinger/Fotolibra; *WWI battle* © Bettmann/Corbis; *gears* © Marilyn Nieves/iStockPhoto.com; *camera* © Bettmann/Corbis; *telephone* © Dorling Kindersley; *Einstein* © Underwood & Underwood/Corbis; *influenza sign* San Francisco Chronicle; *Votes for Women statuette* The Granger Collection, New York; *Jeannette Rankin* © Corbis; *Wilhelm II* © Corbis; *Balkans* © Rikard Larma/AP Images; *soldiers in trench* © Corbis; illustration Chris Costello/Houghton Mifflin Harcourt; *Lusitania* © Three Lions/Hulton Archive/Getty Images; *Eddie Rickenbacker* © Bettmann/Corbis; *I Want You poster* The Granger Collection, New York; *Harlem Hell Fighters* National Archives and Records Administration, Records of the War Department General and Special Staffs (165-WW-127-8); *Joseph D. Lawrence* Houghton Mifflin Harcourt; *John J. Pershing* The Granger Collection, New York; *airplane* Air Team Images; *gas mask* © Dorling Kindersley; *tanks* © Three Lions/Hulton Archive/Getty Images; *Super Dreadnought* Library of Congress Prints & Photographs Division [LC-USZ62-103269]; *Sergeant York* © Bettmann/Corbis; *YMCA WWI poster* Library of Congress Prints and Photographs Division [LC-USZC4-7709]; *Harriet Stanton* Brown Brothers; *victory garden* © Bettmann/Corbis; *food conservation poster* The Granger Collection, New York; *Wake Up America poster* Library of Congress Prints & Photographs Division [LC-USZC4-3802]; *enemy alien political cartoon* © Corbis; *During the World War There Was a Great Migration North by Southern Negroes* (Panel no. 1 from The Migration of the Negro mural series) (1940–1941), Jacob Lawrence. Casein tempera on hardboard, 12" x 18". The Phillips Collection; acquired 1942/© Estate of Gwendolyn Knight Lawrence/ Artists Rights Society (ARS), New York.

Module 8: *American flag* © Izzy Schwartz/Photodisc/Getty Images; *flappers* © Bettmann/Corbis; *Harding button* © David J. & Janice L. Frent Collection/Corbis; *Chinese communist flag* Photograph by Martin Plomer, © Dorling Kindersley; *Stalin* © Bettmann/Corbis; *Jazz band* © Frank Driggs Collection/Getty Images; *King Tut* © Bettmann/Corbis; *Time Magazine* Time Life Pictures/Time Magazine, © Time Inc./Time Life Pictures/Getty Images; *Louis Armstrong* © Hulton Archive/Getty Images; *Charles Lindbergh* © Bettmann/Corbis; *Hirohito* © Bettmann/Corbis; *Ford Model T* © Bettmann/Corbis; *Warren Gamaliel Harding* (Detail) (ca. 1923), Margaret Lindsay William. Oil on canvas, 135.9 x 99.7 cm. National Portrait Gallery, Smithsonian Institution/Art Resource, New York; *Teapot Dome cartoon* Stock Montage; *Calvin Coolidge* (Detail), Charles S. Hopkins. White House Historical Association (White House Collection) (8); *home appliance* © Camerique/Robertstock.com; *Coolidge cartoon* Culver Pictures; *Fajans* Houghton Mifflin Harcourt; *Ku Klux Klan* © Bettmann/Corbis; *female strikers* Library of Congress Prints and Photographs Division [LC-B2-956-14]; *John Llewellyn Lewis* © Bettmann/Corbis; *Billy Sunday* © Bettmann/Corbis; *concealing alcohol (both)* © Underwood & Underwood/Corbis; *Al Capone* © Underwood & Underwood/Corbis; *Scopes cartoon* © The Granger Collection, New York; *woman using washing machine* Library of Congress Prints & Photographs Division, Washington, DC [LC-H822-T01-1999-008]; *flappers* © Hulton Archive/Getty Images; *typesetter* Lewis Wickes Hine (1920) GEH

NEG 16682/Courtesy George Eastman House; *bobbed hair* Library of Congress Prints & Photographs Division; *Tunney/Dempsey* © Bettmann/Corbis; *dance party* © Underwood & Underwood/Corbis; *Cosser radio* © Hulton-Deutsch Collection/Corbis; *radio actors* © Underwood & Underwood/Corbis; *Gertrude Ederle* © Bettmann/Corbis; *Babe Ruth* © New York Times Company/Hulton Archive/Getty Images; *Rube Foster* National Baseball Hall of Fame Library, Cooperstown, New York; *Helen Wills* © Central Press/Hulton Archive/Getty Images; *Red Grange* Library of Congress Prints & Photographs Division, Washington, DC [LC-F8-38629]; *Lou Gehrig, Amelia Earhart, Charles Lindbergh* © Bettmann/Corbis; *Night Windows* Night Windows (1928), Edward Hopper. Oil on canvas, 29" x 34". Museum of Modern Art, New York. Gift of John Hay Whitney [248.1940]. Digital Image © The Museum of Modern Art/Licensed by SCALA/Art Resource, New York; *F. Scott Fitzgerald* © Hulton Archive/Getty Images; *Zora Neale Hurston* Brown Brothers; *James Weldon Johnson* Fisk University, Nashville, Tennessee; *Harlem street, The Hot Five, Duke Ellington* © Frank Driggs Collection/Getty Images; *Cotton Club* © Hulton-Deutsch Collection/Corbis; *Henry Ford* © Underwood & Underwood/Corbis; *screen captures (all)* © 2010 A&E Television Networks, LLC. All rights reserved.

Module 9: *American flag* © Izzy Schwartz/Photodisc/Getty Images; *shantytown* © Photo Collection Alexander Alland Sr./Corbis; *bread line* © American Stock/Hulton Archive/Getty Images; *Manchuria* © Bettmann/Corbis; *Vanity Fair* © 1933 Condé Nast Publications; *World's Fair* Chicago History Museum (Negative number CHi-39026); *Gandhi* © Bettmann/Corbis; *Gordon Parks* © AP Images; *farm equipment auction* © Arthur Rothstein/Corbis; *Day of Wrath* Dies Irae (October 29, 1929), James Naumburg Rosenberg. Lithograph on paper, 13 5/8" x 10 1/2". National Museum of American Art, Washington, DC/Art Resource, New York; *NYSE 1914* © Bettmann/Corbis; *NYSE 2000* © Reuters/Corbis; *Ann Marie Low* Reproduced from *Dust Bowl Diary* by Ann Marie Low, by permission of the University of Nebraska Press; *NYC shantytown* © Franklin D. Roosevelt Library/Bettmann/Corbis; *farmer and sons in Dust Bowl* Library of Congress Prints and Photographs Division [LC-USZC4-4840]; *Boys walking tracks* National Archives and Records Administration (NARA); *Ozark sharecropper* Farm Security Administration/Library of Congress Prints and Photographs Division [LC-USF33-006068-M5]; *Family walks through Texas* Library of Congress Prints and Photographs Division [LC-DIG-ppmsc-00241]; *Herbert Hoover* Herbert Clark Hoover (Detail) (1931), Douglas Chandor. Oil on canvas. National Portrait Gallery, Smithsonian Institution/Art

Resource, New York; *overburdened men cartoon* "Ding" Darling Wildlife Society; *Bonus Army* © Bettmann/Corbis.

Module 10: *American flag* © Izzy Schwartz/Photodisc/Getty Images; *crowd* © Thomas D. McAvoy/Time & Life Pictures/Getty Images; *Civilian Conservation Corps* AP Images; *Vanity Fair* © 1934 Condé Nast Publications; *Mussolini* © Bettmann/Corbis; *Hindenburg disaster* The Granger Collection, New York; *Wizard of Oz* © MGM/The Kobal Collection; *Civilian Conservation Corps* © Archive Photos/Getty Images; *Franklin D. Roosevelt* Franklin Delano Roosevelt (Detail) (1935), Henry Salem Hubbell. Oil on masonite panel, 121.9 x 116.2 cm. National Portrait Gallery, Smithsonian Institution/Art Resource, New York; *Eleanor Roosevelt* White House Historical Association; *Civilian Conservation Corps* National Archives and Records Administration (NARA); *Changing Course* Jay N. "Ding" Darling. © 1937 by the Des Moines Register and Tribune Company. Reprinted with permission/Stock Montage; *Roosevelt Cartoon* The Granger Collection, New York; *Dorothea Lange* Dorothea Lange at Work, Texas (Detail) (1934), Paul Taylor. © The Dorothea Lange Collection, Oakland Museum of California, City of Oakland. Gift of Paul S. Taylor; *farmer with plow* Library of Congress Prints & Photographs Division, Washington, DC [LC-DIG-fsa-8a01823]; *Migrant Mother (close-up)* Migrant Mother, Nipomo, California (1936), Dorothea Lange/Library of Congress [Prints & Photographs Division LC-USZ62-95653]; *Kentucky Bread Line* © Margaret Bourke-White/Time Life Pictures/Getty Images; *Running Water Poster* National Archives and Records Administration (NARA); *Light Poster* Light (1937), Lester Beall. From the series "Rural Electrification Administration." Lithograph, 101.6 x 76.2 cm (40 x 30 in./Library of Congress Prints and Photographs Division [U.S. B415.3]; *Charles Evans Hughes* © Bettmann/Corbis; *strike* © Bettmann/Corbis; *Frances Perkins* © Bettmann/Corbis; *Marian Anderson* © Hulton Archive/Getty Images; *Robert F. Wagner* © Bettmann/Corbis; *Sit-Down Strike* © Bettmann/Corbis; *Organize? Poster*, chromolithograph (mid-1930s), Ben Shahn. The Granger Collection, New York/© Estate of Ben Shahn/Licensed by VAGA, New York, NY; *Memorial Day Massacre* Carl Linde/Courtesy of the Illinois Labor History Society; *movie theater Line* Russell Lee (1941). Library of Congress Prints and Photographs Division [USF34-38814-D]; *Gone With the Wind* © MGM/Fred Parrish/Photofest; *American Gothic* American Gothic (1930), Grant Wood. Oil on beaver board, 30 11/16" x 25 11/16" (78 cm x 65.3 cm) unframed. The Art Institute of Chicago, Friends of American Art Collection [1930.934]. Photography © The Art Institute of Chicago/All rights reserved by the Estate of Nan Wood Graham/